CAMPBELL'S
HIGH SCHOOL/COLLEGE QUIZ
BOOK

By John P. Campbell

Campbell's High School / College Quiz Book

Campbell's Potpourri I of Quiz Bowl Questions

Campbell's Potpourri II of Quiz Bowl Questions

Campbell's Middle School Quiz Book #1

Campbell's Potpourri III of Quiz Bowl Questions

Campbell's Middle School Quiz Book #2

Campbell's Elementary School Quiz Book #1

Campbell's 2001 Quiz Questions

Campbell's Potpourri IV of Quiz Bowl Questions

Campbell's Middle School Quiz Book #3

The 500 Famous Quotations Quiz Book

Campbell's 2002 Quiz Questions

Campbell's 210 Lightning Rounds

CAMPBELL'S
High School/College Quiz
BOOK

The Quiz Contestant's
Vade Mecum

JOHN P. CAMPBELL

Revised and Expanded Edition

PATRICK'S PRESS
Columbus, Georgia

Printed in the United States of America

Campbell, John P., 1942-
Campbell's High school/college quiz book.
Rev. ed. of: Campbell's High school/college bowl bible.
1st ed. 1983.
Includes index.
1. Questions and answers. I. Campbell, John P., 1942-   . High school/college bowl bible. II. Title. III. Title: High school/college quiz book.
AG195.C286 **1988**   031'.02   84-19012
ISBN 0-9609412-3-1

First Edition: 1st Printing, February, 1983/2nd Printing, December 1983/Revised Edition: 1st Printing, October, 1984/2nd Printing, August 1985/3rd Printing, April 1986/4th Printing, February, 1987/5th Printing, October 1988/6th Printing, March, 1990/7th Printing, January 1992.

I am indebted to the following publishers and copyright owners for permission to reproduce their material.

ACKNOWLEDGMENTS

I would like to express my indebtedness to two people who played a major role in the completion of this book. One is Dr. Jay Cliett, the Coordinator in the Department of Mathematics at Georgia Southwestern College, the Coordinator of the High School Academic Bowl Tournament, and the coach of his school's College Bowl team. Dr. Cliett agreed to read all the material and arranged for other staff members to read material in their field. His assistance in this regard and his many suggestions and corrections were invaluable. The other is Rinda Brewbaker, formerly of Brookstone School and now part-time English instructor at Columbus College. I am deeply grateful for her counsel and suggestions and especially for her editing ability that gave organization and focus where it was lacking.

I gratefully acknowledge the following for having contributed a significant number of questions: *Mathematics*: Marie Santry, Brookstone School; Pam Coffield, Brookstone School; Patricia Culpepper, Columbus High; and Dr. Jay Cliett. *Biology*: John Cole, Brookstone School; and Delmarie Vernon, Columbus High; *Physics and Chemistry*: Joe Skinner, Hardaway High.

I thank the staff members of Georgia Southwestern College who so willingly agreed to read the material.

I thank my mother, Mrs. John Campbell, for her support.

I thank the following students for checking the accuracy of the material: Priscilla Faucette, Brookstone School; Tippi Faucette, Queens College; Mona Crawford, Columbus College; and Eric Rowland.

I thank the following for reading the material, for making corrections and suggestions, and possibly for contributing questions: *History*: Dr. Frank Lowrey, Georgia Southwestern; Ron Burkhart, Brookstone School; Nan Pate, Brookstone School; and Howard Mendel, Brookstone School. *U.S. Government*: Kent Sole, Georgia Southwestern; and Nan Pate, Brookstone School. *U.S. Geography*: Don Cope, Columbus College. *American Literature*: Jack Norton, Georgia Southwestern; Tina Cliff, Brookstone School; John Harder, Massanutten Academy; and Dr. Charles Cherry, Villanova University. *English Grammar*: Fred Power, Georgia Southwestern; and Rinda Brewbaker. *Biology*: Dr. Jack Carter, Georgia Southwestern; and Sam Pate, Brookstone School. *Mathematics*: Dr. Albert Van Cleave, Columbus, College. *Chemistry*: Dr. Wayne Counts, Georgia Southwestern; Fred Beal, Brookstone School; and Jim Rutledge, Shaw High. *Physics*: Frank Jones, Georgia Southwestern; Fred Beal, Brookstone School; and Jim Rutledge, Shaw High. *French*: Reggie Comer, Georgia Southwestern. *Spanish*: Reggie Comer, Georgia Southwestern; Martha Mullinax, Brookstone School. *German*: Howard Mendel, Brookstone School; and Jane Frenkel, formerly of Spencer High and Baker High.

I would like to thank the staffs of the W.C. Bradley Memorial Library, the Columbus College Library, and the Columbus *Ledger-Enquirer* Library for their help in research. Also thanks to Clara Ellis, the Brookstone School librarian.

I thank Ben Parsons of Parsons' Productions for most of the lyrics for the ''Columbus Stockade Blues'' and Carroll Lisby of the Columbus *Ledger-Enquirer* for completing the lyrics.

I also thank Tim Randolph, Brookstone School; Keith Abney, Emory University; Anne Pergl, Antilles School; and Waldrup Printing Company, Columbus, Georgia, for the help they provided.

**To the often unknown,
unappreciated, unacknowledged,
unrecognized, unrewarded,
and unheralded . . .**

To songwriters Thomas P. (Tom) Darby of Columbus, Georgia, and Johnny J. (Jimmie) Tarlton of Phenix City, Alabama, who sold their 1927 hit the ''Columbus Stockade Blues'' outright for $150 and who never received any royalties for this work even though their song sold sensationally (more than 1,000,000 copies):

Columbus Stockade Blues

'Way down in Columbus, Georgia,
Wanna be back in Tennessee.
'Way down in Columbus Stockade,
Friends have turned their back on me . . .

Go away and leave me if you wish to;
Never let me cross your mind.
In your heart you love some other,
Leave me darlin', I don't mind.

Many a night with you I rambled,
Many an hour I spent with you.
Thought I gained your heart forever;
No, you have proved false to me.

Go away and leave me if you wish to;
Never let me cross your mind.
In your heart you love some other,
Leave me darlin', I don't mind.

Last night while I lay sleeping,
I dreamed that I was in your arms.
When I woke I was mistaken;
I was peeping through the bars.

Go away and leave me if you wish to;
Never let me cross your mind.
In your heart you love another;
Now, I got those walkin' blues.

And to *alma mater* writers everywhere:

The Brookstone School *Alma Mater*

On the city's northern border
Stalwart stands our Alma Mater.
Thank you for our firm foundation
Sending us forth to lead the nation.
You have been our stepping stone —
Our own Beloved Brookstone.

You sprang forth from Trinity
Shining light of this grand city.
Guiding us as independent
We return as all resplendent.
We know we can stand alone —
Thank you Beloved Brookstone.

John Campbell, lyricist
Sue Allen, composer

CONTENTS

U.S. GEOGRAPHY

AMERICAN LITERATURE

ENGLISH GRAMMAR

(AMERICAN) LANGUAGE

MATHEMATICS

BIOLOGY

CHEMISTRY

PHYSICS

MATHEMATICS, SCIENCE, AND MEDICINE

NATIONS AND CAPITALS

QUESTIONS AND ANSWERS

1. Who are the only 2 fictional heroes of Mediterranean exploration? Name the authors and their works.
ANSWER: Odysseus in Homer's *The Odyssey* and Jason in Apollonius' of Rhodes *Argonautica*.

2. The 8th Century B.C. Greeks were active explorers and 3 of their major colonies were Syracuse in Sicily, Cyrene in Libya, and Massilia (Marseille) in Southern France. Who were their 2 major competitors?
ANSWER: The Phoenicians and the Carthaginians.

3. By what 2 names did Marco Polo describe Japan and China?
ANSWER: Cipangu and Cathay.

4. Who were the Spanish King and Queen who financed Christopher Columbus's voyages? Give the meaning of the phrase ''Columbus's egg.''
ANSWER: King Ferdinand of Aragón and Queen Isabella of Castille/''An easy job once you know how.''

5. What were the names of the 3 ships of Christopher Columbus in 1492? What are the English translations of these Spanish words?
ANSWER: *Niña, Pinta,* and the *Santa María*/A little girl, or child; a spotted mare; and the Mother of Christ.

6. Give the names of the 2 brothers who captained the *Niña* and the *Pinta* for Christopher Columbus.
ANSWER: Martin Alonzo Pinzón *(Pinta)* and Vicente Yáñez Pinzón *(Niña).*

7. In what 3 ways was Christopher Columbus like a politician?
ANSWER: He didn't know where he was going; when he got there he didn't know where he was; and when he got back he didn't know where he had been.

8. Between what 2 countries did the papal Line of Demarcation of 1493 divide the New World? Who set the boundary? What 2 treaties (in 1494 and 1529) changed the boundary?
ANSWER: Spain and Portugal (Spain was given the area 100 leagues west of the Azores and Cape Verde Islands, and Portugal, the area to the east)/Pope Alexander VI in his bull *Inter Caetera* of 1493/The Treaty of Tordesillas of 1494 changed the imaginary north-south line to 370 leagues west of the Cape Verde Islands, and the Treaty of Saragossa of 1529 changed the line to 297½ leagues east of the Moluccas (Spice Islands).

9. Identify the explorers by the following nicknames.

a) Admiral of the Ocean Sea	f) Father of Arctic Discovery
b) Pathfinder of the West	g) Knight in Buckskin
c) Terror of the Spanish Main	h) Dean of Polar Explorers
d) Shepherd of the Ocean	i) Father of New France
e) The Fair God (Quetzalcóatl)	j) The Red

ANSWER: a) Christopher Columbus b) John Charles Frémont c) Sir Francis Drake d) Sir Walter Raleigh e) Hernán Cortés f) John Davis g) Jedediah Strong Smith h) Nils Adolf Erik Nordenskiöld i) Samuel de Champlain j) Eric.

10. Give the 4 dates (years only) of the 4 voyages of Christopher Columbus.
ANSWER: 1492, 1493-1496, 1498, and 1502-1504.

11. What 3 men made the ''Big 3'' voyages during the years 1492-1522, and what 3 Italian artists produced masterpieces during those years?
ANSWER: Christopher Columbus, Vasco da Gama, and Ferdinand Magellan made the voyages while Leonardo da Vinci, Michelangelo, and Raphael produced the masterpieces.

12. Who were the men who captained the first Spanish, the first English, and the first French vessels to explore the New World? Who commanded the first Italian vessel to the New World?

ANSWER: Christopher Columbus for Spain, John Cabot for the English, and Giovanni da Verrazano for the French/No Italian vessels explored the New World.

13. What were the names of the first 5 European nations that were colonial empire builders?
ANSWER: Portugal, Spain, England, France, and the Netherlands.

14. Who suggested the name "America" and why did he do so?
ANSWER: Martin Waldseemüller (Waltzemüller), a Lorraine (German) geographer, suggested the name for the new continent (South America) be named after the discoverer Americus (Amerigo) Vespucci.

15. What were the names of Ferdinand Magellan's 5 ships that he assembled in 1519 for his voyage around the world? Which one was Magellan's flagship and which one finished the voyage? Name the commander who actually was the first to sail around the world. What verb means "to sail around the world?"
ANSWER: The *Trinidad*, the *San Antonio*, the *Concepción*, the *Victoria*, and the *Santiago*/The *Trinidad* and the *Victoria*/Juan Sebastián del Cano/"Circumnavigate."

16. What are the names of and locations for the 3 oldest universities in the New World which were chartered in 1538 and 1551, antedating Harvard by 98 years?
ANSWER: The University of Santo Domingo (1538) in the Dominican Republic; the University of San Marcos (1551) in Lima, Peru; and the University of Mexico (the Royal and Pontifical University, 1551) in Mexico City, Mexico (Harvard was founded in 1636).

17 Name the 2 most important works dealing with the sea that were written by English explorer John Davis.
ANSWER: *The Seaman's Secrets* (1594) and *The Worldes Hydrographical Description* (1595).

18. The expedition of what European explorer in the mid-16th century discovered such natural phenomena in the American Southwest as the Grand Canyon and herds of buffalo (bison)?
ANSWER: Francisco de Coronado.

19. What explorer is associated with the following descriptions?
a) Discovered Florida in 1513
b) Sailed the ocean blue in 1492
c) Discovered the Mississippi in 1541
d) Circumnavigated the globe in 1577-1580 in an English vessel
e) Rounded the Cape of Good Hope in 1488.
f) Discovered Gambia in 1795
g) Named the Sandwich (Hawaiian) Islands
h) Looked for the "7 golden cities of Cíbola" and explored the Southwest of United States in 1540-1542
i) Conquered Mexico in 1519-1521
j) Conquered the Inca Empire in 1533

ANSWER: a) Ponce de León b) Christopher Columbus c) Hernando de Soto d) Sir Francis Drake e) Bartholomeu Diaz f) Mungo Park g) James Cook h) Francisco de Coronado i) Hernán Cortés j) Francisco Pizarro.

20. By what names were the 3 French settlements (areas) in North America in the 16th century and later known?
ANSWER: Acadia (Nova Scotia; Atlantic coast possessions); New France (Canada); and the Louisiana Territory.

21. Name the 3 ships of Henry Hudson in his voyages to the New World in the 17th century.
ANSWER: The *Hopewell*, the *Half Moon*, and the *Discovery*.

22. What 3 geographical locations are named after Henry Hudson?
ANSWER: The Hudson Bay, the Hudson Strait, and the Hudson River.

23. Name the 2 areas named after English explorer William Baffin.
ANSWER: Baffin Bay and Baffin Island.

24. What were the 2 major voyages that opened up the Mississippi River in the 17th century? Who was the first European to discover and cross the Mississippi?
ANSWER: The Jolliet and Marquette expedition in 1673 and the explorations of Sieur

de la Salle in 1682/Hernando de Soto in 1541.

25. Who were the 8 Jesuit martyrs of North America? When were they canonized and what is their feast day? Among what group of Indians did they work and what group killed them?
ANSWER: Saints Jean de Brébeuf, Noël Chabanel, Antoine Daniel, Charles Garnier, Isaac Joques, Gabriel Lalemant, René Goupil, and Jean de Lalande (the last 2 were not Jesuit priests)/1930 and October 19/Huron Indians and the Iroquois.

26. Name the first 3 Europeans to land in Tahiti, and give the years of their landings.
ANSWER: Samuel Wallis in 1767, Louis Antoine de Bougainville in 1768, and Captain James Cook in 1769.

27. What were the 4 aptly named ships of the scientific explorations of the British explorer James Cook? What were the years of his 3 ''Great Voyages''?
ANSWER: The *Endeavour,* the *Resolution,* the *Adventure,* and the *Discovery* /1768-1771; 1772-1775; and 1776-1779.

28. Identify the explorers from the following descriptions.
a) Discovered the Pacific Ocean in 1513
b) Discovered New Caledonia in 1774
c) Completed the circumnavigation of the globe in the *Victoria* in 1522
d) Found David Livingstone in 1871
e) Discovered Victoria Falls in 1855
f) First European to reach India in 1498 by way of the Cape of Good Hope
g) First to reach the South Pole in 1911
h) First to fly over the North Pole in 1926
i) Discovered the St. Lawrence River in 1534
j) Founded the city of Quebec in 1608
ANSWER: a) Vasco Núñez de Balboa b) James Cook c) Juan del Cano d) Sir Henry Stanley e) David Livingstone f) Vasco da Gama g) Roald Amundsen h) Richard E. Byrd i) Jacques Cartier j) Samuel de Champlain.

29. What 2 men were involved in the expedition of 1804-1806 sent to explore the United States to the Pacific? What U.S. President was responsible for organizing this expedition? What 2 major rivers and 1 major mountain range were navigated and crossed along the way? Name the only fatality on this expedition. What was the name of the Indian interpreter and his wife with this group?
ANSWER: (Meriwether) Lewis and (William) Clark/President Thomas Jefferson/The Missouri and the Columbia Rivers and the Rocky Mountains/Sgt. Charles Floyd/Toussaint Charbonneau and Sacagawea (Sacajawea).

30. What were the 3 names given by Lewis and Clark to the 3 forks they encountered in the Missouri River?
ANSWER: The Jefferson, the Madison, and the Gallatin.

31. Name the last 3 rivers the Lewis and Clark expedition had to navigate in order to reach the Pacific.
ANSWER: The Clearwater, the Snake, and the Columbia Rivers.

32. In what city and state is Lewis and Clark College located?
ANSWER: Portland, Oregon.

33. Name the two 19th century explorers, one Scottish and the other Anglo-American, who were celebrated for their exploration of the interior of Africa.
ANSWER: David Livingstone and Sir Henry Morton Stanley.

34. With what explorers are the following ships associated?
a) *Trinidad, Concepción, Victoria*
b) *Gabriel, Michael, Aid*
c) *Matthew*
d) H.M.S. *Beagle*
e) *Judith, Pelican, Golden Hind*
f) *Endeavour, Resolution, Adventure, Discovery*
g) *La Dauphine*
h) *Fram, Gjøa, Norge* (a dirigible)
i) *Hopewell, Half Moon, Discovery*
j) *Roosevelt*
ANSWER: a) Ferdinand Magellan b) Sir Martin Frobisher c) John Cabot d) Charles Darwin e) Sir Francis Drake f) James Cook g) Giovanni da Verrazano h) Roald Amundsen i) Henry Hudson j) Robert E. Peary.

35. Between what countries did the Norwegian Thor Heyerdahl sail in 1947 aboard

the *Kon-Tiki?*

ANSWER: **He sailed from Peru to Polynesia in a balsa-wood raft that was lashed together with hemp rope.**

36. What country did Heyerdahl visit in 1955 which has statues between 10 and 37 feet high? What was the name of this island when James Cook visited there in 1774? What country annexed this island in 1888?

ANSWER: **Easter Island/Paaseiland/Chile.**

37. What was the name of the first Earth-orbiting satellite? When was it launched and by what country? Who was the first person to fly in the first manned orbital flight? Give the date and the aircraft. Who was the first female in an orbital flight? Give the date and the aircraft.

ANSWER: *Sputnik I*/**October 4, 1957, by the Soviet Union/Yuri A. Gagarin of the Soviet Union on April 12, 1961, in** *Vostok I*/**Valentina V. Tereshkova of the Soviet Union on June 16-19, 1963, in** *Vostok 6.*

38. Give the name of the first U.S. satellite program. What was the name of America's first satellite? In what year under which U.S. President was NASA, or the National Aeronautics and Space Administration, formed?

ANSWER: **Project Vanguard/***Explorer I*/**1958 under President Eisenhower.**

39. Name the first 3 U.S. manned space flight projects.

ANSWER: *Mercury, Gemini,* **and** *Apollo* **(followed by** *Skylab,* **a space station, and** *Space Shuttle,* **space craft and airplane).**

40. Who were the first 4 Americans in space (the first 2 were in suborbital flights and the second 2 were in orbital flights)? Give the dates of their flights and name their program and their aircraft.

ANSWER: **Alan B. Shepard, Jr. on May 5, 1961, in** *Mercury-Redstone* **3 -** *Freedom 7*

　　　Virgil I. Grissom on July 21, 1961, in *Mercury-Redstone* **4 -** *Liberty Bell 7*

　　　John H. Glenn, Jr. on Feb. 20, 1962, in *Mercury-Atlas* **6 -** *Friendship 7*

　　　M. Scott Carpenter on May 24, 1962, in *Mercury-Atlas 7 - Aurora 7*

41. What are the names of the first 4 manned American orbital spacecraft?

ANSWER: *Friendship 7* **(Glenn),** *Aurora 7* **(Carpenter),** *Sigma 7* **(Walter M. Schirra, Jr.), and** *Faith 7* **(Gordon Cooper).**

42. What are the 4 manned space flight programs of the Soviets?

ANSWER: *Vostok, Voskhod, Soyuz,* **and** *Salyut.*

43. Name the 7 unmanned planetary and lunar U.S. space programs.

ANSWER: *Ranger* **(Moon),** *Lunar Orbiter* **(Moon),** *Surveyor* **(Moon),** *Mariner* **(Mars, Venus, and Mercury),** *Pioneer* **(most of the planets),** *Viking* **(Mars), and** *Voyager* **(Jupiter, Saturn, Uranus, and Neptune).**

44. Name the 4 unmanned planetary and lunar programs of the Soviets.

ANSWER: *Luna, Mars, Venera,* **and** *Zond.*

45. What are the names of the original 7 U.S. astronauts of Project *Mercury?*

ANSWER: **Malcolm Scott Carpenter, Leroy Gordon Cooper, Jr., John Herschel Glenn, Virgil I. Grissom, Walter M. Schirra, Alan B. Shepard, Jr., and Donald K. Slayton.**

46. Name the 3 astronauts who died together on duty when their *Apollo* space capsule burned in a flash fire in 1967.

ANSWER: **Virgil I. Grissom, Roger Chaffee, and Edward H. White.**

47. What was the name of the spacecraft that took 3 men on the first manned voyage around the Moon, December 21-28, 1968? Name the 3 astronauts involved. What was the name of the spacecraft that took 3 astronauts to the Moon for the first landing there via the Lunar Module on July 20, 1969? Name the 3 astronauts involved.

ANSWER: *Apollo 8*/**Frank Borman, James A. Lovell, Jr. and William A. Anders/** *Apollo 11*/**Edwin E. Aldrin, Jr., Neil A. Armstrong, and Michael Collins**

(Armstrong was the first to walk on the Moon, followed by Aldrin).

48. What were the names of the 2 reed boats Thor Heyerdahl built in 1970 and sailed across the Atlantic proving that the Egyptians could have done the same thing? Between what countries did these 2 expeditions sail?
ANSWER: The *Ra I* and the *Ra II*/From Morocco to the West Indies.

49. In 1977 what was the path of Heyerdahl's ship the *Tigris?*
ANSWER: From the mouth of the Tigris River through the Persian Gulf to the Indus Valley of Pakistan.

50. Name the 3 main technological innovations of Jacques Cousteau.
ANSWER: The aqualung, the bathyscaphe, and underwater photography.

51. Name the astronauts involved in the following Moon flights.
a) *Apollo 12* - Nov., 1969   d) *Apollo 16* - April, 1972
b) *Apollo 14* - Jan.-Feb., 1971   e) *Apollo 17* - Dec., 1972
c) *Apollo 15* - July-Aug., 1971
ANSWER: a) Alan L. Bean, Charles Conrad, Jr., and Richard F. Gordon, Jr. b) Edgar D. Mitchell, Stuart A. Roosa, and Alan B. Shepard, Jr. c) James B. Irwin, David R. Scott, and Alfred M. Worden d) Charles M. Duke, Jr., Thomas K. Mattingly II, and John W. Young e) Eugene A. Cernan, Ronald E. Evans, and Harrison H. Schmitt.

52. Name the astronauts who participated in the 3 manned *Skylab* expeditions listed below.
a) May-June, 1973   c) November, 1973-February, 1974
b) July-September, 1973
ANSWER: a) Charles Conrad, Jr., Joseph P. Kerwin, and Paul J. Weitz b) Alan L. Bean, Owen K. Garriott, and Jack R. Lousma c) Gerald Carr, Edward Gibson, and William Pogue.

53. What 3 astronauts manned the *Apollo 18,* the last manned spaceflight of the Apollo Project? With what spacecraft did they dock? What was the nickname of this space flight?
ANSWER: Vance D. Brand, Donald K. Slayton, and Thomas P. Stafford (the flight was in July, 1975)/The Soviet *Soyuz 19*/"Handshake in Space."

54. There are 5 U.S. space shuttles; the first shuttle was a trainer but the other 4 will go or have gone into orbit. Name the 5 in order.
ANSWER: *Enterprise* (trainer), *Columbia, Challenger, Discovery,* and *Atlantis.*

55. Give the date of the first U.S. space shuttle launch, and list the 8 astronauts who flew in the first 4 *Columbia* missions. Where did the first 2 flights land, and where did the 3rd do so? What was different about the landing of the 4th shuttle flight?
ANSWER: April 12, 1981/Robert L. Crippen and John W. Young; Joe H. Engle and Richard H. Truly; Gordon Fullerton and Jack R. Lousma; and Ken Mattingly and Henry Hartsfield/The first two at Edwards Air Force Base in the Mojave Desert in California, and the 3rd at the White Sands Proving Ground in White Sands, New Mexico/It landed on a concrete runway (Runway 22) at Edwards Air Force Base instead of on the sand.

56. Name the first Western European to fly into space, and give his nationality. With what Soviet spacemen aboard what Soviet spacecraft did he do so?
ANSWER: Jean-Loup Chrétien from France went into orbit with the Soviet's Vladimir Dzhanibekov and Alexander Ivanchenkov aboard a *Soyuz T-6* spacecraft which docked with the *Salyut-7* space station.

57. Valentina Tereshkova became the first woman in space in 1963. What Russian woman in August, 1982, became the 2nd woman in space? Name the pilot and the flight engineer aboard the *Soyuz T-7* spacecraft that took her into space.
ANSWER: Svetlana Savitskaya/Leonid Popov was the pilot and Alexander Serebrov was the flight engineer.

58. Name the 2 Englishmen who from 1979 to 1982 completed a 35,000-mile trip

around the world via the North and South Poles. What was the name of their ship?
ANSWER: Sir Ranulph Fiennes and Charles Burton/*Benjamin Bowring.*

59. *Voyager 2* flew past Saturn in August, 1981. What planet will it fly by in 1986 and what planet in 1989?
ANSWER: Uranus in 1986 and Neptune in 1989.

60. What America space projects do the following represent?

a) S.M.M.   c) HEAO   e) OGO   g) SAS
b) OSO   d) OAO   f) ATS

ANSWER: a) Solar Maximum Mission b) Orbiting Solar Observatory c) High Energy Astronomy Observatory d) Orbiting Astronomical Observatory e) Orbiting Geophysical Observatory f) Applications Technology Satellite g) Small Astronomy Satellite.

61. The November, 1982, voyage of the 5th space shuttle mission included a record number of 4 astronauts. Name the 4 members of the crew. Name the 2 companies whose communications satellites were placed in orbit. What was the motto of the mission?
ANSWER: Vance D. Brand, commander; Col. Robert F. Overmyer; Dr. William B. Lenoir; and Dr. Joseph P. Allen/Satellite Business Systems and Telesat of Canada/"We deliver."

62. Paul Weitz, Karol Bobko, Story Musgrave, and Donald Peterson were the astronauts on the 6th space mission in April, 1983. Identify their space shuttle, which was named after a pioneering 19th century oceanographic ship. What did Peterson and Musgrave do that had not been done since the Skylab mission in 1974? This 6th space mission failed to place the TDRS into the correct orbit (since corrected). What is the meaning of TDRS?
ANSWER: *Challenger*/Walked in space/Tracking and Data Relay Satellite.

63. How many members - the largest crew at that time launched in any space vehicle -were on the 7th shuttle mission? Name the space ship. What is the name of the first American woman in space who was on this flight? Name any of the 4 men in the crew.
ANSWER: 5/*Challenger*/Sally Ride (Hawley)/Robert Crippen, Norm Thagard, John Fabian, and Rick Hauck.

64. Guion S. Bluford, Richard H. Truly, Daniel C. Brandenstein, Dale A. Gardner, and William F. Thornton were the 5 astronauts on the 8th shuttle mission in *Challenger.* Which one is the first black American astronaut, and which one is the oldest astronaut ever in space? What was unusual about the lift-off time? When and on what mission was there a similar lift-off time? For which country was a satellite put into orbit on this shuttle mission?
ANSWER: Bluford and Thornton/At 2:32 a.m., making it the first nighttime space shuttle luanch/December 7, 1972, on *Apollo 17*/India (INSAT, India National Satellite).

65. John Young, Brewster Shaw, Owen Garriott, Byron Lichtenberg, Ulf Merbold, and Robert Parker comprised the crew - the largest one to date - of the 9th shuttle flight. Name this space ship that flew the longest shuttle journey. Name the area on the ship that is a billion-dollar scientific research station. Which crew member flew on his 5th space flight, and which crew member was the first non-American astronaut?
ANSWER: *Columbia*/Spacelab/John Young/Ulf Merbold (from West Germany).

66. Vance D. Brand, Robert L. Gibson, Bruce McCandless, Robert Stewart, and Ronald E. McNair comprised the crew of the 10th shuttle mission in February, 1984. Name the space ship on this mission. Which 2 astronauts made the first untethered space walks? Because of these spacewalks with $10 million computerized backpacks, what nickname did this space flight receive? At which space center was a landing made for the first time? Which astronaut became the second black to fly on an American spaceship? Name the 2 communications satellites that failed to go into the correct orbit.
ANSWER: *Challenger*/Bruce McCandless (first) and Robert Stewart/"Buck Rogers

Flight'' (Rogers used a belt made of invertron)/Kennedy Space Center/Ronald E. McNair/Western Union's Westar VI/Indonesia's Palapa-B2.

67. Who said, ''That may have been one small step for Neil, but it's a heck of a big leap for me''? Who was the first man to ''walk'' in space? Who was the first American to ''walk'' in space? What are the meanings of EVA and MMU?

ANSWER: Bruce McCandless/Aleksei Leonov (Russian) aboard *Voskhod 2* (1965)/Ed White aboard *Gemini IV* (3 months later in 1965)/ExtraVehicular Activity and Manned Maneuvering Unit.

68. Name the first cosmonaut from India who was aboard a Soviet space flight in April, 1984. What did he perform in space as a possible solution to space sickness?

ANSWER: Rakesh Sharma/Yoga.

69. Robert Crippen (his 3rd mission), George ''Pinky'' Nelson, James ''Ox'' van Hoften, Terry Hart, and Dick Scobee comprised the crew of the 11th shuttle mission in April, 1984. Name the space ship on this mission. What was the name of the satellite this mission repaired on this historic flight? What logo did this crew sport on their T shirts? Identify the acronym LDEF, the label for the package of 57 scientific experiments left in space. What does TPAD mean? What is the meaning of WOW WONG as used in reference to a shuttle landing?

ANSWER: *Challenger*/Solar Maximum Mission (Solar Max)/Ace Satellite Repair Co. (''We pick up, repair, and deliver'' - Crippen)/Long-duration Exposure Facility/Trunnion Pin Attachment Device/Weight On Wheels, Weight on Nose Gear.

EXPLORERS: NORTH AMERICA, THE ARCTIC, AND THE ANTARCTIC

Saint Brendan....Irish.... Some believe he may have been the first discoverer of America (in the 6th century A.D.).

Eric the Red (Erik Thorvaldsson)....Norwegian.... He colonized Greenland about A.D. 985.

Leif Ericsson (Leif Eriksson)....Norwegian.... He explored Vinland (Wineland) in North America about A.D. 1000, and he may have sailed to Labrador and Newfoundland.

Christopher Columbus (Christoforo Colombo-Cristóbal Colón)....Italian.... He sailed for King Ferdinand and Queen Isabella of Spain and discovered America in 1492, on October 12. He landed on an island he named San Salvador (called Watlings Island today) in the Bahamas. He also landed on Cuba and Hispaniola in the Caribbean. On his second voyage in 1493 he landed on Dominica and passed by Guadeloupe, Puerto Rico, and the Virgin Islands. He visited Venezuela in 1498, and Honduras in 1502.

John Cabot (Giovanni Caboto)....Italian.... He skirted the New World for Henry VII of England in 1497-1498 in his ship the *Matthew*, and he possibly landed on Cape Breton Island, Newfoundland, or in Maine.

Juan Ponce de León....Spanish.... He settled Puerto Rico and discovered Florida in 1513 while looking for the Fountain of Youth on Bimini Island. He named the land *la florida* because it was Easter Sunday and because of the abundance of flowers.

Diego Velásquez....Spanish.... He conquered Cuba in 1511, and founded Santiago (1514) and Havana (1515).

Giovanni da Verrazano (Verrazzano)....Italian.... In 1524 aboard *La Dauphine* he set out to explore the New World for Francis I of France. He discovered the New York and the Narragansett Bays, and the Verrazano-Narrows Bridge across the New York Bay is named after him. He explored the North American coast to North Carolina.

Jacques Cartier....French.... He discovered Prince Edward Island and the St. Lawrence River as far as Quebec and Montreal (1534-1536).

Álvar Núñez Cabeza de Vaca....Spanish.... He explored the Texas coast and the interior of the area in 1536.

Hernando de Soto....Spanish.... He was sent by Charles I to explore the New World during the years 1538-1542. He explored the southern part of the United States and discovered the Mississippi River (in 1541).

Francisco Vásquez de Coronado....Spanish.... From 1540 to 1542 he explored the Southwest of the United States, especially looking for the ''7 golden cities of Cíbola'' and the wealthy cities of *Gran Quivira*.

Hernando de Alarcón....Spanish.... He explored the southwestern United States and discovered the Colorado River in 1540.

Sir Martin Frobisher....English.... He discovered Frobisher Bay in 1576 and Resolution Island in 1578. His 3 voyages were made in the *Gabriel*, the *Michael*, and the *Aid*.

Sir Humphrey Gilbert....English.... He established the first English colony in North America at St. John's Bay, Newfoundland, in 1583.

John Davis....English.... He discovered Davis Strait (between Greenland and Baffin Island) and Cumberland Sound during the years 1585-1587. He also discovered the Falkland Islands in 1592. Three of his expeditions were aboard the ship *Desire*. He is called the "Father of Arctic Discovery."

Willem Barents....Dutch.... He explored the Arctic and discovered Barents Island and Spitsbergen in 1596. His 3 voyages to the Arctic were made between 1594 and 1596. Barents Sea was also named after him.

Samuel de Champlain....French.... He is the "Father of New France (Canada)." He founded the city of Quebec in 1608 and discovered the Ottawa River and the Lakes Champlain (1609), Ontario, and Huron. He did most of his exploring from 1603 to 1609. He visited the Maine coast in 1604.

John Smith....English.... He was a founder of Virginia and the founder and savior of the colony of Jamestown in 1607. This was the first permanent English colony in North America. He was possibly saved from death by Pocahontas, daughter of Chief Powhatan.

Henry Hudson....English.... He made 4 voyages from 1607 to 1610, during which time he explored the Arctic for the Dutch, while sailing under an English flag. He had the Hudson River, the Hudson Bay, and the Hudson Strait named after him. His ships were the *Hopewell*, the *Half Moon*, and the *Discovery*.

William Baffin....English.... From 1613 to 1616, he explored the Arctic and discovered Baffin Island and Baffin Bay in 1616.

Jean Nicolet....French.... He was the first white man to explore Mackinac Island, Green Bay, and Lake Michigan (1634).

Pierre Esprit Radisson....Canadian (b. France).... His exploration (along with Médard Chouart, Sieur des Groseilliers) of Lake Superior and other areas in 1660 inspired the formation of the Hudson's Bay Company in London in 1670.

Louis Jolliet (Joliet)....French–Canadian.... In 1673, he explored and charted the Mississippi River with the Jesuit missionary, Father Jacques Marquette. They reached the Arkansas River and went no farther but ascertained that the Mississippi emptied into the Gulf of Mexico.

Jacques Marquette....French.... He explored and charted the Mississippi River with Louis Jolliet in 1673. They went as far as the Arkansas River.

Jean Louis Hennepin....Flemish.... From 1678-1680, he explored the Midwest and upper Mississippi River region and discovered and named St. Anthony's Falls.

René Robert Cavelier Sieur de La Salle....French.... In 1679 on the sailing ship *Le Griffon*, he was the first to cross the Great Lakes. He was also the first to navigate the Mississippi to its mouth (1682), and he named the Mississippi Valley region Louisiana after Louis XIV.

Antoine Laumet de la Mothe Cadillac....French.... He explored the Michigan area and founded Detroit in 1701.

Sieur de La Vérendrye (Pierre Gaultier de Varennes)....French-Canadian.... From 1731 to 1743, he expanded New France's influence in present-day western Ontario and Manitoba. He discovered Lake Manitoba in 1739.

Vitus Jonassen Bering....Danish.... He explored the northeastern coast of Asia for Czar Peter I of Russia in 1725. During his other explorations from 1728-1742, he discovered Alaska (1741). The strait between Siberia and Alaska was named the Bering Strait after him. Two of his ships were named *St. Peter* and *St. Paul*.

Daniel Boone....American.... He explored Kentucky in 1767 and 1769, and he opened up the Wilderness Road in 1775.

Robert Gray....American.... He was the first to sail around the world under the American flag (1787-1790), and he named the Columbia River after his ship.

Sir Alexander Mackenzie....Scottish-Canadian.... He discovered the Mackenzie River in 1789, and in 1793, he became the first European to cross North America overland to the Pacific north of Mexico.

Meriwether Lewis....American.... He was asked by Thomas Jefferson to lead an expedition to explore the United States to the Pacific, and he did so from 1804 to 1806 with William Clark. They went northwest from St. Louis by navigating the Missouri, Clearwater, Snake, and Columbia Rivers.

William Clark....American.... He explored the United States to the Pacific with Meriwether Lewis on the Lewis and Clark expedition (1804-1806).

Zebulon Montgomery Pike....American.... He explored the American Southwest in 1806, and he unsuccessfully tried to climb the peak that was later named for him.

Nathaniel Brown Palmer....American.... His ship was the *Hero*, and he was the first man to see the continent of Antarctica (1820). The Palmer Peninsula and the Palmer Archipelago were named after him.

Sir John Franklin....English.... From 1819 to 1827, he explored northern Canada to the Arctic. From 1845 to 1847, he commanded the expedition with the ships *Erebus* and *Terror*, looking for the Northwest Passage. Franklin, along with the entire crew perished.

Jedediah Strong Smith....American.... He was the first white man to cross the Great Salt Lake Desert and the Sierra Nevada (1826-1827).

Charles Wilkes....American.... He explored the Antarctica and the Pacific Islands from 1838 to 1842. Wilkes Land bears his name.

John Charles Frémont....American.... He was nicknamed "the Pathfinder" because of his western explorations. Frémont Peak, named after him, is located in Wyoming.

Kit Carson....American.... He was a frontiersman from 1829 to 1845. From 1842 to 1845, he explored the west as a scout and adviser for John Frémont.

Nils Adolf Erick Nordenskiöld....Swedish.... He was the first to navigate the Northeast Passage (the Arctic Ocean from Europe to the Pacific) in 1878 to 1880 aboard the *Vega*.

Robert Edwin Peary....American.... He discovered the North Pole on April 6, 1909, along with Matthew Henson and four eskimos. His ship was the *Roosevelt*. He also proved that Greenland was an island (1891).

Roald Englebregt Gravning Amundsen....Norwegian.... He was the first to reach the South Pole (1911). His ship was the *Fram*. He was also the first to navigate the Northwest Passage from east to west. He did so aboard the *Gjøa* from 1903 to 1906. He flew over the North Pole in the dirigible the *Norge*.

Richard Evelyn Byrd....American.... He was the first man to fly over the North Pole (1926, aboard the *Josephine Ford*) and the South Pole (1929, aboard the *Floyd Bennett*). He led five expeditions to explore the Antarctica from 1928 to 1956. His base camp was called Little America.

NICKNAMES

Eric (Thorwaldson)	the Red
Leif Ericson	Leif the Lucky
Christopher Columbus	Admiral of the Mosquitos, (Lord) Admiral of the Ocean Sea, Captain General of the Armada
Alvar Núñez Cabeza de Vaca	Cow's Head
John Davis	Father of Arctic Discovery
Samuel de Champlain	Father of New France, Founder of Canada
Jacques Marquette	Père Marquette
Daniel Boone	Sheltowee ("Big Turtle")
Meriwether Lewis	Long Knife, Sublime Dandy
Sacajawea (Sacagawea)	Bird Woman
Jedediah Strong Smith	Knight in Buckskin, Splendid Wayfarer
John Charles Frémont	(Great) Pathfinder, Pathfinder of the West
Nils Adolf Erik Nordenskiöld	Dean of Polar Explorers
Marie Ahnighito Peary (daughter of Robert E. Peary)	Snow Baby

Columbus's project of sailing to
the Orient. . . . . Enterprise of the Indies
St. Lawrence River . . . . La Grande Rivière
Missouri River . . . . Big Muddy
Fur traders and trappers . . . . *coureurs de bois* (runners of the woods)
Mississippi River . . . . Great River
Mackenzie River . . . . River of Disappointment (according to Sir
                                                      Alexander Mackenzie)
Mojave River . . . . The Inconstant
Walruses . . . . Sea horses
Atlantic Ocean . . . . Ocean Sea, Sea of Darkness
Hudson Strait . . . . Mistaken Straits
Yellowstone National Park . . . . Colter's Hell
Guns . . . . Lightning sticks (according to the Indians)
Detroit . . . . City of Straits
England . . . . Mistress of the Seas (after the 1588 defeat
                                                      of the Spanish Armada)

FAMOUS PAIRS

John Smith . . . . Pocahontas
Pocahontas . . . . John Rolfe
Louis Jolliet . . . . Jacques Marquette
Daniel Boone . . . . Rebecca (Bryan)
Meriwether Lewis . . . . William Clark
Lewis and Clark Expedition . . . . Sacajawea
Sacajawea . . . . Toussaint Charbonneau
Sir John Franklin . . . . Lady Franklin
John Frémont . . . . Jessie Benton
Robert Edwin Peary . . . . Josephine Peary

NAMES FROM THE PAST AND CURRENT NAMES

La Isla Española (the Spanish Island) . . . . Hispaniola
Guanahani-San Salvador . . . . Watlings Island (also called San Salvador)
San Juan de Borinquen . . . . Puerto Rico
Rio del Espíritu Santo
(River of the Holy Spirit) . . . . Mississippi River
New France . . . . Canada
Francesca . . . . North American coast named for Francis I
Stadacona . . . . Quebec City
San Miguel . . . . San Diego
New Albion . . . . Pacific Northwest (especially California)
Hochelaga . . . . Montreal

EXPLORERS: SOUTH AND CENTRAL AMERICA

Alonso de Ojeda....Spanish.... He explored the northeastern coast of South America in 1499 and the Gulf of Darien in 1505.

Vicente Yáñez Pinzón....Spanish.... He may have discovered Brazil, January 20-26, 1500.

Pedro Álvares Cabral....Portuguese.... He ostensibly set sail for India and landed in Brazil, April 22, 1500. He is called the discoverer of Brazil, although this title may properly belong to Vicente Yáñez Pinzón.

Amerigo Vespucci....Italian.... He may have discovered South America, but whether he did or not, he did have 'America' named after him by Martin Waldseemüller. (America was originally applied to South America, later to North America). His discovery was in 1499-1500. He may have discovered the Rio de la Plata in 1501-1502.

Vasco Núñez de Balboa....Spanish.... He discovered the Pacific Ocean in 1513 near Panama. Balboa named it the ''South Sea,'' a name later changed to the ''Pacific

Ocean'' by Magellan because of its peaceful nature.

Juan Diaz de Solís....Spanish.... He explored the coasts of Latin America in 1506-1508, and explored the Rio de la Plata and Uruguay in 1515-1516.

Hernán (Hernando) Cortés (Cortez)....Spanish.... He held the Emperor Montezuma II hostage and took Emperor Cuauhtémoc (Guatemotzin), the last Aztec emperor, prisoner in his conquest of Mexico (1519-1521). He discovered Lower California in 1536.

Ferdinand Magellan (Fernão de Magalhães-Fernando de Magallanes)....Portuguese.... He led the first circumnavigation of the globe, and he made the first known crossing of the Pacific (1519-1522). His ship was the *Trinidad*. He died in the Philippines in 1521. Juan Sebastian del Cano completed the circumnavigation of the globe in the ship *Victoria*. The Strait of Magellan in South America is named after him.

Francisco Pizarro....Spanish.... He defeated Atahualpa, the last independent ruler of the Inca empire, and conquered the Inca empire in Peru in 1532-1533. He also founded a new capital at Lima in 1535.

Sebastian Cabot....Italian.... He is the son of John Cabot. He explored the Rio de la Plata estuary and other South American areas from 1526 to 1530.

Francisco de Orellana....Spanish.... He explored the Napo and Amazon Rivers and he was the first man to explore and navigate the entire length of the Amazon (1541-1542).

Pedro de Valdivia....Spanish.... He conquered Chile in 1540-1541 and founded Santiago. He founded Concepción in 1550, and Valdivia in 1552.

Sir Walter Raleigh....English.... He explored the Orinoco River and the interior of Guiana in 1595.

Willem Cornelis Schouten....Dutch.... He discovered Cape Horn and proved that Tierra del Fuego was an island (1615-1616). He also explored New Guinea.

NICKNAMES

Hernán Cortés . . . . The Fair God (or Quetzalcóatl) (called that by Montezuma II)
Sir Walter Raleigh . . . . Shepherd of the Ocean
El Dorado . . . . The Gilded (Golden) One
Patagonia (South Argentina and
South Chile). . . . . Land of the Big-footed Ones
Asuncion . . . . Mohammed's Paradise
Peru. . . . . Land of Cinnamon
Lima, Peru. . . . . City of Kings
Amazon River . . . . El Mar Ducle (''Gentle Sea'')
Venezuela . . . . Little Venice

FAMOUS PAIRS

Hernán Cortés . . . . Malinche (Doña Marina)
Sir Walter Raleigh . . . . Elizabeth Throgmorton

NAMES FROM THE PAST AND CURRENT NAMES

Great South Sea . . . . Pacific Ocean
Tenochtitlán. . . . . Mexico City
Kingdom of Quito . . . . Ecuador
Makanon/''Freshwater Sea'' . . . . Rio de la Plata
Las Hibueras . . . . Honduras
Darien . . . . Panama
Falkland Islands . . . . *Islas Malvinas* (to the Argentineans)
Islas Malvinas . . . . Falkland Islands (to the British)
Isla Sancta **(Holy Island).** . . . . South America

EXPLORERS: OTHER PARTS OF THE WORLD

Hanno....Carthaginian.... He explored the west coast of Africa and especially Sierra Leone about 500 B.C.

Pytheas....Greek.... In the 4th century B.C., he explored Britain and northern Europe.

Nearchus...Greek.... He discovered the mouth of the Tigris and Euphrates Rivers about 325-324 B.C.

Alexander the Great....Greek.... In 327 B.C., he crossed the Hindu Kush and visited Punjab (India).

Giovanni de Piano (John of Plano) Carpini....Italian.... From 1245 to 1246 A.D., he traveled north of the Caspian Sea to Karakorum in Mongolia.

Marco Polo....Venetian.... He visited China from 1271 to 1295, and he served Kublai Khan for 17 years. He was the first European to cross all of Asia.

Prince Henry "the Navigator"....Portuguese.... The Great Age of Discovery dates from 1415, when Henry led the expedition that conquered Ceuta, a Muslim stronghold in Morocco. This event marked the start of Portugese overseas expansion. Henry sent others to explore the Atlantic to the west and he sought to locate Prester John, a legendary priest-king of Africa.

Diogo Cam (Cão)....Portugese.... He was the first European to explore the Congo River and discover its mouth (about 1483).

Bartholomeu (Bartholomew) Diaz (Dias)....Portuguese.... He was sent by John II of Portugal to explore the African coast and find an ocean route to India. He rounded the Cape of Good Hope in 1488.

Vasco da Gama....Portuguese.... He was sent by Manuel II of Portugal to India by way of the Cape of Good Hope. He was the first to reach India (in 1498). He was made Viceroy of India in 1524, and he was the first person to govern a European empire in Asia.

Richard Chancellor....English.... His pioneering in 1553-1554 established the first trade between Russia and England through the English Muscovy Company (1555).

Sir Francis Drake....English.... He was the first Englishman to circumnavigate the globe (1577-1580), but he was notorious for plundering Spanish towns and ships. He was the first English commander to see the Pacific. His first ship was the *Judith*. A later flagship was the *Pelican,* subsequently named the *Golden Hind.*

Pedro Fernández de Queirós (Quirós)....Portuguese.... He was working for Spain when he discovered the New Hebrides and other islands in the South Pacific in 1606-1607.

Abel Janszoon Tasman....Dutch.... He discovered Tasmania, New Zealand, Tonga, and the Fiji Islands in 1642-1643.

Semyon Ivanovich Dezhnev (Dezhnez)....Russian.... He explored Siberia starting about 1641 and became the first European to prove the separation of Asia and North America. Cape Dezhnev, on the northeastern tip of Asia, was named after him.

James Cook....English.... He was the first explorer to navigate the world from west to east, and he is especially noted for using new technology, including a diet plan to avoid scurvy and a chronometer to measure longitude. He discovered New Caledonia and Norfolk Island in 1774. He also discovered Christmas Island (1777) and named the Sandwich (Hawaiian) Islands. He colonized Australia and New Zealand in 1769, and crossed the Antarctic Circle in 1773. He made three voyages from 1768 to 1780, and his four ships were the *Endeavour*, the *Resolution*, the *Adventure*, and the *Discovery.*

Louis-Antoine de Bougainville....French.... He was the first Frenchman to circumnavigate the world (from 1766-1769). His ships were *La Boudeuse* and *L'Etoile.* The plant *bougainvillea* was named after him.

James Bruce....Scottish.... He rediscovered the source of the Blue Nile in 1770.

Mungo Park....Scottish.... He explored the Gambia River in 1795.

Charles Robert Darwin....English.... He traveled aboard the H.M.S. *Beagle* from 1831 to 1836, and later developed his theory of evolution through natural selection. He wrote *On the Origin of Species by Means of Natural Selection* (1859).

Richard Lemon Lander....English.... He explored the lower part of the Niger River in 1830-1831.

David Livingstone....Scottish.... He opened Africa to the West by crossing the Kalahari Desert and exploring the interior of Africa. He discovered and named Victoria Falls.

Sir Richard Francis Burton....English.... He discovered Lake Tanganyika in 1858.

John Hanning Speke....English.... He was the first European to reach Lake Victoria.

Sir Henry Morton Stanley....English-American (Born John Rowlands).... He found David Livingstone in 1871 at Ujiji on the shores of Lake Tangangyika and greeted him with the words: "Dr. Livingstone, I presume?" He was the first to trace the Congo River to its mouth.

NICKNAMES

Marco Polo........................ Il Milione (one who talks in millions)
Sir Francis Drake................... The Dragon, Prince of Buccaneers, Terror of the Spanish Main
James Cook........................ Captain Cook, Great Circumnavigator, Greatest Explorer of the 18th Century
Charles Darwin .... Great Naturalist
Henry Morton Stanley .... Bula Matari ("Rock Breaker")
World of the ancient Greeks and Romans .... Ancient world
Africa.............................. Dark Continent, *Terra Incognita,* White Man's Grave
Zambezi River .... God's Highway
Pamir Knot (Asia)................... Roof of the World

NAMES FROM THE PAST AND CURRENT NAMES

Indies .... Asia
Punjab............................ India
Cipangu........................... Japan
Cathay............................ China
Ch'i, Yen, Yuchow, Nanching (Nanking), Yenching (Yenking), Chungtu, Khanbalik (Cambaluc to Marco Polo), Tatu, Peiping, Peiching (Peking) .... Peiking
Mare Nostrum **(Our Sea — according to the Romans)** .... Mediterranean Sea
Armorican Peninsula .... Brittany
Bagamogo .... Tanzania
Gran Canaria .... Great Canary Island
Abyssinia.......................... Ethiopia
Cape of Storms *(Cabo Tormentoso)*... Cape of Good Hope
Thule (Ultima Thule) .... Iceland or Norway — "Farthest (northernmost) point of the known world"
Magna Graecia.................... Southern Italy
Massilia........................... Marseille, France
Land of Punt .... Somaliland
Iol Caesarea...................... Cherchell, Algeria
Espíritu Santo **Island**............... New Hebrides
Unknown Southern Land *(Terra Australis Incognita)*............... Australia or Antarctica
Great South Land, New South Wales ..... Australia
Van Diemen's Land .... Tasmania
Staten Landt .... New Zealand
Sandwich Islands .... Hawaiian Islands
Gold Coast........................ Ghana

QUESTIONS AND ANSWERS

1. Name the 9 wars in which the United States has participated. Which 2 are technically conflicts?
ANSWER: **The Revolutionary War, the War of 1812, the Mexican War, the Civil War, the Spanish-American War, World War I, World War II, the Korean War, and the Vietnam War/Korea and Vietnam.**

2. What were the major territorial expansions of the United States in the years: 1783, 1803, 1819, 1845, 1846, 1848, 1853, 1867 (2), 1898 (4), 1899 (2), 1903, 1916, and 1947?
ANSWER: **1783—U.S. boundaries to the Mississippi, to the Great Lakes and to Spanish Florida by the Treaty of Paris/1803—the Louisiana Purchase from France/ 1819—the Floridas by the Treaty with Spain/1845—Texas through annexation /1846—the Oregon Territory through the Treaty with Great Britain/1848—the Mexican Cession in the Treaty of Guadalupe Hidalgo/ 1853—the Gadsden Purchase from Mexico/1867—the Purchase of Alaska from the Russians and Midway Island by occupation / 1898—the Hawaiian Islands by annexation; the Philippine Islands, Puerto Rico, and Guam by conquest from Spain/1899—Wake Island by occupation and American Samoa by division with Germany and Great Britain/1903—the Panama Canal Zone by Treaty with Panama/1916—the Virgin Islands by purchase from Denmark/1947—the Trust Territories of the Pacific Islands.**

3. What states make up what was formerly called the Northwest Territory?
ANSWER: **Ohio, Indiana, Illinois, Michigan, Wisconsin, and parts of Minnesota.**

4. Joel Garreau wrote a book called *The Nine Nations of North America*. What are the names of Joel Garreau's 9 nations?
ANSWER: **The Empty Quarter; Ectopia; Breadbasket; Mexamerica; Quebec; New England; The Foundry; Dixie; and The Islands.**

5. Which hero of an important battle in the American Revolution has been honored with a statue that does not bear his name? Name the battle or the site.
ANSWER: **Benedict Arnold/Second Battle of Freeman's Farm on Bemis Heights or Saratoga on October 7, 1777.**

6. Give the names of the 4 American Revolutionary leaders honored with a niche in a monument commemorating the Battle of Saratoga in 1777.
ANSWER: **Horatio Gates, Philip Schuyler, Daniel Morgan, and Benedict Arnold.**

7. Name the American athlete who upset Hitler's ''Aryan'' theories at the 1936 Olympic Games held in Berlin, Germany, in 1936, and name the 4 events he won.
ANSWER: **Jesse Owens/100 meters, 200 meters, long jump, and as a member of the 4 X 100-meter relay team.**

8. What are the names of the 3 main hills in Boston?
ANSWER: **Beacon, Breeds, and Bunker.**

9. Name the top 3 coal mining states in the U.S.
ANSWER: **Kentucky, West Virginia, and Pennsylvania.**

10. What is the name of the first permanent English settlement in North America?
ANSWER: **Jamestown, Virginia, in 1607.**

11. Name the founder of the American Nazi Party.
ANSWER: **George Lincoln Rockwell.**

12. Name the person who leaked the Pentagon Papers and the newspaper that began publishing them on June 13, 1971.
ANSWER: **Daniel Ellsberg, former Deputy Secretary of Defense/*New York Times*.**

13. Who were ''The Big 3'' during World War II?
ANSWER: **Franklin D. Roosevelt, Winston Churchill, and Joseph Stalin.**

14. Name the first American to become the official world chess champion, the year in which he accomplished this feat, and the defending champion he defeated.
ANSWER: **Bobby Fischer/1972/Boris Spassky (of Russia).**

15. In what 3 fields are the Pulitzer Prizes awarded?
ANSWER: Journalism, literature, and music.

16. What were the 4 essentials (all beginning with the letter ''B'') needed for a prospector's success in the Old West?
ANSWER: Brains, Brawn, Burros, and Beans.

17. What were the names of the 2 infantrymen made popular by cartoonist Bill Mauldin during World War II?
ANSWER: Willie and Joe.

18. Name the 2 semi-public/private — but U.S. government financed — railroads.
ANSWER: Amtrak (*American, travel, track*) and Conrail (*Consolidated Rail Corp.*).

19. ''You can't keep a man in the ditch unless you are willing to stay in it with him.'' Who said this, and of what institute was he the founder and president?
ANSWER: Booker T. Washington/Tuskegee Institute (1881-1915).

20. Whose nickname was ''Billy the Kid'' and what sheriff shot him?
ANSWER: William H. Bonney (real name was Henry McCarty)/Was shot by Pat Garrett.

21. In what year did Attorney General Charles J. Bonaparte establish the Bureau of Investigation at the urging of Theodore Roosevelt? Who became the first head of the FBI? Give the year. There have been but 4 heads of the FBI. Name the other 3. Where is the FBI National Academy located?
ANSWER: 1908/J. Edgar Hoover/1924/L. Patrick Gray (1972), Clarence Kelley (1973), and William H. Webster (1978)/Quantico, Virginia.

22. Who said, ''Hold the fort! I am coming!''?
ANSWER: William Tecumseh Sherman at Kennesaw Mountain, Georgia, to General John Corse who was at Allatoona Pass. The date was October 5, 1864.

23. What Frenchman fired the shot that cost the French its American Empire? Why?
ANSWER: Samuel de Champlain/Because he joined the Algonquin and Huron Indians in their fight against the Iroquois. Thus the Iroquois became life-long French-haters, costing France dearly.

24. In what cities do the following Football Bowl Games take place?

a) Stagg Bowl	f) Cotton Bowl	k) Gator Bowl
b) Sugar Bowl	g) Bluebonnet Bowl	l) Sun Bowl
c) Orange Bowl	h) Peach Bowl	m) Florida Citrus Bowl
d) Rose Bowl	i) Hall of Fame Bowl	n) California Bowl
e) Fiesta Bowl	j) Liberty Bowl	o) Holiday Bowl

ANSWER: a) Phenix City, AL   b) New Orleans, LA   c) Miami, FL   d) Pasadena, CA e) Tempe, AZ f) Dallas, TX   g) Houston, TX   h) Atlanta, GA   i) Tampa, FL j) Memphis, TN   k) Jacksonville, FL   l) El Paso, TX   m) Orlando, FL   n) Fresno, CA o) San Diego, CA.

25. Its founder was John Heath and it has a distinctive gold key. What is the name of this society, at what university did it start, and at what university did it become famous?
ANSWER: Phi Beta Kappa originated at William and Mary and became famous at Harvard.

26. Name the only 2 present female U.S. senators (as of July, 1984).
ANSWER: Paula Hawkins from Florida and Nancy Kassebaum from Kansas.

27. Name the last 5 U.S. National Security advisers (as of July, 1984).
ANSWER: R. McFarlane, W. Clark, R. Allen, Z. Brzezinski, and H. Kissinger.

28. Who was known as the ''Son of Sam''? In which state did he commit his murders?
ANSWER: David Berkowitz/New York.

29. What organization started by which U.S. President was headed by Sargent Shriver?
ANSWER: Peace Corps/John F. Kennedy.

30. Who wrote *The Fate of the Earth* (1982)? What are the titles of the 3 sections of the book? What is the subject of this book?
ANSWER: Jonathan Schell/''A Republic of Insects and Grass,'' ''The Second

Death,'' and ''The Choice''/A nuclear holocaust.

31. According to Benjamin Franklin, what are the only 2 things certain in this world?
ANSWER: Death and taxes.

32. What astronauts became the first American female and the first American black in space on flights they made on *Challenger* missions in 1983?
ANSWER: Sally Ride Hawley and Guion S. Bluford, Jr.

33. What American journalist wrote the book *Ten Days That Shook the World* (1919)? What is the subject of the book, and where is the writer buried? What friend of his wrote an introduction for later editions of the book? What film did this book inspire and who directed the film?
ANSWER: John Reed/The Russian (Bolshevik) Revolution/The writer is buried in the Kremlin in Moscow/Lenin/*Reds*/Directed by Warren Beatty.

34. Who wrote *Red Star Over China* (1937)? On what travels is this book based? In what 2 places are the author's ashes buried?
ANSWER: Edgar Snow/On his travels with the Chinese Red Army for 5 months into Soviet China/In a garden on the Peking University campus and at Sneden's Landing near Palisades, New York, near the Hudson River.

35. Who was the American poet who joined the French Foreign Legion as a private at the outbreak of World War I, won the *Croix de Guerre* and the *Médaille Militaire,* and was killed in action in 1916? He is especially remembered for having written ''I Have a Rendezvous with Death.''
ANSWER: Alan Seeger.

36. What former U.S. President called what U.S. President a ''Byzantine logothete''? Explain the allusion and why it was used.
ANSWER: Theodore Roosevelt called Woodrow Wilson a ''Byzantine logothete'' in 1916/A logothete in Byzantium was an accountant. Roosevelt meant that Wilson was pushing a pencil when the U.S. should have intervened in World War I.

37. What are the 3 names of the railroad nicknamed the ''Katy''?
ANSWER: The Missouri, the Kansas, and the Texas.

38. Name the person who headed the investigation of President Kennedy's assassination and the one who headed the Senate Committee which investigated Watergate.
ANSWER: Earl Warren/Sam Irvin.

39. What Civil War general graduated from West Point without receiving a single demerit?
ANSWER: Robert E. Lee.

40. What is the national symbol of the United States that can be found on the Great Seal of the U.S.? What animal did Benjamin Franklin want instead and why? What is the U.S. national symbol clutching in its right and left talons? What is in its beak?
ANSWER: The Bald Eagle/The Turkey because it was a ''respectable bird'' and an American native and because he considered the Bald Eagle to be a ''bird of bad moral character''/An olive branch with 13 olives is in the right talon and 13 arrows are in the left/A banner with the motto *E Pluribus Unum* (''From many, one'').

41. What are the names of the 3 nephews of Donald Duck?
ANSWER: Huey, Dewey, and Louie.

42. Name the U.S. President that graduated from Bowdoin College in Maine in 1824, and name the 2 well-known writers who graduated in Bowdoin's 1825 class.
ANSWER: Franklin Pierce/Henry Wadsworth Longfellow and Nathaniel Hawthorne.

43. Identify the following ''Old's.''

a) Old Faithful	f) Old Fuss and Feathers	k) Old Yeller
b) Old Hickory	g) Old Rough and Ready	l) Old Betsy
c) Old Ironsides	h) Old Blood and Guts	m) old country
d) Old Glory	i) *Old Creole Days*	n) Old Dominion
e) Old Man River	j) *Old Man and the Sea*	o) Old Fox

ANSWER: a) geyser in Yellowstone National Park b) nickname of Andrew Jackson c) nickname of the U.S. frigate *Constitution* d) nickname of the U.S. flag e) nickname for the Mississippi River f) nickname of Gen. Winfield Scott g) nickname of Zachary Taylor h) nickname of Gen. George S. Patton i) 7 short stories by George Washington Cable j) novel by Ernest Hemingway k) friendly watchdog in Disney films l) Davy Crockett's rifle m) the original home country of an immigrant n) nickname for Virginia o) nickname for George Washington.

44. Who said: "Everyone talks about the weather, but nobody does anything about it"?
ANSWER: Mark Twain still receives credit for this phrase, but it was probably said by Charles Dudley Warner, Twain's brother-in-law.

45. Who said, "History is more or less bunk"?
ANSWER: Henry Ford.

46. Fill in the missing sentence from the following speech given by Congressman Willard Duncan Vandiver at a banquet in Philadelphia in 1899: "I come from a state that raises corn and cotton and cockleburs and Democrats, and frothy eloquence neither convinces nor satisfies me. _____. You have got to show me."
ANSWER: The Congressman from Missouri said, "I am from Missouri."

47. Who said, "I never met a man I didn't like"?
ANSWER: Will Rogers.

48. Give the Pledge of Allegiance to the Flag, and tell who wrote it. What 3 changes were made in the Pledge?
ANSWER: "I pledge allegiance to the flag of the United States of America and to the Republic for which it stands, one Nation under God, indivisible, with liberty and justice for all."/Francis Bellamy wrote it in 1892./"the flag of the United States" replaced "my flag"; "of America" and "under God" were added to the original version.

49. Recite the first stanza of "The Star-Spangled Banner." Who wrote it? When? Where was he at the time? Why was he there? What was its original title? To what tune were the words first sung? What U.S. President proclaimed "the Star-Spangled Banner" as the national anthem? In what year did he do so, and in what year did Congress confirm this action?
ANSWER: "Oh! say, can you see, by the dawn's early light,
What so proudly we hailed at the twilight's last gleaming?
Whose broad stripes and bright stars thro' the perilous fight,
O'er the ramparts we watched, were so gallantly streaming?
And the rockets' red glare, the bombs bursting in air,
Gave proof thro' the night that our flag was still there.
Oh! say, does that star-spangled banner yet wave
O'er the land of the free and the home of the brave?"
/Francis Scott Key/1814/Aboard the British ship the *Minden* in the Chesapeake Bay during the bombardment of Fort McHenry, in Baltimore, Maryland/September 13-14, 1814/He was a Washington lawyer accompanied by Colonel John Skinner and he was negotiating the release of a Maryland physician, Dr. William Beanes/The "Defence of Fort M'Henry"/"To Anacreon in Heaven"/Woodrow Wilson/1916 and 1931.

50. Recite the Negro minstrel song "Jim Crow," originated by Thomas D. Rice in 1835, that came to symbolize Negro discrimination and segregation.
ANSWER: "Wheel about, turn about/Do just so/Every time I wheel about/I jump Jim Crow."

51. Who were the 3 U.S. Secretaries of State in the 20th century who resigned their posts in disputes with their administrations? Give the years of their resignations.

ANSWER: William Jennings Bryan in 1915; Cyrus Vance in 1980; and Alexander Haig in 1982.

52. What 2 people are given credit for the line, ''Never give a sucker an even break''?
ANSWER: Wilson Mizner and W.C. Fields.

53. Who said: ''It ain't a fit night out for man or beast,'' and ''It was a woman who drove me to drink—and I never remembered to thank her''?
ANSWER: W.C. Fields.

54. What are the names of the 2 comic strip characters with German names who caused lots of problems for the Captain and his sidekick? What is the name of the comic strip?
ANSWER: Hans and Fritz by Rudolph Dirks/''The Katzenjammer Kids'' or ''The Captain and the Kids'' or ''The Katzies.''

55. What 3 reasons did British soldiers give when asked during WWII why they resented the American troops who were in Britain awaiting the Normandy invasion?
ANSWER: The British troops said the Americans were ''overpaid, oversexed, and over here.''

56. What President said: ''It's just a red herring to get the minds of the voters off the sins of the 80th Congress''? About what was he speaking? Define the phrase ''red herring'' and explain its origin in the sport world. What nickname did this President have for the 80th Congress?
ANSWER: President Harry S Truman/He was speaking about charges of Communist influence in the U.S. government and especially about Whittaker Chambers' assertion that Alger Hiss had been a Communist agent/A ''red herring'' is ''something that diverts attention from the basic issue'';the phrase is from fox hunting and dog trainers pulled smoked herring across the trail of the fox to help train the dogs in scent discrimination/The ''Do-Nothing Congress.''

57. Who is credited with the saying that ''There's a sucker born every minute''?
ANSWER: Phineas Taylor Barnum.

58. What Boston Society was started in 1876 to guard the public against literature damaging to public morals? The founding spirit of this organization has had his name become part of the lexicon meaning ''strict censorship.'' Name him. Name also the person who probably coined this word.
ANSWER: Boston's Watch and Ward Society/Founded by Anthony Comstock/George Bernard Shaw probably coined the word ''comstockery.''

59. What U.S. Vice President said: ''What this country really needs is a good five-cent cigar''? To whom was he the Vice President?
ANSWER: Vice President Thomas Marshall (1913-1921)/To Woodrow Wilson.

60. What woman is credited with all the following quotes, and about whom was she speaking in each case?
a) ''_____was not a bad man, he was just a slob.''
b) ''He was weaned on a pickle.''
c) ''You can't make soufflé rise twice.''
d) ''He looks like the bridegroom (the little man) on the wedding cake.''
ANSWER: Alice Roosevelt Longworth, daughter of Theodore Roosevelt/a) (Warren) Harding b) Calvin Coolidge c) Thomas E. Dewey d) Thomas E. Dewey (Mrs. Longworth is credited with popularizing this quote which may have been by Walter Winchell, Ethel Barrymore, or a Mrs. Flandrau).

61. The titles of what novel by John Steinbeck and what book by Bruce Catton can be found in the first stanza of the ''Battle Hymn of the Republic'' by Julia Ward Howe?
ANSWER: *The Grapes of Wrath* and (The) *Terrible Swift Sword*.

62. Name the volumes in the 3-volume history of the Army of the Potomac during the Civil War written by Bruce Catton.

ANSWER: *Mr. Lincoln's Army* (1951), *Glory Road: The Bloody Route From Fredericksburg to Gettysburg* (1952), and *A Stillness at Appomattox* (1953).

63. Who said: "I'll call her Old Glory, boys, Old Glory," and to what does "Old Glory" refer?

ANSWER: Captain William Driver was given a flag by some Salem, Massachusetts, citizens before embarking on a round-the-world cruise in August, 1831. He made the statement as the flag was being hoisted to the masthead of the *Charles Doggett*. Captain Driver was the one who brought the British mutineers of the ship *Bounty* from Tahiti back to Pitcairn Island/"Old Glory" is the popular name for the U.S. flag.

64. Name the "Big 3" California newspapers.

ANSWER: The Los Angeles *Times*, the Oakland *Tribune*, and the San Francisco *Chronicle*.

65. Identify the persons who said the following last words.
   a) "Let me die in the old uniform in which I fought my battles for freedom. May God forgive me for putting on any other." (1801)
   b) "Tell the men to fire faster and not to give up the ship; fight her till she sinks."
   c) "Thomas Jefferson still survives." (1826)
   d) "The South, the poor South! God knows what will become of her." (1850)
   e) "Strike my (the) tent!" or "Let the tent be struck!" (1870)
   f) "Amen." (1877)
   g) "Glory hallelujah! I'm going to the Lordy!" (1882)
   h) "Now comes the mystery." (1887)
   i, "Make the world better." (1890)
   j) "I killed the President because he was the enemy of the good people, the working people. I am not sorry for my crime." (1901)
   k) "I have tried so hard to do the right." (1908)
   l) "So little done, so much to do." (1922)
   m) "Start the act of contrition."(1944)

ANSWER: a) Benedict Arnold b) Captain James Lawrence c) John Adams d) John C. Calhoun e) Robert E. Lee f) Brigham Young g) Charles Guiteau h) Henry Ward Beecher (clergyman) i) Lucy Stone (suffragette) j) Leon Czolgosz k) Grover Cleveland l) Alexander Graham Bell m) Alfred E. Smith.

66. Name the 2 tallest Sequoias or California redwoods. Give their approximate height within 10 feet. Name the one whose combined girth and height make it the largest living thing on earth. After whom are the Sequoias named? How old is the bristle-cone pine in California named "Methuselah" or "Great-grandad Pickaback"?

ANSWER: The "Howard Libbey" is about 367 feet high and the "General Sherman" about 272 feet/The "General Sherman"/After Sequoya, the Cherokee inventor of the alphabet/4,800 years.

67. What is the only monument erected in the U.S. for a bird, and in what state is it found? Why was this bird so honored?

ANSWER: "The Sea Gull Monument" in Utah/The sea gull saved the Mormons from a cricket plague that was threatening to wipe out their wheat crop.

68. What country and what sculptor gave the Statue of Liberty to the United States? In what year was it given, and in what year was it dedicated? What is the name of the statue in French? Give the author and title of the poem that is on a tablet within the pedestal on which the Statue of Liberty stands. Recite the last 5 lines of the poem (recite the entire poem if you can).

ANSWER: France and Frédéric Auguste Bartholdi/1884/1886/*La Liberté Éclairant le Monde* ("Liberty Enlightening the World")/Emma Lazarus/"The New Colossus"

"Not like the brazen giant of Greek fame,
With conquering limbs astride from land to land;
Here at our sea-washed, sunset gates shall stand
A mighty woman with a torch, whose flame
Is the imprisoned lightning, and her name
Mother of Exiles. From her beacon-hand
Glows world-wide welcome; her mild eyes command
The air-bridged harbor that twin cities frame.
"Keep ancient lands, your storied pomp!" cries she
With silent lips. "Give me your tired, your poor,
Your huddled masses yearning to breathe free.
The wretched refuse of your teeming shore.
Send these, the homeless, tempest-tost to me,
I lift my lamp beside the golden door!"

69. What character in what novel by James Fenimore Cooper has the same nickname as the Republican candidate who lost to James Buchanan in the 1856 election?

ANSWER: Natty Bumppo was nicknamed "The Pathfinder" in the novel by the same name, and that was the nickname of John Charles Frémont.

70. Which company founded the town of Marietta, Ohio? What military leader brought some peace to the region by defeating the Indians at what battle in 1794? By what nickname did this military leader become known because of his reckless courage? Name the states that were formerly part of the Northwest Territory?.

ANSWER: Ohio Company/General Anthony Wayne/Battle of Fallen Timbers/"Mad Anthony"/Ohio (1803), Indiana (1816), Illinois (1818), Michigan (1837), Wisconsin (1848), and part of Minnesota. Minnesota became a state in 1858.

71. Name all the U.S. Presidents Gilbert Stuart painted during his lifetime.

ANSWER: Washington, Adams (John), Jefferson, Madison, Monroe, and Adams (John Quincy).

72. Name in order the 3 capitals of Virginia, and give the dates that they became the capitals.

ANSWER: Jamestown (1607), Williamsburg (1699), and Richmond (1779).

73. What 4 things did Horace Greeley lose in 1872?

ANSWER: His wife (she died on October 30, 1872), the election (to Ulysses S. Grant), his influence at the newspaper (the New York *Tribune*) to Whitelaw Reid, and his life (he died on November 29, 1872). (He also lost all his electoral votes.)

74. Of what curiosity are the beginning dates of the Revolutionary War, the Civil War, the Spanish-American War, and the First World War for the United States?

ANSWER: The United States entered each war in April: April 19, 1775; April 12, 1861; April 25, 1898; and April 6, 1917.

75. Who were the 2 builders of the Brooklyn Bridge? In what year was the bridge started and in what year was it finished?

ANSWER: John Augustus Roebling and Washington Augustus Roebling/1870 and 1883.

76. What are the names of the 2 oldest universities in the United States?

ANSWER: Harvard and William and Mary.

77. John Stark was nicknamed the "Leonidas of America" because of his defense of the pass at the bridge over the Wallomsac (Walloomsack) River in Vermont on August 16, 1777. What is the historical allusion for the nickname?

ANSWER: Leonidas the First defended the pass at Thermopylae against Xerxes and his Persian forces in 80 B.C.

78. Name the 3 U.S. Presidents who graduated from William and Mary. What system and what Greek society were established long ago at the school? After whom is the main building on campus named?

ANSWER: Thomas Jefferson, James Monroe, and John Tyler/The honor system and Phi Beta Kappa/Sir Christopher Wren.

79. In what 3 wars have the most U.S. deaths (total deaths) occurred?

ANSWER: Civil War (525,000 +), World War II (405,000 +), and World War I (116,000 +).

80. According to Harry Truman who were the 4 members of his ''kitchen cabinet''?

ANSWER: Secretary for Inflation, Secretary of Reaction, Secretary for Columnists, and Secretary of **Semantics.**

81. What 2 phrases denote the flag of the U.S.? The red and white stripes of the flag of the U.S. were the same as those of the Grand Union flag of Britain. However, the flag did differ in that the 13 stars in the canton of the U.S. flag replaced the crosses of what 2 saints in the Grand Union flag? Name the countries of these 2 saints.

ANSWER: ''The Stars and Stripes'' and ''Old Glory''/St. George (for England) and St. Andrew (for Scotland).

82. What words are inscribed on the Liberty Bell, and from which book of the Bible do they come? In what city is the Liberty Bell located? In what building of that city was the Liberty Bell first located and in what building (as of 1976) is it now located? When did the crack first appear? What happened to the Bell in 1835?

ANSWER: ''Proclaim Liberty Throughout All the Land Unto All the Inhabitants Thereof''/Leviticus 25:10/In Philadelphia/In Pennsylvania's State House (later named Independence Hall) (1917)/Now located in the Liberty Bell Pavilion (located next to Independence Hall)/On August 27, 1753, when the bell was first rung/The bell cracked again in 1835 announcing the death of Chief Justice John Marshall.

83. What Latin phrase connects the State of Virginia, Abraham Lincoln, and John Wilkes Booth? Why?

ANSWER: *Sic semper tyrannis* (''Thus always to tyrants'')/This phrase is Virginia's motto. It is supposedly the phrase spoken by Booth after he leapt to the stage after assassinating President Lincoln.

84. What Greek word connects Ronald Reagan, Illinois, and the State of California? Why?

ANSWER: *Eureka* [''I have found (it)'']/President Reagan graduated from Eureka College in Illinois, and *Eureka* is the motto of California. *Eureka* was spoken by Archimedes when he placed the crown of King Hiero II in the bathtub and thus discovered how to test the purity of Hiero's golden crown. Gold was discovered in California, thus the state's motto.

85. On the title page of what Journal in 1629 was one of the 3 Latin mottoes on the Great Seal of the United States found? Name the other 2 mottoes (all of which are found on the back of a U.S. one dollar bill) that are on the Great Seal, and give their sources. A committee of 3 men originally proposed a design for the Great Seal in August, 1776, but their design was rejected. Name these 3 men. In what year was the design for the seal adopted?

ANSWER: *E Pluribus Unum* (''From many, one'') was found on *Gentleman's Journal*/*Annuit Coeptis* [''He (God) has favored our undertakings''] is from Vergil's *Aeneid*, Book IX, verse 625, and *Novus Ordo Seclorum* (''A new order of the ages'') is from Vergil's fourth *Eclogue*/ John Adams, Benjamin Franklin, and Thomas Jefferson/1782 (June 20).

86. Name the 3 foreign states which were the first ones to recognize officially the existence of the United States.

ANSWER: France (1778), England and Sweden (1783).

87. What 3 names are involved in the full name of the Santa Fe railroad?

ANSWER: The Atchison, Topeka, and the Santa Fe.

88. Name the members of the Rockefeller family that have served as governors of states and name the states.

ANSWER: Nelson A. Rockefeller was governor of New York from 1959 to 1973; Winthrop Rockefeller was governor of Arkansas from 1967 to 1971; and John Davison Rockefeller, IV was elected governor of West Virginia in 1977 and reelected in 1981.

89. States are represented in Statuary Hall with a statue of one of their most famous citizens. Which state is represented by each of the following?

a) Junípero Serra

b) Alexander Hamilton Stephens

c) Kamehameha I.

d) Lewis Wallace

e) Henry Clay

f) Jefferson Davis

g) William Jennings Bryan

h) Sequoya

i) Robert Fulton

j) Marcus Whitman

ANSWER: a) California b) Georgia c) Hawaii d) Indiana e) Kentucky f) Mississippi g) Nebraska h) Oklahoma i) Pennsylvania j) Washington.

90. What author wrote all the following works, and who is the subject of each one?

a) *Lust for Life* (1934)

b) *Sailor on Horseback* (1938)

c) *Immortal Wife* (1944)

d) *The Passionate Journey* (1947)

e) *Adversary in the House* (1947)

f) *The President's Lady* (1951)

g) *Love is Eternal* (1954)

h) *The Agony and the Ecstasy* (1961)

i) *Those Who Love* (1965)

j) *The Passions of the Mind* (1971)

k) *The Greek Treasure* (1975)

l) *The Origin* (1980)

ANSWER: Irving Stone/a) Vincent Van Gogh b) Jack London c) Jessie B. Frémont d) John Noble e) Eugene V. Debs f) Rachel and Andrew Jackson g) Mary Todd Lincoln h) Michelangelo i) Abigail Adams j) Sigmund Freud k) Heinrich and Sophia Schliemann l) Charles Darwin.

91. For the 5 following U.S. Military Academies, give the year each was started, the present location, and the geographic site (river, mountain) near which or on which it is located.

a) Air Force Academy

b) Coast Guard

c) Merchant Marine Academy

d) Military Academy

e) Naval Academy

ANSWER: a) 1954, Colorado Springs, Colorado, the Rampart Range b) 1876, New London, Connecticut, the Thames River (initially the Revenue Cutter School of Instruction, moved to the present site in 1912) c) 1942, Kings Point, Long Island, New York, Long Island Sound d) 1802, West Point, New York, the Hudson River e) 1845, Annapolis, Maryland, the Severn River (called the Naval School until 1850; was moved to Newport, Rhode Island, during the Civil War).

92. The following mottoes pertain to which branches of the U.S. armed forces?

a) "I want you"

b) *Semper fidelis* (Always Faithful)

c) "Don't give up the ship"

d) "Keep 'em flying"

e) *Semper Paratus* (Always Prepared)

ANSWER: a) U.S. Army b) U.S. Marine Corps c) U.S. Navy d) U.S. Air Force e) U.S. Coast Guard.

93. In *America in Midpassage* (1939) these historians wrote: "At no time, at no place, in solemn convention assembled, through no chosen agents, had the American people officially proclaimed the United States to be a democracy. The

Constitution did not contain the word or any word lending countenance to it, except possibly the mention of 'We, the people,' in the preamble...When the Constitution was framed no respectable person called himself or herself a democrat.'' Name this American husband and wife pair.

ANSWER: Charles Austin and Mary Ritter Beard.

94. Five U.S. Secretaries of State have won the Nobel Prize for Peace. Name them.

ANSWER: Elihu Root (1912), Frank Billings Kellogg (1929), Cordell Hull (1945), George Catlett Marshall (1953), and Henry Alfred Kissinger (shared the prize with Le Duc Tho of North Vietnam, 1973).

95. What Americans won the Nobel Prize for Peace in 1925, 1931, 1946, 1950, 1962, 1964, and 1970?

ANSWER: Charles G. Dawes (1925, shared with Sir J. Austen Chamberlain of Great Britain), Jane Addams and Nicholas Murray Butler (1931), Emily G. Balch and John R. Mott (1946), Ralph J. Bunche (1950), Linus C. Pauling (1962), Martin Luther King, Jr. (1964), and Norman E. Borlaug (1970).

96. Thomas Buchanan Read wrote a poem about the ride of a well-known Civil War general and about his famous ride from Winchester, Virginia, to Cedar Run, Virginia, to rescue his troops from an impending loss to the Confederate army. Name the General and the number of miles by filling in the following line of the poem: ''And _____ _____ miles away.''

ANSWER: ''And *Sheridan twenty* miles away.''

97. On what hill on what island during World War II was the famous photograph taken of the raising of the flag by the 3rd Marine Division? What was the shape of the island? Name the photographer.

ANSWER: Mount Suribachi on Iwo Jima, February 23, 1945/Like a porkchop (Iwo Jima means ''sulfur island'' in Japanese, for whatever that is worth/ Joe Rosenthal.

98. What is the only state named after a U.S. President? What territory was named after Thomas Jefferson, and what state did that territory become? What region named after Benjamin Franklin attempted to become the 14th state? What was the desire of the local residents for naming the state of Washington, and what 3 states were involved?

ANSWER: Washington/The territory in present-day Colorado was the Territory of Jefferson which became the State of Jefferson in 1859 upon the extralegal action of the election of a governor by the mining camp residents. Congress dissolved this government in 1861 and authorized the Colorado Territory, which became in 1876 the state of Colorado/Eastern Tennessee (When the Tennessee territory was ceded by North Carolina to the United States in 1784, Eastern Tennessee residents organized a new state and named it Franklin. A constitution was adopted and a governor elected. North Carolina reestablished its jurisdiction by 1789. The area became part of the state of Tennessee in 1796)/Columbia, and the 3 states were Washington, Idaho, and Montana (The Oregon Territory, which included present-day Washington, was created by Congress in 1848, but the local residents did not want to be governed from Salem, Oregon, and petitioned Congress for a separate Columbia Territory. Congress, in 1853, named the territory after George Washington instead of the Columbia River. This territory included Washington, the northern part of Idaho, and the western part of Montana.) Washington became the 42nd state in 1889.

99. What do the following towns have in common: Quincy, Massachusetts; Fillmore, California; Arthur, Kentucky; Cleveland, Tennessee; Taft, Texas; Trumansburg, New York; and Nixon, Texas?

ANSWER: None of them were named after U.S. Presidents.

100. According to President Franklin D. Roosevelt, who were ''the three greatest minds that America has produced''?
ANSWER: Thomas Jefferson, Benjamin Franklin, and Count Rumford.

101. Who is identified by the following description: born in Woburn, Massachusetts, in 1753, a loyalist during the American Revolution, tried but not acquitted for sedition in 1774, went to England in 1776, became Imperial Count of the Holy Roman Empire in 1792, was noted for his research on heat, helped establish the Royal Institution of London, and returned to America in the 1790's?
ANSWER: Count Rumford or Sir Benjamin Thompson.

102. What U.S. President said: ''If I had to choose between a government without newspapers or newspapers without a government, I would choose the latter''?
ANSWER: Thomas Jefferson.

103. Who was the principal speaker at the dedication of the Civil War cemetery at Gettysburg in 1863 who wrote: ''I wish I could flatter myself that I had come as near to the central idea of this occasion in two hours as you did in two minutes''? To whom did he address those words?
ANSWER: Edward Everett/Abraham Lincoln.

104. Recite Abraham Lincoln's Gettysburg Address.
ANSWER: Fourscore and seven years ago our fathers brought forth on this continent a new nation conceived in liberty and dedicated to the proposition that all men are created equal. Now we are engaged in a great civil war testing whether that nation, or any nation so conceived and so dedicated, can long endure. We are met on a great battlefield of that war. We have come to dedicate a portion of that field as a final resting place for those who here gave their lives that that nation might live. It is altogether fitting and proper that we should do this. But, in a larger sense, we cannot dedicate, we cannot consecrate, we cannot hallow this ground. The brave men, living and dead, who struggled here have consecrated it far above our poor power to add or detract. The world will little note nor long remember what we say here, but it can never forget what they did here. It is for us the living rather to be dedicated here to the unfinished work which they who fought here have thus far so nobly advanced. It is rather for us to be here dedicated to the great task remaining before us—that from these honored dead we take increased devotion to that cause for which they gave the last full measure of devotion—that we here highly resolve that these dead shall not have died in vain, that this nation under God shall have a new birth of freedom, and that government of the people, by the people, for the people shall not perish from the earth.

105. An anonymous Kentuckian answered the question, ''What are the boundaries of the United States?'' in an unusual way. What did he say bound the U.S. on the north, the east, the south, and the west?
ANSWER: On the north by the Aurora Borealis, on the east by the rising sun, on the south by the precession of the Equinoxes, and on the west by the Day of Judgement.

106. What are the 3 words that are found on the seal of the F.B.I.?
ANSWER: Fidelity, Bravery, and Integrity.

107. Name the 3 Progressive Party candidates and the years they ran for election.
ANSWER: Theodore Roosevelt in 1912, Robert M. LaFollette in 1924, and Henry A. Wallace in 1948.

108. Identify the candidate for each of the following political parties in the given year.

a) Libertarian (1976)
b) Socialist (1928)
c) Anti-Masonic (1832)
d) Greenback (1876)
e) Prohibition (1880)
f) Socialist (1904)
g) Union (1936)
h) States' Rights (1948)
i) American Independent (1976)
j) American (1968)

ANSWER: a) Roger Lea MacBride b) Norman M. Thomas c) William Wirt d) Peter Cooper e) Neal Dow f) Eugene V. Debs g) William Lemke h) Strom Thurmond i) Lester G. Maddox j) George C. Wallace.

109. Name the 6 times that the Republicans and Democrats have had their conventions in the same cities.

ANSWER: In Chicago in 1884, 1932, 1944, and 1952; in Philadelphia in 1948; and in Miami Beach in 1972.

110. Who wrote "America"? Recite the first stanza.

ANSWER: Samuel Francis Smith/
My country! 'tis of thee,
Sweet land of liberty,
Of thee I sing.

Land where my fathers died!
Land of the Pilgrims' pride!
From every mountain side,
Let freedom ring!

111. There were 2 Battles of The Wilderness. Briefly explain each one by identifying the commanding officers and by giving the outcome.

ANSWER: General Edward Braddock with 1,400 British regulars and 450 colonials under Lt. Col. George Washington was defeated by 900 French and Indians at the Monongahela River about 8 miles South of Ft. Duquesne on July 9, 1755. The other Wilderness battle took place on May 5-6, 1864, between Robert E. Lee and Ulysses S. Grant. Lee got the best of Grant.

112. From the following excerpt of a speech, identify the speaker, the year, and the name by which the speech is known.

"If they dare to come out in the open field and defend the gold standard as a good thing, we will fight them to the uttermost. Having behind us the producing masses of this nation and the world, supported by the commercial interests, the laboring interests, and the toilers everywhere, we will answer their demand for a gold standard by saying to them: You shall not press down upon the brow of labor this crown of thorns, you shall not crucify mankind upon a cross of gold."

ANSWER: William Jennings Bryan's "Cross of Gold" speech at the Democratic Convention in Chicago on July 9, 1896.

113. Identify each of the railroads by its nickname.
a) "Northern Cross"
b) "Cotton Belt"
c) "Frisco"
d) "Katy"

ANSWER: a) Wabash b) St. Louis-Southwestern c) St. Louis-San Francisco d) Missouri, Kansas, and Texas.

114. Who was speaking about whom in each of the following statements?
a) "I can't spare this man; he fights."
b) "Do men now mourn for him, the great man eloquent? I put on sackcloth long ago."
c) "I have lost my right arm."
d) "That dirty little atheist."
e) "The Barefoot Boy from Wall Street."
f) "Now look, that damned cowboy is President of the United States."
g) "To the memory of the Man, first in war, first in peace, and first in the hearts of his countrymen."

ANSWER: a) Abraham Lincoln of General Ulysses S. Grant b) Theodore Parker of Daniel Webster c) Robert E. Lee of Thomas "Stonewall" Jackson d) Theodore Roosevelt of Thomas Paine e) Harold L. Ickes of Wendell Willkie f) Mark Hanna of Theodore Roosevelt g) Henry Lee of George Washington.

115. Bruce Elliott in *Fantasy and Science Fiction* (1951) created a scenario in

which 15 apes were placed in front of 15 typewriters. After a long wait, each ape typed a single, different word. What are those 15 words?

ANSWER: **Now, Is, The, Time, For, All, Good, Parties, To, Come, To, The, Aid, Of, Man.**

116. What was Charles E. Weller's sentence that was used to test the first typewriter of Christopher L. Sholes in 1867, and that became the campaign slogan of Ulysses S. Grant in 1868?

ANSWER: **''Now is the time for all good men to come to the aid of the party.''**

117. What 3 cities in America did William Sidney Porter (O. Henry) say were ''story cities''?

ANSWER: **''New York, of course, and New Orleans, and best of the lot, San Francisco.''**

118. In terms of U.S. defense capability, what does the term ''triad'' mean?

ANSWER: **It refers to the U.S. strategic deterrent force made up of land-based missles, a strategic bomber force, and the Polaris or Poseidon submarine fleet.**

119. In the Saturday Night Massacre of October 20, 1973, identify the following.
a) President Nixon's chief of staff
b) Attorney General who was ordered by the chief of staff to dismiss the Special Prosecutor, but who resigned instead
c) The Special Prosecutor who wanted the subpoenaed White House tapes
d) The Assistant Attorney General who also resigned because he would not dismiss the Special Prosecutor
e) The Solicitor General who did fire the Special Prosecutor

ANSWER: **a) Alexander Haig b) Elliot Richardson c) Archibald Cox d) William Ruckelshaus e) Robert Bork.**

120. Who wrote ''The American's Creed''? In what year? What is the text of the creed?

ANSWER: **William Tyler Page/1917/''I believe in the United States of America as a government of the people, by the people, for the people; whose just powers are derived from the consent of the governed; a democracy in a republic; a sovereign Nation of many sovereign States; a perfect union, one and inseparable; established upon those principles of freedom, equality, justice, and humanity for which American patriots sacrificed their lives and their fortunes. I therefore believe it is my duty to my country to love it, to support its Constitution, to obey its laws, to respect its flag, and to defend it against all enemies.''**

121. What French architect and engineer said that Jenkins' Hill in Washington, D.C., seemed to be ''a pedestal waiting for a monument''? What was built on this ''pedestal''? Who burned it in 1814? What statue is on its dome? Who is the artist who painted the giant fresco in The Great Rotunda?

ANSWER: **Pierre L'Enfant/U.S. Capitol/The British/Statue of Freedom/Constantino Brumidi.**

122. What Civil War general owned a home at Arlington, Virginia, that later became the site of Arlington National Cemetery? In what year for what war was an Unknown American Soldier first buried? What is the inscription on the Tomb of the Unknown Soldier or the Tomb of the Unknowns?

ANSWER: **Robert E. Lee/1921 for World War I/''Here rests in honored glory an American Soldier known but to God.''**

123. Recite the Preamble and the first paragraph of the Declaration of Independence.

ANSWER: **''When, in the Course of human events, it becomes necessary for one people to dissolve the political bands which have connected them with another, and to assume among the powers of the earth, the separate and equal station to which the Laws of Nature and of Nature's God entitle them, a decent respect to the opinions of mankind requires that they** should declare the causes which impel them to the separation. We hold these truths to be self-evident, that all men are created equal, that they are endowed by their Creator with certain unalienable Rights, that among these are Life, Liberty, and the pursuit of Happiness.''

124. Recite the Preamble of the Constitution of the United States of America.

ANSWER: ''We the people of the United States, in Order to form a more perfect Union, establish Justice, insure domestic Tranquillity, provide for the common defense, promote the general Welfare, and secure the Blessings of Liberty to ourselves and our Posterity, do ordain and establish this Constitution for the United States of America.''

125. Identify the city with which each of the following late 19th early 20th century terms or areas was associated.
a) Gold Coast
b) Beacon Street
c) Nob Hill
d) The Four Hundred

ANSWER: a) Chicago, Illinois b) Boston, Massachusetts c) San Francisco, California d) New York, New York.

126. From the time of George Washington's inauguration, the U.S. had 2 Capitols before Washington, D.C., became the permanent Capitol in 1800. But between 1774 and 1800 the government met in 10 different places. List the Capitols in the Continental Congress and, later, those of the Congress of the United States before Washington, D.C.

ANSWER: Carpenters' Hall, Philadelphia (1774); Independence Hall, Philadelphia (1775-1776; 1777; 1778-1783); Congress Hall, Baltimore (1776-1777); Old Court House, Lancaster, Pennsylvania (1777); York County Court House, York, Pennsylvania (1777-1778); Nassau Hall, Princeton, New Jersey (1783); State House, Annapolis, Maryland (1783-1784); French Arms Tavern, Trenton, New Jersey (1784); Federal Hall, New York City (1785-1790); Congress Hall, Philadelphia (1790-1800).

127. What are the names of the 4 nephews of Popeye the Sailor Man? What are the names of the 3 nieces of Daisy Duck?

ANSWER: Peepeye, Pipeye, Poopeye, and Pupeye/April, May, and June.

128. Name President Taft's Secretary of the Interior from 1909 to 1911 who fired a subordinate, Louis R. Glavis, who had accused him of impeding an investigation of fraudulent coal-land claims in Alaska. What was the name of the Forestry Bureau Chief who was dismissed by Taft for denouncing the Secretary of the Interior? What was Theodore Roosevelt's reaction to this matter? What was ironic about the Secretary of the Interior's middle name?

ANSWER: Richard Ballinger/Gifford Pinchot/Roosevelt was upset at the repudiation of his conservationist policies; this issue was a major reason for the breakup of the Republican Party in 1912 and the formation of the Bull Moose Party/Ballinger's middle name was Achilles, and an ''Achilles' Heel'' is ''a very vulnerable spot.''

129. States originally donated 1 or 2 statues of their most famous citizens to Statuary Hall in Washington, D.C., but as of 1933, one of the two statues is located elsewhere in the Capitol. Which state is represented by each of the following statues not located in Statuary Hall?
a) Father Damien
b) Jacques Marquette
c) Will Rogers
d) George Clinton
e) John Stark
f) William King
g) John Winthrop
h) Crawford Williamson Long

ANSWER: a) Hawaii b) Wisconsin c) Oklahoma d) New York e) New Hampshire f) Maine g) Massachusetts h) Georgia.

130. Who wrote ''America the Beautiful''? Recite the first stanza.

ANSWER: Katharine Lee Bates/

O beautiful for spacious skies,   America! America!
For amber waves of grain;   God shed His grace on thee
For purple mountain majesties   And crown thy good with brotherhood
Above the fruited plain!   From sea to shining sea!

131. The Land of Oz consists of the Emerald City and 4 countries. What are the names of the 4 countries and what colors are associated with them? Who wrote the story? How many sequel books were there? What girl from what state and with what dog dreams of going to the land of Oz? Down which road did the girl travel? What are the names of her aunt and uncle? Name the all-metal man.

ANSWER: **Winkie Country — West (yellow), Munchkin Country — East (blue), Quading Country — South (red), Gillikin Country — North (purple)/L. Frank Baum/38/Dorothy Gale/Kansas/Toto/The Yellow Brick Road/Aunt Em (Emily) and Uncle Henry/Tin Woodsman.**

132. Who is the American legendary super-hero cowboy who dug the Rio Grande? Why did he have such a name? Who raised him? Name his horse, his wife, and the place he worked.

ANSWER: **Pecos Bill/He fell from the family wagon into the Pecos River/Coyotes/ Widow Maker/Slue Foot/Cross-Eyed Ranch.**

133. What is the name of the American folk hero lumberjack who is of considerable size? What did he dig so that he could float logs to the mill? What did he scoop out so that his blue ox could have a drink of water? Name his wife, his son, his daughter, and his blue ox. Name his 3 dogs. What was the name of his time-keeper who became his bookkeeper?

ANSWER: **Paul Bunyan/Puget Sound/The Great Lakes/Minnie/Jean/Teenie/Babe/ Elmer the Moose, a terrier; Nero the Bear, a hound; and Jacko the reversible dog/Johnny Inkslinger.**

134. In 1851, who was the West Texas frontier judge, saloon-keeper, and justice of the peace who ruled by one law book and a six-shooter and said he was the only "Law West of the Pecos"? What did he rename his town of Vinegaroon and why? What was the name of his saloon? What was this judge's nickname?

ANSWER: **Judge Roy Bean/Langtry after English actress Lillie Langtry with whom he was in love/"The Jersey Lily"/"The Texas Hanging Judge."**

135. Who are the only 2 Americans buried in the Kremlin?

ANSWER: **John Reed (journalist) and Bill Haywood (founder of the IWW or the International Workers of the World).**

136. Give the location of each of the following massacres.

a) Americans were slain by British troops (March 5, 1770)

b) Colonial militia was slain by Tory-Indian force July 3, 1778

c) James W. Fannin's men were killed by Santa Anna's men (March, 1836)

d) 20 Mormons were slain by mobs in the fall (1838)

e) Missionary Dr. Marcus Whitman and family were slain by the Cayuse Indians (November, 1847)

f) Quantril's Confederate band killed over 150 (August 21, 1863)

g) Captain William Fetterman and his troops were ambushed by Indians led by High Backbone (December 21, 1866)

h) 200-300 Sioux under Big Foot were slain by the 7th U.S. Cavalry led by Major S.M. Whitside (December 29, 1890)

i) Eight members of "Bugs" Moran's (O'Banion) gang were felled by Al Capone's thugs (February 14, 1929)

j) Vietnamese villagers were killed by American troops led by William Calley (March 16, 1968)

ANSWER: **a) Boston, Massachusetts b) Wyoming Valley, Pennsylvania c) Goliad, Texas d) Haun's Mill, Missouri e) Waiilatpu, Walla Walla Valley , Oregon Territory f) Lawrence, Kansas g) Wyoming h) Wounded Knee, South Dakota i) Chicago, Illinois j) My Lai, Vietnam.**

137. A TV movie, "The Children of An Lac," dealt with the evacuation of hundreds of Vietnamese orphans from South Vietnam during the last days of the war. What military base near Columbus, Georgia, and what woman from Columbus played a significant role in this evacuation? What actress played this Columbus woman in the movie?

ANSWER: **Fort Benning/Betty Tisdale/Shirley Jones.**

138. What American inventor nicknamed the "American Leonardo" painted what famous work that was purchased in 1982 by Daniel J. Terra for $3.25 million? What famous American writer commissioned this work? What is the better-known nickname of this painter-inventor, and what were his 2 main inventions?

ANSWER: Samuel Finley Breese Morse painted *Gallery of the Louvre* (1832)/ James Fenimore Cooper/"Father of the Telegraph"/The telegraph and the Morse code.

139. Name the 2 Nobel Prizes won by Linus Carl Pauling.

ANSWER: The Nobel Prize in chemistry in 1954 (for his research into the nature of the chemical bond) and the Nobel Prize for peace in 1962 (for trying to ban the testing of nuclear weapons).

140. Name the British general who started the Boy Scouts in 1907. Name the British woman who started the British Girl Guides in 1910, and name the American woman who founded the Girl Guides (changed later to Girl Scouts) in 1912. In which city did the American woman start this organization? Arrange the following Boy Scout levels from beginner to the most advanced: First-class, Star, Tenderfoot, Eagle, Life, Second-class.

ANSWER: Sir Robert S.S. Baden-Powell/Agnes Baden-Powell/Juliette Gordon Low/Savannah, Georgia/Tenderfoot, Second-class, First-class, Star, Life, and Eagle.

141. Name the first ship to circumnavigate the globe, and name the first submarine to do the same.

ANSWER: Magellan's ship *Victoria* (1519-1522)/The American *Triton* (1960).

142. He said, "Our policy is directed not against any country or doctrine but against hunger, poverty, desperation and chaos. Its purpose should be the revival of a working economy in the world so as to permit the emergence of political and social conditions in which free institutions can exist." Name this Secretary of State whose European Recovery Plan was also named after him.

ANSWER: George Catlett Marshall.

143. Who made the following remark, "Any man who hates dogs and small children can't be all bad," and about whom was he speaking?

ANSWER: Leo C. Rosten about W.C. Fields.

144. What 2 men wrote *Beyond the Melting Pot* (1963)? What was the book's main contention?

ANSWER: Nathan Glazer and Daniel P. Moynihan/That the various ethnic communities in the U.S. have not become assimilated.

145. What combination of number and letter identifies the Coca-Cola secret ingredient? Who was the druggist who invented it? In what city did he begin work as a pharmacist and sell drinks and his own concoctions at the Eagle Drug and Chemical Company? What was Coca-Cola first called? What was the stimulant in the drink, and what replaced it in 1886?

ANSWER: 7X/Dr. John Styth Pemberton/Columbus, Georgia (The restaurant in the Columbus Hilton is named Pemberton's)/French Wine of Cocoa — Ideal Nerve and Tonic Stimulant/Cocaine/Caffeine.

146. What city is noted for being the birthplace of Royal Crown Cola (RC Cola's local pronunciation is "Aura See")? In the early 20th century, who was the man responsible for developing Royal Crown Ginger Ale and Chero Cola? In the 1930's the company marketed a big 12-ounce bottle of RC Cola. What was its nickname?

ANSWER: Columbus, Georgia/Claud Adkins Hatcher/"Belly Washer."

147. what is the name of the book or what are the names of the 2 characters created by american newspaperman, don marquis, in 1927? what is unusual in this book of blank verse? why is that so? what animals are the 2 characters? what is the motto of the feline animal in the story?

ANSWER: *archy and mehitabel*/no capital letters are used/archy composed the book at night when marquis was absent by falling from above onto each

key/archy is the cockroach and mehitabel is a cat/''wottehell, archy, toujours gai.''

148. Give the locations of the following clinics and name the founders.
a) the Menninger Psychiatric Clinic
b) the Mayo Clinic
c) the Hughston Orthopaedic Clinic (to be complemented by the Hughston Sports Medicine Hospital in 1984)

ANSWER: a) Topeka, Kansas/Charles F. Menninger and sons, Karl Augustus and William Claire b) Rochester, Minnesota/Charles Horace Mayo and brother William James Mayo c) Columbus, Georgia/Jack C. Hughston.

149. He wrote in the *Flag Salute Cases* (1943), ''One who belongs to the most vilified and persecuted minority in history is not likely to be insensible to the freedoms guaranteed by our Constitution....But as judges we are neither Jew nor Gentile, neither Catholic nor agnostic.'' Name this associate Justice of the Supreme Court.

ANSWER: Felix Frankfurter.

150. Name the American woman for whom King Edward VIII of England abdicated his throne in December, 1936. From which city and state was she?

ANSWER: Wallis Warfield Simpson/Baltimore, Maryland.

151. Identify each of the following.
a) The judge who presided over the Watergate trials
b) The town in which Norman Rockwell died
c) The presidential candidate whose campaign slogan was $AuH_2O = 1964$
d) The official communist newspaper sold in the U.S.
e) The German-born physicist who was once offered the presidency of Israel
f) The monthly awards given by Senator William Proxmire for wasteful government spending
g) The doctor who set John Wilkes Booth's broken leg
h) The West Virginia school that lost most of its football team in a 1970 plane crash
i) The town in the sociological study of *Middletown,* USA

ANSWER: a) John J. Sirica b) Stockbridge, Massachusetts c) Barry Goldwater d) *The Daily Worker* e) Albert Einstein f) Golden Fleece Award g) Dr. Samuel Mudd h) Marshall University i) Muncie, Indiana.

152. Who was the most decorated soldier in WWII, and what was the name of his autobiography?

ANSWER: Audie Murphy/*To Hell and Back.*

153. Name the first balloon to cross successfully the Atlantic Ocean (August, 1978). Name any of the 3 men who piloted the balloon.

ANSWER: *Double Eagle II*/Ben Abruzzo, Maxie Anderson, and Larry Newman.

154. Give the number of years between the Declaration of Independence and Lincoln's Gettysburg address.

ANSWER: ''Four score and seven years ago . . .'' (or 87 years).

155. Give the year and the circumstances of each of the following ''first'' messages.
a) ''What hath God wrought!''
b) ''Europe and America are united by telegraph. Glory to God in the highest and on earth peace and good will towards men.''
c) ''Mr. Watson, come here, I want you.''
d) ''Mary had a little lamb.''
e) ''That's one small step for a man, one giant leap for mankind.''

ANSWER: a) First telegraph message — from Washington to Baltimore by Samuel F.B. Morse on May 24, 1844 b) First transoceanic cable message — from Valentina, Ireland, to Hearts Content, Newfoundland, from Queen Victoria to President James Buchanan, on August 16, 1858 c) First telephone message — from Alexander Graham Bell to Thomas Augustus Watson in 1876 d) First recorded message on a phonograph — by Thomas Edison in 1877 e) First sentence from a man on the surface of the moon — by Neil Armstrong in 1969.

156. Name the highest civilian award that a U.S. citizen can receive, and name the President who established it.
ANSWER: The Presidential Medal of Freedom/John F. Kennedy.

157. Name the leader, the Temple, and the town in Guyana involved in the 1978 tragedy that took the lives of 912 people.
ANSWER: Jim Jones/Peoples Temple/Jonestown.

158. Identify the utopian society from each of the following descriptions.
    a) Founded by Johann Conrad Beissel at Ephrata, Pennsylvania, in 1732
    b) Founded by Ann Lee at Watervliet (near Albany), New York in 1774
    c) Founded by George Rapp in Posey County, Indiana, in 1815
    d) Founded by Robert Owen in Posey County, Indiana, in 1825
    e) Founded by George Ripley at West Roxbury, Massachusetts, in 1841
    f) Founded by Christian Metz at Ebenezer, New York, in 1843
    g) Founded by John Humphrey Noyes at Oneida, New York, in 1848
    h) Founded by Étienne Cabet at Nauvoo, Illinois, in 1849
ANSWER: a) The Solitary Brethren of the Community of Seventh Day Baptists (also called Ephrata and Cloister) b) Shakers c) Harmony Society d) New Harmony e) Brook Farm f) Amana Society g) Oneida Community h) Icarians.

159. What British pirate and ship owner in New York was hanged for murder and piracy in 1701? Name both his ship and the Armenian ship he appropriated in 1698.
ANSWER: Captain William Kidd/*Adventure*/*Quedagh Merchant*.

160. Identify each of the following.
    a) The first advocate of daylight saving time
    b) The name of Charles Lindbergh's autobiographical account of his Atlantic crossing written in 1927
    c) The U.S. newspaper with the largest daily circulation
    d) The city where the world's largest airport is located
    e) The only state over whose territory no foreign flag has flown
    f) The least-populated county in the continental United States
    g) The mountain location of the unfinished Crazy Horse Memorial and the sculptor who started the project
    h) The city and state in which the Tennis Hall of Fame is located (in a casino)
    i) The physical characteristic shared by Thomas Jefferson, Bill Walton, Sinclair Lewis, and Dave Cowens
    j) The Supreme Court Justice nicknamed ''Whizzer''
ANSWER: a) Benjamin Franklin b) *We* c) *The Wall Street Journal* d) Atlanta, Georgia e) Idaho f) Loving County, Texas g) Thunderhead Mountain (South Dakota)/Korczak Ziolkowski h) Newport, Rhode Island i) they are all red-headed j) Bryon White.

161. Who said: ''I don't make jokes, I just watch the government and report the facts''?
ANSWER: Will Rogers.

162. Identify each of the following.
    a) The B-29 that dropped the atomic bomb on Hiroshima
    b) The pilot of the B-29 that dropped the atomic bomb on Hiroshima
    c) The first five-star general of the U.S. Air Force
    d) The first U.S. atomic aircraft carrier (1961)
    e) The first U.S. aircraft carrier (1922)
    f) The peace ship of Henry Ford (1915)
    g) The powered ship which in 1952 set a record for the fastest Atlantic crossing
    h) The aircraft Bryan Allen peddled across the English Channel (June, 1979)
    i) The first human-powered aircraft — piloted by Bryan Allen (August, 1977)
    j) The U.S. lieutenant col. who led the first bombing raid on Tokyo (April, 1942)
    k) The person sometimes called Japan's last shogun (1945-1951)
    l) The U.S. general who was court-martialed for insubordination in 1925 for criticism of the neglect of air power by military leaders

m) The American Revolutionary hero of the battle at Saratoga whose statue in that city does not bear his name

ANSWER: a) *Enola Gay* b) Paul Tibbets, Jr. c) Henry "Hap" Arnold d) U.S.S. *Enterprise* e) U.S.S. *Langley* (formerly the U.S.S. *Jupiter*) f) *Oscar II* g) S.S. *United States* h) *Gossamer Albatross* i) *Gossamer Condor* j) James Harold Doolittle k) General Douglas MacArthur l) William Lendrum "Billy" Mitchell m) Benedict Arnold.

163. Who were the 4 Horsemen of Calumny referred to by U.S. Senator Margaret Chase Smith of Maine in a June 1, 1950, speech? Toward which Senator was this speech directed?

ANSWER: Fear, Ignorance, Bigotry, and Smear (she said: "But I don't want to see the Republican Party ride to political victory on the Four Horsemen of Calumny — Fear, Ignorance, Bigotry, and Smear"/Senator Joseph McCarthy.

164. Give in the descending order the 3 largest 1982 populations of Indian reservations.

ANSWER: Navajo (Arizona, New Mexico, Utah), Creek, and Cherokee (both in Oklahoma).

165. What is the name of the architect who designed the Vietnam Veterans Memorial monument? Who is the sculptor who designed the statue and the flagpole that was placed to the side of the V-shaped Vietnam memorial?

ANSWER: Maya Ying Lin/Frederick Hart.

166. Give the date for each of the following special events.

a) Inauguration Day
b) Groundhog Day
c) Lincoln's Birthday
d) Washington's Birthday
e) Memorial/Decoration Day
f) Flag Day
g) Independence Day
h) Labor Day
i) Columbus Day
j) Halloween
k) Election Day
l) Veterans/Armistice Day
m) Forefather's Day (anniversary of the Pilgrims' landing in 1620)

ANSWER: a) January 20 b) February 2 c) February 12 d) February 22 e) last Monday in May f) June 14 g) July 4 h) first Monday in September i) October 12 j) October 31 k) first Tuesday after the first Monday in November l) November 11 m) December 21.

167. Name the first person to describe Santa Claus as a fat and jolly person in his work (1809), and name the first to draw this plump and jolly Santa (1863) as he is known today.

ANSWER: Washington Irving (Diedrich Knickerbocker) in *A History of New York* and Thomas Nast in *Harper's Weekly*.

168. Name the Five-and-Dime store entrepreneur and the city in which he opened up his first store in 1878. After this store failed, in what city did he open a successful store in 1879? Name the building in New York City that was the tallest in the world from 1913 to 1931. What building erected in 1931 became the tallest?

ANSWER: F. (Frank) W. (Winfield) Woolworth/Utica, New York/Lancaster, Pennsylvania/The Woolworth Building/The Empire State Building.

169. Identify each of the following.

a) The first Black man of science
b) The annual NAACP award for the outstanding Black person
c) The first Black to attend the University of Mississippi
d) The Black who accompanied Robert Edwin Peary to the North Pole in 1909, and about whom Peary said, "I can't get along without"
e) The Black who advocated a "Back-to-Africa" movement in the late 1920's, and whose newspaper, *Negro World,* spread his philosophy

ANSWER: a) Benjamin Banneker b) Spingarn Medal c) James Meredith d) Matthew Alexander Henson e) Marcus Mosiah Garvey.

170. Name the 2 highest decorations for gallantry in the United States, and name the medal originally awarded for distinguished military service but reconstituted by Congress in 1932 and now awarded for military men wounded in the line of duty.

ANSWER: The Congressional Medal of Honor (1861-1862) and the Distinguished

Service Medal/Purple Heart.

171. What are the 4 seasons in California according to some wits?
ANSWER: Flood, drought, fire, and earthquake.

172. John Greenleaf Whittier wrote about a Virginia statesman who opposed the war with England in 1812: "Too honest or too proud to feign/A love he never cherished,/Beyond Virginia's border line/His patriotism perished." Name him.
ANSWER: John Randolph.

173. In which city and state is each of the following Halls of Fame located?
a) Hall of Fame for Great Americans
b) National Professional Football Hall of Fame
c) National Football Hall of Fame
d) Women's Hall of Fame
e) Country Music Hall of Fame
f) National Baseball Hall of Fame and Museum
g) National Hall of Fame for Famous American Indians
h) National Cowboy Hall of Fame and Western Heritage Center
ANSWER: a) Bronx Community College of the City University of New York in New York City b) Canton, Ohio c) New Brunswick, New Jersey d) Seneca Falls, New York e) Nashville, Tennessee f) Cooperstown, New York g) Anadarko, Oklahoma h) Oklahoma City, Oklahoma.

174. Identify each of the following facts related to the history of American women.
a) The first coeducational college in the U.S. (1835)
b) The 2 leaders of the 1848 Women's Rights Convention at Seneca Falls, N.Y.
c) The leader of the 1850 National Women's Rights Convention at Worcester, Massachusetts
d) The leader of the Women's National League (1863)
e) The 2 leaders of the National Woman Suffrage Association (May, 1869)
f) The 2 leaders of the American Woman Suffrage Association (November, 1869)
g) The first 3 presidents of the National American Woman Suffrage Association (1890 was the year of amalgamation of the 2 Associations)
h) The founder of the National Woman's Party (1913)
i) The leader of the National Organization for Women (1966)
j) The 3 major leaders of the National Women's Political Caucus (1971)
ANSWER: a) Oberlin College, Oberlin, Ohio b) Elizabeth Cady Stanton and Lucretia Mott c) Lucy Stone d) Susan B. Anthony e) Susan B. Anthony and Elizabeth Cady Stanton f) Lucy Stone and Julia Ward Howe g) Elizabeth Cady Stanton (1890-1892), Susan B. Anthony (1892-1900), and Carrie Chapman Catt (1900-1904) h) Alice Paul i) Betty Friedan j) Gloria Steinem, Bella Abzug, and Shirley Chisholm.

175. What woman was known as "America's First Libber" and "Champion of Women's Rights"? What woman was sometimes known as the "Mother of the Equal Rights Amendment to the U.S. Constitution"?
ANSWER: Susan B. Anthony/Alice Paul.

176. Identify the author of each of the following works.
a) *Woman in the Nineteenth Century* (1845)
b) *The Second Sex* (1953)
c) *A Study of the Sexes in a Changing World* (1955)
d) *The Feminine Mystique* (1963)
e) *Sexual Politics* (1970)
f) *The Female Eunuch* (1971)
g) *Against Our Will: Men, Women, and Rape* (1975)
h) *The Power of the Positive Woman* (1977)
ANSWER: a) Margaret Fuller b) Simone de Beauvoir (Fr.) c) Margaret Mead d) Betty Friedan e) Kate Millett f) Germaine Greer (Aust.) g) Susan Brownmiller h) Phyllis Schlafly.

177. Identify each of the following well-known American women.
a) The first American-born saint and founder of the Sisters of Charity
b) The founder of Christian Science
c) The founder of Hull House in Chicago
d) The first American woman to qualify as a free balloon pilot
e) The woman who is the founder of Mother's Day

f) The accomplished American dancer who was killed when her scarf wrapped around the wheel of an automobile and strangled her

ANSWER: a) Elizabeth Ann Bayley Seton b) Mary Baker Eddy c) Jane Addams d) Jeannette Ridlon Piccard e) Anna Jarvis f) Isadora Duncan.

178. Who was the American journalist who took a trip around the world in 72 days, 6 hours, 11 minutes? Give her real name and her pen name. Whose fictional record did she break? From what songwriter's song did she take her pen name?

ANSWER: Elizabeth Cochrane Seaman's pen name was Nellie Bly/Phileas Fogg who went around the world in 80 days/Stephen Foster's song "Nelly Bly."

179. Who was the legendary Negro steel-driving man who won a bet against a steam drill by driving a deeper hole into a rock but who died in the process? How did he die? On what tunnel was he working? On what railroad? In what state?

ANSWER: John Henry/He burst a blood vessel/Big Bend Tunnel/Chesapeake & Ohio Railroad/West Virginia.

180. Who was the American railroad engineer who gave his life in a train crash to save passengers and crew? How did he save them? What was the name of the train on that fateful day, April 30, 1900?

ANSWER: Casey Jones/He kept his hand on the brake lever, thus minimizing the impact and saving lives/*The Cannonball Express.*

181. What Confederate locomotive belonging to Georgia's Western and Atlantic Railroad was hijacked by 20 Union soldiers during the Civil War? Who led the Union soldiers? What was the name of the Confederate locomotive that chased the stolen one and caught it? Who led the Confederate chasers?

ANSWER: *The General*/James J. Andrews/*The Texas*/William A. Fuller.

182. Who founded Boys Town in 1917? Near what city in what state is it located? What is its motto?

ANSWER: Father Edward Joseph Flanagan/Omaha, Nebraska/"He ain't heavy, he's my brother."

183. What are the 4 H's of the 4H Club, and what are its mottos?

ANSWER: Head, Heart, Hands, and Health/"Make the Best Better" and "We Learn to Do by Doing."

184. Identify the date, name, or nickname of each of the following tariffs.
    a) The date by which the first tariff law is known
    b) The nickname of the 1828 Tariff Act which had excessive rates
    c) The 1833 Tariff which reduced the Tariff of 1832 by 10% over an 8 year period
    d) The 1846 Tariff which reduced average rates to about 25%
    e) The 1861 Tariff which raised rates
    f) The 1890 Tariff which had the highest peacetime rates
    g) The 1894 Tariff law which reduced rates from 48.4% to 41.3%
    h) The 1909 bill which only slightly lowered the Dingley Tariff of 1897
    i) The 1913 Tariff bill which significantly reduced rates
    j) The 1922 Tariff which raised the average duties to about 38.5%
    k) The 1930 Tariff which raised duties to the highest ever in peacetime

ANSWER: a) 1789 b) the "Tariff of Abominations" or the "Black Tariff" c) Compromise Tariff of 1833 d) Walker Tariff e) Morrill Tariff f) McKinley Tariff g) Wilson-Gorman Tariff h) Payne-Aldrich Tariff i) Underwood-Simmons Tariff j) Fordney-McCumber Tariff k) Hawley-Smooth Tariff.

185. What airplane pilot set out for Los Angeles in 1938 and landed his airplane in Dublin, Ireland? What was the newspaper headline recognizing this fact?

ANSWER: Douglas "Wrong Way" Corrigan/"NAGIRROC YAWGNORW OT LIAH" (read it backwards).

186. In what year was the naval battle at Midway which ended the Japanese advance in the Pacific Ocean? What were the names of the 3 U.S. carriers involved? Who was the U.S. commander?

ANSWER: 1942 (June 4-6)/*Enterprise, Hornet,* and *Yorktown*/Admiral Chester Nimitz.

187. What are the service hymns for each of the following branches?
   a) U.S. Marines   c) U.S. Navy
   b) U.S. Air Force   d) U.S. Coast Guard
ANSWER: a) *Marine Hymn* **b)** *Wild Blue Yonder* **c)** *Anchors Away* **d)** *Semper Paratus.*

188. Name the college professor later hired by the "Today" show who participated in the rigging of the TV game show "Twenty-One," and name the emcee.
ANSWER: Charles Van Doren/Jack Barry.

189. Name the Georgia governor who ejected blacks from his restaurant, and name the restaurant where he sold souvenir ax handles.
ANSWER: Lester Maddox/Pickrick.

190. Identify each of the following.
   a) The person who established the Order of the Purple Heart medal
   b) The Indian chief who dined with the pilgrims on the first Thanksgiving in 1621
   c) The motto given the *New York Times* by Adolph S. Ochs
   d) The location of the Statue of Freedom ("Miss Freedom")
   e) The longest running western on television (1955-1975)
   f) The U.S. President who was originally named Leslie Lynch King, Jr.
   g) The name of the mill in California where gold was discovered that started the California gold rush
   h) The American woman who was Helen Keller's teacher
   i) The first "Man of the Year" named by *Time* magazine (1927)
ANSWER: a) George Washington b) Massasoit (real name was Wawmegin, or "Yellow Feather") c) "All the News That's Fit to Print" d) the Capitol Dome in Washington, D.C. e) "Gunsmoke" f) Gerald R. Ford g) Sutter's Mill h) Anne Sullivan i) Charles Lindbergh.

191. "B.V.D.'s" is a common designation for underwear. What names do the initials represent?
ANSWER: Bradley, Voorhees, and Day (a trade name from 1876).

192. Who was the only man executed for war crimes following the Civil War? For what reason? What Private in the U.S. Army was executed on January 31, 1945? For what reason?
ANSWER: Captain Henry Wirz, who was hanged November 10, 1865/He was the commander of the Andersonville Stockade (in Georgia), a Confederate prison in which 12,912 Union prisoners died. He was convicted of cruelty by a federal military commission (a movement is in process to exonerate his name)/Eddie D. Slovik/For desertion.

193. Name the author of the Uncle Remus stories and the newspaper where he worked.
ANSWER: Joel Chandler Harris/*Atlanta Constitution.*

194. Name the 2 well-known American families noted for their feuding in the 1880's and 1890's. In what states did they live and fight? What river separates the 2 states?
ANSWER: The Hatfields and the McCoys/West Virginia (Logan County for the Hatfields) and Kentucky (Pike County for the McCoys)/The Tug River.

195. Who led the U.S. Treasury Department crimefighters called "the Untouchables"?
ANSWER: Eliot Ness.

196. The State College there is nicknamed the "Profs"; *The Underground Grammarian* is published there by Richard Mitchell; and it was the site of the 1967 summit meeting between President Johnson and Soviet Premier Alexei Kosygin at Hollybush. Name the city and state.
ANSWER: Glassboro, New Jersey.

197. Name the husband and wife who were executed on June 19, 1953, at Sing Sing Prison? What was their crime?
ANSWER: Julius and Ethel Rosenberg/Conspiracy to commit espionage for the Soviet Union.

198. Identify the inventor of each of the following inventions.
    a) cotton gin (1793)   f) cylinder lock (1860)
    b) mechanical mower-reaper (1831)   g) barbed wire (1873)
    c) steel plow (1837)   h) fountain pen (1884)
    d) passenger elevator (1852)   i) gyrocompass (1911)
    e) repeating rifle (1860)   j) helicopter (1939)

ANSWER: a) Eli Whitney b) Cyrus McCormick c) John Deere d) Elisha G. Otis e) Oliver
        Winchester f) Linus Yale g) Joseph Glidden h) Lewis Waterman i) Elmer
        Sperry j) Igor Sikorsky.

199. Identify the president, as of February, 1987, of each of the following labor
    unions.
    a) AFL-CIO   f) International Longshoremen's
    b) United Auto Workers   Association
    c) United Mine Workers   g) United Farm Workers of America
    d) United Steelworkers   h) American Federation of Teachers
    e) Industrial Workers of America   i) International Brotherhood of Teamsters

ANSWER: a) Lane Kirkland b) Owen Bieber c) Richard L. (Rich) Trumka d) Lynn Williams
        e) Dominick D'Ambrosio f) Thomas W. Gleason g) Cesar E. Chavez h) Albert Shanker
        i) William J. McCarthy.

200. In what 2 years was an International Exposition held in Chicago, Illinois? In what
    year will a 3rd one be held there? Chicago will actually be one of 2 cities that will
    hold a joint Universal Exposition. What is the other city? What event will be cele-
    brated at that time?

ANSWER: 1893 (World's Columbian Exposition) and 1933-1934 (Century of Progress
        Exposition)/1992/Seville, Spain/The 500th anniversary of Christopher
        Columbus's sailing from Spain and landing in America.

201. Identify each of the following.
    a) American muscleman who sold body-building by mail
    b) "Birdman of Alcatraz"
    c) Tombstone, Arizona's graveyard
    d) 82 settlers from Illinois going to California in 1846-1847, 47 of whom sur-
       vived by cannabilism in a California pass. Led by George and Jacob _____.
    e) 1931 case in Alabama in which 9 Negro boys were accused of raping 2 white
       girls in a railroad freight car
    f) The British pirate who terrorized the Carolina and Virginia coasts in 1716-
       1718 aboard his ship *Queen Anne's Revenge*
    g) Jersey City, New Jersey, mayor whose "Listen, here is the law. I am the law!
       Those boys go to work!" was misinterpreted (1937)
    h) Political boss in Kansas City, Missouri, convicted of income tax evasion
       (1940's)
    i) New York Supreme Court judge who vanished August 6, 1930
    j) Cow that supposedly started the Chicago fire of 1871 after kicking over a
       lantern
    k) First European settlement in the New World (1492)
    l) Longest running television program in the U.S.
    m) The man-ape of the U.S. and Canada similar to the Tibetan Yeti
    n) Leader of a Louisiana band of pirates and smugglers who fought for Andrew
       Jackson at the Battle of New Orleans
    o) Lone survivor of the Little Big Horn massacre (June 25, 1876)
    p) Terrorist group that kidnapped Patty Hearst (1974-1975)
    q) Richest silver vein in the world, and now the site of Virginia City, Nevada
    r) Scene of a famous gunfight between Wyatt Berry Stapp Earp, his two
       brothers, Morgan and Virgil, Doc Holliday, and the Clanton and McLaury
       brothers (gangs)
    s) The oldest state law enforcement agency in the U.S., which was formed by
       Stephen F. Austin to protect American settlers along the Brazos River and
       which later became an official mounted fighting force

t) Company founded by Henry _____ and William G. _____ that handled express service to western states, and merged in 1918 to form the American Railway Express Company
u) Place where witches were hanged in 1692
v) "Old Man River"
w) Old market building and public hall in Boston, Massachusetts, called "the Cradle of Liberty" from its use as a meeting place by American Revolutionary War patriots
x) The name shared by cities in New Hampshire, Massachusetts, North Carolina, and California, possibly named because of the harmony sought by their inhabitants
y) The New Jersey coastal area explored for oil
z) The section of San Francisco connected with the 1960's drug culture

ANSWER: **a) Charles Atlas b) Robert Stroud c) Boot Hill d) Donner Party e) Scottsboro Case f) Blackbeard (Edward Teach) g) Frank Hague h) Thomas Pendergast i) Judge Crater j) Mrs. O'Leary's cow k) La Navidad l) "Meet the Press" m) Big Foot *(Sasquatch)* n) Jean Lafitte (Laffite) o) Comanche, Keogh's horse p) Symbionese Liberation Army q) Comstock Lode r) O.K. Corral (Tombstone, Arizona) s) Texas Rangers t) Wells, Fargo & Company u) Salem, Massachusetts v) the Mississippi River w) Faneuil Hall x) Concord y) Baltimore canyon z) Haight-Ashbury.**

MAJOR U.S. FAIRS AND INTERNATIONAL EXPOSITIONS

1853 Crystal Palace Exposition — New York City

1876 Philadelphia Centennial Exposition — Fairmount Park, Philadelphia, Pennsylvania

1893 World's Columbian Exposition — Jackson Park, Chicago, Illinois

1894 Midwinter International Exposition — San Francisco, California

1898 Trans-Mississippi and International Exposition — Omaha, Nebraska

1901 Pan American Exposition — Buffalo, New York

1904 Louisiana Purchase Exposition — St. Louis, Missouri

1905 Lewis and Clark Centennial Exposition — Portland, Oregon

1907 Jamestown Ter Centennial Exposition — Hampton Roads, Virginia

1909 Alaska-Yukon Pacific Exposition — Seattle, Washington

1915- Panama-Pacific International Exposition — San Francisco, California
1916 Panama-California International Exposition — San Diego, California

1926 Sesqui-Centennial — Philadelphia, Pennsylvania

1933-
1934 Century of Progress International Exposition — Chicago, Illinois

1935 California Pacific International Exposition — San Diego, California

1939- New York World's Fair — New York
1940 Trylon and Perisphere were the symbols for "The World of Tomorrow" theme

1939- Golden Gate International Exposition — Treasure Island, San Francisco,
1940 California

1962 Seattle World's Fair or the Century 21 Exposition—Seattle, Washington
Space Needle was the symbol for the "Man in the Space Age" theme

1964- New York World's Fair—New York City
1965 Unisphere was the symbol for the "Peace Through Understanding" theme

1974 Expo '74 — Spokane, Washington
"Tomorrow's Fresh, New Environment" was the theme

1982 Knoxville World's Fair—Knoxville, Tennessee
Sunsphere was the symbol for the "Energy Turns the World" theme

1984 New Orleans World's Fair—New Orleans, Louisiana Wonderwall was the main structure for "The World of Rivers—Fresh Water as a Source of Life" theme

STATUES CONTRIBUTED BY THE STATES TO STATUARY HALL

Alabama . . . . . Jabez L.M. Curry
    *Joseph Wheeler
Alaska . . . . . .E.L. "Bob" Bartlett
    Ernest Gruening
Arizona . . . . .*John Campbell Greenway
    Eusebio Francisco Kino,
    S.J.
Arkansas . . . James Paul Clarke
    *Uriah Milton Rose
California . . . Thomas Starr King
    *Junípero Serra
Colorado . . . .*Florence Rena Sabin
Connecticut . Roger Sherman
    Jonathan Trumbull
Delaware . . . John Middleton Clayton
    Caesar A. Rodney
Florida . . . . .*John Gorrie
    Edmund Kirby Smith
Georgia . . . . . Crawford Williamson Long
    *Alexander Hamilton
    Stephens
Hawaii . . . . . Joseph Damien de Veuster
    *Kamehameha I.
Idaho . . . . . . William Edgar Borah
    *George Laird Shoup
Illinois . . . . . James Shields
    *Frances Elizabeth Willard
Indiana . . . . . Oliver Perry Morton
    *Lewis Wallace
Iowa . . . . James Harlan
    *Samuel Jordan Kirkwood
Kansas . . . . . . George Washington Glick
    *John James Ingalls
Kentucky . . .*Henry Clay
    Ephraim McDowell
Louisiana . . .*Huey Pierce Long, Jr.
    Edward Douglas White, Jr.
Maine . . . . . .*Hannibal Hamlin
    William King
Maryland . . . .Charles Carroll
    John Hanson
Massachusetts.Samuel Adams
    John Winthrop
Michigan . . . Lewis Cass
    Zachariah Chandler
Minnesota . .*Henry Mower Rice
    Maria L. Sanford
Mississippi. . .*Jefferson Davis
    James Zachariah George

Missouri . . . .*Thomas Hart Benton
    Francis Preston Blair, Jr.
Montana . . . .*Charles Marion Russell
Nebraska . . . .*William Jennings Bryan
    Julius Sterling Morton
Nevada . . . . . . Patrick Anthony McCarran
New
Hampshire . . . John Stark
    *Daniel Webster
New Jersey. . . Philip Kearny
    Richard Stockton
New Mexico . . Dennis Chavez
New York . . . . George Clinton
    Robert R. Livingston
North Carolina. Charles Brantley Aycock
    *Zebulon Baird Vance
North Dakota .*John Burke
Ohio . . . .*William Allen
    James A. Garfield
Oklahoma . . . . Will Rogers
    *Sequoya
Oregon . . . . . *Jason Lee
    John McLoughlin
Pennsylvania .*Robert Fulton
    John P. Muhlenberg
Rhode Island . Nathanael Greene
    Roger Williams
South Carolina. John Caldwell Calhoun
    Wade Hampton
South Dakota .*William Henry H. Beadle
    Joseph Ward
Tennessee . . . Andrew Jackson
    *John Sevier
Texas . . . . Stephen Fuller Austin
    *Sam Houston
Utah . . . .*Brigham Young
Vermont . . . . . Jacob Collamer
    *Ethan Allen
Virginia. . . . . *Robert Edward Lee
    George Washington
Washington . . Mother Joseph
    *Marcus Whitman
West Virginia . John E. Kenna
    *Francis Harrison Pierpont
Wisconsin. . .*Robert Marion LaFollette,
    Sr.
    Jacques Marquette
Wyoming . . . . Esther Hobart Morris

*Asterisk indicates the statue is in Statuary Hall; the other statues are elsewhere in
the Capitol.

AMERICAN INVENTIONS/CREATIONS

INVENTIONS	INVENTORS/CREATORS	DATE
Long rifle	Pennsylvania gunsmiths	1730-1740
Franklin stove	Benjamin Franklin	1740
Lightning rod	Benjamin Franklin	1752
Conestoga wagon	Pennsylvania wainwrights	1750-1760
Submarine	David Bushnell	1776
Bifocal lens	Benjamin Franklin	1780
Steam engine (multitubular boiler)	John Stevens	1783
First successful steamboat	John Fitch	1787
Spinning cotton thread mill	Samuel Slater (b. England)	1790
Cotton gin	Eli Whitney	1793
Lancaster turnpike	Pennsylvania	1795
Cast-iron plow	Charles Newbold	1797
Interchangeable parts	Eli Whitney	1798
First commercially successful steamboat (the *Clermont*)	Robert Fulton	1807
Hand printing press	George Clymer	1816
Cast-iron 3-piece plow	Jethro Wood	1819
U.S. steam locomotive (the *Tom Thumb*)	Peter Cooper	1830
Mechanical mower-reaper	Cyrus McCormick	1831
Revolver	Samuel Colt	1835
Steel plow	John Deere	1837
Steam shovel	William S. Otis	1838
Vulcanization of rubber	Charles Goodyear	1839
Clipper ships	Donald McKay (the most famous builder)	1840's-1850's
Ether for an anesthesia	Crawford Long	1842
Telegraph	Samuel F.B. Morse	1844
Suspension bridge (wire cable)	John A. Roebling	1845
Sewing machine	Elias Howe	1846
Ether as a practical anesthetic	William T.G. Morton	1846
Corliss steam engine	George Corliss	1846-1880
Modern safety pin	Walter Hunt	1849
Practical sewing machine (foot-operated)	Isaac M. Singer	1851
Passenger elevator	Elisha G. Otis	1852
Condensation of milk	Gail Borden	1853
Trans-Atlantic cable	Cyrus Field	1858
Modern oil well	Edwin Drake	1859
Repeating rifle	Oliver F. Winchester	1860
Cylinder lock	Linus Yale	1860
Pony Express	William H. Russell	1860
Revolving machine gun	Richard J. Gatling	1862
Pullman car (sleeping car on a train)	George M. Pullman	1864
First practical typewriter	Christopher Sholes and Carlos Glidden	1867
Air brake	George Westinghouse	1868
Electric voting machine	Thomas Edison	1869
Central Pacific-Union Pacific Railroad	Nebraska-California (Huntington & Stanford)	1869
Barbed wire	Joseph F. Glidden	1873
Telephone	Alexander Graham Bell	1875-1876
Phonograph (cylinder)	Thomas Edison	1877

Half-tone engraving (the
"optical V") . . . . Fredrick Eugene Ives 1878
Electric lighting (light bulb) . . . . Thomas Edison 1879
Cigarette machine production . . . . . . James Buchanan Duke 1880
Camera/roll film/Kodak camera . . . . George Eastman 1880-1888
Fountain pen . . . . Lewis E. Waterman 1884
Motion-picture projector . . . . Thomas Edison 1889
Mayo Clinic . . . . William & Charles Mayo 1889
Browning machine gun . . . . John Moses Browning 1890
Gasoline-powered automobile . . . . . . Charles & Frank Duryea 1893
Safety razor . . . . King Gillette 1895
Yellow fever eradication . . . . Watler Reed 1901
Assembly line for automobiles . . . . . Ransom Eli Olds 1901
Air conditioning . . . . Willis H. Carrier 1902
Airplane . . . . Wilbur & Orville Wright 1903
Theory of relativity and Brownian
Motion (general theory of relativity
in 1916) . . . . Albert Einstein (b. Germany) 1905
Vacuum tube (triode) . . . . Lee De Forest 1906
Gyrocompass . . . . Elmer A. Sperry 1911
Moving assembly line . . . . Henry Ford 1913
Schick test (skin test for
diphtheria . . . . Béla Schick 1913
Thompson submachine gun . . . . John T. Thompson 1916
Browning automatic rifle . . . . John M. Browning 1917
Electronic television . . . . Vladimir K. Zworykin 1923
Fast-frozen food processing . . . . Clarence Birdseye 1924
Liquid-propelled rocket . . . . Robert Goddard 1926
Analog computer . . . . Vannevar Bush 1930
Cyclotron . . . . Ernest O. Lawrence 1930
Electric Razor . . . . Col. Jacob Schick 1931
Split atom in nuclear fission . . . . Enrico Fermi (b. Italy) 1934
Nylon (by Wallace H.
Carothers) . . . . Wallace H. Carothers and
                                              DuPont laboratories 1935
Helicopter . . . . Igor Sikorsky (b. Russia) 1939
Plutonium, curium, americium,
berkelium, californium,
mendelevium, einsteinium, fermium,
and nobelium . . . . Glenn T. Seaborg,
                                              co-discoverer 1940-1955
Atomic chain reaction . . . . Enrico Fermi 1942
Atomic bomb construction by an
international team of scientists
led by . . . . J. Robert Oppenheimer 1943-1945
Digital computer . . . . Howard H. Aiken 1944
Dehydrated food processing . . . . Clarence Birdseye 1949
Hydrogen bomb . . . . Edward Teller (and others) 1953
DNA deciphering (Watson-
Crick model of DNA) . . . . James Watson 1953
Laser-maser principle . . . . Charles H. Townes 1953-1958
Salk polio vaccine . . . . Dr. Jonas Salk 1953
Nuclear reactor . . . . Enrico Fermi/Leo Szilard 1955
Oral polio vaccine . . . . Dr. Albert Sabin 1955
Laser . . . . Gordon Gould 1957
High-energy radiation belts
(Van Allen Belts) . . . . James A. Van Allen 1958
Heart surgery and transplants . . . . . Drs. Michael De Bakey &
                                              Denton A. Cooley 1966

AMERICAN INVENTORS/CREATORS AND THEIR NICKNAMES

Alexander Graham Bell . . . . . . Father of the Telephone
Clarence Birdseye . . . . Father of Frozen Foods
Gail Borden . . . . Father of Condensed Milk
Vannevar Bush . . . . Father of Memex
David Bushnell . . . . Father of the Submarine
Peter Cooper . . . . Father of Cooper Union, Father of Railroads
Nathaniel Currier and James
Merritt Ives . . . . Printmakers to the American People
Michael Ellis De Bakey . . . . . . Texas Tornado
Lee De Forest . . . . Father of Wireless Telegraphy (the Radio)
Benjamin Newton Duke and
James Buchanan Duke . . . . . . Tobacco Kings
Charles Edgar Duryea . . . . Father of the Automobile
George Eastman . . . . Father of the Kodak
Thomas Alva Edison . . . . Electrical Wizard, Father of Light, Father of the
Phonograph, Hugo, Victor, Wizard of Menlo Park,
Wizard of the Wires
Albert Einstein . . . . Father of Relativity
Enrico Fermi . . . . Architect of the A-Bomb, The Columbus to the Atomic
Age
Cyrus West Field . . . . Father of the Submarine Cable, Greatest Wirepuller
of Modern Times
John Fitch . . . . Poor John Fitch
Henry Ford . . . . Automobile Wizard, Father of the Flivver, Father of
the Motor Car, Flivver King, Genius of Motordom
Benjamin Franklin . . . . Father of the Mail Order Catalog, Father of the Stove,
Grand Old Man, Many-sided Franklin, Philomath,
Tamer of Lightning
Robert Fulton . . . . Father of Steamboat Navigation, Father of the
Steamboat, Quicksilver Bob
Richard Jordan Gatling . . . . . . Father of the Gatling Gun
King Camp Gillette . . . . Father of the Safety Razor
Robert Goddard . . . . Father of American Rocketry
Charles Goodyear . . . . Rubber's Goodyear
Elias Howe . . . . Father of the Sewing Machine
Cyrus Hall McCormick . . . . . . Father of the Reaper
Charles Horace Mayo . . . . Doctor Charlie
William James Mayo . . . . Doctor Will
Samuel Finley Breese
Morse . . . . American Leonardo, Father of the Telegraph
Ransom Eli Olds . . . . Father of Oldsmobile and Reo
Julius Robert Oppenheimer . . . Equivocal Hero of Science, Father of the A-Bomb,
Troubled Pied Piper of Los Alamos
George Mortimer Pullman . . . . Father of the Sleeping Car
Walter Reed . . . . Doctor in Uniform
John Augustus Roebling and
Washington Augustus
Roebling . . . . Fathers of the Brooklyn Bridge
Christopher Latham Sholes . . . Father of the Typewriter
Igor Ivan Sikorsky . . . . Father of the Helicopter, Uncle Igor
Isaac Merrit Singer . . . . Father of the Sewing Machine
Samuel Slater . . . . Father of American Manufacturing
John Taliaferro Thompson . . . Father of the Tommy Gun
George Westinghouse . . . . Father of the Air Brake, Inventive Wizard
Eli Whitney . . . . Father of the Cotton Gin, Whittling Boy
Orville and Wilbur Wright . . . . American Pioneers in Aviation
Linus Yale . . . . Father of the Cylinder Lock
Vladimir Kosma Zworykin . . . . Father of Television

INDIAN LORE: QUESTIONS AND ANSWERS

1. Of what tribes were the following Indian chiefs the leaders?

   a) Geronimo
   b) Chief Joseph
   c) Black Hawk
   d) Crazy Horse
   e) Tamanend
   f) Pontiac
   g) Massasoit
   h) Red Eagle
   i) Sitting Bull
   j) Tecumseh

   ANSWER: a) Apache b) Nez Percé c) Sauk (Sac) d) Oglala Sioux e) Delawares f) Ottawas g) Wampanoags h) Creeks i) Hunkpapa Teton Sioux j) Shawnees.

2. What Indians were known by the following names?

   a) Lily of the Mohawk
   b) Matoaka, Lady Rebecca, or Mrs. John Rolfe
   c) Patron Saint of North America or St. Tammany
   d) Bird Woman
   e) Captain Jack
   f) William Henry
   g) the Prophet
   h) Metacomet
   i) William Weatherford
   j) George Guess

   ANSWER: a) Kateri (Katherine) Tekakwitha b) Pocahontas c) Tamanend d) Sacajawea (Sacagawea) e) Keintpoos (Kintpuash) f) Gelelemend or Killbuck g) Tenskwatawa or Lalawethika (Elskwatawa) h) King Philip i) Red Eagle j) Sequoya (Sequoyah).

3. Identify the following Indian related descriptions.

   a) First North American Indian to be a candidate for sainthood
   b) The 3 leaders at the Battle of the Little Bighorn
   c) State and date of the Battle of the Little Bighorn
   d) The author of *The Song of Hiawatha*
   e) The founder of the League of Iroquois (c. 1570)
   f) The part Indian and part Negro who was the first person killed at the Boston Massacre
   g) The Indian nicknamed "Big Tree"
   h) The State in which the Aztec National Monument is located
   i) The Indian nicknamed "Red Sleeves"
   j) The coined word for an individual of one of the native peoples of America

   ANSWER: a) Kateri (Katherine) Tekakwitha b) Gall, Crazy Horse, and Sitting Bull c) Montana, June 25, 1876 d) Henry Wadsworth Longfellow e) Hiawatha f) Crispus Attucks g) Adoeette h) New Mexico i) Mangas Coloradas j) Amerind.

4. Identify the Indian word from the following descriptions.

   a) Peace pipe
   b) Indian corn
   c) Black volcanic glass used by the Indians for making spear and arrow points
   d) Lean dried (deer) meat pounded into a powder and mixed with fat, dried fruits and berries
   e) Indian communal dwelling (Spanish word for village)
   f) Cactus containing a drug that causes dreams and hallucinations; mescal
   g) Beads used as a medium of exchange
   h) Conference with an Indian leader or group; discussion meeting
   i) Primitive sled with 2 poles joined by a frame and pulled by an animal
   j) Long flat-bottomed sled without runners made of thin boards
   k) Indian ritual of lavish giving of gifts by the host as display of social rank requiring reciprocation

   ANSWER: a) calumet b) maize c) obsidian d) pemmican e) pueblo f) peyote g) wampum h) powwow i) travois j) toboggan k) potlatch.

5. What phrase from Indian custom means "to stop fighting, to lay down arms, to make peace"? What arms are usually involved in this process? Recite the 5 lines of Henry Wadsworth Longfellow's *The Song of Hiawatha* that describe the process. What was smoked as a preliminary ritual?

   ANSWER: "Bury the hatchet"/Hatchet, ax, and tomahawk/"Buried was the bloody hatchet./Buried was the dreadful war club;/Buried were all warlike weapons,/And the war cry was forgotten. / There was peace among the nations."/The calumet or peace pipe.

6. What are the names of the 5 Civilized Indian Tribes?
ANSWER: Cherokee, Chickasaw, Choctaw, Creek, and Seminole.

7. Name the 3 largest language groups of Indians along the Atlantic coast south of the Saint Lawrence River in the 1600's. Give the names of the "5 Nations" of the second largest group. What was the name of the tribe that moved north in the early 18th century and joined the league of "5 Nations" to make it "6 Nations"? Also, name the 4 tribes of the 3rd largest group.
ANSWER: Algonquins, Iroquois, and Muskogean/Iroquois: Cayuga, Mohawk, Oneida, Onondaga, and Seneca/The Tuscaroras/Muskogean: Chickasaws, Choctaws, Creeks, and Seminoles.

8. Give in descending order the largest 1984 populations of Indian reservations.
ANSWER: Navajo (Arizona, New Mexico, Utah), Creek and Cherokee (both in Oklahoma).

9. Name the 3 states with the largest Indian populations.
ANSWER: California, Oklahoma, and Arizona.

10. Identify each of the following Indian related descriptions.
    a) The English-speaking Pemaquid Indian chief who made friends with the Pilgrims and who introduced Massasoit to them
    b) The Patuxet Indian who showed the Pilgrims how to plant corn and where the best places to hunt and fish were
    c) The Indian chief of the Wampanoags who was supposedly invited to dine with the Pilgrims on the first Thanksgiving Day in 1621
    d) The Author of *The Last of the Mohicans*
    e) The Indian brigadier general, the leader of the Cherokee Mounted Rifles, who was in the Confederate Army
    f) The only Indian credited with winning a war against the U.S. government, for he caused the government to abandon forts Kearny, Reno, and Smith in Wyoming and Montana in 1868
    g) The founder of the Ghost Dance Religion
    h) The Nez Percé Indian chief whose skillful tactic of retreat through Idaho and Montana in 1877 earned him the nickname of the "Indian Napoleon"
    i) The Indian woman who criticized government mistreatment of the Paiutes, who met with President Hayes in 1880, and who wrote *Life Among the Paiute: Their Claims and Wrongs* (1883)
    j) The American Indian, winner of the pentathlon and decathlon at the 1912 Olympic Games, who became the first president of the American Football Association (the present-day National Football League)
    k) The Indian Industrial School in Pennsylvania attended by Jim Thorpe
    l) The meaning of AIM and CERT
ANSWER: a) Samoset b) Squanto c) Massasoit d) James Fenimore Cooper e) Stand Watie f) Red Cloud g) Wovoka h) Chief Joseph i) Sara Winnemucca (Thoc-me-tony) j) Jim Thorpe k) Carlisle l) American Indian Movement and Council of Energy Resources Tribe.

INDIAN CHIEFS/LEADERS AND THEIR TRIBES

Adoeette . . . . Kiowas
Aspinet . . . . Nausets
Black Hawk (Ma-ka-tae-
mish-kia-kiak). . . . . Sauk (Sac)
Blacksnake . . . . Senecas
Joseph Brant
(Thayendanegea) . . . . . . Mohawks
Buckongahelas . . . . Delawares
Catahecassa . . . . Shawnees
Cochise . . . . Chiricahua Apaches
Cornplanter (John
O'Bail) . . . . Senecas
Crazy Horse (Tashunca-
Uitco) . . . . Oglala Sioux
Gall . . . . Hunkpapa Teton Sioux
Gelelemend (Killbuck,
William Henry) . . . . Delawares
Geronimo (Goyathlay) . . . Chiricahua Apaches
Hiawatha . . . . Mohawks
Chief Joseph (Hinmaton
Yalatkit) . . . . Nez Percé
Junaluska . . . . Cherokee
Keintpoos (Kintpuash,
Captain Jack) . . . . Modoc
Keokuk . . . . Sauk (Sac)
Lappawinze . . . . Delawares
Little Thunder . . . . Brulé Sioux
Little Turtle . . . . Miamis of Indiana
(John or James) Logan
(Tah-gah-jute) . . . . Iroquois Mingo and
                              Cayuga
Lone Wolf . . . . Kiowas
William MacIntosh . . . . . Creeks
Madokawando . . . . Penobscot
Mangas Coloradas . . . . . Apaches
Massasoit . . . . Wampanoags
Mazakutemani . . . . Sisseton Sioux
Negwagon . . . . Ottawas
Old Knife . . . . Pawnees
Osceola . . . . Seminoles
Oshkosh . . . . Menominees
Petalesharo . . . . Pawnees
King Philip (Metacomet) . Wampanoags

Pitchlynn (Peter Perkins
Pitchlynn) . . . . Choctaws
Pokagon . . . . Potawatomi
Pontiac . . . . Ottawas
Powhatan (Wa-hun-
sen-a-cawh) (Wahun-
sonacock) . . . . Powhatan league (Con-
                              federacy of Powhatan)
                              Algonkin (Algonquian)
                              tribes
Queen Anne . . . . Pamunkeys
John W. Quinney . . . . Stockbridges
Red Bird . . . . Winnebagos
Red Cloud (Mahpiua
Luta) . . . . Oglala Teton Sioux
Red Eagle (William
Weatherford) . . . . Creeks
Red Fish . . . . Oglala Sioux
Red Horn . . . . Piegans
Red Jacket (Sagoye-
watha) . . . . Senecas
Red Thunder . . . . Yanktonai Sioux
Redwing . . . . Sioux
Roman Nose (Woqini) . . . Cheyennes
                              (Himoiyogis)
Samoset . . . . Pemaquids
Sequoia (Sequoyah,
Sequoya, George
Guess) . . . . Eastern Cherokees
Setaugya (Satank) . . . . . . Kiowas
Sitting Bull (Tatanka
Iyotake) . . . . Hunkpapa Teton Sioux
Standing Bear . . . . Poncas
Tananend (St.
Tammany) . . . . Delawares
Tecumseh (Tecumtha,
Tecumthe, Tikamthi) . . . . Shawnees
Tenskwatawa (the
Prophet, Lalawethika,
Elskwatawa) . . . . Shawnees
Waneta . . . . Yanktonai Sioux
Yellow Thunder . . . . Winnebagos

THE NINE WORLD WARS AND THEIR PEACE TREATIES

In Europe	In America
1688-1697 War of the League of Augsburg (War of the Grand Alliance)	1689-1697 King William's War
Peace of Ryswick-1697	
1701-1713 War of Spanish Succession	1702-1713 Queen Anne's War
Treaty of Utrecht-1713	
1740-1748 War of Austrian Succession	1744-1748 King George's War
Treaty of Aix-la-Chapelle-1748	
1756-1763 Seven Years' War	1754-1763 French and Indian War
Treaty of Paris-1763	
1778-1783 War of the American Revolution	1775-1783 American Revolution
Treaty of Paris-1783	
1793-1802 Wars of the French Revolution	1798-1800 Undeclared French War
1803-1815 Napoleonic Wars	1812-1814 War of 1812
Treaty of Ghent-1814	
1914-1918 World War I	1917-1918 World War I
Treaty of Versailles-1919	
1939-1945 World War II	1941-1945 World War II
V-E Day May 8, 1945 V-J Day September 2, 1945	

FLAGS: QUESTIONS AND ANSWERS

1. Identify the U.S. states from the following description of their flags.
    a) Has a bison
    b) Has a grizzly
    c) Has a gold beaver on the reverse side
    d) Has the sun of the Zia Indians
    e) Has the motto ''Battle Born''
    f) Has a white palmetto and a crescent

    moon
    g) Has the Union Jack in the upper left
    h) Has the torch of liberty and knowledge and 19 gold stars
    i) Has the dates May 20, 1775, and April 12, 1776
    j) Has a gold anchor with the motto ''Hope''

ANSWER: a) Wyoming b) California c) Oregon d) New Mexico e) Nevada f) South Carolina g) Hawaii h) Indiana i) North Carolina j) Rhode Island.

2. Identify the following U.S. territories (including Washington, D.C.) from the descriptions of their flags.
    a) Has a gold American eagle between blue letters ''V'' and ''I''
    b) Has the territorial seal which has a palm tree and a boat
    c) Has 3 red stars above 2 parallel horizontal red stripes
    d) Has a white triangle bordered with red and an American eagle on the right
    e) Has 3 red and 2 white horizontal stripes and a white star

ANSWER: a) Virgin Islands b) Guam c) Washington, D.C. d) American Samoa e) Puerto Rico.

3. What are the 2 states that have the Confederate flag as part of their flag?
ANSWER: Georgia and Mississippi.

4. What are the 2 states that have a red saltire or X-shaped cross as part of their flag?
ANSWER: Alabama and Florida.

5. What word means the study of flags?
ANSWER: Vexillology.

6. Identify the countries or explorers of America from the following descriptions of their flags or banners.
    a) A raven, which is the Norse symbol of good luck
    b) A castle for the Province of Castile and a crimson lion for the Province of Leon
    c) A green cross with crowns and the letters ''F'' (for Ferdinand) and ''Y'' (for Isabella) (This was the personal banner of a famous explorer)
    d) A red St. George's cross
    e) 3 gold fleurs-de-lis (the Blue Bourbon flag)
    f) 3 yellow fleurs-de-lis (the White Bourbon flag)
    g) Union Jack which combines the crosses of St. George (England) and St. Andrew (Scotland)
    h) Yellow cross on a light blue shield
    i) AOC (for *Algemeene Ost-Indische Compagnie*)
    j) G.W.C. (for *Geoctroyeerde West-Indische Compagnie*)

ANSWER: a) Vikings b) Spain c) Christopher Columbus d) John Cabot and future English explorers e) Giovanni Da Verrazano and future French explorers f) Huguenots g) England h) Sweden i) Dutch East India Company j) Dutch West India Company.

7. Identify the American flags from the following descriptions.
    a) Has a coiled rattlesnake on a yellow field with the words ''Don't tread on me''
    b) Has a single star and a grizzly bear
    c) The Minutemen used it at Concord and it has the motto *Vince Aut Morire* (Conquer or Die)
    d) Bears the motto ''Don't Give Up The Ship''
    e) Has 3 stripes and 7 stars

ANSWER: a) Gadsden Flag b) Flag of California or of the Bear Flag Republic c) Bedford flag d) Oliver Perry's flag e) Stars and Bars or the Confederate flag.

U.S. STATES/TERRITORIES AND BRIEF DESCRIPTIONS OF THEIR FLAGS

Alabama . . . . A saltire or X-shaped red cross.

Alaska . . . . 7 gold stars that represent the Big Dipper and a larger star representing the North Star or Polaris.

Arizona . . . . A large copper star represents the mining industry with 13 rays, alternately red and yellow representing the Spanish flag.

Arkansas . . . . Diamond-shaped center with 4 stars.

California . . . . A grizzly bear and a red star for this "Bear Flag Republic."

Colorado . . . . Red letter C encompassing a golden disk or ball.

Connecticut . . . . State seal, with 3 grape vines, each bearing fruit and, below, the state motto *Qui Transtulit Sustinet.*

Delaware . . . . State coat of arms, with a farmer and a rifleman and the state motto "Liberty and Independence," on a buff-colored diamond above the date December 7, 1787.

Florida . . . . State seal, with the sun's rays illuminating a steamboat and an Indian woman with the state motto "In God We Trust," in a red saltire or X-shaped cross.

Georgia . . . . State seal on the left combined with the Confederate Battle Flag on the right.

Hawaii . . . . Union Jack in upper left with 8 horizontal stripes representing the 8 main islands.

Idaho . . . . State seal, with the Goddess of Justice and a miner with an inscription above a stag's head bearing the state motto *Esto Perpetua,* all of which is above the "State of Idaho" inscription.

Illinois . . . . State seal, with a bald eagle. In its beak is a banner bearing the state motto "State Sovereignty National Union." On a rock beneath the eagle are the dates 1868 and 1818.

Indiana . . . . The torch of knowledge and liberty and 19 gold stars.

Iowa . . . . Blue, white, and red bars (like the French flag) on which in the center there is an eagle with a banner bearing the state motto "Our Liberties We Prize and Our Rights We Will Maintain."

Kansas . . . . Sunflower above the state seal which has a man plowing a field and with the state motto *Ad Astra per Aspera* at the top and 34 stars below

Kentucky . . . . Goldenrod below the state seal, which has two men greeting each other and the state motto "United We Stand, Divided We Fall."

Louisiana . . . . A pelican feeding its young above the state motto "Union, Justice, and, Confidence."

Maine . . . . State seal, which has a pine tree, a moose, a farmer, and a sailor below the state motto *Dirigo.* Above the motto is a star which represents the North Star.

Maryland . . . . Gold-and-black pattern for the Calverts, and red and white ornate crosses for the Crossland family.

Massachusetts . . . . The state coat of arms, which has an Indian in gold and a silver star on the left side of the shield and bears the state motto *Ense Petit Placidam Sub Libertate Quietem.*

Michigan . . . . State seal, which has an elk and a moose supporting a shield. There are 3 mottoes on the seal: *E Pluribus Unum* on the upper scroll, *Tuebor* ("I will defend"), and the state motto *Si Quaeris Peninsulam Amoenam Circumspice* on the scroll under the shield.

Minnesota . . . . State seal, which has a plowman and an Indian along with the state motto "L'Etoile du Nord." The seal is surrounded by 19 gold stars.

Mississippi. . . . . Battle Flag of the Confederacy in the upper left and 3 horizontal blue, white, and red stripes.

Missouri. . . . . Three red, white, and blue stripes, and in the center the state seal surrounded by 24 stars.

Montana. . . . . State seal, which depicts the agricultural and mining wealth of the state by its plow, pick and shovel and on which is the state motto *Oro y Plata.*

Nebraska . . . . State seal, which has a blacksmith, a cabin, a steamboat, and a train and the state motto "Equality Before the Law" along with the date "March 1st, 1867."

Nevada. . . . . Gold and green insignia with the motto "Battle Born" and sagebrush forming a half-wreath for a silver star.

New Hampshire . . . . State seal with the Revolutionary War frigate *Raleigh* and the date 1776. The seal is surrounded by a wreath of laurel leaves, interspersed with 9 gold stars.

New Jersey. . . . . State seal, which has two figures (Ceres and Liberty), the date 1776, and the state motto "Liberty and Prosperity."

New Mexico . . . . Red and yellow colors of the Spanish flag and the ancient sun symbol of the Zia indians.

New York . . . . State coat of arms with Justice and Liberty standing next to a shield, a bald eagle atop a globe, and a banner with the state motto *Excelsior.*

North Carolina . . . . The dates May 20, 1775 (Mecklenburg Declaration of Independence) and April 12, 1776 (Halifax Resolves) are on scrolls on the left with 2 horizontal bands of red and white on the right.

North Dakota . . . . Modified seal of the United States with an eagle grasping in its talons an olive branch and a sheaf of arrows with a streamer in its beak bearing the national motto *E Pluribus Unum.*

Ohio . . . . A pennant with 3 red and 2 white bars for its roads and rivers and a blue triangle for its hills and valleys with 17 white stars surrounding a white circle with a red disk at its center.

Oklahoma. . . . . A shield, peace pipe, and an olive branch.

Oregon . . . . State seal, which has a shield encircled by 33 stars, a bald eagle, and the state motto "The Union." The year 1859 is below the seal. This flag has a different design on the reverse—a gold beaver.

Pennsylvania . . . . State coat of arms which is supported by a horse on either side and bears a bald eagle, a ship, a plow, and three sheaves of wheat.

Rhode Island . . . . Gold anchor with the motto "Hope" below surrounded by 13 gold stars.

South Carolina . . . . A white palmetto tree in the center and a white crescent moon in the upper left corner.

South Dakota . . . . State seal, which has a farmer plowing his field, a steam boat, and a smelting furnace along with the state motto "Under God the People Rule." The state nickname "The Sunshine State" is below.

Tennessee . . . . Three white stars in the center (for the 3 divisions of the state and for the 3rd state to join the Union after the original 13).

Texas . . . . A lone white star on the left and 2 horizontal bars of white and red on the right.

Utah . . . . State seal, which has a beehive flanked by sego lilies along with the state motto ''Industry.'' The dates 1847 and 1896 are for the entrance of the Mormons into Salt Lake Valley and the state's entrance into the Union, respectively.

Vermont . . . . State seal with a pine tree, four sheaves of wheat, a cow and the state motto ''Vermont, Freedom and Unity'' on the scroll in the center.

Virginia. . . . . State seal with Virtue standing over a fallen Tyranny along with the motto *Sic semper tyrannis.*

Washington . . . . State seal, the date (1889), and a picture of the President after whom it was named.

West Virginia . . . . State arms with the date (June 20, 1863) on a rock and the state motto *Montani Semper Liberi.*

Wisconsin. . . . . State seal, which has the state motto ''Forward'' on the upper scroll above a badger, 13 stars on the lower scroll, and a sailor and a workman with a pick supporting the state's coat of arms.

Wyoming . . . . State seal on the ribs of a white bison.

District of Columbia . . . . Three red stars above 2 parallel horizontal stripes.

American Samoa. . . . . White triangle bordered with red and bearing an American eagle on the right.

Guam . . . . Territorial seal (with a palm tree and a boat).

Puerto Rico . . . . Three red and 2 white horizontal stripes with a white star on a triangular-shaped blue field.

Virgin Islands . . . . Gold American eagle between blue letters ''V'' and ''I.''

ADMISSION OF STATES TO THE UNION

Order of Admission	State	Date of Admission	Order of Admission	State	Date of Admission
1	Delaware	December 7, 1787	26	Michigan	January 26, 1837
2	Pennsylvania	December 12, 1787	27	Florida	March 3, 1845
3	New Jersey	December 18, 1787	28	Texas	December 29, 1845
4	Georgia	January 2, 1788	29	Iowa	December 28, 1846
5	Connecticut	January 9, 1788	30	Wisconsin	May 29, 1848
6	Massachusetts (incl. Maine)	February 7, 1788	31	California	September 9, 1850
			32	Minnesota	May 11, 1858
7	Maryland	April 28, 1788	33	Oregon	February 14, 1859
8	South Carolina	May 23, 1788	34	Kansas	January 29, 1861
9	New Hampshire	June 21, 1788	35	West Virginia	June 20, 1863
10	Virginia	June 26, 1788	36	Nevada	October 31, 1864
11	New York	July 26, 1788	37	Nebraska	March 1, 1867
12	North Carolina	November 21, 1789	38	Colorado	August 1, 1876
13	Rhode Island	May 29, 1790	39	North Dakota	November 2, 1889
14	Vermont	March 4, 1791	40	South Dakota	November 2, 1889
15	Kentucky	June 1, 1792	41	Montana	November 8, 1889
16	Tennessee	June 1, 1796	42	Washington	November 11, 1889
17	Ohio	March 1, 1803	43	Idaho	July 3, 1890
18	Louisiana	April 30, 1812	44	Wyoming	July 10, 1890
19	Indiana	December 11, 1816	45	Utah	January 4, 1896
20	Mississippi	December 10, 1817	46	Oklahoma	November 16, 1907
21	Illinois	December 3, 1818	47	New Mexico	January 6, 1912
22	Alabama	December 14, 1819	48	Arizona	February 14, 1912
23	Maine	March 15, 1820	49	Alaska	January 3, 1959
24	Missouri	August 10, 1821	50	Hawaii	August 21, 1959
25	Arkansas	June 15, 1836			

U.S. COLLEGES AND UNIVERSITIES

QUESTIONS AND ANSWERS

1. In which city is each of the following colleges or universities located?

   a) Arizona State   f) Florida   k) Marquette
   b) Boston College   g) Harvard   l) Michigan State
   c) Brigham Young   h) Indiana   m) Missouri
   d) De Paul   i) Iowa State   n) Oklahoma
   e) Duke   j) Kansas   o) Purdue

   ANSWER: a) Tempe, Arizona b) Chestnut Hill, Massachusetts c) Provo, Utah d) Chicago, Illinois e) Durham, North Carolina f) Gainesville, Florida g) Cambridge, Massachusetts h) Bloomington, Indiana i) Ames, Iowa j) Lawrence, Kansas k) Milwaukee, Wisconsin l) East Lansing, Michigan m) Columbia, Missouri n) Norman, Oklahoma o) West Lafayette, Indiana.

2. Each of the following colleges or universities is a member of which conference?

   a) Alabama   f) Austin Peay   k) Indiana State
   b) Washington   g) Colorado   l) Fullerton
   c) Northwestern   h) Dartmouth   m) Ball State
   d) S.M.U.   i) Georgia Tech   n) Southern Mississippi
   e) Hawaii   j) Boise State   o) Georgia

   ANSWER: a) Southeastern (SEC) b) Pac 10 c) Big Ten d) Southwest e) Western Athletic f) Ohio Valley g) Big 8 h) Ivy League i) Atlantic Coast (ACC) j) Big Sky k) Missouri Valley l) Pacific Coast m) Mid-American n) None — an Independent o) Southeastern (SEC).

3. Give the nickname for each of the following colleges or universities.

   a) Yale   f) South Carolina   k) Minnesota
   b) West Virginia   g) Rutgers   l) Maryland
   c) Virginia Tech   h) Purdue   m) James Madison
   d) Tulsa   i) Penn State   n) Georgetown
   e) Stanford   j) Oregon   o) Cornell

   ANSWER: a) Bulldogs, Elis b) Mountaineers c) Hokies/Gobblers d) Golden Hurricanes e) Cardinals f) Fighting Gamecocks g) Scarlet Knights h) Boilermakers i) Nittany Lions j) Ducks k) Golden Gophers l) Terrapins, Terps m) Dukes n) Hoyas o) Big Red.

4. What is the oldest college located in Virginia, and what is the oldest located in Massachusetts?

   ANSWER: William and Mary/Harvard.

5. What schools are competing in each of the following?

   a) Razorbacks vs. Bearcats   d) Cornhuskers vs. Sooners
   b) Tar Heels vs. Flyers   e) Friars vs. Orangemen
   c) Volunteers vs. Black Knights   f) Dons vs. Salukis

   ANSWER: a) Arkansas vs. Cincinnati b) North Carolina vs. Dayton c) Tennessee vs. Army d) Nebraska vs. Oklahoma e) Providence vs. Syracuse f) San Francisco vs. Southern Illinois.

6. In which city is each of the following Texas colleges or universities located?

   a) Texas   e) Southern Methodist   i) West Texas State
   b) Texas A & M   f) Rice   j) North Texas State
   c) Texas Christian   g) Baylor   k) Lamar
   d) Texas Tech   h) Hardin-Simmons   l) Stephen F. Austin

   ANSWER: a) Austin b) College Station c) Fort Worth d) Lubbock e) Dallas f) Houston g) Waco h) Abilene i) Canyon j) Denton k) Beaumont l) Nacogdoches.

7. In which city is each of the following New York colleges or universities located?

   a) Canisius   f) Hartwick   k) St. John's
   b) Colgate   g) Hofstra   l) Sarah Lawrence
   c) Columbia   h) Iona   m) U.S. Merchant Marine Academy
   d) Cornell   i) Long Island   n) U.S. Military Academy
   e) Fordham   j) Rensselaer Tech   o) Vassar

ANSWER: a) Buffalo b) Hamilton c) New York d) Ithaca e) New York f) Oneonta
g) Hempstead h) New Rochelle i) Brooklyn j) Troy k) Jamaica l) Bronxville
m) Kings Point n) West Point o) Poughkeepsie.

8. In which city are all the following colleges located?
Dropsie, Drexel, St. Joseph's, La Salle, Temple, and the University of Penn-
sylvania.
ANSWER: Philadelphia.

9. Give the nickname for each of the following colleges or universities.
a) Yeshiva   g) Brandeis   m) Washington & Jefferson
b) Swarthmore   h) Whittier   n) Austin Peay State
c) Furman   i) Massachusetts   o) Baruch College
d) Pennsylvania   j) Providence   p) North Carolina (Charlotte)
e) Catholic U.   k) Kenyon   q) Virginia
f) Delta State   l) Denver   r) Lewis & Clark
ANSWER: a) Maccabbees b) Little Quakers c) Paladins d) Quakers e) Cardinals
f) Statesmen g) Judges h) Poets i) Minutemen j) Friars k) Lords l) Pioneers
m) Presidents n) Governors o) Statesmen p) 49ers q) Cavaliers r) Pioneers.

10. Name the first 5 state colleges chartered by a state legislature, and give the years
of their charters if possible.
ANSWER: Georgia (the oldest state-chartered university — 1785, although not established until 1801); North Carolina (chartered in 1789, but the first state
university to hold classes — 1795); Vermont (chartered — 1791); South
Carolina (chartered — 1801); and Ohio (chartered — 1804).

11. Identify the state nickname by which each of the following universities is known.
a) Delaware   g) Nebraska   m) Pennsylvania
b) Indiana   h) North Carolina   n) South Dakota
c) Kansas   i) North Dakota   o) Tennessee
d) Maryland   j) Ohio (State)   p) Virginia
e) Michigan   k) Oklahoma   q) Wisconsin
f) Minnesota   l) Oregon (State)   r) Wyoming
ANSWER: a) Blue Hen b) Hoosier c) Jayhawk d) Terrapin e) Wolverine f) Gopher
g) Cornhusker h) Tar Heel i) Sioux j) Buckeye k) Sooner l) Beaver
m) Quaker n) Coyote o) Volunteer p) Cavalier q) Badger r) Cowboy.

12. With which university is each of the following school songs associated?
a) ''Far Above Cayuga's Waters''   f) ''Mother of Men''
b) ''Helen of Troy''   g) ''On the Banks of Old Raritan''
c) ''Horned Frogs''   h) ''(The) Orange and the Black''
d) ''I'm a Jayhawk''   i) ''Roar, Lion, Roar''
e) ''(The) Matador Song''   j) ''Song of the Owls''
ANSWER: a) Cornell U. b) U. of South Carolina c) Texas Christian U. d) Kansas U.
e) Texas Tech U. f) Yale U. g) Rutgers U. h) Princeton U. i) Columbia U.
j) Rice U.

13. What 3 colleges are nicknamed ''The Big 3''?
ANSWER: Harvard, Princeton, and Yale.

14. What 3 New England colleges are called ''The Little 3''?
ANSWER: Amherst, Williams, and Wesleyan.

15. What Colleges are named ''The 7 Sisters''?
ANSWER: Barnard, Bryn Mawr, Mount Holyoke, Radcliffe (merged with Harvard),
Smith, Vassar (now coed), and Wellesley.

16. Name the 8 Ivy League Colleges. Why were these schools named the ''Ivy
League''?
ANSWER: Brown, Columbia, Cornell, Dartmouth, Harvard, University of Pennsylvania,
Princeton, and Yale/Because of the ivy-colored walls of these institutions
(named by Caswell Adams of the New York *Journal American*).

17. The college is nicknamed the ''Brewers,'' and it was founded and endowed by a
brewer. Name it and give its location.
ANSWER: Vassar is in Poughkeepsie, New York.

18. The college is nicknamed the "Chiefs," and it is the site of the Basketball Hall of Fame. Name it and give its location.
ANSWER: Springfield College, Springfield, Massachusetts.

19. Identify each of the following colleges.
    a) The Virginia school originally named the Collegiate School
    b) The New Jersey school originally named Queen's College
    c) The Rhode Island school originally named Rhode Island College
    d) The New Jersey school originally named College of New Jersey
    e) The Pennsylvania school originally named the College and Academy of Philadelphia
    f) The New Hampshire school originally named Moor's Indian Charity School
    g) The New York school originally named King's College
ANSWER: a) William and Mary   b) Rutgers   c) Brown   d) Princeton   e) Pennsylvania   f) Dartmouth   g) Columbia.

20. Identify each of the following colleges.
    a) The California school that takes its name from the "American Quaker Poet"
    b) The Washington, D.C., school that is the world's only liberal arts college for the deaf
    c) The Ohio school which was the site of the slaying on May 4, 1970, of four students and the wounding of 10 others by National Guardsmen during a demonstration over the U.S. involvement in Cambodia and Vietnam
    d) The Florida school named after the manufacturer of a well-known hat
    f) The South Carolina school founded by a northern textile industrialist nicknamed the "All-Stars" after a famous athletic shoe
    f) The South Carolina school named after the Revolutionary War hero nicknamed the "Swamp Fox"
    g) The Washington school named after the protestant missionary in the Walla Walla valley in 1836
ANSWER: a) Whittier   b) Gallaudet   c) Kent State   d) Stetson   e) Converse   f) Francis Marion   g) Marcus Whitman.

21. What is the name of the predominantly black college, nicknamed the "Pirates" and located in Virginia, which was founded in 1868 to help educate slaves freed after the Civil War?
ANSWER: Hampton Institute.

22. What is the name of the college, nicknamed the "Lyon" after the founder Mary Lyon, which became in 1837 the first college for women? This college is located in South Hadley, Massachusetts.
ANSWER: Mount Holyoke College (originally Mount Holyoke Seminary).

U.S. COLLEGES/UNIVERSITIES: THEIR NICKNAMES AND LOCATIONS

Adelphi U	Panthers	Garden City, NY
Air Force Academy	Falcons	Colorado Springs, CO
Akron, U. of	Zips	Akron, OH
Alabama, U. of (Birmingham)	Blazers	Birmingham
Alabama, U. of	Crimson Tide, Red Elephants	University (Tuscaloosa)
Alcorn State U	Braves	Lorman, MS
American U	Eagles	Washington, DC
Amherst College	Lord Jeffs	Amherst, MA
Appalachian State U	Mountaineers	Boone, NC
Arizona State U	Sun Devils	Tempe
Arizona, U. of	Wildcats	Tucson
Arkansas State U	Tomahawks, Indians	State University
Arkansas, U. of	Razorbacks, Hogs	Fayetteville
Ashland College	Eagles	Ashland, OH
Army (U.S. Military Academy)	Black Knights, Cadets	West Point, NY

Auburn U	Plainsmen, Tigers, War Eagles	Auburn, AL
Austin Peay State U	Governors	Clarksville, TN
Baldwin-Wallace College	Yellow Jackets	Berea, OH
Ball State U	Cardinals	Muncie, IN
Barnard College	Bears	New York, NY
Baruch College	Statesmen	New York, NY
Bates College	Bobcats	Lewiston, ME
Baylor U	Bears	Waco, TX
Belmont Abbey College	Crusaders	Belmont, NC
Berea College	Mountaineers	Berea, KY
Berry College	Vikings	Mount Berry, GA
Boise State U	Broncos	Boise, ID
Boston College	Eagles	Chestnut Hill, MA
Boston U	Terriers	Boston, MA
Bowdoin College	Polar Bears	Brunswick, ME
Bowling Green State U	Falcons	Bowling Green, OH
Bradley U	Braves	Peoria, IL
Brandeis U	Judges	Waltham, MA
Brigham Young U	Cougars	Provo, UT
Brown U	Bruins, Bears	Providence, RI
Bucknell U	Bisons	Lewisburg, PA
California State U	Titans	Fullerton
California State U	49ers	Long Beach
California, U. of	Golden Bears	Berkeley
California, U. of (UCLA)	Bruins	Los Angeles
Campbell U	Camels	Buies, NC
Canisius College	Golden Griffins	Buffalo, NY
Carnegie-Mellon U	Tartans	Pittsburgh, PA
Catholic U	Cardinals	Washington, DC
Central Michigan U	Chippewas	Mt. Pleasant
Chicago, U. of	Maroons	Chicago, IL
Cincinnati, U. of	Bearcats	Cincinnati, OH
The Citadel	Bulldogs, Cadets	Charleston, SC
Clemson U	Tigers	Clemson, SC
Cleveland State U	Vikings	Cleveland, OH
Colby College	White Mules	Waterville, ME
Colgate U	Red Raiders	Hamilton, NY
Colorado State U	Rams	Fort Collins
Colorado, U. of	Buffaloes, Buffs	Boulder
Columbia U	Lions	New York, NY
Columbus College	Cougars	Columbus, GA
Connecticut, U. of	Huskies	Storrs
Cornell U	Big Red	Ithaca, NY
Creighton U	Bluejays	Omaha, NE
Dartmouth College	Big Green	Hanover, NH
Davidson College	Wildcats	Davidson, NC
Dayton, U. of	Flyers	Dayton, OH
Delaware, U. of	Fightin' Blue Hens	Newark
Delta State U	Statesmen	Cleveland, MS
Denison U	Big Red	Granville, OH
Denver, U. of	Pioneers	Denver, CO
De Paul U	Blue Demons	Chicago, IL
De Pauw U	Tigers	Greencastle, IN
Detroit, U. of	Titans	Detroit, MI
Dickinson College	Red Devils	Carlisle, PA
Drake U	Bulldogs	Des Moines, IO
Drexel U	Dragons	Philadelphia, PA
Duke U	Blue Devils	Durham, NC
Duquesne U	Dukes	Pittsburgh, PA
East Carolina U	Pirates	Greenville, NC
East Tennessee State U	Bucs	Johnson City
Eastern Kentucky U	Colonels	Richmond
Eastern Michigan U	Hurons	Ypsilanti
Emory U	Eagles	Atlanta, GA
Evansville, U. of	Purple Aces	Evansville, IN
Fairleigh Dickinson U	Knights	Teaneck, NJ
Florida A&M U	Rattlers	Tallahassee
Florida State U	Seminoles	Tallahassee
Florida, U. of	Gators	Gainesville
Fordham U	Rams	Bronx, NY
Fresno State U	Bulldogs	Fresno, CA
Furman U	Paladins	Greenville, SC

Gallaudet College	Bisons	Washington, DC
George Washington U	Colonials	Washington, DC
Georgetown U	Hoyas	Washington, DC
Georgia Tech	Yellow Jackets, Ramblin' Wreck	Atlanta
Georgia Southwestern	Hurricanes	Americus
Georgia, U. of.	Bulldogs	Athens
Gonzaga U	Bulldogs	Spokane, WA
Grambling State U	Tigers	Grambling, LA
Hardin-Simmons U	Cowboys	Abilene, TX
Hartwick College	Warriors, Wicks	Oneonta, NY
Harvard U	Crimson	Cambridge, MA
Hawaii, U. of.	Rainbows, Rainbow Warriors	Honolulu
Hofstra U	Flying Dutchmen	Hempstead, NY
Holy Cross College	Crusaders	Worcester, MA
Houston, U. of.	Cougars	Houston, TX
Howard U	Bisons	Washington, DC
Idaho State U	Bengals	Pocatello
Idaho, U. of.	Vandals	Moscow
Illinois, U. of (Urbana-Champaign)	Fighting Illini	Urbana-Champaign
Indiana State U. (Evansville)	Eagles, Screaming Eagles	Evansville
Indiana State U	Sycamores	Terre Haute
Indiana U	Fightin' Hoosiers	Bloomington
Iona College	Gaels	New Rochelle, NY
Iowa State U.	Cyclones	Ames
Iowa, U. of.	Hawkeyes	Iowa City
Jackson State U.	Tigers	Jackson, MS
Jacksonville U	Dolphins	Jacksonville, FL
James Madison U	Dukes	Harrisonburg, VA
Johns Hopkins U	Blue Jays	Baltimore, MD
Kansas State U	Wildcats	Manhattan
Kansas, U. of.	Jayhawks	Lawrence
Kent State U	Golden Flashes	Kent, OH
Kentucky, U. of	Wildcats	Lexington
Kenyon College	Lords	Gambler, OH
Lamar U	Cardinals	Beaumont, TX
La Salle College	Explorers	Philadelphia, PA
Lehigh U	Engineers	Bethlehem, PA
Lewis & Clark College	Pioneers	Portland, OR
Long Island U	Blackbirds	Brooklyn, NY
Louisiana State U	Fighting Tigers	Baton Rouge
Louisiana Tech U	Bulldogs	Ruston
Louisville, U. of.	Cardinals, Red Rage	Louisville, KY
Loyola College	Greyhounds	Baltimore, MD
Loyola U	Ramblers	Chicago, IL
Maine, U. of	Black Bears	Orono
Marquette U	Warriors	Milwaukee, WI
Marshall U.	Thundering Herd	Huntington, WV
Maryland, U. of.	Terrapins, Terps	College Park
Massachusetts Institute of Technology (MIT)	Engineers, Beavers	Cambridge
Massachusetts, U. of	Minutemen	Amherst
McNeese State U	Cowboys	Lake Charles, LA
Memphis State U	Tigers	Memphis, TN
Mercer U	Bears	Macon, GA
Miami U (Ohio)	Redskins	Oxford, OH
Miami U	Hurricanes	Coral Gables, FL
Michigan State U	Spartans	East Lansing
Michigan, U. of	Wolverines	Ann Arbor
Middlebury College	Panthers	Middlebury, VT
Middle Tennessee State U	Blue Raiders	Murfreesboro
Minnesota, U. of	Golden Gophers	Minneapolis
Mississippi State U	Bulldogs	Mississippi State
Mississippi, U. of.	Rebels, Ole Miss	University
Mississippi Valley State	Delta Devils	Itta Bena
Missouri, U. of	Tigers	Columbia
Montana State U	Bobcats	Bozeman
Montana, U. of	Grizzlies	Missoula
Morehead State U	Eagles	Morehead, KY
Morgan State U	Bears	Baltimore, MD
Mount St. Mary's College	Mountaineers	Emmitsburg, MD
Murray State U	Thoroughbreds	Murray, KY
Navy (U.S. Naval Academy)	Midshipmen	Annapolis, MD

Nebraska, U. of	Cornhuskers	Lincoln
Nevada, U. of (Las Vegas)	Rebels	Las Vegas
Nevada, U. of (Reno)	Wolf Pack	Reno
New Hampshire, U. of	Wildcats	Durham
New Mexico, U. of	Lobos	Albuquerque
Niagara U	Purple Eagles	Niagara University, NY
North Carolina State U	Wolfpack	Raleigh
North Carolina, U. of	Tar Heels	Chapel Hill
North Carolina, U. of (Charlotte)	49ers	Charlotte
North Dakota, U. of	Fighting Sioux	Grand Forks
North Texas State U	Mean Green, Eagles	Denton
Northeast Louisiana U	Indians	Monroe
Northern Arizona U	Lumberjacks	Flagstaff
Northern Illinois U	Huskies	DeKalb
Northwestern State U	Demons	Natchitoches, LA
Northwestern U	Wildcats	Evanston, IL
Notre Dame, U. of	Fighting Irish	Notre Dame (South Bend), IN
Oberlin U	Yeomen	Oberlin, OH
Ohio State U	Buckeyes	Columbus
Ohio U	Bobcats	Athens
Oklahoma State U	Cowboys	Stillwater
Oklahoma, U. of	Sooners	Norman
Old Dominion U	Monarchs	Norfolk, VA
Oral Roberts U	Titans	Tulsa, OK
Oregon State U	Beavers	Corvallis
Oregon, U. of	Ducks	Eugene
Pacific, U. of	Tigers	Stockton, CA
Pan American U	Broncs	Edinburg, TX
Penn State U	Nittany Lions	University Park, PA
Pennsylvania, U. of	Quakers, Red and Blue	Philadelphia
Pepperdine U	Waves	Malibu, CA
Pittsburgh, U. of	Panthers	Pittsburgh, PA
Prairie View A&M U	Panthers	Prairie View, TX
Princeton U	Tigers	Princeton, NJ
Providence U	Friars	Providence, RI
Purdue U	Boilermakers	West Lafayette, IN
Queens College		Charlotte, NC
Randolph-Macon College	Yellow Jackets	Ashland, VA
Rensselaer Poly Tech	Engineers	Troy, NY
Rhode Island, U. of	Rams	Kingston
Rice U	Owls	Houston, TX
Richmond, U. of	Spiders	Richmond, VA
Rider College	Broncs	Lawrenceville, NJ
Rollins College	Tars	Winter Park, FL
Rutgers U	Scarlet Knights	New Brunswick, NJ
St. Bonaventure U	Bonnies	St. Bonaventure, NY
St. John's U	Redmen	Jamaica, NY
St. Joseph's U	Hawks	Philadelphia, PA
St. Louis U	Billikens	St. Louis, MO
St. Peter's College	Peacocks	Jersey City, NJ
San Diego State U	Aztecs	San Diego, CA
San Diego, U. of	Toreros	San Diego, CA
San Francisco, U. of	Dons	San Francisco, CA
San Jose State U	Spartans	San Jose, CA
Seton Hall U	Pirates	South Orange, NJ
Slippery Rock State College	Rockets	Slippery Rock, PA
South, U. of the	Tigers	Sewanee, TN
South Alabama, U. of	Jaguars	Mobile
South Carolina, U. of	Fighting Gamecocks	Columbia
South Dakota, U. of	Coyotes	Vermillion
South Florida, U. of	Bulls, Golden Brahmans	Tampa
Southern California, U. of (USC)	Trojans	Los Angeles
Southern Illinois, U. of	Salukis	Carbondale
Southern Methodist U	Mustangs	Dallas, TX
Southern Mississippi, U of	Golden Eagles	Hattiesburg
Southern U	Black Knights	New Orleans, LA
Southwestern Louisiana, U. of	Ragin Cajuns	Lafayette
Southwestern at Memphis	SAM, Lynx Cats	Memphis, TN
Stanford U	Cardinals	Stanford, CA
Stetson U	Hatters	DeLand, FL
Swarthmore College	Little Quakers	Swarthmore, PA
Sweet Briar College	Vixens	Sweet Briar, VA

School	Mascot	Location
Syracuse U	Orangemen	Syracuse, NY
Temple U	Owls	Philadelphia, PA
Tennessee State U	Tigers	Nashville
Tennessee Tech U	Golden Eagles	Cookeville
Tennessee, U. of (at Chattanooga)	Moccasins	Chattanooga
Tennessee, U. of	Volunteers, Vols	Knoxville
Texas A&M U.	Aggies	College Station
Texas Christian U	Horned Frogs	Fort Worth
Texas Southern U	Tigers	Houston
Texas Tech U	Red Raiders	Lubbock
Texas, U. of (at Arlington)	Mavericks	Arlington
Texas, U. of	Longhorns	Austin
Texas-El Paso	Miners	El Paso
Toledo, U. of	Rockets	Toledo, OH
Trinity U	Tigers	San Antonio, TX
Troy State U	Trojans	Troy, AL
Tufts U	Jumbos	Medford, MA
Tulane U	Green Wave	New Orleans, LA
Tulsa, U. of	Golden Hurricanes	Tulsa, OK
Tuskegee Institute	Golden Tigers	Tuskegee Institute, AL
U.S. Coast Guard Academy	Bears	New London, CT
U.S. Merchant Marine Academy	Mariners	Kings Point, NY
Ursinus College	Bears	Collegeville, PA
Utah State U	Aggies	Logan
Utah, U. of	Utes	Salt Lake City
Vanderbilt U	Commodores	Nashville, TN
Vassar College	Brewers	Poughkeepsie, NY
Vermont, U. of	Catamounts	Burlington
Villanova U	Wildcats	Villanova, PA
Virginia Military Institute (VMI)	Keydets	Lexington
Virginia Tech	Hokies, Gobblers	Blacksburg
Virginia, U. of	Cavaliers	Charlottesville
Wake Forest U	Demon Deacons, Deacs	Winston-Salem, NC
Washington & Jefferson College	Presidents	Washington, PA
Washington & Lee U	Generals	Lexington, VA
Washington State U	Fighting Cougars	Pullman
Washington, U. of	Huskies	Seattle
Wayne State U	Tartars	Detroit, MI
Weber State College	Wildcats	Ogden, UT
West Chester State College	Rams	West Chester, PA
West Georgia College	Braves	Carrollton, GA
West Virginia U	Mountaineers	Morgantown
Western Carolina U	Catamounts	Cullowhee, NC
Western Kentucky U	Hilltoppers	Bowling Green, KY
Western Michigan U	Broncos	Kalamazoo
Westminster College	Blue Jays	Fulton, MO
Whittier College	Poets	Whittier, CA
Wichita State U	Shockers	Wichita, KS
Widener College	Pioneers	Chester, PA
William & Mary, College of	Indians, The Tribe	Williamsburg, VA
Wisconsin, U. of	Badgers	Madison
Wittenberg U	Tigers	Springfield, OH
Wyoming, U. of	Cowboys	Laramie
Xavier U	Musketeers	Cincinnati, OH
Yale U	Bulldogs, Elis	New Haven, CT
Yeshiva U	Maccabbees	New York, NY
Youngstown State U	Penguins	Youngstown, OH
Zaragoza at Zamora	Zodiacs, Zaz	Zion, ZA

SCHOOLS AND THEIR ATHLETIC CONFERENCES

SOUTHEASTERN
Alabama
Auburn
Florida
Georgia
Kentucky
LSU
Mississippi
Mississippi State
Tennessee
Vanderbilt

SOUTHWEST
Arkansas
Baylor
Houston
Rice
S.M.U.
Texas Tech
T.C.U.
Texas
Texas A&M

BIG EIGHT
Colorado
Iowa State
Kansas
Kansas State
Missouri
Nebraska
Oklahoma
Oklahoma State

BIG SKY
Boise State
Idaho
Idaho State
Montana
Montana State
Nevada-Reno
Northern Arizona
Weber State

MID-AMERICAN
Ball State
Bowling Green
Central Michigan
Eastern Michigan
Kent State
Miami (Ohio)
Northern Illinois
Ohio University
Toledo
Western Michigan

PACIFIC-10
Arizona
Arizona State
California
Oregon
Oregon State
Southern California
Stanford
U.C.L.A.
Washington
Washington State

WESTERN ATHLETIC
Air Force
Brigham Young
Colorado State
Hawaii
New Mexico
San Diego State
Texas-El Paso
Utah
Wyoming

IVY LEAGUE
Brown
Columbia
Cornell
Dartmouth
Harvard
Penn
Princeton
Yale

MISSOURI VALLEY
Drake
Illinois State

Indiana State
Southern Illinois
Tulsa
West Texas State
Wichita State

SOUTHERN
Appalachian
The Citadel
Davidson
East Tennessee State
Furman
Marshall
UT Chattanooga
V.M.I.
Western Carolina

BIG TEN
Illinois
Indiana
Iowa
Michigan
Michigan State
Minnesota
Northwestern
Ohio State
Purdue
Wisconsin

OHIO VALLEY
Akron
Austin Peay
Eastern Kentucky
Middle-Tennessee State
Morehead State
Murray State
Tennessee Tech
Youngstown State

ATLANTIC COAST
Clemson
Duke
Georgia Tech
Maryland
North Carolina
North Carolina State
Virginia
Wake Forest

PACIFIC COAST
Fresno State
Fullerton
Long Beach State
Nevada-Las Vegas
New Mexico State
Pacific
San Jose State
Utah State

SOUTHLAND
Arkansas State
Lamar
Louisiana Tech
McNeese State
Northeast Louisiana
North Texas State
Texas-Arlington

SOUTHWESTERN
Alcorn State
Grambling
Jackson State
Mississippi Valley
Prairie View
Southern U.
Texas-Southern

YANKEE
Boston U.
Connecticut
Maine
Massachusetts
New Hampshire
Rhode Island

INDEPENDENTS
Army
Boston College
Cincinnati
Colgate
East Carolina
Florida State
Holy Cross
Louisville
Memphis State
Miami (Florida)
Navy
Northwest Louisiana
Notre Dame
Penn State
Pittsburgh
Richmond
Rutgers
South Carolina
Southern Mississippi
Southwestern Louisiana
Syracuse
Temple
Tennessee State
Tulane
Virginia Tech
West Virginia
Western Kentucky
William & Mary

NICKNAMES OF U.S. GANGSTERS/CRIMINALS/OUTLAWS

Antonino Leonardo
  (Anthony Joseph) Accardo .. Big Tuna, Joe Batty, Mr. Big in Crime
Albert Anastasia .... The Boss, Lord High Executioner of Murder, Inc.
Anthony Anastasio .... Tough Tony
Arizona Clark Barker .... Bloody Mama, Kate, Ma
Leroy Barnes .... Mr. Untouchable, Nicky
Sam Battaglia .... Teets
David Berkowitz........... 44-Caliber Killer, Son of Sam
William Bonney (or Henry
  McCarthy/McCarty, or
  Kid Antrim .... Billy the Kid
William B. Brocius
  (Brocious; William B.
  Graham) .... Curly Bill
Fred Buckminster .... Deacon
Martha Jane Cannary....... Calamity Jane, White Devil of the Yellowstone
Al Capone .... The Beast, The Behemoth, Big Al, Big Guy, Chicago's
                            Master Criminal, Millionaire Gorilla, Real Mayor of
                            Chicago, Scarface
Caryl Chessman........... Red Light Bandit
Vincent Coll .... Mad Dog, Mad Dog of the Underworld
Frank Costello
  (Francesco Saveria)....... Prime Minister of the Underworld, The Politician
Albert Henry DeSalvo .... Boston Strangler, Measuring Man
Jack Diamond (John
  Thomas Noland).......... Clay Pigeon, Legs
John Herbert Dillinger ...... Desperate Dan, Public Enemy Number One
Charles Arthur Floyd .... Pretty Boy
Vito Genovese .... Don Vitone
Sam Giancana .... Momo, Mooney
Lester M. Gillis .... Baby Face Nelson (a.k.a. George Nelson)
Bruno Richard Hauptmann... Cemetery John
John Henry Holliday........ Doc
George R. Kelly .... Machine Gun
Jesse James .... Robin Hood of the Missouri, Robin Hood of the Little
                            Blue
Thomas Lucchese .... Three-Finger Brown
Charles Luciano
  (Salvatore Luciano) .... Charlie Lucky, King of the New York Rackets, Lucky,
                            The Man, Three-Twelve
Victor Lustig
  (Robert Miller)........... The Count, Man Who Sold the Eiffel Tower
Charles Manson........... Demon of Death Valley, Hippie Murderer, Hypnotic Hip-
                            pie
Salvatore Maranzano .... Boss of all Bosses, Father of Cosa Nostra
Giuseppe Masseria .... Joe the Boss
George Moran .... Bugs
George Nelson .... Baby Face
Charles Dion O'Banion ...... Chicago's Arch Criminal, Deanie, Gangland's Favorite
                            Florist
James Earl Ray .... Camouflaged Killer
Dutch Schultz .... Dutchman
Belle Starr (born Myra Belle
  Shirley) .... The Bandit Queen, Female Jesse James, Female Robin
                            Hood, Queen of the Outlaws
Robert Franklin Stroud ..... Bird Man (Birdman) of Alcatraz
William Francis Sutton ...... Babe Ruth of Bank Robbers, Slick Willie, The Actor
Roger Touhy .... Black Roger, Roger the Terrible, Terrible Touhy
Joseph Weil .... Chicago's Minister of Human Cupidity, The Yellow Kid

NICKNAMES OF MUSICIANS/SINGERS

Roy Claxton Acuff .... King of Country Music, King of the Hillbillies, Smoky Mountain Boy
Julian Edwin Adderley ...... Cannonball
Marian Anderson .... Lady from Philadelphia, Voice of the Century
Louis Armstrong .... Gatemouth, King, Satch, Satchmo, Pops
Eddie Arnold .... The Tennessee Plowboy
Chet Atkins .... Mr. Guitar
Joan Baez .... Non-violent Singer
Burt Bacharach .... Father of the New Sound
Mildred Bailey (Norville) .... Rocking Chair Lady
Pearl Bailey .... Pearlie Mae
William Basie .... The Count, Jump King
Ludwig Van Beethoven ..... Great Mogul of Music
Pat Boone .... Mr. Clean
Harry Belafonte .... Restless Troubadour
Louis Hector Berlioz .... Creator of Program Music
James Hubert Blake .... Eubie
James Brown .... King of Soul, Mr. Dynamite
Cabell Calloway .... Cab, King of Hi De Hi De Ho, Hi De Ho Man
Enrico Caruso .... World's Greatest Tenor
Johnny Cash .... King Johnny, King of Country Music, Man in Black
Chubby Checker .... Twist King
Nat Cole .... King
Alice Cooper .... Mr. America, Schlock, Rock's Godzilla
Aaron Copland .... Dean of American Composers, King from Brooklyn
Xavier Cougat .... Cugie, Guy Lombardo of Latin Music
Jimmy Ray Dean .... Dandy of Country Music
Tommy Dorsey .... Sentimentlal Gentleman of Swing
Eddie Duchin .... Magic Fingers of Radio
Bob Dylan .... Radical Prophet of American Youth
Edward Kennedy Ellington ... America's Good Will Music Ambassador, Aristocrat of Swing, The Duke, King of Jazz, King of Swing
Arthur Fiedler .... Mr. Boston, Mr. Pops
Ella Fitzgerald .... First Lady of Swing, First Lady of Jazz
Ernest Jennings Ford .... Cousin Ern, King of the Tennessee Pea Pickers, Tennessee Ernie
George Gershwin .... Mr. Big of Tin Pan Alley, Mr. Tin Pan Alley
Stan Getz .... The Sound
John Birks Gillespie .... Dizzy
Benjamin David Goodman ... Benny, King of Swing
Bill Haley .... The Rambling Yodeler, Rock Around The Clock Haley
W(illiam) C(hristopher)
Handy .... Father of the Blues
Lyle Cedric Henderson ...... Skitch
Woodrow Charles Herman ... Woody
Earl Kenneth Hines .... Fatha
Al Hirt .... Trumpeting Behemoth
Billie Holliday .... Lady, Lady Day
Mahalia Jackson .... Queen of the Gospel Song
Janis Joplin .... Pearl, Queen of the Hippies
Scott Joplin .... King of the Ragtime Composers
Jerome David Kern .... Dean of America's Show Music Composers
B.B. King .... Blues Boy
Eartha Mae Kitt .... That Bad Eartha, Thursday's Child
Eugene Bertram Krupa ...... Ace Drummer Man, King of the Drums
Peggy Lee .... Queen of American Pop Music
Guy Lombardo .... King of Corn, Mr. New Year's Eve, Prince of Wails, Schmaltz King

Loretta Lynn	Coal Miner's Daughter, First Lady of Country Music
Chuck Mangione	Gap
Annunzio Paolo Mantovani	Maestro of Massed Strings
Bette Midler	The Divine Miss M
Thelonious Monk	High Priest of Bebop
Ferdinand Joseph Morton (Ferdinand Joseph La Menthe)	Jelly Roll
Eugene Ormandy	Maestro, Mr. Conductor
Charlie Parker	Bird, Yardbird
Cole Porter	Elegant Hoosier Tunesmith
Elvis Presley	Elvis the Pelvis
Harry Raderman	Man Who Made the Trombone Laugh
Bernard Rich	Baby Taps, Buddy
Arthur (Artur) Rubinstein	Playboy of the Piano
Pete Seeger	Reincarnated Troubadour, Thomas Jefferson of Folk Music
(Carl) Doc Severinsen	World's Greatest Trumpet Player
Beverly Sills	Bubbles
Frank Sinatra	Chairman of the Board, King of Swoon, Ol' Blue Eyes, The Voice
Bessie Smith	Empress of the Blues
Kate Smith	First Lady of Radio, Moon Over the Mountain Girl, Songbird of the South
John Philip Sousa	March King
Eddie South	Dark Angel of the Violin
Joan Sutherland	Glorious Iceberg
Weldon Leo Teagarden	Jack
Mel Tormé	The Velvet Fog
Arturo Toscanini	The Maestro
Sophie Tucker	Last of the Red-Hot Mamas, Queen of Jazz
Rudy Vallee	The Crooner, Vagabond Lover
Sarah Vaughan	The Divine One
Bobby Vinton	Polish Prince of American Pop Music
Thomas Wright Waller	Fats, Black Horowitz
Fred Waring	America's Authentic Music Man
Ethel Waters	Baby Star, Bronze Raquel Welch, Sweet Mama String-bean
Lawrence Welk	Liberace of the Accordion, Mr. Music Maker
Paul Whiteman	Dean of American Popular Music, King of Jazz, Pops
Hank Williams	King of Country Music
Mary Lou Williams	Queen of Jazz

NICKNAMES OF ENTERTAINERS

Fred Allen	King of the Quick Quip
Steve Allen	Steverino
Roscoe Arbuckle	Fatty
Gene Autry	Oklahoma's Yodeling Cowboy, The Singing Cowboy
Lauren Bacall	The Look
Josephine Baker	La Bakhair
Tallulah Bankhead	Darling of the Gods, Tallu
Theda Bara	Original Glamour Girl, Queen of the Vampires, The Vamp
Brigitte Bardot	Bad Little Bad Girl, Eternal Sex Goddess, The Sex Kitten
John Blythe Barrymore	The Great Profile
Lionel Barrymore	Hollywood's Grand Old Man
Edgar Bergen	Noel Coward of Ventriloquists, The Perfect Stooge
Milton Berle	Mr. Saturday Night, Mr. Television, Uncle Milty

Thomas Greene Bethune	Blind Tom, Incredible Imitator
Humphrey Bogart	Bogie (Bogey)
Raymond Wallace Bolger	Mr. Rubberlegs
Clara Bow (Mrs. George Belden)	The It Girl, The Red Head
Carol Burnett	Hot Lips
Eddie Cantor	Banjo-Eyes
Judy Carne	Sock-It-To-Me Girl
Johnny Carson	Great Carsoni, Prince of Darkness
Lon Chaney	Man of a Thousand Faces
Charlie Chaplin	Chapu-rin, Charlot, Little Tramp, Twentieth-Century Moses
Sidney Chayefsky	Paddy
George Michael Cohan	King of Broadway, Man Who Owned Broadway, Mr. Broadway, Prince of the American Theatre, Yankee Doodle Dandy
Perry Como	The Barber, King of the Jukes, Mr. Relaxation
Bing (Harry Lillis) Crosby	Der Bingle, The Groaner, Old Dad
Sammy Davis	Candy Man, Mr. Wonderful
Doris Day	Golden Tonsil, Prettiest Three-Million Dollar Corporation with Freckles in America, The Girl Next Door, Tomboy with the Voice
James Dean	Father of Rock Culture
Bo Derek	The Perfect 10
Marie Dressler	Grand Old Lady of the Movies, Queen Marie of Hollywood, Old Trouper
Isadora Duncan	First of the Modern Women
Irene Dunne	First Lady of Hollywood
Jimmy Durante	Ragtime Jimmy, The Schnozz, Schnozzola
Dale Evans	Queen of the Cowgirls, Queen of the West
Douglas Fairbanks, Sr.	Fourth Musketeer
Stepin Fetchit	White Man's Negro
Jane Fonda	Non-Stop Activist
Clark Gable	King of Hollywood
Judy Garland	Lady Lazarus, Triple Threat Girl
Edward Richard Gibson	Hoot
John Gilbert	Great Lover
Dorothy Gish (De Guiche)	Miss Apprehension
Lillian Gish (De Guiche)	First Lady of the Screen, Iron Horse, Miss Lillian
Jackie Gleason	The Fat One, The Great One, Mr. Saturday Night
George Gobel	Lonesome George
Arthur Godfrey	Red, Red Head
Betty Grable	Number One Pin Up Girl, Soldier's Inspiration, The Legs, Undisputed Queen of the Movies
D(avid) Lewelyn W(ark) Griffith	American Shakespeare, Father of the Film Industry, God of Hollywood
Jean Harlow	Blonde Bombshell
Helen Hayes	First Lady of the American Theatre
Rita Hayworth	Love Goddess
Margaux Hemingway	Fabulous Babe
Alfred Hitchcock	Portly Master of the Involuntary Scream, Master of Suspense
Dustin Hoffman	The Little Big Man, The Midnight Cowboy
Bob Hope	Ski Nose
Harry Houdini	Handcuff King, Monarch of Leg Shackles
Georgie Jessel	Boy Monologuist, Toastmaster General of the U.S.A.
Al Jolson	Jolie, The Immortal Jolson
George S. Kaufman	Gloomy Dean of Broadway
Buster Keaton	Great Stone Face

Emmett Kelly . . . . Weary Willie
Dorothy Kilgallen (Mrs.
 Richard Kollmar) . . . . Voice of Broadway
Veronica Lake . . . . The Peekaboo Girl
Dorothy Lamour . . . . Paratrooper Pet, Sarong Girl, Sweetheart of the Fox-
holes
David Letterman . . . . Prince of Late Night Television
Jeannette MacDonald . . . . The Iron Butterfly
Marie McDonald . . . . The Body
George Emmette McFarland . . Spanky
Victor Mature . . . . Hollywood's Number One Glamour Boy, The Hunk
Louis B. Mayer . . . . King of Hollywood
Burgess Meredith . . . . Bugs, Buzz
David Merrick . . . . Barnum of Broadway Producers
Yvette Mimieux . . . . Hollywood's Little Princess
Tom Mix . . . . America's Favorite Cowboy, World's Champion Cowboy
Vaughn W. Monroe . . . . Modern Generation's Rudy Vallee, The Voice of R.C.A.
Paul Muni . . . . Man of Many Faces
John Ringling North . . . . Greatest Showman since Barnum
Kim Novak . . . . Hollywood's Melancholy Blonde
Annie Oakley . . . . Little Sure Shot
Maureen O'Hara . . . . Queen of Technicolor
Minnie Pearl . . . . Queen of Country Corn
Sam Peckinpah . . . . Master of Violence
Mary Pickford . . . . America's Sweetheart, Queen of the Movies
Molly Picon (Mrs. Jacob
 Kalich) . . . . Sweetheart of Second Avenue
ZaSu Pitts . . . . Girl with the Ginger Snap Name
Sally Rand . . . . Fan-tastic Sally, Her Sexellency
Basil Rathbone . . . . Man with the Finest Sneer in the Movies
Burt Reynolds . . . . The Frog Prince
Don Rickles . . . . Master of Insult Comedy, Merchant of Venom
Luther Robinson . . . . Bojangles, King of the Tap Dancers
Roy Rogers . . . . King of the Cowboys, Top Boots-and-Saddle Star
Billy Rose . . . . Basement Barnum, Midget Maestro of Broadway
Abe Saperstein . . . . Barnum of Basketball
Mack Sennett . . . . King of Comedy
Ann Sheridan . . . . The Oomph Girl
(Richard) Red Skelton . . . . . . Marcel Marceau of Television
(Bernard) James Stewart . . . . Grand Old Man of the Aw Shucks School
Ed Sullivan . . . . Great Stone Face, Unsmiling Irishman
Shirley Temple . . . . Eighth Wonder of the World, Little Goldilocks
Irving Grant Thalberg . . . . Boy Producer
Marlo Thomas . . . . Miss Independent, Princess of Situation Comedy, That Girl
Michael Todd . . . . America's Greatest Showman, New Ziegfield
Spencer Tracy . . . . Old Bucko
Lana Turner . . . . Sweater Girl
Rudy Vallee . . . . The Crooner, Vagabond Lover
Rudolph Valentino . . . . The Sheik
John Wayne . . . . The Duke
Jack Webb . . . . Sergeant Joe Friday
Lawrence Welk . . . . Liberace of the Accordion, Mr. Music Maker
Orson Welles . . . . Boy Wonder
Mae West . . . . Diamond Lil, Screen's Bad Girl, Siren of Sex, Siren of
the Screen

Pearl White . . . . Queen of the Silent Serials
Ed Wynn . . . . Perfect Fool
Loretta (Gretchen) Young . . . The Iron Butterfly, The Steel Butterfly
Darryl Francis Zanuck . . . . . . The Chief
Flo(renz) Ziegfield, Jr. . . . . . . Lorenzo the Magnificent of the Stage, Ziggy

PSEUDONYMS

Eddie Albert . . . . Edward Albert Heimberger
Alan Alda . . . . Alphonso D'Abruzzo
Fred Allen . . . . John Florence Sullivan
Woody Allen . . . . Allen Stewart Konigsberg
June Allyson . . . . Ella Geisman
Julie Andrews . . . . Julia Elizabeth Wells
Ann-Margret . . . . Ann-Margaret Olsson
Eve Arden . . . . Eunice Quedens
Beatrice Arthur . . . . Bernice Frankel
Jean Arthur . . . . Gladys Georgianna Greene
Fred Astaire . . . . Frederick Austerlitz
Lauren Bacall . . . . Betty Joan Perske
Anne Bancroft . . . . Annemarie Italiano
Rona Barrett . . . . Rona Burnstein
John and Lionel Barrymore . . John and Lionel Blythe
Warren Beatty . . . . Warren Beaty
Tony Bennett . . . . Antonio Dominick Benedetto
Robby Benson . . . . Robert Segal
Jack Benny . . . . Benjamin Kubelsky
Ingmar Bergman . . . . Ernst Ingmar Bergman
Milton Berle . . . . Milton Berlinger
Irving Berlin . . . . Israel Baline
Robert Blake . . . . Michael Gubitosi
Blondie . . . . Deborah Harry
Pat Boone . . . . Charles Eugene Boone
David Bowie . . . . David Jones
Fanny Brice . . . . Fanny Borach
Beau Bridges . . . . Lloyd Vernet Bridges, III
Charles Bronson . . . . Charles Buchinsky
Mel Brooks . . . . Melvin Kaminsky
Yul Brynner . . . . Taidje Khan, Jr.
George Burns . . . . Nathan Birnbaum
Ellen Burstyn . . . . Edna Rae Gillooly
Richard Burton . . . . Richard Walter Jenkins, Jr.
Red Buttons . . . . Aaron Chwatt (Schwatt)
Michael Caine . . . . Maurice Micklewhite
Eddie Cantor . . . . Edward Israel Itskowitz
Diahann Carroll . . . . Carol Diahann Johnson
Cyd Charisse . . . . Tula Ellice Finklea
Ray Charles . . . . Ray Charles Robinson
Cher . . . . Cherylynn La Piere
Claudette Colbert . . . . Lily Chauchoin
Perry Como . . . . Pierino Roland Como
Alice Cooper . . . . Vincent Damon Furnier
Joan Crawford . . . . Lucille LeSueur
Tony Curtis . . . . Bernard Schwartz
Vic Damone . . . . Vito Farinola
Bobby Darin . . . . Robert Walden Cassotto

Bette Davis	Ruth Elizabeth Davis
Doris Day	Doris von Kappelhoff
Yvonne De Carlo	Peggy Yvonne Middleton
James Dean	James Byron
John Denver	Henry John Deutschendorf, Jr.
Bo Derek	Mary Cathleen Collins
Angie Dickinson	Angeline Brown
Marlene Dietrich	Maria Magdalena von Losch
Troy Donahue	Merle Johnson, Jr.
Diana Dors	Diana Fluck
Kirk Douglas	Issur Danielovitch Demsky
Mike Douglas	Michael Delaney Dowd, Jr.
Faye Dunaway	Dorothy Faye Dunaway
Bob Dylan	Robert Zimmerman
Dale Evans	Frances Octavia Smith
Douglas Fairbanks	Julius Ullman
Stepin Fetchit	Lincoln Theodore Perry
Rhonda Fleming	Marilyn Louis
Joan Fontaine	Joan de Havilland
Glen Ford	Gwyllyn Ford
Redd Foxx	John Elroy Sanford
Connie Francis	Concetta Franconero
Clark Gable	William Clark Gable
Greta Garbo	Greta Louissa Gustafsson
Judy Garland	Frances Gumm
James Garner	James Baumgarner
Crystal Gayle	Brenda Gail Webb Gatzimos
Janet Gaynor	Laura Gainor
Mitzi Gaynor	Francesca Mitzi von Gerber
John Gilbert	John Pringle
Paulette Goddard	Marian Levy
Marjoe Gortner	Hugh Marjoe Ross Gortner
Elliott Gould	Elliott Goldstein
Betty Grable	Elizabeth Grasle
Stewart Granger	James Stewart
Cary Grant	Archibald Leach
Lee Grant	Lyova Haskell Rosenthal
Buddy Hackett	Leonard Hacker
Jean Harlow	Harlean Carpenter
Rex Harrison	Reginald Carey
Sterling Hayden	John Hamilton
Helen Hayes	Helen Hayes Brown
Susan Hayward	Edythe Marriner
Rita Hayworth	Margarita Cansino
Audrey Hepburn	Edda Hepburn van Heemstra
William Holden	William Franklin Beedle, Jr.
Billie Holiday	Eleanora Gough McKay
Judy Holiday	Judith Tuvim
Bob Hope	Leslie Townes Hope
Hedda Hopper	Elda Furry
Harry Houdini	Ehrich Weiss
Rock Hudson	Roy Scherer/Roy Fitzgerald
Engelbert Humperdinck	Arnold/Gerry Dorsey
Lauren Hutton	Mary Laurence Hutton
Elton John	Reginald Kenneth Dwight
Al Jolson	Asa Yoelson

Jennifer Jones	Phyllis Isley
Tom Jones	Thomas Jones Woodward
Boris Karloff	William Henry Pratt
Danny Kaye	David Daniel Kaminsky
Diane Keaton	Diane Hall
Veronica Lake	Constance Ockleman
Hedy Lamarr	Hedwig Eva Maria Kiesler
Dorothy Lamour	Dorothy Kaumeyer
Elsa Lanchester	Elizabeth Sullivan
Mario Lanza	Alfred Arnold Cocozza
Stan Laurel	Arthur Stanley Jefferson
Steve Lawrence	Sidney Leibowitz
Gypsy Rose Lee	Rose Louise Hovick
Peggy Lee	Norma Delores Jean Engstrom
Janet Leigh	Jeannette Helen Morrison
Vivien Leigh	Vivian Mary Hartley
Jerry Lewis	Joseph Levitch
Liberace	Wladziu Valentino Liberace
Hal Linden	Hal Lipshitz
Carole Lombard	Jane Alice Peters
Sophia Loren	Sofia Scicolone
Peter Lorre	Laszlo Loewenstein
Bela Lugosi	Bela Blasko
Shirley MacLaine	Shirley McLean Beaty
Karl Malden	Mladen Sekulovich
Dorothy Malone	Dorothy Maloney
Jayne Mansfield	Vera Jane Palmer
Fredric March	Frederick McIntyre Bickel
Dean Martin	Dino Crocetti
Tony Martin	Alvin Morris
Walter Matthau	Walter Matuschanskavasky
Ethel Merman	Ethel Zimmerman
Ray Milland	Reginald Truscott-Jones
Ann Miller	Lucille Ann Collier
Joni Mitchell	Roberta Joan Anderson
Marilyn Monroe	Norma Jean Baker/Mortenson
Yves Montand	Ivo Livi
Lola Montez	Maria Gilbert
Robert Montgomery	Henry Montgomery, Jr.
Terry Moore	Helen Koford
Paul Muni	Muni Weisenfreund
Pola Negri	Barbara Appolonia Chapulek
Mike Nichols	Michael Igor Peshkowsky
Kim Novak	Marilyn Pauline Novak
Merle Oberon	Estelle Merle O'Brien Thompson
Hugh O'Brien	Hugh J. Krampe
Maureen O'Hara	Maureen Fitzsimmons
Laurence Olivier	Baron Olivier of Brighton
Tony Orlando	Michael Anthony Orlando Cassavitis
Janis Page	Donna Mae Tjaden
Patti Page	Clara Ann Fowler
Debra Paget	Debralee Griffin
Lilli Palmer	Lillie Marie Peiser
Bernadette Peters	Bernadette Lazzara
Mary Pickford	Gladys Mary Smith

Jane Powell	Suzanne Bruce
Paula Prentiss	Paula Ragusa
George Raft	George Ranft
Tony Randall	Leonard Rosenberg
Basil Rathbone	Philip St. John Basil Rathbone
Donna Reed	Donna Mullenger
Debbie Reynolds	Marie Frances Reynolds
Edward G. Robinson	Emmanuel Goldenberg
Ginger Rogers	Virginia McMath
Roy Rogers	Leonard Slye
Mickey Rooney	Joe Yule, Jr.
Billy Rose	William Samuel Rosenberg
Lillian Russell	Helen Louise Leonard
Telly Savalas	Aristoteles Savalas
Randolph Scott	Randolph Crane
Mack Sennett	Michael Sinnott
Omar Sharif	Michael Shalhoub
Dinah Shore	Frances Rose Shore
Beverly Sills	Belle Silverman
Ann Sothern	Harriette Lake
Barbara Stanwyck	Ruby Stevens
Belle Starr	Myra Belle Shirley
Gale Storm	Josephine Owaissa Cottle
Suzanne Somers	Suzanne Mahoney
Donna Summer	La Donna Andrea Gaines
Robert Taylor	Spangler Arlington Brugh
Danny Thomas	Amos Jacobs
Michael Todd	Avrom Hirsch Goldbogen
Sophie Tucker	Sophie Abuza
Rudolph Valentino	Rodolpho d'Antonguolla
Frankie Valli	Frank Castelluccio
Muddy Waters	McKinley Morganfield
John Wayne	Marion Michael Morrison
Raquel Welch	Raquel Tejada
Shelly Winters	Shirley Schrift
Stevie Wonder	Steveland Morris Hardaway
Natalie Wood	Natasha Gurdin
Jane Wyman	Sarah Jane Fulks
Tammy Wynette	Wynette Pugh

ACADEMY AWARD WINNERS
BEST ACTOR

1927-28 Emil Jannings (The Way of All Flesh, The Last Command)	1956 Yul Brynner (The King and I)
	1957 Alec Guinness (The Bridge on the River Kwai)
1928-29 Warner Baxter (In Old Arizona)	
1929-30 George Arliss (Disraeli)	1958 David Niven (Separate Tables)
1930-31 Lionel Barrymore (A Free Soul)	1959 Charlton Heston (Ben-Hur)
1931-32 Fredric March (Dr. Jekyll and Mr. Hyde), Wallace Beery (The Champ)	1960 Burt Lancaster (Elmer Gantry)
	1961 Maximilian Schell (Judgment at Nuremberg)
1932-33 Charles Laughton (The Private Life of Henry VIII)	1962 Gregory Peck (To Kill a Mockingbird)
1934 Clark Gable (It Happened One Night)	1963 Sidney Poitier (Lilies of the Field)
1935 Victor McLaglen (The Informer)	1964 Rex Harrison (My Fair Lady)
1936 Paul Muni (The Story of Louis Pasteur)	1965 Lee Marvin (Cat Ballou)
	1966 Paul Scofield (A Man for All Seasons)
1937 Spencer Tracy (Captains Courageous)	1967 Rod Steiger (In the Heat of the Night)
1938 Spencer Tracy (Boys Town)	1968 Cliff Robertson (Charly)
1939 Robert Donat (Goodbye, Mr. Chips)	1969 John Wayne (True Grit)
1940 James Stewart (The Philadelphia Story)	1970 George C. Scott (Patton)
	1971 Gene Hackman (The French Connection)
1941 Gary Cooper (Sergeant York)	1972 Marlon Brando (The Godfather)
1942 James Cagney (Yankee Doodle Dandy)	1973 Jack Lemmon (Save the Tiger)
1943 Paul Lukas (Watch on the Rhine)	1974 Art Carney (Harry and Tonto)
1944 Bing Crosby (Going My Way)	1975 Jack Nicholson (One Flew Over the Cuckoo's Nest)
1945 Ray Milland (The Lost Weekend)	
1946 Fredric March (The Best Years of Our Lives)	1976 Peter Finch (Network)
	1977 Richard Dreyfuss (The Goodbye Girl)
1947 Ronald Colman (A Double Life)	1978 Jon Voight (Coming Home)
1948 Laurence Olivier (Hamlet)	1979 Dustin Hoffman (Kramer vs. Kramer)
1949 Broderick Crawford (All the King's Men)	1980 Robert De Niro (Raging Bull)
1950 José Ferrer (Cyrano de Bergerac)	1981 Henry Fonda (On Golden Pond)
1951 Humphrey Bogart (The African Queen)	1982 Ben Kingsley (Gandhi)
	1983 Robert Duvall (Tender Mercies)
1952 Gary Cooper (High Noon)	1984 F. Murray Abraham (Amadeus)
1953 William Holden (Stalag 17)	1985 William Hurt (Kiss of the Spider Woman)
1954 Marlon Brando (On the Waterfront)	1986 Paul Newman (The Color of Money)
1955 Ernest Borgnine (Marty)	1987 Michael Douglas (Wall Street)

BEST ACTRESS

1927-28 Janet Gaynor (Seventh Heaven, Street Angel, Sunrise)	1958 Susan Hayward (I Want to Live!)
	1959 Simone Signoret (Room at the Top)
1928-29 Mary Pickford (Coquette)	1960 Elizabeth Taylor (Butterfield 8)
1929-30 Norma Shearer (The Divorcee)	1961 Sophia Loren (Two Women)
1930-31 Marie Dressler (Min and Bill)	1962 Anne Bancroft (The Miracle Worker)
1931-32 Helen Hayes (The Sin of Madelon Claudet)	1963 Patricia Neal (Hud)
	1964 Julie Andrews (Mary Poppins)
1932-33 Katharine Hepburn (Morning Glory)	1965 Julie Christie (Darling)
1934 Claudette Colbert (It Happened One Night)	1966 Elizabeth Taylor (Who's Afraid of Virginia Woolf?)
1935 Bette Davis (Dangerous)	1967 Katharine Hepburn (Guess Who's Coming to Dinner)
1936 Luise Rainer (The Great Ziegfeld)	
1937 Luise Rainer (The Good Earth)	1968 Katharine Hepburn (The Lion in Winter), Barbra Streisand (Funny Girl)
1938 Bette Davis (Jezebel)	
1939 Vivien Leigh (Gone with the Wind)	1969 Maggie Smith (The Prime of Miss Jean Brodie)
1940 Ginger Rogers (Kitty Foyle)	
1941 Joan Fontaine (Suspicion)	1970 Glenda Jackson (Women in Love)
1942 Greer Garson (Mrs. Miniver)	1971 Jane Fonda (Klute)
1943 Jennifer Jones (The Song of Bernadette)	1972 Liza Minnelli (Cabaret)
	1973 Glenda Jackson (A Touch of Class)
1944 Ingrid Bergman (Gaslight)	1974 Ellen Burstyn (Alice Doesn't Live Here Anymore)
1945 Joan Crawford (Mildred Pierce)	
1946 Olivia de Havilland (To Each His Own)	1975 Louise Fletcher (One Flew Over the Cuckoo's Nest)
1947 Loretta Young (The Farmer's Daughter)	
	1976 Faye Dunaway (Network)
1948 Jane Wyman (Johnny Belinda)	1977 Diane Keaton (Annie Hall)
1949 Olivia de Havilland (The Heiress)	1978 Jane Fonda (Coming Home)
1950 Judy Holliday (Born Yesterday)	1979 Sally Field (Norma Rae)
1951 Vivien Leigh (A Streetcar Named Desire)	1980 Sissy Spacek (Coal Miner's Daughter)
1952 Shirley Booth (Come Back, Little Sheba)	1981 Katharine Hepburn (On Golden Pond)
	1982 Meryl Streep (Sophie's Choice)
1953 Audrey Hepburn (Roman Holiday)	1983 Shirley McClain (Terms of Endearment)
1954 Grace Kelly (The Country Girl)	1984 Sally Field (Places In the Heart)
1955 Anna Magnani (The Rose Tattoo)	1985 Geraldine Page (The Trip to Bountiful)
1956 Ingrid Bergman (Anastasia)	1986 Marlee Martin (Children of a Lesser God)
1957 Joanne Woodward (The Three Faces of Eve)	1987 Cher (Moonstruck)

ACADEMY AWARD WINNERS
BEST PICTURE

1927-28	Wings	1958	Gigi
1928-29	The Broadway Melody	1959	Ben-Hur
1929-30	All Quiet on the Western Front	1960	The Apartment
1930-31	Cimarron	1961	West Side Story
1931-32	Grand Hotel	1962	Lawrence of Arabia
1932-33	Cavalcade	1963	Tom Jones
1934	It Happened One Night	1964	My Fair Lady
1935	Mutiny on the Bounty	1965	The Sound of Music
1936	The Great Ziegfeld	1966	A Man for All Seasons
1937	The Life of Émile Zola	1967	In the Heat of the Night
1938	You Can't Take It with You	1968	Oliver!
1939	Gone with the Wind	1969	Midnight Cowboy
1940	Rebecca	1970	Patton
1941	How Green Was My Valley	1971	The French Connection
1942	Mrs. Miniver	1972	The Godfather
1943	Casablanca	1973	The Sting
1944	Going My Way	1974	The Godfather, Part II
1945	The Lost Weekend	1975	One Flew Over the Cuckoo's Nest
1946	The Best Years of Our Lives	1976	Rocky
1947	Gentleman's Agreement	1977	Annie Hall
1948	Hamlet	1978	The Deer Hunter
1949	All the King's Men	1979	Kramer vs. Kramer
1950	All About Eve	1980	Ordinary People
1951	An American in Paris	1981	Chariots of Fire
1952	The Greatest Show on Earth	1982	Gandhi
1953	From Here to Eternity	1983	Terms of Endearment
1954	On the Waterfront	1984	Amadeus
1955	Marty	1985	Out of Africa
1956	Around the World in 80 Days	1986	Platoon
1957	The Bridge on the River Kwai	1987	The Last Emperor

BEST DIRECTOR

1927-28	Frank Borzage (Seventh Heaven), Lewis Milestone (Two Arabian Knights)	1956	George Stevens (Giant)
		1957	David Lean (The Bridge on the River Kwai)
1928-29	Frank Lloyd (The Divine Lady)	1958	Vincente Minnelli (Gigi)
1929-30	Lewis Milestone (All Quiet on the Western Front)	1959	William Wyler (Ben-Hur)
1930-31	Norman Taurog (Skippy)	1960	Billy Wilder (The Apartment)
1931-32	Frank Borzage (Bad Girl)	1961	Robert Wise and Jerome Robbins (West Side Story)
1932-33	Frank Lloyd (Cavalcade)		
1934	Frank Capra (It Happened One Night)	1962	David Lean (Lawrence of Arabia)
1935	John Ford (The Informer)	1963	Tony Richardson (Tom Jones)
1936	Frank Capra (Mr. Deeds Goes to Town)	1964	George Cukor (My Fair Lady)
		1965	Robert Wise (The Sound of Music)
1937	Leo McCarey (The Awful Truth)	1966	Fred Zinnemann (A Man for All Seasons)
1938	Frank Capra (You Can't Take It with You)		
		1967	Mike Nichols (The Graduate)
1939	Victor Fleming (Gone with the Wind)	1968	Sir Carol Reed (Oliver!)
1940	John Ford (The Grapes of Wrath)	1969	John Schlesinger (Midnight Cowboy)
1941	John Ford ((How Green Was My Valley)	1970	Franklin J. Schaffner (Patton)
		1971	William Friedkin (The French Connection)
1942	William Wyler (Mrs. Miniver)		
1943	Michael Curtiz (Casablanca)	1972	Bob Fosse (Cabaret)
1944	Leo McCarey (Going My Way)	1973	George Roy Hill (The Sting)
1945	Billy Wilder (The Lost Weekend)	1974	Francis Ford Coppola (The Godfather, Part II)
1946	William Wyler (The Best Years of Our Lives)		
		1975	Milos Forman (One Flew Over the Cuckoo's Nest)
1947	Elia Kazan (Gentleman's Agreement)		
1948	John Huston (The Treasure of Sierra Madre)	1976	John Avildsen (Rocky)
		1977	Woody Allen (Annie Hall)
1949	Joseph L. Mankiewicz (A Letter to Three Wives)	1978	Michael Cimino (The Deer Hunter)
		1979	Robert Benton (Kramer vs. Kramer)
1950	Joseph L. Mankiewicz (All About Eve)	1980	Robert Redford (Ordinary People)
1951	George Stevens (A Place in the Sun)	1981	Warren Beatty (Reds)
1952	John Ford (The Quiet Man)	1982	Richard Attenborough (Gandhi)
1953	Fred Zinnemann (From Here to Eternity)	1983	James L. Brooks (Terms of Endearment)
1954	Elia Kazan (On the Waterfront)	1984	Milos Forman (Amadeus)
		1985	Sydney Pollack (Out of Africa)
1955	Delbert Mann (Marty)	1986	Oliver Stone (Platoon)
		1987	Bernardo Bertolucci (The Last Emperor)

SPORTS' NICKNAMES

BASEBALL:

Hank Aaron . . . . Atlanta Slugger, Hammerin' Hank, New Sultan of the Swat

Grover Cleveland
 Alexander . . . . Alexander the Great, Old Pete

Walter Alston . . . . Smokey

Adrian Constantine Anson . . . Cap, Pop

Louis Aparacio . . . . Little Looie, Little Louie

Luke Appling . . . . Old Aches and Pains

Frank Baker . . . . Home Run

Ernie Banks . . . . Mr. Cub, Mr. Sunshine

Red Barber . . . . The Ol' Redhead

Robert Belinsky . . . . Bo

James Thomas Bell . . . . Black Ty Cobb, Papa

Johnny Bench . . . . Swinger from Binger

Lawrence P. Berra . . . . Ugly Duckling, Yogi

Ewell Blackwell . . . . Blackie, The Whip

Jim Bottomley . . . . Sunny Jim

Jim Bouton . . . . Bulldog

Ralph Branca . . . . Hawk

Mordecai P. Brown . . . . Miner, Three-Finger

Roy Campanella . . . . The Happy Warrior

Rod Carew . . . . Sweetest Swinger

Steve Carlton . . . . Lefty

Alexander Cartwright . . . . . . Father of Baseball

Orlando Cepeda . . . . Baby Bull, Cha-Cha

Frank Chance . . . . Husk, Peerless Leader

Albert Benjamin Chandler . . . Happy

Roberto Clemente . . . . The Great One

Tyrus Raymond Cobb . . . . The Georgia Peach, Idol of Baseball Fandom, Ty

Gordon Stanley Cochrane . . . . Black Mike, Mickey

Eddie Collins . . . . Sharpest Second-sacker

Charles A. Comiskey . . . . Commy, The Old Roman

John B. Conlan . . . . Jocko

Donald Eugene Conley . . . . . . Big Brave from Milwaukee, Daddy Long Arms

Clint Courtney . . . . Scrap Iron

Roger Cramer . . . . Doc, Flit

Frank Crosetti . . . . The Crow

Hazen Shirley Cuyler . . . . Kiki

Al Dark . . . . Blackie, Bright Star of the Boston Braves

Loraine Day . . . . First Lady of Baseball

(Jay Hanna) Jerome
 Herman Dean . . . . Dizzy, Great Man, Ol' Diz

Bill Dickey . . . . Baseball's Quiet Man

Joe DiMaggio . . . . Jolting Joe, Yankee Clipper

Walt Dropo . . . . Moose

Donald Scott Drysdale . . . . . . Big D

Leo Durocher . . . . The Lip

Charles Ebbets . . . . Father of the Brooklyn Dodgers

John J. Evers . . . . The Trojan

Bob Feller . . . . Bullet Bob, Rapid Robert

Mark Fidrych . . . . The Bird

Curtis Charles Flood . . . . The Man Who Sued Baseball

Edward C. Ford . . . . The Chairman of the Board, Whitey

James Emory Foxx . . . . The Beast, Double X, Maryland Strongboy

Bob Friend . . . . The Warrior

Frankie Frisch	The Fordham Flash
Carl Furillo	The Reading Rifle, Skoon
Mike Garcia	The Big Bear
Lou Gehrig	Buster, Columbia Lou, The Iron Horse, Pride of the Yankees
Josh Gibson	The Black Babe Ruth
Robert Gibson	Hoot, Old Master
Jim Gilliam	Junior
Vernon Gomez	The Gay Castillon, Goofy, Lefty
Leon A. Goslin	Goose
Richard Michael Gossage	Goose
Jim Grant	Mudcat
Hank Greenberg	Hammerin' Hank
Clark Calvin Griffith	Old Fox
Charlie Grimm	Jolly Cholly
Robert Moses Grove	Lefty, Mose
Ron Guidry	Louisiana Lightning
Stan Hack	Smiling Stan
Harvey Haddix	The Kitten
Stanley Harris	Boy Wonder, Bucky
Charles Leo Hartnett	Gabby, Man in the Iron Mask
Ricky Henderson	New Base-stealing King
Tommy Henrich	Old Reliable
Rogers Hornsby	The Rajah, The Rajah of Swat
Ralph Houk	Major
Frank Howard	The Capital Punisher, Hondo
Charles Waite Hoyt	Schoolboy
Robert Hubbard	Cal
Carl Hubbell	King Carl, The Meal Ticket
James Miller Huggins	Hug, The Mighty Mite
Jim Hunter	Catfish
Reggie Jackson	Mr. October
Joe Jackson	Shoeless Joe
Walter Johnson	Barney, Big Swede, The Big Train, Grand Veteran
Sam Jones	Sad Sam
William H. Keeler	Wee Willie
Charlie Keller	King Kong
Harmon Killebrew	Killer, Muscular Marvel from Idaho
Ralph Kiner	Mr. Home Run
Dave Kingman	King Kong
Sandy Koufax	Man with the Golden Arm
Napoleon Lajoie	Larry, Nap
Kennesaw Mountain Landis	Czar of American Baseball, Czar of the National Pastime, Judge
Harry Arthur Lavagetti	Cookie
Vernon Sanders Law	Deacon
Anthony Michael Lazzeri	Push'em-up Lazzeri
Ernie Lombardi	Bocci, Schnozz
Edmund Walter Lopat	Steady Eddie
Albert Walter Lyle	Sparky
Connie Mack	Mr. Baseball, Patriarch of the Dugout, Tall Tactician
Bill Madlock	Mad Dog
Sal Maglie	The Barber
Mickey Mantle	The Commerce Comet, Everybody's Hero, The Great Mick, Million Dollar Invalid, Wounded Hero

Walter James Maranville .... Rabbit
Juan Marichal .... Manito, The Dominican Dandy
Marty Marion .... The Octopus, Slats
Roger Maris .... New Home Run Champion
Richard W. Marquand ...... Rube
John Martin .... Pepper, Wild Hoss of the Osage
Christy Mathewson .... The Big Six
Willie Mays .... Say-Hey Kid, Willie the Wallop
Joe McCarthy .... Marse Joe
Willie McCovey .... Stretch
Sam McDowell .... Sudden Sam
John J. McGraw .... Father of Inside Baseball, The Little Napoleon
Leland McPhail .... Lord Larry, Wizard of Baseball
Joe Medwick .... Ducky (Duckie), Muscles
Frederick Charles Merkle ... Bonehead
Saturnino Orestes Arieta
  Minoso .... Minnie
Johnny Mize .... The Big Cat
Wilmer D. Mizell .... Vinegar Bend
Thurmon Munson .... Pudge, Round Man
Stan Musial .... Stan the Man, What-a-Man Stan
Don Newcombe .... Newk
Hal Newhouser .... The Gay Reliever, Prince Hal
Norman L. Newsom .... Bobo, Buck
Phil Niekro .... Knucksie, Master of the Knuckleball
Billy O'Dell .... Digger
Johnny Lee Odom .... Blue Moon
Mel Ott .... Master Melvin, Mighty Mite
Arnold Malcolm Owen ...... Mickey
Danny Ozark .... Ozark Ike
Joe Page .... Fireman
Leroy Paige .... Satchel
Milt Pappas .... Gimpy
Mel Parnell .... Dusty
Herb Pennock .... The Knight of Kennett Square
Gaylord Perry .... Master of the Spitball
John Wesley Powell .... Boog
Vic Raschi .... The Springfield Rifle
Harold Henry Reese .... The Little Colonel, Pee Wee
Harold Patrick Reiser .... Pete, Pistol Pete
Allie Reynolds .... The Chief, Wahoo
James Lamar Rhodes .... Dusty
Branch Rickey .... Grand Old Man of Baseball, Mahatma
Bill Rigney .... The Cricket, Specs
Phil Rizzuto .... Little Monkey, Scooter
Robert E. Roberts .... Robin
Brooks Robinson .... Bobby the Robber, Human Vacuum Cleaner, Mr. Impossible
Jackie Robinson .... America's First Negro in Baseball, The Pioneer
Elwin Charles Roe .... Preacher
Robert A. Rolfe .... Red
Pete Rose .... Charlie Hustle
Al Rosen .... Flip
Lynwood Thomas Rowe ..... Schoolboy
Charles H. Ruffing .... Red

George Herman Ruth	Babe, Bambino, Idol of the American Boy, Jidge, King of Swat, Sultan of the Swat
Al Schacht	Clown Prince of Baseball
Albert Fred Schoendienst	Red
Tom Seaver	Tom Terrific
George Selkirk	Twinkletoes
Truett Banks Sewell	Rip
Roy Sievers	Squirrel
Al Simmons	Bucketfoot Al
Harry Leon Simpson	Suitcase
George Sisler	Gorgeous George, The Perfect Ballplayer
Bill Skowron	Moose
Enos Slaughter	Country
Edwin Donald Snider	Duke, Duke of Brooklyn, Silver Fox
Tris Speaker	The Gray Eagle, Spoke
Eddie Stanky	The Brat, Muggsy
Wilver D. Stargell	Gentle Ben, Willie
Charles Stengel	Casey, Dutch, Old Perfessor
Charles Evard Street	Gabby, Old Sarge
Bill Terry	Memphis Bill
Bobby Thompson	The Staten Island Scot
Marv Throneberry	Marvelous Marv
Harold Joseph Traynor	Pie
Paul H. Trout	Dizzy
Bob Turley	Bullet Bob
Fernando Valenzuela	El Toro
C. Arthur Vance	Dazzy
John Vander Meer	Double No-Hit Kid, The Dutch Master
George E. Waddell	Baseball's Greatest Clown, Rube
John P. Wagner	The Flying Dutchman, Hans, Honus
Fred Walker	Dixie, The People's Cherce
Harry W. Walker	The Hat
Ed Walsh	Big Ed, Big Moose
Lloyd Waner	Little Poison
Paul Waner	Big Poison
Lon Warneke	The Arkansas Humming Bird
Zach Wheat	Buck
Ted Williams	The Kid, The Splendid Splinter, Teddy Ballgame, The Thumper
Maury Wills	Base-stealing King
Louis R. Wilson	Hack
Early Wynn	Gus
Jim Wynn	Toy Cannon
Carl Yastrzemski	The Hawk, Yaz
Eddie Yost	The Walking Man
Denton True Young	Cy, Cyclone
Gus Zernial	Ozark Ike

BASKETBALL:

Forrest C. Allen	Phog
Nate Archibald	Little Big Man, Tiny
Arnold Auerbach	Red
Jim Barnes	Bad News
Marvin Barnes	The Eraser, Good News
Zelmo Beatty	Big Z
Larry Bird	The Bird

Joe Caldwell . . . . Pogo
Gene Conley . . . . Daddy Long Legs
Bob Cousy . . . . Houdini of the Hardwood, Magician of the Court
Wilt Chamberlain . . . . The Big Dipper, Wilt the Stilt
Darryl Dawkins . . . . Chocolate Thunder, Mr. Earthquake
Henry Dehnert . . . . Dutch
Julius Erving . . . . The Doctor, Doctor J
Clarence Francis . . . . Bevo
Walter Frazier . . . . Clyde
John Havlicek . . . . Boston's Sixth Man, Hondo
Connie Hawkins . . . . The Hawk
Elvin Hayes . . . . The Big E
Marques Haynes . . . . Best Dribbler in Basketball History
Nat Holman . . . . Mr. Basketball
Kareem Abdul Jabbar (Lew
  Alcindor) . . . . Master of the Skyhook
Earvin Johnson . . . . Magic
Meadowlark Lemon . . . . Clown Prince of Basketball, Comedy King of the Sports
                                   World
Angelo Luisetti . . . . Hank
Pete Maravich . . . . Pistol Pete
George Mikan . . . . Greatest Player of the First-Half Century, Nearsighted
                                   Giant
Earl Monroe . . . . Earl the Pearl
Dr. James A. Naismith . . . . . . Father of Basketball
Oscar Robertson . . . . The Big O, Oz
Len Robinson . . . . Truck
Adolph F. Rupp . . . . Baron of Bluegrass Country
Abraham Saperstein . . . . Barnum of Basketball
Jerry West . . . . Mr. Clutch
Leonard Wilkins . . . . Lennie, Will-o'-the Wisp

BOXING:

Muhammad Ali (Cassius
  Marcellus Clay, Jr.) . . . . Cassius the Brashest, The Greatest, The Louisville Lip
Henry Armstrong (Henry
  Jackson) . . . . Hammerin' Henry, Homicide Hank, King Who Wore
                                   Three Crowns
Max Baer . . . . Clouting Clown, Fistic Harlequin, Madcap Maxie,
                                   Playboy of Pugilism
Carmen Basilio . . . . Canastota Onion Farmer, Uncrowned Champion
James J. Braddock . . . . The Cinderella Man, Forgotten Man
Jack Broughton . . . . Father of Boxing
Georges Carpentier . . . . Orchid Man
Reuben Carter . . . . Hurricane Carter
William Conn . . . . The Pittsburgh Kid
Gerry Cooney . . . . Gentleman Gerry, Killer Bull with the Marshmellow
                                   Heart
James J. Corbett . . . . Dancing Master, Gentleman Jim
Pat De Marco . . . . Paddy
Jack Dempsey . . . . The Champ, Fighter of the Half Century, Jack the Giant
                                   Killer, Kid Blackie, Manassa Mauler
Michael Dokes . . . . Dynamite Dokes
Roberto Duran . . . . Fists of Stone, No Más Man
Luis Angel Firpo . . . . Wild Bull of the Pampas

Robert Prometheus Fitz-
simmons .... Champion of Champions, The Cornishman, The
Australian Blacksmith
George Foreman .... Big George, Lightning Destroyer
Joe Frazier............... Smokin' Joe
Kid Galivan (Geraldo
Gonzalez) .... The Hawk
Rocky Graziano (Rocco
Barbella) .... Atomic Puncher, Rockabye Rocky
Marvin Hagler .... Marvelous Marvin
Thomas Hearns .... Hit Man
Larry Holmes .... Gentle Giant, Giant Killer
John Arthur Johnson .... The Galveston Giant, Jack, Li'l Arthur
Stanley Ketchel .... The Michigan Assassin
Jacob La Motta .... Bronx Bull
Benny Leonard .... Ghetto Wizard, Mama's Boy
Ray Charles Leonard .... America's Darling, Sugar Ray
Joe Louis (Barrow) .... The Brown Bomber
Charles McCoy .... Kid McCoy, The Real McCoy
Lenny and Ray Mancini ..... Boom Boom
Rocky Marciano (Rocco
Francis Marchegiano) ..... Brockton Blockbuster, Brockton Bull
Archie Moore .... Old Mongoose, Magnificent Mongoose
Floyd Patterson .... The Rabbit
Willie Pep................ Old Master, Will-o'-the Wisp
Ray Robinson (Walker
Smith) .... Sugar Ray, Sweet as Sugar
Maxie Rosenbloom......... Slapsie Maxie
Jack Sharkey............. Bay Stater, Boston Sailor, The Lithuanian
John L. Sullivan........... Boston Strong Boy, Great John L.
Gene Tunney .... The Fighting Marine
Joe Walcott (Arnold
Raymond Cream) .... Jersey Joe
Mickey Walker............ Toy Bulldog
Jess Willard.............. Cowboy Jess, Kansas Giant, Pottawatomie Giant

FOOTBALL:

Benjamin Agajanian .... Automatic
Alan Ameche .... The Horse
Sammy Baugh .... Slinging Sammy
Joseph Bellino .... Joe the Jet, Navy Destroyer
Earl Henry Blaik .... Colonel, Red
Felix Blanchard .... Doc, Mr. Inside
James Nathaniel Brown ..... Football Player of the Decade
Paul Bryant .... Bear
Dick Butkus .... Animal
Christian K. Cagle .... Onward Christian Cagle, Red
Walter Camp .... Father of American Football
Hugh Daugherty .... Duffy
Glenn Davis .... Mr. Outside
Mike Ditka .... Hammer Ditka, Monk Ditka
Frank Gifford .... Golden Boy
Carlton Gilchrist........... Cookie
Otto Graham.............. Best Quarterback of All Time
Harold Grange .... The Galloping Ghost, Red
Joe Greene............... Mean Joe Greene

Roosevelt Grier . . . . Big Rosey, The Jolly Giant
Lou Groza . . . . The Toe
George Halas . . . . Father of Professional Football, Father of the National
                                       Football League, Papa Bear
Robert Lee Hayes . . . . Super-flanker Hayes
Elroy Hirsch . . . . Crazylegs
Paul Hornung . . . . Golden Boy
Don Hutson . . . . Alabama Antelope, First Super End, Man with the
                                       Magnetic Mitts
Billy Johnson . . . . White Shoes
David Jones . . . . Deacon
Ed Jones . . . . Too Tall
Charles Justice . . . . Choo Choo
Alex Karras . . . . The Crippler, Tippy-Toe
Earl Lambeau . . . . Curly
Richard Lane . . . . Night Train
Robert Lawrence Layne . . . . . Built-In Timepiece
Gene Lipscomb . . . . Big Daddy
Gino Marchetti . . . . Football's Great Defensive End
Don Meredith . . . . Dandy Don
Earl Morral . . . . Earl the Pearl
Eugene Morris . . . . Mercury
Marion Motley . . . . Otto Graham's Bodyguard
Bronislau Nagurski . . . . Big Ukranian, The Battling Bronk, Bronco
Joe Namath . . . . Broadway Joe, Joe Willie
Ernie Nevers . . . . Big Dog
Vito Parilli . . . . Babe
Roy Riegels . . . . Wrong Way
Knute Rockne . . . . The Bald Eagle of Notre Dame, Rock of Notre Dame
Gayle Sayers . . . . The Comet, Galloping Gale
Allie Sherman . . . . Pedantic Professor
Don Shula . . . . Miami's Unmiraculous Miracle Worker
O(renthal) J(ames)
  Simpson . . . . The Juice, O.J., Orange Juice
Kenny Stabler . . . . The Snake
Roger Staubach . . . . The Dodger
Amos Alonzo Stagg . . . . Dean of Football Coaches, Football's Grand Old Man
Francis Tarkenton . . . . The Scrambler
Jim Thorpe . . . . The Fabulous Indian
Y(elberton) A(braham)
  Tittle . . . . Colonel Slick
Clyde D. Turner . . . . Bulldog, Kid from Sweetwater
Johnny Unitas . . . . Man With the Golden Arm, The Old Master
Doak Walker, Jr. . . . . All-American Mustang, Little Man in Pro Football
Glenn Warner . . . . Pop
Bob Waterfield . . . . Rifle
Claude Young . . . . Buddy
Paul Younger . . . . Tank

GOLF:

Willie Anderson . . . . Silent Scot
Benjamin Crenshaw . . . . Gentle Ben
Babe (Didrickson)
  Zacharias . . . . Athletic Phenomenon of All Time, Marvelous Mildred
Walter Hagen . . . . The Haig
Ben Hogan . . . . Bantam Ben, Golfdom's Mighty Mite, Little Ben

Bobby Jones .... Boy Wonder, Emperor Jones, Grand Slammer, The Immortal Golfer, King of the Links
Tony Lema................ Champagne Tony
Cary Middlecoff .... Doc
Orville Moody............. The Sarge, Unknown Soldier
Jack Nicklaus .... The Bear
Greg Norman .... Great White Shark
Gary Player .... Golf's Black Knight, Man in Black
Juan Rodriguez .... Chi Chi, Clown Prince of Golf
Gene Sarazen .... Squire of the Greens
Charles Sifford............ Jackie Robinson of Golf
Sam Snead .... Slammin' Sam (Sammy)
Lee Trevino .... Supermex
Mary Kathryn Wright .... Mickey

HORSERACING:

Eddie Arcaro .... Banana Nose, Heady Eddie, King of the Little Men, King of the Stakes Riders
Steve Cauthen .... The Kid
James Edward Fitzsimmons .... Dean of American Trainers, Grand Old Man of Racing, Sage of Sheepshead Bay, Sunny Jim
Man o'War................ Big Red
Native Dancer .... Gray Ghost
Earl Sande .... A Handy Guy, Great Jockey of the Golden Age of Sports
Willie Shoemaker .... Silent Shoe, The Shoe

ICE HOCKEY:

Jean Beliveau .... Big Jean, Crown Prince of Hockey, Le Gros Bill
Yvan Cournoyer .... The Road Runner
Alex Delvecchio .... Fats
Marcel Dionne .... Little Beaver
Bernie Geoffrion .... Boom Boom
Wayne Gretzky .... The Great One, The More Than Amazin' One
Bobby Hull............... Golden Boy, The Golden Jet
Ted Lindsay .... Terrible Ted
Howie Morenz .... Babe Ruth of Hockey, Canadien Comet
Bobby Orr .... Greatest Player of Hockey
Lester Patrick .... Old Man in the Net
Henri Richard .... The Pocket Rocket
Maurice Richard .... Babe Ruth of Hockey, The Rocket, The Rocket of the Ice
Dave Schultz .... The Hammer
Eddie Shore .... Firebrand of the Ice
Lorne John Worsley .... Gump

ICE SKATING:

Dick Button .... Poetry on Ice
Jackson Haines .... American Skating King, Father of Figure Skating
Sonja Henie .... Girl in White, Golden Girl, Symphony on Silver Skates
Charlie Tickner .... Mr. Perseverance

POOL:

Ralph Greenleaf . . . . Man with a Cue Stick
Willie Hoppe . . . . The Boy Wonder, Old Master
Rudolf Walter Wanderone,
  Jr. . . . . Minnesota Fats

RACING:

Mario Andretti . . . . The Tiger
Erwing George Baker . . . . Cannonball
Anthony Joseph Foyt . . . . A.J., Hard-nosed Demon of the Ovals, The Houston
                                  Hurricane
Stirling Moss . . . . British Auto Ace
Shirley Muldowney . . . . Cha Cha
Berna E. Oldfield . . . . Barney, America's Speed King
Richard Petty . . . . King of the Road, Stock Car Racing King
Eddie Rickenbacker . . . . Ace of Aces
Robert Unser . . . . The Albuquerque Cowboy

SWIMMING:

Florence Chadwick . . . . Queen of the World's Waterways
Clarence Crabbe . . . . Buster
Gertrude Ederle . . . . Wonderful Trudy
Shane Gould . . . . The Australian Wonder
Vladimir Salnikov . . . . The Russian Machine
Mark Spitz . . . . King of Amateur Swimming, Olympic Gold
Johnny Weissmuller . . . . The Human Fish

TEAMS:

1906 Chicago White Sox . . . . The Hitless Wonders
1910's Philadelphia Athletics $100,000 Infield
1927 New York Yankees . . . . Murderer's Row
1930's St. Louis Cardinals . . Gas House Gang
1940's Chicago Bears . . . . . . Monsters of the Midway
1950 Philadelphia Phillies . . . The Whiz Kids
1960's Los Angeles Rams'
  Defensive Line . . . . The Fearsome Foursome
1969 New York Mets . . . . Amazing Mets, Miracle Mets
1970's Minnesota Vikings'
  Defensive Line . . . . The Purple People Eaters
1970's Dallas Cowboys . . . . . Doomsday Defense
1970's Miami Dolphins . . . . . No-Name Defense
1970's Denver Broncos . . . . . Orange Crush
1976 Philadelphia Flyers . . . . The Broad Street Bullies
1980's Washington Redskins'
  Offensive Line . . . . The Hogs
1980's Detroit Lions . . . . Silver Rush

TENNIS:

Bjorn Borg . . . . The Iceman, Imperturbable Swede, Relentless Borg
Don Budge . . . . Oakland Redhead, Red-headed Comet of the Courts
Maureen Connolly Brinker . . . Mighty Little Mo
Jimmy Connors . . . . Jimbo

Dwight Davis . . . . Father of the Davis Cup
Dr. James Dwight . . . . Father of American Lawn Tennis
Richard Gonzales . . . . Pancho
Billie Jean King . . . . King of the Courts, Old Lady, Tennis Tycoon
Jack Kramer . . . . Big Jake
Rod Laver . . . . The Rocket
Suzanne Lenglen . . . . La Grande Suzanne
Chris Evert Lloyd . . . . Ice Maiden
John McEnroe . . . . The Brat, Fiery American Rebel, Junior, Mr. Sourpuss
Gertrude Augusta Moran . . . . Gorgeous Gussie, Gussie
Bobby Riggs . . . . Queen of the Courts, White Muhammad Ali
Francisco Segura . . . . Pancho
Margaret Court Smith . . . . . . Amazing Amazon
Bill Tilden . . . . Big Bill, Court Jester, Giant of the Court, Wild Bill
Helen Wills (Newington,
  Moody, or Roark) . . . . Little Poker Face, The Princess, Queen Helen
Major Walter Clopton
  Wingfield . . . . Father of Modern Tennis

TRACK AND FIELD:

Donald Bragg . . . . Don Tarzan Bragg
James B. Connolly . . . . First American Olympic Champion
Glenn Cunningham . . . . The Miraculous Miler
Walt Davis . . . . The Kangaroo Kid
Clarence DeMar . . . . The Shuffler
Harrison Dillard . . . . Old Bones
Ray Ewry . . . . The Human Frog
Richard D. Fosbury . . . . Master of the Fosbury Flop
Robert Bruce "Bob"
  Mathias . . . . Champion of Champions, King of the Decathlon
James Randel Matson . . . . . . Gentle Giant, Randy
Edwin Moses . . . . Mr. Consistency
Renaldo Nehemiah . . . . Skeets
Paavo Nurmi . . . . Flying Finn, Phantom Finn
Parry O'Brien . . . . Mighty Muscle Man
Jesse Owens . . . . Athlete of the Half Century, Brown Bombshell, Ebony
                                       Express
Charles Paddock . . . . Golden Boy of the Cinder Track
Wilma Rudolph . . . . Skeeter
Emil Zatopek . . . . Incredible Czech

MISCELLANEOUS:

Avery Brundage . . . . America's Champion Amateur Athlete
Olga Korbut . . . . The Little Russian, The Little Sparrow
Ernie Ladd . . . . King of Wrestling
Pele (Edson Arantes Do
  Nascimento) . . . . The Black Pearl, World's Most Famous Athlete
William Ashley Sunday . . . . . Billy, Hunkster of the Tabernacle
R.E. "Ted" Turner . . . . Captain Courageous, Mouth of the South, Teddy
                                       Ballgame

QUESTIONS AND ANSWERS

1. What are the names of America's 2 oldest cities? Who founded them, and what were the years?

    ANSWER: St. Augustine by Don Pedro Menéndez de Avilés on September 8, 1565 (he landed there on August 28), and Santa Fe in 1609-1610 by Pedro de Peralta (he named it *La Villa Real de la Santa Fe de San Francisco de Asis*, meaning The Royal City of the Holy Faith of St. Francis of Assisi).

2. Two English explorers failed to reach America in 1578, but one reached Newfoundland in 1583 and the other helped found a colony on the American coast in 1587. What were their names? What did the Indians call this colony? What was it named and for whom? In what state is it today? Who was the first child born there? What is the nickname of this colony today? What were the only words—which are still a mystery—found there when a relief ship arrived in 1591?

    ANSWER: Sir Humphrey Gilbert (Newfoundland) and Sir Walter Raleigh (American coast)/Roanoke/Virginia for Elizabeth, the ''Virgin Queen''/North Carolina /Virginia Dare/The ''Lost Colony''/The word ''Cro'' was cut into a tree and ''Croatoan'' was carved on a doorpost.

3. Two trading companies were chartered by King James I in 1606 for trading in and settling the British-held Territory of North America, called Virginia. Name the 2 trading companies.

    ANSWER: The North and South Virginia Companies of London or the Plymouth Company (or the Virginia Company of Plymouth) for the northern territory and the London Company for the southern territory.

4. What were the names of the 3 ships of the London Company that brought settlers to Jamestown (named for James I) on May 24, 1607? What Captain helped the colony survive, and who was the first full governor?

    ANSWER: The *Discovery*, the *Godspeed (Goodspeed)*, and the *Sarah Constant*/Captain John Smith/Lord Thomas De La Warr.

5. Who was the leader of the Indian group that threatened the settlers at Jamestown? What was his daughter's name? Whose life did she supposedly save? Whom did she marry?

    ANSWER: Chief Powhatan (real name was Wahunsonacock)/Pocahontas (real name was Matoaka and her Christian name was Rebecca)/Captain John Smith/ John Rolfe.

6. What boat accompanied the *Mayflower* from Southhampton to Plymouth, England, before it proved to be unseaworthy to travel to the New World on September 16? Who captained the *Mayflower?* What was the name of the child born en route aboard ship? Who was the only person to die on the trip? Who was the leader and historian of the Puritans? On what date did the Pilgrims land and where? What agreement was signed by 41 of the passengers that was the New World's first attempt at democracy?

    ANSWER: The *Speedwell*/Captain Christopher Jones/Oceanus/Will Butten/William Bradford/December 21, 1620, at Plymouth (Rock), Massachusetts/The Mayflower Compact.

7. Which persons were known by the following nicknames?

    a) Father of the American Revolution   f) Father of the Tariff
    b) Father of American History   g) Father of Pennsylvania
    c) Father of the Continental Congress   h) Father of the American Army
    d) Father of Steamboat Navigation   i) Father Wooden Leg
    e) Father of the Gerrymander   j) Father of Massachusetts

    ANSWER: a) Samuel Adams b) William Bradford c) Benjamin Franklin d) Robert Fulton e) Elbridge Gerry f) Alexander Hamilton g) William Penn h) Baron von Steuben i) Peter Stuyvesant j) John Winthrop.

8. What 2 B's were the mainstays of the early pilgrims — one was for the body and the other for the soul?

ANSWER: **The beaver and the Bible.**

9. How would Art Buchwald facetiously explain Thanksgiving to the French in regard to the following words: Thanksgiving; Captain Miles Standish; the *Mayflower*; Plymouth; pilgrims; corn; and redskins?

ANSWER: **Thanksgiving is *le jour du Merci Donnant*; Captain Miles Standish is *le Capitaine Kilomètres Deboutish*; the *Mayflower* is *la Fleur du Mai*; Plymouth is *une voiture américaine*; pilgrims are *pélerins*; corn is *maïze*; and redskins are *les peaux-rouges* (Mr. Buchwald would explain that the only reason the *peaux-rouges* taught the *pélerins* how to grow *maïze* was because the *peaux-rouges* liked *maïze* with their *pélerins*).**

10. During the colonial government period, name the 3 types of colonies that existed.

ANSWER: **Royal, Proprietary, and Corporate or Commercial.**

11. What Dutch leader purchased Manhattan Island from the Indians? In what year and for how much? On what ship did he arrive in America? What name did he give the area the immigrants settled?

ANSWER: **Peter Minuit/He arrived May 4, 1626, and he bought the Island for $24 or about 60 guilders/*Sea-mew*/New Amsterdam.**

12. Name the 2 ships which in 1634 brought about 250 passengers led by Leonard Calvert up the Potomac to Maryland. Name the village the passengers laid out.

ANSWER: **The *Ark* and the *Dove*/St. Mary's.**

13. Name the 4 United Colonies that comprised the New England Confederation in 1643. Then name the other 3 New England settlements that were excluded from this Confederation.

ANSWER: **Massachusetts Bay, Plymouth, Connecticut, and New Haven/Maine, New Hampshire, and Rhode Island.**

14. Who founded Georgia in 1733 as a buffer colony between what 2 rivers? Name the 2 founders of Methodism who visited Georgia in the 1730's.

ANSWER: **James Oglethorpe/The Savannah and Altamaha/John and Charles Wesley.**

15. Who made each of the following statements?
    a) "Give me liberty or give me death"
    b) "Stand your ground"
    c) "Don't fire until you see the whites of their eyes"
    d) "There, I guess King George will be able to read that"
    e) "I regret that I have but one life to lose for my country"
    f) "I have not yet begun to fight"
    g) "Millions for defense, but not one cent for tribute"
    h) "May God forgive me for putting on any other"
    i) "Don't give up the ship"
    j) "We have met the enemy and they are ours"

ANSWER: **a) Patrick Henry b) John Parker c) William Prescott d) John Hancock e) Nathan Hale f) John Paul Jones g) Charles Cotesworth Pinckney (Robert Goodloe Harper) h) Benedict Arnold i) James Lawrence j) Oliver Hazard Perry.**

16. What famous trial took place in 1735? In giving this name you should have named the defendant. Whom was he accused of libeling? Name the lawyer that defended him. And what phrase from this *cause célèbre* is used today? What is the meaning of that phrase? In explaining the meaning of the phrase, explain why it came about?

ANSWER: **The trial of John Peter Zenger, the publisher of the New York *Weekly Journal*/William S. Cosby, the royal governor of New York/Andrew Hamilton, his lawyer, got an acquittal for Zenger in what was considered to be an air-tight libel case/The phrase is "Philadelphia Lawyer"/It means "a clever lawyer skilled in manipulating legal technicalities"/Philadelphia lawyers were considered to be very clever anyway and it was said that "Three Philadelphia lawyers were a match for the devil himself."**

17. Who was instrumental in founding the first learned society in America in 1743, and what was the name of that society?

ANSWER: Benjamin Franklin/The American Philosophical Society.

18. Give the names of the 4 colonial wars between 1689 and 1763 that were extensions of wars which involved European nations.
ANSWER: King Williams' War from 1689-1697; Queen Anne's War from 1702-1713; King George's War from 1744-1748; and the French and Indian War from 1754-1763.

19. In 1760 what were the 5 largest towns in population in America?
ANSWER: Philadelphia; New York; Boston; Charles Town (Charleston), South Carolina; and Newport, Rhode Island.

20. Name the surveyor's line that became the dividing line between slave and free states, give the 2 states separated by the line, and identify the 2 English astronomers/surveyors who drew the line in 1767.
ANSWER: The Mason and Dixon Line/Pennsylvania and Maryland/Charles Mason and Jeremiah Dixon.

21. Name the 3 British ships from which American colonials dumped tea during the "Boston Tea Party." What was the date, and how were the colonials dressed?
ANSWER: The *Eleanor,* the *Beaver,* and the *Dartmouth*/December 16, 1773/As Mohawk Indians.

22. There might have been "Tea Parties" in several more cities in 1773 instead of just in Boston and Annapolis. What 3 cities cancelled their orders for tea?
ANSWER: New York, Philadelphia, and Charleston.

23. In what state did each of the following battles take place?
    a) Fort Ticonderoga   f) Cowpens
    b) Bennington   g) Yorktown
    c) Brandywine Creek   h) Tippecanoe
    d) Saratoga (Freeman's Farm)   i) Bladensburg
    e) Vincennes   j) Fort McHenry
ANSWER: a) New York b) Vermont c) Pennsylvania d) New York e) Indiana f) South Carolina g) Virginia h) Indiana i) Maryland j) Maryland.

24. What are the 2 dates of the 2 Continental Congresses, and where did they meet?
ANSWER: The first met from September 5 to October 26, 1774, in Carpenters' Hall in Philadelphia; the second met on May 10, 1775, in Philadelphia's State House (later Independence Hall).

25. In 1775, what were the 2 "established" tax-supported churches?
ANSWER: The Anglican and the Congregational.

26. Who were the 3 men who gave warning of the coming of the British in 1775? Which one reached Concord?
ANSWER: Paul Revere, William Dawes, and Dr. Samuel Prescott/Samuel Prescott— Revere was the first to reach Lexington. Dawes and Dr. Prescott joined him there. Prescott was the only one to get to Concord. Dawes turned back. Revere was captured and brought back to Lexington. He was later released.

27. In what 2 towns on April 19, 1775, did one hear the "shots heard round the world"? What is the name of Ralph Waldo Emerson's poem which contains the phrase? Recite the 4 lines that contain that phrase.
ANSWER: Lexington and Concord/"Concord Hymn" (or "Concord Monument Hymn")/
                    "By the rude bridge that arched the flood,
                    Their flag to April's breeze unfurled,
                    Here once the embattled farmers stood,
                    And fired the shot heard round the world."

28. Name the 3 British Major Generals who arrived in America on May 25, 1775, aboard the *Cerberus* to give support to General Thomas Gage.
ANSWER: Major Generals Sir William Howe, Sir Henry Clinton, and Johnny Burgoyne.

29. What are the names, locations, and dates of the beginning and ending battles of the American Revolutionary War? What treaty ended this war, and where was it signed?

ANSWER: The Battle of Lexington in Massachusetts on April 19, 1775, was the beginning, and the Battle of Yorktown, October 19, 1781, in Virginia, was the last/The Treaty of Paris, September 3, 1783.

30. What document was sent to George III on July 5, 1775, asking for harmony and a cessation of hostilities?
ANSWER: The Olive Branch Petition.

31. Who were the 5 members appointed by the Continental Congress to draw up the Declaration of Independence? Who was the principal writer? How many days did it take? When did Congress debate it and on what day was the document approved? On what date did most of the signers sign?
ANSWER: John Adams, Benjamin Franklin, Thomas Jefferson, Robert Livingston, and Roger Sherman/Thomas Jefferson/About 18 — from June 11 to June 28, 1776/Congress debated it on July 2 and 3 and it was approved on July 4, 1776/August 2, 1776.

32. Name the 2 signers of the Declaration of Independence who were later to become U.S. Presidents.
ANSWER: John Adams and Thomas Jefferson.

33. Which persons were known by each of the following nicknames?
a) Hero of Fort McHenry   d) Hero of Lake Erie
b) Hero of Vincennes   e) Hero of Chippewa
c) Hero of Saratoga   f) Hero of Stony Point
ANSWER: a) George Armistead b) George Rogers Clark c) Horatio Gates d) Oliver Hazard Perry e) Winfield Scott f) Anthony Wayne.

34. The 13 colonies that seceded from Great Britain and fought in the American Revolution became the 13 original states. Name them.
ANSWER: Connecticut, Delaware, Georgia, Maryland, Massachusetts, New Hampshire, New Jersey, New York, North Carolina, Pennsylvania, Rhode Island, South Carolina, and Virginia.

35. Name the 2 Poles who were officers in the American Army during the Revolutionary War.
ANSWER: Thaddeus Kosciusko and Count Casimir Pulaski.

36. What 3 Americans, chosen by Congress to talk peace, met Admiral Richard Howe on Staten Island on September 11, 1776? Why did the talks fail?
ANSWER: John Adams, Benjamin Franklin, and Edward Rutledge/Howe wanted the Declaration of Independence to be revoked as a basis of negotiations.

37. What was the "Conway Cabal" of September-December, 1777?
ANSWER: It was not a major plot, but apparently there was an effort to remove George Washington as military leader and replace him with General Horatio Gates. General Thomas Conway, an Irish volunteer, wrote letters criticizing Washington's leadership at the Battle of Saratoga. Washington was supported by military and Congressional leaders and nothing further developed.

38. Name the 2 pacts signed by Silas Deane, Benjamin Franklin, and Arthur Lee with the French on February 6, 1778.
ANSWER: A treaty of amity and commerce and a treaty of alliance.

39. In the summer of 1778, what 3 victories were achieved by George Rogers Clark on the Ohio River?
ANSWER: Kaskaskia (Illinois), Cahokia (Illinois), and Vincennes (Indiana).

40. What was ratified on March 1, 1781? Who was the first "President of the United States" before George Washington? Name the other 7 "Presidents of the United States in Congress Assembled."
ANSWER: Articles of Confederation/John Hanson/Elias Boudinot, Thomas Mifflin, Richard Henry Lee, John Hancock, Nathaniel Gorham, Arthur St. Clair, and Cyrus Griffin.

41. Name the 4 main leaders who combined to force Cornwallis' defeat at Yorktown

on October 19, 1781.

ANSWER: **Washington, Lafayette, Rochambeau, and De Grasse.**

42. What 5 Americans were appointed to the Peace Commission at Paris in June, 1781, and what peace treaty did they conclude on what date?

ANSWER: **Benjamin Franklin, John Adams, John Jay, Henry Laurens, and Thomas Jefferson (who did not serve)/Treaty of Paris on September 3, 1783.**

43. Name the 2 important ordinances passed by Congress, one in 1785 and the other in 1787.

ANSWER: **The Land Ordinance of 1785 and the Northwest Ordinance of 1787.**

44. Identify each of the following nicknames.

a) Seminary of Sedition   f) American Cannae
b) Mother of Mischief   g) Old Ironsides
c) Tarring and Feathering Gentlemen   h) Fulton's Folly
d) Bushnell's Turtle   i) Unnecessary War
e) Bloody Year (on the frontier)   j) Unnecessary Battle

ANSWER: **a) Virginia House of Burgesses b) Stamp Act of 1765 c) Liberty Boys d) David Bushnell's submarine e) 1777 f) Cowpens (Jan. 17, 1781) g) the** Constitution **h) the** Clermont **i) War of 1812 j) Battle of New Orleans (Jan. 8, 1815).**

45. Name the 3 persons who wrote *The Federalist* papers, a series of papers aimed at encouraging the adoption of the proposed Constitution. Which 2 were the main writers, and under what pseudonym were these papers published?

ANSWER: **Alexander Hamilton, James Madison, and John Jay/Hamilton and Madison /Publius.**

46. What 6 men signed both the Declaration of Independence and the Constitution of the United States?

ANSWER: **George Clymer, Benjamin Franklin, Robert Morris, George Read, Roger Sherman, and James Wilson.**

47. Name the first 2 constitutions overthrown by the American people.

ANSWER: **The British Constitution and the Articles of Confederation.**

48. Name the first 5 states to ratify the U.S. Constitution in 1787-1788. There were only 3 states to ratify unanimously. Name them.

ANSWER: **Delaware (Dec. 7), Pennsylvania (Dec. 12), New Jersey (Dec. 18), Georgia (Jan. 2), and Connecticut (Jan. 9)/Delaware, New Jersey, and Georgia.**

49. According to the 1790 census, what were the 5 most populous states?

ANSWER: **Virginia, Massachusetts (including Maine), Pennsylvania, North Carolina, and New York.**

50. Name the first 3 states admitted to the Union after the original 13.

ANSWER: **Vermont (March 4, 1791), Kentucky (June 1, 1792), and Tennessee (June 1, 1796).**

51. Give the date on which George Washington was first inaugurated, the city, and the building. Name the 3 capitals of the U.S. in order.

ANSWER: **April 30, 1789, in New York City, at Federal Hall/New York, followed by Philadelphia, then to Washington, D.C.**

52. The XYZ affair, intended to improve relations between France and the United States, involved 3 men sent to France by John Adams. Name them. Who was the Directory's foreign minister?

ANSWER: **Elbridge Gerry, Charles C. Pinckney, and John Marshall/Prince Talleyrand.**

53. Who were the American and British comanders during each of the following battles?

a) Bunker Hill   e) Germantown
b) Trenton   f) *Bonhomme Richard-Serapis*
c) Princeton   g) King's Mountain
d) Saratoga (Freeman's Farm)   h) Yorktown

ANSWER: **a) Prescott-Howe b) Washington-Rall c) Washington-Cornwallis d) Gates-Burgoyne e) Washington-Howe f) Jones-Pearson g) Campbell-Ferguson**

h) **Washington-Cornwallis.**

54. What 2 freedoms guaranteed in the Constitution by the Bill of Rights were taken away by the Sedition Act of 1798?
ANSWER: **Freedom of speech and freedom of the press.**

55. Who were the 2 participants in a duel held in Weehawken, New Jersey, on July 11, 1804, and what were the results?
ANSWER: **Aaron Burr and Alexander Hamilton. Burr wounded Hamilton, and Hamilton died on July 12.**

56. What 2 American envoys to France worked to complete the Louisiana Purchase? Who was Napoleon's Minister of Finance? For how much money was the Louisiana Purchase made, and on what date was the deal made?
ANSWER: **Robert Livingston and James Monroe/Barbé-Marbois/$15,000,000 (60 million francs)/April 30, 1803.**

57. Name the 4 Barbary States of North Africa. What 2 men combined for a land and sea operation that ended the Tripolitan War and led to the peace treaty of June 4, 1805? How much did America pay the pasha of Tripoli in ransom for American prisoners?
ANSWER: **Algiers, Morocco, Tripoli, and Tunis/Captain William Eaton on land and Commodore John Rodgers at sea/$60,000.**

58. What were the names of the 2 ships in the affair off Hampton Roads, Virginia, on June 22, 1807, that ultimately led to the War of 1812? What happened?
ANSWER: **The British ship the *Leopard* fired on the *Chesapeake* under Captain James Barron and killed 3 Americans before impressing 4 sailors.**

59. Which persons were known by each of the following nicknames?
a) Robin Hood of the Forest
b) Traitorous Hero
c) Johnny Appleseed
d) Patriarch of New England
e) French Gamecock
f) Swamp Fox
g) Prophet of the Revolution
h) Light-horse Harry
i) Schoolmaster of the Republic
j) Independent Man
ANSWER: **a) Ethan Allen b) Benedict Arnold c) John Chapman d) John Cotton e) Marquis de Lafayette f) Francis Marion g) Patrick Henry h) Henry Lee i) Noah Webster j) Roger Williams.**

60. What was the name of the great Shawnee chief and his brother who defied whites in 1810 and later? At what battle did the Shawnee chief die?
ANSWER: **Tecumseh and the Prophet (Tenskwatawa)/Battle of the Thames on Oct. 5, 1813.**

61. What were the 3 prongs of America's 3-pronged invasion of Canada in the War of 1812?
ANSWER: **Across the Detroit River at Detroit, across the Niagara River at Fort Niagara, and across Lake Champlain at Montreal.**

62. In what year was the first segment of the Cumberland Road started and in what year was the road finished? What 2 cities did it join? What are 2 other names for this road? What mountains did it cross?
ANSWER: **It was started in 1811 and finished in 1818./It ran from Cumberland, Maryland, to Wheeling (now West Virginia). Later it was extended to Zanesville, Ohio, and later to Vandalia, Illinois (Illinois built the Federal road to St. Louis)/The National Road or the National Turnpike/The Allegheny Mountains.**

63. Name the 4 significant American naval victories on August 19, October 17 and 25, and December 29, which greatly boosted American morale in 1812.
ANSWER: **The *Constitution* over the *Guerrière*, the *Wasp* over the *Frolic*, the *United States* over the *Macedonian*, and the *Constitution* over the *Java*.**

64. The delegates of what 5 states met at Hartford, Connecticut, from December 15, 1814, to January 5, 1815, to seek redress for wrongs from the Federal government?

ANSWER: Connecticut, Massachusetts, Rhode Island, New Hampshire (2 counties sent delegates), and Vermont (1 county sent a delegate).

65. During 1814 the British attempted 3 invasions. What were the names of the 3 battles at which British forces were defeated?
ANSWER: Battles of Lake Champlain, Fort McHenry, and New Orleans.

66. Who were the 5 American peace commissioners in Belgium to sign the Treaty of Ghent in December of 1814?
ANSWER: John Quincy Adams, James A. Bayard, Henry Clay, Albert Gallatin, and Jonathan Russell.

67. Why was the Battle of New Orleans on January 8, 1815, called the ''unnecessary battle''?
ANSWER: Because it was fought 15 days after the Treaty of Ghent had been signed.

68. What was the beginning date for the War of 1812? In order to give the ending date for the war, give the date the Treaty of Ghent was signed, the date of the Battle of New Orleans, and the date the Treaty was ratified by the Senate.
ANSWER: June 18, 1812/December 24, 1814, January 8, 1815, and February 16, 1815.

69. Identify each of the following.
   a) The specific charge against Rhode Island founder Roger Williams in Massachusetts Bay in 1636
   b) The woman convicted of sedition and banished from Massachusetts Bay in 1638 as ''a woman not fit for our society''
   c) The name of the capital and last governor (director general) of New Netherland
   d) The first Medical School in North America (1765; now the U. of Pennsylvania)
   e) The designer of the first political cartoon in the U.S.
   f) The Federal Government unit created by the Connecticut or Great Compromise
ANSWER: a) ''disseminating newe & dangerous opinions'' b) Anne Hutchinson c) New Amsterdam (New York City) and Peter Stuyvesant d) College and Academy of Philadelphia e) Benjamin Franklin f) Congress.

9 COLONIAL COLLEGES FOUNDED BY ROYAL DECREE

COLLEGE	DATE	LOCATION	DENOMINATION	NAMED AFTER
Harvard	1636	Cambridge, Mass.	Congregational	John Harvard
William & Mary	1693	Williamsburg, Va.	Anglican	William and Mary
Yale (Collegiate School)*	1701	New Haven, Conn.	Congregational	Elihu Yale
Princeton (College of New Jersey)	1746	Princeton, N.J.	Presbyterian	—
Columbia (King's College)	1754	New York City	Nonsectarian under Anglican control	—
Pennsylvania (1751) (The College and Academy of Philadelphia)	1755	Philadelphia, Pa.	Nonsectarian	—
Brown (Rhode Island College)	1764	Providence, R.I.	Baptist	Nicholas Brown
Rutgers (Queen's College)	1766	New Brunswick, N.J.	Dutch Reformed	Col. Henry Rutgers
Dartmouth (It grew from Moor's Indian Charity School)	1769	Hanover, N.H.	Congregational	2nd Earl of Dartmouth

*Original names listed, if applicable, in parentheses

AMERICAN QUOTATIONS/SLOGANS/MOTTOES

JOIN OR DIE

This slogan was used by the colonists during the Colonial and Revolutionary War periods. It was originated by Benjamin Franklin in 1754. He wanted the disunited colonies to unite to fight France's influence in the country. He drew a snake in 8 severed parts. These parts represented the colonies of South Carolina, North Carolina, Virginia, Maryland, Pennsylvania, New York, and New Jersey, with the New England colonies as the head of the snake. He was urging the colonies to either unite or die by being destroyed by France and her Indian allies. During the Revolutionary War this slogan was used to unite the colonies against Great Britain.

TAXATION WITHOUT REPRESENTATION IS TYRANNY

This slogan was used by the American colonists in 1765 after the British Parliament raised the Stamp Act tax. The colonists were already heavily taxed and did not want to pay even more for the French and Indian war.

NO TAXATION WITHOUT REPRESENTATION

This phrase was used by the rebelling colonists during the Revolutionary War against the British system of taxation. The Stamp Act of 1765 was highly resented and Patrick Henry voiced this idea in May, 1765, in a speech to the Virginia House of Burgesses. His speech also included these lines: "Caesar had his Brutus; Charles the First his Cromwell; and George the Third may he profit by their example. If this be treason, make the most of it." Some spectators shouted "Treason!" Henry supposedly apologized. (American lawyer and Statesman, James Otis, may have used this phrase in 1763 in Boston in protest over taxation from Britain.)

LIBERTY, PROPERTY, AND NO STAMPS

The Sons of Liberty used this slogan in protest against the Stamp Act of 1765. This group engaged in violent protests and even tarred and feathered their opponents. Samuel Adams was the aggressive leader of this group.

UNITED WE STAND, DIVIDED WE FALL

The line "By uniting we stand, by dividing we fall" in "The Liberty Song" by John Dickinson in July, 1768, became a popular slogan for many orators in the years following. It is now the motto of the state of Kentucky.

GIVE ME LIBERTY OR GIVE ME DEATH

This phrase is from Patrick Henry's speech before the Virginia House of Burgesses on March 23, 1775 at St. John's Church, Richmond, Virginia. Henry wanted the colonists to resist British rule and to provide for the expense of the colony by arming the Virginia militia. His statement was: "Is life so dear, or peace so sweet, as to be purchased at the price of chains and slavery? Forbid it, Almighty God! I know not what course others may take, but as for me, give me liberty or give me death!"

WE MUST ALL HANG TOGETHER

This phrase was used by the signers of the Declaration of Independence during the years 1775 to 1781. Benjamin Franklin said: "We must all hang together, or assuredly we shall all hang separately."

ONE IF BY LAND, AND TWO IF BY SEA

This line was from Henry Wadsworth Longfellow's poem titled "Paul Revere's Ride." The original phrase on April 16, 1775 was that: "If the British went out by water, we would show two lanterns in the North Steeple; and if by land, one." The signal was given from the Old North Church steeple.

STAND YOUR GROUND

Captain John Parker was the commander of a force of 70 Minutemen at the Battle of Lexington, April 19, 1775. He told his men: "Stand your ground! Don't fire unless fired upon. But if they mean to have war, let it begin here!" The British were led by Major John Pitcairn and his phrase to Parker and his men was: "Lay down your arms, you damned rebels, and disperse" (or "Disperse, disperse, ye rebels! Damn you! Why don't you disperse?"). Eight Americans died.

IN THE NAME OF THE GREAT JEHOVAH, AND THE CONTINENTAL CONGRESS

This was Ethan Allen's response when the Fort Ticonderoga leader, Captain De la

Place, questioned the authority he and his Green Mountain Boys had for demanding the surrender of the fort. De la Place surrendered the fort on May 10, 1775.

DON'T FIRE UNTIL YOU CAN SEE THE WHITES OF THEIR EYES

On June 17, 1775, while the Continental soldiers were waiting for British troops under General William Howe to attack Bunker Hill, Colonel William Prescott, who was in charge of the Continentals, supposedly gave this order to his men at Breed's Hill, where the Battle of Bunker Hill was actually fought. The British suffered a sizable loss but won the hill on a bayonet charge as the supply of American powder became depleted. This phrase has also been attributed to Major Israel Putnam. The full quote may have been: "Men, you are all marksmen—don't one of you fire until you see the whites of their eyes! Then, fire low."

DON'T TREAD ON ME

Christopher Gadsden, on February 8, 1776, presented to the Second Continental Congress a yellow flag with this motto and the figure of a coiled rattlesnake ready to strike. The rattlesnake represented the colonists as dangerous when aroused, and it was intended as a warning to the British leaders that if the rights of the colonists were trampled on, they would strike back.

THERE, I GUESS KING GEORGE WILL BE ABLE TO READ THAT

John Hancock said these words on July 4, 1776, as he was signing the Declaration of Independence. His handwriting was very large, and he was the first to sign the Declaration.

ARE THESE THE MEN WITH WHOM I AM TO DEFEND AMERICA?

George Washington said these words in New York at Kip's Bay in September, 1776, in a moment of despair because few men obeyed his commands.

I ONLY REGRET THAT I HAVE BUT ONE LIFE TO LOSE (GIVE) FOR MY COUNTRY

These were the words of 21-year-old Nathan Hale on September 22, 1776, before he was hanged by Major General William Howe on Long Island. He was accused of being a spy and was hanged without a trial.

THESE ARE THE TIMES THAT TRY MEN'S SOULS

These words are part of Thomas Paine's *The American Crisis* that General George Washington read to rally his troops before crossing the Delaware on December 25, 1776. He also read: "The summer soldier and the sunshine patriot will, in this crisis, shrink from the service of their country; but he that stands it now, deserves the love and thanks of man and woman."

THERE, MY BOYS, ARE YOUR ENEMIES—REDCOATS AND TORIES. YOU MUST BEAT THEM—OR MOLLY STARK IS A WIDOW TONIGHT

These words were spoken by General John Stark before the Battle of Bennington, Vermont, August 16, 1777. Stark's statement is also cited as: "My men, yonder are the Hessians. They were bought for seven pounds and ten pence a man. Are you worth more? Prove it. Tonight, the American flag floats from yonder hill or Molly Stark sleeps a widow!"

I HAVE NOT YET BEGUN TO FIGHT

These immortal words became the slogan for the U.S. Navy. These words came from John Paul Jones on September 23, 1779, in the naval battle between the American vessel the *Bonhomme Richard* (named after the "Poor Richard" of Benjamin Franklin's *Poor Richard's Almanac*) and the British ship the *Serapis*. Jones lashed his ship to the British ship to keep his from sinking. One of his sailors asked for quarter, and when the Captain of the *Serapis,* Richard Pearson, asked for verification ("Do you ask for quarter?"), Jones cracked the man's skull by hurling two pistols at him. Jones replied to the Captain: "I have not yet begun to fight!" Jones changed ships to the *Serapis*, and that's how he won the battle.

FREE SHIPS MAKE FREE GOODS

In 1793 Britain was seizing American supplies intended for France. These words became an American rallying cry since the U.S. was neutral in the war and was protesting the British actions of the seizures. However, Britain had the Navy to stop supplies from reaching France and that was that.

FIRST IN WAR, FIRST IN PEACE

Major General Henry Lee used this phrase in his eulogy on General George Washington made in Congress on December 26, 1799. He said: "To the memory of the man, first in war, first in peace, and first in the hearts of his countrymen."

MILLIONS FOR DEFENSE, BUT NOT ONE CENT FOR TRIBUTE

This phrase was used in 1799-1800 to express indignation and resentment toward the French government. The affair was the XYZ affair as three minor French officials of Prince Talleyrand, called Messieurs X, Y, and Z, demanded a $250,000 bribe and a $10,000,000 loan from the United States to France, and threatened to declare war if these demands were not met. President John Adams had sent Elbridge Gerry, John Marshall, and Charles Cotesworth Pinckney to mollify a France bitter because the U.S. refused to help her in war against England. Pinckney's reply to the French spokesman was, "No! No! Not a sixpence, sir." The negotiations ended and this rallying cry provided support for John Adams's policy of armed neutrality. This slogan is often attributed to Pinckney, but Robert Goodloe Harper supposedly made the statement in a toast to John Marshall at a banquet in June, 1798.

MAY GOD FORGIVE ME FOR EVER PUTTING ON ANY OTHER

Possibly Benedict Arnold's dying words uttered on June 14, 1801, in London as he asked for his American uniform. Arnold was a brilliant American military officer who felt slighted in promotions by the Congress. He was reprimanded in 1779 for unprofessional conduct and later betrayed his country and fought for the British.

ONCE AN ENGLISHMAN, ALWAYS AN ENGLISHMAN

This was the English principle by which the British Navy impressed sailors on American ships. The British claimed that the impressed sailors were deserters from the Royal Navy. Some of them were. Yet this principle led to the *Chesapeake* incident of June 22, 1807. Three Americans were killed in the attack and four seamen were taken aboard the English vessel the *Leopard.* Three of the men were American sailors. The British recalled Admiral Berkeley and paid an indemnity for those killed and wounded but still asserted the right to search vessels to reclaim deserters.

FREE TRADE AND SEAMEN'S RIGHTS

This was the slogan of the "War Hawks," those Western and Southern Congressmen who advocated war with Great Britain and who were led by Henry Clay as Speaker of the House (1811-1815). The War Hawks had shouted "On to Canada!" since they wanted Canada as part of the United States. After the victory of the *Constitution* in August, 1812, Henry Clay said: "Strike wherever we can reach the enemy, at sea and on land. But if we fail, let us fail like men, lash ourselves to our gallant tars, and expire together in one common struggle, fighting for free trade and seamen's rights!"

DON'T GIVE UP THE SHIP

These were the dying words of Captain James Lawrence on June 1, 1813. He was in charge of the *Chesapeake* in a battle against the *Shannon* commanded by Captain Philip Broke of Britain. This battle took place just outside Boston Harbor. The *Chesapeake* was destroyed, and the British won the battle. Jones's words became the motto of the U.S. Navy. He said: "Tell the men to fire faster and not give up the ship; fight her till she sinks." He is also quoted as saying: "Keep the guns going! Fight her till she strikes or sinks! Don't give up the ship!"

WE HAVE MET THE ENEMY AND THEY ARE OURS

Oliver Hazard Perry at the Battle of Lake Erie on September 10, 1813, had hoisted a 9-foot standard with Lawrence's last words DON'T GIVE UP THE SHIP displayed on the mast of his flagship the *Lawrence,* which he named after James Lawrence. Perry defeated the British under Captain Robert Barclay in the *Detroit.* But Perry was able to do so only after he abandoned his ship and got to the *Niagara* and took charge. Perry's words in a message sent to General William Henry Harrison on shore were: "We have met the enemy and they are ours, two ships, two brigs, one schooner, and one sloop."

REMEMBER THE RAISIN! REMEMBER THE RIVER RAISIN!

This was the rallying cry for the American dragoons from Kentucky as they faced the British and Tecumseh at the Battle of the Thames on October 5, 1813. The Americans were seeking revenge for the Indian massacres at the Battle of the River Raisin. Tecumseh was killed, the Indians were defeated, and British power in Upper Canada ended as a result of the Battle of the Thames.

NOT ONE INCH OF TERRITORY CEDED OR LOST

This was the slogan used to emphasize that nothing was lost in the settlement of the Treaty of Ghent signed on December 24, 1814, as all land reverted to its original status before the war.

REVOLUTIONARY WAR BATTLES AND AMERICAN/BRITISH COMMANDERS

Lexington and Concord...... Massachusetts .... **April 19, 1775**
American; John Parker and others   British: John Pitcairn, Francis Smith
Ft. Ticonderoga .... New York.............. **May 9-10, 1775**
American: Ethan Allen, Benedict Arnold   British: William Delaplace
Bunker Hill.............. Massachusetts.......... **June 17, 1775**
American: William Prescott   British: Sir William Howe
Montreal............... Canada .... **November 13, 1775**
American: Richard Montgomery   British: Sir Guy Carleton
Quebec................ Canada .... **December 31, 1775**
American: Richard Montgomery   British: Sir Guy Carleton
Long Island .... New York............ **August 27-28, 1776**
American: George Washington   British: Sir William Howe
Trenton.................. New Jersey .... **December 26, 1776**
American: George Washington   British: Johann Rall
Princeton .... New Jersey   **January 3, 1777**
American: George Washington   British: Lord Charles Cornwallis
Oriskany................. New York............. **August 6, 1777**
American: Nicholas Herkimer   British: Barry St. Leger
Bennington.............. Vermont (New York border)**August 16, 1777**
American: John Stark   British: Friedrich Baum, Heinrich von
                                                    Breyman
Brandywine Creek .... Pennsylvania........... **September 11, 1777**
American: George Washington   British: Sir William Howe
Saratoga (Freeman's Farm) .. New York............. **Sept. 19 & Oct. 7, 1777**
American: Horatio Gates   British: John Burgoyne
Germantown............. Pennsylvania........... **October 4, 1777**
American: George Washington   British: Sir William Howe
Monmouth .... New Jersey .... **June 28, 1778**
American: George Washington   British: Henry Clinton
Vincennes .... Indiana .... **February 23-25, 1779**
American: George Rogers Clark   British: Henry Hamilton
Savannah............... Georgia .... **Sept. 15-Oct. 9, 1779**
American: Charles d'Estaing, Benjamin   British: Augustine Prevost
            Lincoln
Bonhomme Richard-.... North Sea .... **September 23, 1779**
Serapis
American: John Paul Jones   British: Richard Pearson
Charleston .... South Carolina.......... **April 11-May 12, 1780**
American: Benjamin Lincoln   British: Henry Clinton
Camden .... South Carolina   **August 16, 1780**
American: Horatio Gates   British: Lord Charles Cornwallis
King's Mountain.......... N-S Carolina .... **October 7, 1780**
American: William Campbell   British: Patrick Ferguson
Cowpens .... South Carolina.......... **January 17, 1781**
American: Nathanael Greene,   British: Lord Charles Cornwallis,
            Daniel Morgan   Banastre Tarleton
Guilford Courthouse .... North Carolina .... **March 15, 1781**
American: Nathanael Greene   British: Lord Charles Cornwallis
Yorktown .... Virginia .... **October 6-19, 1781**
American: George Washington   British: Lord Charles Cornwallis

AMERICAN BATTLES/WARS/NOTABLE INCIDENTS: THEIR SITES AND DATES

Virginia Colony disappeared .. Roanoke Island 1587-1590
Pequot War............... Connecticut area 1636-1637
Iroquois War.............. New York area.......... 1642-1653
King William's War........ .... May 12, 1689-
                                            Sept. 20, 1697
Queen Anne's War .... May 4, 1702-
                                            April 11, 1713
Tuscarora War .... North-South Carolina..... Sept. 22,1711
                                            March 23,1713
War of Jenkins' Ear .... Florida-Georgia 1739-1742
Bloody Marsh
(Bloody Swamp) .... St. Simon's Island....... 1742
King George's War 1744-1748
French and Indian War...... ...... April 17,1754-Feb. 10, 1763
Fort Necessity .... Pennsylvania........... July 3, 1754
The Wilderness (Ft.
Duquesne) .... Pennsylvania........... July 9, 1755
Lake George............. New York............. September 8, 1755
Louisburg................ Cape Breton Island ..... June 8-July 26, 1758
Fort Ticonderoga .... New York............. July 8, 1758
Fort Frontenac .... Canada .... August 27, 1758
Fort Duquesne .... Pennsylvania........... November 25, 1758
Fort Niagara .... New York............. July 25, 1759
Crown Point .... New York............. July 31, 1759
Plains of Abraham.......... Quebec .... Sept. 12-18, 1759
Montreal................. Canada .... September 8, 1760
Detroit .... British Territory........ November 29, 1760
Pontiac's Rebellion (War) .... Detroit area .... May 9-Nov. 28, 1763
Golden Hill .... New York............. January 19, 1770
Boston Massacre .... Massachusetts .... March 5, 1770
Almanance Creek .... North Carolina .... May 16, 1771
Gaspée................. Rhode Island coast ...... June 9-10, 1772
Boston Tea Party........... Massachusetts .... December 16, 1773
Lexington and Concord...... Massachusetts .... April 19, 1775
Ft. Ticonderoga & Crown
Point .... New York............. May 9-10, 1775
Bunker Hill (Breed's Hill) .... Massachusetts .... June 17, 1775
Falmouth (Portland) burned .. Maine .... October 18, 1775
Montreal................. Canada .... November 13, 1775
Quebec.................. Canada .... December 31, 1775
Moore's Creek Bridge....... North Carolina .... February 27, 1776
Charleston Harbor .... South Carolina.......... June 1-28, 1776
Long Island .... New York............. August 27-28, 1776
Valcour Bay-Split Rock...... Lake Champlain......... October 11-13, 1776
Split Rock................ Lake Champlain......... October 13, 1776
White Plains .... New York............. October 28, 1776
Trenton.................. New Jersey .... December 26, 1776
Princeton .... New Jersey .... January 3, 1777
Oriskany................. New York............. August 6, 1777
Bennington............... Vermont.............. August 16, 1777
Brandywine Creek .... Pennsylvania .... September 11, 1777
Paoli Massacre .... Pennsylvania .... September 20-21, 1777
Saratoga (Freeman's Farm) .. New York............. Sept. 19 & Oct. 7, 1777
Germantown.............. Pennsylvania .... October 4, 1777
Winter at Valley Forge....... Pennsylvania 1777-1778
Monmouth .... New Jersey .... June 28, 1778
Wyoming Valley Massacre ... Pennsylvania.......... July 3-6, 1778

Kaskaskia. . . . . Illinois . . . . July 4, 1778
Cherry Valley Massacre . . . . . New York. . . . . November 11, 1778
Savannah . . . . Georgia . . . . December 29, 1778
Vincennes . . . . Indiana . . . . February 23-25, 1779
Portsmouth and Norfolk . . . . . Virginia . . . . May 9-10, 1779
Stony Point . . . . New York. . . . . July 16, 1779
Savannah (Coast and the
City) . . . . Georgia . . . . Sept. 15-Oct. 9, 1779
Bonhomme Richard-
Serapis . . . . England coast . . . . September 23, 1779
Winter at Morristown . . . . New Jersey 1779-1780
Charleston Siege . . . . South Carolina . . . . Apr. 11-May 12, 1780
Mutiny at Morristown . . . . . . New Jersey . . . . May 25, 1780
Camden . . . . South Carolina . . . . August 16, 1780
King's Mountain. . . . . North-South Carolina . . . . October 7, 1780
Cowpens . . . . South Carolina . . . . January 17, 1781
Guilford Courthouse . . . . North Carolina . . . . March 15, 1781
Alliance v. *Mars*
& Minerva . . . . Atlantic Ocean . . . . April 2, 1781
Hobkirk's Hill . . . . South Carolina . . . . April 25, 1781
Ninety-Six . . . . South Carolina . . . . May 22-June 19, 1781
Alliance v. *Atalanta*
& Trepassy . . . . Atlantic Ocean . . . . May 29, 1781
Eutaw Springs . . . . South Carolina . . . . September 8, 1781
Yorktown Campaign . . . . Virginia . . . . Aug. 30-Oct. 19, 1781
Shays' Rebellion . . . . Massachusetts . . . . Aug. 1786-Feb. 1787
Whiskey Rebellion . . . . Pennsylvania . . . . July-November, 1794
Fallen Timbers . . . . Ohio (Maumee River) . . . . August 20, 1794
Tripolitan War. . . . . Barbary States 1801-1805
Philadelphia . . . . Tripoli . . . . February 16, 1804
Essex case (British
court) . . . . Atlantic Ocean . . . . July 23, 1805
Chesapeake-Leopard . . . . Virginia coast. . . . . June 22, 1807
Spitfire-Guerrière . . . . New York Harbor . . . . May 1, 1811
President-Little Belt . . . . Cape Charles . . . . May 16, 1811
Tippecanoe. . . . . Indiana . . . . November 7, 1811
Detroit . . . . Michigan . . . . August 16, 1812
Constitution-Guerrière. . Nova Scotia . . . . August 19, 1812
Niagara Campaign . . . . Niagara River area . . . . Oct. 13-Nov. 28, 1812
Wasp-Frolic . . . . Virginia coast. . . . . October 17, 1812
United States-
Macedonian . . . . Madeira Islands . . . . October 25, 1812
Montreal. . . . . Canada . . . . November 19, 1812
Constitution-Java . . . . . . Brazilian coast . . . . December 29, 1812
Frenchtown . . . . Raisin River . . . . January 22, 1813
York . . . . Canada . . . . April 27, 1813
Fort Meigs . . . . Maumee River . . . . May 1-9, 1813
Sackett's Harbor . . . . Lake Ontario . . . . May 28-29, 1813
Chesapeake-Shannon . . . Boston Harbor area . . . . . . June 1, 1813
Fort Stephenson . . . . Sandusky River . . . . August 2, 1813
Lake Erie . . . . U.S.-Canada . . . . September 10, 1813
Thames . . . . Canada . . . . October 5, 1813
Chateaugay . . . . Canada . . . . October 25, 1813
Chrysler's Farm . . . . Canada . . . . November 10, 1813
Buffalo burned . . . . New York. . . . . December 29-30, 1813
Creek War . . . . Alabama-Florida . . . . Aug. 30, 1813-
                                                        March 27, 1814
Horseshoe Bend . . . . Alabama . . . . March 27, 1814
Chippewa (Chippawa) . . . . . . Niagara frontier . . . . July 5, 1814

Lundy's Lane . . . . Niagara frontier . . . . July 25, 1814
Fort Erie . . . . Niagara frontier . . . . Aug. 2-Sept. 1, 1814
Lake Champlain-Plattsburg . . Lake Champlain area . . . . . September 11, 1814
Saratoga-Confiance . . . . . Lake Champlain . . . . September 11, 1814
Bladensburg . . . . Maryland . . . . August 24, 1814
Washington burned . . . . Washington, D.C. . . . . August 24-25, 1814
Fort McHenry . . . . Maryland . . . . September 12-14, 1814
New Orleans . . . . Louisiana . . . . January 8, 1815
Decatur's Algerine
Expedition . . . . Barbary States . . . . May 10-June 30, 1815

THE THIRTEEN ORIGINAL COLONIES

COLONY	DATE	FOUNDED BY
1. Virginia	1607	The London Company (the Virginia Company of London)
Plymouth	1620	Pilgrims
Maine	1623	Sir Ferdinando Gorges & Capt. John Mason (Gorges took full control of the ''Province of Maine'' in 1629)
2. New Hampshire	1623	Capt. John Mason and others
3. Massachusetts	1630	Puritans
4. Maryland	1634	Lord Baltimore
5. Connecticut	1635	Massachusetts emigrants
6. Rhode Island	1636	Roger Williams
New Haven	1638	Massachusetts emigrants and Puritans led by Theophilus Eaton and the Rev. John Davenport
7. Delaware	1638	Swedes (merged with Pennsylvania in 1682)
8. North Carolina	1653	Virginians
9. New York	1624	Dutch Protestant Walloons
	1664	Duke of York
10. New Jersey	1665	Lord John Berkeley and Sir George Carteret
11. South Carolina	1670	Eight nobles (lords proprietors)
12. Pennsylvania	1681	William Penn
13. Georgia	1733	James Edward Oglethorpe and others

STATES AND THEIR RATIFICATION DATE OF THE CONSTITUTION

STATE	DATE	STATE	DATE
1. Delaware	Dec. 7, 1787	8. South Carolina	May 23, 1788
2. Pennsylvania	Dec. 12, 1787	9. New Hampshire	June 21, 1788
3. New Jersey	Dec. 18, 1787	10. Virginia	June 25, 1788
4. Georgia	Jan. 2, 1788	11. New York	July 26, 1788
5. Connecticut	Jan. 9, 1788	12. North Carolina	Nov. 21, 1789
6. Massachusetts	Feb. 6, 1788	13. Rhode Island	May 29, 1790
7. Maryland	April 28, 1788		

AMERICAN HISTORICAL PERSONAGES AND THEIR NICKNAMES

Samuel Adams . . . . Amendment Monger, American Cato, Brain (Drill Master, Engineer, Father, Firebrand, Penman) of the American Revolution, Chief Incendiary of the House, Cromwell of New England, Father of the American Revolution, Last of the Puritans, Man of the Town Meeting, Psalm Singer, Sam the Maltster, Samuel the Publican, Tribune of the People, Would-be Cromwell

Ethan Allen . . . . Green Mountain Boy, Robin Hood of the Forest

Ira Allen . . . . Founder of Vermont

George Armistead . . . . Hero of Fort McHenry

Benedict Arnold . . . . Dark Eagle, Traitorous Hero

John Jacob Astor . . . . Father of Oregon, Richest Man in America

Nathaniel Bacon . . . . Virginia Rebel

John Barnwell . . . . Tuscarora John

John Barry . . . . Father of the American Navy

James Asheton Bayard . . . . . . Goliath of His Party, High Priest of the Constitution

Richard Bland . . . . Cato of the Revolution, Virginia Antiquary

John Bourgoyne . . . . General Elbow-Room, Gentleman Johnny

Edward Braddock . . . . Braddock of the Coldstream Guards, Bulldog, Ill-starred General

William Bradford . . . . Father of American History

Thomas Butler . . . . Navarre of the American Revolution

John Chapman . . . . Johnny Appleseed, Patron Saint of American Orchards

William Christy . . . . Hero of Fort Meigs

George Rogers Clark . . . . Hannibal of the Missouri, Hero of Vincennes, Washington of the West

Charles Cornwallis . . . . Cobwallis

John Cotton . . . . Father and Glory of Boston, Patriarch of New England

William Crawford . . . . Big Captain

Richard Dale . . . . Fighting Dick Dale

Jonathan Edwards . . . . Artist of Damnation, Elder, Fiery Puritan, Great Awakener

Oliver Ellsworth . . . . Cerberus of the Treasury

John Endicott . . . . Father of New England

Benjamin Franklin . . . . Anthony Afterwit, American Socrates, Busybody, Father of All the Yankees, Father of the Continental Congress, Father of the Mail Order Catalog, Father of the Stove, First Civilized American, Grand Old Man, Liberator of the New World, Many-sided Franklin, Philomath, Sage of America, Tamer of Lightning

Philip Freneau . . . . Poet of the American Revolution

Robert Fulton . . . . Father of Steamboat Navigation, Father of the Steamboat, Folly Fulton, Quicksilver Bob

Christopher Gadsden . . . . Flame of Liberty

Albert Gallatin . . . . Watchdog of the Treasury

Horatio Gates . . . . Hero of Saratoga, Granny Gates

Elbridge Gerry . . . . Father of the Gerrymander

Nathanael Greene . . . . Fighting Quaker

Alexander Hamilton . . . . Alexander the Coppersmith, Caesar, Father of the Tariff, King of the Feds, Little Lion, Prime Minister

Andrew Hamilton . . . . Day-Star of the Revolution, Minister, Philadelphia Lawyer

John Hancock . . . . King Hancock, King of the Smugglers, Yankee Doodle Dandy

John Hawley . . . . Nestor of the Patriots

Patrick Henry . . . . Forest-born Demosthenes, Man of the People, Phrasemaker, Prophet of the Revolution, Trumpeter of Revolt,

Voice of the Revolution

Thomas Hooker	First Democrat, Light of the Western Churches
Samuel Hopkins	Father of Abolition
John Paul Jones	Bayard of the Sea, Father (Founder) of the American Navy, Prince Burliabled
Marquis de Lafayette (Marie Jean Paul Roch Yves Gilbert du Motier Lafayette)	French Gamecock, Grandison Cromwell
Jean Lafitte	Boss, Gentleman Smuggler, Last of the Buccaneers, Pirate (Terror) of the Gulf
John Laurens	Bayard of the Revolution
Henry Lee	Light-horse Harry, Sage of Ashland
Richard Henry Lee	American Cicero, Cicero of the Revolution, Federal Farmer
Robert Livingston	Cato, Cicero of America
Mary Ludwig Hays McCauley	Captain Molly, Molly Pitcher
Francis Marion	Bayard of the South, (Old) Swamp Fox, Swamp Fox of South Carolina
John Mease	Last of the Cocked Hats
Mrs. James Monroe	La Belle Américaine
Robert Morris	Bobby the Cofferer, Bobby the Treasurer, Financier of the American Revolution, Merchant Prince, Patriot Financier
Jedidiah Morse	Father of American Geography
William Penn	Father of Pennsylvania, First American Advertising Man
Oliver Hazard Perry	Hero of Lake Erie
Charles Pinckney	Blackguard Charlie, A South Carolina Federalist
John Pintard	Father of the Historical Societies in America
Israel Putnam	Old Put, Wolf Putnam
John Rolfe	Father of Tobacco
Philip John Schuyler	Great Eye
Samuel Slater	Father of American Manufacturing, Father of the Factory System
John Smith	Father of Virginia
Miles Standish	Captain Shrimp, Hero of New England, Little Indian Fighter
John Stark	Leonidas of America
Baron von Steuben	Father of the American Army
Peter Stuyvesant	Father Wooden Leg, Hard-headed Pete, Headstrong Peter, Hardkopping Piet, Old Silver Leg, Old Silver Nails, One-legged Governor, Wooden Leg
Thomas Sumter	(South) Carolina Gamecock, Gamecock
Jonathan Trumbull	Brother Jonathan, Rebel Governor
Anthony Wayne	Big Thunder, Black Snake, Chief Who Never Sleeps, Dandy Wayne, Hero of Stony Point, Mad Anthony, Tornado, Wind
Noah Webster	Schoolmaster of the Republic, Schoolmaster to America
Roger Williams	Apostle of Toleration, Banished Preacher, Founder of Rhode Island, Independent Man, Indian's Friend, Rebel of Salem
John Winthrop	American Nehemiah, Father of Massachusetts

GENERAL NICKNAMES AND CLAIMS TO FAME

St. Augustine	America's Oldest City
Santa Fe	Lone Star of Civilization (2nd oldest U.S. city — founded in 1609)
Winter of 1609-1610	Starving time
Virginia House of Burgesses	Seminary of Sedition (according to James I)

Tobacco . . . . King Nicotine
White men . . . . Palefaces (according to the Indians)
Plymouth, Massachusetts . . . . First Town of America (Pilgrims made the first permanent settlement, December, 1620)
Leaders aboard the *Mayflower* . . . . Saints
Non-Pilgrims . . . . Strangers
Early settlers to New England . . . . Old Planters
Soldiers with swords or colonial white
men . . . . Long knives, Big knives (according to the Indians)
North Carolinians . . . . Quintessence of Virginia's discontent
Cape Hatteras, North Carolina . . . . Graveyard of the Atlantic
North Carolina . . . . Vale of humility between 2 mountains of conceit (i.e., between Virginia and South Carolina)
1629-1640 voyages to America. . . . . Great Puritan Migration
Connecticut . . . . Constitution State (first written constitution signed there in 1639)
Jesuit priests . . . . Black Robes (Gowns) (according to the Indians)
Rhode Island in the 17th century . . . . Traditional home of the otherwise minded
Pennsylvania . . . . (founded as the) "holy experiment" in 1682
Massachusetts in the 1700's . . . . Bible Commonwealth
New Orleans, Louisiana . . . . Crescent City
John Law's failed financial scheme . . . . . Mississippi Bubble
Indian heaven . . . . Happy Hunting Ground
Indian source of good or bad fortune . . . . The Great Spirit
Savannah, Georgia . . . . Cradle of Georgia, First City of the South (founded February 12, 1733)
French territorial ambitions
in the mid-18th century . . . . Gallic Peril (according to the British)
French and Indian War, 1754-1763 . . . . . . Great War for Empire
Pennsylvania . . . . Penn's Woodland
Quakers . . . . Broad brims
Stamp Act of 1765 . . . . Mother of Mischief
Colonial women who refused to serve
or use English tea . . . . Daughters of Liberty
British Redcoats . . . . Lobster-backs, Bloody-backs
British King . . . . Great White Father with the Red Coat, Royal Brute of Great Britain
Malt Liquor . . . . John Barleycorn
Cotton . . . . King Cotton
Colonial Militia . . . . Minutemen
England . . . . The Mother Country
British musket . . . . Brown Bess, Brown musket
Foreign officers in Continental Army . . . . . Hungry adventurers (according to Washington)
Poorly dressed colonial soldier . . . . Yankee Doodle (according to the British)
British Parliament's 5 acts
of March 31, 1774, against
Massachusetts . . . . Intolerable Acts
First Continental Congress on
September 5, 1774 . . . . Nursery of American Statesmen (according to John Adams)
Liberty Boys . . . . Tarring and Feathering Gentlemen
Lexington, Massachusetts/
Philadelphia, Pennsylvania . . . . Birthplace of American Liberty

Faneuil Hall, Boston. . . . . Cradle of Liberty
David Bushnell's submarine of 1775 . . . . . Bushnell's Turtle
Appeal sent to King George III on
July 5, 1775, by Congress to
offer peace. . . . . Olive Branch Petition
Beverly, Massachusetts . . . . Birthplace of the American Navy (the
                                                    Hannah was the first ship of the
                                                    American Navy — built in 1775)
Hessian soldiers in the British
Army during the American
Revolution . . . . Hessian Flies
Independence Hall, Philadelphia . . . . Birthplace of Liberty, Cradle of American
                                                    Liberty
Pennsylvania . . . . Birth State of the Nation (Declaration
                                                    of Independence signed there on July 4,
                                                    1776)
Philadelphia. . . . . City of Brotherly Love
1777 . . . . Bloody Year (on the frontier)
Dover, Delaware . . . . First City of the First State (May 12, 1777)
Colonial attempt to blow up British
vessels on the Delaware River in
1777 . . . . Battle of the Kegs
Benjamin Cleveland's soldiers at
King's Mountain on Oct. 7, 1780. . . . . Cleveland's Bulldogs (Devils, Heroes)
Cowpens - Jan. 17, 1781 . . . . American Cannae
Paper money . . . . Continentals
Revolutionary War currency notes . . . . Long/Short Bobs
Constitution of the United States
before ratification. . . . . Triple-headed Monster
Delaware . . . . First State (first state to ratify the
                                                    Constitution - December 7, 1787)
Writers and Signers of the Constitution . . . Founding Fathers
The Constitution . . . . Supreme Law of the Land (contemporary
                                                    term)
Negro slaves . . . . Black ivory
Symbol of the people of the United
States . . . . Brother Jonathan
Official residence of the President
of the United States . . . . White House
White House . . . . Yankee Palace (according to the British
                                                    during the War of 1812)
U.S. President. . . . . (Great White) Father (popularized by the
                                                    movies) (according to the Indians)
John Adams's appointees (Judges). . . . . . . Midnight Appointees/Judges
Jefferson's small coastal fleet . . . . Jeffs, Mosquito fleet
The *Constitution*. . . . . Old Ironsides
Embargo Act . . . . Ograbme, Gobarme, Mobrage Acts (O-
                                                    grab-me, Go-bar-me, Mob-rage Acts)
Clermont - 1807 . . . . Fulton's Folly
Republican Party faction led by
John Randolph. . . . . Quids
Life aboard a British naval vessel. . . . . Floating hell
Unkempt Americans . . . . Dirty shirts (according to the British)
Tenskwatawa . . . . The Prophet
Pro-British Americans (Traitors) . . . . Blue-light Federalists
War of 1812. . . . . War of Iniquity, Mr. Madison's War,
                                                    Unnecessary War
Battle of New Orleans. . . . . Unnecessary Battle

QUESTIONS AND ANSWERS

1. From what 2 countries in the 19th century did most of the immigrants to the United States come?
ANSWER: Ireland and Germany.

2. Who were the 2 sons of tragedian Junius Brutus Booth who were also tragedians?
ANSWER: Edwin T. Booth and John Wilkes Booth.

3. How were the 3 R's spelled by the poorly-paid and ill-trained teachers of the 19th century?
ANSWER: Readin', 'Ritin', and 'Rithmetic.

4. What 3 men in the first part of the 19th century were known as the ''Immortal Trio'' or the ''Great Triumvirate''?
ANSWER: John C. Calhoun, Henry Clay, and Daniel Webster.

5. What were the 2 regrets of President Andrew Jackson later in life concerning Henry Clay and John C. Calhoun?
ANSWER: That he hadn't shot Henry Clay or hanged John C. Calhoun.

6. Name the 4 nations that claimed the Oregon Country in the early part of the 19th century. How did 2 of the countries withdraw their claims?
ANSWER: Spain, Russia, Great Britain, and the United States/Spain retreated by signing the Florida Treaty of 1819 and Russia did so by the Treaties of 1824 and 1825 with America and Britain.

7. Name the first 4 new states that were created following the War of 1812.
ANSWER: Indiana (1816), Mississippi (1817), Illinois (1818), and Alabama (1819).

8. In 1818 what 2 important Spanish posts in Florida did General Andrew Jackson seize that brought East Florida under the control of the United States military? Name the 2 British traders who were captured and killed by Jackson.
ANSWER: St. Marks and Pensacola/Alexander Arbuthnot and Robert Ambrister.

9. What 2 states applied for admission to statehood in 1819? In what years were these 23rd and 24th states admitted? Name the 11 slave states and the 11 free states that existed prior to the admission of these states. Also, what were the 3 parts of the Missouri Compromise?
ANSWER: Maine and Missouri/Maine on March 15, 1820, and Missouri on August 10, 1821/The 11 slave states were Alabama, Delaware, Georgia, Kentucky, Louisiana, Maryland, Mississippi, North Carolina, South Carolina, Tennessee, and Virginia; and the 11 free states were Connecticut, Indiana, Illinois, New Hampshire, New Jersey, Pennsylvania, Massachusetts, Ohio, Rhode Island, New York, and Vermont/
1. Missouri was admitted as a slave state
2. Maine as a separate state
3. No more slavery was permitted in the Louisiana Territory north of the 36°30' line.

10. Name the 5 nations that President James Monroe recognized in 1822 in Latin and South America.
ANSWER: Chile, Colombia, La Plata (Argentina), Mexico, and Peru.

11. What were the 2 basic features of the Monroe Doctrine of 1823? To what 3 world powers was this doctrine directed?
ANSWER: Non-colonization and non-intervention on the American continents/Spain, Russia, and France.

12. In what 3 years and for what parties was Henry Clay a candidate for the presidency of the United States?
ANSWER: In 1824 as a Democratic-Republican; in 1832 as a National Republican; and in 1844 as a Whig.

13. Who were the 4 U.S. presidential candidates in the 1824 election? Who had the most electoral votes, and who had the most popular votes, and why did this person fail to win the election? What section of Congress decided the outcome, and why did it do so? Who gave his votes to whom and who was appointed

Secretary of State? Who became President? What post did Henry Clay hold at the time?

ANSWER: **Andrew Jackson, Henry Clay, William H. Crawford, and John Quincy Adams/Andrew Jackson had the most electoral and the most popular votes but failed to win the election because he did not have a majority of the electoral vote/The House of Representatives is directed by the 12th Amendment to decide the issue in the event of a deadlock/Henry Clay gave his votes to Adams and was appointed Secretary of State/John Quincy Adams/Speaker of the House.**

14. For what event in October, 1825, did the words "The Wedding of the Waters" have meaning? Who presided at this "Wedding"? When was the project started? How wide and deep was it? What did the "Wedding" symbolize? What nickname was given to the project?

ANSWER: **The event was the official opening of the Erie Canal which connected the Great Lakes with the Atlantic Ocean/Governor DeWitt Clinton poured 5 gallons of water into the Atlantic Ocean/Started on July 4, 1817/40 feet wide and 4 feet deep/It symbolized the "Wedding" of Lake Erie with the Atlantic Ocean/"Clinton's Ditch" after DeWitt Clinton.**

15. Who made each of the following statements?
    a) "Our country! May she always be in the right."
    b) "Like a fire-bell in the night."
    c) "Thomas Jefferson still survives."
    d) "Liberty and Union, now and forever, one and inseparable."
    e) "Our (Federal) Union! It must be preserved."
    f) "I'd rather be right than be President."
    g) "A House divided against itself cannot stand."
    h) "I can't spare this man, he fights."
    i) "I propose to fight it out on this line if it takes all summer."
    j) "Damn the torpedoes—Full speed ahead."

ANSWER: **a) Stephen Decatur b) Thomas Jefferson c) John Adams d) Daniel Webster e) Andrew Jackson f) Henry Clay g) Abraham Lincoln h) Abraham Lincoln i) Ulysses S. Grant j) David Glasgow Farragut.**

16. Between what 4 cities in Ohio did the construction of 2 canals take place in 1825? On what bodies of water are the towns located?

ANSWER: **Between Portsmouth and Cleveland and between Cincinnati and Toledo (Cleveland and Toledo are on Lake Erie while Portsmouth and Cincinnati are on the Ohio).**

17. Name the railroad that began construction on July 4, 1828. Name the last surviving signer of the Declaration of Independence who dug the shovelful of dirt in the opening ceremonies.

ANSWER: **The Baltimore and Ohio/Charles Carroll of Carrollton.**

18. What 2 trees were the symbols of the 1828 election, and which candidates did each represent?

ANSWER: **The hickory represented Andrew Jackson, and the oak was for John Quincy Adams.**

19. What is a "Kitchen Cabinet"? With which U.S. President was this term first associated? Name any members of this "Cabinet."

ANSWER: **It is a group of informal advisors to the U.S. President/Andrew Jackson/ Francis P. Blair, Andrew J. Donelson, Duff Green, Isaac Hill, Amos Kendall, William B. Lewis, and Martin Van Buren.**

20. Name the first 3rd political party to hold a presidential nominating convention. Where was the convention held, when did it take place, and who was the candidate nominated?

ANSWER: **The Anti-Masonic Party/Baltimore, 1831/William Wirt.**

21. Over what woman did President Jackson dismiss his entire Cabinet and appoint a new one? What No. 2 man in line to be President lost out, and who took his place? What happened to the Secretary of War?

ANSWER: **Peggy (Margaret) O'Neill (O'Neale) Timberlake who had married Secretary** of War John H. Eaton/John C. Calhoun/Jackson supported Martin Van Buren, not John C. Calhoun, as his successor/Secretary Eaton was made governor of Florida (1834-1836) and then he served as minister to Spain (to 1840).

22. Who was the first Vice-President to accede to the presidency by death of the President? Who died and how long had he held office?
ANSWER: **John Tyler/William Henry Harrison died of pleurisy on April 4, 1841, after 30 days in office.**

23. Who invented the telegraph? Between what 2 cities was the first message sent, and what was the first message?
ANSWER: **Samuel F.B. Morse/1844 between Washington and Baltimore/''What hath God wrought?''**

24. Give the 4 points of James K. Polk's 1844 presidential campaign.
ANSWER: **1. Lower the tarrif   3. Acquire California**
2. Restore the independent treasury 4. Settle the Oregon dispute.

25. Name the first ''dark horse'' U.S. presidential candidate in American history. Whom did he defeat, and in what election did he do so?
ANSWER: **James K. Polk of Tennessee/He defeated Henry Clay in the 1844 election by 170 to 105 electoral votes and by 38,000 popular votes.**

26. Give the beginning and ending dates of the Mexican War.
ANSWER: **James K. Polk sent Zachary Taylor to the Rio Grande on January 13, 1846, to provoke the Mexicans to attack. They finally did so on April 25, 1846. Congress declared war on May 13, 1846. The war ended at Chapultepec-Mexico City on September 14, 1847. The Treaty of Guadalupe Hidalgo was signed on February 2, 1848.**

27. What 2 reasons were the basis for Polk's asking Congress to declare war on Mexico before the initial attack was made?
ANSWER: **$3,000,000 in American claims against Mexico, and the rejection of the offer of $25,000,000 for California made by Polk's envoy, John Slidell.**

28. Which persons are known by each of the following nicknames?
    a) Father of Texas
    b) Father of States' Rights
    c) Father of the National Road
    d) Father of Abolitionism
    e) Father of Prohibition
    f) Father of Oregon
    g) Father of the Mormons
    h) Expounding Father of the
       Constitution
ANSWER: **a) Stephen Austin and Samuel Houston b) John C. Calhoun c) Henry Clay d) William Lloyd Garrison e) Neal S. Dow f) John Jacob Astor g) Joseph Smith h) Daniel Webster.**

29. What Proviso of August 8, 1846, stated that in any territory acquired from Mexico neither slavery nor involuntary servitude would exist?
ANSWER: **The Wilmot Proviso (but it was defeated in the Senate).**

30. Name the famous literary recluse who in 1846 refused to pay a poll tax and was arrested. How much was the tax? What was the protest? What essay did he write because of this experience?
ANSWER: **Henry David Thoreau/One dollar/He objected to slavery and the Mexican War/''Civil Disobedience.''**

31. By what name are the Mormons properly known? Who was their first prophet, and who was his successor? Name the 2 towns, and their states, that were at the beginning and the end of the Mormon Trail in 1846-1847. What threatened the Mormon crops in 1848, and what ate that threat?
ANSWER: **The Church of Christ of Latter Day Saints/Joseph Smith and Brigham Young/The Mormons fled from Nauvoo, Illinois, and went to Salt Lake City, Utah/Crickets were destroying their crops, but the sea gulls ate the crickets.**

32. Name the 2 women who led the Seneca Falls, New York, Women's Right's Convention on July 19, 1848.

ANSWER: Lucretia Mott and Elizabeth Cady Stanton.

33. Give the 5 parts of the Compromise of 1850 passed by Congress.
ANSWER: 1. California was admitted as a free state
2. The Territory of New Mexico was to be organized with no restrictions as to slavery
3. The Utah Territory was created with no restrictions as to slavery
4. A more stringent Fugitive Slave Law
5. Abolition of the slave trade in the District of Columbia, and Texas was to be compensated ($10,000,000) for disputed land given to New Mexico.

34. Identify each of the following nicknames.
a) Clinton's Ditch
b) Hydra of Corruption
c) The Alamo City
d) Lucy Stoners
e) Genuine Arkansas Toothpick
f) Beecher's Bibles
g) Battle of the Giants
h) Drake's Folly
i) Quaker guns
j) Lincoln's Great Snake
ANSWER: a) Erie Canal b) Second Bank of the United States c) San Antonio, Texas d) Women who kept their maiden names after marriage e) Bowie knife f) Sharp's rifles g) Lincoln-Douglas debates (1858) h) Oil well in Titusville, Pa. i) Dummy wooden guns (cannons) j) Union blockade of Southern ports.

35. What election year marked the end of the Whig Party as a major power? Who was the Whig candidate that year? What "dark horse" candidate won the election? What 2 Whig leaders died during the election campaign?
ANSWER: 1852/Winfield Scott/Franklin Pierce/Henry Clay and Daniel Webster.

36. Who was the Secretary of War for Franklin Pierce, and what major office did he hold later?
ANSWER: Jefferson Davis/President of the Confederacy.

37. What agreement was concluded on December 30, 1853, by what minister to Mexico with what Mexican leader for what American President that purchased land for $10,000,000 for a southern railway route? What 2 present-day U.S. states were involved?
ANSWER: James Gadsden concluded an agreement for the Gadsden Purchase area with Santa Anna for President Franklin Pierce/Southern Arizona and New Mexico.

38. In 1854 what U.S. ministers to Spain, England, and France met in Belgium to prepare what manifesto that offered Spain $120,000,000 for Cuba? If Spain refused, the U.S. would take it from her. Spain had captured an American steamer on February 28, 1854, and this incident was the basis for the manifesto. Name the ship. The 3 ministers did meet in Belgium initially, but where did they spend the last 6 days and sign the treaty?
ANSWER: Pierre Soulé, James Buchanan, and John Y. Mason/The Ostend Manifesto/ The *Black Warrior*/Aix-la-Chapelle in Rhennish Prussia.

39. From the following words, identify the song and the author.
"Mine eyes have seen the glory of the coming of the Lord:
He is trampling out the vintage where the grapes of wrath are stored;
He hath loos'd the fateful lightning of His terrible swift sword:
His truth is marching on."
ANSWER: "The Battle Hymn of the Republic" by Julia Ward Howe.

40. Between what 2 men was there serious violence on the Senate floor in May, 1856, and what was the outcome?
ANSWER: Charles Sumner of Massachusetts attacked the Pierce administration, the South, and slavery, as well as the personal character of Andrew P. Butler of South Carolina. Butler's nephew, Preston Brooks, was incensed and brutally beat Sumner with a cane.

41. In the 1856 presidential campaign sex appeal was prominent for the first time. Who had the sex appeal and what was his wife's name? Also, what was his nickname? What candidate in the election lacked this sex appeal?
ANSWER: John Charles Frémont was the Republican candidate. He was young (43)

and had a very attractive wife, Jessie/''Pathfinder of the West''/James Buchanan was 65 and a bachelor.

42. What Supreme Court decision of March 6, 1857, ruled that the plaintiff was neither a U.S. nor a Missouri citizen, and thus could not sue in federal courts? Who was the Chief Justice?

ANSWER: **The Dred Scott decision (*Dred Scott v. Sandford (sic-*Sanford*)*/Roger B. Taney.**

43. Who supposedly said: ''You can fool all of the people some of the time, and some of the people all of the time, but you cannot fool all of the people all the time''?

ANSWER: **Abraham Lincoln.**

44. Name the 7 cities in Illinois that were the sites of the Lincoln-Douglas debates between August 21 and October 15, 1858.

ANSWER: **Ottawa, Freeport, Jonesboro, Charleston, Galesburg, Quincy, and Alton.**

45. In which state did each of the following Civil War battles take place?

a) Fort Sumter　　　　　　　　　f) Vicksburg
b) First Bull Run　　　　　　　　g) Chancellorsville
c) Fort Donelson　　　　　　　　h) Chickamauga
d) Shiloh　　　　　　　　　　　i) Spotsylvania
e) Antietam　　　　　　　　　　j) Cold Harbor

ANSWER: **a) South Carolina b) Virginia c) Tennessee d) Tennessee e) Maryland f) Mississippi g) Virginia h) Georgia i) Virginia j) Virginia.**

46. Name the 4 most populous predominantly white nations in the world in 1860.

ANSWER: **Russia, France, Austria, and the United States.**

47. Between what 2 cities 1,980 miles apart was the first Pony Express established? Give the date it was started.

ANSWER: **St. Joseph, Missouri, and Sacramento, California/April 3, 1860.**

48. What were the names of the 4 Parties involved in the presidential election of 1860, and who was the candidate for each Party?

ANSWER: **Abraham Lincoln for the Republican Party; Stephen A. Douglas for the Democratic Party; John C. Breckinridge for the Southern Democrats; and John Bell for the Constitutional Union Party.**

49. How many states had seceded from the Union by the time Lincoln was inaugurated? Name them. On what date and where did they form the Confederate States of America? Who were the President and Vice President? What 2 features prevented the South from seceding geographically from the North?

ANSWER: **Seven/South Carolina, Mississippi, Florida, Alabama, Georgia, Louisiana, and Texas/February 8, 1861, at Montgomery, Alabama/Jefferson Davis was the President and Alexander Stephens the Vice President/The Mississippi River and the Appalachian Mountains.**

50. On what day in what year was the shot fired that started the Civil War? Who gave the orders for the artillery barrage? Who supposedly fired the first shot? Upon what fort in what harbor and state did this event take place? What Major was in charge of the fort? On what date did the fort surrender? How many were killed in the attack?

ANSWER: **April 12, 1861/General Pierre Gustave Toutant Beauregard/Edmund Ruffin/ Fort Sumter in Charleston Harbor in South Carolina/Major Robert Anderson /April 14, 1861/None.**

51. Here's a difficult question: name the 6 Battles during the 7 Days' Battles of June 25-July 1, 1861.

ANSWER: **Mechanicsville (Beaver Dam Creek), Gaines' Mill, Savage's Station, White Oak Swamp, Frayser's Farm (Glendale), and Malvern Hill.**

52. In what year did the *Trent* affair occur? What 2 Confederate emissaries to Britain and France had beaten the Northern blockade, and where did they board the *Trent*? What American frigate captained by what officer stopped the *Trent* and took the commissioners to Boston?

ANSWER: 1861/James M. Mason and John Slidell in Havana, Cuba/The *San Jacinto* and Captain Charles Wilkes.

53. Name the 3 capitals of the Confederate States.

ANSWER: Montgomery, Alabama, and Richmond and Danville, Virginia.

54. How many states were in the Confederacy? Name them.

ANSWER: Eleven/Alabama, Arkansas, Florida, Georgia, Louisiana, Mississippi, North Carolina, South Carolina, Tennessee, Texas, and Virginia.

55. Which persons are known by each of the following nicknames?

a) Old Osawatomie
b) South's Avenging Angel
c) Little Giant
d) Old White Hat
e) Sword of the Confederacy
f) Old Ace of Spades
g) Greatest American Jurist
h) That Vile Wretch in Crinoline
i) Plumed Knight of the Confederacy
j) Rock of Chickamauga

ANSWER: a) John Brown b) John Wilkes Booth c) Stephen A. Douglas d) Horace Greeley e) Thomas Jackson f) Robert E. Lee g) John Marshall h) Harriet Beecher Stowe i) Jeb Stuart j) George Thomas.

56. Give the names of the 2 organized secret societies that acted like fifth columns (traitors) in both the North and the South during the Civil War.

ANSWER: The Knights of the Golden Circle in the North and the Heroes of America in the South.

57. What were the names of the 2 American ironclad ships during the Civil War? Where and when did they meet? What 2 ships had the Confederate ship sunk the day before? What was the other name for the Southern ship. Give the 2 nicknames for the Northern ship.

ANSWER: The *Monitor* and the *Merrimac* (k)/March 9, 1862, at Hampton Roads, Virginia/The *Cumberland* and the *Congress* had been sunk by the *Merrimac* (k)/The *Virginia*/"Tin Can on a Shingle" and "Cheesebox on a Raft."

58. What 2 forts on what 2 rivers in Tennessee had been built by the Confederates to protect the heart of the Confederacy? When did these forts fall?

ANSWER: Fort Henry on the Tennessee and Fort Donelson on the Cumberland/ Henry on February 6, 1862, and Donelson on February 16, 1862.

59. Whose poem contains the lines: "Shoot, if you must, this old gray head,/But spare your country's flag," she said."? Although the story may be apocryphal, according to legend at least who was the woman? What flag was it? To whom was she speaking? What was the response to her comments? How old was the woman in this poem?

ANSWER: John Greenleaf Whittier's/Barbara Frietchie (also the name of the poem)/ The Stars and Stripes/Stonewall Jackson/"'Who touches a hair of yon gray head/Dies like a dog! March on!' he said."/She was "four score years and ten."

60. Many Civil War battles have 2 names. Why do the Southerners call the battles by one name and the Northerners by another?

ANSWER: The Southerners called the battles for the nearest town while the Northerners named them for the nearest river.

61. Who declared that the Civil War was a contest to insure that "government of the people, by the people, and for the people shall not perish from the earth"? What speech was this and in what year? Recite the first sentence.

ANSWER: Abraham Lincoln/His Gettysburg Address on November 19, 1863/ "Fourscore and seven years ago our fathers brought forth upon this continent, a new nation, conceived in Liberty, and dedicated to the proposition that all men are created equal."

62. Who were the 2 leaders of the Armies of Northern Virginia and Carolina during the Civil War?

ANSWER: General Joseph Eggleston Johnston and General Robert E. Lee.

63. What man raised a company of soldiers in 3 days in Indianapolis for the Mexican

War, commanded a division at Crump's Landing near Shiloh under Ulysses Grant, and later wrote the novel *Ben-Hur*?

ANSWER: General Lew Wallace.

64. Name the Generals who were the successive Commanders in Chief of the Army of the Potomac. Name those who were the successive Commanders of the Union Armies.

ANSWER: Generals Irwin McDowell (April 12, 1861), George Brinton McClellan (July 2, 1861), Ambrose E. Burnside (Nov. 7, 1862), Joseph Hooker (Jan. 25, 1863), and George G. Meade (June 28, 1863)/Generals Winfield C. Scott (June 25, 1841), George Brinton McClellan (Nov. 1, 1861), Henry W. Halleck (July 11, 1862), and Ulysses S. Grant (March 9, 1864).

65. Name the 2 railroad companies formed in the 1860's that combined to complete a coast-to-coast railroad.

ANSWER: The Union Pacific and the Central Pacific.

66. Other than Jefferson Davis and Alexander Stephens, President and Vice President respectively of the Confederacy, name anyone else in the Confederate Cabinet during the Civil War.

ANSWER: STATE: Robert Toombs, R.M.T. Hunter, Judah P. Benjamin; WAR: Leroy P. Walker, Judah P. Benjamin, George W. Randolph, Gustavus W. Smith, James A. Seddon, John C. Breckinridge; NAVY: Stephen R. Mallory; TREASURY: Christopher G. Memminger, George A. Trenholm; ATTORNEY GENERAL: Judah P. Benjamin, Thomas Bragg, Thomas H. Watts, George Davis; POSTMASTER GENERAL: John H. Reagan.

67. What was the name of the boat destroyed by a Union boat in 1864 and described as ''Built of English oak in an English yard, armed with English guns, manned by an English crew, and sunk in the English Channel''? This British boat destroyed many Yankee ships.

ANSWER: The *Alabama* (other important cruisers Britain sold the Confederacy were the *Florida* and the *Shenandoah*).

68. Who were the 3 Confederate representatives and the 2 Union representatives who met on February 3, 1865, in peace discussions to end the Civil War? Aboard what boat did the discussions take place, and in what town was this?

ANSWER: Vice President Alexander Stephens, R.M.T. Hunter, and J.A. Campbell were from the South. President Abraham Lincoln and Secretary of War William H. Seward represented the North./The *River Queen*/Hampton Roads, Virginia.

69. In which speech, when, and by whom was the following statement made? ''With malice toward none, with charity for all, with firmness in the right as God gives us to see the right, let us strive on to finish the work we are in, to bind up the nation's wounds, to care for him who shall have borne the battle and for his widow and his orphan, to do all which may achieve and cherish a just and lasting peace among ourselves and with all nations.''

ANSWER: The Second Inaugural Address on March 4, 1865, by Abraham Lincoln.

70. Identify the Civil War Battles by the following nicknames.

a) Gettysburg of the West   d) Burnside's Slaughter Pen
b) High-water Mark of the Confederacy   e) Battle of the Crater
c) Battle Above the Clouds

ANSWER: a) Pea Ridge, Arkansas b) Gettysburg, Pennsylvania c) Lookout Mountain, Tennessee d) Marye's Heights, Fredericksburg, Virginia e) Petersburg, Virginia.

71. On what day was President Abraham Lincoln shot? By whom? In what city and at what theatre? What play was being presented and who wrote the play? What U.S. President-to-be was supposed to have been in the same box with Lincoln? Who were the people in President Lincoln's box? Who was in charge of security? Where was the guard? What were supposedly the words of the assassin as he leapt to the stage? What character in the play has given us what word for a style of whiskers? How did the assassin die and who was responsible? Name the

people who were hanged for the crime as conspirators. What happened to Secretary of State William H. Seward? What doctor who aided Booth was sentenced to a life prison term but pardoned in 1869? What historical first occurred in the hanging of Mary Surratt?

ANSWER: **April 14, 1865 (Lincoln died the next day)/John Wilkes Booth/Washington, D.C. at Ford's Theatre/*Our American Cousin* by Tom Taylor/Ulysses S. Grant/Mrs. Lincoln, Major Rathbone, and his fiancée, Clara Harris/Secretary of War Edwin M. Stanton/Outside the theatre drinking/"*Sic semper tyrannis*—Virginia is avenged"/Lord Dundreary gave us "dundrearies"/Booth was shot by Boston Corbett/Mrs. Mary Surratt (ran a boarding house), Lewis Paine, David Herold, and George Atzerodt (he was supposed to kill Vice President Johnson)/Seward's throat was cut by Paine. Seward did not die/Dr. Samuel Mudd/She was the first woman in U.S. history to be hanged.**

72. What was the beginning date of the Civil War and on what day did the South surrender to the North? Who were the 2 Generals involved in the surrender?

ANSWER: **The Fort Sumter attack on April 12, 1861, was the start and the South surrendered April 9, 1865, at Appomattox Courthouse, Virginia/Robert E. Lee surrendered to Ulysses S. Grant.**

73. Name the 3 Civil War generals who were called "The Immortal 3."

ANSWER: **Ulysses S. Grant, Philip Sheridan, and William T. Sherman.**

74. What 4 slave states remained in the Union throughout the Civil War?

ANSWER: **Delaware, Kentucky, Maryland, and Missouri.**

75. The last important land battle of the Civil War was fought on April 16, 1865, one week after Lee surrendered at Appomattox. What city in Georgia was captured by the Federal forces in this battle?

ANSWER: **Columbus.**

76. Who were the Northern and Southern commanders during each of the following Civil War battles?

a) Antietam	f) Gettysburg
b) Second Bull Run	g) Kennesaw Mountain
c) Chickamauga	h) Nashville
d) Cold Harbor	i) Seven Days
e) Fort Donelson	j) The Wilderness

ANSWER: **a) McClellan and Lee b) Pope and Lee-Jackson c) Rosecrans and Bragg d) Meade-Grant and Lee e) Grant and Buckner-Floyd f) Meade and Lee g) Sherman and Johnston h) Thomas and Hood i) McClellan and Lee j) Meade-Grant and Lee.**

77. Identify each of the following.
   a) The woman who worked to establish public hospitals for the mentally ill
   b) The man noted for his U.S. Civil War photographs
   c) The first Secretary of the Massachusetts Board of Education who reorganized the state's educational system
   d) The historian who wrote the ten-volume *History of the United States* (1834-1882)
   e) The composer who wrote "Oh! Susannah," "My Old Kentucky Home," and "Jeanie with the Light Brown Hair"
   f) The author of 6 graded *Eclectic Readers* (1835-1857)
   g) The founder of Mount Holyoke Seminary in South Hadley, Massachusetts, in 1837
   h) The Maryland-born ex-slave who edited the newspaper, the *North Star*

ANSWER: **a) Dorothea Dix b) Mathew Brady c) Horace Mann d) George Bancroft e) Stephen Foster f) William Holmes McGuffey g) Mary Lyon h) Frederick Douglass.**

AMERICAN QUOTATIONS/SLOGANS/MOTTOES

OUR COUNTRY! MAY SHE ALWAYS BE IN THE RIGHT
After Congress had declared war on Algiers, Commodore Stephen Decatur defeated an Algerine fleet near Spain and he forced Algiers, Tunis, and Tripoli to pay $81,000 for the captured American vessels and give up all future "tribute" (bribes). Algerine officials wanted to continue the tribute in the form of gunpowder. Decatur said: "If you insist on receiving powder as tribute, you must expect to receive *balls* with it." Later at a banquet on April 4, 1816, at Norfolk, Virginia, Decatur made this toast: "Our Country! In her intercourse with foreign nations may she always be in the right, and always successful, right or wrong" (sometimes quoted as, "may she always be in the right; but our country, right or wrong.")

LIKE A FIRE-BELL IN THE NIGHT
Thomas Jefferson said this in 1820 about the Missouri controversy and the passions it stirred. He wrote: "This momentous question, like a fire-bell in the night awakened and filled me with terror. I considered it the knell of the Union. It is hushed, indeed, for the moment. But this is only a reprieve, not a final sentence."

THOMAS JEFFERSON STILL SURVIVES
John Adams supposedly said this on his death bed on July 4, 1826. Ironically Thomas Jefferson's death occurred several hours before that of Adams. Adams was at Quincy, Massachusetts, and Jefferson was at Monticello, Virginia.

LIBERTY AND UNION, NOW AND FOREVER, ONE AND INSEPARABLE
These words were part of Daniel Webster's second speech on January 26, 1830, in Congress in rebuttal to South Carolina Senator Robert Young Hayne. One issue in the debate was states' rights versus national power. Hayne defended the nullification issue, and Webster responded with: "I go for the Constitution as it is, and for the Union as it is. It is, Sir, the people's Constitution, the people's government, made for the people, made by the people, and answerable to the people....What is all this worth?...Liberty first and Union afterward;...Liberty and Union, now and forever, one and inseparable."

OUR (FEDERAL)* UNION! IT MUST BE PRESERVED!
At a banquet on April 13, 1830, President Andrew Jackson delivered a toast aimed at Vice President John C. Calhoun's ideas about states rights. Jackson looked at Calhoun and said: "Our (Federal) Union: it must be preserved!" Calhoun then rose for a toast and said: "The Union, next to our liberty, most dear! May we always remember that it can only be preserved by respecting the rights of the states and by distributing equally the benefits and the burdens of the Union."
*(Jackson amended his toast for publication to include the word "Federal").

JOHN MARSHALL HAS MADE HIS DECISION, NOW LET HIM ENFORCE IT!
These imperious words were said by President Andrew Jackson and directed toward a Supreme Court decision he did not like which supported the rights of the Cherokee Nation when Georgia tried to evict the Indians. The Cherokees had a written language invented by Sequoya in 1821 and were settled as farmers, yet the State of Georgia wanted to remove them. In 1827 the Cherokees adopted a constitution and became independent calling themselves the Cherokee Nation. In the Supreme Court case *Worcester v. Georgia* before Chief Justice John Marshall, the Court held that Indian nations were capable of making treaties, thus ruling that the Cherokee Nation had territorial boundaries within which the laws of Georgia "can have no force." Because of Jackson's attitude, Justice Marshall's ruling was never enforced. The Cherokees were forced to sign a treaty giving them 5 million dollars and a reservation in Oklahoma. General Winfield Scott led an army that drove the Indians westward. This forced march was called the "Trail of Tears."

THE ONLY GOOD INDIAN IS A DEAD INDIAN
An Andrew Jackson belief like that of many Westerners. Jackson showed no sympathy for the Indians either as a General or as a President. This was likewise the motto of white settlers as they pushed westward. Philip Henry Sheridan is usually credited with the statement, for he said, "The only good Indians I ever saw were dead."

I AM IN EARNEST—I WILL NOT EQUIVOCATE—I WILL NOT EXCUSE—I WILL NOT RETREAT A SINGLE INCH—AND I WILL BE HEARD

William Lloyd Garrison, American journalist, wrote these words in 1831 in the first issue of his weekly paper, the *Liberator*, demanding the abolition of slavery. He wrote: ''I will be as harsh as truth, and as uncompromising as justice. On this subject, I do not wish to think, or speak, or write with moderation. No! No!...but urge me not to use moderation in a cause like the present. I am in earnest—I will not equivocate—I will not excuse—I will not retreat a single inch—AND I WILL BE HEARD.''

TO THE VICTOR BELONG THE SPOILS

This remark was made by New York Democrat, Senator William Learned Marcy, in a Senate speech in January, 1832. He made this statement in defense of Andrew Jackson's appointment of Martin Van Buren as ambassador to Great Britain. Marcy said: ''If they (the politicians) are successful, they claim as a matter of right, the advantages of success. They see nothing wrong in the rule, that to the victor belong the spoils of the enemy.'' Even though Jackson changed only about 9% of Federal officeholders during the first year (20% overall), Jackson's name is forever associated with the ''spoils system.''

BE ALWAYS SURE YOU'RE RIGHT—THEN GO AHEAD

Motto of David Crockett. He was a U.S. Congressman from 1827-1831 and from 1833-1835. He fought and died at the siege of the Alamo. He wrote, ''I leave this rule for others when I'm dead, Be always sure you're right—then go ahead.''

REMEMBER THE ALAMO

A Texan war cry after General Antonio Lopez de Santa Anna and 3,000 Mexicans had wiped out nearly 200 Texans in the Spanish mission called the Alamo on March 6, 1836. James Bowie, Davy Crockett, and their leader Colonel William Travis were among the slain Texans. Texas declared its independence from Mexico, and Santa Anna soon laid siege to the Alamo.

REMEMBER GOLIAD

A Texan war cry after about 400 American volunteers under Captain James W. Fannin, Jr., surrendered at the Battle of Coleto to General José Urrea, only to be massacred a week later on March 27, 1836.

FIFTY-FOUR FORTY, OR FIGHT! (54°40' OR FIGHT!)

Senator William Allen of Ohio coined this phrase during the presidential campaign of 1844. This phrase was quite popular with the Western Democrats seeking an Oregon boundary settlement with Great Britain. President James Polk compromised in 1846 and settled on the 49th degree as the Northwest boundary of the United States (Samuel Medary, an Ohio editor, may deserve the credit for coining the phrase).

MANIFEST DESTINY

Andrew Jackson used the term in 1824, but it was newspaper editor John L. O'Sullivan, writing in *The United States Magazine and Democratic Review* in 1845, who popularized the phrase in his editorial. Manifest Destiny was the doctrine advocating the continued territorial expansion of the United States as its duty and fate. O'Sullivan wrote: ''...the inevitable fulfillment of the general law which is rolling our population westward; the connexion...is too evident to leave us in doubt of the manifest design of Providence in regard to the occupation of this continent....'' He also wrote: ''It is our manifest destiny to overspread and to possess the whole of the continent which Providence has given us for the...great experiment of liberty.'' Representative Robert C. Winthrop referred in Congress to ''...the right of our manifest destiny to spread over this whole continent.''

THIS IS THE PLACE

The words of Brigham Young leading his Mormon followers when he saw the Great Salt Lake Valley on July 24, 1847. The Mormons fled Nauvoo, Illinois, after their leader Joseph Smith had been killed by an angry mob.

HO, FOR THE HALLS OF MONTEZUMA!

An American cry at the outbreak of hostilities with Mexico as Congress declared war on May 13, 1846. The Marines' Hymn was written in 1847. The first stanza is:

From the halls of Montezuma,

To the shores of Tripoli,
We fight our country's battles
On the land as on the sea.

FREE SOIL, FREE SPEECH, FREE LABOUR, AND FREE MEN
This was the slogan of the Free-soil Party in the 1848 elections. The Party was for the Wilmot Proviso and against slavery in the territories. Martin Van Buren was the presidential candidate of the Free-soil Party.

I'D RATHER BE RIGHT THAN BE PRESIDENT
Kentucky Senator Henry Clay made this statement after colleagues argued that his defense of the Compromise of 1850 would diminish his chances for the presidency.

AMERICANS TO RULE AMERICANS
This was the slogan of the Know-Nothing Party (also called the American Party and the Order of the Star-Spangled Banner) during the 1850's. Members answered "I know nothing" when asked about their organization. This party was opposed to, (1) unrestricted immigration, (2) the Roman Catholic Church, and (3) the holding of a public office by a foreigner. Members of this party recognized each other by closing one eye, making an O with the thumb and forefinger, and pushing the nose through the circle. This action was read as eye-nose-O or "I know nothing."

GO WEST, YOUNG MAN, GO WEST
Horace Greeley is credited with the expression, but it was John Soulé who coined it in the Terre Haute *Express* in 1851. Greeley apparently did say later, "Go West, young man, and grow up with the country." He encouraged homesteading in the West because of the Gold Rush potential in that part of the country. From the *Life of Horace Greeley* there are these words: "...turn your face to the great West, and there build up a home and fortune."

HEAR ME FOR MY CAUSE
These words were part of Daniel Webster's renowned Seventh of March speech in 1850. This event was the last meeting of the Triumvirate of Clay, Calhoun, and Webster. Clay was seeking his third compromise. Calhoun had to have his speech about leaving slavery alone and respecting Southern rights read by an aide. Calhoun said before he died: "The South! The South! God knows what will become of her!" Webster's speech supported Clay's resolutions. He said in part: "I wish to speak today, not as a Massachusetts man, nor as a Northern man, but as an American....I speak today for the preservation of the Union. Hear me for my cause."

THE SOUTH! THE SOUTH! GOD KNOWS WHAT WILL BECOME OF HER!
John C. Calhoun's words shortly before he died in 1850. Calhoun fought ardently to restore the political balance between the North and the South and he wanted slavery to be left alone. A monument in Charleston, South Carolina, is dedicated to him, and on it is inscribed "Truth, Justice, and the Constitution."

WE EXECRATE IT, WE SPIT UPON IT, WE TRAMPLE IT UNDER OUR FEET
Spoken by William Lloyd Garrison in 1851 about the new Fugitive Slave Law which was considered extremely harsh on Negroes by Northerners.

A HOUSE DIVIDED AGAINST ITSELF CANNOT STAND
These are the words of Abraham Lincoln in a nominating speech as the Republican nominee for the U.S. Senate on June 16, 1858, at the State Convention in Springfield, Illinois. The Dred Scott Decision of March 6, 1857, encouraged Lincoln to seek active leadership in the party. Lincoln said: "A house divided against itself cannot stand. I believe this government cannot endure permanently half slave and half free. I do not expect the Union to be dissolved—I do not expect the house to fall—but I do expect it will cease to be divided. It will become all one thing, or all the other." (The quote is Biblical in origin, Mark 3:25 and 41:35).

ALL WE ASK IS TO BE LET ALONE
Words from a speech by Jefferson Davis in 1861 referring to the desire of Southerners to be left alone to handle the problems of slavery without Northern interference.

DEO VINDICE (GOD MAINTAINS)
This was a motto of the Confederate States meaning that God was favorable to the cause of the rebelling states and that the act of seceding was justified in His sight.

ALL QUIET ALONG THE POTOMAC

This phrase expressed the discontent of the people of the North, especially Abraham Lincoln, with the inactivity of the Army of the Potomac under Major General George McClellan. After taking over from Major General Joseph McDowell, McClellan did nothing. He was nicknamed ''Mac the Unready'' and ''The Little Corporal of Unfought Fields.'' Lincoln was so upset that he wrote: ''If McClellan is not using the army, I should like to borrow it for a while.'' McClellan was finally forced into action by Lincoln, and after taking Yorktown, was repulsed at Richmond. Lincoln replaced him after 15 months. Today the expression is used when Congress has adjourned and the President has left the city.

THERE IS JACKSON, STANDING LIKE A STONE WALL! RALLY BEHIND THE VIRGINIANS!

These words about Thomas Jackson were said by Brigadier General Barnard Elliott Bee at the First Battle of Bull Run, Manassas, Virginia, on July 21, 1861. Jackson got the nickname because he was indifferent to danger and exposed himself to enemy fire. Jackson died at Chancellorsville, Virginia, in May, 1863, as he was mistakenly shot by his own men. Robert E. Lee said of Jackson, ''I have lost my right arm.'' General Bee's full quote is: ''Let us determine to die here, and we will conquer. There is Jackson standing like a stone wall! Rally behind the Virginians!''

NO TERMS EXCEPT AN UNCONDITIONAL AND IMMEDIATE SURRENDER CAN BE ACCEPTED

These were the words of General Ulysses S. Grant to General Simon Bolivar Buckner during the Battle of Fort Donelson in Tennessee on February 16, 1862. Later that morning Buckner surrendered the fort and about 12,000 men. Unconditional Surrender became Grant's nickname since it matched his initials.

I CAN'T SPARE THIS MAN, HE FIGHTS

President Abraham Lincoln said this about General U.S. Grant in April, 1862. When Grant was taken by surprise at the Battle of Shiloh, there were many demands for his dismissal. Lincoln, however, admired the fighting spirit of Grant and kept him.

IT IS WELL THAT WAR IS SO TERRIBLE, OR WE SHOULD GROW TOO FOND OF IT

Robert E. Lee's words at the Battle of Marye's Heights in Fredericksburg on December 13, 1862. His remark was directed at the bravery of the Federal troops as they charged the Confederate position and were repulsed. 7,000 Federal troops died there.

THAT BLOODY OLD MAN HAS MURDERED MY SOLDIERS/ALL THIS HAS BEEN MY FAULT. IT IS I THAT HAVE LOST THIS FIGHT

The first phrase has been attributed to General George E. Pickett, of General Robert E. Lee, after the disastrous (Pickett's) charge at Gettysburg, July 3, 1863/The second phrase is that of Robert E. Lee, as he went to console the survivors of the charge. Lee had ordered the charge, but the support he expected never materialized.

RICH MAN'S WAR, POOR MAN'S FIGHT

Volunteers in the North during the Civil War served no more than their time, and ''bounty jumpers'' frequently deserted. In 1863 a draft was instituted, but draftees could get out by paying a substitute $300. Thus the cry ''Rich man's war, poor man's fight.'' There were draft riots, and the one in New York lasted from July 13-16, 1863. This was also a slogan of protest in the Confederacy against various laws that favored large slave-owners.

A CROW COULD NOT FLY OVER IT WITHOUT CARRYING HIS RATIONS WITH HIM

General Philip Sheridan made this comment about the Shenandoah Valley in Virginia after he ravaged the land as ordered to do so by Ulysses S. Grant in 1864 (sometimes cited as, ''A crow would have had to carry its rations if it had flown across the Valley).

WHEN IN DOUBT FIGHT/I PROPOSE TO FIGHT IT OUT ON THIS LINE IF IT TAKES ALL SUMMER

The first phrase is the personal motto of General Ulysses S. Grant, and he fought indeed in the Wilderness Campaign in 1864. The fighting was of the ''blood and guts'' type and he was called ''Grant the Butcher.''/The second phrase referred to Grant's philosophy of forging ahead and beating the enemy even if he had to trade two lives to get one. Grant wrote these words on May 11, 1864, after 18,000 casualties at

Spotsylvania. Grant failed at Cold Harbor and Petersburg. A nine month struggle resulted.

DAMN THE TORPEDOES—FULL SPEED AHEAD!

At the Battle of Mobile Bay on August 5, 1864, Admiral David Glasgow Farragut's words were: "Damn the torpedoes (mines)! Four bells! Captain Drayton, go ahead! Jouett, full speed!" Farragut was aboard his flagship the *Hartford* sailing into Mobile Bay to destroy the Confederacy's last stronghold on the Gulf of Mexico. He was opposed by the Confederate *Tennessee.*

DELENDA EST ATLANTA (Atlanta must be destroyed)

These words were a Civil War cry in the Northern states as Atlanta was a prominent depot of Confederate supplies since it was a major rail center. On November 17, 1864, General Sherman completed his destruction of Atlanta. These words parallel the "Delenda est Carthago," a saying of Cato the Elder in the 2nd century B.C. who wanted Carthage eliminated as a threat to the Roman Empire.

WAR IS HELL

Supposedly the words of Major General William Tecumseh Sherman although he could never remember having said them. He wrecked and smashed his way through Georgia because he said he wanted to shorten the war by destroying Confederate supplies and morale. He did say that "war is war, and not popularity-seeking." It was reported that at a graduation address at Michigan Military Academy on June 19, 1879, he said: "War is at best barbarish...War is hell." At a convention at Columbus, Ohio, in 1880, he said: "There is many a boy here today who looks on war as all glory, but, boys, it is all hell."

DON'T SWAP HORSES IN THE MIDDLE OF THE STREAM

Abraham Lincoln said this when nominated for reelection as President in 1864. Even though Lincoln was not all that popular, he considered that the people voted for him because he was the incumbent and they thought it best not to change.

THE WAR IS OVER—THE REBELS ARE OUR COUNTRYMEN AGAIN

These were Grant's words at Appomattox Court House in Virginia on April 9, 1865, as General Robert E. Lee surrendered. The Federal troops began to cheer, but Grant silenced them with these words.

SIC SEMPER TYRANNIS — THE SOUTH IS AVENGED!

"Thus always to tyrants" were supposedly the words of John Wilkes Booth on April 14, 1865, at Ford's Theatre in Washington during the performance of *Our American Cousin* after he jumped to the stage from the balcony after shooting President Lincoln. Secretary of State Edwin McMasters Stanton, responsible for the safety of the President, said after Lincoln passed away the following day, "Now he belongs to the ages."

AMERICAN BATTLES/WARS/NOTABLE INCIDENTS: THEIR SITES AND DATES

First Seminole War	Florida	1816-1818
Fort Apalachicola	Florida	July 27, 1816
St. Marks	Florida	April 7, 1818
Pensacola	Florida	May 24, 1818
Vesey Slave Uprising	Charleston, S.C.	May 30, 1822
Nat Turner Insurrection	Virginia	August 13-23, 1831
Black Hawk War	Wisconsin Territory and Illinois	Apr. 6-Aug. 2, 1832
Second Seminole War	Florida	Nov. 1835-Aug.14,1842
The Alamo Siege	San Antonio, Texas	Feb. 23-Mar. 6, 1836
Goliad	Texas	March 27, 1836
San Jacinto	Texas	April 21, 1836
Caroline	Canadian frontier- Niagara River	Dec. 29, 1837
Aroostook "War"	New Brunswick and Maine	Feb.-May, 1839
Antirent War	New York	1839-1846
Creole	Atlantic Ocean	October, 1841
Mexican Attack	Texas	January, 1842
Dorr Rebellion	Providence, R.I.	April-May, 1842
Bear Flag Revolt	California	June 10-July 5, 1846
Palo Alto	Mexico	May 8-9, 1846
Resaca de la Palma	Mexico	May 9, 1846
Mexican War	Mexico-California	May 13, 1846 Sept. 14, 1847
Monterey	Mexico	Sept. 20-24, 1846
San Pascual	California	December 6, 1846
El Brazito	Mexico	December 25, 1846
Los Angeles	California	Jan. 8-10, 1847
The Sacramento	Mexico	February 28, 1847
Buena Vista	Mexico	Feb. 22-23, 1847
Vera Cruz	Mexico	Mar. 22-29, 1847
Cerro Gordo	Mexico	April 17-18, 1847
Contreras	Mexico	Aug. 19-20, 1847
Churubusco	Mexico	Aug. 20, 1847
Molino del Rey	Mexico	September 8, 1847
Chapultepec	Mexico	Sept. 12-13, 1847
Mexico City	Mexico	Sept. 13-14, 1847
Pottawatomie Creek Massacre	Kansas	May 24-25, 1856
John Brown's Raid — Harpers Ferry	(West) Virginia	Oct. 16-18, 1859
Fort Sumter	South Carolina	April 12, 1861
First Bull Run (Manassas Junction)	Virginia	July 21, 1861
Trent	near Cuba	November 8, 1861
Mill Springs	Kentucky	Jan. 19-20, 1862
Fort Henry	Tennessee	Feb. 6, 1862
Fort Donelson	Tennessee	Feb. 12-16, 1862
Pea Ridge (Elkhorn Tavern)	Arkansas	March 7-8, 1862
Monitor v. Merrimac (k)	Hampton Roads, Va.	March 9, 1862
Peninsular Campaign	Virginia	March 17-July 3, 1862
Shiloh (Pittsburg Landing)	Tennessee	April 6-7, 1862
Fair Oaks (Seven Pines)	Virginia	May 31-June 1, 1862
Seven Days' Campaign	Virginia	June 25-July 1, 1862
Second Bull Run	Virginia	Aug. 29-30, 1862
Perryville	Kentucky	October 8, 1862

Antietam	Maryland	September 17, 1862
Fredericksburg	Virginia	December 13,1862
Murfreesboro (Stone's River)	Tennessee	Dec. 31, 1862-Jan. 2, 1863
Vicksburg Campaign	Mississippi	May-June, 1862 (by sea) Dec. 1862-Jan. 1863 (by land) March 29-July 4, 1863
Chancellorsville	Virginia	May 2-4, 1863
Gettysburg	Pennsylvania	July 1-3, 1863
Chickamauga	Georgia	Sept. 19-20, 1863
Battles Around Chattanooga (Lookout Mountain, Orchard Knob, Missionary Ridge)	Tenn.-Georgia	Nov. 23-27, 1863
The Wilderness	Virginia	May 5-7, 1864
Sherman's March through Georgia/Atlanta Campaign	Georgia	May 5-Sept. 2, 1864
Spotsylvania (Court House)	Virginia	May 8-12, 1864
Cold Harbor	Virginia	June 1-3, 1864
Petersburg Campaign	Virginia	June 15, 1864 Apr. 2, 1865
Kennesaw Mountain	Georgia	June 27, 1864
Mobile Bay	Alabama	August 5, 1864
Cedar Creek	Virginia	October 19, 1864
Sherman's March to the Sea	Georgia	Nov. 14-Dec. 2, 1864
Franklin	Tennessee	Nov. 30, 1864
Nashville	Tennessee	Dec. 15-16, 1864
Sherman's March through the Carolinas	Carolinas	Jan. 16-Mar. 21, 1865
Five Forks	Virginia	April 1, 1865
Sayler's (Sailor's) Creek	Virginia	April 6, 1865
Surrender at Appomattox Courthouse	Virginia	April 9, 1865

CIVIL WAR BATTLES AND NORTHERN/SOUTHERN COMMANDERS

First Bull Run (Manassas Junction) ..... Virginia ..... **July 21, 1861**
North: Irvin McDowell   South: Joseph E. Johnston and
                                            P.G.T. Beauregard

Fort Henry ..... Tennessee ..... **February 6, 1862**
North: Andrew Foote and Ulysses S. Grant South: Lloyd Tilghman

Fort Donelson ..... Tennessee ..... **February 12-16, 1862**
North: Ulysses S. Grant   South: Simon Bolivar Buckner and
                                            John Floyd

Peninsular Campaign ..... Virginia ..... **Mar. 17-July 3, 1862**
North: George McClellan   South: Joseph E. Johnston and
                                            Robert E. Lee

Shiloh (Pittsburg Landing) ..... Tennessee ..... **April 6-7, 1862**
North: Ulysses S. Grant   South: Albert Sidney Johnson and
                                            P.G.T. Beauregard

Fair Oaks (Seven Pines) ..... Virginia ..... **May 31-June 1, 1862**
North: George McClellan   South: Joseph E. Johnston

Seven Days' Campaign ..... Virginia ..... **June 25-July 1, 1862**
North: George McClellan   South: Robert E. Lee

Second Bull Run (Manassas Junction) ..... Virginia ..... **Aug. 29-30, 1862**
North: John Pope   South: Robert E. Lee and
                                   Thomas "Stonewall" Jackson

Perryville . . . . Kentucky . . . . **October 8, 1862**
North: Don Carlos Buell   South: Braxton Bragg
Antietam . . . . Maryland . . . . **Sept. 17, 1862**
North: George McClellan   South: Robert E. Lee
Fredericksburg . . . . Virginia . . . . **Dec. 13, 1862**
North: Ambrose Burnside   South: Robert E. Lee
Murfreesboro (Stone's River) . . . . . . Tennessee . . . . **Dec. 31, 1862-Jan. 2,**
                                                   1863
North: William Rosecrans   South: Braxton Bragg
Vicksburg Campaign . . . . Mississippi . . . . **March 29-July 4, 1863**
North: Ulysses S. Grant   South: John Pemberton
Chancellorsville . . . . Virginia . . . . **May 2-4, 1863**
North: Joseph Hooker   South: Robert E. Lee
Gettysburg . . . . Pennsylvania . . . . **July 1-3, 1863**
North: George Meade   South: Robert E. Lee
Chickamauga . . . . Georgia . . . . **Sept. 19-20, 1863**
North: William Rosecrans   South: Braxton Bragg
Battles around Chattanooga . . . . Tenn.-Georgia   **Nov. 23-27, 1863**
North: George Thomas and   South: Braxton Bragg
   Ulysses S. Grant
The Wilderness . . . . Virginia . . . . **May 5-7, 1864**
North: George G. Meade and   South: Robert E. Lee
   Ulysses S. Grant
Sherman's March/
Atlanta Campaign . . . . Georgia . . . . **May 5-Sept. 2, 1864**
North: William Tecumseh Sherman   South: Joseph E. Johnston and
                                           John B. Hood
Spotsylvania (Court House) . . . . Virginia . . . . **May 8-12, 1864**
North: George G. Meade and   South: Robert E. Lee
   Ulysses S. Grant
Cold Harbor . . . . Virginia . . . . **June 1-3, 1864**
North: George G. Meade and   South: Robert E. Lee
   Ulysses S. Grant
Petersburg Campaign . . . . Virginia . . . . **June 15, 1864-**
                                                   Apr. 2, 1865
North: George G. Meade and   South: Robert E. Lee
   Ulysses S. Grant
Kennesaw Mountain . . . . Georgia . . . . **June 27, 1864**
North: William Tecumseh Sherman   South: Joseph E. Johnston
Mobile Bay . . . . Alabama . . . . **August 5, 1864**
North: David Farragut   South: Franklin Buchanan
Franklin . . . . Tennessee . . . . **November 30, 1864**
North: John Schofield   South: John B. Hood
Nashville . . . . Tennessee . . . . **December 15-16, 1864**
North: George Thomas   South: John B. Hood

AMERICAN HISTORICAL PERSONAGES AND THEIR NICKNAMES

William Allen. . . . . Earthquake Allen, Petticoat Allen, Ohio Gong

John Jacob Astor . . . . Father of Oregon, Richest Man in America

John James F. Audubon . . . . . American Woodman

Stephen Fuller Austin . . . . Father of Texas

George Bancroft . . . . Brahmin Rebel, Father of American History, G.B.

P.G.T. Beauregard . . . . Hero of Fort Sumter, Old Alphabet, Old Bore, Old Bory

Henry Louis Benning . . . . Old Rock

Thomas Hart Benton . . . . Gold Bug, Gold Humbug, Old Bullion, Old Humbug, Old Roman

Nicholas Biddle. . . . . Czar Nicholas I, Emperor Nick of the Bribery Bank

John Wilkes Booth . . . . Actor Turned Assassin, South's Avenging Angel

John C. Breckinridge . . . . Beau Sabreur Among Statesmen

Preston Smith Brooks . . . . Bully Brooks

John Brown . . . . God's Angry Man, Martyr Hero, Old Brown of Osawatomie, Old Osawatomie, Osawatomie Brown

Benjamin Franklin Butler . . . . The Beast, Beast Ben, Beast Butler, Bluebeard of New Orleans, Old Cockeye, Silver Spoon, Spoon Butler

John C. Calhoun . . . . Eagle Orator of South Carolina, Father of States' Rights, Great Nullifier, Napoleon of Slavery, Young Hercules

General Lewis Cass . . . . American Minister at Paris, Father of the Old North West, Father of Popular Sovereignty, Great Father at Detroit, Northern Man with Southern Principles

Joshua L. Chamberlain . . . . . . Hero of Little Round Top

Benjamin F. Cheatham . . . . . . Bulldog, Ney of the Confederacy, Old Frank

Henry Clay . . . . Apostle of Liberty, Cock of Kentucky, Corrupt Bargainer, Father of National Road, Father of the Protective Policy, Great Commoner, Great Compromiser, Great Pacificator, Harry of the West, Judas of the West, Millboy of the Slashes, Mr. Whig, Old Chief, President-Maker, Sage of Ashland, Same Old Coon, Second Washington, War Hawk

Tom Corwin . . . . Black Tom, Wagon Boy

William Price Craighill. . . . . . . Father of Our Modern Fortifications

Sam Davis . . . . Boy-hero of the Confederacy, Nathan Hale of the South

Varina A.J. Davis . . . . Daughter of the Confederacy

Dorothea Lynde Dix. . . . . Heaven-sent angel of Mercy and of Prison Reform

Stephen Arnold Douglas . . . . . Little Giant, Steam Engine in Breeches, Traitor to the South

Neal S. Dow . . . . Colonel Dow, Father of Prohibition, Father of the Maine Law, Moral Columbus, Napoleon of Temperance, Sublime Fanatic

Jubal Anderson Early . . . . Crackers, Old Jube, Old Jubilee

Margaret (Peggy) O'Neill
(Mrs. John Eaton) . . . . Bellona, Pothouse Peggy, Gorgeous Hussy

David Glasgow Farragut . . . . . Hero of Mobile Bay, Old Salamander

John Charles Frémont. . . . . . . Gray Mustang, Pathfinder, Pathfinder of the West

William Lloyd Garrison . . . . . . Father of Abolitionism, Massachusetts Madman, Old Bachelor

Francis Granger . . . . Silver Gray

Horace Greeley. . . . . Ghost, Old White Hat, Prince of Journalists, Sage of Chappaqua

Peter Hagner . . . . Watch-dog of the Treasury

Edward Everett Hale . . . . Man Without a Country

Sarah Joseph Hale . . . . Mother of Thanksgiving

Henry Halleck. . . . . Old Brains

Cornelia Hancock . . . . Battlefield Angel

John Bell Hoou . . . . Butcher Hood
Joseph Hooker . . . . Fighting Joe Hooker
Samuel Houston . . . . Father of Texas, the Raven
Samuel Gridley Howe . . . . Lafayette of the Greek Revolution, S.G.H.
Rachel Donelson Jackson . . . . Aunt Rachel, Bonny Brown Wife
Thomas Jonathan Jackson . . . Blue Light Elder, Fool Tom Jackson, Immovable Stonewall, Invincible Stonewall, Old Tom Jackson, Stonewall, Sword of the Confederacy
Robert Edward Lee . . . . Gentle General, Grey General, King of Spades, Marse Robert, Old Ace of Spades, Old Spades Lee, Uncle Robert
Jenny Lind . . . . Swedish Nightingale
James Longstreet . . . . Bulldog, Lee's Old Warhorse, Old Pete, Pete, War Horse of the Confederacy
Elijah Parish Lovejoy . . . . Martyr Abolitionist
Benjamin Lundy . . . . Peter-the-Hermit of the Abolitionist Movement
George Brinton McClellan . . . . General of the Mackerel Brigade, Hero of West Virginia, Little Corporal, Little Corporal of Unfought Fields, Little Mac, Little Mac the Young Napoleon, Little Napoleon, Mac the Unready, Tardy George
Kenneth Mackenzie . . . . King of the Missouri, Emperor Mackenzie, Emperor of the West
Dorothy P.T. Madison . . . . Dolley, Dowager, Queen Dowager, Nation's Hostess, Quaker Dolley, Queen Dolley
John Bankhead Magruder . . . Prince John
John Marshall . . . . Ablest Constitutionalist, Greatest American Jurist, Legal Interpreter of the Constitution, Moulding Father of the Constitution, Silver Heels
George Gordon Meade . . . . . . Four-Eyed George
Lucretia Mott . . . . Advance Agent of Emancipation, Flower of Quakerism, Invincible Warrior in Righteous Causes, Sweet-Spirited Advocate of Justice, Love and Humanity
John Pelham . . . . Boy Major, Gallant Pelham
Matthew Calbraith Perry . . . . . Great Commodore, Old Bruin
Giddeon Pillow . . . . Polk's Spy
Benjamin Mayberry Prentiss . . Hero of the Hornet's Nest
John Randolph
(of Roanoke) . . . . Jack the Giant-Killer, Little David, Man with the Sling, Political Meteor, Sage of Roanoke
Santa Anna . . . . the Liberator, Napoleon of the West
Winfield Scott . . . . Hero of Chippewa, Marshall Tureen, Old Fuss and Feathers
William Henry Seward . . . . . . Higher Law, Sage of Auburn
Philip Sheridan . . . . Jack of Clubs, Little Phil
William Tecumseh Sherman . . Great Marcher, Mad Tom, Old Billy, Old Tecumseh, Sherman the Brute, Uncle Billy
Gilmore Simms . . . . Cooper of the South, Southern Cooper, W.G.S.
Joseph Smith . . . . Father of the Mormons
Alexander H. Stephens . . . . . . Dwarf Statesman, Little Aleck, Little Wizard
Thaddeus Stevens . . . . American Pitt, Arch Priest of Anti-Masonry, Chief Old Woman, Great American Commoner, Old Commoner
Charles Stewart . . . . Old Ironsides
Harriet Beecher Stowe . . . . . . Crusader in Crinoline, That Vile Wretch in Crinoline, Victorian Cinderella
James Ewell Brown Stuart . . . Beauty, Beauty Stuart, Bible-Class Man, Eyes of the Army, Jeb, Knight of the Golden Spurs, Old Jeb, Plumed Knight of the Confederacy, Prince Rupert of the Confederacy
Roger Brooke Taney . . . . King Coody

George Thomas............Lion-Hearted Thomas, Old Pap Safety, Old Reliable Pap, Rock of Chickamauga, Uncle George
Mary Todd Lincoln.........She-Wolf
Harriet Tubman...........Moses, Negro Moses
Denmark Vesey...........Black John Brown, Télémaque Vesey
William Walker............Gray-eyed Man of Destiny, Honey, Missy
Daniel Webster............All Eyes, Benedict Arnold, Black Dan, Black Giant, Defender of the Constitution, Defender of the Union, Eagle, Eagle of the East, Expounder of the Constitution, Expounding Father of the Constitution, Fallen Star, God-like Daniel, Great Interpreter, Great Stone Face, Judas, Illustrious Defender, Immortal Webster, Indian Dan, Little Black Dan, Massachusetts Giant, Massachusetts Thunderer, Modern Sisyphus, New England Cicero, New Hampshire Demosthenes, Old Titanic, Earth-son, Pillar of the Constitution, Union-Territorial Defaulter, Upholder of the Constitution, Voice of New England, Whig Gulliver
Mason Weems.............Parson
Brigham Young...........Mormon Moses

GENERAL NICKNAMES AND CLAIMS TO FAME

Period from 1817 to 1825 during which
James Monroe was President of the U.S...Era of Good Feelings (coined by Benjamin Russell, editor of the Boston *Columbian Centeniel*, in 1817)
Erie Canal........................Clinton's Ditch
Second Bank of the United States.......Hydra of Corruption, Moneyed Monster, the Monster
Mississippi River...................Nile of America
1824 Protective Tariff and nationwide economic improvements proposed by
Henry Clay........................American System
Columbus, Georgia.................South's Oldest Industrial City (founded in 1827; planned in 1828)
Tariff of 1828.....................Black Tariff, Tariff of Abominations
Banknotes........................Old Nick's (Nicholas Biddle) Money
Paper currency without specie backing...........................Greenbacks
Currency based on speculator's notes............................Land-office money
B&O Locomotive...................Iron Horse, Iron Monster, Tom Thumb
Iron tramp steamers.................Teakettles
Andrew Jackson's informal advisers.....Kitchen Cabinet
Powerful closed political party meetings..........................King Caucuses
Forced march of the Indian tribes from Georgia in 1833.................Trail of Tears, Trail Where They Cried
Tobacco chewing and spitting..........That salivary propensity
Gonzales, Texas....................The Lexington of Texas (On Oct. 2, 1835, the first shots fired there against Mexico)
San Antonio, Texas..................The Alamo City (March 6, 1837)
John C. Calhoun, Henry Clay, and Daniel Webster.....................Great Triumvirate, Immortal Trio
Supporters of the original abolitionists........................Garrisonians
Democratic Party members of the

Equal Rights faction - 1835 - opposed
to the regular party organizations . . . . Locofocos
Jackson's state banks in 1836 . . . . Pet banks
United States Flag . . . . Old Glory
Traveling frontier preachers. . . . . Circuit riders
The Alamo . . . . Shrine of Texas Liberty
Theatre . . . . the Devil's Chapel (according to Puritanical minds)
Lynching . . . . Necktie parties
Women who kept their maiden names . . . . Lucy Stoners
Whig minority that supported
Tyler in 1841 . . . . Corporal's Guard
2 antislavery factions of the Democratic
Party in New York in the 1840's . . . . Barnburners and Hunkers
California . . . . Golden State (gold discovered there in 1848)
Bowie knife . . . . Genuwine Arkansas Toothpick
Mexicans . . . . Greasers (according to the Americans)
Texans and other Americans . . . . Bullies of the North, Gringos, Yanquis (according to the Mexicans)
Hard cider . . . . Poor Westerner's Champagne
Mexican War - 1846 to 1848 . . . . Jimmy Polk's War, Mr. Polk's War
U.S. Infantrymen in Mexican War . . . . Adobies (later "dobies" & then "doughboys")
Mexican Cadets who died at the
Battle of Chapultepec defending the
Mexican Military College . . . . *Los Niños*
Gold prospectors in California
in 1849 . . . . Argonauts, 49ers, Sourdoughs
Southern laws that limited
Negro freedom . . . . Jim Crow laws
"Battle Hymn of the Republic" . . . . *Marseillaise* of the Unemotional Yankee
Civil strife in Kansas in the 1850's . . . . Bleeding Kansas
Sharps rifles used in Kansas in the
1850's by the anti-slavery emigrants. . . . . Beecher's Bibles
Southern political leaders with radical
views on slavery and secession . . . . Fire-eaters (pro-slavery prior to the Civil War)
Clipper ship . . . . Most-perfect full-rigged sailing vessel ever conceived by man
Rule by majorities . . . . King Numbers
Secret network for helping fugitive
slaves . . . . Underground Railroad
Laws that protected runaway slaves . . . . . Personal liberty laws
Plantation mansion . . . . The Big House
Excessive cultivation of the land . . . . Land butchery
"Po" (poor) whites . . . . Clay-eaters, Crackers, Hillbillies, Piney wood people, Sand hillers, White trash
Slaves . . . . Human cattle
Trappers . . . . Mountain men
Triple-decked steamboat . . . . Floating palace
Great Plains (as erroneously
described) . . . . Great American Desert
White House . . . . Crown of Thorns (according to James Buchanan 1857-1861)
Lincoln-Douglas debates in 1858 . . . . Battle of the Giants
California settlers and miners . . . . Gold diggers, gold hunters
Elite Southern owners of cotton farms
prior to the Civil War . . . . Cotton Snobs

Northern Whigs unopposed to
slavery............................. Cotton Whigs
Northerners with Southern principles
who favored slavery................. Doughfaces
Slavery .... That peculiar (i.e., special) institution
                                    (according to slaveowners)
Plantation owner .... Massa (according to a Negro slave)
Oil well dug by Edwin L. Drake near
Titusville, Pennsylvania.............. Drake's Folly (he struck oil in 1859)
Oil .... Black gold
Harriet Beecher Stowe............... Little lady who made the big war
                                    (according to Abraham Lincoln)
Gatling machine guns .... Coffee grinders
Irish workers...................... Paddies
Gettysburg, Pennsylvania .... Battlefield City (July 1-3, 1863)
Tented railroad encampments that
followed railroad construction .... Hell-on-wheels
Pullman sleeping cars .... Gorgeous traveling hotels, Wheeled torture
                                    chambers
Camels .... Ships of the desert
Civil War .... The Revolution, Second War of
                                    Independence, War Between the North and
                                    the South, War Between the States, War
                                    of Secession, War of Independence, War
                                    of the Rebellion
Dummy wooden guns (cannons) .... Quaker guns (cannons)
Monitor .... (Yankee) Cheesebox on a Raft, Tin Can on
                                    a Shingle
Bayonets......................... Candlesticks
Land mines .... Infernal machines (i.e., booby traps)
Floating mines..................... Torpedoes
Northern Civil War soldier(s) .... Billy Yank, Boys in Blue, Blue Bellies,
                                    Yankees
Southern Civil War soldier(s).......... Boys in Gray, Graycoats, Graybacks,
                                    Johnny Reb
Anti-war Civil War Democrats in the
North............................. Copperheads
Monetary rewards for enlisting in
army .... Bounties
Enlistees for money who then deserted
and repeated the process............. Bounty-jumpers
Burned railroad rails .... Jeff Davis neckties, Iron donuts,
                                    Sherman's hair pins
Stragglers who looted while
trailing Sherman's army .... Sherman's bummers
Gen. Burnside's Ninth Corps of the
Army of the Potomac .... Burnside's Peripatetic Geography Class
Robert E. Lee's soldiers.............. Dogs of War
Stonewall Jackson's infantrymen .... Foot Cavalry
Ships with protective armor made of
iron plating and as effective as if
made of tin....................... Tin clads
Union blockade of Southern ports .... Lincoln's Great Snake
Civil War Catholic Sisters serving as
nurses........................... Angels of the Battlefield
Northern deserters to the
Southern army..................... Galvanized Yankees
New recruits during the Civil
War .... Baby Boys, Mamma's Pets

Ulysses S. Grant, Philip Sheridan,
and William T. Sherman. . . . . The Immortal Three
Independent Civil War marauders . . . . Border ruffians, Bushwackers
Southern scythe blades used
as knives. . . . . Yankee Slayers
Soldiers from Tennessee . . . . Butternuts
Northern soldiers who enlisted
for $300. . . . . Three-hundred-dollar-men
Cadets at Virginia Military Academy
at Lexington, Va., during the
Civil War . . . . Seed-corn of the Confederacy
Robert E. Lee's and all other
Confederate soldiers in rags upon
returning home after the Civil War . . . . Lee's Ragamuffins

PLACES AND THEIR NICKNAMES

United States. . . . . Brother Jonathan/Mother Lode of
Democracy
Great Britain . . . . John Bull/Mistress of the Seas
New Orleans, Louisiana. . . . . Queen of the South
Cincinnati, Ohio. Porkopolis of the West
Boston, Massachusetts . . . . Hub of the Universe
Ireland. . . . . Land of Famine (1846)
United States. . . . . Colossus of the North (according to Latin
and South Americans)
Tennessee. . . . . Volunteer State (30,000 enlisted for the
Mexican War, 1846-1848)
Camargo, Mexico. . . . . Yawning Graveyard
Texas. . . . . Lone Star State
Charleston, South Carolina . . . . Cradle of Secession
South Carolina. . . . . Hell-hole of Secession
Military prison at Andersonville,
Georgia . . . . Hell upon Earth
Pea Ridge (March 7-8, 1862) . . . . Gettysburg of the West
Violent section of the Shiloh battlefield
(May 5, 1862) . . . . Hornet's Nest
2nd Battle of Bull Run (August 29-
30, 1862) . . . . Battle of the Rocks
Deadly section of the Antietam
battlefield (Sept. 17, 1862) . . . . Dead Man's Corner
Sunken road at Antietam, Maryland
(September 17, 1862). . . . . Bloody Lane
Battle at Marye's Heights,
Fredericksburg, Va. (Dec. 13, 1862) . . . . Burnside's Slaughter Pen
Section at Vicksburg where many
Federals died (March-July, 1863) . . . . Logan's Slaughter Pen
Battle of Gettysburg, Pa. (June 28-
July 4, 1863). . . . . High-water Mark of the Confederacy
Battle of Lookout Mountain, Tenn.
(November 24, 1863) . . . . Battle Above the Clouds
Union soldiers at Chattanooga that
lived mainly on crackers . . . . Cracker Line
Wilderness, Va. (May 5-7, 1864) . . . . Bloody Angle, Hell's Half Acre
Section of battlefield at Spottsylvania
(May 12, 1864) . . . . Bloody Angle, Hell's Half Acre
Battle of Petersburg, Va. (July 30 1864) . . Battle of the Crater and the Petersburg
Mine Assault
Shenandoah Valley, Va. . . . . Valley of Humiliation (according to the
Union soldiers)
Danville, Virginia . . . . Last Capital of the Confederacy

QUESTIONS AND ANSWERS

1. What 3 amendments to the U.S. Constitution were enacted as a result of the Civil War between the years 1865 and 1870?

ANSWER: **The 13th — Abolition of Slavery on December 18, 1865; the 14th — Civil Rights on July 29, 1868; and the 15th — Black Suffrage on February 3, 1870.**

2. What was the name for the renegade white Republican Southerners who collaborated with Northerners during the Reconstruction period? And what was the name for the Northerners who exploited poor Southerners? Explain the origin of these terms.

ANSWER: **Scalawags/Carpetbaggers/Scalawags came possibly from the undersized, useless pony bred on Scalloway, a Shetland Island; carpetbagger comes from the habit these people had of carrying all their possessions in a large cheap bag made of carpet material.**

3. Name the agency created by Congress on March 3, 1865, that was intended to provide for, protect, and educate the newly emancipated Negroes. Against what "Codes" enacted by Southern state legislatures could this agency have offset? Explain these "Codes."

ANSWER: **The Freedmen's Bureau/"Black Codes"/The "Codes" were a body of vagrancy and apprenticeship laws which kept the Negro economically and politically subservient.**

4. What were the dates of the famous "swing around the circle" or "nonpolitical" speeches in 1866? What U.S. President made these speeches en route to what city? What was the topic of discussion? What was the result?

ANSWER: **August 28 to September 15, 1866/President Andrew Johnson on the way to Chicago/The President was opposed to the Radical Congress over Southern Reconstruction and the 14th Amendment/Johnson lost as the Radicals gained more than two-thirds majority in both houses of Congress in the fall of 1866.**

5. The first Reconstruction Act of March 2, 1867, established 5 military districts in the South. What were these 5 districts and who was the Union general in charge of each one who was to prepare them for readmission as states?

ANSWER: **I) Virginia — General John M. Schofield, II) North and South Carolina — General Daniel E. Sickles, III) Alabama, Georgia, and Florida — General John Pope, IV) Arkansas and Mississippi — General E.O.C. Ord, and V) Texas and Louisiana — General Philip H. Sheridan. (Tennessee was not included in the federal supervision).**

6. Who said each of the following quotes?

   a) "Let us have peace"
   b) "The public be damned"
   c) "Genius is one percent inspiration and ninety-nine percent perspiration"
   d) "I will not accept if nominated and will not serve if elected"
   e) "You may fire when you are ready, Gridley"
   f) "It has been a splendid little war"
   g) "Speak softly and carry a big stick"
   h) "We stand at Armageddon, and we battle for the Lord"
   i) "It must be peace without victory" and "The world must be made safe for democracy"
   j) "Lafayette, we are here"

ANSWER: **a) Ulysses S. Grant b) William H. Vanderbilt c) Thomas Alva Edison d) William Tecumseh Sherman e) George Dewey f) John Hay g) Theodore Roosevelt h) Theodore Roosevelt i) Woodrow Wilson j) Charles E. Stanton.**

7. Who purchased Alaska for the United States? Who was the Russian leader at the time? What was the date of the purchase? What time of day did it occur? How much did it cost? What nicknames were given to the purchase?

ANSWER: **Secretary of State William H. Seward/Czar Alexander II/March 30, 1867/ Papers signed at 4:00 a.m./$7,200,000/"Seward's Icebox," "Seward's Polar Bear Garden," and "Seward's Folly."**

8. Name the first 2 states to be readmitted to the Union. What 5 states were all readmitted on June 25, 1868 (Georgia was readmitted but expelled in 1869 for refusing to ratify Amendment 15 of the U.S. Constitution)? Give the names of the last 4 states readmitted in 1870.

ANSWER: Tennessee (July 24, 1866) and Arkansas (June 22, 1868)/North Carolina, Alabama, Florida, Louisiana, and South Carolina/Virginia (Jan. 27), Mississippi (Feb. 23), Texas (Mar. 30), and Georgia (July 15).

9. Who was the only U.S. President ever impeached? What Act passed by Congress prevented him from removing his appointees without Senate approval? Whom did the President dismiss from office? What year was the impeachment trial? What does the vote of 35 to 19 against the President indicate? Whose vote was considered to be the deciding one? What nickname was given to him? Who would have become President?

ANSWER: Andrew Johnson/The Tenure of Office Act/Secretary of War Edwin M. Stanton/1868/It was one short of the required two-thirds needed for dismissal/U.S. Senator from Kansas, Edmund G. Ross/''the man who saved a President''/The president *pro tem* of the Senate, Ben Wade of Ohio.

10. What 2 railroad companies were authorized by Congress in July, 1862, to build a line from Nebraska to California? What were the beginning and ending dates of construction? Where did the 2 railroads meet and what was the event called? What telegraph message was sent?

ANSWER: The Union Pacific R.R. (from Omaha, Nebraska) and the Central Pacific R.R. (from Sacramento, California)/January 8, 1863, and May 10, 1869/ They met at Promontory Point, Utah (near Ogden)/The event was called the ''wedding of the rails'' as a silver sledge drove a golden spike into the adjoining tracks. The Union Pacific had laid 1086 miles and the Central Pacific 689 miles of track/The message was: ''The last rail is laid! The last spike driven! The Pacific Railroad is completed.''

11. There were 4 other transcontinental railroads built in the U.S. during the 19th century. Name them and give their beginning and ending points.

ANSWER: 1) Northern Pacific: Ashland, Wisconsin, to Portland, Oregon
      2) Atchison, Topeka, and Sante Fe: Kansas City, Kansas, to Deming, New Mexico (later from Chicago to San Francisco on its own lines)
      3) Southern Pacific: New Orleans, Louisiana, to San Francisco, California
      4) Great Northern: St. Paul, Minnesota, to Seattle, Washington.

12. What woman is identified by each of the following nicknames?

a) Mother of the Red Cross   f) Advocate of Hatchetation
b) Woman the Germans Shot   g) Little Sure Shot
c) Heaven-sent Angel of Mercy and of   h) Mother of Muckrakers
    Prison Reform   i) First Lady of the World
d) Lemonade Lucy   j) Terrible Siren
e) Typhoid Mary

ANSWER: a) Clara Barton b) Miss Edith Cavell (English) c) Dorothea Lynde Dix d) Lucy Webb Hayes e) Mary Mallon f) Carrie Nation g) Annie Oakley H) Ida Minerva Tarbell i) Edith Boling Wilson j) Victoria Claflin Woodhull.

13. Who were the 3 directors of the Erie Railroad involved in 1867 in the ''Erie Ring''? What New York Central Railroad magnate tried to acquire the Erie Railroad, and what was unloaded on him by the Erie directors? Who was Edward Stokes?

ANSWER: Jay Gould, James Fisk, and Daniel Drew/Commodore Cornelius Vanderbilt bought a lot of illegal stock printed by Gould and Fisk. Fisk said: ''If this printing press don't break down, I'll be damned if I don't give the old hog all he wants of Erie!''/Edward Stokes, a rival lover, shot and killed Jim Fisk (the Erie line went bankrupt in 1875).

14. Give the year, city, and state in which the Ku Klux Klan was founded. Who was the first Grand Wizard? What is the etymological meaning of the name? Give the names of at least 2 other secret societies that were founded in the U.S. about the same time.

ANSWER: 1866 at Pulaski, Tennessee/Nathan Bedford Forrest/From the Greek *kuklos,* a circle/Knights of the White Camellia, White League, Boys of '76, Pale Faces, and Invisible League, Circle, or Empire.

15. Who was the leader of the Tweed Ring? Of what organization was he the boss?

What reporter of what paper started an exposé, and what cartoonist of what publication helped destroy these crooked officials? What New York Attorney General, later Governor of the state, helped overthrow this ring?

ANSWER: **William M. Tweed/Tammany Hall/George Jones of the New York** *Times* **and Thomas Nast of** *Harper's Weekly*/**Samuel J. Tilden.**

16. After whom was The Tammany Society named? What was the symbol of this Society? What cartoonist created not only the symbol of the Tammany Society but also those of the Republican and Democratic Parties?

ANSWER: **The Tammany Society was named after the Delaware Indian leader, Chief Tammany (or possibly after, Tamanend)/The tiger, taken from a tiger's head painted on the engine of an old fire company/Thomas Nast created or popularized not only the Tammany tiger but also the Democratic donkey and the Republican elephant.**

17. List at least 3 of the scandals during the Grant administration 1869-1877 and describe them briefly.

ANSWER: **1) Crédit Mobilier — a construction company for the Union Pacific railroad which fraudulently received money — Crédit Mobilier stock was ''sold'' (given) to Congressmen to block an investigation.**

    2) Congress's ''Salary Grab'' — Congressmen doubled their salary and received two years of retroactive pay as well.

    3) J.D. Sanborn's collections — Sanborn was hired by the Secretary of Treasury to collect overdue taxes. He kept half as a commission for himself and for those who helped him get the position.

    4) Whiskey Ring — Treasury officials and distillers were defrauding the government of taxes on whiskey by filing false reports.

    5) Belknap Scandal — Secretary of War, William W. Belknap, had accepted bribes for the sale of trading-post positions in Indian territories.

18. Give the location with which the following battles or incidents are identified.

a) Rosebud River

b) Little Big Horn

c) Haymarket Square Riots

d) Wounded Knee

e) *Maine*

f) *Lusitania*

g) The Pershing Expedition

h) Belleau-Wood

i) Second Battle of the Marne

j) Meuse-Argonne Offensive

ANSWER: **a) Montana Territory b) Montana Territory c) Chicago, Illinois d) South Dakota e) Havana Harbor, Cuba f) Irish coast g) Mexico h) France i) France j) France.**

19. In what year did the Centennial Exposition take place and in what city? What was the name of the great steam engine there and in what hall was it located?

ANSWER: **1876 in Philadelphia/Corliss steam engine in Machinery Hall.**

20. Name the only 4 territories/states to grant women the right to vote in the 19th century.

ANSWER: **Wyoming Territory (1869), Utah Territory (1870), Colorado (1893), and Idaho (1896).**

21. What election was called the ''Stolen Election'' and why? Name the 3 Southern states where 19 votes were in doubt (Oregon had one vote). What nicknames were given to the President because of this election?

ANSWER: **The election of 1876 because Samuel Jones Tilden had 4,300,000 popular votes and 184 electoral ones (185 were needed to win) to 4,036,000 and 165 popular and electoral votes for Rutherford B. Hayes but lost the election because the votes in the Southern states and the one in Oregon were switched to Hayes due to bribery, forgery, and perjury and an 8 to 7 vote of the Electoral Commission. Hayes won 185 to 184/Louisiana, South Carolina, and Florida/He was nicknamed ''Old 8 to 7'' and ''His Fraudulency.''**

22. From what 2 Southern states did President Hayes withdraw the last federal troops after the Civil War? With what result?

ANSWER: **South Carolina (April 10, 1877) and Louisiana (April 24, 1877)/The South became solidly Democratic for the next 50 years.**

23. Who was the second President of the United States to be assassinated? What was

the date? Where did it happen? Who was responsible? Who became President?

ANSWER: **James A. Garfield/July 2, 1881, and he died on September 19/At a Washington railroad station/Charles J. Guiteau, who was hanged on June 30, 1882/Chester A. Arthur.**

24. What American woman organized the American Red Cross in 1881? What Swiss philanthropist founded the International Red Cross in 1864?

ANSWER: **Clara Barton/Jean Henri Dunant (he set the process in motion).**

25. Name the first 3 U.S. warships in the "New Navy" of steel ships that were completed in 1887. What were these ships nicknamed?

ANSWER: **The *Chicago*, the *Boston*, and the *Atlanta* (and the despatch boat the *Dolphin*)/The "White Squadron."**

26. Who were the 2 candidates in the 1884 presidential election? What letters and what phrase containing 3 R's were instrumental in the defeat of the Republican candidate? Briefly explain why these incidents hurt the candidate.

ANSWER: **Grover Cleveland and James G. Blaine/The "Mulligan letters" of 1876 referred to Blaine's crooked deals as Speaker of the House, and "Rum, Romanism, and Rebellion" was the phrase spoken by Dr. Samuel Burchard, a Republican clergyman, accusing the Democratic Party of these abuses. Blaine did not repudiate this sentiment and alienated the Catholic vote.**

27. Identify each of the following "Fathers."
    a) Father of Our Modern Navy
    b) Father of the Federal Reserve System
    c) Father of Dollar Diplomacy
    d) Father of the Suez Canal
    e) Father of Civil Service Reform
    f) Father of the 18th Amendment
    g) Father of the Volstead Act

ANSWER: **a) William Eaton Chandler b) Carter Glass c) Philander Chase Knox d) Ferdinand de Lesseps e) George Hunt Pendleton f) Morris Sheppard g) Andrew J. Volstead.**

28. What brief song was directed against Grover Cleveland during the campaign (related to his possible fathering of an illegitimate child in his younger days with Maria Halpin)?

ANSWER: **Ma! Ma! Where's my pa?**
Gone to the White House. Ha! Ha! Ha!

29. Who were the 4 pallbearers, 2 Southern and 2 Northern, for the funeral of President Ulysses S. Grant in July, 1885?

ANSWER: **Generals Joe Johnston and Simon B. Buckner of the South, and Generals William T. Sherman and Philip Sheridan of the North.**

30. Name the 4 anarchists who were hanged for the Haymarket Square riot-massacre of May 4, 1886.

ANSWER: **George Engel, Adolph Fischer, and August Spies (all German-born), and Albert Richard Parsons (American-born).**

31. In what year was the American Federation of Labor formed, and who was the first president? What organization preceded this one that was formed in 1881?

ANSWER: **1886/Samuel Gompers/Federation of Organized Trade and Labor Unions of the United States and Canada.**

32. What Act was the first major attempt by Congress to regulate private business for society's benefit? In what year was it enacted, and against whom was it directed? In what year was the Sherman Antitrust Act enacted?

ANSWER: **Interstate Commerce Act/1887/Against the railroads/1890.**

33. Name the 6 states admitted to the Union in 1889-1890 by a Republican Congress seeking more Republican electoral and Congressional votes.

ANSWER: **North Dakota (Nov. 2, 1889), South Dakota (Nov. 2, 1889), Montana (Nov. 8, 1889), Washington (Nov. 11, 1889), Idaho (July 3, 1890), and Wyoming (July 10, 1890).**

34. Name the 3 countries involved in the 3-way protectorate of Samoa as resolved by the Berlin Conference of 1889. What 2 countries were still involved in 1889?

ANSWER: United States, Germany, and Great Britain/Germany and the United States.

35. What object 250 feet high was invented for the 1893 World's Fair in Chicago? What "village" dancers at the Fair were more popular than this object?

ANSWER: The Ferris' Wheel (invented by George Washington Gale Ferris)/The "Egyptian Village" dancers.

36. Identify or explain what is meant by each of the following nicknames.
   a) Seward's Icebox
   b) Literary piano
   c) Old Reliable
   d) Stolen Election
   e) Hog Butcher of the World
   f) Dead man's hand
   g) Gun that Won the West
   h) Liberty Cabbage
   i) Big Bertha
   j) Dreadnaught

ANSWER: a) Alaska — purchased in 1867 for the U.S. by William Seward b) Christopher Sholes's typewriter (1867) c) Sharps Buffalo Rifle d) 1876 Election e) Chicago, Illinois f) "Wild Bill" Hickok's hand of aces and eights when he was shot in 1876 g) Colt revolver h) Sauerkraut in WWI i) German long-range gun during WWI j) Large heavy battleship.

37. Whose "Army" marched on Washington in May, 1894? What group of people were the "soldiers"? What did this "Army" seek?

ANSWER: "General" Jacob S. Coxey's "Army"/The unemployed/A public works relief program.

38. In what year was Hawaii annexed to the United States? Who was in charge of the islands? What happened to Queen Liliuokalani?

ANSWER: July 7, 1898 (sovereignty was formally transferred on August 12, 1898)/ The President of the Republic was Sanford P. Dole/The Queen had been overthrown in 1893 by a group of Americans.

39. What incident was the immediate cause of the Spanish-American War of 1898? On what date was this war formally declared? What were the names of the 3 major battles of this war?

ANSWER: The sinking of the *Maine* on February 15, 1898 /April 25, 1898/Battle of Manila Bay on May 1 led by Commodore George Dewey; Battles of El Caney and San Juan Hill on July 1 led by General William Shafter; and the Battle of Santiago Bay on July 3 by Rear Admiral William T. Sampson and Commodore Winfield S. Schley.

40. What member of McKinley's cabinet said: "McKinley has no more backbone than a chocolate éclair"? What was the issue? What did this Secretary want to do, and what did McKinley do?

ANSWER: Secretary of War Theodore Roosevelt/The sinking of the *Maine*/ Roosevelt wanted an ultimatum sent to Spain immediately after the sinking/ McKinley asked Congress to declare war about 2 months later.

41. On what day was an armistice signed that ended the Spanish-American War, and on what day and where was a peace treaty concluded?

ANSWER: August 12, 1898/December 10, 1898/Paris (Treaty of Paris).

42. What role did the "Yellow Press" play in the Spanish-American War? Who were the 2 editors of "Yellow Journalism"? Explain the meaning and the origin of the phrase "Yellow Press/Journalism."

ANSWER: The press incited resentment against Spain by reporting on Spanish atrocities — real or imagined. Hearst supposedly told a newspaper artist, "You furnish the pictures and I'll furnish the war."/William Randolph Hearst of the New York *Journal* and Joseph Pulitzer of the New York *World*/The phrase means the use of cheaply sensational or distorted newspaper stories to attract readers and had its origin in 1895 in the "Yellow Kid" comic strip in the New York *World* as yellow ink was used for the first time in order to attract readers' attention.

43. What Secretary of State in what year in what U.S. President's Cabinet instituted an "Open Door" policy? What was the meaning of this policy, and toward which country was this directed?

ANSWER: John Hay in 1899 in McKinley's Cabinet/All the great trading powers would have equal trading rights with the Chinese Government.

44. Who killed President McKinley? Where? How? What happened to the assassin?

ANSWER: Leon Czolgosz/September 6, 1901, in the Temple of Music at the Pan-American Exposition in Buffalo/McKinley was shaking hands with visitors when he was shot twice in the stomach. He died on September 14, 1901/ Czolgosz was electrocuted in New York.

45. Who replaced McKinley as President? According to British author John Morley, what did he say this new President was a combination of?

ANSWER: Theodore Roosevelt/St. Paul and St. Vitus.

46. Identify each of the following men by his nickname.
   a) Financial Wizard of Hobcaw Barony   h) Jupiter of Wall Street
   b) Plumed Knight   i) Standard Oil King
   c) Boy Orator of the Platte   j) King of the Muckrakers
   d) Czar of Steel   k) Sage of Gramercy Park
   e) Mephistopheles of Wall Street   l) Boss
   f) Battling (Fighting) Bob   m) Commodore
   g) Destroyer of the League of Nations

ANSWER: a) Bernard Mannes Baruch b) James Gillespie Blaine c) William Jennings Bryan d) Andrew Carnegie e) Jay Gould f) Robert M. La Follette g) Henry Cabot Lodge h) J. Pierpont Morgan i) John Davison Rockefeller j) Joseph Lincoln Steffens k) Samuel Jones Tilden l) William Marcy Tweed m) Cornelius Vanderbilt.

47. What Amendment to Cuba's 1901 Constitution allowed U.S. intervention in Cuban affairs, permitted the sale or lease to the U.S. of 2 naval bases, and forbade changes concerning Cuban sovereignty without U.S. approval?

ANSWER: Platt Amendment (cancelled in 1934 except for the Guantanamo Bay lease).

48. What 2 men were responsible for the eradication of yellow fever from Cuba and then from the Panama Canal Zone?

ANSWER: Walter Reed and his associates proved the method of the transmission of yellow fever through a mosquito (the Washington D.C. Army medical center is named for him) and William Crawford Gorgas destroyed the breeding places of the mosquito.

49. What 2 Central American sites were being considered for an isthmian canal in 1902-1903? What was the name of the treaty of 1901 that gave the U.S. full control of the canal? What treaty was signed with Colombia (for the Panama Canal route) but was rejected by the Colombian Senate? What did the Panamanians do in the fall of 1903? What treaty did the U.S. conclude with Panama in 1903? Who was the chief engineer of the Panama Canal construction? When did the Canal open?

ANSWER: Panama and Nicaragua/Hay-Pauncefote Treaty/Hay-Herrán Treaty/They revolted and broke away from Colombian control/Hay-Bunau-Varilla Treaty/ Lt. Colonel George W. Goethals/August 15, 1914.

50. What was the Roosevelt Corollary to the Monroe Doctrine? What 3 countries had threatened to intervene forcefully in the Dominican Republic to collect debts, thus precipitating Roosevelt's new dictum?

ANSWER: That the United States would intervene in the Americas to keep peace/ Belgium, France, and Italy.

51. In what city and state was the Russo-Japanese Peace Treaty in 1905 signed? Who presided at this meeting? What did he receive for his efforts? Name the Russian Czar and the Japanese ruler at that time.

ANSWER: Portsmouth, New Hampshire/Theodore Roosevelt/The Nobel Peace Prize in 1906/Nicholas II (Russia) and Emperor Mutsuhito (Japan).

52. Identify the author of each of the following "muckraking" works.
   a) *History of the Standard Oil*   c) *The Greatest Trust in the World*
      Company   d) *The Great American Fraud*
   b) *The Shame of the Cities*   e) *The Bitter Cry of the Children*

124 Campbell's High School/College Quiz Book

f) *The Jungle*   *Government*
g) *The Struggle for Self-*   h) *Following the Color Line*

ANSWER: a) Ida M. Tarbell b) Lincoln Steffens c) Charles Edward Russell d) Samuel Hopkins Adams e) John Spargo f) Upton Sinclair g) Lincoln Steffens h) Ray Stannard Baker.

53. In what 3 years did William Jennings Bryan run for the presidency and lose?
ANSWER: 1896, 1900, and 1908 (each year as a Democrat).

54. What is "Dollar Diplomacy," and with what administration is this policy associated?
ANSWER: It was the use of American economic power supported by military and political muscle to create economic opportunities for American businessmen in the Far East and Latin America/William Howard Taft's.

55. What were the 3 parts of Woodrow Wilson's "Triple wall of privilege," and how did he combat them?
ANSWER: 1) The Tariff — Wilson appeared before Congress and got the Underwood - Simmons Tariff Bill passed in 1913.
2) Banking and currency — by the Federal Reserve Act of 1913.
3) Trusts — by the Federal Trade Commission Act of 1914 and by the Clayton Anti-Trust Act of 1914.

56. What 3 countries were called the ABC Powers? Between what 2 countries did they intervene in 1914, and what incident caused this intervention? Where was the meeting held to work out a solution?
ANSWER: Argentina, Brazil, and Chile/Between the United States and Mexico/A German ship unloaded munitions at Vera Cruz, Mexico on April 21, 1914, and the U.S. attacked the city/Niagara Falls, Ontario in 1914.

57. Give another name for the Virgin Islands, and name the country from whom the U.S. purchased these islands. In what year and for how much? What are the 3 main islands in the U.S. Virgins Islands?
ANSWER: Danish West Indies/From Denmark/In 1917 for $25,000,000/St. Croix, St. John, and St. Thomas.

58. Name the 3 hatchets of temperance leader Carrie Moore Nation. For which league was she crusading? What amendment to the U.S. Constitution was ratified on January 16, 1919? What act passed on October 28, 1919, was designed to provide the means for the enforcement of the 18th Amendment?
ANSWER: Faith, Hope, and Charity/Anti-Saloon League/18th Amendment (Prohibition)/The National Prohibition Enforcement Act (or Volstead Act).

59. Identify each of the following by his nickname.
a) Billy the Kid
b) Buffalo Bill
c) Old Yellow Hair
d) Hero of Manila Bay
e) Wild Bill
f) Black Jack
g) Ace of Aces
h) Butcher
i) Fighting Joe
j) Robin Hood of the Little Blue
ANSWER: a) William Bonney b) William Frederick Cody c) George Armstrong Custer d) George Dewey e) James Butler Hickok f) John Joseph Pershing g) Eddie Rickenbacker h) Valeriano Weyler (Sp.) i) Joseph Wheeler j) Jesse James.

60. To what incident does the phrase "the forgotten handshake" refer, and what election did it influence?
ANSWER: Charles Evans Hughes failed to shake the hand of California's favorite son, Governor Hiram W. Johnson, in 1916, when they were both staying in the same hotel/Hughes lost California by 3773 votes and the 1916 election to Woodrow Wilson.

61. What 3 U.S. states were part of the Zimmermann Note? When was it sent? From whom to whom? When did the U.S. declare war on Germany?
ANSWER: Germany offered financial support to Mexico to help reconquer Arizona, New Mexico, and Texas if Mexico entered the fight against the U.S./February 24, 1917/German Foreign Secretary Arthur Zimmermann sent it to the German minister in Mexico, Heinrich von Eckhardt/April 6, 1917.

62. What was the A.E.F., and who commanded it? In what battle in WWI did the U.S. play its first significant role? What battle was considered the turning point of the war? What battle was the first distinctively U.S. offensive? On what day in what year at what hour was the armistice signed? Where and with what French general? At what time did hostilities cease?

ANSWER: **The American Expeditionary Force by General John J. Pershing/Belleau Wood from June 6 to July 1, 1918/2nd Battle of the Marne, July 18 to August 6, 1918/Battle of St. Mihiel of September 12-16, 1918/On November 11, 1918, at 5:00 a.m./In the Forest of Compiegne with General Ferdinand Foch/At 11:00 a.m.**

63. What were the names of the "Big Four" representatives at the peace negotiations in Paris at the end of World War I? When did they meet? What treaty was signed when? Where exactly?

ANSWER: **Woodrow Wilson of the United States, Georges Clemenceau of France, David Lloyd George of England, and Vittorio Orlando of Italy/January 18, 1919/The Treaty of Versailles was signed on June 28, 1919/In the Hall of Mirrors (at Versailles).**

64. How many "points" were in Wilson's peace plan? For what League did he fight? How many "reservations" were there, and whose name was attached to them at the time of Senate approval? Who were the leading 3 "irreconcilables" to the Treaty of Versailles?

ANSWER: **Fourteen/League of Nations/14 and they were called the Lodge Reservations (after Henry Cabot Lodge)/William Borah, Hiram Johnson, and Robert La Follette.**

65. In what 5 years did Eugene V. Debs run for the presidency of the United States as the Socialist candidate and lose?

ANSWER: **1900, 1904, 1908, 1912, and 1920.**

66. With which major industry was each of the following men associated in the last half of the 19th century?

a) John D. Rockefeller
b) James J. Hill
c) Collis P. Huntington
d) Philip Armour
e) James B. Duke
f) Charles A. Pillsbury
g) Andrew Carnegie
h) J.P. Morgan
i) Cornelius Vanderbilt
j) Gustavus F. Swift

ANSWER: **a) petroleum (oil) b) railroads c) railroads d) meatpacking e) tobacco f) flour mills g) steel h) banking i) railroads j) meatpacking.**

67. Identify each of the following.
a) The first billion dollar business corporation
b) The author of *Progress and Poverty* (1879)
c) The leader in the prepared-foods business who condensed milk and founded a town in Texas
d) The outstanding Secretary of State of the Grant administration (1869-1877)
e) The 3 years between 1865 and 1920 in which economic Panics hit the country (there were Panics in 1819, 1837, and 1857)
f) The 2 men, one English and one American, who discovered independently a process by which iron could be transformed into steel
g) The author of the book *The Gospel of Wealth* (1901)
h) The author of *Looking Backward* (1888)
i) The North Carolina site where the Wright brothers made aviation history in 1903

ANSWER: **a) U.S. Steel b) Henry George c) Gail Borden d) Hamilton Fish e) 1873, 1893, and 1907 f) Henry Bessemer and William Kelly (the process is known as the Bessemer process) g) Andrew Carnegie h) Edward Bellamy i) Kitty Hawk.**

AMERICAN QUOTATIONS/SLOGANS/MOTTOES

LET US HAVE PEACE
This phrase was that of Ulysses S. Grant in his letter of acceptance on May 29, 1868, of the Republican nomination for the presidency. This four-word slogan was his major contribution to the campaign. These words are engraved on his tomb on the Hudson River.

WHAT ARE YOU GOING TO DO ABOUT IT?
These were William Marcy Tweed's defiant words to New Yorkers when they denounced him at a meeting. Tweed and the Tweed Ring were swept out of office in 1871. Thomas Nast's cartoon ''The Tammany Tiger Loose — 'What are you going to do about it?' '' was very influential in seeing that Tweed was not reelected. Tweed's complete statement was: ''As long as I count the votes, what are you going to do about it?''

LAW? WHAT DO I CARE ABOUT THE LAW? HAIN'T I GOT THE POWER?
Commodore Cornelius Vanderbilt said these words when told by lawyers that the law blocked his path. The phrase shows his disregard for government or public opinion. He is also well-known for saying: ''Can't I do what I want with my own?''

THE PUBLIC BE DAMNED!
William H. Vanderbilt, son of Cornelius Vanderbilt, made this famous statement in October, 1882. When he was asked by a news reporter why an extra-fare mail train between New York and Chicago was being discontinued without public consultation, Vanderbilt said that it was because it wasn't paying for itself despite the public benefit. The reporter then asked, ''Are you working for the public or for the stockholders?'' Vanderbilt said, ''The public be damned! I am working for my stockholders. If the public wants the train, why don't they pay for it?''

GENIUS IS ONE PERCENT INSPIRATION AND NINETY-NINE PERCENT PERSPIRATION
''The Wizard of Menlo Park,'' Thomas Alva Edison, said these words. Edison had a laboratory at Menlo Park, New Jersey, for 11 years from 1876 to 1887, when he moved his work to West Orange, New Jersey.

I AM A STALWART AND ARTHUR IS NOW PRESIDENT
President James Garfield's assassin, Charles J. Guiteau, said these words after he assassinated him on July 2, 1881.

CHET ARTHUR PRESIDENT OF THE UNITED STATES! GOOD GOD!
These were the words of an unidentified person, but they were the same words reiterated by many who were concerned about Arthur's ability to govern the United States.

I WILL NOT ACCEPT IF NOMINATED AND WILL NOT SERVE IF ELECTED
William Tecumseh Sherman's words to the Republican National Convention on June 5, 1884, as he refused to run for President of the United States.

RUM, ROMANISM, AND REBELLION
These words spelled doom for the candidacy of James G. Blaine in the presidential election of 1884 against Grover Cleveland since Blaine failed to repudiate this religious slur to Catholics. Dr. Samuel Burchard, a spokesman for a group of New York City preachers, said at a meeting that: ''We are not Mugwumps. We are Republicans, and don't propose to leave our party and identify ourselves with the party whose antecedents have been rum, Romanism, and rebellion.''

YES, BUT THIS IS A BILLION DOLLAR COUNTRY
This remark was made by House Speaker, Thomas ''Czar'' Reed, in 1890 in reply to teasing remarks about his ''Billion Dollar Congress.'' The Fifty-first Congress was called the ''Billion Dollar Congress'' since it was the first peacetime Congress to spend a billion tax dollars.

WE HAVE NOTHING TO ARBITRATE
George M. Pullman spoke these words in 1893 as he recoiled from suggestions of arbitration from a committee of workers. A Pullman strike occurred June 21, 1894. President Grover Cleveland broke the strike in July of that year by sending in Federal

troops on the suggestion of Attorney General Richard Olney. Cleveland said: ''If it takes the entire army and navy of the United States to deliver a postal card in Chicago, that card will be delivered.''

LET THERE BE LIGHT
This motto was inscribed on the many library buildings donated to the American public by Andrew Carnegie. The inscription comes from Genesis 1:3.

REMEMBER THE MAINE! TO HELL WITH SPAIN!
This was the slogan in the Spanish-American War after the battleship *Maine* was blown up in the Havana, Cuba, harbor on February 15, 1898, at the cost of 266 American lives.

YOU MAY FIRE WHEN YOU ARE READY, GRIDLEY
Commodore George Dewey's words to the captain of his flagship at the Battle of Manila Bay on May 1, 1898, during the Spanish-American War in the Philippines. Dewey easily defeated the Spanish fleet.

DON'T CHEER, MEN—THE POOR FELLCWS (DEVILS) ARE DYING!
The words of Captain John W. Philip of the American ship the *Texas* to his men about the Spanish sailors aboard the burning *Vizcaya* at Santiago harbor in Cuba on July 3, 1898, during the Spanish-American War. The Spanish fleet under Admiral Pascual Cervera tried to escape from the harbor, but it was destroyed.

IT HAS BEEN A SPLENDID LITTLE WAR
Secretary of State John Hay wrote these words after the Treaty of Paris was ratified on February 6, 1899, ending the Spanish-American War. But in reality the war was costly. The U.S. lost more men to disease than battle wounds, and the long and difficult Philippine Insurrection was just beginning.

THE OPEN DOOR
Secretary of State John Hay announced this new American policy on July 3, 1900. The policy was that all nations would have equal trading rights and financial opportunities in China. Few nations actually supported this idea, and the policy did not originate with Hay; Alfred E. Hippisley, an Englishman, first proposed it; Lord Charles Beresford wrote about it in *The Break-up of China*; and Hay's adviser, W. W. Rockhill, revised a Hippisley memorandum and sent it on to Hay.

WE'LL STAND PAT!
These were supposedly Mark Hanna's words about President William McKinley's reelection campaign. The country had just won a war, and prosperity was evident in the full dinner pail of each worker. However, ''Stand Pat with McKinley'' was apparently not a slogan in the election of 1900. Hanna apparently popularized the expression in 1902.

NOW LOOK, THAT DAMNED COWBOY IS PRESIDENT OF THE UNITED STATES
Mark Hanna uttered these words after the assassination of President William McKinley when Theodore Roosevelt was sworn in as the 26th President on September 14, 1901.

SPEAK SOFTLY AND CARRY A BIG STICK
President Theodore Roosevelt said at the Minnesota State Fair in September, 1901, ''Speak softly and carry a big stick; you will go far.'' He wanted the U.S. to have a very capable Navy to be able to enforce the Monroe Doctrine. By extension, Roosevelt was also brandishing a big stick to deter big business.

PERDICARIS ALIVE, OR RAISULI DEAD
Although arrangements had already been made for the release of Perdicaris, Secretary John Hay, in consultation with President Roosevelt, sent on June 22, 1904, a telegram to the Sultan of Morocco demanding the release of Ion Perdicaris, a Greek subject and a naturalized American, who had been captured and held for $70,000 ransom by Achmed Ben Mohammed Raisuli, a native chief in revolt against the Sultan. Roosevelt sent the telegram primarily to enhance his popularity at the Republican National Convention meeting in Chicago.

I TOOK THE ISTHMUS
Teddy Roosevelt bragged in 1911: ''I took the Canal Zone and let Congress debate; and while the debate goes on, the Canal does also.'' After the rejection of the treaty

with the Colombian government, Roosevelt said: "Damn the law, I want the canal built!" He insisted he had a "mandate from civilization" to get construction started. Work was started in 1904 and the canal opened to traffic on August 15, 1914. It was officially finished in 1921.

THE GREATEST LIBERTY MAN HAS EVER TAKEN WITH NATURE
English writer James Bryce said this about the Panama Canal in 1912.

WE STAND AT ARMAGEDDON, AND WE BATTLE FOR THE LORD
These words concluded Theodore Roosevelt's speech at the Progressive Party Convention in Chicago on June 17, 1912. Roosevelt said: "We fight in honorable fashion for the good of mankind; fearless of the future; unheeding of our individual fates; with unflinching hearts and undimmed eyes; we stand at Armageddon, and we battle for the Lord!" He bragged that he felt "as strong as a bull moose," and the bull moose became the symbol of his party. After being shot in the chest, he said: "There is a bullet in my body, but it takes more than that to kill a Bull Moose." However, Woodrow Wilson easily won the 1912 election with 435 electoral votes to 88 for Roosevelt and 8 for Taft.

HE KEPT US OUT OF WAR
This phrase was the campaign slogan of the Democrats in 1916. The slogan developed out of the answer to the question "What did we do?" which was "We didn't go to war." The phrase refers to Woodrow Wilson's foreign policy vis-à-vis Germany and World War I. Wilson himself, however, never used the slogan, for he thought the U.S. would become involved in the war.

IT MUST BE PEACE WITHOUT VICTORY
These were Woodrow Wilson's words as he appealed to the world in an address to the U.S. Senate on January 22, 1917. He was looking for a lasting peace to be accomplished through a league of nations. Wilson said, "Only a peace between equals can last." His words upset his Allies and Germany declared on January 31 that she would sink all ships around the British Isles.

THE WORLD MUST BE MADE SAFE FOR DEMOCRACY
These words were part of Woodrow Wilson's address to Congress on April 2, 1917, asking for a declaration of war. Besides wanting "a world safe for democracy," he wanted "a war to end war." On April 6, 1917, Congress approved the war declaration.

LAFAYETTE, WE ARE HERE
Colonel Charles E. Stanton speaking for General John Pershing, leader of the American Expeditionary Forces, delivered these words at Lafayette's tomb in Paris on July 4, 1917, as Parisians shouted "Vive l'Amérique." These words represented America's desire to pay tribute to someone who rendered her a great service in the past. (General Pershing may have said these words earlier at Lafayette's tomb on June 24, 1917).

FOOD WILL WIN THE WAR/THE WOLF IS AT THE DOOR
The first phrase was Herbert Hoover's slogan during World War I as administrator of the Council for National Defense. His task was to produce enough food to feed the U.S. and its Allies./Hoover's second phrase illustrated the difficulty of getting food into Central Europe to fight starvation and stop the threat of the spreading of communism.

OVER THE TOP
The order given to American troops in World War I to leave the trenches and charge the German lines.

HEAVEN, HELL, OR HOBOKEN BY CHRISTMAS!
This phrase was attributed to General John J. Pershing and used by American troops in late 1918 in France as they looked forward to an early return home from the war.

HE CAN WALK ON DEAD LEAVES AND MAKE NO MORE NOISE THAN A TIGER
These words describe the *éminence grise* role of Colonel Edward M. House, who was the close adviser and confidant of President Woodrow Wilson.

GOOD PAY OR BUM WORK
This phrase was the motto of the Industrial Workers of the World (the I.W.W. was nicknamed the "Wobblies" or the "I Won't Works") led by William D. "Big Bill"

Haywood. These workers advocated one giant industrial union. They stirred up trouble but suffered many reprisals. Haywood and other associates were convicted in 1918 under the Espionage Act, and he was sentenced to 20 years at Leavenworth.

AMERICAN BATTLES/WARS/NOTABLE INCIDENTS: THEIR SITES AND DATES

Fenian Uprising	Canada	May 31, 1866
Sioux Wars	Dakota Territory	1866-1868/1875-1876
Apache War	New Mexico/Arizona	1871-1886
Virginius	Cuba	October 31, 1873
Rosebud River	Montana Territory	June, 1876
Little Big Horn	Montana Territory	June 25-26, 1876
Railroad Strike		1877
Nez Percé War	Pacific Northwest	1877
Haymarket Square Riots	Chicago	May 4, 1886
Wounded Knee	South Dakota	December 29, 1890
Baltimore	Valpariso, Chile	October 16, 1891
Coxey's Army March	To Washington	March 25-May 1, 1894
Klondike Gold Rush	Canada	August 16, 1896
Maine	Havana Harbor, Cuba	February 15, 1898
Manila Bay	Philippines	May 1, 1898
El Caney, San Juan Hill	Cuba	July 1, 1898
Santiago Bay	Cuba	July 3, 1898
Manila	Philippines	August 13, 1898
Philippine Insurrection	Philippines	Feb. 4, 1899-April, 1902
Boxer Revolt	China	1900
Vera Cruz	Mexico	April 21, 1914
Lusitania	Irish coast	May 7, 1915
Arabic Affair	English coast	Aug. 19-Oct. 5, 1915
Columbus	New Mexico	March 9, 1916
The Pershing Expedition	Mexico	March 15, 1916-Feb., 1917
Sussex	English Channel	March 24, 1916
Zimmermann Note	Germany to Mexico	March 1, 1917
Cantigny	France	May 28, 1918
Aisne Defensive	France	May 27-June 5, 1918
Château-Thierry	France	May 31-June 28, 1918
Belleau-Wood (Bois de la Brigade Marine)	France	June 2-July 7, 1918
Champagne-Marne Operation	France	July 15-18, 1918
Second Battle of the Marne	France	July 15-Aug. 6, 1918
Aisne-Marne Offensive	France	July 18-Aug. 6, 1918
Somme Offensive	France	Aug. 8-Nov. 11, 1918
Amiens	France	Aug. 8-11, 1918
Oise-Aisne Offensive	France	Aug. 18-Nov. 11, 1918
Ypres-Lys Offensive	Belgium	Aug. 19-Nov. 11, 1918
St. Mihiel	France	Sept. 12-16, 1918
Meuse-Argonne Offensive	France	Sept. 26-Nov. 11, 1918

AMERICAN HISTORICAL PERSONAGES AND THEIR NICKNAMES

Horatio Alger . . . . Holy Horatio
William Vincent Allen . . . . Intellectual Giant of Populism
William Backhouse Astor . . . . Landlord of New York
Phineas Taylor Barnum. . . . . . Prince of Humbugs
Clara Barton . . . . Angel of the Battlefield, Mother of the Red Cross
Bernard Mannes Baruch. . . . . Adviser of Presidents, Barney, Financial Wizard of Hobcaw Barony, Park-bench Philosopher (Statesman)
Thomas Greene Bethune . . . . .Blind Tom, Incredible Imitator
James Gillespie Blaine . . . . . . Gladstone of America, Guano Statesman, Henry of Navarre, Magnetic Man, Magnetic Statesman, Man from Maine, Plumed Knight, Premier Blaine, Tattooed (i.e., with political dishonesty) Knight, Uncrowned King
Richard Parks Bland . . . . Father of Free Silver, Silver Dick
William Bonney. . . . . Billy the Kid
James Buchanan Brady . . . . . Diamond Jim
William Jennings Bryan . . . . . Boy Orator of the Platte, Great Commoner, Peerless Leader, Silver-tongued Orator
Joseph Gurney Cannon. . . . . . Foul-mouthed Joe, Uncle Joe, Watchdog of the Treasury
Andrew Carnegie . . . . Czar of Steel, Laird of Skibo (Castle), Library Builder, Napoleon of the Smokestack, Prince of Peace, Steel Baron (King)
George Washington Carver . . . Father of Chemurgy, Peanut Man, Plant Doctor, Negro Burbank, Sweet-potato Man, Wizard of Tuskegee
Miss Edith Cavell (Eng.). . . . . Woman the Germans Shot
William Eaton Chandler. . . . . . Father of our Modern Navy, Stormy Petrel
Salmon Portland Chase. . . . . . Attorney General for Runaway Slaves, Father of Greenbacks, Ferry Boy
George Clinton . . . . Father of the Barge Canal, Father of New York
William Frederick Cody. . . . . . Buffalo Bill, Champion Buffalo Hunter of the Plains, Last of the Great Scouts, Little Billy Cody the Messenger, Pohaska, the Scout, Wagonmaster, Wild Bill the Pony Express Rider
Roscoe Conkling. . . . . Lord Roscoe, Peacock Senator
Jacob S. Coxey. . . . . General
George Armstrong Custer . . . . Boy General, Glory Hunter, Long Hair, Old Yellow Hair, White Chief with Yellow Hair
George Dewey. . . . . Hero of Manila (Bay)
Dorothea Lynde Dix. . . . . Heaven-sent Angel of Mercy and of Prison Reform
Daniel Drew . . . . Great Bear, Sphinx of the Stock Market, Uncle Daniel
Charles Warren Fairbanks . . . Icebanks
James Fisk, Jr. . . . . Colonel Fisk, Jubilee Jim, Prince of Erie
Carter Glass . . . . Father of the Federal Reserve System, Snapping Turtle, Sound Money Glass, Unreconstructed Rebel
William Crawford Gorgas . . . . Conqueror of Yellow Fever
Jay Gould . . . . Mephistopheles of Wall Street, Railroad King, Wizard of Erie
Harlan Halsey. . . . . King of Dime Novelists, Old Sleuth
Winfield Scott Hancock. . . . . . Hancock the Superb
Marcus Alonzo Hanna. . . . . . . Dollar Mark, Uncle Mark
William Hope Harvey. . . . . Coin, Little Professor
Lucy Webb Hayes. . . . . Lemonade Lucy
William Randolph Hearst. . . . . Emperor of Newsprint, Lord of San Simeon, People's Democrat, Poor Little Rich Boy
James Butler Hickok. . . . . Duck Bill, Dutch Bill, Prince of Pistoleers, Shanghai Bill, Wild Bill
James J. Hill. . . . . Empire Builder

Charles Evans Hughes	Bearded Iceberg, Bearded Lady (by Roosevelt), Evasive
Jesse James	Robin Hood of the Little Blue (of the Missouri, and of the U.S.A.)
Philander Chase Knox	Father of Dollar Diplomacy, Sleepy Phil
Robert M. La Follette	Battling Bob, Fighting Bob
Mary Elizabeth Lease	Kansas Pythoness, Mary Yellin
Ferdinand de Lesseps (Fr.) . . .	Father of the Suez Canal, Great Undertaker
Henry Demarest Lloyd	First of the Muckrakers, The Middle-Class Conscience
Henry Cabot Lodge	Destroyer of the League of Nations, Scholar in Politics
William Gibbs McAdoo	Bill the Builder, Crown Prince, Dancing Fool, Daddy Longlegs, World War Croesus
Mary Mallon	Typhoid Mary
Charles Horace Mayo	Doctor Charlie
Willliam James Mayo	Doctor Will
J. Pierpont Morgan	Commodore, Dr. of Wall Street, J.P., Jupiter of Wall Street, Prince of American Financiers
Charles Francis Murphy	Apostle of Temperance, Silent Charley
Carrie Nation (Amelia Moore Gloyd)	Advocate of Hatchetation, Lady with the Hatchet, Little Hatchet
Annie Oakley (Phoebe Anne Oakley Moses)	Little Missy, Little Sure Shot, Peerless Lady Wingshot
Alton B. Parker	Parker the Silent
George Hunt Pendleton	Father of Civil Service Reform, Gentleman George
John Joseph Pershing	Black Jack Pershing
John Sargent Pillsbury	Father of the University of Minnesota
Thomas Collier Platt	Easy Boss Platt, Me Too Platt
Joseph Pulitzer	Blind Publisher
Thomas Brackett Reed	Biddy, Czar Reed, Terrible Turk
Walter Reed	Doctor in Uniform
Edward V. Rickenbacker	Ace of Aces, Captain Eddie, Eddie Rickenbacker
John Davison Rockefeller	John D, Oil Barron, Reckafellow, Standard Oil King
William Henry Seward	Higher Law, Sage of Auburn, Uncle Billy
Morris Sheppard	Father of the 18th Amendment
John Philip Sousa	March King
Joseph Lincoln Steffens	Golden Rule Fellow, King of the Muckrakers
Charles Sherwood Stratton . . .	General Tom Thumb, Tom Thumb, Pet of the Palace
Ida Minerva Tarbell	Dean of Women Authors of America, Miss Tarbarrel, Mother of Muckrakers
Horace A.W. Tarbor	Silver King
Samuel Jones Tilden	Old Usufruct, Sage of Gramercy Park, Sage of Greystone, Slippery Sam, Thrifty Sam, Whispering Sam
William Marcy Tweed	Boss
Cornelius Vanderbilt	Commodore
Andrew J. Volstead	Father of the Volstead Act, Goat of the Wets, The Obscure Mr. Volstead
Daniel Wolsey Voorhees	Tall Sycamore of the Wabash
Ben Wade	Bluff Ben, Old Ben Wade
Booker Taliaferro Washington	Black Messiah, Spokesman for the Negro
Henry Watterson	Henry of Navarre, Light Horse Harry, Marse Henry
Valeriano Weyler (Sp.)	Butcher
Joseph Wheeler	Fighting Joe, Little Hero, Little Joe
Edith Bolling Wilson	First Lady of the World
Victoria Claflin Woodhull	Terrible Siren
Alvin Cullum York	Sergeant, Sergeant York

GENERAL NICKNAMES AND CLAIMS TO FAME

1860 to 1868	The Gilded Age (from Mark Twain's *The Gilded Age*, 1873)
Appealing to wartime emotions	Waving (shaking) the bloody shirt
President Johnson's Reconstruction Plan	Restoration
Reconstruction Period.........................	Age of Hate
The land or states south of the Mason-Dixon Line	Dixie
Southern laws after the Civil War that discriminated against the Negroes	Black Codes, Black Laws
Irish-American miners in Eastern Pennsylvania from 1865 to 1875 who used violence to oppose oppressive industrial-social conditions	Molly Maguires, Sleepers
Charles Crocker, Mark Hopkins, Collis P. Huntington, and Leland Stanford	Big Four (Railroad magnates)
Fight for the Erie Railroad waged by Daniel Drew, Jim Fisk, and Jay Gould against Cornelius Vanderbilt in 1866 and later	Erie War
Daniel Drew, Jim Fisk, and Jay Gould	Erie Ring
Jay Cooke and Company	Financier of the Civil War
Alaska purchased by William Seward for the United States in 1867	Johnson's Polar Bear Garden, Seward's Folly, Seward's Icebox, Walrussia
Christopher Sholes's typewriter (1867)	Literary piano
September 24, 1869, Panic	Black Friday
Industrialists who became wealthy by exploitation in late 19th century..........................	Robber Barons
Erie Railroad	Scarlet Woman
Southern industrialists (or ones-to-be)	Bourbons, Redeemers
Silver	Beloved white metal, Sacred white metal, White gold
Revolvers firing 6 shots before reloading	Six-shooters
Sharps Buffalo Rifle	Old Reliable
Stray unbranded calves; those people independent of party loyalty or groups in general	Mavericks
42nd Congress's voting for an increased salary to members and $5000 in back pay	Salary Grab of 1872
People paid to vote	Voting cattle
Coinage Act of 1873	Crime of 1873
Homesteader who starts a farm..................	Squatter
Homesteader who starts a farm on open range land	Nester
Meat packing firms of Armour, Cudahy, Morris, Swift, and Wilson	Beef Barons, Big Five Packers
Southern states for the Democratic party starting with the 1876 election........................	Solid South
1876 election	Great Fraud, Stolen Election
Rutherford B. Hayes's administration — 1876 to 1880.....................................	Cold Water Administration
Alexander Graham Bell's telephone in 1876	Lover's telegraph
Colorado...................................	Centennial State
Government funds which government officials use for local projects	Pork barrel
Birmingham, Alabama	Pittsburgh of the South
Barnum's (and, later, Bailey's) Circus	Greatest Show on Earth
Chicago, Illinois	Hog Butcher of the World
Steel......................................	The gleaming metal

Shoshoni travois	Prairie Buggy
Indian reservations	Human zoos
Large canvas-covered wagon	Prairie Schooner
Black soldiers	Buffalo soldier (according to the Indians)
Locomotive	Bad medicine wagon, Fire horse (according to the Indians)
A pair of aces and a pair of eights in a poker hand	Dead man's hand (held by "Wild Bill" Hickok when he was shot in 1876)
Boom towns	Helldorados, Hell-on-wheels
Tombstone, Arizona's cemetery	Boot Hill
.45-calibre single action revolver by Colt	Peacemaker
Bad Liquor	Rot gut
Newcomer to ranching and mining in the West	Tenderfoot
Dodge City	Bibulous Babylon of the Frontier, Boothill, Cowboy Capital of the World
Cowboy	Cowpoke, cowpuncher
Law and order in Abilene, Kansas	Judge Colt
Colt revolver	Gun that Won the West
To campaign in small towns and rural areas	Barnstorm
Small backward town in a cattle area	Cow town
Cowboy pistols	Shooting irons
Fraudulent voting	Ballot-box stuffing
Southern Congressmen of the '80's and '90's	Confederate Brigadiers
Stock market speculators	Captains of Industry
Family farm	Backbone of democracy
Red Cross (founded in America in 1881)	Greatest Mother in the World
Pendleton Act of 1883	Magna Carta of Civil Service Reform
Republicans who did not support James Blaine for President in 1884	Mugwumps
Money used to buy votes	Boodle
Expensive, lavish banquet held for James G. Blaine in New York on October 29, 1884	Balshazzar's Feast, Boodle Banquet
Civil War fleet as described in 1886	Floating washtub
Lakewood, New Jersey, home of Grover Cleveland as President	Little White House
Veterans who wanted the military pension that was vetoed by President Cleveland in February, 1887	Blood-suckers, Bums, Rebel Brigadiers
A punched ticket or a free pass	An Annie Oakley
Female prophet of doom	Calamity Jane
Johnstown, Pennsylvania	The Flood City (May 31, 1889)
Late 19th century	Gilded Age
1890 to 1900	Gay Nineties, Mauve Decade
Wyoming	Equality State
51st Congress	Billion Dollar Congress
Columbian Exposition in 1893 in Chicago	Dream of Loveliness
Unemployed followers of "General" Jacob S. Coxey who marched on Washington in 1894	Coxey's Army
William Jennings Bryan's speech of July 7, 1896	Cross of Gold Speech, Crown of Thorns Speech
Those who wanted military rule over the Philippines	Expansionists
Those who opposed McKinley's military rule over all the Philippines	Anti-Expansionists, Anti-Imperialists

Troops organized by Teddy Roosevelt and commanded by Colonel Leonard Wood during the
Spanish-American War . . . . Rough Riders, Teddy's Terrors, Wood's Weary Walkers
Canned rations during the 1898 War . . . . Embalmed beef
Spanish-American War . . . . Splendid Little War (according to John Hay)
Caribbean after the Spanish-American War . . . . An American lake
Philippine Islands . . . . Achilles' heel (according to Theodore Roosevelt)
Filipinos . . . . Little brown brothers (according to William H. Taft)
The Automobile . . . . Horseless Carriage
Wall Street speculators after the passage of the
March 14, 1900, Currency Bill by Congress . . . . Napoleons of Wall Street
1900 Senate . . . . Millionaires' Club
Site of the Permanent Court of Arbitration at the
Hague donated by Andrew Carnegie . . . . Palace of Peace, Temple of Peace
Fictional club of newspaper reporters who publish
information from confidential sources . . . . Ananias Club (Theodore Roosevelt's coinage)
Reporters assigned to the White House during Teddy
Roosevelt's administration . . . . Newspaper Cabinet
Writers who exposed business-political scandals . . . . . Muckrakers
Czar of Russia . . . . Preposterous little creature (according to Theodore Roosevelt)
Teddy Roosevelt's companions from 1901 to 1909
who were very active physically . . . . Tennis Cabinet
Japanese in California . . . . Yellow Peril
Thomas Lawson, Upton Sinclair, Ray Baker, Lincoln
Steffens, and Ida Tarbell . . . . The Muckrakers
William Jennings Bryan, William Travers Jerome,
and Theodore Roosevelt . . . . Three Best Known Men in America
Members of the Industrial Workers of the World
(founded in 1905) . . . . Wobblies
1907 Wall Street Panic . . . . Rich Man's Panic
Model T Ford . . . . Tin Lizzie
Small, cheap automobile (Tin Lizzie) . . . . Flivver
Oklahoma (admitted to the Union in 1907) . . . . Beautiful Land
National nominating conventions . . . . Quadrennial madhouses
U.S. fleet (on its 14-month world cruise in 1907-1909) . . . . Great White Fleet
New Jersey . . . . Mother of Trusts
William Taft's fiscal foreign policy . . . . Dollar Diplomacy
White House . . . . Loneliest Place in the World (according to William H. Taft)
Lobbyists . . . . Third House of Congress
Panama Canal . . . . Big Ditch
Balkan States in early 20th century . . . . Powder keg of Europe
Mann Act of 1910 . . . . White Slave (Traffic) Act
Big battleships . . . . White Elephants of the Sea
William Jennings Bryan's diplomatic procedures in
Woodrow Wilson's Cabinet — 1913 to 1915 . . . . Grape Juice Diplomacy
Clayton Act of October 15, 1914 . . . . Labor's Magna Carta
Pershing's expedition to Mexico in 1916-1917 . . . . Perishing Expedition
Republican Senators seeking their own interests and

not the public's..............................Little Group of Willful Men
(according to Woodrow Wilson
whose arming of merchant
vessels and U.S. entry into
the League of Nations was
blocked by this group)

Dachshunds, German measles, hamburger steak,
and sauerkraut during World War I................Liberty Pups, Measles, Steak,
and Cabbage

German long-range gun ....Big Bertha

Germans during World War I.....................Boches, Huns, Jerries, Krauts

Americans traveling on Allied vessels in WWI........Guardian Angels

To economize, feed the world (later, to pauperize) ....Hooverize

Herbert Hoover's preaching ....Gospel of the Clean Plate

American Airmen during WWI....................Cavaliers of the Clouds

4th U.S. Marine Brigade........................Devil Dogs

38th Infantry of the 3rd U.S. Division ....Rock of the Marne

Deep-dyed Isolationists........................Battalion of Death,
Bitterenders, Irreconcilables

Pilot who shot down at least 5 enemy aircraft ....Ace

94th Pursuit Squadron in WWI ....Hat-in-the-ring squadron

British soldiers in WWI ....Limeys,Tommies

American soldiers in WWI......................Doughboys, Yanks

Large heavy battleship ....Dreadnaught

Interest-bearing bonds during WWI ....Liberty Bonds

U.S. troops surrounded by Germans at Meuse-
Argonne ....Lost Battalion

42nd Division of the A.E.F. during WWI ....Rainbow Division

Land between the trenches of the 2 lines in WWI .....No-man's land

Those who did not want a negotiated peace with the
Central European powers at the end of WWI ....Bitterenders

MUCKRAKING

The official period for muckraking was from 1902 to 1912. Previous to 1902, *Harper's Weekly* crusaded against the corruption of the Tweed Ring, and Henry Demarest Lloyd denounced the Standard Oil Company in *Wealth Against Commonwealth* (1894). Theodore Roosevelt coined the term "muckrakers" in 1906 from John Bunyan's allegory *Pilgrim's Progress.* Bunyan wrote about a man "with a muck-rake in his hand" who would rather rake filth than look upward to see the heavenly crown that was being offered to him from above.

The Arena **(magazine) (1889)** . . . . Benjamin Fowler, Editor
(the first muckraking periodical, which was discontinued in 1909)
McClure's Magazine **(1893)**. . . . . S.S. McClure, founder
(noted for its publication of Ida M. Tarbell's exposé in 1902)
Collier's, Cosmopolitan, Everybody's
(other magazines that engaged in muckraking)
"The World of Graft" (1901) in *McClure's* . . . . .Josiah Flynt Willard
"Standard Oil Company" (1902) in *McClure's* . . . . Ida M. Tarbell
(*History of the Standard Oil Company* was published in 1904)
Frenzied Finance **(1902)** . . . . Thomas W. Lawson
(insurance and stock fraud manipulation — published in *Everybody's* in 1905-1906)
The Shame of the Cities **(1904)** . . . . Lincoln Steffens
(Big Business and municipal government allied in corruption - published in *McClure's* in 1902)
The Greatest Trust in the World **(1905)** . . . . Charles Edward Russell
(the beef trust)
"The Treason of the Senate" (1906) in *Cosmopolitan*. . . . . . David Graham Phillips
(senatorial corruption - appeared in book form in 1964)
The Great American Fraud **(1906)** . . . . Samuel Hopkins Adams
(patent medicine abuse)
The Bitter Cry of the Children **(1906)**. . . . . John Spargo
(child labor abuse)
The Jungle **(1906)**. . . . . Upton Sinclair
(a fictional account of the Chicago stockyards and the meat-packing plants)
"The Railroads on Trial" (1906) in *McClure's* . . . . Ray Stannard Baker
The Struggle for Self-Government **(1906)**. . . . . Lincoln Steffens
(Big Business and municipal government allied in corruption)
Story of Life Insurance **(1907)**. . . . . Burton J. Hendrick
Following the Color Line **(1908)** . . . . Ray Stannard Baker
(racial discrimination)
History of the Great American Fortunes **(1910)** . . . . Gustavus Myers

QUESTIONS AND ANSWERS

1. What were the 2 symbols, one for the women's suffragist movement and the other for their opponents, in 1919 in the U.S.? What amendment to the U.S. Constitution gave women the right to vote, and what was the date? Name the 36th state to ratify that amendment.

ANSWER: The suffragists used yellow jonquils, and their opponents used red roses/ The 19th Amendment on August 18, 1920/Tennessee.

2. With what was the "Big Red Scare" of 1919-1920 concerned? Who was responsible for it? What role did a U.S. transport ship play in this affair?

ANSWER: It was a crusade against suspected Communists. The Bolshevik Revolution had occurred in Russia in 1917, and the Workers' Party was organized in the U.S. in 1919/A. Mitchell Palmer, the U.S. Attorney General/The *Buford* carried 249 aliens to Russia.

3. Who was the only man ever to run for President of the U.S. from a prison cell? What Party did he represent in what year and against whom? What was his crime? In what penitentiary was he, and what was his number?

ANSWER: Eugene V. Debs/Socialists in 1920 against Warren G. Harding/He had violated the Sedition Act of May 16, 1918, which was an amendment to the Espionage Act of June 15, 1917/The Atlanta Penitentiary/Number 9653.

4. What was the name of the first of several naval disarmament conferences held after World War I in Washington in 1921-1922? Who was the U.S. Secretary of State, and what was his startling proposal? Name the 5 countries that signed the Five Power Naval Armaments Treaty in February, 1922. What ratio of capital-ship construction was agreed upon by the 5 countries? What Naval Conference of 1930 extended this agreement to cruisers and destroyers? What country abrogated the treaties in 1934?

ANSWER: The Washington Armament Conference/Charles Evans Hughes proposed a 10-year moratorium on capital-ship construction/The United States, Great Britain, Japan, France, and Italy/5:5:3:1.75:1.75 for the U.S., Great Britain, Japan, France, and Italy, respectively/The London Naval Conference/Japan.

5. Who were the 3 Secretaries, of State, Treasury, and Commerce, of the Harding Administration who had distinguished records of accomplishment?

ANSWER: Charles Evans Hughes, Andrew W. Mellon, and Herbert Hoover.

6. Name the 2 members, the Secretary of the Interior and the Attorney General, of the Harding Administration who were forced to resign because of their involvement in the Teapot Dome Scandal. Who became the new Secretary of the Interior?

ANSWER: Albert B. Fall (Interior) and Harry M. Daugherty (Attorney General)/Hubert Work.

7. What did people jokingly say about the difference between President George Washington and the easy-going President Warren G. Harding?

ANSWER: Washington could not tell a lie and Harding could not tell a liar.

8. Name the 3 countries with which the United States was still technically at war 3 years after the Treaty of Versailles was rejected by the United States. How was this problem resolved?

ANSWER: Germany, Austria, and Hungary/In July, 1921, Congress passed a resolution which declared that the war was officially ended and, in August, 1921, Washington negotiated separate treaties with each country.

9. Who said each of the following?
    a) "Not nostrums but normalcy"
    b) "The business of America is business"
    c) "The hand that held the dagger has struck it into the back of its

    neighbor"
    d) "I shall return"
    e) "Nuts"
    f) "An iron curtain has descended across the continent

g) ''I'm going to give 'em hell''   j) ''I have a dream''
h) ''We will bury you''   k) ''Nattering nabobs of negativism''
i) ''Ich bin ein Berliner''

ANSWER: a) Warren G. Harding b) Calvin Coolidge c) Franklin D. Roosevelt d) Douglas MacArthur e) A.C. McAuliffe f) Winston Churchill g) Harry S Truman h) Nikita S. Khrushchev i) John F. Kennedy j) Martin Luther King, Jr. k) Spiro T. Agnew.

10. What 2 sites were involved in the Teapot Dome Scandal? Give the years and the U.S. President who was in office. What role did the President, Albert B. Fall, and Edwin Denby play in this affair?

ANSWER: The oil reserves at Teapot Dome, Wyoming, and Elk Hills, California/1921-1923, President Harding/President Harding had transferred to Secretary of the Interior Albert B. Fall the administration of these oil reserves with the approval of Secretary of the Navy Edwin Denby. Fall then leased the oil fields to oil operators Harry F. Sinclair and Edward L. Doheny. (Fall was the first Cabinet member ever to be jailed as a criminal. He was sent to prison in 1931. The scandal's notoriety lasted about 10 years).

11. Name the plan of April, 1924, that scheduled German reparation payments to former enemies; the plan of February, 1929, that revised the first plan and reduced the amount of German reparation payments; and name the conference of June, 1932, that cancelled 90% of the reparation payments demanded in the second plan.

ANSWER: The Dawes Plan/The Young Plan/The Lausanne Conference.

12. Who were the 2 Chicago college students who kidnapped and killed a 14-year-old neighbor just for kicks in 1924? Name the boy they killed and the lawyer who defended them.

ANSWER: Richard Loeb and Nathan Leopold/Bobbie Franks/Clarence Darrow.

13. For what reason was John T. Scopes brought to trial in 1925? In what city and state? What was the well-known nickname for this trial? Who defended Scopes, and what famous person assisted the prosecution?

ANSWER: Scopes violated the anti-evolution law of March, 1925/Dayton, Tennessee/ The ''Monkey Trial''/Clarence Darrow and William Jennings Bryan.

14. Name the first man to make a solo nonstop flight across the Atlantic (completed on May 21, 1927). How many hours did it take? In what plane did he fly? From what airfield did he take off, and on what airfield did he land? This same man's child was kidnapped and killed on March 1, 1932. Who was convicted and executed for this crime in 1936?

ANSWER: Charles A. Lindbergh/33½ hours/The Spirit of Saint Louis/Roosevelt Field on Long Island and Le Bourget in Paris/Bruno Richard Hauptmann.

15. Name the 2 Italian anarchists who died in the electric chair on August 23, 1927. What crime had they committed? Why was this case a *cause célèbre*? By what nickname are they known?

ANSWER: Nicola Sacco and Bartolomeo Vanzetti/The murder and robbery of a paymaster and a guard in a Massachusetts shoe factory in 1920/Because many believed there was insufficient evidence and that they were convicted because of their radical beliefs/The ''Braintree Martyrs.''

16. What United States Secretary of State won the Nobel Peace Prize in 1929, and for what reason?

ANSWER: President Coolidge's Secretary Frank B. Kellogg for the Kellogg-Briand Pact of August 27, 1928, with Aristide Briand of France. The countries signing the treaty renounced war as an instrument of national policy.

17. What massacre happened on February 14, 1929?

ANSWER: The St. Valentine's Day Massacre, when 7 members of ''Bugs'' Moran's gang (the O'Banion gang) were murdered by Al Capone's gang.

18. Give the 3 main dates associated with the collapse of the stock market in 1929.

ANSWER: On Thursday, October 24, 13 million shares were sold; on October 29, ''Black Tuesday,'' 16 million shares were sold; and on November 13, stocks had lost over 40 percent in value.

19. What is a "Brain Trust," and with what U.S. President was this term first associated? Name some of the members of this group.

ANSWER: **It is a group of advisers to a candidate who are competent in a field and work closely with that person devising policies and drafting speeches/ Franklin D. Roosevelt/Raymond Moley, Rex Tugwell, Adolf Berle, Hugh Johnson, George Peek, Samuel Rosenman, and Harny L. Hopkins.**

20. Who is known by each of the following nicknames?

a) Father of the U.S. Air Force	f) Mother of the Civil Rights Movement
b) Father of Modern Education	g) Father of the Civil Rights Movement
c) Architect of the "Containing Communism" Policy	h) Father of the Atomic Submarine
	i) Dean of American Governors
d) Father of the United Nations	j) Ambassador of the Air
e) Father of the 20th Amendment to the Constitution	k) First Lady of the Air
	l) Prince of Wit and Wisdom

ANSWER: **a) Henry H. Arnold b) John Dewey c) John Foster Dulles d) Cordell Hull e) George W. Norris f) Rosa Parks g) A. Philip Randolph h) Hyman Rickover i) Nelson Rockefeller j) Charles Lindbergh k) Amelia Earhart l) Will Rogers.**

21. Name the 3 R's of Franklin Roosevelt's New Deal program.

ANSWER: **Relief, Recovery, and Reform.**

22. Who was the "Father of the 20th Amendment"? When was it ratified? What was this amendment nicknamed? What were the 2 main provisions of the amendment?

ANSWER: **George W. Norris/January 23, 1933/"Lame Duck" Amendment/That Congress convene on January 3 and that the President and Vice President begin their term of office on January 20 following the national elections.**

23. Who tried to assassinate President-elect Franklin Roosevelt on February 15, 1933, in Miami, Florida? Who was wounded and later died in this incident? What happened to the assassin?

ANSWER: **Giuseppe Zangara/Anton Cermak, Mayor of Chicago/Zangara died in the electric chair on March 20, 1933.**

24. By what name was the special session of Congress called by Franklin D. Roosevelt from March 9 to June 16, 1933, known? What tradition was started by President Roosevelt on March 12, 1933?

ANSWER: **The "Hundred Days"/"Fireside Chats."**

25. For what during the New Deal did the initials NRA stand? What was the symbol of this agency, what 2 things were clutched in its claws, and what was its motto?

ANSWER: **The National Recovery Administration/A blue eagle was clutching a cogwheel and a thunderbolt/"We Do Our Part."**

26. Who were the first 2 women cabinet members? What positions did they hold and for which U.S. Presidents did they work?

ANSWER: **Frances Perkins and Mrs. Oveta Culp Hobby/Perkins was FDR's Secretary of Labor and Mrs. Hobby was Eisenhower's Secretary of Health, Education, and Welfare.**

27. Name the 7 states included in the Tennessee Valley Authority area. In what year was the TVA established?

ANSWER: **Tennessee, Kentucky, Mississippi, Alabama, Georgia, North Carolina, and Virginia/1933.**

28. What dam on the Colorado River was finished in 1936, and which 2 dams were finished on the Columbia River in 1937 and 1942 respectively?

ANSWER: **The Hoover Dam/Bonneville and Grand Coulee Dams.**

29. What Louisiana Senator and demagogue was assassinated in 1935 by a doctor? Name the doctor and give the popular nickname of the Senator. Name the author of the novel which won the 1947 Pulitzer Prize and which closely paralleled the life of this Senator. What is the name of the main character and the name of the narrator in the novel?

ANSWER: **Huey P. Long/Dr. Carl A. Weiss/"Kingfish"/Robert Penn Warren/***All the King's Men***/Willie Stark and Jack Burden.**

30. How many Supreme Court Justices did Franklin Roosevelt want to add in his "Court Packing" scheme in 1937? Who was his first appointee, and why was this an embarrassing choice? How many Justices did Roosevelt appoint during his term?

ANSWER: **Six/Hugo LaFayette Black was an embarrassing choice because he had been a member of the Ku Klux Klan (Black did become, however, one of the most influential figures in American judicial history)/Eight.**

31. Give the location of each of the following battles or incidents.
    a) St. Valentine's Day Massacre
    b) Guadalcanal Campaign
    c) Eniwetok (Enewetak)
    d) D-Day
    e) Leyte Campaign
    f) Iwo Jima
    g) Okinawa
    h) Nagasaki
    i) Pusan Perimeter
    j) Gulf of Tonkin
    k) Ia Drang Valley
    l) U.S. Mayagüez

ANSWER: **a) Chicago, Illinois b) Solomon Islands c) Marshall Islands d) France (Normandy) e) Philippines f) Volcano Islands g) Ryukyu Islands h) Japan i) Korea j) South China Sea k) Vietnam l) Gulf of Siam.**

32. Name the 8 defense base sites the U.S. received from Britain in 1940 in exchange for 50 old-model destroyers. For how long were they to be controlled?

ANSWER: **Placentia Bay, Newfoundland; Bermuda; Bahamas; Jamaica; Antigua; St. Lucia; Trinidad; and British Guiana/99 years.**

33. What 2 leaders met aboard what boat at what place on August 3, 1941, to write and sign the Atlantic Charter?

ANSWER: **Franklin D. Roosevelt and Winston Churchill/Aboard the U.S.S. *Augusta*/Near Placentia Bay, Newfoundland.**

34. Name the 8 U.S. battleships which were among the 86 naval vessels present during the Japanese attack on Pearl Harbor on December 7, 1941. Name the only ship that was totally and permanently lost. What was Pearl Harbor's nickname?

ANSWER: **U.S.S. *Arizona*, U.S.S. *California*, U.S.S. *Maryland*, U.S.S. *Nevada*. U.S.S. *Oklahoma*, U.S.S. *Pennsylvania*, U.S.S. *Tennessee*, and the U.S.S. *West Virginia*/The U.S.S. *Arizona*/The Gibraltar of the Pacific.**

35. What was the name of the Atomic Bomb project between the years 1942 and 1945? Who was in charge? What scientist coordinated the project? What were the 4 locations of the project, and what was done at each one? What happened and where on July 16, 1945?

ANSWER: **Manhattan (District) Project/Brigadier General Leslie R. Groves/J. Robert Oppenheimer/Oak Ridge, Tennessee, had the U-235 separation plant; Los Alamos, New Mexico, had the bomb development laboratory; Hanford, Washington, had the plutonium production development; and the University of Chicago created the first self-sustaining nuclear reaction/The first atomic bomb was exploded at Alamogordo, New Mexico.**

36. List the 6 international conferences President Roosevelt attended in 1943, the 1 in 1944, and the 1 in 1945, and tell briefly about each one.

ANSWER: — Casablanca, January, 1943 — He met with Churchill and an "unconditional surrender" ultimatum was declared against the enemy.
— Ango-American Conference, May, 1943 — He met with Churchill and many officials to set May 1, 1944, for the Normandy Invasion.
— 1st Quebec Conference, August, 1943 — He met with Churchill and May 1, 1944, was reaffirmed as the Normandy Invasion date.
— 1st Cairo Conference, November, 1943 — Roosevelt met with Churchill and Chiang Kai-shek, and they issued an "unconditional surrender" ultimatum against Japan.
— Teheran Conference, November-December, 1943 — Roosevelt, Churchill, and Stalin met to coordinate plans for a coordinated attack against Germany and Japan.
— 2nd Cairo Conference, December, 1943 — Roosevelt and Churchill met

with Turkey's President Ismet Inönü to reaffirm Turkey's alliance with Great Britain.
- 2nd Quebec Conference, September, 1944 — Roosevelt and Churchill met to finalize plans for a victory over Germany and Japan.
- Yalta Conference, February, 1945 — Roosevelt, Churchill, and Stalin gathered in the Crimea and pledged their support to postwar liberated governments.

37. Identify each of the following by his/her nickname.
   a) Dictator of Louisiana   e) Galahad of the Elderly
   b) Buck Private's Gary Cooper   f) Labor's Rugged Individualist
   c) Bad Boy of Baltimore   g) Poor Little Rich Girl
   d) Old Blood and Guts   h) Simple Barefoot Boy from Wall Street

ANSWER: a) Huey Long b) Douglas MacArthur c) H.L. Mencken d) George S. Patton e) Claude Pepper f) Walter Reuther g) Gloria Vanderbilt h) Wendell Willkie.

38. What conference held where in August-October, 1944, with American, British, Chinese and Soviet representatives served as a basis for later discussions that led to the foundation of the United Nations? On what date in what city with how many nations present was the Charter of the United Nations drafted? Who was the U.S. Secretary of State? On what date was the charter signed and on what date did the U.S. Senate give its approval? On what date, known as United Nations Day, was the U.N. established? What 5 Great Powers became the permanent members of the Security Council? Where was the International Court of Justice to sit, and how many judges were there to be?

ANSWER: The Dunbarton Oaks Conference near Washington, D.C./April 25, 1945, in San Francisco (in the Opera House) with 50 nations present/Edward R. Stettinius/June 26, 1945, and July 28, 1945/October 24, 1945/The United States, the USSR, the United Kingdom, France, and China/The Hague, the Netherlands, and 15 judges.

39. When was it, near what town, and who were the 4 major figures who attended the Potsdam Conference?

ANSWER: From July 17 to August 2, 1945/Near Berlin, Germany, and President Harry S Truman, Premier Joseph Stalin, and Prime Minister Winston Churchill (until July 28 when he was replaced by newly elected Prime Minister Clement R. Attlee).

40. What are the dates for V-E Day (Victory in Europe Day), the bombing of Hiroshima and Nagasaki, and V-J Day (Victory in Japan Day)? On which battleship in Tokyo Bay conducted by which U.S. general were formal ceremonies held ending the war with Japan?

ANSWER: V-E Day was May 8, 1945/Hiroshima was August 6, 1945/Nagasaki was August 9, 1945/V-J Day was September 2, 1945/The U.S.S. *Missouri*/ General Douglas MacArthur.

41. Where in Germany after WWII were the Nazi war crimes trials held? Who was the chief U.S. prosecutor?

ANSWER: At Nuremberg (Nürnberg) (1945-1949)/Associate Justice Robert H. Jackson.

42. Who were the 4 main candidates for the presidency of the U.S. in 1948? Give their party affiliation. What newspaper was held up by the winner, and what were the headlines?

ANSWER: Harry S Truman, Democratic Party; Thomas E. Dewey, Republican Party; J. Strom Thurmond, States' Right Democratic Party; and Henry A. Wallace, Progressive Party/Truman held up the Chicago *Daily Tribune* which proclaimed "DEWEY DEFEATS TRUMAN."

43. What was the Truman Doctrine, and when was it proposed? What was the Marshall Plan, and when was it proposed?

ANSWER: The Truman Doctrine was proposed on March 12, 1947, and it provided for economic and military aid to Greece and Turkey to fight communism/The

Marshall Plan was proposed by Secretary of State George C. Marshall on June 5, 1947, promising that the United States would provide the financial assistance to the European countries that developed a plan for their economic recovery.

44. It began on June 24, 1948, and ended May 12, 1949. What was it that the Soviet Union blockaded, and what means did the U.S. use to break that blockade?

ANSWER: **The Soviet Union blockaded Berlin, and the U.S. airlifted supplies during the 10 month blockade. The airlift was called ''Operation Vittles'' by the pilots.**

45. What treaty was signed on April 4, 1949, and what were the 12 nations involved?

ANSWER: **NATO or the North Atlantic Treaty Organization/The United States, Canada, Great Britain, Belgium, Denmark, France, Iceland, Norway, Luxembourg, Portugal, Italy, and the Netherlands (Greece, Turkey, and West Germany were added later).**

46. What expression by what U.S. President had the words ''heat'' and ''kitchen'' in it? What motto did this President have on his desk?

ANSWER: **''If you can't stand the heat, get out of the kitchen''/Harry S Truman/ ''The buck stops here.''**

47. Name either of the 2 men who attempted to assassinate President Truman on November 1, 1950. What nationality were these 2 men? Where did the attempted assassination take place? What happened to the 2 men?

ANSWER: **Oscar Collazo and Griselio Torresola/Puerto Ricans/At Blair House in Washington, D.C./Torresola was killed immediately, and Collazo's death sentence was commuted to life imprisonment.**

48. Name the former U.S. State Department official who was convicted of perjury in 1950 for denying he was part of a Communist spy network. What former Communist agent denounced this man, and what Republican from California made a reputation in the case? Name the 2 Russian agents who were executed in June, 1953, for passing atomic secrets to the Soviets. Name the Senator from Wisconsin who charged in 1950 that there were Communists in the State Department and who was condemned by the Senate in December, 1954. What does his name mean today?

ANSWER: **Alger Hiss/Whittaker Chambers and Richard Nixon/Julius and Ethel Rosenberg/Joseph R. McCarthy/McCarthyism means ''the misuse of information through accusations and sensationalism that deprives the rights of individuals in order to achieve a goal'' (originally to suppress communism).**

49. What was the beginning date of the Korean War, and on what date was an armistice signed? Whom did President Truman appoint as commander in chief of the forces there in July, 1950, and relieve of that command on April 11, 1951?

ANSWER: **June 25, 1950/July 27, 1953/General Douglas MacArthur.**

50. What famous U.S. Supreme Court decision in May, 1954, reversed what 1896 decision that had interpreted the 14th Amendment as approval of separate but equal facilities for Negroes? Who was Chief Justice of the Supreme Court and who appointed him? Whom had he replaced?

ANSWER: *Brown v. Board of Education of Topeka* **reversed** *Plessy v. Ferguson***/Chief Justice Earl Warren was appointed by President Eisenhower after the death of Chief Justice Frederick Moore Vinson.**

51. What does SEATO stand for, and who were the 8 nations that signed this defensive treaty in September, 1954?

ANSWER: **Southeast Asian Treaty Organization/Australia, Great Britain, France, New Zealand, Pakistan, the Philippines, Thailand, and the United States.**

52. Who is known by each of the following nicknames?

a) Abominable No-Man   e) Modern Knight Errant
b) First Man on the Moon   f) Scoop
c) Little Man on the Wedding Cake   g) Nixon's Svengali
d) Cactus Jack   h) Lone Eagle

ANSWER: a) Sherman Adams b) Neil Armstrong c) Thomas E. Dewey d) John Nance Garner e) J. Edgar Hoover f) Henry Jackson g) Henry Kissinger h) Charles Lindbergh.

53. Who were the leaders of the A.F. of L. and the CIO when these 2 unions merged in December of 1955? Who was elected president of the union? Who is the president today? Name the presidents of the Teamsters from 1952-1984.

ANSWER: George Meany and Walter Reuther/George Meany/Lane Kirkland/Dave Beck, Jimmy Hoffa, Frank Fitzsimmons, Roy Williams, and Jackie Presser.

54. Name the 3 countries that gained control of the Suez Canal in 1956. Who was the President of Egypt? What major country opposed this use of force, and what major country threatened to intervene? What force was installed as a buffer force between Egypt and Israel?

ANSWER: Great Britain, France, and Israel/Gamal Abdel Nasser/The U.S. opposed the use of force and Russia threatened to send "volunteers" to help Egypt/A United Nations Emergency Force acted as a buffer.

55. What was the "Eisenhower Doctrine"?

ANSWER: A doctrine passed by Congress on March 7, 1957, authorizing military and economic aid to any Middle East nation that requested it with the U.S. prepared to use force to repel any communist aggression.

56. Into what city and state in 1957 did President Eisenhower send a thousand U.S. paratroopers to aid desegregation and to place the National Guard under federal control? Who was the governor of this state? What Black over the opposition of what governor was admitted to the University of Mississippi in 1962? What governor blocked integration of the University of Alabama in 1963 until President Kennedy federalized the National Guard?

ANSWER: Little Rock, Arkansas/Governor Orval E. Faubus/James Meredith and Governor Ross Barnett/Governor George C. Wallace.

57. Name the plane and the pilot in the incident in May, 1960, that caused Premier Nikita Khrushchev to cancel the 4-Power Summit Conference in Paris. The pilot's freedom was exchanged for the release of what Soviet spy?

ANSWER: U-2 incident with the pilot Francis Gary Powers/Powers was released in exchange for Rudolf Abel.

58. When, where, and by whom was President John F. Kennedy assassinated? What happened to the assassin? What commission under whose leadership attributed the killing to one assassin?

ANSWER: November 22, 1963, in Dallas, Texas, by Lee Harvey Oswald/Oswald was later shot by Dallas nightclub owner Jack Ruby/The Presidential Commission under Chief Justice Earl Warren.

59. Identify each of the following nicknames.

a) Jazz Age
b) Bible Belt
c) Braintree Martyrs
d) *Spirit of St. Louis*
e) Manhattan Project
f) Day of Infamy
g) Wolf Packs
h) Foggy Bottom
i) Operation Vittles
j) *Corn Pone Special*

ANSWER: a) 1920's b) Southern United States c) Sacco and Vanzetti d) Lindbergh's airplane e) 1940's atomic bomb project f) Pearl Harbor, December 7, 1941 g) German submarine groups in WWII h) U.S. State Department i) Berlin Airlift of supplies in 1948-1949 j) Lyndon Johnson's 1960 campaign train.

60. Who shot and killed the Reverend Martin Luther King, Jr., on April 4, 1968, and Senator Robert P. Kennedy on June 5-6, 1968, and where did these assassinations occur? What is the SCLC and who assumed its leadership after King was killed?

ANSWER: King was shot by James Earl Ray in Memphis, Tennessee, and Kennedy was shot by Sirhan Sirhan in Los Angeles, California/The Southern Christian Leadership Conference/Dr. Ralph Abernathy took charge.

61. Name any of the 5 islands or groups of islands the U.S. returned to Japan in 1968 and 1972.

ANSWER: Iwo Jima, Bonin, Volcano, Okinawa, and Ryukyu Islands.

62. A cease-fire on January 28, 1973, ended the U.S. involvement in the Vietnam War. Briefly list the involvement of and escalation or deescalation by the U.S. Presidents during this war.

ANSWER: Truman...... Sent a 35-man military mission on June 27, 1950, along with economic assistance.

Eisenhower...Sent military advisers, who totaled almost 700 by May, 1960.

Kennedy..... Sent 400 Special Forces soldiers and over a 100 additional military advisers in May, 1961, and sent 5,000 U.S. troops to Thailand in April-May, 1962. There were over 16,000 troops in Southeast Asia at the end of 1963.

Johnson ..... Initiated the Tonkin Gulf Resolution; bombed North Vietnam; sent regular military units; and had over 536,000 troops there by the end of 1968. Started peace talks in May, 1968.

Nixon .... Authorized the bombing of Cambodia; resumed the bombing of North Vietnam; mined Haiphong Harbor; reduced troop levels to 150,000 by the end of 1971; and signed the cease-fire that ended U.S. involvement.

63. Who were the Vice President and President in the 1970's to resign that office? For what reasons did they do so?

ANSWER: Vice President Spiro Agnew did so in October, 1973, for income-tax evasion, and President Richard M. Nixon did so on August 9, 1974, to avoid impeachment and removal from office by Congress for his role in the Watergate scandals.

64. What are the names of the 2 Washington *Post* reporters who exposed the Watergate coverup? What was the name of their book?

ANSWER: Robert Woodward and Carl Bernstein/*All the President's Men.*

65. What was President Ronald Reagan's humorous quip to his wife after being shot on March 30, 1981, by John Hinckley, Jr.?

ANSWER: ''I forgot to duck.''

NEW DEAL AGENCIES

AAA.... Agricultural Adjustment Administration	**NIRA** ... National Industrial Recovery Administration
CCC.... Civilian Conservation Corps	**NLRB**... National Labor Relations Board
CCC.... Commodity Credit Corporation	**NRA**.... National Recovery Administration
CWA ... Civil Works Administration	**NYA**.... National Youth Administration
FCA.... Farm Credit Administration	**PWA** ... Public Works Administration
FCC.... Federal Communications Commission	**RA**..... Resettlement Administration
FCIC ... Federal Crop Insurance Corporation	**REA**.... Rural Electrification Administration
FDIC ... Federal Deposit Insurance Corporation	**SEC**.... Securities and Exchange Commission
FERA... Federal Emergency Relief Administration	**SSA**.... Social Security Administration
FFMC .. Federal Farm Mortgage Corporation	**SSB**.... Social Security Board
FHA.... Federal Housing Administration	**TVA**.... Tennessee Valley Authority
FSA.... Farm Security Administration	**USHA** .. United States Housing Authority
HOLC... Home Owners Loan Corporation	**WPA** ... Works Progress Administration

AMERICAN QUOTATIONS/SLOGANS/MOTTOES

WE DREW TO A PAIR OF DEUCES, AND FILLED
Warren G. Harding's comment to the Press the day after he was nominated by the Republican Party for President in 1920. Harding was not a serious candidate when he entered the race, and the nomination was quite a surprise; the poker long-shot analogy is appropriate.

NOT NOSTRUMS BUT NORMALCY
In May of 1920, President Warren G. Harding's penchant for alliteration led him to coin this phrase and popularize it at a speech in Boston. Harding's ''normalcy'' meant a return to more peaceful, prosperous, and less complicated times. He said: ''America's present need is not heroics but healing; not nostrums but normalcy; not revolution but restoration;...not surgery but serenity;...not submergence in internationality but sustainment in triumphant nationality.''

THE BUSINESS OF AMERICA IS BUSINESS
President Calvin Coolidge made this statement in January, 1925, by which he meant that the government should not interfere in business matters. He thus became the high priest of the great god ''Business.'' He said in full: ''The chief business of the American people is business.''

WELL, THEY HIRED THE MONEY, DIDN'T THEY?
Calvin Coolidge reiterated this American feeling that the Allies in World War I should pay their war debt. U.S. Allies felt that their contribution was the dead of their youth while the U.S. mostly provided the money. The American attitude was intransigent.

I DO NOT CHOOSE TO RUN FOR PRESIDENT IN 1928
This was Calvin Coolidge's line in declining to run for the presidency in 1928.

THE FORGOTTEN MAN
Franklin D. Roosevelt's speech during a campaign radio address on April 7, 1932, included these words: ''These unhappy times call for the building of plans...that build from the bottom up and not the top down, that put their faith once more in the forgotten man at the bottom of the economic pyramid.'' By the ''forgotten man'' Roosevelt meant the man out of work suffering from the Depression.

A NEW DEAL
Franklin D. Roosevelt was nominated for President by the Democrats in Chicago on July 2, 1932, when ''Cactus Jack'' Garner's votes were switched to Roosevelt in exchange for second place on the ticket. Roosevelt's program was enunciated in his acceptance speech when he said: ''Let it be from now on the task of our party to break foolish traditions . . . I pledge you, I pledge myself, to a new deal for the American people.''

THE ONLY THING WE HAVE TO FEAR IS FEAR ITSELF/THIS NATION ASKS FOR ACTION, AND ACTION NOW
Franklin D. Roosevelt was inaugurated on March 4, 1933, and these words were part of his inauguration speech: ''So, first of all, let me assert my firm belief that the only thing we have to fear is fear itself—nameless, unreasoning, unjustified terror which paralyzes needed efforts to convert retreat into advance....This nation asks for action, and action now. Our greatest primary task is to put people to work.'' Roosevelt mentioned what a great nation the U.S. was and that it would revive and prosper. His words comforted and inspired a nation in the middle of economic woes.

AS MAINE GOES, SO GOES THE NATION (UNION)
Elections for State officers in Maine were held in September, and the results in Maine were supposedly an indication of the way the political wind was blowing in the rest of the country. In the 1936 presidential election, Alf Landon carried only 2 states, Maine and Vermont. The aforementioned political adage was changed by James Farley in a statement to the Press to read: ''As Maine goes, so goes Vermont.''

I SEE A NATION ILL-HOUSED, ILL-CLAD, ILL-NOURISHED
Said by President Franklin D. Roosevelt in his second Inaugural Address given on January 20, 1937. Roosevelt concluded a list of ''I sees'' with ''I see one-third of a nation ill-housed, ill-clad, ill-nourished.'' He also said: ''The test of our progress is

not whether we add more to the abundance of those who have much; it is whether we provide enough for those who have too little.''

WAR IS A CONTAGION
President Roosevelt's words on October 5, 1937, at a bridge dedication in Chicago. He said that the peace of the world was being jeopardized by ten percent of the population. He also said: ''War is a contagion, whether it be declared or undeclared....We are determined to keep out of war, yet we cannot insure ourselves against the disastrous effects of war and the dangers of involvement.''

THE HAND THAT HELD THE DAGGER HAS STRUCK IT INTO THE BACK OF ITS NEIGHBOR
Franklin Roosevelt's words on June 10, 1940, the day that Mussolini joined the war and sided with Germany by attacking France.

A DAY OF INFAMY
President Roosevelt's words to Congress concerning Japan's attack on Pearl Harbor. He said: ''Yesterday, December 7, 1941—a date which will live in infamy—the United States of America was suddenly and deliberately attacked by naval and air forces of the Empire of Japan.'' Congress declared war on Japan, December 8, 1941.

GET HIROHITO FIRST
An American war cry after the bombing of Pearl Harbor. Fortunately calmer heads prevailed as American strategists decided on a better plan of defeating Germany first, then moving with force against Japan. Hirohito, the Emperor of Japan, would have to wait.

PRAISE THE LORD, AND PASS THE AMMUNITION
These were supposedly the words of Navy Chaplain Howell M. Forgy, who was aboard the U.S.S. *New Orleans* at Pearl Harbor on December 7, 1941. It was said that he put down his Bible and exhorted the ship's gunners to get the Japanese during the attack. These words became part of a wartime song by Frank Loesser.

I SHALL RETURN
General Douglas MacArthur's words after the surrender of American forces on April 9, 1942, on Bataan. MacArthur returned to Leyte Island on October 20, 1944, and said: ''People of the Philippines, I have returned....Rally to me.''

LAFAYETTE, WE ARE HERE AGAIN
This phrase was spoken by American troops as they entered familiar towns during World War II such as Château-Thierry and Belleau Woods where Americans had fought during World War I.

NUTS
Hitler made one final massive effort in the Ardennes Forest on December 16, 1944. The American troops took a beating and retreated. On December 22, at Bastogne, Belgium, the Germans, having surrounded the U.S. troops, asked the Americans to surrender. Brigadier General Anthony Clement McAuliffe, commander of the 101st Airborne Division, replied, ''Nuts.'' The Americans held on until help arrived and stopped the Germans at the Battle of the Bulge.

AN IRON CURTAIN HAS DESCENDED
Winston Churchill on March 5, 1946, at Westminister College in Fulton, Missouri, said: ''From Stettin in the Baltic to Trieste in the Adriatic, an iron curtain has descended across the Continent.''

WE ARE IN THE MIDST OF A COLD WAR
Bernard Baruch's words in 1947 about the world situation. He said: ''Let us not deceive ourselves, we are in the midst of a cold war.'' He was the first one to use the term ''cold war.''

I'M GOING TO GIVE 'EM HELL
President Harry S Truman's words during the 1948 election campaign. Truman, a heavy underdog, scored an impressive upset victory over Tom Dewey. Truman received 303 electoral votes to Dewey's 189.

THE WRONG WAR, AT THE WRONG PLACE, AT THE WRONG TIME, AND WITH THE WRONG ENEMY

These were General Omar Bradley's words to a U.S. Senate Committee on May 15, 1951, concerning General Douglas MacArthur's desire for war on the China mainland. MacArthur wanted a total war with China and appealed to Congressmen to do so. MacArthur addressed Congress on April 19, 1951, and stated as his main point, "In war there can be no substitute for victory." Truman had relieved MacArthur of his command in Korea on April 11, 1951.

I SHALL NOT BE A CANDIDATE FOR REELECTION
Harry S Truman said these words in March, 1952, announcing that he would not run for the presidency in 1952. Adlai E. Stevenson was nominated by the Democrats to oppose Dwight D. Eisenhower.

I SHALL GO TO KOREA
This was Dwight D. Eisenhower's promise during the 1952 election campaign. He said he would concentrate on the job of ending the Korea War as soon as the election was over, even if that required a personal visit. He said: "I shall go to Korea." He visited there from December 2 to 5, 1952. The armistice that ended the conflict was signed on July 27, 1953.

WHAT'S GOOD FOR GENERAL MOTORS
Charles E. Wilson was the president of General Motors when Dwight Eisenhower asked him to run the Defense Department. Wilson held GM stock, and GM had 60% of the defense contracts. Wilson told the Senate Armed Forces Committee in 1952: "I thought what was good for the country was good for General Motors, and what was good for General Motors was good for the country."

WE WILL BURY YOU
These were Nikita S. Khrushchev's words in November, 1956, directed toward the West. Khrushchev later explained that he meant that Russia would surpass the capitalist countries with superior technology.

WE STAND TODAY ON THE EDGE OF A NEW FRONTIER
John F. Kennedy's words on July 15, 1960, as he accepted the Democratic nomination for President. Kennedy said: "We stand today on the edge of a New Frontier—the frontier of the 1960's, a frontier of unknown opportunities and perils, a frontier of unfulfilled hopes and threats."

LET US NEVER NEGOTIATE OUT OF FEAR, BUT LET US NEVER FEAR TO NEGOTIATE
This phrase was part of John F. Kennedy's inaugural speech on January 20, 1961. Kennedy ended his speech with his now well-known: "And so, my fellow Americans, ask not what your country can do for you; ask what you can do for your country."

VICTORY HAS A THOUSAND FATHERS, BUT DEFEAT IS AN ORPHAN
President John F. Kennedy's words as he accepted the responsibility for the April 17, 1961, Bay of Pigs invasion which ended in failure.

ICH BIN EIN BERLINER
Kennedy's words in West Berlin on June 26, 1963. He said: "All free men, wherever they may live, are citizens of Berlin. And therefore, as a free man, I take pride in the words 'Ich bin ein Berliner.' "

I HAVE A DREAM/WE SHALL OVERCOME
Martin Luther King, Jr.'s words on August 29, 1963, in a speech at the Civil Rights "March on Washington." He said: "I have a dream that one day this nation will rise up and live out the true meaning of its creed: 'We hold these truths to be self-evident, that all men are created equal.'...I have a dream that my four little children will one day live in a nation where they will not be judged by the color of their skin, but by the content of their character."/The highlight of the 1963 March on Washington was the anthem of the Civil Rights movement, "We Shall Overcome," which was sung in front of the Lincoln Memorial.

YOU CAN'T SAY THAT DALLAS ISN'T FRIENDLY TO YOU TODAY
The words were those of the wife of Governor John Connally to President John F. Kennedy as they were riding through Dallas, Texas, and being received by an enthusiastic crowd just moments before he was shot and killed by Lee Harvey Oswald.

LET US CONTINUE
Lyndon B. Johnson's words to the Congress on November 27, 1963, just days after he

took office after the assassination of President Kennedy. He was seeking passage of all of Kennedy's New Frontier programs as a memorial to the late President.

COME NOW, AND LET US REASON TOGETHER
Lyndon B. Johnson's motto which was taken from Isaiah 1:18 and 28:30.

WAR ON POVERTY IN AMERICA
Lyndon B. Johnson's words in his State of the Union Address on January 8, 1964. He said: "This administration, here and now, declares unconditional war on poverty in America." The Office of Economic Opportunity supported Community Action Programs, Youth Programs, and Work Experience Programs. The Vietnam War drained a lot of money from his ambitious program.

I SHALL NOT SEEK AND I WILL NOT ACCEPT THE NOMINATION OF MY PARTY FOR ANOTHER TERM AS YOUR PRESIDENT
Lyndon B. Johnson's words on March 31, 1968, in a televised speech to the nation in which he announced unilateral deescalation of the war and invited North Vietnam to reciprocate in a "series of mutual moves toward peace." So that no one would think his plea was a politically expedient one on his part, he closed his talk with the startling announcement that he would not seek another term of office.

THAT'S ONE SMALL STEP FOR A MAN, ONE GIANT LEAP FOR MANKIND
Astronaut Neil A. Armstrong's words upon stepping on the moon on July 20, 1969. Upon landing on the moon Armstrong said: "Houston, Tranquility Base here. The Eagle has landed."

EFFETE (CORPS OF IMPUDENT) SNOBS/NATTERING NABOBS OF NEGATIVISM
Both phrases were spoken by former Vice President Spiro Agnew. The first phrase was directed at peace demonstrators protesting the Vietnam War. "Effete" means "worn out" or "intellectually barren" and not "effeminate" as many people thought. Agnew used this phrase in a speech in New Orleans in October, 1969, when he said: "A spirit of national masochism prevails encouraged by an effete corps of impudent snobs who characterize themselves as intellectuals."/The second phrase was used in San Diego in September, 1970, in which he denounced the pessimists in the media, and it was especially intended for those reporters and commentators for their criticism and questioning of President Nixon's Vietnam War policy. He said: "In the United States today, we have more than our share of the nattering nabobs of negativism. They have formed their own 4-H Club—the hopeless, hysterical hypochondriacs of history." "Nattering" means "chattering idly" or "complaining"; "nabobs" means "wealthy, (self-) important people."

I AM NOT A CROOK
President Richard Nixon's words proclaiming his lack of guilt in any wrongdoing in the Watergate affair. The Watergate tapes indicated his involvement in the cover-up of the crimes. Nixon believed in his innocence, for in a 1977 interview with David Frost he declared: "Well, when the President does it, that means it is not illegal." Nixon resigned on August 9, 1974, rather than face an impeachment trial.

I AM A FORD, NOT A LINCOLN/OUR LONG NATIONAL NIGHTMARE IS OVER
Gerald R. Ford made the first statement on October 12, 1973, after his nomination as Vice President and repeated the line in his first address as President of the United States/The second phrase referred to the nightmare of "Watergate" and its long-drawn out history culminating with President Nixon's resignation on August 9, 1974. Ford made this statement on August 9, 1974, after being sworn in as the 38th President of the U.S.

THE MORAL EQUIVALENT OF WAR
This phrase was used by President Jimmy Carter in a televised speech on April 18, 1977, as he exhorted the people and the Congress to support his energy program designed to preserve fuel, conserve energy, and develop alternate forms of it so that the U.S. could become self-sufficient and not have to rely on foreign governments to supply U.S. energy needs. He said: "The energy crisis has not yet overwhelmed us, but it will if we do not act quickly," and that this is "the greatest challenge that our country will face in our lifetimes." The phrase was taken from William James's essay "The Moral Equivalent of War" (1910).

AMERICAN BATTLES/WARS/INCIDENTS: THEIR SITES AND DATES

St. Valentine's Day
Massacre .... Chicago .... February 14, 1929
U.S.S. *Panay* .... Yangtze River .... December 12, 1937
Robin Moor .... Coast of Brazil.......... May 21, 1941
U.S.S. *Kearny*......... near Iceland .... October 17, 1941
U.S.S. *Reuben James*... near Iceland .... October 30, 1941
Pearl Harbor .... Hawaii .... December 7, 1941
Battle of the Atlantic .... Jan. 1942-May, 1943
Bataan & Corregidor ...... Philippines .... Jan. 2-May 6, 1942
Java Sea...................................... Feb. 27-March 1, 1942
Tokyo bombed .... Japan .... April 18, 1942
Coral Sea .... May 7-8,1942
Midway............... Pacific Ocean .... June 3-6, 1942
Guadalcanal Campaign .... Solomon Islands .... Aug. 7-Nov. 15, 1942
Savo Island............. Solomon Islands .... August 9, 1942
Cape Esperance .... Solomon Islands .... October 11-12, 1942
Santa Cruz .... Solomon Islands .... October 26-27, 1942
North African Campaign ... North Africa .... Nov. 8, 1942-May 13, 1943
Bismarck Sea .... New Guinea .... March 2-3, 1943
Aleutian Islands .... North Pacific........... Mar. 24-Aug. 15, 1943
Sicily .... July 10-Aug. 17, 1943
Pacific Advance .... Gilbert, Marshall, and
                         Mariana Islands .... Nov. 21, 1943-Apr. 1, 1945
Makin................. Gilbert Islands .... Nov. 21, 1943
Tarawa .... Gilbert Islands .... Nov. 21, 1943
Anzio-Rome .... Italy .... Jan. 22-June 4, 1944
Kwajalein Atoll .... Marshall Islands .... Feb. 1-8, 1944
Truk .... Caroline Islands .... Feb. 17-18, 1944
Eniwetok (Enewetak) ..... Marshall Islands .... Feb. 18-23, 1944
D-Day .... France (Normandy)....... June 6, 1944
Philippine Campaign ...... Philippines .... June 19-Dec. 15, 1944
Philippine Sea........................ June 19-20, 1944
Guam .... Mariana Islands .... July 21-Aug. 10, 1944
Paris liberated........... France .... August 25, 1944
Brussels-Antwerp........ Belgium .... August 28, 1944
Luxembourg liberated .... September 11, 1944
Germany................................ Sept. 12, 1944-Apr. 26, 1945
Leyte Campaign .... Philippines .... Oct. 20, 1944-Jan. 1, 1945
Leyte Gulf .... Philippines .... Oct. 23-25, 1944
Ardennes Forest/Bastogne/
Battle of the Bulge........ France, Belgium, and
                         Luxembourg .... Dec. 1944-Jan. 1945
Philippines Liberation ..... Philippines .... Jan. 9-Aug. 14, 1945
Iwo Jima.............. Volcano Islands .... Feb. 19-Mar. 16, 1945
Okinawa .... Ryukyu Islands.......... April 1-June 21, 1945
Germany surrenders....................... May 1-8, 1945
Hiroshima.............. Japan .... Aug. 6, 1945
Nagasaki .... Japan .... Aug. 9, 1945
Japan surrenders .... August 14, 1945
Berlin Airlift .... Germany............. June 24, 1948-May 12, 1949
Osan................. Korea .... July 5, 1950
Pusan Perimeter .... Korea .... Aug. 5-Sept. 26, 1950
Inchon Landing.......... Korea .... Sept. 15, 1950
Inchon to Seoul to the
Yalu River.............. Korea .... Sept. 15-Nov. 24, 1950
Yalu River to 38th
parallel .... Korea .... Nov. 25-Dec. 15, 1950

38th parallel to
Osan-Han River.......... Korea .... Jan. 1-24, 1950
Osan-Han River to north
of the 38th parallel .... Korea .... Jan. 25-April 22, 1951
North of 38th parallel to
south of 38th parallel ..... Korea .... April 23-May, 1951
Seoul-"Iron Triangle,"
"Punchbowl" .... Korea .... May-June 15, 1951
Little Rock school crisis .... Arkansas .... Sept. 4-25, 1957
U-2 plane shot down...... Russia .... May 1, 1960
Bay of Pigs .... Cuba................. April 17, 1961
Cuban Missile Crisis
(missile bases dismantled
Nov. 20) .... Cuba................. Oct. 22-28, 1962
Gulf of Tonkin .... South China Sea .... Aug. 2-4, 1964
Pleiku .... South Vietnam .... Feb. 7, 1965
Selma to Montgomery
March................. Alabama .... March 21-25, 1965
Watts Riot .... Los Angeles .... Aug. 11-16, 1965
Ia Drang Valley .... Vietnam .... Nov. 3-6, 1965
Chicago Riots .... Illinois................. July 12-15, 1966
Newark Riots .... New Jersey............. July 12-17, 1967
Detroit Riots .... Michigan .... July 23-30, 1967
Khe Sanh .... Vietnam .... April 5, 1968
U.S.S. *Pueblo* .... North Korea .... Jan. 23, 1968
Tet Offensive............ Vietnam .... Jan. 30-Feb. 20, 1968
My Lai Massacre .... Vietnam .... March 16, 1968
Racial riots in 125 cities
in 29 states following the
assassination of Rev.
Martin Luther King, Jr..... United States .... April 4-11, 1968
Kent State .... Ohio .... May 4, 1970
Last U.S. troops leave
Vietnam............... Vietnam .... March 29, 1973
"Saturday Night
Massacre"............. Washington, D.C......... Oct. 20, 1973
Last Americans leave
Saigon................ Vietnam .... April 29, 1975
U.S. Mayagüez.......... Cambodia/Gulf of Siam.... May 14-15, 1975
Three Mile Island .... Harrisburg, Pa........... March 28, 1979
Capture of 53 hostages
and the American Embassy
in Teheran............. Iran .... November 4, 1979
Failure of U.S. attempt to
rescue hostages held by Iran. Iran .... April 24-25, 1980
Release of 52 hostages
by Iran................ Iran .... January 20, 1981
Air Traffic Controllers'
strike and their union,
PATCO, decertified as
a bargaining agent........ U.S.................. Aug. 3-Oct. 22, 1981
Poisoned Tylenol killings ... Illinois .... Sept.-Oct., 1982
Beirut terrorist attack
kills 241 U.S. marines ..... Lebanon .... October 23, 1983
U.S. troops land.......... Granada .... October 25, 1983

AMERICAN HISTORICAL PERSONAGES AND THEIR NICKNAMES

Creighton William Abrams ... Patton's Peer
Bella Savitsky Abzug .... Battling (Bellicose, Hurricane) Bella, Mother Courage
Sherman Adams .... Abominable No-Man
Spiro Agnew .... Spiro T. Eggplant, Nixon's Nixon, White Knight
Edwin Eugene Aldrin, Jr. ..... Buzz, Second Man on the Moon
Jack Anderson .... America's Highest Authority on Eavesdropping, Modern Muckraker, Muckraker with a Mission, Square Courage of Washington, Voice of the Voiceless
Neil Armstrong .... First Man on the Moon
Henry H. Arnold .... Father of the U.S. Air Force, Hap
Francis Lee Bailey .... Head Hunter
Alben William Barkley .... Dear Alben, Little Alby, Veep
David Berkowitz .... 44-Caliber Killer, Son of Sam
William Edgar Borah .... Big Potato, Idaho Lion, Lion of the Senate, Lone Lion
Omar Nelson Bradley .... Doughboy's General, G.I.'s General
Louis Dembitz Brandeis ..... People's Attorney, People's Lawyer
Arthur Bremer .... Boy Who Shut Everyone Out, Misanthrope
Harold Brown .... Dr. No
Art Buchwald .... Washington's Resident Humorist
William F. Buckley, Jr. ...... Conservative Columnist
Tristam Burgess .... Bald Eagle of Rhode Island
Arthur Frank Burns .... Sugar Daddy of Big Bankers
William Calley .... Hero Calley, Rusty Calley, Unlikely Villain
Dale Carnegie .... Man With a Message
Lillian Carter .... Miss Lillian
William Casey .... Wall Street's Favorite Bureaucrat
Whittaker Chambers .... Uncle Whit
Claire Lee Chennault .... Flying Tiger, Old Leather Face
Caryl Chessman .... Red Light Bandit
Frank Church .... Senator Sunday School
William P. Clark, Jr. .... Don't Know Man, Nitwit
Lucius DuBignon Clay .... Great Uncompromiser
Thomas Gardiner Corcoran ... Tommy the Cork, White House Tommy
Archibald Cox .... Blabbermouth, First Watergate Prosecutor, Mr. Impeccable
Charles Curtis .... Big Chief
Angela Davis .... Angela the Red, Enigmatic Angela
John Dean, III .... America's Unsung Hero, Mr. Clean, Secret-Sharer
John Dewey .... Father of Modern Education
Thomas E. Dewey .... Little Man on the Wedding Cake
Everett McKinley Dirksen .... Dirk, Distillery King, Wizard of Ooze
John Foster Dulles .... Architect of the ''Containing Communism'' Policy
Thomas Eagleton .... McGovern's Man From Missouri
Amelia Earhart (Putnam) ..... America's Premier Air Woman, First Lady of the Air
Daniel Ellsberg .... Last Great American Hero, Man Who Started It All
Sam Ervin .... Hyperbolic Historian, Po' Ol' Country Lawyer, Senator Sam, Southern Sam, Uncle Sam
Billie Sol Estes .... Billie Boy from Pecos
Charles W. Fairbanks .... Icebanks
Albert Fall .... Decade's Arch Villain, Patriarch of the Three Rivers
Jim Farley .... Big Jim, Four-job Farley (Spoiler), Genial Jim, Gentleman Jim, Political Thorn, Smiling Jim, That Candid Spoilsman
Henry Ford .... Automobile Wizard, Genius of Motordom
Fanne Foxe .... Argentine Firecracker, Tidal Basin Bombshell
John Kenneth Galbraith ..... Great Mogul, World's Tallest Economist
John Nance Garner .... Cactus Jack, Favorite Son of Texas, Mohair Jack,

	Owl, Poker Face, Sage of Uvalde, Uvalde Jack
Marcus Garvey	Black Nationalist, Provisional President of Africa
Euell Gibbons	Wild Hickory Nut
John Glenn	First American in Orbit, Original Astronaut
Barry Goldwater	Beelzebub M. Goldwater, Monster from Arizona
Billy Graham	Cadillac Evangelist, Most Admired Man in America
Alexander Haig	Man In Charge, Mr. Inside, the New Haldeman, Sir Laurence Olivier of the White House
H.R. Haldeman	First of the Nixon Men, Keeper of the Gates, Lickety-Split Technician, Nixon's Alter Ego, the President's Rasputin, Pride of the Pragmatists
William F. Halsey	Bull
Richard Hanna	Capitol Hill's Premier Junketeer
W. Averell Harriman	Crocodile
Bruno Hauptmann.	Cemetery John
S.I. Hayakawa	Samurai in a Tam O'Shanter, Sleepy-eye
Patricia Hearst	Renegade Newspaper Heiress, Tania
J. Edgar Hoover	Modern Knight Errant
Charles Evans Hughes	Bearded Iceberg
Cordell Hull.	Cord, Father of the United Nations, Old H'ar-Thar'-and-Ev'ry Whar'
Hubert Horatio Humphrey. . . .	HHH, Happy Warrior, Hump, Pinky
E. Howard Hunt	Compulsive Spy, Master Story Teller
Harold LeClaire Ickes	Blunderbuss Ickes, Chicago Chinch-bug, Curmudgeon, Honest Harold, New Deal Blackjack Squad, Old Curmudgeon
Henry Jackson	Last of the Cold War Liberals, Scoop
Hugh Johnson	Babe Ruth of the New Deal, Crackdown Johnson, Crackdown Czar of the N.R.A., Great Thundering Rooster, King of the Never-Made-Good Crack Downs, N.R.A. Czar, Old Iron Pants
Teddy Kennedy.	Chappaquiddick Chicken, Coward of Chappaquiddick, Democrat's Albatross, Hero of Chappaquiddick, Hero of Squaw Island, Last of the Kennedy Brothers
Robert Kennedy	RFK
Martin Luther King, Jr..	Peaceful Warrior
Henry Kissinger	Administration's Marco Polo, Henry the K, Henry-You-Know-Who, Herr Henry, Hustling Henry, Nixon's Svengali, Sammy Glick of the Cold War, Superhenry
Robert La Follette	Battling Bob, Fighting Bob
Fiorello H. La Guardia	Butch, Little Flower
Alf Landon	Coolidge of the West, Horse and Buggy Governor, Kansas Coolidge, Poor Man's Coolidge
William Lemke	Liberty Bell, Moratorium Bill
Charles Lindbergh	Ambassador of Good Will, Ambassador of the Air, Flying Fool, Lindy, Lone Eagle, Lucky Lindy, Slim
Huey Long	Dictator of Louisiana, Hooey Long, Kingfish, Louisiana's Loud Speaker
Alice Roosevelt Longworth . . .	Little Miss Roosevelt, Princess Alice, Queen Alice
Douglas MacArthur.	Beau Brummel of the Army, Buck Private's Gary Cooper, D'Artagnan of the A.E.F., Disraeli of the Chiefs of Staff, Dugout Doug, The Magnificent, Napoleon of Luzon
Lester Maddox	Mr. White Backlash
Malcolm X (Malcolm Little) . . .	Big Red, Detroit Red
Joseph McCarthy	Low-blow Joe, Tail-Gunner Joe
George McGovern	Honest George, Master Wrecker, St. George
Thomas Riley Marshall	Advocate of the Five Cent Cigar, Hoosier Statesman
George Meany	Silver-haired Elderly Statesman of American Labor

Andrew Mellon . . . . Aluminum Baron, Greatest Secretary of the Treasury since Hamilton, Mentor of Aluminum, Ubiquitous Financier of the Universe, World's Second Richest Man, Uncle Andy

H.L. Mencken . . . . Bad Boy of Baltimore, Disturber of the Peace, Great Debunker, Greatest Practicing Literary Journalist, the Irreverent Mr. Mencken, Private Secretary of God Almighty, Ringmaster, Sage of Baltimore

Wilbur Mills . . . . Arkansas Hunkerer, Mr. Taxes

John Mitchell . . . . Big Enchilada, Phantom President of the United States, President's Worst Friend

Martha Mitchell . . . . American Mouth of the Year, Last of the Great Southern Belles, Mouth That Roared, Watergate Warbler

William Mitchell . . . . Angry Eagle of Aviation, Pioneer of Air Power

Walter Mondale . . . . Fritz

Wayne Morse . . . . Lone Wolf of the Senate, The Wrecker

Audie Murphy. . . . . America's Most Decorated Soldier, Baby Murphy

Ralph Nader . . . . Consumer Advocate, Genius of the Negative Approach, National Ombudsman, Open Issue Ralph, People's Lawyer, Premier Public Relations Man of the Age

George William Norris . . . . Dean of the Liberals, Father of the Public Utility Regulation, Great Purist, Father of the 20th Amendment to the Constitution

Thomas P. O'Neill, Jr. . . . . . . Tip

Lee Harvey Oswald . . . . Man Who Killed Kennedy, The Psychopath

A. Mitchell Palmer . . . . Fighting Quaker, Quaking Fighter

Rosa Parks . . . . Mother of the Civil Rights Movement

Wright Patman . . . . Anti-Chain-Store Patman, Father of the Bonus

George S. Patton. . . . . Blood 'n' Guts, Old Blood and Guts, Old Iron Pants, Green Hornet

Drew Pearson . . . . Leading Muckraker of His Time, Pugnacious Pearson, Tenacious Muckraker

Claude Pepper . . . . The Galahad of the Elderly

Asa Frances Perkins. . . . . Fearless Frances, Liberal Politician, Loquacious Linguist Whom Labor Loves

Adam Clayton Powell . . . . King

A. Philip Randolph . . . . The Chief, Father of the Civil Rights Movement, Mr. Black Labor

James Earl Ray . . . . Camouflaged Killer, Lovelorn Killer

Sam Rayburn . . . . Mr. Sam, Grand Old Man

Walter Reuther . . . . Labor's Rugged Individualist, Red-headed Kid from Wheeling

Hyman Rickover . . . . Father of the Atomic Submarine

Nelson Rockefeller . . . . Dean of American Governors, Mr. Clean, Old Nels, Rocky, Spendthrift of Albany

Will Rogers . . . . Ambassador of Good Will, Cherokee Kid, Cowboy Philosopher, Man Who Can Say Anything and Make Everybody Like It, Poet Lariat, Prince of Wit and Wisdom

Eleanor Roosevelt . . . . First Lady of the World, World's Most Admired Woman

Jack Ruby . . . . Assassin's Assassin

Pierre Salinger . . . . Plucky

William Saxbe. . . . . Old Blunderbuss

George Schultz . . . . Supercrat, Washington's Scholar-Athlete

Alfred Emanuel Smith . . . . Assemblyman from the Bowery, Happy Warrior, Hero of the Cities, Newsboy Al, Sidewalk Statesman

Harold Stassen . . . . Secretary for Peace

Joseph Warren Stilwell . . . . . . Old Tu'key Neck, Uncle Joe, Vinegar Joe

Robert Alphonso Taft . . . . Mr. Republican

Herman Talmadge . . . . Humman Talmadge, Ol'Hummon

Gloria Vanderbilt. . . . . Poor Little Rich Girl
Robert Vesco . . . . Bootstrap Kid
James J. Walker. . . . . Beau James, Gentleman Jimmy, Mayor Jimmy, Playboy
of New York, Tammany Tiger, Wisecracker
George C. Wallace . . . . Headless Horseman, Lonesome George
Henry A. Wallace . . . . Lord Corn Wallace, Pied Piper of the Politburo, Plow
'Em Under Wallace
Byron Raymond White . . . . . . Whizzer White
Edward Douglas White . . . . . Mentor of the Rule of Reason
Theodore H. White . . . . Dean of American Reporters
Wendell Willkie. . . . . Rich Man's Roosevelt, Simple Barefoot Boy from Wall
Street, Simple Barefoot Wall Street Lawyer

GENERAL NICKNAMES AND CLAIMS TO FAME

Prohibition Era. . . . . Dry Era
Place in which a small group of politicians
conduct secret negotiations (as with
Warren Harding's nomination on
June 12, 1920) . . . . Smoke-filled Room
Model T . . . . Tin Lizzie
Homemade (inferior) gin . . . . Bathtub gin
1920's. . . . . Dollar Decade, Golden Twenties, Jazz Age,
Roaring Twenties
Early airplanes. . . . . Flying coffins
Post WWI America . . . . Era of Wonderful Nonsense
Making/selling illegal whiskey . . . . Bootlegging
Person who smuggles/sells illegal
whisky. . . . . Bootlegger
Japan . . . . Land of the Cherry Blossom
United States. . . . . Land of Promise (according to the
immigrants)
Flaming youth of the 1920's (according
to Gertrude Stein)/People who did not fit
into the 1920's way of life (according to
Ernest Hemingway) . . . . A Lost Generation *(une génération
perdue)*
Orientals in California. . . . . Yellow horde
Person who smuggles whiskey across
the border by motorized means . . . . Rumrunner
Place that sold illegal whiskey . . . . Speakeasy
Weak beer with 3.2% alcohol . . . . 3.2 beer (near beer)
Southern United States . . . . Bible Belt
Thomas Walsh and Burton Wheeler for
their investigations of the Harding
administration scandals. . . . . Assassins of character, Montana mud-
gunners or scandalmongers
Ku Klux Klan . . . . Knights of the Invisible Empire
Politicians close to Warren Harding who
used their political influence for personal
gain (usually by illegal means). . . . . Ohio Gang
Southern and Western progressive
senators . . . . Sons of the Wild Jackasses (according to
Senator Moses)
1925 Tennessee trial of John Scopes on
the validity of the law on the teaching
of evolution . . . . Monkey Trial
Automobiles. . . . . Houses of prostitutions on wheels
Sacco and Vanzetti (d. 1927) . . . . Braintree Martyrs

Bootleg Liquor . . . . Liquid tonsillectomies

The common people, the rabble . . . . Booboisie (according to H. L. Mencken)

Machine guns . . . . Typewriters

The era which ended in the Wall Street
Crash of 1929 . . . . Era of Wonderful Nonsense (coined by Westbrook Pegler)

Congress and those members who were
not reelected in November, yet served
until March 4 the following year . . . . Lame Duck Congress, Lame Ducks

League of Nations . . . . League of Hallucinations

The U.S. because of the many
immigrants who adopted American ways
after a time . . . . Melting Pot

Prohibition . . . . Noble experiment (according to Herbert Hoover)

Chicago . . . . City of the Big Shoulders (according to Carl Sandburg)

Lindbergh's airplane . . . . *Spirit of St. Louis*

$.05 admission theatres . . . . Nickleodeons

Wall Street . . . . The Street, Street of Sorrows

Self-appointed censors . . . . Bookburners

Shantytowns . . . . Hoovervilles, Hoover Villas

Attorney General of the U.S. . . . . First Lawyer of the Land

Anti-union contracts . . . . Yellow dog contracts

Moratorium on war-debt payments . . . . . . Hoover Holiday

FBI agents . . . . G-men

Franklin Roosevelt's advisers . . . . Brain Trust (Brains Trust)

Common working man during the
Depression . . . . Forgotten Man (according to Franklin Roosevelt)

Closing of the banks by Roosevelt from
March 6 to 9, 1933 . . . . Bank Holiday

Project to create jobs to stimulate the
economy but a waste of government
money . . . . Boondoggle (coined by Samuel Maverick)

Roosevelt's New Deal Agencies . . . . ABC's of the New Deal, Alphabet Agencies, Alphabet Soup

Mid-western states afflicted by severe
drought and strong winds (in the
1930's) . . . . Dust Bowl

Devalued dollar as of April 19, 1933,
when the U.S. went off the gold
standard . . . . Baloney Dollar

The 9 Justices of the U.S. Supreme
Court, most of whom blocked Roosevelt's
New Deal programs in the 1930's . . . . Nine Old Men (according to Franklin Roosevelt)

President Roosevelt's plan to add more
Supreme Court Justices . . . . Court packing

Opponents of Roosevelt's New Deal
program, or those who criticized any of
his policies . . . . Intellectual Termites, Political Gadflies

74th Congress of 1935 according to
critics who objected to its approval of
President Roosevelt's proposals . . . . Rubber Stamp Congress

Munitions manufacturers . . . . Merchants of death

Groups that backed Wendell Willkie in
the 1940 presidential campaign . . . . Unholy Alliance (according to Franklin Roosevelt)

United States in 1940 . . . . Arsenal of Democracy

Howard Hughes's 8-engine wooden
flying boat . . . . Spruce Goose

1940's atomic bomb project . . . . Manhattan (District) Project

Home of Franklin Roosevelt at Warm
Springs, Georgia . . . . Little White House

Pearl Harbor, December 7, 1941 . . . . Day of Infamy

70 mile walk of American prisoners
without food and water in 1942 from
Mariveles to San Fernando on Bataan (a
peninsula on Luzon in the Philippines). . . . Death March, The March of Death

German submarine groups. . . . . Wolf packs

U.S.S. *Franklin* . . . . Big Ben

Roosevelt's New Deal . . . . Raw Deal (according to the critics)

Republicans who accepted New Deal and
Fair Deal domestic and foreign policies,
especially the economic ones. . . . . Me-Too-Ers

Truk . . . . Gibraltar of the Pacific

June 6, 1944. . . . . D-Day, The Longest Day

Liberty Ships . . . . Ugly Ducklings

San Francisco, Calif. (April 25, 1945) . . . . The United Nations' Conference Center

Alamogordo, New Mexico (July 16,
1945) . . . . City where the Atomic Age Dawned

Significant increase in the population of
the U.S. During and after the war . . . . Baby boom

U.S. State Department. . . . . Foggy bottom

1947-1948 Congress. . . . . Do-Nothing Congress, the Republican 80th
(according to President Truman)

Southern democrats in 1948 opposed to
Truman's civil rights platform . . . . Dixiecrats

Berlin airlift in 1948-1949 . . . . Operation Vittles

Marshall Plan. . . . . Martial Plan, Operation Rathole, Share-the-
American-Wealth-Plan

200,000 Chinese troops which entered
the Korean War to help the North
Koreans. . . . . Volunteers

The U.S., according to Mao Tse-tung,
who saw it as a nation with only
imaginary strength . . . . Paper Tiger

Helicopter . . . . Chopper, Egg beater, Whirly bird

Physical abuse and mental torture plus
indoctrination to change someone's
loyalty . . . . Brainwashing

Intellectual supporters of Adlai
Stevenson in 1952. . . . . Eggheads

Eisenhower's original cabinet . . . . Eight millionaires and a plumber

Policy of risking war by forcing an
enemy to retreat from his actions . . . . Brinkmanship

Groton, Connecticut. . . . . World's Submarine Capital (the *Nautilus*,
the first atomic-powered submarine, was
launched there on January 21, 1954)

Belief that Communist control in one
country will be followed in others. . . . . . . Domino Theory

Conference (argument) between Vice
President Richard Nixon and Soviet
Chairman Nikita Khrushchev at the U.S.
exhibition in Moscow in 1959 in a
"typical American home" . . . . Kitchen Debate, Kitchen Conference (Sokol-
niki Summit)

Loss of the more intelligent, most
qualified people of a country to another
one .... Brain Drain

Lyndon Johnson's campaign train
in 1960 .... *Corn Pone Special*

An idealized John F. Kennedy administration .... Camelot

The length of the John F. Kennedy
Administration, from January 20, 1961,
to November 22, 1963 .... Thousand Days (1,037 exactly)

Interracial groups which went South in
the fight for black Civil Rights in 1960's .. Freedom Riders

Interracial groups which marched and
demonstrated in the South for racial
integration .... Freedom Marchers

The bright, rather young executives of
Secretary Robert McNamara's Defense
Department in 1961 .... Whiz Kids

An all-out war advocate in international
affairs .... Hawk

Critics of the Vietnam policy of Lyndon
Johnson.......................... Nervous Nellies (according to President
Johnson)

A peace advocate in international affairs .. Dove

Those coming of age in the 1960's ...... New Generation

Exchange of table-tennis players between
China and the United States in 1971 ..... Ping-Pong Diplomacy

Henry Kissinger's Mid-East peace
negotiations attempts .... Shuttle Diplomacy

Outlandish uniforms of the White House
Drum and Bugle Corps as ordered by
Richard Nixon .... Graustarkian

White House special group who were
instructed to plug leaks during the Nixon
administration .... Plumbers

Those convicted of breaking into the
Democratic National Committee head-
quarters in Washington, D.C., on
June 17, 1972..................... Watergate Seven

The October 20, 1973, dismissal of
Special Prosecutor Archibald Cox by
Richard Nixon .... Saturday Night Massacre

Military satellite used for espionage...... Eye in the sky

Earning money from a salary and
receiving a pension from the government
simultaneously .... Double dipping

Population reeducation to advocate one
birth for one death .... Zero Population Growth

Mostly Southern conservative Democrats
in the House .... Boll Weevils

Eastern and Midwestern Republicans
in the House .... Gypsy Moths

QUESTIONS AND ANSWERS

1. In what 2 cities was George Washington inaugurated as President of the U.S.?
ANSWER: In New York City on April 30, 1789, and in Philadelphia, Pennsylvania, on March 4, 1793.

2. What were the 3 executive departments established by Congress for Washington's administration, and who held those posts initially? Who were the first Postmaster General, the first Attorney General, and the first Chief Justice?
ANSWER: Thomas Jefferson was Secretary of State; Alexander Hamilton was Secretary of the Treasury; and Henry Knox was Secretary of War/Samuel Osgood was Postmaster General (Benjamin Franklin was a Postmaster General, but Osgood was the first to serve a President); Edmund Randolph was Attorney General; and John Jay was the first Chief Justice.

3. Who was the only woman who was wife of one U.S. President and mother of another? Name the 2 Presidents.
ANSWER: Abigail Adams was the wife of John Adams and mother of John Quincy Adams.

4. Name the 2 U.S. Presidents who received the largest percentage of the electoral votes cast in an election.
ANSWER: George Washington received 100% of the votes cast in the 1789 and the 1892 elections, and James Monroe received 99.57% of the votes (all but one) in the 1820 election.

5. Name the 3 U.S. Presidents who died on a July 4.
ANSWER: John Adams, Thomas Jefferson, and James Monroe.

6. Only 2 states fathered the first 6 U.S. Presidents. What 2?
ANSWER: Virginia and Massachusetts.

7. Name the 3 U.S. Presidents who were nicknamed the "Virginia Dynasty."
ANSWER: Thomas Jefferson, James Madison, and James Monroe (sometimes this "Dynasty" has 4 members, with George Washington being the 4th).

8. What is the maximum number of years that a U.S. President may serve?
ANSWER: 10 years.

9. Thomas Jefferson believed in the unofficial rule that no President should serve more than 2 terms. What 2 Presidents tried to win 3rd terms but were defeated?
ANSWER: Ulysses S. Grant (his backers were unable to get him nominated for a 3rd term) and Theodore Roosevelt (he lost in the 1912 election).

10. What U.S. President established a tradition against running for a 3rd term, and who was the first President to win a 3rd term?
ANSWER: Thomas Jefferson and Franklin Delano Roosevelt.

11. Who was the first U.S. President to submit his messages to Congress in writing? Name the 2 Presidents before this one who delivered their messages in person. Who was the next President who, after a long hiatus, revived the practice of addressing Congress in person?
ANSWER: Thomas Jefferson/George Washington and John Adams/Woodrow Wilson.

12. Name the 2 U.S. Presidents who chose to walk rather than ride in their inaugural parade.
ANSWER: Thomas Jefferson and Jimmy Carter. Jefferson walked to the Capitol from Mrs. Conrad's boarding house; Carter walked from the Capitol back to the White House.

13. Name the U.S. President under which each of the following Vice Presidents served.

a) Daniel D. Tompkins	f) Thomas A. Hendricks
b) George M. Dallas	g) Levi P. Morton
c) William R.D. King	h) Adlai E. Stevenson
d) John C. Breckinridge	i) Thomas R. Marshall
e) William A. Wheeler	j) Charles Curtis

ANSWER: a) James Monroe b) James K. Polk c) Franklin Pierce d) James Buchanan

e) Rutherford B. Hayes f) Grover Cleveland g) Benjamin Harrison h) Grover Cleveland i) Woodrow Wilson j) Herbert Hoover.

14. Who was the first U.S. President to live in the White House? Who was the first inaugurated President who lived in the White House? Who was the French architect who designed Washington, D.C.?
ANSWER: **John Adams/Thomas Jefferson/Pierre C. L'Enfant.**

15. Name the first 3 Vice Presidents of the United States. Who was the last Federalist President of the U.S.?
ANSWER: **John Adams, Thomas Jefferson, and Aaron Burr/John Adams.**

16. Name the 2 Vice Presidents of Thomas Jefferson.
ANSWER: **Aaron Burr and George Clinton.**

17. Who were the 3 U.S. Vice Presidents who died on a July 4? Who was the only U.S. President born on a July 4?
ANSWER: **John Adams, Thomas Jefferson, and Hannibal Hamlin/Calvin Coolidge.**

18. What 2 U.S. Presidents died on the same day, July 4, 1826?
ANSWER: **John Adams and Thomas Jefferson.**

19. How many U.S. Presidents are not buried in the United States? Name them.
ANSWER: **Four/Richard Nixon, Gerald Ford, Jimmy Carter, and Ronald Reagan.**

20. Name the 2 U.S. Presidents who were elected by the House of Representatives.
ANSWER: **Thomas Jefferson and John Quincy Adams.**

21. Who were James Madison's 2 Vice Presidents?
ANSWER: **George Clinton and Elbridge Gerry.**

22. How many Vice Presidents of the U.S. later became Presidents? Name them.
ANSWER: **Thirteen/John Adams, Thomas Jefferson, Martin Van Buren, John Tyler, Millard Fillmore, Andrew Johnson, Chester Arthur, Theodore Roosevelt, Calvin Coolidge, Harry Truman, Lyndon Johnson, Richard Nixon, and Gerald Ford.**

23. Who were the 7 Vice Presidents of the U.S. who died while in office?
ANSWER: **George Clinton (1812), Elbridge Gerry (1814), William R.D. King (1853), Thomas A. Hendricks (1885), Garret A. Hobart (1899), Henry Wilson (1875), and James D. Sherman (1912).**

24. Name the 2 Vice Presidents of the U.S. who resigned from office. Give the year and the President at the time. Who was the only President to be impeached? Who was the only President to resign from office? Give the years each of these events occurred.
ANSWER: **John C. Calhoun in 1832 with Andrew Jackson the President, and Spiro Agnew in 1973 with Richard Nixon the President/Andrew Johnson in 1867/ Richard Nixon in 1974.**

25. How many state capitals are named after U.S. Presidents? Name them.
ANSWER: **Four/Jefferson City, Missouri; Madison, Wisconsin; Jackson, Mississippi; and Lincoln, Nebraska.**

26. How many U.S. states have been named after U.S. Presidents? Name them.
ANSWER: **Just 1/Washington.**

27. Who were the 2 Vice Presidents of Andrew Jackson?
ANSWER: **John C. Calhoun and Martin Van Buren.**

28. Who were the candidates, what was the party, in what town and what year was the first party nominating convention held?
ANSWER: **William Wirt and Amos Ellmaker were the candidates of the Anti-Masonic Party, which met in Baltimore, Maryland, on September 26, 1831, for the presidential election of 1832.**

29. Name the 7 U.S. Presidents who were born in a log cabin.
ANSWER: **Andrew Jackson, Zachary Taylor, Millard Fillmore, Franklin Pierce, James Buchanan, Abraham Lincoln, and James Garfield.**

30. There have been 3 U.S. Presidents from Tennessee, but none of them was born in that state. Name the 3 Presidents and give their states of birth.

ANSWER: Andrew Jackson was born in South Carolina, and James K. Polk and Andrew Johnson were both born in North Carolina.

31. Recite the oath that is prescribed by the Constitution for the President of the United States.

ANSWER: "I do solemnly swear that I will faithfully execute the office of President of the United States, and will to the best of my ability, preserve, protect and defend the Constitution of the United States."

32. Name the only 2 times the Democrats did not win the election between 1800 and 1860, and tell who and what party defeated them.

ANSWER: The Democrats lost in 1840 to William Henry Harrison and the Whig Party and again in 1848 to the Whig Party, to Zachary Taylor this time.

33. Name the 6 Secretaries of State who became President of the United States and name the President under whom they served.

ANSWER: Thomas Jefferson (George Washington), James Madison (Thomas Jefferson), James Monroe (James Madison), John Quincy Adams (James Monroe), Martin Van Buren (Andrew Jackson), and James Buchanan (James K. Polk).

34. Name the 8th and 10th U.S. Vice Presidents who became the 8th and 10th Presidents of the U.S.

ANSWER: Martin Van Buren and John Tyler.

35. George Washington was nicknamed "Stepfather of His Country," and Abraham Lincoln was called "Father Abraham." Identify the Presidents from the following nicknames which all contain the word "Father."

a) Father of His Country
b) Father of the Homestead Act
c) Father of the University of Virginia
d) Father of the Constitution
e) Father of Pittsburgh
f) Father of American Independence
g) Father of the American Navy
h) Father of the Declaration of Independence

ANSWER: a) George Washington b) Andrew Johnson c) Thomas Jefferson d) James Madison e) George Washington f) John Adams g) John Adams h) Thomas Jefferson.

36. A minority President in the U.S. is one who received less than 50% of the popular vote. Name the first 5 minority Presidents.

ANSWER: John Quincy Adams, James K. Polk, Zachary Taylor, James Buchanan, and Abraham Lincoln.

37. In one 9 year period of time in United States history there were 6 Presidents. Name those 6 who held office from 1841 to 1850.

ANSWER: Martin Van Buren, William H. Harrison, John Tyler, James K. Polk, Zachary Taylor, and Millard Fillmore.

38. What 2 presidential elections did the Whig party ever win? Who were the Presidents, and what profession did these men have in common? Two other Presidents had this profession. Who were they? Who were the other 2 Whig Presidents, and how did they come to office?

ANSWER: The elections of 1840 and 1848/William Henry Harrison in 1840 and Zachary Taylor in 1848/They were both professional soldiers/Ulysses S. Grant and Dwight D. Eisenhower (Taylor and Grant were farmers before they became soldiers, however)/John Tyler, who took office upon Harrison's death, and Millard Fillmore, who took office upon Taylor's death.

39. Who was the first U.S. President elected without having any prior political experience or training? Who succeeded him?

ANSWER: Zachary Taylor/Millard Fillmore.

40. Name the first 3 Vice Presidents of the U.S. to become President after the death of the President. Give the years and name the Presidents.

ANSWER: John Tyler, Millard Fillmore, and Andrew Johnson/William H. Harrison died in 1841, Zachary Taylor in 1850, and Abraham Lincoln in 1865.

41. Name the 3 Presidents who graduated from William and Mary College.
ANSWER: Thomas Jefferson, James Monroe, and John Tyler.

42. During which 2 years did the U.S. have 3 Presidents each?
ANSWER: 1841 and 1881.

43. Who were the 3 U.S. Presidents during 1841?
ANSWER: Martin Van Buren, William Henry Harrison, and John Tyler.

44. Who were the 3 Presidents during 1881?
ANSWER: Rutherford B. Hayes, James A. Garfield, and Chester A. Arthur.

45. There were only 3 Vice Presidents of the U.S. who succeeded to the presidency who were elected to that post and not because of the death or resignation of the President. Name the 3.
ANSWER: John Adams, Thomas Jefferson, and Martin Van Buren.

46. An important general waging a war during which he had a successful amphibious landing was suddenly removed from his command by a Democratic President after a dispute over the conduct of the war. The general returned home to receive an ovation as a popular hero and was retired with all honors, pay, and rank. The following year the Democratic President declined nomination for another term and a general was elected President of the United States. Since there were 2 almost identical cases, give the 2 examples of this situation in U.S. history.
ANSWER: General Winfield Scott, who, during the Mexican War, made an amphibious landing near Vera Cruz, Mexico, was relieved of his command by James K. Polk in 1847. Polk declined to run again, and General Zachary Taylor was elected President in 1848/General Douglas MacArthur who, during the Korean War, made an amphibious landing at Inchon, South Korea, was relieved of his command by Harry S Truman in 1951. Truman declined to run again, and General Dwight D. Eisenhower was elected President in 1952.

47. There were 15 U.S. Presidents who were minority Presidents, which means that that they did not receive at least 50% of the popular vote. Name the 3 Presidents who actually trailed their opponents in the popular vote, and name their opponents.
ANSWER: John Quincy Adams over Andrew Jackson in 1824; Rutherford B. Hayes over Samuel J. Tilden in 1876; and Benjamin Harrison over Grover Cleveland in 1888.

48. Give the political party of each of the following U.S. Presidents.

a) John Adams
b) John Quincy Adams
c) William H. Harrison
d) Zachary Taylor
e) James Buchanan
f) Rutherford B. Hayes
g) Benjamin Harrison
h) Theodore Roosevelt
i) Woodrow Wilson
j) Harry Truman

ANSWER: a) Federalist b) Democratic-Republican c) Whig d) Whig e) Democrat f) Republican g) Republican h) Republican i) Democrat j) Democrat.

49. Name the U.S. President who appointed each of the following as Chief Justice of the Supreme Court.

a) John Jay
b) John Marshall
c) Roger Brooke Taney
d) William Howard Taft
e) Charles Evans Hughes
f) Frederick Moore Vinson
g) Earl Warren
h) Warren Earl Burger

ANSWER: a) George Washington b) John Adams c) Andrew Jackson d) Warren Harding e) Herbert Hoover f) Harry Truman g) Dwight Eisenhower h) Richard Nixon.

50. How many men have been President of the United States? What 2 positions in the list of numbered Presidents does Grover Cleveland hold? Who defeated him for reelection in 1889?
ANSWER: 39 (although Ronald Reagan is the 40th President)/22nd and 24th/ Benjamin Harrison.

51. Name the 6 Presidents of the U.S. who have been named ''James.''

ANSWER: **Madison, Monroe, Polk, Buchanan, Garfield, and Carter.**

52. Name the 2 Vice Presidents of Abraham Lincoln.
ANSWER: **Hannibal Hamlin and Andrew Johnson.**

53. What President of 11 U.S. states had neither a predecessor nor a successor?
ANSWER: **Jefferson Davis.**

54. What 5 U.S. Presidents wore beards while in office?
ANSWER: **Abraham Lincoln, Ulysses S. Grant, Rutherford B. Hayes, James Garfield, and Benjamin Harrison.**

55. Name the 2 U.S. Presidents who celebrated golden wedding anniversaries and who were related as father and son. What 2 Presidents were related as grandfather and grandson.
ANSWER: **John Adams and John Quincy Adams/William Henry Harrison and Benjamin Harrison.**

56. Name the 2 Vice Presidents of Ulysses S. Grant.
ANSWER: **Schuyler Colfax and Henry Wilson.**

57. What 2 Presidents of the U.S. served the least amount of time as Presidents?
ANSWER: **William Henry Harrison (31 days in 1841) and James A. Garfield (6½ months in 1881).**

58. Name the 3 Vice Presidents of the U.S. whose last names were Johnson, and name the Presidents they served.
ANSWER: **Richard M. Johnson with Martin Van Buren; Andrew Johnson with Abraham Lincoln; and Lyndon B. Johnson with John F. Kennedy.**

59. Who were the only 2 Republican Presidents of the U.S. to serve 2 full terms? What educational experience did these men have in common?
ANSWER: **Ulysses S. Grant and Dwight D. Eisenhower/They both attended West Point.**

60. Name the 5 U.S. Presidents who graduated from Harvard.
ANSWER: **John and John Quincy Adams, Theodore Roosevelt and Franklin Roosevelt, and John F. Kennedy.**

61. Many U.S. Presidents served in both Houses of Congress; who were the 5 who served only in the Senate?
ANSWER: **James Monroe, Martin Van Buren, Benjamin Harrison, Warren Harding, and Harry Truman.**

62. Name the 3 U.S. Presidents who were also governors of Virginia.
ANSWER: **Thomas Jefferson, James Monroe, and John Tyler.**

63. What 4 U.S. Presidents were also governors of New York?
ANSWER: **Martin Van Buren, Grover Cleveland, Theodore Roosevelt, and Franklin D. Roosevelt.**

64. Name the 4 U.S. Presidents who died a natural death in office.
ANSWER: **William H. Harrison, Zachary Taylor, Warren G. Harding, and Franklin D. Roosevelt.**

65. What 4 U.S. Presidents are sculpted on Mount Rushmore?
ANSWER: **George Washington, Thomas Jefferson, Abraham Lincoln, and Theodore Roosevelt.**

66. What 2 Presidents of the U.S. had fathers who signed the Declaration of Independence?
ANSWER: **John Quincy Adams and William Henry Harrison.**

67. Name the 4 generals who lost attempts to become Presidents of the U.S.
ANSWER: **Lewis Cass in 1848; Winfield Scott in 1852; George B. McClellan in 1864; and Winfield Scott Hancock in 1880 (John Charles Frémont, a presidential candidate in 1856, became a major general during the Civil War).**

68. What 3 families have been twice represented in the White House?
ANSWER: **Adams, Harrison, and Roosevelt.**

69. Name the 2 Presidents who were 2nd cousins.

ANSWER: James Madison and Zachary Taylor.

70. Identify the U.S. Presidents from the following nicknames which all have ''Hero'' as part of the nickname.

a) Hero of '77

b) Hero of Fort Donelson

c) Hero of Tippecanoe

d) Hero of New Orleans

e) Hero of San Juan Hill

f) Hero of Appomattox

g) Hero of Buena Vista

h) Land Hero of 1812

ANSWER: a) Rutherford B. Hayes b) Ulysses S. Grant c) William H. Harrison d) Andrew Jackson e) Theodore Roosevelt f) Ulysses S. Grant g) Zachary Taylor h) Andrew Jackson.

71. Name the 3 U.S. Presidents from Ohio who served one after the other.

ANSWER: Ulysses S. Grant, Rutherford B. Hayes, and James Garfield.

72. Who were the 3 U.S. Presidents from Virginia who served one after the other?

ANSWER: Thomas Jefferson, James Madison, and James Monroe.

73. Who were the only 2 elected Democratic Presidents of the U.S. between James Buchanan and Franklin D. Roosevelt (1861-1932)? There was 1 other Democratic President during this time who was not elected. Who was he?

ANSWER: Grover Cleveland and Woodrow Wilson/Andrew Johnson (he was a Democrat, but he was elected with Lincoln on the Union ticket in 1864, which was a temporary label for the Republicans).

74. Name the 4 kinds of office that a U.S. citizen may hold under the Constitution.

ANSWER: Executive, judicial, legislative, and military.

75. Who were the first 2 military men in U.S. history to hold the rank of full general?

ANSWER: George Washington and Ulysses S. Grant.

76. According to Ulysses S. Grant, what were the only 2 tunes he knew?

ANSWER: One was ''Yankee Doodle,'' and the other one wasn't.

77. What 3 U.S. Presidents were in office during the Reconstruction period in the South after the Civil War?

ANSWER: Andrew Johnson, Ulysses S. Grant, and Rutherford B. Hayes.

78. Name the 6 states admitted to the Union during Benjamin Harrison's administration.

ANSWER: South Dakota and North Dakota on November 2, 1889; Montana on November 8, 1889; Washington on November 11, 1889; Idaho on July 3, 1890; and Wyoming on July 10, 1890.

79. In what years were the following women U.S. Presidential nominees?

a) Victoria Claflin Woodhull

b) Belva Ann Bennett Lockwood

c) Victoria Chavez

d) Charlene Mitchell

e) Linda Jenness

f) Margaret Wright

g) Deirdre Griswold

h) Ellen McCormack

i) Maureen Smith

j) Ellen L. Jensen

ANSWER: a) 1872 b) 1884 and 1888 c) 1968 d) 1968 e) 1972 f)1976 g) 1980 h) 1980 i) 1980 j) 1952.

80. What has decorated the office of the U.S. Vice President since Theodore Roosevelt had it removed from the presidential study because of its tinkling?

ANSWER: A chandelier.

81. What was the cause of the death of the following U.S. Presidents?

a) William Henry Harrison

b) Zachary Taylor

c) Warren Harding

d) Franklin Roosevelt

ANSWER: a) pleurisy, pneumonia b) cholera morbus, acute gastroenteritis c) the cause is unknown, pneumonia, cerebral hemorrhage or thrombosis, or poisoning are the best possibilities d) cerebral hemorrhage.

82. What President of the U.S. said, ''Franklin, I hope you never become President'' to what 5-year-old youngster?

ANSWER: Grover Cleveland/Franklin Roosevelt.

83. Who were the 7 U.S. Presidents to become President at less than 50 years of age?

ANSWER: Theodore Roosevelt by succession at 42; John F. Kennedy was the youngest by election at 43; and the others were James K. Polk, Franklin Pierce, Ulysses S. Grant, James A. Garfield, and Grover Cleveland.

84. What 3 U.S. Presidents were wounded in a military conflict?

ANSWER: James Monroe, Rutherford B. Hayes (4 times), and John F. Kennedy/ Monroe at the Battle of Trenton, New Jersey, December 26, 1776/Hayes at Giles Court House, Virginia, May 10, 1862; at the Battle of South Mountain, Maryland, September 14, 1862; at Winchester, Virginia, September 19, 1864; and at the Battle of Cedar Creek, Virginia, October 19, 1864/ Kennedy in 1943 in the Solomon Islands when his PT boat was rammed by the Japanese boat the *Amagiri* (Franklin Pierce was injured in the Mexican War at the Battle of Contreras, August 19, 1847, when his horse threw him).

85. How sage or wise are you? Sage enough to identify the U.S. Presidents by the following nicknames? Try them.

a) Sage of Wheatland
b) Sage of Lindenwald
c) Sage of Montpelier
d) Sage of Mount Vernon
e) Sage of Princeton (2)
f) Sage of Springfield
g) Sage of Kinderhook
h) Sage of The Hermitage
i) Sage of Monticello

ANSWER: a) James Buchanan b) Martin Van Buren c) James Madison d) George Washington e) Grover Cleveland and Theodore Roosevelt f) Abraham Lincoln g) Martin Van Buren h) Andrew Jackson i) Thomas Jefferson.

86. There have been 9 incumbent U.S. Presidents who ran for reelection and were defeated. Name them and give the year each was defeated.

ANSWER: John Adams (1800), John Quincy Adams (1828), Martin Van Buren (1840), Grover Cleveland (1888), Benjamin Harrison (1892), William H. Taft (1912), Herbert Hoover (1932), Gerald Ford (1976), and Jimmy Carter (1980).

87. What 5 incumbent U.S. Presidents were denied the renomination of their party? Give the year and name the person who received the nomination instead. What do 4 of them have in common?

ANSWER: John Tyler (1844, Henry Clay), Millard Fillmore (1852, Winfield Scott), Franklin Pierce (1856, James Buchanan), Andrew Johnson (1868, Horatio Seymour), and Chester Arthur (1884, James Gillespie Blaine)/Tyler, Fillmore, Johnson, and Arthur were Vice Presidents who succeeded to the presidency because of the death of the President.

88. There have been 3 U.S. Presidents who were not incumbents at the time who were defeated for the presidency. Name them and give the year each tried to win the presidency.

ANSWER: Martin Van Buren (1848), Millard Fillmore (1856), and Theodore Roosevelt (1912).

89. What 2 U.S. Presidents were engineers by profession?

ANSWER: Herbert Hoover and Jimmy Carter.

90. Name the only 2 U.S. Presidents to celebrate their 90th birthdays.

ANSWER: John Adams and Herbert Hoover.

91. What amendment of the U.S. Constitution passed in what year specifies one thing the President and the Vice President cannot have in common?

ANSWER: The 12th Amendment of 1804 specifies that they cannot be from the same state.

92. Who were the only 3 bald U.S. Presidents?

ANSWER: John Adams, John Quincy Adams, and Dwight Eisenhower.

93. Who was the youngest elected U.S. President, and who was the youngest person to have held that office?

ANSWER: John F. Kennedy at 43 and Theodore Roosevelt at 42.

94. Every U.S. President except one since 1840 who was elected in a year ending

with 0 died in office. Name the 7 who were elected and who died. Name the one who did not die but almost did so. Also who was elected in 1848 and died in office.

ANSWER: 1840 — William Henry Harrison; 1860 — Abraham Lincoln; 1880 — James A. Garfield; 1900 — William McKinley; 1920 — Warren G. Harding; 1940 — Franklin D. Roosevelt; 1960 — John F. Kennedy/Ronald Reagan in 1980/1848 — Zachary Taylor.

95. How many U.S. Presidents have died by assassination? Name each and his assassin.

ANSWER: Four/Abraham Lincoln by John Wilkes Booth in 1865; James Garfield by Charles Guiteau in 1881; William McKinley by Leon Czolgosz in 1901; and John Kennedy by Lee Harvey Oswald in 1963.

96. What 3 U.S. Presidents were President at the following moments: the beginning of the construction of the Panama Canal by the United States; the day the Canal was opened to traffic; and the day it was officially completed?

ANSWER: Theodore Roosevelt in 1904; Woodrow Wilson in 1914; and Warren Harding in 1921.

97. What was the nickname of Theodore Roosevelt's administration and what name did he give to his progressive program of 1910?

ANSWER: Square Deal and New Nationalism.

98. In 1912, who were the 3 candidates for President? One had been President, one was the President at the time, and one was going to be President.

ANSWER: Theodore Roosevelt, William H. Taft, and Woodrow Wilson.

99. Name the 2 Republican candidates for President of the U.S. in the 20th century who received only 8 electoral votes each. Name the year, who defeated them, and the states whose electoral votes they received.

ANSWER: William Howard Taft in 1912 against Woodrow Wilson received 8 votes from Utah and Vermont, and Alfred Landon in 1936 against Franklin D. Roosevelt won 8 votes from Maine and Vermont.

100. Name the candidate for the presidency who said: "While there is a lower class, I am in it. While there is a criminal element, I am of it. While there is a soul in prison, I am not free."

ANSWER: Eugene V. Debs, Socialist candidate.

101. The word *Duumvirate* or *Duumvirs* refers to 2 Roman officers who were united in the administration of one public office. What U.S. President and his assistant were thus nicknamed?

ANSWER: Woodrow Wilson and Edward Mandell House.

102. Who were the only 4 Vice Presidents of the U.S. who took office after the death of the President who were then elected to office?

ANSWER: Theodore Roosevelt, Calvin Coolidge, Harry Truman, and Lyndon Johnson.

103. Name the U.S. President, the U.S. Vice President, and the 4-time governor of New York and defeated Democratic candidate for the presidency who were nicknamed the "Happy Warrior."

ANSWER: Theodore Roosevelt, Hubert Humphrey, and Alfred E. Smith.

104. How many times, in what years, and against whom did William Jennings Bryan lose an election?

ANSWER: Three/1896 to William McKinley; 1900 to William McKinley; and 1908 to William H. Taft.

105. What were the names of the 2 Vice Presidents of William McKinley?

ANSWER: Garret A. Hobart and Theodore Roosevelt.

106. Identify the U.S. Presidents from the following nicknames/sobriquets.
a) Hermit Author of Palo Alto
b) Centennial President
c) Era of Good Feeling President
d) Old Rough and Ready
e) Butcher from Galena
f) Bachelor President
g) Canal Boy
h) Coiner of Weasel Words
i) Old Eight to Seven
j) Little Magician

ANSWER: a) Herbert Hoover b) Benjamin Harrison c) James Monroe d) Zachary Taylor e) Ulysses S. Grant f) James Buchanan g) James A. Garfield h) Woodrow Wilson i) Rutherford B. Hayes j) Martin Van Buren.

107. A President-to-be introduced a Democratic candidate for President in 1924 and 1928. Name the President-to-be, the candidate, and the nickname he used to describe this person. The nickname he used was a reference to what poem by what English poet? Finally, the English poet wrote the poem in honor of his brother John, but the death of what famous English Admiral was at least partly responsible for the poem?

ANSWER: Franklin D. Roosevelt introduced Alfred E. Smith and used the nickname "The Happy Warrior" (Roosevelt took the Democratic nomination from Smith in 1932)/The poem was "Character of the Happy Warrior" by William Wordsworth/Lord Nelson.

108. Name the 7 U.S. Presidents born in Ohio.

ANSWER: Ulysses S. Grant, Rutherford B. Hayes, James A. Garfield, Benjamin Harrison, William McKinley, William H. Taft, and Warren G. Harding.

109. Name the 2 U.S. Presidents who graduated from Princeton.

ANSWER: James Madison and Woodrow Wilson.

110. What 2 Presidents of the U.S. have been awarded the Nobel Peace Prize?

ANSWER: Theodore Roosevelt and Woodrow Wilson.

111. Zachary Taylor in 1848 failed to carry either the House or the Senate when he was elected; who was the next President who failed to do so?

ANSWER: Dwight Eisenhower in 1956.

112. What were the names of the 2 dogs of Calvin Coolidge?

ANSWER: Rob Roy and Prudence Prim.

113. Who was the first U.S. President from a seceded Southern state to be elected since Zachary Taylor?

ANSWER: Woodrow Wilson (he was born in Virginia).

114. Name the 3 U.S. Republican Presidents in the 20th century who were reelected to that office.

ANSWER: William McKinley, Dwight Eisenhower, and Richard Nixon.

115. Who are the only 2 U.S. Presidents buried in Arlington National Cemetery?

ANSWER: William H. Taft (1930) and John F. Kennedy (1963).

116. Name the 9 U.S. Presidents who did not attend college.

ANSWER: George Washington, Andrew Jackson, Martin Van Buren, Zachary Taylor, Millard Fillmore, Abraham Lincoln, Andrew Johnson, Grover Cleveland, and Harry Truman.

117. What 3 U.S. Presidents graduated from military academies?

ANSWER: Ulysses S. Grant and Dwight D. Eisenhower from West Point, and Jimmy Carter from the Naval Academy.

118. Give the names of the 2 canaries of Calvin Coolidge.

ANSWER: Nip and Tuck.

119. What 4 Republicans were defeated by Franklin D. Roosevelt in presidential elections? Give each of the years.

ANSWER: Herbert Hoover in 1932; Alfred M. Landon in 1936; Wendell L. Willkie in 1940; and Thomas E. Dewey in 1944.

120. On January 6, 1941, President Roosevelt made a speech to Congress in which he referred to the "4 Freedoms." What were these "Freedoms"? He also recommended a program with the Allies. What was it called?

ANSWER: Freedom of speech and expression; Freedom of worship; Freedom from want; and Freedom from fear/The Lend-Lease Pact.

121. "If the convention should nominate me, I shall accept. If the people elect me, I will serve." At what Democratic national convention (give the year) was the preceding statement made, and by whom?

ANSWER: In 1944 by Franklin D. Roosevelt.

122. With what 2 U.S. Presidents were the phrases "Clear it with Sidney" and "Clear it with Sherm" associated? Name the men involved.

ANSWER: **The first one was Franklin Roosevelt and "Sidney" was Sidney Hillman, the first U.S. labor leader to have a post with true executive responsibility in the federal government; the second was Dwight Eisenhower and "Sherm" was Sherman Adams, Eisenhower's chief executive assistant from 1953 to 1958.**

123. Who were the 3 Vice Presidents who served under Franklin D. Roosevelt?

ANSWER: **John Nance Garner, Henry A. Wallace, and Harry S Truman.**

124. What were the 3 R's of Franklin Roosevelt's New Deal program?

ANSWER: **Relief, Recovery, and Reform.**

125. You probably know where you live, but can you identify the U.S. Presidents with the homes or residences in which they lived?

a) The Beeches
b) Spiegel Grove
c) Monticello
d) Wheatland
e) Sagamore Hill
f) Lindenwald
g) Mount Vernon
h) Gettysburg farm
i) The Hermitage
j) Sherwood Forest

ANSWER: **a) Calvin Coolidge b) Rutherford B. Hayes c) Thomas Jefferson d) James Buchanan e) Theodore Roosevelt f) Martin Van Buren g) George Washington h) Dwight D. Eisenhower i) Andrew Jackson j) John Tyler.**

126. Since Franklin Roosevelt, name the 5 times the Republicans won the presidency and name the President.

ANSWER: **1952 and 1956 with Dwight Eisenhower, 1968 and 1972 with Richard Nixon, and 1980 with Ronald Reagan.**

127. Three U.S. Presidents in this century have received more than 500 Electoral College votes. Name the Presidents and the years they won these votes.

ANSWER: **FDR (523; 1936); R. Nixon (520; 1972); R. Reagan (525; 1984).**

128. Other than FDR, Nixon, and Reagan, (who received more than 500 Electoral College votes), 4 U.S. Presidents in this century have received more than 450 Electoral College votes. Name the Presidents and the years of their victories.

ANSWER: **Ronald Reagan (489) in 1980; Lyndon B. Johnson (486) in 1964; Franklin D. Roosevelt (472) in 1932; and Dwight D. Eisenhower (457) in 1956.**

129. What literary magazine in 1936 picked what U.S. presidential winner based on the results of several million mailed ballots?

ANSWER: **The *Literary Digest's* poll picked Alfred Landon as the overwhelming winner against Franklin Roosevelt.**

130. What U.S. President said: "When they told me yesterday what had happened, I felt like the moon, the stars and all the planets had fallen on me. If you fellows (the reporters) ever pray, pray for me"? When did he say it?

ANSWER: **Harry S Truman on April 13, 1945, the day after he became President as a result of Franklin Roosevelt's death.**

131. About whom was he speaking and who said: "I just cannot sit with that fellow"?

ANSWER: **Harry S Truman said that about Richard Nixon.**

132. Name the 4 Secretaries of State in the Truman administration.

ANSWER: **Edward Stettinius, Jr., James F. Byrnes, George C. Marshall, and Dean Acheson.**

133. Who were the 4 main candidates for President of the U.S. in 1948? Name their parties.

ANSWER: **Harry Truman, Democrat; Thomas Dewey, Republican; J. Strom Thurmond, States' Rights (or Dixiecrat); and Henry A. Wallace, Progressive.**

134. Name the 2 daughters of Richard M. Nixon.

ANSWER: **Patricia Nixon Cox and Julie Nixon Eisenhower.**

135. What 4 cabinet posts under what 2 U.S. Presidents did Elliot Richardson hold?

ANSWER: Attorney General, Secretary of Defense, and Secretary of Health, Education, and Welfare under Richard Nixon; and Secretary of Commerce under Gerald Ford.

136. Where was the Democratic Party National Convention held in each of the following years?

a) 1968   c) 1976   e) 1984
b) 1972   d) 1980   f) 1988

ANSWER: a) Chicago, Ill. b) Miami Beach, Fla. c) New York, N.Y. d) New York, N.Y. e) San Francisco, Calif. f) Atlanta, Ga.

137. Where was the Republican Party National Convention held in each of the following years?

a) 1968   c) 1976   e) 1984
b) 1972   d) 1980   f) 1988

ANSWER: a) Miami Beach, Fla. b) Miami Beach, Fla. c) Kansas City, Mo. d) Detroit, Mich. e) Dallas, Tex. f) New Orleans, La.

138. Name the presidential and vice presidential candidates of either the Republican or Democratic Party which lost in the following elections.

a) 1960   c) 1968   e) 1976
b) 1964   d) 1972   f) 1980

ANSWER: a) Richard Nixon and Henry Cabot Lodge b) Barry Goldwater and William E. Miller c) Hubert Humphrey and Edmund S. Muskie d) George McGovern and Sargent Shriver e) Gerald Ford and Robert Dole f) Jimmy Carter and Walter Mondale.

139. In Richard Nixon's book about the 6 crises, what were the 6?

ANSWER: The Hiss Case; The Fund; The Heart Attack (of President Eisenhower); The Caracas Trip; The Khruschev Debate; and The Campaign of 1960.

140. Who were the 2 Vice Presidents who served under Richard Nixon?

ANSWER: Spiro Agnew and Gerald Ford.

141. Who were the 2 females who attempted to assassinate President Gerald Ford?

ANSWER: Lynette "Squeaky" Fromme and Sara Jane Moore.

142. What President and Vice President of the U.S. were nicknamed "Fritz and Grits"?

ANSWER: Jimmy Carter and Walter Mondale.

143. What are the maiden names of the 2 wives of Ronald Reagan?

ANSWER: Jane Wyman and Nancy Davis.

144. What 2 men were the oldest at the time they served as President of the U.S.?

ANSWER: Ronald Reagan (70 years 98 days made him the oldest) and Dwight Eisenhower.

145. Who were the 2 oldest men ever sworn in as Presidents of the U.S.?

ANSWER: Ronald Reagan (69 years 349 days) and William Henry Harrison.

146. There were 2 Vice Presidents of the U.S. who were never elected to that post. Who were they?

ANSWER: Gerald Ford and Nelson Rockefeller.

147. Name the 4 children of President Ford.

ANSWER: Michael, John (Jack), Steven, and Susan (married name is Vance).

148. Name the 4 children of President Carter.

ANSWER: John (Jack), James (Chip), Donnel (Jeff), and Amy.

149. Name the 4 children of Ronald Reagan and identify them according to who their mother was.

ANSWER: Maureen (married name is Revell) and Michael (adopted) were by Jane Wyman, and Patricia (Patti Davis) and Ronald were by Nancy Davis Reagan.

150. Identify the Presidents who wrote the following books.

a) *Plain Speaking: An Oral   c) *Where's the Rest of Me?*
   Biography* (1974)   (1965)
b) *Six Crises* (1962)   d) *Rough Riders* (1899)

e) *Crusade in Europe* (1951)
f) *A Time for Action* (1964)
g) *Principles of Mining* (1909)
h) *A Time to Heal* (1979)
i) *Why Not the Best?* (1975)
j) *Why England Slept* (1940)
k) *Happy Warrior, Alfred E. Smith* (1928)

ANSWER: a) Harry S Truman b) Richard M. Nixon c) Ronald Reagan d) Theodore Roosevelt e) Dwight D. Eisenhower f) Lyndon B. Johnson g) Herbert Hoover h) Gerald R. Ford i) James E. Carter j) John F. Kennedy k) Franklin D. Roosevelt.

151. At what 3 colleges did President Jimmy Carter do his undergraduate work?

ANSWER: Georgia Southwestern College in Americus, Georgia Tech in Atlanta, and the U.S. Naval Academy in Annapolis, Maryland, from which he graduated.

152. Name the 3 U.S. Presidents who started a 2nd term in office but did not complete it.

ANSWER: Abraham Lincoln, William McKinley, and Richard M. Nixon.

153. What are the 2 rivers in the U.S. named after U.S. Presidents? In which state are they located? With what river do they join to form what river?

ANSWER: The Jefferson and the Madison are located in Montana/They join with the Gallatin to form the Missouri.

154. Each state has placed 1 statue of a most famous citizen in Statuary Hall in Washington, D.C. A statue of another prominent member of the state is located (as of 1933) elsewhere in the Capitol. There are but 3 Presidents, whose statues are located elsewhere in the Capitol, among these many famous citizens. Name them and name their state.

ANSWER: James Garfield from Ohio, Andrew Jackson from Tennessee, and George Washington from Virginia.

155. Franklin Roosevelt won 4 consecutive elections for the Democrats but who won the 4 Democratic victories prior to Roosevelt's triumphs? Give the person each defeated.

ANSWER: 1916 - Woodrow Wilson defeated Charles Evans Hughes; 1912 - Wilson defeated William Howard Taft; 1892 - Grover Cleveland defeated Benjamin Harrison; and 1884 - Cleveland defeated James Gillespie Blaine.

156. Who are the 6 living wives of Presidents of the U.S.?

ANSWER: Jacqueline Kennedy Onassis, Lady Bird Johnson, Patricia Nixon, Betty Ford, Rosalynn Carter, and Nancy Reagan (Jane Wyman could be included in this group).

157. What 3 U.S. Presidents were territorial governors, and what territories did they govern?

ANSWER: Andrew Jackson in Florida, William H. Harrison in Indiana, and William H. Taft in the Philippines.

158. What are the full names of the following U.S. Presidents?
a) Grant
b) Wilson
c) Cleveland
d) Coolidge

ANSWER: a) Hiram Ulysses Simpson Grant b) Thomas Woodrow Wilson c) Stephen Grover Cleveland d) John Calvin Coolidge.

159. What are the middle names of the following U.S. Presidents?
a) William Harrison
b) James Polk
c) Rutherford Hayes
d) James Garfield
e) Chester Arthur
f) Herbert Hoover
g) Richard Nixon
h) Gerald Ford
i) James Carter
j) Ronald Reagan

ANSWER: a) Henry b) Knox c) Birchard d) Abram e) Alan f) Clark g) Milhous h) Rudolph i) Earl j) Wilson.

160. Name the 3 U.S. Presidents against whom articles of impeachment were drawn up.

ANSWER: John Tyler, Andrew Johnson, and Richard Nixon.

161. What are the 3 largest religious affiliations of U.S. Presidents?

ANSWER: Episcopalian, Presbyterian, and Unitarian.

162. Identify the U.S. Presidents and their religious affiliations from the following.

a) 3 Baptists
b) 3 Methodists
c) 3 Disciples of Christ
d) 2 Dutch Reformed
e) 2 Quakers
f) 1 Congregationalist
g) 1 Roman Catholic

ANSWER: a) Warren Harding, Harry Truman, and Jimmy Carter b) James Polk, Ulysses Grant, and William McKinley c) James Garfield, Lyndon Johnson, and Ronald Reagan d) Martin Van Buren and Theodore Roosevelt e) Herbert Hoover and Richard Nixon f) Calvin Coolidge g) John Kennedy.

163. In what years were the following Blacks U.S. presidential nominees?

a) Clennon King
b) Clifton De Berry
c) Eldrige Cleaver
d) Dick Gregory
e) Charlene Mitchell
f) Margaret Wright

ANSWER: a) 1960 b) 1964 and 1980 c) 1968 d) 1968 e) 1968 f) 1976.

164. Identify the Presidents from the following descriptions.

a) Only President born in a hospital
b) First President not born a British subject
c) First President born outside the original 13 states
d) First President to survive a wound from an assassin
e) Only President whose temporary official residence was the Octagon House
f) President who escaped possible death by explosion aboard the U.S.S. *Princeton*
g) President whose daughter had the ''Baby Ruth'' candy bar named for her
h) First President to appoint a brother to a cabinet post

ANSWER: a) Jimmy Carter b) Martin Van Buren c) Abraham Lincoln d) Ronald Reagan e) James Madison f) John Tyler g) Grover Cleveland (daughter was named Ruth) h) John Kennedy (appointed brother Robert to be the Attorney General).

165. Identify the following from the descriptions.

a) Only Vice President buried in Washington, D.C., and the only Vice President whose name has become part of the English language
b) First Vice President elected by the Senate
c) The President of the U.S. for a day (maybe) on March 4, 1849
d) First Congress to appropriate a billion dollars

ANSWER: a) Elbridge Gerry and ''gerrymander'' is part of the language b) Richard Mentor Johnson (1836) c) David Rice Atchison d) 52nd Congress (1891-1893).

166. Who was the only U.S. President preceded and succeeded by the same man?
ANSWER: Benjamin Harrison.

167. If a landslide victory in a presidential election is 60% or more of the popular vote, then name the 4 Presidents who won by landslides and give the year.
ANSWER: Lyndon Johnson (61.1%) in 1964; Franklin D. Roosevelt (60.8%) in 1936; Richard Nixon (60.7%) in 1972; and Warren Harding (60.4%) in 1920.

168. Which U.S. Presidents are connected with each of the following political labels?

a) The New Freedom
b) The Great Society
c) The New Deal
d) The New Frontier
e) The Square Deal
f) The Fair Deal

ANSWER: a) Woodrow Wilson b) Lyndon Johnson c) Franklin Roosevelt d) John Kennedy e) Theodore Roosevelt f) Harry Truman.

169. Who was the first U.S. Vice President to be nominated at a national political convention? This Vice President later became President. His Vice President became the first Vice President elected by the Senate because there was no clear choice as Francis Granger, John Tyler, and William Smith shared the electoral votes. Who was he?
ANSWER: Martin Van Buren/Richard Mentor Johnson.

170. Who was the youngest U.S. Vice President to be inaugurated and how old was he? Who was the oldest Vice President to be inaugurated and how old was he?

Both of these men were natives of the same state. Name it.

ANSWER: John Cabell Breckinridge at 36/Alben Barkley at 71/Kentucky.

171. An act of Congress in 1949 made the Vice President a regular member of the National Security Council. What Vice President became the first regular member of this Council?

ANSWER: Alben Barkley.

172. What state could be called "the Mother of Vice Presidents"? There were 11 Vice Presidents from this state. Name any 6 of them.

ANSWER: New York/Aaron Burr, George Clinton, Daniel D. Tompkins, Martin Van Buren, Millard Fillmore, William Almon Wheeler, Chester A. Arthur, Levi Parsons Morton, Theodore Roosevelt, James Schoolcraft Sherman, and Nelson Aldrich Rockefeller.

173. Identify each of the following.
   a) The number of individuals who have held the office of Vice President
   b) The 2 Vice Presidents who each served under different Presidents
   c) The first woman vice presidential nominee of a major political party (1924)
   d) The first Black candidate for the vice presidency (1880)
   e) The Vice President who presided over the Senate with a pistol at his side
   f) The Vice President-elect who died before performing any of the duties of office
   g) The Vice President who took the oath of office in another country
   h) The first Vice President to attend meetings of the Cabinet regularly
   i) The first Vice President to marry while in office (1949)
   j) The first Vice President to be called "The Veep"
   k) The youngest Vice President to succeed to the presidency upon the death of the President
   l) The oldest Vice President to succeed to the presidency upon the death of the President
   m) The first Vice President sworn in by the Speaker of the House

ANSWER: a) 43 b) George Clinton and John C. Calhoun c) Mrs. Leroy Springs d) Blanche Kelso Bruce e) Martin Van Buren f) William Rufus De Vane King g) William Rufus De Vane King (Havana, Cuba) h) Calvin Coolidge i) Alben William Barkley j) Alben William Barkley k) Theodore Roosevelt l) Harry Truman m) Lyndon B. Johnson (by Sam Rayburn).

174. Name the 6 Presidents who carried their Vice Presidents into office for a second term, and name the Vice Presidents.

ANSWER: Washington (Adams), Monroe (Tompkins), Wilson (Marshall), Franklin Roosevelt (Garner), Eisenhower (Nixon), and Nixon (Agnew).

175. Give the year of occurrence and the U.S. President in office for each of the following events. (The answers for the dates and the Presidents are to the right of the event.)

   a) Teapot Dome Scandal . . . . 1923 . . . . Warren Harding
   b) Pony Express began . . . . 1860 . . . . James Buchanan
   c) Wilmot Proviso defeated . . . . 1846 . . . . James Polk
   d) Peary discovered North Pole . . . . 1909 . . . . William Taft
   e) Bay of Pigs . . . . 1961 . . . . John Kennedy
   f) Spanish-American War . . . . 1898 . . . . William McKinley
   g) Black Hawk War began . . . . 1832 . . . . Andrew Jackson
   h) Library of Congress established . . . . 1800 . . . . John Adams
   i) American Red Cross organized . . . . 1881 . . . . James Garfield
   j) Social Security Act passed . . . . 1935 . . . . Franklin Roosevelt
   k) Erie Canal opened for traffic . . . . 1825 . . . . John Quincy Adams
   l) Dedication of Washington Monument . . . 1885 . . . . Chester Arthur
   m) Korean War ended . . . . 1953 . . . . Dwight Eisenhower
   n) Marshall Plan passed . . . . 1948 . . . . Harry Truman
   o) Cotton gin patented by Eli Whitney . . . . . 1793 . . . . George Washington
   p) *Chesapeake v. Leopard*
      confrontation . . . . 1807 . . . . Thomas Jefferson

q)	Commodore Perry's Japan expedition...	1852	Millard Fillmore
r)	Fourteenth Amendment ratified	1868	Andrew Johnson
s)	Twenty-fourth Amendment ratified	1964	Lyndon Johnson
t)	American hostages taken in Iran	1979	Jimmy Carter
u)	Hawley-Smooth Tariff passed	1930	Herbert Hoover
v)	Panama Canal opened to traffic	1914	Woodrow Wilson
w)	Wright brothers' airplane flight	1903	Theodore Roosevelt
x)	British captured Washington, D.C.	1814	James Madison
y)	Haymarket Square Riot	1886	Grover Cleveland
z)	American hostages released	1981	Ronald Reagan
aa)	National Road began	1811	James Madison
bb)	Dred Scott decision	1857	James Buchanan
cc)	Homestead Act enacted	1862	Abraham Lincoln
dd)	Firing on Fort Sumter	1861	Abraham Lincoln
ee)	First 7 states secede from Union	1860-1861	James Buchanan
ff)	First transcontinental RR finished	1869	Ulysses Grant
gg)	Mayagüez incident	1975	Gerald Ford
hh)	Berlin airlift organized	1948	Harry Truman
ii)	Mexican War began	1846	James Polk
jj)	Kellogg-Briand Pact	1928	Calvin Coolidge
kk)	Stock market crashed	1929	Herbert Hoover
ll)	*Sussex* ultimatum	1916	Woodrow Wilson
mm)	Last U.S. troops left Vietnam	1973	Richard Nixon
nn)	Taft-Hartley Act passed	1947	Harry Truman
oo)	First man walked on the moon	1969	Richard Nixon
pp)	*Savannah* crossed the Atlantic	1819	James Monroe
qq)	Mt. Saint Helens erupted (19th cent.)	1842	John Tyler
rr)	Whitey grazed on White House lawn	1849	Zachary Taylor
ss)	Kansas-Nebraska Act enacted	1854	Franklin Pierce
tt)	Gadsden Purchase completed	1853	Franklin Pierce
uu)	Pendleton Act passed	1883	Chester Arthur
vv)	Federal Reserve Act passed	1913	Woodrow Wilson
ww)	Treaty of Ghent signed	1814	James Madison
xx)	Klondike Gold rush began	1896	Grover Cleveland
yy)	Louisiana Purchase completed	1804	Thomas Jefferson
zz)	Hiroshima and Nagasaki bombed	1945	Harry Truman

176. Use the mnemonic device WILL A JOLLY MAN MAKE A JOLLY VISITOR, and name the first 8 U.S. Presidents.
ANSWER: **Washington, Adams (John), Jefferson, Madison, Monroe, Adams (John Quincy), Jackson, and Van Buren.**

177. Five of the first 7 U.S. Presidents served 8 consecutive years in office. Who were they?
ANSWER: **Washington, Jefferson, Madison, Monroe, and Jackson.**

178. Since Andrew Jackson there have been but 4 U.S. Presidents who served 8 consecutive years in office. Who were they?
ANSWER: **Ulysses S. Grant, Woodrow Wilson, Franklin D. Roosevelt, and Dwight D. Eisenhower.**

179. Who was the only U.S. President/Commander-In-Chief during 2 wars and what were the names of those wars?
ANSWER: **Harry S Truman/The wars were World War II and the Korean War.**

180. What are the names of the 2 living widows of U.S. Presidents?
ANSWER: **Jacqueline Kennedy Onassis and Lady Bird Johnson.**

181. Name the 5 Civil War generals who later became U.S. Presidents.
ANSWER: **Grant, Hayes, Garfield, Arthur, and Harrison.**

182. The following U.S. Presidents played Varsity sports in college. Name their sports and their colleges. Which of the following was nicknamed "The Kansas Cyclone"?

a) Dwight D. Eisenhower   c) Gerald Ford
b) John F. Kennedy   d) Jimmy Carter

ANSWER: a) Football at the U.S. Military Academy at West Point b) Swimming at Harvard c) Football at the University of Michigan d) Cross-country at the U.S. Naval Academy/Dwight Eisenhower.

183. What U.S. President with a group of Nobel Prize winners at a dinner in their honor at the White House in 1962 said about what U.S. President: ''I think this is the most extraordinary collection of talent, of human knowledge, that has ever been gathered together at the White House, with the possible exception of when _____dined alone''?

ANSWER: John F. Kennedy/Thomas Jefferson.

184. The motto on President Eisenhower's Oval Office desk plaque was ''Suaviter in modo, fortiter in re.'' What is its meaning?

ANSWER: ''Gently in Manner, Strongly in Deed,'' or ''Gentle of Manner, Strong in Action.''

185. Name the 3 U.S. Presidents whose last names have just 4 letters.

ANSWER: James K. Polk, William H. Taft, and Gerald R. Ford.

186. Name the 2 left-handed U.S. Presidents.

ANSWER: James A. Garfield and Gerald Ford.

PRESIDENTS AND STATES IN WHICH THEY WERE GOVERNORS

Thomas Jefferson........ Virginia	**William McKinley**...... Ohio
James Monroe........... Virginia	**Theodore Roosevelt**.... New York
Martin Van Buren........ New York	**Woodrow Wilson**...... New Jersey
John Tyler............. Virginia	**Calvin Coolidge**....... Massachusetts
James K. Polk........... Tennessee	**Franklin D. Roosevelt**.. New York
Rutherford B. Hayes....... Ohio	**Jimmy Carter**......... Georgia
Andrew Johnson......... Tennessee	**Ronald Reagan**....... California
Grover Cleveland........ New York	

PRESIDENTS ELECTED TO PHI BETA KAPPA

John Quincy Adams	**Chester A. Arthur**	**Calvin Coolidge**
Martin Van Buren	**Grover Cleveland**	**Franklin D. Roosevelt**
Franklin Pierce	**Theodore Roosevelt**	**Harry Truman**
Rutherford B. Hayes	**William H. Taft**	**Dwight Eisenhower**
James A. Garfield	**Woodrow Wilson**	

(Only Adams, Arthur, T. Roosevelt, and Taft won their gold keys because of scholastic achievement.)

U.S. PRESIDENTS AND THEIR VICE PRESIDENTS

TERM	PRESIDENT (Birth)	STATE	PARTY	VICE PRESIDENTS
1789-1797	1) George Washington	Va.	Fed.	John Adams
1797-1801	2) John Adams	Mass.	Fed.	Thomas Jefferson
1801-1809	3) Thomas Jefferson	Va.	D-R*	Aaron Burr and George Clinton
1809-1817	4) James Madison	Va.	D-R*	George Clinton (d. 1812) and Elbridge Gerry (d. 1814)
1817-1825	5) James Monroe	Va.	D-R*	Daniel D. Tompkins
1825-1829	6) John Quincy Adams	Mass.	D-R*	John C. Calhoun
1829-1837	7) Andrew Jackson	S.C.	Dem.	John C. Calhoun (resigned 1832) and Martin Van Buren
1837-1841	8) Martin Van Buren	N.Y.	Dem.	Richard M. Johnson
1841-1845	9) William H. Harrison (d.1841)	Va.	Whig	John Tyler
	10) John Tyler	Va.	Whig	
1845-1849	11) James K. Polk	N.C.	Dem.	George M. Dallas
1849-1853	12) Zachary Taylor (d. 1850)	Va.	Whig	Millard Fillmore
	13) Millard Fillmore	N.Y.	Whig	
1853-1857	14) Franklin Pierce	N.H.	Dem.	William R.D. King (d. 1853)
1857-1861	15) James Buchanan	Pa.	Dem.	John C. Breckinridge
1861-1869	16) Abraham Lincoln (d. 1865)	Ky.	Rep.	Hannibal Hamlin and Andrew Johnson
	17) Andrew Johnson	N.C.	Dem.**	
1869-1877	18) Ulysses S. Grant	Ohio	Rep.	Schuyler Colfax and Henry Wilson (d. 1875)
1877-1881	19) Rutherford B. Hayes	Ohio	Rep.	William A. Wheeler
1881-1885	20) James A. Garfield (d.1881)	Ohio	Rep.	Chester A. Arthur
	21) Chester A. Arthur	Vt.	Rep.	
1885-1889	22) Grover Cleveland	N.J.	Dem.	Thomas A. Hendricks (d. 1885)
1889-1893	23) Benjamin Harrison	Ohio	Rep.	Levi P. Morton
1893-1897	24) Grover Cleveland	N.J.	Dem.	Adlai E. Stevenson
1897-1905	25) William McKinley (d. 1901)	Ohio	Rep.	Garret A. Hobart (d. 1899) and Theodore Roosevelt
	26) Theodore Roosevelt	N.Y.	Rep.	
1905-1909	Theodore Roosevelt			Charles W. Fairbanks
1909-1913	27) William H. Taft	Ohio	Rep.	James S. Sherman (d. 1912)
1913-1921	28) Woodrow Wilson	Va.	Dem.	Thomas R. Marshall
1921-1925	29) Warren G. Harding (d. 1923)	Ohio	Rep.	Calvin Coolidge
	30) Calvin Coolidge	Vt.	Rep.	
1925-1929	Calvin Coolidge			Charles G. Dawes
1929-1933	31) Herbert C. Hoover	Iowa	Rep.	Charles Curtis
1933-1949	32) Franklin D. Roosevelt (d. 1945)	N.Y.	Dem.	John N. Garner, Henry A. Wallace and Harry S Truman
	33) Harry S Truman	Mo.	Dem.	
1949-1953	Harry S Truman			Alben W. Barkley
1953-1961	34) Dwight D. Eisenhower	Tex.	Rep.	Richard M. Nixon
1961-1964	35) John F. Kennedy (d. 1963)	Mass.	Dem.	Lyndon B. Johnson
	36) Lyndon B. Johnson	Tex.	Dem.	
1964-1969	Lyndon B. Johnson			Hubert H. Humphrey
1969-1977	37) Richard M. Nixon (resigned 1974)	Cal.	Rep.	Spiro T. Agnew (resigned 1973) and Gerald R. Ford
	38) Gerald R. Ford	Neb.	Rep.	Nelson A. Rockefeller
1977-1981	39) James E. Carter, Jr.	Ga.	Dem.	Walter F. Mondale
1981-	40) Ronald W. Reagan	Ill.	Rep.	George Bush

*Democratic—Republican

**Johnson was a Democrat but a member of the National Union Party which consisted of Republicans and War Democrats (the party was formed in 1864).

PRESIDENTIAL ELECTIONS

YEAR	CANDIDATES	PARTY	ELECTORAL VOTES
1789	GEORGE WASHINGTON	None	69
	John Adams	None	34
	John Jay	None	9
1792	GEORGE WASHINGTON	Federalist	132
	John Adams	Federalist	77
	George Clinton	Democratic-Republican	50
	Thomas Jefferson	Democratic-Republican	4
	Aaron Burr	Democratic-Republican	1
1796	JOHN ADAMS	Federalist	71
	Thomas Jefferson	Democratic-Republican	68
	Thomas Pinckney	Federalist	59
	Aaron Burr	Democratic-Republican	30
1800	THOMAS JEFFERSON	Democratic-Republican	73
	Aaron Burr	Democratic-Republican	73
	John Adams	Federalist	65
	Charles C. Pinckney	Federalist	64
1804	THOMAS JEFFERSON	Democratic-Republican	162
	Charles C. Pinckney	Federalist	14
1808	JAMES MADISON	Democratic-Republican	122
	Charles C. Pinckney	Federalist	47
	George Clinton	Democratic-Republican	6
1812	JAMES MADISON	Democratic-Republican	128
	DeWitt Clinton	Federalist	89
1816	JAMES MONROE	Democratic-Republican	183
	Rufus King	Federalist	34
1820	JAMES MONROE	Democratic-Republican	231
	John Quincy Adams	Independent Republican	1
1824	JOHN QUINCY ADAMS*	None	84
	Andrew Jackson	None	99
	William H. Crawford	None	41
	Henry Clay	None	37
1828	ANDREW JACKSON	Democratic	178
	John Quincy Adams	National Republican	83
1832	ANDREW JACKSON	Democratic	219
	Henry Clay	National Republican	49
	John Floyd	Independent	11
	William Wirt	Anti-Masonic	7
1836	MARTIN VAN BUREN	Democratic	170
	William H. Harrison	Whig	73
	Hugh L. White	Whig	26
	Daniel Webster	Whig	14
	W.P. Mangum	Independent Democrat	11
1840	WILLIAM H. HARRISON	Whig	234
	Martin Van Buren	Democratic	60
	James G. Birney	Liberty	--
1844	JAMES K. POLK*	Democratic	170
	Henry Clay	Whig	105
	James G. Birney	Liberty	--
1848	ZACHARY TAYLOR*	Whig	163
	Lewis Cass	Democratic	127
	Martin Van Buren	Free Soil	--

*Minority President, i.e., one who received less than 50% of the popular vote.

1852	FRANKLIN PIERCE	Democratic	254
	Winfield Scott	Whig	42
	John P. Hale	Free Soil	--
1856	JAMES BUCHANAN*	Democratic	174
	John C. Frémont	Republican	114
	Millard Fillmore	American	8
1860	ABRAHAM LINCOLN*	Republican	180
	John C. Breckinridge	Southern Democratic	72
	John Bell	Constitutional Union	39
	Stephen A. Douglas	Democratic	12
1864	ABRAHAM LINCOLN	Republican	212
	George B. McClellan	Democratic	21
1868	ULYSSES S. GRANT	Republican	214
	Horatio Seymour	Democratic	80
1872	ULYSSES S. GRANT	Republican	286
	Horace Greeley	Democratic, Liberal Republican	66**
1876	RUTHERFORD B. HAYES*	Republican	185
	Samuel J. Tilden	Democratic	184
	Peter Cooper	Greenback	--
1880	JAMES A. GARFIELD*	Republican	214
	Winfield S. Hancock	Democratic	155
	James B. Weaver	Greenback	--
	Neal Dow	Prohibition	--
1884	GROVER CLEVELAND*	Democratic	219
	James G. Blaine	Republican	182
	Benjamin F. Butler	Greenback	--
	John P. St. John	Prohibition	--
1888	BENJAMIN HARRISON*	Republican	233
	Grover Cleveland	Democratic	168
	Clinton B. Fisk	Prohibition	--
	Anson J. Streeter	Union Labor	--
1892	GROVER CLEVELAND*	Democratic	277
	Benjamin Harrison	Republican	145
	James B. Weaver	Populist	22
1896	WILLIAM McKINLEY	Republican	271
	William Jennings Bryan	Democratic-Populist	176
	John M. Palmer	National Democratic	--
	Joshua Levering	Prohibition	--
1900	WILLIAM McKINLEY	Republican	292
	William Jennings Bryan	Democratic	155
	John G. Wooley	Prohibition	--
1904	THEODORE ROOSEVELT	Republican	336
	Alton B. Parker	Democratic	140
	Eugene V. Debs	Socialist	--
1908	WILLIAM H. TAFT	Republican	321
	William Jennings Bryan	Democratic	162
	Eugene V. Debs	Socialist	--
	Eugene W. Chafin	Prohibition	--
1912	WOODROW WILSON*	Democratic	435
	Theodore Roosevelt	Progressive	88
	William H. Taft	Republican	8

*Minority President, i.e., one who received less than 50 percent of the popular vote.

**Greeley died before the Electoral College met and his electoral votes were given to other candidates.

	Eugene V. Debs	Socialist	--
	Eugene W. Chafin	Prohibition	--
1916	WOODROW WILSON*	Democratic	277
	Charles E. Hughes	Republican	254
	Allan L. Benson	Socialist	--
	J.F. Hanly	Prohibition	--
1920	WARREN G. HARDING	Republican	404
	James M. Cox	Democratic	127
	Eugene V. Debs	Socialist	--
1924	CALVIN COOLIDGE	Republican	382
	John W. Davis	Democratic	136
	Robert M. LaFollette	Progressive	13
1928	HERBERT C. HOOVER	Republican	444
	Alfred E. Smith	Democratic	87
	Norman M. Thomas	Socialist	--
1932	FRANKLIN D. ROOSEVELT	Democratic	472
	Herbert C. Hoover	Republican	59
	Norman M. Thomas	Socialist	--
1936	FRANKLIN D. ROOSEVELT	Democratic	523
	Alfred M. Landon	Republican	8
	William Lemke	Union	--
1940	FRANKLIN D. ROOSEVELT	Democratic	449
	Wendel L. Willkie	Republican	82
1944	FRANKLIN D. ROOSEVELT	Democratic	432
	Thomas E. Dewey	Republican	99
1948	HARRY S. TRUMAN*	Democratic	303
	Thomas E. Dewey	Republican	189
	J. Strom Thurmond	States' Right Democratic	39
	Henry A. Wallace	Progressive	--
1952	DWIGHT D. EISENHOWER	Republican	442
	Adlai E. Stevenson	Democratic	89
1956	DWIGHT D. EISENHOWER	Republican	457
	Adlai E. Stevenson	Democratic	73
1960	JOHN F. KENNEDY*	Democratic	303
	Richard M. Nixon	Republican	219
1964	LYNDON B. JOHNSON	Democratic	486
	Barry Goldwater	Republican	52
1968	RICHARD M. NIXON*	Republican	301
	Hubert H. Humphrey	Democratic	191
	George C. Wallace	American Independent	46
1972	RICHARD M. NIXON	Republican	520
	George McGovern	Democratic	17
	John G. Schmitz	American	--
	John Hospers	Libertarian	1
1976	JIMMY CARTER	Democratic	297
	Gerald R. Ford	Republican	240
	Eugene J. McCarthy	Independent	--
	Lester G. Maddox	American Independent	
1980	RONALD REAGAN	Republican	489
	Jimmy Carter	Democratic	49
	John B. Anderson	Independent	--
	Ed Clark	Libertarian	--
	Barry Commoner	Citizens	--

*Minority President, i.e., one who received less than 50 percent of the popular vote.

PRESIDENTIAL NICKNAMES/SOBRIQUETS

George Washington ...... American Caesar, American Fabius, Atlas of America, Cincinnatus of the West, Deliverer of America, Farmer President, Father of His Country, Father of Pittsburgh, Old Fox, Sage of Mount Vernon, Savior of His Country, Step-father of His Country, Surveyor President, Sword of the Revolution

John Adams .... Atlas of Independence, Colossus of Debate, Colossus of (American) Independence, Duke of Braintree, Father of American Independence, Father of the American Navy, His Rotundity, Machiavelli of Massachusetts, Old Sink or Swim, Partisan of Independence, President by Three Votes

Thomas Jefferson .... Father of the Declaration of Independence, Father of the University of Virginia, Long Tom, Man of the People, Pen of the Revolution, Philosopher of Democracy, Red Fox, Sage of Monticello, Scribe of the Revolution

James Madison .... Father of the Constitution, Sage of Montpelier

James Monroe .... Era of Good Feeling President, Last Cocked Hat, Last of the Cocked Hats

John Quincy Adams ...... Accidental President, Minority President, Old Man Elo-quent, Second John

Andrew Jackson .... Duel Fighter, Hero of New Orleans, King Andrew, King Andrew the First, Land Hero of 1812, Mischievous Andy, Old Hickory, People's President, Pointed Arrow, Sage of the Hermitage, Sharp Knife

Martin Van Buren .... American Talleyrand, Enchanter, First-class Second-rate Man, Flying Dutchman, The Fox, Kinderhook Fox, King Martin the First, Little Magician, Little Van, Machiavellian Belshazzar, Mistletoe Politician, Petticoat Pet, Red Fox of the Kinderhook, Sage of Kinderhook, Sage of Lindenwald, Whiskey Van, The Wizard, Wizard of Kinderhook, Wizard of the Albany Regency.

William Henry Harrison .... Farmer of North Bend, Farmer President, Hard Cider, Hero of Tippecanoe, Log Cabin Candidate (President), Old Granny, Old Tip, Old Tippecanoe, Tippecanoe, Washing-ton of the West

John Tyler .... Accidental President, His Accidency, Young Hickory

James K. Polk. .... First Dark Horse, Napoleon of the Stump, People's Choice, Polk the Purposeful, Young Hickory

Zachary Taylor .... Hero of Buena Vista, Old Buena Vista, Old Rough and Ready, Old Zach

Millard Fillmore .... Accidental President, American Louis Philippe, His Accidency, Wool-carder President

Franklin Pierce .... Dark Horse President, Doughface President, Fainting General, Handsome Frank, Hero of Chippewa, Hero of Many a Well-fought Bottle, Old Chapultepec, Purse, Young Hickory, Young Hickory of the Granite Hills

James Buchanan .... Bachelor President, Old Buck, Old Fogy, Old Public Func-tionary, Sage of Wheatland, Ten-cent Jimmy

Abraham Lincoln .... The Ancient, The Baboon, The Buffoon, Caesar, Emanci-pation President, Father Abraham, Flatboat Man, Grand Wrestler, Great Emancipator, Honest Abe (Lincoln), Illi-nois Baboon, Jester, Long 'Un, Man of the People, Martyr President, Massa Linkum, Old Abe, Railsplitter, Sage of Springfield, Sectional President, Tycoon, Tyrant, Uncle Abe

Andrew Johnson. .... Andy Veto, Daddy of the Baby, Father of the Homestead Act, His Accidency, King Andy the First, Old Andy, Old

Veto, Sir Veto, Tailor of the Potomac, Tennessee Tailor, Veto President

Ulysses S. Grant . . . . American Caesar, The Butcher, Butcher from Galena, Butcher Grant, Galena Tanner, Great Hammerer, Great Peacemaker, Hero of Appomattox, Hero of Fort Donelson, Hog Grant, Lyss, Old Three Stars, Sam, Silent Man, Tanner President, Texas, Uncle Sam (Grant), Unconditional Surrender, Uniformed Soldier, Union Safeguard, United States (Grant), Unprecedented Strategist, Unquestionably Skilled, Useless Grant

Rutherford B. Hayes . . . . . . Dark Horse President, Eight to Seven, The Fraud, Fraud President, Goody Two-shoes, Granny Hayes, Great Unknown, Hero of '77, His Fraudulency, Old Eight to Seven, President De Facto, Queen Victoria in Breeches

James A. Garfield . . . . Boatman Jim, Canal Boy, Dark Horse, Martyr President, Preacher President, Teacher President

Chester A. Arthur . . . . America's First Gentleman, Arthur the Gentleman, The Dude, Dude President, Elegant Arthur, First Gentleman of the Land, Gentleman Boss, His Accidency, Our Chet, Prince Arthur

Grover Cleveland . . . . Beast of Buffalo, Buffalo Hangman, Buffalo Sheriff, Claimant, Dumb Prophet, Grover the Good, Hangman of Buffalo, His Accidency, Man of Destiny, Morgan's Errand-boy, Old Grover, Old Veto, Our Grover, People's President, Perpetual President, Pretender, Reform Governor, Sage of Princeton, Stuffed Prophet, Uncle Jumbo, Veto Governor, Veto Mayor, Veto President

Benjamin Harrison . . . . Baby McKee's, Centennial President, Chinese Harrison, Grandfather, Grandfather's Hat, Grandpa's Grandson, Kid Gloves Harrison, Little Ben, Son of His Grandfather, White House Ice Chest

William McKinley . . . . High Priest of High Protection, High Priest of Protective Tariffs, Idol of Ohio, Napoleon of Protection, Prosperity's Advance Agent, Stocking-foot Orator, Wobbly Willie

Theodore Roosevelt . . . . . . Bull Moose, Cowboy President, Damn Cowboy, Driving Force, Dynamo of Power, Four Eyes, Great White Chief, Happy Warrior, Haroun-al-Roosevelt, Hero of San Juan Hill, His Accidency, Mad Messiah, Man on Horseback, Master of the Obvious, Meddler, Old Lion, Roosevelt I, Rough Rider, Sage of Princeton, Teddy, Teddy (Theodore) the Meddler, Telescope Teddy, T.R., Trust-busting President, Trust Buster, Typical American

William Howard Taft . . . . . . Big Bill, Big Chief, Big Will Taft, Good Old Will

Woodrow Wilson . . . . Coiner of Weasel Words, Drum Major of Civilization, The Phrasemaker, Phrasemaker of Versailles, The Professor, The Schoolmaster, Schoolmaster in Politics

Warren G. Harding . . . . Dark Horse Candidate, Teapot Dome, Winnie

Calvin Coolidge . . . . Cautious Cal, Red, Silent Cal, Sphinx of the Potomac

Herbert Hoover . . . . Boy Wonder, The Chief, Friend of Helpless Children, Great Engineer, Great Humanitarian, Hermit Author of Palo Alto, Knight of the Clean Garbage Can, Man of Great Heart, Miracle Man, Wonder Boy

Franklin D. Roosevelt . . . . . American Dictator, Boss, The Champ, FDR, F.D.R., Featherduster of Dutchess County, Franklin Deficit Roosevelt, Gallant Leader, Gideon of Democracy, Houdini in the White House, Kangaroosevelt, New Deal Caesar, Raw Dealocrat, Roosevelt II, Sphinx, Squire of Hyde Park, That Fellow Down in Washington, That Madman in the White House, That Man in the White House

Harry S Truman . . . . Average Man's Average Man, Give 'Em Hell Harry, Haber-
dasher Harry, High Tax Harry, HST, (Little) Man from
Missouri, Man of Independence
Dwight D. Eisenhower . . . . General Ike, Ike
John F. Kennedy . . . . Jack, JFK, That Wit in the White House
Lyndon B. Johnson . . . . . . Accidental President, Big Daddy, Landslide Johnson,
Landslide Lyndon, LBJ, Light Bulb Johnson, Prodigious
Spender, Uncle Cornpone
Richard M. Nixon . . . . The Czar, Embattled President, The Godfather, Ike's
Kissinger, King Richard, Nation's No. 1 Football Fan,
President Truthful, Tarnished President, Tricky Dick
Gerald R. Ford . . . . Jerry, Junie, His Accidency, Mr. Clean, Mr. Middle
America
Jimmy Carter . . . . Don Quixote in the White House, Peanut Farmer
Ronald Reagan . . . . Dutch, Great Communicator, Mr. Clean, Most Happy
Fellow, Not-So-Favorite Son, Ronald the Right, Teflon
President

NOTABLE PRESIDENTIAL HOMES/RESIDENCES

George Washington . . . . . . Mount Vernon - Mount Vernon, Virginia
Thomas Jefferson . . . . Monticello - Monticello (near Charlottesville), Virginia
James Madison . . . . Montpelier - Montpelier Station, Virginia
James Monroe . . . . Ashfield (Ash Lawn) - near Charlottesville, Virginia (Oak
Hill, Virginia)
John Quincy Adams . . . . . . The Old Mansion (Old House) or Peacefield - Braintree
(now Quincy) Massachusetts
Andrew Jackson . . . . The Hermitage - near Nashville, Tennessee
Martin Van Buren . . . . Lindenwald - near Kinderhook, New York
William Henry Harrison
and Benjamin Harrison . . . . Berkeley Plantation (Harrison's Landing) - birthplace of
William Henry and ancestral home of Benjamin - between
Richmond and Williamsburg, Virginia (Charles City
County, Virginia)
John Tyler . . . . Sherwood Forest Plantation - Charles City County, Virginia
James Buchanan . . . . Wheatland - Wheatland (Lancaster), Pennsylvania
Rutherford B. Hayes . . . . . . Spiegel Grove - near Fremont, Ohio
Grover Cleveland . . . . Westland - Princeton, New Jersey
Little White House - Lakewood, New Jersey
Theodore Roosevelt . . . . . . Sagamore Hill - Oyster Bay, New York
Woodrow Wilson . . . . Shadow Lawn (ancestral home) - Staunton, Virginia
Calvin Coolidge . . . . The Beeches - Northampton, Massachusetts
Franklin Roosevelt . . . . Hyde Park - Hyde Park, New York
Little White House - Warm Springs, Georgia
Dwight D. Eisenhower . . . . Gettysburg farm - Gettysburg, Pennsylvania
Lyndon Johnson . . . . Texas White House - LBJ Ranch near Johnson City, Texas
Richard Nixon . . . . Western White House - San Clemente, California
Southern White House - Key Biscayne, Florida

PRESIDENTS AND THEIR PROGRAMS/SLOGANS

Theodore Roosevelt . . . . Square Deal
Theodore Roosevelt . . . . New Nationalism (1910 Progressive Party program)
Woodrow Wilson . . . . New Freedom
Franklin Roosevelt . . . . New Deal
Harry S Truman . . . . Fair Deal
Dwight D. Eisenhower . . . . Great Crusade
John Kennedy . . . . New Frontier
Lyndon Johnson . . . . Great Society
Richard Nixon . . . . New Federalism
Jimmy Carter . . . . New Foundation
Ronald Reagan . . . . Reaganomics/New Federalism

PRESIDENTIAL FIRSTS, LASTS, ONLYS, AND SOME SECONDS

George Washington . . . . . . Only President inaugurated in 2 cities (New York City and Philadelphia)

Only President unanimously elected by electoral votes

First and only President who did not live in Washington, D.C.

John Adams . . . . First President to live in the White House

Only President inaugurated at Philadelphia both as a President and as a Vice President

First President defeated for reelection

Thomas Jefferson . . . . First President to be elected by the House of Representatives

First President inaugurated in Washington, D.C.

Only President to write his own epitaph ("Here was buried Thomas Jefferson, author of the Declaration of American Independence, of the statute of Virginia for religious freedom, and father of the University of Virginia.")

James Madison . . . . Last surviving signer of the Constitution

Only President to have 2 Vice Presidents who died in office (George Clinton and Elbridge Gerry)

James Monroe . . . . First President to make a goodwill tour of the states

First President who had been a senator

First President to ride on a steamboat (the *Savannah*)

John Quincy Adams . . . . . . First minority President

Only son of a President who became a President

Second President whose election was decided by the House of Representatives

Andrew Jackson . . . . . . First presidential candidate to be named by a national nominating convention

First President born in a log cabin

First President to have an assassination attempt directed at him

First President to ride on a railroad train

Martin Van Buren . . . . Last President who was a Vice President and succeeded to the presidency through an election and not because of the death of a President

First President born a U.S. citizen and not a British subject

William Henry Harrison . . . . First President to die in office (April 4, 1841)

Served the shortest term as President

Last President born before the American Revolution

John Tyler . . . . First Vice President to succeed to the presidency because of the death of the President

First President to be married while in office

James K. Polk . . . . First "dark horse" presidential candidate elected

First Speaker of the House of Representatives to become President

Zachary Taylor . . . . First person to become President who was not previously elected to public office

First President to die in office while Congress was in session (2nd President to die in office)

Last Whig President who was elected to that office

Millard Fillmore . . . . Last Whig President

First President born in the 19th century

Franklin Pierce . . . . Only President who completed his term without making any changes in his cabinet

Only elected President who was not renominated by his

party for a second term

James Buchanan . . . . First bachelor elected as President

Only President to remain a bachelor

Abraham Lincoln . . . . First President who was assassinated

First President not born in the 13 original states (he was born in Kentucky)

Andrew Johnson. . . . . Only President to be impeached

First President to receive a queen (Queen Emma of the Sandwich, later Hawaiian, islands)

First former President elected to the U.S. Senate

Ulysses S. Grant. . . . . First President to receive a king (King David Kalakaua of the Sandwich, later Hawaiian, Islands)

Only President buried in Grant's tomb (Riverside Park in New York City)

Rutherford B. Hayes . . . . . . First President to have a phone installed in the White House

First President to visit the west coast

James A. Garfield . . . . Last President born in a log cabin

First left-handed President

Second President to be assassinated

Chester A. Arthur . . . . First President born in Vermont

Grover Cleveland . . . . First Democratic President after the Civil War

Only President to serve 2 nonconsecutive terms

Only President married in the White House

Only President to have hanged a man (as sheriff in Buffalo, N.Y. — Andrew Jackson may have hanged a man before he became President)

Benjamin Harrison . . . . First President to have electric lights in the White House

More states were admitted to the Union during his administration than during any other

Only President preceded and succeeded by the same man

William McKinley . . . . Last President to have served in the Civil War

Last President to engage in a war for territorial expansion

Theodore Roosevelt . . . . . . First President to travel outside the U.S. (to Panama)

First President (and first American) to win the Nobel Peace Prize

First President to fly in an airplane

First President to ride in a gasoline-powered automobile

Youngest person to become President (42)

William H. Taft . . . . First President of the 48 states (Arizona in 1912)

Only President to serve as Chief Justice of the Supreme Court (or on the Supreme Court)

First President buried in Arlington National Cemetery

First President to throw out a baseball to start the professional baseball season (1910 between Washington and Philadelphia)

First President to get stuck in a bathtub

Woodrow Wilson. . . . . First President to earn a doctoral degree

First President who was president of a major university

Only President to defeat 2 former Presidents in an election

First President to hold a press conference (1913)

First President to visit Europe

Only President buried in Washington, D.C. (in the National Cathedral)

Warren Harding . . . . First newspaper publisher to be elected President

First President to visit Canada and Alaska

First President to have a cabinet member convicted and sent to prison (Albert B. Fall)

First President to make a radio broadcast

First President to ride to his inauguration in an automobile

Calvin Coolidge . . . . First President to be sworn in by his father

Only President born on a July 4

Only President nicknamed for his taciturnity

Herbert Hoover . . . . Last "lame duck" President or the last one whose term of office ended on March 3

First President born west of the Mississippi (in Iowa)

Franklin D. Roosevelt . . . . . First President elected for a 3rd term (and a 4th as well)

First President to visit South America while in office

First President to make a television appearance (at the New York World's Fair - April 30, 1939)

First President to take office on January 20 (1937)

Harry S Truman . . . . First President to take office during a war

First President to make an address on TV from the White House (1947)

First President to travel underwater in a submarine (1946)

Dwight D. Eisenhower . . . . First President to have a pilot's license

Only Republican President in the 20th century to serve 2 full terms

Only President who was a 5-star general

John F. Kennedy . . . . First President to win a Pulitzer Prize for a book (*Profiles in Courage*)

Youngest person ever elected as President (43)

First President born in the 20th century

First President who was a Roman Catholic

First President to have served in the U.S. Navy

Lyndon B. Johnson . . . . First President to be sworn in on an airplane and the first sworn in by a woman

Richard M. Nixon . . . . First President to resign the office of President

First President to appoint another Vice President by using Amendment 25 (Spiro Agnew resigned)

First President to visit China

Gerald R. Ford . . . . First Vice President and President without being elected to either office (appointed Vice President to replace Spiro Agnew and became President after Richard Nixon resigned)

Jimmy Carter . . . . First President to have graduated from the U.S. Naval Academy

First President to walk from the Capitol to the White House after his inauguration

First President to be attacked by a bunny

Ronald Reagan . . . . Oldest President to be elected to office (69 years and 349 days old)

First President elected who had been divorced

First President to have been a professional actor

First President to have worked with Bonzo

First President to have been head of a union (the Screen Actors Guild)

PRESIDENTS AND THEIR GROUPS

Andrew Jackson	Kitchen Cabinet
Theodore Roosevelt	Tennis Cabinet
Warren Harding	Ohio Gang; Poker Cabinet
Herbert Hoover	Medicine Ball Cabinet
Franklin D. Roosevelt	Brain Trust
Harry S Truman	Cronies
Dwight Eisenhower	Eight Millionaires and a Plumber; the Palace Guard
John F. Kennedy	Irish Mafia
Richard M. Nixon	Plumbers
Jimmy Carter	Georgia Mafia
Ronald Reagan	California Mafia

PRESIDENTIAL ASSASSINATIONS, ASSASSINATION ATTEMPTS, AND DEATHS WHILE IN OFFICE

Andrew Jackson......... January 30, 1835 — Jackson was in the rotunda of the
Capitol when he was attacked by Richard Lawrence. Law-
Attempt   rence fired two pistols at close range but both weapons
                           misfired. Lawrence was committed to jail and mental in-
                           stitutions for life. He was found to be insane at the time of
                           his act.

William H. Harrison ...... March, 1841 — Harrison was in the White House when a
                           man entered the Red Room by the window. Two door-
Attempt   keepers seized the man. Harrison arrived and helped tie
                           the man up (probably not an assassination attempt).

Death   Died on April 4, 1841, after he developed pneumonia from
                           spending two hours in the open without an overcoat on a
                           cold rainy Inauguration Day, March 4, 1841.

Zachary Taylor .... Died July 9, 1850, of cholera morbus after eating cherries
Death   and wild berries.

Abraham Lincoln .... Shot on April 14, 1865, by John Wilkes Booth, a Southern
                           sympathizer, in Washington, D.C., at Ford's Theatre,
Assassination   while attending the play *Our American Cousin.* Lin-
                           coln died on April 15, 1865. Booth was shot on April 26,
                           1865, in a barn near Port Royal, Virginia.

                           William H. Seward, Lincoln's Secretary of State, was
                           stabbed several times on April 14, 1865, by an accom-
                           plice of John Wilkes Booth, Lewis Paine. Seward survived.

                           Ulysses S. Grant was supposed to have been in atten-
                           dance in the same lodge with Lincoln. Booth supposedly
                           had a knife to use on Grant.

James A. Garfield .... Shot on July 2, 1881, in the Baltimore and Potomac Rail-
                           road Depot in Washington, D.C., by Charles J. Guiteau.
Assassination   Garfield died on September 19, 1881. Guiteau had been
                           denied a job for a government office. Guiteau was tried,
                           convicted, and later hanged (June 30, 1882), at a
                           Washington, D.C. jail.

William McKinley .... Shot on September 6, 1901, at the Pan-American Exposi-
                           tion in Buffalo, New York, by Leon Czolgosz, a factory
Assassination   worker and an anarchist. Czolgosz fired 2 shots from a
                           pistol hidden in a handkerchief. McKinley died on Sep-
                           tember 14, 1901. Czolgosz was tried and convicted. He
                           was electrocuted (October 29, 1901) at the Auburn State
                           Prison, Auburn, New York.

Theodore Roosevelt ...... Shot in the chest while campaigning in Milwaukee, on
(as a former President) October 14, 1912. John Nepomuk Schrank, a saloon
                           keeper, shot him because he objected to Roosevelt's
Attempt   seeking a 3rd term as President. Schrank was committed
                           to a State Hospital for the insane and died there on Sep-
                           tember 15, 1943. Roosevelt completed his speech before
                           seeking medical help at the hospital.

Warren Harding .... Died on August 2, 1923, after becoming ill following a trip
                           to Alaska. He died in San Francisco from pneumonia ac-
Death   cording to his doctors, from food poisoning according to
                           others. His wife refused permission to have an autopsy
                           performed and the exact cause of his death is unknown.

Franklin D. Roosevelt ..... On February 15, 1933, at Miami, Florida, Giuseppe
(as President-elect)   Zangara, a bricklayer, tried to kill President Roosevelt. He
Attempt   missed Roosevelt but killed Anton J. Cermak, Mayor of

Chicago, Illinois, and wounded 5 other persons. Cermak died on March 6. Zangara was executed on March 20, 1933, at the Florida State Prison.

Death   Roosevelt died of a cerebral hemmorrhage on April 12, 1945 at the Little White House in Warm Springs, Georgia.

Harry S Truman . . . . Truman was unhurt when 2 Puerto Rican nationalists tried to shoot their way into Blair House, November 1, 1950.
Attempt   Oscar Collazo and Griselio Torresola made the assassination attempt. Torresola was killed and Collazo was wounded. Two White House guards were wounded, and Leslie Coffelt, another guard, was killed. Collazo was sentenced to die, but his sentence was commuted to life imprisonment.

John F. Kennedy . . . . Kennedy was shot and killed on November 22, 1963, in Dallas, Texas, by Lee Harvey Oswald. Governor John B.
Assassination   Connally, Jr., of Texas was injured in the same incident. Jack Ruby shot and killed Oswald two days later in a Dallas Police Station. Oswald was also accused of shooting police officer, J. D. Trippett.

Gerald R. Ford . . . . Two assassination attempts were made on Ford's life, one in Sacramento, California, on September 5, 1975, and
Attempts   another in San Francisco, California, on September 22, 1975. Lynette "Squeaky" Fromme was prevented from firing her .45-caliber pistol (the gun was empty anyway) on September 5. On the 22nd, Sara Jane Moore shot once with a .38-caliber pistol but missed. Fromme and Moore were sentenced to life in prison.

Ronald Reagan . . . . President Reagan was shot in the chest on March 30, 1981, in Washington, D.C., by John W. Hinckley, Jr.
Attempt   Reagan was seriously injured, but made a quick recovery. Three others were also injured including James Brady, White House Press Secretary, who was the most seriously injured. Hinckley was found to be not guilty by reason of insanity.

MIDDLE NAMES OF PRESIDENTS

John **Quincy** Adams
William **Henry** Harrison
James **Knox** Polk
Ulysses **Simpson** Grant
Rutherford **Birchard** Hayes
James **Abram** Garfield
Chester **Alan** Arthur
William **Howard** Taft
Warren **Gamaliel** Harding
Herbert **Clark** Hoover

Franklin **Delano** Roosevelt
Harry **S** Truman
Dwight **David** Eisenhower
John **Fitzgerald** Kennedy
Lyndon **Baines** Johnson
Richard **Milhous** Nixon
Gerald **Rudolph** Ford
James **Earl** Carter
Ronald **Wilson** Reagan

RARELY USED FIRST NAMES OF PRESIDENTS

Hiram Ulysses Simpson Grant
Stephen Grover Cleveland

Thomas Woodrow Wilson
John Calvin Coolidge

PRESIDENTS AND THEIR MILITARY EXPERIENCE

George Washington ...... Lieutenant colonel in the French and Indian War and Commander-in-Chief of the Continental Army during the Revolutionary War.

James Monroe .... Became a major during the Revolutionary War.

Andrew Jackson........ Fought in the American Revolution, was a major general in the Tennessee state militia, fought in the Creek and Seminole Wars, and became a major general during the War of 1812.

William Henry Harrison.... Was in the Army from 1791 to 1798, fought Indians at the Battle of Tippecanoe and, during the War of 1812, became supreme commander of the Army of the Northwest.

Zachary Taylor .... Commissioned a first lieutenant in 1808, fought in the War of 1812, the Seminole War, the Black Hawk War, and commanded the army of Texas during the Mexican War.

John Tyler .... Captain of a military company during the war of 1812.

Franklin Pierce........... Became a brigadier general during the Mexican War.

James Buchanan .... Volunteer cavalry soldier during the War of 1812.

Abraham Lincoln .... Elected a captain during the Black Hawk War.

Ulysses S. Grant........ Graduated from West Point and served in the Mexican War. Became supreme commander of the Union army during the Civil War. Appointed a full general after the war.

Rutherford B. Hayes ...... Commissioned a major in the Ohio volunteers during the Civil War and became a major general during the war.

James A. Garfield .... Commissioned a lieutenant colonel during the Civil War and rose to the rank of major general.

Chester A. Arthur .... Brigadier general of the New York State Militia during the Civil War.

Benjamin Harrison .... Colonel of the 70th Indiana Regiment during the Civil War and achieved the rank of brigadier general.

William McKinley .... Was a major in the Union army during the Civil War.

Theodore Roosevelt ...... Became a colonel in the Spanish-American War and helped lead the ''Rough Riders'' at San Juan Hill.

Harry S Truman .... Rose to the rank of major during World War I.

Dwight D. Eisenhower .... Graduated from West Point, was a training officer during WWI, and became the Supreme Allied Commander to Europe during WWII, Chief of Staff of the U.S. Army, and a five-star general.

John F. Kennedy .... Commanded a Navy PT-boat in the Pacific Theatre during World War II.

Lyndon B. Johnson....... Served as a naval officer during World War II and was once decorated by General Douglas MacArthur.

Richard M. Nixon .... Served as a naval officer in the Pacific during World War II and rose to the rank of lieutenant commander.

Gerald R. Ford .... Commissioned as an ensign in the Navy during World War II and rose to the rank of lieutenant commander.

Jimmy Carter .... Graduated from the Naval Academy (1946) and was on submarine duty as a naval officer but did not take part in war during the Korean War.

Ronald Reagan .... Served 3 years in the U.S. Army Air Corps' First Motion Picture Unit during WWII making training films. Was discharged with the rank of captain. He was also a reserve officer in the Army cavalry.
Played a serviceman in *Voice of the Turtle;* a cavalryman in *Sergeant Murphy;* a Navy flier in *Submarine D-1;* a VMI Cadet in *Brother Rat;* Lieutenant Custer in the *Santa Fe Trail;* an R.A.F. pilot in *International Squadron;* and an R.A.F. pilot in *Desperate Journey.*

U.S. PRESIDENTS AND THEIR WIVES

George Washington . . . . Martha Dandridge Custis
John Adams . . . . Abigail Smith
Thomas Jefferson . . . . Martha Wayles Skelton
James Madison . . . . Dolley Payne Todd
James Monroe . . . . Elizabeth Kort(w)right
John Quincy Adams . . . . Louisa Catherine Johnson
Andrew Jackson . . . . Rachel Donelson Robards
Martin Van Buren . . . . Hannah Hoes
William H. Harrison . . . . Anna Symmes
John Tyler . . . . Letitia Christian; Julia Gardiner
James K. Polk . . . . Sarah Childress
Zachary Taylor . . . . Margaret Mackall Smith
Millard Fillmore . . . . Abigail Powers; Caroline Carmichael McIntosh
Franklin Pierce . . . . Jane Means Appleton
James Buchanan . . . . none
Abraham Lincoln . . . . Mary Todd
Andrew Johnson . . . . Eliza McCardle
Ulysses S. Grant . . . . Julia Dent
Rutherford B. Hayes . . . . Lucy Ware Webb
James A. Garfield . . . . Lucretia Rudolph
Chester A. Arthur . . . . Ellen Lewis Herndon
Grover Cleveland . . . . Frances Folsom
Benjamin Harrison . . . . Caroline Lavina Scott; Mary Scott Lord Dimmick
William McKinley . . . . Ida Saxton
Theodore Roosevelt . . . . Alice Hathaway Lee; Edith Kermit Carow
William H. Taft . . . . Helen Herron
Woodrow Wilson . . . . Ellen Louise Axson; Edith Bolling Galt
Warren G. Harding . . . . Florence Kling DeWolfe
Calvin Coolidge . . . . Grace Anna Goodhue
Herbert Hoover . . . . Lou Henry
Franklin D. Roosevelt . . . . . . Anna Eleanor Roosevelt
Harry S Truman . . . . Elizabeth Virginia Wallace
Dwight D. Eisenhower . . . . . . Mamie Geneva Doud
John F. Kennedy . . . . Jacqueline Lee Bouvier
Lyndon B. Johnson . . . . Claudia Alta Taylor
Richard M. Nixon . . . . Thelma Patricia Ryan
Gerald R. Ford . . . . Elizabeth Bloomer (Warren)
Jimmy Carter . . . . Rosalynn Smith
Ronald W. Reagan . . . . Jane Wyman; Nancy Davis

U.S. PRESIDENTS, THEIR BIRTHPLACES AND BURIAL SITES

George Washington . . . . Westmoreland County, Va./Mount Vernon, Va.
John Adams . . . . Braintree, Mass./Quincy, Mass.
Thomas Jefferson . . . . Shadwell, Va./Monticello, Va.
James Madison . . . . Port Conway, Va./Montpelier, Va.
James Monroe . . . . Westmoreland County, Va./Richmond, Va.
John Quincy Adams . . . . Braintree, Mass./Quincy, Mass.
Andrew Jackson . . . . Waxhaw (New Lancaster County), S.C./Hermitage, Tenn.
Martin Van Buren . . . . Kinderhook, N.Y./Kinderhook, N.Y.
William H. Harrison . . . . Berkeley, Va./North Bend, Oh.
John Tyler . . . . Greenway, Va. (Charles City County, Va.)/Richmond, Va.

James K. Polk . . . . Pineville (Mecklenberg County), N.C./Nashville, Tenn.
Zachary Taylor . . . . Orange County, Va./Louisville, Ky.
Millard Fillmore . . . . Summer Hill, Cayuga County, N.Y. (Locke, N.Y.)/Buffalo, N.Y.
Franklin Pierce . . . . Hillsboro, N.H./Concord, N.H.
James Buchanan . . . . Mercersburg (nearby), Pa./Lancaster, Pa.
Abraham Lincoln . . . . Hardin County, Ky./Springfield, Ill.
Andrew Johnson . . . . Raleigh, N.C./Greeneville, Tenn.
Ulysses S. Grant . . . . Point Pleasant, Oh./New York City, N.Y.
Rutherford B. Hayes . . . . Delaware, Oh./Fremont, Oh.
James A. Garfield . . . . Orange, Oh./Cleveland, Oh.
Chester A. Arthur . . . . Fairfield, Vt./Albany, N.Y.
Grover Cleveland . . . . Caldwell, N.J./Princeton, N.J.
Benjamin Harrison . . . . North Bend, Oh./Indianapolis, Ind.
William McKinley . . . . Niles, Oh./Canton, Oh.
Theodore Roosevelt . . . . New York City, N.Y./Oyster Bay, N.Y.
William H. Taft . . . . Cincinnati, Oh./Arlington National Cemetery, Va.
Woodrow Wilson . . . . Staunton, Va./Washington, D.C.
Warren G. Harding . . . . Corsica, Oh. (Blooming Grove, Oh.)/Marion, Oh.
Calvin Coolidge . . . . Plymouth, Vt./Plymouth, Vt.
Herbert Hoover . . . . West Branch, Ia./West Branch, Ia.
Franklin D. Roosevelt . . . . Hyde Park, N.Y./Hyde Park, N.Y.
Harry S Truman . . . . Lamar, Mo./Independence, Mo.
Dwight D. Eisenhower . . . . . . Denison, Tex./Abilene, Kans.
John F. Kennedy . . . . Brookline, Mass./Arlington National Cemetery, Va.
Lyndon B. Johnson . . . . Stonewall (nearby), Tex./Johnson City (nearby), Tex.
Richard M. Nixon . . . . Yorba Linda, Calif.
Gerald R. Ford . . . . Omaha, Neb.
Jimmy Carter . . . . Plains, Ga.
Ronald W. Reagan . . . . Tampico, Ill.

U.S. PRESIDENTS AND THE COLLEGES THEY ATTENDED

George Washington . . . . Did not attend
John Adams . . . . Harvard
Thomas Jefferson . . . . William and Mary
James Madison . . . . Princeton
James Monroe . . . . William and Mary
John Quincy Adams . . . . Harvard
Andrew Jackson . . . . Did not attend
Martin Van Buren . . . . Did not attend
William H. Harrison . . . . Hampden-Sydney, left before graduation
John Tyler . . . . William and Mary
James K. Polk . . . . North Carolina
Zachary Taylor . . . . Did not attend
Millard Fillmore . . . . Did not attend
Franklin Pierce . . . . Bowdoin
James Buchanan . . . . Dickinson
Abraham Lincoln . . . . Did not attend
Andrew Johnson . . . . Did not attend
Ulysses S. Grant . . . . U.S. Military Academy
Rutherford B. Hayes . . . . Kenyon
James A. Garfield . . . . Williams
Chester A. Arthur . . . . Union
Grover Cleveland . . . . Did not attend
Benjamin Harrison . . . . Miami
William McKinley . . . . Allegheny, left before graduation
Theodore Roosevelt . . . . Harvard
William H. Taft . . . . Yale
Woodrow Wilson . . . . Princeton

Warren G. Harding . . . . Ohio Central, left before graduation
Calvin Coolidge . . . . Amherst
Herbert Hoover . . . . Stanford
Franklin D. Roosevelt . . . . Harvard
Harry S Truman . . . . Did not attend
Dwight D. Eisenhower . . . . . . U.S. Military Academy
John F. Kennedy . . . . Harvard
Lyndon B. Johnson . . . . Southwest Texas State
Richard M. Nixon . . . . Whittier
Gerald R. Ford . . . . Michigan
Jimmy Carter . . . . Georgia Southwestern; Georgia Institute of Technology;
U.S. Naval Academy
Ronald W. Reagan . . . . Eureka

U.S. PRESIDENTS AND WORKS THEY HAVE WRITTEN

George Washington . . . . *Farewell Address,* 1796
John Adams . . . . *Thoughts on Government,* 1776; *Discourses on Davila,* 1805
Thomas Jefferson . . . . *A Summary View of the Rights of British America,* 1774; *Notes on the State of Virginia,* 1785
James Madison . . . . *Letters of Helvidus,* 1796; *Journal of the Federal Convention,* 1840
James Monroe . . . . *A View of the Conduct of the Executive in the Foreign Affairs of the United States,* 1798
John Quincy Adams . . . . *Jubilee of the Constitution,* 1789; *An Answer to Paine's Rights of Man,* 1793; *Letters on Silesia,* 1804; *Social Compact,* 1842
Martin Van Buren . . . . *Inquiry into the Origin and Course of Political Parties in the United States,* 1867
William Henry Harrison . . . . . *Discourses on the Aborigines of the Valley of Ohio,* 1839
James Buchanan . . . . *The Administration on the Eve of the Rebellion,* 1865
Abraham Lincoln . . . . *Legacy of Fun,* 1865
Ulysses Simpson Grant . . . . . *Personal Memoirs* (2 volumes), 1885-1886
Grover Cleveland . . . . *Principles and Purposes of Our Form of Government,* 1892; *Self Made Man in American Life,* 1897; *Independence of the Executive,* 1900; *Presidential Problems,* 1904
Benjamin Harrison . . . . *This Country of Ours,* 1897
Theodore Roosevelt . . . . *Naval War of 1812,* 1882; *Personal Experieces of Life on a Cattle Ranch,* 1885; *Winning of the West,* 1889; *The Wilderness Hunter,* 1893; *Rough Riders,* 1899; *Strenuous Life,* 1900; *African Game Trails,* 1910; *New Nationalism,* 1910; *Great Adventure,* 1918
William Howard Taft . . . . *Four Aspects of Civic Duty,* 1906; *Popular Government,* 1913; *The United States and Peace,* 1914
Woodrow Wilson . . . . *When a Man Comes to Himself,* 1901; *New Freedom,* 1913; *On Being Human,* 1916
Warren Gamaliel Harding . . . . *Rededicating America,* 1920; *Our Common Country,* 1921
Calvin Coolidge . . . . *Have Faith in Massachusetts,* 1919; *Price of Freedom,* 1924; *Foundations of the Republic,* 1926
Herbert Clark Hoover . . . . *Principles of Mining,* 1909; *New Day,* 1928; *Challenge to Liberty,* 1934; *America's First*

	Crusade, 1942; *Problems of a Lasting Peace*, 1942; *On Growing Up*, 1962
Franklin Delano Roosevelt	... *Happy Warrior, Alfred E. Smith*, 1928; *Records of the Town of Hyde Park*, 1928; *Looking Forward*, 1933; *On Our Way*, 1934
Harry S Truman	*Mr. Citizen*, 1960; *Plain Speaking: An Oral Biography*, 1974
Dwight David Eisenhower	... *Crusade in Europe*, 1951; *The White House Years* - Volume I, *Mandate for Change, 1953-1956*, 1963; Volume II, *Waging Peace, 1956-1961*, 1965
John Fitzgerald Kennedy	.... *Why England Slept*, 1940; *Profiles in Courage*, 1956; *A Nation of Immigrants*, 1959; *The Strategy of Peace*, 1960; *To Turn the Tide*, 1962; *The Burden and the Glory*, 1964
Lyndon Baines Johnson	..... *My Hope for America*, 1964; *A Time for Action*, 1964; *This America*, 1966
Richard Milhous Nixon	...... *Six Crises*, 1962; *The Real War*, 1980
Gerald Rudolph Ford	.... *A Time to Heal*, 1979
Jimmy (James Earl) Carter	.... *Why Not the Best?*, 1975; *Keeping Faith*, 1982
Ronald Wilson Reagan	...... *Where's the Rest of Me?* 1965

PRESIDENTIAL POLITICAL CAMPAIGN SLOGANS

1828 - Bargain and Corruption; Jackson and Reform; Huzza for Jackson; All Hail Old Hickory; Hurrah for Jackson!

1832 - Jackson Forever; Go the Whole Hog; Freedom and Clay; Hurrah for Jackson!

1836 - Rumpsey Dumpsey, Rumpsey Dumpsey, Colonel Johnson Killed Tecumseh; Rumpsey Dumpsey Who Killed Tecumseh?

1840 - Tippecanoe and Tyler Too; Down with Van Burenism; Free Trade and Sailors Rights; Van, Van is a Used-up Man; The Union of the Whigs for the Sake of the Union; With Tip and Tyler We'll Bust Van's Biler; Van's Policy, Fifty Cents a Day and French Soup - Our Policy, Two Dollars a Day and Roast Beef; Tip and Ty; Out With the Old and in With the New; Harrison and Reform; Log Cabin and Hard Cider

1844 - The Northwest and the Southwest; Polk and the Tariff of '42; Polk, Dallas, Texas, Oregon and the Tariff of '42; Who is James K. Polk?; Polk and the Democratic Tariff of 1842; James K. Polk and the Tariff of 1842; Young Hickory, Dallas, and Victory; All of Oregon or None; Polk, Slavery, and Texas; Clay, Union, and Liberty; Hooray for Clay; Fifty-Four Forty or Fight

1848 - Free Soil, Free Speech, Free Labor, and Free Men; General Taylor Never Surrenders

1852 - We Polked 'em in '44, we'll Pierce 'em in '52

1852 - Give 'em Jessie; Free Speech, Free Press, Free Soil, Free Men, Frémont and Victory; Frémont and Jessie; Free Soil, Free Speech, Free Men, and Frémont; Jessie Bent-on Being Free; We are Buckhunting; We Follow the Pathfinder; We shall Be Redeemed from the Rule of Nigger Drivers, and Give 'em Jessie; Free Soil, Free Speech, and Frémont

1860 - The Constitution and the Union, Now and Forever; Free Homes for Free Men; Free Territory for a Free People; A House Divided Against Itself Cannot Stand; Intervention is Disunion; Let Liberty Be National and Slavery Sectional; Millions for Freedom, Not One Cent for Slavery; Popular Sovereignty and National Union; Slavery is a Moral and Political Wrong; The Union, the Constitution, and the Enforcement of the Laws; Vote Yourself a Farm; Land for the Landless; We Want a Statesman, Not a Rail Splitter, as President

1864 - Don't Swap Horses in the Middle of a Stream; Old Abe Removed McClellan, Now We'll Remove Old Abe; Mac Will Win the Union Back; Vote as You Shot; Uncle Abe and Andy

1868 - Let Us Have Peace; The Party That Saved the Union Must Rule It; Waving the

Bloody Shirt; Scratch a Democrat and You Will Find A Rebel; Grant - The Man Saved a Nation; Vote as You Shot; Repudiate the Republicans; Now is the Time for All Good Men to Come to the Aid of the Party

1872 - Universal Amnesty and Universal Enfranchisement; Turn the Rascals Out, Grant Beat Davis - Greeley Bailed Him; Waving the Bloody Shirt

1876 - Waving the Bloody Shirt; Democracy, the Last Refuge of Personal and Political Rights, Will Give Us Back the Ancient Purity of Govermnent; Grantism Means Poor People Made Poorer; Let Us Have a Clean Sweep; Reform is Necessary In Civil Service; Reform Is Necessary to Establish a Sound Currency; Tilden and Reform; We Demand that Our Customhouse Taxation Shall Be for Revenue Only; We Demand a Rigorous Frugality in Every Department of the Government; Invisible in War, Invincible in Peace; Vote as You Shot; Turn the Rascals Out; The Boys in Blue Will See it Through; Hurrah! For Hayes and Honest Ways

1880 - Anything to beat Grant

1884 - No more '76; A Public Office is a Public Trust, Turn the Rascals Out; We Love Him for the Enemies He Has Made; Aut Caeser aut Nihil (Either Caesar or Nothing); Burn, Burn, Burn This Letter; Ma, Ma, Where's My Pa? Gone to the White House, Ha, Ha, Ha; No, No, No Free Trade; Blaine! James G. Blaine! The Contintental Liar From the State of Maine; Rum, Romanism, and Rebellion

1888 - A Surplus is Easier to Handle Than a Deficit; Tippecanoe and Tariff, Too!; Grandpa's Pants Won't Fit Benny; Yes, Grandfather's Hat Fits Ben

1896 - Elect McKinley, the Advance Agent of Prosperity; Sixteen to One; No Crown of Thorns, No Cross of Gold; In God We Trust, With Bryan We Bust; McKinley and the Full Dinner Pail; We'll Have Our Pockets Lined with Silver; Stop Bryan, Save America

1900 - The Flag of the Republic Forever, of an Empire Never; Mckinley and the Full Dinner Pail; A Repubic Can Have No Colonies; The Constitution and the Flag, One and Inseperable, Now and Forever; Governments Derive Their Just Powers From the Consent of the Governed; We'll Stand Pat; Four More Years of the Full Dinner Pail; Let Well Enough Alone; Immediate Freedom for the Philippines; Stand Pat With McKinley

1904 - We Want Teddy for Four More Years; Theodore Roosevelt, One and Indivisible; Three Cheers for the Rough Rider; Government of Law, Not of Men; Square Deal

1908 - Stand Pat

1912 - A Covenant With the People; The Moose is Loose; We're Ready for Teddy Again; New Freedom; New Nationalism; I Am as Strong as a Bull Moose

1916 - Don't Swap Horses in the Middle of the Stream; He Kept Us Out of War; Let us Keep This Honest Man; Let Us Keep This Proven Man; War in the East: Peace in the West: Thank God for Wilson; Wilson's Wisdom Wins Without War

1920 - Back to Normalcy With Harding; Let's Have Done With Wiggle and Wobble; Return to Normalcy; Not Nostrums But Normalcy

1924 - Coolidge or Chaos; Entrenched Greed; Honest at Home - Honor Abroad; Keep Cool with Coolidge; Entrenched Wealth; Keep Cool and Keep Coolidge

1928 - A Vote For Al Smith is a Vote for the Pope; Hoover and Happiness, or Smith and Soup Houses; Let's Look at the Record; A Chicken in Every Pot, a Car in Every Garage (said about Hoover in 1932)

1932 - Down With Hoover; Throw the Spenders Out; The Forgotten Man; Happy Days Are Here Again; The New Deal; Everything Will Be Rosy With Roosevelt; Prosperity is Just Around the Corner; The Worst is Past; It Might Have Been Worse; Don't Swap Barrels Going Over Niagara; Swap Horses or Drown; In Hoover We Trusted, Now We Are Busted

1936 - Defeat the New Deal and Its Reckless Spending; Don't Swap Horses in the Middle of the Stream; For Three Long Years; Life, Liberty and Landon; Let's Get Another Deck; Up With Alf - Down With the Alphabet; Land Landon With a Landslide; Land a Job With Landon

1940 - Americe Calls; Don't Swap Horses in the Middle of the Stream; Just Roosevelt; Love Thine Enemy; FDR Carry On; Stick With Roosevelt; Reelect Our President, Franklin D. Roosevelt; We Want Willkie; Wendell Willkie for Prosperity; I Am a

Democrat for Willkie; No Third Term; We Don't Want Eleanor Either; Roosevelt for Ex-President; Win With Willkie; Roosevelt? No! No! A Thousand Times No!; Away with the New Deal and Its Inefficency; America Wants Willkie; No Fourth Term Either; Better a Third Term Than a Third-Rater; There's No Indispensable Man; Two Good Terms Deserve Another; Martin, Barton, and Fish

1944 - Time for a Change; Don't Swap (Change) Horses in the Middle of the Stream

1948 - Time for a Change; Save What's Left; Give 'Em Hell Harry; Don't Let Them Take It Away; Do-Nothing Congress; Don't Waste Your Vote; Fair Deal

1952 - I Like Ike; You Never Had It So Good; All the Way With Adlai; It's Time for a Change; We Like Ike; Don't Let Them Take It Away; I Shall Go To Korea; $K_1 C_2$

1956 - I Like Ike; All the Way With Adlai

1960 - Experience Counts; They Understand What Peace Demands; Get America Moving Again; The New Frontier; America Cannot Stand Still

1964 - $AuH_2 0 = 1964$; $AuH_2 0 + 1964 =$; All the Way With LBJ; Extremism in the Pursuit of Liberty is No Virtue; A Choice Not an Echo; Love That Lyndon; In Your Heart You Know He's Right

1968 - Who But Hubert; Nixon's the One; Clean for Gene; Spiro Who?; Stop the War!; Spiro Agnew — Who's He?

1972 - Acid, Amnesty, and Abortion

1976 - The Grin Will Win; Why Not the Best?; Jimmy Who?

1980 - Vote for the Oldest and the Wisest; Are You Better Off Than You Were Four Years Ago?

1984 - Four More Years; Let's Make America Great Again and Let the Eagle Soar

QUESTIONS AND ANSWERS

1. What are the 2 basic rules that determine citizenship by birth? Which of the 2 is specifically provided for by one of the amendments to the Constitution, and which amendment is that?

ANSWER: *Jus soli* — which is the law of the soil, that is, being born on the soil of the United States or its possessions, and *jus sanguinis* — which is the law of the blood, that is, having one parent who is a U.S. citizen/*Jus soli* and the 14th Amendment.

2. What 3 requirements must a person meet according to the Constitution in order to become President?

ANSWER: The President must be a natural-born citizen, be at least 35 years of age, and have been a resident of the United States for at least 14 years.

3. What article of the Constitution or what amendment provides for the presidential succession? What is the line of succession as provided for by the President Act of 1886, amended in 1947?

ANSWER: Article II/20th Amendment (1933)

1. Vice President	10. Secretary of Commerce
2. Speaker of the House	11. Secretary of Labor
3. President *pro tem* of the Senate	12. Secretary of Health and Human
4. Secretary of State	Services
5. Secretary of the Treasury	13. Secretary of Housing and Urban
6. Secretary of Defense	Development
7. Attorney General	14. Secretary of Transportation
8. Secretary of the Interior	15. Secretary of Energy
9. Secretary of Agriculture	16. Secretary of Education

4. What is the absolute maximum number of years that a President may hold office? What amendment regulates this time and in what year was it passed? How might Gerald Ford have been affected by this amendment? What President could have served an unlimited time in office and why?

ANSWER: 10 years — a maximum of 2 full terms (8 years) plus 2 years by succession to the office to which some other person was elected/The 22nd Amendment of 1951/Gerald Ford completed about 2½ years of Richard Nixon's term of office and, if he had been elected in 1976, would have been ineligible to seek another term of office in 1980/Harry Truman, for he was specifically exempted from the new restriction and because *ex post facto* laws are prohibited under the Constitution.

5. What was the former name for each of the following Cabinet posts?
   a) Department of State (1789)   d) Department of Labor (1913)
   b) Department of Defense (1949)   e) Department of Health and Human Services
   c) Department of Commerce (1913)   (1953; name changed in 1979)

ANSWER: a) Department of Foreign Affairs (1781) b) National Military Establishment (1947 — name changed to Department of Defense in 1949 — Department of War was started in 1789) c) Department of Commerce and Labor (1903) d) Department of Commerce and Labor (1903) e) Department of Health, Education, and Welfare.

6. Who are the only 2 honorary citizens of the United States?

ANSWER: The Marquis de Lafayette and Winston Churchill (Raoul Wallenberg, Swedish attache to Budapest who disappeared in 1945, may be a third).

7. Identify the person who in 1754 proposed a plan to unify the colonies under a central government, and name his plan.

ANSWER: Benjamin Franklin/Albany Plan of Union.

8. Name the 3 statutes enacted by the U.S. Congress in the 1930's that are called ''labor's bill of rights.''

ANSWER: The Norris-LaGuardia (Anti-Injunction) Act of 1932, the Wagner (National Labor Relations) Act of 1935, and the Fair Labor Standards Act of 1938.

9. Name the 4 statutes that form the foundation of the national regulation of labor-management relations.

ANSWER: The Norris-LaGuardia Act of 1932, the Wagner Act of 1935, the Taft-Hartley Act of 1947, and the Landrum-Griffin (Labor-Management Reporting and Disclosure) Act of 1959.

10. Give the dates (year only) for the creation of each of the following Cabinet posts.
    a) Secretary of State
    b) Secretary of the Treasury
    c) Secretary of Defense
    d) Attorney General
    e) Secretary of the Interior
    f) Secretary of Agriculture
    g) Secretary of Commerce
    h) Secretary of Labor
    i) Secretary of Health and Human Services
    j) Secretary of Housing and Urban Development
    k) Secretary of Transportation
    l) Secretary of Energy
    m) Secretary of Education

ANSWER: a) 1789 b) 1789 c) 1947 (1789) d) 1789 e) 1849 f) 1889 g) 1913 h) 1913 i) 1953 j) 1965 k) 1966 l) 1977 m) 1979.

11. What 2 states have the largest number of counties? What 2 states do not have organized county governments? What are counties in Louisiana and Alaska called? What are counties in Delaware called?

ANSWER: Texas has 254 and Georgia has 159/Connecticut and Rhode Island (Connecticut has no counties. Rhode Island has judicial districts — but there is no organized county government)/In Louisiana counties are called parishes, and in Alaska they are boroughs/Hundreds.

12. How old must a person be in order to serve as a U.S. Congressman, a U.S. Senator, and a U.S. Supreme Court Justice?

ANSWER: 25 for a Congressman, 30 for a Senator, and no age is specified for a Supreme Court Justice.

13. How many votes are needed in the following situations?
    a) Pass a Congressional bill over the President's veto
    b) Successful ratification of an amendment to the U.S. Constitution
    c) Congressional proposals of amendments to the Constitution
    d) Conviction of the President, etc. in an impeachment case

ANSWER: a) Two-thirds in each house (290 in the House of Representatives and 67 in the Senate b) Three-fourths of the state legislatures, or 38 (there are 2 other alternate methods) c) Two-thirds vote in each house d) Two-thirds vote of the Senators present.

14. Since Presidents do not vote in Washington, D.C., but in their home states where they are registered, name the Presidents since Franklin D. Roosevelt, their native states, and the states where they voted while President, if different from the states of their birth.

ANSWER: Dwight D. Eisenhower was born in Texas, grew up in Kansas, but voted in Texas; Gerald R. Ford was born in Nebraska but voted in Michigan; and Ronald Reagan was born in Illinois but voted in California.

15. What are the only 2 crimes specified in the U.S. Constitution?

ANSWER: Treason and bribery (The President, Vice President, and all civil officers of the U.S. shall be removed from office on impeachment for, and conviction of, treason, bribery, or other high crimes and misdemeanors).

16. What are the 3 formal duties of the Vice President of the U.S.?

ANSWER: To preside over the Senate and to help decide the question of presidential disability (and, of course, to assume the office of Acting President if necessary).

17. Who were the writers of the following sources for the U.S. Constitution?
    a) *Commentaries on the Laws of England*
    b) *The Spirit of the Laws*
    c) *Two Treatises of Government*
    d) *The Social Contract*

ANSWER: a) Sir William Blackstone b) Baron de Montesquieu c) John Locke d) Jean-Jacques Rousseau.

18. What are the names of the 2-part process to formally add an amendment to the Constitution? There are 2 methods for each part of the 2-part process. Name the 2 methods for each part.

ANSWER: Proposal and ratification/An amendment may be formally proposed by a two-thirds vote of both houses of Congress or by the application of two-thirds of the state legislatures to the Congress. To be ratified, an amendment must be approved by three-fourths of the states by legislative action or by state conventions. Only the 21st Amendment has been ratified by state conventions.

19. What are 4 major expenditures of state governments in the U.S.?

ANSWER: Education, public welfare, highways, and social insurance (trusts, pensions).

20. What are the 3 major branches of the U.S. government? What phrase represents the restraining powers imposed upon these 3 separate and distinct branches? What system serves as a check on the popular election of the President and the Vice President?

ANSWER: Legislative (Congress), executive (President), and the judicial (courts)/ *Checks and balances*/The Electoral College.

21. What are the 3 largest sources of revenue for the U.S. government?

ANSWER: Individual income taxes, social insurance taxes and contributions, and corporation income taxes.

22. What powers are being described by the following?
   a) Powers that are held by the states under the U.S. Constitution
   b) Powers of both the national government and the states
   c) Powers that are exercised only by the national government

ANSWER: a) reserved (residual) powers b) concurrent powers c) exclusive powers.

23. What is the number of electoral votes needed to win the election for President of the United States? The 11 largest states have 2 more than the minimum number of votes needed to win. Name these 11 states in order of largest to smallest and give the number of electoral votes each has.

ANSWER: 270/California (47), New York (36), Texas (29), Pennsylvania (25), Illinois (24), Ohio (23), Florida (21), Michigan (20), New Jersey (16), Massachusetts (13), North Carolina (13), and Georgia, Indiana, or Virginia (each has 12).

24. 49 of 50 state legislatures can be described by what 1 word? What state legislature is different and what word describes it? In what year did the voters of this state approve this type of legislature? What 3 states until what years had the same type of legislature?

ANSWER: Bicameral (that is, two-chambered)/Nebraska is unicameral (one-chambered)/1934/Georgia until 1789, Pennsylvania until 1790, and Vermont until 1836.

25. What are the 3 general types of power possessed by the U.S. Congress?

ANSWER: Those *expressed* in the Constitution, those *implied* from the expressed powers, and those that are *inherent* in the running of a national government.

26. What are the 3 qualifications required by the Constitution to become a U.S. Senator? What amendment changed the election process of senators? How so?

ANSWER: A Senator must be at least 30 years of age, a citizen for at least 9 years, and an inhabitant of the state from which elected/The 17th Amendment in 1913/From being elected by state legislatures to being elected by the people.

27. What are the 3 qualifications required by the U.S. Constitution to become a member of the U.S. House of Representatives?

ANSWER: A Representative must be at least 25 years of age, a citizen for at least 7 years, and an inhabitant of the state from which elected (by statute, an inhabitant of the district to be represented).

28. What is the term of office for a member of the U.S. House, the U.S. Senate, a President of the U.S., and a U.S. Supreme Court Justice?

ANSWER: 2 years for a Representative (no limit on being reelected), 6 years for a Senator (no limit on being reelected), 4 years for a President (can be reelected for a second term), and Supreme Court Justices are chosen for life and there is no retirement age.

29. How many members of the U.S. Congress are there? How many members are in the U.S. Senate and how many in the U.S. House?
ANSWER: 535/100 in the Senate and 435 in the House.

30. Name the only U.S. constitutional amendment that has been repealed and name the amendment that repealed it.
ANSWER: The 18th or Prohibition Amendment was passed in 1919 and repealed in 1933 by the 21st Amendment.

31. What are the 3 inalienable rights of the people guaranteed by the Declaration of Independence? (Note that the Declaration of Independence has no legal validity).
ANSWER: Life, Liberty, and the pursuit of Happiness.

32. During what 2 periods of U.S. history has the U.S. had a Confederate government?
ANSWER: The period from 1781 to 1789 under the Articles of Confederation and the time from 1861 to 1865 with the Confederate States in the South.

33. What French phrase is the foundation of the capitalistic system? What does it mean literally and practically? Who expounded on this theory and in what book did he do so?
ANSWER: *Laissez-faire*/Literally it means ''(to) allow to do,'' which means that the government does not interfere in society/Adam Smith in *The Wealth of Nations* (1776).

34. The U.S. Senate has refused 9 times to approve of a presidential Cabinet appointee. Name the person the Senate rejected in each of the following situations.
    a) Jackson's appointment of the Secretary of the Treasury in 1834
    b) Tyler's appointment of the Secretary of the Treasury in 1843
    c) Tyler's appointment of the Secretary of the Treasury in 1844
    d) Tyler's appointment of the Secretary of the Navy in 1844
    e) Tyler's appointment of the Secretary of War in 1844
    f) Andrew Johnson's appointment of the Attorney General in 1868
    g) Andrew Johnson's appointment of the Secretary of the Treasury in 1869
    h) Coolidge's appointment of the Attorney General in 1925
    i) Eisenhower's appointment of the Secretary of Commerce in 1959
ANSWER: a) Roger B. Taney b) Caleb Cushing c) James Green d) David Henshaw e) James M. Porter f) Henry Stanberry g) Alexander Stewart h) Charles B. Warren (rejected twice) i) Lewis Strauss.

35. Who was the U.S. President who appointed the first Black to a Cabinet post? Name the Black and the Cabinet post. Who was the first President to appoint both a woman and a Black to Cabinet positions? Name the 2 people and the Cabinet posts.
ANSWER: Lyndon B. Johnson appointed Robert C. Weaver as the Secretary of Housing and Urban Development (1966)/Gerald R. Ford appointed Carla Hills as Secretary of Housing and Urban Development (1975) and William T. Coleman as Secretary of Transportation (1975).

36. Name the 3 women Jimmy Carter appointed to Cabinet level status, and name the positions they held.
ANSWER: Juanita M. Kreps was Secretary of Commerce, Patricia R. Harris (the first Black woman appointee) was Secretary of Housing and Urban Development (and, in 1979, Secretary of Health and Human Services), and Shirley Hufstedler was the Secretary of Education (1979).

37. On which day in which month does Federal law now require states to hold national elections?
ANSWER: The first Tuesday after the first Monday/November (in even-numbered years).

38. Name the 6 states that have but 1 Representative in the U.S. House of Representatives.

ANSWER: Alaska, Delaware, North Dakota, South Dakota, Vermont and Wyoming.

39. 7 states have but 2 members in the U.S. House of Representatives. Name them.

ANSWER: Hawaii, Idaho, Maine, Montana, Nevada, New Hampshire, and Rhode Island.

40. Name the 3 states that have the largest number of Representatives in the U.S. House of Representatives and give the number for each state.

ANSWER: California (45), New York (34), and Texas (27).

41. Who presides at a Senate impeachment when the U.S. President is on trial, and how many members present must concur to convict the President?

ANSWER: Chief Justice of the Supreme Court/two-thirds.

42. What 3 powers have been delegated exclusively to the U.S. House of Representatives?

ANSWER: It originates all bills for raising revenue; it elects the President if there is no electoral majority; and it impeaches federal officials.

43. Explain the meaning of the phrase ''Dean of the House.'' Who is the Democrat and who are the 2 Republicans holding this position?

ANSWER: The ''Dean of the House'' is the member who has served the longest/The senior Democrat (and the senior of the 3) is Jamie L. Whitten of Mississippi, who has served since November 4, 1941. The 2 senior Republicans are William Broomfield of Michigan and Robert Michel of Illinois, who have served since January 3, 1957 (John J. Rhodes of Arizona was the senior Republican — from January 3, 1953 to January 3, 1983).

44. Who were the first 3 Speakers of the U.S. House and who, including the present Speaker, are the last 3 to hold that post? Of the 47 Speakers, who served the longest?

ANSWER: Frederick A.C. Muhlenburg (Pennsylvania) was first from 1789 to 1791 and third from 1793 to 1795, and Jonathan Trumbull (Connecticut) was second from 1791 to 1793. John W. McCormack (Massachusetts) served from 1963 to 1971, Carl Albert (Oklahoma) served from 1971 to 1977, and Thomas P. O'Neill, Jr. (Massachusetts), the current Speaker, began in 1977/Sam Rayburn (Texas) served for 17 years and 62 days from 1940 to 1961 except for 1947-1949 and 1953-1955.

45. Sam Rayburn served the longest time as Speaker of the House, but his tenure was interrupted twice. Who were the 3 men who had the longest continuous service as Speakers of the House?

ANSWER: John McCormack (Massachusetts) served for 8 years, 11 months, and 23 days, Champ Clark (Missouri) served for 7 years, 10 months, and 29 days, and Joseph G. Cannon (Illinois) served for 7 years, 3 months, and 24 days.

46. 3 colors are associated with the electronic voting system in the U.S. Congress. What is the significance of the green, the red, and the amber colors?

ANSWER: Green is for ''yea,'' red is for ''nay,'' and amber is for ''present.''

47. What is the record for the longest filibuster in the U.S. Congress and who holds that record?

ANSWER: 24 hours and 18 minutes and it is held by Strom Thurmond, a South Carolina Republican (he spoke against the Civil Rights Act of 1957).

48. How many days (not counting Sundays) does it take for a bill to become law after the President of the U.S. receives it if he does not act upon it? What is a pocket veto?

ANSWER: Ten days/An indirect veto of a legislative bill if the bill remains unsigned and Congress has adjourned within those 10 days.

49. What are the only 2 qualifications imposed by states on all voters?

ANSWER: All voters must be citizens of the United States and they must reside in a state for a period of time (this time period varies from state to state).

50. What are the 2 basic forms of the direct primary that are used in most states today?

ANSWER: The closed primary (only for those registered voters for a specific party) and the open primary (for any registered voter who can vote for the candidate of any party).

51. Name the only 3rd party to achieve the level of a major party in the U.S., and in what year did this party come into being?
ANSWER: **The Republican Party, and it was born in 1854.**

52. What were the names of the first 2 political parties in the U.S., and who were the leaders of these parties?
ANSWER: **The Federalists were led by Alexander Hamilton, and the Anti-Federalists were organized by Thomas Jefferson (later called the Jeffersonian Republicans or the Democratic-Republicans, and in 1828, renamed the Democratic Party).**

53. It is very difficult for 3rd party candidates for the presidency to be on the ballots in every state. Name the last three 3rd party candidates to accomplish this feat.
ANSWER: **Ed Clark of the Libertarian Party and John Anderson running independently in 1980, and George Wallace (American Independent Party) in 1968.**

54. Name the first 2 women to serve as National Chairpersons, one for the Democratic Party in 1972 and 1973 and the other for the Republican Party from 1974 to 1977.
ANSWER: **Jean Westwood for the Democrats and Mary Louise Smith for the Republicans.**

55. The right to vote has been expanded in several stages. Identify the legislative action through the following descriptions.
a) The test to decide voting rights which was finally dropped as of 1810
b) Proposed in 1869 and ratified in 1870
c) Proposed in 1919 and ratified in 1920
d) The 1965 Act
e) Proposed in March of 1971 and ratified in July of 1971
ANSWER: **a) Religious test b) 15th Amendment c) 19th Amendment d) Voting Rights Act e) 26th Amendment.**

56. What pieces of legislation are known by the following nicknames?
a) White Slave Traffic Act of 1910
b) Lame Duck Amendment
c) Doctrine of Residual Powers
d) Due Process Amendment
e) Prohibition Amendment
f) Crime of '73
g) Blanket Code
h) Magna Carta of civil service reform
i) Labor's Magna Carta
j) Susan B. Anthony Amendment
ANSWER: **a) Mann Act b) 20th Amendment c) 10th Amendment d) 5th Amendment e) 18th Amendment f) Congressional Act of 1873 discontinuing the coinage of silver dollars g) President Roosevelt's Re-Employment Agreement of 1933 h) Pendleton Act of 1883 i) Clayton Act of 1914 j) 19th Amendment.**

57. How many members of the U.S. Senate have been expelled? What were the circumstances?
ANSWER: **Fifteen/William Blount of Tennessee was expelled in 1797 for conspiring to lead Indian tribes and British warships in an attack on Spanish Florida and Louisiana, and 14 senators were expelled in 1861 and 1862 for supporting the Confederacy.**

58. Identify each of the following (independent) agencies/departments of the U.S. government from the given acronyms.
a) CIA
b) CEA
c) OMB
d) CAB
e) EPA
f) FBI
g) FDIC
h) FTC
i) GSA
j) ICC
k) NASA
l) NLRB
m) NSF
n) NRC
o) SEC
p) SBA
q) TVA
r) VA
s) AID
t) EEOC
ANSWER: **a) Central Intelligence Agency b) Council of Economic Advisers c) Office of Management and Budget d) Civil Aeronautics Board e) Environmental Protection Agency f) Federal Bureau of Investigation g) Federal Deposit Insurance Corporation h) Federal Trade Commission i) General Services Administration j) Interstate Commerce Commission k) National Aeronautics and Space Administration l) National Labor Relations Board m) National Science**

Foundation n) Nuclear Regulatory Commission o) Securities and Exchange Commission p) Small Business Administration q) Tennessee Valley Authority r) Veterans Administration s) Agency for International Development t) Equal Employment Opportunities Corporation.

59. The British government can be characterized as parliamentary, unitary, and monarchal. What 3 words can characterize the U.S. government?
ANSWER: **Presidential, federal, and republican (representative).**

60. In what way are William Plumer, James Monroe, and the Electoral College connected?
ANSWER: **George Washington was the only President to be unanimously elected by the Electoral College, but James Monroe would have been had one elector, William Plumer, voted for him in the 1820 election. Plumer considered Monroe a weak President, and he objected to Monroe ''on account of his financial embarrassments.''**

61. In the U.S., if the President-elect were to die before the Electoral College had voted, who would become President? If the President-elect were to die after the Electoral College had voted, who would become President?
ANSWER: **The party organization would name a new presidential candidate/The Vice President-elect.**

62. Identify each of the following members of Congress by the given descriptions.
    a) First Black to serve in the House, December, 1870 to March, 1879
    b) First Black to serve in the Senate, February, 1870 to March, 1871
    c) First Black woman to serve in Congress, elected in 1968
    d) First woman elected to the Congress, 1916
    e) First woman elected to the U.S. Senate without having been preceded in Congress by a spouse or appointed to fill an unexpired term, 1979
    f) First woman to serve in both the House and the Senate
    g) First woman elected to the U.S. Senate, November, 1932 (and the first to preside over a Senate session)
    h) First woman member of the U.S. Senate, appointed October 3, 1922
ANSWER: **a) Joseph H. Rainey b) Hiram R. Revels c) Shirley Chisholm d) Jeannette Rankin e) Nancy Landon Kassebaum f) Margaret Chase Smith g) Hattie Caraway h) Rebecca Latimer Felton.**

63. What number constitutes a quorum in the U.S. House of the Representatives, the Senate, and the Supreme Court?
ANSWER: **218, 51, and 6 respectively.**

64. Who are the first 6 women who have been elected governor of a state? Give their states. Who was the first woman in the U.S. to be elected governor of a state in her own right, and not as a successor to her husband? Name the 3 who followed their husbands in office.
ANSWER: **Nellie T. Ross of Wyoming (1925-1927); Miriam A. Ferguson of Texas (1925-1927 and 1933-1935); Lurleen Wallace of Alabama (1967-1968); Ella T. Grasso of Connecticut (1974-1980); Dixie Lee Ray of Washington (1977-1980); and Martha Layne Collins of Kentucky (1984-   )/Ella T. Grasso/Ross, Ferguson, and Wallace followed their husbands in the office.**

65. Identify the state or states from the following descriptions.
    a) Only state with a unicameral legislature
    b) Only state whose governor does not have the power to veto acts of the legislature
    c) Only state whose legislature cannot remove public officials by impeachment
    d) Only 2 states that do not have county governments
    e) Only state that does not have ratification of constitutional changes by popular vote
    f) Only state that requires the governor to be over 30 years of age (35)
ANSWER: **a) Nebraska b) North Carolina c) Oregon d) Rhode Island and Connecticut e) Delaware f) Oklahoma.**

66. Name the 3 states whose present constitutions are the oldest state constitutions.

ANSWER: Massachusetts (1780), New Hampshire (1784), and Vermont (1793).

67. Most governors are elected for 4 year terms. Only 4 states still have a 2 year term for the governor. Name them.
ANSWER: Arkansas, New Hampshire, Rhode Island, and Vermont.

68. In 4 states governors are not allowed to serve more than 1 consecutive term. Name the 4.
ANSWER: Kentucky, Mississippi, New Mexico, and Virginia.

69. Name the 5 governors in the 20th century who have been removed from office by being impeached. Name their states.
ANSWER: William Sulzer of New York (1913); James E. Furguson of Texas (1917); J.C. Walton of Oklahoma (1923); Harvey S. Johnston of Oklahoma (1929); and Evan Mecham of Arizona (1988).

70. Who served as Senate Majority Leader from 1961 to 1977? Who served as Senate Minority Leader in 1953 and 1954 and as Majority Leader from 1955 to 1960?
ANSWER: Mike Mansfield (Montana)/Lyndon B. Johnson (Texas).

71. What Majority leader of the U.S. Senate was Minority leader from 1977 to 1981? Who served as Senate Minority leader from 1969 to 1977? Who served as Minority leader from 1959 to 1969?
ANSWER: Howard H. Baker, Jr. (Tennessee)/Hugh Scott (Pennsylvania)/Everett M. Dirksen (Illinois).

72. How many states did the following Presidents win in the presidential elections in the year given?
   a) Nixon - 1968   c) Carter - 1976   e) Reagan - 1984
   b) Nixon - 1972   d) Reagan - 1980
ANSWER: a) 32 b) 49 c) 23 d) 44 e) 49.

73. What is the total number of presidential electors according to states? How is the figure calculated? What is the total number of presidential electors? How do you explain the difference?
ANSWER: 535/Based on the number of Senators (100) and Representatives (435)/ 538/Because Washington, D.C., is considered a state for the election of the President and Vice President and given 3 electoral votes.

74. What is the difference in the impeachment process and the 25th Amendment concerning the removal of a President who is unfit for the office?
ANSWER: Impeachment concerns moral unfitness ("treason, bribery, or other high crimes and misdemeanors") for the office while the 25th Amendment allows his removal for physical and mental unfitness.

75. Identify each of the following.
   a) Lyndon Johnson's first Attorney General
   b) The 2 Presidents Dean Rusk served as Secretary of State
   c) Lyndon Johnson's first Secretary of Defense
   d) The last Postmaster General (in the Nixon administration)
   e) The 2 Presidents Henry Kissinger served as Secretary of State
   f) The Secretary of the Treasury to both Nixon and Ford
   g) The 4 Attorneys General of the Nixon administration
ANSWER: a) Bobby Kennedy b) John Kennedy and Lyndon Johnson c) Robert McNamara d) Winton Blount e) Richard Nixon and Gerald Ford f) William Simon g) John Mitchell, Richard Kleindienst, Elliot Richardson, and William Saxbe.

76. Identify each of the following.
   a) The States' Rights candidates in the 1948 election
   b) The American Party candidates in the 1968 election
   c) The American Party candidates in the 1972 election
   d) The Independent Party candidates in the 1980 election
ANSWER: a) J. Strom Thurmond and Fielding Wright b) George C. Wallace and Curtis

E. LeMay c) John Schmitz and Thomas Anderson d) John Anderson and Patrick Lucey.

77. Explain each of the following terms.
   a) Writ of *Habeas Corpus*   c) *ex post facto* law
   b) cloture (or closure)   d) *stare decisis*

ANSWER: a) to keep people from being held in jail indefinitely without being brought to trial (in full, *habeas corpus subjiciendum*) b) a parliamentary procedure taken by either house of Congress to stop a debate or filibuster and put the measure under discussion to an immediate vote c) legislation passed to punish a person for an act that was not illegal before the act was passed (Congress and the states are prohibited under the Constitution from enacting such laws) d) a policy of law that requires courts to abide by laws and precedents announced in former decisions as applicable to a similar set of facts.

78. What 5 states do not levy a general sales tax?
ANSWER: Alaska, Delaware, Montana, New Hampshire, and Oregon.

79. What types of taxes, regressive or progressive, are sales taxes and individual income taxes?
ANSWER: Sales taxes are regressive, and individual income taxes are progressive.

80. The Department of State was created in 1789. By what 3 different names, in 1775, 1777, and 1781, was this office known?
ANSWER: The Committee of Secret Correspondence (1775-1777), the Committee for Foreign Affairs (1777-1781), and the Department of Foreign Affairs (1781-1789).

81. What 1 word precedes "Extraordinary and Plenipotentiary" in the official title of a U.S. foreign service officer? A Committee on Secret Correspondence was established by the Continental Congress in 1775. Who was the first Chairman of the Committee (in essence, a Secretary of State)? Who were the 3 secret agents designated by this Committee to be the first U.S. representatives abroad? After the Declaration of Independence, who were the 3 men appointed by the Continental Congress to negotiate a Treaty of Alliance with France (signed in 1778)?
ANSWER: Ambassador/Benjamin Franklin/Arthur Lee of Virginia — to London; Charles W. F. Dumas of Switzerland — to The Hague; and Silas Deane of Connecticut — to Paris/Silas Deane, Arthur Lee, and Benjamin Franklin.

82. Name the 3 largest federal agencies with respect to the number of employees.
ANSWER: Department of Defense (960,000), Postal Service (655,000), and the Veterans Administration (235,000).

83. Who were the well-known Secretaries of State (as identified by their initials) under the following Presidents?
   a) Jefferson - JM   f) T. Roosevelt - ER
   b) J.Q. Adams - HC   g) Harding and Coolidge - CH
   c) W.H. Harrison, Tyler, and   h) F.D. Roosevelt - CH
      Fillmore - DW   i) Truman - GM
   d) Lincoln and Johnson - WS   j) Eisenhower - JD
   e) McKinley and Roosevelt - JH   k) Kennedy and Johnson - DR
ANSWER: a) James Madison b) Henry Clay c) Daniel Webster d) William H. Seward e) John Hay f) Elihu Root g) Charles E. Hughes h) Cordell Hull i) George C. Marshall j) John Foster Dulles k) Dean Rusk.

84. What are the 3 main sources of revenue for local governments?
ANSWER: Property taxes, general (selective) sales taxes, and individual and corporation income taxes.

85. How many departments of the government take orders directly from the President?
ANSWER: 13 (the Cabinet).

86. Identify the President elected in each of the following years who received less than 50% of the popular vote.

a) 1824	e) 1860	i) 1888	m) 1948
b) 1844	f) 1876	j) 1892	n) 1960
c) 1848	g) 1880	k) 1912	o) 1968
d) 1856	h) 1884	l) 1916	

ANSWER: a) John Quincy Adams b) James K. Polk c) Zachary Taylor d) James Buchanan e) Abraham Lincoln f) Rutherford B. Hayes g) James A. Garfield h) Grover Cleveland i) Benjamin Harrison j) Grover Cleveland k) Woodrow Wilson l) Woodrow Wilson m) Harry S. Truman n) John F. Kennedy o) Richard M. Nixon.

87. Which state did each of the following represent as senator?

a) Robert A. Taft	e) Mike Mansfield	i) Henry M. Jackson
b) Lyndon Johnson	f) Everett Dirksen	j) Hattie Caraway
c) John F. Kennedy	g) Howard Baker	k) Rebecca L. Felton
d) Alben Barkley	h) Barry Goldwater	l) Margaret C. Smith

ANSWER: a) Ohio b) Texas c) Massachusetts d) Kentucky e) Montana f) Illinois g) Tennessee h) Arizona i) Washington j) Arkansas k) Georgia l) Maine.

88. Which state did each of the following represent as governor?

a) George Romney	f) Franklin Roosevelt
b) Ronald Reagan	g) Nelson Rockefeller
c) Nellie T. Ross	h) Alfred E. Smith
d) Miriam Ferguson	i) Earl Warren
e) Jimmy Carter	j) John B. Connally

ANSWER: a) Michigan b) California c) Wyoming d) Texas e) Georgia f) New York g) New York h) New York i) California j) Texas.

89. Of which city was each of the following the mayor?

a) Dianne Feinstein	f) Tom Bradley	k) Maynard Jackson
b) Andrew Young	g) Harold Washington	l) Jane Byrne
c) Coleman Young	h) John F. Fitzgerald	m) Henry Cisneros
d) Edward Koch	i) Kathy Whitmire	n) Richard Hatcher
e) James Walker	j) W. Wilson Goode	o) Donald Schaefer

ANSWER: a) San Francisco, CA b) Atlanta, GA c) Detroit, MI d) New York, NY e) New York, NY f) Los Angeles, CA g) Chicago, IL h) Boston, MA i) Houston, TX j) Philadelphia, PA, k) Atlanta, GA l) Chicago, IL m) San Antonio, TX n) Gary, IN o) Baltimore, MD.

90. Three members of the House of Representatives have been elected to Congress on a write-in vote. Name any of the 3. There has been but 1 person ever elected to the U.S. Senate as a write-in candidate. Name him.

ANSWER: Dale Alford (D) of Arkansas in 1958; Joe Skeen (R) of New Mexico in 1980; and Ron Packard (R) of California in 1982/Senator Strom Thurmond of South Carolina in 1954 as an independent after leaving the Democratic Party.

91. Name the 1 court mentioned in the U.S. Constitution. What are the 3 levels of the regular federal court structure?

ANSWER: The Supreme Court/The Supreme Court, 12 courts of appeal, and 91 district courts.

92. Name the 7 special courts or legislative courts.

ANSWER: The Court of Claims, Customs Court, Court of Customs and Patent Appeals, Territorial Courts, Courts of the District of Columbia, Court of Military Appeals, and the United States Tax Court.

93. Name the constitutional amendment which is before the states for approval with the possibility that it may become the 27th Amendment.

ANSWER: A D.C. Representation Amendment which would give Washington, D.C.

representation in Congress as if it were a state (The Equal Rights Amendment's deadline has passed).

94. Who were the well-known Secretaries of the Treasury (as identified by their initials) under the following Presidents?

a) George Washington - AH
b) Jefferson and Madison - AG
c) Jackson - RT (not confirmed by the Senate)
d) Lincoln - SC
e) Wilson - WM
f) Wilson - CG
g) Harding, Coolidge, and Hoover - AM
h) Roosevelt and Truman - HM
i) Truman - FV
j) Nixon - GS
k) Ford - WS

ANSWER: a) Alexander Hamilton b) Albert Gallatin c) Roger B. Taney d) Salmon P. Chase e) William McAdoo f) Carter Glass g) Andrew Mellon h) Henry P. Morgenthau, Jr. i) Fred M. Vinson j) George Shultz k) William Simon.

95. In what cities are the 3 U.S. mints located? Where is the Bullion Depository for gold located? Where is the depository for silver located?

ANSWER: Philadelphia, Pennsylvania; Denver, Colorado; and San Francisco, California/Fort Knox, Kentucky/West Point, New York.

96. In what year was the Federal Reserve Act passed? How many Federal Reserve Districts are there? Name the cities in which the Federal Reserve Banks are located?

ANSWER: 1913/12/Boston, New York, Philadelphia, Cleveland, Richmond, Atlanta, Chicago, St. Louis, Minneapolis, Kansas City, Dallas, and San Francisco.

97. In what year was the Federal Home Loan Bank System created by Congress? How many regional Federal Home Loan Banks are there? Name the cities in which they are located.

ANSWER: 1932/12/Boston, New York, Pittsburgh, Atlanta, Cincinnati, Indianapolis, Chicago, Des Moines, Little Rock, Topeka, San Francisco, and Seattle.

98. On U.S. Federal Reserve Notes there is a letter of the alphabet that designates the Federal Reserve District. Tell which city is designated by each of the following letters.

a) "D"
b) "I"
c) "L"
d) "A"
e) "K"
f) "C"
g) "E"
h) "H"
i) "F"
j) "G"
k) "J"
l) "B"

ANSWER: a) Cleveland b) Minneapolis c) San Francisco d) Boston e) Dallas f) Philadelphia g) Richmond h) St. Louis i) Atlanta j) Chicago k) Kansas City l) New York.

99. Who were the first 2 Presidents to deliver their annual messages personally before the joint sessions of the House and Senate? Who discontinued this practice? What President revived the practice? Every President since except one has gone to the Congress to personally deliver his annual message. Who was the exception?

ANSWER: George Washington and John Adams/Thomas Jefferson/Woodrow Wilson/ Herbert Hoover.

100. Name the 2 delegates to the Constitutional Convention who later became U.S. Presidents.

ANSWER: George Washington and James Madison.

101. Provide the answer to each of the following descriptions.

a) Actual "writer of the U.S. Constitution"
b) Nicknamed the "Father of the Constitution"
c) State that was not represented at the Constitutional Convention
d) Delegates of this state signed the Constitution first according to protocol
e) Delegates of this state signed the Constitution last according to protocol
f) Number of delegates who signed the Constitution
g) Original Constitution is displayed at this site

ANSWER: a) Gouverneur Morris b) James Madison c) Rhode Island d) New Hampshire e) Georgia f) 39 g) National Archives Building in Washington, D.C.

102. What is the name of the document adopted by the Connecticut Colony in 1639 that is considered to be the world's first written constitution?

ANSWER: The *Fundamental Orders*.

AN OUTLINE OF THE CONSTITUTION OF THE UNITED STATES

PREAMBLE

ARTICLE I. LEGISLATIVE BRANCH

Section 1. Legislative Powers; the Congress
Section 2. House of Representatives
Section 3. Senate
Section 4. Elections of Senators and Representatives
Section 5. Legislative Proceedings
Section 6. Compensation, Privileges, and Disabilities of Members
Section 7. Revenue Bills; President's Veto
Section 8. Powers Granted to Congress
Section 9. Powers Denied to Congress
Section 10. Powers Forbidden to the States

ARTICLE II. EXECUTIVE BRANCH

Section 1. Executive Power; the President; Election and Qualifications of the President
Section 2. Powers of the President
Section 3. Powers and Duties of the President

Section 4. Impeachment

ARTICLE III. JUDICIAL BRANCH

Section 1. Judicial Power; Terms of Office
Section 2. Jurisdiction
Section 3. Treason and Punishment

ARTICLE IV. RELATIONS OF STATES

Section 1. Full Faith and Credit Among States
Section 2. Privileges and Immunities of Citizens
Section 3. Admission of New States; Territories
Section 4. Guarantee of a Republican Form of Government

ARTICLE V. PROVISIONS FOR AMENDMENT OF THE CONSTITUTION

ARTICLE VI. PUBLIC DEBTS; SUPREMACY OF NATIONAL LAW; OATH

ARTICLE VII. RATIFICATION OF CONSTITUTION

AMENDMENTS TO THE CONSTITUTION (I—X, the Bill of Rights, ratified December 15, 1791)

1ST .... Freedom of Religion, Speech, and the Press; Rights of Assembly and Petition
2ND.... Right to Bear and Keep Arms
3RD .... Quartering of Soldiers
4TH .... Searches and Seizures
5TH .... Rights of the Accused in Criminal Cases
6TH .... Right to a Fair Trial
7TH .... Rights in Civil Trials
8TH .... Bail, Fines, and Punishments
9TH .... Enumeration of the Rights of the People
10TH ... Powers Reserved to the States
11TH ... Lawsuits Against States (1795)
12TH ... Election of President and Vice President (1804)
13TH ... Abolition of Slavery (1865)
14TH ... Civil Rights of Citizens, Especially Negroes (1868)
15TH ... Negro Suffrage (1870)

16TH ... Income Taxes (1913)
17TH ... Popular Election of Senators (1913)
18TH ... Prohibition of Intoxicating Liquors (1919)
19TH ... Woman Suffrage (1920)
20TH ... Terms of the President and Congress; Death of the President-elect (1933)
21ST ... Repeal of 18th Amendment (1933)
22ND... Presidential Tenure (1951)
23RD ... Suffrage in the District of Columbia (1961)
24TH ... Right to Vote in Federal Elections - Poll Taxes Abolished (1964)
25TH ... Presidential Succession; Vice Presidential Vacancy; Presidential Disability (1967)
26TH ... Suffrage for 18-Year-Olds (1971)

SIGNERS OF THE DECLARATION OF INDEPENDENCE

John Hancock: *President*

NEW HAMPSHIRE
Josiah Bartlett
Wm. Whipple
Matthew Thornton

RHODE ISLAND
Step. Hopkins
William Ellery

CONNECTICUT
Roger Sherman
Sam'el Huntington
Wm. Williams
Oliver Wolcott

NEW YORK
Wm. Floyd
Phil. Livingston

Frans. Lewis
Lewis Morris

NEW JERSEY
Richd. Stockton
Jno. Witherspoon
Fras. Hopkinson
John Hart
Abra. Clark

PENNSYLVANIA
Robt. Morris
Benjamin Rush
Benj. Franklin
John Morton
Geo. Clymer
Jas. Smith

Geo. Taylor
James Wilson
Geo. Ross

MASSACHUSETTS BAY
Saml. Adams
John Adams
Robt. Treat Paine
Elbridge Gerry

DELAWARE
Caesar Rodney
Geo. Read
Tho. M'Kean

MARYLAND
Samuel Chase
Wm. Paca

Thos. Stone
Charles Carroll of Carrollton
VIRGINIA
George Wythe
Richard Henry Lee
Th. Jefferson
Benj. Harrison
Ths. Nelson, Jr.

Francis Lightfoot Lee
Carter Braxton
NORTH CAROLINA
Wm. Hooper
Joseph Hewes
John Penn
SOUTH CAROLINA
Edward Rutledge

Thos. Heyward, Junr.
Thomas Lynch, Junr.
Arthur Middleton
GEORGIA
Button Gwinnett
Lyman Hall
Geo. Walton

SIGNERS OF THE CONSTITUTION OF THE UNITED STATES
George Washington: *President and Deputy from Virginia*

NEW HAMPSHIRE
John Langdon
Nicholas Gilman
MASSACHUSETTS
Nathaniel Gorham
Rufus King
CONNECTICUT
Wm. Saml. Johnson
Roger Sherman
NEW YORK
Alexander Hamilton
NEW JERSEY
Wil. Livingston
David Brearley
Wm. Paterson
Jona. Dayton
PENNSYLVANIA

B. Franklin
Robt. Morris
Thos. Fitzsimons
James Wilson
Thomas Mifflin
Geo. Clymer
Jared Ingersoll
Gouv. Morris
DELAWARE
Geo. Read
John Dickinson
Jaco. Broom
Gunning Bedford Jun.
Richard Bassett
MARYLAND
James McHenry
Danl. Carroll

Dan. of St. Thos. Jenifer
VIRGINIA
John Blair
James Madison, Jr.
NORTH CAROLINA
Wm. Blount
Hu. Williamson
Richd Dobbs Spaight
SOUTH CAROLINA
J. Rutledge
Charles Pinckney
Charles Cotesworth Pinckney
Pierce Butler
GEORGIA
William Few
Abr. Baldwin

UNITED STATES COINS

COIN	PORTRAIT/DESIGN ON BACK
Cent	Abraham Lincoln/Lincoln Memorial
Nickel	Thomas Jefferson/Monticello
Dime	Franklin D. Roosevelt/Torch; Laurel and Oak Leaves
Quarter	George Washington/Eagle
Half Dollar	John F. Kennedy/Presidential Seal
Dollar	Dwight D. Eisenhower/Eagle (Apollo 11 insignia)
Dollar	Susan B. Anthony/Eagle (Apollo 11 insignia)

UNITED STATES CURRENCY

$1	George Washington	. . . . Great Seal of the U.S.
$2[1]	Thomas Jefferson	. . . . . . Monticello
$2[2]	Thomas Jefferson	. . . . . . John Trumbull's ''Signing of the Declaration of Independence''
$5	Abraham Lincoln	. . . . . . Lincoln Memorial
$10	Alexander Hamilton	. . . . U.S. Treasury Building
$20	Andrew Jackson	. . . . The White House
$50	Ulysses S. Grant	. . . . U.S. Capitol
$100	Benjamin Franklin	. . . . . Independence Hall
$500[3]	William McKinley	. . . . . . Ornate FIVE HUNDRED
$1,000	Grover Cleveland	. . . . . . Ornate ONE THOUSAND
$10,000	Salmon P. Chase	. . . . . . Ornate TEN THOUSAND
$100,000	Woodrow Wilson	. . . . Ornate ONE HUNDRED THOUSAND

[1]Discontinued in 1966. [2]Issued in 1976. [3]Denominations of $500 and higher were discontinued in 1969.

GOVERNMENT LEADERS

AS OF 9/88

President . . . . Ronald Reagan
Vice President . . . . George Bush

The Cabinet - Secretaries of

State . . . . George Shultz
Treasury . . . . Nicholas Brady
Defense . . . . Frank Carlucci
Attorney General . . . . Richard Thornburgh
Interior . . . . Donald P. Hodel
Agriculture . . . . Richard Lyng
Commerce . . . . C. William Verity
Labor . . . . Ann Dore McLaughlin
Health and Human Services . . . . Otis "Doc" Bowen
Housing and Urban Development . . . . . . Samuel Pierce
Transportation . . . . James H. Burnley
Energy . . . . John Herrington
Education . . . . Lauro Cavazos

Senate

President of the Senate . . . . George Bush
President Pro Tempore . . . . John Stennis (Dem. — Mississippi)
Majority Leader . . . . Robert C. Byrd (Dem. — West Virginia)
Majority Whip . . . . Alan Cranston (Dem. — California)
Minority Leader . . . . Robert Dole (Rep. — Kansas)
Minority Whip . . . . Alan K. Simpson (Rep. — Wyoming)

House of Representatives

Speaker . . . . Jim Wright (Dem. — Texas)
Majority Leader . . . . Thomas Foley (Dem. — Washington)
Majority Whip . . . . Tony Coelho (Dem. — California)
Minority Leader . . . . Robert H. Michel (Republican — Illinois)
Minority Whip . . . . Trent Lott (Republican — Mississippi)

Presidential Troika

Chief of Staff . . . . Kenneth Duberstein

U.N. Ambassador . . . . Vernon Walters
Director of the Office of Management and Budget . . . . James Miller
Press Secretary . . . . James Brady
Special Trade Representative . . . . Clayton Yeutter
Chief Economist — Chairman of the Council of
Economic Advisers . . . . Beryl Sprinkel
White House Congressional Liaison . . . . Max Friedersdorf
Chief of "Crisis Management" . . . . George Bush
Treasurer of the United States . . . . Katherine Ortega
National Security Adviser . . . . Colin Powell
FBI Director . . . . William Sessions
CIA Director . . . . William Webster
Federal Reserve Board Chairman . . . . Alan Greenspan
Environmental Protection Agency . . . . Lee Thomas
Chairman of the Joint Chiefs of Staff . . . . Adm. William Crowe, Jr.
Acting White House Spokesman . . . . Marlin Fitzwater

SENATORS / GOVERNORS AND THEIR STATES
As of 10/1/1991

STATES	SENATORS (Senior Senator listed first)	GOVERNORS
Alabama	Howell T. Heflin (D) / Richard Shelby (D)	Guy Hunt (R)
Alaska	Ted Stevens (R) / Frank H. Murkowski (R)	Walter Hickel (I)
Arizona	Dennis DeConcini (D) / John McCain (R)	Fife Symington (R)
Arkansas	Dale Bumpers (D) / David H. Pryor (D)	William Clinton (D)
California	Alan Cranston (D) / John Seymour (R)	Pete Wilson (R)
Colorado	Timothy Wirth (D) / Hank Brown (R)	Roy Romer (D)
Connecticut	Christopher Dodd (D) / Joseph Lieberman (D)	Lowell Weicker (I)
Delaware	William V. Roth Jr. (R) / Joseph Biden, Jr. (D)	Michael N. Castle (R)
Florida	Bob Graham (D) / Connie Mack (R)	Lawton Chiles (D)
Georgia	Sam Nunn (D) / Wyche Fowler (D)	Zell Miller (D)
Hawaii	Daniel K. Inouye (D) / Daniel Akaka (D)	John Waihee (D)
Idaho	Steven D. Symms (R) / Larry Craig (R)	Cecil Andrus (D)
Illinois	Alan J. Dixon (D) / Paul Simon (D)	Jim Edgar (R)
Indiana	Richard G. Lugar (R) / Dan Coats (R)	Birch E. Bayh (D)
Iowa	Charles E. Grassley (R) / Tom Harkin (D)	Terry Branstad (R)
Kansas	Robert J. Dole (R) / Nancy Landon Kassebaum (R)	Joan Finney (D)
Kentucky	Wendell H. Ford (D) / Mitch McConnell (R)	Wallace Wilkinson (D)
Louisiana	J. Bennett Johnston (D) / John Breaux (D)	Charles Roemer (D)
Maine	William S. Cohen (R) / George J. Mitchell (D)	John McKernan (R)
Maryland	Paul S. Sarbanes (D) / Barbara Mikulski (D)	Donald Schaefer (D)
Massachusetts	Edward M. Kennedy (D) / John F. Kerry (D)	William Weld (R)
Michigan	Donald W. Riegel, Jr. (D) / Carl Levin (D)	John Engler (R)
Minnesota	David F. Durenberger (R) / Paul Wellstone (D)	Arne Carlson (R)
Mississippi	Thad Cochran (R) / Trent Lott (R)	Ray Mabus (D)
Missouri	John C. Danforth (R) / Christopher Bond (D)	John Ashcroft (R)
Montana	Max Baucus (D) / Conrad Burns (D)	Stan Stephens (R)
Nebraska	J. James Exon (D) / Bob Kerrey (D)	Ben Nelson (D)
Nevada	Harry Reid (D) / Richard Bryan (D)	Bob Miller (D)
New Hampshire	Warren R. Rudman (R) / Robert Smith (R)	Judd Gregg (R)
New Jersey	Bill Bradley (D) / Frank Lautenberg (D)	James Florio (D)
New Mexico	Pete V. Domenici (R) / Jeff Bingaman (D)	Bruce King (D)
New York	Daniel P. Moynihan (D) / Alfonse M. D'Amato (R)	Mario Cuomo (D)
North Carolina	Jesse Helms (R) / Terry Sanford (D)	James G. Martin (R)
North Dakota	Quentin D. Burdick (D) / Kent Conrad (D)	George A. Sinner (D)
Ohio	John H. Glenn Jr. (D) / Howard M. Metzenbaum (D)	George Voinovich (R)
Oklahoma	David L. Boren (D) / Don Nickles (R)	David Walters (D)
Oregon	Mark O. Hatfield (R) / Bob Packwood (R)	Barbara Roberts (D)
Pennsylvania	Arlen Specter (R) / Harris Wofford (R)	Robert Casey (D)
Rhode Island	Claiborne Pell (D) / John H. Chafee (R)	Bruce Sundlun (D)
South Carolina	Strom Thurmond (R) / Ernest F. Hollings (D)	Carroll Campbell (R)
South Dakota	Larry Pressler (R) / Thomas Daschle (D)	George Mickelson (R)
Tennessee	James R. Sasser (D) / Albert Gore, Jr. (D)	Ned Ray McWherter (D)
Texas	Lloyd Bentsen (D) / Phil Gramm (R)	Ann Richards (D)
Utah	E.J.(Jake) Garn (R) / Orrin G. Hatch (R)	Norman Bangerter (R)
Vermont	Patrick Leahy (D) / James Jeffords (R)	Howard Dean (R)
Virginia	John W. Warner (R) / Chuck Robb (D)	L. Douglas Wilder (D)
Washington	Brock Adams (D) / Slade Gorton (R)	Booth Gardner (D)
West Virginia	Robert C. Byrd (D) / Jay Rockefeller, IV (D)	Gaston Caperton (D)
Wisconsin	Robert W. Kasten, Jr. (R) / Herb Kohl (D)	Tommy Thompson (R)
Wyoming	Malcolm Wallop (R) / Alan K. Simpson (R)	Mike Sullivan (D)

SUPREME COURT

QUESTIONS AND ANSWERS

1. One President appointed 3 Supreme Court Chief Justices. Name him and name the 3 Chief Justices. What was unusual about the 2nd one he appointed?
ANSWER: George Washington/The Chief Justices were John Jay, John Rutledge, and Oliver Ellsworth/Washington appointed Rutledge in July, 1795, when the Congress was not in session, and Rutledge presided over the August, 1795, term of the Supreme Court. The Senate rejected his appointment in December, 1795.

2. Name the 4 men who served as Associate Justice before being appointed as Chief Justice.
ANSWER: John Rutledge, Edward D. White, Charles E. Hughes, and Harlan F. Stone.

3. What Supreme Court Justice served the longest term and how many years did he serve? Three Justices served for 34 years. Name them.
ANSWER: William Orville Douglas served for 36 years/John Marshall, Stephen Johnson Field, and Hugo Lafayette Black.

4. Name the 2 present Supreme Court Justices from the state of Arizona.
ANSWER: William Hubbs Rehnquist and Sandra Day O'Connor.

5. Identify the Supreme Court Justices from the following descriptions.
   a) Only Supreme Court Justice to resign under the threat of impeachment (1969)
   b) First Black Justice
   c) First woman Justice
   d) First Jewish Justice
   e) First Chief Justice
   f) Associate Justice known as "the Great Dissenter"
   g) Associate Justice who was impeached but later acquitted
   h) Chief Justice who headed the commission that investigated the Kennedy Assassination
   i) Associate Justice who resigned to run for the Presidency and who was later appointed Chief Justice
   j) The Lyndon Johnson appointee whose nomination for Chief Justice was rejected by the Senate
   k) Chief Justice who presided over the Senate impeachment trial of President Johnson in 1868
   l) Chief Justice who succeeded in fighting President Franklin Roosevelt's "court packing" plan
   m) Chief Justice during the *Marbury v. Madison* decision in 1803
ANSWER: a) Abe Fortas b) Thurgood Marshall c) Sandra Day O'Connor d) Louis Brandeis e) John Jay f) Oliver Wendell Holmes g) Samuel Chase h) Earl Warren i) Charles Evans Hughes j) Abe Fortas k) Salmon Portland Chase l) Charles Evans Hughes m) John Marshall.

6. What Justice appointed by Dwight Eisenhower resigned during Ronald Reagan's term of office after 23 years on the bench? Whom did the President name to take his place?
ANSWER: Potter Stewart/Sandra Day O'Connor.

7. Name the Chief Justice and the other 8 members of the U.S. Supreme Court (as of 12/82).
ANSWER: Warren Earl Burger/William Joseph Brennan, Jr., Byron Raymond White, Thurgood Marshall, Harry Andrew Blackmun, Lewis Franklin Powell, Jr., William Hubbs Rehnquist, John Paul Stevens, and Sandra Day O'Connor.

8. What are the salaries of the Chief Justice of the U.S. Supreme Court and of the Associate Justices?
ANSWER: $96,800 and $93,000 respectively.

9. Name the first 2 cases in which the U.S. Supreme Court declared a Congressional Act to be unconstitutional.
ANSWER: *Marbury v. Madison* in 1803 and the *Dred Scot Case* in 1857.

10. Identify the following U.S. Supreme Court cases by the given description.
    a) First use of the power of judicial review
    b) First example of the doctrine of implied powers

c) First example of the "one-man, one-vote" rule
d) Nicknamed the "Sick Chicken Case"
e) Known as the "Pentagon Papers Case"

ANSWER: a) *Marbury v. Madison* **(1803) b)** *McCulloch v. Maryland* **(1819)**
c) *Baker v. Carr* **(1962) d)** *Schecter v. United States* **(1935)**
e) *New York Times v. United States* **(1971).**

11. Who was the youngest Supreme Court Justice to serve on the Court? Name the 3 Justices who were named to the Court before their 40th birthdays.

ANSWER: Joseph Story (at 32 who served from 1811 to 1845)/James Iredell, Bushrod Washington, and William Johnson.

CHIEF JUSTICES OF THE SUPREME COURT

CHIEF JUSTICES OF THE SUPREME COURT	STATE OF RESIDENCE	PRESIDENT WHO APPOINTED THEM	YEARS OF SERVICE
1. John Jay	New York	Washington	1789-1795
2. John Rutledge	South Carolina	Washington	1795
3. Oliver Ellsworth	Connecticut	Washington	1796-1800
4. John Marshall	Virginia	John Adams	1801-1835
5. Roger Brooke Taney	Maryland	Jackson	1836-1864
6. Salmon Portland Chase	Ohio	Lincoln	1864-1873
7. Morrison Remick Waite	Ohio	Grant	1874-1888
8. Melville Weston Fuller	Illinois	Cleveland	1888-1910
9. Edward Douglass White	Louisiana	Taft	1910-1921
10. William Howard Taft	Ohio	Harding	1921-1930
11. Charles Evans Hughes	New York	Hoover	1930-1941
12. Harlan Fiske Stone	New York	F.D. Roosevelt	1941-1946
13. Frederick Moore Vinson	Kentucky	Truman	1946-1953
14. Earl Warren	California	Eisenhower	1953-1969
15. Warren Earl Burger	Minnesota	Nixon	**1969-1986**
16. William H. Rehnquist	**Arizona**	**Reagan**	**1986**

SUPREME COURT JUSTICES

SUPREME COURT JUSTICES	PRESIDENT WHO APPOINTED THEM
1. John Jay	Washington
2. John Rutledge	Washington
3. William Cushing	Washington
4. James Wilson	Washington
5. John Blair	Washington
6. James Iredell	Washington
7. Thomas Johnson	Washington
8. William Paterson	Washington
9. John Rutledge	Washington
10. Samuel Chase	Washington
11. Oliver Ellsworth	Washington
12. Bushrod Washington	John Adams
13. Alfred Moore	John Adams
14. John Marshall	John Adams
15. William Johnson	Jefferson
16. Henry Brockholst Livingston	Jefferson
17. Thomas Todd	Jefferson
18. Gabriel Duvall	Madison
19. Joseph Story	Madison
20. Smith Thompson	Monroe
21. Robert Trimble	J.Q. Adams
22. John McLean	Jackson
23. Henry Baldwin	Jackson
24. James Moore Wayne	Jackson
25. Roger Brooke Taney	Jackson
26. Philip Pendleton Barbour	Jackson
27. John Catron	Jackson
28. John McKinley	Van Buren
29. Peter Vivian Daniel	Van Buren
30. Samuel Nelson	Tyler
31. Levi Woodbury	Polk
32. Robert Cooper Grier	Polk
33. Benjamin Robbins Curtis	Fillmore
34. John Archibald Campbell	Pierce
35. Nathan Clifford	Buchanan
36. Noah Haynes Swayne	Lincoln
37. Samuel Freeman Miller	Lincoln
38. David Davis	Lincoln
39. Stephen Johnson Field	Lincoln
40. Salmon Portland Chase	Lincoln
41. William Strong	Grant
42. Joseph P. Bradley	Grant
43. Ward Hunt	Grant
44. Morrison Remick Waite	Grant
45. John Marshall Harlan	Hayes
46. William Burnham Woods	Hayes
47. Stanley Matthews	Garfield
48. Horace Gray	Arthur
49. Samuel Blatchford	Arthur
50. Lucius Quintus Cincinnatus Lamar	Cleveland
51. Melville Weston Fuller	Cleveland
52. David Josiah Brewer	B. Harrison
53. Henry Billings Brown	B. Harrison

SUPREME COURT JUSTICES	PRESIDENT WHO APPOINTED THEM
54. George Shiras, Jr. . . . . B. Harrison	80. Felix Frankfurter . . . . F. Roosevelt
55. Howell Edmunds Jackson. . . . . . B. Harrison	81. William Orville Douglas . . . . F. Roosevelt
56. Edward Douglass White . . . . . . Cleveland	82. Frank Murphy . . . . F. Roosevelt
(raised to Chief Justice in 1910 . . Taft)	83. James Francis Byrnes . . . . F. Roosevelt
57. Rufus Wheeler Peckham. . . . . . Cleveland	84. Robert Houghwout Jackson . . . . F. Roosevelt
58. Joseph McKenna . . . . McKinley	85. Wiley Blount Rutledge . . . . F. Roosevelt
59. Oliver Wendell Holmes . . . . T. Roosevelt	86. Harold Hitz Burton . . . . Truman
60. William Rufus Day . . . . T. Roosevelt	87. Frederick Moore Vinson . . . . Truman
61. William Henry Moody . . . . T. Roosevelt	88. Tom Campbell Clark . . . . Truman
62. Horace Harmon Lurton . . . . Taft	89. Sherman Minton. . . . . Truman
63. Charles Evans Hughes . . . . Taft	90. Earl Warren . . . . Eisenhower
64. Willis Van Devanter . . . . Taft	91. John Marshall Harlan . . . . Eisenhower
65. Joseph Rucker Lamar. . . . . Taft	92. William Joseph Brennan, Jr. . . . Eisenhower
66. Mahlon Pitney . . . . Taft	93. Charles Evans Whittaker . . . . . . Eisenhower
67. James Clark McReynolds . . . . . . Wilson	94. Potter Stewart . . . . Eisenhower
68. Louis Dembitz Brandeis . . . . Wilson	95. Byron Raymond White . . . . Kennedy
69. John Hessin Clarke . . . . Wilson	96. Arthur Joseph Goldberg . . . . Kennedy
70. William Howard Taft . . . . Harding	97. Abe Fortas . . . . L. Johnson
71. George Sutherland . . . . Harding	98. Thurgood Marshall. . . . . L. Johnson
72. Pierce Butler. . . . . Harding	99. Warren Earl Burger. . . . . Nixon
73. Edward Terry Stanford . . . . Harding	100. Harry Andrew Blackmun . . . . Nixon
74. Harlan Fiske Stone . . . . Coolidge	101. Lewis Franklin Powell, Jr. . . . Nixon
75. Charles Evans Hughes . . . . Hoover	102. William Hubbs Rehnquist . Nixon
76. Owen Josephus Roberts . . . . Hoover	103. John Paul Stevens . . . . Ford
77. Benjamin Nathan Cardozo . . . . Hoover	104. Sandra Day O'Connor . . . . Reagan
78. Hugo Lafayette Black . . . . F. Roosevelt	**105. Antonin Scalia. . . . . Reagan**
79. Stanley Forman Reed . . . . F. Roosevelt	**106. Anthony Kennedy. . . . . Reagan**

HISTORIC SUPREME COURT DECISIONS

1793 — *Chisholm v. Georgia* — Led to the enactment of the 11th Amendment (1798), which established that federal courts have no authority in suits by citizens against a state, thus preventing a citizen of another state from suing a state.

1803 — *Marbury v. Madison* — Declared the Judiciary Act of 1789 unconstitutional and void. The principle of "judicial review" was first asserted and established with this decision, although the Court first exercised the power of judicial review in *Hylton v. United States* in 1796 when it upheld the constitutionality of a Congressional tax.

1810 — *Fletcher v. Peck* — Court first found a state law to be unconstitutional.

1816 — *Martin v. Hunter's Lessee* — Established the Court's appellate power when "federal questions" are involved. (See *Cohens v. Virginia*)

1819 — *McCulloch v. Maryland* — Upheld the doctrine of implied powers of the Constitution and allowed for a liberal interpretation by Congress.

1819 — *Dartmouth College v. Woodward* — Ruled that a charter is a contract, which the Constitution protects against state legislative interference.

1821 — *Cohens v. Virginia* — Along with *Martin v. Hunter's Lessee*, established that a uniform interpretation applied for "federal questions," and that the court's scope of jurisdiction was founded on the doctrine of national supremacy.

1824 — *Gibbons v. Ogden* — Established the basis for federal regulatory powers in the area of interstate commerce. Also established the precedent that Congress can invalidate contradictory laws of the states, especially concerning the granting of monopoly privileges.

1827 — *Brown v. Maryland* — Established the "original package" doctrine of goods if the "original package" were imports and subject to congressional and not state regulation.

1831 — *Cherokee Nation v. Georgia* — Court ruled that it had no jurisdiction since the Cherokee Nation was a "domestic dependent nation" with no standing in court either as citizens or as a foreign nation, thus upholding Georgia's laws over the territory it claimed as its own.

1832 — *Worcester v. Georgia* — Declared a Georgia law to be unconstitutional, for Georgia laws were not applicable within the territorial boundaries of the Cherokee nation. The Court ruled that Federal jurisdiction over the Cherokee was exclusive.

1857 — *Dred Scott v. Sanford* — Declared a Congressional Act to be unconstitutional. The Court stated that Congress could not pass a law depriving citizens of their property without due process of law.

1866 — *Ex Parte Milligan* — Court declared that neither Congress nor the President could institute military tribunals to try civilians, even during wartime, in areas where civil courts were available as the Constitution ''is a law for rules and people equally in war and in peace.''

1883 — *Civil Rights Cases* — 5 cases in which the Court restricted the scope of federal authority by holding that the 14th Amendment did not protect the invasion of civil rights by individuals. In effect the Court allowed racial discrimination against blacks by private persons.

1896 — *Plessy v. Ferguson* — Established a constitutional foundation for the ''separate-but-equal'' doctrine in upholding a Louisiana law requiring segregated railroad facilities since the separate black facilities were equal to the facilities for others.

1905 — *Lochner v. New York* — Ruled that a 10-hour-day law for bakers was unconstitutional because it violated ''freedom of contract'' between employer and employee (reversed in 1937).

1911 — *Standard Oil Co. of New Jersey et al. v. United States* — Court upheld the dissolution of the mighty company as it applied the ''rule of reason'' to the Sherman Anti-Trust Act of 1890.

1911 — *U.S. v. American Tobacco Co.* — Court ordered the reorganization rather than the dissolution of the company based on the ''rule of reason.''

1919 — *Schenck v. United States* — Court ruled that the government cannot restrict freedom of speech unless the speech creates a ''clear and present danger'' leading to evils that Congress is empowered to protect against.

1925 — *Gitlow v. New York* — This case and many others from 1925 to 1932 established that most of the guarantees in the Bill of Rights of the Constitution were applicable to the states.

1935 — *Schechter Poultry Corporation v. United States* — The ''Sick Chicken Case.'' The Court unanimously invalidated the National Industrial Recovery Act by ruling that Congress could not ''delegate legislative'' powers to the Executive and could not regulate wholly intrastate business.

1937 — *National Labor Relations Board v. Jones and Laughlin Steel Corporation* — Decided that the federal government is empowered to regulate local labor union activities. The Wayne Act was upheld.

1952 — *Youngstown Sheet and Tube Company v. Sawyer* — Ruled that President Truman's seizure of the nation's steel mills to prevent a strike was unconstitutional. This was the first time a presidential action was ruled unconstitutional.

1954 — *Brown v. Board of Education of Topeka* — Reversed the *Plessy v. Ferguson* (1896) decision that established the ''separate but equal'' doctrine and thus declared for the first time that segregation was unconstitutional.

1957 — *Roth v. United States* — Defined obscenity and ruled that the 1st Amendment to the Constitution does not protect the publication of obscene material.

1961 — *Mapp v. Ohio* — Eliminated the use of evidence obtained by illegal means from criminal trials.

1962 — *Baker v. Carr* — Allowed courts to listen to citizens' complains about unequal election districts. Ended reapportionment of political districts in favor of rural areas and led to reapportionment decisions based on a ''one man, one vote'' basis.

1962 — *Engel v. Vitale* — Court ruled a non-denominational prayer by the New York Board of Regents to be unconstitutional.

1963 — *School District of Abington Township v. Schempp* — Struck down the state law requiring the reading of the Bible and the recitation of the Lord's Prayer.

1964 — *New York Times v. Sullivan* — Held that public officials acting in an official capacity could not sue for libel unless they proved actual malice.

1964 — *Gideon v. Wainright* — Extended coverage of the 14th Amendment to indigent defendants for court-appointed counsel.

1964 — *Reynolds v. Sims* — Declared that all state legislators must be elected by the rule of ''one person, one vote,'' meaning that election districts must be roughly equal in population.

1964 — *Escobedo v. Illinois* — Prohibited a confession from being used as evidence if the accused person has been denied permission to see a lawyer.

1966 — *Miranda v. Arizona* — Established the Miranda Rule that suspects must be informed of their rights.

1971 — *New York Times Company v. United States* — ''Pentagon Papers Case.'' Court held that prior censorship by the government was unconstitutional and any attempt to block publication would violate the 1st Amendment.

1972 — *Furman v. Georgia* — Ruled that the death penalty imposed by state courts was unconstitutional under the 8th and 14th Amendments.

1972 — *Branzburg v. Hayes* — Held that reporters were not constitutionally privileged under the 1st Amendment to refuse to reveal their sources to a valid grand jury during an investigation or criminal trial.

1973 — *Roe v. Wade* and *Doe v. Bolton* — Struck down two state laws banning abortion during the first six months of pregnancy as a violation of privacy based on the 14th Amendment, and, by implication, overturned restrictive abortion laws in 44 other states.

1973 — *Miller v. California* — Court established a detailed set of standards for evaluating obscenity and thus gave more power to states and local governments to determine what material is obscene.

1973 — *Roe v. Wade* and *Doe v. Bolton* — Struck down all state laws banning abortion during the first 6 months of pregnancy as a violation of privacy based on the 14th Amendment.

1974 — *United States v. Richard Nixon* — Court held that the Supreme Court and not the President is the final judge of the Constitution.

1978 — *Regents of the University of California v. Allan Bakke* — Prohibited specific quotas from being used by university and college admission programs to achieve racial balance.

1980 — *Diamond v. Chakrabarty* — Court upheld patent of creating new life forms from manmade microorganisms.

QUESTIONS AND ANSWERS

1. Name the 7 most commonly accepted major sections of the United States.
ANSWER: New England, Middle Atlantic States, Southern States, Midwestern States, Rocky Mountain States, Southwestern States, and Pacific States (this is an arbitrary listing, for there is no agreement on these divisions).

2. What are the names of the 6 New England States?
ANSWER: Connecticut, Maine, Massachusetts, New Hampshire, Rhode Island, and Vermont.

3. Name the 5 Middle Atlantic States (some would place only 3 states here).
ANSWER: Delaware, Maryland, New Jersey, New York, and Pennsylvania (Delaware and Maryland are sometimes placed in the South; the District of Columbia or Washington, D.C., is frequently included here).

4. Name the 8 South Atlantic States.
ANSWER: Delaware, Maryland, Virginia, West Virginia, North Carolina, South Carolina, Georgia, and Florida (Washington, D.C., is frequently included here).

5. What are the names of the 11 Southern States (these are the 11 states of the Old Confederate States of America)?
ANSWER: Alabama, Arkansas, Florida, Georgia, Louisiana, Mississippi, North Carolina, South Carolina, Tennessee, Texas, and Virginia (Delaware, Kentucky, Maryland, and West Virginia are frequently placed here, and Texas is considered to be a Southwestern State).

6. Name the 12 Midwestern States.
ANSWER: Illinois, Indiana, Iowa, Kansas, Michigan, Minnesota, Missouri, Nebraska, North Dakota, Ohio, South Dakota, and Wisconsin (sometimes this is an area called the Middle West and Kentucky and West Virginia are included but not Kansas, Nebraska, North Dakota, and South Dakota; sometimes there is an area called the Great Plains, and the 5 states included are Kansas, Nebraska, North Dakota, Oklahoma, and South Dakota).

7. What are the names of the 6 Rocky Mountain States?
ANSWER: Colorado, Idaho, Montana, Nevada, Utah, and Wyoming (sometimes Arizona, New Mexico, and Nevada are included here).

8. Name the 4 Southwestern States.
ANSWER: Arizona, New Mexico, Oklahoma, and Texas (if Texas is placed with the 11 Confederate States, then it is not listed here; sometimes Arizona and New Mexico are grouped with the Rocky Mountain States).

9. What are the names of the Pacific Coast States or what are the names of the Pacific States?
ANSWER: California, Oregon, and Washington/Alaska, California, Hawaii, Oregon, and Washington.

10. According to the 1982 census report, what are the 5 largest U.S. states by population?
ANSWER: California, New York, Texas, Pennsylvania, and Illinois.

11. According to the 1982 census report, what are the 5 largest U.S. cities in population?
ANSWER: New York, Los Angeles, Chicago, Houston, and Philadelphia.

12. Name the 5 smallest states with respect to population.
ANSWER: Alaska, Wyoming, Vermont, Delaware, and North Dakota.

13. Name the 5 largest U.S. states with respect to area in square miles.
ANSWER: Alaska, Texas, California, Montana, and New Mexico.

14. Name the 5 smallest states with respect to area in square miles.
ANSWER: Rhode Island, Delaware, Connecticut, Hawaii, and New Jersey.

15. Fifteen U.S. state capitals are also the largest cities by population in the state. Name at least 10.
ANSWER: Phoenix, Arizona; Little Rock, Arkansas; Denver, Colorado; Atlanta, Georgia; Honolulu, Hawaii; Boise, Idaho; Indianapolis, Indiana; Des Moines, Iowa; Boston, Massachusetts; Jackson, Mississippi; Oklahoma City, Oklahoma;

Providence, Rhode Island; Columbia, South Carolina; Salt Lake City, Utah; and Charleston, West Virginia.

16. Seventeen U.S. state capitals are not even in the top 3 of the largest cities by population in the state. Name at least 12.

ANSWER: **Sacramento, California; Tallahassee, Florida; Springfield, Illinois; Frankfort, Kentucky; Augusta, Maine; Annapolis, Maryland; Lansing, Michigan; Jefferson City, Missouri; Helena, Montana; Carson City, Nevada; Trenton, New Jersey; Albany, New York; Harrisburg, Pennsylvania; Pierre, South Dakota; Austin, Texas; Montpelier, Vermont; and Olympia, Washington.**

17. How many states were named in honor of royal personages? List the state and the person for whom each was named.

ANSWER: **Seven/Georgia for King George II of England; Maryland for Queen Henrietta Maria, wife of King Charles I of England; Louisiana for King Louis XIV of France; North and South Carolina for King Charles I of England (from *Carolinus*, Latin for "Charles"); and Virginia and West Virginia for Queen Elizabeth I of England (the "Virgin Queen").**

18. What 4 states were named for people other than Kings and Queens?

ANSWER: **Delaware for the Delaware River and Bay which were named after Thomas West, Lord De La Warr, the first governor of the Virginia colony; New York for James, Duke of York (he later became King James II); Pennsylvania for William Penn's father; and Washington for George Washington (the only state named after a U.S. President).**

19. For what 2 people were Washington and the District of Columbia named?

ANSWER: **George Washington and Christopher Columbus.**

20. What 2 states were named for English localities?

ANSWER: **New Hampshire by John Mason, who was previously governor of the town of Portsmouth in Hampshire, England; and New Jersey by Lord Berkeley and Sir George Carteret after the island of Jersey in the English Channel.**

21. What 2 states were named from the French language?

ANSWER: **Vermont, from the words for "green mountain" (*vert* and *mont*), and Louisiana (after Louis XIV). Maine may have been named from the French province of Maine but more likely from "the Mayn Land of New England" in the 1629 patent. Oregon may be from the French word *ouragon* for "hurricane."**

22. What 4 states were named from the Spanish language?

ANSWER: **California, meaning "an imaginary land of gold and jewels," probably from the name of an island in García Ordóñez de Montalvo's 16th century work, *The Exploits of Explandián*; Colorado, meaning "reddish, reddish-brown" from the color of the Colorado River; Florida, meaning "flowery," and named by Ponce de León on Easter Sunday when the area was covered with flowers; Nevada, meaning "snowy" or "snow-covered"; and Montana, meaning "mountainous."**

23. What state name was coined by new American settlers to describe the original inhabitants of the area? What state name is derived from the Dutch language?

ANSWER: **Indiana, which means "land of the Indians"/The Rhode in Rhode Island is Dutch for "red" (although the name may come from the island of Rhodes in Greece).**

24. Identify each of the following, all of which are related to New England.
   a) The 2 largest states in area
   b) The smallest state in area
   c) The 2 largest states in population
   d) The smallest state in population
   e) The only state that does not lie along the Atlantic Ocean
   f) The 2 largest cities
   g) The only National Park located there
   h) The most northern and most eastern state

i) The state once named New Connecticut
j) The southernmost and westernmost state
k) The city described as "a state of mind almost entirely surrounded by water"
l) The river which separates Vermont from New Hampshire

ANSWER: a) Maine and Vermont b) Rhode Island c) Massachusetts and Connecticut d) Vermont e) Vermont f) Boston and Providence g) Acadia (Maine) h) Maine i) Vermont j) Connecticut k) Boston l) Connecticut River.

25. Name the 9 states that were named after Indian tribes.
ANSWER: Alabama, Arkansas, Illinois, Iowa, Kansas, Missouri, North Dakota, South Dakota, and Utah.

26. Name the states whose mottoes are from the language of the American Indian, French, Greek, Hawaiian, Spanish, and Italian.
ANSWER: Washington's motto, *Al-Ki* (By and By), is American Indian; Minnesota's *L'Etoile du Nord* (The North Star) is French; California's *Eureka* (I have found it) is Greek; Hawaii's *Ua Mau Ke Ea O Ka Aina I Ka Pono* (The life of the land is preserved by righteousness) is Hawaiian or Polynesian; Montana's *Oro y Plata* (Gold and Silver) is Spanish; and Maryland's *Fatti Maschii, Parole Femine* (Manly deeds, womanly words) is Italian.

27. What 2 rivers join to form the Ohio in Pittsburgh? What is the area near the fork of these rivers called? What is the name of the stadium that is the home of the Pittsburgh Steelers and Pirates?
ANSWER: The Monongahela and the Allegheny Rivers/The Golden Triangle/ Three Rivers Stadium (on the Allegheny River).

28. Name the 3 different rivers surrounding Manhattan Island in New York.
ANSWER: The East, the Harlem, and the Hudson.

29. Name the 5 boroughs into which New York City is divided.
ANSWER: The Bronx (Bronx County), Brooklyn (Kings County), Manhattan (New York County), Queens (Queens County), and Staten Island (Richmond County).

30. List the 5 New York boroughs from the largest to the smallest according to population.
ANSWER: Brooklyn, Queens, Manhattan, the Bronx, and Staten Island.

31. Name the 3 federally-owned islands in upper New York Bay.
ANSWER: Liberty Island (formerly Bedloe's Island); Ellis Island; and Governor's Island.

32. Identify the Square or Circle formed in New York when Broadway crosses each of the following streets.
a) Park Avenue
b) Fifth Avenue
c) Sixth Avenue
d) Seventh Avenue
e) Eighth Avenue
f) Columbus Avenue
g) Amsterdam Avenue at West 72nd Street
ANSWER: a) Union Square b) Madison Square c) Herald Square d) Times Square e) Columbus Circle f) Lincoln Square g) Verdi Square.

33. Identify each of the following tunnels in New York.
a) The tunnel under the Hudson River which connects Canal Street in Manhattan with Twelfth Street in Jersey City, New Jersey.
b) The tunnel under the Hudson River which connects 38th Street in Manhattan with Weekawken, New Jersey.
c) The tunnel under the East River which connects Manhattan with Queens
d) The tunnel under the East River which connects Manhattan with Brooklyn
ANSWER: a) Holland Tunnel b) Lincoln Tunnel c) Queens-Midtown Tunnel d) Brooklyn-Battery Tunnel.

34. What 2 states does the George Washington Bridge connect? Which river does this bridge span? Name the 2 cities connected by the bridge.
ANSWER: New York and New Jersey/Hudson River/New York City and Fort Lee, New Jersey.

35. Identify each of the following New York bridges.

a) The bridge which connects Manhattan Island at 178th Street with Fort Lee, New Jersey
b) The 3 bridges which connect Staten Island with New Jersey
c) The bridge over the Kill Van Kull which connects Staten Island with Bayonne, New Jersey
d) The bridge over the Hudson River which connects Manhattan with Riverdale, New Jersey
e) The bridge, named for an Italian navigator, which connects Fort Hamilton, Brooklyn, with Fort Wadsworth, Staten Island
f) The 3 bridges over the East River which connect Brooklyn with Manhattan
g) The bridge over the East River which connects Queens with Manhattan
h) The bridge with 3 spans which connects the Bronx, Queens, and Manhattan
i) The bridge over the Harlem River which connects the Bronx with Manhattan

ANSWER: a) George Washington Bridge b) Goethals, Outerbridge, and the Bayonne c) Bayonne Bridge d) Henry Hudson Bridge e) Verrazano-Narrows Bridge f) Brooklyn (1883), Williamsburg (1903), and the Manhattan Bridge (1909) g) Queensboro Bridge h) Triborough Bridge i) Alexander Hamilton Bridge.

36. What are the names of the 5 tallest buildings in the world in descending order from the tallest? (In answering this question you will be naming the 5 tallest buildings in the U.S.; the 3 tallest in Chicago; and the 2 tallest in New York City).
ANSWER: Sears Tower, Chicago; World Trade Center, New York City; Empire State Building, New York City; Standard Oil Building, Chicago; and the John Hancock Center, Chicago. Helmut Jahn's Houston tower will become the world's 4th tallest when it is finished in 1986.

37. In what state (outside of Alaska) are the highest and lowest points in the United States, and what are the names of these points? What is the name of the highest point in the United States?
ANSWER: California/The highest is Mount Whitney and the lowest is Death Valley/Mount McKinley.

38. Name the 2 great mountain ranges of the U.S. Which one is the largest? Which one is the oldest?
ANSWER: The Rocky Mountains and the Appalachian Mountains/Rocky Mountains/ Appalachian Mountains.

39. Name the last 3 states to become part of the United States before Alaska (1/3/1959) and Hawaii (8/21/1959).
ANSWER: Oklahoma (11/16/1907), New Mexico (1/6/1912), and Arizona (2/14/1912).

40. Identify the state capitals from each of the following nicknames.
a) Birthplace of Dixie
b) City of 3 Capitols
c) Mile High City
d) Capital of the First State
e) Beantown
f) Deseret
g) Capital of the Evergreen State
h) Music City, U.S.A.
i) Cornhusker Capital City
j) Bluegrass Capital

ANSWER: a) Montgomery, Alabama b) Little Rock, Arkansas c) Denver, Colorado d) Dover, Delaware e) Boston, Massachusetts f) Salt Lake City, Utah g) Olympia, Washington h) Nashville, Tennessee i) Lincoln, Nebraska j) Frankfort, Kentucky.

41. Name the 5 Great Lakes using the traditional mnemonic device.
ANSWER: HOMES—Huron, Ontario, Michigan, Erie, and Superior.

42. Name the 5 Great Lakes in the descending order of size.
ANSWER: Superior, Huron, Michigan (Huron is larger in area, but Michigan is larger in length and depth), Erie, and Ontario.

43. Name the 5 Great Lakes in order from west to east.
ANSWER: Superior, Michigan, Huron, Erie, and Ontario.

44. The 5 Great Lakes together form the world's largest body of what? Which Great Lake is the only one contained entirely in the U.S.? Which of the Great Lakes extends the

farthest south? Which U.S. state has coastal areas that border on 4 of the 5 Great Lakes? What is the name of the one it does not touch?

ANSWER: The largest body of freshwater/Lake Michigan/Lake Erie/Michigan/ Lake Ontario.

45. Between what 2 lakes is Niagara Falls located? Name the 2 waterfalls that comprise Niagara Falls. What island is located between the 2 falls? What is the name of the steamer that takes sightseers close to the base of the Falls?

ANSWER: Lake Ontario and Lake Erie/The American Falls and Horseshoe (or Canadian) Falls/Goat Island/*The Maid of the Mist*.

46. Name the pairs of Great Lakes that are connected by each of the following.
    a) The St. Marys River and the Soo, or Sault Sainte Marie, Canals
    b) The Mackinac Straits
    c) The St. Clair River, Lake Saint Clair, and the Detroit River
    d) The Niagara River and the Welland Canal

ANSWER: a) Lake Superior and Lake Huron b) Lake Michigan and Lake Huron c) Lake Huron and Lake Erie d) Lake Erie and Lake Ontario.

47. What 3 bodies of water form the world's greatest inland waterway system? Which bodies of water are at the ends of this great system?

ANSWER: The Mississippi River, the Great Lakes, and the St. Lawrence Seaway/The Gulf of Mexico at the Mississippi and the Atlantic Ocean at the St. Lawrence.

48. Identify each of the following, all of which pertain to the Great Lakes.
    a) The shallowest
    b) The one farthest north
    c) The one on which Isle Royale National Park is located
    d) The one on which Mackinac Island is located
    e) The 6th lake that makes up the Great Lakes System of North America
    f) The one connected by rivers, lakes, or canals to 3 other Great Lakes
    g) The one called *Lac du Chat* (Lake of the Cat) by French Explorers
    h) The city where the Great Lakes connect with the Mississippi River system
    i) The lake on which Split Rock Lighthouse and the Apostle islands are located

ANSWER: a) Lake Erie b) Lake Superior c) Lake Superior d) Lake Huron e) Lake St. Clair f) Lake Huron g) Lake Erie h) Chicago i) Lake Superior.

49. Why was the Detroit River called the "Dardanelles of the New World," or why is it now called the "Dardanelles of America"?

ANSWER: Because it connects Lake St. Clair with Lake Erie just as the Dardanelles connects 2 bodies of water, the Sea of Marmara (Marmora) and the Aegean Sea.

50. What 2 cities are connected by a tunnel between the U.S. and Canada which was opened in 1930? What is the name of the tunnel? These 2 cities are also connected by a bridge. Name the bridge across the St. Marys River at Sault Ste. Marie, completed in 1962, which links Michigan with Ontario.

ANSWER: Detroit, Michigan, and Windsor, Ontario/The Detroit-Windsor Tunnel/ The International Bridge.

51. There are 4 U.S. capital cities that begin with the same letter as the first letter of the state in which they are the capitals. Name them.

ANSWER: Dover, Delaware; Honolulu, Hawaii; Indianapolis, Indiana; and Oklahoma City, Oklahoma.

52. In which state is each of the following scenic sites located?

a) Painted Desert	f) Valley Forge State Park
b) La Brea Tar Pits	g) Kill Devil Hills
c) Stone Mountain	h) Martha's Vineyard
d) Pike's Peak	i) Mesabi Range
e) Black Hills	j) Carlsbad Caverns

ANSWER: a) Arizona b) California c) Georgia d) Colorado e) South Dakota f) Pennsylvania g) North Carolina h) Massachusetts i) Minnesota j) New Mexico.

53. What 3 rivers combine to form the Missouri River? At what site do these 3 rivers form the Missouri? For whom was the Gallatin named?

ANSWER: **The Jefferson, the Madison, and the Gallatin/Three Forks, Montana/ For Albert Gallatin, Thomas Jefferson's Secretary of the Treasury (1801-1809).**

54. Name the 9 pairs of states that have the Mississippi River as their boundary between them.

ANSWER: **Minnesota and Wisconsin; Wisconsin and Iowa; Iowa and Illinois; Illinois and Missouri; Missouri and Kentucky; Missouri and Tennessee; Tennessee and Arkansas; Arkansas and Mississippi; and Mississippi and Louisiana.**

55. In what 2 states are the 2 largest natural bridges located? What is the name of the larger of the 2?

ANSWER: **Utah and Virginia/Rainbow Arch (Bridge) in Utah.**

56. With what state is each of the following cities usually associated?

a) Paducah
b) Pocatello
c) Sylacauga
d) Apalachicola
e) Peoria
f) Bogalusa
g) Oshkosh
h) Ottumwa
i) Ogallala
j) Poughkeepsie

ANSWER: **a) Kentucky (and Texas) b) Idaho c) Alabama d) Florida e) Illinois f) Louisiana g) Wisconsin h) Iowa i) Nebraska j) New York.**

57. What is the motto of Georgia? What one word is on the arch which is supported by 3 columns, and what 3 branches of government do the 3 pillars represent?

ANSWER: **Wisdom, Justice, and Moderation/Constitution and the 3 pillars are the legislative, judicial, and executive branches.**

58. In which state is each of the following the highest point?

a) Mt. Katahdin
b) Brasstown Bald
c) Mt. Whitney
d) Mt. Rainier
e) Mt. McKinley
f) Mt. Washington
g) Clingmans Dome
h) Mt. Hood
i) Mt. Mitchell
j) Mauna Kea

ANSWER: **a) Maine b) Georgia c) California d) Washington e) Alaska f) New Hampshire g) Tennessee h) Oregon i) North Carolina j) Hawaii.**

59. How many states combined do Alaska and Hawaii touch? How many does Maine touch? Name the 2 states that touch 8 others.

ANSWER: **None/1—New Hampshire/Tennessee and Missouri.**

60. Name the 8 states that touch Tennessee.

ANSWER: **Kentucky, Virginia, North Carolina, Georgia, Alabama, Mississippi, Arkansas, and Missouri.**

61. Name the 8 states that touch Missouri.

ANSWER: **Iowa, Illinois, Kentucky, Tennessee, Arkansas, Oklahoma, Kansas, and Nebraska.**

62. According to South Carolinians, what 2 rivers in South Carolina did they facetiously say joined "to form the Atlantic Ocean"?

ANSWER: **The Ashley and the Cooper.**

63. On which lakes are the following cities located?

a) Buffalo, New York
b) Chicago, Illinois
c) Cleveland, Ohio
d) Gary, Indiana
e) Milwaukee, Wisconsin
f) New Orleans, Louisiana
g) Rochester, New York
h) Seattle, Washington

ANSWER: **a) Lake Erie b) Lake Michigan c) Lake Erie d) Lake Michigan e) Lake Michigan f) Lake Pontchartrain g) Lake Ontario h) Lake Washington.**

64. What national park is located in parts of 3 states, and what are the names of those states?

ANSWER: **Yellowstone National Park/Wyoming, Idaho, and Montana.**

65. In what state are the following national parks located?

a) Grand Teton   f) Mammoth Cave
b) Hot Springs   g) Sequoia
c) Denali   h) Zion
d) Arches   i) Lassen Volcanic
e) Carlsbad Caverns   j) Petrified Forest

ANSWER: a) Wyoming b) Arkansas c) Alaska d) Utah e) New Mexico f) Kentucky g) California h) Utah i) California j) Arizona.

66. Identify the national park in which each of the following sites is located.

a) Painted Desert   g) Blackfoot Glacier   l) Harding Icefield
b) Mount McKinley   h) Chisos Mountains   m) Paradise Valley
c) Old Faithful   i) Landscape Arch   n) Nevada and Ribbon Falls
d) Mount Whitney   j) The Maze   o) Valley of Ten Thousand
e) Bridalveil Falls   k) Skyline Drive   Lakes
f) Clingmans Dome

ANSWER: a) Petrified Forest (Ariz.) b) Denali (Alas.) c) Yellowstone (Wyo., Mont., and Ida.,) d) Sequoia (Calif.) e) Yosemite (Calif.) f) Great Smoky Mountains (N.C. and Tenn.) g) Glacier (Mont.) h) Big Bend (Tex.) i) Arches (Ut.) j) Canyonlands (Ut.) k) Shenandoah (Va.) l) Kenai Fiords (Alas.) m) Mount Rainier (Wash.) n) Yosemite (Calif.) o) Katmai (Alas.).

67. What are the 3 largest national parks in the U.S. in gross acreage?
ANSWER: Wrangell-St. Elias (Alaska), Gates of the Arctic (Alaska), and Denali (Alaska).

68. What 6 states have geographical formations called "panhandles"? Which state is nicknamed "The Panhandle State"?
ANSWER: Alaska, Florida, Idaho, Oklahoma, Texas, and West Virginia/ West Virginia.

69. Identify each of the following national monuments with the state in which it is located.

a) Aztec Ruins   f) Scotts Bluff
b) Devils Tower   g) Pinnacles
c) Custer Battlefield   h) Rainbow Bridge
d) Muir Woods   i) Montezuma Castle
e) Grand Portage   j) Ocmulgee

ANSWER: a)New Mexico b) Wyoming c) Montana d) California e) Minnesota f) Nebraska g) California h) Utah i) Arizona j) Georgia.

70. Between what 2 rivers was Philadelphia laid out? What are the meanings of the words "Philadelphia" and "Pennsylvania"?
ANSWER: The Delaware and the Schuylkill/"Brotherly love" and "Penn's woodland."

71. Name the 5 longest bridges in the U.S. and give their locations.
ANSWER: Verrazano-Narrows in New York City; Golden Gate in San Francisco; Mackinac Straits in Mackinaw City, Michigan; George Washington in New York City; and the Tacoma Narrows in Washington.

72. What are the 5 rivers over 1,000 miles long that have the same names as U.S. states?
ANSWER: The Ohio, Arkansas, Missouri, Mississippi, and Colorado.

73. What man created the name "United States of the America"?
ANSWER: Thomas Paine.

74. What lakes on what river have been formed by the following Arizona dams?

a) Glen Canyon Dam   c) Davis Dam
b) Hoover Dam   d) Parker Dam

ANSWER: a) Lake Powell b) Lake Mead c) Lake Mohave d) Lake Havasu/All the dams were built on the Colorado River (Hoover and Davis dams are on the Arizona-Nevada border and Parker Dam is on the Arizona-California border. Glen Canyon Dam is in northern Arizona near the Utah border).

75. What dams on what rivers in Arizona have been named after the 26th, the 30th, and the 31st U.S. Presidents? On what river is the Bartlett Dam? By what other name is the Hoover Dam known?
ANSWER: Theodore Roosevelt Dam—Salt River/Coolidge Dam—Gila River/ Hoover Dam—Colorado River/Verde River/Boulder (Canyon) Dam.

76. Name the pairs of states in which Lakes Powell, Mead, Mohave, and Havasu are located.
ANSWER: Arizona and Utah/Arizona and Nevada/Arizona and Nevada/Arizona and California.

77. Identify each of the following, all of which pertain to U.S. National Parks.
   a) The Arkansas city which has most of a national park within its city limits
   b) The island in the U.S. Virgin Islands on which two-thirds of the Virgin Islands National Park is located
   c) The only national park in Michigan
   d) The national park whose name in Spanish means "green table"
   e) The national park originally named Mount McKinley National Park
   f) The 2 national parks that lie north of the Arctic Circle
   g) The largest national park and the smallest
   h) The national park through which the Colorado River flows
   i) The location of the *First, Second, Third, Black, Blue,* and *Rainbow* "forests"
   j) The national park in which "Bathhouse Row" is located
   k) The 2 oldest national parks
   l) The national park located on Mount Desert Island
ANSWER: a) Hot Springs b) St. John c) Isle Royale d) Mesa Verde (Colo.) e) Denali (Alas.) f) Gates of Arctic and Kobuk Valley (Alas.) g) Wrangell-St. Elias (Alas.)/Hot Springs (Ark.) h) Grand Canyon (Ariz.) i) Petrified Forest (Ariz.) j) Hot Springs (Ark.) k) Yellowstone, 1872 (Wyo., Mont., and Ida.) and Sequoia, 1890 (Calif.) l) Acadia (Me.).

78. What 3 U.S. national parks lie across the Continental Divide?
ANSWER: The Yellowstone, Glacier, and Rocky Mountain National Parks.

79. Give the names of the 3 national parks located in the Sierra Nevada.
ANSWER: Yosemite, Kings Canyon, and Sequoia.

80. Identify the national park in which each of the following sites is located.
   a) General Sherman Tree
   b) Grizzly Giant Tree
   c) Cliff Palace and Spruce Tree House
   d) Emerald Pool
   e) Santa Elena Canyon
   f) Muldrow Glacier
   g) Great White Throne
   h) Jackson Hole and Jackson Lake
   i) Floyd Collins Crystal Cave
   j) Mauna Loa and Kilauea volcanoes
   k) Ten Thousand Islands and Big Cypress Swamp
   l) the General Grant, the General Lee, and the Hart Tree
ANSWER: a) Sequoia (Calif.) b) Yosemite (Calif.) c) Mesa Verde (Colo.) d) Yellowstone (Wyo., Mont., and Ida.) e) Big Bend (Tex.) f) Denali (Alas.) g) Zion (Ut.) h) Grand Teton (Wyo.) i) Mammoth Cave (Ken.) j) Hawaii Volcanoes (Haw.) k) Everglades (Fla.) l) Kings Canyon (Calif.).

81. What 4 states begin with the letter "W"?
ANSWER: Washington, West Virginia, Wisconsin, and Wyoming.

82. Name the 2 states that were originally a part of Virginia.
ANSWER: Kentucky and West Virginia.

83. Between what 2 states does the Sabine River form most of the boundary?
ANSWER: Texas and Louisiana.

84. How long is it and between what points does the Alaskan pipeline stretch?
ANSWER: 800 miles/It goes from Prudhoe Bay to Valdez (it was begun in 1974 and was finished in 1977).

85. On which rivers are the following cities located?
   a) Cincinnati, Ohio
   b) Jacksonville, Florida
   c) Baltimore, Maryland
   d) Dallas, Texas
   e) Nashville, Tennessee
   f) Phoenix, Arizona
   g) Washington, D.C.
   h) Omaha, Nebraska
   i) El Paso, Texas
   j) Baton Rouge, Louisiana
ANSWER: a) Ohio b) St. Johns c) Patapsco d) Trinity e) Cumberland f) Salt g) Potomac

h) Missouri i) Rio Grande j) Mississippi.

86. In what 2 states is the Dinosaur National Monument located?
ANSWER: Colorado and Utah.

87. What 4 states carry the official designation of "Commonwealth"?
ANSWER: Kentucky, Massachusetts, Pennsylvania, and Virginia.

88. How many states begin with the letter "M"? Name them.
ANSWER: Eight/Maine, Maryland, Massachusetts, Michigan, Minnesota, Mississippi, Missouri, and Montana.

89. In what 3 are the Ozark Mountains principally located?
ANSWER: Arkansas, Missouri, and Oklahoma (with an Eastern section in Southern Illinois).

90. Into which bodies of water do the following rivers empty?
a) Mississippi
b) Missouri
c) Rio Grande
d) Arkansas
e) Colorado
f) Columbia
g) Snake
h) Pecos
ANSWER: a) Gulf of Mexico b) Mississippi River c) Gulf of Mexico d) Mississippi River e) Gulf of California f) Pacific Ocean g) Columbia River h) Rio Grande.

91. What 4 states touch the same point? What is this location called?
ANSWER: New Mexico, Arizona, Utah, and Colorado/The "4 Corners."

92. How many states have completely man-made, arbitrary borders, and which ones are they?
ANSWER: Four/New Mexico, Wyoming, Utah, and Colorado.

93. In what Hills and in what state is Mt. Rushmore located? Who sculpted the faces of the 4 Presidents on Mount Rushmore? Name the 4 Presidents.
ANSWER: The Black Hills in South Dakota/Gutzon Borglum (from 1927 to 1941; his son Lincoln finished the work in 1941)/George Washington, Thomas Jefferson, Abraham Lincoln, and Theodore Roosevelt.

94. What is Georgia's answer to Mount Rushmore? What sculptor started the work in 1923, and who continued it? Who finally finished it in 1970? What 3 Confederate heroes are carved on this mountain?
ANSWER: Stone Mountain/Gutzon Borglum (1923)/Augustus Lukeman (1925-1928; whose work was discontinued until 1964)/Finished by Walker K. Hancock (1964-1970)/Robert E. Lee, Jefferson Davis, and Thomas "Stonewall" Jackson.

95. Name the 13 states that border Canada in order going from West to East.
ANSWER: Alaska, Washington, Idaho, Montana, North Dakota, Minnesota, Michigan, Ohio, Pennsylvania, New York, Vermont, New Hampshire, and Maine.

96. Name the 4 states bordering Mexico.
ANSWER: California, Arizona, New Mexico, and Texas.

97. Name the 5 states that touch the Gulf of Mexico.
ANSWER: Texas, Louisiana, Mississippi, Alabama, and Florida.

98. What are the 5 states that touch the Pacific Ocean?
ANSWER: California, Oregon, Washington, Alaska, and Hawaii.

99. In which city and state is each of the following sites located?
a) Disneyland
b) Joe Louis Arena
c) The Loop
d) Copley Square
e) Rittenhouse Square
f) Inner Harbor
g) Little White House (Georgia)
h) Ghirardelli Square
i) Opryland, U.S.A.
j) Redstone Arsenal
ANSWER: a) Anaheim, California b) Detroit, Michigan c) Chicago, Illinois d) Boston, Massachusetts e) Philadelphia, Pennsylvania f) Baltimore, Maryland g) Warm Springs, Georgia h) San Francisco, California i) Nashville, Tennessee j) Huntsville, Alabama.

100. Name the 5 states that touch West Virginia.
ANSWER: Pennsylvania, Maryland, Virginia, Kentucky, and Ohio.

101. Name the 5 states that touch Nevada.
ANSWER: Oregon, Idaho, Utah, Arizona, and California.

102. What are the 6 states that touch Oklahoma?
ANSWER: Kansas, Missouri, Arkansas, Texas, New Mexico, and Colorado.

103. Tell which states have the following mottoes.
   a) North to the Future   f) *Eureka*
   b) *L'Étoile du Nord*   g) Equal Rights
   c) United We Stand, Divided We Fall   h) *Montani semper liberi*
   d) Wisdom, Justice, and Moderation   i) In God We Trust
   e) *Sic semper tyrannis*   j) Live Free or Die
ANSWER: a) Alaska b) Minnesota c) Kentucky d) Georgia e) Virginia f) California g) Wyoming h) West Virginia i) Florida j) New Hampshire.

104. What river did Stephen Collins Foster immortalize in his ballad "Old Folks at Home"? In what swamp does this river rise? Through what 2 states does it flow? What comic strip by what artist takes place in this swamp? Name 3 of the characters in the comic strip.
ANSWER: The Suwannee River/The Okefenokee Swamp/Georgia and Florida/"Pogo" by Walt Kelly/Pogo Possum, Albert the Alligator, Churchy La Femme, Wiley Catt, Seminole Sam, Beauregard, Howland Owl.

105. The Potomac River forms the boundary between what 3 states?
ANSWER: Virginia, Maryland, and West Virginia.

106. Each of the following scenic sites is located in 2 states. Name the 2 states.
   a) Mojave Desert   f) Dismal Swamp
   b) Land Between the Lakes   g) Death Valley
   c) Lake Tahoe   h) Clingmans Dome
   d) Hells Canyon   i) Black Hills National Forest
   e) Lake Mead   j) Columbia River Gorge
ANSWER: a) California and Nevada b) Kentucky and Tennessee c) California and Nevada d) Idaho and Oregon e) Arizona and Nevada f) Virginia and North Carolina g) California and Nevada h) North Carolina and Tennessee i) South Dakota and Wyoming j) Washington and Oregon.

107. Name the 2 states in which most of the Civil War battles were fought.
ANSWER: Virginia and Tennessee.

108. Name the 3 major unincorporated territories of the United States.
ANSWER: The U.S. Virgin islands, American Samoa, and Guam.

109. From which states were the following 5 states created: Vermont, Kentucky, Tennessee, Maine, and West Virginia?
ANSWER: Vermont from New York, New Hampshire, and Massachusetts; Kentucky and West Virginia from Virginia; Tennessee from North Carolina; and Maine from Massachusetts.

110. The Wild and Scenic Rivers Act of 1968 was established to preserve some of the nation's rivers in their pristine state and affected each of the following. Identify the states in which these rivers are principally located.
   a) Salmon and Clearwater   f) Saint Croix
   b) Rogue   g) Allagash
   c) Feather   h) Little Miami
   d) Eleven Point   i) Chattooga
   e) Rio Grande   j) Wolf
ANSWER: a) Idaho b) Oregon c) California d) Missouri e) New Mexico f) Minnesota and Wisconsin g) Maine h) Ohio i) Georgia j) Wisconsin.

111. Name the highest and lowest points in the National Park System and identify the state in which each is located.

ANSWER: Mt. McKinley in Alaska (Denali National Park)/Crater Lake in Oregon (Crater Lake National Park).

112. There are 6 federal penitentiaries. Give the city in the following states in which these penitentiaries are located.

a) Georgia   c) Indiana   e) Pennsylvania
b) Illinois   d) Kansas   f) Washington

ANSWER: a) Atlanta b) Marion c) Terre Haute d) Leavenworth e) Lewisburg f) McNeil Island.

113. Name the largest and the smallest counties in terms of area in the U.S.

ANSWER: San Bernardino County in Southern California is the largest with 20,131 square miles/New York County in New York is the smallest with 20 square miles.

114. Identify each of these geographic items from literature.

a) The camp in Calaveras County, California, immortalized in the stories of Bret Harte and Mark Twain, especially in Twain's *The Celebrated Jumping Frog of Calaveras County*
b) The island in the Spanish romance *Las Sergas de Esplandián* (1510) by García Ordóñez de Montalvo, from which the name of a U.S. state probably came
c) The Nevada city that was the setting for Mark Twain's *Roughing It*
d) The mountains in which *Dunderberg* of Washington Irving's "Rip Van Winkle" is located
e) The New York city that was the setting for the *Leatherstocking Tales* of James Fenimore Cooper
f) The lake in Cooperstown, New York, that is the site of "Glimmerglass" in James Fenimore Cooper's novels
g) The state known as the Rip Van Winkle State until 1834
h) The state from which "dust bowl" refugees head west to California in John Steinbeck's *The Grapes of Wrath*
i) The area in Charleston, South Carolina, that was the inspiration for Heywood and Gershwin's *Porgy and Bess*
j) The Rhode Island city in which the Old Stone Mill inspired Henry W. Longfellow's *Skelton in Armor*

ANSWER: a) Angels Camp b) California c) Virginia City d) Catskills e) Cooperstown f) Lake Otsego g) North Carolina h) Oklahoma i) Catfish Row j) Newport.

115. Name the 3 capes of North Carolina.
ANSWER: Cape Hatteras, Cape Lookout, and Cape Fear.

116. Through what 4 states does the Arkansas River flow?
ANSWER: Colorado, Kansas, Oklahoma, and Arkansas.

117. What 7 states do the Tennessee River and its tributaries drain?
ANSWER: Tennessee, Mississippi, Alabama, Kentucky, Virginia, North Carolina, and Georgia.

118. What rock formation on what mountain in New Hampshire inspired what short story by what American writer? In what range in New Hampshire can the peaks Mt. Washington, Adams, Jefferson, Clay, Monroe, Madison, and Franklin be found?
ANSWER: The Old Man of the Mountain on Profile or Cannon Mountain inspired "The Great Stone Face" by Nathaniel Hawthorne/In the Presidential Range.

119. Name the 2 highest peaks in eastern North America (east of the Mississippi River).
ANSWER: Mt. Mitchell in North Carolina and Mt. Washington in New Hampshire.

120. What mountain range forms (contains) the Continental Divide? What is another name for the Continental Divide? Through which 5 states does the Divide run? What are the only 2 states that have the Divide as part of their border?
ANSWER: The Rocky Mountains/The "Great Divide"/Montana, Wyoming, Idaho, Colorado, and New Mexico/Idaho and Montana.

121. Name the only 4 U.S. states which were once independent republics. Which one was the only one that was an independent monarchy?

ANSWER: Hawaii, Texas, California, and Vermont/Hawaii.

122. Between what 2 states is Lake Champlain located?
ANSWER: Vermont and New York.

123. What are the 3 largest islands of the United States in square miles?
ANSWER: Hawaii, Kodiak, and Puerto Rico.

124. Identify the boundaries (coasts) of the United States from the given mileage.
    a) 1,060   b) 1,631   c) 2,069   d) 3,987   e) 7,623
ANSWER: a) Arctic Coast b) Gulf Coast c) Atlantic Coast d) Canadian frontier e) Pacific
    Coast.

125. Give the location of the following U.S. Capes.
    a) Cape Cod   e) Cape Lookout
    b) Cape Fear   f) Cape Canaveral
    c) Cape Girardeau   g) Cape May
    d) Cape Hatteras
ANSWER: a) Massachusetts b) North Carolina c) Missouri d) North Carolina e) North
    Carolina f) Florida g) New Jersey.

126. What does the Greek alphabet have in common with Mississippi?
ANSWER: A Delta.

127. Name the 3 rivers that serve as parts of the boundary of Illinois.
ANSWER: The Mississippi, the Ohio, and the Wabash.

128. Name the 2 rivers that serve as parts of the boundary of Indiana.
ANSWER: The Ohio and the Wabash.

129. Name the 3 rivers that serve as parts of the boundary of Iowa.
ANSWER: The Mississippi, the Missouri, and the Big Sioux.

130. Name the 5 states that have compass points in their names.
ANSWER: North and South Carolina, North and South Dakota, and West Virginia.

131. One continental U.S. state, which has the highest overall elevation of all the states, has
    55 mountain peaks which all measure more than 14,000 feet in altitude. Name this
    state and give its nickname. Then name its 2 highest peaks.
ANSWER: Colorado is nicknamed the "Highest State"/Mount Elbert and Mount Massive.

132. What is the capital or administrative center of each of the following U.S. controlled
    areas?
    a) Guam   d) Trust Territory of the Pacific Islands
    b) Puerto Rico   e) U.S. Virgin Islands
    c) American Samoa
ANSWER: a) Agana b) San Juan c) Pago Pago d) Saipan e) Charlotte Amalie.

133. Identify the following U.S. possessions as self-governing, non-self-governing, or part
    of the Trust Territory of the Pacific Islands.
    a) Guam   c) American Samoa   e) U.S. Virgin Islands
    b) Puerto Rico   d) Marshall Islands   f) Midway Islands
ANSWER: a) self-governing b) self-governing c) self-governing d) Trust Territory of the
    Pacific e) non-self-governing f) non-self-governing.

134. What are the capitals of the following states?
    a) Arizona   f) North Dakota
    b) California   g) Oregon
    c) Delaware   h) South Dakota
    d) Idaho   i) Texas
    e) Kentucky   j) Washington
ANSWER: a) Phoenix b) Sacramento c) Dover d) Boise e) Frankfort f) Bismarck
    g) Salem h) Pierre i) Austin j) Olympia.

135. Identify the following states by their nicknames.
    a) Yellowhammer State
    b) Centennial State
    c) Gem State
    d) Free State
    e) Magnolia State
    f) Silver State
    g) Excelsior State
    h) Modern Mother of Presidents
    i) Keystone State
    j) Equality State

ANSWER: a) Alabama b) Colorado c) Idaho d) Maryland e) Mississippi f) Nevada g) New York h) Ohio i) Pennsylvania j) Wyoming.

136. In what state is Punxsutawney located? What well-known animal lives there? Where exactly? What day is his special day? What happens if he sees his shadow?

ANSWER: Pennsylvania/Punxsutawney Phil—a groundhog/Gobbler's Knob/ February 2/ Six more weeks of winter.

137. What states are being described in the following quotes?
    a) "The figure of a camel attempting to rise" (by Irvin S. Cobb)
    b) "A rum keg being tapped at both ends" (by Benjamin Franklin)
    c) "A vale of humility between two mountains of conceit"
    d) "The loveliest fleet of islands that lies anchored in any ocean" (by Mark Twain)

ANSWER: a) Kentucky b) New Jersey c) North Carolina d) Hawaii.

138. Identify each state from the following descriptions.
    a) The only state bisected by the Mississippi River
    b) The only state bordered by a single state
    c) The only state with a one syllable pronunciation
    c) The state with the longest shoreline of any inland state
    e) The state that contains Lake Itasca, the source of the Mississippi
    f) The only state that touches the Atlantic Ocean and the Great Lakes
    g) The only state that touches the Atlantic Ocean and the Gulf of Mexico

ANSWER: a) Louisiana b) Maine c) Maine d) Michigan e) Minnesota f) New York g) Florida.

139. Texas is the only state to have lived under 6 different flags. Name the 6 nations whose flags have flown over Texas.

ANSWER: Spain, France, Mexico, the Republic of Texas, the Confederate States of America, and the United States.

140. What 2 cities in Minnesota are nicknamed the "Twin Cities"? Name the river that separates them.

ANSWER: Minneapolis and St. Paul/Mississippi.

141. Identify the place in New Jersey called New Jersey's "Westminster Abbey." Besides the 4 signers of the Declaration of Independence who are buried there, name the U.S. President and Vice President who are buried there.

ANSWER: Princeton Cemetery/Grover Cleveland and Aaron Burr.

142. Identify each of the following rivers from the nickname or description.
    a) Means "Great River" in Spanish
    b) Nicknamed the "Father of Waters"
    c) Nicknamed the "Big Muddy"
    d) Named by the Indians the "red river"

ANSWER: a) Rio Grande b) Mississippi c) Missouri d) Colorado.

143. Name the 5 longest U.S. rivers in descending order.

ANSWER: Mississippi, Missouri, Rio Grande, Arkansas, and the Colorado (most sources list the Mississippi at 2,348 miles and the Missouri at 2,315).

144. Identify the location of each of the following U.S. ships.
    a) USS *Yorktown*
    b) USS *Texas*
    c) USS *Constitution*
    d) USS *Constellation*
    e) USS *Missouri* (now in active service)
    f) USS *Arizona*
    g) USS *Alabama*
    h) USS *Niagara*
    i) USS *North Carolina*

ANSWER: a) Charleston, South Carolina b) Houston, Texas c) Boston, Massachusetts

d) Baltimore, Maryland e) Bremerton, Washington f) Honolulu, Hawaii
g) Mobile, Alabama h) Erie, Pennsylvania i) Wilmington, North Carolina.

145. Name in descending order the 3 largest U.S. cities in square mile area. What city in Florida was once the largest U.S. city in area?
ANSWER: Juneau, Alaska; Sitka, Alaska; and Anchorage, Alaska/Jacksonville.

146. Name in descending order the 3 largest contiguous U.S. cities in square mile area.
ANSWER: Jacksonville, Florida; Oklahoma City, Oklahoma; and Houston, Texas.

147. Identify the city or location from the meaning of its French name.
a) "middle" or "monks"
b) "red stick" or "red pole"
c) "big breast"
d) "strait" or "narrows"
e) "the barn"
f) "clear water"
g) "end of the lake"
h) "lake that speaks"
i) "prairie of the dog"
j) "root"
ANSWER: a) Des Moines, Iowa b) Baton Rouge, Louisiana c) Grand Teton Mountain, Wyoming d) Detroit, Michigan e) LaGrange, Georgia and Illinois f) Eau Claire, Wisconsin g) Fond du Lac, Minnesota h) Lac qui Parle, Minnesota i) Prairie du Chien, Wisconsin j) Racine, Wisconsin.

148. Identify each of the cities from the following descriptions.
a) Only state capital with 3 capitol buildings
b) City that is 5,280 feet in altitude and has an appropriate nickname
c) Alabama's only port city
d) Birthplace of night baseball (June 2, 1882)
e) First landing place of the pilgrims (November 11, 1620)
f) Named for a Greek city and known as the home of the Georgia Bulldogs
g) Nicknamed "The Waterloo of the American Revolution" (October 19, 1781)
h) Known as "Paul Bunyan's Capital"
i) Nicknamed the "Home of the Comstock Lode" (gold and silver mines)
j) Nicknamed "The Fountain City" and the location of Patrick's Press
ANSWER: a) Little Rock, Arkansas b) Denver ("The Mile High City"), Colorado c) Mobile d) Ft. Wayne, Indiana e) Provincetown, Massachusetts f) Athens g) Yorktown, Virginia h) Brainerd, Minnesota i) Virginia City, Nevada j) Columbus, Georgia.

149. Hampton and what other 3 Virginia cities make up the Port of Hampton Roads?
ANSWER: Norfolk, Portsmouth, and Newport News.

150. The flags of what 5 countries have flown over Mobile, Alabama?
ANSWER: Spain, France, Great Britain, the Confederate States of America, and the United States.

151. What 3 cities are known as the "Atomic Cities"?
ANSWER: Los Alamos, New Mexico; Oak Ridge, Tennessee; and Richland, Washington.

152. What is the name of the deepest canyon in the United States? In what 2 states is it located? What river has carved this gorge?
ANSWER: Hells Canyon/Idaho and Oregon/Snake River.

153. In what 2 adjoining states are nearby towns named after Lewis and Clark, and what are the names of those towns?
ANSWER: Lewiston, Idaho, and Clarkston, Washington.

154. Name the 8 time zones for the United States and its possessions.
ANSWER: Atlantic, Eastern, Central, (Rocky) Mountain, Pacific, Yukon, Alaska-Hawaii, and Bering Time.

155. There is 1 royal palace in the United States. What is its name and where is it located? Who were the King and Queen who reigned there? How were they related?
ANSWER: The Iolani Palace in Honolulu, Hawaii (built 1882)/King Kalakaua (1874-1891) and Queen Liliuokalani (1891-1892)/They were brother and sister.

156. Between what points does the Appalachian Trail extend? Within 200 miles, about how long is it? Through which 2 national parks does it pass?
ANSWER: From Mt. Katahdin in Maine to Mt. Springer (near Dahlonega) in Georgia/

About 2000 miles/Great Smoky Mountains (N.C. and Tenn.) and Shenandoah.

157. The 2000 mile Appalachian Trail extends through 14 states. Name all 14.
ANSWER: **Maine, New Hampshire, Vermont, Massachusetts, Connecticut, New York, New Jersey, Pennsylvania, Maryland, West Virginia, Virginia, North Carolina, Tennessee, and Georgia.**

158. The Appalachian Trail in the East extends for 2000 miles and is located in 14 states. How long is it, and in what states is the Pacific Crest Trail located?
ANSWER: **2350 miles/Washington, Oregon, and California.**

159. From the following postal zip code abbreviations give the state each represents.
a) ME   c) MO   e) MI   g) MS
b) MA   d) MT   f) MD   h) MN
ANSWER: **a) Maine b) Massachusetts c) Missouri d) Montana e) Michigan f) Maryland g) Mississippi h) Minnesota.**

160. Name the most populous city in each of the following states.
a) Alabama   f) Montana
b) Connecticut   g) New Hampshire
c) Delaware   h) North Carolina
d) Kansas   i) Oregon
e) Mississippi   j) Tennessee
ANSWER: **a) Birmingham b) Bridgeport c) Wilmington d) Wichita e) Jackson f) Billings g) Manchester h) Charlotte i) Portland j) Memphis.**

161. Identify the state in which each of the following counties is located.
a) Dade County   d) Suffolk County
b) Nassau County   e) Anne Arundel County
c) Alameda County   f) Arlington County
ANSWER: **a) Florida, Georgia, or Missouri b) New York or Florida c) California d) New York e) Maryland f) Virginia.**

162. Identify each of the following locations.
a) The city and the building from which Lee Harvey Oswald shot President John Kennedy on November 22, 1963
b) The All-American Soap-Box Derby City
c) The city the swallows return to on March 19 of each year
d) The first national monument in the U.S. (September 24, 1906) and its location
e) The state in which Mauch Chunk, the borough that changed its name to Jim Thorpe in 1954, is located
f) The former name of Helena, Montana
g) The world's largest cathedral
h) The state in which Cairo, Thebes, Karnak, and Little Egypt are located
i) The location of Sarah Winchester's Unfinished Mansion
j) The present location of the great American hoax, the Cardiff Giant
ANSWER: **a) Texas School Book Depository in Dallas, Texas b) Akron, Ohio c) San Juan Capistrano, California d) Devil's Tower, Wyoming e) Pennsylvania f) Last Chance Gulch g) St. John the Divine in New York h) Illinois i) San Jose, California j) Cooperstown, New York.**

163. Identify the location of each of the following U.S. deserts.
a) Black Rock   d) Great Salt Lake   f) Painted Desert
b) Colorado   e) Mojave   g) Sonoran (or Sonora)
c) Death Valley
ANSWER: **a) Nevada b) California c) California and Nevada d) Utah e) California f) Arizona g) Arizona and California (and Mexico).**

164. Give the location of each of the following U.S. caves or caverns.
a) Carlsbad Caverns   c) Mammoth Cave   e) Wyandotte Cave
b) Luray Caverns   d) Wind Cave
ANSWER: **a) New Mexico b) Virginia c) Kentucky d) South Dakota e) Indiana.**

165. Off the coastline of which states are the following areas (all explored for their oil potential) located?
     a) Georges Bank   c) Prudhoe Bay   e) Diapir Field
     b) Baltimore Canyon   d) Santa Maria Basin
ANSWER: a) Massachusetts b) New Jersey c) Alaska d) California e) Alaska.

166. Identify each of the following geographical locations, each one named after an individual in American history.
     a) The towns in Mississippi and Indiana named after a Polish engineering officer who served with the Revolutionary forces from 1776 to 1783
     b) The towns in Georgia, Tennessee, and Virginia (and several other states) named after the Polish military officer killed in the battle of Savannah, Georgia, in 1779
     c) The state capital named after an Irish born American Revolutionary War general killed in the assault on Quebec on December 31, 1775
     d) The 2 islands in Vermont named after Revolutionary War heroes Ethan and Ira Allen
     e) The towns in Florida, Georgia, Pennsylvania and many other states named after this French major general in the Continental Army who was a close adviser to General George Washington
     f) The towns in Indiana, Missouri, and Nevada named after an early 20th century U.S. general whose *My Experiences in the World War* won the 1932 Pulitzer Prize
     g) The town in Alabama named after an Indian chief who was killed in 1540 in a battle against Hernando do Soto and his Spanish troops
     h) The towns in Georgia, Iowa, Nebraska, Utah, and many other states named after the Revolutionary War general who was nicknamed "Mad Anthony"
     i) The towns in Kansas, Michigan, Nebraska, and Oklahoma named after a Shawnee chieftain killed at the Battle of the Thames on October 5, 1813
     j) The towns in Indiana, Maine, Michigan, New York, and Wisconsin named after a Prussian officer whom George Washington appointed Inspector General of the Continental Army
ANSWER: a) Kosciusko (Thaddeus b) Pulaski (Casimir) c) Montgomery (Richard), Alabama d) North Hero and South Hero Islands e) Lafayette, Fayette, or Fayetteville (Marquis de Lafayette) f) Pershing (John J.) g) Tuscaloosa h) Wayne (Anthony) i) Tecumseh j) Steuben (Friedrich von).

167. One of the nicknames of Virginia is "Mother of States." The state recieved this nickname because all or part of 8 other states were formed from western territory once claimed by Virginia. Name these 8 states.
ANSWER: Illinois, Indiana, Kentucky, Michigan, Minnesota, Ohio, West Virginia, and Wisconsin.

168. Name the only 2 inland states among the 11 states of the Confederate States of America.
ANSWER: Arkansas and Tennessee.

169. Identify each of the following geographical locations named after famous people.
     a) The mountain in Colorado named after Martha Washington
     b) The pass in Oregon named after the 18th U.S. President (named for him after he captured Vicksburg on July 4, 1863)
     c) The mountain in Alaska named after the 25th U.S. President
     d) The dam in Arizona named after the 30th U.S. President
     e) The lake in Washington named after the 32nd U.S. President
     f) The peak in Colorado named after a U.S. explorer and army general
     g) The mountain in California named after the U.S. essayist who edited *The Dial*
     h) The mountain in Alaska named after the 1921 Nobel Prize winner in physics
ANSWER: a) Mount Lady Washington b) Grants Pass c) Mount McKinley d) Coolidge Dam e) Roosevelt Lake f) Pikes Peak g) Mount Emerson h) Mount Einstein.

170. Name the 8 sizable (main) islands that make up the state of Hawaii. Which island is the largest?
ANSWER: Hawaii, Maui, Oahu, Kauai, Molokai, Lanai, Niihau, and Kahoolawe (largely uninhabited)/Hawaii (the islands are listed in order from largest to smallest).

171. Name the 8 Hawaiian Islands from east to west.

ANSWER: Hawaii, Maui, Kahoolawe, Molokai, Lanai, Oahu, Kauai, and Niihau (Kahoolawe has no permanent residents).

172. Identify each of the following Hawaiian islands from its nickname.
    a) Orchid Island, Volcano Island, or Big Island
    b) Valley Island
    c) Aloof, or Forbidden Island
    d) Garden Island (Isle)
    e) Gathering Place
    f) Pineapple Island
    g) Friendly Island

ANSWER: a) Hawaii b) Maui c) Niihau d) Kauai e) Oahu f) Lanai g) Molokai.

173. Identify each of the following, all of which are related to Hawaii.
    a) The island which is owned by the Dole Company
    b) The island on which Father Damien de Veuster located his leper colony
    c) The location (port and island) the Japanese attacked on December 7, 1941
    d) The only 2 active volcanoes on Hawaii
    e) The most famous extinct volcano on Hawaii
    f) The island on which Honolulu is located
    g) The most southern of the Hawaiian Islands
    h) The volcano that discharges more lava than any other active volcano in the world
    i) The world's highest mountain if measured from the edge of its base on the ocean floor to the summit
    j) The Hawaiian city nicknamed the "Gateway to the Kilauea Volcano"
    k) The Hawaiian mountain whose name means "House of the Sun"
    l) The Hawaiian canyon nicknamed the "Grand Canyon of the Pacific"

ANSWER: a) Lanai b) Molokai c) Pearl Harbor on Oahu d) Mauna Loa and Kilauea e) Diamond Head f) Oahu g) Hawaii h) Mauna Loa i) Mauna Kea j) Hilo k) Mt. Haleakala (Maui) l) Waimea Canyon.

174. What did Captain James Cook name the Hawaiian Islands when he landed on them on January 18, 1778, and after whom did he name them?

ANSWER: Sandwich Islands/After the Earl of Sandwich, First Lord of the British Admiralty.

175. Name the twin volcanoes on Hawaii. Which one is the world's highest island peak?

ANSWER: Mauna Loa and Mauna Kea/Mauna Kea.

176. In which city and state is each of the following airports located?
    a) Logan
    b) O'Hare
    c) La Guardia
    d) Hartsfield
    e) Richard E. Byrd
    f) Stapleton
    g) John F. Kennedy
    h) Love Field
    i) Hopkins
    j) John Wayne
    k) Mitchell Field
    l) Lockheed Air Terminal
    m) Sky Harbor
    n) William P. Hobby
    o) McCarran

ANSWER: a) Boston, Mass. b) Chicago, Ill. c) New York, N.Y. d) Atlanta, Ga. e) Richmond, Va. f) Denver, Colo. g) New York N.Y. h) Dallas, Tex. i) Cleveland, O. j) Santa Ana, Calif. k) Milwaukee, Wis. l) Burbank, Calif. m) Phoenix, Ariz. n) Houston, Tex. o) Las Vegas, Nev.

177. Identify each of the following U.S. rivers.
    a) The river on which the Robert Moses hydroelectric plant, the largest one in the eastern U.S., is located
    b) The river that forms almost two-thirds of the border between Mexico and the U.S.
    c) The name or names by which the Mexicans call the Rio Grande
    d) The river that forms the boundary between New Hampshire and Vermont
    e) The river formed at Franklin, New Hampshire, where the Winnepesaukee and Pemigewasset streams meet
    f) The river in Maine sometimes called the "Rhine of America"
    g) The river formed by the confluence of the Alabama and Tombigbee rivers
    h) The principal river of New Mexico

i) The 300 mile long river that forms the entire eastern boundary of Pennsylvania

j) The river that has been described by farmers as being "too thick to drink and too muddy to plow"

ANSWER: a) Niagara River b) Rio Grande c) *Rio Bravo* (bold river) or *Rio Bravo del Norte* (Old river of the north) d) Connecticut River e) Merrimack River f) Saint John River g) Mobile River h) Rio Grande i) Delaware River j) Missouri.

178. What mountain range in Washington divides the western part of the state from the central and eastern part, and what river unites this same region?

ANSWER: Cascade Mountains/Columbia River.

179. What is the name of the line between the Piedmont Plateau and the Atlantic coastal plain stretching from New Jersey to Alabama along which a series of waterfalls provides electric power to major cities? What are the names of the 4 capital cities along this line?

ANSWER: Fall Line/Columbia, South Carolina; Raleigh, North Carolina; Richmond, Virginia; and Washington D.C.

180. The Columbia River between Washington and Oregon provides by means of many dams one-third of the hydroelectric energy produced in the U.S. Name any 4 of the 9 most important dams on the river. Then name the largest dam and the lake formed by this dam.

ANSWER: Bonneville, The Dalles, John Day, McNary, Priest Rapids, Rock Island, Rocky Reach, Chief Joseph, and Grand Coulee/Grand Coulee/Franklin D. Roosevelt Lake.

181. Identify each of the following.

a) The world's largest earthen structure and the state in which it is located

b) The world's largest private research foundation

c) The gorge known as "Pennsylvania's Grand Canyon"

d) The largest municipal park in the U.S.

e) The only borough of the 5 New York boroughs that is part of the mainland

f) The New York stadium known as the "House that Ruth Built"

g) The New York building that served as the first U.S. Capitol

h) The world's longest suspension bridge

i) The world's largest indoor theatre

j) The county in which Cincinnati, Ohio, is located, named after George Washington's successor as president-general of the Cincinnati Society

k) The only 2 active volcanoes in the contiguous U.S.

l) The largest of New York's Finger Lakes

m) The body of water into which the Housatonic and the Thames rivers empty

n) The body of water into which the Connecticut River empties

ANSWER: a) New Cornelia Tailings Dam/Arizona b) Battelle Memorial Institute (Columbus, Ohio) c) Pine Creek Gorge d) Fairmount Park (Philadelphia) e) Bronx f) Yankee Stadium g) Federal Hall h) Verrazano-Narrows Bridge (New York) i) Radio City Music Hall j) Hamilton (Alexander) k) Mt. St. Helens (Washington) and Mt. Lassen (California) l) Seneca m) Long Island Sound n) Long Island Sound.

182. Name the 3 great river systems which drain the state of Pennsylvania. Which one does not have a major port because it is only partly navigable? Name the 3 major ports of Pennsylvania, and tell on which body of water each is located.

ANSWER: Delaware, Susquehanna, and the Ohio/Susquehanna/Erie (on Lake Erie), Pittsburgh (on the Ohio, Monongahela, and the Allegheny), and Philadelphia (on the Delaware).

183. Identify each of the following U.S. cities.

a) The California city described as "a hundred suburbs in search of a city"

b) The Missouri city nicknamed the "Heart of America" because it is almost at the center of the U.S.

c) The Montana city called the "Richest Hill on Earth"

d) The Arizona town nicknamed the "Cowboy Capital of the World"

f) The Arizona town said to be "the town too tough to die"

g) The Montana city described as being "a mile high and a mile deep"

ANSWER: a) Los Angeles b) Kansas City c) Butte d) Scottsdale e) Dodge City f) Tombstone g) Butte.

184. Name the 3 highest falls in the U.S.

ANSWER: Yosemite Falls, Ribbon Falls, and the Silver Strand Falls (all are located in Yosemite National Park).

185. Identify each of the following U.S. cities from the description.
   a) The Wisconsin town named after a game first played by North American Indians who used a long-handled racket with a pouch and a hard rubber ball
   b) The South Carolina city named after the poetical term for the U.S. personified as a woman and derived from the explorer Christopher Columbus
   c) The Ohio town named after a society formed by Revolutionary War Army officers who named their society after a Roman statesman and general who became commander in chief, defeated the enemy, marched back to Rome, and returned to farming after 16 days in office
   d) The Missouri city named after the Carthaginian general who crossed the Alps with his elephants to invade Italy in the 2nd Punic War
   e) The Rhode Island city meaning divine guidance or care and so named by Roger Williams because he believed that God had guided him there
   f) The Ohio city named after a Spanish city which was the capital from 1085 to 1561 and noted as the city where El Greco lived
   g) The Ohio city named for Queen Marie Antoinette of France in appreciation for France's help during the American Revolutionary War
   h) The North Carolina city named after a famous English statesman, soldier, explorer, and poet who sent settlers to the present-day North Carolina area he named *Virginia*
   i) The Illinois city named after an Egyptian city because it, like an Egyptian city on the Nile, is located on a low-lying delta formed by the Ohio River

ANSWER: a) La Crosse b) Columbia c) Cincinnati (after the Society of Cincinnati after Lucius Quinctius Cincinnatus) d) Hannibal e) Providence f) Toledo g) Marietta h) Raleigh i) Cairo.

186. Name the city located at the confluence of the Mad, Great Miami, and the Stillwater rivers.

ANSWER: Dayton, Ohio.

187. Identify each of the following U.S. cities: the smallest capital city in area; the smallest capital city in population; the largest capital city in area; the largest capital city in population.

ANSWER: Frankfort (Ky.)/Montpelier (Vt.)/Juneau (Alas.)/Phoenix (Ariz.).

188. Identify each of the following U.S. cities from the description.
   a) The North Carolina city named for the Queen of Mecklenburg-Strelitz, the wife of King George III of Great Britain
   b) The Ohio city named for the youngest signer of the United States Constitution
   c) The Oregon city named after Francis Pettygrove's home town (Asa Lovejoy wanted to call it Boston, but when he and Petty flipped a coin, Pettygrove won and named it after his home town in Maine.)
   d) The South Carolina city named after King Charles II of England
   e) The California suburb of Los Angeles named after an ancient mountainous pastoral district in central Peloponnesus whose name means "any place of rural peace and simplicity"
   f) The Alaskan town originally named Carroll after the last surviving signer of the Declaration of Independence, Charles Carroll of Carrollton (Maryland), but now named after the ancient city in Phocis on the slopes of Mount Parnassus in Greece, the site of an oracle of Apollo

ANSWER: a) Charlotte b) Dayton (Jonathan) c) Portland d) Charleston (originally, Charles Town) e) Arcadia f) Delphi.

189. Name any 3 of Georgia's Golden Isles.

ANSWER: Tybee, Ossabaw, St. Catherines, Blackbeard, Sapelo, Sea Island, St. Simons, Jekyll, and Cumberland.

190. Identify each of the following U.S. states.
   a) The state in the contiguous U.S. which has a longer coastline than any other state
   b) The state which has more lakes than any other state
   c) The last settled state of the l3 original English colonies
   d) The 2 U.S. states that have the longest coastline
   e) The only state that lies outside of North America
   f) The youngest U.S. state
   g) The 2 smallest states in area west of the Appalachian Mountains
   h) The state in which the biggest known earthquake in North America occurred (1964)
   i) The largest state east of the Mississippi River
   j) The 2 most densely populated states
   k) The state almost bisected by the Chesapeake Bay
   l) The state which has a small part of the state separated from the rest by a double hairpin turn in the Mississippi

ANSWER: a) Florida b) Florida c) Georgia d) Alaska and Florida e) Hawaii f) Hawaii g) Indiana and Hawaii h) Alaska i) Georgia j) New Jersey and Rhode Island k) Maryland l) Kentucky.

191. Give the year for each of the following U.S. disasters.
   a) Great Chicago Fire   c) Johnstown (Pa.) flood
   b) San Francisco Earthquake   d) Baltimore Fire

ANSWER: a) 1871 b) 1906 c) 1889 d) 1904.

192. Identify each of the following U.S. cities based on the description.
   a) The city in North Carolina named after American Revolutionary War Major General Nathanael _____ who commanded the Continental Army at the Battle of Guilford Courthouse in March, 1781
   b) The Tennessee city on the Mississippi named after the ancient Egyptian capital which was located on the Nile River just south of Cairo
   c) The North Dakota city renamed after the Prussian chancellor of the German Empire who was nicknamed the "Iron Chancellor"
   d) The city in New York on the Mohawk River named after an ancient city in North Africa just north of modern Tunis
   e) The city in Minnesota named after a Civil War general who commanded a corps at Gettysburg and was the losing Democratic presidential candidate in 1880
   f) The city in Pennsylvania named after the ancient town in Judea, Palestine, that was the birthplace of Jesus
   g) The Oregon seaport on the Columbia River which was the site of the first American settlement in the Northwest (1811) and was named from a fur-trading post established by U.S. fur merchant and financier John Jacob _____
   h) The Missouri city founded in 1827 whose name was inspired by patriotic feelings developed during the fiftieth anniversary celebration of the Declaration of Independence in 1826
   i) The Minnesota city once known as Pig's Eye and named on November 1, 1841, by Father Lucien Galtier, who dedicated the new basilica to an early Christian missionary nicknamed the "Apostle of Nations"

ANSWER: a) Greensboro (Nathanael Greene) b) Memphis c) Bismarck d) Utica e) Hancock f) Bethlehem g) Astoria h) Independence i) St. Paul.

193. In what 2 states and between what 2 lakes is the Land Between the Lakes Recreation Area located?
ANSWER: Tennessee and Kentucky/Lake Barkley and Kentucky Lake.

194. Identify the following, each of which is related to mountains.
   a) The state in which the Berkshire Hills are located
   b) The state in which the Green Mountains are principally located

c) The state in which the Adirondacks are located

d) The mountain range located in central Pennsylvania, western Maryland, eastern West Virginia, and western Virginia

e) The state in which the Catskill Mountains are located

f) The California mountain range named "snowy mountain ridge" in Spanish

g) The largest stone mountain in North America

h) The mountains so named because they are frequently covered by a haze of smoky mist

i) The mountains that form the boundary between Tennessee and North Carolina

j) The highest point in California's Sierra Nevada

ANSWER: a) Massachusetts b) Vermont c) New York d) Allegheny Mountains e) New York f) Sierra Nevada g) Stone Mountain, Georgia h) Great Smoky Mountains i) Great Smoky Mountains j) Mount Whitney.

195. Name the 2 largest salt water lakes in the U.S.
ANSWER: Great Salt Lake, Utah, and Lake Pontchartrain, Louisiana.

196. Identify each of the following.

a) The dam on the Columbia River that is the largest dam and greatest single source of water power in the U.S.

b) The lowest point in Death Valley

c) The deposits discovered in Death Valley and the number of mules in a mule team that brought the deposits out of the valley

d) The island off Georgia which may have been a lair for Edward Teach, the pirate, for whom it is appropriately named

e) The names of the 2 major swamp areas in Florida

f) The largest underseas park in the U.S. (off the Florida Keys)

g) The oldest permanent European settlement in the U.S.

h) The tallest trees in the world and the state in which they are located

i) The largest land bird on the North American Continent

j) The road along which Junipero Serra established his 21 missions in California

k) The name of the oldest road in the U.S.

l) The world's only 3-tube underwater vehicular tunnel

m) The meaning of *Nova Albion*, the name given to the California area by Sir Francis Drake

n) The largest wildlife preserve in the U.S.

o) The northernmost ice-free port in North America that is the southern terminal of the Trans-Alaskan pipeline

p) The oldest seat of government in the U.S.

q) The bridge (1962) across the St. Marys River at Sault Ste. Marie which connects Michigan with Ontario

r) The name of the Water Gap that separates New Jersey from Pennsylvania

ANSWER: a) Grand Coulee b) near Badwater, California c) borax/20-mule teams d) Blackbeard e) Everglades and Okefenokee f) John Pennekamp Coral Reef State Park g) St. Augustine, Florida h) ancient redwoods/California i) California condor j) *El Camino Real* (The Royal Road) k) *El Camino Real*, New Mexico) l) Lincoln Tunnel m) New England n) Yellowstone National Park o) Valdez, Alaska p) Santa Fe, New Mexico q) International Bridge r) Delaware Water Gap.

197. Name the 5 longest rivers that rise (that is, for which the Rockies supply the headwater streams and tributaries) in the Continental Divide. Indicate whether they flow to the east or to the west.
ANSWER: Missouri (east), Rio Grande (east), Arkansas (east), Colorado (west), and Columbia (west).

198. Name the 2 largest freshwater lakes that are wholly within the United States.
ANSWER: Lake Michigan and Lake Okeechobee (in Florida).

199. Identify each of the following U.S. states.

a) The state that was originally the "Three Lower Counties" of Pennsylvania

b) The only 2 states that do not share boundaries with other states
c) The state known as *Russian America* before being purchased by the U.S.
d) The only diamond producing state
e) The state sometimes called a "state on wheels" because of the many tourists using automobiles there
f) The largest state in the contiguous U.S.
g) The state bounded on the northwest by Lake Michigan and on all of the southern border by the Ohio River
h) The name of the 15th state and the first state west of the Alleghenies
i) The state described by Robert Frost as "a state in a very natural state"
j) The state that lies midway between the Atlantic and Pacific oceans and is nicknamed "Midway, U.S.A"

ANSWER: a) Delaware b) Hawaii and Alaska c) Alaska d) Arkansas e) California f) Texas g) Indiana h) Kentucky i) Vermont j) Kansas.

200. Identify each of the following bodies of waters, each of which is associated with Alaska.
a) It is north of the Aleutian Islands between Alaska and Siberia.
b) It is between Alaska and the Soviet Union and separates the Bering Sea from the Arctic Ocean.
c) It is a sea north of Alaska, the Yukon, and the Northwest Territories.
d) It is the gulf south of the Alaskan mainland.
e) It is the smallest ocean in the world and lies north of Alaska.

ANSWER: a) Bering Sea b) Bering Strait c) Beaufort Sea d) Gulf of Alaska e) Arctic Ocean.

201. Give the name of the animals and the U.S. location from which they usually leave on St. John's Day (October 23) and return on St. Joseph's Day (March 19).

ANSWER: Swallows at San Juan Capistrano (California).

202. Name any of the 7 largest of New York's Finger Lakes (listed from west to east).

ANSWER: Canandaigua, Keuka, Seneca, Cayuga, Owasco, Skaneateles, and Otisco.

203. Identify each of the following.
a) The oldest formal garden (1741) in the U.S., which is located in Charleston, S.C.
b) The State House which has a statue of "The Independent Man"
c) The Texas landmark nicknamed the "Cradle of Texas Liberty"
d) The highest point on the entire eastern seaboard of the U.S.
e) The world's longest natural arch
f) The Nebraska landmark described as a "haystack with a pole stuck in the top"
g) The 2nd largest military building in the U.S. (after the Pentagon)
h) The channel in Alaska that separates Juneau from Douglas Island

ANSWER: a) Middleton b) Providence, Rhode Island c) The Alamo d) Cadillac Mountain, Maine e) Landscape Arch, Utah f) Chimney Rock g) Army Finance Center at Ft. Benjamin Harrison (Indiana) h) Gastineau Channel.

204. Name the large U.S. western desert region with its own streams and lakes inside it, and give the 6 states in which it is located.

ANSWER: Great Basin/California, Nevada, Utah, Wyoming, Idaho, and Oregon.

205. Identify each of the following, all of which are rivers in the U.S.
a) The river in New York that has sometimes been called the "Rhine of America"
b) The river between New York City and Albany
c) The river that flows through the Grand Canyon
d) The river that generates (produces) about one-third of the hydro-electric power produced in the U.S.
e) The river named by Captain Robert Gray after his ship
f) The longest river that flows into the Mississippi-Missouri River system (Joliet and Marquette turned back when they reached it)
g) The longest river in Maine
h) The river that forms part of the boundary between Quebec and Maine

ANSWER: a) Hudson b) Hudson c) Colorado d) Columbia e) Columbia f) Arkansas g) Penobscot River h) St. John River.

206. Identify each of the following, all of which are U.S. lakes.
    a) The lake that was formed by the Grand Coulee Dam
    b) The largest high-altitude lake in North America
    c) The largest artificial lake in the U.S.
    d) The largest natural freshwater lake west of the Mississippi in the contiguous U.S.
    e) The deepest lake in the U.S. and the crater of the inactive volcano in which this lake was formed
    f) The deepest freshwater lake in the U.S.

ANSWER: a) Franklin D. Roosevelt Lake b) Yellowstone Lake (Yellowstone National Park) c) Lake Mead, Arizona and Nevada (largest in volume)/ Lake Sakakawea, North Dakota (largest in area) d) Flathead Lake, Montana (Iliamna Lake, Alaska, is largest) e) Crater Lake/Mount Mazama f) Crater Lake, Oregon.

207. Name the 7 Wonders of American engineering as compiled by the American Society of Civil Engineers.

ANSWER: Chicago's Sewage Disposal System; Colorado River Aqueduct; Empire State Building; Grand Coulee Dam; Hoover Dam; Panama Canal; and the San Francisco-Oakland Bay Bridge.

208. Identiy each of the following U.S. cities.
    a) The Alaskan city voted upon in 1976 to be the future new capital
    b) The Arkansas city called *la petite roche* in 1722 by French explorer Bernard de la Harpe
    c) The North Dakota city called the *Les Grandes Fourches* by French explorers
    d) The West Virginia city founded by railroad magnate Collis P. _____
    e) The South Carolina city at which the Ashley and the Cooper rivers meet and as some have said facetiously join "to form the Atlantic"

ANSWER: a) Willow (near Anchorage) b) Little Rock c) Grand Forks d) Huntington e) Charleston.

209. Identify the U.S. locations named after the following: Louis XIV; Louis XV and his patron saint, Louis IX; and Louis XVI.
ANSWER: Louisiana; St. Louis, Missouri; and Louisville, Kentucky.

210. Identify each of the following U.S. sites.
    a) The pass between Kentucky and Tennessee that was called the "Gateway to the West"
    b) The valley between the U.S. and Mexico that was nicknamed the "Valley Between Two Worlds"
    c) The New York area called the "Capital of Black America"
    d) The valley in Virginia that was called the "Granary of the Confederacy"
    e) The Delaware Beach that is called the "Nation's Summer Capital"
    f) The highest point east of the Mississippi River
    g) The first English colony in the New World located on an island in North Carolina, formerly a part of Virginia
    h) The area of North Dakota called *des mauvaises terres à traverser* by French pioneers because of the roughness of the terrain
    i) The founder of the first English settlement on the Atlantic coast
    j) The name of the bridge linking Fort Erie, Ontario, with Buffalo, New York

ANSWER: a) Cumberland Gap b) Rio Grande Valley c) Harlem d) Shenandoah Valley e) Rehoboth Beach f) Mount Mitchell g) Roanoke Island h) Badlands i) Sir Walter Raleigh j) Peace Bridge.

211. Identify the 7 letters of the alphabet which do not begin the name of a U.S. state.
ANSWER: b, e, j, q, x, y, and z.

212. Identify each of the following U.S. cities from the description.
    a) The city in which Pine, Chestnut, Walnut, and Locust streets are located—names recalling the founder's love for woods and found in a state part of whose name means "woodland"

b) The city in which John F. Kennedy Stadium, the Spectrum, and Veterans Stadium are located back-to-back

c) The city in which *The Pioneer* statue is atop the dome of the state capitol

d) The present-day Pennsylvania city which George Washington once described as the "Land in the Fork"

e) The Ohio city Winston Churchill described as "the most beautiful of the inland cities of the Union"

f) The Ohio city that is the largest on the Ohio River

g) The Texas city called "the town that built a port that built a city"

h) The Texas city that William Sydney Porter (O. Henry) called the "City of the Violet Crown"

i) The city in which the First and Second U.S. Banks (1791-1811 and 1816-1836) are located

ANSWER: a) Philadelphia b) Philadelphia c) Salem, Oregon d) Pittsburgh e) Cincinnati f) Cincinnati g) Houston h) Austin i) Philadelphia.

213. Name any 3 of the wealthy and fashionable Main Line communities near Philadelphia which developed along the "main line" of the old Pennsylvania Railroad which ran from Philadelphia to Paoli.

ANSWER: Paoli, Daylesford, Berwyn, Devon, Stratford, Wayne, St. Davids, Radnor, Villanova, Rosemont, Bryn Mawr, Haverford, Ardmore, Wynnewood, Narbert, Merion, and Overbrook.

214. Identify each of the following states.

a) The state whose entire eastern boundary is formed by the Mississippi and whose western boundary is formed by the Missouri and the Big Sioux rivers

b) The northernmost state of the Great Plains-Rocky Mountain region

c) The 3 states with the most national parks

d) The state in which the 1964 earthquake occurred

e) The state in which New Sweden was the first permanent colony

f) The state that is the driest

g) The state with the least amount of inland water

h) The most densely populated state

i) The state lying between the Delaware River on the west and the Hudson River on the east

j) The state which is shaped like a boot heel and is bisected by the Missouri River until its confluence with the Mississippi River

k) The longest state east of the Mississippi River

l) The state whose nickname may have come from the pioneers' traditional greeting to visitors: "Who's yere?"

m) The state bordered by Minnesota, Lake Superior, Michigan, Lake Michigan, Illinois, and Iowa

n) The state whose name was originally applied to a valley in Pennsylvania

ANSWER: a) Iowa b) Montana c) Alaska (8), California (6), and Utah (5) d) Alaska e) Delaware f) Nevada g) Hawaii h) New Jersey i) New Jersey j) Missouri k) North Carolina l) Indiana (Hoosier State) m) Wisconsin n) Wyoming.

215. Name the 7 consecutive governments that have ruled over Baton Rouge, Louisiana.

ANSWER: France, Great Britain, Spain, Republic of West Florida, United States, Confederate States of America, and the U.S. (again).

216. Identify the statue of the female atop the capitol buildings from each of the following descriptions.

a) The statue of the Roman goddess of agriculture in Montpelier, Vermont

b) The statue of a woman personifying freedom from despotism in Helena, Montana

ANSWER: a) Ceres b) Liberty.

217. Identify each of the following U.S. sites.

a) The Kentucky falls that are the largest south of the Niagara Falls and east of the Rockies

b) The largest natural bridge in the world and its location

c) The low-lying coral and sand bars in Florida where Fort Jefferson National Monument is located and where Dr. Samuel Mudd was imprisoned (1865-1869)

d) The easternmost possession of the U.S.

e) The capital of Russian America until 1867

f) The closest point to Asia in the U.S.

g) The northernmost point in Alaska

h) The oldest and largest national military park in the U.S.

i) The region of the U.S. once referred to as the "hotbed of the American Revolution"

j) The 2 other names by which Hells (Hell's) Canyon is known

k) The island in New York Harbor which was nicknamed "The Gateway to the New World" and which was used as a U.S. immigration station until 1954

l) The island in New York Bay on which the Statue of Liberty is located and the name of this island prior to 1956

ANSWER: a) Cumberland Falls b) Landscape Arch/Utah c) Dry Tortugas d) U.S. Virgin Islands e) Sitka, Alaska f) Little Diomede Island, Alaska (Bering Strait) g) Point Barrow h) Chickamauga and Chattanooga Military Park i) New England j) Grand Canyon of the Snake and the Snake River Canyon k) Ellis Island l) Liberty Island/Bedloe's Island.

218. Identify each of the following U.S. locations from the Spanish translations of their names.

a) "great (or large) river"

b) "the crosses"

c) "the meadows"

d) "ash tree"

e) "the angels"

f) "tall tree"

g) "yellow"

h) "the pass"

ANSWER: a) Rio Grande b) Las Cruces, N.M. c) Las Vegas, Nev. d) Fresno, Calif. e) Los Angeles, Calif. f) Palo Alto, Calif. g) Amarillo, Tex. h) El Paso, Tex.

219. Identify each of the following U.S. cities from the given description.

a) The Texas city that may have been named after President James K. Polk's Vice President who served from 1845 to 1849

b) The Alaskan city named after a U.S. Senator from Indiana who served as Vice President from 1905 to 1909 under President Theodore Roosevelt

c) The Massachusetts town named for the battle at which King Charles II of England suffered a humiliating defeat during the English Civil War

d) The city in Nevada founded as Eagle Station and renamed for a frontiersman nicknamed

e) The North Dakota city named for William George _____, a pioneer in the shipment of goods by an express company

f) The Texas city named after the "Father of Texas" who was the hero of the Texas War for independence (1835-1836) and who defeated and captured Santa Anna in the Battle of San Jacinto

g) The Texas city named for the "Father of Texas" who started a colony in 1821

h) The Tennessee city named after George Washington's Secretary of War (1789-1795)

i) The Kentucky town named for an American Revolutionary War battle that took place in Massachusetts on April 19, 1775

ANSWER: a) Dallas b) Fairbanks c) Worcester d) Carson City e) Fargo f) Houston g) Austin h) Knoxville (after Henry Knox) i) Lexington.

220. Name the races, the racetracks, the cities, and the states that comprise the Triple Crown of Horseracing.

ANSWER: Kentucky Derby, Churchill Downs, Louisville, Kentucky/Preakness, Pimlico, Baltimore, Maryland/Belmont Stakes, Belmont, Elmont, New York.

221. Name the 4 "Great Lakes" of South Dakota formed by each of the following massive rolled-earth dams. On which river are these dams located?

a) Oahe Dam

b) Big Bend Dam

c) Fort Randall Dam

d) Gavins Point Dam

ANSWER: a) Lake Oahe b) Lake Sharpe c) Lake Francis Case d) Lewis and Clark Lake/ Missouri River.

222. Identify each of the following U.S. cities from the description.
    a) The southernmost city in the continental U.S.
    b) The highest state capital in the U.S.
    c) The U.S. city that is farthest to the east
    d) The Ohio city named after the Greek word for "highest point"
    e) The city that was the first U.S. capital under the Constitution
    f) The North American city closest to the Arctic Circle
    g) The U.S. city which is the 2nd largest city in area in the world
    h) The U.S. city with back-to-back football and baseball stadiums at the Harry S Truman Sports Complex
    i) The city that was the first capitol of the Confederacy
    j) The New Hampshire city called Derryfield and renamed in 1810 after an English textile city
ANSWER: **a) Key West, Fla. b) Santa Fe, N.M. c) Lubec, Me. d) Akron e) New York f) Fairbanks, Alas. g) Juneau, Alas. h) Kansas City, Mo. i) Montgomery, Ala. j) Manchester.**

223. Name the 4 main resort centers along Florida's "Gold Coast."
ANSWER: **Miami Beach, Palm Beach, Daytona Beach, and Fort Lauderdale.**

224. Identify the following multiple sites.
    a) The 3 Virginia towns sometimes called the "historic triangle"
    b) The 3 North Carolina universities that form the North Carolina Research Triangle
    c) The "Tri-Cities" in the state of Washington
    d) The 4 cities in the Calumet District
    e) The Quad cities of the Iowa-Illinois area
    f) The 2 U.S. states that are known as the "Twin Sisters"
    g) The "Tri-Cities" or "Triple Cities" of New York
    h) The 3 states in the "Tri-State Area"
    i) The 3 states in the "Tri-State Area" known as the Panhandle region
ANSWER: **a) Jamestown, Williamsburg, and Yorktown b) Duke (Durham), North Carolina (Chapel Hill), and North Carolina State (Raleigh) c) Kennewick, Pasco, and Richland d) East Chicago, Gary, Hammond, and Whiting (Indiana) e) Davenport (Iowa), Rock Island, Moline, and East Moline (Illinois) f) North and South Dakota or North and South Carolina g) Binghamton, Endicott, and Johnson City h) Connecticut, New Jersey, and New York i) Texas, Oklahoma, and New Mexico.**

225. Identify each of the following "Twin Cities," "Sister-Cities," or "Bi-Cities."
    a) The North Dakota cities separated by the Missouri River
    b) The Georgia and Alabama cities separated by the Chattahoochee River
    c) The Florida cities separated by the Tampa Bay
    d) The Maine cities separated by the Androscoggin River
    e) The Minnesota cities separated by the Mississippi River
    f) The Tennessee and Virginia cities with the same name separated by the state line
ANSWER: **a)Bismarck and Mandan b) Columbus and Phenix City c) Tampa and St. Petersburg d) Lewiston and Auburn e) Minneapolis and St. Paul f) Bristol and Bristol.**

226. Give the name of the Arizona city named for a bird of Egyptian mythology which lived in the Arabian desert for 500-600 years and then consumed itself in fire, only to ressurect itself from its ashes to begin another long life. Give the name of the California city that has this bird as its symbol representing the city's rebirth after the earthquake and fire which destroyed it in 1906.
ANSWER: **Phoenix, Arizona/San Francisco.**

227. Identify each of the following.
    a) The meaning of PATH in the New York-New Jersey area
    b) The name of the only island located in Crater Lake, Oregon
    c) The Wyoming rock formation featured in the movie *Close Encounters of the Third Kind*
    d) The area in Florida called the "river of grass"

e) The world's largest single freshwater lake that is partly in the U.S.

f) The Indian name for Mount McKinley meaning "The High One"

g) The Cliff Palace in Colorado whose name means "green table" in Spanish

h) The world's largest natural bridge

i) The name of the 700 mile fault in California

j) The largest gypsum dune field in the world

k) The house in Montgomery, Alabama, used as the first White House of the Confederacy

ANSWER: a) Port Authority Trans-Hudson b) Wizard Island c) Devils Tower d) Everglades e) Lake Superior f) Denali g) Mesa Verde h) Landscape Arch (Utah) i) San Andreas Fault j) White Sands (New Mexico) k) Jefferson Davis' house.

228. Identify each of the following winds associated with the U.S.

a) A warm moist southwest wind on the coast of Oregon, Washington, and southwest Canada in the winter and spring

b) A warm dry wind that blows down the eastern slopes of the Rocky Mountains

c) A cold northern wind that causes temperatures to drop rapidly in the Kansas, Oklahoma, and Texas region, and which frequently brings three days of wind and rain (named from the color which accompanies the cloud bank)

d) A sudden strong cold gale from the north over the Plains or across Texas or other Gulf Coast states which moves into the Gulf of Mexico and the western Caribbean

e) A gale or wind blowing from the northeast

f) A gale or wind blowing from the northwest

g) A strong, hot dry dust-bearing wind of southern California from the Mohave Desert during the winter (named for the Mexican general who liked to make attacks sweeping down from the hills)

h) A northerly windstorm in the Juneau, Alaska, area between October and March (named for the _____ River and the hurricane like winds produced at its mouth)

i) A sudden violent gust of cold land air rushing down snow-covered mountain passes toward the coast in Alaska

j) A violent tropical cyclone with winds of 73 miles an hour or greater occurring in the western North Atlantic and the Gulf of Mexico

ANSWER: a) wet chinook b) chinook c) blue norther d) norther e) northeaster (nor'easter) f) northwester (nor'wester) g) Santa Ana (Santa Anna) h) taku i) williwaw (willywaw) j) hurricane.

229. Identify each of the following states from the state bird, state flower, and state tree.

a) Mockingbird...Apple blossom...Pine

b) American robin...Mountain laurel...White oak

c) Mockingbird...Magnolia...Magnolia

d) Roadrunner...Yucca flower...Piñon, or nut pine

e) Sea gull...Sego lily...Blue spruce

f) Robin...Wood violet...Sugar maple

ANSWER: a) Arkansas b) Connecticut c) Mississippi d) New Mexico e) Utah f) Wisconsin.

230. Identify the state in which each of the following was once a former capital.

a) Vincennes   c) Natchez   e) Milledgeville

b) Guthrie   d) Sitka   f) New Bern

ANSWER: a) Indiana b) Oklahoma c) Mississippi d) Alaska e) Georgia f) North Carolina.

231. Identify the state for which each of the following is a state song.

a) "Where the Columbine Grows"   e) "On the Banks of the Wabash, Far Away"

b) "Yankee Doodle"

c) "Swanee River"   f) "The Old North State"

d) "Home on the Range"   g) "You Are My Sunshine"

ANSWER: a) Colorado b) Connecticut c) Florida d) Kansas e) Indiana f) North Carolina g) Louisiana.

U.S. EXTREMITIES—LOCATIONS IN 50 STATES (left) AND 48 STATES (right)

Point Barrow, Alaska	North	Lake of the Woods/Northwest Angle, Minnesota
South Cape (Ka Lae), Hawaii	South	Key West, Florida
West Quoddy Head, Maine	East	West Quoddy Head, Maine
Cape Wrangel, Attu Island, Alaska	West	Cape Alava, Washington
Mount McKinley, Alaska	Highest	Mount Whitney, California
Death Valley, California	Lowest	Death Valley, California

ROUTES/TRAILS

Boston Post Road . . . . Boston to New York City

Bozeman Trail . . . . Fort Laramie, Wyoming, to Virginia City, Montana

Braddock's Road . . . . Cumberland, Maryland, to Fort Duquesne (present-day Pittsburgh), Pennsylvania

California Trail (from many routes) . . . especially Council Bluffs, Missouri, to Sacramento-San Francisco, California (breaking off the Oregon Trail at Fort Hall in present-day Idaho)

Chisholm Trail . . . . San Antonio, Texas, to Abilene, Kansas (with extensions south to Mexico)

Desert Trail . . . . Santa Fe, New Mexico (south through Colorado), to Los Angeles, California

El Camino Real . . . . San Diego to Sonoma, California

Lancaster Turnpike . . . . Philadelphia to Lancaster, Pennsylvania

Lewis and Clark Route . . . . St. Louis, Missouri, to Portland, Oregon (Columbia River at the Pacific Ocean)

Mohawk Trail . . . . Along the Mohawk River from the Albany, New York, area, to the Great Lakes and the Buffalo, New York, area

Mormon Trail . . . . Nauvoo, Illinois, to Salt Lake City, Utah

Natchez Trace Route . . . . Nashville, Tennessee, to Natchez, Mississippi

National Road (Cumberland Road or the Great National Pike) . . . . Cumberland, Maryland, to Vandalia, Illinois (later to Saint Louis)

Oregon Trail . . . . Near Independence, Missouri, to Fort Vancouver, Washington (Oregon Territory) or Fort William, Portland (The Oregon Trail and the California Trail were sometimes called the Overland Trail)

Pennsylvania State Road (also called Forbes' Road) . . . . Philadelphia to Fort Duquesne (Pittsburgh)

Pony Express Line . . . . St. Joseph, Missouri, to Sacramento, California (by boat from Sacramento to San Francisco)

Santa Fe Trail . . . . Independence (near Kansas City), Missouri, to Santa Fe, New Mexico

(Old Spanish Trail--a continuation of the Santa Fe Trail) . . . . Santa Fe, New Mexico, to Los Angeles, California, and then to San Francisco (north through Colorado, Utah, the Colorado River, and the Mohave Desert)

Southern Trail . . . . Galveston, Texas, to El Paso, Texas

Wilderness Road . . . . Halston River at the Block House in Virginia through the Cumberland Gap to the Kentucky River in central Kentucky to Boonesborough (near Lexington) and to Harrodsburgh and thence to the Ohio and beyond

STATES AND THEIR CAPITALS

Alabama	Montgomery	Montana	Helena
Alaska	Juneau	Nebraska	Lincoln
Arizona	Phoenix	Nevada	Carson City
Arkansas	Little Rock	New Hampshire	Concord
California	Sacramento	New Jersey	Trenton
Colorado	Denver	New Mexico	Santa Fe
Connecticut	Hartford	New York	Albany
Delaware	Dover	North Carolina	Raleigh
Florida	Tallahassee	North Dakota	Bismarck
Georgia	Atlanta	Ohio	Columbus
Hawaii	Honolulu	Oklahoma	Oklahoma City
Idaho	Boise	Oregon	Salem
Illinois	Springfield	Pennsylvania	Harrisburg
Indiana	Indianapolis	Rhode Island	Providence
Iowa	Des Moines	South Carolina	Columbia
Kansas	Topeka	South Dakota	Pierre
Kentucky	Frankfort	Tennessee	Nashville
Louisiana	Baton Rouge	Texas	Austin
Maine	Augusta	Utah	Salt Lake City
Maryland	Annapolis	Vermont	Montpelier
Massachusetts	Boston	Virginia	Richmond
Michigan	Lansing	Washington	Olympia
Minnesota	St. Paul	West Virginia	Charleston
Mississippi	Jackson	Wisconsin	Madison
Missouri	Jefferson City	Wyoming	Cheyenne

STATES AND THEIR ABBREVIATIONS

Alabama	Ala. or AL	Montana	Mont. or MT
Alaska	Alas. or AK	Nebraska	Neb., Nebr., or NE
Arizona	Ariz. or AZ	Nevada	Nev. or NV
Arkansas	Ark. or AR	New Hampshire	N.H. or NH
California	Calif., Cal., or CA	New Jersey	N.J. or NJ
Colorado	Colo. or CO	New Mexico	N.M., N. Mex., or NM
Connecticut	Conn. or CT	New York	N.Y. or NY
Delaware	Del. or DE	North Carolina	N.C. or NC
Florida	Fla. or FL	North Dakota	N.D., N. Dak., or ND
Georgia	Ga. or GA	Ohio	O. or OH
Hawaii	Haw. or HI	Oklahoma	Okla. or OK
Idaho	Ida. or ID	Oregon	Ore., Oreg., or OR
Illinois	Ill. or IL	Pennsylvania	Pa., Penn., or PA
Indiana	Ind. or IN	Rhode Island	R.I. or RI
Iowa	Ia. or IA	South Carolina	S.C. or SC
Kansas	Kan., Kans., or KS	South Dakota	S.D., S. Dak., or SD
Kentucky	Ky., Ken., or KY	Tennessee	Tenn. or TN
Louisiana	La. or LA	Texas	Tex. or TX
Maine	Me. or ME	Utah	Ut. or UT
Maryland	Md. or MD	Vermont	Vt. or VT
Massachusetts	Mass. or MA	Virginia	Va. or VA
Michigan	Mich. or MI	Washington	Wash. or WA
Minnesota	Minn. or MN	West Virginia	W. Va. or WV
Mississippi	Miss. or MS	Wisconsin	Wis., Wisc., or WI
Missouri	Mo. or MO	Wyoming	Wyo. or WY

STATES AND THEIR NICKNAMES

Alabama . . . . Cotton State/Cornucopia of the South/Heart of the Deep South/ Heart of Dixie/Star of the South/Yellowhammer State

Alaska . . . . Arctic Treasureland/Gibraltar of the North/Great Land/Land of the Midnight Sun/Land Where the Summer Sun Never Sets/The Last Frontier

Arizona . . . . Apache State/Aztec State/Grand Canyon State/Italy of America/ Jewel in the West/Sunset State/Valentine State (February 14, 1912)

Arkansas . . . . Bear State/Bowie State/Hot Water State/Land of Majestic Beauty/ Land of Opportunity/Nation's Cool Green Paradise/Wonder State

California . . . . Cornucopia of the World/Eureka State/El Dorado State/Gateway to the Pacific/Golden State/Sunshine Empire/Wine Land of America

Colorado . . . . Centennial State (1876)/Highest State/Land of Contrasts/Rocky Mountain Empire/Silver State/Ski Country U.S.A./Switzerland of America/Top of the Mountain State

Connecticut . . . . Arsenal of the Nation/Blue Law State/Brownstone State/Constitution State/Insurance State/Land of Steady Habits/Nutmeg State/ Provision State

Delaware . . . . Blue Hen State/Diamond State/First State/New Sweden/State that Started a Nation/Uncle Sam's Pocket Handkerchief

Florida . . . . Alligator State/Everglade State/Gulf State/Land of Sunshine and Flowers/Orange State/Peninsula State/Sunshine State

Georgia . . . . Buzzard State/Cracker State/Empire State of the South/Goober State/Land of Adventure/Land of Peanuts, Pecans, and Peaches/ Peach State/Yankee Land of the South

Hawaii . . . . Aloha State/Crossroads of the Pacific/Gateway to the Orient (Pacific)/50th State of Enchantment/Gem (Paradise, Playground) of the Pacific/Island State

Idaho . . . . Gem of the Mountains/Gem State/Panhandle State/Spud State/ State of Shining Mountains

Illinois . . . . Corn Belt State/Garden of the West/Heart (Hub) of the Nation/ Land of Lincoln/Prairie State/Tall State

Indiana . . . . Center of the Commercial Universe/Crossroads of America/ Hoosier State/Peerless State/State of Surprises

Iowa . . . . Breadbasket of the Nation/Corn State/Food Market of the World/ Hawkeye State/Land of the Rolling Prairie/Land Where the Tall Corn Grows

Kansas . . . . Battleground of Freedom/Breadbasket of America/Garden of the West/Jayhawker State/Midway, U.S.A./Salt of the Earth/Sunflower State/Wheat State

Kentucky . . . . Bluegrass State/Corncracker State/Dark and Bloody Ground State/Hemp State/Pioneer Commonwealth/Tobacco State

Louisiana . . . . Bayou State/Child of the Mississippi River/Creole State/Holland of America/Magnolia State/Nature's Cornucopia/Pelican State/ Sportsman's Paradise/Sugar State

Maine . . . . Angler's Paradise/Border State/Lobsterland/Lumber State/Pine Tree State/Polar Star State/Vacationland

Maryland . . . . America in Miniature/Cockade State/Free State/Monumental State/Old Line State/Oyster State/Queen State/Star-Spangled Banner State/Terrapin State

Massachusetts . . . . Baked Bean State/Bay State/Birthplace of American Freedom/ Custodian of the Nation's Heritage/Hub of the Universe/Old Colony State/Puritan State

Michigan . . . . Automobile State/Great Lake State/Lady of the Lakes/Peninsula State/Wolverine State/Wonderland of 11,000 Lakes

Minnesota . . . . Bread and Butter State/Gopher State/Land of 10,000 Lakes/Land of Sky-Blue Waters/New England of the West/North Star State

Mississippi . . . . Bayou State/Border-Eagle State/Gateway to the Southland/Hospitality State/Magnolia State/Mud-Cat State/Tadpole State

Missouri . . . . Center State/Gateway to the West/Heartland of Hospitality/Iron Mountain State/Mother of the West/Pennsylvania of the West/Show Me State

Montana . . . . Big Sky (Ski) Country/Bonanza State/Land of Enchantment/Land of Shining Mountains/Land of Scenic Splendor/Treasure State

Nebraska . . . . Antelope State/Beef State/Cornhusker State/Cowboy Country/Land of the Pioneer/Land Where the West Begins/Tall Corn State/Tree Planters State

Nevada . . . . Battle-Born State/Entertainment Capital of the World/Sagebrush State/Silver State/State Where Man and Nature Gamble

New Hampshire . . . . Granite State/Land of Peace and Beauty/Mother of Rivers/Old Man of the Mountain State/White Mountain State/Yankee Playground

New Jersey . . . . Cockpit of History (of the Revolution)/Crossroads State/Garden State/Hub of Commerce/Industrial Park State/Pathway of the Revolution/Workshop of the Nation

New Mexico. . . . . Cactus State/Land of Enchantment/Space Age Research Center for the Free World/Sunshine State/Unspoiled Empire

New York . . . . Apple State/Empire State/Excelsior State/Knickerbocker State/Nation's Showcase/Seat of Empire

North Carolina. . . . . Graveyard of the Atlantic/First in Freedom/Ireland of America/Land of Beginnings/Old North State/Tar Heel State/Year-Round Mid-South

North Dakota . . . . Flickertail State/Gateway to the Big Country/Land of the Dakotas/Land of Theodore Roosevelt and General Custer/Sioux State

Ohio . . . . Buckeye State/Gateway to the Northwest Territory/Modern Mother of Presidents/Oldest State West of the Thirteen Original Colonies

Oklahoma . . . . Boomer State/Buckle of the Sunbelt/Heart of Cow Country/Land of the Red Men/Sooner State

Oregon . . . . Beaver State/End of the Trail/Land of Exciting Contrasts/Pacific Wonderland/Sunset State/Web-foot State

Pennsylvania . . . . Birthplace of a Nation/Coal State/Keystone State/Quaker State/State Where American Industry Began/Workshop of the World

Rhode Island . . . . American Venice/Land of Roger Williams/Little Rhody/Ocean State/Plantation State/Smallest State

South Carolina . . . . Keystone of the South Atlantic Seaboard/Palmetto State/Swamp State/Wonderful Iodine State

South Dakota. . . . . Artesian State/Blizzard State/Coyote State/Land of Infinite Variety/Pheasant Capital of the World/Sunshine State

Tennessee . . . . Big Bend State/Butternut State/Hog and Hominy State/Lion's Den State/Mother of Southwestern Statesmen/Volunteer State

Texas . . . . Beef State/Blizzard State/Jumbo State/Lone Star State/State of the Confederacy/World Cotton Center

Utah . . . . Beehive State/Deseret State/Honey State/Land of the Saints/Mormon State/Salt Lake State

Vermont . . . . Beckoning State/Country with a Heritage/Green Mountain State/Land of Marble, Milk, and Honey/Ski State of the East

Virginia . . . . Battlefield of the Civil War/Birthplace of 8 Presidents/Birthplace of the Nation/Cavalier State/Commonwealth/Mother of Presidents/Mother of States and Statesmen/Old Dominion

Washington . . . . Chinook State/Clam State/Evergreen State/Gateway to Alaska and the Orient/State of Exciting Contrasts

West Virginia .... Appalachian State/Free State/Fuel State/Glass Center of the World/Mountain State/Panhandle State/Switzerland of America
Wisconsin .... America's Dairyland/Badger State/Cheese Capital of the Nation/Copper State/Land o' Lakes/Playground of the Middle West
Wyoming .... Cowboy State/Equality State/Land of Cattle, Sheep, Song, and Story/Land of the Purple Sage/Sagebrush State/Sanctuary of Peace

NICKNAMES OF STATES THAT ARE TITLES OF BOOKS

Alaska .... *The Land of Now* by D.A. Noonan
Montana .... *The Big Sky* by A.B. Guthrie, Jr.
New Mexico .... *The Land of the Delight-Makers* by Adolph Bandelier
South Carolina .... *The State That Forgot* by W. Ball
Texas .... *The Land of Promise* by Joseph Lynn Clark

U.S. CAPITALS AND THEIR NICKNAMES

Montgomery, AL ...... Birthplace of Dixie, City of Opportunity, Cradle of the Confederacy
Juneau, AK .... Alaska's Scenic Capital, Capital of an Empire, Gateway to Glacier Bay National Moument
Phoenix, AZ .... City Where Summer Winters, Heart of the Sun Country, Metropolis of the Desert, Miracle City in the Valley of the Sun
Little Rock, AR .... Arkopolis, City of Roses, City of 3 Capitols
Sacramento, CA ...... Camellia Capital of the World, Golden City, Heart of California, City Where California Began (1839)
Denver, CO .... Convention City, Gateway to the Rockies, Mile High City, Queen City of the Plains (the Rockies; the West)
Hartford, CT .... Charter Oak City, City Beautiful, Gateway to Connecticut, Insurance Capital of the World
Dover, DE .... Capital of the First State, First City of the First State
Tallahassee, FL ...... Florida's Beginning Point, Center of Florida, Southland at Its Best
Atlanta, GA .... Big A, Big Peach, (Business) Hub of the Southeast, City Too Busy to Hate, Dogwood City, Gate City (Paris) of the South
Honolulu, HI .... Center of Pineapple Industry, Crossroads of the Pacific, Exciting City of Welcome
Boise, ID .... City of Trees, Pioneer Log Cabin Village, The Woods
Springfield, IL .... Flower City, Great American Shrine, Home of Abraham Lincoln
Indianapolis, IN ...... Circle City, Crossroads of America, Hoosier Capital, Railroad City
Des Moines, IA ...... City of Certainties, Farm Capital of America, Hartford of the West
Topeka, KS .... Center of the Nation
Frankfort, KY .... Bluegrass Capital, Heart of Kentucky, Historic Frankfort
Baton Rouge, LA ...... Chemical Center of the South, City Where the Sea Starts, Growth Center of the Mississippi
Augusta, ME .... City of Manifold Advantages, City of Year-Round Recreation
Annapolis, MD .... Ancient City, Athens of America, Crabtown-on-the-Bay, Home of the U.S. Naval Academy, Venice of America
Boston, MA .... Athens of America, Beantown, Birthplace of Freedom, Cradle of Liberty (of the American Revolution), Hub of American Culture, Hub of the Universe, Literary Emporium, Puritan City, Tri-Mountain City
Lansing, MI .... City in the Forest
St. Paul, MN .... Boston of the West, Gateway to the Famed Northwoods, North Star City, Saintly City
Jackson, MS .... Chimneyville, Crepe Myrtle City, Crossroads of the Old and New South, Oil Center for Mississippi

Jefferson City, MO . . . . . Convention City, Jeff City

Helena, MT . . . . Last Chance Gulch, Queen City of the Mountains

Lincoln, NE . . . . Cornhusker Capital City, Hartford of the West, Lilac City

Carson City, NV . . . . Gateway to Lake Tahoe and Yosemite Valley

Concord, NH . . . . Cradle of Liberty

Trenton, NJ . . . . Capital City, City of Iron and Clay, "Trenton Makes, The World Takes"

Santa Fe, NM . . . . Ancient City, City Different, Oldest and Quaintest City in the U.S., Royal City

Albany, NY . . . . Cradle of the American Union, Edinburgh of America, Historic and Colorful Capital of the Empire State

Raleigh, NC . . . . City of Oaks, Trading Center

Bismarck, ND . . . . City Beside the Broad Missouri, Skyscraper City of the Prairies

Columbus, OH . . . . Middle of Marketing America, Rose Capital of the World

Oklahoma City, OK . . . . . Capital of Soonerland, City of 1000 Lakes, Sedate Capital of the Bible Belt

Salem, OR . . . . Cherry City, Fisherman's Paradise, Heart of the Pacific Wonderland

Harrisburg, PA . . . . Courteous Capital City, Heart of the Commonwealth, State City

Providence, RI . . . . Bee-Hive of Industry, Roger Williams City, Southern Gateway of New England

Columbia, SC . . . . Gateway to the South, Golden Rule City

Pierre, SD . . . . City in the Center of Hunting Lands, Gateway to the Black Hills, Home of the Giant Oahe Dam

Nashville, TN . . . . Athens of the South, Country Music Capital of the World, Dimple of the Universe, Iris City, Music City, U.S.A., Rock City

Austin, TX . . . . Big Heart of Texas, Boom Town Without Oil, City of the Violet Crown

Salt Lake City, UT . . . . . Deseret, City of the Saints, Mormon Capital, Mormon Metropolis, New Jerusalem, Utah Zion

Montpelier, VT . . . . Capital City of the Green Mountain State, Insurance and Granite Center

Richmond, VA . . . . Capital of the Confederacy, Capital of the Old South, City of 7 Hills, Cockade City

Olympia, WA . . . . Bear's Place, Capital of the Evergreen State

Charleston, WV . . . . Charley West, Chemical City, Kanawha River City

Madison, WI . . . . City Built on an Isthmus, City of 4 Lakes, Recreation City

Cheyenne, WY . . . . Hell on Wheels, Home of Frontier Days, Magic City of the Plains (the West)

Washington, D.C. . . . . . Capital City, City of Magnificent Distances, City of Receptions, Executive City, Federal City

Euphoria, U.S.A. . . . . . . Fat City

3 LARGEST CITIES BY POPULATION IN EACH STATE BASED ON THE 1980 CENSUS

Alabama
Birmingham
Mobile
Montgomery (Capital)
Alaska
Anchorage
Fairbanks
Juneau (Capital)
Arizona
Phoenix (Capital)
Tucson
Mesa
Arkansas
Little Rock (Capital)
Fort Smith
North Little Rock
California
Los Angeles
San Diego
San Francisco
Colorado
Denver (Capital)
Colorado Springs
Aurora
Connecticut
Bridgeport
Hartford (Capital)
New Haven
Delaware
Wilmington
Newark
Dover (Capital)
Florida
Jacksonville
Miami
Tampa
Georgia
Atlanta (Capital)
Columbus
Savannah
Hawaii
Honolulu (Capital)
Pearl City
Kailua
Idaho
Boise (Capital)
Pocatello
Idaho Falls
Illinois
Chicago
Rockford
Peoria
Indiana
Indianapolis (Capital)
Fort Wayne
Gary
Iowa

Des Moines (Capital)
Cedar Rapids
Davenport
Kansas
Wichita
Kansas City
Topeka (Capital)
Kentucky
Louisville
Lexington (Fayette)
Owensboro
Louisiana
New Orleans
Baton Rouge (Capital)
Shreveport
Maine
Portland
Lewiston
Bangor
Maryland
Baltimore
Rockville
Hagerstown
Massachusetts
Boston (Capital)
Worcester
Springfield
Michigan
Detroit
Grand Rapids
Warren
Minnesota
Minneapolis
St. Paul (Capital)
Duluth
Mississippi
Jackson (Capital)
Biloxi
Meridian
Missouri
St. Louis
Kansas City
Springfield
Montana
Billings
Great Falls
Butte (Silver Bow)
Nebraska
Omaha
Lincoln (Capital)
Grand Island
Nevada
Las Vegas
Reno
North Las Vegas
New Hampshire
Manchester

Nashua
Concord (Capital)
New Jersey
Newark
Jersey City
Paterson
New Mexico
Albuquerque
Santa Fe (Capital)
Las Cruces
New York
New York
Buffalo
Rochester
North Carolina
Charlotte
Greensboro
Raleigh (Capital)
North Dakota
Fargo
Bismarck (Capital)
Grand Forks
Ohio
Cleveland
Columbus (Capital)
Cincinnati
Oklahoma
Oklahoma City (Capital)
Tulsa
Lawton
Oregon
Portland
Eugene
Salem (Capital)
Pennsylvania
Philadelphia
Pittsburgh
Erie
Rhode Island
Providence (Capital)
Warwick
Cranston
South Carolina
Columbia (Capital)
Charleston
Greenville
South Dakota
Sioux Falls
Rapid City
Aberdeen
Tennessee
Memphis
Nashville (Davidson)(Capital)
Knoxville
Texas
Houston

Dallas	**Virginia**	Huntington
San Antonio	Norfolk	Wheeling
Utah	Virginia Beach	**Wisconsin**
Salt Lake City (Capital)	Richmond (Capital)	Milwaukee
Provo	**Washington**	Madison (Capital)
Ogden	Seattle	Green Bay
Vermont	Spokane	**Wyoming**
Burlington	Tacoma	Casper
Rutland	**West Virginia**	Cheyenne (Capital)
Barre	Charleston (Capital)	Laramie

NICKNAMES IF APPLICABLE OF THE 3 LARGEST CITIES IN EACH STATE
(Capital cities not included--see section on capital cities and their nicknames)

Birmingham, Ala. . . . . . . City Where the Mighty Smith Stands (Vulcan statue), City with a Heart in the Heart of Dixie, Magic City, Pittsburgh of the South

Mobile, Ala. . . . . Alabama's Only Port City, City of Six Flags, Queen City of the Gulf

Anchorage, Alas. . . . . Air Crossroads of the World, Chicago of the North, Largest City in the Largest State

Fairbanks, Alas. . . . . Centennial City (1867 Exposition), Gateway to the Arctic, Heart of the Golden North

Tucson, Ariz. . . . . The Old Pueblo (Arizona's oldest city, 1776), Retirement City of the Nation, Southwest Sun Center, Western Gateway to Mexico

Mesa, Ariz. . . . . City Where It's June in January Along the Romantic Apache Trail

Fort Smith, Ark. . . . . Gateway to the Beautiful Ozark Playground, Little Gibraltar on the Arkansas

Los Angeles, Calif. . . . . . Angel City, Big Orange, Glamor Capital of the World, Motion Picture Capital of the World

San Diego, Calif. . . . . Birthplace of California (1542), Cradle of Californian Civilization, Plymouth of the Pacific Coast, World-famous Zoo City

San Francisco, Calif. . . . . Baghdad by the Bay, City by the Bay, City of a Hundred Hills, City by the Golden Gate, United Nations' Conference Center (April 25, 1945)

Colorado Springs, Colo. . . Little Lunnon (London), Newport of the West

Aurora, Colo. . . . . Gateway to the Rockies

Bridgeport, Conn. . . . . . . Essen of America, Industrial Capital of Connecticut, Park City

New Haven, Conn. . . . . . . City of Elms, Connecticut's Elm City, The Yankee Athens

Wilmington, Del. . . . . Chemical Capital of the World, Dupont Town, First City of the First State (first settlement established there by the Swedes)

Jacksonville, Fla. . . . . . . Jax, Hartford of the South

Miami, Fla. . . . . Gateway of the Americas, Jewel City of the Sunshine State, Twin Cities (with Miami Beach)

Tampa, Fla. . . . . Cigar Capital of America, Gateway to the Caribbean, Industrial Hub of Florida

Columbus, Ga. . . . . The Fountain City, South's Oldest Industrial City (1828)

Savannah, Ga. . . . . City of Historical Charm, Cradle of Georgia, First City of the South, Georgia's Colonial Capital, Georgia's Oldest City (1733), Mother City of Georgia

Pocatello, Ida. . . . . The Gate City to the Great Northwest

Chicago, Ill. . . . . City of the Big Shoulders, Hog Butcher for the World, Home of the Loop, Meat-Packing Capital of the World, The Second City, The Windy City

Rockford, Ill. . . . . City at the Top in Illinois

Peoria, Ill. . . . . City Pledged to Progress, Whiskey Town (former site of Hiram Walker & Sons)

Fort Wayne, Ind. . . . . Birthplace of Night Baseball, Center of the World's Magnet Wire Production

Gary, Ind.	America's Magic City, Gateway to the Indiana Dunes, Steel City
Cedar Rapids, Ia.	The Rapid City
Davenport, Ia.	Eastern Gateway of Iowa, Quad-Cities (with Moline, East Moline, and Rock Island, Illinois)
Wichita, Kan.	Air Capital of the World, Cow Capital, Great Airplane Manufacturing Center, Kansas' Premier City
Kansas City, Kan.	Gateway to Kansas, Heart of America
Louisville, Ky.	City by the Falls, Home of the Kentucky Derby
Lexington, Ky	Belle City of the Bluegrass Regions, Capital of the Horse World
Owensboro, Ky.	Heart of the Big River Country
New Orleans, La.	America's Most Interesting City, City of Jazz and the Mardi Gras, Cradle of Jazz, Creole City, Crescent City, Great South Gate, Paris of America, Superdome City
Shreveport, La.	Capital City (Queen City) of the Land of Ark-La-Tex
Portland, Me.	America's Sunrise Gateway, Vacation City on Casco Bay
Lewiston, Me.	Industrial Heart of Maine, Spindle City
Bangor, Me.	Gateway to the North Woods, Penobscot River City
Baltimore, Md.	Birthplace of the Star-Spangled Banner, Monument City
Worcester, Mass.	Birthplace of Modern Rocketry, Faithful City
Springfield, Mass.	Dean of the 27 U.S.A. Springfields, Rifle City (National Armory established there in 1794)
Detroit, Mich.	Automobile Capital, City of Straits, Motor City, Motown, Renaissance City
Grand Rapids, Mich.	Furniture Center of the World, Gateway to the Water Wonderland
Minneapolis, Minn.	City of Lakes, Twin City (with St. Paul), Vacation Capital
Duluth, Minn.	Air-Conditioned City, City Where the Prairie Meets the Sea (Lake Superior), Westernmost Port on America's Fourth Seacoast
Biloxi, Miss.	America's Riviera, Mother of New Orleans, Oldest French City in the U.S.A.
Meridian, Miss.	Heart of the New South
St. Louis, Mo.	Gateway Arch City, Home of the World's Largest Brewery (Anheuser-Busch), Queen of the Mississippi
Kansas City, Mo.	Heart of America, Mushroomopolis, Overgrown Cow Town, Steak Center of the Nation
Springfield, Mo.	Paris of the Ozarks, Queen City to the Southern Ozarks
Billings, Mont.	Capital of the Midland Empire
Great Falls, Mont.	The Electric City, Niagara of the West
Butte, Mont.	City That is a Mile High and a Mile Deep, Copper City, Richest Hill on Earth
Omaha, Neb.	Boy's Town, Crossroads of the Nation, Insurance Capital, Livestock and Meat Packing Capital
Las Vegas, Nev.	Broadway of the Desert, City of Little Wedding Churches, City of Destiny, City Without Clocks, Gambler's Mecca
Reno, Nev.	Biggest Little City in the World, Twin City by the Truckee (with Sparks, Nevada)
Manchester, N.H.	City in the Very Heart of New England, Queen City of the Merrimack Valley
Nashua, N.H.	Gate City of New Hampshire
Newark, N.J.	Birmingham of America, Milwaukee of the East
Jersey City, N.J.	City That Has Everything for Industry
Paterson, N.J.	Cradle of American Industry (1791), Federal City (planned capital of the U.S. by Alexander Hamilton and others), Lyons of America, Silk City
Albuquerque, N.M.	Duke City, Hot Air Balloon Capital of the World
New York, N.Y.	Babylonian Bedlam, Baghdad on the Hudson, The Big Apple, City That Never Sleeps, Financial Capital, Gotham, Modern Gomorrah, Seat of Empire

Buffalo, N.Y.	Bison City, Queen City of the Great Lakes
Rochester, N.Y.	Film City, Lake Ontario's Westernmost American Seaport, Photographic Capital
Charlotte, N.C.	Carolina's Queen City, Heart of the Piedmont
Greensboro, N.C.	Pivot of the Piedmont
Fargo, N.D.	Mainline City, Metropolis of North Dakota, Transportation Hub of the Northwest
Grand Forks, N.D.	The Only Grand Forks in the Nation
Cleveland, O.	Forest City, Lighting Capital of the World (GE plant), Queen of Lake Erie
Cincinnati, O.	Porkopolis, Queen City of the Ohio River, Ragtown
Tulsa, Okla.	Home of Diamond Products, Home of the International Petroleum Exposition, Main Street of America, Oil Capital of the World
Lawton, Okla.	Fort Sill Artillery and Missile Center, Post City
Portland, Ore.	City of Roses, City on the Willamette, City in the Evergreen Playground, Little Stumptown
Eugene, Ore.	Skinner's Mudhole, Spokane of Oregon
Philadelphia, Penn.	America's Bicentennial City, Birthplace of American Liberty (of American Independence; July 4, 1776), City of Brotherly Love, City of Homes, City of Penn (1682), Quaker City
Pittsburgh, Penn.	Arsenal of the World, Birmingham of America, City of Steel, Hearth of the Nation, Iron City, Smoky City, Workshop of the World
Erie, Penn.	Gem City of the Lakes, Harbor City
Warwick, R.I.	Growing City Convenient to Recreation Areas
Charleston, S.C.	City of Secession, Earthquake City, Palmetto City
Greenville, S.C.	Textile Center of the World
Sioux Falls, S.D.	Gateway to the Dakotas, Pheasant City, U.S.A.
Rapid City, S.D.	Denver of South Dakota, Eastern Gateway to the Black Hills
Aberdeen, S.D.	Quint City (Fisher quintuplets' birthplace--1963), Hub City of the Dakotas
Memphis, Tenn.	Babylon on the Bluff, City of the Blues, City of Churches, Home of King Cotton, Tri-State Capital (Ark., Tenn., and Miss.)
Knoxville, Tenn.	City Where Lakes and Mountains Meet, Gateway to the Great Smoky Mountains
Houston, Tex.	Astrodome City, Space Headquarters, U.S.A., World's Heart Transplant Capital
Dallas, Tex.	All-American Town, Big "D," City Deep in the Heart of Texas
San Antonio, Tex.	Alamo City (March 6, 1837), Cradle of Texas Liberty, St. Anthony's Town (1716), Venice of the Prairie
Provo, Ut.	Gateway to Utah's Famous Mountainland, Pioneer Mormon City, Steel Center of the West
Ogden, Ut.	West's Fastest-Growing Transportation and Industrial Center
Burlington, Vt.	Queen City of Vermont
Rutland, Vt.	Heart of the Green Mountains, Marble City
Norfolk, Va.	Center of the Mid-Atlantic, Dismal Swamp City
Virginia Beach, Va.	Virginia's Atlantic City
Seattle, Wash.	American Gateway to Alaska and the Orient, Little Portage, Skidrow on the Sound
Spokane, Wash.	Gateway to the Inland Empire, Home of the Mining Barons
Tacoma, Wash.	Gateway to Mount Rainier, Second Major City on the Puget Sound
Huntington, W. Va.	Gateway City
Wheeling, W. Va.	City of Historic Lore, Nail City
Milwaukee, Wis.	The American Munich, City of Old World Charm
Green Bay, Wis.	Cheese Storage Capital of the World, Lion of the Fox River Valley
Casper, Wyo.	Oil Capital of the Rockies
Laramie, Wyo.	Center for Medicine, Gateway to the Snowy Range

STATES AND THEIR NOTABLE SITES

Alabama . . . . Boll Weevil Monument (Enterprise); Browns Ferry Nuclear Plant (near Belle Mina); Cathedral Caverns (near Grant); Ivy Green (Helen Keller's birthplace in Tuscumbia); Mound State Monument (Moundsville); Muscle Shoals; Sequoyah Cave (Valley Head); Talladega National Forest; Wilson Dam (Muscle Shoals)

Alaska . . . . Aleutian Islands; Ballistic Missile Early Warning System (BMEWS); Distant Early Warning System (DEW Line); Gastineau Channel (Juneau); Joint Surveillance System (JSS); Kodiak Islands; Malaspina Glacier; Marine Highway; Mendenhall Glacier (near Juneau); Muir Glacier; Muldrow Glacier; Pribilof Islands; Prudhoe Bay; Totem Pole Lane (near Sitka); Totem Village (Haines); Valley of Ten Thousand Smokes; Will Rogers and Wiley Post Monument (near Barrow)

Arizona . . . . Coolidge, Davis, Glen Canyon, Hoover, Parker, and Roosevelt dams; "Ear of the Wind" (Monument Valley); Fort Apache; Giant Saguaro Cactus; Grand Canyon; Hopi and Navajo Indian reservations; Lakes Havasu, Mead, Mohave, and Powell; London Bridge (Lake Havasu City); Meteor Crater; Monument Valley; Oak Creek Canyon; O.K. Corral (Tombstone); Painted Desert; Picacho Peak and Pass; Superstition Mountain; Tombstone

Arkansas . . . . Blanchard Springs Caverns and Recreation Area; Crater of Diamonds Mine (near Murfreesboro); Diamond Cave (near Jasper); Dogpatch, U.S.A. amusement park (near Harrison); Eureka Springs; Hot Springs; Magnet Cove (near Hot Springs); Mammoth Spring; Mystic Caverns (Harrison); Ouachita and Ozark national forests and mountains

California . . . . Big Sur Coast; Cascade, Klamath, and Sierra Nevada mountains; Death Valley; Donner Pass; Edwards Air Force Base (Rosamond); El Camino Real ("The Royal Road"); El Capitan (Yosemite); Fort Ord (near Monterey); Imperial Valley; Lake Merritt (Oakland); Lassen Peak; Marineland (Redondo Beach); Mojave Desert; Monterey Bay; Mount Palomar and Mount Wilson observatories; Mount Shasta; Mount Whitney; Napa Valley; Palm Springs; *Queen Mary* (Long Beach); Redwood Highway; Ribbon Falls (Yosemite); Salton Sea; San Antonio Plaza (San Jose); San Bernardino, San Gabriel, and San Luis valleys; San Juan Capistrano; San Simeon; Scotty's Castle (Death Valley); Sierra Nevada; Silicon and Salinas valleys; Squaw Valley; Vandenberg Air Force Base (Lompoc); Zabriskie Point

Colorado . . . . Alva B. Adams Tunnel; Arapahoe Basin, Aspen, Crested Butte, Loveland Pass, Vail, and Winter Park ski resorts; Bent's Old Fort (near La Junta); Curecanti National Recreation Area; Durango-Silverton Narrow-gauge Railroad; Estes Park; National Bureau of Standards (Boulder); Royal Gorge of the Arkansas River (near Canon City)

Connecticut . . . . Mystic Seaport Museum of Maritime America (Mystic); Nathan Hale Homestead (Coventry); Newgate Prison (East Granby); U.S. Naval Submarine bases (Groton and New London); Whitfield House (Guilford)

Delaware . . . . Bethany Beach; Delaware Memorial Bridge (near New Castle); Delmarva Peninsula; Dover Air Force Base; Fenwick Island; Fort Delaware (Pea Patch Island); John Dickinson Mansion (near Dover); Rehoboth Beach

Florida . . . . Amelia Island; Apalachicola, Ocala, and Osceola national forests; Box Singing Tower (near Lake Wales); Circus World (near Haines City); Cypress Gardens (near Winter Haven); Daytona Beach;

Daytona International Speedway; De Soto National Memorial (near Bradenton); Eglin Air Force Base (Valparaiso); Ernest Hemingway's and John James Audubon's homes (Key West); Fort Caroline National Memorial (near Jacksonville); Fort Lauderdale; John F. Kennedy Space Center (Cape Canaveral); Key West; Marineland; Miami Beach; Overseas Highway (Key West); Palm Beach; Salvador Dali Museum (St. Petersburg); Silver Springs; Stephen Foster Memorial (White Springs); Tamiami Trail; Thomas Edison's home (Fort Myers); Wakulla Springs (near Tallahassee)

Georgia . . . . Alexander H. Stephens Memorial State Park (Crawfordsville); Callaway Gardens; Crawford Long Medical Museum (Jefferson); Dahlonega; Etowah (Indian) Mounds (Cartersville); Fort Pulaski (Cockspur Island); Franklin D. Roosevelt Memorial (near Warm Springs); Helen; Little White House (Warm Springs); Okefenokee National Wildlife Refuge; Providence Canyon; Robert Toombs' home (Washington); Robins Air Force Base (Warner Robins); Sea Islands (Saint Simons, °Jekyll, and Sea Island); Suwanee River; Westville (Lumpkin)

Hawaii . . . . Barking Sands (Kauai); Diamond Head (Oahu); Haleakala Crater (Maui); Iolani Palace (Honolulu); James Cook Monument (Kealakekua Bay on Hawaii); the "Needle"--Iao Valley (Maui); Pearl Harbor (Oahu); Royal Mausoleum (Honolulu); USS *Arizona* Memorial (Pearl Harbor); Waikiki Beach (Oahu); Waimea Canyon (Kauai)

Idaho . . . . Blackfoot Mountains; Bunker Hill Mine (near Kellogg); Cataldo Missions (near Kellogg); Coeur d'Alene Lake; Crystal Ice Cave (near American Falls); Gospel-Hump Wilderness Area; Hells Canyon; Lava Hot Springs; Lewis and Clark Highway; Little City of Rocks (near Gooding); Saw-tooth National Recreational Area; Shoshone Falls (near Twin Falls); Shoshone Ice Caves; Steamboat Spring, Hooper Spring, Soda Springs, and Champagne Springs; Sun Valley

Illinois . . . . Abraham Lincoln Home and Gravesite (Springfield); Argonne National Laboratory (Lemont); Baha'i Temple (Wilmette); Bishop Hill (near Galva); Black Hawk, Cahokia Mounds, Mississippi Palisades, and Pere Marquette state parks; Chain O'Lakes; Dickson Mounds Indian Burial Grounds (near Lewistown); Fermi National Accelerator Laboratory (near Batavia); Joseph Smith Home (Nauvoo); Lincoln Log Cabin State Park (near Charleston); Morton Arboretum (near Lisle); Shawnee National Forest; Spoon River; Ulysses S. Grant Home (Galena)

Indiana . . . . Army Finance Center (Ft. Benjamin Harrison); Beverly Shores (Lake Michigan); Eugene V. Debs Home (Terre Haute); Hoosier National Forest; James Whitcomb Riley Home (Greenfield); Lincoln Boyhood National Memorial (near Lincoln City); Marengo Cave; mineral springs at French Lick, Martinsville, and West Baden; Mounds Park (Anderson); New Harmony; Santa Claus; Tippecanoe; Wyandotte Cave (near Leavenworth)

Iowa . . . . Amana Colonies (near Cedar Rapids); Dodge House (Council Bluffs); Dvořák Memorial (Spillville); Floyd Monument (Sioux City); Grotto of the Redemption (West Bend); Herbert Hoover Birthplace (West Branch); Little Brown Church (near Nashua); Spirit Lake Massacre Monument (near West Okoboji)

Kansas . . . . Chalk Beds; Civic Plaza (Kansas City); Dodge City with its Boot Hill; Flint Hills; Forbes Air Force Base (near Topeka); Fort Larned; Fort Leavenworth (near Leavenworth); Fort Riley (near Junction City); Front Street (Dodge City); Hollenberg Pony Express Station (Hanover); Huron Indian Cemetery (Kansas City); John

Brown Memorial State Park (Osawatomie); Menninger Foundation (Topeka); Pawnee Rock

Kentucky . . . . Abraham Lincoln's ancestral home at Sinking Creek Farm (Hodgenville); Bluegrass Region; "Corner of Celebrities" District (Frankfort); Cumberland Falls and Gap; Cumberland Gap National Historical Park; Daniel Boone National Forest; Fort Harrod (Harrodsburg); George Rogers Clark Memorial (Harrodsburg); Henry Clay's home, Ashland (Lexington); International Museum of the Horse (Lexington); Jackson Purchase Region; John James Audubon Memorial Museum; Knobs Region; Liberty Hall (Frankfort); Mammoth Cave; My Old Kentucky Home (Federal Hill near Bardstown); Natural Bridge; Pennyroyal Plateau; Shakertown (near Lexington); U.S. Army Armor Center (Fort Knox); U.S. Gold Bullion Depository (Fort Knox)

Louisiana . . . . Audubon Memorial State Monument (near St. Francisville); Bayou Country; Cajun Country; Evangeline Oak (St. Martinville); Kisatchie National Forest (near St. Martinville); Lake Pontchartrain; Lake Pontchartrain Causeway; Longfellow-Evangeline Memorial Park; Louisiana Downs (Shreveport); Salt Mine (Avery Island)

Maine . . . . Allagash Wilderness Waterway; Bar Harbor (Mount Desert Island); Baxter State Park; Black Mansion (Ellsworth); Boothbay Harbor; Burnham Tavern (Machias); Brunswick Naval Air Station; Monhegan Island; Moosehead Lake; Old Gaol Museum (York); Roosevelt Campobello International Park (New Brunswick near Lubec); Quoddy Head; Thunder Hole (Acadia National Park); Wedding Cake House (Kennebunk)

Maryland . . . . Aberdeen Proving Ground; Andrews Air Force Base (Camp Springs); Barbara Frietchie House (Frederick); Catoctin Recreational Demonstration Area and Camp David (near Thurmont); Columbia; Harbor Tunnel; National Institutes of Health (Bethesda); Ocean City; St. Marys' City (near Leonardtown); State House (Annapolis); William P. Lane, Jr., Memorial Bridge (formerly the Chesapeake Bay Bridge)

Massachusetts . . . . Adams House (Quincy); Cape Cod; Fairbanks House (Dedham); Gloucester; Harvard University (Cambridge); John Greenleaf Whittier House (Amesbury); John and Priscilla Alden House (Duxbury); Martha's Vineyard; Naismith Basketball Hall of Fame (Springfield); Nantucket Island; Nathaniel Hawthorne Birthplace and House of the Seven Gables (Salem); Old Sturbridge Village (Sturbridge); Pilgrim House Tavern and Pilgrim Monument (Provincetown); Quadrangle (Springfield); Witch House (Salem)

Michigan . . . . Big Spring (near Manistique); Dutch Village (Holland); Fort Michilimackinac; Hiawatha National Forest; Isle Royale; Kellogg Bird Sanctuary (near Battle Creek); Lake Michigan; Lake of the Clouds; Mackinac Bridge; Mackinac Island; Sleeping Bear Dune; Soo Canals (Sault Sainte Marie); Tahquamenon Falls (near Newberry); United States Ski Hall of Fame (Ishpeming); Vandenberg Center (Grand Rapids)

Minnesota . . . . Boundary Waters Canoe Area; Charles A. Lindbergh's boyhood home (Little Falls); Grand Mound (near International Falls); High Falls; Lake Itasca; Lake of the Woods; Lumbertown U.S.A. (Brainerd); Mesabi Range; Mayo Clinic and Foundation (Rochester); Statues of Paul Bunyan and Babe (Bemidji); Superior and Chippewa national forests

Mississippi . . . . De Soto National Forest; Elvis Presley Birthplace (Tupelo); Fort Massachusetts (Ship Island); Jefferson Davis' Home *Beauvoir* (Biloxi); Natchez Trace Parkway; Old Capitol and New Capitol

(Jackson); Old Spanish Fort (Pascagoula); Piney Woods Country; *Rosemont* (Jefferson Davis' boyhood home; near Woodville); Vicksburg

Missouri .... Elephant Rocks State Park; Harry S Truman Library and Museum (Independence); Jesse James' home (St. Joseph); Lake of the Ozarks; Mark Twain National Forest; Meramec Cavern (near Sullivan); Ozark National Scenic Riverways; Pioneer Mother statue (Lexington); Pony Express Stables Museum (St. Joseph); Silver Dollar City (near Branson); Winston Churchill Memorial and Library at Westminster College (Fulton)

Montana .... Beartooth Highway; Bighorn Canyon National Recreation Area; Custer, Gallatin, and Lewis and Clark national forests; Flathead Lake Recreation Area; Gallery '85 (Billings); Gates of the Mountains Gorge; Grinnell Glacier Crevasse; Grinnell Lake; Giant Springs (near Great Falls); Lewis and Clark Caverns State Park (near Three Forks); Lolo Hot Springs; Museum of the Plains Indians (Browning); Medicine Rocks State Park (near Ekalaka); National Bison Range (Moiese); Three Forks; Virginia City (near Dillon)

Nebraska .... Arbor Lodge (Nebraska City); Buffalo Bill's home at Scouts Rest Ranch (near North Platte); Chimney Rock; Courthouse Rock; Harold Warp Pioneer Village (Minden); Jail Rock; Sand Hills; Scotts Bluff; Toadstool Park (near Crawford); Willa Cather Pioneer Memorial (Red Cloud); William Jennings Bryan Home (Lincoln)

Nevada .... Carson City; Cathedral Gorge State Park; Davis and Hoover dams; Elephant Rock (Valley of Fire State Park); Lake Mead Recreational Area; Lake Tahoe; Las Vegas; MGM Grand Hotel (Reno); Newlands Irrigation Project (near Reno); Pyramid Lake; Virginia City (1859 Comstock Lode discovery site); Valley of Fire State Park

New Hampshire ...... Bretton Woods; Canterbury Shaker Village; Crawford Notch; Daniel Webster's Birthplace (near Franklin); the Flume (Franconia Notch); Franklin Pierce Homestead (near Hillsboro); Lake Winnipesaukee (Center Harbor); Lost River (North Woodstock); Mary Baker Eddy's birthplace (Concord); MacDowell Colony (Peterborough); Merrimack Valley; Mt. Monadnock; Mt. Washington; Presidential Range; Profile, or Cannon, Mountain with its "Old Man of the Mountain" formation (Franconia Notch); Strawberry Banke (Portsmouth); White Mountains; Winter Carnival (Dartmouth College)

New Jersey .... Atlantic City boardwalk; Asbury Park; Barnegat Lighthouse (Long Beach Island); Cape May; Convention Hall (Atlantic City-- site of the Miss America Pageant); Delaware Water Gap (near Columbia); Garden State Parkway; Grover Cleveland Museum and Birthplace (Caldwell); Hoboken; Liberty State Park; Lincoln Tunnel (Weehawken to Manhattan); McGuire Air Force Base; "Molly Pitcher's Well" (Monmouth); Sandy Hook Lighthouse; Thomas Edison State Park (Menlo Park); Thomas Edison Museum (West Orange); Walt Whitman House (Camden); Wildwood

New Mexico .... Alamogordo; Apache, Carson, Cibola, Coronado, Gila, Lincoln, and Santa Fe national forests; Acoma-Zuni Trail; Bradley Science Hall and Museum (Lost Alamos); Carlsbad Caverns; *El Camino Real*; Fort Union Ruins; Gila Wilderness (near Silver City); Gran Quivira National Monument; Hopi, Navajo, and Zuni reservations (near Gallup); Kit Carson House (Taos); Inscription Rock (at the El Moro Monument); Los Alamos Scientific Laboratory; Old Town (Albuquerque); Palace of the Governors (Santa Fe); Powder

Puff ski area; Sandia Base and Kirtland Air Force Base (Albuquerque); Santa Fe; Ship Rock Peak; Taos Ski Valley; Temple of the Sun; Truth or Consequences; White Sands Missile Range and Proving Grounds (near Alamogordo)

New York . . . . Adirondack Mountains; Alfred E. Smith State Office Building (Albany); Ausable Chasm; Catskills; Delaware River Valley; Empire State Plaza (Albany); Fort Ticonderoga; Franklin D. Roosevelt's home (Hyde Park); Hudson River Valley; Lake Placid; Love Canal; Mark Twain's grave (Elmira); Mohawk River and Valley; Niagara Falls (near Buffalo); Saint Lawrence Seaway; Saratoga Springs; Sleepy Hollow Restoration (Tarrytown); Steuben Memorial (near Remsen); Theodore Roosevelt's home (*Sagamore Hill*, near Oyster Bay); Thomas Paine's home (New Rochelle); Walt Whitman's birthplace (near Huntington, Long Island); Washington Irving's *Sunnyside* (near Tarrytown); Watkins Glen (Seneca Lake)

North Carolina . . . . Alamance Battlefield (near Burlington); Andrew Johnson House (Raleigh); Biltmore Estate (near Asheville); Camp Lejeune Marine Base; Cape Hatteras, Cape Lookout, and Cape Fear; Carl Sandburg Home, *Connemara* (Flatrock); Chapel Hill; Chimney Rock; Croatan and Pisgah national forests; Dismal Swamp; Ft. Bragg; Grandfather Mountain (Linville); Kill Devil Hill (near Kitty Hawk); *Lost Colony* Drama (Fort Raleigh, near Mateo); Nags Head; Ocracoke Island; Old Salem (Winston-Salem); Outer Banks; Pinehurst; Research Triangle Park (between Raleigh, Durham, and Chapel Hill); Roanoke Island; Thomas Wolfe's home *Dixieland* (near Asheville); Tryon Palace (New Bern); U.S.S. *North Carolina* (Wilmington); William Sydney Porter's, Dolley Madison's, and Edward R. Morrow's birthplaces (Greensboro)

North Dakota . . . . Badlands; Drift Prairie; Fort Abercrombie; Fort Abraham Lincoln Park and Museum (near Mandan); International Peace Garden (between Boissevain, Manitoba, and Dunseith, N.D.); Lake Sakakawea; Lewis and Clark State Park; Pioneer Family statue (Bismarck); Red River Valley; "Skyscraper of the Plains" (State Capitol Building in Bismarck); Theodore Roosevelt's Elkhorn Ranch; Theodore Roosevelt National Memorial Park; Writing Rock (near Grenora)

Ohio . . . . All-American Soap Box Derby Site (Akron); Blue Hole (near Castalia); Cascade Plaza (Akron); Fort Ancient (near Lebanon); Fort Recovery; Great Serpent Mound (near Hillsboro); Kelleys Island (Lake Erie); McKinley Memorial and Gravesite (Canton); Mound City Group; National Monument (Chillicothe); National Professional Football Hall of Fame (Canton); Neil Armstrong Air and Space Museum (Wapakoneta); Perry's Victory and International Peace Memorial (South Bass Island, Lake Erie); Rutherford B. Hayes Library and Museum (Fremont); Schoenbrunn Village (near New Philadelphia); Thomas Edison's birthplace (Milan); tombs of Presidents Harrison, Hayes, Garfield, McKinley, and Harding; Wayne National Forest; Zoar Village (near New Philadelphia)

Oklahoma . . . . Broken Bow Resevoir; Chickasaw National Recreation Area; Creek Capitol (Okmulgee); Fort Sill (near Lawton); Geronimo's grave site (Lawton); Lake Eufaula; Lake Texoma (near Madill); Lake O'the Cherokees; National Hall of Fame for Famous American Indians (Anadarko); Ouachita Mountains and National Forest; Pioneer Woman Monument and Memorial (Ponca City); Sequoyah's home (near Sallisaw); *Trail of Tears* drama (Tahlequah); Washita Battlefield (near Cheyenne); Wichita Mountains National Wildlife Refuge (near Lawton); Will Rogers Memorial (Claremore); Woolaroc Museum (near Bartlesville)

Oregon .... Bonneville Dam; Cascade Range; *The Circuit Rider* (Salem); Columbia River Gorge; Crater Lake; Hells Canyon (Snake River); Hellgate Canyon (Rogue River); Methodist Mission Parsonage (Salem); Mount Hood; Mount Jefferson; Mount Mazama; Mount Washington; Oregon Dunes National Recreation Area; Picture Gorge (near Dayville); Sea Lion Caves; Three Sisters Mountain; Timberline ski resort; Wallowas; Willamette Valley and National Forest

Pennsylvania .... Allegheny National Forest; Daniel Boone Homestead (near Reading); Delaware Water Gap; Drake Well Park (Titusville); Eisenhower farm and home (near Gettysburg); Ephrata Cloisters (Ephrata); Fort Necessity (near Uniontown); Hershey Chocolate World (Hershey); James Buchanan's home *Wheatland* (Lancaster); Lehigh Valley; Oliver Hazard Perry's flagship *Niagara* (Erie); Pine Creek Gorge (near Wellsboro); Pocono Mountains; Rockville Bridge (near Harrisburg); Three Mile Island (Harrisburg); U.S. Army War College (Carlisle); Valley Forge National Historical Park; Washington Crossing State Park; General "Mad Anthony" Wayne Blockhouse (Erie); Wyoming Valley

Rhode Island .... Bishop George Berkeley's *Whitehall* (Middletown); Casimir Pulaski and Goddard Memorial state parks; Gaspee Point (Warwick); General Nathanael Greene Homestead (Coventry); Gilbert Stuart Birthplace (North Kingstown); Narragansett Bay (near Warwick); Roger Williams Park Museum (Providence); Slater Mill Historic Site (Pawtucket)

South Carolina .... Francis Marion and Sumter National forests; Hilton Head Island; John C. Calhoun's *Fort Hill* (Clemson); Myrtle Beach; Table Rock State Park; U.S. Marine Corps training center at Parris Island (near Beaufort)

South Dakota .... Badlands; Belle Fourche; Black Hills National Forest; Brandon Mounds (near Sioux Falls); Bureau of Indian Affairs; Corn Palace (Mitchell); Crazy Horse Memorial and Crazy Horse Mountain (near Custer); Custer National Forest; Deadwood; Dinosaur Park (Rapid City); Ellsworth Air Force Base (near Rapid City); Fort Wadsworth; Homestake Gold Mine (Lead); Jewel Cave; Mt. Rushmore (near Rapid City); Petrified Wood Forest; Prairie Hills; Sylvan Lake; Wild Bill Hickok's and Calamity Jane's gravesites (Deadwood); Wind Cave; World War I Soldier's and Sailor's War Memorial (Pierre); Wounded Knee

Tennessee .... American Museum of Science and Energy (Oak Ridge); Andrew Johnson National Monument (Greeneville); Cherokee National Forest; Cumberland Gap National Historic Park; David Crockett Park (near Lawrenceburg); Great Smoky Mountains; James K. Polk's home (Columbia); Land Between the Lakes National Recreation Area; Lookout Mountain (near Chattanooga); Natchez Trace Parkway; Oak Ridge National laboratories; Obed Wild and Scenic River; Railroad Museum (Jackson); Reelfoot Lake; Rock City Gardens

Texas .... Alpine-Big Bend Scenic Drive; *The Cowboy* statue (Austin); Dallas-Fort Worth Airport; Davy Crockett, Sabine, and Sam Houston national forests; Dwight D. Eisenhower birthplace (Denison); Fannin Battlefield (near Goliad); Fort Bliss (El Paso); Lyndon B. Johnson Library (Austin); O. Henry Museum (Austin); Odessa Meteor Crater; Palo Duro Canyon State Park; Sam Houston Steamboat House (Huntsville); Sheppard Air Force

Base (Wichita Falls); Six Flags Over Texas (Arlington); Spindletop Oil Field (Beaumont); Will Rogers Memorial Complex (Fort Worth)

Utah .... Angel Arch; Bonneville Salt Flats Speedway (near Wendover); Flaming Gorge Dam; Golden Spike National Historic Site; Kimball's Stage Station (near Kimball's Junction); Lake Powell; Landscape Arch; Monument Valley; Mount Timpanogos; Promontory Point; Provo Canyon; Rainbow Ridge; Wasatch Range

Vermont .... Appalachian Gap; Bennington Battle Monument; Calvin Coolidge's birthplace (Plymouth); Chester A. Arthur Memorial (Fairfield); Green Mountain National Forest; Lake Champlain; The Long Trail; Mt. Mansfield State Forest; Middlebury College (attended by the author); Old Constitution House (Windsor); granite statue of Robert Burns (Barre); Stowe, Sugarbush, Killington, Bromley, and Mt. Snow ski areas; *Ticonderoga* (Shelburne)

Virginia .... Arlington National Cemetery; Appomattox Court House National Historic Park; Benjamin and William Henry Harrison's *Berkeley* (near Charles City); Blue Ridge Mountains; Busch Gardens (near Williamsburg); Chesapeake-Bay Bridge Tunnel; Cumberland Gap; Great Dismal Swamp; George Mason's home *Gunston Hall* (near Lorton); George Washington's *Mt. Vernon* (near Alexandria); George Washington and Jefferson national forests; Great Appalachian Valley; James Madison's *Montpelier* (near Orange); James Monroe's *Ash Lawn* (near Charlottesville); Langley Air Force Base (Hampton); Luray, Grand, and Endless caverns; McLean House (Appomattox); Marine Corps Air Station (Quantico); Natural Bridge (near Lexington); Natural Chimneys (near Mount Solon); Robert E. Lee's birthplace at Stratford Hall (near Montross); Robert E. Lee Memorial Chapel (Lexington); Shenandoah Valley; Skyline Drive and Blue Ridge Parkway; Thomas "Stonewall" Jackson's grave site (Lexington); Thomas Jefferson's *Monticello* (Charlottesville); Tidewater Region; Virginia Beach; Williamsburg; Wolf Trap Farm Park for the Performing Arts; Woodrow Wilson's birthplace (Staunton); Yorktown

Washington .... Bonneville Dam; Puget Sound Naval Shipyard; Cascade Mountain Range; Cascade Tunnel; Columbia River; Dry Falls; Fort Lewis (near Tacoma); Fort Nisqually (Tacoma); Grand Coulee Dam; Ice Caves; Lake Chelan; Lake Franklin D. Roosevelt; Lake Washington; Lewis and Clark Interpretative Center (near Ilwaco); Mount Adams; Mount St. Helens; Mount Rainier; Olympic Mountains; Olympic National Park; Point Defiance Park (Tacoma); Polaris Missile Submarine Base (Bangor); San Juan Islands; U.S.S. *Missouri* (Bremerton; back in active service as of 1984)

West Virginia .... Berkeley Springs and White Sulphur Springs resorts; Blackwater Falls State Park; Blennerhasset Island (near Parkersburg); Chief Cornstalk Monument in Tu-Endie-Wei Park (Point Pleasant); Grave Creek Mound (Moundsville); Harpers Ferry; Ice Mountain; Jackson's Mill (near Weston); John Brown Gallows (Charles Town); Monongahela National Forest; Spruce Knob-Seneca Rocks Recreational Area; Sleepy Creek State Forest

Wisconsin .... Castle Rock; Cave of the Mounds (Blue Mounds); Devil's Lake State Park; Door County Peninsula; Horicon Marsh; House on the Rock (near Dodgeville); Lake Winnebago; Nicolet National Forest; *Taliesin* (Frank Lloyd Wright's home near Spring Green); United States Armed Forces Institute (Madison); Villa Louis (Prairie du Chien); Wisconsin Dells

Wyoming	Bighorn Canyon and Flaming Forge Recreational Areas; Buffalo Bill Historic Center (Cody); Devil's Tower; Fort Laramie; Grand Canyon of the Yellowstone; Jackson Hole Museum (near Moran Junction); Mammoth Hot Springs; National Elk Refuge (near Jackson); Old Faithful (Yellowstone Park); Shoshone, Bighorn, Teton, and Medicine Bow national forests; Teapot Dome and Salt Creek fields; Teton Range; Warren Air Force Base (near Cheyenne); Yellowstone Falls

CITIES AND THEIR NOTABLE SITES

Birmingham, AL	Statue of the Roman god Vulcan (on Red Mountain); Woodrow Wilson Park
Huntsville, AL	Alabama Space and Rocket Center; George C. Marshall Space Flight Center; Redstone Arsenal; Von Braun Civic Center
Mobile, AL	Azalea Trail; Bankhead Tunnel; Bellingrath Home and Gardens (nearby); Dauphin Island (Mobile Bay); U.S.S. *Alabama* (Mobile Bay); U.S.S. *Drum* (a submarine; Mobile Bay)
Montgomery, AL	First White House of the Confederacy (Jefferson Davis' home); Gunter and Maxwell Air Force bases
Tuskegee, AL	Booker T. Washington Home; George Washington Carver Museum
Anchorage, AK	Elmendorf Air Force Base (nearby); Fort Richardson (nearby)
Phoenix, AZ	Apache Trail (nearby); Taliesin West (Frank Lloyd Wright's home, now an architectural school; nearby)
Tucson, AZ	Arizona-Sonora Desert Museum (nearby); Kitt Peak National Observatory and McMath Solar Telescope (nearby); San Xavier del Bac Mission--"White Dove of the Desert" (nearby)
Little Rock, AR	MacArthur Park; War Memorial Park
Los Angeles, CA	Bel Air; Beverly Hills; Burbank; Century City -- "City within a City"; Culver City; Disneyland (Anaheim); Forest Lawn Memorial Park (Glendale); Mann's (formerly Graumann's) Chinese Theatre; Griffith Park; Hanna-Barbera's Marineland (Palos Verdes Estates); J. Paul Getty Museum (Malibu); Johnny Carson (Burbank); Hollywood Boulevard, Bowl, Hills, and Park; Knott's Berry Farm (Buena Park); La Brea Tar Pits; Long Beach; MacArthur Park; Malibu; Olvera Street; Pacific Ocean Park; Pacific Palisades; Pershing Square; Redondo Beach; San Fernando Valley; Santa Ana; Santa Anita (Arcadia); Santa Monica; Sunset Boulevard with its "Sunset Strip"; Tournament of Roses (Pasadena); Warner Brothers Studio (Burbank); Watts; Wilshire Boulevard with its "Miracle Mile"
Sacramento, CA	Capitol Park; State Capitol Building and Mall; Mather and McClellan Air Force Base (nearby); Sutter's Fort
San Diego, CA	Balboa Park; Community Concourse; Coronado; La Jolla; Mission Bay and Beach; Mission Valley; North Island Naval Air Station; Old Town District; Presidio Park; San Diego Zoo; *Star of India* (San Diego Bay)
San Francisco, CA	Alcatraz (prison from 1933-1963; in San Francisco Bay); Bank of America; Bay Area Rapid Transit (to Oakland; known as BART); Candlestick Park; The Cannery; Chinatown; Coit Tower; Embarcadero; Fisherman's Wharf; Ghirardelli Square; Golden Gate Bridge and Park; Market Street; Nob, Russian, and Telegraph hills; Portsmouth Square; Presidio; Transamerica Pyramid; Treasure Island
Colorado Springs, CO ..	Cave of the Winds (nearby); Cheyenne Mountain Combat Operations Center of the North American Defense Command (NORAD); Fort Carson (nearby); Garden of the Gods; Pike National Forest; Pikes Peak; Professional Rodeo Hall of Fame; Will Rogers Shrine of the Sun Memorial (Cheyenne Mountain)

Denver, CO . . . . William F. ("Buffalo Bill") Cody's grave (Lookout Mountain); Buffalo Bill Cody Museum; Eisenhower Memorial Tunnel (nearby); Lowry Air Force Base (nearby); Moffat Tunnel; Red Rocks Park; Rocky Mountain Arsenal (nearby); United States Mint

Bridgeport, CT . . . . Barnum Museum; Beardsley Park; Elias Howe Statue; P.T. Barnum Statue; Seaside Park

Hartford, CT . . . . American School for the Deaf; The Charter Oak Monument; Constitution Plaza; Harriet Beecher Stowe House; Mark Twain House and Memorial; Old State House; Wadsworth Atheneum

New Haven, CT . . . . Center Church; Judges' Cave; Yale Bowl

Stratford, CT . . . . American Shakespeare Festival Theatre; Connecticut Theatre for the Performing Arts

Wilmington, DE . . . . . . Caesar Rodney Statue; E.I. Du Pont de Nemours & Company; Fort Christina with its Kalmar Nyckel Monument commemorating the landing of the Swedes in 1638 on The Rocks; Henry Francis du Pont Winterthur Museum (nearby); Holy Trinity (Old Swedes) Church; Old Town Hall

Miami, FL . . . . Biscayne Boulevard; Coral Gables; Coconut Grove; Fort Dallas; Hialeah Park; Villa Viscaya, James Deering's estate (nearby)

Orlando, FL . . . . Epcot Center (nearby); Sea World (nearby); Walt Disney World (nearby)

St. Augustine, FL . . . . . Castillo de San Marcos (1672); City Gate; Fort Matanzas National Memorial (nearby); Oldest House

Sarasota, FL . . . . Circus Hall of Fame; Ringling Circus Museum; John and Mable Ringling Museum of Art

Tampa, FL . . . . Busch Gardens; MacDill Air Force Base (nearby); Ybor City (Latin Quarter)

Atlanta, GA . . . . Cyclorama (Grant Park); Dobbins Air Force Base (nearby); Five Points; Hartsfield International Airport; Martin Luther King, Jr., tomb; The Omni; Peachtree Center and Peachtree Street; Six Flags Over Georgia; Stone Mountain (nearby); U.S. Center for Disease Control; World Congress Center; *Wren's Nest* (Joel Chandler Harris' home)

Augusta, GA . . . . Augusta National Golf Course (site of the Masters Golf Tournament); Fort Gordon (nearby); the Manse (Woodrow Wilson's boyhood home)

Columbus, GA . . . . Columbus Iron Works Convention and Trade Center; Confederate Naval Museum; Fort Benning (nearby); Springer Opera House (state theatre of Georgia)

Savannah, Ga . . . . Factor's Walk; Fort McAllister; Fort Pulaski (nearby); Fort Stewart (nearby); Juliette Gordon Low's birthplace (founder of the Girl Scouts of America); Ships of the Sea Museum; Yamacraw Bluff

Honolulu, HI . . . . Aloha Tower; Hickam Air Force Base; Iolani Palace (the capitol from 1959 to 1969); Makaha; Punch Bowl; Waikiki Beach

Chicago, IL . . . . Adler Planetarium; Chicago Board of Trade; Chicago Picasso; Field Museum of Natural History; Gold Coast; Grant Park; Jackson Park and Jackson Drive; Lincoln Park; the Loop; Madison Street; "Magnificient Mile" (Michigan Ave. to Oak St.); Merchandise Mart; Museum of Science and Industry; O'Hare International Airport; Sears Tower; State Street

Indianapolis, IN . . . . . . Benjamin Harrison Memorial Home; Conner Prairie Pioneer Settlement and Museum (nearby); Eagle Creek Park; Indiana World War Memorial Plaza; Indianapolis Motor Speedway and Racing Hall of Fame; Mile Square; Monument Circle with its Soldiers and Sailors Monument; Scottish Rite Cathedral

Vincennes, IN . . . . George Rogers Clark Memorial; *Grouseland* (William Henry Harrison's home as territorial governor)

Abilene, KS . . . . Eisenhower Presidential Library, Memorial Museum, boyhood home, and "Place of Meditation"

Wichita, KS . . . . A. Price Woodard, Jr., Memorial Park; Century II; Historic Wichita Cow Town; McConnell Air Force Base (nearby); Mid-American All Indian Center

Louisville, KY . . . . *Belle of Louisville*; Churchill Downs (home of the Kentucky Derby); Founders Square; *Locust Grove*, George Rogers Clark's home; Zachary Taylor National Cemetery

New Orleans, LA . . . . . Basin, Bourbon, Canal, and Royal streets; The French Quarter (the *Vieux Carré*, "The Old Square"); Grand Isle (nearby); Jackson Square; Louisiana Purchase Memorial; Mardi Gras parades; Superdome

Portland, ME . . . . Deering's Oaks Park; Lincoln Park; Portland Head Light (nearby); Tate House; Wadsworth-Longfellow House

Baltimore, MD . . . . Basilica of the Assumption of the Blessed Virgin Mary; Battle Monument; The Block; Catholic Cathedral of Mary Our Queen; Charles Center; Edgar Allan Poe House; Flag House; Fort McHenry; Francis Scott Key Monument; Inner Harbor; Johns Hopkins University and medical center; Loyola High (Towson) and Loyola College (attended by the author); National Aquarium; Preakness Stakes (Pimlico); U.S.S. *Constellation*; Washington Monument

Boston, MS . . . . Back Bay; Beacon Hill; Boston Common; Breed's Hill; Bunker Hill Monument (Breed's Hill); Copley Square; Faneuil Hall; Freedom Trail; Franklin Park; Heartbreak Hill; John F. Kennedy Library; Lafayette Place; Liberty Tree; Old North Church; Old State House; Paul Revere's House and Monument; Prudential Tower; Scollay Square; U.S.S. *Constitution* ("Old Ironsides")

Concord, MS . . . . Hawthorne's *The Wayside*; Hawthorne's and Emerson's *Old Manse*; Louisa May Alcott's *Orchard House*; Minute Man statue; Old North Bridge; Sleepy Hollow Cemetery (nearby); Walden Pond (nearby)

Plymouth, MS . . . . Massasoit statue; *Mayflower II*; Plimoth Plantation (first Pilgrim plantation); Plymouth Rock

Dearborn, MI . . . . *Fair Lane* (Henry Ford's estate); Greenfield Village; Henry Ford Museum; Thomas A. Edison's laboratory

Detroit, MI . . . . Belle Isle Park; Cadillac Square; Detroit to Windsor Tunnel/Bridge; Joe Louis Arena; Renaissance Center; River Rouge Park; Silverdome (Pontiac); Woodward Avenue

Minneapolis, MN . . . . . Falls of Saint Anthony; Guthrie Theatre; Hennepin, Marquette, and Nicollet avenues; Lake District; The Midway; Minnehaha Falls and Park; Theodore Wirth Park

St. Paul, MN . . . . Capital Centre; Cathedral of St. Paul; Indian Mounds Park; Landmark Center; Town Square Park; Winter Carnival

Hannibal, MO . . . . Mark Twain's Boyhood Home and Museum; Mark Twain Cave (nearby); Tom Sawyer and Huckleberry Finn statues

Kansas City, MO . . . . . . Crown Center; Freeway Loop; Harry S Truman Sports Complex; Liberty Memorial; Livestock Exchange; Pershing Square; Swope Park

St. Louis, MO . . . . Aloe Plaza; Climatron (at the Missouri Botanical Garden); Forest Park; Gateway Arch; Grant's Farm (Grantwood); Jefferson National Expansion Memorial; Memorial Plaza; Old Court House (site of the 1846 Dred Scott Trial); *Santa Maria* replica

Helena, MT . . . . "Guardian of the Gulch" fire tower; Last Chance Gulch (main street); Statue of Liberty reproduction (on dome of the state capitol)

Omaha, NE . . . . Father Flanagan's Boys Town (nearby); Strategic Air Command at Offutt Air Force Base (nearby)

Las Vegas, NV .... Hoover Dam (nearby); Lake Mead (nearby); Nellis Air Force Base Test Site; "The Strip"

Jersey City, NJ .... Holland Tunnel (to Manhattan); Journal Square Transportation Center; Port Jersey

Newark, NJ .... The Gateway; Military Park with its "The Wars of America" monument; Plume House; Trinity Cathedral

Trenton, NJ .... Battle Monument; Capital Place; Fort Dix (nearby); Soldiers' and Sailors' War Memorial Building; Trent House

Buffalo, NY .... Ansley Wilcox Mansion (now the Theodore Roosevelt Inaugural Historic Site); Commodore Perry Monument (Front Park); Martin House; Milburn House; Niagara Square; Peace Bridge (to Fort Erie, Ontario); Red Jacket Monument (Forest Lawn Cemetery); William McKinley Memorial (Niagara Square)

Cooperstown, NY ..... Cardiff Giant Site (Farmer's Museum); Fenimore House; National Baseball Hall of Fame and Museum

New York, NY .... American Museum of Natural History; Battery Park; Bedford-Stuyvesant; Bronx; Broadway; Brooklyn Bridge; Carnegie Hall; Cathedral of St. John the Divine; Central Park; Chelsea; Coney Island; Ellis Island; Empire State Building; Federal Hall; Flatiron Building; Flushing Meadows-Corona Park; Franklin D. Roosevelt (formerly Welfare) Island; Garment District; Governor's Island; Gracie Mansion; Gramercy Park; Grand Central Station; Grant's Tomb (Riverside Park); Greenwich Village; Guggenheim Museum; Harlem; Herald Square; John F. Kennedy International Airport; La Guardia Field; Liberty Island; Lincoln Center for the Performing Arts; Madison Avenue; Madison Square Garden; Manhattan Island; Metropolitan Opera House; Morningside Heights; Museum of Modern Art (MOMA); Park Avenue; Pelham Bay Park; Pennsylvania Station; Prospect Park; RCA Building; Radio City Music Hall; Randalls Island; Riker's Island; Rockefeller Center; Roosevelt Park; St. Patrick's Cathedral; SoHo; Staten Island; Statue of Liberty; Times Square; United Nations; U.S. Coast Guard headquarters (Governor's Island); Van Cortlandt Park; Verrazano-Narrows Bridge; Wall Street; World Trade Center

Rochester, NY .... Clock of the Nations; Eastman Kodak Company; Lincoln First Tower; Susan B. Anthony Memorial and House; Xerox Corporation and Square

Cincinnati, OH .... The Basin; Eden Park; Fountain Square; Kings Island amusement park (nearby); Mount Airy Forest; Mt. Auburn; Riverfront Stadium; Tyler-Davidson Fountain; Union Terminal

Cleveland, OH .... Civil War's Soldiers' and Sailors' Monument (Public Square); Emerald Necklace; Euclid Avenue; the "Flats"; Monumental Park (Public Square); Rockefeller Park; Terminal Tower Building; Washington Park

Columbus, OH .... American Rose Society Park of Roses; Avenue of Flags; Battelle Memorial Institute; Capitol Square; Christopher Columbus statue

Dayton, OH .... Dunbar House; Orville and Wilbur Wright Home; U.S. Air Force Museum and Institute of Technology; Wright-Patterson Air Force Base

Oklahoma City, OK .... *The Cowboy* statue; Lincoln Park Zoo; National Cowboy Hall of Fame and Western Heritage Center; National Softball Hall of Fame; Tinker Air Force Base

Tulsa, OK .... Council Oak; Mohawk Park; Williams Center

Portland, OR .... Forest Park; International Rose Test Gardens; Mount Tabor Park; Sanctuary of Our Sorrowful Mother; Washington Park

Philadelphia, PA ...... Academy of Natural Sciences; American Philosophical Society; Benjamin Franklin Parkway and gravesite; Betsy Ross House; Carpenters' Hall; Congress Hall; Elfreth's Alley; Fairmount Park;

First and Second banks of the United States; Franklin Institute; Independence Hall; Liberty Bell; Penn Center; Rittenhouse Square; Rodin Museum with *The Burghers of Calais*; Society Hill; Southwark; U.S. Mint; Washington Square with its Revolutionary War Memorial; William Penn statue

Pittsburgh, PA . . . . Fort Pitt Blockhouse; Gateway Center; Golden Triangle; Mellon Institute; Point State Park; Stephen Collins Foster Memorial; Three Rivers Stadium; United States Steel Building

Newport, RI . . . . Bowen's Wharf; Cliff Walk; Cornelius Vanderbilt's home *The Breakers*; International Tennis Hall of Fame; Newport Jazz Festival; Old Colony House; Old Stone Mill; Touro Synagogue; United States Naval War College; Washington Square; White Horse Tavern; William K. Vanderbilt's *Marble House*

Charleston, SC . . . . The Battery; Catfish Row; Charles Towne Landing; Cypress, Magnolia, and Middleton Place gardens (nearby); Dock Street Theatre; Fort Moultrie; Fort Sumter; John C. Calhoun statue; Old Charles Towne; Polaris Submarine Base; U.S.S. *Yorktown*

Columbia, SC . . . . Fort Jackson (nearby); Strom Thurmond Federal Office Building; Woodrow Wilson Boyhood Home

Knoxville, TN . . . . Atomic Energy Commission (AEC) Oak Ridge Installation; *Bleak House* (Gen. James Longstreet's headquarters in 1863); Sunsphere; Tennessee Valley Authority; William Blount Mansion

Memphis, TN . . . . Beale Street; *Graceland* (Elvis Presley's home); Libertyland; McKellar Park; Pink Palace; Presidents Island (Mississippi River); W.C. Handy Park

Nashville, TN . . . . Andrew Jackson's *The Hermitage* (nearby); Country Music Hall of Fame and Museum; Fort Nashborough replica; Grand Ole Opry; Opryland, U.S.A.; Parthenon replica in Centennial Park

Dallas, TX . . . . Dealey Plaza (John F. Kennedy Memorial plaque site); First International Building; Nieman-Marcus; Reunion Tower; State Fair Park (nearby)

Houston, TX . . . . Astrodome; Astrohall; Astroworld Amusement Park; Hermann Park; Lyndon B. Johnson Space Center (formerly the Manned Spacecraft Center); Old Market Square; Pennzoil Place; San Jacinto Battleground State Park; San Jacinto Monument (nearby); U.S.S. *Texas*

San Antonio, TX . . . . . . The Alamo; Brackenridge Park; Brooke Army Medical Center; Brooks, Kelly, Lackland, and Randolph Air Force Bases; Fort Sam Houston; Hemisfair; Mission San José; *Paseo del Rio* ("River Walk"); Tower of the Americas; *La Villita* ("Little Village")

Salt Lake City, UT . . . . . Brigham Young's *Beehive House* and *Lion House*; Brigham Young Monument; Bingham Canyon Copper Pit (nearby); Dead Horse Point (near Moab); Eagle Gate; Great Salt Lake; Hot Pots (near Heber); Mormon Temple; Pioneer Trails State Park; Salt Lake Tabernacle; Latter Day Saints Church Office Building; Salt Palace; Sea Gull Monument; Temple Square; "This is the Place" Monument; Trolley Square

Arlington,VA . . . . *Arlington House* (Robert E. Lee's House and Memorial); Arlington National Cemetery; Pentagon; Tomb of the Unknowns

Norfolk, VA . . . . General Douglas MacArthur Memorial; Norfolk Naval Base and Air Station; Norfolk Naval Shipyard; St.Paul's Church; Scope

Richmond, VA . . . . Battle Abbey (Confederate Memorial Institute); Capitol Square; Edgar Allan Poe Museum; Hollywood Cemetery (burial site of Jefferson Davis, James Monroe, and John Tyler); John Marshall House; Kings Dominion (nearby); Maggie Walker House; Monument Avenue; Museum of the Confederacy; St.John's Church; "White House" of the Confederacy

Seattle, WA . . . . Boeing Field; Kingdome; Lake Union; Green Lake; Monorail; Pacific Science Center; Pike Place markets; Pioneer Square; Seattle Center; Space Needle

Milwaukee, WI . . . . Blatz Temple of Music (Washington Park); Greek Orthodox Church of the Annunciation (Wauwatosa); Lincoln Memorial; Menomonee Drive Valley; Mitchell Park Conservatory; War Memorial Center; Whitnall Park

NATIONAL PARKS AND THEIR LOCATIONS

Denali . . . . Alaska
Gates of the Arctic . . . . . Alaska
Glacier Bay . . . . Alaska
Katmai . . . . Alaska
Kenai Fiords . . . . Alaska
Kobuk Valley . . . . Alaska
Lake Clark . . . . Alaska
Wrangell-St. Elias . . . . . Alaska
Grand Canyon . . . . Arizona
Petrified Forest . . . . Arizona
Hot Springs . . . . Arkansas
Channel Islands . . . . California
Kings Canyon . . . . California
Lassen Volcanic . . . . California
Redwood . . . . California
Sequoia . . . . California
Yosemite . . . . California
Mesa Verde . . . . Colorado
Rocky Mountain . . . . Colorado
Biscayne . . . . Florida
Everglades . . . . Florida
Haleakala . . . . Hawaii
Hawaii Volcanoes . . . . . Hawaii
Mammoth Cave . . . . Kentucky
Acadia . . . . Maine

Isle Royale . . . . Michigan
Voyageurs . . . . Minnesota
Glacier . . . . Montana
Carlsbad Caverns . . . . . New Mexico
Great Smoky Mts . . . . . . North Carolina, Tennessee
Theodore Roosevelt . . . North Dakota
Crater Lake . . . . Oregon
Badlands . . . . South Dakota
Wind Cave . . . . South Dakota
Big Bend . . . . Texas
Guadalupe Mountains . . Texas
Arches . . . . Utah
Bryce Canyon . . . . Utah
Canyonlands . . . . Utah
Capitol Reef . . . . Utah
Zion . . . . Utah
Virgin Islands . . . . Virgin Islands
Shenandoah . . . . Virginia
Mount Rainier . . . . Washington
North Cascades . . . . Washington
Olympic . . . . Washington
Grand Teton . . . . Wyoming
Yellowstone . . . . Wyoming, Montana, Idaho

NATIONAL MILITARY PARKS/BATTLEFIELDS/BATTLEFIELD PARKS/SITES

Horseshoe Bend . . . . . . Alabama
Pea Ridge . . . . Arkansas
Chickamauga and
Chattanooga . . . . Georgia, Tennessee
Kennesaw Mountain . . . Georgia
Antietam . . . . Maryland
Monocacy . . . . Maryland
Brice Cross Roads . . . . . Mississippi
Tupelo . . . . Mississippi
Vicksburg . . . . Mississippi
Wilson's Creek . . . . Missouri
Big Hole . . . . Montana
Guilford Courthouse . . . North Carolina

Moores Creek . . . . North Carolina
Fort Necessity . . . . Pennsylvania
Gettysburg . . . . Pennsylvania
Cowpens . . . . South Carolina
Kings Mountain . . . . South Carolina
Fort Donelson . . . . Tennessee
Shiloh . . . . Tennessee
Stones River . . . . Tennessee
Fredericksburg and
Spotsylvania County
Battlefields Memorial . . Virginia
Manassas . . . . Virginia
Petersburg . . . . Virginia
Richmond . . . . Virginia

NATIONAL MONUMENTS AND THEIR LOCATIONS

Russell Cave .... Alabama
Admiralty Island ...... Alaska
Aniakchak .... Alaska
Cape Krusenstern ..... Alaska
Misty Fiords.......... Alaska
Canyon de Chelly...... Arizona
Casa Grande .... Arizona
Chiricahua .... Arizona
Hohokam Pima .... Arizona
Montezuma Castle..... Arizona
Navajo .... Arizona
Organ Pipe Cactus..... Arizona
Pipe Spring .... Arizona
Saguaro (Giant Cactus). Arizona
Sunset Crater......... Arizona
Tonto .... Arizona
Tumacacori .... Arizona
Tuzigoot .... Arizona
Walnut Canyon........ Arizona
Wupatki .... Arizona
Cabrillo .... California
Death Valley .... California,
Nevada
Devils Postpile .... California
Joshua Tree .... California
Lava Beds .... California
Muir Woods .... California
Pinnacles .... California
Black Canyon of the
Gunnison .... Colorado
Colorado .... Colorado
Dinosaur .... Colorado, Utah
Florissant Fossil Beds.. Colorado
Great Sand Dunes ..... Colorado
Hovenweep .... Colorado, Utah
Yucca House .... Colorado
Castillo de San Marcos. Florida
Fort Jefferson .... Florida
Fort Matanzas .... Florida
Fort Frederica .... Georgia
Fort Pulaski .... Georgia
Ocmulgee............ Georgia
Craters of the Moon.... Idaho
Effigy Mounds .... Iowa
Saint Croix Island ..... Maine

Fort McHenry......... Maryland
Pipestone............ Minnesota
Grand Portage .... Minnesota
George Washington
Carver .... Missouri
Custer Battlefield...... Montana
Agate Fossil Beds ..... Nebraska
Homestead........... Nebraska
Scotts Bluff .... Nebraska
Lehman Caves........ Nevada
Aztec Ruins .... New Mexico
Bandelier .... New Mexico
Capulin Mountain ..... New Mexico
Chaco Canyon .... New Mexico
El Morro............. New Mexico
Gran Quivira .... New Mexico
Fort Union .... New Mexico
Gila Cliff Dwellings .... New Mexico
Pecos .... New Mexico
Salinas.............. New Mexico
White Sands .... New Mexico
Statue of Liberty ...... New Jersey,
New York
Castle Clinton .... New York
Fort Stanwix.......... New York
Mound City Group ..... Ohio
John Day Fossil Beds .. Oregon
Mount St. Helens
Volcano .... Oregon
Oregon Caves .... Oregon
Congaree Swamp ..... South Carolina
Fort Sumter .... South Carolina
Jewel Cave........... South Dakota
Alibates Flint Quarries . Texas
Cedar Breaks......... Utah
Natural Bridges .... Utah
Rainbow Bridge....... Utah
Timpanogos Cave ..... Utah
Buck Island Reef ...... Virgin Islands
Booker T. Washington .. Virginia
George Washington
Birthplace .... Virginia
Devils Tower .... Wyoming
Fossil Butte .... Wyoming

NATIONAL LAKESHORES/SEASHORES AND THEIR LOCATIONS

Point Reyes .... California
Canaveral............ Florida
Gulf Islands .... Florida,
Mississippi
Cumberland Island .... Georgia
Indiana Dunes .... Indiana
Assateague Island..... Maryland,
Virginia

Cape Cod .... Massachusetts
Pictured Rocks........ Michigan
Sleeping Bear Dunes... Michigan
Fire Island .... New York
Cape Hatteras .... North Carolina
Cape Lookout......... North Carolina
Padre Island .... Texas
Apostle Islands .... Wisconsin

NATIONAL HISTORICAL PARKS AND THEIR LOCATIONS

Klondike Gold Rush....	Alaska, Washington
Sitka................	Alaska
Chesapeake and Ohio Canal..........	District of Columbia, Maryland, West Virginia
War in the Pacific	Guam
Kalaupapa	Hawaii
Kaloko-Honokohau	Hawaii
Puuhonua o Honaunau .	Hawaii
Nez Percé...........	Idaho
George Rogers Clark...	Indiana
Cumberland Gap	Kentucky, Tennessee, Virginia
Jean Lafitte	Louisiana
Harpers Ferry.........	Maryland, West Virginia
Boston	Massachusetts
Lowell	Massachusetts
Minute Man	Massachusetts
Morristown..........	New Jersey
Chaco Culture	New Mexico
Saratoga	New York
Women's Rights.......	New York
Independence	Pennsylvania
Valley Forge..........	Pennsylvania
Lyndon B. Johnson	Texas
San Antonio Missions ..	Texas
Appomattox Court House	Virginia
Colonial	Virginia
San Juan Island.......	Washington

NATIONAL HISTORIC SITES AND THEIR LOCATIONS

Tuskegee Institute	Alabama
Fort Bowie	Arizona
Hubbell Trading Post...	Arizona
Fort Smith	Arkansas, Oklahoma
Eugene O'Neil	California
Fort Point............	California
John Muir............	California
Bent's Old Fort........	Colorado
Ford's Theatre	District of Columbia
Sewall-Belmont House .	District of Columbia
Andersonville.........	Georgia
Martin Luther King, Jr. .	Georgia
Puukohola Heiau	Hawaii
Lincoln Home	Illinois
Herbert Hoover	Iowa
Fort Larned	Kansas
Fort Scott	Kansas
Abraham Lincoln Birthplace	Kentucky
Clara Barton..........	Maryland
Hampton	Maryland
Thomas Stone	Maryland
U.S.S. *Constellation* ...	Maryland
Adams	Massachusetts
Boston African American	Massachusetts
Frederick Law Olmstead	Massachusetts
John Fitzgerald Kennedy	Massachusetts
Longfellow...........	Massachusetts
Salem Maritime.......	Massachusetts
Saugus Iron Works	Massachusetts
Springfield Armory	Massachusetts
Jefferson National Expansion Memorial ...	Missouri
Fort Union Trading Post	Montana, North Dakota
Grant-Kohrs Ranch	Montana
Saint-Gaudens........	New Hampshire
Edison	New Jersey
Georgia O'Keefe	New Mexico
Eleanor Roosevelt	New York
Home of Franklin D. Roosevelt	New York
Martin Van Buren	New York
Sagamore Hill	New York
Theodore Roosevelt Birthplace	New York
Theodore Roosevelt Inaugural	New York
Vanderbilt Mansion	New York
Carl Sandburg Home...	North Carolina
Fort Raleigh..........	North Carolina
Knife River Indian Villages	North Dakota
James A. Garfield	Ohio
William Howard Taft ...	Ohio
Allegheny Portage Railroad	Pennsylvania
Edgar Allan Poe.......	Pennsylvania
Eisenhower	Pennsylvania
Friendship Hill........	Pennsylvania
Hopewell Village	Pennsylvania
San Juan	Puerto Rico
Ninety Six	South Carolina
Andrew Johnson	Tennessee
Fort Davis	Texas
Palo Alto Battlefield ...	Texas
Golden Spike	Utah
Christiansted	Virgin Islands
Maggie L. Walker	Virginia
Fort Vancouver	Washington
Whitman Mission	Washington
Fort Laramie	Wyoming

NATIONAL MEMORIALS AND THEIR LOCATIONS

Coronado	Arizona
Arkansas Post	Arkansas
John F. Kennedy Center for the Performing Arts .	District of Columbia
LBJ Memorial Grove on the Potomac	District of Columbia
Lincoln Memorial	District of Columbia
Theodore Roosevelt Island	District of Columbia
Thomas Jefferson Memorial	District of Columbia
Vietnam Veterans Memorial	District of Columbia
Washington Monument .	District of Columbia
De Soto	Florida
Fort Caroline	Florida
U.S.S. *Arizona*	Hawaii
Lincoln Boyhood	Indiana
Federal Hall	New York
General Grant	New York
Hamilton Grange	New York
Wright Brothers	North Carolina
Fort Clatsop	Oregon
Johnstown Flood	Pennsylvania
Thaddeus Kosciuszko . .	Pennsylvania
Mount Rushmore	South Dakota
Roger Williams	Rhode Island
Chamizal	Texas
Arlington House, Robert E. Lee Memorial	Virginia

NATIONAL RECREATION AREAS AND THEIR LOCATIONS

Glen Canyon	Arizona, Utah
Lake Mead	Arizona, Nevada
Golden Gate	California
Santa Monica Mountains	California
Whiskeytown-Shasta-Trinity	California
Curecanti	Colorado
Chattahoochee River . . .	Georgia
Bighorn Canyon	Montana, Wyoming
Delaware Water Gap . . .	New Jersey, Pennsylvania
Gateway	New Jersey, New York
Cuyahoga Valley	Ohio
Chickasaw	Oklahoma
Amistad	Texas
Lake Meredith	Texas
Coulee Dam	Washington
Lake Chelan	Washington
Ross Lake	Washington

NATIONAL PRESERVES AND THEIR LOCATIONS

Aniakchak	Alaska
Bering Land Bridge	Alaska
Denali	Alaska
Gates of the Arctic	Alaska
Glacier Bay	Alaska
Katmai	Alaska
Lake Clark	Alaska
Noatak	Alaska
Wrangell-St. Elias	Alaska
Yukon-Charley Rivers . .	Alaska
Big Cypress	Florida
Big Thicket	Texas

PARKWAYS AND OTHER NATIONAL PARKLANDS AND THEIR LOCATIONS

Natchez Trace Parkway	Alabama, Mississippi, Tennessee
Buffalo National River	Arkansas
Frederick Douglass Home	District of Columbia
National Capitol Parks	District of Columbia, Maryland, Virginia
National Mall	District of Columbia
National Visitor Center	District of Columbia
Rock Creek Park	District of Columbia
White House	District of Columbia
Big South Fork National River and Recreation Area	Kentucky, Tennessee
Appalachian National Scenic Trail	Maine to Georgia

Catoctin Mountain Park . . . . Maryland
Fort Washington Park . . . . Maryland
George Washington Memorial Parkway . . Maryland, Virginia
Greenbelt Park . . . . Maryland
Piscataway Park . . . . Maryland
Lower Saint Croix National Scenic River . Minnesota, Wisconsin
Saint Croix National Scenic River . . . . Minnesota, Wisconsin
Ozark National Scenic Riverways . . . . Missouri
Fort Benton . . . . Montana
Delaware National Scenic River . . . . New Jersey, New York, Pennsylvania
Upper Delaware Scenic and
Recreational Area . . . . New York, Pennsylvania
Blue Ridge Parkway . . . . North Carolina, Virginia
Perry's Victory and International
Peace Memorial . . . . Ohio
Obed Wild and Scenic River . . . . Tennessee
Rio Grande Wild and Scenic River . . . . . . Texas
Prince William Forest Park . . . . Virginia
Wolf Trap Farm Park for the Performing Arts Virginia
New River Gorge National River . . . . West Virginia
John D. Rockefeller, Jr., Memorial
Parkway . . . . Wyoming

SCENIC SITES LOCATED IN SEVERAL STATES

Apache National Forest . . . . Arizona and New Mexico
Appalachian Scenic Trail . . . . Maine to Georgia (in 14 states)
Assateague Island Seashore . . . . Maryland and Virginia
Bighorn Canyon Recreational Area . . . . . . Wyoming and Montana
Big South Fork National River and
Recreational Area . . . . Kentucky and Tennessee
Bitterroot National Forest . . . . Idaho and Montana
Black Hills National Forest . . . . South Dakota and Wyoming
Blue Ridge Mountain Range . . . . S. Pennsylvania to N. Georgia
Blue Ridge Mountains . . . . N. Virginia to N. Georgia
Blue Ridge National Parkway . . . . Virginia and North Carolina
Caribou National Forest . . . . Idaho, Utah, and Wyoming
Chesapeake and Ohio Canal . . . . Maryland, West Virginia, and Washington,
                                                  D.C.
Chickamauga and Chattanooga
National Military Parks . . . . Georgia and Tennessee
Chimney Topps Mountain . . . . North Carolina and Tennessee
Clingmans Dome . . . . North Carolina and Tennessee
Columbia River(Gorge) . . . . Washington and Oregon (and British Colum-
                                                  bia)
Coronado National Forest . . . . Arizona and New Mexico
Cumberland Gap . . . . Kentucky, Tennessee, and Virginia
Custer National Forest . . . . Montana and South Dakota
Death Valley . . . . California and Nevada
Delaware Water Gap . . . . Pennsylvania and New Jersey
Delmarva Peninsula . . . . Delaware, Maryland, and Virginia
Dinosaur National Monument . . . . Colorado and Utah
Dismal Swamp . . . . Virginia and North Carolina
Flaming Gorge Recreational Area . . . . Utah and Wyoming
Fort Smith Historic Site . . . . Arkansas and Oklahoma
Fort Union Trading Post Historic Site . . . . North Dakota and Montana
Gateway Recreational Area . . . . New York and New Jersey
George Washington Bridge . . . . New York and New Jersey
George Washington Memorial Parkway . . Maryland and Virginia

George Washington National Forest . . . . . Virginia and West Virginia
Glen Canyon Recreational Area . . . . Arizona and Utah
Great Smoky Mountains . . . . Tennessee and North Carolina
Green River . . . . Utah, Wyoming, and Colorado
Gulf Islands National Seashore . . . . Florida and Mississippi
Harpers Ferry Historical Park . . . . West Virginia and Maryland
Hell's Canyon . . . . Idaho and Oregon
Hoover Dam . . . . Arizona and Nevada
Hovenweep National Monumet . . . . Utah and Colorado
Hudson Valley . . . . New York and New Jersey
Jefferson National Forest . . . . Kentucky, Virginia, and West Virginia
Kaniksu National Forest . . . . Idaho, Montana, and Washington
Klamath National Forest . . . . California and Oregon
Klondike Gold Rush Historical Park . . . . . . Alaska and Washington
Kootenai National Forest . . . . Idaho and Montana
Lake Mead Recreational Area . . . . Arizona and Nevada
Lake Mohave . . . . Arizona and Nevada
Lake Tahoe . . . . California and Nevada
Land Between the Lakes Recreation Area . Kentucky and Tennessee
Lookout Mountain . . . . Tennessee, Georgia, and Alabama
Mississippi Palisades . . . . Iowa, Illinois, and Wisconsin
Mojave Desert . . . . California, Nevada, and Arizona
Monument Valley . . . . Arizona and Utah
Natchez Trace Parkway . . . . Alabama, Mississippi, and Tennessee
Ouachita National Forest . . . . Arkansas and Oklahoma
Ozark Mountains . . . . Arkansas, Missouri, and Oklahoma
Red River . . . . Louisiana, Oklahoma, Texas, and Arkansas
Rogue River National Forest . . . . California and Oregon
Saint Croix River Scenic Waterway . . . . . . Wisconsin and Minnesota
Sawtooth National Forest . . . . Idaho and Utah
Snake River . . . . Idaho, Oregon, Wyoming, and Washington
Statue of Liberty National Monument . . . . New York and New Jersey
Targhee National Forest . . . . Idaho and Wyoming
Umatilla National Forest . . . . Oregon and Washington
Wasatch National Forest . . . . Utah and Wyoming
White Mountain National Forest . . . . Maine and New Hampshire
Yellowstone National Park . . . . Idaho, Montana, and Wyoming

STATES AND THEIR MOTTOES

Alabama . . . . *Audemus jura nostra defendere* ("We dare defend our rights")
Alaska . . . . North to the Future
Arizona . . . . *Ditat Deus* ("God enriches")
Arkansas . . . . *Regnat Populus* ("The People rule")
California . . . . *Eureka* ("I have found [it]")
Colorado . . . . *Nil Sine Numine* ("Nothing without the divine will [the deity]")
Connecticut . . . . *Qui Transtulit Sustinet* ("He who transplanted still sustains")
Delaware . . . . Liberty and Independence
Florida . . . . In God We Trust
Georgia . . . . Wisdom, Justice, and Moderation
Hawaii . . . . *Ua Mau Ke Ea O Ka Aina I Ka Pono* ("The life of the land is
perpetuated in [preserved by] righteousness")
Idaho . . . . *Esto Perpetua* ("May she [it] endure forever")
Illinois . . . . State Sovereignty--National Union
Indiana . . . . (The) Crossroads of America
Iowa . . . . Our liberties we prize and our rights we will maintain
Kansas . . . . *Ad Astra Per Aspera* ("To the Stars through Difficulties")
Kentucky . . . . United We Stand, Divided We Fall

Louisiana	Union, Justice, and Confidence
Maine	*Dirigo* ("I direct")
Maryland	*Fatti Maschii, Parole Femine* ("Manly deeds, womanly words" or "Deeds are males, words are females")
Massachusetts	*Ense Petit Placidam Sub Libertate Quietem* ("By the sword we seek peace, but peace only under liberty")
Michigan	*Si Quaeris Peninsulam Amoenam Circumspice* ("If you seek a pleasant peninsula, look around you")
Minnesota	*L'Étoile Du Nord* ("The North Star")
Mississippi	*Virtute et Armis* ("By Valor and Arms")
Missouri	*Salus Populi Suprema Lex Esto* ("The welfare of the people shall be [should be] the supreme law")
Montana	*Oro y Plata* ("Gold and Silver")
Nebraska	Equality Before the Law
Nevada	All for Our Country
New Hampshire	Live Free or Die
New Jersey	Liberty and Prosperity
New Mexico	*Crescit Eundo* ("It grows as it goes")
New York	*Excelsior* ("Ever Upward" or "Still Higher")
North Carolina	*Esse Quam Videri* ("To be rather than to seem")
North Dakota	Liberty and Union, Now and Forever, One and Inseparable
Ohio	With God, all things are possible
Oklahoma	*Labor Omnia Vincit* ("Labor conquers all things")
Oregon	The Union
Pennsylvania	Virtue, Liberty, and Independence
Rhode Island	Hope
South Carolina	*Animis Opibusque Parati* ("Prepared in soul [mind] and resources") and *Dum Spiro, Spero* ("While I breathe, I hope")
South Dakota	Under God the People Rule
Tennessee	Agriculture and Commerce and "Tennessee--America at its best"
Texas	Friendship
Utah	Industry
Vermont	Freedom and Unity
Virginia	*Sic semper tyrannis* ("Thus always to tyrants")
Washington	*Al-Ki* (Chinook for "By and By")
West Virginia	*Montani semper liberi* ("Mountaineers are always free [freemen]")
Wisconsin	Forward
Wyoming	Equal Rights
Washington, D.C.	*Justitia Omnibus* ("Justice to all")
United States	*E Pluribus Unum* ("One out of many" or "From many, one") and "In God We Trust"
On the reverse of the Great Seal of the United States	*Annuit Coeptis* ("He [God] has smiled on our undertakings") and *Novus Ordo Seclorum* ("A new order of the ages")

STATE BIRDS/FLOWERS/TREES

Alabama	Yellowhammer	Camellia	Southern (longleaf) pine
Alaska	Willow ptarmigan	Forget-me-not	Sitka spruce
Arizona	Cactus wren	Saguaro (cactus) blossom	Paloverde
Arkansas	Mockingbird	Apple blossom	Pine
California	California valley quail	Golden poppy	California redwood
Colorado	Lark bunting	Rocky Mountain columbine	Blue spruce

Connecticut	American robin	Mountain laurel	White oak
Delaware	Blue hen chicken	Peach blossom	American holly
Florida	Mockingbird	Orange blossom	Sabal palmetto palm
Georgia	Brown thrasher	Cherokee rose	Live oak
Hawaii	Nene (Hawaiian goose)	Hibiscus	Kukui (Candlenut)
Idaho	Mountain bluebird	Syringa (Mock Orange)	Western white pine
Illinois	Eastern cardinal	Native violet	White oak
Indiana	Cardinal	Peony	Tulip tree, or yellow poplar
Iowa	Eastern goldfinch	Wild rose	Oak
Kansas	Western meadowlark	Sunflower	Cottonwood
Kentucky	Kentucky cardinal	Goldenrod	Kentucky coffee tree
Louisiana	Eastern brown pelican	Magnolia	Bald cypress
Maine	Chickadee	White pine cone and tassel	Eastern white pine
Maryland	Baltimore oriole	Black-eyed Susan	White Oak
Massachusetts	Chickadee	Arbutus (Mayflower)	American elm
Michigan	Robin	Apple blossom	White pine
Minnesota	Common loon	Pink and white lady's slipper	Norway, or red pine
Mississippi	Mockingbird	Magnolia	Magnolia
Missouri	Bluebird	Hawthorn	Flowering dogwood
Montana	Western meadowlark	Bitteroot	Ponderosa pine
Nebraska	Western meadowlark	Goldenrod	Cottonwood
Nevada	Mountain Bluebird	Sagebrush	Single-leaf piñon
New Hampshire	Purple finch	Purple lilac	White birch
New Jersey	Eastern goldfinch	Purple violet	Red oak
New Mexico	Roadrunner	Yucca flower	Piñon, or nut pine
New York	Bluebird	Rose	Sugar maple
North Carolina	Cardinal	Flowering dogwood	Pine
North Dakota	Western meadowlark	Wild prairie rose	American elm
Ohio	Cardinal	Scarlet carnation	Buckeye
Oklahoma	Scissor-tailed flycatcher	Mistletoe	Redbud
Oregon	Western meadowlark	Oregon grape	Douglas fir
Pennsylvania	Ruffed grouse	Mountain laurel	Hemlock
Rhode Island	Rhode Island red	Violet	Red maple
South Carolina	Carolina wren	Carolina jessamine	Palmetto
South Dakota	Ring-necked pheasant	American pasqueflower	Black Hills spruce
Tennessee	Mockingbird	Iris	Tulip poplar
Texas	Mockingbird	Bluebonnet	Pecan
Utah	Sea gull	Sego lily	Blue spruce
Vermont	Hermit thrush	Red clover	Sugar maple
Virginia	Cardinal	American dogwood	Flowering dogwood
Washington	Willow goldfinch	Western rhododendron	Western hemlock
West Virginia	Cardinal	Rhododendron	Sugar maple
Wisconsin	Robin	Wood violet	Sugar maple
Wyoming	Meadowlark	Indian paintbrush	Cottonwood

STATES AND THEIR STATE SONGS

Alabama	"Alabama"
Alaska	"Alaska's Flag"
Arizona	"Arizona"
Arkansas	"Arkansas"
California	"I Love You, California"
Colorado	"Where the Columbine Grows"
Connecticut	"Yankee Doodle"
Delaware	"Our Delaware"
Florida	"Swanee River"
Georgia	"Georgia on My Mind"
Hawaii	"Hawaii Ponoi" ("Hawaii's Own")
Idaho	"Here We Have Idaho"
Illinois	"Illinois"
Indiana	"On the Banks of the Wabash, Far Away"
Iowa	"The Song of Iowa"
Kansas	"Home on the Range"
Kentucky	"My Old Kentucky Home"
Louisiana	"Give Me Louisiana"; "You Are My Sunshine"

Maine	"State of Maine Song"	Pennsylvania	none
Maryland	"Maryland, My Maryland"	Rhode Island	"Rhode Island"
Massachusetts	"All Hail to Massachusetts"	South Carolina	"Carolina"
Michigan	"Michigan, My Michigan"	South Dakota	"Hail, South Dakota"
Minnesota	"Hail Minnesota"	Tennessee	"The Tennessee Waltz";
Mississippi	"Go Mis-sis-sip-pi"		"When It's Iris Time in Ten-
Missouri	"Missouri Waltz"		nessee"; "My Tennessee"
Montana	"Montana"	Texas	"Texas, Our Texas"
Nebraska	"Beautiful Nebraska"	Utah	"Utah, We Love Thee"
Nevada	"Home Means Nevada"	Vermont	"Hail, Vermont!"
New Hampshire	"Old New Hampshire"	Virginia	"Carry Me Back to Old Vir- ginia (Virginny)"
New Jersey	none	Washington	"Washington, My Home"
New Mexico	"O, Fair New Mexico"	West Virginia	"The West Virginia Hills";
New York	"I Love New York"		"This is My West Virginia";
North Carolina	"The Old North State"		"West Virginia My Home
North Dakota	"North Dakota Hymn"		Sweet Home"
Ohio	"Beautiful Ohio"	Wisconsin	"On, Wisconsin"
Oklahoma	"Oklahoma!"	Wyoming	"Wyoming"
Oregon	"Oregon, My Oregon"		

CITIES AND BODIES OF WATER ON WHICH THEY ARE LOCATED

(The bodies of water are rivers unless otherwise noted)

Mobile, Ala. .... Mobile and Mobile Bay (north of the Gulf of Mexico)
Montgomery, Ala. .... Alabama
Phenix City, Ala. .... Chattahoochee
Anchorage, Alas. ...... Cook Inlet
Fairbanks, Alas. .... Chena
Juneau, Alas. .... Gastineau Channel
Mesa, Ariz. .... Salt
Phoenix, Ariz. .... Salt
Tucson, Ariz. .... Santa Cruz
Fort Smith, Ark. .... Poteau and Arkansas
Little Rock, Ark. .... Arkansas
North Little Rock, Ark. ... Arkansas
Los Angeles, Calif. ..... Santa Monica Bay, San Pedro Bay, and the Pacific Ocean
Sacramento, Calif. ..... Sacramento and American
San Diego, Calif. ...... San Diego Bay and the Pacific Ocean
San Francisco, Calif. ... Golden Gate and San Francisco Bay and the Pacific Ocean
Aurora, Colo. .... Sand Creek
Denver, Colo. .... South Platte and Cherry Creek
Bridgeport, Conn. ...... Long Island Sound and the Pequonnock
Hartford, Conn. .... Connecticut
New Haven, Conn. ..... Long Island Sound and New Haven Harbor
Dover, Del. .... St. Jones
Wilmington, Del. ...... Brandywine Creek, Christina, and the Delaware
Jacksonville, Fla. ...... St. Johns River (Atlantic Ocean)
Miami, Fla. .... Biscayne Bay and the Miami (Atlantic Ocean)
Tampa, Fla. .... Tampa Bay and the Hillsborough (Gulf of Mexico)
Honolulu, Haw. .... Mamala Bay and the Pacific Ocean
Kailua, Haw. .... Kailua Bay and the Pacific Ocean
Hilo, Haw. .... Hilo Bay and the Pacific Ocean
Boise, Ida. .... Boise
Idaho Falls, Ida. .... Snake
Chicago, Ill. .... Chicago and Lake Michigan
Peoria, Ill. .... Illinois (Lake Peoria)
Rockford, Ill. .... Rock
Springfield, Ill. .... Lake Springfield

Fort Wayne, Ind. . . . . St. Marys and St. Joseph, which form the Maumee
Gary, Ind. . . . . Lake Michigan
Indianapolis, Ind. . . . . . . White (West Fork)
Cedar Rapids, Ia. . . . . . . Cedar
Davenport, Ia. . . . . Mississippi
Des Moines, Ia. . . . . Des Moines and Raccoon
Kansas City, Kans. . . . . . Kansas and Missouri
Topeka, Kans. . . . . Kansas (Kaw)
Wichita, Kans. . . . . Arkansas
Frankfort, Ky. . . . . Kentucky
Louisville, Ky. . . . . Ohio
Owensboro, KY. . . . . Ohio
Baton Rouge, La. . . . . . . Mississippi
New Orleans, La. . . . . . . Mississippi and Lake Pontchartrain
Shreveport, La. . . . . Red
Augusta, Me. . . . . Kennebec
Bangor, Me. . . . . Penobscot
Lewiston, Me. . . . . Androscoggin
Portland, Me. . . . . Casco Bay
Annapolis, Md. . . . . Severn and the Chesapeake Bay
Baltimore, Md. . . . . Patapsco and the Chesapeake Bay
Hagerstown, Md. . . . . . . Antietam Creek (nearby)
Boston, Mass. . . . . Massachusetts Bay, Charles, Neponset, Chelsea, and Mystic
Springfield, Mass. . . . . . Connecticut
Worcester, Mass. . . . . . . Lake Quinsigamond and the Blackstone
Detroit, Mich. . . . . Detroit and Lake St. Clair
Grand Rapids, Mich. . . . Grand
Lansing, Mich. . . . . Grand, Red Cedar, and Sycamore
Duluth, Minn. . . . . St. Louis Bay and Lake Superior
Minneapolis, Minn. . . . . Mississippi and the Falls of St. Anthony
St. Paul, Minn. . . . . Mississippi at the mouth of the Minnesota
Biloxi, Miss. . . . . Biloxi Bay and Mississippi Sound (Gulf of Mexico)
Jackson, Miss. . . . . Pearl
Jefferson City, Mo. . . . . . Missouri
Kansas City, Mo. . . . . . . Kansas (Kaw) and the Missouri
St. Louis, Mo. . . . . Mississippi
Billings, Mont. . . . . Yellowstone
Butte, Mont. . . . . Clark Fork
Great Falls, Mont. . . . . . Missouri
Grand Island, Neb. . . . . . Platte (nearby)
Lincoln, Neb. . . . . Salt Creek
Omaha, Neb. . . . . Missouri
Reno, Nev. . . . . Truckee
Concord, N.H. . . . . Merrimack
Manchester, N.H. . . . . . . Merrimack at the mouth of the Piscataquog
Nashua, N.H. . . . . Merrimack and Nashua
Jersey City, N.J. . . . . Hudson and Hackensack and Newark Bay
Newark, N.J. . . . . Newark Bay and the Passaic
Patterson, N.J. . . . . Passaic
Trenton, N.J. . . . . Delaware and Assunpink Creek
Albuquerque, N.M. . . . . . Rio Grande
Las Cruces, N.M. . . . . . . Rio Grande
Santa Fe, N.M. . . . . Santa Fe
Albany, N.Y. . . . . Hudson
Buffalo, N.Y. . . . . Niagara and Lake Erie
New York, N.Y. . . . . Hudson, East, Long Island Sound, Atlantic Ocean
Rochester, N.Y. . . . . Genesee, New York State Barge Canal, and Lake Ontario
Bismark, N.D. . . . . Missouri
Fargo, N.D. . . . . Red River of the North

Grand Forks, N.D....... Red and Red Lake rivers
Cincinnati, O. .... Ohio
Cleveland, O. .... Lake Erie and the Cuyahoga
Columbus, O. .... Olentangy and the Scioto
Lawton, Okla. .... Cache Creek
Oklahoma City, Okla. ... North Canadian
Tulsa, Okla............ Arkansas
Eugene, Oreg.......... Willamette
Portland, Oreg......... Willamette and Columbia (nearby)
Salem, Oreg. .... Willamette
Erie, Penn. .... Lake Erie
Harrisburg, Penn....... Susquehanna
Philadelphia, Penn. .... Delaware and the Schuylkill
Pittsburgh, Penn. ...... Allegheny and the Monongahela, which form the Ohio
Cranston, R.I.......... Pawtuxet
Providence, R.I. .... Narragansett Bay
Warwick, R.I. .... Pawtuxet, East Greenwich Bay, and Narragansett Bay
Charleston, S.C........ Ashley and the Cooper
Columbia, S.C......... Broad and the Saluda, which form the Congaree
Greenville, S.C. .... Reedy
Pierre, S.D............ Missouri
Rapid City, S.D. .... Rapid Creek
Sioux Falls, S.D. ...... Big Sioux
Knoxville, Tenn. .... Holton and French Broad, which form the Tennessee
Memphis, Tenn. .... Mississippi and the Wolf
Nashville, Tenn. .... Cumberland
Austin, Tex............ Colorado
Dallas, Tex............ Trinity
Houston, Tex. .... Houston Ship Channel
San Antonio, Tex....... San Antonio
Odgen, Ut............. Weber and the Ogden
Provo, Ut. .... Provo
Burlington, Vt. .... Lake Champlain
Montpelier, Vt. .... Winooski and the North Branch
Norfolk, Va............ Elizabeth and Hampton Roads Channel at the Chesapeake Bay
Richmond, Va. .... James
Virginia Beach, Va...... Atlantic Ocean
Olympia, Wash. .... Puget Sound and the Deschutes
Seattle, Wash. .... Elliot Bay (Puget Sound) and Lake Washington
Spokane, Wash. .... Spokane
Tacoma, Wash......... Commencement Bay, Puget Sound, and the Puyallup
Charleston, W. Va. ..... Great Kanawha at the mouth of the Elk
Huntington, W. Va...... Ohio and the Guyandotte (nearby)
Wheeling, W. Va. ...... Ohio
Green Bay, Wis. .... Green Bay at the mouth of the Fox
Madison, Wis. .... Between Lakes Menona and Mendota and Lake Wingra, Lake
                       Kegonsa, Lake Waubesa, and the Yahara
Milwaukee, Wis........ Lake Michigan at the mouth of the Menomonee, the Milwaukee,
                       and the Kinnickinnic
Casper, Wyo........... North Platte
Laramie, Wyo. .... Laramie

RIVERS AND BODIES OF WATER INTO WHICH THEY EMPTY

(The rivers are listed from the longest to the shortest)

Mississippi	Gulf of Mexico	Colorado	Gulf of California
Missouri	Mississippi	Brazos	Gulf of Mexico
Rio Grande	Gulf of Mexico	Ohio-Allegheny	Mississippi
Arkansas	Mississippi	Columbia	Pacific Ocean

Red	Mississippi	White (Mo.-Ark)	Mississippi
Snake	Columbia	Tennessee	Ohio
Ohio	Mississippi	Gila	Colorado
Pecos	Rio Grande	Tombigbee	Mobile
Green (Wyo.-Col.-Utah)	Colorado	Apalachicola-	
James (N.D.-S.D.)	Missouri	Chattahoochee	Gulf of Mexico
Cimarron	Arkansas	White (S. Dak.-Neb.)	Missouri
Cumberland	Ohio	Susquehanna	Chesapeake Bay

CITIES AND THEIR FORMER NAME OR NAMES

Montgomery, Alabama	East Alabama and New Philadelphia
Anchorage, Alaska	Ship Creek/Woodrow
Sitka, Alaska	New Archangel
Yuma, Arizona	Colorado City/Arizona City/San Dionisio
San Francisco, California	Yerba Buena (Good Herb)
Bridgeport, Connecticut	Stratfield/Newfield
New Haven, Connecticut	Quinnipiac
Jacksonville, Florida	Cow Ford
Atlanta, Georgia	Terminus/Marthasville
Frankfort, Kentucky	Frank's Ford
Louisville, Kentucky	Falls of the Ohio
Owensboro, Kentucky	Yellow Banks
Augusta, Maine	Cushnoc (trading post)/Hallowell/Harlington
Bangor, Maine	Keduskeag
Portland, Maine	Machigonne/Falmouth
Cambridge, Massachusetts	Newtowne
Worcester, Massachusetts	Quinsigamond
Detroit, Michigan	Fort Pontchartrain/Fort Lernoult
St. Paul, Minnesota	Fort Saint Anthony/Fort Snelling/Pig's Eye
Jackson, Mississippi	LeFleur's Bluff
Kansas City, Missouri	Chouteau's Landing/Westport
Helena, Montana	Last Chance Gulch
Lincoln, Nebraska	Lancaster
Concord, New Hampshire	Penacook/Rumford/Plantation of Penny Cook
Manchester, New Hampshire	Harrytown/Derryfield
Nashua, New Hampshire	Dunstable
Albany, New York	Fort Orange
Kingston, New York	Wiltwyck
New York, New York	New Amsterdam
Bismarck, North Dakota	Edwinton
Cincinnati, Ohio	Losantiville
Salem, Oregon	Chemeketa
Newark, Rhode Island	Aquidneck
Warwick, Rhode Island	Shawomet
Greenville, South Carolina	Pleasantburg
Chattanooga, Tennessee	Ross' Landing
Memphis, Tennessee	Fort Prudhomme
Nashville, Tennessee	Fort Nashborough
Austin, Texas	Waterloo
Barre, Vermont	Wildersburgh
Roanoke, Virginia	Big Lick
Williamsburg, Virginia	Middle Plantation
Olympia, Washington	Smithfield
Tacoma, Washington	Commencement City
Casper, Wyoming	Platte Bridge Station

STATES AND SOME OF THEIR CAPITALS
(including territorial ones)

Alabama . . . . St. Stephens, Huntsville, Cahaba, Tuscaloosa, Montgomery (1846)

Alaska . . . . Sitka, Juneau (1959; district capital in 1900), Willow (future)

Arizona . . . . Fort Whipple, Prescott, Tucson, Prescott, Phoenix (1889)

Arkansas . . . . Arkansas Post, Little Rock (1821)

California . . . . Monterey, San Jose, Vallejo, Benicia, San Francisco, Sacramento (1854)

Colorado . . . . Colorado City (Colorado Springs), Golden, Denver (1867)

Connecticut . . . . New Haven and Hartford, Hartford (1875)

Delaware . . . . New Castle, Dover (1777)

Florida . . . . Tallahassee (1824)

Georgia . . . . Savannah, Augusta, Louisville, Milledgeville, Atlanta (1868)

Hawaii . . . . Honolulu (1959)

Idaho . . . . Lewiston, Boise (1864)

Illinois . . . . Kaskaskia, Vandalia, Springfield (1839)

Indiana . . . . Vincennes, Corydon, Indianapolis (1825)

Iowa . . . . Burlington, Iowa City, Des Moines (1857)

Kansas . . . . Fort Leavenworth, Shawnee Mission, Pawnee, Lecompton, Topeka (1861)

Kentucky . . . . Lexington, Frankfort (1793)

Louisiana . . . . New Orleans (3 times), Donaldsonville, Baton Rouge, Opelousas, Shreveport, Baton Rouge (1882)

Maine . . . . Portland, Augusta (1832)

Maryland . . . . St. Marys City, Annapolis (1694)

Massachusetts . . . . . . Boston (1630)

Michigan . . . . Detroit, Lansing (1847)

Minnesota . . . . St. Paul (1849)

Mississippi . . . . Natchez, Washington, Natchez, Columbia, Jackson (1822)

Missouri . . . . St. Louis, St. Charles, Jefferson City (1826)

Montana . . . . Bannack, Virginia City, Helena (1875)

Nebraska . . . . Omaha, Lincoln (1867)

Nevada . . . . Carson City (1861)

New Hampshire . . . . . . Portsmouth, Exeter, Concord (1808)

New Jersey . . . . Perth Amboy and Burlington, Trenton (1790)

New Mexico . . . . San Gabriel, Santa Fe (1610)

New York . . . . Kingston, Poughkeepsie, New York City, Albany (1797)

North Carolina . . . . . . New Bern, Raleigh (1792)

North Dakota . . . . Bismarck (1889)

Ohio . . . . Chillicothe, Zanesville, Chillicothe, Columbus (1816)

Oklahoma . . . . Guthrie, Oklahoma City (1910)

Oregon . . . . Oregon City, Salem, Corvallis, Salem (1855)

Pennsylvania . . . . Chester, Philadelphia, Lancaster, Harrisburg (1812)

Rhode Island . . . . Newport, East Greenwich, Bristol, South Kingston, Providence, Newport and Providence, Providence (1900)

South Carolina . . . . . . Charleston, Columbia (1790)

South Dakota . . . . Yankton, Pierre (1889)

Tennessee . . . . Knoxville, Murfreesboro, Nashville (1826)

Texas . . . . (many capitals during the Texas Revolution), Houston, Austin, Washington-on-the-Brazos, Austin (1845)

Utah . . . . Fillmore, Salt Lake City (1856)

Vermont . . . . (many earlier capitals), Montpelier (1805)

Virginia . . . . Jamestown, Williamsburg, Richmond (1780)

Washington . . . . Olympia (1889)

West Virginia . . . . Wheeling, Charleston (1885)

Wisconsin . . . . Belmont, Burlington (Iowa), Madison (1848)

Wyoming . . . . Cheyenne (1869)

STATES AND THEIR HIGHEST POINTS

Alabama . . . . . . Cheaha Mountain	Montana . . . . Granite Peak
Alaska . . . . Mt. McKinley	Nebraska . . . . Johnson T.
Arizona . . . . Humphreys Peak	Nevada . . . . Boundary Peak
Arkansas . . . . . Magazine Mountain	New Hampshire . . . Mt. Washington
California . . . . . Mt. Whitney	New Jersey . . . . . . High Point
Colorado . . . . . . Mt. Elbert	New Mexico . . . . . . Wheeler Peak
Connecticut . . . Mt. Frissell	New York . . . . Mt. Marcy
Delaware . . . . . Ebright Road	North Carolina . . . . Mt. Mitchell
Florida . . . . Sec. 30, T6N, R20'W	North Dakota . . . . . White Butte
Georgia . . . . . . Brasstown Bald	Ohio . . . . Campbell Hill
Hawaii . . . . Mauna Kea	Oklahoma . . . . Black Mesa
Idaho . . . . Borah Peak	Oregon . . . . Mt. Hood
Illinois . . . . Charles Mound	Pennsylvania . . . . . Mt. Davis
Indiana . . . . Franklin T	Rhode Island . . . . . Jerimoth Hill
Iowa . . . . Sec. 29, T100N, R41W	South Carolina . . . . Sassafras Mountain
Kansas . . . . Mt. Sunflower	South Dakota . . . . . Harney Peak
Kentucky . . . . . Black Mountain	Tennessee . . . . Clingmans Dome
Louisiana . . . . . Driskill Mountain	Texas . . . . Guadalupe Peak
Maine . . . . Mt. Katahdin	Utah . . . . Kings Peak
Maryland . . . . . Backbone Mountain	Vermont . . . . Mt. Mansfield
Massachusetts . Mt. Greylock	Virginia . . . . Mt. Rogers
Michigan . . . . . Mt. Curwood	Washington . . . . . . Mt. Rainier
Minnesota . . . . Eagle Mountain	West Virginia . . . . . Spruce Knob
Mississippi . . . . Woodall Mountain	Wisconsin . . . . Timms Hill
Missouri . . . . . . Taum Sauk Mountain	Wyoming . . . . Gannett Peak

QUESTIONS AND ANSWERS IN GENERAL

1. Name the 10 American Nobel Prize winners in literature.
ANSWER: Sinclair Lewis (1930)   Ernest Hemingway (1954)
Eugene Gladstone O'Neill (1936)   John Ernst Steinbeck (1962)
Pearl Sydenstricker Buck (1938)   Saul Bellow (1976)
Thomas Stearns Eliot (1948)   Isaac Bashevis Singer (1978) (b. Poland)
William Faulkner (1949)   Czeslaw Milosz (1980) (b. Poland)

2. What 2 writers in what years for what works have won 2 Pulitzer Prizes for fiction? In what year was the Pulitzer Prize for fiction first awarded? Who won it that year? Give the 10 years in which no award was given.
ANSWER: Booth Tarkington in 1919 for *The Magnificent Ambersons* and in 1922 for *Alice Adams,* and William Faulkner in 1955 for *A Fable* and in 1963 for *The Reivers*/1917/No award was given in 1917, 1920, 1941, 1946, 1954, 1957, 1964, 1971, 1974 and 1977.

3. Identify the literary person from each of the following nicknames.
a) The American Wordsworth   f) The American Goldsmith
b) Chekhov of the Suburbs   g) The American Kipling
c) The American Scott   h) The Burns of America
d) The American Montaigne   i) Münchausen in Modern Dress
e) The American Balzac   j) The American Socrates
ANSWER: a) William Cullen Bryant b) John Cheever c) James Fenimore Cooper d) Ralph Waldo Emerson e) William Faulkner f) Washington Irving g) Jack London h) James Whitcomb Riley or John Greenleaf Whittier i) Theodore Dreiser j) Benjamin Franklin.

4. Identify the source by giving the quotation, the work, and the author from which each of the following takes its title.
a) *For Whom the Bell Tolls* by Ernest Hemingway
b) *From Here to Eternity* by James Jones
c) *Of Mice and Men* by John Steinbeck
d) *The Sun Also Rises* by Ernest Hemingway
e) *Tender is the Night* by F. Scott Fitzgerald
ANSWER: a) "...and therefore never send to know for whom the bell tolls; it tolls for thee." From *Devotions Upon Emergent Occasions* by John Donne
b) "Gentleman-rankers out on the spree,/Damned from here to Eternity..." From "Gentleman-Rankers" by Rudyard Kipling
c) "The best-laid schemes o' mice and men/Gang aft a-gley." From *To A Mouse* by Robert Burns
d) "The sun also ariseth, and the sun goeth down, and hasteth to his place where he arose (ariseth)." From Ecclesiastes 1:5
e) "Already with thee; tender is the night..." From "Ode to a Nightingale" by John Keats

5. You probably know many writers by their first 2 initials, but do you know their full names? Give the full names of the following writers.
a) E.E. Cummings or e.e. cummings   f) H.L. Mencken
b) E.L. Doctorow   g) S.J. Perelman
c) J.P. Donleavy   h) J.D. Salinger
d) T.S. Eliot   i) E.B. White
e) J.P. Marquand   j) A.B. Guthrie, Jr.
ANSWER: a) Edward Estlin b) Edgar Lawrence c) James Patrick d) Thomas Stearns e) John Phillips f) Henry Louis g) Sidney Joseph h) Jerome David i) Elwyn Brooks j) Alfred Bertram.

6. Give the title of the literary work in which each of the following female characters appears.
a) Amy March   d) Carrie Meeber
b) Hester Pyrnne   e) Nicole Diver
c) Antonia Shimerda   f) Miss Hepzibah Pyncheon

g) Catherine Barkley
h) Melanie Wilkes
i) Montana Wildhack
j) Rose of Sharon

ANSWER: a) *Little Women* **b)** *The Scarlet Letter* **c)** *My Ántonia* **d)** *Sister Carrie* **e)** *Tender is the Night* **f)** *The House of the Seven Gables* **g)** *A Farewell to Arms* **h)** *Gone With the Wind* **i)** *Slaughterhouse-Five* **j)** *The Grapes of Wrath.*

7. Give the title of the literary work in which each of the following male characters appears.
   a) Billy Pilgrim
   b) Brother Juniper
   c) Jody Baxter
   d) Tom Canty
   e) Dr. Will Kennicott
   f) Jake Barnes
   g) McMurphy
   h) Thomas Sutpen
   i) Henry Fleming
   j) Jeeter Lester

ANSWER: a) *Slaughterhouse-Five* **b)** *The Bridge of San Luis Rey* **c)** *The Yearling* **d)** *The Prince and the Pauper* **e)** *Main Street* **f)** *The Sun Also Rises* **g)** *One Flew Over the Cuckoo's Nest* **h)** *Absalom, Absalom!* **i)** *The Red Badge of Courage* **j)** *Tobacco Road.*

8. Give the city and state (or just city or just state if appropriate) for the locations of the following literary works.
   a) *Babbit*
   b) *Jurgen*
   c) *Looking Backward*
   d) *Studs Lonigan*
   e) *In Cold Blood*
   f) *The House of the Seven Gables*
   g) *The Virginian*
   h) *Light in August*
   i) *The Heart is a Lonely Hunter*
   j) *Go Tell it on the Mountain*

ANSWER: a) Zenith (Winnemac) **b)** Poictesme **c)** Boston, Mass. **d)** Chicago, Ill. **e)** Kansas **f)** Salem, Mass. **g)** Wyoming **h)** Mississippi **i)** Georgia **j)** Harlem, New York.

9. What 2 writers spent time in prison, one for his opposition to the poll tax that would support the Mexican War and the other for embezzlement of funds from an Austin, Texas, bank?

ANSWER: Henry David Thoreau and William Sidney Porter (he took the name O. Henry while he was in prison).

10. An American literary tradition of expatriation, that is, American writers living abroad because of the dissatisfaction with America's lack of civilization and culture, has been well established. In what brief manner did Nathaniel Hawthorne, Gertrude Stein, and Theodore Roosevelt each differently describe this phenomenon?

ANSWER: Hawthorne talked about the pilgrimage to ''Our Old Home''; Stein called the writers ''a lost generation'' (une génération perdue); and Roosevelt called the writers ''hyphenated Americans.''

11. With what group was ''the Hedge Club'' associated? What magazine did they found in 1840? Who were the 2 editors? What did George Ripley found in 1841, and Bronson Alcott in 1843?

ANSWER: The Transcendentalists/the *Dial*/Margaret Fuller and later Ralph Waldo Emerson/Ripley founded Brook Farm in West Roxbury, Massachusetts, and Alcott founded Fruitlands in Harvard, Massachusetts.

12. For what work did each of the following authors in the year given win the Pulitzer Prize in fiction?
   a) Marjorie Kinnan Rawlings - 1939
   b) John Hersey - 1945
   c) Herman Wouk - 1952
   d) McKinlay Kantor - 1956
   e) Harper Lee - 1961

ANSWER: a) *The Yearling* **b)** *A Bell for Adano* **c)** *The Caine Mutiny* **d)** *Andersonville* **e)** *To Kill a Mockingbird.*

13. What story by Stephen Vincent Benét features a Massachusetts senator who said, ''Liberty and Union, now and forever, one and inseparable''?

ANSWER: The senator is Daniel Webster, and Benét's story is ''The Devil and Daniel Webster.''

14. Who wrote each of the following works?
    a) *The Electric Kool-Aid Acid Test* (1968).
    b) *Cat's Cradle* (1963)
    c) *Myra Breckinridge*(1968)
    d) *The Confessions of Nat Turner* (1967)
    e) *Franny and Zooey* (1961)
    f) *Stranger in a Strange Land* (1961)
ANSWER: a) Tom Wolfe b) Kurt Vonnegut c) Gore Vidal d) William Styron e) J.D. Salinger f) Robert Heinlein.

15. Who said?
    a) ''Laugh, and the world laughs with you; Weep, and you weep alone.''
    b) ''Everybody talks about the weather, but nobody does anything about it.''
    c) ''The difference between the right word and the almost right word is the difference between lightning and lightning bug.''
    d) ''Nothing is certain but death and taxes.''
    e) (about Katherine Hepburn) ''She ran the whole gamut of emotions from A to B.''
ANSWER: a) Ella Wilcox b) Mark Twain gets the credit, but Charles Dudley Warner said it c) Mark Twain d) Benjamin Franklin e) Dorothy Parker.

16. Who wrote each of the following works?
    a) *Gentlemen Prefer Blondes* (1925)
    b) ''The Lottery'' (1949)
    c) *The Executioner's Song* (1979)
    d) ''Everything That Rises Must Converge'' (1965)
    e) *The Thin Red Line* (1962)
ANSWER: a) Anita Loos b) Shirley Jackson c) Norman Mailer d) Flannery O'Connor e) James Jones.

17. Identify the author of each of the following works of literature. All of them are concerned with death.
    a) ''Because I Could Not Stop for Death''
    b) ''The Death of the Hired Man''
    c) *A Death in the Family*
    d) *Death in the Afternoon*
    e) *Death Comes for the Archbishop*
    f) ''Thanatopsis''
    g) *As I Lay Dying*
    h) *Death of a Salesman*
    i) *Murder by Death*
    j) *From Death to Morning*
ANSWER: a) Emily Dickinson b) Robert Frost c) James Agee d) Ernest Hemingway e) Willa Cather f) William Cullen Bryant g) William Faulkner h) Arthur Miller i) Neil Simon j) Thomas Wolfe.

18. From the following descriptions taken from mystery detective field, provide the answers.
    a) The physical deformity of Dan Fortune of Dennis Lynds' fame
    b) The detective whose residence was No. 33 Rue Dunot, Paris
    c) The name of the first detective story
    d) The inventor of the detective story (if you knew ''c,'' you know ''d'')
    e) The creator of the pejoratively called ''Had-I-But-Known'' School of detective novels
    f) The author of *The Blackboard Jungle*
    g) The Best Detective Novel award
    h) The writer whose pseudonym used the abbreviation of ''steamship'' as his initials
    i) The author of *In the Heat of the Night* (1965)
    j) The pulp magazine founded by H.L. Mencken and George Jean Nathan
    k) The author of *Psycho* (1959)
ANSWER: a) He had one arm b) C. Auguste Dupin c) ''The Murders in the Rue Morgue'' d) Edgar Allan Poe e) Mary Roberts Rinehart f) Evan Hunter g) the Edgar h) Willard Huntington Wright used S.S. Van Dine as his pseudonym i) John Ball j) *Black Mask* k) Robert Bloch.

19. Who wrote the following line, in what poem, and what word in the quote is the motto of what U.S. state?

"A banner with the strange device, Excelsior!"
ANSWER: Henry Wadsworth Longfellow in "Excelsior." "Excelsior" is the motto of New York.

20. Identify the 2 poets and their poems from the following lines, and supply the identical 2 words that have been omitted in each poem.
    a) "In this world a man must either be _____ or _____."
    b) "When you are the _____, bear/When you are the _____, strike."

    And give the 2 similar words that are in the opening song of the "Laverne and Shirley Show" on TV — similar in the sense that one does the action and the other receives it. Give the classical Yiddish explanation regarding "soup" for these last 2 words.
ANSWER: "Hyperion" by Henry Wadsworth Longfellow and "Preparedness" by Edwin Markham/The 2 words are "anvil" and "hammer"/"Schlemiel" and "schlimazl" are the 2 words in the "Laverne and Shirley Show" song/A schlemiel is a man who is always spilling hot soup, and he's spilling it down the neck of a schlimazl.

21. Identify the authors of the following 1982 prize-winning books.
    a) Pulitzer Prize for Fiction: *Rabbit is Rich*
    b) Pulitzer Prize for Poetry: *The Collected Poems*
    c) Pulitzer Prize for Biography: *Grant*
    d) Pulitzer Prize for General Nonfiction: *The Soul of a New Machine*
    e) The American Book Award for First Novel: *Dale Loves Sophie to Death*
    f) The American Book Award for Autobiography/Biography: *Mornings on Horseback*
    g) The American Book Award for Science: *Lucy: The Beginnings of Humankind*
    h) The National Book Critics Circle Award for General Nonfiction: *The Mismeasure of Man*
    i) The Pen/Faulkner Award for Fiction: *The Chaneysville Incident*
ANSWER: a) John Updike b) Sylvia Plath c) William S. McFeely d) Tracy Kidder e) Robb Forman Dew f) David McCullough g) Donald C. Johanson and Maitland A. Edey h) Stephen Jay Gould i) David Bradley.

22. From the following descriptions taken from the mystery-detective field, provide the answers.
    a) The "mother, grandmother, and godmother of the detective story"
    b) The first detective novel written by a woman
    c) The author of *The Postman Always Rings Twice*
    d) The detective of Jacques Futrelle nicknamed "The Thinking Machine"
    e) The detective of Leslie Charteris known as the Saint
    f) The detective of Phoebe Atwood Taylor known as the "Codfish Sherlock"
    g) The character created by Frank Gruber known as the "Human Encyclopedia"
    h) The detective whose calling card was a stick figure of a person with a halo over his head
ANSWER: a) Anna Katharine Green b) *The Dead Letter* (1867) by Seeley Regester (the pseudonym of Metta Victoria Fuller Victor), although *The Leavenworth Case* (1878) by Anna Katharine Green is sometimes recognized as the first because it is better known c) James M. Cain d) Professor S.F.X. Van Dusen e) Simon Templar f) Asey Mayo g) Oliver Quade h) The Saint, Simon Templar.

23. What is the first novel of each of the following writers?
    a) Louisa May Alcott
    b) James Fenimore Cooper
    c) Stephen Crane
    d) Theodore Dreiser
    e) William Faulkner
    f) Nathaniel Hawthorne
    g) Sinclair Lewis
    h) Herman Melville
    i) Kurt Vonnegut
    j) Thomas Wolfe
ANSWER: a) *Moods* (1865) b) *Precaution* (1820) c) *Maggie: A Girl of the Streets* (1893) d) *Sister Carrie* (1900) e) *Soldier's Pay* (1926) f)

Fanshawe (1828) g) *Our Mr. Wrenn* (1914) h) *Typee* (1846) i)
Player Piano (1960) j) *Look Homeward, Angel* (1929).

24. The following are first novels. Name the author of each one.
    a) *Windy McPherson's Son* (1916)
    b) *The Floating Opera* (1956)
    c) *Alexander's Bridge* (1912)
    d) *The Ginger Man* (1955)
    e) *This Side of Paradise* (1920)
    f) *Williwaw* (1946)
    g) *The Unspeakable Gentleman* (1922)
    h) *The Torrents of Spring* (1926)
    i) *The Young Lions* (1948)
    j) *Cup of Gold* (1929)

ANSWER: a) Sherwood Anderson b) John Barth c) Willa Cather d) J.P. Donleavy e) F. Scott Fitzgerald f) Gore Vidal g) J.P. Marquand h) Ernest Hemingway i) Irwin Shaw j) John Steinbeck.

25. Identify the literary works from the following subtitles.
    a) *The Sources of the Susquehanna*
    b) *A Tale of Acadie*
    c) *Life Among the Lowly*
    d) *Life in the Woods*
    e) *A Tale of the Christ*
    f) *The White Whale*
    g) *A Reminiscence*
    h) *In Search of America*
    i) *The Children's Crusade*
    j) *A Gothic Western*

ANSWER: a) *The Pioneers* (Cooper) b) "Evangeline" (Longfellow) c) *Uncle Tom's Cabin* (Stowe) d) *Walden* (Thoreau) e) *Ben-Hur* (Wallace) f) *Moby Dick* (Melville) g) *The Reivers* (Faulkner) h) *Travels With Charley* (Steinbeck) i) *Slaughterhouse-Five* (Vonnegut) j) *The Hawkline Monster* (Brautigan).

26. Identify each writer from the following pseudonyms.
    a) Artemus Ward
    b) Nathanael West
    c) Mark Twain
    d) O. Henry
    e) Richard Saunders
    f) Ellery Queen
    g) Diedrich Knickerbocker
    h) Jack Keefe
    i) Cornelius Littlepage
    j) A.A. Fair

ANSWER: a) Charles Farrar Browne b) Nathan Weinstein c) Samuel Langhorne Clemens d) William Sidney Porter e) Benjamin Franklin f) Frederick Dannay and Manfred Lee g) Washington Irving h) Ring Lardner i) James Fenimore Cooper j) Erle Stanley Gardner.

27. Who wrote *The Fountainhead* (1943), *Atlas Shrugged* (1957), and *We the Living* (1936)?
ANSWER: Ayn Rand.

28. Who wrote The Education of H*y*m*a*n K*a*p*l*a*n (1937) and *The Joys of Yiddish* (1968)?
ANSWER: Leo Calvin Rosten.

29. Identify the author, and name the work in which each of the following lines is found.
    a) "I 'spect I grow'd."
    b) "Call me Ishmael."
    c) "I kid you not."
    d) "When you call me that, smile."
    e) "The world is a fine place and worth fighting for."
    f) "A whale-ship was my Yale College and my Harvard."
    g) "Tar-baby ain't sayin' nuthin', en Brer Fox, he lay low."
    h) "I think I can — I think I can — I think I can . . . I thought I could — I thought I could — I thought I could."
    i) "The victor belongs to the spoils."
    j) "It is awfully easy to be hard-boiled about everything in the daytime, but at night it is another thing."

ANSWER: a) Harriet Beecher Stowe in *Uncle Tom's Cabin* b) Herman Melville in *Moby-Dick* c) Herman Wouk in *The Caine Mutiny* d) Owen Wister in *The Virginian* e) Ernest Hemingway in *For Whom the Bell Tolls* f) Herman Melville in *Moby-Dick* g) Joel Chandler Harris in *Nights with Uncle Remus* h) Frances M. Ford in *The Little Engine That Could* i) F. Scott Fitzgerald in *The Beautiful and the Damned* j) Ernest Hemingway in *The Sun Also Rises*.

30. Titus Maccius Plautus wrote *The Pot of Gold,* Lucius Apuleius wrote *The Golden Asse of Lucius Apuleius,* and *The Golden Bough* was written by Sir James George Frazer; but who wrote each of the following "Golden" works?
    a) *Golden Boy* (1937) c) *The Golden Apples* (1949)
    b) *The Golden Bowl* (1904) d) "The Gold Bug" (1843)
    ANSWER: a) Clifford Odets b) Henry James c) Eudora Welty d) Edgar Allan Poe.

31. Browning said that April is "a time to be in England," and Chaucer wrote of April "as having sweet showers." Identify the poets from the following lines of poetry about April.
    a) "April is the cruelest month."
    b) "To what purpose, April, do you return again?"
    c) "April this year, not otherwise/Than April of a year ago"
    ANSWER: a) T.S. Eliot in "The Wasteland" b) Edna St. Vincent Millay in "Spring" c) Edna St. Vincent Millay in "Song of a Second April."

32. If you have a song in your heart, you may be able to identify the following literary "Songs" and their authors.
    a) *The Song of Hiawatha* (1855)
    b) "Song of Myself" (1855)
    c) "Song of the Broad-Axe" (1856)
    d) *The Song of the Lark* (1915)
    e) *Songs for Eve* (1954)
    f) *The Executioner's Song* (1979)
    g) "Song of Slaves in the Desert" (1847)
    h) "Evening Song," "Song of the Chattahoochee"
    i) "The Liberty Song" (1768)
    j) "The Love Song of J. Alfred Prufrock" (1917)
    k) "Song of a Second April" (1921)
    l) "Song for a Dark Girl" (1927)
    ANSWER: a) Henry Wadsworth Longfellow b) Walt Whitman c) Walt Whitman d) Willa Cather e) Archibald MacLeish f) Norman Mailer g) John Greenleaf Whittier h) Sidney Lanier i) John Dickinson j) T.S. Eliot k) Edna St. Vincent Millay l) Langston Hughes.

33. Identify the authors of the following works beginning with "Of."
    a) *Of Mice and Men* (1937) d) *Of a Fire on the Moon* (1970)
    b) *Of Time and the River* (1935) e) *Of the Farm* (1965)
    c) *Of Plimouth Plantation* (1856)
    ANSWER: a) John Steinbeck b) Thomas Wolfe c) William Bradford d) Norman Mailer e) John Updike.

34. Many American writers have held a variety of jobs. Associate a writer with each of the following positions.
    a) Chief editor of the *Atlantic Monthly* in 1881
    b) Editor of the *Northern Californian* and the *Overland Monthly*
    c) First flutist in the Peabody Symphony Orchestra in Baltimore
    d) Editor-in-chief of the New York *Evening Post* in 1829
    e) Professor of Anatomy at Dartmouth (1838-1840) and Parkman Professor of Anatomy and Physiology at Harvard (1847-1882)
    f) Manager of an Ohio paint factory
    g) Wrote for the New Orleans *Picayune* under the pseudonym "Drop Shot"
    h) Executive with a Hartford, Connecticut, insurance company
    i) Reviewed books for *Newsweek* and worked as a café dish-washer and night porter
    j) Founded *The Rolling Stone* magazine in 1894
    k) Pediatrician in Rutherford, New Jersey
    ANSWER: a) William Dean Howells b) Bret Harte c) Sidney Lanier d) William Cullen Bryant e) Oliver Wendell Holmes f) Sherwood Anderson g) George Washington Cable h) Wallace Stevens i) Allen Ginsberg j) William Sidney Porter k) William Carlos Williams.

35. Who was the first American poet to have been memorialized by a bust in Westminster Abbey?
    ANSWER: Henry Wadsworth Longfellow.

36. Identify each American poet by each of the following descriptions.
    a) Nicknamed "Poet of the Marshes" b) First important black poet

c) Vermont's Poet Laureate and 4 time Pulitzer Poetry Prize winner
d) Committed suicide; *Ariel* was published posthumously; and wrote the novel *The Bell Jar* (1966)
e) Wrote "Ulalume"
f) Owned the City Lights Bookshop in San Francisco and wrote *A Coney*

Island of the Mind (1958)
g) His poem "Howl" is called "The Waste Land of Our Age"
h) Called the "First Lady of American Poetry"; won the Bollingen, the National Book Award, and the Pulitzer Prize for poetry in 1952

ANSWER: a) Sidney Lanier b) Paul Laurence Dunbar c) Robert Frost d) Sylvia Plath e) Edgar Allan Poe f) Lawrence Ferlinghetti g) Allen Ginsberg h) Marianne Moore.

37. Writers are sometimes identified with specific geographic locations. Give the name of the state with which each of the following was concerned in his writings.
a) George Washington Cable
b) Edward Eggleston
c) Mary Noailles Murfree
d) William Faulkner
e) Willa Cather
f) Sarah Orne Jewett
g) Joel Chandler Harris
h) Erskine Caldwell
i) James Whitcomb Riley
j) John Hay

ANSWER: a) Louisiana (New Orleans) b) Indiana c) Tennessee d) Mississippi e) Nebraska f) Maine g) Georgia h) Georgia i) Indiana j) Illinois.

38. Several American writers died at a relatively early age. Thirteen of the following writers died at 40 years of age or before. Identify them.
a) Hart Crane
b) Stephen Crane
c) Sidney Lanier
d) Jack London
e) Eugene Field
f) Frank Norris
g) Henry Timrod
h) Artemus Ward
i) Nathanael West
j) Thomas Wolfe
k) Ambrose Bierce
l) Robert Frost
m) Wallace Stevens
n) Upton Sinclair
o) Charles Brockden Brown
p) Paul Laurence Dunbar
q) Flannery O'Connor
r) Edgar Allan Poe
s) F. Scott Fitzgerald
t) Henry David Thoreau
u) Booth Tarkington

ANSWER: a) Crane (33) b) Crane (29) c) Lanier (39) d) London (40) f) Norris (32) g) Timrod (39) h) Ward (33) i) West (36) j) Wolfe (38) o) Brown (39) p) Dunbar (35) q) O'Connor (39) r) Poe (40).

39. Name the distinguished American poetess of the latter part of the 18th century who was born in Africa, sold as a slave in Boston in 1761 at the age of 8, and about whom Voltaire once wrote that she was "une Negresse qui a fait de très bons vers anglais."
ANSWER: Phyllis Wheatley.

40. What American bookseller and writer wrote *Familiar Quotations* in 1855?
ANSWER: John Bartlett.

41. Identify not only the American author of each of the following works but also the country in which he was born.
a) *The Age of Anxiety* (1947)
b) *Bells in Winter* (1978)
c) *Lolita* (1955)
d) *All Quiet on the Western*
Front (1929)
e) *A Crown of Feathers* (1973)
f) *Satan in Goray* (1935)

ANSWER: a) W. H. Auden, England b) Czeslaw Milosz, Poland c) Vladimir Nabokov, Russia d) Erich Maria Remarque, Germany e) Isaac Bashevis Singer, Poland f) Isaac Bashevis Singer, Poland.

42. Who wrote each of the following works?
a) *Riders of the Purple Sage* (1912)
b) *Pale Fire* (1962)
c) *Pale Horse, Pale Rider* (1939)
ANSWER: a) Zane Grey b) Vladimir Nabokov c) Katherine Anne Porter.

43. Associate each of the following characters with the author who created the character.
a) Long Tom Coffin
b) Ligeia
c) Diedrich Knickerbocker
d) Morella

e) Natty Bumppo
f) Harvey Birch
g) Baltus Van Tassel
h) Berenice
i) Ichabod Crane
j) Eleanora

ANSWER: a) James Fenimore Cooper b) Edgar Allan Poe c) Washington Irving d) Edgar Allan Poe e) James Fenimore Cooper f) James Fenimore Cooper g) Washington Irving h) Edgar Allan Poe i) Washington Irving j) Edgar Allan Poe.

44. Name the literary movement associated with each of the following authors.
    a) James Fenimore Cooper
    b) Henry James
    c) Theodore Dreiser
    d) William Cullen Bryant
    e) Frank Norris
    f) Nathaniel Hawthorne
    g) William Dean Howells
    h) Stephen Crane
    i) Hamlin Garland
    j) Mark Twain

ANSWER: a) Romanticism b) Realism c) Naturalism d) Romanticism e) Naturalism f) Romanticism g) Realism h) Naturalism i) Veritism j) Realism.

45. Give the last name of the Charleston, South Carolina, literary group of the 1850's whose first names were Henry (poet), Paul Hamilton (poet), J.M. (poet), and William Gilmore (novelist).

ANSWER: Henry Timrod, Paul Hamilton Hayne, J.M. Legare, and William Gilmore Simms.

46. From the 1910-1911 Harvard class, give the last name for a poet and playwright named T.S., a literary historian named Van Wyck, a columnist named Walter, a poet and novelist named Conrad, and a humorist named Robert.

ANSWER: T.S. Eliot, Van Wyck Brooks, Walter Lippmann, Conrad Aiken, and Robert Benchley (all graduated in 1911 except for Lippmann — 1910).

47. Give the last names of several members of a Chicago group of Thirties writers named Sherwood, Carl, Theodore, Ben, and Floyd.

ANSWER: Sherwood Anderson, Carl Sandburg, Theodore Dreiser, Ben Hecht, and Floyd Dell.

48. In what decade were several writers known as the "Beat Generation"? Give the last names of Allen, Jack, William, Peter, Gregory, and Lawrence.

ANSWER: 1950's/Allen Ginsberg, Jack Kerouac, William Burroughs, Peter Orlovsky, Gregory Corso, and Lawrence Ferlinghetti.

49. In the 1950's "Beat Generation" writers were located in several Bohemias. Give the city for the following: Greenwich Village, Venice West, and North Beach.

ANSWER: New York, Los Angeles, and San Francisco.

50. What authors wrote the following: *On the Road, Gasoline,* "Howl," *Pictures from the World Gone Wild,* and *The Naked Lunch?*

ANSWER: Jack Kerouac, Gregory Corso, Allen Ginsberg, Lawrence Ferlinghetti, and William Burroughs.

51. What haven for artists has produced such magazines as the *Little Review,* the *Masses,* the *Seven Arts,* the *Quill,* and the *Village Voice?*

ANSWER: Greenwich Village.

52. In 1871 Lewis Carroll wrote *Through the Looking-Glass.* Fill in the missing phrase in the following quote, define it, and tell what American short-story writer used it as the title of his first collection of stories in 1904:
    "The time has come," the Walrus said,
    "To talk of many things:
    Of shoes — and ships — and sealing-wax —
    Of _____ and _____
    And why the sea is boiling hot —
    And whether pigs have wings."

ANSWER: "Cabbages and kings" means a mixture, an assortment, an amalgam of various topics or items/O'Henry's work was entitled *Cabbages and Kings.*

53. Give the authors of the following works.

a) *Up from Slavery* (1901)
b) *Porgy* (1927)
c) *Porgy and Bess* (1935)
d) *Soul on Ice* (1968)
e) *Stride Toward Freedom* (1958)
ANSWER: a) Booker T. Washington b) DuBose and Dorothy Heyward c) George Gershwin d) Eldridge Cleaver e) Martin Luther King, Jr.

54. Identify the author of each of the following U.S. bestsellers.
a) *How Green Was My Valley* (1940)   f) *The Shoes of the Fisherman* (1963)
b) *The Song of Bernadette* (1942)   g) *The Arrangement* (1967)
c) *The Robe* (1943 and 1953)   h) *Airport* (1968) and *Wheels* (1971)
d) *The Silver Chalice* (1952)   i) *The Silmarillion* (1977)
e) *Advise and Consent* (1960)   j) *The Matarese Circle* (1979)
ANSWER: a) Richard Llewellyn b) Franz Werfel c) Lloyd C. Douglas d) Thomas B. Costain e) Allen Drury f) Morris L. West g) Elia Kazan h) Arthur Hailey i) J.R.R. Tolkien j) Robert Ludlum.

55. Name the author, the story, and the 2 characters, one who sold his watch to buy a pair of combs for her hair, while the other sold her hair to buy a platinum fob chain for his watch.
ANSWER: O. Henry/"The Gift of the Magi"/Jim and Della Young.

56. Identify each of the following.
a) The secretary of Gertrude Stein, or the complete title of *The Autobiography of* _____
b) The writer who created The Cisco Kid character
c) The school from which the 8 members of Mary McCarthy's "The Group" graduated in 1933
d) The person who was the subject of Norman Mailer's *The Executioner's Song* (1979)
e) The person whose body lies "a-mouldering in the grave"
f) The person whose ivory leg is made from the jaw bone of a whale
g) The name of Mark Twain's the "jumping frog of Calaveras County"
h) The name of the store Rhett Butler suggested to Scarlet O'Hara in *Gone With the Wind*
ANSWER: a) Alice B. Toklas b) O. Henry (William Sidney Porter) c) Vassar d) Gary Gilmore e) John Brown f) Captain Ahab g) Dan'l Webster h) "Caveat Emptorium" (a play on the phrase "let the buyer beware")

57. Identify the characters who said each of the following.
a) "Damn the United States. I wish I may never hear of this United States again."
b) "For the love of God! Montresor!"
c) "I'd prefer not to."
d) "Stella!"
e) "A salesman is got to dream, boy. It comes with the territory."
f) "Bred en bawn in a brier-patch, Brer Fox!"
ANSWER: a) Philip Nolan in Edward Everett Hale's *The Man Without a Country* b) Fortunato in Edgar Allan Poe's "A Cask of Amontillado" c) Bartleby in Herman Melville's "Bartleby the Scrivener" d) Stanley Kowalski in Tennessee Williams' *A Streetcar Named Desire* e) Willy Loman in Arthur Miller's *A Death of a Salesman* f) Brer Rabbit in *Uncle Remus: His Songs and His Sayings*.

58. What is the temperature at which book paper catches fire? Who wrote the book with that title? Name the fire department's motto in the story.
ANSWER: Fahrenheit 451/Ray Bradbury/"We burn them to ashes and then burn the ashes."

59. Whose famous last words were?
a) "On the whole I'd rather be in Philadelphia." (1946) (epitaph)
b) "So here it is at last, the distinguished thing." (1916)
c) "It's so good to get home." (1910)

d) "Turn up the lights; I don't want to go home in the dark." (1910)
e) "Excuse my dust." (1967) (witty composition of an epitaph)
f) "What's the answer? _____ In that case, what is the question?" (1945)
g) "God bless . . . God damn . . ." (1961)
h) "God bless Captain Vere." (1891)

ANSWER: a) W.C. Fields b) Henry James c) William James d) O. Henry e) Dorothy Parker f) Gertrude Stein g) James Thurber h) Herman Melville (quoting Billy Budd).

AMERICAN NOVEL/SHORT STORY
QUESTIONS AND ANSWERS

1. What was the name of the first book printed in the colonies in Boston, Massachusetts, in 1640? What was printed in 1639?

ANSWER: The *Bay Psalm Book*/"The Freeman's Oath" and an almanac were printed in 1639.

2. Who was responsible for the publication of the *Pennsylvania Gazette?* Into what magazine did this publication evolve? Under what pseudonym did he write *Poor Richard's Almanack?* How does his epitaph read?

ANSWER: Benjamin Franklin/The *Saturday Evening Post*/Richard Saunders/ "Benjamin Franklin, Printer."

3. What was the name of the first American novel, and who wrote it? Who is considered to be the first American professional man of letters? Name any of his novels. Who was the first writer to use the American Indian as a character in a fictional work? And who was the first person to make a living as a professional writer?

ANSWER: *The Power of Sympathy* (1789) by William Hill Brown/ Charles Brockden Brown/*Wieland: or, The Transformation* (1798), *Ormond: or, The Secret Witness* (1799), *Edgar Huntley: or, Memoirs of a Sleep-Walker* (1799), and *Arthur Mervyn: or, Memoirs of the Year 1793* (1799-1800). He also wrote *Clara Howard: In a Series of Letters* (1801) and *Jane Talbot* (1801). *Wieland* is considered to be the first American Gothic novel/Charles Brockden Brown/Washington Irving (Brown tried but failed to support himself after less than 10 years).

4. Who wrote *A History of New York by Diedrich Knickerbocker?* What was the name of the home and the town in which the author lived? In this *History,* who were the 3 governors of New Amsterdam, and what were their nicknames?

ANSWER: Washington Irving/"Sunnyside" in Tarrytown, New York/Wouter Van Twiller, "Walter the Doubter"; Wilhelmus Kieft, "William the Testy"; and Peter Stuyvesant, "the Headstrong."

5. In *A History of New York by Diedrich Knickerbocker,* who were the 4 explorers who passed through Hell Gate and arrived at the Island of Manna-hata?

ANSWER: Van Kortlandt (Lack-Land), Van Zandt (Earth-born), Harden Broeck (Tough Breeches), and Ten Broeck (Ten [Thin] Breeches).

6. What is an *annus mirabilis?* The year 1819 was considered one since 3 well-known writers were born that year. Who were they?

ANSWER: "A wonderful year"/James Russell Lowell, Herman Melville, and Walt Whitman.

7. Who wrote *The Sketch Book of Geoffrey Crayon,* and what are the 2 best-known stories in this work?

ANSWER: Washington Irving/"Rip Van Winkle" and "The Legend of Sleepy Hollow."

8. What was the first American novel to become popular in a foreign country? Who wrote it, and with what was the novel concerned?

ANSWER: *The Spy* (1821)/James Fenimore Cooper/The American Revolution.

9. What novel did Cooper write about the sea with the intention of challenging the accuracy of what novel by what Scottish writer?

ANSWER: Cooper wrote *The Pilot* challenging Sir Walter Scott's *The Pirate.*

10. Name the 5 Leatherstocking novels by James Fenimore Cooper. Who is the hero of these novels? By what 6 names is he known? What is unusual about the chronological sequence of these novels?

ANSWER: *The Pioneers, The Last of the Mohicans, The Prairie, The Pathfinder,* and *The Deerslayer*/Natty Bumppo/Hawkeye, Leatherstocking, Pathfinder, Deerslayer, Trapper, and *la longue carabine*/The series starts with the old age of Natty Bumppo.

11. Name the major characters created by James Fenimore Cooper in each of the

following novels.

a) *The Spy* (1821) b) *The Pioneers* (1823) c) *The Pilot* (1824)

ANSWER: a) Harvey Birch b) Natty Bumppo c) Long Tom Coffin.

12. What is the name of the trilogy written by James Fenimore Cooper and what are the 3 novels in this trilogy? On what were these novels based?

ANSWER: The *Littlepage Trilogy/Satanstoe* **(1845),** *The Chainbearer* **(1846), and** *The Redskins* **(1846)/The novels were based on the "Anti-Rent War" which occurred in New York during the years 1839-1846, although** *Satanstoe* **was concerned with land tenure from the colonial period to the 1840's,** *The Chainbearer* **with the Revolutionary War, and** *The Redskins* **with the Indians' rescue of the Littlepage family from exploiters.**

13. Name Natty Bumppo's 3 Indian friends in the Leatherstocking Tales.

ANSWER: Uncas, Chingachgook, and Hardheart.

14. List the novels in James Fenimore Cooper's the "Leatherstocking Tales" in the chronological order of their publication and explain each one in the chronology of Natty Bumppo's life.

ANSWER: *The Pioneers* **(1823), Natty as an old man;** *The Last of the Mohicans* **(1826), Natty as a youth during the French and Indian War period and the siege of Fort Henry in 1757;** *The Prairie* **(1827), the old age and death of Natty about 1805;** *The Pathfinder* **(1840), Natty as a youth in the 1760's; and** *The Deerslayer* **(1841), Natty's first contact with Indians and the Wilderness.**

15. List the "Leatherstocking Tales" in the order in which they should have been written for a chronological arrangement of Natty Bumppo's life.

ANSWER: *The Deerslayer, The Last of the Mohicans, The Pathfinder, The Pioneers,* **and** *The Prairie.*

16. What novel by Cooper uses a nickname for the main character that is the same nickname used on a popular TV program, and what is that nickname? What state has the same nickname?

ANSWER: *The Last of the Mohicans* **and** M*A*S*H **uses the nickname "Hawkeye"; Natty Bumppo has the nickname in the novel and Captain Pierce uses it on TV/Iowa is known as the Hawkeye State, a name taken from the Sauk chief, Black Hawk, who was defeated in the Black Hawk War of 1832.**

17. What was Natty Bumppo's last word before he died? Who was the object of his affection the only time he fell in love?

ANSWER: "Here"/Mabel Dunham.

18. Who wrote the short stories "Young Goodman Brown," "Rappaccini's Daughter," "My Kinsman, Major Molineaux," "The Maypole of Merrymount," and "Ethan Brand"?

ANSWER: Nathaniel Hawthorne.

19. Name the 3 major characters in Hawthorne's *The Scarlet Letter*. What was the name of the child? What sin was committed in the novel for which the Scarlet Letter is worn? Who wears the letter?

ANSWER: Hester Prynne, Roger Chillingworth, and Arthur Dimmesdale/Pearl/The sin of adultery/Hester Prynne.

20. What was the inscription Hester Prynne in *The Scarlet Letter* wanted on her tombstone?

ANSWER: The letter "A."

21. What American author's Brook Farm experience was recalled in a fictional account in one of his novels? Name the novel.

ANSWER: Nathaniel Hawthorne/*The Blithedale Romance* **(1852).**

22. Herman Melville wrote about South Seas adventures (twice), navy service, life on a whaling ship, a Liverpool voyage, and life among the cannibals. Link these subjects with the following novels.

a) *Typee* (1846)   d) *Mardi* (1849)
b) *Omoo* (1847)   e) *White-Jacket* (1850)
c) *Redburn* (1849)   f) *Moby-Dick* (1851)

ANSWER: a) life among the cannibals b) South Seas adventures c) Liverpool voyage
d) South Seas adventures e) navy service f) life on a whaling ship.

23. Herman Melville became a sailor at 20 on a merchant ship headed for Liverpool
and sailed on whalers and frigates to the South Seas before returning 5 years
later. To what 2 university programs did he compare his education aboard ship?

ANSWER: Harvard and Yale. The quote from *Moby-Dick* is: "A whale ship was my
Yale College and my Harvard."

24. Aboard what ship did Richard Henry Dana travel in *Two Years Before the
Mast*, and what was the route the ship traveled? To what ship did he change, and
what was he planning to do upon his return home?

ANSWER: The *Pilgrim* went from Boston to the ports of California/He changed to the
Alert, and planned to reenter Harvard on his return to Boston.

25. In *Moby-Dick,* what ship is destroyed by the whale and what is the name of the
ship that comes to the rescue? What were the names of the first and second mates
who ran the ship when Captain Ahab remained in his cabin?

ANSWER: The *Pequod* and the *Rachel*/Starbuck and Stubb.

26. In *Moby Dick,* Captain Ahab's Parsee servant prophesied that the Captain
would die? What were the 3 parts of this prophecy? Who was the only character in
the novel who was rescued?

ANSWER: The Captain would die after he had seen 2 strange hearses, one not constructed by mortal hands and the other made of wood grown in America,
and that the Captain would have neither hearse nor coffin for his burial/
Ishmael.

27. What 2 characters are "bosom friends" in Twain's *Huckleberry Finn*? What 2
similar characters are there in Melville's *Moby Dick*?

ANSWER: Huck Finn and Jim/Ishmael and Queequeg.

28. In what American novel is the first Negro as hero featured, and who wrote that
novel? The hero's name is a term of contempt today; define his name as it is now
used. Whose name in the novel means a "stern taskmaster"? Also whose name
in the novel represents "spontaneity and aimless development," and what related
phrase means "to grow without notice and without help"?

ANSWER: *Uncle Tom's Cabin* written by Harriet Beecher Stowe/"Uncle Tom"
means a Black who acts in a humiliating subservient or servile manner to
Whites. Uncle Tomism is a kind but condescending attitude on the part of
Whites toward Blacks and a fawning and submissive attitude of Blacks
toward Whites/Simon Legree/Topsy/"To grow like Topsy."

29. What are the names of the 4 girls in Louisa May Alcott's work *Little Women*?
Which one is gentle, which one is tall and tomboyish, which one is the oldest and
is plump, and which one is the youngest and curly-haired? Name the girl that died
and name the husbands of the other 3. In what 2 sequels are the adventures of the
March girls and their children continued?

ANSWER: Meg, Jo, Beth, and Amy March/Beth, Jo, Meg, and Amy/Beth died; Meg
married John Brooke; Amy married Theodore Laurence (Laurie); and Jo
married Professor Bhaer/*Little Men* (1871) and *Jo's Boys* (1886).

30. Name the 2 most memorable short stories of Francis Brett Harte?

ANSWER: "The Luck of Roaring Camp" and "The Outcasts of Poker Flats."

31. In *Tom Sawyer,* who was the girl Tom Sawyer was sweet on before the new girl
arrived, and what was the name of the new arrival? What 3 people did Tom and
Huck see sneaking into the graveyard to rob a grave? For what 3 characters, who
were not dead, were funeral services held?

ANSWER: Amy Lawrence before Becky Thatcher arrived/Injun Joe, Muff Potter, and
Doctor Robinson/Thomas Sawyer, Joseph Harper, and Huckleberry Finn.

32. In *Tom Sawyer,* what does Tom answer when asked by his Sunday School

teacher to name the first 2 apostles?

ANSWER: **David and Goliath.**

33. Name Mark Twain's 3 most memorable characters. What is the real name of Mark Twain? What does the name Mark Twain mean? Twain wrote a story about ''The Celebrated Jumping Frog of'' what county? In what state is this county? What other well-known writer wrote about this county?

ANSWER: **Tom Sawyer, Huckleberry Finn, and Pudd'nhead Wilson/Samuel Langhorne Clemens/''Two fathoms''/''Calaveras County''/California/Bret Harte.**

34. What are the names of the 3 Tom Sawyer books of Mark Twain?

ANSWER: *The Adventures of Tom Sawyer* **(1876),** *Tom Sawyer Abroad* **(1893), and** *Tom Sawyer, Detective* **(1896).**

35. What novelist served in the Mexican War and the Civil War, was Governor of the Territory of New Mexico, and was later Ambassador to Turkey? What was the name of his novel which was made into a well-known motion picture in 1926 and 1959?

ANSWER: **Lew Wallace/***Ben-Hur* **(1880).**

36. Who were the 2 suitors, one American and one English, of Isabel Archer in Henry James's *The Portrait of a Lady?*

ANSWER: **Caspar Goodwood and Lord Warburton.**

37. Who wrote *The Prince and the Pauper,* and what are the names of the Prince and the Pauper?

ANSWER: **Mark Twain/The Prince is Edward Tudor, Prince of Wales, and the Pauper is Tom Canty.**

38. In *The Prince and the Pauper,* what was interesting about the birthdays of the Prince and the Pauper? What was the basic difference between the 2 children in their parents' eyes? What were the names of the sisters of Edward Tudor in this novel?

ANSWER: **They were both born on the same day in London/Tom was not wanted and the Prince's arrival was eagerly awaited/Princesses Mary and Elizabeth.**

39. What American writer wrote ''Old Creole Days'' and in 1880 a novel located in New Orleans called *The Grandissimes?* In which dialect did he write? With what writer in 1884 did he tour the United States making speeches, and what did they call themselves?

ANSWER: **George Washington Cable/Creole/Mark Twain and ''Twins of Genius.''**

40. Fill in the blanks with the missing words and identify the novel by Ernest Hemingway written in 1935 from which the following quote is taken: ''All modern American literature comes from one book by _____ called _____. If you read it you must stop where the _____ _____ is stolen from the boys. That is the real end. The rest is just cheating. But it's the best book we've had. All American writing comes from that. There was nothing before. There has been nothing as good since.''

ANSWER: **Mark Twain/***Huckleberry Finn***/Nigger Jim/The novel is** *Green Hills of Africa.*

41. Between what 2 families in *Huckleberry Finn* was there a feud? Who were the 2 men who pretended they were royalty? Give the names of Peter Wilks' 3 daughters.

ANSWER: **The feud was between the Grangerfords and the Shepherdsons/The Duke and the King/Mary Jane, Susan, and Joanna.**

42. What American writer born in Eatonville, Georgia, in 1848, who wrote for the Atlanta *Constitution* for 24 years, is well-known for his tales of *Uncle Remus* (1880-1910)? In what dialect were the tales written?

ANSWER: **Joel Chandler Harris/Southern Negro of the 1800's.**

43. Name any of the regional romance novels or tales of Sarah Orne Jewett? In which state was she born and about which state does she write?

ANSWER: *A Country Doctor, The Country of the Pointed Firs, Deephaven, Tales of New England,* **and** *Old Friends and New/***South**

Berwick, Maine, and she writes about Maine.

44. Who were the 2 children of the house the Governess was in charge of in *The Turn of the Screw?* What were the names of the 2 apparitions in this novelette? Who wrote this work?
ANSWER: **Miles and Flora/Peter Quint and Miss Jessel/Henry James.**

45. Two brothers, one a philosopher and one a novelist, were said to write the opposite of their profession; that is, the philosopher wrote like a novelist and the novelist like a philosopher. Who were they?
ANSWER: **William James, the philosopher, and Henry James, the novelist.**

46. What American novelist received the French Legion of Honor in 1925 for her World War I relief work in France? She also wrote a fictional biography of a famous Secretary of the Treasurer. Name this man, the novel, and the name of the man who shot him in a duel.
ANSWER: **Gertrude Atherton/Alexander Hamilton in *The Conqueror* (1902) and Aaron Burr.**

47. Name the American writer who wrote *Main-Travelled Roads* in 1891 and received the Pulitzer Prize for biography in 1921 for his *A Daughter of the Middle Border.*
ANSWER: **Hamlin Hannibal Garland.**

48. What short story writer, who began writing in the Federal Penitentiary in Columbus, Ohio, wrote *Cabbages and Kings* and such well-known stories as "The Gift of the Magi," "The Furnished Room," and "Mammon and the Archer"? What was his real name? From what French pharmacist may he have taken his pseudonym? For what does the initial "O." stand?
ANSWER: **O. Henry/William Sidney Porter/Etienne-Ossian Henry (although a friendly penitentiary guard, Orrin Henry, may have inspired the name)/Oliver (Porter used Oliver Henry as a pseudonym).**

49. Name what may be America's first full-fledged naturalistic novel. America's first important naturalistic writer may be the novelist who also wrote 2 novels of a proposed trilogy *Epic of Wheat* (some critics feel that Stephen Crane may be America's first important naturalistic novelist). In any case, name this writer, name the 2 works in the trilogy that he did write, and name the work that was not written.
ANSWER: **McTeague: A Story of San Francisco (1899)/Frank Norris (Benjamin Franklin Norris)/The Octopus (1901) and The Pit (1903)/The Wolf was not written.**

50. Who wrote, "A rose is a rose is a rose is a rose."
ANSWER: **Gertrude Stein (in *Sacred Emily* — 1913).**

51. Who said, "You are all a lost generation"? Who used this quote as an epigraph for which novel?
ANSWER: **Gertrude Stein (maybe given to her by a French garage mechanic)/Ernest Hemingway in *The Sun Also Rises.***

52. Name the 3 works that comprise the trilogy of Theodore Dreiser. Name the trilogy.
ANSWER: ***The Financier* (1912), *The Titan* (1914), and *The Stoic* (1947 — posthumously)/*Cowperwood Trilogy* or *Trilogy of Desire.***

53. What American writer, who disappeared in Mexico in 1913 without a trace, wrote "Tales of Soldiers and Civilians" and *The Devils Dictionary?* What was the original name for *The Devil's Dictionary?*
ANSWER: **Ambrose Gwinnett Bierce/*The Cynic's Word Book.***

54. Name the writer who has had 2 towns named after one of his creations, and name the 2 towns. For what stories is he famous?
ANSWER: **Edgar Rice Burroughs/Tarzana, Texas, and Tarzana, California/Stories of Tarzan (*Tarzan of the Apes*, 1914, was the first Tarzan book) and of Mars (*A Princess of Mars*, 1917).**

55. What similar military experience did Ernest Hemingway, E.E. Cummings, and John Dos Passos have during World War I?

ANSWER: They all served in the Ambulance Corps.

56. What 3 well-known novels by Willa Cather deal with immigrants in Nebraska?

ANSWER: *O Pioneers!* (1913), *My Antonia* (1918), and *A Lost Lady* (1933).

57. Name the Big 5 novels of Harry Sinclair Lewis.

ANSWER: *Main Street* (1920), *Babbitt* (1922), *Arrowsmith* (1925), *Elmer Gantry* (1927), and *Dodsworth* (1929).

58. For what member of his father's family was F. Scott Fitzgerald named?

ANSWER: Francis Scott Key (Fitzgerald).

59. Who wrote the novel and what are the names of the 2 women's clubs in *Main Street*?

ANSWER: Sinclair Lewis/The Jolly Seventeen and the Thanatopsis Club.

60. Who wrote the novel whose name and principal character has come to mean ''a middle class American who is a model of narrow-mindedness and self-satisfaction''?

ANSWER: Sinclair Lewis wrote *Babbitt*/The principal character is George F. Babbitt.

61. In *The Enormous Room* by E.E. Cummings, what were the specific names of the group called the ''Delectable Mountains''?

ANSWER: The Wanderer, Zoo Loo, and Surplice.

62. Herman Melville died in 1891; what novel of his was published in 1924? What was the original name of this novel?

ANSWER: *Billy Budd/Billy Budd, Foretopman.*

63. What were the names of the ships in *Billy Budd,* the one that was carrying him and the one that impressed him aboard? Who was responsible for Billy's death, and how did he die? What was the Captain's name and what was his role in Billy's death?

ANSWER: *Rights-Of-Man* and the H.M.S. *Indomitable* (the *Bellipotent,* "powerful in war," was the name Melville finally preferred)/Claggart, the master-at-arms, was responsible because he falsely accused Billy of fomenting a mutiny, and Billy was hanged/Captain Vere, according to the laws of the sea, convened a court-martial which found Billy guilty and sentenced him to be hanged.

64. What persons made *Billy Budd* into a one-act opera in 1949, a 4-act opera in 1951, a 3-act play in 1951, and a movie in 1962? Who directed the movie *Billy Budd* in 1930 and 1956? Who played Captain Ahab in the 1930 and 1956 movie versions?

ANSWER: Giorgia Ghedini/Benjamin Britten/Louis Coxe and Robert Chapman/Peter Ustinov/Lloyd Bacon (1930) and John Huston (1956)/John Barrymore (1930) and Gregory Peck (1956).

65. Who were the 2 girls to whom Martin Arrowsmith in *Arrowsmith* was engaged at the same time? How did he choose between them?

ANSWER: Madeline Fox and Leora Tozer/He invited them both to lunch and explained the situation. Madeline left in a huff and Leora stayed.

66. What city in Spain is famous for the ''running of the bulls''? What novel by Ernest Hemingway partly takes place there?

ANSWER: Pamplona/*The Sun Also Rises.*

67. Name the 2 mules of Father Latour and Father Vaillant in *Death Comes for the Archbishop*? Who wrote this novel?

ANSWER: Contento and Angelica/Willa Cather.

68. Who were the 5 people who died in the novel of *The Bridge of San Luis Rey* when the bridge collapsed? Who wrote the book? What Spanish Friar was burned at the stake for writing a book? What about the book offended Church authorities?

ANSWER: The Marquesa de Montemayor, Pepita, Esteban, Uncle Pio, and Jaime/ Thornton Wilder/Brother Juniper/Brother Juniper explained why God had killed these people at that moment.

69. What 1927 novel of Sinclair Lewis was made into a movie? What 2 actors, the one

who played the principal character and the one who played the jilted-girlfriend-turned prostitute, Lulu Baines, won Oscars for their roles in the film version directed by Richard Brooks?

ANSWER: *Elmer Gantry*/**Burt Lancaster and Shirley Jones.**

70. Name the 3 important novels, by Hemingway, Wolfe, and Faulkner, which were published in 1929.

ANSWER: *A Farewell to Arms* **by Ernest Hemingway;** *Look Homeward, Angel* **by Thomas Wolfe; and** *The Sound and the Fury* **by William Faulkner.**

71. What were the names of the 4 Compson children in *The Sound and the Fury* by William Faulkner?

ANSWER: Benjamin, Quentin, Candace, and Jason.

72. Give the names of the titles of the U.S.A. trilogy by John Dos Passos.

ANSWER: *The 42nd Parallel* **(1930),** *1919* **(1932), and** *The Big Money* **(1936).**

73. In his trilogy, *U.S.A.,* what 3 technical devices does John Dos Passos employ to make his cross-section of America so complete?

ANSWER: The Newsreel, the Camera Eye, and biographies of public figures.

74. What was the name of the theatre that was nationally sponsored by the Works Progress Administration during the New Deal?

ANSWER: The Federal Theatre.

75. Who wrote the Danny O'Neill pentalogy, the Bernard Carr trilogy, and *Studs Lonigan: A Trilogy?* Name the novels in the latter trilogy.

ANSWER: James T. Farrel/*Young Lonigan* **(1932),** *Young Manhood of Studs Lonigan* **(1934), and** *Judgment Day* **(1935).**

76. In *The Mutiny on the Bounty,* what was the ruthless Captain's name, and who led the revolt against him? What 2 men wrote this novel? What are the names of the 2 other books in this trilogy? What island became the home of the mutineers of the *Bounty?*

ANSWER: Captain Bligh and Fletcher Christian/Charles Nordhoff and James Norman Hall/*Men Against the Sea* **and** *Pitcairn's Island*/**Pitcairn's Island.**

77. Who wrote *Gone With the Wind?* In which state and on what plantation does much of the action take place? Give the names of the 3 husbands of Scarlet O'Hara.

ANSWER: Margaret Mitchell/Georgia/Tara Plantation/Charles Hamilton, Frank Kennedy, and Rhett Butler.

78. Who was the first American woman to win the Nobel Prize for literature? In what year did she win it? What was the name of her trilogy and the 3 works in it?

ANSWER: Pearl Sydenstricker Buck/1938/*The House of Earth* **(1935)/The 3 works are** *The Good Earth* **(1931),** *Sons* **(1932), and** *A House Divided* **(1935).**

79. What are the full names of the 2 main characters in Steinbeck's *Of Mice and Men?* What was the swamper's name on the ranch? What was the name of the girl whom Lennie killed at the end?

ANSWER: Lennie Small and George Milton/Candy/Curley's wife (her name is not given).

80. In Steinbeck's *The Grapes of Wrath,* in what state did the Joad's first live and to what state did they travel?

ANSWER: Oklahoma/California.

81. Identify the English author of the following quote and the American author who used part of it for the title of his novel: " . . . any man's death diminishes me, because I am involved in Mankinde; and therefore never send to know for whom the bell tolls; it tolls for thee." Name the novel.

ANSWER: John Donne and Ernest Hemingway/*For Whom the Bell Tolls.*

82. Give the 3 novels in Conrad Richter's trilogy. Which one won the Pulitzer Prize in 1951?

ANSWER: *The Trees* **(1940),** *The Fields* **(1946), and** *The Town* **(1950)/***The Town.*

83. What author started publishing the first of 11 novels in 1940 starring his "hyperthyroid" hero Lanny Budd? By what name were these novels known?
ANSWER: Upton Beall Sinclair/*World's End.*

84. What novel by William Faulkner and which one by Ralph Ellison have the theme of "keep the coloured boy running"?
ANSWER: *Light in August* **and** *Invisible Man.*

85. What county of what state is William Faulkner known for writing about? What are the novels in his trilogy? What family is featured in this trilogy?
ANSWER: Yoknapatawpha County in Mississippi/*The Hamlet* **(1940),** *The Town* **(1957), and** *The Mansion* **(1959)/Snopes Family.**

86. What are the 3 main works of autobiographical fiction that deal with Henry Miller's adventures in the Bohemian underworld of Paris? What is the name of his trilogy and what are the names of the 3 works in the trilogy?
ANSWER: *Tropic of Cancer* **(1934),** *Tropic of Capricorn* **(1938), and** *Black Spring* **(1939)/***The Rosy Crucifixion* **of** *Sexus* **(1949),** *Plexus* **(1953), and** *Nexus* **(1960).**

87. What is an interesting point about the writing of the novel *The Human Comedy* by William Saroyan?
ANSWER: He wrote and directed the film first and wrote the novel later from the manuscript.

88. Whose first book, which won the Pulitzer Prize in 1948 and later was made into a movie, became the basis for what musical play by Rodgers and Hammerstein?
ANSWER: James Michener's *Tales of the South Pacific* **was the basis for** *South Pacific* **by Rodgers and Hammerstein.**

89. In what city and state was the author born who wrote *Reflections in a Golden Eye* (1941), *The Ballad of the Sad Café* (1951), and *Clock Without Hands* (1961)? What professor at what college in this city wrote what nationally acclaimed biography of this writer?
ANSWER: Carson McCullers was born in Columbus, Georgia/Virginia Spencer Carr of Columbus College wrote *The Lonely Hunter: A Biography of Carson McCullers* **(1975).**

90. In Katherine Anne Porter's *Ship of Fools,* what is the name of the German ship, and what route is it traveling? What are the 3 divisions of the book? What are the epigraphs at the beginning of each division? What was her source for the book *Ship of Fools?*
ANSWER: The *Vera* **is going from Veracruz, Mexico, to Bremerhaven, Germany/ Embarkation, High Sea, and The Harbors/"Quand partons-nous vers le bonheur?" (When are we setting forth toward happiness?); "Kein Haus, Keine Heimat" (No house, no home); and from St. Paul, "For here we have no continuing city...."/***The Ship of Fools* **(***Das Narrenschiff,* **1494) by Sebastian Brant.**

91. Who wrote *Letting Go* (1962), *Goodbye Columbus* (1959), and *Portnoy's Complaint* (1969)?
ANSWER: Philip Roth.

92. In Truman Capote's *In Cold Blood,* what was the name of the family that was brutally murdered, and what were the names of the murderers? In what state did the work take place? What did Capote name the genre he invented?
ANSWER: The 4 members of the Clutter family were murdered by Richard Hickock and Perry Smith/Kansas/A non-fiction novel.

93. Who were the 4 men in James Dickey's *Deliverance* who left the city to take a 3-day canoe trip down a roaring river? Name the location (the state) for the novel.
ANSWER: Ed Gentry, Lewis Medlock, Bobby Trippe, and Drew Ballinger/Georgia.

94. Name the first 3 novels of John Cheever. His fourth novel was the occasion for a *Newsweek* cover story in 1977. Name the novel. For what work did he receive

both the Pulitzer Prize and the National Book Critics Circle Award in 1979?

ANSWER: *The Wapshot Chronicle* **(1957),** *The Wapshot Scandal* **(1964),** **and** *Bullet Park* **(1969)/***Falconer* **(1977)/***The Stories of John Cheever.*

95. The author spent 11 years looking for a publisher. His mother spent another 11 years doing the same. What did the author do in 1969? Name the work and the author of the work that won the Pulitzer Prize for fiction in 1981. Name the University Press that finally published this marvelous book.

ANSWER: He committed suicide/*A Confederacy of Dunces* **by John Kennedy Toole/Louisiana State University Press.**

AMERICAN POETRY

QUESTIONS AND ANSWERS

1. Who wrote the first book of original poetry in the U.S., and what was the title of work? By what nickname is this poet known? She came to America with her husband and father aboard what ship that brought settlers who established the Massachusetts Bay Colony?

ANSWER: Anne Bradstreet/*The Tenth Muse Lately Sprung Up in America*/"The Tenth Muse"/The *Arbella* in 1630.

2. What poet was nicknamed the "poet laureate of New England Puritanism"? Name his religious best-seller published in 1662. What at Harvard bears his name?

ANSWER: Michael Wigglesworth/*The Day of Doom*/A dormitory.

3. What colonial poet, considered to be the first major American poet, ordered his heirs to leave his poetry unpublished, which it was until discovered in the Yale library in 1937? What are the names of his 2 major poetic works?

ANSWER: Edward Taylor/*Preparatory Meditations* and *God's Determinations Touching His Elect.*

4. What were the names of the 3 main poets who comprised the first American school of poets? What were the 2 names for this group? From which college did all 3 graduate? During what years were they most active as a group?

ANSWER: John Trumbull, Timothy Dwight, and Joel Barlow/The Connecticut Wits or the Hartford Wits/Yale/During the 1780's and 1790's.

5. Who wrote "the first memorable American poem about nature"? What is the name of that poem written in 1786? His "The House of Night" (1799) on death and the grave has the same theme as the poetry of what group of English poets?

ANSWER: Philip Freneau/"The Wild Honeysuckle"/The Graveyard Poets.

6. What "Victory" is the subject of Philip Freneau's poem "On the Memorable Victory"? Give the date and names of the 2 Captains. What spelling error did Freneau make, and what famous quote was not part of the poem?

ANSWER: The victory of the American *Bon Homme Richard* over the *Serapis*/September 23, 1779/Captain John Paul Jones commanded the American ship and Captain James Pearson the British one/Freneau spelled *Serapis*, *Seraphis*/Jones's "I have not yet begun to fight."

7. Who wrote the following lines, and from what poem do they come? How is the title of this poem from the Greek translated?

> "When thoughts
> Of the last bitter hour come like a blight
> Over thy spirit, and sad images
> Of the stern agony, and shroud, and pall,
> And breathless darkness, and the narrow house,
> Make thee to shudder, and grow sick at heart, —
> Go forth, . . .

ANSWER: William Cullen Bryant/From "Thanatopsis" (1811-1821)/"View of Death."

8. Name the author and the poem from which the following quote is taken.

> "So live, that when thy summons comes to join
> The innumerable caravan, which moves
> To that mysterious realm, where each shall take
> His chamber in the silent halls of death, . . ."

ANSWER: William Cullen Bryant/"Thanatopsis."

9. Identify the poet who wrote the following lines, and name the poem in which they appear.

> "He who, from zone to zone,
> Guides through the boundless sky thy certain flight,
> In the long way that I must tread alone,
> Will lead my steps aright."

ANSWER: William Cullen Bryant/"To a Waterfowl" (1815).

10. Identify the poem from which the following lines are taken, and name the poet of these lines. Explain the name of the poem. Then, explain the connection with the last word of the title and Jules Verne, Robert Fulton, the U.S. Navy, the North Pole, and Andrew Wyeth.

> "Let each new temple, nobler than the last,
>   Shut thee from heaven with a dome more vast,
>   Till thou at length art free,
>   Leaving thine outgrown shell by life's unresting sea!"

ANSWER: **"The Chambered Nautilus" by Oliver Wendell Holmes/A chambered nautilus is a cephalopod mollusk of the Pacific and Indian Oceans which is also called "pearly nautilus." It has a spiral, chambered shell lined with a pearly layer/*Nautilus* is the name of Captain Nemo's submarine in Jules Verne's *20,000 Leagues under the Sea*. The name was taken from Robert Fulton's submarine built in 1798. It is also the name of the world's first atomic submarine (January 21, 1954), which became the first ship to cross under the North Pole from the Atlantic to the Pacific. It is also the name of a tempera painting by Andrew Wyeth.**

11. In what poem by whom do the following lines appear?

> "Have you heard of the wonderful one-hoss shay,
>   That was built in such a logical way
>   It ran a hundred years to a day, . . ."

ANSWER: **"The Deacon's Masterpiece" or, "The Wonderful One-Hoss Shay"/Oliver Wendell Holmes.**

12. In which poem by whom do the following lines appear?

> "Alas for those two loving ones! She waked not from her swound,
>   And he was taken with the cramp, and in the waves was drowned;
>   But Fate has metamorphosed them, in pity of their woe,
>   And now they keep an oyster-shop for mermaids down below."

ANSWER: **"The Ballad of the Oysterman" (1830)/Oliver Wendell Holmes.**

13. What occasioned the writing of the following lines? Identify the poem from which the following lines are taken, and name the poet of these lines.

> "Ay, tear her tattered ensign down!
>   Long has it waved on high,
> And many an eye has danced to see
>   That banner in the sky;
> Beneath it rung the battle shout,
>   And burst the cannon's roar; —
> The meteor of the ocean air
>   Shall sweep the clouds no more."

ANSWER: **The frigate *Constitution* was going to be destroyed in 1830 by the Department of the Navy because it was old and unseaworthy/"Old Ironsides" (1830)/Oliver Wendell Holmes.**

14. The lines below are the last stanza of a poem. About whom is the poem written? What was this person's nickname? What is the name of the poem from which the lines are taken? Who wrote the poem?

> "And if I should live to be
> The last leaf upon the tree
>   In the spring,
> Let them smile, as I do now,
> At the old forsaken bough
>   Where I cling."

ANSWER: **Major Thomas Melville/Nicknamed "The Last of the Cocked Hats"/"The Last Leaf" (1831)/Oliver Wendell Holmes.**

15. The first stanza of the following poem is missing the first line. Give the first line of the poem. Then give the name of the poem and the poet. Name the woman who inspired the poem. To the poet she is like what beauty, and he is like what wanderer?

``
_____

Like those Nicean barks of yore,
That gently, o'er a perfumed sea,
   The weary, way-worn wanderer bore
   To his own native shore.''

ANSWER: ''Helen, thy beauty is to me''/''To Helen'' (1831) by Edgar Allan Poe/Mrs. Jane Stith Stanard/Helen of Troy and Ulysses.

16. In what poem by Poe are the following famous lines found: ''To the glory that was Greece,/And the grandeur that was Rome''?

ANSWER: ''To Helen.''

17. What one word from what poem by what poet completes the 2 blanks in the following lines?
   ''From my books surcease of sorrow — sorrow for the lost _____ —
   For the rare and radiant maiden whom the angels name _____ —
      Nameless here for evermore.''
And what well-known word in the same poem completes the following line —
''Quoth the Raven '_____' ''?

ANSWER: ''Lenore''/''The Raven'' (1842-1844)/Edgar Allan Poe/''Nevermore.''

18. Fill in the name of the woman in the following stanza and you will have the name of the poem. Who wrote it, and who is being idealized?
   ''It was many and many a year ago,
     In a kingdom by the sea,
   That a maiden there lived whom you may know
     By the name of _____ —
   And this maiden she lived with no other thought
     Than to love and be loved by me.''

ANSWER: ''Annabel Lee'' (1849)/Edgar Allan Poe and Virginia Clemm, his wife.

19. Identify the poem from which the following lines are taken, name the author of the lines, and tell what figures of speech are prominent in the poem.
   ''Hear the sledges with the bells —
     Silver bells!
What a world of merriment their melody foretell! . . .
   Keeping time, time, time,
   In a sort of Runic rhyme,
To the tintinnabulation that so musically wells
   From the bells, bells, bells, bells,
    Bells, bells, bells —
From the jingling and the tinkling of the bells.''

ANSWER: ''The Bells'' (1848-1849)/Edgar Allan Poe/Onomatopoeia and alliteration.

20. Who wrote all the following lines? Identify the works from which they come?
  a) ''All mankind love a lover.''
  b) ''A foolish consistency is the hobgoblin of little minds.''
  c) ''For everything you have missed, you have gained something else.''
  d) ''The frolic architecture of the snow.''
  e) ''Good-bye, proud world! I am going home.''
  f) ''Happy is the house that shelters a friend.''
  g) ''He builded better than he knew.''
  h) ''Hitch your wagon to a star.''
  i) ''I am the doubter and the doubt.''
  j) ''Shallow men believe in luck.''
  k) ''Trust thyself: every heart vibrates to that iron string.''
  l) ''Whoso would be a man must be a nonconformist.''

ANSWER: Ralph Waldo Emerson/a) ''Love'' b) ''Self-Reliance'' c) ''Compensation'' d) ''The Snow-Storm'' e) ''Good-Bye'' f) ''Friendship'' g) ''The Problem'' h) ''Civilization'' i) ''Brahma'' j) ''Worship'' k) ''Self-Reliance'' l) ''Self-Reliance.''

21. Identify the author of the following lines, and name the poem from which they are taken.

"Tell them, dear, that if eyes were made for seeing,
Then Beauty is its own excuse for being:
Why thou wert there, O rival of the rose!
I never thought to ask, I never knew:
But, in my simple ignorance, suppose
The self-same Power that brought me there brought you."

ANSWER: Ralph Waldo Emerson/"The Rhodora."

22. Name the poem from which the following lines have been taken, and name the author of the lines.

"By the rude bridge that arched the flood,
    Their flag to April's breeze unfurled,
Here once the embattled farmers stood
    And fired the shot heard round the world."

ANSWER: "Concord Hymn"/Ralph Waldo Emerson.

23. Identify the poet who wrote the following lines, and name the poem from which the lines are taken.

"So nigh is grandeur to our dust,
So near is God to man,
When Duty whispers low, *Thou must,*
The youth replies, *I can.*

ANSWER: Ralph Waldo Emerson/"Voluntaries."

24. What 3 young poets lived in Cambridge, Massachusetts, in the 1830's and were called the "New England Triumvirate," the "Cambridge Poets," or the "Brahmins"?

ANSWER: Henry Wadsworth Longfellow, Oliver Wendell Holmes, and James Russell Lowell.

25. Who wrote all the following lines? Identify the works from which they come?
a) "As unto the bow the cord is, so unto the man is woman."
b) "By the shores of Gitche Gumee,/By the shining Big-Sea-Water."
c) "The fate of the nation was riding that night."
d) "Footsteps echo through the corridors of time."
e) "God has sifted three kingdoms to find the wheat for this planting."
f) "I shot an arrow into the air,/It fell to earth, I knew not where."
g) "Into each life some rain must fall."
h) "Nothing is too late till the tired heart shall cease to palpitate."
i) "Something attempted, something done."
j) "Why don't you speak for yourself, John?"

ANSWER: Henry Wadsworth Longfellow/a) "The Song of Hiawatha" b) "The Song of Hiawatha" c) "Paul Revere's Ride" d) "The Day is Done" e) "The Courtship of Miles Standish" f) "The Arrow and the Song" g) "The Rainy Day" h) "Morituri Salutamus" i) "The Village Blacksmith" j) "The Courtship of Miles Standish."

26. To whom was Hiawatha married in Longfellow's poem *The Song of Hiawatha* (1855)? What was his grandmother's name? Give the names of his father and mother.

ANSWER: Minnehaha/Nokomis/Mudjekeewis, the West Wind, and Wenonah.

27. Who asked whom to propose marriage in his behalf to what lovely girl in *The Courtship of Miles Standish*? (1858) by Longfellow? What was the girl singing and what was she doing when John approached and opened her door?

ANSWER: Miles Standish asked John Alden to propose marriage for him to Priscilla Mullens/She was singing the 100th psalm and spinning.

28. In *The Courtship of Miles Standish,* who married whom? From the following line of the poem, which is a description of their wedding day, the names of what 2 Biblical characters should be in the blanks, "Fresh with the youth of the world, recalling _____ and _____ . . ."?

ANSWER: John Alden married Priscilla Mullens/Rebecca and Isaac (Genesis 24:67).

29. Fill in the 3 blanks; identify the poem from which the following lines are taken; and name the poet who wrote them.

''Under a spreading chestnut-tree
    The _____ _____ stands;
    The _____, a mighty man is he,
      With large and sinewy hands;
    And the muscles of his brawny arms
      Are strong as iron bands.''

ANSWER: ''village smithy''/''smith''/''The Village Blacksmith'' (1839)/Henry Wadsworth Longfellow.

30. Fill in the blank; identify the poem from which the following lines are taken; and name the poet who wrote the lines. What did the skipper do to his little daughter during the storm?
    ''It was the schooner _____,
      That sailed the wintry sea;
    And the skipper had taken his little daughter,
      To bear him company.''

ANSWER: ''Hesperus''/''The Wreck of the Hesperus'' (1839)/Henry Wadsworth Longfellow/''He wrapped her warm in his seaman's coat/Against the stinging blast,/He cut a rope from a broken spar,/And bound her to the mast.''

31. Recite the first stanza of Longfellow's ''The Landlord's Tale: Paul Revere's Ride,'' or give the time and the date of it according to the poem. This poem was the first ''tale'' in which work by Hawthorne?

ANSWER: ''Listen, my children, and you shall hear
    Of the *midnight* ride of Paul Revere,
    On the *eighteenth of April, in Seventy-five;*
    Hardly a man is now alive
    Who remembers that famous day and year.''/*Tales of a Wayside Inn.*

32. Name the poem from which the following lines are taken, and name the poet of these lines. Name the lady, then name the war in which she played an important role.
    ''Lo! in that house of misery
    A lady with a lamp I see
      Pass through the glimmering gloom,
      And flit from room to room.''

ANSWER: ''Santa Filomena''/Henry Wadsworth Longfellow/The lady is Florence Nightingale/The Crimean War.

33. Identify the poet who wrote the following lines, and name the poem from which the lines are taken.
    ''Tell me not, in mournful numbers,
      Life is but an empty dream! —
    For the soul is dead that slumbers
      And things are not what they seem.''

ANSWER: Henry Wadsworth Longfellow/''A Psalm of Life.''

34. In what city and state is the Arsenal in the following lines located? Name the author of these lines. What timely plea is made in the poem?
    ''This is the Arsenal. From floor to ceiling,
      Like a huge organ, rise the burnished arms;
    But from their silent pipes no anthem pealing
      Startles the villages with strange alarms.''

ANSWER: ''The Arsenal at Springfield'' (1844) in Massachusetts/Henry Wadsworth Longfellow/A plea for peace.

35. Identify the poem from which the lines below are taken. In the poem what was being built, what was it to be named, and what does the title symbolize? Name the poet of these lines.
    ''Our hearts, our hopes, are all with thee,
      Our hearts, our hopes, our prayers, our tears,

Our faith triumphant o'er our fears,
Are all with thee, — are all with thee!''

ANSWER: ''The Building of the Ship'' (1849)/A sailing ship and it was to be named *Union*/The title symbolizes the country, the Ship of State, (''Thou, too, sail on, O Ship of State!/Sail on, O UNION, strong and great!'')/Henry Wadsworth Longfellow.

36. What were the last names of the betrothed lovers, Evangeline and Gabriel, and what is the translation of their last names in Longfellow's ''Evangeline'' (1847)? Evangeline was what in what city when she found Gabriel after a long separation?

ANSWER: Evangeline Bellefontaine (''beautiful fountain'') and Gabriel Lajeunesse (''youth'')/A Sister of Mercy in Philadelphia.

37. What is the first line of Longfellow's ''Evangeline''?

ANSWER: ''This is the forest primeval.''

38. Identify the poem from which the following lines are taken, and name the poet who wrote them. About whom was the poem written? From where in the Bible was it taken? Whose son in the Bible was he? What is the popular etymology for the name?

> *1st stanza:*
> So fallen! so lost! the light withdrawn
> Which once he wore!
> The glory from his gray hairs gone
> Forevermore!
>
> *8th stanza:*
> All else is gone; from those great eyes
> The soul has fled:
> When faith is lost, when honor dies,
> The man is dead!

ANSWER: ''Ichabod'' by John Greenleaf Whittier/About Daniel Webster who disappointed many, including the author, by not making a strong antislavery stand in the 1850 Senate debate about slavery in the new territories/Taken from I Samuel 4:21, ''Then they named the boy Ichabod, saying 'Glory has departed from Israel';. . ./Ichabod was the son of Phineas and grandson of Eli/Ichabod's father had just died, and his mother died giving birth to him. His name means ''inglorious'' which is based on the loss of the Ark of God.

39. Fill in the blank in the following lines and name the poem by doing so. Who wrote it?

> ''Blessings on thee, little man,
> _____, with cheek of tan!
> With thy turned-up pantaloons,
> And thy merry whistled tunes;''

ANSWER: ''The Barefoot Boy'' (1855)/John Greenleaf Whittier.

40. Identify the poem from which the following lines are taken, and name the poet who wrote them.

> ''The sun that brief December day
> Rose cheerless over hills of gray,
> And, darkly circled, gave at noon
> A sadder light than waning moon.''

ANSWER: ''Snow-Bound'' (1866) by John Greenleaf Whittier.

41. Who wrote each of the following lines? Identify the poem in which each appears.
a) ''Angel of the backward look.''
b) ''Cheerily, then, my little man,/Live and laugh, as boyhood can!''
In the following lines by the same author, complete the missing line. Name the poem and tell who didn't get married.

> ''Of all the sad words of tongue or pen, the saddest are these: ''_____
> _____!''

ANSWER: John Greenleaf Whittier/a) ''Snow-Bound b) ''The Barefoot Boy''/''It might have been!''/''Maud Muller,'' and it was Maud and the Judge who didn't get married to each other.

42. Who wrote a parody of ''Maud Miller,'' and what's its title? Who gets married in the poem? What is the last line of the stanza below?

> ''If, of all words of tongue and pen,
> The saddest are, ''It might have been,''
> More sad are these, we daily see,''
> ''It is, _____.''

ANSWER: Bret Harte/''Mrs. Judge Jenkins''/Maud and the Judge/'' . . . but hadn't ought to be.''

43. In which poem by which poet do the following lines appear?

> ''I celebrate myself, and sing myself,
> And what I assume you shall assume,
> For every atom belonging to me as good belongs to you.''

ANSWER: ''Song of Myself''/Walt Whitman.

44. Identify the poem from which the following lines are taken, and name the poet of these lines. About whom is the poem written and for what occasion?

> ''My Captain does not answer, his lips are pale and still,
> My father does not feel my arm, he has no pulse nor will,
> The ship is anchor'd safe and sound, its voyage closed and done,
> From fearful trip the victor ship comes in with object won:''

ANSWER: ''O Captain! My Captain!'' (1865)/Walt Whitman/About Abraham Lincoln after he had been assassinated.

45. Identify the poem in which the following lines appear, and name the author who wrote these lines. About whom is the poem written and what was the reason for the title? What word is a symbol of this person?

> ''When lilacs last in the dooryard bloom'd,
> And the great star early droop'd in the western sky in the night,
> I mourn'd, and yet shall mourn with ever-returning spring.''

ANSWER: ''When Lilacs Last in the Dooryard Bloom'd'' (1865)/Walt Whitman/About Abraham Lincoln after he had been assassinated/Whitman was in Brooklyn the day after the assassination and many lilacs were in bloom. He was always reminded of that day by the sight and odor of the lilacs/''star.''

46. There are 3 symbols in Walt Whitman's ''When Lilacs Last in the Dooryard Bloom'd.'' For what do the symbols — ''star,'' ''lilacs,'' and ''the song of the hermit thrush'' stand? Recite the last 2 lines of the poem.

ANSWER: The ''star'' is Abraham Lincoln, the ''lilacs'' are youth, love, and life (resurrection), and ''the song of the hermit thrush'' is the gift of feeling and expression (a love song that offers the author comfort)/''Lilac and star and bird twined with the chant of my soul,/There in the fragrant pines and the cedars dusk and dim.''

47. In which poem by which poet do the following lines appear? Which state is the setting for the poem?

> ''Out of the hills of Habersham,
> Down the valleys of Hall,
> I hurry amain to reach the plain, . . .
> Far from the hills of Habersham,
> Far from the valleys of Hall.''

ANSWER: ''Song of the Chattahoochee'' (1877)/Sidney Lanier/Georgia.

48. In the same poem by Sidney Lanier, what is the name of the private school in Columbus, Georgia, which was named from the following lines?

> ''And oft in the hills of Habersham,
> And oft in the valleys of Hall,
> The white quartz shone, and the smooth brook-stone...''

ANSWER: Brookstone School (The author taught there).

49. The following lines are taken from what poem? Who wrote the poem? What state serves as the setting of the poem? (The word omitted is part of that title).

> ''Oh, like to the greatness of God is the greatness within
> The range of the marshes, the liberal marshes of _____.

ANSWER: ''The Marshes of Glynn'' (1878)/Sidney Lanier/Georgia.

50. Who wrote the following lines, all from different poems?

''To fight aloud, is very brave—
But *gallanter,* I know
Who charge within the bosom
The Cavalry of Woe—''

''My life had stood—a Loaded Gun—
In Corners—till a Day
The Owner passed—identified—
And carried Me away—''

''I know that He exists.
Somewhere—in Silence—
He has hid his rare life
From our gross eyes.''

''I never saw a Moor—
I never saw the Sea—
Yet know I how the Heather looks
And what a Billow be.''

''Because I could not stop for Death—
He kindly stopped for me—
The Carriage held but just Ourselves—
And Immortality.''

''There is no Frigate like a Book
To take us Lands away
Nor any Coursers like a Page
Of prancing Poetry—''

ANSWER: Emily Dickinson.

51. Who wrote the following lines?

''If I can stop one Heart from breaking
I shall not live in vain
If I can ease one Life the Aching
Or cool one Pain

Or help one fainting Robin
Unto his Nest again
I shall not live in Vain.''

ANSWER: Emily Dickinson.

52. Identify the first line of the poem from which the following lines are taken, name the poet, and give the meaning of the word ''Boanerges.''

''And neigh like Boanerges—
Then—prompter than a Star
Stop—docile and omnipotent
At its own stable door—''

ANSWER: ''I like to see it lap the Miles''/Emily Dickinson/''Boanerges,'' the name Christ gave to James and John (Mark 3:17), means ''sons of thunder.''

53. Identify the poets who penned the following lines, and name the poems in which they are found.
   a) ''All that we see or seem is but a dream within a dream.''
   b) ''And death i think is no parenthesis.''
   c) ''Behold I will build me a nest on the greatness of God.''
   d) ''Build thee more stately mansions, O my soul.''
   e) ''The Fiercest agonies have shortest reign.''
   f) ''Good fences make good neighbors.''
   g) ''A great victor, in defeat as great.''
   h) ''Home is the place where, when you have to go there, they have to take you in.''

ANSWER: a) Edgar Allan Poe in ''A Dream Within a Dream'' b) E.E. Cummings in ''Since Feeling is First'' c) Sidney Lanier in ''The Marshes of Glynn'' d) Oliver Wendell Holmes in ''The Chambered Nautilus'' e) William Cullen Bryant in ''Mutation'' f) Robert Frost in ''Mending Wall'' g) Stephen Vincent Benét in ''John Brown's Body'' h) Robert Frost in ''The Death of the Hired Man.''

54. Name the American poet who wrote ''A Dutch Lullaby.'' Another name for the poem would be the same as the answer to ''Who were the 3 characters who sailed off in a wooden shoe?'' Give this name or name the 3 characters. What did they come to fish for? Of what were their nets made? In the poem, identify the ''two little eyes''; ''a little head''; and ''a wee one's trundle-bed.''

ANSWER: Eugene Field/Wynken, Blynken, and Nod/The herring fish/Silver and gold/Wynken and Blynken are the 2 little eyes; Nod is the little head; and a wooden shoe is the wee one's trundle-bed.

55. Name the poet who wrote "Little Boy Blue." Name the animal that is "covered with dust" and the object that is "red with rust."
ANSWER: **Eugene Field/The little toy dog is "covered with dust," and the little toy soldier is "red with rust."**

56. What poet wrote about such characters as Cliff Klingenhagen, Miniver Cheevy, Luke Havergal, Eben Flood, and Richard Cory?
ANSWER: **Edwin Arlington Robinson.**

57. In Robinson's poem "Richard Cory," what did Richard Cory do "one calm summer night"?
ANSWER: **He "Went home and put a bullet through his head."**

58. In Robinson's poem "Miniver Cheevy," after "Miniver coughed, and called it fate," what did he keep on doing?
ANSWER: **"Drinking."**

59. Name the 3 narrative poems of Edwin Arlington Robinson that were based on medieval legends?
ANSWER: **"Merlin" (1917), "Launcelot" (1920), and "Tristram" (1927).**

60. Edwin Arlington Robinson grew up in Gardiner, Maine. What is the name of the fictitious town in his poems?
ANSWER: **Tilbury Town.**

61. Identify the poets who penned the following lines, and name the poems in which they appear.
   a) "I believe a leaf of grass is no less than the journey-work of the stars."
   b) "I dote on myself."
   c) "I forgot in Camelot/The man I loved in Rome."
   d) "In the long way that I must tread alone."
   e) "This is the way the world ends, not with a bang but a whimper."
   f) "Truth, crushed to earth, shall rise again."
   g) "We loved with a love that was more than love—/I and my _____—"
      (fill in the blank and you will have the name of the poem)
   h) "When the evening is spread out against the sky."
   i) "In the room the women come and go/Talking of Michelangelo."
ANSWER: **a) Walt Whitman in "Song of Myself" (*Leaves of Grass*) b) Walt Whitman in "Song of Myself" c) Edna St. Vincent Millay in "Fugitive" d) William Cullen Bryant in "To a Waterfowl" e) T.S. Eliot in "The Hollow Men" f) William Cullen Bryant in "The Battlefield" g) Edgar Allan Poe in "Annabel Lee" h) T.S. Eliot in "The Love Song of J. Alfred Prufrock" i) T.S. Eliot in "The Love Song of J. Alfred Prufrock."**

62. Who is the only poet to have won the Pulitzer Prize 4 times and the only one to have won it exactly 3 times?
ANSWER: **Robert Frost for *New Hampshire: A Poem with Notes and Grace Notes* (1924), *Collected Poems* (1931), *A Further Range* (1937), and *A Witness Tree* (1943)/Edwin Arlington Robinson for *Collected Poems* (1922), *The Man Who Died Twice* (1925), and *Tristram* (1928).**

63. In which poem by which poet do the following lines appear?
   "The woods are lovely dark and deep,
   But I have promises to keep,
   And miles to go before I sleep,
   And miles to go before I sleep."
ANSWER: **"Stopping by Woods on a Snowy Evening" (1923)/Robert Frost.**

64. Who penned the following lines and from what poem are they?
   "I shall be telling this with a sigh
   Somewhere ages and ages hence:
   Two roads diverged in a wood, and I—
   I took the one less traveled by,
   And that has made all the difference."

ANSWER: Robert Frost/''The Road Not Taken'' (1915).

65. In which poem by whom do the following lines appear?
    ''We keep the wall between us as we go.
    To each the boulders that have fallen to each.
    And some are loaves and some so nearly balls
    We have to use a spell to make them balance:
    'Stay where you are until our backs are turned!' ''
ANSWER: ''Mending Wall'' (1913)/Robert Frost.

66. Who was the poet who read a poem at John F. Kennedy's inauguration in 1960? Name the poem he read?
ANSWER: Robert Frost/''The Gift Outright'' (1942).

67. What poetic movement flourished in the United States (in England as well) between the years 1912 and 1917? What are the last names of some of the poets associated with this movement: Ezra, Ford, Hilda, William, and Amy?
ANSWER: ''Imagism''/Ezra Pound, Ford Madox Ford, Hilda Doolittle (H.D.), William Carlos Williams, and Amy Lowell.

68. Whose major works of poetry include *Hugh Selwyn Mauberly* (1920) and the *Cantos* (1925)?
ANSWER: Ezra Pound.

69. Identify the poem and the poet from the following lines. What was the title of her work for which she posthumously won the Pulitzer Prize in 1926?
    ''I walk down the garden-paths,
    And all the daffodils
    Are blowing, and the bright blue squills.
    I walk down the patterned garden-paths
    In my stiff, brocaded gown.''
ANSWER: ''Patterns'' (1915)/Amy Lowell/*What's O'Clock*.

70. What river that runs through the central part of Illinois is the name of an anthology of poems that appeared in 1915? Give the name of the anthology and the poet. What is unusual about this collection of poems?
ANSWER: Spoon River/*Spoon River Anthology*/Edgar Lee Masters/The poems are graveyard epitaphs spoken by the dead from their cemetery in a small Illinois community.

71. Name the Southern poetry magazine published in Nashville, Tennessee, from 1922 to 1925, the contributors to which were either students or teachers at Vanderbilt University. By what name was this group known? Give the full names of the following members of the group named John, Allen, and Robert.
ANSWER: The *Fugitive*/The Fugitives/John Crowe Ransom, Allen Tate, and Robert Penn Warren.

72. Who wrote the following lines and in what poem do they appear? Fill in the blanks with the names of the 4 foreign and one Civil War battle sites.
    ''Pile the bodies high at _____ and _____.
    Shovel them under and let me work —
        I am the grass; I cover all.

    And pile them high at _____
    And pile them high at _____ and _____.
    Shovel them under and let me work.''
ANSWER: Carl Sandburg/''Grass''/Austerlitz and Waterloo/Gettysburg/Ypres and Verdun.

73. What American poet said: ''Here is the difference between Dante, Milton, and me. They wrote about hell and never saw the place. I wrote about Chicago after looking the town over for years and years''?
ANSWER: Carl Sandburg.

74. Who wrote the following and what is the name of the poem?
    ''The fog comes
    on little cat feet.

It sits looking
over harbor and city
on silent haunches
and then moves on.''
ANSWER: Carl Sandburg/''Fog'' (1916).

75. Who wrote the following lines and in what poem do the lines appear?
''Hog Butcher for the World,
Tool Maker, Stacker of Wheat,
Player with Railroads and the Nation's Freight Handler;
Stormy, husky, brawling,
City of the Big Shoulders:''
ANSWER: Carl Sandburg/''Chicago'' (1914).

76. Name the works on the life of Abraham Lincoln written by Carl Sandburg.
ANSWER: *Abraham Lincoln, The Prairie Years* (2 volumes, 1926) and *Abraham Lincoln, The War Years* (4 volumes, 1939).

77. On what Biblical verse and British poet's work is Robinson Jeffers' *Tamar* based?
ANSWER: On Samuel 11:13 and on Percy Bysshe Shelly's *The Cenci*.

78. What are Robinson Jeffers' 2 favorite symbols?
ANSWER: The stone, for the enduring earth, and the hawk, for the wild free spirit of man which is marked for destruction.

79. Identify the poem from which the following lines are taken, and name the poet who wrote these lines.
''It was not so dreadful
As she had feared; she kissed the stained mouth,
And brought smooth stones from the shore until she had covered
Her love against vultures and salty gulls;
Then climbed up, rock to rock, bush to bush.''
ANSWER: ''Give Your Heart to the Hawks''/Robinson Jeffers.

80. Who wrote the lines ''We have lingered in the chambers of the sea by seagirls wreathed with seaweed''? In which poem do these lines appear? What is the literary allusion in the poem's Italian epigraph?
ANSWER: T.S. Eliot/''The Love Song of J. Alfred Prufrock''/From Dante's *Inferno*.

81. In T.S. Eliot's *The Wasteland* (1922), who is the central speaker and what was his role in Homer's *Odyssey*? On what event in whose life was T.S. Eliot's verse drama, *Murder in the Cathedral* (1935), based? What medal did Eliot win in 1964? What role did Irving Babbitt, Barrett Wendell, and Santayana play in his life?
ANSWER: Tiresias/The Theban Seer/The martyrdom of Thomas à Becket in Canterbury Cathedral in 1170/The American Medal of Freedom/They were among his teachers.

82. Who wrote ''Gerontion,'' *Ash Wednesday, Four Quartets,* ''Whispers of Immortality,'' and ''Sweeny among the Nightingales''?
ANSWER: T.S. Eliot.

83. Who wrote the following lines, and in what poem do they appear? What is the poet lamenting in the poem written in 1936, and why is he critical of his own generation? Who ''sowed dragon's teeth'' in Greek mythology, and what is the definition of the phrase?
''Now the boar and the asp have power in our time.
Now the night rolls back on the West and the night is solid.
Our fathers and ourselves sowed dragon's teeth.
Our children know and suffer the armed men.''
ANSWER: Stephen Vincent Benét/''Litany for Dictatorships''/He is lamenting the suffering of peoples by dictatorial governments and his own generation for not obtaining a lasting peace/Cadmus (He slayed a dragon and, on Athena's advice, sowed dragon's teeth. Fully armed soldiers were produced from the teeth and they fought among themselves.)/The phrase means ''to plant seeds of strife or to stir up trouble, especially by peaceful intent.''

84. Identify the poem from which the following lines are taken; name the poet who wrote the lines; and name the ''master'' in these lines.
    "And now at last,
    Comes Traveller and his master. Look at them well.''
ANSWER: **"John Brown's Body''/Stephen Vincent Benét/Robert E. Lee, ''master'' of his horse Traveller.**

85. In what poem by whom do the following lines appear? What post did this poet hold under President Franklin Roosevelt? For what works did he win the Pulitzer Prize for poetry in 1933 and 1953?
    "A poem should be palpable and mute
    As a globed fruit, . . .
    A poem should not mean
    But be.''
ANSWER: **"Ars Poetica''/Archibald MacLeish/Librarian of Congress/*Conquistador* and *Collected Poems 1917-1952*.**

86. Who were the 2 founders of the Salvation Army? How was the man nicknamed since he was the leader of the ''army''? What poet wrote a poem about this leader in 1912, and what is the name of that poem? The poem is to be sung. To what tune and for what reason?
ANSWER: **William and Catherine Booth/''General''/Vachel Lindsay/''General William Booth Enters into Heaven''/''The Blood of the Lamb'' because it is a popular song of the Salvation Army.**

87. Who wrote the following lines and in which poem do they appear?
    "I saw and heard, and knew at last
    The How and Why of all things, past,
    And present, and forevermore.''
ANSWER: **Edna St Vincent Millay/''Renascence'' (1912).**

88. Identify the poem and the poet from the following lines.
    "My candle burns at both ends;
        It will not last the night;
    But ah, my foes, and oh, my friends —
        It gives a lovely light!''
ANSWER: **Edna St Vincent Millay in ''First Fig'' from *A Few Figs from Thistles*.**

89. Name the poet who studied medicine at the University of Pennsylvania, became a General Practitioner in Rutherford, New Jersey, and delivered more babies than any other poet. What is the first line of his poem ''The Artist'' that is the same as a major character in the film *Rocky III?*
ANSWER: **William Carlos Williams/''Mr. T.''**

90. Identify the poet and the poem from the following words: ''mud-luscious,'' ''lame balloonman,'' ''eddieandbill,'' ''puddle-wonderful,'' ''bettyandisbel,'' ''hopscotch and jump-rope,'' and ''goat-footed.''
ANSWER: **e.e. cummings/''chanson innocente.''**

91. Identify the poets who wrote the following lines and the poems in which they appear.
    a) "Doubting, dreaming dreams no mortal ever dared to dream before.''
    b) "Come lovely and soothing death.''
    c) "Footprints on the sands of time.''
    d) "Thou go not, like the quarry-slave at night.''
    d) "I hear America singing.''
    f) "Let him not boast who puts his armor on.''
    g) "Nail to the mast her holy flag.''
ANSWER: **a) Edgar Allan Poe from ''The Raven'' b) Walt Whitman from ''When Lilacs Last in the Dooryard Bloom'd'' c) Henry Wadsworth Longfellow from ''A Psalm of Life'' d) William Cullen Bryant from ''Thanatopsis'' e) Walt Whitman from ''I Hear America Singing'' f) Henry Wadsworth Longfellow from ''Morituri Salutamus'' g) Oliver Wendell Holmes from ''Old Ironsides.''**

AMERICAN DRAMA

QUESTIONS AND ANSWERS

1. What are the names of the 3 separate parts of the trilogy *Mourning Becomes Electra* (1929-1931) by Eugene O'Neill?
ANSWER: *Homecoming, The Hunted,* **and** *The Haunted.*

2. What are the names of the 3 wives of Eugene O'Neill? Which wife was the mother of the daughter who married Charlie Chaplin? Name the daughter.
ANSWER: Kathleen Jenkins, Agnes Boulton, and Carlotta Monterey/Agnes Boulton/ Oona.

3. What were the dying words of Eugene O'Neill?
ANSWER: ''Born in a goddam hotel room and dying in a hotel room!''

4. Name the 3 sons of Ephraim Cabot in Eugene O'Neill's *Desire Under the Elms.* Name the stepmother.
ANSWER: Sim, Peter, and Eben/Abbie.

5. Give the title of the play in which each of the following characters appears.
   a) Ezra Mannon   d) Birdie Hubbard   g) Amanda Wingfield
   b) Brutus Jones   e) John Proctor   h) Blanche DuBois
   c) Willy Loman   f) Harry Hope   i) Dr. Gibbs
ANSWER: a) *Mourning Becomes Electra* **b)** *Emperor Jones* **c)** *Death of a Salesman* **d)** *The Little Foxes* **e)** *The Crucible* **f)** *The Iceman Cometh* **g)** *The Glass Menagerie* **h)** *Streetcar Named Desire* **i)** *Our Town.*

6. Who is the only American playwright to win 4 Pulitzer Prizes for drama? Name the works for which he won the Pulitzers.
ANSWER: Eugene O'Neill/*Beyond the Horizon* **(1920),** *Anna Christie* **(1922),** *Strange Interlude* **(1928), and** *Long Day's Journey Into Night* **(1957).**

7. What American playwright has won the Pulitzer Prize for drama exactly 3 times? Name the plays for which he won the Pulitzers.
ANSWER: Robert E. Sherwood/*Idiot's Delight* **(1936),** *Abe Lincoln in Illinois* **(1939), and** *There Shall Be No Night* **(1941).**

8. On the case of what 2 Italian anarchists is Maxwell Anderson's *Winterset* (1935) based?
ANSWER: The case of Nicola Sacco and Bartolomeo Vanzetti.

9. What number was associated with George Pierce Baker's Harvard Workshop?
ANSWER: 47.

10. In Thornton Wilder's *The Skin of Our Teeth,* what are the periods of the play?
ANSWER: An ice age, a great flood, and a devastating war.

11. Give the Broadway play which is based on each of the following works.
   a) *The Matchmaker*   d) *Green Grow the Lilacs*
   b) *Pygmalion*   e) *The Taming of the Shrew*
   c) *7½ Cents*   f) *The Trapp Family Singers*
ANSWER: a) *Hello, Dolly* **b)** *My Fair Lady* **c)** *Pajama Game* **d)** *Oklahoma* **e)** *Kiss Me, Kate* **f)** *The Sound of Music.*

12. What is the address of the Kowalski family in Thomas Lanier ''Tennessee'' Williams' *Streetcar Named Desire?* What is the mythological explanation for the name? What 2 streetcars brought Blanche to see her sister Stella?
ANSWER: The Elysian Fields/The abode of virtuous people after death/Desire and Cemeteries.

13. The name of the 3rd Act of Williams' *Streetcar Named Desire* was once the title of the play. Name it.
ANSWER: ''The Poker Night.''

14. What playwright in 1965 was the first American elected international president of

P.E.N.? For what do the initials P.E.N. stand?

ANSWER: Arthur Miller/International Association of Poets, Playwrights, Editors, Essayists, and Novelists.

15. For what film did Arthur Miller write a script in 1960 and who directed that film? What wife of Miller played a leading role?

ANSWER: *The Misfits* **and John Huston/Marilyn Monroe.**

16. Name the 4 characters in Edward Albee's *Who's Afraid of Virginia Woolf?*. What are the titles of the 3 Acts? Which one did Albee once plan to use as a title for the entire play? Explain the meaning of the name of the second Act.

ANSWER: Martha, George, Honey, and Nick/"Fun and Games," "Walpurgisnacht," and "Exorcism"/"Exorcism"/*Walpurgisnacht* **or "Walpurgis Night" is "the time of the gathering of witches on Brocken mountain for a demonic orgy; hence, any wild event with a nightmarish quality" (the feast day of St.** *Walpurgis,* **an English missionary in Germany in the 8th century, is April 30.**

17. Identify each of the following dramatists based on the given description.
    a) Wrote a column for the *Washington Times* entitled "This and That and a Little of the Other"
    b) Worked as a Western Union messenger in New York (1955-1958)
    c) Wrote his autobiography entitled *Minority Report* (1963)
    d) Was the Charles E. Norton Professor of Poetry at Harvard
    e) Wrote on public themes such as isolationism, fascism, and labor agitation
    f) Worked as a reporter in New London, Connecticut, and spent six months in a tuberculosis sanatorium

ANSWER: a) George Kaufman b) Edward Albee c) Elmer Rice d) Thornton Wilder e) Lillian Hellman f) Eugene O'Neill.

AMERICAN DRAMATISTS, THEIR PLAYS, AND MAIN CHARACTERS

ALBEE, Edward . . . . *Who's Afraid of Virginia Woolf?* . . . Martha, George, Honey, Nick

ANDERSON, Maxwell . . . . *Winterset* . . . Esdras, Garth, Miriamne, Trock, Mio, Shadow, Judge Gaunt

BEHRMAN, S.N. . . . . *End of Summer* . . . Leonie Frothingham, Dr. Kenneth Rice, Dennis McCarthy, Paula Frothingham, Will Dexter

HELLMAN, Lillian . . . . *The Little Foxes* . . . Regina and Horace Giddens, Benjamin and Oscar Hubbard, Alexandra, Birdie Bagtry Hubbard

INGE, William . . . . *Come Back Little Sheba* . . . Doc, Lola, Marie, Turk

KAUFMAN, George S. . . . . *You Can't Take It with You* . . . Vanderhof family, Alice Vanderhof, Tony Kirby

MILLER, Arthur Ashur . . . . *The Crucible* . . . John Proctor, Abigail Adams, Elizabeth Proctor

Death of a Salesman . . . Willy Loman, Linda Loman, Biff and Happy Loman

ODETS, Clifford . . . . *Golden Boy* . . . Joe Bonaparte, Tom Moody, Lorna Moore, Mr. Bonaparte, Eddie Friseli

O'NEILL, Eugene . . . . *Desire Under the Elms* . . . Ephraim Cabot, Simeon, Peter, Eben, Abbie

Emperor Jones . . . Brutus Jones, Smithers, Lem

The Iceman Cometh . . . Harry Hope, Hickey, Larry

Long Day's Journey Into Night . . . James Tyrone, Mary Cavan Tyrone, James and Edmund Tyrone, Cathleen

Mourning Becomes Electra . . . Ezra, Christine,

Orin and Lavinia Mannon, Captain Adam Brant, Seth, Hazel and Peter Niles

Strange Interlude . . . Nina Leeds, Professor Henry Leeds, Charles Marsden, Dr. Edmund Darrell, Sam Evans, Gordon Evans

RICE, Elmer . . . . *Street Scene* . . . Rose Maurrant, Anna and Frank Maurrant, Sankey, Sam Kaplan, Abe Kaplan, Harry Easter, Shirley Kaplan

SAROYAN, William . . . . *The Time of Your Life* . . . Nick, Joe, Dudley, Elsie, Willie, Harry, Wesley, Kitty Duval, Tom, Blick, Kit

WILDER, Thornton . . . . *Our Town* . . . Dr. and Mrs. Gibbs, George and Rebecca Gibbs, Emily and Wally Webb, Simon Stinson

The Skin of Our Teeth . . . Mr. and Mrs. George Antrobus, Gladys and Henry Antrobus, Sabina

WILLIAMS, Tennessee . . . . *Cat on a Hot Tin Roof* . . . Big Daddy, Big Mamma, Brick, Margaret, Gooper (Brother Man), Mae (Sister Man)

The Glass Menagerie . . . Amanda Wingfield, Tom and Laura Wingfield, Jim O'Connor

A Streetcar Named Desire...Blanche DuBois, Stella Kowalski, Stanley Kowalski

AMERICAN PLAYS, THEIR PUBLICATION DATES, AUTHORS, AND SETTINGS

Emperor Jones . . . 1920 . . . O'Neill . . . . **West Indies**

Desire Under the Elms . . . 1924 . . . O'Neill . . . . . . **Cabot farm house (New England)**

Strange Interlude . . . 1928 . . . O'Neill . . . . **New England and New York**

Street Scene . . . 1929 . . . Rice . . . . **New York**

Mourning Becomes Electra . . . 1931 . . . O'Neill . . **New England**

Winterset . . . 1935 . . . Anderson . . . . **New York**

End of Summer . . . 1936 . . . Behrman . . . . **Maine**

You Can't Take It with You . . . 1936 . . .
Kaufman (with Moss Hart) . . . . **New York**

Golden Boy . . . 1937 . . . Odets . . . . **New York**

Our Town . . . 1938 . . . Wilder . . . . **Grover's Corners, New Hampshire**

The Little Foxes . . . 1939 . . . Hellman . . . . **Deep South**

The Time of Your Life . . . 1939 . . . Saroyan . . . . . . **San Francisco**

The Skin of Our Teeth . . . 1942 . . . Thornton . . . . **Excelsior, New Jersey; Atlantic City**

The Glass Menagerie . . . 1945 (wr. 1940) . . .
Williams . . . . **St. Louis, Missouri**

The Iceman Cometh . . . 1946 . . . O'Neill . . . . **New York's Lower West Side**

A Streetcar Named Desire . 1947 . . . Williams . . . . **New Orleans, Louisiana**

Death of a Salesman . . . 1949 . . . Miller . . . . **New York**

Come Back Little Sheba . . . 1950 . . . Inge . . . . **Midwestern city**

The Crucible . . . 1953 . . . Miller . . . . **Salem, Massachusetts**

Cat on a Hot Tin Roof . . . 1955 . . . Williams . . . . . . **Mississippi Delta**

Long Day's Journey Into Night . . . 1957 . . .
O'Neill . . . . **New London, Connecticut**

Who's Afraid of Virginia Woolf? . . . 1963 . . .
Albee . . . . **New Carthage (New England college campus)**

BROADWAY PLAYS AND THE WORKS ON WHICH THEY ARE BASED

Applause.....................movie *All About Eve* and original story by Mary Orr

Cabaret......................*I am a Camera* by John van Druten and stories by Christopher Isherwood

Camelot ....*The Once and Future King* by T.H. White

Candide ....*Candide* by Voltaire

Carmen Jones ....''Carmen'' by Prosper Mérimée, music by Georges Bizet

Carousel ....play adapted by Glazer from Ferenc Molnar's *Liliom*

Damn Yankees ....*The Year the Yankees Lost the Pennant* by Douglass Wallop

Fanny ....*Marius, Fanny, and César* by Marcel Pagnol

The Fantastiques ....*Les Romantiques* by Edmund Rostand

Fiddler on the Roof ....stories by Sholom Aleichem

Flower Drum Song............*Flower Drum Song* by C.Y. Lee

Gentlemen Prefer Blondes ....*Gentlemen Prefer Blondes* by Anita Loos

Golden Boy ....*Golden Boy* by Clifford Odets

Guys & Dolls................short story ''The Idyll of Miss Sarah Brown'' by Damon Runyan

Gypsy ....*Gypsy* by Gypsy Rose Lee (her memoirs)

Hello, Dolly.................*The Matchmaker* by Thornton Wilder

I Do! I Do! ....*The Fourposter* by Jan de Hartog

The King and I ....*Anna and the King of Siam* by Margaret Landon

Kismet......................*Kismet* by Edward Knoblock

Kiss Me, Kate ....*The Taming of the Shrew* by William Shakespeare

Li'l Abner...................characters created by Al Capp in his comic strip

A Little Night Music ....movie *Smiles of a Summer Night* by Ingmar Bergman

Mame ....*Auntie Mame* by Patrick Dennis

Man of La Mancha...........life and works of Miguel de Cervantes y Saavedra

The Me Nobody Knows ....*The Me Nobody Knows* by Stephen Joseph

The Most Happy Fella ....*They Knew What They Wanted* by Sidney Howard

My Fair Lady................*Pygmalion* by George Bernard Shaw

No, No, Nanette.............*My Lady Friends* by Frank Mandel

Oklahoma!..................*Green Grow the Lilacs* by Lynn Riggs

Oliver!......................*Oliver Twist* by Charles Dickens

Pajama Game ....*7 1/2 Cents* by Richard Bissell

Promises, Promises ....movie *The Apartment* by Wilder and Diamond

Purlie ....*Purlie Victorious* by Ossie Davis

Raisin ....*A Raisin in the Sun* by Lorraine Hansberry

Show Boat ....*Show Boat* by Edna Ferber

The Sound of Music..........*The Trapp Family Singers* by Maria Augusta Trapp

South Pacific................*Tales of the South Pacific* by James Michener

The Student Prince ....Mansfield's adaptation of *Old Heidelberg* by Wilhelm Meyer-Forster

Sugar ....*Some Like It Hot* from Wilder's and Diamond's screenplay

Sweet Charity ....movie *Nights of Cabiria* by Fellini, Pinelli, and Flaiano

West Side Story..............on an idea by Jerome Robbins which was somewhat related to *Romeo and Juliet* by William Shakespeare

Where's Charley?............*Charley's Aunt* by Brandon Thomas

The Wiz ....*The Wonderful World of Oz* by L. Frank Baum

Wish You Were Here ....*Having Wonderful Time* by Arthur Kober

Wonderful Town ....*My Sister Eileen* by Jerome Chodorov and stories by Ruth McKenney

FIRST PLAYS BY AMERICAN DRAMATISTS

Edward Franklin Albee ....*The Zoo Story* (1958)

Maxwell Anderson ....*White Desert* (1923)

Samuel Nathaniel Behrman....*The Second Man* (1927)

Lillian Hellman ....*The Children's Hour* (1934)

William Motter Inge..........*Farther Off from Heaven* (1947)

George Simon Kaufman.......*Some One in the House* (1918, with L. Evans and W. Percival)

Arthur Ashur Miller..........*The Grass Still Grows* (1936, first play); *The Man Who Had All the Luck* (1944, first performed play)

Clifford Odets ....*Waiting for Lefty* (1933)

Eugene Gladstone O'Neill .....*The Web* (1913-1914, first play); *Bound East for Cardiff* (1916, first performed play)

Elmer Rice ....*On Trial* (1914)

William Saroyan ....*The Hungeres: A Short Play* (1939)

Thornton Niven Wilder ....*The Trumpet Shall Sound* (1919-1920)

Tennessee Williams ....*Cairo! Shanghai! Bombay!* (1936, with B.D. Shapiro)

AMERICAN AUTHORS, THEIR NOVELS/SHORT STORIES AND MAIN CHARACTERS

AGEE, James . . . . *Death in the Family* . . . Rufus Follet, Mary and Jay Follet, Catherine Follet

ALCOTT, Louisa May . . . . *Little Women* . . . Meg, Jo, Beth, and Amy March, Theodore Lawrence (Laurie), Mrs. March (Marmee), Professor Bhaer, John Brooke

ALLEN, Hervey . . . . *Anthony Adverse* . . . Anthony Adverse, Don Luis, Marquis Da Vincitata, Maria, Angela Guiseppe, Florence Udney, Dolores de la Fuente

ANDERSON, Sherwood . . . . *Winesburg, Ohio* . . . George Willard, Elizabeth Willard, Dr. Reefy

BALDWIN, James . . . . *Go Tell It on the Mountain* . . . John Grimes, Elizabeth Grimes, Gabriel Grimes, Florence

BARTH, John . . . . *Giles Goat-Boy* . . . George Giles (Billy Bockfuss the Goat-Boy), Max Spielman, Hedda, Lady Creamhair, Redfearn's Tom
The Sot-Weed Factor . . . Ebenezer Cooke, Henry Burlingame III, Joan Toast (Susan Warren), Anna Cooke, Andrew Cooke

BELLAMY, Edward . . . . *Looking Backward* . . . Julia West, Edith Bartlett, Dr. Leete, Edith Leete

BELLOW, Saul . . . . *Augie March* . . . Augie March, Simon March, Georgie March, Stella (Chesney) March
Herzog . . . Moses E. Herzog, Madeleine Herzog, June Herzog, Ramona and Sono Oguki
Humboldt's Gift . . . Charlie Citrine, Renata Koffritz, Denise Citrine, Rinaldo Cantabile, Von Humboldt Fleisher

BUCK, Pearl . . . . *The Good Earth* . . . Wang Lung, O-Lan, Lotus Blossom

CABELL, James Branch . . . . *Jurgen, A Comedy of Justice* . . . Jurgen, Dame Lisa, Dorothy La Désirée

CALDWELL, Erskine . . . . *Tobacco Road* . . . Jeeter Lester, Ada, Dude, Ellie May, Pearl, Lov Bensey, Sister Bessie

CAPOTE, Truman . . . . *In Cold Blood* . . . Herbert William and Bonnie Clutter, Kenyon and Nancy Clutter, Richard Hickock, Perry Smith

CATHER, Willa . . . . *Death Comes for the Archbishop* . . . Father Jean Marie Latour, Father Joseph Vaillant, Kit Carson, Jacinto
My Ántonia . . . Jim Burden, Antonia Shimerda

CHEEVER, John . . . . *Wapshot Chronicle* . . . Leander and Sarah Wapshot, Moses and Melissa Wapshot, Coverly and Betsey Wapshot

CLARK, Walter Van Tilburg . . . . *The Ox-Bow Incident* . . . Gil Carter, Croft, Tetley, Gerald, Davies, Martin, Canby

COOPER, James Fenimore . . . . *The Deerslayer* . . . Natty Bumppo, Hurry Harry, Chingachgook, Thomas Hutter
Last of the Mohicans . . . Natty Bumppo, Chingachgook, Magua, Cora and Alice Munro
The Pathfinder . . . Sergeant Dunham, Mabel Dunham, Natty Bumppo, Jasper Western
The Pilot . . . Lieutenant Richard Barnstable, Mr. Gray, the Pilot (John Paul Jones), Long Tom Coffin, Katherine Plowden, Edward Griffith
The Pioneers . . . Judge Temple, Elizabeth

Temple, Natty Bumppo, Oliver Edwards
The Prairie . . . Natty Bumppo, Ishmael and Esther Bush, Paul Hover, Ellen Wade, Hard-Heart
The Spy . . . Harvey Birch, Major Peyton Dunwoodie, Frances Wharton, Mr. Harper, Mr. Wharton

COZZENS, James Gould . . . . *By Love Possessed* . . . Arthur Winner, Clarissa Winner, Julius Penrose, Helen Detweiler, Noah Tuttle, Marjorie Penrose
Guard of Honor . . . Major General Ira "Bus" Beal, Sal Beal, Colonel Norman Ross

CRANE, Stephen . . . . *The Red Badge of Courage* . . . Henry Fleming, Jim Conklin, Wilson

CUMMINGS, E.E. . . . . *The Enormous Room* . . . E.E. Cummings, W.S.B., Apollyon, Jean le Nègre

DANA, JR., Richard Henry . . . . *Two Years Before the Mast* . . . Richard Henry Dana, Jr.

DICKEY, James . . . . *Deliverance* . . . Ed Gentry, Lewis Medlock, Bobby Trippe, Drew Ballinger

DONLEAVY, J.P. . . . . *The Ginger Man* . . . Sebastian Dangerfield, Marion Dangerfield, Kenneth O'Keefe, Percy Cocklan, Mary

DOS PASSOS, John . . . . *Manhattan Transfer* . . . Ellen Thatcher, Congo, Joe Harland, George Baldwin, Jimmy Herf
U.S.A. . . . . Fainy McCreary, Janey Williams, Joe Williams, Anne Elizabeth Trent, Margo Dowling

DREISER, Theodore . . . . *An American Tragedy* . . . Clyde Griffiths, Roberta Alden, Samuel Griffiths, Sondra Finchley
Sister Carrie . . . Carrie Meeber, Charles Drouet, G.W. Hurstwood

ELLISON, Ralph . . . . *Invisible Man* . . . The Narrator-Hero, Dr. Bledsoe, Ras the Destroyer, Rinehart

FARRELL, James T . . . . *Studs Lonigan: A Trilogy* . . . William "Studs" Lonigan, Frances Lonigan, Lucy Scanlan, Catherine Banahan

FAULKNER, William . . . . *Absalom, Absalom!* . . . . Thomas Sutpen, Ellen Coldfield Sutpen, Henry and Judith Sutpen, Rosa Coldfield, Charles Bon
As I Lay Dying . . . Anse and Addie Bundren, Cash, Darl, Jewel and Vardaman Bundren, and Dewey Dell Bundren
Light in August . . . Joe Christmas, Doc Hines, Mr. McEachern, Joanna Burden, Joe Brown
Sanctuary . . . Popeye, Horace Benbow, Lee Goodwin, Ruby Lamar, Temple Drake
The Sound and the Fury . . . Mrs. Compson, Benjamin, Quentin, Candace, and Jason Compson

FERBER, Edna . . . . *So Big*... Selina Peake DeJong, Dirk "So Big" DeJong, Roelf Pool, August Hempel, Pervus DeJong

FITZGERALD, F. Scott . . . . *The Great Gatsby* . . . Nick Carraway, Daisy and Tom Buchanan, Myrtle Wilson, Jay Gatsby
Tender is the Night . . . Dick and Nicole Diver, Rosemary Hoyt, Tommy Barban

HALE, Edward E. . . . . "The Man Without a Country" . . Philip Nolan

HAMMETT, Dashiell . . . . *The Maltese Falcon* . . . Sam Spade, Brigid

O'Shaughnessy, Joel Cairo

HAWTHORNE, Nathaniel .... *The House of the Seven Gables* . . . Miss Hepzibah Pyncheon, Clifford Pyncheon, Mr. Holgrave, Phoebe Pyncheon
The Marble Faun . . . Miriam, Hilda, Kenyon, Donatello
The Scarlet Letter . . . Hester Prynne, Arthur Dimmesdale, Roger Chillingworth, Pearl

HEMINGWAY, Ernest .... *A Farewell to Arms* . . . Frederic Henry, Catherine Barkley
For Whom the Bell Tolls . . . Robert Jordan, Pablo and Pilar, Maria, Anselmo
The Old Man and the Sea . . . Santiago, Manolin
The Sun Also Rises . . . Jake Barnes, Lady Brett Ashley, Robert Cohn, Mike Campbell, Pedro Romero

HELLER, Joseph .... *Catch-22* . . . Captain John Yossarian, Colonel Cathcart, Major Major Major

HERSEY, John .... *A Bell for Adano* . . . Major Victor Joppolo, Sergeant Borth

HOLMES, Oliver Wendell .... *The Autocrat of the Breakfast Table* . . . The Autocrat, The Schoolmistress, The Old Gentleman

HOWELLS, William Dean .... *The Rise of Silas Lapham* . . . Silas Lapham, Mrs. Lapham, Penelope and Irene Lapham, Mr. Rogers, Tom Corey

IRVING, Washington .... *A History of New York* . . . Hendrick Hudson, Peter Stuyvesant
"The Legend of Sleepy Hollow" . . . Ichabod Crane, Katrina Van Tassel, Abraham Van Brunt
"Rip Van Winkle" . . . Rip Van Winkle, Dame Van Winkle

JAMES, Henry .... *The Ambassadors* . . . Chad Newsome, Lambert Strether, Comtesse de Vionnet, Maria Gostrey
The American . . . Christopher Newman, Claire de Cintré, Valentin de Bellegarde
Daisy Miller . . . Daisy Miller, Winterbourne, Giovanelli
The Portrait of a Lady . . . Isabel Archer, Gilbert Osmond, Henrietta Stackpole, Caspar Goodwood, Lord Warburton, Ralph Touchett, Madame Merle, Pansy Osmond
The Turn of the Screw . . . The Governess, Mrs. Grose, Miles and Flora, Peter Quint, Miss Jessel

KEROUAC, Jack .... *On the Road* . . . Salvatore "Sal" Paradise, Dean Moriarty, Marylou, Bull Lee

KESEY, Ken .... *One Flew Over the Cuckoo's Nest* . . . McMurphy, Miss Ratched, Chief Bromden, Billy Bibbit, Harding

KNOWLES, John .... *A Separate Peace* . . . Phineas (Finny), Gene Forrester

LEWIS, Sinclair .... *Arrowsmith* . . . Martin Arrowsmith, Leora Arrowsmith, Dr. Max Gottlieb
Babbitt . . . George F. Babbitt, Myra Babbitt, Ted, Verona, Paul Riesling, Zilla Riesling
Dodsworth . . . Sam and Fran Dodsworth,

Kurt Obersdorf, Clyde Lockert, Edith Cortright
Elmer Gantry . . . Elmer Gantry, Jim Lefferts, Judson Roberts, Mrs. Gantry, Lulu Bains, Frank Shallard, Eddie Fislinger
Main Street . . . Dr. Will Kennicott, Carol (Milford) Kennicott

LONDON, Jack . . . . *The Call of the Wild* . . . Buck, a spitz, John Thornton
The Sea Wolf . . . Humphrey Van Weyden, Wolf Larsen, Maud Brewster, Mugridge

LOWELL, James Russell . . . . *The Biglow Papers* . . . Hosea Biglow, Bir-dofredum Sawin, Homer Wibur

McCULLERS, Carson . . . . *The Heart is a Lonely Hunter* . . . Mr. Singer, Jake Blount, Mick Kelly, Biff Brannon, Dr. Copeland
The Member of the Wedding . . . . . Frankie Addams, Berenice Sadie Brown, John Henry West, Jarvis, Janice Evans

MAILER, Norman . . . . *The Naked and the Dead.* . . General Cummings, Sgt. Croft, Lieut. Hearn

MALAMUD, Bernard . . . . *The Fixer* . . . . Yokov and Raisl Bok, Schmuel

MELVILLE, Herman . . . . *Billy Budd* . . . Billy Budd, Captain Vere, Claggart
Moby-Dick . . . Ishmael, Queequeg, Ahab, Starbuck, Stubb, Fedallah

MITCHELL, Margaret . . . . *Gone With the Wind* . . . Scarlett O'Hara, Rhett Butler, Ashley Wilkes, Melanie Wilkes, Miss Pittypat, Mammy, Bonnie Blue

NORDHOFF, Charles Bernard, and
HALL, James Norman . . . . *Mutiny on the Bounty* . . . William Bligh, Fletcher Christian, Roger Byam

OATES, Joyce Carol . . . . *Them.* . . Loretta (Botsford) Wendall, Jules Wendall, Maureen Wendall

POE, Edgar Allan . . . . "The Fall of the House of Usher" . . . Roder-ick Usher, Madeline Usher, Narrator

PORTER, Katherine Anne . . . . *Ship of Fools* . . . Captain Thiele

PYNCHON, Thomas . . . . *V.* . . . Benny Profane, Herbert Stencil, Sidney Stencil, V., the eternal woman

RAWLINGS, Marjorie Kinnan . . . . . . *The Yearling* . . . Jody Baxter, Penny Baxter, Ora Baxter, Fodder-wing Forrester

ROTH, Philip . . . . *Portnoy's Complaint* . . . Alexander Port-noy, Sophie Portnoy, Jack Portnoy, the Monkey

SALINGER, J.D. . . . . *The Catcher in the Rye* . . . Holden Caul-field, Phoebe Caulfield, Stradlater, Ackley

SAROYAN, William . . . . *The Human Comedy* . . . Katey Macauley, Homer, Ulysses, and Marcus Macauley, Bess Macauley, Tobey George

SINCLAIR, Upton . . . . *The Jungle* . . . Jurgis Rudkus, Ona Rudkus, Antanas Rudkus

STEINBECK, John . . . . *East of Eden* . . . Adam and Cathy (Ames) Trask, Caleb and Aron Trask, Charles Trask, Lee
The Grapes of Wrath. . . . Tom Joad, Pa and Ma Joad, Rose of Sharon, Jim Casy
Of Mice and Men . . . Lennie Small, George Milton, Candy, Curley

STOWE, Harriet Beecher . . . . *Uncle Tom's Cabin* . . . Uncle Tom, Eva St. Clare, Simon Legree, Eliza, Topsy

TARKINGTON, Booth . . . . *Seventeen* . . . William Sylvanus Baxter, Mrs. Baxter, Jane Baxter, Miss Pratt

THOREAU, Henry David . . . . *Walden* . . . Henry David Thoreau

TWAIN, Mark (Samuel Clemens) ... *The Adventures of Huckleberry Finn* ... Huckleberry Finn, Tom Sawyer, Jim
The Adventures of Tom Sawyer ... Tom Sawyer, Aunt Polly, Huckleberry Finn, Joe Harper, Becky Thatcher, Injun Joe, Muff Potter
A Connecticut Yankee at King Arthur's Court ... The Connecticut Yankee, King Arthur, Clarence, Sandy, Merlin
The Prince and the Pauper ... Tom Canty, Edward (Prince of Wales)

UPDIKE, John .... *Rabbit, Run* ... Harry "Rabbit" Angstrom, Janice Angstrom, Ruth Leonard, Jack and Lucy Eccles

VONNEGUT, Kurt .... *Slaughterhouse-Five* ... Billy Pilgrim, Bernard V. O'Hare, Montana Wildhack, Roland Weary, Kilgore Trout, Wild Bob

WALLACE, Lew .... *Ben-Hur.* .. Ben-Hur, Balthasar, Simonides, Messala, Esther

WARREN, Robert Penn.......... *All the King's Men* ... Jack Burden, Willie Stark, Sadie Burke, Anne Stanton, Adam Stanton, Judge Irwin

WEST, Nathanael.............. *Miss Lonelyhearts* ... Miss Lonelyhearts, Betty, Willie and Mary Shrike, Peter and Fay Doyle

WHARTON, Edith .... *The Age of Innocence* ... Newland Archer, May Welland, Countess Ellen Olenska
Ethan Frome ... Ethan Frome, Zenobia (Zeena) Frome, Mattie Silver

WILDER, Thornton .... *The Bridge of San Luis Rey* ... Brother Juniper, La Périchole, Uncle Pio, the Marquesa de Montemayor

WISTER, Owen................ *The Virginian* ... The Virginian, Trampas, Molly Wood, Judge Henry

WOLFE, Thomas .... *Look Homeward, Angel.* ... Eugene Gant, Eliza Gant, Oliver Gant, Margaret Leonard, Laura James
Of Time and the River ... Eugene Gant, Bascom Pentland, Frances Starwick, Robert Weaver

WRIGHT, Richard.............. *Native Son* ... Bigger Thomas, Mary Dalton, Bessie Mears, Jan Erlone, Mr. and Mrs. Dalton

AMERICAN NOVELS/SHORT STORIES, THEIR PUBLICATION DATES, AUTHORS, AND SETTINGS

A History of New York ... 1809 ... Irving ... **New Amsterdam (New York)**
"Rip Van Winkle" ... 1819-1820 ... Irving...... **New York State**
"The Legend of Sleepy Hollow" ... 1819-1820 ...
    Irving .... **New York State**
The Spy ... 1821 ... Cooper .... **New York State**
The Pilot ... 1823 ... Cooper .... **Coast of England**
The Pioneers ... 1823 ... Cooper .... **New York State**
The Last of the Mohicans ... 1826 ...Cooper. **New York State**
The Prairie ... 1827 ... Cooper .... **Western United States**
"The Fall of the House of Usher" ... 1839 ... Poe. **House of Usher**
The Pathfinder ... 1840 ... Cooper .... **Lake Ontario area**
Two Years Before the Mast ... 1840 ...
    Dana................................. **California and the high seas**
The Deerslayer ... 1841 ... Cooper .... **New York State**

The Biglow Papers . . . 1848 and 1867. . .
    Lowell . . . . **New England**
The Scarlet Letter . . . 1850 . . . Hawthorne . . . . **Boston**
The House of the Seven Gables . . . 1851 . . .
    Hawthorne . . . . **Salem, Massachusetts**
Moby-Dick . . . 1851 . . . Melville . . . . **The high seas**
Uncle Tom's Cabin . . . 1852 . . . Stowe . . . . . **Kentucky and Mississippi**
Walden . . . 1854 . . . Thoreau . . . . **Walden Pond, near Concord, Massachusetts**
The Autocrat of the Breakfast Table . . .
    1858 . . . Holmes . . . . **Boston**
The Marble Faun . . . 1860 . . . Hawthorne . . . . . **Rome, Italy**
"The Man Without a Country" . . . . . .1863. . . Hale. . **United States and the high seas**
Little Women . . . 1868 . . . Alcott . . . . **New England village; New York City; Italy**
The Adventures of Tom Sawyer . . . 1876 . . .
    Twain . . . . **St. Petersburg on the Mississippi**
The American . . . 1877 . . . James . . . . **Paris, France**
Daisy Miller . . . 1878 . . . James . . . . **Vevey, Switzerland; Rome**
Ben-Hur . . . 1880 . . . Wallace . . . . **Antioch and Jerusalem**
The Portrait of a Lady . . . 1881 . . . James . . . . **England, France, Italy**
The Prince and the Pauper . . . 1882 . . .
    Twain . . . . **England**
The Rise of Silas Lapham . . . 1885 . . .
    Howells . . . . **New England**
The Adventures of Huckleberry Finn . . .
    1885 . . . Twain . . . . **Mississippi River**
Looking Backward . . . 1888 . . . Bellamy . . . . . **Boston, Massachusetts**
A Connecticut Yankee at King Arthur's
Co   . . . 1889 . . . Twain . . . . **England**
The Red Badge of Courage . . . 1895. . .
    Crane . . . . **A Civil War battlefield**
The Turn of the Screw . . . 1898 . . . James . . **England**
Sister Carrie . . . 1900 . . . Dreiser . . . . **Chicago and New York**
The Virginian . . . 1902 . . . Wister . . . . **Wyoming**
The Ambassadors . . . 1903 . . . James . . . . **Paris, France**
The Call of the Wild . . . 1903 . . . London . . . . **Alaska**
The Sea Wolf . . . 1904 . . . London . . . . **Pacific Ocean, Bering Sea**
The Jungle . . . 1906 . . . Sinclair . . . . **Chicago**
Ethan Frome . . . 1911 . . . Wharton . . . . **Starkfield, Massachusetts**
Seventeen . . . 1916 . . . Tarkington . . . . **Small Midwestern town**
My Antonia . . . 1918 . . . Cather . . . .'. . **Nebraska prairie land**
Jurgen . . . 1919 . . . Cabell . . . . **Poictesme, a medieval and imaginary land**
Winesburg, Ohio . . . 1919 . . . Anderson . . . . . . **Winesburg, Ohio**
Main Street . . . 1920 . . . Lewis . . . . **Gopher Prairie, Minnesota**
The Age of Innocence . . . 1920 . . . Wharton . . **New York City**
Babbitt . . . 1922 . . . Lewis . . . . **Zenith "in the State of Winnemac"**
The Enormous Room . . . 1922 . . . Cummings . **France**
Billy Budd . . . 1924 . . . Melville . . . . **Aboard the *Indomitable***
So Big . . . 1924 . . . Ferber . . . . **Illinois**
Arrowsmith . . . 1924 . . . Lewis . . . . **United States and West Indies**
An American Tragedy . . . 1925 . . . Dreiser . . . **Kansas City; Chicago; and Lycurgus, New York**
Manhattan Transfer . . . 1925 . . . Dos Passos . . **New York City**
The Great Gatsby . . . 1925 . . . Fitzgerald . . . . . **New York City and Long Island**

The Sun Also Rises . . . 1926 . . . Hemingway . . **Paris, France, and Pamplona, Spain**

Elmer Gantry . . . 1927 . . . Lewis . . . . **Midwest America**

Death Comes for the Archbishop . . . 1927 . . .
    Cather. . . . . **New Mexico and Arizona**

The Bridge of San Luis Rey . . . 1927 . . .
    Wilder. . . . . **Peru**

Look Homeward, Angel . . . 1929 . . . Wolfe . . **North Carolina**

A Farewell to Arms . . . 1929 . . . Hemingway . . **Northern Italy and Switzerland**

The Sound and the Fury . . . 1929 . . .
    Faulkner. . . . . **Mississippi**

Dodsworth . . . 1929 . . . Lewis . . . . **U.S. and Europe**

As I Lay Dying . . . 1930 . . . Faulkner. . . . . **Mississippi**

The Maltese Falcon . . . 1930 . . . Hammett . . . . **San Francisco**

The Good Earth . . . 1931 . . . Buck . . . . **Northern China**

Sanctuary . . . 1931 . . . Faulkner . . . . **Mississippi and Memphis, Tennessee**

Light in August . . . 1932 . . . Faulkner . . . . **Mississippi**

Mutiny on the Bounty . . . 1932 . . . Nordhoff
    and Hall. . . . . **South Pacific and Tahiti**

Tobacco Road . . . 1932 . . . Caldwell . . . . **Georgia**

Miss Lonelyhearts . . . 1933 . . . West . . . . . . **New York City**

Anthony Adverse . . . 1933 . . . Allen . . . . **Western Europe, Africa, and North America**

Tender is the Night . . . 1934 . . . Fitzgerald . . . **Europe**

Of Time and the River . . . 1935 . . . Wolfe . . . . **Harvard; New York; France**

Studs Lonigan: A Trilogy . . . 1935 . . . Farrell . **Chicago**

Absalom, Absalom! . . . 1936 . . . Faulkner . . . . **Mississippi River**

Gone With the Wind . . . 1936 . . . Mitchell . . . **Atlanta, and Tara Plantation, Georgia**

U.S.A. . . . 1930, 1932, 1936 . . . Dos Passos . . . . **U.S.A.**

Of Mice and Men . . . 1937 . . . Steinbeck . . . . . **Salinas Valley, California**

The Yearling . . . 1938 . . . Rawlings . . . . **Florida scrub country**

The Grapes of Wrath . . . 1939 . . . Steinbeck . **Oklahoma and Southwest, U.S.A., and California**

For Whom the Bell Tolls . . . 1940 . . .
    Hemingway. . . . . **Spain**

The Heart is a Lonely Hunter . . . 1940 . . .
    McCullers. . . . . **Georgia mill town**

The Ox-Bow Incident . . . 1940 . . . Clark . . . . . **Nevada**

Native Son . . . 1940 . . . Wright . . . . **An American City**

The Human Comedy . . . 1943 . . . Saroyan . . . **Ithaca, California**

A Bell for Adano . . . 1944 . . . Hersey . . . . **Adano, Italy**

The Member of the Wedding . . . 1946
    McCullers. . . . . **Georgia**

All the King's Men . . . 1946 . . . Warren . . . . . . **Southern U.S.A.**

Guard of Honor . . . 1948 . . . Cozzens . . . . . . **Ocanara, Florida Air Force base**

The Naked and the Dead . . . 1948 . . . Mailer . **Anopopei, a Pacific Island**

The Catcher in the Rye . . . 1951 . . . Salinger . **Pencey Prep in Pennsylvania; and New York City**

East of Eden . . . 1952 . . . Steinbeck . . . . **California**

The Old Man and the Sea . . . 1952 . . .
    Hemingway. . . . . **Cuba and the Gulf Stream**

Invisible Man . . . 1952 . . . Ellison . . . . **Southern U.S.A., and New York City**

Augie March . . . 1953 . . . Bellow . . . . **Chicago**

Go Tell It on the Mountain . . .1953 . . .
    Baldwin . . . . **Harlem, New York**

The Ginger Man . . . 1955 . . . Donleavy . . . . . . **Dublin and London**

Wapshot Chronicle . . . 1957 . . . Cheever. . . . . **St. Botolphs, Massachusetts; Washington; New York**

On the Road . . . 1957 . . . Kerouac . . . . **The United States**

Death in the Family . . . 1957 . . . Agee. . . . . . **Knoxville, Tennessee**

By Love Possessed . . . 1957 . . . Cozzens. . . . . **Brocton, in the Delaware Valley**

A Separate Peace . . . 1960 . . . Knowles. . . . . . . **Devon, a New England prep school**

Rabbit, Run . . . 1960 . . . Updike . . . . **Mount Judge, Pennsylvania**

The Sot-Weed Factor . . . 1960 . . . Barth . . . . **England and Maryland Province**

Catch-22 . . . 1961 . . . Heller . . . . **Pianosa, a mythical Italian island**

One Flew Over the Cuckoo's Nest . . .1962 . . .
Kesey . . . . **Western U.S.A. mental hospital**

Ship of Fools . . . 1962 . . . Porter. . . . . **On board the North German Lloyd S.A. V**era

V. . . . 1963 . . . Pynchon . . . . **Norfolk; New York; Malta; Paris; Florence; Alexandria; Cairo**

Herzog . . . 1964 . . . Bellow . . . . **Montreal; Chicago; New York; Massachusetts**

In Cold Blood . . . 1965 . . . Capote. . . . . **Western Kansas**

The Fixer . . . 1966 . . . Malamud . . . . **The Ukraine**

Giles Goat-Boy . . . 1966 . . . Barth . . . . **Realm of the Imagination**

Slaughterhouse-Five . . . 1969 . . . Vonnegut. . . **Dresden, East Germany; Ilium, New York; the planet of Tralfamaodre**

Them . . . 1969 . . . Oates . . . . **Detroit**

Portnoy's Complaint . . . 1969 . . . Roth . . . . . . **New York City; New Hampshire; Athens; Israel**

Deliverance . . . 1970 . . . Dickey. . . . . **Georgia**

Humboldt's Gift . . . 1975 . . . Bellow . . . . **Chicago; New York; Madrid; Paris**

FIRST NOVELS OF AMERICAN AUTHORS

James Agee . . . . *The Morning Watch* (1951)
Louisa May Alcott. . . . . *Moods* (1865)
Nelson Algren . . . . *Somebody in Boots* (1935)
Sherwood Anderson. . . . . *Windy McPherson's Son* (1916)
Louis Auchincloss . . . . *The Indifferent Children* (1947)
James Baldwin. . . . . *Go Tell It On the Mountain* (1953)
John Barth . . . . *The Floating Opera* (1956)
Lyman Frank Baum . . . . *Father Goose: His Book* (1899)
Edward Bellamy . . . . *Six to One: A Nantucket Idyll* (1878)
Saul Bellow . . . . *Dangling Man* (1944)
Ray Bradbury. . . . . *Fahrenheit 451* (1953)
Richard Brautigan . . . . *A Confederate General from Big Sur* (1965)
Charles Brockden Brown. . . . . *Alcuin: A Dialogue* (1798)
Pearl Sydenstricker Buck. . . . . *East Wind, West Wind* (1930)
Edgar Rice Burroughs . . . . *Tarzan of the Apes* (1914)
James Branch Cabell . . . . *The Eagle's Shadow* (1904)
George Washington Cable . . . . *The Grandissimes* (1880)
Erskine Caldwell . . . . *The Bastard* (1929)
Truman Capote. . . . . *Other Voices, Other Rooms* (1948)
Willa Cather . . . . *Alexander's Bridge* (1912)
John Cheever . . . . *The Wapshot Chronicle* (1957)
Walter van Tilburg Clark. . . . . *The Ox-Bow Incident* (1940)
James Fenimore Cooper. . . . . . *Precaution* (1820)

James Gould Cozzens .... *Confusion* (1924)
Stephen Crane .... *Maggie: A Girl of the Streets* (1893)
Richard Henry Dana, Jr. ...... *Two Years Before the Mast* (1840)
James Dickey .... *Deliverance* (1970)
J.P. Donleavy .... *The Ginger Man* (1955)
John Dos Passos .... *One Man's Initiation — 1917* (1919)
Theodore Dreiser .... *Sister Carrie* (1900)
Ralph Ellison .... *Invisible Man* (1952)
James T. Farrell .... *Young Lonigan* (1932)
William Faulkner .... *Soldier's Pay* (1926)
F. Scott Fitzgerald .... *This Side of Paradise* (1920) (originally called
                              The Romantic Egoist)
Hamlin Garland .... *Jason Edwards: An Average Man* (1892)
Ellen Glasgow .... *The Descendant* (1897)
Zane Grey .... *Betty Zane* (1904)
Joel Chandler Harris .... *Uncle Remus: His Songs and His Sayings*
                              (1880)
Nathaniel Hawthorne .... *Fanshawe* (1828)
Robert Heinlein .... *Space Cadet* (1948)
Joseph Heller *Catch-22* (1961)
Ernest Hemingway .... *The Sun Also Rises* (1926)
John Hersey .... *A Bell for Adano* (1944)
William Dean Howells .... *Their Wedding Journey* (1872)
Henry James .... *Watch and Ward* (1870)
James Jones .... *From Here to Eternity* (1951)
MacKinlay Kantor .... *Diversey* (1928)
Jack Kerouac .... *The Town and the City* (1950)
Ken Kesey .... *One Flew Over the Cuckoo's Nest* (1962)
Sinclair Lewis .... *Our Mr. Wrenn* (1914)
Jack London .... *A Daughter of the Snows* (1902)
Mary McCarthy .... *The Oasis* (1949)
Carson McCullers .... *The Heart is a Lonely Hunter* (1940)
Norman Mailer .... *The Naked and the Dead* (1948)
Bernard Malamud .... *The Natural* (1952)
J.P. Marquand .... *The Unspeakable Gentleman* (1922)
Herman Melville .... *Typee* (1846)
James N. Hall .... *The Lafayette Flying Corps* (1920)
Benjamin Franklin Norris ..... *McTeague* (1899)
Flannery O'Connor .... *Wise Blood* (1952)
John O'Hara .... *Appointment in Samarra* (1934)
Katherine Anne Porter .... *Ship of Fools* (1962)
Thomas Pynchon .... *V.* (1963)
Philip Roth .... *Goodbye, Columbus* (1959)
J.D. Salinger .... *The Catcher in the Rye* (1951)
Irwin Shaw .... *The Young Lions* (1948)
Upton Sinclair .... *Saved by the Enemy* (1898)
Susan Sontag .... *The Benefactor* (1963)
John Steinbeck .... *Cup of Gold* (1929)
William Styron .... *Lie Down in Darkness* (1951)
Booth Tarkington .... *The Gentleman from Indiana* (1899)
Mark Twain .... *The Gilded Age* (1873)
John Updike .... *The Poorhouse Fair* (1959)
Gore Vidal .... *Williwaw* (1946)
Kurt Vonnegut .... *Player Piano* (1960)
Lew Wallace .... *The Fair God* (1873)
Robert Penn Warren .... *Night Rider* (1939)
Eudora Welty .... *The Robber Bridegroom* (1942)
Nathanael West .... *The Dream Life of Balso Snell* (1931)
Edith Wharton .... *The Valley of Decision* (1902)
Thornton Wilder .... *The Cabala* (1926)

AMERICAN WORKS AND THEIR SUBTITLES

The Age of Reason: "An Investigation of True and Fabulous Theology" . . . 1794-1795 . . . Thomas Paine

Salmagundi, or, The Whim Whams and Opinions of Launcelot Langstaff, Esq., and Others . . . 1807-1808 . . . Washington Irving

The Spy: A Tale of the Neutral Ground . . . 1821 . . . James Fenimore Cooper

The Pioneers, Or The Sources of the Susquehanna . . . 1823 . . . James Fenimore Cooper

Horseshoe Robinson, A Tale of Tory Ascendency . . . 1835 . . . John P. Kennedy

Outre-Mer: A Pilgrimage Beyond the Sea . . . 1835 . . . Henry Wadsworth Longfellow

Nick of the Woods, Or, The Jibbenainosay . . . 1837 . . . Robert Montgomery Bird

The Pathfinder, or The Inland Sea . . . 1840 . . . James Fenimore Cooper

Satanstoe, or The Littlepage Manuscripts . . . 1845 . . . James Fenimore Cooper

The Chainbearer, or The Littlepage Manuscripts . . . 1845 . . . James Fenimore Cooper

The Redskins, or, Indian and Injin . . . 1846 . . . James Fenimore Cooper

Evangeline: Or A Tale of Acadie . . . 1847 . . . Henry Wadsworth Longfellow

Moby-Dick: Or The White Whale . . . 1851 . . . Herman Melville

Uncle Tom's Cabin: Or Life Among the Lowly . . . 1852 . . . Harriet Beecher Stowe

Pierre, Or, The Ambiguities . . . 1852 . . . Herman Melville

Walden: Or Life in the Woods . . . 1854 . . . Henry David Thoreau

The Marble Faun: Or The Romance of Monte Beni . . . 1860 . . . Nathaniel Hawthorne

Little Women: Or Meg, Jo, Beth, and Amy . . . 1868 . . . Louisa May Alcott

Septimus Felton: or, The Elixir of Life . . . 1872 . . . Nathaniel Hawthorne

Six to One: A Nantucket Idyll . . . 1878 . . . Edward Bellamy

Uncle Remus, His Sayings and His Songs . . . 1880 . . . Joel Chandler Harris

Ben Hur: A Tale of the Christ . . . 1880 . . . Lewis Wallace

Looking Backward: 2000-1887 . . . 1888 . . . Edward Bellamy

Maggie: A Girl of the Streets . . . 1893 . . . Stephen Crane

The Prince of India, or Why Constantinople Fell . . . 1893 . . . Lew Wallace

McTeague: A Story of San Francisco . . . 1899 . . . Frank Norris

Jurgen, A Comedy of Justice . . . 1919 . . . James Branch Cabell

John Brown, the Making of a Martyr . . . 1929 . . . Robert Penn Warren

Studs Lonigan: A Trilogy . . . 1935 . . . James T. Farrell

Of Time and the River: A Legend of Man's Hunger in His Youth . . . 1935 . . . Thomas Wolfe

The Late George Apley, "A Novel in the Form of a Memoir" . . . 1937 . . . J.P. Marquand

Chicago: City on the Make . . . 1951 . . . Nelson Algren

The Sot-Weed Factor . . . 1960 . . . John Barth (Barth took the title of his book from the following poem by Ebenezer Cooke)

"The Sot-Weed Factor: Or, A Voyage to Maryland, A satyr, In which is describ'd the Laws, Government, Courts and Constitutions of the Country; and also the Buildings, Feasts, Frolicks, Entertainments and Drunken Humours of the Inhabitants of that Part of America. By Eben, Cooke, Gent."

Bid Me to Live, a Madrigal . . . 1960 . . . H.D. (Hilda Doolittle)

Nobody Knows My Name: More Notes of a Native Son . . . 1961 . . . James Baldwin

Going Away, A Report, A Memoir, Going Away . . . 1962 . . . Clancy Sigal

The Reivers, A Reminiscence . . . 1962 . . . William Faulkner

Travels With Charley, In Search of America . . . 1962 . . . John Steinbeck
Boswell, "A Modern Comedy" . . . 1964 . . . Stanley Elkin
God Bless You, Mr. Roosevelt, or Pearls Before Swine . . . 1965 . . . Kurt Vonnegut
Giles Goat-Boy: Or The Revised New Syllabus . . . 1966 . . . John Barth
The Abortion: An Historical Romance . . . 1966 . . . Richard Brautigan
In Cold Blood, A True Account of a Multiple Murder and Its Consequences . . . 1966 . . . Truman Capote
Rochelle: Or Virtue Rewarded . . . 1967 . . . David Slavitt
Vanity of Duluoz: An Adventurous Education, 1935-46 . . . 1968 . . . Jack Kerouac
The Armies of the Night, History as a Novel, the Novel as History . . . 1968 . . . Norman Mailer
Ada Or Ardor, A Family Chronicle . . . 1969 . . . Vladimir Nabokov
Slaughterhouse-Five, Or The Children's Crusade . . . 1969 . . . Kurt Vonnegut, Jr.
Hermaphrodeity: The Autobiography of a Poet . . . 1972 . . . Alan Friedman
Breakfast of Champions, Or, Goodbye, Blue Monday! . . . 1973 . . . Kurt Vonnegut, Jr.
The Hawkline Monster, A Gothic Western . . . 1974 . . . Richard Brautigan
Beyond the Bedroom Wall, A Family Album . . . 1975 . . . Larry Woiwode
Yonnondio, From the Thirties . . . 1977 . . . Tillie Olsen

FIRST AND LAST LINES OF AMERICAN NOVELS

First — It was a feature peculiar to the colonial war of North America, that the toils and dangers of the wilderness were to be encountered before the adverse hosts could meet.
Last — "In the morning I saw the sons of Unamis happy and strong; and yet, before the night has come, have I lived to see the last warrior of the wise race of the Mohicans."
The Last of the Mohicans by James Fenimore Cooper

First — A throng of bearded men, in sad-colored garments and gray, steeple-crowned hats, intermixed with women, some wearing hoods, others bareheaded, was assembled in front of a wooden edifice, the door of which was heavily timbered with oak, and studded with iron spikes.
Last — It bore a device, a herald's wording of which might serve for a motto and brief description of our now concluded legend; so sombre is it, and relieved only by one ever-glowing point of light gloomier than the shadow: —
          "ON A FIELD, SABLE, THE LETTER A, GULES."
The Scarlet Letter by Nathaniel Hawthorne

First — Call me Ishmael.
Last — Now small fowls flew screaming over the yet yawning gulf; a sullen white surf beat against its steep sides; then all collapsed, and the great shroud of the sea rolled on as it rolled five thousand years ago.
Moby Dick by Herman Melville

First — Late in the afternoon of a chilly day in February, two gentlemen were sitting alone over their wine, in a well-furnished dining parlor in the town of P_____, in Kentucky.
Last — Not by combining together, to protect injustice and cruelty, and making a common capital of sin, is this Union to be saved — but by repentance, justice, and mercy; for, not surer is the eternal law by which millstone sinks in the ocean, than that stronger law by which injustice and cruelty shall bring on nations the wrath of Almighty God!
Uncle Tom's Cabin by Harriet Beecher Stowe

First — Under certain circumstances there are few hours in life more agreeable than the hour dedicated to the ceremony known as afternoon tea.

Last — ''Look here, Mr. Goodwood,'' she said; ''just you wait!'' On which he looked up at her.

The Portrait of a Lady by Henry James

First — In the ancient city of London, on a certain autumn day in the second quarter of the sixteenth century, a boy was born to a poor family of the name of Canty, who did not want him.

Last — Now that we are taking leave of him let us try to keep this in our minds, to his credit.

The Prince and the Pauper by Mark Twain

First — You don't know about me without you have read a book by the name of *The Adventures of Tom Sawyer*; but that ain't no matter.

Last — I been there before.

The Adventures of Huckleberry Finn by Mark Twain

First — The cold passed reluctantly from the earth, and the retiring fogs revealed an army stretched out on the hills, resting.

Last — Over the river a golden ray of sun came through the hosts of leaden rain clouds.

The Red Badge of Courage by Stephen Crane

First — When Caroline Meeber boarded the afternoon train for Chicago, her total outfit consisted of a small trunk, a cheap imitation alligator-skin satchel, a small lunch in a paper box, and a yellow leather snap purse, containing her ticket, a scrap of paper with her sister's address in Van Buren Street, and four dollars in money.

Last — In your rocking-chair, by your window, shall you dream such happiness as you may never feel.

Sister Carrie by Theodore Dreiser

First — Some notable sight was drawing the passengers, both men and women, to the window; and therefore I rose and crossed the car to see what it was.

Last — Their eldest boy rides the horse Monte; and, strictly between ourselves, I think his father is going to live a long while.

The Virginian by Owen Wister

First — Buck did not read the newspapers, or he would have known that trouble was brewing, not alone for himself, but for every tidewater dog, strong of muscle and with warm, long hair, from Puget Sound to San Diego.

Last — When the long winter nights come on and the wolves follow their meat into the lower valleys, he may be seen running at the head of the pack through the pale moonlight or glimmering borealis, leaping gigantic above his fellows, his great throat a-bellow as he sings a song of the younger world, which is the song of the pack.

The Call of the Wild by Jack London

First — I first heard of Ántonia on what seemed to me an interminable journey across the great midland plain of North America.

Last — Whatever we had missed, we possessed together the precious, the incommunicable past.

My Ántonia by Willa Cather

First — The towers of Zenith aspired above the morning mist; austere towers of steel and cement and limestone, sturdy as cliffs and delicate as silver rods.

Last — Arms about each other's shoulders, the Babbitt men marched into the living-room and faced the swooping family.

Babbitt by Sinclair Lewis

First — In my younger and more vulnerable years my father gave me some advice that I've been turning over in my mind ever since.

Last — So we beat on, boats against the current, borne back ceaselessly into the past.

The Great Gatsby by F. Scott Fitzgerald

First — Robert Cohn was once middleweight boxing champion of Princeton.

Last — ''Yes,'' I said. ''Isn't it pretty to think so?''

The Sun Also Rises by Ernest Hemingway

First — On Friday noon, July the twentieth, 1714, the finest bridge in all Peru broke and precipitated five travellers into the gulf below.

Last — There is a land of the living and a land of the dead and the bridge is love, the only survival, the only meaning.

The Bridge of San Luis Rey **by Thornton Wilder**

First — A destiny that leads the English to the Dutch is strange enough; but one that leads from Epsom into Pennsylvania, and thence into the hills that shut in Altamont over the proud coral cry of the cock, and the soft stone smile of an angel, is touched by that dark miracle of chance which makes new magic in a dusty world.

Last — Yet, as he stood for the last time by the angels of his father's porch, it seemed as if the Square already were far and lost; or, I should say, he was like a man who stands upon a hill over the town he has left, yet does not say "The town is near," but turns his eyes upon the distant soaring ranges.

Look Homeward, Angel **by Thomas Wolfe**

First — In the late summer of that year we lived in a house in a village that looked across the river and the plain to the mountains.

Last — After a while I went out and left the hospital and walked back to the hotel in the rain.

A Farewell to Arms **by Ernest Hemingway**

First — Through the fence, between the curling flower spaces, I could see them hitting.

Last — The broken flower drooped over Ben's fist and his eyes were empty and blue and serene again as cornice and facade flowed smoothly once more from left to right; post and tree, window and doorway, and signboard, each in its ordered place.

The Sound and the Fury **by William Faulkner**

First — The British are frequently criticized by other nations for their dislike of change, and indeed we love England for those aspects of nature and life which change the least.

Last — Two fishing boats were working out to sea, their sails hanging slack, and the men at the sweeps. I was watching them creeping laboriously toward the Atlantic when I heard Tom's chirrup to the horses, and the sound of the wheels on the drive.

Mutiny on the Bounty **by Charles Nordhoff and James Hall**

First — Scarlett O'Hara was not beautiful, but men seldom realized it when caught by her charm as the Tarleton twins were.

Last — "I'll think of it all tomorrow, at Tara. I can stand it then. Tomorrow, I'll think of someway to get him back. After all, tomorrow is another day."

Gone With the Wind **by Margaret Mitchell**

First — To the red country and part of the gray country of Oklahoma, the last rains came gently, and they did not cut the scarred earth.

Last — She looked up across the barn, and her lips came together and smiled mysteriously.

The Grapes of Wrath **by John Steinbeck**

First — In the town there were two mutes, and they were always together.

Last — And when at last he was inside again he composed himself soberly to await the morning sun.

The Heart is a Lonely Hunter **by Carson McCullers**

First — Gil and I crossed the eastern divide about two by the sun.

Last — Then Gil said, "I'll be glad to get out of here," as if he'd let it all go. "Yeh," I said.

The Ox-Bow Incident **by Walter Van Tilburg Clark**

First — To get there you follow Highway 58, going northeast out of the city, and it is a good highway and new.

Last — But that will be a long time from now, and soon now we shall go out of the house and go into the convulsion of the world, out of history into history and the awful responsibility of Time.

All the King's Men **by Robert Penn Warren**

First — Nobody could sleep.
Last — Hot Dog!
The Naked and the Dead by Norman Mailer

First — If you really want to hear about it, the first thing you'll probably want to know is where I was born, and what my lousy childhood was like, and how my parents were occupied and all before they had me, and all that David Copperfield kind of crap, but I don't feel like going into it, if you want to know the truth.
Last — Don't ever tell anybody anything. If you do, you start missing everybody.
The Catcher in the Rye by J.D. Salinger

First — He was an old man who fished alone in a skiff in the Gulf Stream and he had gone eighty-four days now without taking a fish.
Last — The old man was dreaming about lions.
The Old Man and the Sea by Ernest Hemingway

First — I am an invisible man.
Last — Who knows but that, on the lower frequencies, I speak for you?
The Invisible Man by Ralph Ellison

First — At supper that night, as many times before, his father said, ''Well, spose we go to the picture show.''
Last — But he did not ask, and his uncle did not speak except to say, after a few minutes, ''It's time to go home,'' and all the way home they walked in silence.
Death in the Family by James Agee

First — I went back to the Devon School not long ago, and found it looking oddly newer than when I was a student there fifteen years before.
Last — All of them, all except Phineas, constructed at infinite cost to themselves these Maginot Lines against this enemy, they thought they saw across the frontier, this enemy who never attacked that way — if he ever attacked at all; if he was indeed the enemy.
A Separate Peace by John Knowles

First — It was love at first sight.
Last — The knife came down, missing him by inches, and he took off.
Catch-22 by Joseph Heller

First — The village of Holcomb stands on the high wheat plains of western Kansas, a lonesome area that other Kansans call ''out there.''
Last — Then, starting home, he walked toward the tree, and under them, leaving behind him the big sky, the whisper of wind voices in the wind — bent wheat.
In Cold Blood by Truman Capote

First — George is my name; my deeds have been heard of in Tower Hall, and my child-hood has been chronicled in the *Journal of Experimental Psychology.*
Last — Nonetheless I smiled, leaned on my stick, and, no troubleder than Mom, gimped in to meet the guards halfway.
Giles Goat-Boy by John Barth

First — She was so deeply imbedded in my consciousness that for the first year of school I seem to have believed that each of my teachers was my mother in disguise.
Last — PUNCH LINE So (said the doctor). Now vee may perhaps to begin. Yes?
Portnoy's Complaint by Philip Roth

First — It unrolled slowly, forced to show its colors, curling and snapping back whenever one of us turned loose.
Last — One big marina is already built on the south end of the lake, and my wife's younger brother says that the area is beginning to catch on, especially with the new generation, the one just getting out of high school.
Deliverance by James Dickey

PULITZER PRIZES FOR FICTION

1917 No award
1918 *His Family* by Ernest Poole
1919 *The Magnificent Ambersons* by Booth Tarkington
1920 No award
1921 *The Age of Innocence* by Edith Wharton
1922 *Alice Adams* by Booth Tarkington
1923 *One of Ours* by Willa Cather
1924 *The Able McLaughlins* by Margaret Wilson
1925 *So Big* by Edna Ferber
1926 *Arrowsmith* by Sinclair Lewis
1927 *Early Autumn* by Louis Bromfield
1928 *The Bridge of San Luis Rey* by Thornton Wilder
1929 *Scarlet Sister Mary* by Julia M. Peterkin
1930 *Laughing Boy* by Oliver LaFarge
1931 *Years of Grace* by Margaret Ayer Barnes
1932 *The Good Earth* by Pearl S. Buck
1933 *The Store* by T.S. Stribling
1934 *Lamb in His Bosom* by Caroline Miller
1935 *Now in November* by Josephine W. Johnson
1936 *Honey in the Horn* by Harold L. Davis
1937 *Gone with the Wind* by Margaret Mitchell
1938 *The Late George Apley* by J.P. Marquand
1939 *The Yearling* by Marjorie Kinnan Rawlings
1940 *The Grapes of Wrath* by John Steinbeck
1941 No award
1942 *In This Our Life* by Ellen Glasgow
1943 *Dragon's Teeth* by Upton Sinclair
1944 *Journey in the Dark* by Martin Flavin
1945 *A Bell for Adano* by John Hersey
1946 No award
1947 *All the King's Men* by Robert Penn Warren
1948 *Tales of the South Pacific* by James A. Michener
1949 *Guard of Honor* by James Gould Cozzens
1950 *The Way West* by A.B. Guthrie, Jr.
1951 *The Town* by Conrad Richter
1952 *The Caine Mutiny* by Herman Wouk
1953 *The Old Man and the Sea* by Ernest Hemingway
1954 No award
1955 *A Fable* by William Faulkner
1956 *Andersonville* by MacKinlay Kantor
1957 No award
1958 *A Death in the Family* by James Agee
1959 *The Travels of Jaimie McPheeters* by Robert Lewis Taylor
1960 *Advise and Consent* by Allen Drury
1961 *To Kill A Mockingbird* by Harper Lee
1962 *The Edge of Sadness* by Edwin O'Connor
1963 *The Reivers* by William Faulkner
1964 No award
1965 *The Keepers of the House* by Shirley Ann Grau
1966 *The Collected Stories of Katherine Anne Porter* by Katherine Anne Porter
1967 *The Fixer* by Bernard Malamud
1968 *The Confessions of Nat Turner* by William Styron
1969 *House Made of Dawn* by N. Scott Momaday
1970 *Collected Stories* by Jean Stafford
1971 No award
1972 *Angle of Repose* by Wallace E. Stegner
1973 *The Optimist's Daughter* by Eudora Welty

1974 No award
1975 *The Killer Angels* by Michael Shaara
1976 *Humboldt's Gift* by Saul Bellow
1977 No award
1978 *Elbow Room* by James Alan McPherson
1979 *The Stories of John Cheever* by John Cheever
1980 *The Executioner's Song* by Norman Mailer
1981 *A Confederacy of Dunces* by John Kennedy Toole
1982 *Rabbit is Rich* by John Updike

PULITZER PRIZES FOR POETRY

1918 *Love Songs* by Sara Teasdale
1919 *Corn Huskers* by Carl Sandburg and *Old Road to Paradise* by Margaret
     Widdemar
1920 No award
1921 No award
1922 *Collected Poems* by Edwin Arlington Robinson
1923 *The Ballad of the Harp-Weaver; A Few Figs from Thistles;* eight
     sonnets in *American Poetry, 1922, a Miscellany* by Edna St. Vincent
     Millay
1924 *New Hampshire: A Poem with Notes and Grace Notes* by Robert Frost
1925 *The Man Who Died Twice* by Edwin Arlington Robinson
1926 *What's O'Clock* by Amy Lowell
1927 *Fiddler's Farewell* by Leonora Speyer
1928 *Tristram* by Edwin Arlington Robinson
1929 *John Brown's Body* by Stephen Vincent Benét
1930 *Selected Poems* by Conrad Aiken
1931 *Collected Poems* by Robert Frost
1932 *The Flowering Stone* by George Dillon
1933 *Conquistador* by Archibald MacLeish
1934 *Collected Verse* by Robert Hillyer
1935 *Bright Ambush* by Audrey Wurdemann
1936 *Strange Holiness* by R.P. Tristram Coffin
1937 *A Further Range* by Robert Frost
1938 *Cold Morning Sky* by Marya Zaturenska
1939 *Selected Poems* by John Gould Fletcher
1940 *Collected Poems* by Mark Van Doren
1941 *Sunderland Capture* by Leonard Bacon
1942 *The Dust Which Is God* by William Benét
1943 *A Witness Tree* by Robert Frost
1944 *Western Star* by Stephen Vincent Benét
1945 *V-Letter and Other Poems* by Karl Shapiro
1946 No award
1947 *Lord Weary's Castle* by Robert Lowell
1948 *The Age of Anxiety* by W.H. Auden
1949 *Terror and Decorum* by Peter Viereck
1950 *Annie Allen* by Gwendolyn Brooks
1951 *Complete Poems* by Carl Sandburg
1952 *Collected Poems* by Marianne Moore
1953 *Collected Poems 1917-1952* by Archibald MacLeish
1954 *The Waking* by Theodore Roethke
1955 *Collected Poems* by Wallace Stevens
1956 *Poems — North & South* by Elizabeth Bishop
1957 *Things of This World* by Richard Wilbur
1958 *Promises: Poems 1954-1956* by Robert Penn Warren
1959 *Selected Poems 1928-1958* by Stanley Kunitz
1960 *Heart's Needle* by W.D. Snodgrass
1961 *Times Three: Selected Verse from Three Decades* by Phyllis McGinley

1962 *Poems* by Alan Dugan
1963 *Pictures from Breughel* by William Carlos Williams
1964 *At the End of the Open Road* by Louis Simpson
1965 *77 Dream Songs* by John Berryman
1966 *Selected Poems* by Richard Eberhart
1967 *Live or Die* by Anne Sexton
1968 *The Hard Hours* by Anthony Hecht
1969 *Of Being Numerous* by George Oppen
1970 *Untitled Subjects* by Richard Howard
1971 *The Carrier of Ladders* by W.S. Merwin
1972 *Collected Poems* by James Wright
1973 *Up Country* by Maxine Winokur Kumin
1974 *The Dolphin* by Robert Lowell
1975 *Turtle Island* by Gary Snyder
1976 *Self-Portrait in a Convex Mirror* by John Ashberry
1977 *Divine Comedies* by James Merrill
1978 *Collected Poems* by Howard Nemerov
1979 *Now and Then* by Robert Penn Warren
1980 *Selected Poems* by Donald Rodney Justice
1981 *The Morning of the Poem* by James Schuyler
1982 *Collected Poems* by Sylvia Plath (awarded posthumously)

PULITZER PRIZES IN DRAMA

1918 *Why Marry?* by Jesse Lynch Williams
1919 No award
1920 *Beyond the Horizon* by Eugene O'Neill
1921 *Miss Lulu Bett* by Zona Gale
1922 *Anna Christie* by Eugene O'Neill
1923 *Icebound* by Owen Davis
1924 *Hell-Bent For Heaven* by Hatcher Hughes
1925 *They Knew What They Wanted* by Sidney Howard
1926 *Craig's Wife* by George Kelly
1927 *In Abraham's Bosom* by Paul Green
1928 *Strange Interlude* by Eugene O'Neill
1929 *Street Scene* by Elmer L. Rice
1930 *The Green Pastures* by Marc Connelly
1931 *Alison's House* by Susan Glaspell
1932 *Of Thee I Sing* by George S. Kaufman, Morrie Ryskind, and Ira Gershwin
1933 *Both Your Houses* by Maxwell Anderson
1934 *Men in White* by Sidney Kingsley
1935 *The Old Maid* by Zoe Akins
1936 *Idiot's Delight* by Robert E. Sherwood
1937 *You Can't Take It with You* by Moss Hart and George S. Kaufman
1938 *Our Town* by Thornton Wilder
1939 *Abe Lincoln in Illinois* by Robert E. Sherwood
1940 *The Time of Your Life* by William Saroyan
1941 *There Shall Be No Night* by Robert E. Sherwood
1942 No award
1943 *The Skin of Our Teeth* by Thornton Wilder
1944 No award
1945 *Harvey* by Mary Chase
1946 *State of the Union* by Russel Crouse and Howard Lindsay
1947 No award
1948 *A Streetcar Named Desire* by Tennessee Williams
1949 *Death of a Salesman* by Arthur Miller
1950 *South Pacific* by Richard Rodgers, Oscar Hammerstein II, and Joshua Logan
1951 No award

1952 *The Shrike* by Joseph Kramm
1953 *Picnic* by William Inge
1954 *The Teahouse of the August Moon* by John Patrick
1955 *Cat on a Hot Tin Roof* by Tennessee Williams
1956 *The Diary of Anne Frank* by Frances Goodrich and Albert Hackett
1957 *Long Day's Journey Into Night* by Eugene O'Neill
1958 *Look Homeward, Angel* by Ketti Frings
1959 *J.B.* Archibald MacLeish
1960 *Fiorello!* by George Abbott, Jerome Weidman, Jerry Bock and Sheldon Harnick
1961 *All the Way Home* by Tad Mosel
1962 *How to Succeed in Business Without Really Trying* by Frank Loesser
    and Abe Burrows
1963 No award
1964 No award
1965 *The Subject Was Roses* by Frank D. Gilroy
1966 No award
1967 *A Delicate Balance* by Edward Albee
1968 No award
1969 *The Great White Hope* by Howard Sackler
1970 *No Place to Be Somebody* by Charles Gordone
1971 *The Effect of Gamma Rays on Man-in-the-Moon Marigolds* by Paul
    Zindel
1972 No award
1973 *That Championship Season* by Jason Miller
1974 No award
1975 *Seascape* by Edward Albee
1976 *A Chorus Line* conceived by Michael Bennett
1977 *The Shadow Box* by Michael Cristofer
1978 *The Gin Game* by Donald L. Coburn
1979 *Buried Child* by Sam Shepard
1980 *Talley's Folly* by Lanford Wilson
1981 *Crimes of the Heart* by Beth Henley
1982 *A Soldier's Play* by Charles Fuller

AMERICAN AUTHORS AND THEIR PEN NAMES/PSEUDONYMS/NOMS DE PLUME

Isaac Asimov . . . . Paul French
Zenith Jones Brown . . . . Leslie Ford
Charles Farrar Browne . . . . Artemus Ward
John Dickson Carr . . . . Carter Dickson
John Franklin Carter . . . . Diplomat
Samuel Langhorne Clemens . . . . Mark Twain
James Fenimore Cooper . . . . Cornelius Littlepage, Amabel Penfeather
Frederick Dannay and
Manfred B. Lee . . . . Ellery Queen, Barnaby Ross
David Dresser . . . . Brett Halliday
Gloria and Forrest E. Flickling . . . G.G. Flickling
Benjamin Franklin . . . . Richard Saunders, Alice Addertongue, Anthony
    Afterwit
Erle Stanley Gardner . . . . A.A. Fair, Charles J. Kenny, Charles M. Green,
    Charleton Kendrake
Walter B. Gibson . . . . Maxwell Grant
George Goetz . . . . V. (Victor) F. (Francis) Calverton
John Patrick Goggan . . . . John Patrick
Irving Granich . . . . Michael Gold
E. Howard Hunt . . . . David St. John, Robert Dietrich
Evan Hunter . . . . Ed McBain
Washington Irving . . . . Diedrich Knickerbocker, Geoffrey Corson, Geoffrey
    Crayon (Gent.)

Ring Lardner . . . . Jack Keefe
Elizabeth Linington . . . . Dell Shannon
David Ross Locke . . . . Petroleum Vesuvius Nasby
Dennis Lynds . . . . Michael Collins
Jane McElheney . . . . Ada Clare
Kenneth Millar . . . . (John) Ross MacDonald
Mary NoAilles Murfree . . . . Charles Egbert Craddock
Judson Pentecost Philips . . . . Hugh Pentecost
William Sidney Porter . . . . O. Henry
Georgiana Ann Randolph . . . . Craig Rice
Leo Calvin Rosten . . . . Leonard Q. Ross
Henry Wheeler Shaw . . . . Josh Billings
Frank Morrison Spillane . . . . Mickey Spillane
Edward L. Stratemeyer . . . . Carolyn Keene
Phoebe Atwood Taylor . . . . Alice Tilton
Gore Vidal . . . . Edgar Box
Robert Wade and Bill Miller . . . . . Wade Miller
Edward Hamilton Waldo . . . . Theodore Sturgeon
Nathan Wallenstein Weinstein . . . Nathanael West
Donald E. Westlake . . . . Richard Stark
William Anthony Parker White . . . Anthony Boucher
Raoul Whitfield . . . . Ramon Decolta
Willard Huntington Wright . . . . . . S.S. Van Dine
Leonard Zinberg . . . . Ed Lacy

NICKNAMES OF AMERICAN NOVELISTS, POETS, PLAYWRIGHTS

Edward Bellamy . . . . The Village Utopian
Ambrose Gwinnett Bierce . . . . . . Bitter Bierce, Devil's Lexicographer
Anne Bradstreet . . . . The Tenth Muse
Charles Brockden Brown . . . . The American Gothic Novelist, C.B.B., Pioneer Voice of America
William Cullen Bryant . . . . The American Wordsworth, Father of American Poets
Edgar Rice Burroughs . . . . Normal Bean, Norman Bean, Tarzan Burroughs
Sidney Chayefsky . . . . Paddy Chayefsky
John Cheever . . . . Chekhov of the Suburbs
Ada Clare . . . . Queen of Bohemia
George Michael Cohan . . . . Mr. Broadway, First Actor of the American Theatre, King (Prince) of Broadway, Man who owned Broadway, Prince of the American Theatre, Uncle George, Yankle Doodle Dandy
James Fenimore Cooper . . . . The American Scott, A Travelling Bachelor
E.E. Cummings (e.e. cummings) . . Lower Case Cummings, Magic-maker
Richard Henry Dana, Jr. . . . . Avenging Angel for Seamen's Rights, Sailor's Lawyer
John Dewey . . . . America's Philosopher, Father of Modern Education, The Last Protestant
Theodore Dreiser . . . . Balzac or Zola of American Fiction, Münchausen in Modern Dress, Our Bitter Patriot
Ralph Waldo Emerson . . . . American Montaigne, Columbus of Modern Thought, Prophet of America, Sage of Concord
William Faulkner . . . . American Balzac, Sage of Yoknapatawpha
F. Scott Fitzgerald . . . . Last Laocoön, Spokesman of the Jazz Age
Benjamin Franklin . . . . American Socrates, Philomath, Poor Richard, Sage of America
Robert Frost . . . . Voice of New England
Margaret Fuller . . . . Queen of Cambridge
Allen Ginsberg . . . . Gentle Guru of the Flower People, One of the Crazies, Wild Shaman of the Beat Generation

Joel Chandler Harris . . . . Uncle Remus
Nathaniel Hawthorne . . . . Genius of Romance
Ernest Hemingway . . . . Monarch of American Arts, Papa, Spokesman for the Lost Generation
Oliver Wendell Holmes . . . . The Autocrat (of the Breakfast Table), O.W.H., Professor of Dead and Living Languages
William Dean Howells . . . . Dean of American Letters, Father of Realism, Gentleman from Altruria, Master of Realism
Washington Irving . . . . American Goldsmith, Father of American Literature, Father of American Prose, First Man of Letters, Prince of American Letters
Henry James and sons William
James and Henry James . . . . A Family of Minds
Henry James . . . . Scholar of the Novel
Jack Kerouac . . . . Spokesman for the Beat Generation
Sidney Lanier . . . . Poet of the Marshes, Sunrise Poet
Sinclair Lewis . . . . Bad Boy of National Letters
Jack London . . . . American Kipling, Kipling of the Klondike, Prince of Oyster Pirates, Prophet of the Strenuous Life
Henry Wadsworth Longfellow . . . Children's Poet, H.W.L., Laureate of Song, Poet of the Commonplace
James Russell Lowell . . . . Best Read Man of the Century
Mary McCarthy . . . . First Lady of Letters
H.L. Mencken . . . . Bad Boy of Baltimore, Disturber of the Peace, Great Debunker, Greatest Practicing Literary Journalist, The Irreverent Mr. Mencken, Private Secretary of God Almighty, Ringmaster, Sage of Baltimore
Edna St. Vincent Millay . . . . Poetic Voice of Flaming Youth, Symbol of Flaming Youth
Henry Miller . . . . The Expatriate
Joaquin Miller . . . . Byron of the Sierras
Julia Moore . . . . Sweet Singer of Michigan
Marianne Moore . . . . First Lady of American Poetry
Frederick Ogden Nash . . . . Poet Laureate of Light Verse, Undisputed Master of Light Verse
Dorothy Parker . . . . Constant Reader, Helene Rousseau
Francis Parkman . . . . Historian of the Wilderness
Edgar Allan Poe . . . . Father of Detection, Wizard of Word Music
Ezra Loomis Pound . . . . Expatriate American Poet, Perpetual Adolescent of American Poetry
James Whitcomb Riley . . . . Burns of America, Children's Poet, Hoosier Poet, People's Laureate, Poet of the Common People
Alfred Damon Runyan . . . . Sentimental Cynic
Abraham Joseph Ryan . . . . Father Ryan, Poet of the Confederacy, Poet of the Lost Cause, The Tom Moore of the Confederacy
Gertrude Stein . . . . The Mother Goose of Montparnasse
Harriet Beecher Stowe . . . . Crusader in Crinoline, That Vile Wretch in Crinoline, Victorian Cinderella
Booth Tarkington . . . . Gentleman from Indianapolis
Edward Taylor . . . . The American Metaphysical
Henry David Thoreau . . . . Concord Rebel, Hermit of Walden, Poet Naturalist, Sage of Walden Pond
Henry Timrod . . . . The Poet Laureate of the Confederacy
Mark Twain (Samuel
Langhorne Clemens) . . . . Man from Missouri, Master Pilot of the Mississippi, Moralist of the Main, People's Author, Prince of Humorists, Washoe Giant, Wild Humorist of the Pacific Slope
Gore Vidal . . . . Masked Marvel of Modern Letters

Artemus Ward . . . . Genial Showman
Nathaneal West . . . . Ironic Prophet
Walt Whitman . . . . Good Gray Poet, Poet Laureate of Democracy, Solitary Singer
John Greenleaf Whittier . . . . Burns of America, Poet Laureate of New England, Puritan Poet, Quaker Poet, Wood-Thrush of Essex
Michael Wigglesworth . . . . Poet Laureate of New England Puritanism
Thornton Wilder. . . . . Grand Old Novelist

FULL NAMES OF THOSE LITERARY AMERICANS KNOWN BY THE FIRST 2 INITIALS

S. (Samuel) N. (Nathaniel) Behrman
R. (Richard) P. (Palmer) Blackmur
W. (William) C. (Crary) Brownell
W. (William) R. (Riley) Burnett
V. (Victor) F. (Francis) Calverton
R. (Ronald) S. (Salmon) Crane
E. (Edward) E. (Estlin) Cummings
E. (Edgar) L. (Lawrence) Doctorow
J. (James) P. (Patrick) Donleavy
T. (Thomas) S. (Stearns) Eliot
A. (Alfred) B. (Bertram) Guthrie, Jr.
A. (Abbott) J. (Joseph) Liebling
J. (John) P. (Phillips) Marquand

F. (Francis) O. (Otto) Matthiessen
H. (Henry) L. (Louis) Mencken
W. (William) S. (Stanley) Merwin
S. (Sidney) J. (Joseph) Perelman
J. (James) F. (Farl) Powers
W. (William) H. (Hickling) Prescott
O. (Ole) E. (Edvart) Rølvaag
J. (Jerome) D. (David) Salinger
W. (William) D. (De Witt) Snodgrass
T. (Thomas) S. (Sigismund) Stribling
E. (Elwyn) B. (Brooks) White
W. (William) K. (Kurty) Wimsatt

DETECTIVES AND THEIR AMERICAN CREATORS

DETECTIVES   **AUTHORS** (PSEUDONYMS IN PARENTHESES)
Pat and Jean Abbott . . . . Frances Crane
Uncle Abner . . . . Melville Davisson Post
Dr. Alcazar . . . . Philip MacDonald (an Anglo-American author)
Lew Archer . . . . Kenneth Millar [(John) Ross MacDonald]
Simon Ark . . . . Edward D. Hoch
Oliver Armiston (a raconteur
of Godahl's adventures) . . . . Frederick Irving Anderson
Batman (Bruce Wayne) . . . . Bob Kane
Bert Bayliss . . . . Carolyn Wells
Ned Beaumont. . . . . Dashiell Hammett
Henri Bencolini . . . . John Dickson Carr
Steve Bentley . . . . E. Howard Hunt (Robert Dietrich)
Boston Blackie . . . . Jack Boyle
Theodolinda ("Dol") Bonner. . . . Rex Todhunter Stout
Inspector Blunt . . . . Samuel Langhorne Clemens (Mark Twain)
Brock "The Rock" Callahan . . . . William Campbell Gault
Kenneth Carlisle . . . . Carolyn Wells
Nick Carter . . . . Nicholas Carter (Ormond G. Smith was the actual creator of Nick Carter. John Russell Coryell first wrote about him. Nicholas Carter was the final pseudonym used. The books, done by many writers, were mostly written by Frederick Van Rensselaer Dey)
Jack "Flashgun" Casey . . . . George Harmon Foxe
Pierre Chambrun . . . . Judson Pentecost Philips (Hugh Pentecost)
Charlie Chan . . . . Earl Derr Biggers
Nick and Nora Charles. . . . . Dashiell Hammett
Terry Clane . . . . Erle Stanley Gardner
Dr. Daniel Webster Coffee . . . . . . Lawrence G. Blochman
The Continental Op . . . . Dashiell Hammett
Bertha Cool . . . . Erle Stanley Gardner (A.A. Fair)

Thatcher Colt . . . . Anthony Abbot
Bill Crane . . . . Jonathan Latimer
Uncle George Crowder . . . . Judson Pentecost Philips (Hugh Pentecost)
Jefferson Dimarco . . . . Doris Miles Disney
Earl Drake . . . . Dan J. Marlowe
Nancy Drew . . . . Edward L. Stratemeyer (Carolyn Keene)
Sam Durell . . . . Edward S. Aarons
C. Auguste Dupin . . . . Edgar Allan Poe
87th Precinct Squad . . . . Evan Hunter, born Salvatore A. Lombino (Ed McBain)
Dr. Gideon Fell . . . . John Dickson Carr
Johnny Fletcher and Sam Cragg . Frank Gruber
Dan Fortune . . . . Dennis Lynds (Michael Collins)
Tecumseh Fox . . . . Rex Todhunter Stout
Reynold Frame . . . . Herbert Brean
Henry Gamadge . . . . Elizabeth Daly
Jo Gar . . . . Raoul Whitfield (Ramon Decolta)
Col. Anthony Gethryn . . . . Philip MacDonald
Ebenezer Gryce . . . . Anna Katharine Green
The Green Hornet (Britt Reid) . . . Fran Striker and George W. Trendle
Mike Hammer . . . . Frank Morrison Spillane (Mickey Spillane)
Matt Helm . . . . Donald Hamilton
Ed and Am Hunter . . . . Fredric Brown
Sarah Keate and Lance O'Leary . . Mignon G. Eberhart
Craig Kennedy . . . . Arthur B. Reeve
Francis X. Kerrigan . . . . Joseph Harrington
Donald Lam . . . . Erle Stanley Gardner (A.A. Fair)
Drury Lane . . . . Frederic Dannay, born Daniel Nathan, and Manfred
                                         B. Lee, born Manfred Lepofsky (Barnaby Ross)
Grace Latham and Colonel
John Primrose . . . . Zenith Jones Brown (Leslie Ford)
Michael Lord . . . . C. Daly King
Captain Duncan Maclain . . . . Baynard H. Kendrick
Sergeant Ivor Maddox . . . . Elizabeth Linington
John J. Malone . . . . Georgiana Ann Randolph (Craig Rice)
Philip Marlowe . . . . Raymond Chandler
Perry Mason . . . . Erle Stanley Gardner
Asey Mayo . . . . Phoebe Atwood Taylor
Travis McGee . . . . John D. MacDonald
Lt. Luis Mendoza . . . . Elizabeth Linington (Dell Shannon)
Sir Henry Merrivale . . . . John Dickson Carr (Carter Dickson)
Toussaint Moore . . . . Leonard Zinberg (Ed Lacy)
Mr. I.O. Moto . . . . J.P. Marquand
Kent Murdock . . . . George Harmon Coxe
Ed Noon . . . . Michael Avallone
Hugh North . . . . Van Wyck Mason
Mr. and Mrs. North . . . . Frances and Richard Lockridge
Joe Puma . . . . William Campbell Gault
Fergus O'Breen . . . . William Anthony Parker White (Anthony Boucher)
"Miss Pinkerton" (Nurse
Adams) . . . . Mary Roberts Rineheart
Professor Henry Poggioli . . . . T.S. Stribling
Paul Pry . . . . Erle Stanley Gardner
Oliver Quade . . . . Frank Gruber
Ellery Queen . . . . Frederic Dannay and Manfred B. Lee (Ellery Queen)
Miles Standish Rice . . . . Baynard H. Kendrick
John Ripley . . . . The Gordons (Mildred and Gordon)
Peter Cutler Sargeant II . . . . Gore Vidal (Edgar Box)
Doug Selby . . . . Erle Stanley Gardner (A.A. Fair)
Frank Sessions . . . . Hillary Waugh

The Shadow (Lamont Cranston) . Walter B. Gibson (Maxwell Grant)
Michael Shayne. . . . . David Dresser (Brett Halliday)
Rabbi David Small . . . . Harry Kemelman
Sam Spade . . . . Dashiell Hammett
"Uncle" Gavin Stevens . . . . William Faulkner
Fleming Stone . . . . Carolyn Wells
Peter Styles. . . . . Judson Pentecost Philips
Simon Templar . . . . Leslie Charles Bowyer Yin (his original name before
                                        legally changing it to Leslie Charteris)
Max Thursday . . . . Robert Wade and Bill Miller (Wade Miller)
Virgil Tibbs . . . . John Ball
Dick Tracy. . . . . Chester Gould
Ephraim Tutt . . . . Arthur Train
Dennis Tyler . . . . John Franklin Carter (Diplomat)
Lieutenant Valcour . . . . Rufus King
Philo Vance . . . . Willard Huntington Wright (S.S. Van Dine)
Professor S.F.X. Van Dusen . . . . Jacques Futrelle
J. Rufus Wallingford . . . . George Randolph Chester
Peter Ward . . . . E. Howard Hunt (David St. John)
Peter Wennick. . . . . Erle Stanley Gardner
Honey West. . . . . Gloria and Forrest E. Flickling (G.G. Flickling)
Dr. Basil Willing . . . . Helen McCloy
Pennington Wise . . . . Carolyn Wells
Leonidas Witherall. . . . . Phoebe Atwood Taylor (Alice Tilton)
Hildegarde Withers . . . . Stuart Palmer
Nero Wolfe . . . . Rex Todhunter Stout

ROGUES AND HELPERS AND THEIR AMERICAN CREATORS

Fritz Brenner. . . . . Rex T. Stout
Hamilton Burger . . . . Erle Stanley Gardner
Sam Catchem . . . . Chester Gould
Orrie Cather. . . . . Rex T. Stout
Inspector L.T. Cramer. . . . . Rex T. Stout
Deadwood Dick . . . . Edward L. Wheeler
Blackie Dow . . . . George Randolph Chester
Paul Drake. . . . . Erle Stanley Gardner
Fred Durkin. . . . . Rex T. Stout
The Infallible Godahl . . . . Frederick Irving Anderson
Archie Goodwin . . . . Rex T. Stout
Caspar Gutman (The Fat Man). . . Dashiell Hammett
Sergeant Ernest Heath . . . . Willard Huntington Wright (S.S. Van Dine)
Kato . . . . Fran Striker and George W. Trendle
The Lone Wolf (Michael
Lanyard) . . . . Louis Joseph Vance
Paul Madvig . . . . Dashiell Hammett
Malvino the Magician . . . . Frederick Irving Anderson
John F.X. Markham . . . . Willard Huntington Wright (S.S. Van Dine)
Randolph Mason . . . . Melville Davisson Post
Dr. Motilal Mookerji. . . . . Lawrence Blochman
Brigid O'Shaughnessy . . . . Dashiell Hammett
"The Pack" . . . . Louis Joseph Vance
Saul Panzer. . . . . Rex T. Stout
Parker. Donald E. Westlake (Richard Stark)
Robin (Dick Grayson) . . . . Bob Kane
Rena Savage . . . . Baynard H. Kendrick
Samuel "Spud" Savage . . . . Baynard H. Kendrick
Sgt. Purley Stebbins . . . . Rex T. Stout
Della Street . . . . Erle Stanley Gardner
Jimmy Valentine . . . . William Sidney Porter (O. Henry)

QUESTIONS AND ANSWERS

1. According to the number of clauses they contain, what are the 4 grammatical kinds of sentences?
    ANSWER: Simple, compound, compound-complex, and complex.

2. Which type of sentence is being defined in each of the following?
    a) A sentence with 2 or more independent clauses and 1 or more dependent (subordinate clauses)
    b) A sentence with 1 independent clause and 1 or more dependent clauses
    c) A sentence with only 1 subject and 1 predicate (either or both of which may be compound)
    d) A sentence with 2 or more independent clauses
    ANSWER: a) compound-complex b) complex c) simple d) compound.

3. Identify each of the following sentences as simple, compound, complex, or compound-complex.
    a) If it snows today, we shall go to the mountains for the weekend.
    b) Since it snowed today, we stayed inside; my wife and I painted the kitchen and the kids played video games.
    c) Seniors, juniors, and sophomores worked on raffles, washed cars, and held a barbecue to raise money for their dances.
    d) During the weekend I skied, and Paul ice skated.
    ANSWER: a) complex b) compound-complex c) simple d) compound.

4. In the following sentences, which ones, if any, contain errors in subject-verb agreement?
    a) It is I who, together with Mary and Marty, am going to the show.
    b) She is one of those teachers who give a lot of homework.
    c) Politics has been good to me.
    d) Behind the house stands a fir tree and a garage.
    e) Neither Mary nor Marty is going to the ballgame.
    ANSWER: Sentence d is incorrect (the verb should be ''stand'').

5. Give the 3 parts of a deductive argument known as a syllogism.
    ANSWER: Major premise, minor premise, and the conclusion.

6. Identify the figures of speech found in the following examples.
    a) ''How they clang, and clash, and roar!'' From ''The Bells'' by Edgar Allan Poe
    b) ''The pleasing plague stole on me . . . In short, 'tis that provoking charm . . .'' From the ''Je Ne Sais Quoi'' by William Whitehead
    c) ''The fair breeze blew, the white foam flew'' From ''The Rime of the Ancient Mariner'' by Samuel Taylor Coleridge
    d) ''I am a man which am a Jew of Tarsus, a city in Cilicia, a citizen of *no mean city*.'' From Saint Paul asserting his Hebrew lineage
    e) ''Give us this day our daily bread.'' From the Book of Matthew
    ANSWER: a) onomatopoeia or alliteration b) oxymoron or alliteration c) alliteration d) litotes e) synecdoche.

7. In the following sentences, which ones, if any, contain errors in subject-verb agreement?
    a) She is the only one of our teachers who gives homework on weekends.
    b) Twenty-five miles is quite a distance to travel.
    c) The brother, as well as all his sisters, were lonely.
    d) My best friend and baseball teammate were my college roommate.
    e) Either my brother or my sister are going with us.
    ANSWER: a and b are correct; c is ''was''; d is ''was''; and e is ''is.''

8. According to grammarians, how many parts of speech are there? Name them.
    ANSWER: Eight/Noun, pronoun, adjective, adverb, verb, preposition, conjunction, and interjection.

9. Name the 3 verbals.
    ANSWER: Gerund, infinitive, and participle.

10. Identify each of the following definitions as a gerund, infinitive, or participle.

a) It is a verbal noun ending in -ing.
b) It is a verb form which can serve only as an adjective.
c) It is a verb form which serves as a noun or adjective.
ANSWER: a) gerund b) participle c) infinitive.

11. What are the principal parts of the following verbs?

a) to arise	f) to go
b) to bear (carry)	g) to know
c) to choose	h) to ride
d) to do	i) to shake
e) to drive	j) to stride

ANSWER: a) arise, arose, arisen b) bear, bore, borne c) choose, chose, chosen d) do, did, done e) drive, drove, driven f) go, went, gone g) know, knew, known h) ride, rode, ridden i) shake, shook, shaken j) stride, strode, stridden.

12. Identify the form of each of the following participles.
a) Walked
b) Having walked
c) Walking
ANSWER: a) past participle b) perfect participle c) present participle.

13. In the following sentences, tell whether the infinitive is being used as a noun, adjective, or adverb.
a) I came to get the books you promised me.
b) He lacked the money and means to survive.
c) To study seduously is the key to success.
d) We studied diligently to achieve an ''A.''
ANSWER: a) adverb b) adjective c) noun d) adverb.

14. Into what 3 groups are conjunctions divided?
ANSWER: Coordinating (same as simple), subordinating, and correlative.

15. Name the 7 coordinating conjunctions.
ANSWER: And; but; for; or; nor; yet; so.

16. Give the 4 pairs of correlative conjunctions.
ANSWER: Both-and; either-or; neither-nor; not only-but also.

17. Identify each of the following words as a correlative conjunction, a conjunctive adverb, a coordinating conjunction, or a subordinating conjunction.

a) although	e) either-or	i) besides
b) unless	f) however	j) because
c) and	g) in order that	k) for
d) whenever	h) but	l) nevertheless

ANSWER: A, b, d, g, and j are subordinating conjunctions; c, h, and k are coordinating conjunctions; e is a correlative conjunction; and f, i, and l are conjunctive adverbs.

18. Recite the familiar jingle learned by most schoolchildren concerning the spelling of -*ie*- and -*ei*- words.
ANSWER: ''Write *i* before *e* except after *c*, or when sounded as *a* as in *neighbor* and *weigh*.''

19. State the 2 more formal explanations concerning the spelling of -*ie*- and -*ei*- words.
ANSWER: Write *ie* when the sound is $\bar{e}$ (except after *c*, in which case write *ei*), and write *ei* when the sound is not $\bar{e}$, especially when the sound is $\bar{a}$.

20. Insert *ie* or *ei* in each of the following:

a) ach____ve	g) n____ce	m) w____ld
b) fr____ght	h) l____sure	n) c____ling
c) p____ce	i) s____ge	o) conc____t
d) w____rd	j) w____gh	p) dec____ve
e) sl____gh	k) s____ze	q) hyg____ne
f) ch____ftain	l) for____gn	r) spec____s

ANSWER: a) achieve b) freight c) piece d) weird e) sleigh f) chieftain g) niece h) leisure i) siege j) weigh k) seize l) foreign m) wield n) ceiling o) conceit p) deceive q) hygiene r) species.

21. Give the principal parts of the transitive verbs: to lay, to raise, and to set.
ANSWER: Lay,laid, laid; raise, raised, raised; and set, set, set.

22. Give the principal parts of the intransitive verbs: to lie (to be at rest), to rise, and to sit.
ANSWER: Lie, lay, lain; rise, rose, risen; and sit, sat, sat.

23. Identify the correct verb form from the choices in parentheses in the following sentences.
   a) Please (lay, lie) down.
   b) Last night I (laid, lay) down for half an hour.
   c) As instructed Paul (sat, set) the books on the shelf.
   d) After resting a while, I (raised, rose) and went on my way.
ANSWER: a) lie b) lay c) set d) rose.

24. Identify the correct usage from the choices in the parentheses in the following sentences.
   a) Did she (imply, infer) by those words that he was mad at her?
   b) What (affect, effect) does pornography have on crime?
   c) The two brothers were pushing, shoving, and (raising cane, raising Cain).
   d) The horsethief was tried, convicted, and (hanged, hung) for his crime.
   e) Since he was playing for the first time, he is a/an (acolyte, neophyte, cenobite) in the field.
ANSWER: a) imply b) effect c) raising Cain d) hanged e) neophyte.

25. Identify in the following sentences the type of faulty modifier: misplaced modifier; squinting modifier; or dangling participial, prepositional gerund, or infinitive phrases.
   a) Everyone said during the game John acted in an absurd manner.
   b) Driving down the road, his radio blared.
   c) To play well in a match, good equipment is necessary.
   d) We washed the car with our neighbor's children.
   e) In preparing for a match, it is best to practice well.
ANSWER: a) squinting modifier b) dangling participle c) dangling infinitive phrase d) misplaced modifier e) dangling prepositional gerund phrase.

26. Identify the correct answer from the choices in the parentheses in the following sentences.
   a) Some (venal, venial) officials will help you if your bribe is $500 or more.
   b) Does the prophet (prophecy, prophesy) another earthquake?
   c) Mark's remarks were (ambiguous, equivocal), for he knew exactly what he was saying.
   d) He was a perfect (archetype, linotype, prototype) of what an athlete should be.
   e) He ate two (desserts, deserts) after eating a big meal.
ANSWER: a) venal b) prophesy c) equivocal d) either archetype or prototype e) desserts.

27. What is the kind of grammatical error in each of the following?
   a) I can't hardly believe he ate the whole thing.
   b) He hoped to eventually make enough money to buy the car.
   c) When just a baby, my grandfather died.
   d) I was delighted to win the scholarship. Which helped me pay the tuition.
ANSWER: a) double negative b) split infinitive c) dangling elliptical clause d) sentence fragment.

28. What figure of speech is found in each of the following sentences?
   a) Her eyelids felt as heavy as lead.
   b) At his office he was a roaring lion, but at his home he was a yelping puppy.
   c) The orchards wept when the horticulturist died.
   d) He was called ''pretty boy''; he had a hook nose, buck teeth, cauliflower ears, sunken cheeks, and small beady bloodshot eyes.

e) There were a million people at the dance last night.
ANSWER: a) simile b) metaphor c) personification d) irony e) hyperbole.

29. As what 3 parts of speech may infinitives be used?
ANSWER: As nouns, adjectives, and adverbs.

30. Name the functions of a participial phrase and a gerund phrase.
ANSWER: A participial phrase functions as an adjective and a gerund phrase as a noun.

31. Give the 5 possible endings for a past participle.
ANSWER: -*ed*, -*d*, -*t*, -*en*, or -*n*.

32. Name the 3 parts of an essay.
ANSWER: Introduction, body, and conclusion.

33. According to meaning and purpose, in what 4 ways are sentences classified?
ANSWER: Declarative, exclamatory, imperative, and interrogative sentences.

34. What type of sentence is being defined in each of the following?
   a) A sentence that gives a command or makes a request
   b) A sentence that expresses strong feeling either by a word, phrase, or a dependent clause
   c) A sentence that asks a question
   d) A sentence that makes a statement
ANSWER: a) imperative b) exclamatory c) interrogative d) declarative.

35. According to the arrangement of their content, in what 3 ways are sentences classified?
ANSWER: Periodic, loose, and balanced.

36. According to the arrangement of their content, what types of sentences are being defined in the following?
   a) Complete meaning is obtained well before the sentence ends.
   b) The meaning is not clear until near the end or at the end of the sentence.
   c) Parallel ideas have similar grammatical phrasing.
ANSWER: a) loose b) periodic c) balanced.

37. What are the only 3 English words that end in -*ceed*? What's the only English word that ends in -*sede*? The other words that end with this sound are spelled with what ending?
ANSWER: Exceed, proceed, and succeed/Supersede/-*cede*.

38. Identify the correct answer from the choices in the parentheses in the following sentences.
   a) He has (already, all ready) eaten his dinner.
   b) The entire family was (altogether, all together) for the reunion.
   c) The U.S. (consul, council, counsel) in Cairo was recalled to Washington.
   d) Having borrowed heavily and now unemployed, the geologist was in (dire straits, dire straights).
   e) The (indigenous, indigent) visitors (flouted, flaunted) the local laws against pandering.
ANSWER: a) already b) all together c) consul d) dire straits e) indigent and flouted.

39. What part of speech is being defined by the following definitions?
   a) It is a word that modifies a verb, an adjective, or another adverb.
   b) It is a word used before a noun or pronoun to show its relationship to some other word in the sentence
   c) It is a word that is used in an exclamatory or parenthetical way and has little or no grammatical relationship with the other words in the sentence.
   d) It is a word that substitutes for a noun or nouns or, sometimes, for a pronoun.
   e) It is a word that denotes a person, place, thing, or idea.
   f) It is a word that modifies a noun or a pronoun.
   g) It is a word that expresses action or being.
ANSWER: a) adverb b) preposition c) interjection d) pronoun e) noun f) adjective g) verb.

40. What grammatical structures come to mind when you think of Santa's helpers?

ANSWER: Subordinate clauses.

41. Identify the correct answer from the choices in the parentheses in the following sentences.
    a) Atlanta is the (capital, capitol) of Georgia. The (Capital, Capitol) dome in Atlanta is covered with 43 ounces of gold from Dahlonega.
    b) Do you know where (they're, their, there) going?
    c) The dog ate (its, it's) bone.
    d) Paul (passed, past) the ball to Bill on the fast break for the score.
    e) A student should see his guidance (counselor, councilor) when he has a problem.

ANSWER: a) capital - Capitol b) they're c) its d) passed e) counselor.

42. Give the answers to the following questions.
    a) The subject of an infinitive is always in what case?
    b) The pronouns *you* and *your* are in what person?
    c) A gerund is always used as what part of speech?
    d) A predicate nominative is in what case?
    e) The subject of a gerund is in what case?

ANSWER: a) objective b) second person c) noun d) nominative e) possessive.

43. Answer "Yes" or "No" in the following cases regarding the use of an apostrophe.
    a) It is used to form the possessive case of personal and relative pronouns.
    b) It is used to form the possessive case of indefinite pronouns.
    c) It is used in forming the plural of nouns.
    d) It is used to form the possessive of a plural noun ending in *s*.
    e) It is used to show where letters or figures have been omitted.

ANSWER: a) no b) yes c) no d) yes e) yes.

44. Name the 8 kinds of pronouns.

ANSWER: **Demonstrative, indefinite, intensive, interrogative, personal, reciprocal, reflexive, and relative (reciprocal are sometimes not listed and numeral pronouns sometimes are).**

45. What are the 3 principal parts of verbs in English? What is the 4th "principal part" that is sometimes included? Give the principal parts of the verb "eat."

ANSWER: **Present tense or present infinitive, past tense, and the past participle/ Present participle/Eat, ate, (have) eaten/The present participle is "(is) eating."**

46. Name the 3 endings that form the past tense and the past participle of regular verbs.

ANSWER: *d, ed,* or *t.*

47. Name the 3 divisions of time (as indicated by the tense) of verbs.

ANSWER: **Present, past, and future.**

48. Three of them are primary or simple, and 3 of them are secondary, compound, or perfect; name the 6 tenses of verbs in English.

ANSWER: **Present tense, past tense, future tense, present perfect tense, past perfect tense, and future perfect tense.**

49. Give the present and past indicative mood of the verb "be."

ANSWER:
I am	we are	I was	we were
you are	you are	you were	you were
he, she, it is	they are	he, she, it was	they were.

50. Name the 3 tones of verbs and give an example of each in the present tense with the verb "work."

ANSWER: **Simple tone, progressive tone, and emphatic tone — I work, I am working, and I do work.**

51. What are the 2 voices of verbs?

ANSWER: **Active and passive.**

52. What are the 3 moods (modes) of modern English verbs?

ANSWER: **Indicative, imperative, and subjunctive.**

53. Give the present and the past subjunctive of the verb "be."

ANSWER: (if) I be   (if) we be   (if) I were   (if) we were
         (if) you be   (if) you be   (if) you were   (if) you were
         (if) he, she, it be (if) they be   (if) he, she, it were   (if) they were.

54. Give the tense and voice of each of the following verbs.
   a) They had been seen.
   b) You were seen with that woman again.
   c) He has worked as well as anyone.
   d) I ran to the store.
   e) They will have been sent to prison for the crime.

ANSWER: a) past perfect tense, passive voice b) past tense, passive voice c) present perfect tense, active voice d) past tense, active voice e) future perfect tense, passive voice.

55. Identify the correct answers from the choices in the parentheses in the following sentences.
   a) The bar mitzvah is a (right of passage, rite of passage).
   b) The money was apportioned into (discrete, discreet) allocations.
   c) She wanted to go to the movies, (to, too, two).
   d) The president of the company ordered all the office desks to be made (stationary, stationery).
   e) What is your (principal, principle) goal in life?

ANSWER: a) rite of passage b) discrete c) too d) stationary e) principal.

56. What 2 parts of speech do adjectives modify?
ANSWER: Nouns or pronouns.

57. What are the 2 general types of adjectives?
ANSWER: Descriptive and limiting.

58. Name the 2 indefinite articles.
ANSWER: *A* and *an*.

59. Give the correct form of the relative or interrogative pronoun "who" in the following sentences. (Remember that formal grammar is needed, for the distinction between "who" and "whom" is sometimes not made in current spoken usage).
   a) _____ do you love the most?
   b) _____ was she talking to?
   c) _____ do you think made this egregious faux pas?
   d) I told him _____ I felt would make the best candidate.
   e) They would like to get tickets for _____ wants them.
   f) She said that she could not remember _____ it was.
   g) He said that that's the man _____ he saw at her apartment.
   h) He said, "God bless you," to _____ he encountered on the street.
   i) The scouts spoke to the player _____ no one thought they had selected in the first round of the draft.

ANSWER: a) whom b) whom c) who d) who e) whoever f) who g) whom h) whomever i) whom.

60. What are the 3 degrees of comparison of both adjectives and adverbs?
ANSWER: Positive, comparative, and superlative.

61. Name the 3 parts of speech an adverb modifies.
ANSWER: Verb, adjective, or adverb.

62. Give the comparative and superlative forms of the following positive forms.
   a) little   c) bad   e) helpful
   b) good   d) well   f) short

ANSWER: a) little, less (littler, lesser), least (littlest) b) good, better, best c) bad, worse, worst d) well, better, best e) helpful, more or less helpful, most or least helpful f) short, shorter, shortest.

63. Name the 2 types of clauses.
ANSWER: Independent (or main, or principal) and subordinate (or dependent).

64. In the following sentences, tell whether the dependent clause is used as a noun,

adjective, or adverbial clause.
a) The city where he was born has doubled in size.
b) Whoever has the most courage can swim across the lake.
c) He plays tennis everyday because he needs the exercise.
d) During her pregnancy she played more tennis than I did.
e) No one cares why she didn't come to the party.
ANSWER: a) adjective b) noun c) adverb d) adverb e) noun.

65. Identify the correct answer from the choices in the parentheses in the following sentences.
a) Do you know (who's, whose) going on the trip?
b) The student was (complemented, complimented) on his perfect 4.0 average.
c) The seventeen-year-old needed her parents' permission since she was still a (miner, minor).
d) The dog was too dangerous to be let (loose, lose) from its leash.
e) The punishment fit the crime and he received his just (deserts, desserts).
ANSWER: a) who's b) complimented c) minor d) loose e) deserts.

66. Give the answers to the following questions.
a) In what case is the objective complement of an infinitive?
b) In what case is the subject of a sentence?
c) In what case is a predicate or subjective complement?
d) In what case is the object of a preposition?
e) In what case is an appositive?
ANSWER: a) objective b) nominative c) nominative d) objective e) same case as the word with which it is in apposition.

67. Give all the forms of the personal pronoun asked for in the following.
a) 1st person singular, nominative, possessive, and objective case.
b) 3rd person masculine singular, nominative, possessive, and objective case.
c) 3rd person feminine singular, nominative, possessive, and objective case.
d) 1st person plural, nominative, possessive, and objective case.
e) 3rd person plural, nominative, possessive, and objective case.
ANSWER: a) I; my, mine; me b) he; his; him c) she; her, hers; her d) we; our, ours; us e) they; their, theirs, them.

68. Give the singular and plural forms of the interrogative pronoun ''who'' in the nominative, possessive, and objective case.
ANSWER: Who, whose, and whom.

69. Tell whether the italicized word in the following sentences is a participle or a gerund.
a) The students did not like the teacher's *singing*.
b) *Asking* the teacher for permission was a silly thing to do.
c) A *smiling* candidate has a significant advantage in an election.
d) *Getting* an early start, the early bird got the worm.
e) *Seeing* is *believing*.
ANSWER: a) gerund b) gerund c) participle d) participle e) both words are gerunds.

70. Identify the correct answer from the choices in the parentheses in the following sentences.
a) The phone rang non-stop for 10 minutes. It rang (continually, continuously).
b) The Mayor gave the (counsel, council) some advice.
c) The money was to be divided equally (among, between) the two brothers.
d) If you believe that a magician can really levitate a person, you are suffering from a/an (allusion, delusion, illusion).
e) His mail-order campaign brought (fewer, less) contributions than he had hoped.
ANSWER: a) continuously b) council c) between d) delusion e) fewer.

71. Identify the error in the following sentences.
a) The Pep Committee will meet today at Break, plans will be made for Friday's football game.
b) I told my friends about stealing the car they thought I was dumb.

   c) They studied French, Spanish, German, and played tennis.

   d) She neither had the money nor the desire to visit Paris.

   e) Santa Claus treated the family at Christmas. A bike for Sally and a basketball for me.

ANSWER: a) comma splice b) fused, blended, or run-on sentence c) faulty parallelism (coordination) d) faulty parallelism e) sentence fragment.

72. What are the only 3 cases of English nouns or pronouns?

ANSWER: Nominative or subjective; objective or accusative; and possessive or genitive.

73. Name the 3 ways in which a pronoun agrees with its antecedent.

ANSWER: In person, number, and gender.

74. Name the 3 persons of personal pronouns.

ANSWER: 1st, 2nd, and 3rd persons.

75. For which personal pronouns is gender the same?

ANSWER: 1st and 2nd persons.

76. Identify the type of pronouns in the following groups.

   a) such, this, that, these, those

   b) many, anyone, someone, everybody, any

   c) myself, yourself, himself, ourselves, themselves

   d) that, which, who, whose, whom

   e) who, which, what, whoever, whatever

ANSWER: a) demonstrative b) indefinite c) reflexive or intensive d) relative e) interrogative.

77. What grammatical structure do you have with a man convicted of 2 crimes?

ANSWER: A compound sentence.

78. Name the 4 types of writing.

ANSWER: Argumentation, description, exposition, and narration.

79. Identify the correct answer from the choices in the parentheses in the following sentences.

   a) He was so (credible, creditable, credulous) that he believed everything he read in the racy tabloid.

   b) People who drink alcohol frequently are (apt, liable, likely) to become addicted.

   c) A rifle is usually shot by a person in a (prone, supine) position.

   d) She (learned, taught) me tennis during her free time.

   e) What (kind of, kind of a) car did he want to buy?

ANSWER: a) credulous b) liable c) prone d) taught e) kind of.

80. Tell whether the following words are either always or usually used with singular or plural verbs.

a) remains (corpse)	f) scissors
b) linguistics	g) four liters
c) everyone	h) somebody
d) mumps	i) stamina
e) the number	j) *The Adventures of Tom Sawyer*

ANSWER: a) plural b) singular c) singular d) singular e) singular f) plural g) singular (used as a unit) h) singular i) singular j) singular.

81. What are the 2 ways verbs are classified?

ANSWER: Transitive and intransitive.

82. What do the principal parts of the verbs *burst, cut, hurt,* and *put* have in common?

ANSWER: All 3 principal parts of each verb have the same form.

83. Which punctuation marks would be used for each of the following?

   a) For an intentional omission

   b) To separate independent clauses joined by *and, but,* or *nor*

   c) To separate independent clauses not joined by coordinating conjunctions

   d) To separate a chapter from a verse in the Bible

   e) To make possessive the form of personal and relative pronouns

ANSWER: a) ellipsis or three periods b) comma c) semicolon d) colon e) nothing is needed.

84. Give the 5 parts of a business letter.

ANSWER: The heading; the inside address; the greeting or salutation; the body; and the complimentary close (the signature, also).

85. Identify the figures of speech found in the following examples.
    a) Bunyan's *Pilgrim's Progress*
    b) He ate the whole can.
    c) "Gather ye rosebuds while ye may,/Old Time is still a-flying; And this same flower that smiles today, Tomorrow will be dying." From "To the Virgins, to Make Much of Time" by Robert Herrick.
    d) "As headstrong as an allegory on the banks of the Nile." From Richard Brinsley Sheridan's *The Rivals.*
    e) "Man proposes, but God disposes." From *The Imitation of Christ* by Thomas à Kempis.

ANSWER: a) allegory b) metonymy c) symbolism and *carpe diem* d) malapropism (the line was said by Mrs. Malaprop) e) antithesis.

86. Identify the figure of speech in the following examples.
    a) "A man, a plan, a canal, Panama."
    b) "So, it's kisstomary to cuss the bride"; "Sheats and Kelly."
    c) "I came, I saw, I conquered" (*Veni, vidi, vici*).
    d) "A superman in physique but in intellect a fool."
    e) "His conduct was — but I would be embarrassed to tell you."

ANSWER: a) palindrome b) spoonerism c) asyndeton d) chiasmus e) aposiopesis.

87. Identify the correct answer from the choices in the parentheses in the following sentences.
    a) Judge Martin, known for his impartiality, was typically (disinterested, uninterested) in his latest case.
    b) Sue and Anne are (alumnae, alumni) of State University.
    c) John visited the (oculist, optician, optometrist, ophthalmologist) for an eye operation.
    d) Did you see that cute (praying mantis, preying mantis) in church devouring that insect?
    e) The wife was upset with the (childlike, childish) actions of her husband.

ANSWER: a) disinterested b) alumnae c) oculist or ophthalmologist d) praying mantis e) childish.

88. Give the conjugated form of the verb "ask" according to the following requirements.
    a) first person, plural, future tense, progressive form, passive voice
    b) third person, singular, present tense, progressive form, passive voice
    c) second person, plural, past tense, progressive form, active voice
    d) third person, plural, future perfect tense, progressive form, active voice

ANSWER: a) We will be being asked b) He is being asked c) You were asking d) They will have been asking.

89. Identify the correct answer from the choices in the parentheses in the following sentences.
    a) No one but (he, him) scored 1600 on the SAT test.
    b) Was it (she, her) they were talking to?
    c) They thought the ballplayer to be (he, him) but they decided they were wrong.
    d) He's a better player than (I, me).
    e) Just between you and (I, me), I don't like grits.

ANSWER: a) him b) she c) him d) I e) me.

90. Spell the singular of each of the following words.

a) opera	e) graffiti	i) them
b) cacti	f) ellipses	j) libretti
c) apices	g) dice	k) nuclei
d) errata	h) data	l) stigmata

ANSWER: a) opus b) cactus c) apex d) erratum e) graffito f) ellipsis g) die h) datum i) him, her, or it j) libretto k) nucleus l) stigma.

91. Give the plural form of each of the following nouns.

    a) baby sitter   e) child   i) mouse
    b) cupful   f) tooth   j) passer-by
    c) father-in-law   g) shambles   k) ox
    d) half   h) salary   l) man-of-war

ANSWER: a) baby sitters b) cupfuls c) fathers-in-law d) halves e) children f) teeth g) shambles h) salaries i) mice j) passers-by k) oxen (rarely ox) l) men-of-war.

92. What are the 3 most common inflectional endings for noun plurals in English?
ANSWER: *s, es,* and *en.*

93. Answer each of the following.
    a) Give the term for 2 or more words that have the same sound but different meanings.
    b) Which of the homonyms, *to, too, two,* is an adverb?
    c) What is the central thought of a paragraph called?
ANSWER: a) homonyms b) too c) topic sentence or statement.

94. Give the possessive plural of each of the following words.

    a) attorney-at-law   e) Jones
    b) commander-in-chief   f) P.S.
    c) Bell and Howell   g) 1972
    d) ox   h) woman

ANSWER: a) attorneys-at-law's b) commanders-in-chief's c) Bell and Howell's d) oxen's e) the Joneses' f) P.S.'s g) 1972's h) women's.

95. Identify the correct answer from the choices in the parentheses in the following sentences.
    a) His last proposal was no (different from, different to, different than) his first proposal.
    b) His first car (differs with, differs from) his second car in color only.
    c) Any President will at times (differ with, differ from) the members of his own party on certain issues.
    d) (Compared to, Compared with) the huge medical bills, the car repair bill was insignificant.
    e) *The Fate of the Earth* by Jonathan Schell (consists in, consists of) three chapters.
    f) He dived (in, into) the river from the bridge and aided the rescue.
    g) The school system's appeal for applicants demonstrated its need (of, for) teachers.
ANSWER: a) different from b) differs from c) differ with d) Compared with e) consists of f) into g) for.

96. What are the 4 purposes of punctuation?
ANSWER: To terminate, to introduce, to separate, and to enclose.

97. What are the 3 ways to close a sentence?
ANSWER: With a period, with an exclamation point, or with a question mark.

98. Identify the correct answer from the choices in the parentheses in the following sentences.
    a) They thought (us, we) to be (them, they).
    b) (Who, Whom) did they think (he, him) to be?
    c) They (robbed, stole) my bike.
    d) He hates marriage. He's a (misanthrope, misogynist, misogamist).
    e) What he wants (is, are) more pictures.
    f) He acts as if he (was, were) someone of importance.
    g) What's the sense (of, in) watching television?
    h) Three-fourths of my paper (is, are) finished.
    i) The old man collapsed in the snow and died of (hypothermia, hyperthermia).
    j) The rebels (fomented, fermented) the revolution.

k) The (apogee, perigee) is the highest point, the farthest from the earth.

l) Europe and the USA are considered to be (oriental, occidental) countries.

ANSWER: a) us/them b) whom/him c) stole d) misogamist e) is f) were g) in h) is i) hypothermia j) fomented k) apogee l) occidental.

99. Give the Latin prefix for each of the following.

a) around, both

b) before, previous

c) against

d) beyond, outside

e) below, beneath

f) after, behind, later

g) back, backward

h) beyond, excessively

ANSWER: a) ambi- b) ante- c) contra- d) extra-, extro- e) infra- f) post- g) retro- h) ultra-.

100. Give the Latin root for each of the following.

a) love

b) body

c) belief, faith

d) flow

e) bad

f) death

g) blood

h) life

ANSWER: a) AM- b) CORPOR-, CORP- c) FID- d) FLU-, FLUX- e) MAL-, MALIGN- f) MOR-, MORT- g) SANGUIN- h) VIV-.

101. Give the Greek prefix for each of the following.

a) both, on both sides of

b) against, opposing

c) bad, disordered

d) within

e) good, pleasant

f) over, excessive

g) around, near

h) before, in front of

ANSWER: a) ambi- b) anti- c) dys- d) endo-, ento- e) eu- f) hyper- g) peri- h) pro-.

102. Give the Greek root for each of the following.

a) man, mankind

b) book

c) woman

d) other, different

e) large

f) straight, correct

g) love

h) wise, wisdom

ANSWER: a) ANTHROP- b) BIBLI- c) GYN- d) HETER- e) MEGA- f) ORTH- g) PHIL- h) SOPH-.

103. Give the Greek suffix for each of the following.

a) ruler

b) surgical removal of

c) inflammation of

d) science, study of

e) abnormal preoccupation about

f) diseased condition of

g) one who suffers from

h) abnormal fear of

ANSWER: a) -arch b) -ectomy c) -itis d) -logy e) -mania f) -osis g) -path h) -phobia.

104. Whose famous last words were?

a) ''I am about to, or, I am going to die; either expression is used.'' (1702)

b) ''I am perishing, expiring, passing away, petering out, departing this life, quitting this world, making my exit, going the way of the flesh, shuffling off this mortal coil, meeting my fate, giving up the ghost, taking my last breath, taking my last step, paying my debt to nature, going out with the ebb, going the way of all life, returning to dust, going to meet my Maker, going to glory, going to kingdom come, going to the happy hunting grounds, going to my rest or my reward, going to my long account, joining the majority, being gathered to my fathers, joining my ancestors, joining the choir invisible or the angels, going to Abraham's bosom, passing over Jordan, walking through the valley of the shadow of death, crossing the Stygian ferry, giving an abolus to Charon, dropping dead, croaking, coming to an untimely end, kicking the bucket, going to the wall, shoving off, pegging out, taking the last count, cashing in my chips or checks,...

ANSWER: a) Dominique Bonhours (he's French but such an appropriate quote) b) Roget Thesaurus — who was perfectly healthy but who died of exhaustion.

SYMBOLS AND SIGNS

.	period
,	comma
;	semicolon
:	colon
?	interrogation or question mark
!	exclamation point
'	apostrophe, single quotation mark
-	hyphen
—	dash
··	diaeresis (as in Noël)
	the
˄	caret (as in see‸book)
*	asterisk
#	number
%	per cent
&	ampersand
?!	interrobang
ə	schwa
∴	therefore
∵	because
†	dagger
‡	double dagger
(	open parenthesis
)	close parenthesis
( )	parentheses; curves
" "	quotation marks; quotes
' '	quotation marks, single
[] or <>	brackets (square or angle)
. . . or	ellipsis; leaders
´	acute accent (*accent aigu*, as in *touché*)
`	grave accent (*accent grave,* as in Adèle)
^	circumflex (*accent circumflex*, as in *fenêtre*)
¸	cedilla (*cédille*, as in *garçon*)
~	tilde (as in señor)
¯	macron (pronunciation symbol indicating long vowel, as in bāke)
˘	breve (pronunciation symbol indicating short vowel, as in cŭt)
/	virgule; slash; solidus

GREEK ALPHABET

Alpha
Beta
Gamma
Delta
Epsilon
Zeta
Eta
Theta
Iota
Kappa
Lambda
Mu
Nu
Xi
Omicron
Pi
Rho
Sigma
Tau
Upsilon
Phi
Chi
Psi
Omega

LATIN PREFIXES

PREFIXES	MEANING	EXAMPLES
ab-, a-, abs-	away, from	abduct, abject
ad-, etc	to, toward	admire, adhesive
ambi-	around, both	ambidextrous, ambivert
ante-	before, previous	antecedent, antedate
circum-	around	circumlocution, circumvent
com-, con-, etc	together, very, with	complicate, conduct
contra-	against	contradict, contravene
de-	down, from, off	descend, describe
dis-, di-, dif-	apart, away, off	dispel, diffuse
ex-, e-, ef-	away from, not, out	evade, excise
extra-, extro-	beyond, outside	extramural, extrovert
in-, im-, etc	not, opposing	incapable, immoral
in-, im-, etc	in, into, within	induct, impel
infra-	below, beneath	infrared, infrasonic
inter-	among, between	intercede, interrupt
intra-, intro-	inward, within	intramural, introvert

non-	not	nonentity, nonresident
ob-, etc.	against, over, toward	obstruct, occlude
per-	completely, through	permeate, persecute
post-	after, behind, later	postpone, postscript
pre-	before, earlier, in front of	preclude, prevent
pro-	forward, in front of	proceed, produce
re-	again, back, backward	renew, revoke
retro-	back, backward	retroactive, retrospect
se-	aside, away	secede, segregate
sub-, etc.	beneath, under	subjugate, submarine
super-	above, extra, over	supercede, superfluous
trans-, tran-, tra-	across, beyond	transcend, transport
ultra-	beyond, excessively	ultramodern, ultraviolet

LATIN ROOTS

ROOTS	MEANING	EXAMPLES
AC-, ACR-	sharp	acumen, acrid
AG-, ACT-	do, drive, impel	agent, active
AM-	love	amorous, amicable
ANIM-	mind, life, spirit	animal, inanimate
ANN-, ENNI-	year	annual, perennial
AQU-	water	aquarium, aqueduct
AUD-, AUDIT-	hear	audience, auditorium
BEL-, BELL-	war	bellicose, belligerent
BEN-, BENE-,	well, good	benediction, benefactor
CAD-, CAS-	fall, befall	cadence, casual
CAP- (CIP-), CAPT- (CEPT-)	take, seize	capture, reception
CAPIT-	head	decapitate, precipitate
CARN-	flesh	carnage, incarnate
CED-, CESS-	go, yield	secede, recession
CERN-, CRET-	separate, distinguish	discern, excrete
CID-, CIS-	cut, kill	homicide, incision
CLAM- (CLAIM-)	cry out, shout	clamor, proclaim
CLUD-, CLUS-	close, shut	conclude, recluse
CORPOR-, CORP-	body	incorporate, corpulent
CRE-, CRESC-, CRET-	grow	crescent, excrescence
CRED-, CREDIT-	believe, trust	credible, discredit
CULP-	blame, fault	culpable, exculpate
CUMB-, CUB-	lie down	incumbent, incubator
CUR-, CURR-, CURS-	run, go	concur, excursion
DENT-	tooth	dentist, denture
DIC-, DICT-	say, speak	dictionary, contradict
DOC-, DOCT-	teach	docile, indoctrinate
DUC-, DUCT-	lead	adduce, conduct
EGO-	I, self	egoist, egocentric
EQU-	equal	equity, equidistant
ERR-	wander	aberration, errata
FAC- (FIC-), FACT- (FECT-)	do, make	factory, efficacious
FER-	bear, carry	fertile, transfer
FERV-	boil, bubble	fervent, effervescent
FID-	belief, faith	fidelity, infidel
FIN-	end, limit	infinite, final
FLECT-, FLEX-	bend, twist	genuflect, flexible
FLU-, FLUX-	flow	confluence, influx
FRANG- (FRING-), FRACT-	break	frangible, infraction
GEN-, GENIT-	give birth to, produce	ingenious, genital
GRAD-, GRESS-	step, go	gradual, progression
GRAT-	pleasing, grateful	gratuitous, gratuity

GRAV-................	heavy	gravity, aggravate
GREG-................	flock, herd	congregate, egregious
HER-, HES-............	cling, stick	adhere, cohesion
I-, IT-................	go, travel	ambient, transition
JAC-, JECT-...........	hurl, throw	ejaculate, projectile
JUDIC-...............	judgment	judicious, adjudicate
JUNCT- (JOIN-)	join...............	juncture, disjoin
JUR-.................	swear	adjure, perjury
LATER-...............	side	bilateral, multilateral
LEG-, LIG-, LECT-......	choose, read........	legible, lectern
LEV-.................	light, rise	elevate, levitation
LOC-.................	place.............	locale, dislocate
LOQU-, LOCUT-........	talk, speak	eloquent, colloquial
LUC-.................	light	elucidate, translucent
MAGN-...............	great.............	magnitude, magnanimous
MAL-, MALIGN-........	bad	malevolent, malignant
MAN-, MANU-.........	hand	manipulate, manuscript
MATR-, MATERN-......	mother	matricide, maternity
MEDI-...............	middle	median, immediate
MINOR-, MINUS-, MINUT-...	small, smaller	minority, diminutive
MIT-, MISS-...........	send	transmitter, missile
MON-, MONIT-.........	warn	admonish, premonition
MOR-, MORT-..........	death	moribund, immortal
MULTI-...............	many	multitude, multifarious
MUT-................	change	immutable, mutation
NASC-, NAT-..........	be born	nascent, prenatal
NOMEN-, NOMIN-.......	name	nomenclature, nominate
OMNI-...............	all	omnivorous, omniscient
PATERN-, PATR-........	father	paternal, patrimony
PECUNI-..............	money............	impecunious, pecuniary
PED-.................	foot	centipede, pedestrian
PEL-, PULS-...........	drive, push	propel, impulsion
PEND-, PENS-..........	hang, weigh	suspend, dispense
PLAC-................	please, appease	placate, placid
PLIC-, PLICIT-, PLEX-.....	fold	duplicity, complex
PON-, POSIT-..........	place, put	proponent, deposit
PORT-................	carry.............	deport, portage
POT-.................	power	omnipotent, potential
PUNG-, PUNCT-........	prick, point..........	puncture, punctual
QUIR-, QUIS-..........	ask, seek	inquire, inquisition
REG-, RIG-, RECT-.......	rule, straight, right	regicide, erect
ROG-................	ask	derogatory, interrogate
RUPT-................	break	rupture, interrupt
SANCT-...............	holy	sanctuary, sanctimonious
SANGUIN-.............	blood	sanguine, consanguineous
SCI-.................	know	science, nescient
SCRIB-, SCRIPT-........	write.............	transcribe, transcription
SEC-, SEG-, SECT-.......	cut	sector, bisect
SED-, SID-, SESS-........	sit, seat	sedentary, session
SEN-.................	old	senate, senile
SENT-, SENS-..........	feel	sentiment, sensuous
SEQU-, SECUT-........	follow	sequel, consecutive
SIMIL-, SIMUL-.........	like	assimilate, simulate
SOL-.................	alone.............	solitude, desolate
SOLV-, SOLU-, SOLUT-....	loosen, free..........	absolve, solution
SON-.................	sound	dissonance, supersonic
SPEC-, SPIC-, SPECT-.....	look, see...........	specimen, circumspect
SPIR-................	breathe	conspire, perspiration
STRING-, STRICT-........	draw tight	stringent, stricture

```
STRU-, STRUCT- .......... build ............... instrument, structure
TANG-, TING-, TACT- ....... touch .............. tangible, contact
TEMPOR- ................. time .............. contemporary, temporal
TEN-, TIN-, TENT- ......... hold .............. tenure, detention
TEND-, TENS-, TENT- ....... stretch, strive ........ distend, contentious
TENU- .................... thin ................. tenuous, extenuate
TORQU-, TORT- ........... twist ............. torque, contortion
TRACT- ................... drag, pull ........... contract, extraction
TRUD-, TRUS- ............ push, thrust .......... obtrude, intrusion
TURB- .................... agitate, disturb ....... disturb, turbid
UND- ..................... wave ............... inundate, undulant
VEN-, VENT- .............. come ............... intervene, prevent
VERB- .................... verb, word ........... verbose, verbiage
VERT-, VERS- ............. turn ............... divert, aversion
VID-, VIS- ................ see ............... provident, vision
VINC-, VICT- ............. conquer ............. evince, victorious
VIV- ..................... life ............... vivid, revive
VOC-, VOK- .............. call, voice ........... invocation, revoke
VOL- ..................... wish ............... volition, malevolent
VOLV-, VOLU-, VOLUT- ..... roll, turn ............. evolve, revolution
VOR- ..................... devour ............. voracious, devour
```

LATIN NUMERICAL ROOTS

ROOTS	MEANING	EXAMPLES
SEMI-	half	semicentennial
UN-	one	uniform, unanimous
PRIM-	first	primer, primeval
DU-	two	duet, duplicate
BI-	two, twice	bicycle, bisect
TRI-	three	triangle, tripod
QUADR-	four	quadrangle, quadruped
QUART-	fourth	quarter, quartic
QUINT-	fifth	quintuplet, quintet
SEXT-	six, sixth	sextet, sextant
SEPT-, SEPTEM-	seven	septet, September
OCT-	eight	octet, October
OCTAV-	eighth	octave, octavo
DECI-, DECIM-	tenth	deciliter, decimal
CENT-	hundred	century, centennial
MILL-	thousand	millipede, millimeter

GREEK PREFIXES

PREFIXES	MEANING	EXAMPLES
a- (an-)	lacking, without	amorphous, anemia
amphi-	both, on both sides of	amphibious, amphitheatre
ana-	against, back, up	analysis, anatomy
anti-	against, opposing	antipathy, antithesis
apo-	from, off, separate	apostate, aphelion
cata- (cat-, cath-)	down, against, thoroughly	cataclysm, catholic
dia-	through, across, apart	diameter, diaphanous
dys-	bad, disordered	dysentery, dysphoria
ec- (ex-)	out, out of	eccentric, exodus
en- (em-)	in, within, among	endemic, emphasize
endo-, ento-	within	endogamy, entophyte
epi-	on, upon, in addition to	epidermis, epitaph
eu-	good, pleasant	eugenics, euphemism
exo-, ecto-	outside, external	exogamy, ectoparasite
hyper-	over, excessive	hyperbole, hypercritical

hypo-	below, under, less	hypodermic, hypothesis
meta-	later, changed, over	metabolism, metamorphosis
para-	beside, beyond	paradox, paralysis
peri-	around, near	perimeter, periscope
pro-	before, in front of	prognosis, prologue
pros-	toward, in addition to	proselyte, prosthetic
syn- (sym-, syl-, sys-)	with, together	synchronize, sympathy

GREEK ROOTS

ROOTS	MEANING	EXAMPLES
ACR-	highest	acrobat, acropolis
AESTHE-, ESTHE-	feel, perceive	aesthete, anesthetic
AGOG-, AGOGUE-	lead, leader	demagogue, pedagogue
AGON-	struggle, contest	agony, antagonist
ALG-	pain	cardialgia, nostalgia
ANDR-	man, male	gynandrous, philanderer
ANTHROP-	man, mankind	misanthrope, philanthropy
ARCH-	ancient, primitive, chief	archaeology, monarch
ASTR-, ASTER-	star	asterisk, disaster
AUT-	self	automaton, autonomy
BALL-, BOL-, BLE-	throw, put	ballistics, problem
BI- (as in BIO-)	life	biology, biography
BIBLI-	book	bibliography, bibliophile
CAC-	bad	cacography, cacophony
CAL-, KAL-	beauty	calisthenics, kaleidoscope
CHIR- (CHEIR-)	hand	chiropractor, chirography
CHROM-	color	chromatic, monochrome
CHRON-	time	chronic, synchronize
CLA-	break	iconoclast, clastic
COSM-	world, order, universe	cosmology, cosmetic
CRYPT-	hidden, secret	cryptic, cryptograph
CYCL-	circle, wheel	cyclic, cyclone
DEM-	people	demagogue, epidemic
DERM-	skin	dermatitis, pachyderm
DOX-, DOG-	belief, opinion, teaching	heterodox, orthodox
DYN-, DYNAM-	strength, power	dynamic, dynasty
ER-, EROT-	love	erotic, erotomania
ERG-, URG-	work, power	energy, metallurgy
ETHN-	race, cultural group	ethnic, ethnology
GAM-	marriage	monogamy, misogamy
GEN(E)-, GON-	originate, produce	genesis, theogony
GEN(E)-	kind, race, source	genocide, genealogy
GE-	earth	geology, geodetic
GLOSS-, GLOT-	tongue, language	glossolalia, polyglot
GNO-	know	agnostic, diagnosis
GON-	corner, angle	pentagon, trigonometry
GYN-	woman	gynarchy, misogynist
HEM-, HEMAT-	blood	hemorrhage, hemophilia
HETER-	other, different	heterodox, heterogeneous
HIER-	sacred	hierarchy, hieroglyphic
HOM-, HOME-	same	homogeneous, homonym
HYDR-	water	dehydrate, hydraulic
IATR-	cure, medicine, physician	iatrogenic, pediatric
IS-	same, equal	isosceles, isotope
LATR-, LATER-	worship excessively	idolater, idolatry
LITH-	stone	lithograph, monolith
LOG-	speech, word, reason	epilogue, prologue
MACR-	large, long	macron, macrocosm

MANC-	divine by means of	astramancy, mantic
MEGA-	large	megalomania, megaphone
MICR-	small	microscope, microbe
MIS-	hatred	misanthropy, misandrist
MORPH-	form	amorphous, metamorphosis
NAUT-	sailor	nautical, cosmonaut
NECR-	dead, die, corpse	necrology, necropolis
NE-	new	neologism, neophyte
ODONT-	tooth	odontology, mastodon
ONYM-	name, word	synonym, pseudonym
OP-, OPT-	eye, see	optical, autopsy
ORTH-	straight, correct	orthodox, orthodontist
PALE-	old	paleontology, paleolithic
PAN-	all, entire	panorama, pantheon
PATH-	feel, suffer, disease	empathy, psychopath
PED-	child, boy	pediatrician, pedagogue
PEP-, PEPT-	digest	peptic, eupepsia
PETR-	rock	petrology, petrify
PHIL-	love	philology, philosophy
PHON-	sound, voice	euphony, cacophony
PHOS-, PHOT-	light	phosphorescent, photo
POD-	foot	podium, podiatrics
POL-, POLIS-	city, state	metropolis, Annapolis
POLY-	many, much	polyglot, polytheistic
PSEUD-	false	pseudonym, pseudoscience
PSYCH-	mind	psychic, psychosis
PYR-	fire	pyre, pyromania
SOM-, SOMAT-	body	chromosone, psychosomatic
SOPH-	wise, wisdom	sophomore, theosophy
STOL-, STAL-, STLE-	send, draw	epistolary, epistle
TACT-, TAX-	arrange, put in order	tactics, taxidermy
TAPH-	tomb	cenotaph, epitaph
TAUT-	same	tautology, tautonym
TECHN-	art, craft, technique	polytechnical, technician
TELE-	far, distant	telegram, telepathy
THE-	god	atheist, monotheism
THERM-	heat	thermal, thermometer
TOM-	cut	atom, entomology
TROP-	turn	phototropic, tropic
TROPH-	nourish, grow	atrophy, trophoplasm
XEN-	stranger, foreigner	xenophobia, xenogamy
ZO-	animal	zoophile, zoology

GREEK NUMERICAL ROOTS

ROOTS	MEANING	EXAMPLES
HEMI-	half	hemisphere, hemiplegia
MON-	one, single	monocle, monocracy
PROT-	first, original	prototype, protein
DI-	twice, double, twofold	dicotyledon, dioxide
DICH-	in two	dichotomy, dichogamy
DEUTER-, DEUTERO-	second	deuteragonist, Deuteronomy
TRI-	three	trisect, trilingual
TETR-	four	tetrachord, tetrabrach
PENT-	five	pentarchy, pentagon
HEX-	six	hexagram, hexad
HEPT-	seven	heptagon, heptahedron
OCT-	eight	octamerous, octopus
DEC-	ten	Decalogue, decathlon
HECT-	hundred	hectogram, hectokilo
KILO-	thousand	kilohertz, kilometer

GREEK SUFFIXES

SUFFIXES	MEANING	EXAMPLES
-arch	ruler	matriarch, monarch
-archy	that which is ruled	matriarchy, monarchy
-cracy	rule by, type of government	autocracy, aristocracy
-crat	advocate of or participant in a (specified) theory of government	autocrat, aristocrat
-ectomy	surgical removal of	appendectomy, tonsillectomy
-emia	condition or disease of the blood	leukemia, hypoglycemia
-gram	thing written down	telegram, diagram
-graph	something that writes, something written	telegraph, monograph
-graphy	method of writing, art or science of writing	calligraphy, geography
-itis	inflammatory disease of or inflammation of	neuritis, arthritis
-logy	science, doctrine, theory of, systematic study of	biology, theology
-mania	abnormal preoccupation about, passion for	kleptomania, bibliomania
-maniac	one having a preoccupation about or passion for	kleptomaniac, bibliomaniac
-meter	instrument for measuring, having metrical feet in poetry	barometer, pentameter
-metry	process, art, or science of measuring	geometry, trigonometry
-nomy	science of, system of laws governing	astronomy, economy
-osis	diseased condition of, state or condition of	psychosis, hypnosis
-path	one who suffers from or treats a disease	psychopath, osteopath
-pathy	feeling, suffering, disease of, treatment of disease	antipathy, hydropathy
-phobe	one who fears or hates	Francophobe, Russophobe
-phobia	abnormal fear or hatred of	claustrophobia, pyrophobia
-scope	instrument for viewing	telescope, microscope
-tomy	surgical operation on or cutting of	gastrotomy, lobotomy

PLURALS

SINGULAR	FOREIGN PLURAL	ENGLISH PLURAL
addendum	addenda	addendums
adieu	adieux	adieus
agendum	agenda	agendums
alumnus	alumni	
alumna	alumnae	
analysis	analyses	
antenna	antennae (Zoology)	antennas (TV only)
apex	apices	apexes

apparatus	apparatus	apparatuses
appendix	appendices	appendixes
aquarium	aquaria	aquariums
auditorium	auditoria	auditoriums
automaton	automata	automatons
axis	axes	
baby sitter		baby sitters
bacterium	bacteria	
bandeau	bandeaux	
bandit	banditti	bandits
basis	bases	
beau	beaux	beaus
bolshevik	bolsheviki	bolsheviks
bourgeois	bourgeois	
cactus	cacti	cactuses
campus		campuses
cherub	cherubim	cherubs
chief		chiefs
child		children
concerto	concerti	concertos
congeries		congeries
crisis	crises	
criterion	criteria	criterions, criteria
cupful		cupfuls
curriculum	curricula	curriculums
datum	data	datums (Math only)
desideratum	desiderata	
die	dice	dies (Arch. & Mach. only)
dilettante	dilettanti	dilettantes
echo		echoes
elf		elves, elfs
ellipsis	ellipses	
emphasis	emphases	
emporium	emporia	emporiums
erratum	errata	erratums
father-in-law		fathers-in-law
focus	foci	focuses
foot	foot (British)	feet (foots—material deposited)
formula	formulae	formulas
fox		foxes or fox
gladiolus, gladiola	gladioli	gladioluses
graffito	graffiti	
gymnasium	gymnasia	gymnasiums
half		halves
hero		heroes
hiatus	hiatus	hiatuses
hippopotamus	hippopotami	hippopotamuses
hoof		hooves, hoofs
index	indices	indexes
iris	irides	irises
knife		knives
kibbutz	kibbutzim	
kudos	kudos	
larva	larvae	larvas
larynx	larynges	larynxes
leaf		leaves
libretto	libretti	librettos
lily		lilies
literatus	literati	

loaf. . . . . loaves
maid of honor. . . . . maids of honor
man-of-war . . . . men-of-war
matrix . . . . matrices . . . . matrixes
matzo . . . . matzot, matzoth . . . .
maximum . . . . maxima . . . . maximums
medium. . . . . media . . . . mediums
media (communication) . . . . medias
media (anatomy) . . . . mediae . . . .
medico . . . . medicos . . . .
memento. . . . . mementoes . . . . mementos
metamorphosis . . . . metamorphoses. . . . .
minimum. . . . . minima . . . . minimums
minutia . . . . minutiae . . . .
mouse . . . . mice
nebula. . . . . nebulae. . . . . nebulas
nucleus. . . . . nuclei . . . . nucleuses
oasis . . . . oases . . . .
opus . . . . opera. . . . . opuses
ox. . . . . oxen, ox
passer-by. . . . . passers-by
phenomenon . . . . phenomena . . . . phenomenons
piano. . . . . pianos. . . . .
pic . . . . pics, pix
picador . . . . picadores . . . . picadors
plateau . . . . plateaux . . . . plateaus
portmanteau . . . . portmanteaux . . . . portmanteaus
president-elect. . . . . presidents-elect
radius . . . . radii . . . . radiuses
salary. . . . . salaries
scarf . . . . scarves, scarfs
secretary-general. . . . . secretaries-general
seraph, seraphim . . . . seraphim. . . . . seraphs
shambles. . . . . shambles
sheep. . . . . sheep
solo . . . . solos . . . . solos
son-in-law . . . . sons-in-law
spectrum. . . . . spectra . . . . spectrums
spoonful. . . . . spoonfuls
stigma. . . . . stigmata . . . . stigmas
stimulus . . . . stimuli. . . . .
streptococcus . . . . streptococci . . . .
strongbox. . . . . strongboxes
synthesis . . . . syntheses . . . .
tableau . . . . tableaux . . . . tableaus
tablespoonful. . . . . tablespoonfuls
ten-year-old . . . . ten-year-olds
thesaurus . . . . thesauri. . . . . thesauruses
thesis . . . . theses. . . . .
thief . . . . thieves
tooth . . . . teeth
ultimatum . . . . ultimata. . . . . ultimatums
vertebra . . . . vertebrae. . . . . vertebras
virtuoso. . . . . virtuosi . . . . virtuosos
wharf. . . . . wharves, wharfs

PRINCIPAL PARTS OF VERBS

PRESENT	PAST	PAST PARTICIPLE
arise	arose.	arisen

ask	asked	asked
awake	awaked, awoke	awaked, awoke (awoken)
awaken	awakened	awakened
bare	bared	bared
be (am, are, is)	was	been
bear (carry)	bore	borne
bear (give birth to)	bore	borne, born
beat	beat	beaten, beat
become	became	become
begin	began	begun
bid (command)	bade, bid	bidden, bid
bid (offer)	bid	bid
bind	bound	bound
bite	bit	bitten, bit
blow	blew	blown
break	broke	broken
bring	brought	brought
build	built	built
burn	burned, burnt	burned, burnt
burst	burst	burst
buy	bought	bought
cast	cast	cast
catch	caught	caught
choose	chose	chosen
cleave (split)	cleaved, cleft, clove	cleft, cloven, cleaved
climb	climbed	climbed
come	came	come
creep	crept	crept
cut	cut	cut
deal	dealt	dealt
dig	dug	dug
dive	dived, dove	dived, dove
do	did	done
drag	dragged	dragged
draw	drew	drawn
dream	dreamed, dreamt	dreamed, dreamt
drink	drank	drunk, drunken
drive	drove	driven
drown	drowned	drowned
drug	drugged	drugged
dwell	dwelt, dwelled	dwelt, dwelled
eat	ate	eaten
fall	fell	fallen
feel	felt	felt
find	found	found
flee	fled	fled
fling	flung	flung
flow	flowed	flowed
fly	flew	flown
fly (baseball)	flied	flied
forecast	forecast, forecasted	forecast, forecasted
forget	forgot	forgotten, forgot
forsake	forsook	forsaken
freeze	froze	frozen
get	got	got, gotten
give	gave	given
go	went	gone
grow	grew	grown
hang (object)	hung	hung

hang (person)	hanged	hanged
happen	happened	happened
hear	heard	heard
heave	heaved, hove	hove, heaved
help	helped	helped
hide	hid	hidden, hid
hold	held	held
hurt	hurt	hurt
know	knew	known
lay (place)	laid	laid
lead	led	led
leave (allow to remain)	left	left
leave (bear leaves)	leaved	leaved
lend	lent	lent
let (allow)	let	let
let (tennis)	letted	letted
lie (falsehood)	lied	lied
lie (recline)	lay	lain
light	lighted, lit	lighted, lit
loose	loosed	loosed
loosen	loosened	loosened
lose	lost	lost
mean	meant	meant
meet	met	met
pass	passed	passed, past
pay	paid	paid
prove	proved	proved, proven
put	put	put
raise	raised	raised
ravel	raveled, ravelled	raveled, ravelled
read	read	read
ride	rode	ridden
ring	rang, rung	rung
rise	rose	risen
row	rowed	rowed
run	ran	run
say	said	said
see	saw	seen
seek	sought	sought
set	set	set
shake	shook	shaken
shed	shed	shed
shine (beam)	shone, shined	shone, shined
shine (polish)	shined, shone	shined, shone
show	showed	shown, showed
shrink	shrank, shrunk	shrunk
sing	sang, sung	sung
sink	sank, sunk	sunk, sunken
sit	sat	sat
slay	slew	slain
sleep	slept	slept
slide	slid	slid
sow	sowed	sowed, sown
speak	spoke	spoken
spit (saliva)	spit, spat	spat, spit
spit (impale)	spitted	spitted
spring	sprang, sprung	sprung
stand	stood	stood
steal	stole	stolen

sting	stung	stung
stink	stank, stunk	stunk
stride	strode	stridden
strive	strove, strived	striven, strived
suppose	supposed	supposed
swear	swore	sworn
swim	swam, swum	swum
swing	swung	swung
take	took	taken
teach	taught	taught
tear	tore	torn
tell	told	told
think	thought	thought
thrive	throve, thrived	thrived, thriven
throw	threw	thrown
use	used	used
wake	waked, woke	waked, woke
wear	wore	worn
weave	wove	woven
win	won	won
wind	wound	wound
wring	wrung	wrung
write	wrote	written

DIFFICULT WORDS TO SPELL

abnegate	anoint	bracelet	consistency
abyss	anonymous	buffet	consummacy
academically	aphrodisiac	bureaucrat	continuous
accessible	apparatus	business	contretemps
accidentally	appearance	cacophony	convivial
acclimated	archipelago	calculation	coolly
accommodation	arousing	calendar	coup de grâce
accompaniment	asinine	calligraphy	courteous
accumulate	atelier	camouflage	criticism
accuracy	atheistic	carburetor	croissant
achievement	athletics	Caribbean	cruelty
acquaintance	attendance	caricature	curriculum
acumen	auricular	catalogue (catalog)	debacle
address	autonomy	catastrophe	decadent
admittance	auxiliary	cellar	decease
adolescent	avuncular	cemetery	deceitful
adroit	awfully	changeable	décolletage
adulation	bachelor	chauvinist	deference
advantageous	badinage	chicanery	deity
aeronautics	bagatelle	chiropody	dénouement
agoraphobia	bankruptcy	chiropractor	descendant
aggregate	barbarous	circumlocutory	desiccate
agnosticism	battalion	circumstantial	detrimental
aisle	beggar	clandestine	devastation
allege	believe	clientele	dexterous (dextrous)
allegiance	benediction	colossal	diagnostician
alleviate	beneficial	commiserate	dictionary
allotting	bibliography	competition	dilemma
alma mater	bibulous	complexion	dilettante
altercation	billet doux	conceivable	diligence
ambidextrous	biscuit	conglomerate	dining room
anachronism	blasphemy	connoisseur	diphtheria
animus	bon vivant	conscientious	disappearance
annihilate	bookkeeper	consciousness	disastrous

discernible
discrimination
disparage
dissatisfied
dissemble
dissimulate
dissipate
drunkenness
ebullience
ecstasy
efficiency
egomaniacal
egregious
eighth
embarrassment
emphasize
emphysema
enervate
ennui
environment
epaulet (epaulette)
ephemeral
equanimity
equestrian
equestrienne
equinox
equipment
espionage
eulogy
euphemism
euthanasia
evanescent
exaggerate
exhilaration
extremely
exuberant
familiar
fascinate
fascism
February
feminine
femme fatale
financier
fission
foreign
forfeit
fulfill (fulfil)
gaiety
galaxy
garrulous
gauche
gaucherie
grammatically
graphology
handkerchief
harassment
harridan
haute couture
height

helpfulness
hemorrhage
hereditary
hermaphrodite
hierarchy
hippopotamous
homophonous
hygiene
hypochondriac
hypocrisy
iconoclast
illegible
illiterate
imbroglio
immanent
immediately
imminent
impecunious
implacable
incendiary
incidentally
incongruity
incorrigible
indefatigable
indigence
indigenous
indispensable
inexplicable
infinitesimal
ingenious
ingenuous
inimitable
iniquitous
initiative
innocuous
inoculate
insouciant
interference
intransigent
irrelevant
irresistible
joie de vivre
judgment (judgement)
kerosene (kerosine)
laborious
lackadaisical
larynx
legible
leisurely
libidinous
license (licence)
licentious
likable (likeable)
literature
litigious
livelihood
lubricous (lubricious)
luxurious
magnanimous

magnificence
maintenance
maleficent
malicious
manageable
maneuver (manoeuvre)
marriageable
martinet
martyrdom
medicine
Mediterranean
melancholy
mellifluous
melodious
métier
militate
millennium
miniature
misanthrope
miscegenation
mischievous
misogamist
misogynist
misspelled
monotonous
mortgage
mosquito
municipal
mysterious
naïve (naive)
naïveté (naiveté)
nescience
neuralgia
neurotic
noticeable
noxious
nucleus
nuisance
nutritious
obedience
obsequies
obsequious
obstreperous
occasionally
occurrence
ocular
omitting
omniscient
ophthalmologist
orchestra
oscillate
ovulation
pageant
panegyric
paralysis
paraphernalia
parliament
paroxysm
parricide

parsimony
particularly
pastime
pathos
patronymic
pedestal
pedodontia
pejorative
penicillin
perambulate
perceive
permanent
permissible
perseverance
persiflage
personnel
perspicacious
petulant
phenomenon
philanthrope
philatelist
picnicking
pied-à-terre
piscine
placative
playwright
pneumonia
possession
precede
prejudice
prerogative
prescience
presence
prestige
prestidigitator
prevalent
privilege
probably
profligate
pronunciation
propagate
propeller (propellor)
prophecy
prophesy
prurient
psychoanalysis
ptomaine
pungent
pusillanimous
querulous
received
recommendation
reference
referred
relief (Rolaids)
relieve
reminiscent
remittance
repertoire

repetition	sovereign (sovran)	temperament	vacuum
resemblance	sphygmomanometer	tendency	valedictory
rhythm	statistics	theoretical	valiant
ridiculous	stoical	therapeutic	valuable
sabbatical	strength	titillation	variegate
sacrilegious	stubbornness	tolerance	varieties
savoir-faire	succeed	tortoise	vaudeville
schedule	succession	transcend	vehicle
schizophrenia	supercilious	trompe l'oeil	vengeance
scintillating	superintendent	truly	versatile
seize	supersede	twelfth	vicarious
senescent	surreptitious	tyranny	vigilance
separate	susceptible	ubiquitous	villain
septuagenarian	sycophant	ukulele	virago
sergeant	syllable	unconscionable	vis-à-vis
siege	symbiotic	undoubtedly	vociferous
similar	symmetrical	unnatural	weird
soliloquize	symphonic	unnecessary	wheedle
somnambulism	synchronize	unscrupulous	whistle
sophomore	synergistically	uxoricide	xylophone
soporific	synonymous	vaccine	yacht
soupçon	taciturn	vacillate	zoology

FUMBLERULES OF GRAMMAR

- Thimk!
- Never make misteaks.
- Remember to never split an infinitive.
- The passive voice should never be used.
- Avoid run-on sentences they are hard to read.
- Don't use no double negatives.
- Use the semicolon properly, always use it where it is appropriate; and never where it isn't.
- Reserve the apostrophe for it's proper use and omit it when its not needed.
- Do not put statements in the negative form.
- Verbs has to agree with their subjects.
- No sentence fragments.
- Proofread carefully to see if you any words out.
- If any word is improper at the end of a sentence, a linking verb is.
- Steer clear of incorrect forms of verbs that have snuck in the language.
- Take the bull by the hand and avoid mixed metaphors.
- Avoid trendy locutions that sound flaky.
- Never, ever use repetitive redundancies.
- Everyone should be careful to use a singular pronoun with singular nouns in their writing.
- If I've told you once, I've told you a thousand times, resist hyperbole.
- Also, avoid awkward or affected alliteration.
- Don't string too many prepositional phrases together unless you are walking through the valley of the shadow of death.
- Always pick on the correct idiom.
- ''Avoid overuse of 'quotation ''marks.'' ' ''
- The adverb always follows the verb.
- Avoid commas, that are not necessary.
- If you reread your work, you will find on rereading that a great deal of repetition can be avoided by rereading and editing.
- A writer must not shift your point of view.
- Eschew dialect, irregardless.
- And don't start a sentence with a conjunction.
- Don't overuse exclamation marks!!!
- Place pronouns as close as possible, especially in long sentences, as of ten or more words, to their antecedents.
- Hyphenate between syllables and avoid un-necessary hyphens.
- Write all adverbial forms correct.
- Don't use contractions in formal writing.
- Writing carefully, dangling participles must be avoided.
- It is incumbent on us to avoid archaisms.
- Last but not least, avoid clichés like the plague; seek viable alternatives.

QUESTIONS AND ANSWERS

1. In 1661 what Dutch governor bought a "farm" that was located between what is now 5th and 17th streets in New York City? This area was connected by a road to what town located to the South? Name and define this area of land settled by the Dutch governor as it is used today.

ANSWER: Peter Stuyvesant/New Amsterdam/The Bowery, which is "a section of the city, especially New York city, noted for cheap bars, flophouses, and homeless derelicts."

2. What phrase from the American Revolutionary War means "something with no value at all"? A similar phrase means "to be totally contemptuous of something." What is it? Explain the reason for these phrases.

ANSWER: Not worth a continental/Not care or give a continental/A continental, the script issued by the Continental Congress, became worthless by the end of the war since there were no gold or silver reserves to support it.

3. What phrase from Henry David Thoreau's *Walden, or Life in the Woods* means "to act according to the dictates of one's own conscience"? Give the entire passage from Thoreau's work.

ANSWER: March to the beat of a different drummer/"If a man does not keep pace with his companions, perhaps it is because he hears a different drummer. Let him step to the music he hears, however measured or far away."

4. Identify each of the following words or phrases, each of which is the nickname of a well-known American.
   a) "elaborate or ostentatious display; exaggerated bother and excitement; exaggerated concern with one's appearance" (General Winfield Scott was nicknamed "Old _____")
   b) "one who is undiscouraged or undaunted by difficulties or adversities" (Theodore Roosevelt, Al Smith, and Hubert Humphrey were so nicknamed)
   c) "rough or crude, but effective; characterized by rough vigor rather than refinement; lacking in politeness" (General Zachary Taylor was nicknamed "Old _____" for his conduct during the Seminole and Mexican Wars in the early 19th century)
   d) "to play a defensive game (Australian cricket); to filibuster (British); to refuse to answer or cooperate with; to be obstructive" (popularized during the Watergate scandal; the nickname given by General Bernard Elliott Bee at the First Battle of Bull Run, July 21, 1861, to General Thomas Jonathan Jackson)
   e) "a veteran, as a soldier or politician, who has been in many struggles; a musical composition performed excessively; a horse used in combat; a charger" (Samuel Medary was known as "The _____ of Democracy"; General James Longstreet was called "The _____ of the Confederacy")
   f) "energy, vitality, courage and stamina" (General George S. Patton was nicknamed "Old _____")

ANSWER: a) fuss and feathers b) happy warrior c) rough and ready d) stonewall e) war horse f) blood and guts.

5. There are a number of theories associated with the origin of *O.K.* For which President did a group supporting him found the O.K. Club? What does the *O.K.* stand for in this case? With what state is the *K* associated and why?

ANSWER: Martin Van Buren/Old Kinderhook/Kinderhook, New York, is the birthplace of Martin Van Buren.

6. For what 2 Allied offensives, one in World War I and one in World War II, was the phrase *D-day* used? Define the phrase (as used today).

ANSWER: In WWI, it was for the offensive at Saint-Mihiel (September 12-16, 1918), and in WWII, it was for the Allied invasion of France in Normandy (June 6, 1944)/"The day on which a military operation or an important event is to take place; decision day."

7. First, identify the word that describes the plain of central North America — the level or rolling grassland in the Mississippi Valley. Then give the meaning of the

following descriptions each of which begins with the already identified word.
   a) A large covered wagon used by pioneers
   b) Another name for a coyote
   c) The nickname of a state (identify the state)
   d) The 3 "_____ provinces" of Canada
   e) A plow that cuts a wide shallow furrow and turns the earth completely over
   f) Either of 2 birds resembling a grouse and a pheasant
   g) A burrowing rodent of North America
   h) A raw egg drink for a hangover, or the testicles of a bull calf cooked and served as food (a delicacy, honest)
   i) A Leather-Stocking Tale novel (1827) by James Fenimore Cooper
   j) A town with a French name in SW Wisconsin
   k) A city in East Kansas, near Kansas City

ANSWER: Prairie/a) prairie schooner (also called prairie frigate or prairie ship) b) prairie wolf c) "The Prairie State" is Illinois d) the "Prairie Provinces" are Manitoba, Saskatchewan, and Alberta e) prairie breaker f) prairie chicken (also called prairie fowl or prairie grouse) g) prairie dog h) prairie oyster i) *The Prairie* j) Prairie du Chien k) Prairie Village.

8. What name did the Mormons want to use to name the land they settled in the West? Who suggested the name, and what did it mean to him? Congress rejected the name and chose another. What was it, and for what reason did Congress choose it?

ANSWER: Deseret/Joseph Smith, founder of the Mormons, and to him it meant "honeybee"/Utah because of the name of an Indian tribe (Yutta, Ute, Uta, and Utah).

9. What was the relationship between the nickname given to the South and the ten dollar notes issued before the Civil War? From what French word did this name possibly come? Who wrote the song that popularized the nickname?

ANSWER: Before the Civil War, banks in Louisiana issued 10 dollar notes which had *dix* on one side. These notes were called "Dixies" and the South became known as the "land of Dixies" from the French word *dix* for "10"/Dan Emmett wrote the song "Dixie" ("I wish I was in Dixie's Land") in 1859.

10. What is the word referred to in each of the following descriptions?
   a) The longest word in the OED or the *Oxford English Dictionary*
   b) The nonsense word from the movie *Mary Poppins*, which is also the longest word in *The Random House Dictionary of the English Language*
   c) The longest word in Webster's *Third New International Dictionary*
   d) The word that is a "foot and a half long"
   e) The word describing a 150th anniversary, such as the one Columbus, Georgia, celebrated in 1978 (founded in 1827 but chartered in 1828)
   f) The word describing a 250th anniversary, such as the one Georgia celebrated on February 12, 1983 (James Oglethorpe landed in what is now Savannah in 1733)
   g) The longest word with a mile between the s's

ANSWER: a) floccinaucinihilipilification (the art [action] of estimating as worthless) b) supercalifragilisticexpialidocious c) pneumonoultramicroscopicsilicovolcanoconiosis (a lung disease of miners) d) sesquipedalian — *sesqui* is 1½ and *ped* is a foot e) sesquicentennial f) semiquincentenary g) smiles.

11. What is probably the longest street in the world? It stretches 150 miles from Manhattan Island to Albany, New York. What nickname for the street with the snow covering it was the same as the title of a 1901 novel?

ANSWER: Broadway/"The Great White Way."

12. What nickname of what state comes from a horse chestnut that looks like the eye of a buck?

ANSWER: The Buckeye State is Ohio.

13. Translate each of the following sentences into a well-known figurative expression.
   a) The stylus is more important than the claymore.
   b) Surveillance should precede saltation.

c) Neophyte's serendipity.

d) A vocable to the sapient is adequate.

e) Permit the amercement to coincide with the malfeasance.

ANSWER: a) The pen is mightier than the sword b) Look before leaping c) Beginner's luck d) A word to the wise is sufficient e) Let the punishment fit the crime.

14. What American Indians were known as the ''pierced-nose ones''?
ANSWER: Nez Percé.

15. What breed of horse was named through either a corruption of the French word *pelouse* (the French-Canadians called this horse *à palousé*, meaning ''from the grassy plains'') or from the Palouse Indians who lived on the grassy plains?
ANSWER: Appaloosa.

16. Identify each of the following phrases, each of which has the word ''degree'' in it.
   a) ''slightly sick'' (from the slight variation of normal body temperature of 98.6°)
   b) ''to the greatest power possible; to an extreme; very much so'' (from the field of mathematics in which n represents a number, especially a very large number)
   c) ''step by step; a little at a time; gradually''
   d) ''to a considerable extent; somewhat''
   e) ''a unit representing one degree of deviation, on a single day, of the daily mean temperature, from a standard temperature'' (used in determining fuel and power consumption, based on the mean temperature below 65°F)
   f) ''any of the independent variables, such as pressure, temperature, or composition, needed to specify a system with a given number of phases and components (from the fields of chemistry and physics)
   g) the minutes in a° (degree)/the number of degrees in a right angle/the number of degrees in a straight angle/the number of degrees in a circle

ANSWER: a) one degree under b) to the nth degree c) by degrees d) to a degree e) degree-day f) degree of freedom g) 60 minutes/90 degrees/180 degrees/360 degrees.

17. What are the 3 periods in the development of the English language? Give the beginning date for each.
ANSWER: Old English (A.D. 450); Middle English (1150); and Modern English (1500).

18. What are the first 5 letters of the Greek alphabet?
ANSWER: Alpha, beta, gamma, delta, and epsilon.

19. What are the last 5 letters of the Greek alphabet?
ANSWER: Upsilon, phi, chi, psi, and omega.

20. Identify each of the following phrases, each of which contains a number.
   a) ''a military discharge or the soldier discharged for mental incompetence or military inaptitude'' (from the former section number of the U.S. Army regulations which governed this situation)
   b) ''to dispose of; to bury'' (from the U.S. Navy expression for burial at sea. It became a well-known phrase in the Watergate testimony when John Dean testified that John Ehrlichman told him to ''_____ the briefcase in the Potomac'')
   c) ''mental or physical torture in the questioning of a prisoner to obtain information or a confession'' (popularized in the U.S. by the grueling questioning of a prisoner by the police)
   d) ''the precise time established for the beginning of an attack, a military operation, or a notable event; critical point'' (from WWI for the moment when an attack was to begin)
   e) ''in a highly unfavorable position'' (from the game of Kelly pool)
   f) ''nothing; no more left; an undesirable person at a restaurant or bar who is not to be served'' (possibly from a number code used by bartenders, waiters, etc.)
   g) ''a wide-brimmed felt hat having an exceptionally tall crown'' (popular in Texas and previously worn by American cowboys)

ANSWER: a) Section eight b) deep-six c) third degree d) zero-hour e) behind the eight ball f) eighty-six g) ten-gallon hat (or a Stetson or a John B).

21. Give the phrase that means "a total all-out effort that ends in total failure." Give the date, the location, and the general in charge of this humiliating defeat. Name the 3 Indian chiefs who led the attack. What was the name of the battle?

ANSWER: Custer's last stand/June 25, 1876/Montana Territory/General George Armstrong Custer/Crazy Horse, Sitting Bull, and Gall/Little Bighorn.

22. What phrase means "a meltdown in a nuclear reactor"? Explain the relationship between the name of the country and the phrase. What is the antipodal point of the Pennsylvania reactor where this phenomenon almost occurred? What is the name of the site in Pennsylvania just alluded to? In what year did it happen?

ANSWER: China syndrome/From the proverbial explanation given to a youngster that if he were to dig down through the earth he would reach China/The Diamantina Trench in the Indian Ocean/Three Mile Island/(March 28) 1979.

23. Identify each of the following political words or phrases.

   a) "mutual trading of favors by politicians, as by voting for each other's projects of interest, for political advancement" (from an early practice of neighbors' helping each other in rolling heavy logs)

   b) "to support a cause or political candidate, especially when success seems certain and personal gain is anticipated" (from the wagon carrying musicians publicizing an event, frequently ridden by politicians whose supporters would climb aboard)

   c) "those people who are the very foundation, especially of a political party or movement; the common people; the voters" (from its origins denoting the peasantry in agricultural regions since they are figuratively rooted in the earth)

   d) "a government project or appropriation for legislators to satisfy their constituents" (possibly from the meaning from the Reconstruction period of "pork" as graft or patronage)

   e) "pointless, time-wasting work," or "to engage in pointless, time-wasting work" (frequently a project in which government funds are wasted; from the pleated leather lanyard worn by Boy Scouts and coined by scoutmaster R.H. Link, from a Scottish word for a marble obtained as a gift, without having worked for it)

   f) "a false or slanderous story published to gain a political advantage" (after the imaginary author, Baron von _____, of a nonexistent book, *A Tour Through the Western and Southern States.* A passage from the book stated that Democratic presidential candidate James K. Polk had bought 43 slaves and branded his initials on their shoulders)

   g) "to defeat an opponent, especially a political one in an election with trickery possibly being used" (although the expression is older than the 1832 election, the apocryphal story that has been told is that Henry Clay, going to Louisville, Kentucky, for a speech by way of the Ohio River, was intentionally rowed up the _____ River by the boatman, a Jacksonian supporter, and therefore was unable to make the speech which might have prevented his loss in the election)

   h) "to travel about the country performing plays or giving speeches, especially campaign speeches" (from the custom of traveling troupes which used barns as theatres in small towns)

   i) "a camp of shacks and crates, at the edge of a city, housing the jobless during the Great Depression of the 1930's" (named after the U.S. President who was blamed for the country's financial collapse)

   j) "to achieve a victory" (from hunting; the skin of this animal is hung on a wall or a barndoor to be stretched and cured. President Johnson made an unfortunate statement using a similar phrase at Cam Ranh Bay in South Vietnam in October, 1966, to U.S. troops. He said, "I salute you. Come home with that _____ on the wall.")

   k) "a Republican in 1884 who did not support James G. Blaine's presidential candidacy; an independent, especially in politics; a fence-sitter, or a person who is unable to make up his mind; one who takes a neutral position in controversial matters'' (from an Algonquian word for ''chief'' or ''great man'' as those who supported Grover Cleveland were scorned as those wanting to be ''big chiefs''; also described as an animal or person with its ''_____'' on one side of a fence and its ''_____'' on the other)

l) ''Someone who receives less attention than he should'' (from a 1932 Franklin Roosevelt speech for a New Deal plan that started at the bottom of the economic pyramid)

ANSWER: a) logrolling b) climb (jump) on the bandwagon c) grass roots d) pork barrel e) boondoggle f) roorback (or roorbach) g) row one up Salt River h) barnstorm i) Hoovervilles j) nail the coonskin to the wall k) mugwump l) forgotten man.

24. The group consisted among others of a Mr. Interlocutor, a Mr. Tambo, and a Mr. Bones. Dan Emmett of ''Dixie''-fame organized ''The Virginia'' group in 1843, but a more famous group was ''The Christy'' group organized by Edwin Christy about the same time. What word or phrase describes this blackface variety show?

ANSWER: The Minstrels or a minstrel show.

25. Who wrote?

''The cow is of the bovine ilk;
One end is moo, the other, milk.''

ANSWER: Ogden Nash in *Free Wheeling*.

26. The wife of Noah Webster caught him kissing the maid and said, ''I am surprised.'' How did the great lexicographer correct her?

ANSWER: He said, ''My dear, *I* am surprised; *you* are astonished.'' (In Webster's day, surprise meant ''taken by surprise.'')

27. Identify each of the following political phrases.
    a) President Johnson's domestic social welfare program
    b) ''an intensive investigation supposedly to uncover subversive activity but actually a ploy to harass political opposition'' (from an allusion to the Salem, Massachusetts, witch trials in the 17th century)
    c) ''left exposed to political attack'' (popularized from the Watergate era with an allusion to a corpse dangling in the wind)
    d) ''a harmless, bumbling, incompetent public official'' (named after Alexander _____, who was the Vice President to President John P. Wintergreen in the 1932 musical comedy by George S. Kaufman and Morris Ryskind called *Of Thee I Sing*. The character had to join a guided tour to gain entrance to the White House.)
    e) ''those Southern states that traditionally solidly support the Democratic Party, its programs, and candidates'' (popularized by Confederate General John Singleton Mosby during the Hayes-Tilden 1876 presidential election)
    f) ''place in which a small group of politicians conduct secret negotiations'' (from Harry Daugherty's prediction about how Warren G. Harding's nomination in 1920 for the presidency would be decided)
    g) ''final and unalterable statement of a candidate that he will not run for office'' (from the statement made by General William _____ at the Republican National Convention in Chicago on June 5, 1884: ''I will not accept if nominated, and will not serve if elected'')
    h) ''any of the high officials of the Tammany Society; the chief of a confederation or tribe among some North American Indian tribes'' (from the Algonquian word for ''chief'')
    i) ''the strongly conservative element of a political party, especially the Republican party'' (from the *Vieille Garde* created in 1804 by Napoleon, a group that made the last French charge at Waterloo)
    j) ''the large number of people of moderate opinions who rarely make their social and political feelings known by demonstrating, and whose collective opinion can possibly influence an election'' (a phrase popularized by President Nixon's November 3, 1969, speech in which he diffused demonstrations

against his Vietnam policy)

k) "the foremost woman in a particular field; the wife of the head of any country; the wife of the President of the United States" (popularized by Charles Nirdlinger's 1911 comedy *The* _____ *in the Land*)

l) "any idyllic time, site, or period having excitement, purpose, and style (from the description given to the John F. Kennedy administration and derived from the mythical court of King Arthur)

m) "money, especially counterfeit money; a bribe; graft; stolen goods" (popularized during the 1884 election campaign when the dinner in honor of James G. Blaine by very wealthy supporters was called the "_____ banquet"; from a Dutch word for "riches, property")

n) "a combination of the military and industries producing military hardware, viewed as a powerful political force exerting control over or influence on foreign and economic policy" (coined by Harold Lasswell in 1941 in *The Garrison State* and popularized by Dwight Eisenhower in his farewell address on January 17, 1961)

o) "the misuse of information through accusations and sensationalism that deprives individuals of their rights in order to reach a goal" (originally to suppress communism; named after Wisconsin Senator Joseph _____, who engaged in such practices, 1946-1957)

p) "a scandal that involves officials who violate a public trust through perjury, bribery, burglary, and other abuses of power in order to maintain their elective or appointive positions" (from _____, the building complex in Washington, D.C., housing the Democratic Party headquarters, burglarized on June 17, 1972, under orders of government officials)

q) "to participate in a race or contest, especially to run for public office" (from a Western boxing phrase popularized by Theodore Roosevelt when he decided to run for President in 1912)

r) "any signer of the U.S. Constitution in 1787; any person who founds an institution, movement, or nation" (possibly coined and popularized by Warren G. Harding)

s) "a candidate nominated, often as an honory gesture, for political office by the delegates of his state at a national political convention"

t) "a member of the dissident group of Democrats in the South who formed the States Rights Party in 1948 to oppose the civil rights program of the regular Democratic Party" [from _____ + (DEMO)CRAT]

u) "a relaxation or lessening of tension, especially between nations" (a French word which characterized American-Russian relations during the 1970's)

v) "a movement (and motto) among American Blacks organized to achieve political and economic power in the struggle for civil rights" (popularized by Stokely Carmichael on a Student Nonviolent Coordinating Committee [SNCC] sponsored march through Mississippi in 1966)

w) "a suggestion for a policy of watchful inactivity toward the Black civil rights movement" (a misinterpreted phrase of Daniel P. Moynihan in 1970 as President Nixon's urban affairs adviser; originally phrased by the Earl of Durham, who wrote Queen Victoria in 1839 that Canada should be granted self-government since she had prospered "through a period of _____ _____" by the mother country)

ANSWER: a) War on Poverty b) witch hunt c) twisting slowly in the wind d) Throttlebottom e) Solid South f) smoke-filled room g) Sherman statement h) sachem i) the Old Guard j) silent majority k) First Lady l) Camelot m) boodle n) military-industrial complex o) McCarthyism p) Watergate q) throw (toss) one's hat into the ring r) Founding Father s) favorite son t) Dixiecrat u) détente (detente) v) Black Power w) benign neglect.

28. What is a *Quonset Hut*? The first ones were used at a naval air station during WWII at what place in what state?

ANSWER: A prefabricated structure used as a temporary shelter/Quonset Point, Rhode Island.

29. What 2 eponymous words now in the English language have been contributed

by the Theodore Roosevelt family?

ANSWER: President Roosevelt contributed *teddy bear* partly from his nickname of "Teddy," and partly from his refusal to shoot a bear cub on a leash/Roosevelt's daughter, Alice Roosevelt Longworth, contributed *alice blue*, a pale blue, to the language. A popular song of the time, "In My Sweet Little Alice-Blue Gown," solidified its usage.

30. What 2 words, 1 from the German and 1 from the French, mean "twice baked" or twice cooked"?

ANSWER: Zwieback and biscuit.

31. Identify each of the following phrases, each of which has a U.S. location in it.
    a) "to meet a standard of acceptability" (from the idea that this Illinois town represents Middle America with its traditional values; probably from the traveling theatre groups that played there)
    b) "a clever lawyer who is skilled in manipulating legal technicalities" (from the New England saying that 3 _____ _____ were a match for the devil; and from Andrew Hamilton's brilliant defense of John Peter Zenger in 1735)
    c) "skeptical; needing proof to believe" (from a speech by Congressman Willard D. Vandiver in an 1899 speech in which he said: "I'm _____: you've got to show me")
    d) "the loss of hometown roots" (coined by Oregon Senator Richard L. Neuberger and William Safire from a small Idaho town about politicians in Washington who get defeated and can't return to small town life; its current usage is "They never go back to _____" because of the attraction of Washington, D.C.'s lifestyle)
    e) "to make an insincere or empty speech, especially that of a politician to satisfy his hometown constituents; to talk nonsense" (from Congressman Felix Walker's speech in 1820. Walker was from _____ County, North Carolina. When asked about his nonsensical speech, he said, "I was not speaking to the House, but to _____.")

ANSWER: a) to play in Peoria b) a Philadelphia lawyer c) from Missouri d) you can't go back to Pocatello e) to talk or speak for (to) Buncombe.

32. What is the meaning of the German phrase *Des Landes Vater,* and to what U.S. President does this phrase refer?

ANSWER: "Father of the Country" applies to George Washington.

33. What 2 words did Charles Hoag use in 1852 to coin the name Minneapolis?

ANSWER: Hoag used Minnehaha (Laughing Water) and *polis* (city). There was a waterfall near the town.

34. What is the meaning of the word *Podunk,* and in what 2 states would one find cities of that name?

ANSWER: A small, unimportant, and insignificant town/Massachusetts and Connecticut.

35. Identify each of the following eponymous words or phrases.
    a) "a stale joke; a chestnut" (from a book, _____'s *Jest-Book* by John Mottley containing the jokes of a deceased comedian)
    b) "a life of luxury and idleness" (from the name of the person mentioned in popular 1900 songs such as "The Best of the House is None Too Good for _____," or from the song of the 1880's by Pat Rooney, "Are you the O'Reilly?")
    c) "the humorous theorem that each person in a hierarchy will be promoted until he reaches his level of incompetence" (from a 1968 book of the same name by L.J. Peter and R. Hull)
    d) "an overly complicated machine used for a simple task; something complex and impractical" (from the name of an American cartoonist Reuben _____)
    e) "one's signature, especially on legal documents" from the name of the first person to sign the Declaration of Independence)
    f) "the all-American boy" (from a 1930's radio serial program called "_____ _____, the All-American Boy")

g) "the real thing or person; the genuine article" (possibly from the name of the world's welterweight boxing champion, 1898-1900, nicknamed "the Kid," or maybe from the Scottish name of a clan, and later a whisky)

h) "a traitor" (from the name of an American Revolutionary War general)

i) "a single-edge hunting knife" (named after the brother of the hero of the Alamo, but popularized by Colonel James _____.)

j) "*trademark* — for close-fitting pants of heavy denim reinforced at the seams and pockets with copper rivets" (after _____ Strauss, who first made them in San Francisco after the 1849 gold strike)

k) "humbug" and "to play one for sucker" (from the quintessential showman and the person who believed that "There is a sucker born every minute")

l) "a worker in a railroad section gang; an itinerant worker" (possibly from using tools of the now defunct _____ Manufacturing Company of Chicago, Illinois)

m) a yeast-leavened roll shaped by folding over a flat, round piece of dough (from the _____ hotel in Boston, Massachusetts)

n) "to murder by mob action without legal action, as by hanging"/"the punishment of suspected offenders by private persons without due process of law" (possibly from Captain William _____, of Virginia's vigilance committee)

o) "the idealized American girl of the 1890's (as depicted in the illustrations of Charles Dana _____, U.S. illustrator)

p) a raised setting, as in a ring, in which a gem is held in place by prongs (named after Charles Lewis _____, an American jeweler)

q) a glass jar with a wide mouth and an airtight screw top, used in home canning (named after John L. _____ of New York in 1858)

r) a scale measuring the intensity of an earthquake using a scale from 1 to 10 (named after Charles F. _____, American seismologist)

s) "a handbook of navigation" (from the *American Practical Navigator* originally prepared by U.S. mathematician, astronomer, and navigator, Nathaniel _____ in 1802)

ANSWER: a) Joe Miller b) life of Riley c) Peter Principle d) Rube Goldberg e) John Hancock f) Jack Armstrong g) the real McCoy h) Benedict Arnold i) Bowie knife j) levis k) barnum/barnumize l) gandy-dancer m) Parker House roll n) lynch/lynch law o) Gibson girl p) Tiffany setting or mounting q) Mason jar r) Richter scale s) Bowditch.

36. Between what dates were 53 (later 52) American hostages held by Iran? How many days were they held in captivity? Who was the hostage released for medical reasons? What phrase-symbol was used to celebrate the return of the hostages? Define the phrase. Name the folk song in which the phrase was featured. What is the name of the modern version of this song that in 1973 became an enormous hit? Who were the 2 composers of this song?

ANSWER: From November 4, 1979, to January 20, 1981/444 days/Richard I. Queen/Yellow Ribbon/"An American symbol of separated sweethearts"/ "Round Her Neck She Wore a Yellow Ribbon"/"Tie a Yellow Ribbon Round the Ole Oak Tree"/Irwin Levine and L. Russell Brown.

37. Name the U.S. physician who devised a grip used to save a choking victim, and name the phrase that describes this grip. What is the phrase that means "death from food stuck in the throat"?

ANSWER: H.J. Heimlich/Heimlich maneuver/Café coronary.

38. Give each of the following phrases, all of which are related to the animal world.

a) "very nervous, uneasy, or worried, but also able to move swiftly if necessary" (from the title of a 1955 play by Tennessee Williams)

b) "to change one's opinion, make new plans, or change leaders during an activity or during a crisis" (from a June 9, 1864, comment to the National Union League at the Republican convention by Abraham Lincoln explaining why he was reelected President despite his unpopularity — usually used in the negative)

c) "a pleasure seeking man; ladies' man; social parasite" (from the handsome men hired to entertain older women in fancy clubs in the 1920's)

d) "words or statements that are ambiguous or misleading" (popularized by Theodore Roosevelt in 1916 in a speech criticizing Woodrow Wilson — in reference to words that "suck" the meaning out of words they are juxtaposed with just as this animal is able to suck the egg and leave the shell)

e) "to get everything ready for action" (from American bowling where the pins are called ducks)

f) "usually an elected public official still in office but who has not been reelected; a disabled or helpless person; a stock market speculator who has lost a great deal of money" (from the British for a bankrupt businessman but popularized in America in 1933 by the 20th Amendment which changed the presidential inauguration from March 4 to January 20 and Congressional inauguration to January 3)

g) "a venomous snake; any treacherous person; during the Civil War, a Northener who sympathized with the South" (from the nature of this snake which strikes without warning)

h) "a stripteaser" (word coined by H.L. Mencken in 1920 from the Greek *ecdysis,* the process of molting or shedding an outer layer, as a snakeskin or carapace of insects and crustaceans)

i) "to pretend to be asleep, ill, or dead in order to deceive" (from the only North American marsupial which feigns death when attacked)

ANSWER: a) like a cat on a hot tin roof b) (don't) swap (change) horses in the middle of the stream (in midstream, while crossing a stream) c) lounge lizard d) weasel words e) to get one's ducks in a row f) lame duck g) copperhead/Copperhead h) ecdysiast i) to play possum.

39. What phrase is defined as "petty rules; dance music that is sentimental, insincere, or corny; college courses that are oversimplified and childish; any political candidate who could run and win against an unpopular opponent"? What phrase means "to avoid the issue by fooling around, doing things of minor significance in order to avoid facing a serious problem"? Name the company that produced a $2-4 watch on which the character in the two above phrases appeared? What was this character's original name? Who created him in what film in 1928? Name this character's dog, his girlfriend, and his 2 nephews.

ANSWER: Mickey Mouse/To Mickey Mouse around/Ingersoll Watch Company/Mortimer Mouse/Walt Disney in *Steamboat Willie* (the first Disney talkie which appeared before the first silent *Plane Crazy*)/Pluto/Minnie Mouse/Ferdy and Morty.

40. What proper name means "the personification of the U.S. government and its citizens," a name which was the nickname of chief army inspector Samuel Wilson at Elbert Anderson's stockyard in Troy, New York, in 1812, in reference to the "E.A. — U.S." stamped on pork barrels? What name had been formerly used to personify the United States and its citizens, which probably came from Jonathan Trumbull, first governor of Connecticut, upon whom George Washington relied for supplies during the Revolution? What name popularized by the title character in John Arbuthnot's *Law is a Bottomless Pit* (1712), and republished as *The History of* _____, means "the personification of England or the English people"?

ANSWER: Uncle Sam/Brother Jonathan/John Bull.

41. Identify each of the following words or phrases associated with geographic locations.

a) "continuous watch or vigilance; narrow-minded moral censorship of literature and art" (from the night and day guarding of medieval towns, and also the name of Anthony Comstock's Boston Society of 1876)

b) "a squalid section of the city frequented by vagrants, derelicts, and society's outcasts" (from an unpaved logging road in Washington, especially Seattle, and Oregon in the 19th century)

c) "a cheapskate; a person who does things in a petty way, especially one who gambles cautiously" (possibly a term applied by the California Gold Rushers to those from Pike County, Missouri, considered to be the home of lazy farmers)

d) "a Mexican immigrant who has illegally entered the U.S. in California or Texas" (from the fact that many cross the border by swimming or wading the Rio Grande looking for work in the U.S.)

e) "a puritanical person, especially one who advocates rigorous moral behavior" (possibly from the U.S. colonial period with Connecticut becoming known as The Blue Law State from the blue, or puritanical, laws restricting commerce and recreation)

f) "a small gift given to a customer with his purchase; a gratuity" (from the habit of New Orleans store owners who gave a gift to regular customers)

g) "to betray or be disloyal to a person; to give one's secrets to one's enemies" (from the time when American owners sold uncooperative slaves into harsh servitude to plantation owners of the lower Mississippi)

h) "an impoverished migrant farm worker, especially one from Oklahoma and other areas of the Great Plains forced to migrate because of drought during the Depression of the late 1930's" [from OK(LAHOMA) + IE]

i) "area of the South noted for its rich black soil"

j) "a farmer" (a derogatory Western term used by ranchers, herders, and cowboys possibly for the tillers of the soil who broke up the sods of the virgin buffalo grass in the plains)

k) "a very heavy rainstorm" (from the type of downpour resulting in an onrush of water through gullies, a common occurrence in the Texas and Oklahoma areas)

l) "a main railroad route"; "a fashionable residential district west of Philadelphia, along the railroad line to Paoli"

m) "a poor white, rural Southerner who is usually bigoted and intolerant" (from the sunburned neck acquired by working in the fields in the South)

n) "a prospector or pioneer in Alaska, Canada, and western U.S., especially one living alone" (from leaven, especially fermented bread which was the staple of these old-time prospectors)

o) "a person who took part in the 1849 California gold rush"

p) "an isolated rocky mass or mountain rising above a peneplain" (from a New Hampshire mountain)

q) "a native of Louisiana descended from Acadian French exiles" (from a corruption of the word *Acadian*)

r) "the nouveaux riches" (used disparagingly by the elite first families of Massachusetts referring to those who had become wealthy in the _____ industry and moved into the Back Bay area of Boston)

s) "a whiskey distilled from a mash of at least 50% of corn, rye, and malted barley" (from _____ County, Kentucky)

t) "a devastating surprise attack" (from the sneak attack by Japan that took place on December 7, 1941)

u) the boundary line between Pennsylvania and Maryland, considered to be, before the Civil War, the line separating the free states from the slave states, or, now, between the North and the South (from the names of surveyors Charles _____ and Jeremiah _____ who surveyed it between 1763 and 1767)

v) a rich, irrigated agricultural region in SE California and NE Baja California, Mexico, reclaimed from the Colorado desert (after the Imperial Land Company which developed the region)

ANSWER: a) watch and ward **b)** skid row (originally Skid Road) **c)** piker **d)** wetback **e)** bluenose **f)** lagniappe **g)** to sell down the river **h)** Okie **i)** Black Belt **j)** sodbuster **k)** gulley washer **l)** main line/Main Line **m)** redneck **n)** sourdough **o)** forty-niner (Forty-Niner) **p)** monadnock (Mt. Monadnock) **q)** Cajun (Caijan, Cajan) **r)** codfish aristocracy (codfish gentility) **s)** bourbon (Bourbon) **t)** Pearl Harbor **u)** Mason-Dixon Line **v)** Imperial Valley.

42. In two psychological studies, one by Richard L. Dugdale in 1877 and the other by Henry Herbert Goddard in 1912, a New York family and a New Jersey family were

given pseudonyms. The studies showed that heredity, rather than environment, was the cause of disease and the feeble-mindedness, poverty, delinquency, and crime frequently resulting from it. Give the pseudonyms and their common definition today.

ANSWER: **Jukes and Kallikaks (from the Greek** *kalli-,* **beauty, and** *kak-,* **ugly, bad)/ "Inherently inferior stupid people."**

43. What popular 1920's phrase means "don't be fooled into taking anything that has no value"? In what year were the first five-cent coins containing nickle minted? For what events were these coins used as souvenirs?

ANSWER: **Don't take any wooden nickles/1866/American centennial celebrations.**

44. Describe briefly the following sections of "The Big Apple" (New York City — the phrase originated among Black jazz musicians of New Orleans. *Manzana* in Spanish means "apple" or "tract of land." "Apple" came to mean "city," specifically the downtown area where all the action took place. To play in the "Big Apple" meant to play in the "big town," or New York).

a) The Bowery   g) Wall Street
b) Greenwich Village   h) Broadway
c) Tin Pan Alley   i) Park Avenue
d) Fifth Avenue   j) SoHo (*S*outh of *Ho*uston Street)
e) Seventh Avenue   k) Hell's Kitchen (midtown Manhattan)
f) Madison Avenue   l) Tenderloin (between 23rd and 42nd streets)

ANSWER: **a) area for saloons, flophouses, and derelicts b) haven for artists and writers c) haven for songwriters and publishers d) shopping district e) fashion center f) advertising industry area g) financial district h) theatre district i) wealthy residential area j) Bohemian district; center for arts and crafts k) district known for its slums and crime l) area of vice and corruption.**

45. What member of what President's Cabinet resigned his post and said, "I am against government by crony"? What is the meaning of "government by crony"? This man was nicknamed "(Old) Curmudgeon." What is a *curmudgeon*?

ANSWER: **Secretary of the Interior Harold L. Ickes was in President Truman's Cabinet/"A government (an administration) in which those in power are there because they are close companions of the President and were not chosen for their capability"/"A crusty, ill-tempered, ill-mannered person; a cantankerous person."**

46. What word means "to divide a voting area (state, county, or city) into election districts so as to give one political party an electoral majority in as large a number of districts as possible"? Who was governor of Massachusetts in 1812 when this method was developed and the word coined? What 2 words combined to form this word? What position did this man hold under which President in 1813 and 1814? What did he become the 2nd person to do (George Clinton was the first)?

ANSWER: **Gerrymander/Elbridge Gerry/Gerry was combined with (sala)mander, because the shape of the new district of Essex County, which favored the Democrats over the Federalists, looked like a salamander. Benjamin Russell, editor of the Boston** *Centinel* **coined this word with the help of Gilbert Stuart, who drew the shape of a salamander on a map/Vice President under James Madison/He died in 1814 and became the 2nd Vice President to die in office.**

47. Identify each of the following words or phrases, each of which is related to Indian tradition or history.

a) "to cease hostilities; make peace; become reconciled" (from the American Indian custom of burying all war-like weapons as a sign of good intentions when concluding a peace treaty)

b) "to hide or conceal one's actions or any evidence of any involvement; to wipe out one's footprints" (from the American Indians' practice of erasing their footprints to avoid being followed)

c) "an exclamation of exhilaration" (used as a battle cry by U.S. paratroopers during WWII and derived from the name of an American Apache Indian Chief who possibly used it during a daring leap to freedom off a cliff)

d) ''a metal or wooden club shaped like a bowling tenpin and used for gymnastic exercise''

e) ''a single file'' (from the American Indian habit of secretly walking a trail so as to leave but a single set of tracks which are erased by the last man)

f) ''hostile, seeking a fight; preparing for or engaged in war'' (from the route used by American Indians on warlike forays)

g) ''a pleasant, calm final period of one's life occurring during a state of general decline'' or ''a temporary return to mild, dry, and hazy summer weather during the late fall following the first frosts''

h) ''a person who gives something and then demands it back'' (from the Indian custom of giving a gift and expecting its equivalent in return)

i) ''a contest in which two persons compete by trying to force another's leg down, another's hand down, or to force another off balance''

j) the name of a 1918 novel by John Galsworthy

k) the state in which 31,000 square miles called Indian Territory was reserved for the Indians (1834-1890)

l) ''to curse or jinx, or place a magic spell on to bring bad luck'' (from the Indian custom of marking their territories and sacred sites with symbols as a warning to trespassers)

m) ''a wooden statue of an Indian formerly placed in front of a cigar store''

n) ''honestly; truthfully'' (an intensive used to emphasize the truth of a statement as in, ''Me _____ _____. Speak with straight tongue'' used by Indians during powwows with white men)

o) ''a person who is silent, dull, spiritless, and unresponsive'' (from the standing wooden image of the statue of an Indian holding a cluster of cigars outside of a tobacco store)

p) ''place where a person finds an abundant variety of what he wants or is very successful'' (from the Indian belief in a warrior's abode of happiness after death)

q) ''a group of gangsters or thugs in Paris at the end of the 19th century; a violent Parisian cabaret dance imitative of the manner of an Indian handling his woman in a rough, masterful way'' (from the Southwestern American Indians led by Geronimo)

r) ''the lowest person in a hierarchy; an inexperienced person or one of least importance'' (from the carved and painted post erected in front of the dwellings of Indian tribes of the NW coast of North America; possibly popularized by H. Allen Smith's comic novel whose title is the same as this phrase)

s) ''an American Indian ceremonial headdress consisting of a headband with a tail studded with feathers''

t) ''an American Indian ceremonial dance before battle or after victory''

u) ''a pigment applied by American Indians to their faces and bodies before going into battle''

v) ''a movement and motto among American Indians urging the achievement of social equality through political power''

w) ''to speak in a lying or deceitful manner'' (probably a translation of an American Indian expression dependent upon the description for a river or path that divides into two branches)

x) ''strange, unintelligible speech, talk, or language; gibberish; jargon'' (from the dialect of the Muskogean tribe of North American Indians who now live in Oklahoma)

y) ''the principal deity in the religion of many North American Indian tribes''

z) ''the President of the United States'' (name given to him by the American Indians — frequently used facetiously)

ANSWER: a) to bury the hatchet (ax, tomahawk) b) to cover one's tracks c) ''Geronimo-o-o'' d) Indian club e) Indian file f) on the warpath g) Indian summer h) Indian giver i) Indian wrestling j) *Indian Summer of a Forsyte* k) Oklahoma l) to put the Indian sign on m) cigar-store Indian n) honest Injun (Indian) o) wooden Indian p) happy hunting ground q) Apache r) low man on the totem pole s) war bonnet t) war dance u) war paint v) red power w) to speak with forked tongue x) Choctaw y) Great Spirit z) Great White Father.

48. What phrase means "the use of cheaply sensational or distorted newspaper stories to attract readers"? When this phrase was coined, 2 newspapers were battling for readers at the turn of the century. Name the papers and name the owners. What is the origin of the phrase?

ANSWER: Yellow Journalism or Yellow Press/*The New York World* of Joseph Pulitzer and the *Journal* of William Randolph Hearst/In 1895, Richard Felton Outcault created for *The World* the comic strip "Hogan's Alley" featuring a young boy called the Yellow Kid, so named because yellow ink was used. This innovative use of color was designed to attract new readers. In 1896, the strip was renamed "The Yellow Kid." Outcault then changed newspapers and took his strip with him to the *Journal*, but *The World* ran a similar Yellow Kid comic strip.

49. Gelett Burgess, an American humorist, coined many words in his *Burgess Unabridged: A New Dictionary of Words You Have Always Needed*. He coined a word for "an advertisement, as on a book jacket," and another for "an ill-mannered person; a clod." Name the 2 words. He also popularized a word that means "a sedative; a platitude" to describe a person addicted to the use of clichés (the word also means "a tiresome person; a bore"). Name it. Burgess also wrote a poem about a "Purple Cow." Quote it. Years later he wrote another poem lamenting the earlier "Purple Cow" poem. Recite it.

ANSWER: Blurb/Goop/Bromide/"I never saw a *purple cow.*
I never hope to see one.
But I can tell you anyhow,
I'd rather see one than be one."/

"Ah, yes, I wrote the '*purple cow.*'
I'm sorry now I wrote it.
But I can tell you anyhow,
I'll kill you if you quote it."

50. Identify each of the following phrases, each of which has the word "dollar" in it.
    a) "to be completely certain or absolutely sure" (from the game of poker in which one would bet all that he has, including the bottom chip)
    b) "to pay the full value for something" (from the game of poker in which one uses the highest stack of chips)
    c) "the most important question upon which everything is riding" (based on the WWII radio quiz program which had $64 for the top prize, or on its 1950's imitation TV game show)
    d) "to feel or look great and be in the best of spirits" (as if one were worth an enormous sum of money)
    e) "money as the object of idolatrous worship" (first used by Washington Irving in *The Creole Village*, 1837, describing the Louisiana settlements on the Mississippi)
    f) "the use of American economic power supported by military and political muscle to create opportunities for American businessmen in the Far East and Latin America" (from President Taft's fiscal foreign policy)
    g) "a U.S. federal appointee serving for a token salary for patriotic reasons" (from the minimum amount of money to ensure the existence of a binding contract)

ANSWER: a) to bet one's bottom dollar b) to pay top dollar (for) c) ($64 question) $64,000 question d) to feel like a million dollars e) the almighty dollar f) dollar diplomacy g) dollar-a-year man.

51. Identify the author of the following lines, name the poem, and define the phrase "the mills of God grind slowly."

"Though the mills of God grind slowly, yet
they grind exceedingly small;

Though with patience He stands waiting,
with exactness grinds He all.''

ANSWER: Henry Wadsworth Longfellow/''Retribution''/Retribution (or reward) for one's actions may be delayed, but in the end everyone will get what is merited.

52. Name the region of Pennsylvania settled by expert German wagonmakers who were famous for the wagons they made. What nickname for a cigar comes from this name?

ANSWER: Conestoga (wagons)/''Stogie'' from Conestoga cigars.

53. Name the slang phrase which means ''to go at top speed; go for broke,'' which comes from the railroad signal, a raised pole with a metal ball attached to it, to accelerate to full speed. The phrase is also the name of a song and dance popular in the early 1900's.

ANSWER: To ball the jack (jack means locomotive).

54. Name the author and the title of the book which means ''a no-win paradox in a law, regulation, or practice; a dilemma from which there is no escape.'' According to regulations, a pilot could be released from combat duty only on grounds of insanity, an impossible provision, for only the insane would willingly choose to risk their lives in combat. Who is the main character in this novel? What is the name of the airman who was promoted by a computer error to become the 256th squadron commander?

ANSWER: Joseph Heller/*Catch-22*/Captain John Yossarian/Major Major Major.

55. What phrase means ''a promise of future benefits or rewards that will not be realized''? It comes from the song ''The Preacher and the Slave'' (1910) by Joe Hill? Fill in the last line of the following verse and you will have the phrase.

''You will eat, bye and bye,
In the glorious land above the sky!
Work and pray,
Live on hay,
You'll get _____when you die!''

ANSWER: Pie in the sky.

56. Identify each of the following political words or phrases.
   a) ''the art or practice of pursuing an extremely dangerous policy to the edge of catastrophe (to the brink of war) before stopping'' (a policy associated with President Eisenhower's Secretary of State John Foster Dulles, 1953-1959)
   b) ''a Northern politician or adventurer who went South after the Civil War seeking political or financial gain; any non-native politician who meddles in local affairs for political self-interest'' (from the habit of those during the Civil War who carried all their possessions in a single bag so they could move quickly)
   c) ''a white Republican Southerner during reconstruction after the Civil War; a scamp; rascal; reprobate'' (used disparagingly by Southern Democrats after the Civil War — possibly from the undersized, useless pony bred on Scalloway, a Shetland Island)
   d) ''a closed meeting of a political party to establish policy and select candidates for public office'' (from an Algonquian Indian word meaning ''elder,'' or ''counselor,'' and from the powwows held by Indian tribal leaders)
   e) ''nonsense; foolish talk or behavior'' (from Claire Booth Luce's coinage in referring to Vice President Henry Agard Wallace's foreign aid programs in 1943; a portmanteau combination of *global* and *baloney*)
   f) ''a thriving, booming, rapidly expanding business'' (from the U.S. Government Land Office being overwhelmed with requests from families and speculators for low-cost land after passage of the Homestead Act of 1862)
   g) ''to incite retaliatory action; to stir up party or sectional animosity'' (an action popularized in post Civil War days to exacerbate sectional hostilities; the use of an ensanguined article of clothing with retribution and vengeance as a goal is ancient, however)
   h) ''gossips and defeatists'' (phrase used by President Roosevelt during WWII — modeled on the *fifth column* [''traitors''] of General Mola)

i) "an intellectual; a highbrow" (frequently used disparagingly; used by Owen Johnson in an early 20th century novel; popularized during the 1952 presidential campaign by Stewart Alsop in reference to Adlai Stevenson and his followers)

j) "an adventurer who engages in private military activity in a foreign country" (the 19th century Americans who engaged in fomenting insurrections in Latin America, especially William Walker of Tennessee, who was temporarily successful in Nicaragua in 1855-1857) and "the use of obstruction tactics by a member of a legislative body to delay or prevent passage of generally favored legislation by introducing irrelevant material"

k) The nickname of the U.S. State Department (from Washington *Post's* Edward Folliard's description. State Department offices were built on land where the gasworks once stood and miasma emanated from the area. The nickname eventually became applied to the fogginess of the official language of the State Department)

l) "a clever, unscrupulous person; shyster; any devious or disreputable person" (an obsolete word until popularized by President Harry Truman. He defined it in a 1952 speech as "a person born out of wedlock," especially directing its use to unscrupulous politicians who try to win votes by any means possible)

m) "members of a group who are fanatical or irrational, especially in a political, social, or religious movement" (popularized by Theodore Roosevelt in 1913 in reference to left-leaning radicals; now the meaning refers to right-leaning radicals)

n) "a theory that if one country, as in SE Asia, should come under Communist domination, nearby nations would naturally follow" (from a row of dominoes set on edge which would follow one after the other if the first were toppled; popularized by Dwight Eisenhower in 1954 in his decision to support the South Vietnam government)

o) "a list of opponents who have been targeted for reprisals because of their opposition to the Administration" (popularized by Richard Nixon's list while President which was used to punish political opponents; a list which had been named by John Dean)

p) "colossal fiasco" (from a U.S. sponsored invasion of Cuba, April 17-21, 1971, which ended in defeat)

q) "political, economic, military, and ideological tension and rivalry just short of actual warfare, especially between Soviet and American blocs of nations" (coined by Herbert Bayard Swope after WWII, 1946, to describe U.S.-Soviet relations and popularized by Walter Lippmann)

ANSWER: a) brinkmanship b) carpetbagger c) scalawag d) caucus e) globaloney f) land-office business g) wave the bloody shirt h) sixth column i) egghead j) filibuster k) Foggy Bottom l) snollygoster m) lunatic fringe n) domino theory o) enemies list p) Bay of Pigs q) cold war.

57. Name the phrase that means "a last attempt, as in politics; a final fling; a swan song." Who coined the phrase in using it as the title of his 1956 novel? Upon the life of which mayor of which town was this novel apparently based? What was the name of the group associated with which U.S. President in 1828 and 1832 from which the title of the book was taken? How was this group characterized?

ANSWER: A last hurrah/Edwin O'Connor in *The Last Hurrah*/Major James Curley of Boston/"Hurrah boys" with Andrew Jackson/"A noisy group of campaign supporters."

58. "Two bits, four bits, six bits a dollar" the first person to give the correct amount of money in this phrase, gets to stand up and holler. The Mexican *real* in the 18th century was worth one bit. How many cents was it worth? What is the meaning of the phrase *two-bits*, and what is the meaning of *two-bit*?

ANSWER: $2.50/12½ cents/"A petty sum"/"Inferior; small-time; cheap; insignificant."

59. Identify each of the following eponymous words or phrases.

a) "rules (laws) favoring or encouraging the segregation of Blacks" (from

Thomas D. Rice's plantation song and dance in 1825)

b) ''a drink to which a narcotic, barbituate, or purgative has been added to in-
duce diarrhea or to render the drinker unconscious'' (from a generic name
for an Irishman or possibly from a 19th century Chicago gangster; originally
a horse laxative)

c) ''a person who habitually makes excuses and always has a ready alibi for his
actions'' (from the main character of a 1924 Ring Lardner short story of the
same title)

d) ''a bed that folds or swings into a cabinet or closet'' (designed by American
William Lawrence _____)

ANSWER: a) Jim Crow rules (laws) b) a Mickey (Finn) c) Alibi Ike d) Murphy bed.

60. Identify each of the following words or phrases.

a) ''a small, cheap automobile'' (the nickname for a Model T Ford, from an
analogy with the common food can and either a pet form of Elizabeth or a corruption of the word ''limousine'')

b) ''a wealthy farmer; a rich, unsophisticated farmer or businessman who goes
to the big city and acts like a big spender'' (from a reference to a dairy
farmer based on money he made from the henhouse and the churn; coined
by nightclub entertainer Texas Guinan and popularized by George S. Kaufman's 1925 play)

c) ''a person who deals in illegal liquor'' (from a smuggler's practice of carrying
liquor in tall boots; a phrase popularized during the Prohibition era, 1920-
1933)

d) ''a discordant gathering or parade'' (from a common New Year's practice in
the 19th century of making a great deal of racket with a variety of objects/
instruments — possibly a combination of ''calliope'' and ''thumping'')

e) ''a small, cheap automobile, especially an old one'' (the nickname for a Tin
Lizzie — a Tin Lizzie was a Model T Ford)

f) ''young people of the late 1950's, 1960's mind-expansion drug culture whose
unconventional dress and behavior was an expression of social philosophy''
(from the phrase ''I'm beat,'' meaning ''tired, exhausted'')

g) ''a class of the population composed of the uneducated, the uncultured, the
gullible'' (from an H.L. Mencken coinage, [_____ + (BOURGE)OISIE])

h) ''an inexperienced person; a novice; a newcomer to the ranching and mining
area of the West, especially one unaccustomed to outdoor life; a beginner in
the Boy Scouts'' (from Western U.S. description of cattle which arrived trail-
weary and foot-sore after a long drive)

i) ''an inexperienced person; a novice; a naive immigrant; an easily victimized,
easily deceived person; a dupe'' (after the immature horns of certain
animals)

j) ''an insignificant, conscientious, and hard-working member of the Socialist
Party or of the rank and file of a labor union'' (from Socialist Party use in the
early 20th century for someone who willingly performed menial tasks. Also
popularized by the title of a 1919 Upton Sinclair novel)

k) ''nothing; zero; an insignificant person'' (from the name of a character in a
Playboy-type magazine, *Ballyhoo*, of the 1930's. Scantily clad women
exclaimed, ''Oh, _____!'' Mr. _____, however, was never
seen and his presence was only hinted at. He was in effect a ''nothing'' man.

l) ''the 1890's as a social and cultural period, characterized by prosperity and
complacency'' (from the title of Thomas Beer's work)

m) ''excellent, first-rate; completely satisfactory'' (popularized by Bill ''Bojangles'' Robinson)

n) ''a cowboy's signature'' (in the West, an altered form of John Hancock)

o) ''an indefinitely long period of time'' (from the endless Sunday services and
restrictions of certain denominations, especially the Puritan congregations
which met for 6 to 8 hours on Sundays and forbade other entertainment)

**ANSWER: a) Tin Lizzie b) butter-and-egg man c) bootlegger d) callithumpian band
e) flivver f) beat generation (beatniks) g) booboisie h) tenderfoot i) green-
horn j) Jimmy Higgins k) zilch l) mauve decade m) copacetic (copasetic,**

copesetic) n) John Henry o) month of Sundays.

61. What are the 3 key factors in reporting as dictated by journalism schools?
ANSWER: Acuracy, accruacy, accuarcy.

62. What person of trick-shot fame has a name that means "a free pass to a performance," "a meal ticket," or, in baseball, "a walk"? What is the relationship between her name and "a free pass," or "a meal ticket"? What was her maiden name, and whom did she marry?
ANSWER: Annie Oakley/The free pass had a hole in it and a meal ticket had many more as it was used up, and the meal ticket especially resembled cards that were shot full of holes by Annie Oakley in her sharpshooting act/Anne Mozee/Frank Butler.

63. Identify each of the following words or phrases, each of which has a literary connection.
   a) "a Black who acts in a humiliating or servile manner to Whites" (from the main character, a slave, in an 1852 work by Harriet Beecher Stowe)
   b) "a kind but condescending attitude on the part of Whites toward Blacks and a fawning and submissive attitude of Blacks toward Whites" (based on the main character of Harriet Beecher Stowe's 1852 work)
   c) "a stern taskmaster" (from the cruel slave dealer in Harriet Beecher Stowe's *Uncle Tom's Cabin*)
   d) "a symbol of spontaneity and aimless development"; similarly, "to grow without notice and without help" (from the name of the slave girl in Harriet Beecher Stowe's *Uncle Tom's Cabin*; she answered her "Aunt Ophelia's" question about her parents by remarking "I 'spect I grow'd," being the explanation for being in the world without a mother or father)
   e) "an imaginary, never-never land of high romance; a very romantic piece of writing" (from a 1901 novel by George Barr McCutcheon about the imaginary kingdom of _____ — its adjective form was popularly used in reference to the ornate and exaggerated costumes used by President Nixon in outfitting the White House Drum and Bugle corps)
   f) "a mischievous boy" (from the main character in George W. Peck's 1883 novel, _____ *and His Pa*)
   g) "an emblem for designating human fallibility, particularly adultery" (from Nathaniel Hawthorne's 1850 novel)
   h) "enemy sympathizers within a beleaguered country; traitors" (coined by General Emilio Mola during the Spanish Civil War, 1933-1939, in reference to the sympathizers of Francisco Franco within the city of Madrid who would rise up and capture it. The phrase was popularized, however, by the title of a 1937 play by Ernest Hemingway)
   i) "a country, especially the U.S., or any locality, in which immigrants of various racial groups and nationalists with different social and cultural values are assimilated" (from Israel Zangwill's 1910 play of that name derived from the container, especially at a mint, in which metals and other substances are melted to make an alloy)
   j) a nickname for New York City (from Washington Irving's *Salmagundi*, 1807. The nickname referred to a village in Nottinghamshire, England, in the 13th century where the inhabitants were known as "wise fools" because they feigned stupidity in order to thwart King John from building a hunting lodge, or a castle, an action that would have raised taxes and imposed restrictions)
   k) "a person out of touch with the present" (from a character in Washington Irving's *Sketch Book* who slept for 20 years)
   l) "an excessively and foolishly optimistic person" (after the title character of a 1913 novel by Eleanor Porter)
   m) "a middle class American who is a model of narrow-mindedness and self-satisfaction" (after the title character of a 1922 novel by Sinclair Lewis)
   n) "a person who leads a very commonplace daily life but who seeks escape from reality through daydreaming about courageous feats performed in exciting

adventures'' (from the title character of James Thurber's ''The Secret Life
of _____,'' 1942)

o) ''a person who achieves a rags to riches success through self-reliance and determination'' (from the name of an American author, 1832-1899, who wrote books for boys)

p) ''authentic; true; real; the genuine article'' (from the name of a Pennsylvania Quaker in English woman Susanna Cantilivre's play *A Bold Stroke For a Wife*, 1716. This Quaker of good repute had to prove his identity after the imposter Colonel Feignwell had taken his name and won the hand of Miss Lovely)

q) ''a view of or meditation upon death'' (coined by William Cullen Bryant and the name of one of his poems, 1817)

r) ''a grotesque black doll; a grotesque person'' (from the name of a doll used in illustrations in a series of children's books by Bertha and Florence Upton in the early 20th century)

s) ''the principal street of any small American town or city; an environment characterized by smug, materialistic provincialism (the second definition is from a 1920 novel by Sinclair Lewis)

t) ''a mystery, novel, play, etc.'' (coined in 1930 by D. Gordon in *American News of Books* from the jocular formation of the question ''Who done it?'')

u) ''the refusal to obey government policy or laws that are considered unjust, usually by nonviolent passive resistance'' (popularized by an 1848 essay of that title by Henry David Thoreau)

v) ''chance acquaintances who likely will not meet again'' (from Henry Wadsworth Longfellow's *Tales of a Wayside Inn*, 1863: ''_____
_____, and speak each other in passing . . . '')

w) ''to aim high; to have high aspirations'' (from Ralph Waldo Emerson's essay *Civilization*)

ANSWER: a) Uncle Tom b) Uncle Tomism c) Simon Legree d) Topsy/to grow like Topsy e) Graustark f) Peck's bad boy g) scarlet letter h) fifth column i) melting pot j) Gotham k) Rip Van Winkle l) Pollyanna (called the ''Glad Girl'') m) Babbitt n) Walter Mitty o) Horatio Alger p) Simon Pure q) thanatopsis r) golliwogg (goliwog) s) main street/Main Street t) a whodunit u) civil disobedience v) ships that pass in the night w) to hitch one's wagon to a star.

64. What phrase is a motto that means that ''the speaker is prepared to take responsibility for any of his actions''? This phrase was popularized by being the motto of a U.S. President who kept a sign with these words on his desk. Name the President. This phrase is based on another phrase which means ''to evade responsibility by blaming another person.'' What is this phrase? From what object in the game of poker does this phrase take its origin?

ANSWER: The buck stops here/Harry Truman/To pass the buck/A knife with a buckhorn handle was used to mark the next dealer who could pass the deal if he so desired (sometimes a silver dollar was used as a marker or counter, thus the word ''buck'' for a dollar).

65. To what insect is there a monument in Enterprise, Coffee County, Alabama? Why did the people of Enterprise erect a monument to something that infested and destroyed their cotton industry? What is the meaning of this insect in present-day political terms? What is the name of the insect of the order *lepidoptera*, genus *porthetria*, species *dispar*, which also serves as the name of Eastern and Midwestern Republicans in Congress who may vote Democratic on budget proposals?

ANSWER: Boll weevil/Because after the boll weevil infested the crops, the community raised other crops and became more prosperous than before/Boll weevils are Conservative Southern Democratic members of Congress who vote with Republicans/Gypsy moth(s).

66. Identify each of the following phrases, each of which has the word ''American'' in it.

a) a perennial plant bearing large, long-stemmed crimson flowers

b) the U.S. troops in Europe in WWI
c) a federation of labor unions of the U.S. and Canada, founded in 1886, which merged with the Congress of Industrial Organizations in 1955
d) an organization of veterans of the U.S. armed forces founded in 1919
e) system of hotel operation in which guests pay a fixed price that covers room, service, and meals
f) "an American social ideal that stresses equality among all, especially material prosperity"
g) the fourth Friday in September
h) a large North American deer — the wapiti
i) seven islands in the South Pacific administered by the Department of the Interior since 1951
j) the trophy awarded to the yacht race winner between a selected challenger and a selected American yacht (so named from the prize, the Hundred-Guinea Cup, won by the yacht *America* in 1851, off the Isle of Wight in England)
k) a 1925 novel by Theodore Dreiser
l) "American troops, especially when they are fighting abroad or about to be sent abroad"
m) "Americans abroad who are unappreciative and critical of the native culture" (from Eugene Burdick's and William Lederer's 1955 book, *The* _____)

ANSWER: a) American Beauty b) American Expeditionary Force c) American Federation of Labor d) American Legion e) American Plan f) American dream g) American Indian Day h) American Elk i) American Samoa j) America's Cup k) *An American Tragedy* l) American boys m) ugly Americans.

67. Give the 3 words in West Point's motto.
ANSWER: Duty, Honor, Country.

68. Name the 4 parts in the motto of the Future Farmers of America.
ANSWER: Learning to do; doing to learn; earning to live; and living to serve.

69. What 3 Latin words make up the Olympic motto, and what do these words mean in English?
ANSWER: *Citius, Altius, Fortius,* meaning "Faster, Higher, Braver," or "Swifter, Higher, Stronger."

70. Identify each of the following phrases, each of which comes from the name of an American woman.
    a) "a patrol wagon" (probably from the name of a Boston boarding house owner, Maria Lee, who helped police handle unruly prisoners)
    b) "a prophetess of doom; a woman with a tale of woe or one who is accompanied by trouble" (from a frontierswoman noted for her marksmanship who was named Martha Jane Canary and whose married name was Martha Burke)
    c) "an advocate of retaining maiden names by married women and of women's rights in general" (from Lucy _____, a well known U.S. suffragette who kept her maiden name after marrying Henry Brown Blackwell)
    d) "an inflatable life jacket used especially by aviators downed at sea" (after the name of a buxom American movie actress since the vests were usually inflated by a CO_2 cartridge)

ANSWER: a) black maria b) Calamity Jane c) Lucy Stoner d) Mae West.

71. Define the italicized words in the following quote and tell which historian made the comment the day after Vice President Spiro Agnew's resignation on October 10, 1973: "Never has there been an administration so versed in *mendacity, duplicity, chicanery* and corruption."
ANSWER: *Mendacity* means "lying or dishonesty"; *duplicity* is "deliberate deception" or "double-dealing"; and *chicanery* means "deception by trickery, especially tricky talk or action"/Henry Steele Commager.

72. What phrase means "two people who try to outdo each other in politeness, especially in regards to not taking precedence"? Who is the creator of the comic strip *Happy Hooligan* in which these two characters were portrayed in the 1920's and 1930's? What nationality were the characters? What was the typical wording of the ending of each comic strip?

ANSWER: Alphonse and Gaston/Frederick Burr Opper/French/''After you my dear Alphonse — no, after you, my dear Gaston.''

73. Identify each of the following words or phrases, each of which is associated in some manner with New York State.
    a) ''fine wood shavings used for packing, padding, and stuffing'' (from the past participle of the Latin verb meaning ''to excel,'' which is the motto of New York State meaning ''Ever Upward,'' or ''Still Higher'')
    b) ''a raspberry, or vulgar noise made by a vibration of the lips and tongue to show contempt'' (from a New York borough)
    c) ''an overwhelming torrent; a flood; a cascade'' (from the name of a famous waterfall located on the U.S.-Canadian border in New York and Ontario)
    d) ''a gangster; any of a gang of criminals in a Chinese-American secret society who acted as hired assassins and blackmailers; unprincipled or deceitful person, especially a demagogic politican'' (from the name of a New York city gang organized about 1806)
    e) ''overzealous moral censorship of books, plays, and the fine arts because of alleged immorality'' (after American self-appointed censor, Anthony _____, a leader of the New York Society for the Suppression of Vice. The word was probably coined by George Bernard Shaw.)
    f) ''move away; get going'' (possibly from the policeman's orders at Twenty-third Street in New York City at the turn of the century to the young male flirts hanging out there)
    g) ''the most exclusive social set of the community'' (from 1889 when Ward McAllister decided that there were but a set number of people truly elite enough to be invited to George Washington's centenary inaugural celebration at Mrs. William Astor's New York City townhouse — popularized by C.J. Allen in the New York *Sun*)
    h) ''to smash; to hit repeatedly'' (from the name of a rough, pugilistic New York City cop, John Joseph _____)
    i) ''resort hotels in the Catskill region of New York State'' (so named by the entertainers because of the Jewish cuisine which featured Russian beet soup called borscht)
    j) ''to send or sentence to prison'' (from the fact that Sing Sing is up the Hudson River from New York)
    k) ''a person of either sex who spreads disease or infection (or corruption) to which that person is immune'' (from Mary Mallon, an Irish immigrant who was a typhoid-carrying cook in New York. She died in 1938.)
    l) ''a failure; a blunder; a complete fabrication''; or, ''to make a suicidal leap but fail to die; to fabricate a story'' (after Steve _____, who said he jumped from the Brooklyn Bridge — July, 1886)
    m) ''luxurious, fashionable, elegant, posh'' (after a chain of luxury hotels, especially after the New York *Ritz*, the *Ritz*-Carlton, established by Caesar Ritz)
    n) ''a radical; an extremist who will not compromise, even at the risk of total loss'' (from the radical faction of the Democratic Party in New York State, 1840's-1850's, who opposed the extension of slavery in the territories at all cost — with references to burning down the barn to get rid of the rats)
    o) ''a member of a faction of the Democratic party in New York in 1835 and later, called the Equal Rights Party'' (from the name of the self-igniting matches which were used to hold a meeting in Tammany Hall after the lights were extinguished by the opposition)
    p) ''an educational and entertaining assembly, especially a traveling one that met in tents or outdoors'' (from a county and lake in southwestern New York where the first such assembly was held in 1874. Public lectures, concerts, and plays were part of the summer educational program)
    q) ''any organization, especially a big-city one, which exercises political control through corruption and bossism'' (after a New York City political machine, founded in 1789, and named after a 17th century friendly Delaware Indian chief named Tamanend)

r) "a tax-free allowance made to legislators for expenses in lieu of a salary" (from the New York State legislature's approval of such a plan, and named by Al Smith from a play on the phrases *in lieu of* this and *in lieu of* that, or from a nickname for Louise meaning "something extraordinary; a humdinger; a corker; a beaut'')

s) a salad made of diced apples, celery, walnuts, and mayonnaise (after the _____-Astoria Hotel in New York City)

t) "professional drama produced in New York City outside the main theatrical district and characterized by experimental and low-cost productions" (from being produced in smaller theatres not located on the Main Street of the theatre district)

u) "a lawless, secret society organized for acts of blackmail and violence" (from the Italian *La Mano Nera*, for a group of Sicilians active in the United States in the early 20th century, especially in New York)

v) "a person who is unscrupulous or unethical, especially in law or politics; a pettifogger" (possibly after Scheuster, an unscrupulous New York criminal lawyer who was frequently rebuked for pettifoggery)

ANSWER: a) excelsior b) Bronx cheer c) Niagara d) highbinder e) comstockery f) twenty-three skiddoo g) the Four Hundred h) to broderick i) Borscht (Borsch) Belt (Circuit) j) to send up the river k) Typhoid Mary l) a brodie/to do a brodie m) ritzy (*ritz* means "a pretentious display''; *put on the ritz, acting ritzy*, and *don't get ritzy with me* all refer to an ostentatious display of one's wealth n) barnburner o) locofoco p) chautauqua q) Tammany or Tammany Hall r) lulu s) Waldorf salad t) off-Broadway u) Black Hand v) shyster.

74. What is the phrase in politics that means "an informal group of personal advisers to an elected official"? Who was the first President associated with such a group? What phrase associated with what President means "a group of expert advisers originally to a candidate or incumbent or later to a President"?

ANSWER: Kitchen Cabinet/Andrew Jackson/Brain Trust (coined by James M. Kieran or by Louis Howe)/Franklin Roosevelt.

75. The Roosevelt family gave 2 eponyms, *teddy bear* and *alice blue*, to the English language. What Texas family has also given 2 words, one an eponym and the other not? Define the terms.

ANSWER: Samuel Maverick has contributed *maverick*, originally "an unbranded animal," and now meaning "a nonconformist"/Samuel's grandson, Maury Maverick, a Congressman, contributed *gobbledygook*, meaning "pompous, wordy, and complex talk or writing."

76. Identify each of the following foreign words or phrases, adopted for use in the English language.

a) "a derogatory term for a person of importance and in a position of authority" (from Chinook jargon, for "plenty to eat," especially one who is overbearing)

b) "extremely zealous or enthusiastic" (from the Chinese for "work together"; which was the slogan of the WWII marine raiders, nicknamed "Carlson's Raiders" from its leader Colonel Evans F. Carlson)

c) "wild, rough, heavily wooded, isolated country; wilderness, remote rural regions" and "to compaign the rural regions for votes" (from WWII military slang in the Philippines from a Tagalog word meaning "mountain"; and used by the U.S. soldiers to refer to an inaccessible area of the Philippines)

ANSWER: a) high muck-a-muck (high muckamuck, high muckety-muck) b) gung-ho c) boondocks/to stump the boondocks.

77. Identify each of the following words or phrases, each of which comes from a cartoon or comic strip series.

a) "to try to remain social equals with one's neighbors" (from Arthur R. "Pop" Momand's comic strip in the New York *Globe* from 1913 to 1941)

b) "a person who is timid, meek, or unassertive" (after Caspar _____, A detective character of Harold Tucker Webster's newspaper cartoon series *The Timid Soul* started in 1924; the name was taken from a bland dish of

hot buttered toast in warm milk, often associated with frail persons)
- c) "a person who means well but is inept and frequently in trouble" (popularized by "The Sad_____" comic strip drawn by George Baker during WWII)
- d) "an average, uncompetitive person, especially an inept boxer; a stupid, clumsy, oafish fellow; a born loser" (coined by sports writer Jack Conway in *Variety* and used as the name of a comic strip by Ham Fisher in 1931)
- e) "a man of superhuman powers" (from a translation of the German *Ubermensch* based upon Nietzsche's philosophy of the ideal superior man. Popularized in England by G.B. Shaw's play *Man and* _____ in 1903, and in the U.S. by Jerry Siegel's and Joe Schuster's comic strip bearing the same name)
- f) "a virile and agile man of superior physical strength" (after the hero of the jungle stories of Edgar Rice Burroughs and popularized as well by the comic strip of Harold Foster, started in 1929)
- g) "a state of extreme nervousness; the jitters; the willies" (coined by William De Beck in his comic strip *Barney Google*, 1916)
- h) "a hired thug used to intimidate, terrorize, or eliminate the opposition"; "a stupid, awkward, or oafish person" (popularized by the grotesque comic strip character Alice the _____, in the *Thimble Theatre* series created by E.C. Segar)

ANSWER: a) to keep up with the Joneses b) Milquetoast c) Sad Sack d) palooka/ Joe Palooka e) Superman f) Tarzan g) heebie-jeebies h) goon.

78. Identify each of the following awards.
- a) A prize awarded annually for notable achievement in cartoon artistry (named for Rube [Reuben Lucius] Goldberg)
- b) A statuette awarded by the Academy of Motion Picture Arts and Sciences for achievement in motion pictures (from an Academy employee in 1931 who said, about the statuette, "He reminds me of my Uncle _____")
- c) Any of the awards made annually by the American Theatre Wing for achievement in the theatre (named after the nickname for U.S. theatrical figure Antoinette Perry)
- d) Any of the statuettes awarded annually by the Academy of Television Arts and Sciences for achievement in television (from a variation of *Immy*, engineering slang for the image-orthicon camera, coined in 1948 by U.S. TV engineer Harry R. Lubcke)
- e) A statuette awarded annually for notable achievement in mystery writing (named after Edgar Allan Poe)
- f) Any of the statuettes awarded anually for notable achievement in the recording industry (from the name given to the earliest record player)
- g) Any of several statuettes awarded annually for notable achievement in radio and TV commercials (from the Greek muse of history)

ANSWER: a) Reuben b) Oscar c) Tony d) Emmy e) Edgar f) Grammy [GRAM(OPHONE) + -*my* (as in Emmy)] g) Clio.

79. What name means "an anonymous, average person," or "a fictitious name used in legal proceedings to refer to any person whose name is unknown," and is used in legal proceedings as the first name when two or more persons are involved? What are the names used in legal proceedings for the second, the third, and the fourth person when the names are unknown? What is the name for "the female party to legal proceedings whose real name is unknown"?

ANSWER: John Doe/Richard Roe, John Stiles, and Richard Miles/Jane Doe.

80. Identify each of the following "names."
- a) "a personification of the typical U.S. male college student"
- b) "a name used informally for the average citizen"
- c) "a name used informally for the average man"
- d) "a personification of a Confederate soldier during the Civil War"
- e) "a personification of a Union soldier during the Civil War"
- f) "a name used informally for the average policeman"
- g) "any American" (used by foreigners familiar with WWII U.S. soldiers)

h) "any sailor; any midshipman" (from usage in Annapolis)

i) "an average man; any man at all" (a synonym for John Doe)

ANSWER: a) Joe College (Joe Yale, with Ivy League characteristics) b) John Q. Public (Joe Public) c) Joe Doakes d) Johnny Reb [Johnny + Reb(el)] e) Billy Yank [Billy + Yank(ee)] f) John Law g) G.I. Joe h) Joe Gish i) Joe Blow.

81. Identify the following 2 phrases from horse racing. One means "a finish in which the winner comes out from behind at the last moment" and comes from the last name of a 19th century jockey, Snapper _____, who won races in this manner. The other means "a long lead in a race, especially a long lead early in the race," and comes from the name of "Father _____," a well-known jockey instructor, who counseled his students to take the lead and hold on to it.

ANSWER: Garrison finish/Bill Daley.

82. What phrase means "an unexpected winner; an unknown who makes an unexpectedly good showing; an obscure person in politics who gets the nomination for office unexpectedly, usually by a compromise after a deadlock in the selection process"? Who was the first U.S. President to fit this description? Who were the 2 candidates for the office whose selection ended in this deadlock in 1844? Who was the 2nd U.S. President to fit the description? The answer to both Presidents can be ascertained by completing the following Democratic slogan: "We _____ you in 1844, We'll _____ you in 1852." What British statesman wrote *The Young Duke* (1831) in which the phrase was first used?

ANSWER: Dark horse/James K. Polk/Martin Van Buren and Lewis Cass/Franklin Pierce/Polked — Pierce/Benjamin Disraeli.

83. Identify each of the following phrases.

a) "to act with courage and fortitude in a painful situation; make a difficult decision" (from standard procedure for wounded soldiers prior to the use of anesthesia; a phrase popularized by Lyndon Johnson in relation to tough decisions about Vietnam and by Gerald Ford referring to difficult economic times)

b) "the residents of a college town and the students and faculty of the college" (from the two sections of a university town; those connected with the university and those not)

c) "to have an ulterior or selfish motive" (from a story frequently attributed to Benjamin Franklin. Supposedly, Franklin, as a young man, was questioned by an old-timer about how the grindstone worked. Franklin discovered the joke was on him when, following the man's encouragement, he kept working until the man's axe was ground)

d) "a state of total emergency which requires the help of everyone present" (from the western U.S. when the herds were so restless or wild that everyone, including the cook, had to ride to settle them down or round them up)

e) "a cheap easily obtainable and concealable handgun" (possibly named by the Detroit police for the activity generated by Saturday night passions)

f) "fine; in excellent working condition; everything quite satisfactory" (coined by NASA official Colonel "Shorty" Powers in 1961 during a conversation with Alan Shepard)

ANSWER: a) bite the bullet b) town and gown c) have an axe to grind d) all hands and the cook e) Saturday night special f) A-O.K.

84. What is the name of the spice from the hard, aromatic seed of an evergreen tree? What state has a nickname named after the fruit of this tree? What phrase means "don't purchase any worthless items" based on the 19th century peddlars' practice of selling wooden imitations? The official nickname for this state is connected with the towns of Hartford, Windsor, and Wethersfield in 1639. What is it and why?

ANSWER: Nutmeg/Connecticut/Don't take any wooden nutmegs/The Constitution State/Because these 3 towns adopted the world's first written constitution called the Fundamentals of Connecticut.

85. Even though there is disagreement about its proper pronunciation, what is the meaning of *orthoëpy*?

ANSWER: "The study of pronunciation."

86. In ordinary written English, name the most frequently used vowel and consonant.
ANSWER: *E/T* (phone home).

87. Which of the following words does not belong in the group?
   a) uncle   c) mother   e) father
   b) cousin   d) sister   f) aunt
ANSWER: b) cousin, for sex is not indicated.

88. Identify each of the following words or phrases, each of which is related to war-time.
   a) "keep fighting or trying regardless of the difficulty" (popularized by Commodore Oliver Hazard Perry at the September 10, 1813, Battle of Lake Erie)
   b) "a peaceful period, especially the absence of fighting during wartime" (from the bulletins issued by the Secretary of War Simon Cameron about the absence of action by General George McClellan during the Civil War)
   c) "an informal means of relaying information; rumor; unfounded report" (from the Civil War, the often secret means of transmitting information, gossip, or rumor from person to person)
   d) "a dummy gun made of wood; empty threats" (from the Civil War guns made of wood and named from a religious doctrine of nonviolence)
   e) "a pack mule, especially when young and newly broken in; an inexperienced person; a second lieutenant, especially a newly appointed one" (from the U.S. cavalry custom of marking mules as raw recruits by shaving their tails)
   f) "to fight off attackers; to remain on duty; to maintain a state of affairs when someone is absent" (from General William Tecumseh Sherman's statement, "_____! I am coming!" He sent the message to General John Murray Corse at Allatoona Pass on October 5, 1864)
   g) "to be resourceful and brave, to have confidence in one's ability and to accomplish an assigned task without fanfare" (from the feat of Lieutenant Major Andrew S. Rowan of the U.S. Army, who, during the Spanish-American War, 1898, carried out an order to get through the Spanish blockade into Cuba, deliver a message to the Cuban insurgent leader, General Calixto Garcia, and report back to Washington)
   h) "not in working order" (from the World War I name for a German from the nickname for Friedrich, pertaining to cheap, easily broken, German goods exported to the U.S. before the war. Also possibly related to the comic strip *The Katzenjammer Kids* and the antics of Hans and Fritz)
   i) "the delirium tremens; the heebie-jeebies; excessive nervous tension" (from the American soldier's nickname for the whine made by World War I German artillery shells)
   j) "peaceful; a peaceful period, especially the absence of fighting during wartime" (from the War Department's bulletins during the lulls of trench warfare during World War I. Also the title of a 1929 novel by Erich Marie Remarque)
   k) "a 2nd lieutenant or an officer commissioned after only 3 months at an officer candidate school" (WWII usage for officers commissioned in such a brief period of time, especially when compared to the years of training required of graduates of the Naval Academy or West Point)
   l) "a small, durable automotive vehicle with a quarter-ton capacity and four-wheel drive, used as an all-purpose vehicle by U.S. Armed Forces in WWII" (originally G.P. for "general purpose," and originally military slang for E.C. Segar's Eugene the Jeep, a comic strip character with extraordinary powers)
   m) "a partial curtailment of electric power in a city, especially lights" (coined during WWII as a defensive measure against possible bombing attacks)
   n) "exceeding a goal or quota; out of the trenches and against the enemy, as in attacking" (the original meaning refers to WWI soldiers climbing out of their trenches to attack the enemy)
ANSWER: a) don't give up the ship b) all quiet along the Potomac c) grapevine telegraph d) Quaker gun e) shavetail f) to hold the fort g) to take (carry) a message to Garcia h) on the fritz i) screaming-meemies j) all quiet on the Western Front k) ninety-day wonder l) jeep m) brownout n) over the top.

89. What phrase from the game of poker means "holding two aces and two eights"? Who was murdered at the time he was holding these cards? What was his profession at the time? By whom was he murdered? In what saloon in what city in what year did it happen?

ANSWER: Dead man's hand/Wild Bill Hickok/Sheriff/Jack McCall/Calamity Jane's Saloon/Deadwood City (Dakota Territory)/(August 2) 1876.

90. Give the word or phrase for each of the following, each of which is associated with the alphabet.
    a) "the basic facts, the simplest elements, or the principles of (a subject)" (from the type of child's book which was used to teach the rudiments of the alphabet and reading skills)
    b) "a beginner; novice" (based on the first 4 letters of the alphabet)
    c) "a finisher" (based on the last 4 letters of the alphabet)
    d) "a middle-of-the-roader" (based on the middle 6 letters of the alphabet)

ANSWER: a) the ABC of b) abecedarians c) zyexewarians d) kelemenoparians (Note: the first 2 answers are legitimate, the next 2 are fictitious).

91. Identify each of the following.
    a) "the loss of intellectuals or professional people to other countries via emigration" (although this phrase applies to many countries, it was particularly applied to Britain's loss of professionals who in the early 1960's emigrated to the United States seeking money and better working conditions)
    b) "courage, nerve, pluck; energy, pep" (a trademark for a soft drink popular in New England)
    c) "an agent of the FBI" (popularly associated with a shortened form of *government man*)
    d) "a law-enforcement agent of the U.S. Department of the Treasury" (from a shortened form of *Treasury man*)
    e) "a system of cooperation established in the U.S. before the Civil War to assist fugitive slaves in reaching safety in free states or in Canada"
    f) "industrialists who became wealthy by exploitation in the late 19th century" (the name of a noble of feudal times who robbed travelers passing through his domain)
    g) "a renewal of basic human values by shunning the prevailing commercial attitudes" (after *The Greening of America*, 1970, by Charles A. Reich)
    h) "any motion picture about the American West made by the Italian movie industry" (from pasta of Italian origin)
    i) "an old-fashioned, extremely conservative, or reactionary person; a backwoodsman; a wild range cow or bull; a Civil War draft evader who fled to the swamps and woods" (from an old shellfish or turtle with a greenish growth of algae on its back)
    j) "the youth of the 1960's and 1970's wanting instant gratification and easy solutions to personal and world problems" (possibly from the phrase *here and now* meaning "without delay; immediately")
    k) "the milieu in which most people are relatively wealthy and living comfortably" (from the title of a 1958 book of that name by John Kenneth Galbraith)
    l) "distress suffered by people overwhelmed by and unable to cope with the rapid and myriad social and technological changes of modern society" (from the 1970 work of that title by Alvin Toffler)
    m) a form of pneumonia affecting the internal body organs and the nervous system (had its origin at a 1976 American Legion convention in Philadelphia, Pennsylvania)
    n) "a member or supporter of an extreme rightist, militant anti-communist organization" (founded in December, 1958, by Robert Welch, Jr., and named after John _____, a USAF captain, who died at the hands of Chinese Communists in 1945)
    o) "a member of a militant religious organization of American Negroes advocating the teachings of Islam, especially self-discipline and self-denial, and racial separation"
    p) "a member of an American Negro organization advocating black nationalism"

q) ''a secret crime syndicate in the United States associated with the Sicilian Mafia'' (from the Italian for ''our family,'' or ''our enterprise'')

ANSWER: a) brain drain b) moxie c) G-man d) T-man e) underground railway (railroad) f) robber barons g) greening h) spaghetti western i) mossback j) now generation k) affluent society l) future shock m) legionnaire's disease n) bircher o) Black Muslim p) Black Panther q) Cosa Nostra.

92. What is ''etaoin shrdlu''?
ANSWER: The letters that form the two left-hand vertical rows of a linotype keyboard.

93. What are the only 4 words in the English language that end in -*dous*?
ANSWER: Hazardous, horrendous, stupendous, and tremendous.

94. What are the 2 letters not on a telephone dial?
ANSWER: Q and Z.

95. Identify each of the following

a) ACLU	f) L.A.K.A.O.I.S.	k) P.E.N.
b) AID	g) LASER	l) POSSLQS
c) ASPCA	h) MADD	m) RADAR
d) CARE	i) NORAD	n) START
e) GORK	j) PAC	o) WATS (line)

ANSWER: a) American Civil Liberties Union b) Agency for International Development c) American Society for the Prevention of Cruelty to Animals d) Cooperative for American Relief (Remittances) to Everywhere e) God only really knows f) love and kisses and other indoor sports g) light amplification by stimulated emission of radiation h) Mothers Against Drunk Drivers i) North American Air Defense Command j) Political Action Committee k) Poets, Playwrights, Editors, Essayists, and Novelists l) persons of the opposite sex sharing living quarters m) Radio Detection And Ranging n) Strategic Arms Reduction Talks o) Wide Area Telephone Service.

96. Identify each of the following abbreviations.

a) B.I.D.	f) et seq.	k) pfc.
b) cf.	g) i.e.	l) p.m.
c) cir.	h) n.b.	m) P.S.
d) e.g.	i) op. cit.	n) Q.I.D.
e) et al.	j) p.d.	o) viz.

ANSWER: a) *bis in die* (twice a day) b) *confer* (compare) c) *circa* (about) d) *exempli gratia* (for example) e) *et alibi* (and elsewhere); *et alii* (and others) f) *et sequens* (and the following) g) *id est* (that is) h) *nota bene* (mark well, take notice) i) *opere citato* (in the work cited) j) *per diem* (by the day) k) private first class l) *post meridiem* (after noon) m) *post scriptum* (postscript) n) *quarter in die* (four times a day) o) *videlicet (namely)*.

97. What 2 words, one meaning ''moderation in eating and drinking,'' and the other meaning ''witty; jocular, especially at an inappropriate time,'' have all the vowels in alphabetical order?
ANSWER: *Abstemious* and *facetious*.

98. Identify each of the following geographical locations.
   a) The town in Georgia whose name means ''something hard to understand or explain; mystery; riddle''
   b) The towns in Ohio and Virginia whose name means ''secret or hidden knowledge; elixir; the supposedly great secret of nature that alchemists sought to discover''
   c) The town in Alabama whose name means ''composed of elements drawn from various sources; selected from various systems or sources''
   d) The towns in Georgia and Oregon whose name means ''a scholar; a lover of learning''
   e) The towns in Georgia, Nebraska, and Ohio whose name means ''the last (of a series); the end''
   f) The town in Vermont whose name means ''a paradise; any delightful place; a

state of bliss''
ANSWER: a) Enigma b) Arcanum c) Eclectic d) Philomath e) Omega f) Eden.

99. Identify each of the following words or phrases, each of which is a proper name.
    a) A person who never tells a lie
    b) A person who is very brilliant; a mathematical genius
    c) A person who is a fearless explorer; a knowledgeable backwoodsman
    d) A person who is a notorious robber
    e) A person who is a private detective
    f) A person who is an expert horseman, scout, and sharpshooter
ANSWER: a) a George Washington b) an Einstein c) a Daniel Boone d) a Jesse James
    e) a Pinkerton f) a Buffalo Bill.

100. What word or phrase was coined after or is identified with each of the following?
    a) Amelia Jenks Bloomer   h) Loammi Baldwin
    b) Gen. Ambrose E. Burnsides   i) Enoch Bartlett
    c) E. C. Benedict   j) Jack Bibb
    d) Eddie Cantor   k) Dwight D. Eisenhower
    e) Franklin D. Roosevelt   l) Howard T. Ricketts
    f) Henry I. Shaw and Kate Butler m) John Philip Sousa
    g) Buckminster Fuller   n) Judge James H. Logan
ANSWER: a) bloomers b) sideburns c) eggs benedict d) March of Dimes e) United
    Nations f) scofflaw (a flagrant law violator) g) spaceship earth and geodesic
    dome h) Baldwin apple i) Bartlett pear j) Bibb lettuce k) Eisenhower jacket
    l) rickettsia (a microorganism) m) sousaphone n) loganberry.

101. In which city and state are each of the following language journals published?
    (The editor's name is in parenthesis).
    a) AMERICAN SPEECH: *A Quarterly*   c) VERBATIM: *The Language*
       of Linguistic Usage (Ronald   *Quarterly* (Laurence Urdang)
       Butters)   d) WORD WAYS: *The Journal of*
    b) MALEDICTA: *The International*   *Recreational Linguistics* (A.
       Journal of Verbal Aggression*   Ross Eckler)
       (Reinhold Aman)
ANSWER: a) University, Alabama b) Waukesha, Wisconsin, c) Essex, Connecticut
    d) Morristown, New Jersey.

ABBREVIATIONS/ACRONYMS

AA—Alcoholics Anonymous
AAA—Agricultural Adjustment Administration; Amateur Athletic Association; American Automobile Association
AAAL—American Academy of Arts and Letters
AAU—Amateur Athletic Union
A.B.—*Artium Baccalaureus* (Lat.), Bachelor of Arts
ABA—American Bar Association
ABC—American Broadcasting Company
abr.—abridged; abridgement
AC, A.C., a.c.— alternating current
A/C, a/c—account (bookkeeping)
accel.—*accelerando* (It.), more quickly (music)
acct.—account; accountant; accounting
ACLU—American Civil Liberties Union
ACTION—American Council to Improve Our Neighborhoods
A.D.—*anno Domini* (Lat.), in the year of the Lord; after dark
adag.—*adagio* (It.), slowly and expressively (music)
ADC, a.d.c.—*aide-de-camp* (Fr.)
ADCO—after Daddy cut out
add.—addenda; addendum; addition; additional; address
ad lib., ad libit.—*ad libitum* (Lat.), at one's pleasure
ad val.—*ad valorem* (Lat.), according to the value
ae., aet., aetat.—*aetatis* (Lat.), of age, aged
AEC—Atomic Energy Commission
AFB—Air Force Base
AFL-CIO—American Federation of Labor-Congress of Industrial Organizations
Ag.—*argentum* (Lat.), silver
A.H.—*anno Hegirae* (Lat.), in the year of the Hegira (era of Mohammed)
AID—Agency for International Development
ALA—American Library Association
AM—amplitude modulation
A.M., a.m.—*ante meridiem* (Lat.), before noon
A.M.—*Artium Magister* (Lat.), Master of Arts
AMA—American Medical Association
AMCO—after Mommy cut out
AMVETS— American Veterans of World War II, Korea, and Vietnam
and.—*andante* (It.), slowly and gracefully (music)
anon.—anonymous
AP—Associated Press
APO—Army Post Office
ARC—American Red Cross
ARM—adjustable rate mortgage
ARRA—Association of Road Racing Athletes
ASCAP—American Society of Composers, Authors, and Publishers
ASPCA—American Society for the Prevention of Cruelty to Animals
ATM—Automated Teller Machine
at. no.—atomic number
atty.—attorney
Atty. Gen.—Attorney General
at. wt.—atomic weight
A.U., a.u.—angstrom unit
AUS—Army of the United States
A.V.—Authorized Version (of the Bible)
advp., avoir.—*avoirdupois* (Fr.), weight, heaviness

AWACS— Airborne Warning and Control System
AWOL, A.W.O.L.—absent without (official) leave
B.A.—*Baccalaureus Artium* (Lat.), Bachelor of Arts
B.B.—barn burner
B.B.A.—Bachelor of Business Administration
BBB—Better Business Bureau
BBC—British Broadcasting Corporation
bbl—barrel, barrels
B.C.—before Christ
B.D.—Bachelor of Divinity
B.Ed.—Bachelor of Education
BEF—British Expeditionary Force(s)
BENELUX—BE(lgium), NE(therlands), LUX (embourg): the economic union of
bf—boldface
B.I.D.—*bis in die* (Lat.), twice a day (medicine)
B.L.—*Baccalaureus Legum* (Lat.), Bachelor of Laws
bldg.—building
B. Lit(t).—*Baccalaureus Lit(t)erarum* (Lat.), Bachelor of Literature (or Letters)
BM—basal metabolism
B. Mus.—*Baccalaureus Musicae* (Lat.), Bachelor of Music
b.p., bp—boiling point; bill of parcels
BPOE, B.P.O.E.—Benevolent and Protective Order of Elks
B.S.—Bachelor of Science
BSA—Boy Scouts of America
B.Sc.—*Baccalaureus Scientiae* (Lat.), Bachelor of Science
B.T.U., Btu., b.t.u., btu.—British thermal unit
bu—bushel
B.V.M.—Blessed Virgin Mary
B.Y.O.B.—Bring Your Own Bible, Bottle, Boy, or Bread
B.Y.O.B.B.B.—Bring Your Own Bottle, Buns, and Burgers
CAB—Civil Aeronautics Board; Consumers' Advisory Board
CAP—Civil Air Patrol
CARE—Cooperative for American Relief (Remittances) to Everywhere
CAT—California Achievement Test
CATV—community antenna television
CAVU—ceiling and visibility unlimited
CBP—child-bearing potential
CBS—Columbia Broadcasting System
cc., c.c.—cubic centimeters
CCC—Commodity Credit Corporation
CEA—Council of Economic Advisers
cent—centigrade; centimeter; central; century
CENTO—Central Treaty Organization
CETA—Comprehensive Employment and Training Act
cf.—*confer* (Lat.), compare
chg.—charge; change
chm.—chairman; chamber
CIA—Central Intelligence Agency
CINC, CinC, C. in C.—Commander in Chief
cir., circ.—circular; *circa* (Lat.), about
cit.—citation; cited; citizen
CLI, C.L.I., cli—cost of living index; cost of loving index
C.M.—*Chirurgiae Magister* (Lat.), Master of Surgery
c/o—care of; cash order
COBOL—Common Business Oriented Language
COD, c.o.d.—cash on delivery; collect on delivery

C. of C.—Chamber of Commerce

C. of S.—Chief of Staff; Chief of Service

COLA—cost of living allowance

colloq.—colloquial; colloquialism; colloquium

COMECON—Council for Mutual Economic Assistance (of Communist countries)

C.O.B.Q.—*cum omnibus bonis quiescat* (Lat.), May he rest with all good souls

CORE—Congress of (Committee on) Racial Equality

CPA, C.P.A.—Certified Public Accountant

CPI, C.P.I., cpi—consumer price index

CPO—chief petty officer

CQ—call to quarters

cres., cresc.—*crescendo* (It.), increasingly loud

CROC—Crusade for the Recognition of Obnoxious Commercials (TV)

CROP—Committee for the Recognition of Obnoxious Programs (TV)

CS—civil service

CSA—Confederate States of America

CSC—Civil Service Commission

CST, C.S.T.—Central Standard Time

ct.—carat; cent; county; court

CTBS—comprehensive test of basic skills

cts.—centimes; cents; certificates

cwt—hundredweight

DA, D.A.—delayed action; District Attorney

DAR—Daughters of the American Revolution

DAV—Disabled American Veterans

DC, D.C., d.c., d-c—direct current

d.c., D.C.—*da capo* (It.), repeat; District of Columbia

D.D.—*Divinitatis Doctor* (Lat.), Doctor of Divinity

D.D.S.—Doctor of Dental Surgery

DDT—dichlorodiphenyltrichloroethane (an insecticide)

DEW—distant early warning (system)

DFC—Distinguished Flying Cross

D.G.—*Dei gratia* (Lat.), by the grace of God

dim.—*diminuendo* (It.), diminishing in loudness (music)

D.I.Y.—do-it-yourself

D. Lit., D. Litt.—Doctor Lit(t)erarum (Lat.), Doctor of Literature (or, Letters)

D.L.S.—Doctor of Library Science

DNA—deoxyribonucleic acid

D.O.—Doctor of Optometry; Doctor of Osteopathy

do.—*ditto* (It.), the same

DOA—dead on arrival

DSC, D.S.C.—Distinguished Service Cross

DSM—Distinguished Service Medal

d.s.p.—*decessit sine prole* (Lat.), died without issue

DST, D.S.T.—Daylight Saving Time

D.T.'s—*delirium tremens* (Lat.)

D.V.—*Deo volente* (Lat.), God willing

dwt—pennyweight

ECG, EKG—electrocardiogram

Ed.D—Doctor of Education

EDT—Eastern Daylight Time

EEC—European Economic Community

EEG—electroencephalogram

EEOC—Equal Employment Opportunity Commission

EFT—electronic fund transfer

e.g.—*exempli gratia* (Lat.), for example

ELF—extremely low frequency

Ens.—Ensign

EPA—Environmental Protection Agency

esp.—especially

ESP—extrasensory perception

Esq., Esqr.—Esquire

est.—established, estimated

EST—Eastern Standard Time

ETA—estimated time of arrival

et. al.—*et alibi* (Lat.), and elsewhere; *et alii* (Lat.), and others

etc.—*et cetera* (Lat.), and so forth

et seq.—*et sequens* (Lat.), and the following

ex. lib.—*ex libris* (Lat.), belonging to the library of

f., ff—and the following (page[s])

f—*forte* (It.), loud (music)

FAA—Federal Aviation Administration

FASGROLIA—FAStGROwing Language of Initialisms and Acronyms

FBI—Federal Bureau of Investigation

FCC—Federal Commerce Commission; Federal Communications Commission

FDA—Food and Drug Administration

FDIC—Federal Deposit Insurance Corporation

fec.—*fecit* (Lat.), he (she, it) did, or made it

ff—*fortissimo* (It.), very loud (music)

FFA—Future Farmers of America

F.F.V.—First Families of Virginia

FHA—Federal Housing Administration; Future Homemakers of America

F.I.F.O.—first in, first out

FM, fm—frequency modulation

fn.—footnote

FOB, f.o.b.—free on board

FOF—friend of a friend

FORTRAN—*For*mula plus *Tran*slation

fps—feet per second; foot-pound second

FRB—Federal Reserve Board/Bank

FTC—Federal Trade Commission

FUBAR—fouled-up beyond all recognition

FUBB—fouled-up beyond belief

FUMTU—fouled-up more than usual

fwd—forward

F.Y.I.—for your information

GAO—General Accounting Office

GATT—General Agreement on Tariffs and Trade

GHQ—General Headquarters

GI—general (government) issue

GIGO—garbage in, garbage out

GMT—Greenwich Mean Time

G.O.P.—Grand Old Party (Republican Party)

GORK—God only really knows

GP—general practitioner

GPO—General Post Office; Government Printing Office

GSA, G.S.A.—General Services Administration; Girl Scouts of America

g.t.d.h.d.—give the devil his due

G.T.T.—Gone To Texas

hab. corp.—*habeas corpus* (Lat.), that you have the body (that you produce the body)

H.C.—House of Commons

h.c.l., hcl—high cost of living, high cost of loving

HF—high frequency

HH, H.H.—His (Her) Highness; His Holiness (the Pope)

hhd—hogshead

HIS—human intelligence source

H.J.S.—*hic jacet sepultus* (Lat.), here lies buried

H.M.S.—His Majesty's Service, Ship, or Steamer

H.P., HP, h.p., hp—high pressure; horsepower

HQ, H.Q., hq, h.q.—headquarters

H.R.H., HRH—His (Her) Royal Highness

H.R.I.P.—*hic requiescit in pace* (Lat.), here rests in peace
IAAF—International Amateur Athletic Federation
I.A.E.A.—International Atomic Energy Agency
ib., ibid.—*ibidem* (Lat.), in the same place
I.B.F.—International Banking Facilities
ICBM—intercontinental ballistic missile
ICC—Interstate Commerce Commission
ICJ—International Court of Justice
id.—*idem* (Lat.), the same
i.e.—*id est* (Lat.), that is; that is to say
ILA—International Longshoreman's Association
ILO—International Labor Organization
IMF—International Monetary Fund
in loc. cit.—*in loco citato* (Lat.), in the place cited
INRI—*Iesus Nazarenus, Rex Iudaeorum* (Lat.), Jesus of Nazareth, King of the Jews
I.N.S.—Immigration and Naturalization Service
I.O.—initials only
IOC—International Olympic Committee
IOU—I owe you
I.Q.—intelligence quotient
IRA—Irish Republican Army
IRS—Internal Revenue Service
ITBS—Iowa Test of Basic Skills
IWW—Industrial Workers of the World
J.D.—*Juris Doctor* (Lat.), Doctor of Law
jg., j.g.—junior grade
JUAD—jumping up and down
KBP—king's bishop's pawn (chess)
kg—kilogram
KISS, K.I.S.S.—Keep it short and sweet; keep it short (simple), Stupid
KKK—Ku Klux Klan
KO, K.O., k.o.—knockout (boxing)
kw—kilowatt
k.w.h.—kilowatt-hour
L, L., l., lb—*libra* (Lat.), pound
L.A.K.A.O.I.S.—love and kisses and other indoor sports
LASER—light amplification by stimulated emission of radiation
L.C.—Library of Congress
l.c., loc. cit.—*loco citato* (Lat.), in the place cited
ldc—less developed country
LIDAR—light detection and ranging
L.I.F.O.—last in, first out
loq.—*loquitor* (Lat.), he (she, it) speaks
LPGA—Ladies Professional Golf Association
l.s.—*locus sigilli* (Lat.), place of the seal
LSD—lysergic acid diethylamide
Ltd. ltd.—limited
M—*monsieur* (Fr.), Sir
M.A.—*Magister Artium* (Lat.), Master of Arts
MAD—Mutual Armed Destruction; (Mutually Assured Destruction)
MADD—Mothers Against Drunk Drivers
MBFR—Mutual and Balanced Force Reduction
mdse.—merchandise
MECE—movement, ethyl chloride, and elevation
Messrs.—*Messieurs* (Fr.), gentlemen
mf—*mezzo forte* (It.), moderately loud (music)
mfg.—manufacturing
MFR—Mutual Force Reduction
M.I.—Military intelligence
MIA—missing in action
MLA—Modern Language Association
Mlle.—*Mademoiselle*, (Fr.), Miss
Mme.—*Madame* (Fr.), Madam
Monsig.—*monseigneur* (Fr.), Monsignor (It.),

my Lord
M.O., MO—*modus operandi* (Lat.), method of operation; Medical Officer
mp—*mezzo piano* (It.), moderately soft (music)
MP, M.P., m.p.—Military Police; melting point
mpg., m.p.g.—miles per gallon
MS, Ms, ms.—manuscript
MSS, Mss, mss.—manuscripts
NAACP—National Association for the Advancement of Colored People
NAEP—National Assessment of Educational Progress
NAS—National Academy of Sciences
NASA—National Aeronautics and Space Administration
NASCAR—National Association for Sports Car Auto Racing
NASL—North American Soccer League
NATO—North Atlantic Treaty Organization
N.B., n.b.—*nota bene* (Lat.), mark well, take notice
NBC—National Broadcasting Corporation
NCAA—National Collegiate Athletic Association
NCO, n.c.o.—noncommissioned officer
N.D., n.d.—no date
NED—New English Dictionary
NFL—National Football League
NLRB—National Labor Relations Board
N.M.I.—no middle initial
N.O.C.D.—not our class, dear
non obst.—*non obstante* (Lat.), notwithstanding
non pros.—*non prosequitur* (Lat.), he does not prosecute
non. seq.—*non sequitur* (Lat.), it does not follow
NORAD—North American Air Defense Command
NORML—National Organization for the Reform of Marijuana Laws
NOW—National Organization for Women
N.P.—*nisi prisus* (Lat.), no protest (banking); Notary Public
NPDA—no public display of affection
N.Q.O.K.D.—not quite our kind, dear
N.Q.O.S.—not quite our sort
NRC—National Regulatory Commission
NSC—National Security Council
NSF—National Science Foundation
NSPCA—National Society for the Prevention of Cruelty to Animals
NSPCC—National Society for the Prevention of Cruelty to Children
OAS—Organization of American States
obit.—obituary
OCS—Officer Candidate School
O.D.—Officer of the Day
OED—Oxford English Dictionary
OEO—Office of Economic Opportunity
OHIM—Oh hell it's Monday
O.H.M.S.—On His (Her) Majesty's Service
O.K., OK—correct or approved
op cit.—*opere citato* (Lat.), in the work cited
OPEC—Organization of Petroleum Exporting Countries
OSHA—Occupational Safety and Health Administration
O.S.S.—obligatory sex scene
oz.—ounce
PA—public address (system); power of attorney
PAC—Political Action Committee
PAKISTAN—Punjab, Afghan border states, Kashmir, Sind, and Baluchistan
PBW—particle-beam weaponry

pct.—percent

p.d.—*per diem* (lat.), by the day

P.E.N.—Poets, Playwrights, Editors, Essayists, and Novelists (the International Association of)

per an.—*per annum* (Lat.), by the year

pfc.—private first class

PHA—Public Housing Administration

Ph.D—*Philosophiae Doctor* (Lat.), Doctor of Philosophy

PHTC—putting hubby through college

pizz.—*pizzicato* (It.), plucked (music)

PLU—preservation of local uncertainty

P.L.U.—people like us

P.M., PM, p.m.—*post meridiem* (Lat.), after noon

POSSLQS—persons of the opposite sex sharing living quarters

POW, P.O.W.—prisoner of war

pp—*pianissimo* (It.), very soft (music)

P.P.C.—*pour prendre congé* (Fr.), to take leave

p.q.—previous question

p.r.n.—*pro re nata* (Lat.), as the situation demands (medicine)

PRO—public relations officer

pro tem.—*pro tempore* (Lat.), for the time being

prox.—*proximo mense* (Lat.), next month

P.S., p.s.—*post scriptum* (Lat.), postscript

pseud.—pseudonym

psi—pounds per square inch

PTA—Parent-Teacher Association

P.T.O., PTO—please turn over

PW—Prisoner of War

pwt—pennyweight

PX—Post Exchange

Q—*quasi* (Lat.), as it were, almost

Q.E.D.—*quod erat demonstrandum* (Lat.), that which was to be proved

Q.E.F.—*quod erat faciendum* (Lat.), that which was to be done

Q.I.D.—*quarter in die* (Lat.), four times a day (medicine)

Q.P., q. pl.—*quantum placet* (Lat.), as much as you please

qq.v.—*quae vide* (Lat.), which see

q.s.—*quantum sufficit* (Lat.), as much as may suffice/*quantum satis* (Lat.), as much as is sufficient

q.t.—quiet (on the q.t.)

q.v.—*quod vide* (Lat.), which, or whom, see

RADAR—RAdio Detection and Ranging

RAF—Royal Air Force

RBC—red blood cells; red blood count

RBI, r.b.i., rbi—run(s) batted in (baseball)

R.D.—Rural Delivery

re—reference, regarding

recd.—received

R.F.D.—Rural Free Delivery

RFP—request for proposal

R.I.P.—*requiescat in pace* (Lat.), let him, or her, rest in peace

rit., ritard.—*ritardando* (It.), more slowly (music)

R.N.—Registered Nurse; Royal Navy

ROTC—Reserve Officers Training Corps

rpm, r.p.m.—revolutions per minute

rps—revolutions per second

R.S.V.P.—*répondez s'il vous plaît* (Fr.), answer if you please; please reply

r.t.b.s.—remains to be seen

R.V.S.V.P.—*répondez vite s'il vous plaît*

(Fr.), answer quickly if you please; reply quickly, please

S & L—Savings and Loan

S.A.—Salvation Army

SAC—Strategic Air Command

SAFFU—surpassing all previous foul-ups

SALT—Strategic Arms Limitation Talks

SAM—surface-to-air missile

SAR—Sons of the American Revolution

SBA—Small Business Administration

S.A.S.E.—self-addressed stamped envelope

S.C.L.C.—Southern Christian Leadership Conference

s.d.—*sine die* (Lat.), without appointing a day

SEABEES-C.B.—short for construction battalion

SEATO—Southeast Asia Treaty Organization

SEC—Securities and Exchange Commission

S.E.C.—Southeastern Conference

seq., seqq.—*sequentia* (Lat.), following; sequence

sf., sfz.—*sforzando* (It.), sudden strong accent

SHAPE—Supreme Headquarters Allied Powers (Europe)

S.I.D.—*semel in die* (Lat.), once a day (medicine)

S.J.—Society of Jesus (Jesuits)

SNAFU—situation normal all fouled up

SONAR—SOund NAvigation and Ranging

S.O.P.—standard operating procedure

s.p.—*sine prole* (Lat.), without issue

SPLU—self-paced learning unit

SPQR—*Senatus Populusque Romanus* (Lat.), the Senate and people of Rome

S.R.O., SRO—standing room only

S.S.—steamship

SSA—Social Security Administration

SSE—Selective Service System

S.S.S.—*su segura servidor* (Sp.), your faithful servant

s.s.s.—*stratum super stratum* (Lat.), layer upon layer

stacc.—*staccato* (It.), detached (music)

START—Strategic Arms Reduction Talks

Ste.—*Sainte* (Fr., fem. of saint), saint

SUSFU—situation unchanged, still fouled-up

SWAK—sealed with a kiss

SWALBAKWS—sealed with a lick because a kiss wouldn't stick

T.B., Tb., t.b.—*tubercle bacillus* (Lat.), tuberculosis

TAC—The Athletic Congress

TACAS—Threat Alert and Collision Avoidance System

TARFU—things are really fouled-up

tbs., tbsp.—tablespoon

TF—Task Force

TGIF, T.G.I.F.—thank God it's Friday

TGIM, T.G.I.M.—thank God it's Monday

TGIW, T.G.I.W.—thank God it's Wednesday

T.I.D.—*ter in die* (Lat.), three times a day (medicine)

TKO—technical knockout (boxing)

TLC—tender loving care

TNT—trinitrotoluene, trinitrotoluol

TOT—tip of the tongue

tsp.—teaspoon

TTFN—ta, ta, for now

T.T.F.W.—too tacky for words

TUIFU—the ultimate in foul-ups

TVA—Tennessee Valley Authority

UAW—United Automobile Workers

UFO, U.F.O.—unidentified flying object

UHF—ultrahigh frequency

UMW—United Mine Workers

UNESCO—United Nations Educational, Scientific and Cultural Organization

UNICEF—United Nations Children's Emergency Fund

UNIVAC—Universal Automatic Computer

UPI—United Press International

USMA—United States Military Academy

USMC—United States Marine Corps

USN—United States Navy

U.S.S.—United States Ship

USSR—Union of Soviet Socialist Republics

USW, U.S.W.—*und so weiter* (G.), and so forth

VA—Veterans' Administration

VD—venereal disease

VFW—Veterans of Foreign Wars

VHF—very high frequency

VIP, V.I.P.—very important person

VISTA—Volunteers in Service to America

viz.—*videlicet* (Lat.), namely

vox pop.—*vox populi* (Lat.), voice of the people

V.R.—*Victoria Regina* (Lat.), Queen Victoria

vs.—*versus* (Lat.), against

v.s.—*vide supra* (Lat.), see above

VTOL—vertical take off and landing

VUP, V.U.P.—very unimportant person

WAC—Women's Army Corps

WAF—Women in the Air Force

WATS (line)—Wide Area Telephone Service

WAVES—Women Accepted for Volunteer Emergency Service (Navy)

WBC—white blood cells; white blood count

WCTU—Woman's Christian Temperance Union

WHO—World Health Organization

x—an abscissa (math.); an unknown quantity (many letters of the alphabet are used as unknowns)

Y., YMCA—Young Men's Christian Association

YAVIS—Young, adaptable (attractive), verbal, intelligent, and successful

YDLTPFTYSIE—you didn't like this program the first time you saw it, either

Z—atomic number; zenith distance

ZIP—Zone Improvement Plan

ZOO—zero on originality

ZPG—Zero Population Growth

WORDS AND EXPRESSIONS FROM FRENCH, SPANISH AND GERMAN

ENGLISH	FRENCH	SPANISH	GERMAN
1 6	un . . . . six	uno . . . . seis	eins . . . . sechs
2 7	deux . . . . sept	dos . . . . siete	zwei. . . . . sieben
3 8	trois . . . . huit	tres . . . . ocho	drei . . . . acht
4 9	quatre . . . . . . neuf	cuatro . . . . . . nueve	vier . . . . neun
5 10	cinq . . . . dix	cinco . . . . diez	fünf . . . . zehn
Monday	lundi.	lunes	Montag
Tuesday	mardi	martes	Dienstag
Wednesday.	mercredi	miércoles	Mittwoch
Thursday	jeudi	jueves	Donnerstag
Friday.	vendredi	viernes	Freitag
Saturday.	samedi	sábado	Sonnabend, Samstag
Sunday.	dimanche	domingo	Sonntag
January	janvier	enero	Januar
February.	février.	febrero	Februar
March.	mars	marzo	März
April	avril	abril	April
May	mai	mayo	Mai
June	juin.	junio	Juni
July	juillet	julio	Juli
August	août	agosto	August
Sept.-Oct.	september, octobre	septiembre, octubre	September, Oktober
Nov.-Dec.	novembre, décembre	noviembre, diciembre	November, Dezember
What time is it?.	Quelle heure est-il?.	Qué hora es?	Wieviel Uhr ist es?
a day	un jour	un día.	ein Tag
a week	une semaine	una semana	eine Woche
a month	un mois	un mes	ein Monat
a year	un an/une année	un año	ein Jahr
today	aujourd'hui.	hoy	heute
tomorrow	demain	mañana	morgen
yesterday	hier.	ayer	gestern
north	nord	norte.	Nord (en)
east	est	este	Ost (en)
south	sud	sur	Süd (en)
west	ouest	oeste	West(en)
spring.	le printemps	la primavera	der Frühling
summer	l'été	el verano.	der Sommer
fall	l'automne	el otoño.	der Herbst
winter.	l'hiver.	el invierno.	der Winter
Hello, how do you do? . . .	Bonjour.	Hola, ?Qué tal?	Guten Tag.
How are you?	Comment allez-vous?	¿Cómo está Usted?.	Wie geht es Ihnen? Wie
	(Comment ça va? Ça va?)		geht's?
Very well, thanks,	Très bien, merci,	¿Muy bien, gracias,	Sehr gut, danke,
and you?	et vous?	¿y Usted?.	und Ihnen?
What's the matter?.	Qu'est-ce qui se passe? . .	¿Qué pasa?	Was ist los?
What's your name?	Comment vous appelez-		
	vous?	¿Cómo se llama Usted? . .	Wie heissen Sie?
My name is.	Je m'appelle.	Me llamo.	Ich heisse . . .
What's this?.	Qu'est-ce que c'est ça? . .	¿Qué es esto?	Was ist das?
Where is	Où est?	¿Dónde está . . . ¿ . . .	Wo ist . . . ?
Do you speak English? . . .	Parlez-vous anglais?	¿Habla Usted inglés?	Sprechen Sie Englisch?
Yes, a little	Oui, un peu.	Sí, un poco.	Ja, ein wenig.
What time is it?.	Quelle heure est-il?.	¿Qué hora es?	Wieviel Uhr ist es?
What's the weather?	Quel temps fait-il?	¿Qué tiempo hace?	Was für Wetter haben wir?
			Wie ist das Wetter?
Do you understand?	Comprenez-vous?	¿Comprende Usted?	Verstehen Sie?
I don't understand.	Je ne comprends pas	No comprendo.	Ich verstehe nicht.
What? (What did you	Quoi? Comment?		
say?)	Pardon?	¿Cómo? ¿Perdone?	Wie, bitte?
Good-bye	Au revoir.	Adiós	Auf Wiedersehen.
So long (see you soon) . . .	A bientôt.	Hasta la vista	Bis gleich. Bis später.
Good morning.	Bonjour.	Buenos días.	Guten Morgen.
Good afternoon.	Bonjour.	Buenas tardes.	Guten Tag.
Good evening.	Bonsoir.	Buenas noches.	Guten Abend.
Good night.	Bonne nuit.	Buenas noches.	Gute Nacht.
Please.	S'il vous plaît.	Por favor.	Bitte.
Thank you.	Merci.	Gracias.	Danke.
Thank you very much. . . .	Merci beaucoup.	Muchas gracias.	Danke Schön. Vielen dank.
Yes . . . No.	Oui . . . Non.	Sí . . . No.	Ja . . . Nein.

You're welcome.	De rien (Il n'y a pas de quoi.) Je vous en prie.	De nada. Por nada. No hay de que.	Bitte. Bitte schön. Gern geschehen.
Agreed.	D'accord.	De acuerdo.	Abegemacht! Einverstanden!
It's too bad.	C'est dommage.	Es lástima.	Es ist schade.
To your health! Cheers!	A votre santé!	!Salud!	Prosit! (Zum Wohl!)
I love you.	Je t'aime.	Te quiero. Te amo.	Ich liebe dich.
I don't know.	Je ne sais pas.	No sé.	Ich weiss nicht.
on the right.	à droite.	a la derecha	nach rechts
on the left.	à gauche.	a la izquierda	nach links
I want.	Je veux.	Quiero.	Ich möchte.
I would like.	Je voudrais.	Quisiera	Ich möchte.
I am sick.	Je suis malade.	Estoy mal. Estoy enfermo	Ich bin krank.
I am tired.	Je suis fatigué.	Estoy cansado.	Ich bin müde.
I am cold.	J'ai froid.	Tengo frío.	Mir ist kalt.
I am hot.	J'ai chaud.	Tengo calor.	Mir ist heiss.
I am hungry.	J'ai faim.	Tengo hambre.	Ich habe Hunger.
I am thirsty.	J'ai soif.	Tengo sed.	Ich habe Durst.
I need.	J'ai besoin de.	Necesito.	Ich brauche.
How much does it cost?	C'est combien?	¿Cuánto cuesta?	Was kostet es? Wieviel kostet das?
clothing	(des)vêtements	la ropa	die Kleider
a dress	une robe.	un vestido.	ein Kleid
a blouse	une blouse	una blusa	eine Bluse
stockings	les bas	medias	die Strümpfe
a hat.	un chapeau.	un sombrero.	ein Hut
a shirt.	une chemise.	una camisa.	ein Hemd
a tie	une cravate.	una corbata	eine Krawatte
pants	un pantalon	pantalones	eine Hose
shoes	les souliers.	zapatos.	ein Paar Schuhe
socks	les chaussettes.	calcetines	die Socken
an umbrella	un parapluie	un paraguas	ein Regenschirm
What color?	Quelle couleur?	¿Qué color? ¿De que color?	Welche Farbe?
red	rouge	rojo, roja.	rot
green	vert, verte.	verde	grün
blue	bleu, bleue	azul	blau
black	noir, noire.	negro, negra.	schwarz
white	blanc, blanche	blanco, blanca	weiss
brown.	marron	marrón, pardo, color café	braun
yellow.	jaune	amarillo, amarilla	gelb
orange	orange	anaranjado, anaranjada	orange
gray	gris, grise.	gris.	grau
What is it made of?	De quoi est-il fait?	¿De qué es?	Woraus ist es gemacht?
wood	bois	madera	(das) Holz
iron.	fer	hierro	(das) Eisen
steel.	acier.	acero	(der) Stahl
silver.	argent.	plata	(das) Silber
gold	or	oro	(das) Gold
copper	cuivre.	cobre	(das) Kupfer
leather	cuir.	cuero	(das) Leder
glass	verre.	vidrio	(das) Glas
cotton	coton	algodón	(die) Baumwolle
wool	laine	lana	(die) Wolle
to see	voir.	ver	sehen
to run	courir.	correr.	laufen
to buy	acheter.	comprar	kaufen
to answer	répondre.	contestar	antworten
to speak, talk	parler	hablar	sprechen
to understand	comprendre	comprender	verstehen
to be.	être.	ser/estar	sein
to have	avoir.	tener.	haben
to come.	venir.	venir.	kommen
to listen	écouter.	escuchar	zuhören
to eat.	manger.	comer.	essen
to drink.	boire.	beber	trinken
to do, make	faire.	hacer	tun(do), machen (make)
to sleep.	dormir	dormir.	schlafen
to write.	écrire.	escribir.	schreiben
to give	donner.	dar.	geben

a book	un livre	un libro	ein Buch
a newspaper	un journal	un periódico	eine Zeitung
a pencil	un crayon	un lápiz	ein Bleistift
a pen	un stylo	una pluma	ein Füllfeder
a stamp	un timbre	un sello, una estampilla	eine Briefmarke
a driver's license	un permis de conduire	un permiso de conducir	ein Führerschein
water	l'eau	el agua	das Wasser
the man	l'homme	el hombre	der Mensch; der Mann
the woman	la femme	la mujer	die Frau
the father	le père	el padre	der Vater
the mother	la mère	la madre	die Mutter
the son	le garçon	el hijo	der Sohn
the daughter	la fille	la hija	die Tochter
the boy	le garçon	el muchacho (niño)	der Junge
the girl	la jeune fille	la muchacha (niña)	das Mädchen
the brother	le frère	el hermano	der Bruder
the sister	la soeur	la hermana	die Schwester
the uncle	l'oncle	el tío	der Onkel
the aunt	la tante	la tía	die Tante
the cousin	le/la cousin/cousine	el primo, la prima	der Vetter (die Base)
the nephew	le neveu	el sobrino	der Neffe
the niece	la nièce	la sobrina	die Nichte
the grandfather	le grand-père	el abuelo	der Grossvater
the grandmother	la grand-mère	la abuela	die Grossmutter
the head	la tête	la cabeza	der Kopf
the ear	l'oreille	la oreja	das Ohr
the eye (the eyes)	l'oeil (les yeux)	el ojo (los ojos)	das Auge (die Augen)
the nose	le nez	la nariz	die Nase
the mouth	la bouche	la boca	der Mund
the arm	le bras	el brazo	der Arm
the hand	la main	la mano	die Hand
the leg	la jambe	la pierna	das Bein
the foot	le pied	el pie	der Fuss
the dog	le chien	el perro	der Hund
the cat	le chat	el gato	die Katze
the horse	le cheval	el caballo	das Pferd
the cow	la vache	la vaca	die Kuh
the bird	l'oiseau	el pájaro	der Vogel
the tree	l'arbre	el árbol	der Baum
the sun	le soleil	el sol	die Sonne
the moon	la lune	la luna	der Mond
the star	l'étoile	la estrella	der Stern
the sky	le ciel	el cielo	der Himmel
the rain	la pluie	la lluvia	der Regen
the snow	la neige	la nieve	der Schnee
Do you know?	Savez-vous?	¿Sabe Usted?	Wissen Sie?
I don't know	Je ne sais pas.	No sé.	Ich weiss nicht.
I think so	Je le crois.	Creo que sí.	Ich glaube es.
Do you have?	Avez-vous?	¿Tiene Usted?	Haben Sie?
How old are you?	Quel âge avez-vous?	¿Cuántos años tiene usted?	Wie alt sind Sie?
the market	le marché	el mercado	der Markt
the library	la bibliothèque	la biblioteca	die Bibliothek
the post office	le bureau de poste	la casa de correos	das Postamt
the church	l'église	la iglesia	die Kirche
I am	Je suis (être)	Soy (ser) Estoy (estar)	Ich bin (sein)
I have	J'ai (avoir)	Tengo (tener)	Ich habe (haben)
I go	Je vais (aller)	Voy (ir)	Ich gehe (gehen) Ich fahre (fahren)
I do	Je fais (faire)	Hago (hacer)	Ich tue (tun) Ich mache (machen)
I see	Je vois (voir)	Veo (ver)	Ich sehe (sehen)
I can	Je peux (pouvoir)	Puedo (poder)	Ich kann (können)
I drink	Je bois (boire)	Bebo (beber)	Ich trinke (trinken)
I live	Je vis (vivre)	Vivo (vivir)	Ich lebe (leben)
I come	Je viens (venir)	Vengo (venir)	Ich komme (kommen)
I want	Je veux (vouloir)	Quiero (querer)	Ich will (wollen)
and	et	y	und
but	mais	pero	aber
why	pourquoi	por qué	warum
because	parce que	porque	weil
when	quand	cuándo	wann

already	déjà	ya	schon, bereits
always	toujours	siempre	immer
here	ici	aquí	hier

QUESTIONS AND ANSWERS

1. Answer these questions about the set A whose elements are 1, 2, 3, 4, and 5.
    a) How many elements are there in the Cartesian product of A with itself?
    b) How many subsets does A have?
    c) Is 1 a subset of A?
ANSWER: a) 25 b) 2^5 or 32 c) No, 1 is an element of A.

2. What are the center and radius of the circle whose equation is $x^2 + y^2 - 2x + 4y + 1 = 0$?
ANSWER: The center is $(1, -2)$/The radius is 2.

3. What is the coefficient of the x^2 term in the product of $2x^2 + 3x - 2$ and $3x^2 - 5x + 1$?
ANSWER: -19.

4. What is the remainder when $x^2 - 3x - 4$ is divided into x^4?
ANSWER: $51x + 52$.

5. What is the area inside $(x + 1)^2 + (y - 3)^2 = 16$ that is outside $x^2 + (y - 2)^2 = 1$?
ANSWER: 15π.

6. Which of the following are divisible by 2?
    a) 168,764   b) 43,105   c) 867,000   d) 178,401
ANSWER: a and c.

7. "Twin primes" is the name given to consecutive prime numbers that differ by 2. For example, 3 and 5 are twin primes as are 5 and 7. Find 2 other sets of twin primes which are less than 20.
ANSWER: 11 and 13; 17 and 19.

8. In Statistics, the Pearson r correlation coefficient is used for quantitative expression of the extent to which 2 variables are related.
    a) Between what 2 values does the Pearson r vary?
    b) What value indicates the absence of a relationship?
ANSWER: a) between $+1$ and -1 b) 0.

9. What is:
    a) the simplified form of the square root of 72?
    b) the area of a right triangle with legs of length 4 and 5?
    c) the absolute value of $3 + 2i$?
    d) the volume of a carton whose dimensions are 2 feet by 3 feet by 4 feet?
    e) the x-intercept of the line $y - 2 = 0$?
    f) longer: one yard, one meter, or 40 inches?
    g) half of the sum of $\frac{1}{2}$ and $\frac{1}{4}$?
    h) the thousandths digit of the decimal representation of the fraction four-sevenths?
    i) the sum of the first twelve positive integers?
**ANSWER: a) 6 square root of 2 $(6\sqrt{2})$ b) 10 c) square root of 13 $(\sqrt{13})$
          d) 24 cubic feet e) none f) 40 inches g) 3/8 h) one i) 78.**

10. What are the 5 distinct solutions of the equation x to the fifth power minus x equals zero?
ANSWER: $0, 1, -1, i, -i$.

11. Identify each of the following by its description or by its equation.
    a) A series of numbers possibly formulated from the question: "How many pairs of rabbits can be produced from a single pair in one year if each pair produces a new pair each month and every pair reproduces every month and no rabbit dies?"
    b) $x^2 y = a^2(a - y)$
    c) $(\cos x + i \sin x)^n = \cos nx + i \sin nx$
    d) The expansion of $(a + b)^n$
    e) $(x^2 + y^2)^2 = 2a^2(x^2 - y^2)$
**ANSWER: a) Fibonacci Series b) Witch of Agnesi c) Demoivre's Theorem
          d) Binomial Theorem e) Lemniscate of Bernoulli.**

12. What property of the real numbers is exhibited in each of the following mathematical statements?

a) $a + (b + c) = (b + c) + a$

b) $a \times (b + c) = (b + c) \times a$

c) $a \times [b + (c + d)] = a \times [(b + c) + d]$

d) $a \times [b + (c + d)] = a \times b + a \times (c + d)$

e) $a \times [b \times (c + d)] = [a \times b] \times (c + d)$

ANSWER: a) commutative property of addition b) commutative property of multiplication c) associative property of addition d) distributive property e) associative property of multiplication.

13. If $\frac{(x^2 \cdot y^{-3} \cdot z^5)^3}{(x^4 \cdot y^{-2} \cdot z^{-11})^2}$ is expressed in the form $x^m \cdot y^n \cdot z^k$, the $m + n + k$ is what integer?

ANSWER: 30.

14. $|7 - \sqrt{50}|$ equals which of the following?

a) $7 - \sqrt{50}$ b) $7 + \sqrt{50}$ c) $\sqrt{50} - 7$

ANSWER: $\sqrt{50} - 7$.

15. Tell whether each of the following is true or false.

a) $(x^{-1} + y^{-1})^{-1} = x + y$

b) $x^6 \cdot x^5 = x^{30}$

c) $\sqrt{x^2} = x$

d) $-4^{-2} = -1/16$

e) $(x^{-2})^{-3} = x^6$

ANSWER: a) false b) false c) false d) true e) true.

16. What is the quotient when $x^3 + 27$ is divided by $x + 3$?

ANSWER: $x^2 - 3x + 9$.

17. Tell whether each of the following is true or false.

a) $\sqrt{x^2} = x$ for all real numbers x

b) $x^0 = 1$ for all real numbers x

c) $\frac{0}{x} = 0$ for all real numbers x

ANSWER: a) false b) false c) false(because 0 divided by 0 is undeterminable).

18. An urn contains 3 blue chips, 2 red chips, and 1 white chip.

a) If one chip is drawn from the urn, what is the probability that it is blue or white?

b) If 2 chips are drawn without replacement from the urn, what is the probability that the first one is red and the second one is blue?

ANSWER: a) 4/6 or 2/3   b) 6/30 or 1/5.

19. For each of the following, determine which quantity is smaller.

a) a meter or a yard

b) a mile or a kilometer

c) a liter or a quart

d) a gram or an ounce

ANSWER: a) yard   b) kilometer   c) quart   d) gram.

20. What is the next number in each of these sequences?

a) 1, ½, ¼, 1/8, 1/16, ___?___

b) 1, 4, 7, 10, 13, ___?___

c) 1, 2, 3, 5, 8, 13, ___?___

ANSWER: a) 1/32   b) 16   c) 21.

21. How many real numbers satisfy the equations?

a) $x = \sqrt{x}$

b) $x = x - 3$

c) $x = |x|$

d) $x = $ sgn x (reads "x equals signum x")

ANSWER: a) two   b) none   c) infinitely many   d) three.

22. In each of the following, which is larger?

a) sine of $\pi/2$ or sine or $4\pi/9$

b) the number of edges of a tetrahedron or the number of edges of a cube

c) the number of real roots to the equation $x^4 + 2x^2 + 1 = 0$ or the number of real roots to the equation $x^2 - 4 = 0$

ANSWER: a) sine of $\pi/2$ b) edges of a cube   c) # of real roots to the equation $x^2 - 4 = 0$.

23. What is a Barney with a 100 zeroes after it?

ANSWER: A Barney Google.

24. A rectangular box measures 2 ft. by 3 ft. by 4 ft.

a) What is the volume?

b) What is the length of a diagonal of this box?

c) What is its total surface area?

ANSWER: a) 24 cubic ft.   b) $\sqrt{29}$ ft.   c) 52 sq. ft.

25. For all real numbers a and b, indicate whether each of the following is true or false.

a) $|a| = a$

c) $|a+b| \leq |a| + |b|$

b) $|a-b| = |a| - |b|$

ANSWER: a) false   b) false   c) true.

26. If A is the set whose elements are 1, 3, 5, and 7 and B is the set whose elements are 4, 6, and 8, name
    a) the elements of $A \cup B$ (read A union B)
    b) the elements of $A \cap B$ (read A intersect B)
    c) the elements of $A - B$

ANSWER: a) 1, 3, 4, 5, 6, 7, and 8   b) There are no elements   c) 1, 3, 5 and 7.

27. Concerning the line whose equation is $2x - 3y = 15$, what is
    a) the slope?   c) the X-intercept?
    b) the Y-intercept?

ANSWER: a) 2/3   b) (0, −5)   c) (7.5, 0).

28. Concerning the function $f(x) = 2\sin 3x$, what is
    a) the amplitude of f?   c) the minimum value of this function?
    b) the period of f?

ANSWER: a) 2   b) $\frac{2\pi}{3}$ c) −2.

29. Which of the following are functions?
    a) $y = |x^2 + 1|$ c) $x^2 + y^2 = 4$
    b) $y = \sqrt{4 - x^2}$

ANSWER: a) function   b) function   c) not a function.

30. Which of the following are rational and which are irrational?
    a) The square root of four-ninths   c) The fifth root of 64
    b) The cube root of −8   d) Pi

ANSWER: a) rational   b) rational   c) irrational   d) irrational.

31. Indicate how many times the graph of these parabolas intersects the x-axis
    a) $f(x) = x^2 - 6x + 11$ c) $f(x) = x^2 + 8x + 16$
    b) $f(x) = -3x^2 + 6x - 2$

ANSWER: a) none   b) twice   c) once.

32. Simplify each of the following completely.
    a) i^{58} b) $\sqrt{108}$ c) $\sqrt[5]{96}$

ANSWER: a) −1   b) $6\sqrt{3}$ c) $2\sqrt[5]{3}$

33. Find all the integral factors of the following polynomials.
    a) $16x^4 - y^4$ b) $x^3 - y^3$ c) $2x^2y - 12xy + 18y$

ANSWER: a) $(4x^2 + y^2)(2x+y)(2x-y)$ b) $(x-y)(x^2+xy+y^2)$ c) $2y(x-3)^2$.

34. a) How many distinct ways are there to arrange 5 people in a line?
    b) How many distinct ways are there to arrange 5 people around a circular table?

ANSWER: a) 120   b) 24.

35. If $\sin x = 4/5$ and $0 \leq x \leq \frac{\pi}{2}$, find:
    a) $\cos x$ b) $\tan x$ c) $\csc x$

ANSWER: a) 3/5   b) 4/3   c) 5/4

36. What is the measure of each angle in the following figures?
    a) equilateral triangle   c) regular pentagon
    b) rectangle   d) regular octagon

ANSWER: a) 60°   b) 90°   c) 108°   d) 135°

37. a) What is the arithmetic mean of 7 and 11?
    b) What is the geometric mean of 7 and 11?

ANSWER: a) 9   b) $\sqrt{77}$

38. Name the mathematician principally responsible for each of the following areas of mathematics.
    a) topology   c) analytic geometry
    b) calculus   d) probability

ANSWER: a) Leonard Euler   c) René Descartes
**   b) Sir Isaac Newton or Gottfried Leibniz   d) Blaise Pascal**

(Anecdote: In a "Funky Winkerbean" comic strip about Philosophy II,

it was pointed out that of the great philosophers, Descartes, Plato, Nietzsche, Sartre, and Dehorst, Dehorst is thought to be the greatest, although many people put Descartes before Dehorst.)

39. Consider the ellipse $\frac{x^2}{9} + \frac{y^2}{25} = 1$.
    a) What are the x-intercepts?
    b) What are the y-intercepts?
    c) What are the coordinates of the foci?
ANSWER: a) (3,0), (−3, 0)   b) (0,5), (0, −5)   c) (0, 4), (0, −4)

40. For the complex number 3−4i, find
    a) the conjugate   c) the multiplicative inverse expressed in a+bi form
    b) the additive inverse
ANSWER: a) 3+4i   b) −3+4i   c) 3/25 + (4/25)i

41. Identify as specifically as possible, the following.
    a) A quadrilateral with 4 congruent sides
    b) A quadrilateral with diagonals that bisect each other
    c) A parallelogram with perpendicular diagonals
ANSWER: a) rhombus   b) parallelogram   c) rhombus.

42. Identify the domain of each of the following functions.
    a) $f(x) = \sqrt{9 - x^2}$ c) $h(x) = \frac{1}{x^2 - 3x - 18}$
    b) $g(x) = \frac{1}{\sqrt{x}}$
**ANSWER: a) all real numbers greater than or equal to −3 and less than or equal to 3
        b) all real numbers greater than 0   c) all real numbers except 6 and −3.**

43. Find the numerical value for each of the following:
    a) Tan $\pi/2$ c) csc $\pi/4$
    b) sec π d) ctn $\pi/6$
ANSWER: a) undefined   b) −1   c) $\sqrt{2}$ d) $\sqrt{3}$

44. If the vertex angle of an isosceles triangle measures 120° and each leg measures 6 cm, find each of the following.
    a) The measure of each base angle
    b) The height of the isosceles triangle
    c) The length of the base of the isosceles triangle
ANSWER: a) 30° each   b) 3 cm   c) 6 $\sqrt{3}$ cm.

45. Which is larger?
    a) 4 inches or 10 centimeters.   b) 2 kilograms or 5 pounds.
ANSWER: a) 4 inches   b) 5 pounds.

46. Identify the graph of each of the following.
    a) $2x^2 - 6y^2 = 24$ c) $x^2 + 6y^2 = 4$
    b) $3x^2 + 3y^2 = 8$ d) $x^2 + 3x + 2y^2 = 10$
ANSWER: a) hyperbola   b) circle   c) ellipse   d) ellipse.

47. For each of the following functions, find f(0).
    a) $f(x) = 2x + 3$ b) $f(x) = \sin x$ c) $f(x) = 2^x$
ANSWER: a) 3   b) 0   c) 1.

48. Find the mean, mode, and median of the following set of statistics.
    5, 9, 4, 2, 3, 9, 7, 4
ANSWER: 5 3/8; 4 and 9; 4½.

49. In mathematics, what do the numbers 32-32-32 represent?
ANSWER: A plane (plain) figure.

50. Solve each of the following for x.
    a) $4^x = 2$ b) $\log_x 81 = 4$ c) $|2x + 3| = 4$
ANSWER: a) ½   b) 3   c) ½ and −7/2.

51. For 0 ≤ x < 360, find the angles x (measured in degrees) for which
    a) Sin x = 0   b) Cos x = 0
ANSWER: a) 0°; 180°   b) 90°; 270°.

52. Express each of the following in terms of at most one radical in simplest form.
   a) $\sqrt{2} \cdot \sqrt[3]{2}$ b) $\sqrt[4]{2} \cdot \sqrt[6]{x}$ c) $\sqrt[3]{x} \sqrt{x}$
   ANSWER: a) $\sqrt[6]{32}$ b) $\sqrt[12]{8x^2}$ c) $\sqrt{x}$.

53. Use the fundamental theorem of arithmetic to write the following as a product.
   a) 12   b) 10   c) 32
   ANSWER: a) $3 \times 2 \times 2$ ($2 \times 3 \times 2$ or $2 \times 2 \times 3$ are also acceptable)
   **   b) 5×2 (2×5 is also acceptable)   c) $2 \times 2 \times 2 \times 2 \times 2$.**

54. What comes next?
   a) 1, 3, 5, 7, ?   c) 1, 2, 3, 4, 5, 666, ?
   b) 17, 14, 11, 8, ?   d) 1, 9, 25, 49, ?
   ANSWER: a) 9   b) 5   c) just kidding   d) 81.

55. Tell whether the following series are convergent or divergent.
   a) $1 + 2^2 + 3^2 + 4^2 + \ldots$
   b) $1/2^2 + 1/4^2 + 1/6^2 + 1/8^2 + \ldots$
   c) $1 + \frac{\sqrt{2}}{2} + \frac{\sqrt{3}}{3} + \frac{\sqrt{4}}{4} + \ldots$
   ANSWER: a) divergent b) convergent c) divergent.

56. Supply the missing values.
   a) $e^{i\pi} + 1 = ?$ d) $\int e^x \, dx = ?$ (read the integral of e to the
   b) $3^2 + 4^2 = 5$ to what power?   x with respect to x)
   c) $\sin^2 x + \cos^2 x = ?$
   ANSWER: a) 0   b) 2   c) 1   d) $e^x + c$.

57. Find the greatest common divisor of:
   a) 77 and 91   b) 21 and 54   c) 29 and 47
   ANSWER: a) 7   b) 3   c) 1.

58. Answer true or false to the following.
   a) The diagonals of an isosceles trapezoid bisect each other.
   b) It is possible to draw a triangle whose sides have lengths 18, 9, and 9.
   c) It is possible for a trapezoid to have exactly two right angles.
   ANSWER: a) false   b) false   c) true.

59. The area of one face of a cube is 16 square centimeters.
   a) What is the length of the edge of the cube?
   b) What is the total surface area of the cube?
   c) What is the volume of the cube?
   ANSWER: a) 4 cm.   b) 96 square centimeters   c) 64 cubic centimeters.

60. What is the name given to the following?
   a) A 3-sided polygon   d) A 9-sided polygon (give an answer other
   b) An 11-sided polygon   than nonagon)
   c) A 15-sided polygon
   ANSWER: a) triangle   b) undecagon   c) pentadecagon   d) enneagon.

61. Answer true or false to the following.
   a) Two concentric circles can be internally tangent.
   b) Two lines that are tangent to the same circle must intersect.
   c) Many circles can be tangent to a given line at a given point on the line.
   d) A tangent to a circle is perpendicular to the radius drawn to the point of tangency.
   ANSWER: a) false   b) false   c) true   d) true.

62. Given that x is negative and y is positive, state whether each of the following is
   always, sometimes, or *never* true.
   a) xy is positive   b) $x - y$ is negative   c) $-x - y$ is negative
   ANSWER: a) never   b) always   c) sometimes.

63. Name the following.
   a) The mathematical term for a straight line which is approached but never
      reached by an infinite branch of a curve.
   b) A four-sided plane figure exactly two of whose sides are parallel.
   c) In a right triangle the side opposite the right angle.
   ANSWER: a) asymptote   b) trapezoid   c) hypotenuse.

64. What integer does each of the following equal?
    a) the square root of 256   b) the cube root of 343   c) the fifth root of minus 32
ANSWER: a) 16   b) 7   c) −2 (minus 2 or negative 2).

65. Name the following branches of mathematics.
    a) The study of points, lines, planes and their relationships.
    b) The study of the properties of geometric figures that remain unchanged even when such figures are distorted.
    c) The study of the most general way to deal with properties and relations of numbers.
ANSWER: a) geometry   b) topology   c) algebra.

66. Find these limits:
    a) $\lim_{x \to 0} (x^3 + 5x)$

    b) $\lim_{x \to \infty} \dfrac{1}{x}$

    c) $\lim_{x \to \pi} (x \cdot \cos x)$

    d) $\lim_{x \to 0} \dfrac{\sin x}{x}$
ANSWER: a) 0   b) 0   c) −π d) 1.

67. The Witch of Agnesi, the Folium of Descartes, and the Rhind Papyrus are familiar to many mathematics students. Two of them are curves and one is a mathematical document.
    a) Name the curves.   b) Name the mathematical document.
ANSWER: a) Witch of Agnesi and the Folium of Descartes   b) Rhind Papyrus.

68. Sinh x, cosh x, tanh x, coth x, sech x, and csch x are familiar functions in mathematics.
    a) What is the collective name given to these functions?
    b) $Y = a \cdot \cosh\frac{x}{a}$ is the general equation for what curve?
ANSWER: a) hyperbolic   b) catenary.

69. Name the following.
    a) The oldest mathematical document   b) The value of x which maximizes $\sqrt[x]{x}$
ANSWER: a) Rhind Papyrus   b) e.

70. What is:
    a) the number that is the sin $\pi/3$?
    b) the probability of rolling a sum of 5 with a pair of dice?
    c) the measure of each exterior angle of an equilateral triangle?
    d) the sum of the measures of the interior angles of a pentagon?
    e) the number of distinct 2-man committees that can be formed with 6 people to choose from?
    f) the square root of a googol, or 10^{100}?
    g) the decimal form of the trinary number 2102?
ANSWER: a) $\sqrt{3}/2$ b) 1 in 9   c) 120°   d) 540 degrees   e) 15   f) 10^{50} g) 65.

71. Within the set of real numbers, what is the domain of these functions?
    a) $y = 7x - 4$ b) $y = 1/x$ c) $y = \sqrt{x}$ d) $y = \sqrt{-x}$
ANSWER: a) all real numbers   b) all real numbers except 0   c) all real numbers greater than or equal to 0   d) all real numbers less than or equal to 0.

72. Write the output for this program.
```
10 let A = 4                 30 Print A − B
20 let B = 3 ∗ A             40 End
```
ANSWER: −8.

73. In computer science, an algorithm is a list of step-by-step instructions by which the computer carries out a process.
    a) What is the term for diagrams of algorithms?
    b) What is the term for correcting faulty algorithms?
ANSWER: a) flow charts   b) debugging.

74. Give the output of this program.
```
10 Let M = 2                 40 Next N
20 For N = M to 20 Step 3    50 End
30 Print N
```
ANSWER: 2, 5, 8, 11, 14, 17, 20.

75. Which two of these functions are symmetric with respect to the origin?
    a) $y = x^2 - 7$ b) $y = -7x$ c) $y = -x^3$

ANSWER: b and c.

76. Centi-, as in centimeter, is a prefix meaning one-hundredth. What do the following prefixes mean?
    a) deci-   b) deka-   c) hemi-   d) pico-
ANSWER: a) one-tenth b) ten c) half d) one-trillionth.

77. Goldbach's Conjecture states that every even number greater than 4 is the sum of two odd prime numbers. Give the number 12 as the sum of two odd primes.
ANSWER: $12 = 5 + 7$.

78. Name the curve traced by a point
    a) that moves around a fixed point, called the pole, from which the point continually moves away.
    b) on the rim of a wheel rolling along a straight line.
ANSWER: a) spiral b) cycloid.

79. Which of the following numbers is the largest?
    a) 100^4 b) $1,000^3$ c) $10,000^2$
ANSWER: b) 1000^3.

80. Euler's Formula is a formula which relates the numbers of vertices (v), faces (f), and edges (e) of a polyhedra. State Euler's Formula.
ANSWER: Vertices plus faces = edges plus two ($v + f = e + 2$).

81. Tell whether each of the following is true or false.
    a) A line is a subset of a line segment.
    b) The intersection of a segment and a ray must be a segment.
    c) The intersection of two segments may be a segment.
    d) The union of two rays cannot be a point.
ANSWER: a) false b) false c) true d) true.

82. When 2 parallel lines are cut by a transversal,
    a) how many pairs of corresponding angles are formed?
    b) how many angles are formed?
    c) how many pairs of vertical angles are formed?
ANSWER: a) 4 b) 8 c) 4.

83. Complete the analogies.
    a) Square is to cube as circle is to _____?_____.
    b) Perimeter is to polygon as _____?_____ is to circle.
ANSWER: a) sphere b) circumference.

84. Identify each of the following by its description.
    a) The smallest natural number
    b) The largest natural number
    c) The multiplicative inverse of any number except 0
    d) A group of 5
    e) The only even prime number
    f) The first 4 prime numbers
    g) The angle formed when 2 planes meet
    h) The branch of mathematics that uses letters as symbols instead of numbers
    i) The number of hours in a week; the number of minutes in a day
    j) A triangle having unequal sides and angles
    k) The slope of a horizontal line
    l) A plane figure bounded by straight lines
    m) The irrational numbers which are not the roots of ordinary algebraic equations (e.g. π or pi)
    n) A number 1 followed by 100 zeroes; 10^{100}
    o) The number 1 followed by a googol of zeroes
    p) The identity element of multiplication.
ANSWER: a) 1 b) there is none c) the reciprocal of that number d) pentad e) 2 f) 2, 3, 5, and 7 g) dihedral h) algebra i) 168; 1440 j) scalene triangle k) 0 l) polygon m) transcendental numbers n) googol o) googolplex p) 1.

85. Two numbers have a product of 75, a quotient of 3, a difference of 10, and a sum of 20. What are the 2 numbers?
ANSWER: 15 and 5.

86. Within each set of numbers, select the largest.
    a) 3, 3½, π, 3.1   c) $\sqrt{35}$, $\sqrt{37}$, 6¼, 6
    b) 2, 2.01, e, 1.9   d) 1, 1.07, $\sqrt{2}$, 1.4
ANSWER: a) 3½ b) e c) 6¼ d) $\sqrt{2}$.

87. How many centimeters are in these lengths?
    a) 2 meters   b) 3 decimeters   c) 1200 millimeters   d) ½ meter
ANSWER: a) 200 cm b) 30 cm c) 120 cm d) 50 cm.

88. Between what two consecutive integers do the following lie?
    a) $\sqrt{3}$ b) $\sqrt{47}$ c) $-\sqrt{18}$ d) $\sqrt{.6}$
ANSWER: a) 1, 2, b) 6, 7 c) -5, -4 d) 0, 1.

89. Give the value of these Roman numerals.
    a) D b) X c) DC d) MCM e) XCIX f) DCCCLIX g) $\overline{V}$XCV h) $\overline{MDLV}$CMLXXXIX
ANSWER: a) 500 b) 10 c) 600 d) 1900 e) 99 f) 859 g) 5,095 h) 1,555,989.

90. Answer each of the following.
    a) Who is the Founder of the Arithmetic of Infinity?
    b) What symbol represents the cardinal number of all the integers?
    c) Which has more points on it: a line segment 1'' long or a line segment 2'' long?
ANSWER: a) Georg Cantor b) Aleph Null($\aleph_0$) c)Both have the same number of points.

91. Consider the numbers 2 and 4. What is their
    a) harmonic mean?   b) arithmetic mean?   c) geometric mean?
ANSWER: a) 8/3 b) 3 c) $\sqrt{8}$ or $2\sqrt{2}$.

92. William Hamilton is famous for his development of an algebra which provided a systematic treatment of rotations in three-dimensional space.
    a) What is the name given to the quantities with which this algebra deals?
    b) Are operations on these quantities commutative?
ANSWER: a) quarternions b) no.

93. Boole, Briggs, Cardano, and Galois are common names in mathematics. Boole, for example, is remembered for his work in symbolic logic. The other three are remembered for their feats in group theory, solving cubic equations, and base 10 logarithms. Match the mathematician with his specialty.
ANSWER: Briggs for base 10 logarithms/Cardano for solution of cubic equations/ Galois for group theory.

94. Using any digits, give
    a) the largest possible 4-digit number.
    b) the smallest possible 4-digit number.
    c) the smallest possible 4-digit multiple of 11.
ANSWER: a) 9,999 b) 1,000 c) 1,001.

95. Name the plane region bounded
    a) between 2 concentric circles.
    b) by 2 radii of a circle and the arc of the circle.
    c) by an arc of a circle and the chord of that arc.
ANSWER: a) annulus b) sector (of a circle) c) segment (of a circle).

96. Match the figure with the formula for its area.
    a) rectangle   1) A = base $\times$ height
    b) parallelogram   2) A = πr^2
    c) triangle   3) A = ½ base $\times$ height
    d) circle   4) A = ½ πr^2
ANSWER: a) 1 b) 1 c) 3 d) 2 (4 is a distractor).

97. What is being described in the definition ''a surface with only one side, formed by giving a simple twist to a long, narrow, rectangular strip of paper and then pasting its 2 ends together''?
ANSWER: A Möbius strip after the German mathematician August Ferdinand Möbius.

98. What are the first 3 perfect numbers? Explain why the first of these numbers is a perfect number. Name the first 2 amicable numbers.
ANSWER: 6, 28, and 496 (the next 4 perfect numbers are 8128, 130816, 2096128, and 33550336)/The sum of its positive divisors excluding itself equals the

number itself $(1 + 2 + 3 = 6)/220$ and 284.

99. While a member of the House of Representatives, this later President of the U.S. invented an original proof in 1876 for the Pythagorean Theorem. Who was he?
ANSWER: James A. Garfield.

100. Find each of the following products.
   a) 20×36 b) $(-3)^3$ c) $(-2)^2$ d) -2^2
ANSWER: a) 720   b) -27 c) 4   d) -4.

101. Answer each of the following questions.
   a) Girolamo Saccheri, Nicholas Lobachevsky, and Bernhard Riemann all contributed to the development of what branch of geometry?
   b) In Riemann's geometry, through a point not on a line, how many parallels are there to the given line?
   c) In Lobachevskian geometry, what is the sum of the measures of the angles of a triangle?
ANSWER: a) non-Euclidean   b) none   c) less than 180°.

102. Tell whether each of the following statements is *always, sometimes,* or *never* true.
   a) The sum of 2 integers is an integer.
   b) The difference of 2 irrational numbers is an irrational number.
   c) The square root of a real number is a real number.
   d) The sum of a rational number and an irrational number is a rational number.
ANSWER: a) always   b) sometimes   c) sometimes   d) never.

103. If $a = -2$ and $b = -3$, find the value of:
   a) $a^2 + b^2$ b) $-2ab^2$ c) $\frac{a^2 + b}{b}$
ANSWER: a) 13   b) 36   c) $-1/3$.

104. Each of the following four mathematicians is remembered for first using certain algebraic symbols. The mathematicians are Diophantus, Thomas Harriot, Robert Recorde, and Gottfried Leibniz. The symbols are as follows: greater than (>), integral symbol, minus sign, and the equal sign. Match the mathematician with the symbol he first used.
ANSWER: Diophantus, the minus symbol; Harriot, greater than; Recorde, the equal sign; and Leibniz (Leibnitz), the integral symbol.

105. Translate the following into an algebraic expression.
   a) The product of 7 and N.
   b) The number of cents in N nickels.
   c) A CB radio originally cost d dollars. If the price is reduced by 1/3, represent the new price.
ANSWER: a) 7n   b) 5n   c) $d - \frac{1}{3}d$ or $\frac{2}{3}d$.

106. The formula for the area of a rectangle is $A = l \times w$. If the length is doubled and the width is tripled, then the area of the new rectangle is 6 times the area of the original rectangle. How does the area change if the length is multiplied by 4 and the width is divided by 8?
ANSWER: The original area is multiplied by one-half.

107. If $\tan x = 4/3$, sin 2x equals which of the following?
   a) 8/5   b) 24/25   c) 4/5   d) 12/25
ANSWER: 24/25.

108. The slope of the perpendicular bisector of the line segment joining (2,1) and (6,9) is:
   a) 2   b) -2 c) ½   d) $-½$
ANSWER: d) $-½$.

109. What is the equation of the tangent line to the curve $y = x^2 - 3x$ at the point $(1, -2)$?
   a) $y = x - 1$ b) $y = -x - 1$ c) $y = x + 1$ d) $y = -x + 1$
ANSWER: b) $y = -x - 1$.

110. The edges of a rectangular parallelepiped are 6, 8, & 10. Find the length of a diagonal.
   a) 24   b) $10\sqrt{3}$ c) $10\sqrt{2}$ d) 12
ANSWER: c) $10\sqrt{2}$.

111. The roots of the equation $x^2 - 2x - 6 = 0$ are:

a) complex   b) real and unequal   c) equal   d) rational and unequal.
ANSWER: b) real and unequal.

112. Find the value printed by the following program.

```
10 Let A = 1                    50 Let B = A/B
20 Let B = 2                    60 Next I
30 For I = 1 to 2               70 Print B
40 Let A = B*A                  80 End
Is it 2, 1, ½, or 0?
```

ANSWER: a) 2.

113. V varies directly as the square of s. If s = 2, V = 12, find the value of V when s = 4.
   a) 24   b) 48   c) 14   d) 12.
ANSWER: b) 48.

114. Factor the sum of $x - y$ and $x^2 - y^2$.
   a) $x^2 + x - y^2 - y$ c) $(x - y)(x + 1)(y + 1)$
   b) $x(x + 1) - y(y + 1)$ d) $(x + y + 1)(x - y)$
ANSWER: d.

115. If $4^x = 2^5$, then x is equal to
   a) 2   b) 10   c) 5/2   d) 2.4
ANSWER: c) 5/2.

116. If $\frac{x}{¼} = 25$, then
   a) x = 100   b) 4x = 100   c) .25 x = 25   d) x = 6.25
ANSWER: d) x = 6.25.

117. The four scores on a test were 99, 95, 95, and 87. Find the
   a) mode.   b) mean.   c) median.   d) range.
ANSWER: a) 95   b) 94   c) 95   d) 12.

118. Which of the following sets are closed under the operation of addition?
   a) $\{0, 1\}$ b) {integers}   c) {rational nos.}   d) {irrational nos.}
ANSWER: b) closed under + and c) closed under +.

119. Name the 5 solids which are often called the Platonic solids. Why are these special?
**ANSWER: Regular tetrahedron, regular hexahedron (cube), regular octahedron, regular
       dodecahedron, and regular icosahedron/They are the only regular polyhedra.**

120. Read the following and then answer the question.
   a) All Cyclopses have only one eye.
   b) People cannot get a driver's license unless they have depth perception.
   c) A one-eyed creature does not have depth perception.
   d) Clyde is a Cyclops.
   Is Clyde eligible to receive a driver's license?
ANSWER: No.

121. Simplify each of the following.
   a) $8i(-3i)$ b) $(\sqrt{-4})(\sqrt{-9})$ c) $i^3(i^4 + i)$ d) $6/i$
ANSWER: a) 24   b) −6   c) 1 − i (or 1 + (−i) or −i + 1)   d) −6i.

122. Which of the following quantities could be used to rationalize the denomina-
tion of the fraction $\frac{2}{1 - \sqrt[3]{2}}$?

   a) $1 + \sqrt[3]{2}$ c) $1 + \sqrt[3]{2} + \sqrt[3]{4}$

   b) $1 + \sqrt[3]{4}$ d) $1 - \sqrt[3]{2} + \sqrt[3]{4}$

ANSWER: c) $1 + \sqrt[3]{2} + \sqrt[3]{4}$

123. Which of the following could be used as the lengths of the sides of a triangle if $a > b > 0$?
   a) a, b, a + b   b) a, b, a, −b   c) a, b, a + ½b   d) a, b, a − ½b
ANSWER: a) no   b) no   c) yes   d) yes.

124. Name the point which represents the intersection of
   a) the 3 medians of a triangle.
   b) the 3 altitudes of a triangle.
   c) the 3 angle bisectors of a triangle.

ANSWER: a) centroid   b) orthocenter   c) incenter.

125. Which of the following are acceptable ways to prove two triangles congruent?
a)side, side, side   b)angle, angle, angle   c)side, side, angle   d)angle, angle, side
ANSWER: a) yes   b) no   c) no   d) yes.

126. What is the measure of one interior angle of a rectangular convex
a) quadrilateral?   b) pentagon?
ANSWER: a) 90°   b) 108°

127. What name is given to the two angles described in each of the following?
a) Two angles whose measures have a sum of $90°$
b) Angles whose sides form two pairs of opposite rays
c) Two angles whose measures have a sum of $180°$
d) Two angles in the same plane that have a common vertex and a common side but have no interior points in common
**ANSWER: a) complementary angles   b) vertical angles   c) supplementary angles
d) adjacent angles.**

128. If $\sin x = 3/5$ and $\pi/2 < x < \pi$, find the value of each of the following.
a) $\cos x$ b) $\csc x$ c) $\sec x$ d) $\tan x$
ANSWER: $-4/5$ b) 5/3   c) $-5/4$ d) $-3/4$.

129. Evaluate each of the following.
a) $\sin \pi/6$ b) $\cos \frac{5\pi}{4}$ c) $\tan \frac{4\pi}{3}$ d) $\sec 4\pi$
ANSWER: a) ½   b) $-\frac{\sqrt{2}}{2}$ c) $\sqrt{3}$ d) 1.

130. How many times will the graph of $y = \sin 8x$ intersect the x-axis from 0 to 2π inclusive?
ANSWER: 17.

131. Evaluate each of the following.
a) $\sin (\text{Arccos}\frac{\sqrt{3}}{2})$ c) $\cos (\text{Arcsin} (-\frac{\sqrt{2}}{2})$

b) $\tan (\text{Arctan} 1)$ d) $\sec (\text{Arccos} ½)$
ANSWER: a) ½   b) 1   c)$\frac{\sqrt{2}}{2}$ d) 2.

132. Find the remainder obtained when the polynomial $x^5 - 32$ is divided by
a) $x - 1$ b) $x + 1$ c) $x + 2$ d) $x - 2$
ANSWER: a) -31 b) -33 c) -64 d) 0.

133. Find the value of n if
a) the coefficients in the expansion of $(2a+6)^n$ are 8, 12, 6, 1 respectively.
b) the first two coefficients of $(x+y)^n$ are 1 and 4.
c) the last term in the expanson of $(a + 2b^2)^n$ is $32b^{10}$.
d) the sum of the coefficients in the expansion of $(x + y)^n$ is 128.
ANSWER: a) 3   b) 4   c) 5   d) 7.

134. Using Descartes' Rule of Signs, determine the possible numbers of positive and negative real roots for the following equation.
$2x^3 - 2x^2 + x + 8 = 0$
**ANSWER: Either no positive real roots or two positive real roots. Exactly one negative
real root.**

135. If $f(x) = x^2$, then $f'(x)$, $\lim\limits_{\triangle x \to 0} \frac{\triangle y}{\triangle x}$, and $\lim\limits_{h \to 0} \frac{f(x + h) - f(x)}{h}$ all represent what function?
ANSWER: $\dot{y} = 2x$ or $f'(x) = 2x$, the derivative of f(x).

136. Write each of the following complex numbers in polar form.
a) $4 + 0i$ b) $0 - 3i$ c) $½ + (\frac{\sqrt{3}}{2})i$ d) $-2\sqrt{2} - 2\sqrt{2}\,i$
ANSWER: a) 4 cis 0   b) 3 cis $\frac{3\pi}{2}$ c) 1 cis $\frac{\pi}{3}$ d) 4 cis $\frac{5\pi}{4}$.

137. Name the conic section associated with each of the following pairs of terms.
a) focus, directrix   c) center, radius
b) transverse axis, asymptotes   d) vertices, major axis
ANSWER: a) parabola   b) hyperbola   c) circle   d) ellipse.

138. Label each of the following as true or false.

a) $|a| \cdot |b| = |ab|$ b) $\dfrac{|a|}{|b|} = \left|\dfrac{a}{b}\right|$

ANSWER: a) true   b) true.

139. Which of the following operations are commutative?

a) ordinary addition   d) $*$ such that $a * b = (1 + a) + b$
b) ordinary subtraction   e) $\odot$ such that $a \odot b = a + 2b$
c) ordinary multiplication   f) ordinary division

ANSWER: a, c, and d.

140. For what real values of x is each of the following expressions undefined?

a) $\dfrac{1}{x + 2}$ c) $\dfrac{x + 2}{x^4 + 1}$

b) $\dfrac{x}{x^2 - 9}$ d) $\dfrac{x - 5}{x^2 - 25}$

ANSWER: a) -2 b) ± 3 c) none, defined for all of the real numbers   d) ± 5.

141. What name is given to each of the following properties?

a) If $a = b$ and $b = c$, then $a = c$.
b) If $a, b \in R$, then $a = b$, $a > b$, or $a < b$.
c) If $a \in R$, there exists a real number $-a$, such that $a + (-a) = 0$.
d) Any real number is equal to itself.

ANSWER: a) Transitive Property of Equality   b) The Trichotomy Axiom or Comparison Property   c) Additive Inverse Property   d) Reflexive Property of Equality.

142. What word with the word "math" in it but not directly related to mathematics is defined as "a person of great and diversified learning"?

ANSWER: Polymath.

143. Which of the following are equivalence relations?

a) less than   b) equal to   c) parallel to   d) congruent to

ANSWER: a) no   b) yes   c) no   d) yes.

144. If n represents a number, name an expression to represent each of the following.

a) 3 more than the number   c) 2 less than 5 times the number
b) 5 less than the number   d) 6 more than one-half the number

ANSWER: a) $n + 3$ b) $n - 5$ c) $5n - 2$ d) $(½)n + 6$.

145. What kind of variation exists between x and y in each of the following?

a) $y = 6x$ b) $2y/3x = 1$ c) $xy = 1200$ d) $8/y = 4x$

ANSWER: a) directly proportional   b) directly proportional   c) inversely proportional   d) inversely proportional.

146. Find the x and y intercepts for the graph of each of the following.

a) $-2x + 3y = 12$ c) $x^2 = 3y^2 + 36$
b) $x^2 + y^2 = 16$ d) $x/2 + y/4 = 1$

ANSWER: a) x(-6, 0), y(0, 4)   b) x(± 4, 0), y(± 0, 4)   c) x(± 6, 0), y none   d) x(2, 0), y(0, 4).

147. Evaluate the following numerical expression.

$\{3\,[4\,(9 + 6)^2 - 8] + 5^3\}$ all raised to the zero power is what?

ANSWER: 1.

148. Completely factor each of the following over the integers.

a) $4x + 28$ c) $(x + y)^2 - 7(x + y) + 10$
b) $9x^2 - 16y^2$ d) $ax - ay - bx + by$

ANSWER: a) $4(x + 7)$ b) $(3x - 4y)(3x + 4y)$ c) $(x+y-5)(x+y-2)$ d) $(a - b)(x - y)$ (the order of the factors is not significant).

149. What is the determinant of each of the following matrices?

a) $\begin{vmatrix} 3 & 4 \\ 7 & 9 \end{vmatrix}$ b) $\begin{vmatrix} 1 & 2 & 3 \\ 0 & 0 & 0 \\ 4 & 5 & 6 \end{vmatrix}$ c) $\begin{vmatrix} 8 & -2 \\ 6 & 4 \end{vmatrix}$ d) $\begin{vmatrix} 1 & -1 & 2 & 3 \\ 0 & 4 & -2 & 5 \\ 2 & -2 & 4 & 6 \\ -1 & 1 & 1 & -1 \end{vmatrix}$

ANSWER: a) -1 b) 0   c) 44   d) 0.

150. Which of the following pairs of lines have a single point of intersection?

a) $3x - 2y = -4$
$\quad -6x + 4y = 8$
b) $x + 2y = 10$
$\quad 3x + 4y = 8$

c) $4x - 2y = 3$
$\quad -6x + 3y = 1$
d) $x = 4$
$\quad y = 6$

ANSWER: The lines in b and d have a single point of intersection.

151. Which one of the following lines passes through $(-2, 4)$ and is parallel to $y = 2x + 3$?
a) $y = -\frac{1}{2}x + 5$ b) $y = -\frac{1}{2}x + 4$ c) $y = 2x + 4$ d) $y = 2x + 8$
ANSWER: d) $y = 2x + 8$.

152. Which of the following pairs of statements represents the converse and contra-positive of the statement "If $x < 3$, then $x < 5$"?
a) converse:
   contrapositive:
b) converse:
   contrapositive
c) converse
   contrapositive:
d) converse:
   contrapositive:

If $x < 5$, then $x < 3$
If $x \not< 3$, then $x \not< 5$
If $x < 5$, then $x < 3$
If $x \not< 5$, then $x \not< 3$
If $x \not< 3$, then $x \not< 5$
If $x \not< 5$, then $x \not< 3$
If $x < 5$, then $x < 3$
If $x < 3$, then $x < 5$

ANSWER: b) converse: If $x < 5$, then $x < 3$
contrapositive: If $x \not< 5$, then $x \not< 3$.

153. Label each of the following statements as true or false.
a) All rectangles are squares.
b) Every square is a rectangle.
c) If a parallelogram is a square, then it is a rhombus.
d) Every quadrilateral is a parallelogram.
ANSWER: a) false   b) true   c) true   d) false.

154. Find the maximum area of a rectangle whose perimeter is 36 inches.
ANSWER: 81 square inches.

155. Name the number of sides in each of the following polygons.
a) hexagon   b) octagon   c) dodecagon   d) n - gon
ANSWER: a) 6   b) 8   c) 12   d) n.

156. Describe in words the locus of points
a) that are equidistant from two given points.
b) that are equidistant from two parallel planes.
c) at a given distance k from a fixed point 0.
d) that are 4 inches from a given line l.
ANSWER: a) The plane that bisects the segment joining the two given points and is perpendicular to that segment.
b) A plane parallel to the two given planes and midway between them.
c) A sphere with center 0 and radius k.
d) A cylinder with radius 4 inches.

157. Label each of the following as true or false.
a) $\log_a x + \log_a y - \log_a z = \log_a \frac{xy}{z}$
b) $\log_a x - \log_a y - \log_a z = \log_a \frac{x}{yz}$
c) $4 \log_a x + 3 \log_a y = \log_a 12xy$
d) $-\log_a x - \log_a x^3 = -4 \log_a x$

ANSWER: a) true   b) true   c) false   d) true.

158. Find the value of x in each of the following.
a) $5 = \log_2 x$ b) $\log_{10} 1000 = x$ c) $\log_x 9 = 4$ d) $\log_4 x = -2$
ANSWER: a) 32   b) 3   c) $\sqrt{3}$ d) 1/16

159. If $\log 3 = .4771$ and $\log 2 = .3010$, what is the value of $\log 12$?
ANSWER: 1.0791.

160. If $f(x) = \sqrt{x}$ and $g(x) = x^2$, find the value of each of the following.
a) $f[g(4)]$ b) $g[f(9)]$ c) $f[g(-2)]$ d) $g[f(\frac{1}{4})]$

410   *Campbell's High School/College Quiz Book*

ANSWER: a) 4 b) 9 c) 2 d) ¼.

161. Find the missing terms in the following arithmetic progressions.
   a) 3, ___?___ , 7, ___?___   c) ___?___ , x, ___?___ , −x
   b) 2, ___?___ , ___?___ , 17   d) ___?___ , x, 4x, ___?___

ANSWER: a) 5, 9 b) 7, 12 c) 2x, 0 d) −2x, 7x.

162. Express each of the following repeating decimals as the ratio of two integers.
   a) .$\overline{4}$ b) .$\overline{26}$ c) .$\overline{07}$ d) .$\overline{121}$

ANSWER: a) 4/9 b) 26/99 c) 7/90 d) 121/999.

163. Give the meaning of each of the following mathematical symbols.
   a) ∈   b) ∅   c) ∩   d) ∨   e) ∪

ANSWER: a) is an element of (is contained in, is a member of) b) empty or null set c) intersection d) or e) union.

164. How many 3-digit even numbers less than 400 can be formed if no digit repeats? Are there 216, 108, 72, or 112?

ANSWER: 112.

165. How many 3-digit numbers less than 400 can be formed if no digit repeats? Are there 216, 300, 288, or 168?

ANSWER: 216.

166. If the number of elements in the union of sets A and B is 12, the number in set A is 7 and the number in set B is 10, how many elements are in the intersection of sets A and B?

ANSWER: 5.

167. Identify the 3 trigonometric functions in a right triangle by using *Some officers have curly auburn hair to offer attraction.* Then give the other 3 trigonometric functions in a right triangle.

ANSWER: Sine = opposite side/hypotenuse; cosine = adjacent side/hypotenuse; and tangent = opposite side/adjacent side . . . / . . . Cotangent = adjacent side/opposite side; secant = hypotenuse/adjacent side; and cosecant = hypotenuse/opposite side.

168. Find the range of each of the following.
   a) $y = \sqrt{x^2}$ b) $y = -\sqrt{x^2}$ c) $x^2 + y^2 = 9$ d) $x^2 - y^2 = 9$

ANSWER: a) $y \geq 0$ (all non-negative numbers) b) $y \leq 0$ (all non-positive numbers) c) $-3 \leq y \leq 3$ (all real numbers greater than or equal to −3 and less than or equal to 3) d) all real numbers.

169. Find the maximum value of $f(x) = -x^2 - 2x + 4$.

ANSWER: 5.

170. Name the geometric figure defined by each of the following.
   a) $x^2 + 2y^2 = 16$ b) $y^2 - x^2 = 4$ c) $y^2 = 25 - x^2$ d) $x^2 + y^2 = 0$

ANSWER: a) ellipse b) hyperbola c) circle d) point.

171. In which of the following are the three points collinear?
   a) x (0,0) y (2,4) z(4,8)   c) A (−1,1) B(2,−2) c (−3,3)
   b) M (0,0) N(½,½) 0(1,1)   d) P (1,−1) Q (−1,−3) R (4,2)

ANSWER: a, b, c, and d all contain collinear points.

172. Identify the poem and the author from the following lines.
   "O blinding hour, O holy, terrible day,
   When first the shaft into his vision shone
   Of light anatomized! Euclid alone
   Has looked on Beauty bare."

ANSWER: "Euclid Alone Has Looked on Beauty Bare"/ Edna St Vincent Millay.

173. What is the next number in the following series? Identify the sequence by name.
   0, 1, 1, 2, 3, 5, 8, 13, 21, 34, ___?___

ANSWER: 55/The Fibonacci Sequence.

174. Name the 2 branches of statistics.

ANSWER: Descriptive and inferential.

175. Name the "theorem" for which the most incorrect proofs have been published.

ANSWER: Fermat's last "Theorem" (There exist no positive integers a, b, c, and n such that $a^n + b^n = c^n$, where n is greater than 2.

176. What is Skewes's number?

ANSWER: $10^{10^{10^{34}}}$

177. Each of the following algebraic expressions is factorable over the reals by one of these methods: common factor, difference of two squares, trial-and-error, sum of two cubes, difference of two cubes, and grouping. By which method is each algebraic expression factorable?
a) $4x^2 - 27$ d) $ax - 3ay + 2bx - 6by$
b) $x^3 + x$ e) $2x^2 - 7x - 9$
c) $27x^3 + 1$ f) $8 - 125z^3$

ANSWER: a) difference of two squares   b) common factor   c) sum of two cubes   d) grouping   e) trial-and-error   f) difference of two cubes.

178. Through which quadrants does the graph of $y + 3x - 5 = 0$ pass?
ANSWER: Quadrants I, II, and IV (all must be given for the answer to be correct).

179. Factor completely $x^2 + 2xy + y^2 - 4$.
ANSWER: $(x + y - 2)(x + y + 2)$ or $(x + y + 2)(x + y - 2)$ (either answer is correct).

180. What integer does $128^{5/7}$ equal?
ANSWER: 32.

181. For what value of K will $Kx^2 + 5x - 7 = 0$ have exactly one distinct solution?
ANSWER: $K = -25/28$.

182. Which of the following sets contains both solutions of the equation $x^2 + 7x - 8 = 0$?
a) $\{-1, 0, 2, 6, 8, 11, 13\}$ d) $\{-9, -4, 4, 9, 17, 23\}$
b) $\{-6, -5, 1, 3, 12, 19\}$ e) $\{\frac{1}{2}, 1/3, -\frac{1}{4}, 1/17, 1/21, 93\}$
c) $\{-8, -7, -2, 1, 15\}$

ANSWER: c.

183. K must be bigger than what number for $2x^2 + 11x - K = 0$ to have solutions which are real and unequal?
ANSWER: $-121/8$.

184. What is the sum of the solutions of the equation $x^{2/3} - x^{1/3} - 2 = 0$?
ANSWER: 7.

185. The midpoint of a line segment whose endpoints are A and B is $(4, -2)$. If the x-coordinate of A is 1 and the y-coordinate of A is -7, what are the x and y coordinates of B?
ANSWER: The x-coordinate is 7 and the y-coordinate is 3.

186. Tell whether or not each of the following statements is true or false
a) The sum of two third degree polynomials is a third degree polynomial.
b) The distance between $(2, 5)$ and $(-1, 9)$ is 5.
c) The point $(1, 4)$ is above the graph of $y = 3x + 2$.

ANSWER: a) false   b) true   c) false.

187. Name the phrase from the field of mathematics that means "to do an about-face; to make a complete reversal of opinion or attitude to one's previous position or point of view." Explain the mathematical reason for such a phrase.
ANSWER: To do a 180° turn/180° is half of a circle's 360° and by turning halfway around a circle, one would have made an about-face.

188. 1,001 is the product of three consecutive primes. Name them.
ANSWER: 7, 11, and 13.

189. The endpoints of a diameter of a circle are $(3, 5)$ and $(7, 1)$. Which of the following equations is the equation of that circle?
a) $x^2 + y^2 - 10x - 6y - 26 = 0$ d) $x^2 + y^2 + 10x - 6y + 26 = 0$
b) $x^2 + y^2 - 10x + 6y - 26 = 0$ e) $x^2 + y^2 - 10x - 6y + 26 = 0$
c) $x^2 + y^2 - 10x + 6y + 26 = 0$

ANSWER: e.

190. Which of the following is the equation of the line passing through the point (3, 5) that is perpendicular to $3y - x - 3 = 0$?

    a) $y = -3x + 8$ d) $y = -3x + 10$
    b) $y = -3x + 6$ e) $y = -3x + 12$
    c) $y = -3x + 14$

ANSWER: c.

191. Which of the following functions is increasing everywhere?

    a) $y = 1$ d) $y = x^2 + 2$
    b) $y = -x + 2$ e) $y = -x^2 + 2$
    c) $y = x + 2$

ANSWER: c.

192. What real number is not in the range of $y = \dfrac{4x}{2x - 7}$?

ANSWER: 2.

193. What is the equation of the line passing through the point (5, 7) that has no slope?

ANSWER: $x = 5$.

194. If f is the function whose ordered pairs are (1, 3), (2, 7), and (5,6) and g is the function whose ordered pairs are (3, 11), (7, 4), and (6, 9), what is

    a) $g(f(1))$?   b) $g(f(2))$?   c) $g(f(5))$?

ANSWER: a) 11   b) 4   c) 9.

195. Which of the following functions is the inverse of $f(x) = 3x + 7$?

    a) $g(x) = 1/3\,x + 1/7$ d) $g(x) = \dfrac{1}{3x + 7}$
    b) $g(x) = \dfrac{x + 7}{3}$ e) $g(x) = 3x - 7$
    c) $g(x) = \dfrac{x - 7}{3}$

ANSWER: c.

196. If $f(x) = x^2 + 3$, what is $\dfrac{f(x + h) - f(x)}{h}$?

ANSWER: $2x + h$.

197. What American mathematician coined the word ''googol,'' and what inspired this arbitrary coinage?

ANSWER: Edward Kasner/A sound made by his nine-year old nephew.

198. Tell whether each of the following functions is even, odd, or neither even nor odd.

    a) $f(x) = x^2 + 4x + 6$ d) $f(x) = 4x^3 + 6x$
    b) $f(x) = x^3 + 5$ e) $f(x) = 3x^6$
    c) $f(x) = x^4 + 3x^2 - 7$

ANSWER: a) neither even nor odd   b) neither even nor odd   c) even   d) odd   e) even.

199. If h of x equals f composed with g of x where $f(x) = x^2 + 2x - 3$ and $g(x) = 3x - 4$, then h is which of the following functions?

    a) $h(x) = 3x^2 + 6x - 13$ d) $h(x) = 9x^2 - 18x - 5$
    b) $h(x) = 3x^2 + 6x + 13$ e) $h(x) = 9x^2 + 18x - 5$
    c) $h(x) = 9x^2 - 18x + 5$

ANSWER: c.

200. Which of the following functions are one-to-one?

    a) $y = 3x - 11$ d) $y = 3x^4 - 11$
    b) $y = 3x^2 - 11$ e) $y = -11$
    c) $y = 3x^3 - 11$

ANSWER: a and c are one-to-one.

201. The graph of which of the following equations has the lowest point?

    a) $y = x$ d) $y = x^2 + 3x + 2$
    b) $y = -x^2 - 3x - 2$ e) $x = y^2 + 3y + 2$
    c) $x = -y^2 - 3y - 2$

ANSWER: d.

202. Which of the following is the equation of a rational function whose vertical asymptotes are $x = 1$ and $x = -2$ and whose horizontal asymptote is $y = 2$?

    a) $y = \dfrac{4x^2 + 3x - 11}{2x^2 + 2x - 4}$ b) $y = \dfrac{2x^2}{x^2 + x + 2}$ c) $y = \dfrac{2x^2 + 3x + 5}{x^2 - x + 2}$

ANSWER: a.

203. What is the solution of the following system of equations?
$$2y + 3x = 5 \qquad \text{and} \qquad 4x - 3y = -16$$
ANSWER: $(-1, 4)$.

204. Give π to 13 decimal places. Use *How I wish I could recollect of circle round the exact relation Archimede unwound* if you need help.
ANSWER: 3.1415926535897.

205. Tell which of the following are factors of $g(x) = 2x^{100} - x^{50} + 3x^{20} - 4$.
a) $x + 1$ b) $x - 2$ c) $x - 1$ d) $x + 3$ e) $x + 7$.
ANSWER: a and c.

206. What is the only solution of the equation $\log(x + 4) - \log(x + 2) = \log x$?
ANSWER: $\dfrac{-1 + \sqrt{17}}{2}$

207. Tell whether each of the following is always true, always false, or sometimes true and sometimes false.
a) If tan (T) is positive then sin(T) is positive
b) If cos(T) is negative then cos$(-T)$ is negative
c) If sec(T) is positive then cos$(-T)$ is negative
d) If sin(T) is positive then sin$(-T)$ is negative
ANSWER: a) sometimes true and sometimes false   b) always true   c) always false   d) always true.

208. Which of the following is not an identity?
a) $\tan^2(a) + 1 = \sec^2(a)$
b) $1 + \cot^2(B) = \csc^2(B)$
c) $\cos(\pi/2 - T) = \sin(T)$
d) $\sin(a + b) = \sin(a)\cos(b) + \cos(a)\sin(b)$
e) $\tan(x - y) = \dfrac{\tan x - \tan y}{1 - \tan x \tan y}$
ANSWER: e (note: $\tan(x - y) = \dfrac{\tan x - \tan y}{1 + \tan x \tan y}$).

209. In the standard normal distribution of statistics:
a) give the values of the mean and the standard deviation.
b) how many standard deviations above and below the mean are there in 95% of all cases?
c) name the 3 measures of central tendency which are equal.
ANSWER: a) 0,1 b) 2 c) mean, median, and mode.

210. Who wrote *Euclid and His Modern Rivals* (1879), *Curiosa Mathematica* (1888-1893, 2 volumes), and *Symbolic Logic* (1896)?
ANSWER: Charles Lutwidge Dodgson.

211. Identify the correct order for algebraic operations. Use *Bless my dear Aunt Sally* if you need help.
ANSWER: Brackets, multiply, divide, add, and subtract.

212. "I'm forming a mnemonic to remember a function in analysis" is a mnemonic device to remember the value of e to nine places. Give the value of e to 9 places.
ANSWER: 2.718281828.

213. If you drive in a straight line from point A to point B at 40 km per hour and return from point B to point A at 60 km per hour, what is the average speed for the whole trip?
ANSWER: 48 km per hour (not 50 km per hour).

214. Why is there no Nobel Prize in mathematics?
ANSWER: Because the prime candidate for the prize was Swedish mathematician, Gosta Mittag-Leffler, and he either had a feud with Alfred Nobel or stole the woman with whom Nobel was in love.

215. Wrap a sheet of paper around a cylindrical candle several times. Cut diagonally through both the paper and the candle. When the paper is unrolled, the cut edge of each piece will be in the form of what curve?
ANSWER: Sine curve.

216. Identify each of the following.
a) The maximum area obtained by a planar cross section of a unit cube

   b) The first woman mentioned in mathematical history
   c) The radius of the inscribed circle of a 3-4-5 triangle
   d) The mathematician jailed for giving the horoscope of Jesus Christ
   e) The branch of biology in which organisms are studied according to their geo-
      metrical forms.
ANSWER: a) $\sqrt{2}$ b) **Hypatia**   c) **1**   d) **Girolamo Cardano (1501-1576)**   e) **Promor-
   phology.**

217. If the entries in any of the first 5 rows of Pascal's triangle are read as a number in
   base ten, the result is a power of what number?
ANSWER: **11.**

218. The points of intersection of the trisectors of the angles of any triangle determine the vertices of what kind of triangle?
ANSWER: **Equilateral.**

219. Identify each of the following.
   a) The number of dimples on a regulation golf ball.
   b) The total number of gifts given in *The Twelve Days of Christmas*.
   c) The greatest number of knights that can be placed on a standard chess board
      so that no knight attacks another.
   d) The minimum number of colors necessary to color any map such that the
      regions with a common boundary are colored differently.
ANSWER: **a) 336   b) 364   c) 32   d) 4.**

220. What phrase from the field of geometry means "to digress suddenly from a line
   of action or train of thought and turn to another"?
ANSWER: **Go fly off at (on) a tangent.**

221. What are the 3 classical problems that are impossible to solve using only a
   straight edge and compasses?
ANSWER: **Squaring the circle, doubling the cube, and trisecting an angle.**

222. The definition of the phrases *to square the circle, to double the cube,*
   and *to trisect an angle* can be defined as "*to engage in a useless
   behavior.*" Explain the mathematical reason why each cannot be solved.
ANSWER: *To square the circle* **is impossible with straight-edge and compass
   alone because the number** π **is not the solution of any algebraic equation at
   all (it is a transcendental number), and it especially cannot satisfy one
   whose degree is a power of 2 which is needed to change a circle into a
   square of equal value/** *To double the cube* **is impossible because the
   volume of the cube must be doubled, and if the volume of the original cube
   is** x^3**, the volume of the second cube would be** $2x^3$**. Hence, the side of the
   second cube would be S** $= \sqrt[3]{2x^3} = X\sqrt[3]{2}$**. But** $\sqrt[3]{2}$ **cannot be constructed
   using straight-edge and compass/** *To trisect an angle* **is impossible
   because the degree of the equation using a straight-edge and compass
   must be a power of 2, but the degree of the equation belonging to the problem of trisecting an angle is 3. (If the above brief descriptions of very complex material is not satisfactory,** *tant pis*).

COMPUTERS
QUESTIONS AND ANSWERS

1. What are the names of the 2 basic types of computers?

ANSWERS: Analog and Digital.

2. Identify each of the following.
   a) The oldest known mechanical computing aid and the country in which it was used as early as the 6th century B.C.
   b) The non-mechanical device which multiplied only (1617)
   c) The inventor of a more mechanical adding machine in 1642
   d) The builder of a more advanced calculator in 1694
   e) The mechanical calculator invented in 1834, which was a forerunner of the digital computer
   f) The developer of the first successful punched-card data processing system in about 1886
   g) The person who conceived the first large-scale automatic digital computer in 1937, and the name of this machine built by IBM in 1944
   h) The name of the first large electronic digital computer designed by John W. Mauchly and J. Presper Eckert and completed in 1945
   i) The first computer, designed by Eckert and Mauchly, to be built for commercial purposes
   j) The developer of the first cathode-ray-tube memory in 1950-1951

ANSWER: a) abacus/China b) Napier's bones (by John Napier) c) Blaise Pascal d) Gottfried Wilhelm von Leibniz e) Babbage's analytic engine (by Charles Babbage) f) Herman Hollerith g) Howard A. Aiken/Mark 1 or Automatic Sequence Controlled Calculator h) Eniac (Electronic Numerical Integrator And Calculator, or Computer) i) Univac 1 (UNIVersal Automatic Computer) j) Frederick C. Williams.

3. What is the name of the smallest component of storage in a digital computer, and for what is it an abbreviation?

ANSWER: Bit/binary digit.

4. In what 4 kinds of functional units is a digital computer normally organized?

ANSWER: Control unit, arithmetic and logical unit, memory (storage) units, and input/output units.

5. Identify each of the following acronyms of the computer field.

   a) PLATO   d) ALGOL   g) ALU   j) CRT
   b) FORTRAN   e) BASIC   h) SSI   k) CPU
   c) COBOL   f) PL/1   i) RAM   l) LSI

ANSWER: a) Programmed Logic for Automatic Teaching Operations b) FORmula TRANslation c) COmmon Business Oriented Language d) ALGebraically Oriented Language e) Beginner's All-Purpose Symbolic Instruction Code f) Programming Language One g) Arithmetic and Logical Unit h) Small Scale Integrated circuitry i) Random Access Memory j) Cathode-Ray Tube k) Central Processing Unit l) Large Scale Integrated circuitry.

6. Identify each of the following computer related words.

   a) A computer with features of analog and digital machines
   b) Unit of binary digits
   c) Miniaturized disc of silicon on which an integrated circuit is printed.
   d) SNOBOL
   e) The arithmetic-logical operational part of a microcomputer
   f) CODAP
   g) COGO
   h) Program that translates source program from a high-level language into an object program
   i) OCR
   j) The system for selecting a compatible companion for romance by matching personalities through a computer program
   k) GIGO

ANSWER: a) hybrid computer b) byte c) chip d) String Oriented Symbolic Language e) microprocessor f) Control Data Assembly Program g) Coordinate Geometry h) compiler i) Optical Character Recognition j) computer dating k) Garbage In, Garbage Out.

MATHEMATICIANS

Thales of Miletus....Greek.... Invented deductive mathematics. Predicted an eclipse of the sun based on geometry.

Pythagoras (Of Samos)....Greek.... Developed ''Pythagoras' theorem'' on right triangles, which is that any triangle whose sides are in the ratio 3:4:5 is a right-angled triangle. The ''Pythagorean theorem'' states that the square of the hypotenuse of a right triangle is equal to the sum of the squares of the other two sides.

Eudoxus of Cyzicus....Greek.... Introduced many geometric proofs. Formulated definitions of proportions.

Euclid (Of Alexandria)....Greek.... Published the first geometry textbook *Elements*. Well-known for his fifth, or parallel, postulate that one and only one line can be drawn through a point parallel to a given line. Demonstrated that there are five and only five regular solids. Known as the ''Father of Geometry.''

Archimedes....Greek.... Known for his approximation for the value of π, that is between $3\ 10/70 > \pi > 3\ 10/71$.

Ptolemy....Greek.... Helped develop trigonometry.

Diophantus (Of Alexandria)....Greek.... Sometimes called the ''Father of Algebra.'' Wrote *Arithmetica.*

Omar Khayyám....Persian.... First one to generalize the binomial theorem.

Bhaskara....Hindu.... Wrote *Lilavati.* Developed the principles of the additive inverse and the multiplicative inverse. Known as Bhaskara Acarya or ''Bhaskara the Learned.''

Leonardo Fibonacci....Italian.... Established the Hindu-Arabic numbers as the standard computational symbolism, causing the Roman abacus to become obsolete. Known for the Fibonacci Sequence of 0, 1, 1, 2, 3, 5, 8, 13, 21, 34, 55 . . . . .

Girolamo Cardano....Italian.... Wrote *Ars Magna* (1545), the first Latin treatise devoted exclusively to algebra.

Henry Briggs....English.... Proposed a logarithm system to the base 10.

John Napier....Scottish.... Inventor of logarithms. Wrote *Rabdologiae* (1617). Devised method of multiplication by using sliding rods known as ''Napier's rods'' or ''Napier's bones'' (since they were sometimes made of ivory).

René Descartes....French.... Co-founder of analytical geometry (with Fermat). Published *Dioptrics, Meteors, and Geometry* (1637). Known for his Cartesian coordinates.

Blaise Pascal....French.... Invented the calculating machine (1641). Published *Essay on Conic Sections* (1639). Contributed to the development of differential calculus. Invented with Fermat the mathematical theory of probability. Known for ''Pascal's arithematical triangle,'' ''Pascal's law'' (principle), and ''Pascal's mystic hexagram.''

Pierre de Fermat....French.... Co-founder of analytical geometry (with Descartes). Fermat's last theorem is that the equation $x^n + y^n = z^n$, where x, y, and z are positive integers, has no solution in the rational integers for $n > 2$. Known as the founder of the modern theory of numbers. Co-founder of the theory of probability (with Pascal).

Sir Isaac Newton....English.... Invented differential calculus (1665) and integral calculus (1665). Known for his idea on ''the direct and inverse method of fluxions.'' Discovered the binomial theorem.

Gottfried Wilhelm von Leibniz....German.... Developed differential and integral calculus (later but independent of Newton), the calculus of variations, and topology. Also invented a calculating machine (1671) superior to Pascal's.

Abraham Demoivre....French.... Known for the Demoivre theorem $(\cos x + i \sin x)^n = (\cos nx + i \sin nx)$ when n is rational and i equals square root of -1. Known as the ''Founder of Analytic Trigonometry.''

Leonhard Euler....Swiss.... Founder of pure mathematical analysis.

Johann or Jean Bernoulli....Swiss.... Discoverer of exponential calculus. Coined the term ''integral.'' Published *Opera Omnia* (1742).

Maria Gaetana Agnesi....Italian.... Known for the Witch of Agnesi $x^2y = a^2(a-y)$.

Pierre Simon de Laplace....French.... Founder of the theory of probability and contributed to the development of celestial mechanics.

Adrien Marie Legendre....French.... Simplified Euclid's geometry. Discovered the law of quadratic reciprocity ("the gem of arithmetic").

Karl Friedrich Gauss....German.... Founder of the modern theory of numbers. Wrote *Disquisitiones Arithmeticae* (1801). Founder of non-Euclidean geometry whose work was published posthumously.

Jean Baptiste Joseph Fourier, Baron....French.... Discovered Fourier's theorem which states that any periodic oscillations can be expressed as a mathematical series in which the terms are comprised of trigonometric functions. Wrote *Analytic Theory of Heat* (1822).

Nikolai Ivanovich Lobachevsky....Russian.... Non-Euclidean geometry is sometimes known as Lobachevskian geometry. Wrote "Geometriya" (1826) and *Pangeometry* (1855). Founder of non-Euclidean geometry with János Bolyai of Hungary (who had not published his work). Sometimes called the "Copernicus of Geometry."

Sir William Rowan Hamilton....Irish.... Known for the development of quaternions. Wrote the *Theory of Systems of Rays* (1827).

Niels Henrik Abel....Norwegian.... Known for his theory of elliptic functions in his *Investigations on Elliptic Functions* (1827).

János Bolyai....Hungarian.... Developer of non-Euclidean geometry with Nikolai Lobachevsky.

Evariste Galois....French.... Known for his Galois theory of groups.

Charles Babbage....English.... Developed the fundamental idea of a mechanical digital computer in the 1830's with his machine called the analytic engine. Known as the "Grandfather of the Modern Computer."

George Boole....English.... Developed Boolean algebra. Founder of symbolic logic. Wrote *An Investigation of the Laws of Thought* (1854).

Georg Friedrich Bernhard Riemann....German.... Invented elliptic form of non-Euclidean geometry.

August Ferdinand Möbius....German....A founder of topology. Developed the Möbius strip, a paradoxical one-sided figure formed by joining the two ends of a rectangular strip of paper after giving it a half twist. (1865).

Richard Dedekind....German.... Known for pioneering work in logical and philosophical analysis of mathematical structure. Originated the Dedekind "cuts."

Charles Hermite....French.... Contributed to the theory of numbers and to the theory of continued fractions. Showed that e is a transcendental number and not an algebraic one.

Georg F.L.P. Cantor....German.... Developed the theory of sets (1874) and discovered the transfinite numbers.

Josiah Willard Gibbs....American.... Creator of vector analysis.

David Hilbert....German.... Wrote *Foundations of Geometry* (1899).

Bertrand Arthur William Russell....English.... Wrote *The Principles of Mathematics* (1903) and *Principia Mathematica* (the latter with Alfred North Whitehead) through which he aided the development of mathematical logic.

Alfred North Whitehead....English.... Wrote *A Treatise on Universal Algebra* (1898). Collaborated with Bertrand Russell on *Principia Mathematica* (1910-1913).

Richard Buckminster Fuller....American.... Developed energetic-synergetic geometry. Known for his geodesic dome.

Howard Hathaway Aiken....American.... Invented the first large-scale automatic computer, the Mark I (1937-1944). Completed work on the Mark IV in 1952.

John von Neumann....Hungarian-American.... Wrote his *Mathematical Foundations of Quantum Mechanics* (1932). Helped develop high-speed computers as director of the Electronic Computer Project in Princeton, New Jersey.

Norbert Wiener....American.... Developed the mathematical theory of cybernetics (1948). Wrote *Cybernetics, or Control and Communication in the Man and the Machine* (1948).

MATHEMATICAL FORMULAS

TRIANGLES

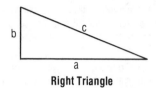

Right Triangle

Pythagorean Theorem
$$a^2 + b^2 = c^2$$

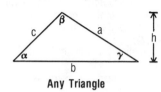

Any Triangle

Angles $\alpha + \beta + \gamma = 180°$

CIRCUMFERENCE OF A CIRCLE

CIRCLE: $C = \pi d$, in which π is 3.1416....and d the diameter of the circle or $C = 2\pi r$ where π is the same as above and r is the radius of the circle.

AREA

TRIANGLE: $A = ab/2$, in which a is the length of the base and b the height.
PARALLELOGRAM: $A = bh$, in which b is the length of the base, and b the height.
SQUARE: $A = a^2$, in which a is the length of one of the sides.
RECTANGLE: $A = ab$, in which a is the length of the base, and b the height.
TRAPEZOID: $A = \frac{h(a+b)}{2}$, in which h is the height, a the length of the longer parallel side, and b the length of the shorter parallel side.
REGULAR POLYGON: $A = ap/2$, in which a is the apothem, and p the perimeter.
REGULAR PENTAGON: $A = 1.720a^2$, in which a is the length of one of the sides.
REGULAR HEXAGON: $A = 2.598a^2$, in which a is the length of one of the sides.
REGULAR OCTAGON: $A = 4.828a^2$, in which a is the length of one of the sides.
CIRCLE: $A = \pi r^2$, in which r is the radius of the circle.

VOLUME

CUBE: $V = a^3$, in which a is the length of one of the edges.
RECTANGULAR PRISM: $V = abc$, in which a is the length, b the width, and c the depth.
PYRAMID: $V = Ah/3$, in which A is the area of the base and h the height.
CYLINDER: $V = \pi r^2 h$, in which r is the radius of the base, and h the height.
CONE: $V = \frac{\pi r^2 h}{3}$, in which r is the radius of the base, and h the height.
SPHERE: $V = \frac{4\pi r^3}{3}$, in which r is the radius.

SURFACE AREA

CYLINDERS   CONES   SPHERES

Surface Area
$$S = 2\pi r^2 + 2\pi rh$$

Surface Area
$$S = \pi r^2 + \pi r\sqrt{r^2 + h^2}$$

Surface Area
$$S = 4\pi r^2$$

STATISTICS

SAMPLE MEAN: $\bar{x} = \frac{\Sigma_i x}{n}$
SAMPLE STANDARD DEVIATION: $s = \sqrt{\frac{\Sigma(x - \bar{x})^2}{n-1}}$

TRIGONOMETRIC IDENTITIES

$$\sin^2 x + \cos^2 x = 1 \qquad \sec^2 x = 1 + \tan^2 x \qquad \csc^2 x = 1 + \cot^2 x$$

$$\sin x = \frac{2 \tan \frac{x}{2}}{1 + \tan^2 \frac{x}{2}} \qquad \cos x = \frac{1 - \tan^2 \frac{x}{2}}{1 + \tan^2 \frac{x}{2}} \qquad \tan x = \frac{2 \tan \frac{x}{2}}{1 - \tan^2 \frac{x}{2}}$$

$$\sin^2 x = \tfrac{1}{2}(1 - \cos 2x) \qquad \cos^2 x = \tfrac{1}{2}(1 + \cos 2x)$$

$$\sin 2x = 2 \sin x \cos x \qquad \cos 2x = \cos^2 x - \sin^2 x$$
$$= 2 \cos^2 x - 1 = 1 - 2 \sin^2 x$$

$$\sin 3x = 3 \sin x - 4 \sin^3 x \qquad \cos 3x = 4 \cos^3 x - 3 \cos x$$

$$\tan 2x = \frac{2 \tan x}{1 - \tan^2 x} \qquad \tan 3x = \frac{3 \tan x - \tan^3 x}{1 - 3 \tan^2 x}$$

$$\sin (A + B) = \sin A \cos B + \cos A \sin B.$$
$$\sin (A - B) = \sin A \cos B - \cos A \sin B$$
$$\cos (A + B) = \cos A \cos B - \sin A \sin B$$
$$\cos (A - B) = \cos A \cos B + \sin A \sin B$$

$$\tan (A + B) = \frac{\tan A + \tan B}{1 - \tan A \tan B} \qquad \tan (A - B) = \frac{\tan A - \tan B}{1 + \tan A \tan B}$$

$$2 \sin A \cos B = \sin (A + B) + \sin (A - B)$$
$$2 \cos A \sin B = \sin (A + B) - \sin (A - B)$$
$$2 \cos A \cos B = \cos (A + B) + \cos (A - B)$$
$$2 \sin A \sin B = \cos (A - B) - \cos (A + B)$$

$$\sin A + \sin B = 2 \sin \frac{A + B}{2} \cos \frac{A - B}{2}$$

$$\sin A - \sin B = 2 \cos \frac{A + B}{2} \sin \frac{A - B}{2}$$

$$\cos A + \cos B = 2 \cos \frac{A + B}{2} \cos \frac{A - B}{2}$$

$$\cos A - \cos B = -2 \sin \frac{A + B}{2} \sin \frac{A - B}{2}$$

Basic Identities

$$\tan x = \frac{\sin x}{\cos x} \qquad\qquad \cot x = \frac{\cos x}{\sin x} = \frac{1}{\tan x}$$

$$\sec x = \frac{1}{\cos x} \qquad\qquad \csc x = \frac{1}{\sin x}$$

Cofunction Identities

$$\sin (\pi/2 - x) = \cos x \qquad \cos (\pi/2 - x) = \sin x \qquad \tan (\pi/2 - x) = \cot x$$

Odd-even Identities

$$\sin (-x) = -\sin x \qquad \cos (-x) = \cos x \qquad \tan (-x) = -\tan x$$

Half Angle Formulas

$$\sin \frac{x}{2} = \pm \sqrt{\frac{1 - \cos x}{2}} \qquad \cos \frac{x}{2} = \pm \sqrt{\frac{1 + \cos x}{2}} \qquad \tan \frac{x}{2} = \frac{1 - \cos x}{\sin x}$$

Laws of Sines and Cosines

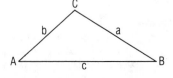

$$\frac{\sin A}{a} = \frac{\sin B}{b} = \frac{\sin C}{c}$$

$$a^2 = b^2 + c^2 - 2bc \cos A$$

Determinants

$$\begin{vmatrix} a_1 & a_2 \\ b_1 & b_2 \end{vmatrix} = a_1 b_2 - a_2 b_1$$

$$\begin{vmatrix} a_1 & a_2 & a_3 \\ b_1 & b_2 & b_3 \\ c_1 & c_2 & c_3 \end{vmatrix} = a_1 \begin{vmatrix} b_2 & b_3 \\ c_2 & c_3 \end{vmatrix} - a_2 \begin{vmatrix} b_1 & b_3 \\ c_1 & c_3 \end{vmatrix} + a_3 \begin{vmatrix} b_1 & b_2 \\ c_1 & c_2 \end{vmatrix}$$

$$= a_1(b_2 c_3 - b_3 c_2) - a_2(b_1 c_3 - b_3 c_1) + a_3(b_1 c_2 - b_2 c_1)$$

Analytic Geometry

Distance Between Two Points (x_1, y_1) and (x_2, y_2) $\quad d = \sqrt{(x_2 - x_1)^2 + (y_2 - y_1)^2}$

Slope of Line Joining Two Points (x_1, y_1) and (x_2, y_2) $\quad m = \dfrac{y_2 - y_1}{x_2 - x_1}$

Midpoint Formulas for the Line Whose Endpoints are (x_1, y_1) and (x_2, y_2)

$$x = \frac{x_1 + x_2}{2}, \quad y = \frac{y_1 + y_2}{2}$$

Exponents

$a^m a^n = a^{m+n}$

$(a^m)^n = a^{mn}$

$\dfrac{a^m}{a^n} = a^{m-n}$

$(ab)^n = a^n b^n$

$\left(\dfrac{a}{b}\right)^n = \dfrac{a^n}{b^n}$

Radicals

$(\sqrt[n]{a})^n = a$

$\sqrt[n]{a^n} = a$, if $a \geq 0$

$\sqrt[n]{ab} = \sqrt[n]{a}\,\sqrt[n]{b}$

$\sqrt[n]{\dfrac{a}{b}} = \dfrac{\sqrt[n]{a}}{\sqrt[n]{b}}$

$\sqrt[n]{\sqrt[m]{a}} = \sqrt[n \cdot m]{a}$

Equation of a Straight Line

Point-slope form: $y - y_1 = m(x - x_1)$
Slope-intercept form: $y = mx + b$

Two-point form: $\dfrac{y - y_1}{\ \ x_1} = \dfrac{y_2 - y_1}{x_2 - x_1}$

Intercept form: $\dfrac{x}{a} + \dfrac{y}{b} = 1$

Distance from a Line to a Point

$$d = \frac{y_1 - mx_1 - b}{\sqrt{m^2 + 1}}$$

Equations of Curves

Circle with center (h,k) and radius r: $(x - h)^2 + (y - k)^2 = r^2$

Parabola with vertex at the origin and with focus on the x-axis: $y^2 = 2px$

Ellipse with center at the origin and with foci on the x-axis: $\dfrac{x^2}{a^2} + \dfrac{y^2}{b^2} = 1$

Hyperbola with center at the origin and with foci on the x-axis: $\dfrac{x^2}{a^2} - \dfrac{y^2}{b^2} = 1$

Logarithms

$$\log_a MN = \log_a M + \log_a N$$
$$\log_a(M/N) = \log_a M - \log_a N$$
$$\log_a(N^p) = p \log_a N$$

Factoring Formulas

$x^2 - y^2 = (x - y)(x + y)$

$x^3 - y^3 = (x - y)(x^2 + xy + y^2)$

$x^3 + y^3 = (x + y)(x^2 - xy + y^2)$

$x^2 + 2xy + y^2 = (x + y)^2$

$x^2 - 2xy + y^2 = (x - y)^2$

$x^3 + 3x^2y + 3xy^2 + y^3 = (x + y)^3$

TRIGONOMETRIC FUNCTIONS

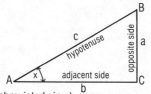

sine of x (abbreviated sin x)

$$= \frac{\text{side opposite the angle x}}{\text{hypotenuse}} = a/c$$

cosine of x (abbreviated cos x)

$$= \frac{\text{side adjacent to the angle x}}{\text{hypotenuse}} = b/c$$

tangent of x (abbreviated tan x)

$$= \frac{\text{side opposite the angle x}}{\text{side adjacent to the angle x}} = a/b$$

cotangent of x (abbreviated cot x)

$$= \frac{\text{side adjacent to the angle x}}{\text{side opposite the angle x}} = b/a$$

secant of x (abbreviated sec x)

$$= \frac{\text{hypotenuse}}{\text{side adjacent to the angle x}} = c/b$$

cosecant of x (abbreviated csc x)

$$= \frac{\text{hypotenuse}}{\text{side opposite the angle x}} = c/a$$

ROMAN NUMERALS

I	1	XL	40	CD	400
II	2	XLIX	49	D	500
III	3	L	50	DC	600
IV	4	LV	55	DCC	700
V	5	LIX	59	DCCC	800
VI	6	LX	60	CM	900
VII	7	LXX	70	M	1000
VIII	8	LXXX	80	MMMM	4000
IX	9	XC	90	$\overline{V}$	5000
X	10	XCV	95	$\overline{X}$	10,000
XV	15	XCIX	99	$\overline{L}$	50,000
XIX	19	C	100	$\overline{C}$	100,000
XX	20	CI	101	$\overline{D}$	500,000
XXIX	29	CC	200	$\overline{M}$	1,000,000
XXX	30	CCC	300		

DATES

MD	1500	MCMLX	1960
MDCC	1700	MCMLXXX	1980
MCM or MDCCCC	1900	MCMLXXXII	1982
MCMXX	1920	MCMXC	1990
MCMXL	1940	MM	2000

GENERAL RULES FOR ROMAN NUMERALS

a) Repeating a letter repeats its value: XXX = 30
b) A letter placed after one of greater value adds thereto: VIII = 8; DCC = 700
c) A letter placed before one of greater value subtracts therefrom: IX = 9; CM = 900
d) A dash over a numeral multiplies the value by 1,000: $\overline{X}$ = 10,000

THE ARCHIMEDEAN SOLIDS

NAME	NO. OF FACES	NO. OF VERTICES	NO. OF EDGES
Truncated tetrahedron	8	12	18
Truncated cube	14	24	36
Truncated octahedron	14	24	36
Truncated dodecahedron	32	60	90
Truncated icosahedron	32	60	90
Cuboctahedron	14	12	24
Small rhombicuboctahedron	26	24	48
Icosidodecahedron	32	30	60
Snub cube	38	24	60
Snub dodecahedron	92	60	150
Great rhombicuboctahedron	26	48	72
Great rhombicosidodecahedron	62	120	180
Small rhombicosidodecahedron	62	60	120

TABLE OF PRIME NUMBERS FROM 1 TO 1000

2	61	149	239	347	443	563	659	773	887
3	67	151	241	349	449	569	661	787	907
5	71	157	251	353	457	571	673	797	911
7	73	163	257	359	461	577	677	809	919
11	79	167	263	367	463	587	683	811	929
13	83	173	279	373	467	593	691	821	937
17	89	179	271	379	479	599	701	823	941
19	97	181	277	383	487	601	709	827	947
23	101	191	281	389	491	607	719	829	953
29	103	193	283	397	499	613	727	839	967
31	107	197	293	401	503	617	733	853	971
37	109	199	307	409	509	619	739	857	977
41	113	211	311	419	521	631	743	859	983
43	127	223	313	421	523	641	751	863	991
47	131	227	317	431	541	643	757	877	997
53	137	229	331	433	547	647	761	881	
59	139	233	337	439	557	653	769	883	

NUMBERS AND THEIR NUMBER OF ZEROES

million	6	undecillion	36
billion	9	duodecillion	39
trillion	12	tredecillion	42
quadrillion	15	quatturodecillion	45
quintillion	18	quindecillion	48
sextillion	21	sexdecillion	51
septillion	24	septendecillion	54
octillion	27	octodecillion	57
nonillion	30	novemdecillion	60
decillion	33	vigintillion	63

POLYGONS AND THE NUMBER OF THEIR SIDES

Triangle	3	Octagon	8
Quadrilateral	4	Nonagon	9
Pentagon	5	Decagon	10
Hexagon	6	Dodecagon	12
Heptagon	7		

PREFIXES AND THEIR MULTIPLES

Prefix	Symbol	Equivalent
atto-	a	quintillionth part
femto-	f	quadrillionth part
pico-	p	trillionth part
nano-	n	billionth part
micro-	μ	millionth part
milli-	m	thousandth part
centi-	c	hundredth part
deci-	d	tenth part
deka-	da	tenfold
hecto-	h	hundredfold
kilo-	k	thousandfold
mega-	M	millionfold
giga-	G	billionfold
tera-	T	trillionfold

Natural Numbers

$$1 + 2 + 3 + \ldots + n = (\tfrac{1}{2})n(n+1)$$
$$1^2 + 2^2 + 3^2 + \ldots + n^2 = (1/6)\,n\,(n+1)(2n+1)$$
$$1^3 + 2^3 + 3^3 + \ldots + n^3 = \tfrac{1}{4}n^2(n+1)^2$$

Arithmetic Progression

$$a + (a + d) + (a + 2d) + \ldots + [a + (n-1)d]$$
$$= \tfrac{n}{2}[2a + (n-1)\,d]$$

Arithmetic mean of n quantities $a_1, a_2 \ldots a_n$

$$= \frac{a_1 + a_2 + a_3 \ldots + a_n}{n}$$

Geometric Progression

$$a + ar + ar^2 + \ldots + ar^{n-1} = a\frac{1 - r^n}{1 - r}$$

If r^2 is less than 1 the sum to infinity is $\dfrac{a}{1 - r}$.

Geometric mean of n quantities $a_1, a_2 \ldots a_n$

$$= \sqrt[n]{a_1 a_2 a_3 \cdots a_n}$$

HISTORIC CURVES

catenary $\quad y = \dfrac{a}{2}(e^{\frac{x}{a}} + e^{-\frac{x}{a}})$

cissoid $\quad y^2(2a - x) = x^3$

conchoid $\quad x^2 y^2 = (y + a)^2(b^2 - y^2)$

cubical parabola $\quad y = ax^3$

cycloid $\quad x = a(x - \sin x), y = a(1 - \cos x)$

folium $\quad x^3 + y^2 - 3axy = 0$

lemniscate $\quad (x^2 + y^2)^2 = a^2(x^2 - y^2)$

probability curve $\quad y = e^{-x^2}$

semicubical parabola $\quad y^2 = ax^3$

strophoid $\quad (a - x)y^2 = (a + x)x^2$

witch $\quad Y = \dfrac{8a^3}{x^2 + 4a^2}$

COMPLEX NUMBERS

Multiplication: $(a + bi)(c + di) = (ac - bd) + (ad + bc)i$

Polar form: $a + bi = r(\cos x + i \sin x)$ where $r = \sqrt{a^2 + b^2}$

Powers: $[r(\cos x + i \sin x)]^n = r^n (\cos nx + i \sin nx)$

Roots: $U_k = \sqrt[n]{r} \left[\cos\left(\frac{x + k \cdot 360^\circ}{n}\right) + i \sin\left(\frac{x + k \cdot 360^\circ}{n}\right)\right]$ $k = 0, 1, 2, \ldots, n-1$

and U_k represents the nth roots of r cis x

BINOMIAL FORMULA

$$(x + y)^n = {}_nC_0 x^n y^0 + {}_nC_1 x^{n-1} y^1 + \ldots + {}_nC_{n-1} x^1 y^{n-1} + {}_nC_n x^0 y^n$$

QUADRATIC FORMULA

The solutions to $ax^2 + bx + c = 0$ are $x = \dfrac{-b \pm \sqrt{b^2 - 4ac}}{2a}$

GRAPHS

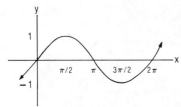

$y = \sin x$

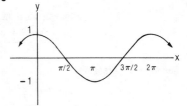

$y = \cos x$

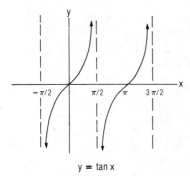

$y = \tan x$

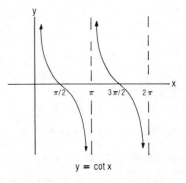

$y = \cot x$

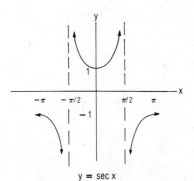

$y = \sec x$

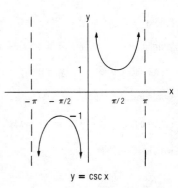

$y = \csc x$

MATHEMATICAL SYMBOLS

+ plus, the sign of addition
− minus, the sign of subtraction
± plus or minus
× multiplication (times)
÷ divided by
= equal to
≠ not equal to
≡ identically equal to
> greater than (or remainder)
< less than
≯ not greater than
≮ not less than
≥ equal to or greater than
≤ equal to or less than
≈ approximately equal to
| | absolute value
∪ logical sum; union
∩ logical product; intersection
⊆ is a subset of
⊂ is a proper subset of
→ approaches the limit of
⇔ equivalent to
≅ congruent to
∼ difference; similar to
∝ varries as; is directly proportional to
∷ geometric proportion
: is to; the ration of
:: as; equals; used between ratios
∞ indefinitely great: the symbol for infinity
−∞ the symbol for minus infinity, infinitely small
! the factorial of
∴ therefore
∵ since;because
... and so on
( ) the ordered pair (a, e)

[ ] square brackets
( ) enveloping brackets, the set of
∥ parallel
∦ not parallel
numbers to follow
% per cent
√ square root
$\sqrt[n]{}$ nth Root
r^n r to the power n, r to the nth power
∠ angle
∟ right angle
⊥ perpendicular
○ circle; circumference; 360°
⌒ arc of a circle
△ triangle
□ square
▭ rectangle
▱ parallelogram
∅ diameter
o ellipse
⍋ sector
⌒ segment
X quantic
° ′ ″ degree, minute, second
   ($1° = 60′$, $1′ = 60″$)
Σ summation
∫ integration sign
′, ″, ‴ prime, double(second) prime, triple (third) prime
— vinculum (above letter)
π Pi (3.14159+)
e 2.7182818828459----
ε an element of, is contained in, is a member of
′ complement (i.e., A' is read the complement of A)

GENERAL BIOLOGY
QUESTIONS AND ANSWERS

1. What 3 simple sugars have the empirical formula $C_6H_{12}O_6$? How many carbon atoms does each sugar have?
ANSWER: Glucose, fructose, and galactose/6.

2. Identify the organelle responsible for or associated with each of the following functions.

    a) respiration
    b) photosynthesis
    c) protein synthesis
    d) protein digestion
    e) water or food storage
    f) information storage
    g) possible storehouse for substances secreted by cells of glands (named for an Italian)
    h) mitotic pole formation in animal cells

ANSWER: a) mitochondrion b) chloroplast c) endoplasmic reticulum d) lysosomes e) vacuole f) nucleus or chromosome g) Golgi bodies h) centriole.

3. What term means ''having two chromosomes of every homologous chromosome pair''? What term means ''having one chromosome of each homologous chromosome pair''? Which of these terms can be used to indicate the chromosome content of a sex cell?
ANSWER: Diploid/Haploid (monoploid)/Haploid (monoploid).

4. Identify the important biological processes described in each of the following.

    a) Involves light and dark reactions
    b) Involves transcription and translation
    c) Involves glycolysis, citric acid cycle, and electron, or hydrogen, transport
    d) Involves use of energy from inorganic chemical reactions to produce sugar, or organic compounds

ANSWER: a) photosynthesis b) protein synthesis c) cell respiration d) chemosynthesis.

5. What term refers to the division of a cell into two approximately equal parts? What term refers to division of the nuclear material, and what term refers to division of the cytoplasm?
ANSWER: Binary fission/Karyokinesis/Mitosis or cytokinesis.

6. Name the 4 nitrogenous bases found in DNA and tell which base is replaced by uracil in RNA.
ANSWER: Adenine, guanine, cytosine, and thymine/Thymine.

7. Identify each of the biological sciences from the given descriptions.

    a) the application of statistics to the study of biological problems
    b) the study of engineering systems based on principles found in living things
    c) the study of a germ-free environment
    d) the study of the land and its animals
    e) the classification and naming of living things
    f) the science of communication and control theory concerned with the relationships between living things and mechanical devices
    g) the study of the land and its plants
    h) the study of ethical problems involved in biological research
    i) the use of physics in studying living things

ANSWER: a) biometrics b) bionics c) gnotobiotics d) zoogeography e) taxonomy f) cybernetics g) phytogeography h) bioethics i) biophysics.

8. What are the 4 imaginary humors (liquids) that the ancient philosophers thought made up the human body and determined the health of that body by the proper balance of the 4 humors? Give a descriptive adjective for each humor and explain its meaning.
ANSWER: Blood, phlegm, (yellow) bile, and black bile/Sanguine (blood) means ''cheerful, confident, and optimistic''; phlegmatic means ''sluggish, slow, unexcitable, and stolid''; ''bilious or choleric — bilious means ''bad-tempered or cross,'' and choleric means ''quick-tempered or irritable''; and melancholic (black bile was really a non-existent fluid thought to come from the spleen or kidney) means ''gloomy, sad, or depressed.''

9. Give the proper name for each of the following subject areas.
    a) the study of plants
    b) the study of tissues
    c) the study of insects
    d) the study of animals
    e) the study of biological inheritance
    f) the study of an organism reacting with its environment
    g) the study of life
    h) the gross study of the human body
    i) the study of immunity from diseases
    j) the study of early animal development
    k) the study of micro-organisms
    l) the study of pond life or fresh water
    m) the science or art of growing flowers, fruits, vegetables, or ornamental shrubs

ANSWER: a) botany b) histology c) entomology d) zoology e) genetics f) ecology g) biology h) anatomy i) immunology j) embryology k) microbiology l) limnology m) horticulture.

10. Name the following cell processes.
    a) getting rid of metabolic waste
    b) breaking down materials
    c) releasing energy by breaking down food
    d) production and release of chemicals

ANSWER: a) excretion (exocytosis) b) digestion c) respiration d) secretions.

11. Identify each of the following with a biological term.
    a) "little organs"
    b) "blood suckers"
    c) "harvestman"
    d) "suicide sacs"
    e) "gardener's friend"
    f) "living jelly"
    g) "pond scum"
    h) "bleeder's disease"
    i) "the cross-eyed worm"
    j) "mother-of-pearl"
    k) "naked seed"
    l) "the key of life"
    m) "Indian's friend" (since they act as a natural compass)

ANSWER: a) organelles b) leeches c) daddy longlegs d) lysosomes e) toad f) the amoeba g) spirogyra h) hemophilia i) planarian j) nacre k) gymnosperm l) DNA m) pleurococcus.

12. Name the following parts of the modern compound microscope.
    a) part used to vary the light intensity
    b) two parts that contain lens, or the two major lenses
    c) part used for focusing

ANSWER: a) diaphragm b) objective and eyepiece (ocular) c) adjustment knobs.

13. What type of man is identified by each of the following?
    a) *homo sapiens*
    b) *homo loquens*
    c) *homo boobiensis* (H.L. Mencken's coinage)

ANSWER: a) "thinking man" b) "speaking man" c) "boob man."

14. How many chromosomes does a normal human cell contain? How many chromosomes does a normal human sex cell contain? How many chromosomes does a normal human fertilized egg contain?

ANSWER: 46/23/46.

15. What term refers to sex cell division? What technical term refers to sex cells, and what term means "union of sex cells"?

ANSWER: Meiosis/Gametes/Fertilization.

16. List the 5 stages (phases) of cell division and tell which stage is the "resting stage."

ANSWER: Interphase, prophase, metaphase, anaphase, and telophase (arranged in the order of occurence)/Interphase is the "resting stage." (Cell division can be considered to have just 4 stages as interphase can be considered as a separate stage).

17. Tell whether each of the following chemicals make up more or less than ten percent of a cell's chemical makeup.
    a) nucleic acid
    b) water
    c) protein
    d) carbohydrate

ANSWER: a) less b) more c) more d) more.

18. Give the technical term for organisms having each of the following methods of getting food.
    a) Make their own food
    b) Get food from other organisms
    c) Get food from a living host
    d) Get food from dead or nonliving organic matter

ANSWER: a) autotrophs b) heterotrophs c) parasites d) saprophytes.

19. What term refers to imprints or preserved remains of organisms that lived in the past? What type of rock provides a clue to the age of these imprints or remains? What other method do scientists have for determining the age of these imprints or remains?

ANSWER: Fossils/Sedimentary rock/Radioactive decay dating.

20. Tell whether each of the following is found in plant cells, animal cells, or both plant and animal cells.
   a) plastids   b) centriole   c) endoplasmic reticulum   d) cell wall

ANSWER: a) plant b) animal c) both plant and animal d) plant.

21. What is the name of the mysterious timing system in plants and animals which regulates the biological rhythms of the organisms? What is the name of the internal cycles that most, if not all, living things seem to have? Name the type of rhythms that are based on a 24 hour cycle.

ANSWER: Biological clock/Biorhythms/Circadian rhythms.

22. Identify each scientist from the description.
   a) Thought human beings evolved   smallpox in 1796
      from fish   f) Known for his theory of cellular
   b) Discovered how the blood circulates   pathology expounded in 1855
      in the human body   g) U.S. Army Major who led the
   c) Standardized terminology and   conquest of yellow fever
      nomenclature for plants and animals   h) Discovered penicillin in 1928
   d) Wrote *On the Origin of Species*   i) Wrote *The Sea Around Us* in 1951
   e) Vaccinated James Phipps against

ANSWER: a) Anaximander b) William Harvey c) Carolus Linnaeus d) Charles Darwin
        e) Edward Jenner f) Dr. Rudolf Virchow g) Walter Reed h) Sir Alexander
        Fleming i) Rachel Carson.

23. Name the bacillus found in the intestinal system, in which a pure gene has been isolated.

ANSWER: E coli or Escherichia coli.

24. What is the name of the condition that describes the retention of heat from sunlight at the earth's surface, caused by an accumulation of carbon dioxide and water vapor in warm air trapped by a mass of cold air?

ANSWER: Greenhouse effect.

25. What are the 2 major areas into which biology has been divided?

ANSWER: Botany, the study of plants, and zoology, the study of animals.

26. Name the organic compounds for which each of the following are building blocks.
   a) glycerol and fatty acid   c) amino acid
   b) nucleotide   d) monosaccharide

ANSWER: a) fat b) nucleic acid c) protein d) carbohydrate (sugar).

27. What biological term identifies each of the following?
   a) organisms that eat plants   c) organisms that eat both plants and meat
   b) organisms that eat meat

ANSWER: a) herbivores b) carnivores c) omnivores.

28. What 2 types of sex chromosomes do humans have? What combination of sex chromosomes produces a male, and what combination produces a female?

ANSWER: X and Y/XY/XX.

29. Name the 2 substances of which chromosomes are made. Name the area of the cell in which chromosomes are located. Give the technical term for duplication of chromosomes.

ANSWER: Nucleic acid (DNA) and protein (Histone)/Nucleus/Replication.

30. What are the names of the 2 kingdoms in a two kingdom classification system? What kingdom is added to make a three kingdom system? What kingdom is added to a three kingdom system to make a four kingdom system?

ANSWER: Plant and animal/Protista/Monera (Protista and monera are interchangeable; a 5th kingdom could be Fungi).

31. Name the following biological chemicals:
    a) energy transfer molecule or universal energy molecule
    b) major hereditary chemical
    c) photosynthesis pigment
    d) biological catalyst

ANSWER: a) ATP (adenosine triphosphate) b) DNA (deoxyribonucleic acid) c) chlorophyll d) enzyme.

32. What term refers to the relationship between organisms and their environment? What term refers to the area on earth where life is possible? What term refers to an environment in which living and nonliving things interact and materials are used in a cyclic fashion?

ANSWER: Ecology/Biosphere/Ecosystem.

33. What term refers to a group of individuals of any one kind of organism in a given ecosystem? What term refers to the place where an organism lives? What term refers to the occupation of an organism?

ANSWER: Population/Habitat/Niche.

34. What term refers to the transmission of characteristics from parents to offspring? What term refers to the study of this phenomenon? What biologist developed some basic laws and principles that govern this phenomenon? What was his nationality? With what plant did he primarily work?

ANSWER: Heredity/Genetics/Gregor Mendel/Austrian/(garden) pea or English pea.

35. What term refers to the non-sex chromosomes of an organism? How many non-sex chromosomes and how many sex chromosomes do normal human cells have?

ANSWER: Autosomes/44 (22 pair)/2 (1 pair).

36. Name the 7 basic taxonomic classifications used to classify living organisms (use ''King Philip, Come Out For God's Sake,'' if you wish). Identify which one of the groups is composed of organisms that are essentially alike and can successfully reproduce.

ANSWER: Kingdom, phylum, class, order, family, genus, and species/Species.

37. What term refers to genetic changes that occur in organisms over many generations of time? What scientist developed the most widely accepted scientific explanation for this phenomenon? What is the name given to the explanation for the phenomenon?

ANSWER: Evolution/Charles Darwin/(Natural) selection.

38. What term refers to sections of the DNA molecule that contain information governing the characteristics of an organism? What term refers to alterations that may occur in the sections of the DNA molecules?

ANSWER: Gene/Mutation.

39. How many words usually comprise modern scientific names for organisms? What basic classification group is represented by this name? What scientist developed this system of naming organisms? What is the scientific name for modern man?

ANSWER: Two/Genus/Carolus Linnaeus/*Homo sapiens*.

40. If 2 hybrid parents are crossed, and only 1 gene pair is considered, what is the expected genotypic ratio of the offspring? If long stems are dominant to short stems in the hybrid parents, what 2 kinds of long-stems will the offspring produce?

ANSWER: 1:2:1/Homozygous (pure) and Heterozygous (hybrid).

41. What would be the possible blood types of offspring from the following parents?
    a) Type A mother, type AB father   c) Type B mother, type A father
    b) Type O mother, type A father   d) Type AB mother, type AB father

ANSWER: a) types AA (Ai), AB, Bi (A, AB, B) offspring b) types Ai, O (ii) (A, O) offspring c) types AB, Ai, Bi, ii (AB, A, B, O) offspring d) types AA, AB; BB (A, AB, B) offspring.

42. What blood type in human beings is always heterozygous? What blood type is always homozygous?

ANSWER: Type AB/Type O.

43. When abnormal cell division occurs, a condition known as nondisjunction may

cause human sex cells to have 3 sex chromosomes. What would be the sex of each of the following occurrences?

a) xxx   b) xxy   c) xyy

ANSWER: a) female b) male c) male (super male).

44. What genetic term refers to each of the following occurrences?
    a) Identical paired genes for a particular trait
    b) Outward appearance as a result of gene action
    c) Different paired genes for a particular trait
    d) Hereditary make-up for a particular trait

ANSWER: a) homozygous (pure) b) phenotype c) heterozygous (hybrid) d) genotype.

45. Name the factor in human blood independent of the A, B, AB, and O blood groups. If this factor is present, the person is said to be _____ ; if this factor is absent, the person is said to be _____.

ANSWER: Rh factor/Rh positive/Rh negative.

46. What is the expected phenotype ratio from crossing a pure dominant with a hybrid and a pure recessive with a hybrid?

ANSWER: 4:0 or all dominant/2:2 or 1:1.

47. Name the type of reproduction described in the following.
    a) Outgrowth formed on the mother   c) Union of isogametes
       cell or unequal division   d) Division of cells
    b) Union of heterogametes

ANSWER: a) budding (asexual) b) sexual c) sexual d) fission (asexual).

48. What sex-linked trait appearing in about 8% of the male population causes those with this condition to see the colors red and green as shades of gray? What fact confirms that this is a sex-linked trait? What sex-linked trait is an abnormal condition of males characterized by a failure of the blood to clot? What plasma protein is essential to the normal clotting of blood?

ANSWER: Red-green color blindness/Because it appears more often in males than in females/Hemophilia (free-bleeder disease)/Fibrinogen.

49. What reduction in chromosome number will occur in the production of sperms and eggs in normal human beings?

ANSWER: Half (or 23), i.e. from 46 to 23.

50. How many mature eggs (ova) are produced in the formation of eggs by meiosis from ogonium? How many mature sperms are produced in the formation of sperms by meiosis from each spermatogonium?

ANSWER: One/Four.

51. What term is used to refer to the chromosome number of somatic (body) cells in humans? What term refers to the chromosome number of sex cells in humans?

ANSWER: Diploid (2n) number/Haploid (n) number.

52. If a mother cell containing 48 chromosomes divides by normal mitotic division, how many chromosomes will each of the 2 daughter cells have? If the daughter cells divide by normal meiotic division, what will be the chromosome number of the resulting cells?

ANSWER: 48/24.

53. Identify the important genetic relationships.
    a) Linear arrangement of genes on chromosomes
    b) Genes present on sex chromosomes
    c) Genes present in a given population
    d) The extent to which genes occur in a population

ANSWER: a) gene linkage b) sex linkage c) gene pool d) gene frequency.

54. Which of Mendel's principles or hypothesis are described in the following?
    a) Hereditary characteristics are controlled by a pair of factors
    b) A pair of factors will separate (segregate) during gamete formation
    c) One factor in a pair may prevent expression of the other

ANSWER: a) concept of unit character b) Law of segregation c) principle of dominance and recessiveness.

55. If the mother is homozygous for a trait and the father is homozygous for the same trait, what is the genotype of the offspring for that trait? If the mother is pure for the trait *tall* and the father is pure for the same trait, what is the phenotype of the offspring?

ANSWER: Homozygous/Tall.

56. If a red bull were mated to a white cow and the offspring are pink, which principle of heredity is shown? What would be the expected ratio if the pink offspring were mated?

ANSWER: Principle of incomplete dominance (nondominance/codominance)/1:2:1 (1/4 red, 2/4 mixed, 1/4 white).

57. What term is used to designate the offspring of a cross between 2 parents that differ in one or more traits? If one parent is red for the color trait and the other parent is white for color, and the offspring produced are all red, which principle of heredity is shown in the offspring?

ANSWER: Hybrid/Principle of dominance and recessiveness.

58. What phrase from the field of Zoology means ''a social hierarchy in which each person's status is determined by one's aggressiveness, wealth, or power as compared to others''? This phrase alludes to the status created when more aggressive birds peck dominated birds without fear of retaliation.

ANSWER: Pecking order or peck order.

59. The following mnemonic device may be known by anatomy students: ''Never lower Tillie's pants; Mother might come home.'' This device is used to remember the 8 carpal (wrist) bones. Name them in order.

ANSWER: Navicular, lunate, triangular, pisiform, multiangular (greater), multiangular (lesser), capitate, and hamate.

60. Identify each of the following biological terms, each of which contains a proper name, from the given descriptions.
   a) Irregular masses of endocrine cells located in the interstitial tissue of the pancreas that secrete insulin: their degeneration may be the cause of diabetes mellitus
   b) A membranous, double-walled, cuplike end of a nephric tubule surrounding the glomerulus of a vertebrate nephron
   c) The part of the vertebrate nephron that lies between the proximal and distal convoluted tubules and that extends, in a loop, from the cortex into the medulla of the kidney and plays a part in water resorption
   d) A mass of arterial capillaries, consisting of a glomerulus and its surrounding Bowman's capsule
   e) The soft, deepest layer of the epidermis from which the outer layers develop
   f) One of the long, slender excretory tubes leading from the digestive tract in most insects and some other arthropods
   g) A bony and cartilaginous tube extending from the middle ear to the pharynx that equalizes air pressure on both sides of the eardrum
   h) Either of two small glands lying along side and discharging into the male urethra
   i) Either of two slender tubes that carry the egg from the ovary to the uterus
   j) Any of the small canals through which blood vessels pass in bone
   k) The random, constant motion created by bombardment by other molecules of small particles as they are dispersed in a fluid
   l) A cytoplasmic organelle believed to function in the formation of secretions within the cell
   m) A series of oxidation-reduction reactions in the living organism which produce carbon dioxide and water to provide energy in the form of phosphate-rich ATP

ANSWER: a) islets, or islands of Langerhans (after Paul Langerhans, German) b) Bowman's capsule (after Sir William Bowman, English) c) loop of Henle, or Henle's loop (after F.G.J. Henle, German) d) Malpighian corpuscle, or Malpighian body (after Marcello Malpighi, Italian) e) Malpighian layer f) Malpighian tube (or Malpighian tubule, Malpighian vessel) g) Eustachian tube (after Bartolommeo Eustachio, Italian) h) Cowpers glands, also called *bourethral gland* (after William Cowper, English) i) Fallopian tube (after Gabriel Fallopius or Fallopio, Italian) j) Haversian canal (after Clopton Havers, English) k) Brownian motion, or Brownian movement (after Robert Brown, Scottish) l) Golgi apparatus, or Golgi body (after Camillo Golgi, Italian) m) Krebs cycle, also called *citric acid cycle* or *tricarboxylic acid cycle* (after Sir Hans Adolf Krebs, German).

61. What 2 words were popularized by Carolus Linnaeus in 1745-1746, one meaning "the plants of a particular area or time" after the Roman goddess of flowers, the other meaning "the animals of particular area or time" after the sister or wife of the Roman god of nature, the patron of farming and animals?
ANSWER: Flora and fauna.

HUMAN ANATOMY AND PHYSIOLOGY

1. Give the technical term for each of the following body planes.
   a) crosswise plane   b) side to side   c) front to rear
ANSWER: a) transverse or horizontal b) coronal or frontal c) sagittal.

2. Name the 2 basic types of glands found in the body, and tell which gland type secretes substances into the blood.
ANSWER: Endocrine and exocrine (ductless or duct) glands/Endocrine (ductless) glands.

3. Name the 5 accessory organs of the skin.
ANSWER: Hair, nails, sebaceous glands (oil glands), sweat glands, and ceruminous glands (wax glands).

4. List the 2 basic skin layers, and tell which layer contains keratinized cells.
ANSWER: Epidermis and dermis/Epidermis.

5. List, in order from simplest to most complex, the 4 levels of body structure organization.
ANSWER: Cell, tissue, organ, and organ system.

6. Name the 3 shapes of epithelial cells.
ANSWER: Squamous or flat, columnar, and cuboidal or cube.

7. Give the common names for each of the following cell types.
   a) neuron   f) chondrocyte
   b) gamete   g) plexus
   c) osteocyte   h) erythrocyte
   d) ganglion   i) rod
   e) leucocyte   j) phagocytes
ANSWER: a) nerve cell b) male or female reproductive cell c) bone cell d) nerve cells or mass of nerve cells e) white blood cell f) cartilage cell g) nerve cells or mass of nerve cell bodies h) red blood cell i) eye cell j) engulfing cells.

8. Identify the basic tissue category for each of the following.
   a) cardiac   b) adipose   c) squamous   d) bone
ANSWER: a) muscle b) connective c) epithelial d) connective.

9. Name the 4 basic types of tissues.
ANSWER: Epithelial, connective, nervous, and muscular.

10. Name the main pigment that is responsible for skin color, and name the condition characterized by a lack of the pigment. Also, tell what external factor normally stimulates production of this pigment.
ANSWER: Melanin and albinism/Ultraviolet radiations.

11. Give the term for the location of each of the following body fluids.
    a) Fluid within cells   b) Fluid outside of cells   c) Fluid between cells
ANSWER: a) intracellular b) extracelluar c) intercelluar.

12. Name the 2 protein filaments found in the contractile fibers of muscle cells, and tell which filament is the thicker of the two filaments.
ANSWER: Actin and myosin/Myosin.

13. Identify the following types of muscle tissues.

a) Tissue located in internal organs   c) Tissue located in muscles attached to
b) Tissue located in the heart   bones
ANSWER: a) smooth or visceral muscle b) cardiac or heart muscle c) skeletal or striated muscle.

14. Give the technical name for each of the following glands.
    a) master gland   b) tear gland   c) oil gland   d) stomach gland
ANSWER: a) pituitary b) lacrimal c) sebaceous d) gastric.

15. What are the 3 enzymes in the pancreas?
ANSWER: Trypsin, amylase, and lipase.

16. Name 4 enzymes of the intestinal glands of the small intestine?
ANSWER: Erepsin, maltase, lactase, and sucrase.

17. Identify the endocrine gland that performs each of the following functions.
    a) Produces adrenalin
    b) Produces growth hormone
    c) Produces a hormone that controls body metabolic rate
    d) Produces a hormone called insulin
ANSWER: a) adrenal gland b) pituitary c) thyroid d) pancreas (islets of Langerhans).

18. Name the following endocrine gland disorders.
    a) Lack of the pancreatic hormone insulin
    b) Overproduction of pituitary growth hormone during development
    c) Enlargement of the thyroid gland causing a swelling of the neck
    d) Underproduction of thyroid hormone during development
ANSWER: a) sugar diabetes (diabetes mellitus) b) giantism c) goiter d) thyroid dwarfism, cretinism, or infantile myxedema.

19. Identify each ''-ology'' from the following descriptions.
    a) the study of blood vessels   f) the study of joints
    b) the study of blood   g) the study of old age
    c) the study of cells   h) the study of the eyes
    d) the study of the head   i) the study of teeth
    e) the study of the nose   j) the study of ulcers
ANSWER: a) angiology b) hematology c) cytology d) cephalogy e) rhinology and nasology f) arthrology g) gerontology and nostology h) ophthalmology i) odontology j) helcology.

20. Metabolism consists of both the breakdown and the synthesis of compounds. What is the technical name for each process?
ANSWER: Catabolism is the breakdown or destructive metabolism, and anabolism is the synthesis or constructive metabolism.

21. Give the technical term or answer for each of the following descriptions.
    a) A high-energy compound common to all living organisms that functions in energy storage and transfer
    b) The normal pH of human blood
    c) A substance which stimulates the production of antibodies
    d) A protein that acts as a catalyst
    e) Chemical secretion of a ductless gland transported to another organ or tissue where it has a specific effect
ANSWER: a) ATP (Adenosine TriPhosphate) b) 7.4 c) antigen d) enzyme e) hormone.

22. Give the full meaning of the following abbreviations.
    a) ACTH   d) LH   g) TSH
    b) TRF   e) FSH   h) D.T.'s
    c) LSD   f) ADH
ANSWER: a) adrenocorticotropic hormone b) thyrotropin releasing factor c) lysergic acid d-iethylamide d) luteinizing hormone e) follicle stimulating hormone f) antidiuretic hormone g) thyroid stimulating hormone h) delirium tremens.

23. Identify the following glands as endocrine or exocrine or both endocrine and exocrine.
    a) pancreas   b) testes   c) liver   d) pituitary

ANSWER: a) endocrine and exocrine b) endocrine c) exocrine d) endocrine.

24. Name the glands of the body that produce each of the following hormones.

a) thyroxine

b) estrogen

c) insulin

d) cortin

e) oxytocin

f) testosterone

g) epinephrine, or adrenalin

h) aldosterone

i) growth and trophic

j) progesteron

ANSWER: a) thyroid b) ovary c) pancreas or islets of langerhans d) adrenal cortex e) pituitary posterior lobe f) testes g) adrenal medulla h) adrenal cortex i) pituitary j) ovary.

25. With which glands are the following enzymes associated?

a) maltase

b) pepsin

c) erepsin

d) sucrase

e) amylase

f) ptyalin

g) trypsin

h) lipase

ANSWER: a) intestinal b) pancreas c) intestinal d) intestinal e) salivary and pancreas f) salivary g) pancreas h) pancreas.

26. What are the names of the 2 lobes of the pituitary gland?
ANSWER: The anterior lobe and the posterior lobe.

27. What term refers to the ''internal steady state'' that must be maintained within the body? What French physiologist developed this concept, and what American physiologist coined the term?
ANSWER: Homeostasis/Christian Bernard/Walter Cannon.

28. What are the 3 parts of the body that form the thoracic cavity which holds the lungs, the trachea, the heart and the esophagus?
ANSWER: Ribs, breastbone, and spine.

29. Name the 6 parts of the breathing organs of man that make up the respiratory system.
ANSWER: Nose, mouth, windpipe (trachea), 2 bronchi (bronchial tubes), bronchioles, and air sacs.

30. Identify the major organ of the human body associated with each of the following terms.

a) hepatic

b) pulmonary

c) gastric

d) encephalon

e) cardiac

ANSWER: a) liver b) lung c) stomach d) brain e) heart.

31. Name the 3 body cavities.
ANSWER: Cranial cavity, thoracic cavity, and abdominal cavity.

32. Name in order the 3 parts of the small intestine.
ANSWER: Duodenum, jejunum, and ileum.

33. Name the 5 divisions of the alimentary canal. List them in order from first to last as they function in the digestive system.
ANSWER: Mouth, esophagus, stomach, small intestine, and large intestine.

34. Name the following body parts.

a) Master gland of the body

b) Molecule in red blood cells that carries oxygen

c) Largest organ in the human body

d) Building blocks of proteins

e) Chief artery in the human body

f) Secretions of ductless glands

g) Muscular contractions of the esophagus that push food through in swallowing

h) Muscular wall that divides the heart lengthwise

i) Main nerve trunk of the parasympathetic nervous system

ANSWER: a) pituitary b) hemoglobin c) skin d) amino acids e) aorta f) hormones g) peristalsis h) septum i) vagus nerve.

35. Name the following parts of the digestive system.

a) Two large glands that produce digestive substances for the small intestine

b) Sack structure in which bile is stored

c) Protrusion at the end of the caecum of the large intestine

ANSWER: a) liver and pancreas b) gall bladder c) appendix.

36. Name the following parts of the respiratory system.

a) Region in the back of the mouth that is a passageway for food and air
b) Voice box
c) Windpipe
d) Protruding pouches of the air sacs where gas exchange occurs

ANSWER: a) pharynx b) larynx c) trachea d) alveoli.

37. Answer the following questions concerning the mechanics of breathing.
    a) Does the chest size increase or decrease during inhalation?
    b) Does the chest pressure increase or decrease during inhalation?
    c) What 2 muscles play the major role in breathing?

ANSWER: a) increases b) decreases c) rib (intercostal) muscles and the diaphragm.

38. Name the following parts of the excretory system.
    a) Bean shaped organ where waste is removed from the blood
    b) Place where urine accumulates before removal from the body
    c) Tube that carries urine out of the body
    c) Tube that connects the kidneys with the urinary bladder

ANSWER: a) kidney b) urinary bladder c) urethra d) ureter.

39. Answer each of the following questions concerning the lymphatic system.
    a) What other body system is closely associated with the lymphatic system?
    b) What is the technical term for the lymphatic fluid?
    c) What is the term applied to the numerous enlarged areas of the lymphatic system where white blood cells destroy germs?
    d) What is the name of the two large lymphatic structures located on the sides of the back of the mouth?

ANSWER: a) circulatory system b) lymph c) lymph nodes d) tonsils.

40. Name the following parts of the digestive system.
    a) Covers the opening to the trachea or windpipe during swallowing
    b) Digestive glands in the mouth region
    c) Place where digestion is completed
    d) Place where water is removed from unabsorbed digested food to form feces

ANSWER: a) epiglottis b) salivary glands c) small intestine d) large intestine.

41. Answer each of the following questions concerning the kidneys.
    a) What is the name of the tiny filters found in the kidneys?
    b) What is the technical term for the substance formed in the kidneys?
    c) What two things do the kidneys remove from blood in order to regulate the volume and osmotic pressure of the blood?

ANSWER: a) nephrons b) urine c) salts and water.

42. What are the names of the 2 female hormones secreted by the ovary cells?
ANSWER: Estrogen and progesterone.

43. What are the 4 stages in the uterine cycle of the female?
ANSWER: Menstruation, follicle stage, ovulation, and the corpus luteum stage.

44. Give the names of the 4 extraembryonic membranes.
ANSWER: Chorion, amnion, yolk sac, and allantois.

45. Name the following parts of the female reproductive system.
    a) Structure in which eggs are formed
    b) Structure that serves as the place where fertilized eggs normally develop
    c) Tube that connects each ovary to the uterus
    d) Tube that connects the uterus to the body surface

ANSWER: a) ovary b) uterus c) fallopian tube or oviduct d) vagina.

46. Name the following parts of the male reproductive system.
    a) Structure in which sperm is formed
    b) The three glands that add activating secretions to sperm
    c) Tube that carries sperm through the penis

ANSWER: a) testes b) Cowper's gland, prostate gland, seminal vesicle c) urethra.

47. Answer the following questions concerning human development.
    a) What term means the union of sperm and egg?
    b) What term is applied to the developing human before it becomes recognizable

as a human?

c) What term is applied to the developing human after it becomes recognizable as a human?

d) In what structure does the exchange of material occur between the mother's blood and the baby's blood?

ANSWER: a) fertilization b) embryo c) fetus d) placenta.

48. Identify the blood solids that perform each of the following functions.

a) Transports oxygen   b) Destroys germs   c) Forms blood clots

ANSWER: a) red blood cells (erythrocytes — hemoglobin) b) white blood cells (leucocytes) c) platelets (thrombocytes).

49. Name the liquid part of the blood, and name the 3 blood solids.

ANSWER: Plasma/The 3 blood solids are red blood cells (erythrocytes), white blood cells (leucocytes) and platelets (thrombocytes).

50. Name the chemical in blood that attacks foreign protein in the body and give the name for the foreign proteins that are attacked. Name the body chemical that defends the body cells against viral attack.

ANSWER: Antibody (agglutinin) and antigen (agglutinogen)/Interferon (this answer has not been proven conclusively).

51. Name the 3 branches of the aortic arch.

ANSWER: Innominate artery, left common carotid, and the left subclavian.

52. Give the names of the 2 sets of one-way valves in the heart.

ANSWER: Atrioventricular valves and semilunar valves.

53. What are the names of the 2 phases of a heartbeat?

ANSWER: Systole and diastole.

54. Name the blood vessels having the following descriptions.

a) Microscopic blood vessels

b) Vessels that carry blood away from the heart

c) Vessels that carry blood toward the heart

d) Vessels that have valves

ANSWER: a) capillaries b) arteries c) veins d) veins.

55. Name the blood vessels having the following descriptions.

a) Carries blood to the lungs

b) Carries blood out of the heart to the body

c) Carries blood from the body directly into the heart

c) Carries blood to the heart muscle

ANSWER: a) pulmonary arteries b) aorta c) vena cavas d) coronary artery.

56. Identify each of the following heart structures.

a) Thin walled chamber that receives blood

b) Thick walled chamber that pumps blood out of the heart

c) Place where heart beat originates

d) Wall that separates the ventricles

ANSWER: a) atrium (auricle) b) ventricle c) pacemaker (sinoatrial node) d) septum.

57. Name each of the following body disorders.

a) Swelling and fusion of the joints

b) Hardening of the arteries

c) Destruction of the mucous membrane of the air passages of the respiratory tract

d) Destruction of alveoli

ANSWER: a) arthritis b) arteriosclerosis c) chronic bronchitis d) emphysema.

58. Identify each of the following phrases in relation to the human anatomy or its conditions.

a) hardening of the arteries

b) "the river of life"

c) "soldiers"

d) "chemical messengers"

e) white of the eye

f) "system for fight or flight"

g) low blood sugar

h) "glands of combat" or "emergency glands"

ANSWER: a) arteriosclerosis b) blood c) white corpuscles d) hormones e) sclerotic layer f) sympathetic nervous system g) hypoglycemia h) paired adrenal glands.

59. What are the 4 types into which all human blood can be classified?
ANSWER: **A, B, AB, or O.**

60. Name the 3 proteins found in plasma.
ANSWER: **Fibrinogen, serum albumin, and serum globulin.**

61. Associate a number with each of the following.

a) teeth in a normal adult
b) milk or deciduous teeth
c) pairs of spinal nerves
d) pairs of ribs
e) quarts of blood in the human body

f) parathyroid glands
g) ventricles in the brain
h) per cent of water in the human body
i) teeth in each jaw
j) pairs of cranial nerves

ANSWER: **a) 32 b) 20 c) 31 d) 12 e) 6 f) 4 g) 4 h) 60 i) 16 j) 12.**

62. What are the 3 body types ending in -*morph*? Define or describe each one.
ANSWER: **Endomorph (abdominal physical type); ectomorph (slender physical type); and mesomorph (athletic physical type).**

63. Identify the vitamin deficiency for each of the following.

a) rickets
b) pellagra
c) night blindness (nyctalopia)
d) scurvy

e) beriberi
f) premature aging
g) hemorrhages
h) pernicious anemia

ANSWER: **a) D (calciferol) b) PP (niacin) c) A (axerophthol) c) C (ascorbic acid) e) B_1 (thiamin) f) B_2 or G (riboflavin) g) K phylloquinone h) B_{12} (cyanocobalamin).**

64. What parts of the human body contains the following structures?

a) aqueous humor
b) arachnoid matter
c) rods and cones
d) dentine
e) epiglottis

f) tympanic membrane
g) fovea
h) solar plexus
i) hypothalmus
j) nephrons

ANSWER: **a) eye b) brain and spinal cord c) eye d) tooth e) trachea f) ear g) eye h) abdomen i) brain j) kidney.**

65. Identify the parts of the brain which control various processes as described in each of the following.

a) Equilibrium and muscular coordination
b) The activity of internal organs
c) Many basic body functions such as temperature, water balance, etc.
d) Seats of emotions, responsible for intelligence

ANSWER: **a) cerebellum b) medulla oblongata c) hypothalamus d) cerebrum.**

66. Name the 5 human sense organs.
ANSWER: **Eyes, ears, nose, tongue, and skin.**

67. Name the 4 common flavors that can be distinguished by a human's taste buds.
ANSWER: **Sour, sweet, salt, and bitter.**

68. What are the 3 distinct layers of the eyeball?
ANSWER: **Sclerotic layer, choroid layer, and the retina.**

69. What are the names of the 2 humors of the eye?
ANSWER: **The aqueous humor and the vitreous humor.**

70. Name the 2 types of photoreceptors (nerve cells) of the eyeball.
ANSWER: **Cones and rods.**

71. Through what 5 areas of the eye must light rays pass before striking the retina?
ANSWER: **Cornea, aqueous humor, pupil, lens, and vitreous humor.**

72. What are the 3 most frequent eye defects?
ANSWER: **Astigmatism, nearsightedness, and farsightedness.**

73. Name the 4 types of teeth in the human mouth.
ANSWER: **Incisors (8), canines (cuspids, 4), premolars (bicuspids, 8), and Molars (12).**

74. What are the 3 parts of the general structure of teeth?
ANSWER: **Crown, neck, and root.**

75. Name the 12 pairs of cranial nerves stemming from man's brain, and name them in order from the first pair to the 12th pair. Medical interns may use the following mnemonic device to help recall these nerves: ''On old Olympus' treeless tops/A fat-arsed Goth vends some hops.''
ANSWER: **Olfactory, optic, oculomotor, trochlear, trigeminal, abducens, facial, acoustic, glossopharyngeal, vagus, spinal-accessory, and hypoglossal.**

76. The outer ear, the middle ear, and the inner ear are the 3 divisions of the human ear. What are the 3 movable little bones of the middle ear?
ANSWER: **Hammer, anvil, and stirrup.**

77. There are 6 bones that make up the ears. Name the 3 types that have 2 bones each. Arrange them in correct order from the ear drum toward the middle ear.
ANSWER: **Malleus, incus, and stapes.**

78. What are the names of the 2 delicate structures of the inner ear?
ANSWER: **The cochlea and the semicircular canals.**

79. What 2 parts of the body does the Eustachian tube connect?
ANSWER: **The middle ear with the throat.**

80. Name the part of the human body associated with each of the following terms.
   a) renal
   b) buccal
   c) pectoral
   d) dorsal
   e) ventral
   f) optical
   g) rectal
   h) nasal
   i) cranial
   j) tarsal
ANSWER: **a) kidney b) mouth c) chest d) back e) belly f) eye g) rectum h) nose i) skull j) foot or ankle.**

81. Name the 2 antagonistic divisions of the autonomic nervous system, and name the part of the central nervous system that controls simple reflexes.
ANSWER: **Parasympathetic and sympathetic/The spinal cord.**

82. Name the specific structure of the nervous system that is described by each of the following.
   a) Snail-like structure in the ear that has nerve endings for hearing
   b) Three ringed structure in the ear that has nerve endings for balance
   c) Inner lining of the eye that has nerve endings for vision
ANSWER: **a) cochlea b) semicircular canals d) retina.**

83. Give the technical term for a nerve cell, and give the 3 basic parts of a nerve cell.
ANSWER: **Neuron/Axon, dendrite, and cell body.**

84. Name the 3 types of neurons based on the direction they conduct impulses, and identify which type lies within the brain and spinal cord.
ANSWER: **Sensory (afferent), motor (efferent), and interneuron (associative or connector/The interneuron (associative or connector).**

85. Give the technical name for each of the following divisions of the nervous system.
   a) Brain and spinal cord
   b) Nerves located outside the brain and spinal cord
   c) Nerves that control various involuntary body functions
ANSWER: **a) central nervous system b) peripheral nervous system c) autonomic nervous system.**

86. Give the technical word for the membrane that covers the brain and spinal cord, and name the 3 layers of this membrane.
ANSWER: **Meninges/The dura mater, the arachnoid membrane, and the pia mater.**

87. Identify the part of the brain that performs each of the following functions.
   a) Controls balance and muscular coordination
   b) Controls involuntary body functions such as heart beat rate and breathing
   c) Controls voluntary actions and contains centers for sensory impressions, intelligence, and memory
ANSWER: **a) cerebellum b) medulla oblongata c) cerebrum.**

88. Identify the general body area where each of the following skeletal muscles is located.
    a) biceps   b) gastrocnemeus   c) pectoralis   d) masseter
ANSWER: a) upper arm b) lower leg c) chest d) jaw (face).

89. List 4 of the 5 functions provided by the skeletal system.
ANSWER: Support, protection, movement, reservoir (mineral storage), and hemo-poiesis (blood tissue formation) or hematopoiesis.

90. Identify the following parts of the skeletal system.
    a) Tissue that connects bones together
    b) Place where bones meet
    c) Covering on the ends of long bones
    d) Tissue that connects muscle to bone
ANSWER: a) ligament b) joint c) (articular) cartilage d) tendon.

91. Name the 4 types of bones.
ANSWER: Long, short, flat, and irregular.

92. Identify the type of bone for each of the following bones.
    a) ribs   b) vertebrae   c) phalanges   d) wrist bones
ANSWER: a) flat bone b) irregular bone c) long bone d) short bone.

93. Name the 3 types of movable joints in the human body.
ANSWER: Ball and socket, hinge, and mixed.

94. Name the blood forming tissue found in bone, and name the 2 varieties of this tissue.
ANSWER: Marrow/Red and yellow marrow.

95. Arrange the following 5 bones of the vertebrae in order from the head downward: sacral, cervical, coccyx, lumbar, and thoracic.
ANSWER: Cervical, thoracic, lumbar, sacral, and coccyx.

96. Give the term for each of the following body parts.
    a) Ends of a long bone   c) Membrane covering the outside of a bone
    b) Shaft of a long bone   d) Hollow cavity in the shaft of a long bone
ANSWER: a) epiphysis b) diaphysis c) periosteum d) medullary (marrow) cavity.

97. Give the name for the body part which contains each of the following bones.
    a) maxilla   d) radius   g) scapula
    b) lumbar   e) incus   h) ischium
    c) fibula   f) manubrium   i) palatine
ANSWER: a) skull b) vertebrae c) leg d) lower arm e) ear f) sternum (breast plate) g) pectoral girdle (shoulder) h) pelvic girdle i) skull.

98. Give the total number of bones found in the human skeleton. Name the 2 divisions of the human skeleton, and give the number of bones found in each division.
ANSWER: 206/Appendicular has 126, and axial has 80.

99. Give the common name for each of the following bones.
    a) clavicle   d) patella   g) carpi
    b) scapula   e) tarsi   h) coccyx
    c) sternum   f) humerus
ANSWER: a) collarbone b) shoulder blade c) chestbone d) kneecap e) ankle bones f) upper arm bone g) wrist bones h) bones at the base of the spine.

100. Name the 7 bones in the leg of a human being.
ANSWER: Femur, patella, fibula, tibia, tarsal bones, metatarsals, and phalanges.

101. What are the 2 bones of the lower leg?
ANSWER: The fibula and the tibia.

102. Name the 6 bones of the arm and hand.
ANSWER: Humerus, ulna, radius, carpals, metacarpals, and phalanges.

103. What are the 3 bones that make up the pelvis in the human body?
ANSWER: Ilium, ischium, and pubis.

104. Name the 2 bones in the lower arm.
ANSWER: The radius and the ulna.

105. There are 206 bones in the human body. Give the total number of bones in each of the following sections of the body.

a) skull
b) the ears
c) vertebrae
d) vertebral ribs
e) sternum
f) upper arms (extremities)
g) lower legs (extremities)
h) pelvic girdle

ANSWER: a) 22 b) 6 c) 26 d) 24 e) 4 f) 60 g) 58 h) 2. There are also 4 bones in the pectoral girdle.

106. There are 22 bones in the human skull. Name 8 of the 13 different types.

ANSWER: Occipital, parietal, sphenoid, ethmoid, inferior nasal conchae, frontal, nasal, lacrimal, temporal, maxilla, zygomatic, palatine, and mandible.

107. There are 26 bones in the vertebrae of the human body. Name the 5 different major bones.

ANSWER: Cervical (7), thoracic (12), lumbar (5), sacral (5 are fused to form the sacrum), and the coccyx (3 to 5 are fused to form the coccyx).

108. Name the 4 bones in the sternum.

ANSWER: Manubrium, sternebrae (''The Body''), xiphisternum, and hyoid.

ZOOLOGY

1. What is the literal meaning of the word *protozoa*? Give the scientific name for the 4 protozoan phyla.

ANSWER: ''First animals''/Sarcodina, ciliophora (ciliata), mastigophora, and sporozoa.

2. Give the protozoan phylum to which each of the following organisms belongs.

a) euglena
b) ameba (amoeba)
c) paramecium
d) plasmodium (malaria parasite)

ANSWER: a) mastigophora (euglenophyta) b) sarcodina c) ciliata (ciliophora) d) sporozoa.

3. What is the literal meaning of the term ''*pseudopodia*?'' What term refers to whiplike cellular projections used for locomotion? What term refers to ''hairlike cellular projections used for locomotion''?

ANSWER: ''False feet''/Flagella/Cilia.

4. What term refers to animals that do not have backbones? What term refers to animals that have backbones? How many phyla of animals have backbones?

ANSWER: Invertebrates/Vertebrates/1.

5. Give the phylum name for each of the following animals.

a) pore bearing animals
b) flatworms
c) joint footed animals
d) stinging cell animals

ANSWER: a) porifera (sponges) b) platyhelminthes c) arthropoda d) coelenterata (onidaria).

6. Give the phylum name for each of the following animals.

a) roundworms
b) segmented worms
c) spiny skin animals
d) soft bodied animals usually with a shell

ANSWER: a) nematoda b) annelida c) echinodermata d) mollusca.

7. Name the 3 phyla of worms giving their common and scientific names.

ANSWER: Flatworms (platyhelminthes)/Roundworms (nematoda)/Segmented worms (annelida).

8. Give the animal phylum to which each of the following organisms belongs.

a) earthworm   b) insect   c) squid   d) coral

ANSWER: a) annelida b) arthropoda c) mollusca d) coelenterata (cnidaria).

9. Give the animal phylum to which each of the following organisms belongs.

a) tapeworm   b) commercial sponge   c) hookworm   d) starfish

ANSWER: a) platyhelminthes b) porifera c) nematoda d) echinodermata.

10. Asymmetrical, bilateral, and radial describe the 3 common types of symmetry

found among animals. Give the type of symmetry found in each of the following animals.

a) insects   b) ameba   c) starfish   d) man

ANSWER: a) bilateral and asymmetrical b) asymmetrical c) radial d) bilateral.

11. What term refers to a digestive system which has two openings? What term refers to a digestive system that has one opening? What type of digestive system do fish have?

ANSWER: One way or complete/Two way or incomplete/One way or complete.

12. Name the animal phylum that is being described in each of the following.

a) Animals that have radial symmetry, tentacles, and incomplete digestive systems
b) Animals that have radial symmetry, tube feet, and complete digestive systems
c) Animals that have spicules, no means of locomotion, are symmetrical, and do not have a digestive system
d) Animals that have bilateral symmetry, an exoskeleton, and a complete digestive system

ANSWER: a) coelenterata (cnidaria) b) echinodermata c) porifera d) arthropoda.

13. Turbellaria, trematoda, and cestoda are three classes of the flatworm phylum called platyhelminthes. Answer the following questions concerning these classes.

a) Which one of the three classes is not completely parasitic?
b) To which class do tapeworms belong?
c) To which class do flukes belong?

ANSWER: a) turbellaria b) cestoda c) trematoda.

14. Answer each of the following questions concerning earthworms.

a) How many aortic arches, or hearts, do they have?
b) What digestive organ do they possess which grinds food using sand?
c) What term refers to the bristles on the body that aid in locomotion?

ANSWER: a) 10 b) gizzard c) setae.

15. Give the scientific name for the class to which each of the following arthropods belongs.

a) crayfish   d) millipede
b) spider   e) grasshopper
c) centipede

ANSWER: a) crustacea b) arachnida c) chilopoda d) diplopoda e) insecta.

16. Name the arthropod classes for animals with the following numbers of legs.

a) 3 pairs   d) many pairs arranged in two pairs per
b) 5 pairs   segment
c) 4 pairs

ANSWER: a) insecta b) crustacea c) arachnida d) diplopoda.

17. Name the segments of an arthropod having a body composed of 3 segments. Name the segments of an arthropod having a body composed of 2 segments. What scientific name is used to describe arthropods having many body segments?

ANSWER: Head, thorax, and abdomen/Cephalothorax and abdomen/Myripod.

18. Give the number of body segments for animals in the following classes.

a) insects   b) arachnids   c) crustaceans   d) centipedes

ANSWER: a) 3 b) 2 c) 2 d) many.

19. Name the stages in incomplete metamorphosis. Name the stages in complete metamorphosis. Which type of metamorphosis do grasshoppers have?

ANSWER: Egg, nymph, and adult/Egg, larva, pupa, and adult/Incomplete.

20. What term means going through several distinct stages in insect development? What type of chemical substance controls this process? What class of vertebrate animals has members that go through this process?

ANSWER: Metamorphosis/Hormone/Amphibia.

21. Give the 3 main characteristics of chordates. Name the 3 subphyla of chordates.

ANSWER: Dorsal tubular nerve cord, notochord, and gill slits/Hemichordata tunicata (or urochordata), cephalochordata, and vertebrata.

22. Give the common and scientific names for the 3 classes of vertebrates that are fishlike.
ANSWER: **Jawless fish — cyclostomata (agnatha), cartilagenous fish — chondrichthyes (elasmobranchii), and bony-fish — osteichthyes (pisces).**

23. To what class of fish does each of the following groups belong?
    a) lamprey and hagfish   b) perch, eel, and bass   c) shark and ray
ANSWER: **a) jawless fish (cyclostomata or agnatha) b) bony fish (osteichthyes or pisces) c) cartilagenous fish (chondrichthyes or elasmobranchii).**

24. What technical term means "cold-blooded or variable temperature"? What technical term means "warm-blooded"? What term means "to have a body temperature that remains constant"?
ANSWER: **Poikilothermic/Homoiothermic/Homoiothermic.**

25. Tell whether each of the following animals is cold-blooded or warm-blooded.
    a) fish   b) birds   c) amphibians   d) mammals
ANSWER: **a) cold-blooded b) warm-blooded c) cold-blooded d) warm-blooded.**

26. Vertebrates have 2, 3, or 4 chambered hearts. How many chambers does each of the following possess?
    a) fish   b) mammal   c) reptiles   d) bird
ANSWER: **a) 2 b) 4 c) 3 d) 4.**

27. Vertebrates breathe by lungs, gills, skin, or a combination of these. Give the breathing devices used by the following animals.
    a) fish   b) reptiles   c) amphibians   d) mammals
ANSWER: **a) gills b) lungs c) lungs, gills, and skin d) lungs.**

28. Vertebrates have skin that is bare or covered with scales, hair, or feathers. For each of the following types of vertebrates, tell whether their skin is bare or is covered with scales, hair, or feathers.
    a) mammals   b) amphibians   c) reptiles   d) cartilagenous fish
ANSWER: **a) hair b) bare c) scales d) skin.**

29. Tell the vertebrate class to which each of the following belongs.
    a) frog   b) dog   c) snake   d) whale
ANSWER: **a) amphibia b) mammalia c) reptilia d) mammalia.**

30. What term refers to producing young from eggs that hatch outside the female's body? What term refers to producing young that hatch inside the female's body? What term refers to giving birth to live young that have been nourished by a placenta inside the female's body?
ANSWER: **Oviparous/Ovoviviparous/Viviparous.**

31. What is the scientific name for birds? What specialization do birds have in their forelimbs? What type of eggs do reptiles and birds have that allows them to reproduce and develop out of water?
ANSWER: **Aves/Wings/Amniote (land) egg.**

32. The three basic types of mammals based on their early development are egg-laying, pouched, and placental mammals. Tell whether the following mammals are egg-laying, pouched, or placental.
    a) duckbilled platypus   b) kangaroo   c) man   d) spiny anteater
ANSWER: **a) egg-laying b) pouched c) placental d) egg-laying.**

33. Name the order of mammal for each of the following descriptions.
    a) flying mammals   c) flesh eating mammals
    b) aquatic mammals   d) erect mammals
ANSWER: **a) chiroptera b) cetacea or (sirenia) c) carnivora d) primate.**

34. Give the technical term for a period of winter inactivity during which an animal's metabolic rate slows down and the animal loses consciousness. Give the technical term for a period of summer dormancy. Which one of the following animals does not undergo a period of winter inactivity described in the first part of this question: bear, snake, or squirrel.
ANSWER: **Hibernation/Estivation (aestivation)/Bear.**

35. What term refers to a body cavity that is lined by a membrane and contains internal organs suspended from the membrane? What term refers to a false body cavity that is not lined by a special membrane? What type of body cavity does man have?

ANSWER: Coelom/Pseudocoelom/Coelom.

36. Identify the type of arthropod that transmits each of the following diseases.

a) Yellow fever virus

b) Typhus

c) Malaria

d) Bubonic plague

e) Venezulean equine encephalomyelitis

f) African sleeping sickness

g) Rocky Mountain spotted fever

ANSWER: a) Aedes mosquito b) human body louse c) Anopheles mosquito d) rat flea e) mosquito f) tsetse fly g) tick.

37. Name in correct order the parts of the leg of an insect from anterior to posterior.

ANSWER: Coxa, trochanter, femur, tibia, and tarsi (tarsus).

38. Arrange the following 7 parts of the digestive system of a bird in descending order starting from the mouth: stomach, rectum, cloaca, gizzard, intestine, esophagus, and crop.

ANSWER: Esophagus, crop, stomach, gizzard, intestine, rectum, and cloaca.

39. Identify the animal described in each of the following.

a) World's fastest animal

b) World's slowest-moving land mammal

c) World's fastest dog

d) World's tallest animal

e) World's longest snake

f) World's largest animal ever

g) World's largest living land animal

h) World's longest-living vertebrate animal

i) World's largest living primate

j) World's smallest breed of dog

k) World's smallest bird

l) World's longest venomous snake

ANSWER: a) cheetah (the antelope is faster at distances over 1,000 yards) b) sloth c) greyhound d) giraffe e) python f) blue whale g) elephant h) tortoise i) gorilla j) chihuahua k) hummingbird l) king cobra.

40. Name the 4 orders of anthropoid apes.

ANSWER: Gorillas, orang-outangs, chimpanzees, and gibbons.

41. Name the 2 largest varieties of snakes.

ANSWER: The anacondas and the pythons.

42. What are the 4 types of poisonous snakes commonly found in the U.S.?

ANSWER: Rattlesnake, cotton mouth (moccasin), copperhead, and coral.

43. What are the 4 families of poisonous snakes?

ANSWER: Cobras, coral snakes, vipers, and pit vipers.

44. Name the only 2 poisonous snakes found in the Eastern United States.

ANSWER: Rattlesnakes and copperheads.

45. Identify the ''-ology'' that deals with each of the following.

a) the study of snakes

b) the study of fish

c) the study of lice and ticks

d) the study of intestinal worms

e) the study of insects

f) the study of whales

g) the study of birds

h) the study of bees

i) the study of reptiles

j) the study of horses

ANSWER: a) ophiology b) ichthyology c) acarology d) helminthology e) entomology f) cetology g) ornithology h) apiology i) herpetology j) hippology.

46. Identify each of the following ''-ptera'' from the given description.

a) sheath-winged

b) like-winged

c) scale-winged

d) membrane-winged

e) half-winged

f) equal-winged

g) two-winged

h) skin-winged

i) nerve-winged

j) straight-winged

ANSWER: a) coleoptera b) homoptera c) lepidoptera d) hymenoptera e) hemiptera f) isoptera g) diptera h) dermaptera i) neuroptera j) orthoptera.

47. List the 9,000 species of birds and the 27 orders in which they are grouped.

ANSWER: Just kidding.

48. What are the 4 scientific groups in which all birds can be classified?

ANSWER: Kingdom — animal; phylum — chordata; subphylum — vertebrata; class — aves.

49. Name the 2 classes of homoiothermic animals.

ANSWER: Aves and mammalia (birds and mammals).

50. Name the 3 common genera of mosquitoes found in the United States. Which one carries yellow fever germs and which one malaria-fever germs?

ANSWER: Culex, Anopheles, and Aedes (Stegomyia)/Aedes and Anopheles.

51. Which phylum is being described in each of the following?

a) ''jointed-footed''   e) ''stomach-footed''
b) ''many-footed''   f) ''lip-footed''
c) ''double-footed''   g) ''head-footed''
d) ''hatchet-footed''   h) ''arm (upper part)-footed''

ANSWER: a) arthropoda b) myriapoda c) diplopoda d) pelecyopoda e) gastropoda f) chilopoda g) cephalopoda h) brachiopoda.

52. Arrange the following 4 mouth parts of a grasshopper from upper to lower.

a) mandibles   b) labium   c) labrum   d) maxillae

ANSWER: Labrum, mandibles, maxillae, and labium.

53. Give the number of legs for each of the following.

a) spider   e) grasshopper
b) lobster   f) crayfish
c) butterfly   g) scorpion
d) tick   h) beetle

ANSWER: a) 8 b) 10 c) 6 d) 8 e) 6 f) 10 g) 8 h) 6.

54. In the hydra's body what are the 2 cell layers that are separated by the mesoglea?

ANSWER: The ectoderm and the endoderm.

55. What are the 2 different types of body forms of the coelenterates?

ANSWER: Polyp and medusa.

56. Into what 3 classes is the flatworm phylum divided?

ANSWER: Turbellaria, trematoda, and cestoda.

57. What are the 3 segments of the thorax of the grasshopper?

ANSWER: Prothorax, mesothorax, and metathorax.

58. What phrase alluding to a fish so hungry it swallows not only the bait but the fishhook, the weight, and some of the fishing line means ''completely or in every way''?

ANSWER: Hook, line, and sinker.

59. Name the 2 kinds of paired fins on fishes.

ANSWER: Pectoral fins and pelvic fins.

60. Name the 3 kinds of single fish fins.

ANSWER: Caudal fin, dorsal fin, and anal fin.

61. What are the 3 chambers of the frog's heart?

ANSWER: 2 atria (auricles) and a muscular ventricle.

62. What is the name of the order of insects for each of the following?

a) silverfish   f) butterflies, moths
b) Mayfly   g) houseflies, mosquitoes
c) dragonflies, damsel flies   h) bedbugs, stink bugs
d) mantis, crickets   i) cicada, aphids
e) termites   j) aphis lion, lacewings

ANSWER: a) thysanura b) ephemeroptera c) odonata d) orthoptera e) isoptera f) lepidoptera g) diptera h) hemiptera i) homoptera j) meuroptera.

63. Parasitism, mutualism, and commensalism are 3 different kinds of what type of relationships?

ANSWER: Symbiosis or ''living together'' relationships.

64. Identify the type of symbiosis in which each of the following organisms participates.

a) remora and the shark
b) alga and fungus in lichen
c) tapeworms
d) protists and termites

e) chicken louse
f) lamprey
g) insects that pollinate flowers

ANSWER: a) commensalism b) mutualism c) parasitism d) mutualism e) parasitism parasitism g) mutualism.

65. What are the 3 distinct forms of a bee?
ANSWER: A queen, a drone, and a worker.

66. Name the 3 different habitats in which mollusks live.
ANSWER: Land, fresh water, and salt water.

67. Name the 5 features that characterize arthropoda.
ANSWER: Jointed appendages, hard external skeleton (or exoskeleton), segmented body, dorsal heart, and ventral nervous system.

68. Into what 2 regions is the body of a crayfish divided?
ANSWER: The cephalthorax and the abdomen.

69. Name the 5 main classes of arthropods.
ANSWER: Crustacea, chilopoda, diplopoda, arachnida, and insecta.

70. What 3 characteristics distinguish chordates from all other animals?
ANSWER: They have a rod of connective tissue called the notochord, a tubular nerve chord, and paired gill slits.

71. What are the 4 subphyla of the phylum Chordata?
ANSWER: Vertebrata, hemichordata, urochordata, and cephalochordata.

72. What are the 7 classes of modern vertebrates? List them in their order of complexity from a structural point of view beginning with the simplest.
ANSWER: Cyclostomata, chondrichthyes, osteichthyes, amphibia, reptilia, aves, and mammalia.

73. What are the 10 organ systems composing the vertebrate bodies? List them in the order that will spell MRS. DC ERNIE.
ANSWER: Muscular, Reproductive (or Respiratory), Skeletal, Digestive, Circulatory, Excretory (or Endocrine), Respiratory (or Reproductive), Nervous Integumentary, and Endocrine (or Excretory) systems.

74. Name the 4 orders of reptiles.
ANSWER: Rhynchocephalia, chelonia (testudinata), squamata, and crocodilia.

75. Using the terms *anterior, posterior, ventral* and *dorsal*, describe each of the following parts of a cat.
a) tail   b) spine   c) belly   d) nose
ANSWER: a) posterior b) dorsal c) ventral d) anterior.

76. Name the 4 classes of land-inhabiting vertebrates.
ANSWER: Amphibians, birds, mammals, and reptiles.

77. Tell whether each of these common words is flat, round, or divided into body segments.
a) nematoda   b) annelida   c) platyhelminthes
ANSWER: a) round and unsegmented b) body divided into segments c) flat and unsegmented.

78. What is the larvae of each of the following called?
a) fly   c) beetle   e) butterfly
b) moth   d) mosquito
ANSWER: a) maggot b) caterpillar c) grub d) wiggler e) caterpillar.

79. What is the weasel called when its fur is white?
ANSWER: Ermine.

BOTANY

1. What 2 basic parts make up the structure of the simplest viruses? Which of the following units are used in measuring viruses: microns, millimicrons, or angstroms?
ANSWER: **Nucleic acid core and protein coat/Millimicrons (micrometers).**

2. What 3 basic shapes do bacteria have? Which of the following units are used in measuring bacteria: microns, millimicrons, or angstroms?
ANSWER: **Coccus (cocci) is sphere-shaped; bacillus (bacilli) is rod-shaped; and spirillum (spirilla) is cork-screw shaped/Millimicrons.**

3. Mycoplasmas, rickettsiae, and spirochetes are three organisms which do not seem to fall within the virus or bacteria groups. Identify each of the following as a description of a mycoplasma, rickettsiae, or spirochete.
    a) Similar to viruses in form and size but has a cellular structure
    b) Seems to be between bacteria and viruses in size and have some characteristics of both groups
    c) Seems to lie between bacteria and larger single-celled organisms
ANSWER: **a) mycoplasma b) rickettsiae c) spirochete.**

4. Tell whether each of the following diseases is caused by a virus, rickettsiae, bacterium, or spirochete.
    a) rocky mountain spotted fever   d) food poisoning
    b) syphilis   e) tuberculosis
    c) polio   f) common cold
ANSWER: **a) rickettsiae b) spirochete c) virus d) bacteria e) bacteria f) virus.**

5. What is the term for the sticky, protective coating surrounding bacteria cells? What name is given to a thick form of this coating? What whiplike structure do some bacteria possess that help them to move?
ANSWER: **Slime layer/Capsule/Flagellum.**

6. What term refers to cells that do not have an organized nucleus? What term refers to cells that have an organized nucleus? Which of these two terms applies to bacteria cells?
ANSWER: **Prokaryotic/Eukaryotic/Prokaryotic.**

7. Name the process by which bacteria make alcohol and lactic acid from sugar. What is the chemical name for the ''swamp (marsh) gas'' produced by some types of bacteria? What term refers to poisonous chemicals produced by bacteria?
ANSWER: **Fermentation/Methane/Toxins.**

8. What term is given to the branching filaments that comprise the body of a fungus? Give the technical term for a mass of these filaments? By what form of asexual reproduction do all fungi reproduce?
ANSWER: **Hyphae/Mycelium/Sporulation (spore formation).**

9. What is the phylum name for true-fungi? Name the 4 classes of true-fungi using common or scientific terms.
ANSWER: **Eumycophyta/Phycomycete (algalike fungi), ascomycete (sac fungi), basidiomycete (club fungi), and deuteromycete (imperfect fungi).**

10. What technical term is given to the plant body of algae? What term is given to a threadlike group of algae cells? What process carried on by algae separates them from fungi?
ANSWER: **Thallus (mycelium)/Filament (hyphae)/Photosynthesis.**

11. There are six phyla of algae. Name any 4 of the algae phyla using common or scientific terms. Which algae phylum has members with cells that do not have organized nuclei?
ANSWER: **Cyanophyta (blue-green algae), chlorophyta (green algae), chrysophyta (yellow-green algae), pyrrophyta (dinoflagellates or fire algae), phaeophyta (brown algae), and rhodophyta (red algae)/Cyanophyta (blue-green algae).**

12. Give the scientific names of the 2 plant phyla? To which phyla do vascular plants belong? To which group do liverworts and mosses belong?

ANSWER: Bryophytes and tracheophytes/Tracheophytes/Byrophytes.

13. Plants have a two-stage life cycle in which a sexual reproduction stage alternates with an asexual reproduction stage. What phrase describes this type of life cycle? What technical terms refer to diploid and what to haploid?

ANSWER: Alternation of generations/Sporophyte stage (diploid)/Gametophyte state (haploid).

14. List the 3 vegetative organs of a plant. Name the vegetative organ that anchors the plant and absorbs water and minerals. Name the vegetative organ that is the main site of photosynthesis.

ANSWER: Root, stem, and leaf/Root/Leaf.

15. Name the 2 subclasses of flowering plants. Name the flowering plant subclass that has parallel leaf veination and flower parts in threes or multiples of three. Name the flowering plant subclass that has netted leaf veination and flower parts in fours or fives.

ANSWER: Monocots and dicots/Monocots/Dicots.

16. Name the class of vascular plant described by each of the following.
   a) Produces seed inside an ovary
   b) Produces seed on the surface of a reproductive structure
   c) Consists of a leafy frond having sori that forms spores

ANSWER: a) angiosperms (flowering plants) b) gymnosperms (naked seed plants) c) ferns (fiicinae).

17. Give the technical term for the plant tissue that is composed of cells that constantly divide to allow the plant to grow. Give the technical term for the thin-walled tissue that provides storage and photosynthesis areas in the plant. Give the technical term for the strengthening tissue in plants.

ANSWER: Meristematic/Parenchyma/Sclerenchyma and/or collenchyma.

18. Give the technical term for plant conduction tissue. Name the type of tissue that conducts food downward in a plant. Name the type of tissue that conducts water and minerals (upward) in a plant.

ANSWER: Vascular tissue/Phloem/Xylem.

19. What term is used to describe plants that live for one growing season? What term is used to describe plants that live for two growing seasons? What term is used to describe plants that live for more than two growing seasons?

ANSWER: Annuals/Biennials/Perennials.

20. What type of plant has a lot of strengthening and conducting tissue? What type of plant has relatively small amounts of strengthening and conducting tissue? Trees belong to which of these types of plants?

ANSWER: Woody/Herbaceous or nonwoody/Woody.

21. What type of tissue comprises the top and bottom surfaces of a leaf? What type of tissue comprises the middle area of a leaf? Which of these leaf tissues contains photosynthesis cells and conducting tissue?

ANSWER: Epidermis/Mesophyll/Mesophyll.

22. Give the name of the pores in the epidermis of a leaf. Name the type of cells that form these pores. Name 3 substances that enter and leave the plant through these pores.

ANSWER: Stoma/Guard cells/Water, carbon dioxide, and oxygen (O_2).

23. Give the technical term for the loss of water from leaves. Give the technical term for the movement of materials in a plant.

ANSWER: Transpiration/Translocation.

24. What 3 basic parts make up a seed? What is the technical term for the seed leaves that serve as food reservoirs?

ANSWER: Embryo plant, stored food, seed coats/Cotyledons.

25. Identify each of the following nonreproductive parts of a flower.
   a) Flower stalk
   b) Petal-like structures that form a ring at the outer end of the stalk

    c) Expanded region at the outer end of the stalk in which the main part of the flower rests

ANSWER: a) pedicel b) sepals c) receptacle.

26. Identify each of the following reproductive parts of a flower.
    a) Male structure consisting of a filament with a knob on the end
    b) Female part consisting of a flask shaped structure with a slender stalk
    c) Swollen base of the female part where ovules are formed

ANSWER: a) stamen b) pistil c) ovary.

27. What term refers to the male sex cells of a plant? What specific knoblike structure produces male sex cells in plants? When the male sex cell is transferred to the female part of the flower, what is the name of the sticky top of the female part on which the pollen becomes stuck?

ANSWER: Pollen/Anther/Stigma.

28. What term refers to a matured, fertilized ovule? What term refers to a ripened ovary? What term refers to the movement of a mature ovule away from the plant that produces it?

ANSWER: Seed/Fruit/Seed dispersal.

29. What term refers to the tiny projections on the surface of plant roots which aid in absorption? Name the 3 primary tissues in a plant root. Which of these primary tissues functions as a storage area?

ANSWER: Root hairs/Epidermis, cortex, and vascular cylinder (stele)/Cortex.

30. Name the following parts of a young, woody stem.
    a) Outer area composed of cork
    b) Middle area composed of vascular xylem and strengthening tissue
    c) Center area composed of primary tissue

ANSWER: a) bark b) wood c) pith.

31. What kind of plant growth lengthens a root or stem and establishes the first tissues? What kind of plant growth increases the diameter of a root or stem? Give the technical term for the tissue area that provides growth in diameter.

ANSWER: Primary growth/Secondary growth/Cambium.

32. What term refers to points along the plant stem where leaves and branches form? What term refers to the space between these points on a stem? What term refers to pores in the bark of a young twig?

ANSWER: Nodes/Internodes/Lenticels.

33. What term refers to the light and dark areas that form circles seen on the end of cut wood? What term refers to the dark, inner wood of a tree? What term refers to the light and functioning, outer wood of a tree?

ANSWER: Annual rings/Heartwood/Sapwood.

34. What class of substances formed in plants regulates plant growth? Name 2 specific types of plant growth regulators that belong to this class. A variety of which of these two types is in synthetic form the most common lawn weed-killer?

ANSWER: Hormones/Auxins and gibberillins/Auxins.

35. What term refers to a plant response to varying periods of light and darkness? What term refers to plant growth responses directly related to environmental stimuli? What term refers to plant movement reactions to external stimuli?

ANSWER: Photoperiodism/Tropism/Nastic movements.

36. Name the 2 general types of fermentation.

ANSWER: Alcohol fermentation and lactic acid fermentation.

37. What are the 2 stages of photosynthesis?

ANSWER: Light or photo phase, and dark or synthetic phase.

38. Name the 2 types of plants that compose a lichen.

ANSWER: Algae and fungi.

39. What are the 2 Phylums of the Plant Kingdom?

ANSWER: Bryophyta and tracheophyta.

40. In the field of flowering plants, what are the 2 kinds of stems?

ANSWER: Monocotyledon (herbaceous) and dicotyledon (woody).

41. Name the 2 kinds of cones produced by conifers.

ANSWER: Seed cones and pollen cones (or ovulate and pistulate or male and female).

42. Name the 2 kinds of mesophyll of most leaves.

ANSWER: Palisade mesophyll and spongy mesophyll.

43. Name the 3 well-defined regions of the primary tissues of the root.

ANSWER: Epidermis, the cortex, and the vascular cylinder or stele.

44. Identify the following plant responses with a type of biological tropism or periodism.
    a) The tendrils of a climbing plant wrap around an object they touch
    b) The roots of seeds planted upside down grow down and the shoot grows away from the earth
    c) Some roots grow toward water
    d) Leaves bend toward the light
    e) Plants are produced as a response to varying periods of day and night length

ANSWER: a) thigmotropism b) geotropism c) hydrotropism d) phototropism e) photoperiodism.

45. Give the biological term for each of the following.
    a) Plant hormone that causes cells to become longer and larger
    b) The terminal (tip) cell of a growing plant
    c) The plant cell, dead when functional, which transports water and dissolved minerals upward
    d) The poisonous, colorless substance found in tobacco leaves
    e) Any tree which sheds its leaves seasonally
    f) The green pigment in plants essential to photosynthesis
    g) The first leaves formed from a seed that acts as a food reservoir
    h) A cell plastid in plants containing chlorophyll responsible for photosynthesis
    i) The process which moves water from cell to cell through a semi-permeable membrane from an area of greater water concentration to one of lesser concentration
    j) The vascular tissue in a plant that conducts dissolved food substances

ANSWER: a) auxin or IAA (Indole Acetic Acid) b) apical or meristem cell c) xylem d) nicotine e) deciduous f) chlorophyll g) cotyledon h) chloroplast i) osmosis j) phloem.

46. Which of the following are the 4 parts found in the dicot seed?
    a) mesocarp   c) hypocotyl   e) stipe
    b) epicotyl   d) radicle   f) cotyledon

ANSWER: b, c, d, and f.

47. Identify the ''-ology'' that is concerned with each of the following areas.
    a) the study of mosses   e) the study of plant diseases
    b) the study of pollen   f) the study of seeds
    c) the study of ferns   g) the study of fruits
    d) the study of seaweed   h) the study of trees and shrubs

ANSWER: a) bryology or muscology b) palynology c) pteridology d) algology or phycology e) epiphytology or phytopathology f) spermology g) pomology h) dendrology.

48. Which 2 of the following are cell organelles found in plant cells but not in animal cells?
    a) lysosomes   b) cell wall   c) nuclei   d) chloroplasts   e) mitochondria

ANSWER: b and d.

49. Which 2 of the following trophic levels are necessary for every ecosystem?
    a) producers   b) heterotrophs   c) consumers   d) carnivores   e) decomposers

ANSWER: a and e.

50. List in order the layers of xylem and phloem in a woody stem, starting from the outside of the stem and going to the center of the stem.

ANSWER: Primary phloem, secondary phloem, secondary xylem, primary xylem.

450   Campbell's High School/College Quiz Book

NOTABLE BIOLOGISTS

Anaximander....Greek.... Developed a theory that human beings evolved from fish.

Hippocrates....Greek...."Father of Modern Medicine." The Hippocratic Oath was named for him. Wrote *Corpus Hippocraticum.*

Aristotle....Greek.... Observed and classified animals. Wrote *Parts of Animals, On Plants, History of Animals,* and *Generation of Animals.* Known as the "Father of Biology " and the "Founder of Zoology."

Pliny the Elder....Roman.... Collected data about plants and animals. Wrote *Natural History.*

Galen....Greek...."Father of Experimental Physiology." Wrote *On the Natural Faculties.* Established the idea of pulmonary circulation.

Rhazes (or Ibn Zakariya al-Razi)....Persian.... First to describe measles and smallpox, use mercurial purgatives, and publish a book on children's diseases.

Leonardo da Vinci....Italian.... Helped formulate modern anatomical study through his notebooks.

Paracelsus or **Theophrastus Philippus Aureolus Bombastus von Hohenheim.... Swiss....**Pioneer in the application of chemistry to medicine and believed that diseases had specific causes of external origin rather than an imbalance of bodily "humors." Believed that the 3 principles of the Arabs (mercury, salt, and sulfur) had to be in balance in the body for good health.

Andreas Vesalius....Flemish...."Father of Anatomy" because of his work, *Concerning the Fabric of the Human Body,* or *Fabrica* (1543).

William Harvey....English.... Discovered how the blood circulates in the human body. Wrote *An Anatomical Treatise on the Motion of the Heart and Blood in Animals* (1628). Known as the "Founder of Modern Physiology."

Marcello Malpighi....Italian.... Called the "Founder of Microscopic Anatomy." Discovered capillaries on the surface of the lung and demonstrated that they connect arteries with veins, confirming William Harvey's explanation for blood circulation.

Thomas Sydenham....English.... The "English Hippocrates." Did the first major work on epidemiology since Hippocrates. Known as the "Founder of Modern Epidemiology."

Robert Hooke....English.... First person to observe cells. Wrote *Micrographia* (1665), which was a milestone in the history of microscopy. He introduced the term *cells* in this work.

Anton van Leeuwenhoek (Leuwenhoek)....Dutch.... Discovered bacteria with a microscope. Known as the "Father of Microbiology."

Jethro Tull....English.... Invented machine drill for sowing seed and a horse-drawn row cultivator, and introduced a system of sowing in drills (c. 1701). Developed the modern system of planting crops in rows with regular cultivation between rows to control weeds.

Stephen Hales....English.... Founder of plant physiology. Wrote *Vegetable Staticks* (1727) and *Haemastaticks* (1733).

Carolus Linnaeus (Carl von Linné)....Swedish.... Classified all known plants and animals and standardized terminology and nomenclature. First to use the scientific name *homo sapiens* for humans and the signs ♂ and ♀ for male and female. His binomial nomenclature for species is the starting point for all nomenclature. Wrote *Species Plantarum* (1753) and *Systema Naturae* (1758).

Giovanni Battista Morgagni....Italian.... Published *On the Seats and Causes of Disease* (1761) which demonstrated that diseases start in specific organs of the body and are scattered throughout the body. He also described many diseases of the heart and blood vessels. "Founder of Pathological Anatomy."

Albrecht von Haller....Swiss.... Wrote the first standard textbook of physiology (1757-1765), the 8-volume *Elementa Physiologiae.*

James Lind....Scottish.... Proved that citrus fruits would cure scurvy.

John Hunter....Scottish....A major comparative anatomist. Known as the "Founder of Scientific Surgery" and the "Father of Experimental Surgery."

Edward Jenner....English.... Performed the first vaccination against smallpox, on James Phipps, in 1796. He was a pioneer in immunology and virology.

Marie François Xavier Bichat....French.... Pioneer in scientific histology and pathological anatomy. Known as the "Founder of Histology."

Baron Georges Cuvier....French.... First to compare the anatomy of various animals with that of human beings. Founder of comparative anatomy and developer of vertebrate paleontology. Wrote *Lectures on Comparative Anatomy* (1799-1805).

Jean Baptiste Chevalier de Lamarck....French.... Forerunner of Darwinian evolutionary theory. First to classify animals into vertebrates and invertebrates. His theory of Lamarckism (later proved fallacious) was that plants and animals evolve by adjusting to changes in their environment. Wrote *Zoological Philosophy* (1809).

Jean Louis Agassiz....Swiss-American.... Pioneered in classification of animals, especially fossil fish, and originated ice ages concept.

Asa Gray....American.... Specialized in the classification and description of plants. Wrote *Manual of Botany of the Northern United States* (1848).

Rudolf Virchow....German.... Established the science of pathology and is known as the "Father of Pathology," or the "Father of Cellular Pathology."

Matthias Schlieden and **Theodor Schwann....German....**Developed theory that all living organisms are composed of cells and cell products.

Charles Robert Darwin....English.... Noted for his theory of evolution through the process of natural selection. Wrote *On the Origin of Species by Means of Natural Selection, or the Preservation of Favoured Races in the Struggle for Life* (1859).

Alfred Russel Wallace....English.... Known for his independent discovery of evolutionary change at the same time as Darwin. His travels took him up the Amazon River and the Rio Negro and to the Malay Archipelago.

Johann Gregor Mendel....Austrian.... Discovered the basic principles of heredity through a breeding experiment with peas in the monastery garden. His work laid the foundation for the new science of genetics.

Thomas Henry Huxley....English.... Supported Darwin's theory of evolution. Observed marine life aboard the H.M.S. *Rattlesnake*. Became an expert on Medusae. Wrote *Evidence as to Man's Place in Nature* (1863), which related man to anthropoid apes.

Louis Pasteur....French.... Pioneer in bacteriology. Killed microbes by heat and saved the French wine industry in 1864. Later his method, pasteurization, helped preserve milk, beer, and food. In 1865, he saved the silk industry by eliminating the microbe which caused the disease. Proved the value of vaccination by vaccinating sheep against a disease called anthrax, thus founding the science of immunity. Developed a cure for rabies. Disproved the theory of spontaneous generation.

Hugo de Vries....Dutch.... Discovered and revealed (along with Carl Correns and Erich Tschermak) the importance of Gregor Mendel's work (1900) and advanced the theory of hereditary mutations.

Jean Henri Casimir Fabre....French.... Pioneer in entomology. Published *Souvenirs Entomologiques* (10 vols., 1879-1907).

Walter Reed....American.... Led an investigation that proved that mosquitoes carried the yellow fever virus from person to person. Helped show how to control typhoid fever and yellow fever.

Ivan Petrovich Pavlov....Russian.... Won the Nobel Prize for physiology or medicine in 1904 for his work on digestion and the nervous system. Famous for his conditioned reflex work with dogs.

Robert Koch....German.... Pioneer in bacteriology. Won the Nobel Prize for physiology or medicine in 1905 for his discovery of the germ causing tuberculosis (sometimes known as Koch's bacillus).

Paul Ehrlich....German.... Pioneer in immunology and chemotherapy. Researched histology of the blood. Shared the Nobel Prize for physiology or medicine in 1908 with Elie Metchnikoff for research on immunity.

Luther Burbank....American.... Developed and improved over 800 kinds of trees, plants, and flowers.

Casimir Funk....Polish-American.... Discovered vitamins. Isolated B_{11}, or thiamine (1911).

George Washington Carver....American.... Revolutionized Southern agriculture. Developed numerous products from peanuts, sweet potatoes, and pecans. Called the "Plant Doctor," and kown as the "Father of Chemurgy."

Thomas Hunt Morgan....American.... Demonstrated that living things pass on characteristics from generation to generation through genes. Won the Nobel Prize for physiology or medicine in 1933 for his work on heredity described in *The Theory of the Gene* (1926). Used the fruit fly, *Drosophilla Melangaster*, to study the laws of heredity.

Karl Landsteiner....American (b. Austria).... Won the Nobel Prize for physiology or medicine in 1930 for his discovery of the 4 types of human blood — A, B, AB, and O. Discovered (with A.S. Wiener) the Rh blood factor in 1940.

Sir Alexander Fleming.... Scottish... Discovered penicillin in 1928. Shared the Nobel Prize in medicine or physiology in 1945 for the development of this drug.

Hermann Joseph Muller...American... Won the Nobel Prize for physiology or medicine in 1946 for his discovery that X-rays can produce mutations.

Paul Hermann Muller....Swiss.... Won the Nobel Prize in physiology or medicine (1948) for developing DDT to kill insects.

Rachel Louise Carson....American.... Known for her concern for the ecology and the environment, and especially for her opposition to the indiscriminate use of pesticides. Wrote *The Sea Around Us* (1951) and *Silent Spring* (1966).

Trofim Denisovich Lysenko....Russian.... His philosophy of the treatment of seeds called vernalization had an adverse effect on Soviet biological and agricultural research.

Selman Abraham Woksman....Russian-American.... Received the Nobel Prize for physiology or medicine in 1952 for the discovery of the antibiotic streptomycin, effective against tuberculosis.

Arthur Kornberg....American.... Produced DNA artificially. Shared the Nobel Prize for physiology or medicine in 1959 for his work on the understanding of the enzymatic synthesis of DNA.

Severo Ochoa....Spanish-American.... Produced RNA artificially. Shared the Nobel Prize for physiology or medicine in 1959 for the test-tube synthesis of nucleic acids.

James D. Watson and **Francis H.C. Crick....American....**Discovered the structure of DNA, for which they shared the Nobel Prize for physiology or medicine in 1962. Wrote *The Double Helix* (1953). The double helix is the two intertwined coils that form the crystalline structure of DNA.

SCIENCES AND STUDIES OF

acarology....... lice and ticks
acology .... therapeutic agents
            (remedies)
adenology .... glands
aesthophysiology.. organs of sensation
algology......... seaweeds
andrology .... male diseases
angiology........ blood vessels
apiology......... bees
arachnology...... spiders
arthrology .... joints
atmology .... aqueous vapor
audiology........ hearing
auxology .... growth
bacteriology..... bacteria
bioecology....... plant and animal
            interrelationship
biology .... living things
bromotology ..... food
bryology .... mosses
caliology .... birds' nests
carcinology ...... crustaceans
cardiology .... heart
carpology .... fruits
cephalology...... head
cetology......... whales
chololology....... bile
chondrology ..... cartilage
coleopterology.... beetles
conchology ...... shells

craniology .... skull
cryobiology ...... living things in a very cold
            environment
cytology......... cells
dactylology ...... fingers
dendrochronology . tree ring dating
dendrology ...... trees and shrubs
dermatology ..... skin
desmology....... ligaments
dipteriology...... flies
ecology .... environment
embryology ...... formation and development of
            living things
endocrinology .... endocrine glands
entomology ...... insects
enzymology...... enzymes and their actions
epidemiology..... epidemics
epiphytology ..... plant disease
etiology .... causes of disease
faunology .... animal distribution
fungology .... fungi
gynecology ...... female functions and diseases
helcology........ ulcers
helminthology .... worms
hematology ...... blood
hepatology....... liver
herpetology ..... reptiles
hippology .... horses
histology .... tissues, organs
hygiology........ health and hygiene

hymenopterology . . ants, wasps, etc.
hysterology . . . . . . uterus
iatrology . . . . medicine
ichthyology . . . . . . fishes
immunology . . . . . immunity from diseases
laryngology . . . . . larynx
limnology . . . . pond life, lakes
loimology . . . . infectious diseases
mammaology . . . . mammals
mastology . . . . . . mammals
microbiology . . . . . micro-organisms
morphology . . . . . form and shape of living things
muscology . . . . . . mosses
mycology . . . . fungi
myrmecology . . . . ants
myology . . . . muscles
nasology . . . . nose
nephrology . . . . . kidneys
neurology . . . . . . nervous system
nosology . . . . classification of diseases
nyctology . . . . night-blindness
odontology . . . . . . teeth
olfactology . . . . . . smells
oncology . . . . tumors
oology . . . . eggs
ophiology . . . . snakes
ophthalmology . . . . eyes
ornithology . . . . . birds
osteology . . . . bones
otology . . . . ears

palynology . . . . pollen
pathology . . . . essential nature of diseases
phlebology . . . . veins
phycology . . . . seaweed
physiology . . . . function of organs
phytology . . . . botany
phytopathology . . . disease in plants
piscology . . . . fish
plasmology . . . . . . corpuscles of living matter
pomology . . . . fruit
proctology . . . . rectum, hemorrhoids
protozoology . . . . . one-celled animals
pteridology . . . . . . ferns
pterology . . . . insect wings
rhinology . . . . nose
serology . . . . blood
siphonapterology . . fleas
soteriology . . . . hygiene
spermology . . . . . . seeds
splenology . . . . spleen
stomatology . . . . . mouth diseases
therology . . . . mammals
threpsology . . . . . nutrition
tocology . . . . obstetrics
trichology . . . . hair
vermiology . . . . . . worms
virology . . . . viruses
zoology . . . . animals
zymology . . . . fermentation

BONES OF THE BODY

Top of the head . . . . **cranial bones (cranium)**
Cheekbone . . . . **zygoma**
Collarbone . . . . **clavicle**
Shoulder blade . . . . **scapula**
Breastbone . . . . **sternum**
12 pairs of ribs . . . . **ribs**
Upper arm . . . . **humerus**
2 bones in lower arm . . . . . **radius and ulna**
Of the spinal column . . . . . **vertebrae**
Hipbones . . . . **pelvis**

Tailbone . . . . **coccyx**
Upper leg or thigh . . . . **femur**
2 bones of lower leg . . . . . **tibia and fibula**
Kneecap . . . . **patella**
Of the wrist . . . . **carpi**
Of the fingers . . . . **phalanges**
Of the ankles . . . . **tarsi**
Of the toes . . . . **phalanges**
Anklebone . . . . **talus**
Heelbone . . . . **calcaneus**

SPECIALIZED LANGUAGE

Temporary stopping
of breathing . . . . **apnea**
Armpit . . . . **axilla**
Blister . . . . **bleb**
Slow heartbeat . . . . **bradycardia**
Bad teeth . . . . **cacodontia**
Kidney stone . . . . **renal calculus**
Decay . . . . **caries**
Headache . . . . **cephalalgia**
Scar . . . . **cicatrix**
Limping . . . . **claudication**
Perspiration (profuse) . . . . **diaphoresis**
Speech impairment . . . . . . **dysarthria**
Defective bone formation . . **dysostosis**
Indigestion . . . . **dyspepsia**
Difficulty in swallowing . . . **dysphagia**
Shortness of breath . . . . . . **dyspnea**
Painful urination . . . . **dysuria**
Black-and-blue mark . . . . **ecchymosis**
Nosebleed . . . . **epistaxis**

A boil . . . . **furunculus**
Buttock . . . . **gluteus**
Bad breath . . . . **halitosis**
Voice box . . . . **larynx**
Low back pain . . . . **lumbago**
Nose . . . . **nasus**
Back of the head . . . . **occiput**
Artificial limb . . . . **prosthesis**
Itching . . . . **pruritus**
Fever . . . . **pyrexia**
Heartburn . . . . **pyrosis**
Runny nose . . . . **rhinorrhea**
German measles . . . . **rubella**
Scarlet fever . . . . **scarlatina**
Hiccups . . . . **singultus**
Rapid heartbeat . . . . **tachycardia**
Cough . . . . **tussis**
Chicken pox . . . . **varicella**
Smallpox . . . . **variola**

INFLAMMATORY CONDITIONS

adenitis . . . . lymphatic glands
angiitis . . . . blood or lymph vessel
appendicitis . . . . . . vermiform appendix

arthritis . . . . joints
blepharitis . . . . eyelid
bronchitis . . . . bronchial tubes

bursitis . . . . bursa (connecting tissue in vacinity of joints)
carditis . . . . heart
cheilitis . . . . lip
cholecystitis . . . . . gall bladder
chondritis . . . . cartilage
colitis . . . . colon
coxitis . . . . hip joint
cystitis . . . . bladder
dermatitis . . . . skin
diverticulitis . . . . . diverticulae of the colon
encephalitis . . . . . . brain
enteritis . . . . bowels
enterocolitis . . . . . colon and small intestine
esophagitis . . . . . . esophagus
gastritis . . . . stomach
gingivitis . . . . gums
glossitis . . . . tongue
gnathitis . . . . jaw
hepatitis . . . . liver
hyalitis . . . . vitreous humor of the eye
hysteritis . . . . uterus
keratitis . . . . cornea
laryngitis . . . . larynx
lymphadenitis . . . . lymph gland
mastitis . . . . the female breast
meningitis . . . . meninges (membranes of spinal cord and brain)
meningomyelitis . . spinal cord and its surrounding membranes
metritis . . . . uterus
myelitis . . . . spinal cord
myositis . . . . muscle
nephritis . . . . kidneys

neuritis . . . . nerves
omphalitis . . . . navel
oophoritis . . . . ovary
ophthalmitis . . . . . whole eye
orchitis . . . . testes
osteitis . . . . bone
otitis . . . . ear
parotitis . . . . parotid glands (supply saliva to the mouth)
pericarditis . . . . . . pericardium
periodontists . . . . . jaw (area around the tooth)
peritonitis . . . . peritoneum (the bowels)
phlebitis . . . . vein
pneumonitis . . . . . lungs
poliomyelitis . . . . . gray matter of the spinal cord
pyonephritis . . . . kidney accompanied by the presence of pus
rachitis . . . . spine
rectitis . . . . rectum
rhinitis . . . . nose
sclerotitis . . . . sclera (white or outer coat of eye)
sinusitis . . . . sinus
sphenoiditis . . . . . . air cavity of the sphenoid bone (large bone at base of skull)
stomatitis . . . . mouth
tonsilitis . . . . tonsils
tympanitis . . . . ear-drum
typhilitis . . . . caecum (cecum — the pouch at the beginning of the large intestine)
ulitis . . . . gums
uteritis . . . . womb

GESTATION OR INCUBATION PERIOD OF ANIMALS

bear	180-240 (days)	giraffe	400-481	porcupine	58- 74
cat	52- 69	goat	136-160	rabbit	29- 36
chicken	22	hippopotomus	220-255	rat	18- 27
chimpanzee	240-271	horse	327-346	reindeer	202-216
cow	280	kangaroo	32- 42	sheep	146-158
coyote	61- 63	leopard	85- 99	tiger	96-116
deer	197-305	lion	102-113	whale	360-545
dog	53- 71	man	253-303	wolf	58- 66
duck	21-35	monkey	137-272	zebra	340-400
elephant	510-735	mouse	18- 32		
fox	51- 63	pig	100-132		

ANIMAL NAMES: MALE, FEMALE, AND THEIR YOUNG

Antelope	Buck	Doe	Fawn	**Horse**	Stallion	Mare	Colt/Foal
Ass	Jack	Jenny	Foal/Hinny	**Lion**	Lion	Lioness	Cub
Bear	Boar	Sow	Cub	**Moose**	Bull	Cow	Calf
Cat	Tom	Queen	Kitten	**Peafowl**	Peacock	Peahen	Poult
Cattle	Bull	Cow	Calf	**Rabbit**	Buck	Doe	Bunny
Chicken	Rooster	Hen	Chick/Poult	**Red deer**	Stag, Hart	Hind	Fawn
Deer	Buck	Doe	Fawn	**Rhinoceros**	Bull	Cow	Calf
Dog	Dog	Bitch	Pup	**Sheep**	Ram	Ewe	Lamb
Duck	Drake	Duck	Duckling	**Swan**	Cob	Pen	Cygnet
Elephant	Bull	Cow	Calf	**Swine**	Boar	Sow	Piglet
Fox	Dog	Vixen	Cub/Pup/Kit	**Tiger**	Tiger	Tigress	Cub
Goat	Billy goat	Nanny goat	Kid	**Whale**	Bull	Cow	Calf
Goose	Gander	Goose	Gosling	**Wolf**	Dog	Bitch	Pup

[a **bullock** is a young bull or a castrated bull steer
a **heifer** is a young cow that has not born a calf
a **sire** is a male animal, especially the four-legged kind
a **dam** is a female animal, especially the four-legged kind
a **colt** is a young male horse, donkey, etc., especially a male racehorse four years of age or younger
a **filly** is a young female horse, especially under five years of age
a **tabby** is any domestic cat, especially a female]

ANIMALS AND THEIR OFFSPRING

Beaver	kit, kitten	Insect	nymph, pupa
Bird	nestling, fledgling	Otter	whelp
Eagle	eaglet	Oyster	spat
Eel	elver	Pheasant	poult
Fish	fry, fingerling	Salmon	parr
Frog	tadpole, polliwog	Seal	pup
Hare	leveret	Turkey	poult
Hawk	eyas, eyess	Wolf	whelp, cub
Hog	shoat, shote	Zebra	colt

ANIMAL GROUP TERMINOLOGY

ants	colony	kine	drove
apes	shrewdness	kittens	kindle, litter
asses	pace	larks	exaltation, ascension
badgers	cete	leopards	leap
bass	shoal	lions	pride
bears	sleuth, sloth	locusts	plague, swarm
bees	grist, hive, swarm	magpies	tidings
birds	dissimulation, flight, flock, volery	mallard	sord
		martens	richness
boars	singular	monkeys	tribe, troop
buffalo	herd	mules	barren, span
caterpillars	army	nightingales	watch
cats	cluster, clutter, clowder, litter	owls	parliament
		oxen	yoke, span
cattle	drove	oysters	bed
chicks	brood, clutch, peep	parrots	company
clams	bed	partridges	covey
colts	rag	peacocks	muster, ostentation
coots	cover	penguins	colony
cottontails	nest	pheasants	bouquet, nest, nide, nye
cranes	sedge, seige, siege	pigs	litter
crows	murder	ponies	string
curs	cowardice	porpoises	pod
dogs	pack, litter	quail	bevy, covey
doves	dule	rabbits	covey, nest
ducks	brace, flock, paddling, team	racehorses	string
eagles	convocation	rats	rabble
eels	swarm	raven	unkindness
eggs	clutch	rhinoceroses	crash
elephants	herd	rooks	clamor
elks	gang	sardines	family
ferrets	business	seals	pod
finches	charm	sheep	drove, flock
fish	school, shoal, draught	snipe	wisp
foxes	leash, skulk	sparrows	host
frogs	army	squirrels	dray
geese	flock, gaggle, skein (in flight)	starlings	murmuration
gnats	cloud, horde	storks	mustering
goats	trip, tribe	swallows	flight
gorillas	band	swans	bevy, wedge
hares	down, husk, leash	swine	sounder, farrow, drift
hawks	cast	toads	knot
hens	brood	trout	hover
herons	siege	turkeys	rafter, raft
hogs	drift	turtledoves	eule, pitying
horses	harras, herd, pair, team, span	turtles	bale
		vipers	nest
hounds	cry, mute, pack	whales	gam, pod
hummingbirds	charm	wildcats	clowder
jackrabbits	husk	wolves	pack, route
jays	band, party	woodcocks	fall
jellyfish	smack, smush	woodpeckers	descent
kangaroos	troop		

A CLASSIFICATION OF LIVING THINGS

KINGDOM MONERA

DIVISION SCHIZOMYCETES. Bacteria*
    Class Myxobacteria. *Myxococcus, Chondromyces*
    Class Spirochetes. *Leptospira, Cristispira, Spirocheta, Treponema*
    Class Eubacteria. *Staphylococcus, Escherichia, Salmonella, Pasteurella, Streptococcus, Bacillus, Spirillum, Caryophanon*
    Class Rickettsiae. *Rickettsia, Coxiella*
    Class Bedsonia. *Chlamydia*
DIVISION CYANOPHYTA. Blue-green algae. *Gloeocapsa, Microcystis, Oscillatoria, Nostoc, Scytonema*

KINGDOM PLANTAE

DIVISION EUGLENOPHYTA. Euglenoids. *Euglena, Eutreptia, Phacus, Colacium*
DIVISION CHLOROPHYTA. Green algae
    Class Chlorophyceae. True green algae. *Chlamydomonas, Volvox, Ulothrix, Spirogyra, Oedogonium, Ulva*
    Class Charophyceae. Stoneworts. *Chara, Nitella, Tolypella*
DIVISION CHRYSOPHYTA
    Class Xanthophyceae. Yellow-green algae. *Botrydiopsis, Halosphaera, Tribonema, Botrydium*
    Class Chrysophyceae. Golden-brown algae. *Chrysamoeba, Chromulina, Synura, Mallomonas*
    Class Bacillariophyceae. Diatoms. *Pinnularia, Arachnoidiscus, Triceratium, Pleurosigma*
DIVISION PYRROPHYTA. Dinoflagellates. *Gonyaulax, Gymnodinium, Ceratium, Gloeodinium*
DIVISION PHAEOPHYTA. Brown algae. *Sargassum, Ectocarpus, Fucus, Laminaria*
DIVISION RHODOPHYTA. Red algae. *Nemalion, Polysiphonia, Dasya, Chondrus, Batrachospermum*
DIVISION MYXOMYCOPHYTA. Slime molds
    Class Myxomycetes. True slime molds. *Physarum, Hemitrichia, Stemonitis*
    Class Acrasiae. Cellular slime molds. *Dictyostelium*
    Class Plasmodiophoreae. Endoparasitic slime molds. *Plasmodiophora*
    Class Labyrinthuleae. Net slime molds. *Labyrinthula*
DIVISION EUMYCOPHYTA. True fungi
    Class Phycomycetes. Algal fungi. *Rhizopus, Mucor, Phycomyces*
    Class Oömycetes. Water molds, white rusts, downy mildews. *Saprolegnia, Phytophthora, Albugo*
    Class Ascomycetes. Sac fungi. *Neurospora, Aspergillus, Penicillium, Saccharomyces, Morchella, Ceratostomella*
    Class Basidiomycetes. Club fungi. *Ustilago, Puccinia, Coprinus, Lycoperdon, Psalliota, Amanita*
DIVISION BRYOPHYTA
    Class Hepaticae. Liverworts. *Marchantia, Conocephalum, Riccia, Porella*
    Class Anthocerotae. Hornworts. *Anthoceros*
    Class Musci. Mosses. *Polytrichum, Sphagnum, Mnium*
DIVISION TRACHEOPHYTA. Vascular plants
    Subdivision Psilopsida. *Psilotum, Tmesipteris*
    Subdivision Lycopsida. Club mosses. *Lycopodium, Phylloglossum, Selaginella, Isoetes, Stylites*
    Subdivision Sphenopsida. Horsetails. *Equisetum*
    Subdivision Pteropsida. Ferns. *Polypodium, Osmunda, Dryopteris, Botrychium, Pteridium*
    Subdivision Spermopsida. Seed plants
        Class Pteridospermae. Seed ferns. No living representatives
        Class Cycadae. Cycads. *Zamia*
        Class Ginkgoae. *Ginkgo*
        Class Coniferae. Conifers. *Pinus, Tsuga, Taxus, Sequoia*
        Class Gneteae. *Gnetum, Ephedra, Welwitschia*
        Class Angiospermae. Flowering plants
            Subclass Dicotyledoneae. Dicots. *Magnolia, Quercus, Acer, Pisum, Taraxacum, Rosa, Chrysanthemum, Aster, Primula, Ligustrum, Ranunculus*
            Subclass Monocotyledoneae. Monocots. *Lilium, Tulipa, Poa, Elymus, Triticum, Zea, Ophyrys, Yucca, Sabal*

KINGDOM ANIMALIA

SUBKINGDOM PROTOZOA

PHYLUM PROTOZOA. Acellular animals
    Subphylum Plasmodroma
    Class Flagellata (or **Mastigophora**). Flagellates. *Trypanosoma, Calonympha, Chilomonas* (also *Euglena, Chlamydomonas*, and other green flagellates included in Plantae as well)
    Class Sarcodina. Protozoans with pseudopods. *Amoeba, Globigerina, Textularia, Acanthometra*
    Class Sporozoa. *Plasmodium, Monocystis*
    Subphylum Ciliophora
    Class Ciliata. Ciliates. *Paramecium, Opalina, Stentor, Vorticella, Spirostomum*

SUBKINGDOM PARAZOA

PHYLUM PORIFERA. Sponges
    Class Calcarea. Calcareous (chalky) sponges. *Scypha, Leucosolenia, Sycon, Grantia*
    Class Hexactinellida. Glass sponges. *Euplectella, Hyalonema, Monoraphis*
    Class Demospongiae. *Spongilla, Euspongia, Axinella*

SUBKINGDOM MESOZOA

PHYLUM MESOZOA. *Dicyema, Pseudicyema, Rhopalura*

*There is no generally accepted classification for bacteria at the class level. The system used here is based on R. Y. Stanier, M. Doudoroff, and E. A. Adelberg, *The Microbial World* (3rd ed.; Prentice-Hall, 1970), though these authors do not formally designate their categories as classes. Other systems usually recognize more classes, some of them very small.

SUBKINGDOM METAZOA

SECTION RADIATA

PHYLUM COELENTERATA (or Cnidaria)
Class **Hydrozoa.** Hydrozoans. *Hydra, Obelia, Gonionemus, Physalia*
Class **Scyphozoa.** Jellyfishes. *Aurelia, Pelagia, Cyanea*
Class **Anthozoa.** Sea anemones and corals. *Metridium, Pennatula, Gorgonia, Astrangia*
PHYLUM CTENOPHORA. Comb jellies
Class **Tentaculata.** *Pleurobrachia, Mnemiopsis, Cestum, Velamen*
Class **Nuda.** *Beroe*

SECTION PROTOSTOMIA

PHYLUM PLATYHELMINTHES. Flatworms
Class **Turbellaria.** Free-living flatworms. *Planaria, Dugesia, Leptoplana*
Class **Trematoda.** Flukes. *Fasciola, Schistosoma, Prosthogonimus*
Class **Cestoda.** Tapeworms. *Taenia, Dipylidium, Mesocestoides*
PHYLUM NEMERTINA (or **Rhynchocoela**). Proboscis worms. *Cerebratulus, Lineus, Malacobdella*
PHYLUM ACANTHOCEPHALA. Spiny-headed worms. *Echinorhynchus, Gigantorhynchus*
PHYLUM ASCHELMINTHES
Class **Rotifera.** Rotifers. *Asplanchna, Hydatina, Rotaria*
Class **Gastrotricha.** *Chaetonotus, Macrodasys*
Class **Kinorhyncha** (or **Echinodera**). *Echinoderes, Semnoderes*
Class **Nematoda.** Round worms. *Ascaris, Trichinella, Necator, Enterobius, Ancylostoma, Heterodera*
Class **Nematomorpha.** Horsehair worms. *Gordius, Paragordius, Nectonema*
PHYLUM ENTOPROCTA. *Urnatella, Loxosoma, Pedicellina*
PHYLUM PRIAPULIDA. *Priapulus, Halicryptus*
PHYLUM ECTOPROCTA (or **Bryozoa**). Bryozoans, moss animals
Class **Gymnolaemata.** *Paludicella, Bugula*
Class **Phylactolaemata.** *Plumatella, Pectinatella*
PHYLUM PHORONIDA. *Phoronis, Phoronopsis*
PHYLUM BRACHIOPODA. Lamp shells
Class **Inarticulata.** *Lingula, Glottidia, Discina*
Class **Articulata.** *Magellania, Neothyris, Terebratula*
PHYLUM MOLLUSCA. Molluscs
Class **Amphineura**
Subclass **Aplacophora.** Solenogasters. *Chaetoderma, Neomenia, Proneomenia*
Subclass **Polyplacophora.** Chitons. *Chaetopleura, Ischnochiton, Lepidochiton, Amicula*
Class **Monoplacophora.** *Neopilina*
Class **Gastropoda.** Snails and their allies (univalve molluscs). *Helix, Busycon, Crepidula, Haliotis, Littorina, Doris, Limax*
Class **Scaphopoda.** Tusk shells. *Dentalium, Cadulus*
Class **Pelecypoda.** Bivalve molluscs. *Mytilus, Ostrea, Pecten, Mercenaria, Teredo, Tagelus, Unio, Anodonta*

Class **Cephalopoda.** Squids, octopuses, etc. *Loligo, Octopus, Nautilus*
PHYLUM SIPUNCULIDA. Sipunculus, Phascolosoma, Dendrostomum
PHYLUM ECHIURIDA. *Echiurus, Urechis, Thalassema*
PHYLUM ANNELIDA. Segmented worms
Class **Polychaeta** (including Archiannelida). Sandworms, tubeworms, etc. *Nereis, Chaetopterus, Aphrodite, Diopatra, Arenicola, Hydroides, Sabella*
Class **Oligochaeta.** Earthworms and many fresh-water annelids. *Tubifex, Enchytraeus, Lumbricus, Dendrobaena*
Class **Hirudinea.** Leeches. *Trachelobdella, Hirudo, Macrobdella, Haemadipsa*
PHYLUM ONYCHOPHORA. *Peripatus, Peripatopsis*
PHYLUM TARDIGRADA. Water bears. *Echiniscus, Macrobiotus*
PHYLUM PENTASTOMIDA. *Cephalobaena, Linguatula*
PHYLUM ARTHROPODA
Subphylum **Trilobita.** No living representatives
Subphylum **Chelicerata**
Class **Eurypterida.** No living representatives
Class **Xiphosura.** Horseshoe crabs. *Limulus*
Class **Arachnida.** Spiders, ticks, mites, scorpions, whipscorpions, daddy longlegs, etc. *Archaearanea, Latrodectus, Argiope, Centruroides, Chelifer, Mastigoproctus, Phalangium, Ixodes*
Class **Pycnogonida.** Sea spiders. *Nymphon, Ascorhynchus*
Subphylum **Mandibulata**
Class **Crustacea.** *Homarus, Cancer, Daphnia, Artemia, Cyclops, Balanus, Porcellio*
Class **Chilopoda.** Centipeds. *Scolopendra, Lithobius, Scutigera*
Class **Diplopoda.** Millipeds. *Narceus, Apheloria, Polydesmus, Julus, Glomeris*
Class **Pauropoda.** *Pauropus*
Class **Symphyla.** *Scutigerella*
Class **Insecta.** Insects
Order **Collembola.** Springtails. *Isotoma, Achorutes, Neosminthurus, Sminthurus*
Order **Protura.** *Acerentulus, Eosentomon*
Order **Diplura.** *Campodea, Japyx*
Order **Thysanura.** Bristletails, silverfish, firebrats. *Machilis, Lepisma, Thermobia*
Order **Ephemerida.** Mayflies. *Hexagenia, Callibaetis, Ephemerella*
Order **Odonata.** Dragonflies, damselflies. *Archilestes, Lestes, Aeshna, Gomphus*
Order **Orthoptera** (including **Isoptera**). Grasshoppers, crickets, walking sticks, mantids, cockroaches, termites, etc. *Schistocerca, Romalea, Nemobius, Megaphasma, Mantis, Blatta, Periplaneta, Reticulitermes*
Order **Dermaptera.** Earwigs. *Labia, Forficula, Prolabia*
Order **Embiaria** (or **Embiidina** or **Embioptera**). *Oligotoma, Anisembia, Gynembia*
Order **Plecoptera.** Stoneflies. *Isoperla,*

Taeniopteryx, Capnia, Perla
Order Zoraptera. *Zorotypus*
Order Corrodentia. Book lice. *Ectopso-cus, Liposcelis, Trogium*
Order Mallophaga. Chewing lice. *Cuclotogaster, Menacanthus, Menopon, Trichodectes*
Order Anoplura. Sucking lice. *Pediculus, Phthirius, Haematopinus*
Order Thysanoptera. Thrips. *Heliothrips, Frankliniella, Hercothrips*
Order Hemiptera (including **Homoptera**). Bugs, cicadas, aphids, leafhoppers, etc. *Belostoma, Lygaeus, Notonecta, Cimex, Lygus, Oncopeltus, Magicicada, Circulifer, Psylla, Aphis*
Order Neuroptera. Dobsonflies, alderflies, lacewings, mantispids, snakeflies, etc. *Corydalus, Hemerobius, Chrysopa, Mantispa, Agulla*
Order Coleoptera. Beetles, weevils. *Copris, Phyllophaga, Harpalus, Scolytus, Melanotus, Cicindela, Dermestes, Photinus, Coccinella, Tenebrio, Anthonomus, Conotrachelus*
Order Hymenoptera. Wasps, bees, ants, sawflies. *Cimbex, Vespa, Glypta, Scolia, Bembix, Formica, Bombus, Apis*
Order Mecoptera. Scorpionflies. *Panorpa, Boreus, Bittacus*
Order Siphonaptera. Fleas. *Pulex, Nosopsyllus, Xenopsylla, Ctenocephalides*
Order Diptera. True flies, mosquitoes. *Aedes, Asilus, Sarcophaga, Anthomyia, Musca, Chironomus, Tabanus, Tipula, Drosophila*
Order Trichoptera. Caddisflies. *Limnephilus, Rhyacophila, Hydropsyche*
Order Lepidoptera. Moths, butterflies. *Tinea, Pyrausta, Malacosoma, Sphinx, Samia, Bombyx, Heliothis, Papilio, Lycaena*

SECTION DEUTEROSTOMIA
PHYLUM CHAETOGNATHA. Arrow worms. *Sagitta, Spadella*
PHYLUM ECHINODERMATA
Class Crinoidea. Crinoids, sea lilies. *Antedon, Ptilocrinus, Comactinia*
Class Asteroidea. Sea stars. *Asterias, Ctenodiscus, Luidia, Oreaster*
Class Ophiuroidea. Brittle stars, serpent stars, basket stars, etc. *Asteronyx, Amphioplus, Ophiothrix, Ophioderma, Ophiura*
Class Echinoidea. Sea urchins, sand dollars, heart urchins. *Cidaris, Arbacia, Strongylocentrotus, Echinanthus, Echinarachnius, Moira*
Class Holothuroidea. Sea cucumbers. *Cucumaria, Thyone, Caudina, Synapta*
PHYLUM POGONOPHORA. Beard worms. *Siboglinum, Lamellisabella, Oligobrachia, Polybrachia*
PHYLUM HEMICHORDATA
Class Enteropneusta. Acorn worms. *Saccoglossus, Balanoglossus, Glossobalanus*
Class Pterobranchia. *Rhabdopleura,*

Cephalodiscus
PHYLUM CHORDATA. Chordates
Subphylum Urochordata (or **Tunicata**). Tunicates
Class Ascidiacea. Ascidians or sea squirts. *Ciona, Clavelina, Molgula, Perophora*
Class Thaliacea. *Pyrosoma, Salpa, Doliolum*
Class Larvacea. *Appendicularia, Oikopleura, Fritillaria*
Subphylum Cephalochordata. Lancelets, amphioxus. *Branchiostoma, Asymmetron*
Subphylum Vertebrata. Vertebrates
Class Agnatha. Jawless fishes. *Cephalaspis,* Pteraspis,* Petromyzon, Entosphenus, Myxine, Eptatretus*
Class Placodermi. No living representatives
Class Chondrichthyes. Cartilaginous fishes. *Squalus, Hyporion, Raja, Chimaera*
Class Osteichthyes. Bony fishes
Subclass Sarcopterygii
Order Crossopterygii (or **Coelacanthiformes**). Lobe-fins. *Latimeria*
Order Dipnoi (or **Dipteriformes**). Lungfishes. *Neoceratodus, Protopterus, Lepidosiren*
Subclass Brachiopterygii. Bichirs. *Polypterus*
Subclass Actinopterygii. Higher bony fishes. *Amia, Cyprinus, Gadus, Perca, Salmo*
Class Amphibia
Order Anura. Frogs and toads. *Rana, Hyla, Bufo*
Order Urodela. Salamanders. *Necturus, Triturus, Plethodon, Ambystoma*
Order Apoda. *Ichthyophis, Typhlonectes*
Class Reptilia
Order Chelonia. Turtles. *Chelydra, Kinosternon, Clemmys, Terrapene*
Order Rhynchocephalia. Tuatara. *Sphenodon*
Order Crocodylia. Crocodiles and alligators. *Crocodylus, Alligator*
Order Squamata. Snakes and lizards. *Iguana, Anolis, Sceloporus, Phrynosoma, Natrix, Elaphe, Coluber, Thamnophis, Crotalus*
Class Aves. Birds. *Anas, Larus, Columba, Gallus, Turdus, Dendroica, Sturnus, Passer, Melospiza*
Class Mammalia. Mammals
Subclass Prototheria
Order Monotremata. Egg-laying mammals. *Ornithorhynchus, Tachyglossus*
Subclass Theria. Marsupial and placental mammals
Order Marsupialia. Marsupials. *Didelphis, Sarcophilus, Notoryctes, Macropus*
Order Insectivora. Insectivores (moles, shrews, etc.). *Scalopus, Sorex, Erinaceus*
Order Dermoptera. Flying lemurs. *Galeopithecus*
Order Chiroptera. Bats. *Myotis, Eptesicus, Desmodus*
Order Primates. Lemurs, monkeys,

*Extinct.

apes, man. *Lemur, Tarsius, Cebus, Macacus, Cynocephalus, Pongo, Pan, Homo*
Order Edentata. Sloths, anteaters, armadillos. *Bradypus, Myrmecophagus, Dasypus*
Order Pholidota. Pangolin. *Manis*
Order Lagomorpha. Rabbits, hares, pikas. *Ochotona, Lepus, Sylvilagus, Oryctolagus*
Order Rodentia. Rodents. *Sciurus, Marmota, Dipodomys, Microtus, Peromyscus, Rattus, Mus, Erethizon, Castor*
Order Cetacea. Whales, dolphins, porpoises. *Delphinus, Phocaena, Monodon, Balaena*

Order Carnivora. Carnivores. *Canis, Procyon, Ursus, Mustela, Mephitis, Felis, Hyaena, Eumetopias*
Order Tubulidentata. Aardvark. *Orycteropus*
Order Proboscidea. Elephants. *Elephas, Loxodonta*
Order Hyracoidea. Coneys. *Procavia*
Order Sirenia. Manatees. *Trichechus, Halicore*
Order Perissodactyla. Odd-toed ungulates. *Equus, Tapirella, Tapirus, Rhinoceros*
Order Artiodactyla. Even-toed ungulates. *Pecari, Sus, Hippopotamus, Camelus, Cervus, Odocoileus, Giraffa, Bison, Ovis, Bos*

QUESTIONS AND ANSWERS

1. Name the 10 elements that were either known to or discovered by ancient man.
ANSWER: Carbon, copper, gold, iron, lead, mercury, silver, sulfur, tin, and antimony (zinc is sometimes listed as having been known to ancient man).

2. Give the freezing and boiling points of water as represented by the 3 temperature scales.
   a) °C   b) °K   c) °F
ANSWER: a) 0°C and 100°C b) 273°A(K) and 373°A(K) c) 32°F and 212°F.

3. Give the charge on each of the following radicals.
   a) ammonium   b) peroxide   c) acetate   d) permanganate
ANSWER: a) +1 b) -2 c) -1 d) -1.

4. The raw materials used in a blast furnace for the making of steel are ore, limestone, and coke. Give the elements or compound that will represent the various raw materials.
   a) ore   b) limestone   c) coke
ANSWER: a) iron ore (iron oxide) b) calcium carbonate c) carbon.

5. The numbers on a fertilizer bag like 13-13-13 represent 3 elements. What are these elements?
ANSWER: Nitrogen, phosphorus, and potassium (generally known as N, K_2O, and P_2O_5).

6. Which one of the following scientists was the first to submit a proof of established theory concerning the existence of atoms?
   a) Robert Boyle   b) Isaac Newton   c) John Dalton   d) Niels Bohr
ANSWER: John Dalton.

7. Name the phrase from the field of chemistry that means "a stern, final test that proves the value, genuineness, quality or worth of someone or something." In chemistry what object was being tested by what chemical to have led to the coining of such a phrase?
ANSWER: Acid test/Gold was tested by using nitric acid or aqua fortis. Gold was not decomposed by the acid, but inferior metals were.

8. Identify each of the following elements from the given description.
   a) Formerly named wolfram   structure of all biological (organic)
   b) Has the largest electro-negative   compounds
      value   g) The only non-metal that is liquid at
   c) Most abundant element in the   room temperature
      universe   h) The element in the halogen family
   d) Named for one of the U.S. States   with the smallest atomic weight
   e) Weighs less than helium   i) The element whose symbol is Cm
   f) Serves as the basis for the   j) The element whose symbol is No
ANSWER: a) tungsten b) fluorine c) hydrogen d) californium e) hydrogen f) carbon g) bromine h) flourine i) curium (named after Madame Marie Curie j) nobelium (named after Alfred Nobel).

9. Identify each of the following chemical elements from its Latin name.
   a) *argentum*   c) *ferrum*   e) *aurum*
   b) *stannum*   d) *plumbum*   f) *hydrargyrum*
ANSWER: a) silver b) tin c) iron d) lead e) gold f) mercury.

10. In a continuous spectrum the color red will be on one end while the color violet will be on the other end. Which color represents the longest wavelength? Which color has the highest frequency? Which color will bend the most through a prism?
ANSWER: Red/Violet/Violet.

11. The following statements describe various processes used to make organic chemicals. Give the name for each process that is described.
   a) Breaking of large molecules into smaller molecules
   b) Joining together of molecules so that compounds with chains of very large molecular size are produced
ANSWER: a) cracking b) polymerization.

12. Of the following gases, which one may be used in a light bulb?

    a) hydrogen   b) oxygen   c) argon   d) helium

ANSWER: c) argon.

13. The following terms represent different types of chemical reactions. For each reaction give the number of products that are produced by each type.

    a) single displacement   b) double displacement   c) composition reaction

ANSWER: a) 2 products b) 2 products c) 1 product.

14. Give the chemical names for each of the following compounds.

    a) $HC_2H_3O_2$ d) Na_2CO_3 g) BaO_2

    b) $NaHCO_3$ e) H_2O_2 h) H_2SO_4

    c) HNO_3 f) Cs_2S i) $MgCO_3$

ANSWER: a) acetic acid b) sodium bicarbonate c) nitric acid d) sodium carbonate e) hydrogen peroxide f) cesium sulfide g) barium peroxide h) sulfuric acid i) magnesium carbonate.

15. Hydrolysis is used to describe a chemical reaction. Give the reactant needed for any hydrolysis.

ANSWER: Water.

16. Which one of the following terms is used to describe the separation of ions from the crystals of ionic compounds.

    a) dissociation   b) electrolysis   c) ionization   d) synthesis

ANSWER: a) dissociation.

17. Non-metal elements tend to form what type of ions?

ANSWER: Negative ions.

18. Which one of the following statements best describes the behavior of metallic elements?

    a) They act as reducing agents.   c) They acquire negative oxidation numbers.

    b) They share electrons.   d) They donate protons.

ANSWER: a.

19. The atomic weight of potassium is 39.0983. This number is established as described by which of the following statements?

    a) The atomic weight is obtained from an average atomic weight of all the isotopes for potassium.

    b) The atomic weight is obtained from an average atomic weight of the radioactive isotopes for potassium.

    c) The atomic weight is obtained from an average atomic weight of the non-radioactive isotopes.

    d) The atomic weight is obtained from the atomic weight of the one isotope that is most abundant.

ANSWER: a.

20. Which of the following statements is correct when describing the most stable state of an atom's electrons?

    a) The most stable state is when the electrons have moved to a higher energy level.

    b) The most stable state is when the electrons are in the ground state.

    c) The most stable state is when the electrons are in the excited state.

ANSWER: b.

21. The atomic weight of the atom calcium is 40.08. Which one of the following statements is incorrect?

    a) One atom of calcium is 40.08 amu.

    b) One mole of calcium is 40.08 grams.

    c) One atom of calcium is a little over 3 times as heavy as the atom carbon.

    d) One atom of calcium is 40.08 grams.

ANSWER: d.

22. Isotopes of an element are best described by which of the following statements?

    a) Different symbols but same atomic weights

    b) Different symbols but same atomic numbers

c) Same symbols but different number of neutrons

d) Same symbols but different number of protons

ANSWER: c.

23. The terms Tyndall, dialysis, coagulation, and electrophoresis represent a specialized field of chemistry. What is this specialized field?

ANSWER: Chemistry of colloidal systems (colloids) or protein chemistry.

24. Special chemicals like phenothelien, methyl orange, and litmus are used to test for acids or bases. What are these special chemicals called?

ANSWER: Indicators.

25. Of the following formula terms, which one represents the smallest possible ratio?

a) empirical formula   c) polyatomic formula

b) molecular formula   d) diatomic formula

ANSWER: a.

26. All of the following except one are features of Dalton's theory. Which is the one statement that does not fit in his theory?

a) Atoms of different elements are different.

b) Each element is composed of like atoms.

c) Different types of atoms exist for each material in the world.

d) Atoms unite in simple whole number ratios to form compounds.

ANSWER: c.

27. Which region of an atom represents the greatest density?

ANSWER: Nucleus.

28. The spectrum emitted by excited atoms and observed through a spectroscope represents which one of the following motions?

a) Protons leaving the nucleus

b) Electrons moving to higher energy levels

c) Neutrons leaving the nucleus

d) Electrons moving to lower energy levels

ANSWER: d.

29. An element's symbol may be written as $^{239}_{93}X$.

a) What is the atomic number?

b) What is the number of electrons?

c) What is the number of neutrons?

ANSWER: a) 93 b) 93 c) 146.

30. When a neutral metal atom becomes an ion, the radius of the ion will be different from that of the neutral metal atom. Which one of the following statements is correct?

a) The ionic radius of the metal is greater than its atomic radius.

b) The ionic radius of the metal is less than its atomic radius.

ANSWER: b.

31. Which 3 of the following terms represent physical properties of substances?

a) porosity   b) density   c) reactivity   d) expandibility

ANSWER: a, b, and d.

32. In a given period of the periodic chart, which of the following are true statements?

a) Nonmetal atoms have a large atomic radius compared to metal atoms.

b) Nonmetal atoms have higher electronegative values than the metal ion.

c) Nonmetal atoms have higher ionization energies than the metal ion.

d) Nonmetal atoms tend to acquire electrons more readily than the metal ion.

ANSWER: b, c, and d.

33. A chemical change occurs when mercuric oxide is decomposed into mercury and oxygen. Which statement does *not* show that a chemical change took place?

a) Properties of the starting substance appeared to change.

b) New products are formed.

c) A different state of matter was produced.

d) New combinations of atoms were made.

ANSWER: c.

34. Each sublevel within an atom is divided into orbitals. For each of the following sublevels give the correct number of orbitals.
    a) p sublevel   b) s sublevel   c) f sublevel   d) d sublevel

ANSWER: a) 3 orbitals b) 1 orbital c) 7 orbitals d) 5 orbitals.

35. The element phosphorus may be in the red, the yellow, or the white form. What chemical term is used to describe these elements which exist in different forms and exhibit different properties?

ANSWER: Allotropic states.

36. There are a number of ways to express the concentration of a chemical solution. Two of the methods are molality and molarity. For each of the following mathematical ratios, identify the unit of concentration.

a) $\dfrac{\text{moles of solute}}{\text{liters solution}}$ b) $\dfrac{\text{moles of solute}}{\text{kg of solvent}}$

ANSWER: a) Molarity (M) b) molality (m).

37. Define each of the following chemical terms.
    a) oxidizer   b) alloy   c) pyrotechnics

ANSWER: a) A substance that causes another substance to give up one or more electrons b) A solution in which solute and solvent are both solids c) The art of making and using fireworks.

38. Which 2 items in the following list of approximate conversion factors are most incorrect?
    a) 1 m = 39.37 inch   d) 1 inch = 2.54 cm
    b) 1 l = .946 qt   e) 1 metric ton = 1000 lbs
    c) 1 mile = 1.6 km

ANSWER: b and e.

39. STP conditions represent what temperature and pressure?

ANSWER: 0°C (273°K), 760 mm, 1 atm or 760 torr (all are acceptable).

40. Which chemical element may have the name stannous or stannic depending on its oxidation number in the compound named?

ANSWER: Tin.

41. Some chemical reactions are reversible and form stable equilibrium systems. In some systems a change in conditions places a stress on the system that is relieved by a shift in the position of the equilibrium. This principle is known as whose principle?

ANSWER: Le Chatelier's.

42. There are various theories that are used to determine if a substance is an acid or a base. The theories are the Brönsted-Lowry theory and the Lewis theory. Relate each of the following statements to the correct theory.
    a) An acid is an electron-pair acceptor.   b) An acid is a proton donor.

ANSWER: a) Lewis theory b) Brönsted-Lowry theory.

43. Classify each of the following elements as a metal or nonmetal.
    a) chromium   c) gold   e) iron
    b) fluorine   d) helium

ANSWER: a) metal b) nonmetal c) metal d) nonmetal e) metal.

44. Name the more reactive element expected in each of the following pairs.
    a) lithium, sodium   c) chlorine, bromine
    b) potassium, calcium

ANSWER: a) sodium b) potassium c) chlorine.

45. A chemical reaction may or may not go to completion depending on the type of products produced. From the following possible products that may be produced in a chemical reaction, which one type will not allow the reaction to go to completion?
    a) A gas is formed.   c) Water is formed.
    b) Precipitation occurs.   d) Soluble ionic products are formed.

ANSWER: d.

46. Organic compounds may contain single, double, or triple covalent bonds. For each of the following types of organic compounds, give the number of bonds that it

contains.
a) alkene compounds   c) alkane compounds
b) alkyne compounds
ANSWER: a) double b) triple c) single.

47. Water may contain various ions. Of the following ions, which 2 determine the hardness of the water?
a) sodium ion   c) magnesium ion
b) calcium ion   d) lithium ion
ANSWER: Calcium and magnesium.

48. The following 2 chemical reactions contain salt, base, acid, and water compounds. What chemical process (term) describes each reaction?
a) acid + base→water + salt   b) water + salt→acid + base
ANSWER: a) neutralization b) hydrolysis.

49. Which one of the following bases is used as a medicinal antacid?
a) ammonia   c) calcium hydroxide
b) sodium hydroxide   d) magnesium hydroxide
ANSWER: d) magnesium hydroxide.

50. Sulfuric acid has the following properties. Which property allows it to be used to prepare other acids?
a) highly ionized   c) high density
b) excellent dehydrating agent   d) high boiling point
ANSWER: d) high boiling point.

51. The following compounds are all electrolytes. Which substance has a low degree of ionization?
a) sodium hydroxide   c) sodium chloride
b) hydrochloric acid   d) ammonium hydroxide
ANSWER: d) ammonium hydroxide.

52. Each of the following compounds has a different type of bond holding the elements together. Name the bond type for each compound.
a) calcium chloride   b) water   c) sugar
ANSWER: a) ionic bond b) covalent c) covalent.

53. One of the following mathematical processes will convert a difference in water levels inside and outside a gas collecting tube to the mercury equivalent in mm. Which is the correct mathematical process?
a) Water level difference must be added to 13.6
b) Water level difference must be subtracted from 13.6
c) Water level difference must be divided by 13.6
d) Water level difference must be multiplied by 13.6
ANSWER: c.

54. Which of the following has the least effect on the rate of solution of a solid in a liquid?
a) surface area   b) agitation   c) pressure   d) temperature
ANSWER: c) pressure.

55. Which of the following is a correct expression for STP?
a) The celsius temperature of melting ice
b) The celsius temperature of boiling water
c) Zero degrees Celsius and 760 mm or 273 Kelvin and 760 mm
d) 100°C and 760 mm
ANSWER: c.

56. The mercury level inside a gas collecting tube is 10 mm lower than that outside. The measured room pressure is 760 mm. Which of the following equals the gas inside the tube?
a) 770 mm   b) 760 mm   c) 750 mm   d) 740 mm
ANSWER: a) 770 mm.

57. The element sodium reacts with water. Which of the following gives the products of this reaction?

a) sodium oxide and hydrogen gas   c) sodium peroxide and hydrogen gas
b) sodium hydroxide and hydrogen gas   d) sodium hydroxide
ANSWER: b.

58. Which of the following is *not* a possible unit for measuring the pressure of a gas?
a) cm of mercury   c) pounds per square foot
b) ounces per square inch   d) pounds per millimeter
ANSWER: d) pounds per millimeter.

59. Give the formulas for each of the following compounds.
a) sodium sulfate   f) sodium chloride
b) barium carbonate   g) hydrochloric acid
c) argon gas   h) sucrose
d) nitric acid   i) sodium bicarbonate
e) chlorine gas   j) glucose
**ANSWER: a) Na_2SO_4 b) $BaCO_3$ c) Ar d) HNO_3 e) Cl_2 f) NaCl g) HCl h) $C_{12}H_{22}O_{11}$
i) $NaHCO_3$ j) $C_6H_{12}O_6$.**

60. Convert each of the following metric numbers to millimeters (mm).
a) 12 cm   b) 2 dm   c) 3 km   d) 5 m
ANSWER: a) 120 mm b) 200 mm c) 3,000,000 mm d) 5000 mm.

61. What is the term that refers to the quantitative calculations of chemical elements or compounds involved in chemical reactions?
ANSWER: Stoichiometry (also spelled, stoicheiometry or stoechiometry).

62. In a solution there is a substance that does the dissolving and a substance that is dissolved. Distinguish between the 2 substances.
a) solvent   b) solute
ANSWER: a) the substance that does the dissolving b) the substance that is dissolved.

63. How many liters does one mole of a gas at STP conditions occupy?
ANSWER: 22.4 liters.

64. Which one of the following formulas does not represent a radical?
a) OH   c) HCO_3 e) CH_4
b) CO_3 d) NH_4
ANSWER: e) CH_4.

65. Which one of the following quantity numbers represents one amu?
a) 1.66×10^{-24} gm   c) 6.40×10^{23} gm
b) 6.02×10^{23} gm   d) 1.9×10^{-23} gm
ANSWER: a.

66. The following compounds, when dissolved in water, are electrolytes. Indicate which compounds are strong electrolytes and which ones are weak electrolytes.
a) sodium hydroxide   d) acetic acid
b) ammonium hydroxide   e) sulfuric acid
c) hydrochloric acid
ANSWER: a) strong b) weak c) strong d) weak e) strong.

67. What is the classification of an element that gives up electrons when forming a binary compound?
ANSWER: Metal.

68. Indicate which of the following pH's show an acidic or basic solution.
a) pH 3.5   b) pH 5   c) pH 8.3
ANSWER: a) acid b) acid c) base.

69. An active metal reacting with an acid will produce 2 products. Which of the following identifies the products of this reaction?
a) salt and water products   c) salt and gas products
b) two salt products
ANSWER: c.

70. What is the number of electrons in the outer shell of each of the following families of elements?
a) Noble gas family   b) Alkali family   c) Boron family
ANSWER: a) 8 electrons b) 1 electron c) 3 electrons.

71. Some nonmetal oxide compounds and some metal oxide compounds are known as anhydrides. When they are added to water a one product reaction results. Give the type of compound that is produced in each of the following reactions.
    a) nonmetal oxide plus water   b) metal oxide plus water
ANSWER: a) acid b) base.

72. Which 3 of the following substances are colloidal systems?
    a) dust in air   d) milk
    b) salt in water   e) whipped cream
    c) antifreeze in water
ANSWER: a, d, and e.

73. Two of the following processes are physical characteristics. Name them.
    a) souring of milk   d) photosynthesis
    b) tarnishing   e) ductility
    c) malleability
ANSWER: c and d.

74. Which one of the following terms does not represent a chemical property?
    a) The substance is a reducing agent.
    b) The substance has a high tensil strength.
    c) The substance is unstable.
ANSWER: b.

75. Give the charge on each of the following radicals.
    a) ammonium   d) sulfite
    b) nitrite   e) nitrate
    c) chromate
ANSWER: a) +1 b) -1 c) -2 d) -2 e) -1.

76. Depending on the structure of a compound, one of the following statements may be used to describe the compound. Give the correct term that may be used instead of the statement.
    a) The compound contains water held in loose chemical combination.
    b) The compound is without water.
    c) The compound has no definite crystalline shape.
ANSWER: a) hydrate b) anhydrous c) amorphous.

77. Which of the following compounds may be used in photographic film?
    a) sodium chloride   c) sodium bicarbonate
    b) silver bromide   d) calcium chloride
ANSWER: b) Silver bromide.

78. Name the 7 diatomic elements.
ANSWER: Bromine, chlorine, fluorine, hydrogen, iodine, nitrogen, and oxygen.

79. The 3 main types of radiation are Alpha, Beta, and Gamma. Name the kind of radiation described in each of the following.
    a) High energy, short wavelength and very penetrating
    b) Harmful if inside the body and is described as a fast moving electron
    c) Least penetrating and is described as a helium nucleus
ANSWER: a) Gamma b) Beta c) Alpha.

80. Give the letter that represents each of the 4 quantum numbers.
ANSWER: n, l, m, and s.

81. Which 2 of the following elements are noble gases?
    a) hydrogen   c) argon   e) oxygen
    b) helium   d) nitrogen
ANSWER: b) helium and c) argon.

82. The value of $+\frac{1}{2}$ or $-\frac{1}{2}$ may be used by which of the following quantum numbers?
    a) l   b) n   c) s   d) m
ANSWER: c) s (known as the spin quantum number).

83. Explain the following symbols used in the writing of chemical equations.
    a) $\rightarrow$ b) $\triangle$ c) $\uparrow$ d) $\rightleftarrows$
ANSWER: a) yields b) heat c) gas d) equilibrium or reversible.

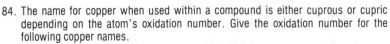

84. The name for copper when used within a compound is either cuprous or cupric depending on the atom's oxidation number. Give the oxidation number for the following copper names.
    a) cupric   b) cuprous
ANSWER: a) +2 b) +1.

85. What type of bonding always produces ionization when water is added?
    a) ionic bonding   c) covalent bonding
    b) polar covalent bonding
ANSWER: a.

86. The number 6.02 x 10^{23} can represent atoms, ions, or molecules. What term is used to represent this quantity of particles?
ANSWER: One mole.

87. Name the physical property of a specific substance described by each of the following.
    a) The substance is 2.7 *times as heavy* as water of equal volume.
    b) The substance may be drawn into a wire.
    c) The maximum temperature for changing gas to a liquid is 120°C.
ANSWER: a) specific gravity b) ductility c) critical temperature.

88. The following formulas represent various inorganic radicals. Give the correct name for each radical.
    a) SO_4^{-2} c) NH_4^{+1} e) OH^{-1}
    b) ClO_3^{-1} d) PO_4^{-3}
ANSWER: a) sulfate b) chlorate c) ammonium d) phosphate e) hydroxide.

89. Two of the following elements are known as halogens. Name them.
    a) fluorine   c) sodium   e) argon
    b) neon   d) chlorine   f) lithium
ANSWER: a) fluorine and d) chlorine.

90. The following mathematics relationships represent 2 different gas laws. Give the names of the laws.
    a) $\dfrac{V2}{V1} = \dfrac{T2}{T1}$ b) $\dfrac{V1}{V2} = \dfrac{P2}{P1}$
ANSWER: a) Charles' Law b) Boyle's Law.

91. From the following ions, name the 3 with a positive charge of two.
    a) sodium ion   d) lithium ion
    b) magnesium ion   e) chloride ion
    c) zinc ion   f) barium ion
ANSWER: b) magnesium c) zinc ion and f) barium ion.

92. Give the names for the following compounds using the needed prefix.
    a) PCl_3 b) CO_2 c) CCl_4
ANSWER: a) phosphorus trichloride b) carbon dioxide c) carbon tetrachloride.

93. Name the 5 elements that have names beginning with the letter "L."
ANSWER: Lanthanum, lawrencium, lead, lithium, and lutetium.

94. Name the 2 types of chemical reactions in which heat is absorbed or given off. Which is which?
ANSWER: Exothermic (given off) and endothermic (absorbed).

95. What 3 elements are in the chemical compound H_2SO_4?
ANSWER: Hydrogen, oxygen, and sulfur.

96. Name at least 8 of the elements whose names begin with the letter "C."
ANSWER: Cadmium, calcium, californium, carbon, cerium, cesium, chlorine, chromium, cobalt, copper, and curium.

97. Name the 6 elements whose names begin with the letter "B."
ANSWER: Barium, berkelium, beryllium, bismuth, boron, and bromine.

98. Name the 6 elements that are in the alkaline earth family Group IIA. What valence or change do they exhibit? Which one is found in lime? Which one has the

smallest atomic weight? Which one is strongly radioactive?

ANSWER: Beryllium(4), magnesium(12), calcium(20), strontium(38), barium(56), radium(88)/ + 2/Calcium/Beryllium/Radium.

99. Name the 3 elements whose names begin with the letter "E."

ANSWER: Einsteinium, erbuim, and europium.

100. Name the 5 elements that are in the sulfur group VIA family of the periodic table. Three of them are solids. Which one is a gas? Which one was known in Biblical times as "brimstone"? Give the number of electrons each has in its valence shell.

ANSWER: Oxygen(8), sulfur(16), selenium(34), tellurium(52), and polonium(84)/ Oxygen/Sulfur/6.

101. Name the 2 elements named by association with the state of California.

ANSWER: Berkelium(97) is named in honor of Berkeley, California, and californium (98) is named in honor of the state of California.

102. Elements 99 and 100 were named in honor of 2 great scientists. Name the elements and the scientists. Elements 101 and 102 were also named after 2 well-known men. Name the elements and the men. For what is the scientist associated with 101 known? What product did the scientist connected with 102 develop? What well-known prizes are named after him?

ANSWER: 99 is einsteinium after Alfred Einstein/Fermium(100) is after Enrico Fermi/ 101 is mendelevium for Dmitri Mendeleev/102 is nobelium for Alfred Nobel/The periodic table/Dynamite/The Nobel Prizes.

103. After whom was element 103 named? Name the element. What did this man invent? Element 104 has not been officially recognized. Russian scientists named it after whom? What did this man do? How did the Russian scientists prepare this element?

ANSWER: Ernest Orlando Lawrence/Lawrencium/The cyclotron/Igor Kurchatov and the proposed element is kurchatovium/Pioneered in nuclear physics/By bombarding plutonium with neon.

104. What is the name of the system in which all 3 states of matter — solid, liquid, and gas — exist in contact and in equilibrium with one another? What is the one for water on the Kelvin scale?

ANSWER: Triple point/273.16°K.

105. Name the famous physicist and chemist who won not only the 1903 Nobel Prize in physics but also the 1911 Nobel Prize in chemistry.

ANSWER: Marie Curie.

106. Name the recipients, the years, and the fields in which the Curie family won Nobel Prizes.

ANSWER: Pierre and Marie Curie in 1903 for physics; Marie Curie in 1911 for chemistry; and Irène Joliot Curie (with Frédéric Joliot) in 1935 for chemistry.

107. Identify each of the following laws or principles.
   a) Equal volumes of all gases under the same conditions of temperature and pressure contain equal numbers of molecules.
   b) If the temperature remains constant, the volume of a given weight of gas is inversely proportional to the pressure.
   c) If a system in equilibrium is disturbed by external factors, such as a change in temperature, pressure, or concentration, the system will adjust to a new equilibrium that will counteract the disturbing factors.
   d) If the pressure remains constant, the volume of a gas varies directly with the Absolute temperature.
   e) In a mixture of two or more gases, the total pressure exerted by a gas is the same as if each gas alone occupied the volume.
   f) At a given temperature and pressure the rate of diffusion of a gas is inversely proportional to the square root of its density: $\frac{R_1}{R_2} = \sqrt{\frac{D^2}{D^1}}$
   g) At a constant temperature the concentration of a gas dissolved by a liquid is

proportional to the pressure of the gas.

h) The heat of a chemical reaction is the same whether the reaction takes place in one or several steps.

i) The chemical and physical properties of the chemical elements are periodic functions of their atomic weights.

ANSWER: a) Avogadro's law b) Boyle's law c) Le Chatelier's principle (law) d) Charles' law or Gay-Lussac's law e) Dalton's law (Dalton's law of partial pressure or law of additive pressure f) Graham's law of diffusion g) Henry's law h) Hess's law (law of constant heat summation) i) Mendeleev's law.

108. Each of the following is a definition for a word ending in -on. Give the word which best fits each definition.

a) The antiparticle of the electron

b) An electrically neutral sub-atomic particle

c) An electrically charged atom or group of atoms

d) An apparatus that will give high energy to particles such as protons, deuterons, and helium ions until they achieve high enough velocities to disrupt the nuclei of atoms

e) The nucleus of a deuterium atom

f) A negatively charged particle carrying a negative charge of 1.602×10^{-19} coulomb and a mass of $1/1837$ of the hydrogen atom

g) A unit (particle) of light having no charge or mass but an indefinitely long lifetime

h) A unit charge of positive electricity having a mass 1,836 times that of the electron

ANSWER: a) positron b) neutron c) ion d) cyclotron e) deuteron f) electron g) photon h) proton.

109. The following formulas, copied verbatim from the scientist's private papers, identify whose work on his mass-energy theorem?

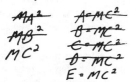

ANSWER: Albert Einstein.

110. Each of the following defines a word ending in -ion. Give the word which best fits the definition.

a) A mixture in which one liquid is scattered in small globules throughout another, such as milk fats in milk, kerosene in water

b) Originally, the combination of oxygen with another substance; the loss of electrons by an atom or group of atoms

c) The opposite of oxidation; the removal of oxygen from a compound; the gain of electrons by an atom or group of atoms

d) The process by which a solid substance is vaporized (changed into a gas), without first becoming a liquid

e) A chemical change, especially oxidation, producing heat and light

f) The physical process by which a substance changes from a gas into a liquid

g) The adhesion of the molecules of gas, liquid, or dissolved matter to the surface of a solid

h) The amount of a specified substance per unit volume

i) A refining process of separating gold and silver from a base metal such as lead

j) The separation of a substance into simpler substances by chemical reaction

k) The process in which a liquid is vaporized and then condensed into a more nearly pure or refined substance

l) The changing of a liquid into vapor by heat

m) The absorption of gases by solids

n) The alleged conversion of base metals into gold and silver by alchemy

o) The hydrolysis of fats or oils by an alkali

ANSWER: a) emulsion b) oxidation c) reduction d) sublimation e) combustion f) con-

densation g) absorption h) concentration i) cupellation j) decomposition
k) distillation l) evaporation m) occlusion n) transmutation o) saponification.

111. What is the name for the process of changing neutral atoms or molecules to ions?
What are the names of a negatively charged ion and a positively charged ion?
Toward what is each attracted in electrolysis?
ANSWER: Ionization/Anion and cation/Anion to the anode and cation to the cathode.

112. What is the name of the process in which there is a movement of molecules from
a place of greater concentration to a place of lesser concentration? What is the
relative speed of this process in solids, liquids, and gases?
ANSWER: Diffusion/Rapid in gases, slow in liquids, and very slow in solids.

113. Identify the person(s) who discovered each of the following elements.
a) oxygen   d) molybdenum   g) iodine
b) hydrogen   e) polonium   h) magnesium
c) radium   f) nitrogen   i) calcium
**ANSWER: a) Joseph Priestly and Carl Wilhelm Scheele b) Henry Cavendish c) Pierre
and Marie Curie d) Carl Wilhelm Scheele e) Pierre and Marie Curie f) Daniel
Rutherford g) Bernard Courtois h) Sir Humphry Davy i) Sir Humphry Davy.**

114. Give the common names for each chemical name and its formula.
a) Nitric acid HNO_3 (hepta hydrated)
b) Nitric acid and hydrochloric acid,   g) Nitrous oxide N_2O
$_1HNO_3 + _3HCl$ h) Magnesium hydroxide $Mg(OH)_2$
c) Acetyl-salicylic acid   i) Calcium sulfate $(CaSO_4)_2 \cdot H_2O$
$C_6H_4 (OCOCH_3)COOH$ (hemi hydrated)
d) Sodium bicarbonate $NaHCO_3$ j) Mercury Hg
e) Mercurous chloride Hg_2Cl_2 k) Sucrose $C_{12}H_{22}O_{11}$
f) Magnesium sulfate $MgSO_4 \cdot 7H_2O$
**ANSWER: a) aqua fortis b) aqua regia c) aspirin d) baking soda e) calomel f) epsom
salts g) laughing gas h) milk of magnesia i) plaster of Paris j) quicksilver
k) sugar.**

115. Name the 5 chemical elements that comprise the Nitrogen group VA family.
Which one is a gas? Which element occurs in nature in the form of gray, brittle
flakes? Which element is the first word of the title of a play by Joseph Kesselring,
"_____ *and Old Lace*"?
**ANSWER: Nitrogen (7), phosphorus (15), arsenic (33), antimony (51), bismuth (83)/
Nitrogen/Arsenic/Arsenic.**

116. What substance ranges in color from black to brown and is a radioactive material
consisting primarily of uranium oxide? What substance does it contain that is
more radioactive than pure uranium? Name the 2 scientists who found this
substance.
ANSWER: Pitchblende/Radium/Pierre and Marie Curie.

117. With what 2 classes of compounds were Svante Arrhenius, G.N. Lewis, and
Brönsted and Lowry concerned?
ANSWER: Acids and bases.

118. Identify each of the following from the description.
a) The forerunners of chemists who permits it to be hammered, pounded,
sought to change baser metals into or rolled into sheets
gold   f) PCB
b) The heat required to raise the   g) "fool's gold"
temperature of 1 gram of water 1°C   h) Atoms having the same chemical
c) The quantity of heat required to   properties and atomic number but
raise the temperature of one pound   different atomic weights
of water one degree Fahrenheit   i) A chemical reaction of a salt with
d) The unit of radioactivity equal to the   water to form an acid and base
quantity of any radioactive substance   j) The common name for solid carbon
in which the number of dis-   dioxide
integrations per second is $3.7x10^{10}$ k) Atoms which have different atomic
e) The property of a substance that   numbers but the same mass number

ANSWER: a) alchemists b) calorie c) B.T.U. or British Thermal Unit d) curie e) malleability f) polychlorinated biphenyls g) pyrite h) isotopes i) hydrolysis j) dry ice k) isobars.

119. Name the type of compound formed by each of the following reactions.
   a) Metal oxide plus water   c) Non-metal oxide plus water
   b) Active metal plus acid
ANSWER: a) base b) salt and hydrogen c) acid.

120. Which of the following is the molecular weight of $(NH_4)_2CO_3$?
   a) 92   b) 94   c) 96   d) 98
ANSWER: c) 96.

121. Identify each of the following.
   a) The maximum number of electrons existing in the 4th shell of any element
   b) The maximum number of electrons possible in any atomic orbital
   c) The factor which determines the atomic number of an element
   d) In any given atom, the number of electrons that can have a principal quantum number of 4
ANSWER: a) 32 b) 2 c) the number of protons in the nucleus d) 32.

122. What are the names of the 3 noble metals or elements in group IB of the periodic table? Which one has the greatest density? Name the elements in group IIB.
ANSWER: Copper (29), silver (47), and gold (79)/Gold/Zinc (30), cadmium (48), and mercury (80).

123. Identify the person who discovered or isolated each of the following.
   a) the electron   d) the neutron
   b) deuterium   e) radioactive decay
   c) the positron   f) the proton
ANSWER: a) Joseph J. Thomson (1895) b) Harold C.F.G. Urey (1931) c) Carl D. Anderson (1932) d) James Chadwick (1932) e) Antoine Henri Becquerel (1896) f) Ernest Rutherford (1911).

124. Russian scientists claim to have created a radioactive element, element 105. What did they call it? After whom? American scientists made the same claim. What did they call it, and after whom did they name it?
ANSWER: Nielsbohrium/Niels Bohr, a Danish physicist who is known for his theory of the structure of the atom/Hahnium/Otto Hahn, a German radiochemist who discovered nuclear fission.

125. Russian and American scientists have also claimed to have artificially created radioactive element number 106. No name was given to the element and neither side's claim has been accepted officially. However, the International Union of Pure and Allied Chemicals has given element 106 a Latin name. What is that name and what is its meaning?
ANSWER: *Unnilsexium*/Latin for ''one-zero-six.''

126. The following prefixes may be used at times when naming compounds. The prefixes represent a definite quantity of atoms. Give the number that each prefix represents.
   a) penta-   c) hepta-   e) tetra-
   b) octa-   d) hexa-   f) mono-
ANSWER: a) 5 b) 8 c) 7 d) 6 e) 4 f) 1.

127. Three of the following elements are classified as transition elements. Name them.
   a) carbon   c) iron   e) chromium
   b) copper   d) xenon   f) silicon
ANSWER: Copper, iron, and chromium.

128. Give the mathematical relationship for converting centigrade degree to kelvin degree.
ANSWER: $C° + 273°$.

129. A substance that increases the rate of a chemical reaction but is not consumed in the reaction is known by what term?
ANSWER: Catalyst.

130. Which one of the following statements describe the reduction of an atom?
     a) The loss of electrons from that atom, therefore an increase in oxidation number
     b) The gain of electrons by that atom, therefore an increase in oxidation number
     c) The loss of electrons from that atom, therefore a decrease in oxidation number
     d) The gain of electrons by that atom, therefore a decrease in oxidation number
ANSWER: d.

131. Of what 2 elements is bronze made? Of what 2 elements is brass made? Solder is an alloy of what 2 metals? Electrum is a light-yellow alloy of what 2 metals?
ANSWER: Copper and tin/Copper and zinc/Tin and lead/Gold and silver (and copper).

132. What 4 elements exist in liquid form near room temperature?
ANSWER: Mercury, bromine, cesium, and gallium.

133. Name the 7 elements that begin with the letter ''N.''
ANSWER: Neodymium, neon, neptunium, nickel, niobium, nitrogen, and nobelium.

134. What are the 3 states of matter? What is the now commonly accepted 4th state?
ANSWER: Solid, liquid, and gas/Plasma.

135. What 2 elements combine to make table salt?
ANSWER: Sodium and chlorine (or chloride).

136. Name the 10 transition elements whose atomic numbers are 21-30 inclusive.
ANSWER: Scandium, titanium, vanadium, chromium, manganese, iron, cobalt, nickel, copper, and zinc.

137. What are the 3 methods by which heat is transferred?
ANSWER: Convection, conduction, and radiation.

138. What are the 5 most common elements by weight in the earth's crust?
ANSWER: Oxygen (49.2%), silicon (25.7%), aluminum (7.4%), iron (4.7%), and calcium (3.4%).

139. Name the 3 most electronegative elements. Name the 3 least electronegative elements not including the rare gases.
ANSWER: Fluorine (4.0), oxygen (3.5), and nitrogen (3.0)/Cesium (0.7), rubidium (0.8), and potassium (0.8).

140. Give the name for each of the following formulas.
     a) H_2O c) $H_2(SO_4)$ e) $H(NO_3)$
     b) HCl   d) $H(C_2H_3O_2)$ f) $H_3(PO_4)$
ANSWER: a) Hydrogen oxide (water) b) hydrogen chloride (hydrochloric acid) c) hydrogen sulfate (sulfuric acid) d) acetic acid e) hydrogen nitrate (nitric acid) f) tri-hydrogen phosphate (phosphoric acid).

141. Depending upon whether 1, 2, or 3 protons are supplied by the molecule or ion, in what 3 ways are acids classified? Tell the classification for each of the following formulas.
     a) H_2SO_4 b) H_3PO_4 c) HNO_3
ANSWER: Monobasic, dibasic, or tribasic (or monoprotic, diprotic, and triprotic)/ a) dibasic b) tribasic c) monobasic.

142. Depending upon whether the molecule or ion is capable of accepting 1, 2, or 3 protons, in what 3 ways are bases classified? Identify the class to which each of the following belongs.
     a) $Al(OH)_3$ b) KOH   c) $Ca(OH)_2$
ANSWER: Monoacid, diacid, or triacid/a) triacid b) monoacid c) diacid.

143. Name the 5 elements that comprise group IVA. Which 2 are nonmetals? Which 2 are important in the computer field in transistors and semiconductors?
ANSWER: Carbon (6), silicon (14), germanium (32), tin (50), and lead (82)/Carbon and silicon/Silicon and germanium.

144. What are the names of the 6 alkali metals in group IA of the periodic table? Which ones occur free in nature?
ANSWER: Lithium (3), sodium (11), potassium (19), rubidium (37), cesium (55), and francium (87)/None of them.

145. Name the 5 elements in group IIIA of the periodic table. Which one has a low melting point (29.8°C)? Which one is a nonmetal?
ANSWER: Boron (5), aluminum (13), gallium (31), indium (49), and thallium (81)/ Gallium/Boron.

146. According to the ancient and medieval philosophers, what were the 4 elements from which all other substances were composed? What was the 5th element that was added later, and what does this word mean today?
ANSWER: Fire, air, water, and earth/"Quintessence," (or "ether" according to Aristotle), supposed to be the constituent matter of the heavenly bodies/"The perfect manifestation of something."

147. Of what 3 things are "little girls" made?
ANSWER: "Sugar and spice and everything nice."

148. What are the 2 most abundant elements in the universe?
ANSWER: Hydrogen and helium.

149. What are the 3 most abundant elements in the lithosphere (or on land, based on igneous rock) and the 3 most abundant in the hydrosphere (in the sea)?
ANSWER: Oxygen, silicon (sand), and aluminum/Oxygen, hydrogen, and chlorine.

150. An atom which loses (an) electron(s) from its outer shell is called what? An atom which gains (an) electron(s) in its outer shell is called what?
ANSWER: Positive ion (cation)/Negative ion (anion).

151. Identify the pairs of qualities Aristotle linked to the 4 elements.
ANSWER: Fire was hot and dry; air was hot and moist; water was cold and moist; and earth was cold and dry.

152. Identify each of the following.
a) Joseph Black's "fixed air"
b) Henry Cavendish's "inflammable air" (called phlogiston by some chemists)
c) Joseph Priestly's "dephlogisticated air"
d) Carl Wilhelm Scheele's "fire air"
e) Antoine Lavoisier's "acid former" (from the Greek)
f) Antoine Lavoisier's "water former" (from the Greek)
g) Carl Wilhelm Scheele's "dephlogisticated marine acid air"
ANSWER: a) carbon dioxide b) hydrogen c) oxygen d) oxygen e) oxygen f) hydrogen g) chlorine.

153. What is the name of the hypothetical substance, stone, or chemical preparation alchemists believed would convert all baser metals into gold? What, according to alchemists, were the 2 main elements of this substance? From Ripley's *The Compound of Alchemie* (c. 1471), name any of the 12 stages in the transmutation of metals.
ANSWER: The philosopher's stone/Sulphur and mercury/Calcination, dissolution, separation, conjunction, putrefaction, congelation, cibation, sublimation, fermentation, exaltation, multiplication, and projection.

154. Name 2 general types of solids dispersed in liquids, and name the 2 general methods of preparing colloidal systems.
ANSWER: Lyophobic and lyophilic/Condensation and dispersion.

155. What is the name of the scattering and polarization of a light beam passing through a system of particles, such as a solution of colloidal particles? What is the name of the random, zigzag motion of microscopic particles dispersed in a fluid medium, and caused by collision with molecules of the fluid?
ANSWER: Tyndall effect/Brownian motion or movement.

156. What is the symbol for each of the following elements?
a) tin
b) tungsten
c) gold
d) arsenic
e) lead
f) sodium
g) mercury
h) iron
i) cobalt
j) potassium
k) magnesium
l) antimony
m) silver
n) hydrogen
o) platinum
ANSWER: a) Sn b) W c) Au d) As e) Pb f) Na g) Hg h) Fe i) Co j) K k) Mg l) Sb m) Ag n) H o) Pt.

157. Name each of the following based on the number of C atoms in each.
     a) CH_4 d) C_4H_{10} g) C_6H_6
     b) C_2H_6 e) C_4H_8 h) C_7H_8
     c) C_3H_8 f) C_4H_6
**ANSWER: a) methane b) ethane c) propane d) butane(s) e) butene(s) f) butyne(s)
g) benzene h) toluene (or cycloheptatriene).**

158. Name the 3 isotopes of hydrogen.
ANSWER: Hydrogen, deuterium, and tritium.

159. In the early periodic classification of the elements with what name was each of
     the following terms associated?
     a) The "triads"   c) The "periodic law"
     b) The "law of octaves"
ANSWER: a) Dobereiner b) Newlands c) Mendeleev.

160. Identify each of the following by the description.
     a) The acronym A.M.U.   compound
     b) The horizontal rows in the periodic   g) The number of metalloids
        table   h) The elements called "rare earths"
     c) The simplest form of matter   i) The basis for the modern classifi-
     d) The number of known elements   cation of elements
     e) The vertical columns in the   j) The 2nd series of elements placed
        periodic table   separately at the bottom of the
     f) The sum of the atomic weights in a   periodic table
**ANSWER: a) Atomic Mass Unit b) periods or series c) element d) 103 (but claims are
in for 4 more — 107 may now be known) e) groups or families f) molecular
weight g) 8 or 9 h) lanthanides i) atomic numbers j) lanthanides and acti-
nides (also inner transition elements).**

161. Name the 8 elements generally referred to as the metalloids.
**ANSWER: Antimony, arsenic, astatine, beryllium, boron, polonium, silicon, and
tellurium (aluminum is sometimes included).**

162. Name the members of the zero group or VIIIA group known as the inert or Nobel
     gases. Which one has the smallest atomic weight? Which one is used to prevent
     Caisson Disease? Which one is used in electric signs? Which one is used in
     regular electric light bulbs and electric signs? Which 2 are not prepared for
     normal commercial use? Name the only nobel gas with no stable isotopes.
**ANSWER: Helium, neon, argon, krypton, xenon, and radon/Helium/Helium/Neon/
Argon/Krypton and xenon/Radon.**

163. Name the 5 chemical elements that comprise the Halogen group VIIA and give
     their atomic number. What is the meaning of the word *halogen*? What is the
     only one that does not form oxyacids? Which 2 have 2 stable isotopes? Which
     halogen was first prepared from salts obtained by the evaporation of sea water?
**ANSWER: Fluorine (9), chlorine (17), bromine (35), iodine (53), astatine (85)/Salt-
former/Fluorine/Chlorine and bromine/Bromine.**

164. By what slang term is a user of LSD (d-lysergic acid) known? What term defines
     natural precipitation falling through atmosphere containing sulfur dioxide and
     nitrogen oxide pollutants, thus forming an acid bias in the atmosphere and in the
     soil? What phrase describes rock music with lyrics and sound suggestive of
     drug-induced-experiences? What phrase means "to ask for a loan; to place
     excessive demands on," and refers to something that is sharp and biting to the
     taste as well as full of destructive power? From the area of finance, what phrase
     means the degree of an organization's liquidity capacity, that is, its ability to
     convert its assets into cash?
ANSWER: Acid head/Acid fallout (rain)/Acid rock/To put the acid on/Acid test ratio.

165. You're the king — a chess king, to be exact — and you're standing on the
     periodic table, squarely on Arsenic. Name any of the 8 elements to which you can
     legally move.
**ANSWER: Silicon (14), phosphorus (15), sulfur (16), germanium (32), selenium
(34), tin (50), antimony (51), and tellurium (52). (Arsenic is 33).**

166. Identify each of the following items that would be found in a chemistry lab from the given description.
    a) A graduated glass tube with fine gradations and a stopcock at the bottom, used for measuring small amounts of liquid or gas
    b) A closed glass vessel with a long tube, used to distill or decompose substances by heat
    c) A very shallow, cylindrical glass dish with a loose-fitting cover, used especially for cultures in bacteriology
    d) A slender glass tube into which fluid is taken up by suction, used especially for measuring or transferring

ANSWER: a) burette b) retort c) petri dish d) pipette (pipet).

167. What phrase from the field of chemistry means in political terms ''an issue that indicates the ideological purity of a candidate,'' and in chemistry comes from the organic dye that turns blue in bases and red in acids?

ANSWER: Litmus-test issue.

168. What is the name of the Nobel Prize winner in chemistry in 1920 whose Third Law of Thermodynamics implies that pressure, volume, and surface tension would all become independent of temperature at absolute zero?

ANSWER: Walther Hermann Nernst.

169. Take a trip across the U.S.A. by means of the chemical elements. Identify each of the following elements from its atomic number, give its symbol, and then give the state whose postal abbreviation is the same as the chemical symbol.

a) 10	d) 20	g) 27	j) 49	m) 91
b) 13	e) 21	h) 31	k) 57	n) 101
c) 18	f) 25	i) 42	l) 60	

ANSWER: a) Neon, Ne, Nebraska b) Aluminum, Al, Alabama c) Argon, Ar, Arkansas d) Calcium, Ca, California e) Scandium, Sc, South Carolina f) Manganese, Mn, Minnesota g) Cobalt, Co, Colorado h) Gallium, Ga, Georgia i) Molybdenum, Mo, Missouri j) Indium, In, Indiana k) Lanthanum, La, Louisiana l) Neodymium, Nd, North Dakota m) Protactinium, Pa, Pennsylvania n) Mendelevium, Md, Maryland.

170. After E.T. got home, his one desire was to ''15, 1, 8, 10   56, 6, 19.'' Decipher the message by means of the atomic numbers and symbols of the chemical elements.

ANSWER: P (Phosphorus), H (Hydrogen), O (Oxygen), Ne (Neon) = Phone
        Ba (Barium), C (Carbon), K (Potassium)   = Back

171. Identify each of the following elements from the given description.
    a) Named after the Roman goddess of the earth
    b) Named after the personification of the heavens, the husband or son of Gaea (Earth) who was overthrown by his son Cronus (Saturn)
    c) Named after a Greek king, son of Zeus, who was condemned in Hades to stand in water that receded when he tried to drink, and with fruit hanging above him that receded when he reached for it
    d) Named after the Greek sun god, the son of Hyperion
    e) Named after the Greek goddess of the rainbow and messenger of the gods
    f) Named after the Roman god of the dead and the ruler of the underworld
    g) Named after the Roman goddess of agriculture
    h) Named after the Greek goddess of wisdom and the arts
    i) Named after the Greek goddess of the moon
    j) Named after any of the race of Greek giant deities who were overthrown by the Olympian gods
    k) Named after the queen of Thebes, daughter of Tantalus, who was turned to stone while weeping over the loss of her children (give the former name for this element which was based on the U.S. personified as a woman)
    l) Named after the Titan in Greek mythology who stole fire from heaven and gave it to man, an action for which he was severely punished by Zeus.

ANSWER: a) tellurium (Tellus) b) uranium (Uranus) c) tantalum (Tantalus) d) helium (Helios) e) iridium (Iris) f) plutonium (Pluto) g) cerium (Ceres) h) palladium

(Athena or Athene; also called Pallas Athena or Pallas Athene) i) selenium (Selene) j) titanium (Titan) k) niobium (Niobe — columbium, Columbia) l) promethium (Prometheus).

172. With which planets did the alchemists of the Middle Ages associate each of the following metals?

a) gold   c) copper   e) tin   g) quicksilver
b) silver   d) iron   f) lead

ANSWER: a) the sun b) the moon c) Venus d) Mars e) Jupiter f) Saturn g) Mercury.

NOTABLES IN CHEMISTRY

Thales of Miletus....Greek.... Believed that water was the one element from which the world was formed. Founder of Greek Science, Mathematics, and Philosophy.

Empedocles of Agrigentum....Greek.... Believed that there were 4 elements — earth, air, fire, and water.

Democritus....Greek.... Developed a theory that the world consisted of tiny, indivisible particles called atoms.

Roger Bacon....English.... Laid the foundation for the experimental method of chemical research. Known as the "Founder of Experimental Science." Finished his *Opus maius (Longer Work)* about 1267.

Jan Baptista van Helmont....Flemish.... Sometimes called the "Father of Biochemistry" for using quantitative methods with a biological problem. Invented the word *gas*.

Robert Boyle....Irish.... Developed Boyle's law of gases (volume of a gas varies inversely with pressure). Known as the "Father of Chemistry." First to separate chemistry from alchemy. First to clearly define element. Wrote the *Sceptical Chymist* (1661).

Joseph Black....Scottish.... Defined specific heat and formed the concept of latent heat. Showed that carbon dioxide differs from ordinary air.

Lord Henry Cavendish....English.... Discovered hydrogen (1766), and showed that water is a compound of oxygen and hydrogen.

Joseph Priestly....English.... Discovered hydrochloric acid (1772), laughing gas (1772), and oxygen (1774), and prepared carbon monoxide and amonia.

Carl Wilhelm Scheele....Swedish.... Discovered oxygen (1771) and chlorine (1774), molybdenum (1778), manganese, tungsten, and other chemical elements and substances.

Antoine Laurent Lavoisier....French...."Father of Modern Chemistry." Wrote the first modern textbook of chemistry, *Elements of Chemistry* (1789). Discovered the role of oxygen in combustion and respiration and overthrew G. E. Stahl's theory on combustion.

Martin Heinrich Klaproth....German.... Sometimes called the "Father of Analytic Chemistry." Discovered uranium and zirconium (1789).

Sir Humphry Davy....English.... Discovered the chemical elements sodium, potassium, magnesium, barium, calcium, and strontium.

Joseph Louis Gay-Lussac....French.... Pioneered work in gases. Formulated the law that all gases expand by equal amounts when subjected to equal increments in temperature (Jacques Alexandre César Charles had discovered the same law but had not published it). First to isolate the element boron and to introduce the terms pipette and burette.

John Dalton....English.... Formulated the law of partial pressure in gases (1802) and developed the atomic theory and explained its application (1803).

Amedeo Avogadro....Italian.... Developed Avogadro's law of gases (1811), which is that equal volumes of all gases at the same temperature and pressure contain equal numbers of molecules. Coined the term molecule and is regarded as one of the founders of physical chemistry.

Bernard Courtois....French.... Discovered the element iodine (1811).

Jöns Jakob Berzelius....Swedish.... Co-discovered the element cerium and discovered selenium and thorium. Originated the system of writing modern chemical symbols and formulas.

Friedrich Wöhler....German.... Founder of the science of organic chemistry. Synthesized organic compounds from inorganic material (1828), thus refuting the prevailing "vital force" theory.

Thomas Graham....Scottish.... Founder of colloid chemistry and a principal founder of physical chemistry. Known for Graham's law (1833) of diffusion.

Michael Faraday....English.... Discovered a mathematical relationship between electricity and the valence of a chemical element. These laws of electrolysis bear his name. A pioneer in the liquefaction of gases.

Robert Wilhelm Bunsen....German.... Developed the foundations of spectroscopy (1859) with Gustav Kirchnoff. Developed the Bunsen burner (1855). Discovered cesium and rubidium.

Sir William Crookes....English.... Discovered thallium (1861). Invented the radiometer (1875).

Dmitri Ivanovich Mendeleev....Russian.... Devised the periodic table. Wrote *Elements of Chemistry* (1868).

Julius Lothar Meyer....German.... Developed a periodic table of 57 elements (1868) independent of Dmitri Mendeleev.

Friedrich August Kekulé von Stradonitz ....German.... Suggested the molecular structure for benzene. Called "Founder of the Structure Theory of Organic Chemistry."

Hillaire Chardonnet....French.... Patented a fiber (1884) that was later named rayon.

Josiah Willard Gibbs....American.... Founded the science of chemical thermodynamics. Contributed his famous phase rule, which is applicable to all systems of equilibrium.

Louis Pasteur....French.... Founder of microbiology. Laid the foundation of the germ theory of disease. Developed pasteurization. Developed a vaccine against rabies (1885). Founder of preventive medicine.

Henry Gwyn-Jeffreys Moseley....English.... Helped determine the relationship between the atomic number of an element and its properties and helped arrange the elements in their correct places in the periodic table.

Henry L. Le Chatelier....French.... Known for Le Chatelier's principle (law) concerning the shifting of directions by chemical reactions.

Antoine Henri Becquerel....French.... Shared the Nobel Prize for physics in 1903 with Pierre and Marie Curie for the discovery of natural radioactivity.

Marie Sklodowska Curie....Polish-French.... Discovered radium and polonium while working in conjunction with Pierre Curie and Henri Becquerel and shared with them the Nobel Prize for physics in 1903. She won the Nobel Prize for chemistry in 1911 for the discovery of radium and polonium and isolation and study of radium.

Svante August Arrhenius....Swedish.... Developed the theory of electrolytic dissociation (or ionization) and won the Nobel Prize for chemistry in 1903.

Mikhail Tswett....Russian.... Developed chromatography (1903).

Sir Joseph John Thomson....English.... Won the Nobel Prize for physics in 1906 for his research on the conduction of electricity by gases. Discovered the electron (1897).

Ernest Rutherford....English.... Developed the theory of the atom (1911). Discovered alpha and beta rays and protons. Known as the "Father of Nuclear Science." Won the Nobel Prize in chemistry in 1908 for work on the disintegration of elements and the chemistry of radioactive substances.

Max von Laue....German.... First used X ray crystallography (1912).

Niels Bohr....Danish.... Developed a theory of atomic structure (1913).

Theodore William Richards....American.... First American chemist to receive the Nobel Prize (1914) — for his exact determination of the atomic weights of chemical elements.

Sir William Bragg and son Sir W. Lawrence Bragg....English.... Used X rays to determine the structure of crystals for which they won the Nobel Prize in physics in 1915.

Fritz Haber....German.... Invented the Haber Process of producing ammonia from nitrogen and hydrogen for which he won the Nobel Prize in chemistry in 1918.

Albert Einstein....German-American.... Developed the theory of relativity and demonstrated the relationship between matter and energy ($E = mc^2$).

Gilbert Newton Lewis....American.... Helped develop the modern electric theory of valence, thermodynamics, and acid-base theory.

Walther Hermann Nernst....German.... Won the 1920 Nobel Prize in chemistry for his formulation of the third law of thermodynamics which states that entropy approaches zero as temperature approaches zero.

Francis William Aston....English.... Invented the mass spectrograph (1919). Received the Nobel Prize in chemistry in 1922 for the discovery of isotopes in non radioactive elements.

Johannes Nicolaus Brönsted....Danish.... Known for his theory on acids and bases (1922).

Thomas Martin Lowry....English.... Known for this theory of acids and bases developed independently of Brönsted.

Theodor Svedberg....Swedish.... Developed the ultracentrifuge. Won the Nobel Prize in chemistry in 1926 for work on dispersion systems and colloid chemistry.

Friedrich Bergius....German.... Shared the Nobel Prize for chemistry in 1931 with Carl Bosch for work on chemical high-pressure methods.

Irving Langmuir....American.... Won the Nobel Prize in chemistry in 1932 for his discoveries about molecular films absorbed on surfaces. Invented the gas-filled electric light bulb.

Carl David Anderson....American.... Discovered the positron, or anti-electron (1932). Won the Nobel Prize in physics in 1936. During 1936-38, he discovered the existence of mesons in cosmic rays.

Harold Clayton Urey....American.... Won the Nobel Prize in chemistry in 1934 for the discovery of deuterium (''heavy water''), a rare hydrogen isotope.

Sir James Chadwick....English.... Won the Nobel Prize for physics in 1935 for his discovery of the neutron (1932).

Ernest Orlando Lawrence....American.... Invented the cyclotron.

Otto Hahn....German.... Received the Nobel Prize for chemistry in 1944 for the discovery of the fission of heavy nuclei.

Glenn Theodore Seaborg....American.... Shared the Nobel Prize for chemistry in 1951 with Edwin M. McMillan for the discoveries in the chemistry of transuranium elements. Co-discovered elements with atomic numbers 94-102 of the periodic table (plutonium, americium, curium, berkelium, californium, einsteinium, fermium, mendelevium, and nobelium). These discoveries were made with the aid of a cyclotron.

Linus Carl Pauling....American.... Won the Nobel Prize for chemistry in 1954 for his research into the nature of the chemical bond.

Willard Frank Libby....American.... Won the Nobel Prize in chemistry in 1960 for developing a method of using radioactive carbon to determine the age of objects.

Melvin Calvin....American.... Received the Nobel Prize in chemistry in 1961 for discoveries concerning photosynthesis.

INTERNATIONAL ATOMIC WEIGHTS

Element	Symbol	Atomic Number	Atomic Weight	Element	Symbol	Atomic Number	Atomic Weight
Actinium	Ac	89	(227)	Mercury	Hg	80	200.59
Aluminum	Al	13	26.9815	Molybdenum	Mo	42	95.94
Americium	Am	95	(243)	Neodymium	Nd	60	144.24
Antimony	Sb	51	121.75	Neptunium	Np	93	237.0482
Argon	Ar	18	39.948	Neon	Ne	10	20.179
Arsenic	As	33	74.9216	Nickel	Ni	28	58.70
Astatine	At	85	(210)	Niobium	Nb	41	92.9064
Barium	Ba	56	137.33	Nitrogen	N	7	14.0067
Berkelium	Bk	97	(247)	Nobelium	No	102	(259)
Beryllium	Be	4	9.0122	Osmium	Os	76	190.2
Bismuth	Bi	83	208.9804	Oxygen	O	8	15.9994
Boron	B	5	10.811	Palladium	Pd	46	106.4
Bromine	Br	35	79.904	Phosphorus	P	15	30.9737
Cadmium	Cd	48	112.41	Platinum	Pt	78	195.09
Calcium	Ca	20	40.08	Plutonium	Pu	94	(244)
Californium	Cf	98	(251)	Polonium	Po	84	(209)
Carbon	C	6	12.011	Potassium	K	19	39.0983
Cerium	Ce	58	140.12	Praseodymium	Pr	59	140.9077
Cesium	Cs	55	132.9054	Promethium	Pm	61	(145)
Chlorine	Cl	17	35.453	Protactinium	Pa	91	231.0359
Chromium	Cr	24	51.996	Radium	Ra	88	226.0254
Cobalt	Co	27	58.9332	Radon	Rn	86	(222)
Copper	Cu	29	63.546	Rhenium	Re	75	186.207
Curium	Cm	96	(247)	Rhodium	Rh	45	102.9055
Dysprosium	Dy	66	162.50	Rubidium	Rb	37	85.4678
Einsteinium	Es	99	(254)	Ruthenium	Ru	44	101.07
Erbium	Er	68	167.26	Samarium	Sm	62	150.35
Europium	Eu	63	151.96	Scandium	Sc	21	44.956
Fermium	Fm	100	(257)	Selenium	Se	34	78.96
Fluorine	F	9	18.9984	Silicon	Si	14	28.0855
Francium	Fr	87	(223)	Silver	Ag	47	107.868
Gadolinium	Gd	64	157.25	Sodium	Na	11	22.9898
Gallium	Ga	31	69.72	Strontium	Sr	38	87.62
Germanium	Ge	32	72.59	Sulfur	S	16	32.064
Gold	Au	79	196.967	Tantalum	Ta	73	180.948
Hafnium	Hf	72	178.49	Technetium	Tc	43	(97)
Helium	He	2	4.0026	Tellurium	Te	52	127.60
Holmium	Ho	67	164.9304	Terbium	Tb	65	158.9254
Hydrogen	H	1	1.0079	Thallium	Tl	81	204.37
Indium	In	49	114.82	Thorium	Th	90	232.0381
Iodine	I	53	126.9045	Thulium	Tm	69	168.9342
Iridium	Ir	77	192.22	Tin	Sn	50	118.69
Iron	Fe	26	55.847	Titanium	Ti	22	47.90
Krypton	Kr	36	83.80	Tungsten	W	74	183.85
Lanthanum	La	57	138.9055	Uranium	U	92	238.029
Lawrencium	Lr	103	(260)	Vanadium	V	23	50.942
Lead	Pb	82	207.19	Xenon	Xe	54	131.30
Lithium	Li	3	6.941	Ytterbium	Yb	70	173.04
Lutetium	Lu	71	174.97	Yttrium	Y	39	88.9059
Magnesium	Mg	12	24.305	Zinc	Zn	30	65.38
Manganese	Mn	25	54.9380	Zirconium	Zr	40	91.22
Mendelevium	Md	101	(258)				

Values in parentheses are estimated for isotopes of longest half-life.

INTERNATIONAL ATOMIC WEIGHTS

Atomic Number	Element	Symbol	Atomic Weight	Atomic Number	Element	Symbol	Atomic Weight
1	Hydrogen	H	1.0079	53	Iodine	I	126.9045
2	Helium	He	4.0026	54	Xenon	Xe	131.30
3	Lithium	Li	6.941	55	Cesium	Cs	132.9054
4	Beryllium	Be	9.0122	56	Barium	Ba	137.33
5	Boron	B	10.811	57	Lanthanum	La	138.9055
6	Carbon	C	12.011	58	Cerium	Ce	140.12
7	Nitrogen	N	14.0067	59	Praseodymium	Pr	140.9077
8	Oxygen	O	15.9994	60	Neodymium	Nd	144.24
9	Fluorine	F	18.9984	61	Promethium	Pm	(145)
10	Neon	Ne	20.179	62	Samarium	Sm	150.35
11	Sodium	Na	22.989	63	Europium	Eu	151.96
12	Magnesium	Mg	24.305	64	Gadolinium	Gd	157.25
13	Aluminum	Al	26.9815	65	Terbium	Tb	158.9254
14	Silicon	Si	28.0855	66	Dysprosium	Dy	162.50
15	Phosphorus	P	30.9737	67	Holmium	Ho	164.9304
16	Sulfur	S	32.064	68	Erbium	Er	167.26
17	Chlorine	Cl	35.453	69	Thulium	Tm	168.9342
18	Argon	Ar	39.948	70	Ytterbium	Yb	173.04
19	Potassium	K	39.0983	71	Lutetium	Lu	174.97
20	Calcium	Ca	40.08	72	Hafnium	Hf	178.49
21	Scandium	Sc	44.956	73	Tantalum	Ta	180.948
22	Titanium	Ti	47.90	74	Tungsten	W	183.85
23	Vanadium	V	50.942	75	Rhenium	Re	186.207
24	Chromium	Cr	51.996	76	Osmium	Os	190.2
25	Manganese	Mn	54.9380	77	Iridium	Ir	192.22
26	Iron	Fe	55.847	78	Platinum	Pt	195.09
27	Cobalt	Co	58.9332	79	Gold	Au	196.967
28	Nickel	Ni	58.70	80	Mercury	Hg	200.59
29	Copper	Cu	63.546	81	Thallium	Tl	204.37
30	Zinc	Zn	65.38	82	Lead	Pb	207.19
31	Gallium	Ga	69.72	83	Bismuth	Bi	208.9804
32	Germanium	Ge	72.59	84	Polonium	Po	(209)
33	Arsenic	As	74.9216	85	Astatine	At	(210)
34	Selenium	Se	78.96	86	Radon	Rn	(222)
35	Bromine	Br	79.904	87	Francium	Fr	(223)
36	Krypton	Kr	83.80	88	Radium	Ra	226.0254
37	Rubidium	Rb	85.4678	89	Actinium	Ac	(227)
38	Strontium	Sr	87.62	90	Thorium	Th	232.0381
39	Yttrium	Y	88.9059	91	Protactinium	Pa	231.0359
40	Zirconium	Zr	91.22	92	Uranium	U	238.029
41	Niobium	Nb	92.9064	93	Neptunium	Np	237.0482
42	Molybdenum	Mo	95.94	94	Plutonium	Pu	(244)
43	Technetium	Tc	(97)	95	Americium	Am	(243)
44	Ruthenium	Ru	101.07	96	Curium	Cm	(247)
45	Rhodium	Rh	102.9055	97	Berkelium	Bk	(247)
46	Palladium	Pd	106.4	98	Californium	Cf	(251)
47	Silver	Ag	107.868	99	Einsteinium	Es	(254)
48	Cadmium	Cd	112.41	100	Fermium	Fm	(257)
49	Indium	In	114.82	101	Mendelevium	Md	(258)
50	Tin	Sn	118.69	102	Nobelium	No	(259)
51	Antimony	Sb	121.75	103	Lawrencium	Lr	(260)
52	Tellurium	Te	127.60				

Values in parentheses are estimated for isotopes of longest half-life.

PERIODIC TABLE OF THE ELEMENTS

IA	IIA	IIIB	IVB	VB	VIB	VIIB	VIII	VIII	VIII	IB	IIB	IIIA	IVA	VA	VIA	VIIA	Zero
1 H																1 H	2 He
3 Li	4 Be											5 B	6 C	7 N	8 O	9 F	10 Ne
11 Na	12 Mg											13 Al	14 Si	15 P	16 S	17 Cl	18 Ar
19 K	20 Ca	21 Sc	22 Ti	23 V	24 Cr	25 Mn	26 Fe	27 Co	28 Ni	29 Cu	30 Zn	31 Ga	32 Ge	33 As	34 Se	35 Br	36 Kr
37 Rb	38 Sr	39 Y	40 Zr	41 Nb	42 Mo	43 Tc	44 Ru	45 Rh	46 Pd	47 Ag	48 Cd	49 In	50 Sn	51 Sb	52 Te	53 I	54 Xe
55 Cs	56 Ba	57-71 *La	72 Hf	73 Ta	74 W	75 Re	76 Os	77 Ir	78 Pt	79 Au	80 Hg	81 Tl	82 Pb	83 Bi	84 Po	85 At	86 Rn
87 Fr	88 Ra	89-103 **Ac															

*LANTHANIDE SERIES

57 La	58 Ce	59 Pr	60 Nd	61 Pm	62 Sm	63 Eu	64 Gd	65 Tb	66 Dy	67 Ho	68 Er	69 Tm	70 Yb	71 Lu

**ACTINIDE SERIES

89 Ac	90 Th	91 Pa	92 U	93 Np	94 Pu	95 Am	96 Cm	97 Bk	98 Cf	99 Es	100 Fm	101 Md	102 No	103 Lr

THE ELEMENTS AND THEIR DISCOVERERS

Element	Atomic Number	Date	Discoverer	Country of Discovery
Carbon	6	—	Known to the ancients	—
Sulfur	16	—	Known to the ancients	—
Iron	26	—	Known to the ancients	—
Copper	29	—	Known to the ancients	—
Silver	47	—	Known to the ancients	—
Tin	50	—	Known to the ancients	—
Antimony	51	—	Known to the ancients	—
Gold	79	—	Known to the ancients	—
Mercury	80	—	Known to the ancients	—
Lead	82	—	Known to the ancients	—
Arsenic	33	1250	Albertus Magnus, or possibly known to the ancients, or discovered by Georg Brandt in 1733	—
Phosphorus	15	1669	Hennig Brand	Germany
Zinc	30	1721	Johann Friedrich Henckel	Germany
Cobalt	27	1735	Georg Brandt	Sweden
Platinum	78	1735	Antonio De Ulloa	Colombia
Bismuth	83	1739	Johann Hein Pott	Germany
Nickel	28	1751	Axel Cronstedt	Sweden
Hydrogen	1	1766	Henry Cavendish	England
Nitrogen	7	1772	Daniel Rutherford	Scotland
Oxygen	8	1774	Joseph Priestly; Carl Wilhelm Scheele	England; Sweden
Chlorine	17	1774	Carl Wilhelm Scheele	Sweden
Manganese	25	1774	Johann Gottlieb Gahn	Sweden
Molybdenum	42	1778	Carl Wilhelm Scheele	Sweden
Tellurium	52	1782	Franz Müller von Reichenstein	Romania
Tungsten	74	1783	Fausto and Juan José de Elhuyar	Spain
Zirconium	40	1789	Martin H. Klaproth	Germany
Uranium	92	1789	Martin H. Klaproth	Germany
Titanium	22	1791	William Gregor	England
Yttrium	39	1794	Johann Gadolin	Finland
Chromium	24	1797	Louis N. Vauquelin	France
Beryllium	4	1798	Louis N. Vauquelin	France
Niobium	41	1801	Charles Hatchett	England
Tantalum	73	1802	Anders G. Ekeberg	Sweden
Iridium	77	1802	Smithson Tennant	England
Rhodium	45	1803	William Wollaston	England
Palladium	46	1803	William Wollaston	England
Cerium	58	1803	W. von Hisinger; Jöns Berzelius; Martin Klaproth	Sweden; Germany
Osmium	76	1804	Smithson Tennant	England
Sodium	11	1807	Sir Humphry Davy	England
Potassium	19	1807	Sir Humphry Davy	England
Boron	5	1808	Joseph Louis Gay-Lussac; Louis Jacques Thenard	England; France
Magnesium	12	1808	Sir Humphry Davy	England
Calcium	20	1808	Sir Humphry Davy	England
Strontium	38	1808	Sir Humphry Davy	England
Barium	56	1808	Sir Humphry Davy	England
Iodine	53	1811	Bernard Courtois	France
Lithium	3	1817	Johann Arfvedson	Sweden
Selenium	34	1817	Jöns Berzelius	Sweden
Cadmium	48	1817	Friedrich Stromeyer	Germany
Silicon	14	1824	Jöns Berzelius	Sweden

Aluminum	13	1825	Hans Christian Oersted	Denmark
Bromine	35	1826	Antoine J. Balard	France
Thorium	90	1828	Jöns Berzelius	Sweden
Vanadium	23	1830	Nils G. Sefström	Sweden
Lanthanum	57	1839	Carl Mosander	Sweden
Terbium	65	1843	Carl Mosander	Sweden
Erbium	68	1843	Carl Mosander	Sweden
Ruthenium	44	1844	Karl Ernst Klaus	Russia
Cesium	55	1860	Gustav R. Kirchhoff, Robert Bunsen	Germany
Rubidium	37	1861	Gustav R. Kirchhoff, Robert Bunsen	Germany
Thallium	81	1861	Sir William Crookes; Claude Auguste Lamy	England; France
Indium	49	1863	Ferdinand Reich; Theodor Richter	Germany
Gallium	31	1875	Paul Emile Lecoq de Boisbaudran	France
Holmium	67	1878	Per Theodor Cleve	Sweden
Scandium	21	1879	Lars F. Nilson	Sweden
Samarium	62	1879	Paul Emile Lecoq de Boisbaudran	France
Thulium	69	1879	Per Theodor Cleve	Sweden
Gadolinium	64	1880	Jean Charles de Marignac	Switzerland
Praseodymium	59	1885	C.F. Auer von Welsbach	Austria
Neodymium	60	1885	C.F. Auer von Welsbach	Austria
Fluorine	9	1886	Henri Moissan	France
Germanium	32	1886	Clemens Winkler	Germany
Dysprosium	66	1886	Paul Emile Lecoq de Boisbaudran	France
Argon	18	1894	Sir William Ramsay; Baron Rayleigh	England
Helium	2	1895	Sir William Ramsay; Nils Langlet; P.T. Cleve	England Sweden
Europium	63	1896	Eugène Demarçay	France
Neon	10	1898	Sir William Ramsay; Morris W. Travers	England
Krypton	36	1898	Sir William Ramsay; Morris W. Travers	England
Xenon	54	1898	Sir William Ramsay; Morris W. Travers	England
Polonium	84	1898	Pierre and Marie Curie	France
Radium	88	1898	Pierre and Marie Curie	France
Actinium	89	1899	André Debierne	France
Radon	86	1900	Friedrich Ernst Dorn	Germany
Ytterbium	70	1907	Georges Urbain	France
Lutetium	71	1907	Georges Urbain	France
Protactinum	91	1917	Otto Hahn; Lise Meitner; Frederick Soddy; John Cranston	Germany; England
Hafnium	72	1923	Dirk Coster; Georg von Hevesy	Denmark
Rhenium	75	1925	Walter Noddack; Ida Tacke; Otto Berg	Germany
Technetium	43	1937	Carlo Perrier; Émilio Segrè	Italy
Francium	87	1939	Marguerite Perey	France
Astatine	85	1940	D.R. Corson; K.R. MacKenzie; Émilio Segrè	United States
Neptunium	93	1940	Edwin M. McMillan; Philip H. Abelson	United States
Plutonium	94	1940	G.T. Seaborg; J.W. Kennedy; E.M. McMillan; A.C. Wahl	United States
Americium	95	1944	G.T. Seaborg; R.A. James; L.O. Morgan; A. Ghiorso	United States

Curium . . . . 96 . . . . . 1944 . . G.T. Seaborg; R.A. James;
A. Ghiorso . . . . United States

Promethium . . . . 61 . . . . . 1945 . . J.A. Marinsky; Lawrence E.
Glendenin; Charles D. Coryell . . . . United States

Berkelium . . . . . . 97 . . . . . 1949 . . G.T. Seaborg, S.G. Thompson;
A. Ghiorso . . . . United States

Californium . . . . . 98 . . . . . 1950 . . G.T. Seaborg, S.G. Thompson;
A. Ghiorso; K. Street, Jr. . . . . United States

Einsteinium . . . . 99 . . . . . 1952 . . Albert Ghiorso and associates . . . . United States

Fermium . . . . 100 . . . . . 1953 . . Albert Ghiorso and associates . . . . United States

Mendelevium . . . 101 . . . . . 1955 . . G.T. Seaborg; A. Ghiorso; B.G.
Harvey; G.R. Choppin;
S.G. Thompson . . . . United States

Nobelium . . . . . . 102 . . . . . 1958 . . G.T. Seaborg, A. Ghiorso,
T. Sikkeland, J.R. Walton . . . . United States

Lawrencium . . . . 103 . . . . . 1961 . . A. Ghiorso; T. Sikkeland;
A.E. Larsh; R.M. Latimer . . . . United States

Kurchatovium* . . 104 . . . . . 1964 . . Claimed by G. Flerov and
associates . . . . Russia

Rutherfordium* . 104 . . . . . 1969 . . Claimed by A. Ghiorso and
associates . . . . United States

Nielsbohrium* . . 105 . . . . . 1968 . . Claimed by G. Flerov and
associates . . . . Russia

Hahnium* . . . . . . 105 . . . . . 1970 . . Claimed by A. Ghiorso and
associates . . . . United States

Element* . . . . . . 106 . . . . . 1974 . . Claimed by G. Flerov and   Russia and
A. Ghiorso and associates . . . . United States

*Not officially recognized.

TABLE OF COMMON CHEMICALS, THEIR CHEMICAL NAMES, AND THEIR FORMULAS

Common Name	Chemical Name	Formula
Aniline	Phenylamine (Aminobenzine)	$C_6H_5NH_2$
Aqua fortis	Nitric Acid	HNO_3
Aqua regia	Nitric acid and hydrochloric acid (nitrohydrochloric acid)	$_1HNO_3 + _3HCl$
Aspirin	Salicylic Acid	$C_9H_8O_4$
Aspirin	Acetyl-salicylic acid	$C_6H_4(OCOCH_3)COOH$
Baking soda	Sodium bicarbonate	$NaHCO_3$
Bleaching powder	Calcium hypochlorite — chloride	$Ca(OCl)Cl$
Blue vitriol	Copper sulfate	$CuSO_4 \bullet 5H_2O$
Bone black	Carbon (animal charcoal)	C
Boric acid (orthoboric acid)	Boric acid	H_3BO_3
Borax	Sodium tetraborate (Sodium borate)	$Na_2B_4O_7 \bullet 10H_2O$
Brimstone	Sulfur	S
Calomel	Mercurous chloride	Hg_2Cl_2
Camphor (artificial)	Pinene hydrochloride	$C_{10}H_{17}Cl$
Carbolic acid	Phenol	C_6H_5OH
Carborundum	Silicon carbide	SiC
Caustic (or caustic soda)	Sodium hydroxide	$NaOH$
Chile saltpeter	Sodium nitrate	$NaNO_3$
Chloroform	Trichlormethane	$CHCl_3$
Chrome yellow	Lead chromate	$PbCrO_4$
Copperas (Green/iron vitriol)	Ferrous sulfate	$FeSO_4 \bullet 7H_2O$
Corrosive sublimate	Mercuric chloride	$HgCl_2$
Cream of Tartar	Potassium acid tartrate	$KHC_4H_4O_6$
Dextrose (corn/grape sugar)	Glucose	$C_6H_{12}O_6 \bullet H_2O$
Emery powder	Aluminum oxide	Al_2O_3
Epsom salt(s)	Magnesium sulfate (hepta hydrated)	$MgSO_4 \bullet 7H_2O$
Ether	Ethyl ether	$(C_2H_5)_2O$
Formalin (formol)	40% solution of formaldehyde in water	$HCHO$
Fusel oil	Mixed amyl alcohols	$C_5H_{11}OH$
Glauber's salt	Sodium sulfate	$Na_2SO_4 \bullet 10H_2O$
Glucose	Dextrose	$C_6H_{12}O_6$
Glycerin	Glycerol	$C_3H_5(OH)_3$
Gypsum	Calcium sulfate	$CaSO_4 \bullet 2H_2O$
Horn silver	Silver chloride	$AgCl$
Hypo	Sodium thiosulfate	$Na_2S_2O_3 \bullet 5H_2O$
Kaolin(e)	Aluminum silicate	$Al_2O_3 \bullet 2SiO_2O_2 \bullet 2H_2O$
Kieselguhr (diatomite)	Silica	SiO_2
Lampblack	Impure carbon	C
Laughing gas	Nitrous oxide	N_2O
Magnesia	Magnesium oxide	MgO
Marble	Calcium carbonate	$CaCO_3$
Methanol	Methyl alcohol	CH_3OH
Microcosmic salt	Sodium ammonium hydrogen phosphate	$Na(NH_4)HPO_4 \bullet 4H_2O$
Milk of magnesia	Magnesium hydroxide	$Mg(OH)_2$
Muriatic acid	Hydrochloric acid	HCl
Norwegian Saltpeter	Calcium nitrate	$Ca(NO_3)_2$
Paris green	Copper acetoarsenite	$Cu_5(C_2H_3O_2)_2 \bullet 3CuAs_2O_4$
Plaster of Paris	Calcium sulfate (hemi hydrated)	$(CaSO_4)_2 \bullet H_2O$

Prussic acid	Hydrocyanic acid	HCN
Quicklime	Calcium oxide	CaO
Quicksilver	Mercury	Hg
Rochelle salts	Potassium sodium tartrate	$KNaC_4H_4O_6$
Spirit of hartshorn (ammonia water)	Ammonia solution	NH_4OH
Silica	Silicon dioxide	SiO_2
Sugar	Sucrose	$C_{12}H_{22}O_{11}$
Sugar of lead	Lead acetate	$Pb(C_2H_3O_2)_2 \cdot 3H_2O$
Superphosphate	Calcium acid phosphate	$CaH_4(PO_4)_2$
Table salt	Sodium chloride	NaCl
Washing soda	Sodium carbonate	$Na_2CO_3 \cdot 10H_2O$
Water glass	Sodium silicate	Na_2SiO_3
White lead	Basic lead carbonate	$Pb(OH)_2 \cdot 2PbCO_3$
Wood alcohol	Methyl alcohol	CH_3OH
Zinc white	Zinc oxide	ZnO

QUESTIONS AND ANSWERS

1. In order to measure the resistance of a circuit component, the necessary connections for the meters will have which one of the following set-ups?
    a) Both ammeter and voltmeter in series
    b) Both ammeter and voltmeter in parallel
    c) Ammeter in series and voltmeter in parallel
    d) Ammeter in parallel and voltmeter in series
    ANSWER: c.

2. Which one of the following statements is correct about lamps connected in a series circuit?
    a) If one goes out, they all go out.
    b) Each lamp operates separately.
    c) The resistance of each lamp must be identical.
    ANSWER: a.

3. Voltage may correctly be expressed in which one of the following ways?
    a) coulombs/charge   c) dynes/cm
    b) coulombs/second   d) joules/coulomb
    ANSWER: d) joules/coulomb.

4. The potential difference between 2 points in an electric field is known by what term?
    ANSWER: Voltage.

5. Which of the following units is the unit of capacitance?
    a) volt   c) farad
    b) coulomb   d) newton
    ANSWER: c) farad.

6. Which one of the following electromagnetic radiations has the longest wavelengths?
    a) gamma rays   c) x-rays
    b) radio waves   d) infrared rays
    ANSWER: b) radio waves.

7. What term describes the ejection of electrons from a metal surface when light falls on it?
    ANSWER: Photoelectric effect.

8. Which one of the following mathematical relationships represents power?
    a) (force) times (distance)   c) (work) divided by (time)
    b) (work) times (distance)   d) (force) divided by (time)
    ANSWER: c.

9. Name the 2 types of images formed by mirrors or lenses.
    ANSWER: Real and virtual.

10. Name the 3 primary colors of paints, pigments, etc. Name the 3 primary colors of light (of the spectrum). Name the 3 colors of television screen phosphors. Name the 3 colors that are often called the achromatic colors.
    ANSWER: Red, yellow, and blue/Red, green, and blue/Red, green, and blue/Black, white, and gray.

11. Name the 3 fundamental particles of the atom. Which one is positively charged? Which one has no charge? What is the name for high speed electrons?
    ANSWER: Neutron, proton, and electron/Proton/Neutron/Beta or Alpha particles.

12. What are the 7 items associated with the mnemonic device "Roy G. Biv," or what what are the 7 distinct colors of the visible spectrum?
    ANSWER: Red, orange, yellow, green, blue, indigo, and violet.

13. Which 3 of the following examples represent kinetic energy?
    a) A rock rolls down a cliff.   c) A car travels along a level road.
    b) A stretched rubberband.   d) An airplane flies on a level course.
    ANSWER: a, c, and d.

14. The law of universal gravitation, Newton's second law, centripetal force, and

weight are all concepts in physics that have mathematical relationships. Relate the following mathematical statements to their respective concepts.

a) $F = (M)(g)$

b) $F = \dfrac{G\,(M_1)(M_2)}{R^2}$

c) $F = (M)(a)$

d) $F = \dfrac{(M)(v^2)}{R}$

ANSWER: a) weight b) universal gravitation c) Newton's second law d) centripetal force.

15. From the following list of units give the correct representation of units for the terms *impulse, momentum, weight, period, acceleration of gravity* and *work*.

a) newton-meter

b) seconds

c) kilogram-meter/sec

d) newtons

e) newton-sec

f) meter/sec/sec

ANSWER: a) work b) period c) momentum d) weight e) impulse f) acceleration of gravity.

16. Newton's laws are known as the First Law of Motion, Second Law of Motion, and the Third Law of Motion. For each of the following descriptions give the correct law that is described.

a) Law of interaction or momentum, or equal and opposite reactions ($p = mv$)

b) Law of inertia

c) Law of acceleration ($F = ma$)

ANSWER: a) Third Law b) First Law c) Second Law.

17. Which one of the following statements is correct for explaining the concept of mass?

a) The mass of an object is equal to the weight of an object.

b) The mass of an object is a measure of the hardness of the object.

c) The mass of an object is a measure of its resistance to a change in its state of real or uniform motion.

d) The mass of an object is a measure of its density.

ANSWER: c.

18. Which one of the following is not needed to determine the time it takes for an object to fall to the ground?

a) Height of the object above the ground

b) Gravitational acceleration

c) Initial downward velocity of the object

d) Horizontal velocity of the object

ANSWER: d.

19. Which of the following factors does not influence the period of a pendulum's motion?

a) Length of the pendulum

b) Mass of the pendulum bob

c) Arc of the initial motion of the pendulum

ANSWER: b.

20. From the following units (labels) determine the one that correctly represents a newton force.

a) $Kg - \dfrac{m}{n}$

b) $Kg - \dfrac{m}{sec^2}$

c) $Kg - \dfrac{m}{sec}$

d) $\dfrac{m}{cm^3}$

e) $\dfrac{m}{sec^2}$

ANSWER: b.

21. When 2 velocities acting at an angle to each other are constructed into a vector system, the resultant will be determined by which one of the following operations?

a) The scalēr sum of the two velocity vectors

b) The vector product of two velocity vectors

c) The diagonal of the parallelogram constructed from the velocity vectors

ANSWER: c.

22. Identify each of the following terms from the description.

a) The measure of a body's resistance to acceleration

b) The tendency of a body to maintain its state of motion
c) The capacity for work
d) The time-rate of change of position
e) The agent that produces an acceleration of an object from a state of rest or constant velocity
f) The force that gravitation exerts on a body

ANSWER: a) mass b) inertia c) energy d) velocity e) force f) weight.

23. Which 2 of the following are vector quantities?

a) velocity   c) speed   e) time
b) mass   d) force

ANSWER: a and d.

24. Explain what physical quantity each of the following relationships will determine.

a) mass times acceleration   c) mass times speed of light squared
b) distance/time   d) mass/volume

ANSWER: a) determines force b) determines speed c) determines energy d) determines mass density or density.

25. Based on significant figures, determine the best answer to the problem: divide 2.21 by 1.2.

a) 1.841   b) 1.8   c) 1.84   d) 2.0

ANSWER: b) 1.8

26. For the optical equation $\frac{1}{S_0} + \frac{1}{S_i} = \frac{1}{f}$ explain what each system will represent.

a) S_0 b) S_i c) f

ANSWER: a) object distance b) image distance c) focal length.

27. Give the force unit (label) within each of the systems of measurements.

a) CGS   c) English
b) MKS

ANSWER: a) dyne b) newton c) pound.

28. Determine the number of significant figures in each of the following.

a) 0.0467   c) 2.4×10^{-3} e) 40400
b) 2304   d) 0.04060

ANSWER: a) 3 b) 4 c) 2 d) 4 e) 3.

29. Which 2 of the following give the correct answer for the multiplication of (6×10^{-7}) (3×10^{-3})?

a) 18×10^{-10} c) 1.8×10^{-9} e) 18×10^{-4}
b) 1.8×10^{-10} d) 1.8×10^{-11}

ANSWER: a and c.

30. Give the correct conversion factors for each of the following metric to English factors.

a) 1 meter to inches   d) 1 kilogram to pounds
b) 1 meter to yards   e) 1 kilometer to miles
c) 1 liter to quarts

ANSWER: a) 39.37 inches b) 1.09 yards c) 1.06 quarts d) 2.2 pounds e) .62 miles.

31. What are the 3 characteristics of sound? Which one is defined by the logarithmic expression $\beta = 10 \log \frac{1}{I_0}$? Which one is measured in vibrations per second? What is the name of the unit that measures the intensity of sound?

ANSWER: Loudness, pitch, and quality/Loudness/Pitch/Decibel.

32. Identify the following types of energy.

a) The energy of a body with respect to position
b) The energy of a body with respect to motion
c) The energy equivalent of the rest mass of a body, and equal to the rest mass multiplied by the speed of light squared

ANSWER: a) potential energy or gravitational potential energy b) kinetic energy c) rest energy.

33. Identify the terms from the following descriptions concerned with the surface effects of liquids.

a) The molecular force between like molecules of a substance that acts to unite them
b) The molecular force between unlike molecules of a substance that acts to hold them together .
c) The tendency of liquids to rise in small glass tubes
ANSWER: a) cohesion b) adhesion c) capillarity.

34. A ball is tossed vertically upward with a velocity of 10 m/sec. At the peak of its path, the ball has
a) zero velocity.
b) maximum gravitational attraction.
c) maximum acceleration.
d) no forces acting on it.
ANSWER: a.

35. Einstein's formula, $E = mc^2$ states that mass and energy are
a) directly proportional to each other.
b) independent of each other.
c) equal.
d) inversely proportional to each other.
ANSWER: a.

36. Explain the conversion of matter into energy of Einstein's theorem, $E = mc^2$.
ANSWER: E is the energy in ergs, m is the mass of the matter in grams, and c is the speed of light in centimeters per second ($c^2 = 9 \cdot 10^{20}$).

37. Each of the following units represents either mass or force. For each unit indicate the measurement of mass or force.
a) grams
b) dynes
c) newtons
d) pounds
e) slugs
ANSWER: a) mass b) force c) force d) force e) mass.

38. Which 3 units represent the correct units for density?
a) g/cm^2
b) g/cm^3
c) lbs/cubic inch
d) cm^3/g
e) 40 tons/sq inch
f) kg/mm^3
ANSWER: b, c, and f.

39. Which 2 of the following mathematical expressions represent the correct mathematical relationship for the speed of a wave?
a) $v = \frac{1}{2}mv^2$
b) $v = \frac{\lambda}{f}$
c) $v = (f)(\lambda)$
d) $v = \frac{f}{\lambda}$
e) $\lambda = \frac{v}{f}$
ANSWER: c and e.

40. What power of 10 is represented by each of the following prefixes?
a) hecto-
b) milli-
c) kilo-
d) mega-
e) micro-
ANSWER: a) 2 [(100) 10^2] b) -3[(.001) 10^{-3}] c) 3[(1000) 10^3] d) 6 [(1,000,000) 10^6] e) -6 [(.000001) 10^{-6}]

41. Express the answers to each of the following problems as a power of ten.
a) $(2 \times 10^{-4})(4 \times 10^{-2})$
b) $(6 \times 10^4) \div (3 \times 10^2)$
c) $(6 \times 10^{-4}) \div (3 \times 10^2)$
ANSWER: a) 8×10^{-6} b) 2×10^2 c) 2×10^{-6}

42. Which 2 of the following are possible ways to use the Law of Sines?
a) $\frac{\sin A}{a}$ = angle
b) $\frac{a}{\sin A} = \frac{b}{\sin B} = \frac{c}{\sin C}$
c) $\frac{a^2}{\sin A} = \frac{c^2}{\sin C}$
d) $\frac{a}{\sin A} = \frac{b}{\sin B}$
ANSWER: b and d.

43. What are the 3 methods by which heat may be transferred? Which one is the only method by which energy may be transmitted through empty space (vacuum)?
ANSWER: Conduction, convection, and radiation/Radiation.

44. If the price of real gold were quoted as $300 per ounce, what would be the cost of 5 pounds of gold?
ANSWER: $18,000 (Gold is measured in Troy weight and 1 pound = 12 ounces).

45. Which one of the following reduces to the units of acceleration?

a) kg - newton/meter
b) newton/kg
c) newton-sec/kg
d) kg-meter/newton

ANSWER: b.

46 A body in equilibrium
a) must have no forces acting on it.
b) has no unbalanced force acting on it.
c) must not have inertia.
d) may be accelerating.

ANSWER: b.

47. Which 3 of the following processes give off heat?
a) cooling of a vapor
b) fusion
c) condensation
d) liquid converted to solid
e) vaporization

ANSWER: a, c, and d.

48. Which of the following factors determine the speed/velocity of a wave?
a) The amplitude of the wave
b) The medium in which the wave is propagating
c) The wavelength of the wave
d) The frequency of the wave

ANSWER: b, c, and d.

49. Which one of the following properties of a wave determines the wave's energy energy content?
a) frequency
b) wavelength
c) amplitude
d) period

ANSWER: c) amplitude.

50. The following descriptions of a wave represent various properties of the wave. Give the correct property for each description.
a) Cycles per second
b) Distance between two successive crests
c) Maximum displacement from the rest position
d) Time required for a single complete wave to pass a given point

ANSWER: a) frequency b) wavelength c) amplitude d) period.

51. Which 2 of the following waves do not need a medium to travel through?
a) electromagnetic waves
b) mechanical waves
c) radio waves
d) sound waves

ANSWER: a and c.

52. Waves can be classified by the way they travel. The following statements describe the 2 methods of travel. For each method give the correct term used to classify the method of travel.
a) The particles of the medium vibrate at right angles to the path along which the wave travels through the medium.
b) The displacement of particles of the medium are parallel to the direction of the propagation of the wave.

ANSWER: a) transverse b) longitudinal.

53. Which one of the following methods is currently used for the calibration of thermometers?
a) freezing point oi water
b) triple point of water
c) boiling point of water
d) boiling point of helium

ANSWER: b.

54. Name the person(s) responsible for each of the following.
a) galvanometer (1820)
b) barometer (1643)
c) electric battery (1800)
d) cyclotron (1930)
e) pendulum clock (1657)
f) electrostatic generator (1931)
g) synchrocyclotron (1944)
h) betatron (1939)
i) geiger counter (1911)

ANSWER: a) Johann S.C. Schweigger b) Evangelista Torricelli c) Count Alessandro Volta d) Ernest Orlando Lawrence e) Christian Huygens f) Robert J. Van de Graaff g) Vladimir I. Veksler/Edwin M. McMillan (independently) h) Donald W. Kerst i) Hans Geiger and Ernest Rutherford.

55. In what year did Albert Einstein win the Nobel Prize for physics, and for what reason did he do so? What were the subjects of the 3 papers he contributed to *Annalen der Physik* (Annals of Physics) in 1905?

ANSWER: 1921/For his work in the domain of theoretical physics, especially for his discovery of the law of photoelectric effect/Quanta, theory of relativity (''The Electrodynamics of Moving Bodies''), and Brownian movement.

56. Identify each of the following SI units from the description.
   a) The SI unit of capacitance
   b) The SI unit of pressure or stress
   c) The SI unit of energy, work, or quantity of heat
   d) The SI unit of electric resistance
   e) The SI unit of frequency
   f) The SI unit of inductance
   g) The SI unit of electric charge or quantity of electricity
   h) The SI unit of force
   i) The SI unit of electrical potential, potential difference, or electro-motive force
   j) The SI unit of magnetic flux

ANSWER: a) farad b) pascal c) joule d) ohm e) hertz f) henry g) coulomb h) newton i) volt j) weber.

57. Which 3 of the following units measure length?
   a) dram
   b) liter
   c) rod
   d) meter
   e) chain
   f) sievert

ANSWER: c, d, and e.

58. Give in ascending order the 5 units of quantity from pint to bushel.

ANSWER: Pint, quart, peck, half-bushel, bushel.

59. Identify each of the following terms of light from the description.
   a) A unit of luminous flux in the International System, equal to the light emitted in a unit solid angle by a point source of one-candle power
   b) A unit (particle) of light having no charge or mass but an indefinitely long lifetime
   c) A unit of luminance equal to $1/\pi$ candle per square centimeter
   d) A unit of luminance equal to one lumen per square foot
   e) A unit of intensity expressed in standard candles

ANSWER: a) lumen b) photon c) lambert d) foot-candle or candle-foot e) candle power.

60. Which 2 of the following waves are mechanical waves?
   a) radio waves
   b) sound waves
   c) water waves
   d) light waves
   e) x-rays

ANSWER: b and c.

61. What is the formula for the speed of sound in feet per second through any given temperature of air?

ANSWER: $V = \dfrac{1087\sqrt{273+t}}{16.52}$ **(t is the temperature in Centigrade)**

62. Which one of the following temperatures represents absolute zero of temperature?
   a) 0°C
   b) 0°F
   c) -273.16°K
   d) -273.16°C

ANSWER: d) -273.16°C.

63. What term is used to describe the process when two or more waves meet and their displacements are superimposed?

ANSWER: Interference.

64. Which 3 of the following properties are physical properties of sound waves?
   a) intensity
   b) frequency
   c) loudness
   d) harmonic content

ANSWER: a, b, and d.

65. Which one of the following laws states that a ray of light bends in such a way that the ratio of the sine of the angle of incidence to the sine of the angle of refraction is a constant?
   a) Law of Reflection
   b) Charles' Law
   c) Snell's Law
   d) Index of Refraction Law
   e) Ohm's Law

ANSWER: c) Snell's Law.

66. A laser is a device used to produce coherent light. The word laser is an acronym. Explain what each letter represents.
   a) l   b) a   c) s   d) e   e) r
ANSWER: a) light b) amplification c) stimulated d) emission e) radiation.

67. The image seen in a plane mirror appears to be behind the mirror. What type of image is produced by the plane mirror?
ANSWER: Virtual image.

68. From the following frequency ratings of sound, which one would produce a sound audible to most humans?
   a) 400,000 cycles/second   c) 4,000 cycles/second
   b) 40,000 cycles/second   d) 4 cycles/second
ANSWER: c.

69. Explain what each of the following heat constants represents.
   a) 80 calories/gram   b) 540 calories/gram
ANSWER: a) heat of fusion for ice b) heat of vaporization for water.

70. What type of nuclear reaction is thought to be the source of energy in stars?
ANSWER: Fusion.

71. Which one of the following descriptions best explains radioactivity?
   a) Changes in the number of orbital electrons
   b) Changes in the crystal structure
   c) Changes in molecular structure
   d) Changes within the nucleus
ANSWER: d.

72. Which one of the following lists the emissions from radioactive substances in the order of increasing penetrating powers?
   a) gamma, beta, alpha   c) alpha, beta, gamma
   b) gamma, alpha, beta   d) beta, alpha, gamma
ANSWER: c.

73. A battery made of cells connected in series has all of the following characteristics except which one?
   a) The negative terminal of one cell is connected to the positive terminal of a second cell.
   b) The emf of the battery is the same as the emf of a single cell.
   c) The internal resistance of the battery is equal to the sum of the internal resistances of individual cells.
ANSWER: b.

74. Give the device that measures each of the following.
   a) feeble electric currents   d) thickness   g) ductility
   b) energy   e) specific gravities   h) speed
   c) distance walked   f) electric currents   i) a tuning fork
ANSWER: a) galvanometer b) dynamometer c) pedometer d) micrometer or pachymeter e) densimeter f) ammeter g) extensometer h) tachometer i) tonometer.

75. What are the 3 family names of subatomic particles?
ANSWER: Lepton, meson, and baryon.

76. What are the 2 particle names of the meson family and the 4 particle names of the lepton family?
ANSWER: Pion and kaon/Electron's neutrino, muon's neutrino, electron, and muon.

77. Identify each of the following laws or principles from the given descriptions.
   a) An increase in the velocity of a fluid results in a decrease in pressure, and a decrease in the velocity results in an increase in pressure.
   b) For steady current the mass of any substance deposited at the cathode is proportional to the quantity of electricity that has been conducted through an electrolyte.
   c) External pressure applied to an enclosed fluid is uniformly transmitted without change to each part of the fluid.
   d) When an electric current is established in a conductor, heat is developed at a

rate that is proportional to the square of the intensity of the current.
e) Any point on an advancing wavefront acts as the source of new wavelets whose envelope constitutes a new wave front at every successive stage of the process.
f) The apparent change in the frequency of sound, light, or radio waves is caused by a change in the distance between the source of the wave and the receiver.
g) The steady current through any portion of an electric circuit is directly proportional to the applied electromotive force.
h) The force of attraction between two charged particles is directly proportional to the product of their charges and inversely proportional to the square of the distance between them.

ANSWER: a) Bernouilli's Principle b) Faraday's Law c) Pascal's Law d) Joule's Law e) Huygens' Principle f) Doppler's Principle g) Ohm's Law h) Coulomb's Law.

78. Identify each of the following units of measure from the given definitions.
a) A unit of frequency equal to one cycle per second
b) A unit of energy or work equal to 10^7 ergs or one newton-meter
c) A unit of energy equal to one dyne-centimeter
d) The cgs unit of force, equal to the force which will produce an acceleration of one centimeter per second per second on a mass of one gram
e) A unit of force which will give one kilogram an acceleration of one meter per second per second
f) A unit of mass that is accelerated at the rate of one foot per second per second when acted upon by a force of one pound weight, equivalent to approximately 32.2 pounds

ANSWER: a) hertz b) joule c) erg d) dyne e) newton f) slug.

79. At what temperature do Celsius and Fahrenheit thermometers read the same?
ANSWER: 40° below zero or -40 degrees.

80. What phrase from physics means "an abrupt sizable step forward, especially because of new information or technology"? In the field of physics, what does this phrase represent exactly?
ANSWER: *Quantum leap (jump)*/The jumping of an electron from one energy state to another.

81. Which 3 of the following mathematical relationships represent a parallel electrical circuit?
a) $V_t = V_1 + V_2 + V_3 \cdots$
b) $V_t = V_1 = V_2 = V_3 \cdots$
c) $\frac{1}{R_t} = \frac{1}{R_1} + \frac{1}{R_2} + \frac{1}{R_3} \cdots$
d) $R_t = R_1 + R_2 + R_3 \cdots$
e) $I_t = I_1 = I_2 + I_3 \cdots$
f) $I_t = I_1 + I_2 + I_3 \cdots$

ANSWER: b, c, and f.

82. Which 3 of the following mathematical relationships represent a series electrical circuit?
a) $V_t = V_1 + V_2 + V_3 \cdots$
b) $\frac{1}{V_t} = V_1 + V_2 + V_3 \cdots$
c) $R_t = R_1 + R_2 + R_3 \cdots$
d) $I_t = I_1 = I_2 = I_3 \cdots$
e) $I_t + I_1 + I_2 + I_3 \cdots$
f) $\frac{1}{R_t} = \frac{1}{R_1} + \frac{1}{R_2} + \frac{1}{R_3} \cdots$

ANSWER: a, c and d.

83. Assuming that an object is in a state of free fall near the earth's surface, what is the formula for the speed in feet per second acquired by the falling body, and what is the formula for the distance in feet traveled by the falling body?
ANSWER: v = 32t (t is the time in seconds)/d = 16t² (t is the time in seconds).

84. Which one of the following velocities represents the speed of sound in air at 0°C?
a) 332 m/sec
b) 400 m/sec
c) 344 m/sec
d) 532 m/sec
ANSWER: a.

85. The intensity of a sound of fixed frequency is independent of which of the following factors?
a) Power of the source
b) Distance from the source

c) Wavelength of the sound   d) Amplitude of the sound
ANSWER: c.

86. The speed of sound is determined by the medium it travels through. Arrange the following in order of their influence on the speed of sound from slow to fast.
    a) water   b) aluminum   c) air   d) steel
ANSWER: Air, water, aluminum, and steel.

87. Which one of the following emissions from a radioactive atom brings about no change in the nucleus?
    a) alpha   b) gamma   c) beta
ANSWER: b) gamma.

88. Which one of the following radioactive emissions is an electron ?
    a) alpha particle   b) gamma ray   c) beta particle
ANSWER: a) alpha particle .

89. Which one of the following isotopes of uranium is fissionable?
    a) uranium -238   b) uranium -235   c) uranium -239
ANSWER: b.

90. What is the customary energy unit used to measure energy exchanges involving subatomic particles?
ANSWER: Electronvolt (10^n, N = integer, electron volts such as Mev, Kev, Gev).

91. Which of the following scientists developed the uncertainty principle within the concepts of quantum mechanics.
    a) Compton   c) Heisenberg
    b) Louis de Broglie   d) Bohr
ANSWER: c) Heisenberg.

92. Which one of the following types of radiation is only a release of excess energy from the nucleus?
    a) beta   b) alpha   c) gamma
ANSWER: c) gamma.

93. For each of the following systems of measurement, give the unit (label) for mass.
    a) MKS   b) CGS   c) English
ANSWER: a) kilogram b) gram c) slug.

94. Which concept — IMA, AMA, and Efficiency — is represented by each of the following mathematical relationships?
    a) $\frac{AMA}{IMA} \times 100$ b) $\frac{S_e}{S_r}$ c) $\frac{R}{E}$
ANSWER: a) Efficiency b) IMA c) AMA.

95. What does each of the following motion concepts solve?
    a) $(V_i)(\triangle t) + \frac{1}{2}at^2$ c) $V_i \pm at$
    b) $\frac{V_f - V_i}{t_f - t_i}$ d) $\sqrt{Rg}$
ANSWER: a) distance b) acceleration c) final velocity d) critical velocity.

96. Identify each of the following terms related to heat from the given definition.
    a) The amount of heat needed to raise the temperature of 1 gram of water 1 degree centigrade
    b) The particular temperature-pressure combination at which the solid, liquid, and gaseous states of a substance are all at equilibrium with one another
    c) The mathematical quantity which measures thermodynamic degeneration
    d) The temperature at which air becomes saturated producing dew, or the point at which vapor condenses into a liquid
    e) The direct change of a solid to a gas or a gas to a solid without becoming a liquid
    f) The temperature at which all molecular motion ceases, equal to —273.15°C or —459.67°F
    g) The amount of heat required to raise the temperature of one pound of water one degree Fahrenheit
ANSWER: a) calorie b) triple point c) entropy d) dew point e) sublimation f) absolute

zero g) British thermal unit or BTU.

97. Identify the scientist responsible for or primarily associated with each of the following accomplishments.

a) Discovered U-235 (1935)
b) Discovered x-rays (1895)
c) Achieved the first successful nuclear chain reaction (1942)
d) Developed the quantum theory of energy (1900)
e) Developed the hydrogen bomb (1952)
f) Discovered electromagnetic induction (1831)
g) Launched the first successful liquid-fueled rocket (1926)
h) Formulated the first explanation of radioactivity (1902)
i) Developed a unified field theory (1929)

ANSWER: a) Arthur Jeffrey Dempster b) Wilhelm Conrad Roentgen c) Enrico Fermi d) Max Planck e) Edward Teller f) Michael Faraday g) Robert Hutchings Goddard h) Ernest Rutherford i) Albert Einstein.

98. Identify each of the following terms from the field of electricity and magnetism from the given definition.

a) A unit of electricity in electrolysis which will dissolve 1 gram equivalent weight of a substance, equal to 96,500 coulombs
b) In an electrolytic cell, the negative electrode, from which current flows
c) In an electrolytic cell, the positively charged electrode, toward which current flows
d) A quantum of sound or vibrational energy
e) Any of several unstable subatomic particles having a mass between that of the electron and the proton
f) The splitting of the nucleus of an atom into nuclei of lighter atoms, accompanied by the release of energy
g) A thermonuclear reaction in which nuclei combine to form more massive nuclei with the simultaneous release of energy

ANSWER: a) faraday b) cathode c) anode d) phonon e) meson (mesotron) f) nuclear (fission) g) nuclear (fusion).

99. In which direction would a person be facing if he stood at the North Pole? If an object is pulled northward with a force of 10 pounds and southward with a force of 5, what are the magnitude and the direction of the net force on the object?

ANSWER: A person would be looking south in every direction from the North Pole/ Magnitude is 5 pounds/Direction is north.

100. The concept of work is represented by the formula *force times distance*. For each of the following sets of units, what would be another unit (label) for work?

a) (newton) (meter)
b) (dyne) (centimeter)

ANSWER: a) joule b) ergs.

101. What are the 3 accepted states of matter? Most of the universe is made up of a theoretical fourth state of matter. What is the fourth state called and describe this state of matter?

ANSWER: Solid, liquid, and gas/Plasma. Plasma state, mass of positive atoms (ions), and free moving electrons.

102. Which one of the following theories explains light in terms of its polarizing properties?

a) Wave Theory
b) Quantum Theory
c) Particle Theory

ANSWER: a) Wave Theory.

103. Arrange the following electromagnetic waves in order from the shortest to the longest wavelength.

a) ultraviolet
b) microwaves
c) gamma rays
d) infrared
e) radio waves

ANSWER: gamma, ultraviolet, infrared, microwaves, and radio waves.

104. Which one of the following descriptions is correct for images formed by diverging mirrors (rear view mirrors)?

a) Images are virtual, erect, and smaller than the object.

b) Images are real, erect, and smaller than the object.

c) Images are real, inverted, and larger than the object.

ANSWER: a.

105. Which one of the following types of lenses may be used for magnifying an object?

a) diverging lenses   b) converging lenses

ANSWER: b.

106. What is the property of a medium that determines the speed of light in that medium?

ANSWER: Index of refraction (or optical density).

107. According to Einstein's formula, $E = mc^2$, in what 2 ways can matter be converted into energy? What is the name of the machine at Princeton's Plasma Physics Laboratory that uses magnetic fields to hold and compress hydrogen gases until temperatures of about 100 million° Celsius are reached? What Russian scientist suggested the idea?

ANSWER: By fission (the nuclei of large atoms are split, thus releasing the energy that binds them together) and by fusion (the nuclei of hydrogen are squeezed together to form helium, thus releasing energy)/The Tokamak Fusion Test Reactor (Tokamak is a Russian acronym for a toroidal, or doughnut-shaped, magnetic chamber)/Andre Sakharov.

108. Name the 2 commercial classes of plastics.

ANSWER: Thermoplastics and thermosetting plastics.

109. In electronics, what is the source of a supply of charged particles, usually electrons?

ANSWER: A cathode.

110. What temperature in Centigrade is required for 1 mole of a gas under 1 atmosphere of pressure to occupy 22.4 liters of volume?

ANSWER: 0° Centigrade.

111. What is known as the amount of heat required to melt 1 kg of a crystalline solid?

ANSWER: The heat of fusion of that solid.

112. How many times is the capacity of a pipe increased if its inside diameter is doubled?

ANSWER: 4 times.

113. Name the American who was the first person to win 2 Nobel Prizes in physics, and give the reasons for which he won those Prizes.

ANSWER: John Bardeen/Bardeen shared the 1956 Prize with Walter Brattain and William Shockley for the discovery of the transistor effect, and he shared the 1972 Prize with Leon N. Cooper and John R. Schrieffer for developing the theory of superconductivity.

114. The index of refraction represents a constant for light passing from one medium (air) into another medium. Which one of the following mathematical ratios represents the index of refraction?

a) $\dfrac{\text{sine } i}{\text{sine } r}$ b) $\dfrac{\text{sine } r}{\text{sine } i}$

ANSWER: a.

115. The slope of a graph is the measure of its steepness. Explain what each of the following graphs of motion will determine.

a) Distance-Time Graph   b) Velocity-Time Graph

ANSWER: a) speed b) acceleration.

116. What is the force which keeps an object in a circular path?

ANSWER: Centripetal force.

117. What 2 commonly known forces are in effect when a bucket of water is swung in a vertical circle?

ANSWER: Centrifugal (away from the center) and centripetal (toward the center)

118. Give the unit of measure for each of the following characteristics in the mks system of units.

a) electrical resistance   b) power   c) current

ANSWER: a) ohms b) watts (or joule/sec) c) ampere (or coulomb/sec).

119. Which 3 of the following may be represented by a vector quantity?
    a) velocity   c) force   e) speed
    b) mass   d) weight
ANSWER: a, c, and d.

120. Give the mathematical equations that represent the following concepts.
    a) Acceleration
    b) Final velocity of a uniformly accelerating object
    c) Distance traveled with no acceleration
ANSWER: a) $a = \frac{\triangle v}{t}$ b) $V_f = V_0 + at$ or $V_f = V_i + at$ c) $S = (V)(t)$.

121. Light has the property of bending around the edges of a barrier. What term describes this property?
ANSWER: Diffraction.

122. What allows a charged object to feed all of its excess charge into the earth?
ANSWER: Grounding.

123. Which of the following are characteristics of parallel circuits?
    a) Each resistor (load) can be operated independently.
    b) As additional resistors (loads) are added in parallel the total load resistance decreases.
    c) Parallel circuits are used for house wiring.
ANSWER: All of them.

124. A single vector force may be broken up into components. What is this process called?
ANSWER: Resolution of a vector.

125. Many bridges are developed from the concepts of parallel forces. Parallel force and its relationship to the pivot point must be considered. What term describes the force times its distance from the pivot point?
ANSWER: Torque.

126. Give the term defined by each of the following statements.
    a) Devices in a nuclear reactor used to regulate the rate of the nuclear reaction
    b) A force needed to balance a resultant force
    c) Gravitational attraction of the earth for an object
    d) A wave whose nodes are stationary
ANSWER: a) control rods b) equilibriant c) weight or gravitional force d) standing
        wave.

127. Which of the following scientists showed that accelerated charged particles generate electromagnetic waves?
    a) Einstein   c) Faraday
    b) Thompson   d) Maxwell
ANSWER: d) Maxwell.

128. Which 3 of the following mathematical relationships represent Ohm's Law?
    a) $V = I/R$ c) $I = V/R$ e) $V = (I)(R)$
    b) $I = (V)(R)$ d) $R = V/I$ f) $R = I/V$
ANSWER: c, d, and e.

129. In the International System of Units what are the 7 bases of measurement?
ANSWER: Length, mass, time, electric current, thermodynamic temperature, amount
        of substance, and luminous intensity.

130. Give the definitive unit of measurement for each of the following 7 bases of measurement.
    a) length   e) thermodynamic temperature
    b) mass   f) amount of substance
    c) time   g) luminous intensity
    d) electric current
ANSWER: a) meter b) kilogram c) second d) ampere e) degrees Kelvin f) mole
        g) candela.

131. Give the unit of measure defined by each of the following.
    a) A unit of electric current equal to a constant current that when maintained in two straight parallel conductors of infinite length and negligible circular sections one meter apart in a vacuum produces between the conductors a force equal to 2×10^{-7} newton per meter of length.
    b) A unit of luminous intensity equal to 1/60 of the luminous intensity of one square centimeter of a blackbody surface at the solidification temperature of platinum.
    c) A unit of time equal to the duration of 9 192 631 770 periods of radiation corresponding to the transition between two hyperfine levels of the ground state of the cesium-133 atom.
    d) A unit of measurement equal to 1 650 763.73 wavelengths in vacuum of the radiation corresponding to the transition between the levels $2p_{10}$ and $5d_5$ of the krypton-86 atom.
    e) A unit of temperature equal to the fraction 1/273.16 of the thermodynamic temperature of the triple point of water.
    f) A quantity of a chemical substance having a weight in grams numerically equal to its molecular weight: one _____ of a substance contains 6.02257 $\times 10^{23}$ molecules.
    g) A unit of weight and mass equal to the mass of the international prototype made of platinum-iridium and nearly equal to 1000 cubic centimeters of water at the temperature of its maximum density.

ANSWER: a) ampere b) candela c) second d) meter e) kelvin f) mole g) kilogram.

132. For what does the abbreviation SI stand? In what countries are the National Bureau of Standards and the National Physical Laboratory located?

ANSWER: International System of Measurement (French: *Le Système International d'Unités*)/United States and England.

133. Identify the following 2 units of measurement.
    a) The plane angle with its vertex at the center of a circle that is subtended by an arc equal in length to the radius.
    b) The solid angle with its vertex at the center of a sphere that is subtended by an area of the spherical surface equal to that of a square with sides equal in length to the radius.

ANSWER: a) radian b) steradian.

134. Give the formulas for converting from Fahrenheit degrees to Celsius and from Celsius to Fahrenheit.

ANSWER: $F° = (C° \times 1.8) + 32$ and $C° = (F° - 32) \times 5 \div 9$ (or to convert Fahrenheit to Celsius, subtract 32 from the Fahrenheit temperature and multiply by 5/9; to convert Celsius to Fahrenheit, multiply the Celsius temperature by 9/5 and add 32).

135. Who is known as the "Father of Experimental Science"? In which town was he when he was slain? During which war? By whom? What was he doing and what were his last words? How did this person complete the following: "Give me a place to stand on, and I will _____"? What instrument is being referred to in this quote: "If there were another world and he could go to it, he would move this one"?

ANSWER: Archimedes/Syracuse/Second Punic War/By a Roman soldier/He was drawing geometric figures in the sand/"Disturb not my circle"/"move the earth"/Lever.

136. What is the name of the principle that a body wholly or partially immersed in a fluid is buoyed up by a force (buoyant force) equal to the weight of the fluid displaced by the body? What is the name of the device made up of a spiral tube coiled about a shaft and used to lift water for irrigation?

ANSWER: Archimedes' principle/Archimedean (Archimedes') screw.

137. What term is being described by each of the following?
    a) The bending of light as it enters a new material obliquely
    b) The bending of light rays after striking a surface
    c) The bending of light rays as they move around edges due to interference

effects
d) The process in which two or more waves combine to reinforce or neutralize each other according to their relative phases on meeting

ANSWER: a) refraction b) reflection c) diffraction d) interference.

138. With which scientist is each of the following theories associated?
    a) corpuscular theory
    b) wave theory
    c) three-component theory
    d) theory of electromagnetism
    e) quantum theory
    f) opponent color theory

ANSWER: a) Sir Isaac Newton b) Christian Huygens c) Thomas Young and Hermann von Helmholtz d) James Clerk Maxwell e) Max Planck f) Ewald Hering.

139. Many scientists have contributed to the body of knowledge concerning the measurement of ''c,'' the speed of light. Identify the scientist described in each of the following.
    a) He stationed two observers at various distances apart, opened shutters to lanterns, and timed the intervals to see if there was an increase in elapsed time.
    b) He observed the eclipse of one of Jupiter's satellites.
    c) He observed the fixed position of stars during a year's time.
    d) He used mirrors and a rotating cogged wheel to pulse light and measured the duration of each pulse.
    e) He used a rotating mirror instead of a cogged wheel and became the first to come close to the present measurement of the speed of light. He estimated it at 298,000 km/sec. (within 1% of the present calculation).
    f) In the 1880's he used a rotating prism of four or more faces. In 1926 he used several rotating mirrors of 8, 12, or 16 sides and measured light at a distance of 22 miles between Mt. Wilson and Mt. San Antonio in Southern California.
    g) He used a Kerr cell in 1926.
    h) His indirect method used a radio-frequency transmitter to produce electric standing waves along two adjacent parallel wires.

ANSWER: a) Galileo Galilei b) Ole Rømer (Olaus Roemer) c) James Bradley d) Armand Fizeau e) Jean L. Foucault f) Albert Michelson g) Enrique Gaviola h) J. Mercier.

140. Identify each of the following.
    a) The U.S. Atomic Energy Commission's highest award
    b) The first recipient of the U.S. Atomic Energy Commission's highest award (1956)
    c) The author of *Mathematical Foundations of Quantum Mechanics* (1932)
    d) The discoverer of the fundamental constant h, the quantum of action
    e) The person known for his Christmas lecture, ''The Chemical History of the Candle''
    f) The name of the superconductor device built by IBM in 1973 that can perform a switching operation in one one hundred-billionth of a second

ANSWER: a) Enrico Fermi Award b) John von Neumann c) John von Neumann d) Max Planck e) Michael Faraday f) Josephson junction.

141. Name the type of pendulum invented in 1851 that can demonstrate the rotation of the earth. Upon what principle is it dependent?

ANSWER: The Foucault pendulum (after Jean Bernard Léon Foucault)/Upon Newton's first law of motion, that a mass moving uniformly in a straight line or in a state of rest will remain in uniform motion in a straight line or in a state of rest unless acted upon by some external force.

NOTABLE PHYSICISTS

Democritus....Greek.... Developed a theory that the world consisted of tiny, indivisible particles called atoms.

Aristotle....Greek.... Wrote $Physics$ (8 books). Using deduction and logic he formed theories concerning change in many areas of physics.

Archimedes....Greek.... Devised Archimedes' screw, a device for raising water, and discovered Archimedes' principle concerning buoyancy.

Galileo Galilei....Italian.... Demonstrated from the Leaning Tower of Pisa that bodies of different weights accelerate uniformly (1589). Discovered the law of the pendulum (1584). Formed the 3 laws of motion later stated by Isaac Newton. Wrote *Discourses Concerning Two New Sciences* (1636).

William Gilbert....English....In 1600, published *De Magnete (Concerning Magnetism)*, the first serious study of magnetism.

Evangelista Torricelli....Italian.... Developed the barometer (1643) and improved the microscope and telescope.

Christiaan Huygens....Dutch.... Discovered the wave theory of light (1678) and invented the pendulum clock (1657).

Sir Isaac Newton....English.... Conceived of the theory of universal gravitation in *Principia* (1687) supposedly after seeing an apple fall in his garden. Formulated 3 laws of motion. Laid the foundation for the modern study of optics.

Gabriel Daniel Fahrenheit....German-Dutch.... Invented first practical mercury thermometer (1714). Devised the Fahrenheit temperature scale (c. 1720) in which the melting point of ice is 32° and the boiling point of water is 212°.

René Antoine Ferchault de Réaumur....French.... Developed the Reaumur scale with a freezing point of water at 0° and a boiling point at 80°.

Daniel Bernoulli....Swiss.... Developed the theory of the pressure of gases on the walls of a container. Wrote *Hydrodynamica* (1738). Known for Bernoulli's Law (Principle) on pressure and liquids and gases.

Anders Celsius....Swedish.... Developed a temperature scale (1742) which placed the boiling point at 0° and the freezing point at 100° (later reversed).

Henry Cavendish....English.... Determined the specific gravity of hydrogen (known as "inflammable air") and carbon dioxide (known as "fixed air"; 1766). Discovered hydrogen (1766). Demonstrated that water is a compound of oxygen and hydrogen. Showed that "common air" (the atmosphere) is 4/5ths nitrogen and 1/5th oxygen.

Charles Augustin de Coulomb....French.... Formulated Coulomb's Law, which states that the force of attraction between two charged particles is directly proportional to the product of their charges and inversely proportional to the square of the distance between them. A unit for the quantity of electricity, the *coulomb,* was named in his honor.

Jacques Alexandre Charles....French.... Discovered Charles' Law, that different gases all expand by the same amount with a given rise in temperature. This law is better known as Gay-Lussac's Law, for Charles did not publish his work.

Sir Benjamin Thompson....English (b. America).... Stated that heat was not a substance of a body but the result of the motion of the particles in that substance.

Alessandro Volta....Italian.... Invented the voltaic pile, the electric battery (1800). An electromagnetic unit, the *volt*, is named in his honor (1881).

John Dalton....English.... Formulated the law of partial gases (1802) and developed an atomic theory about the structure of matter (1803).

Hans Christian Oersted....Danish.... Discovered that magnetic fields surround any wire containing electricity (1819). Founder of the science of electromagnetism (1820). He was thus the first to establish the connection between magnetism and electricity. A unit of magnetic field intensity, the *oersted*, is named in his honor.

André Marie Ampère....French.... Developed principles of electromagnetism using electric currents (1820). The *ampere*, a unit of intensity of an electric current is named in his honor. Formulated Ampère's law.

Georg Simon Ohm....German.... Discovered Ohm's Law, that the steady current through any portion of an electric current is directly proportional to the applied electromotive force.

Michael Faraday....English.... Discovered electromagnetic induction (1831). Formulated laws of electrolysis. *Farad,* a unit of capacitance, and *faraday,* a unit of electricity, were named in his honor.

Joseph Henry....American.... Invented the electric relay (1835). In effect, invented the telegraph but his work was not patented and Morse received credit. Discovered the principle of induction. A unit of induction, the *henry,*is named after him.

Christian Johann Doppler....Austrian.... Discovered the Doppler effect (1842), that the apparent change in the frequency of sound, light, or radio waves is caused by a change in the distance between the source of the wave and receiver.

Rudolf Clausius....German.... Helped create the science of thermodynamics (1850).

Jean Bernard Léon Foucault....French.... Demonstrated the rotation of the Earth with Foucault's pendulum (1851) and built the first gyroscope (1852). Proved that the velocity of light is greater in the air than in the water. The eddy current, or Foucault current, is named after him.

Gustav Robert Kirchovv....German.... Discovered a fundamental law of electromagnetic radiation (1859). Used a spectroscope to discover cesium (1860).

James Prescott Joule....English.... Formulated Joule's law on the relationship between heat and mechanical energy. The unit of work energy, the *joule,* is named in his honor.

James Clerk Maxwell....Scottish.... Developed the mathematical explanation of the electromagnetic theory of light. His treatise on *Electricity and Magnetism* (1873) is the foundation of present-day electromagnetic theory.

Henry Augustus Rowland....American.... Determined the value of the *ohm*, the unit for measuring resistance to electric current.

Heinrich Rudolph Hertz....German.... Discovered electromagnetic radio waves, called Hertzian waves (1887). A *hertz*, a unit of frequency equal to one cycle per second, is named in his honor.

Ernest Mach....Austrian.... Established the study of the philosophy of sciences. Known for his Mach number, a unit relating speed to the velocity of sound (1887).

Wilhelm Konrad Roentgen....German.... Discovered X-rays (1895), for which he was awarded in 1901 the first Nobel Prize for physics.

Hendrick Antoon Lorentz....Dutch.... Developed electron theory and shared with Pieter Zeeman the 1902 Nobel Prize for physics for the discovery of the phenomena called the *Zeeman effect* (the effects of magnetism on light).

Antoine Henri Becquerel....French.... Co-discoverer with Pierre and Marie Curie of natural radioactivity (1896), for which he shared with them the 1903 Nobel Prize for physics. One of the creators of electromagnetism.

Marie (Sklodowska) et Pierre Curie....French.... Pioneered work in radioactivity and discovered radium and polonium in 1898. They shared the Nobel Prize for physics in 1903 with Henri Becquerel. Known for the Curie point, the temperature at which ferromagnetic substances lose their magnetism, and for Curie's law.

Sir Joseph John Thomson....English.... Discovered the electron in 1897 and won the 1906 Nobel Prize for physics for the study of the conduction of electricity by gases. gases.

Albert Abraham Michelson....German-American....Edward Williams Morely....American.... Michelson won the 1907 Nobel prize in physics for this precision spectroscopic and metrological investigations. Was the first person to measure with accuracy the diameter of a star. Michelson and Morely collaborated on various aspects of the wave light theory.

Marchese Guglielmo Marconi....Italian.... Known as the ''Father of Wireless Telegraphy.'' Founded his wireless telegraph company in 1897. Shared the Nobel Prize for physics in 1909 with Carl Ferdinand Braun (German) for the development of wireless telegraphy.

Hans Wilhelm Geiger....German.... Developed the Geiger counter (c. 1911) with Ernest Rutherford.

Ernest Rutherford....British....''Father of Nuclear Physics'' because he formulated the first explanation of radioactivity. Best known for his description of the nuclear structure of the atom (1911).

Max Planck....German.... Developed the quantum theory of energy (1900), for which he won the Nobel Prize for physics in 1918. Known also for Planck's constant.

Albert Einstein....German-American.... Developed theory of relativity (1905). Awarded the Nobel Prize for physics in 1921 for his work on the photoelectric effect. Developed a unified field theory (1929).

Sir William Henry and Sir William Lawrence Bragg, *père et fils.*...**British....**Shared the Nobel Prize for physics in 1915 for using X-ray diffraction methods to determine the structure of crystals. Sir William Henry developed the X-ray spectrometer to explore atomic structure, and, with Sir William Lawrence, developed a new science of X-ray analysis.

Lise Meitner....Austrian.... Co-discovered protactinium (1917) with Otto Hahn. Developed the theory of fission energy (1939), which helped develop the atomic bomb.

Niels Henrik David Bohr....Danish.... Won the Nobel Prize for physics in 1922 for his investigation of atomic structure and radiation. Founder of the modern quantum theory of matter and modern theory of atomic and molecular structure.

Robert Hutchings Goddard....American.... Launched the first successful liquid-fueled rocket (1926). The Goddard Space Flight Center in Greenbelt, Maryland, is named in his honor. Known as the "Father of Modern Rocketry and Space Flight."

Arthur Holly Compton....American.... Helped prove quantum theory with discovery that X-rays act as atomic particles (the Compton effect), for which he shared the Nobel Prize for physics in 1927 with Charles Wilson. Also helped develop the atomic bomb.

Louis Victor de Broglie....French....Founder of wave mechanics. Received the Nobel Prize for physics in 1929 for the discovery of the wave-like nature of electrons.

Werner Heisenberg....German.... Received the 1932 Nobel Prize for physics for his work in the development of quantum mechanics. Famous for his "uncertainty principle," which holds that the position and momentum of a subatomic particle cannot be precisely determined at the same time. This principle is also called the "principle of indeterminacy."

Erwin Schrödinger....Austrian.... Provided the basis for quantum theory with his Schrödinger equation, a mathematical formulation of wave mechanics, for which he shared the Nobel Prize for physics with Paul Dirac in 1933.

Frédéric Joliot-Curie and Iréne Joliot-Curie....French.... Won the Nobel Prize in chemistry in 1935 for their discovery of artificial radioactivity.

Sir James Chadwick....British.... Discovered the neutron (1932), for which he was awarded the Nobel Prize for physics in 1935.

Carl David Anderson....American.... Discovered the existence of the positron, or antielectron, a unit of matter (1932). Shared with Victor F. Hess the Nobel Prize for physics is 1936 for his discovery of the positron. During 1936-1938 he discovered the existence of mesons in cosmic rays.

Enrico Fermi....Italian-American.... Split the atom in nuclear fission (1934). Received the Nobel Prize in physics in 1938 for his discovery of nuclear reactions brought about by slow neutrons. Produced the first chain reaction, and helped develop the atomic bomb in the 1940's.

Ernest Orlando Lawrence....American.... Inventor of the cyclotron (1930), for which he won the 1939 Nobel Prize for physics.

J. Robert Oppenheimer....American.... Directed construction of the first atomic bomb (1943-1945) as part of the Manhattan Project. Known as the "Father of the Atomic Bomb."

Edward Teller....American.... Developed the hydrogen bomb (1952). Worked on the Manhattan Project to develop the atomic bomb. Known as the "Father of the Hydrogen Bomb."

Isidor Isaac Rabi....Austrian-American.... Supervised the development of radar (1940-45). Received the Nobel Prize for physics in 1944 for developing the molecular-beam resonance method for recording the magnetism of atomic nuclei.

Arthur Jeffrey Dempster....American.... Discovered U-235, which is the isotope of uranium basic to atomic bombs.

Sir Edward Victor Appleton....British.... Won the 1947 Nobel Prize for his discovery that the Appleton layer or F-region, the upper layer of the ion-sphere, bounces radio waves back to Earth. His work made possible the development of radar and radio communication over long distances.

Sir John D. Cockcroft and Ernest T.S. Walton....British and Irish.... Shared the Nobel Prize for physics in 1951 for their work on the transmutation of atomic nuclei by their method of accelerating protons with high voltages and bombarding the nuclei with them.

Andrey Dmitriyevich Sakharov....Russian.... Known as the "Father of the Hydrogen Bomb." Won the Nobel Prize for peace in 1975.

Max Born....German.... Pioneered research in quantum mechanics, for which he shared the Nobel Prize for physics in 1954 with Walther Bothe.

John Bardeen....Walter Brattain....William Shockley....American.... Shared the Nobel Prize for physics in 1956 for their research on semiconductors and the development of the transistor. Bardeen also shared the 1972 Nobel Prize in physics, this time with Leon N. Cooper and John P. Schrieffer for their work on the theory of super-conductivity.

Tsung-Dao Lee....Chen Ning Yang....Chinese-Americans.... Received the 1957 Nobel Prize for physics for their investigation of the laws of parity, which led to significant discoveries regarding elementary particles.

James Alfred Van Allen....American.... Discovered (1958) the Van Allen belts, two zones of electrically charged particles that surround the earth. He comfirmed his belief of high-energy radiation in nearby space by means of a counter aboard *Explorer IV*.

Owen Chamberlain....Emilio Segrè....American.... Discoverers of the antiproton and winners of the Nobel Prize for physics in 1959.

Johannes Hans Jensen....German.... Discovered nuclear shell structure of atomic nuclei. Shared Nobel Prize for physics in 1963 with Maria Goeppert Mayer (American) for their nuclear shell theory.

Charles Hard Townes....American.... Invented the maser (1951) and shared the Nobel Prize for physics (1964) with Nikolai G. Basov and Aleksandr M. Prochorov for their work in the development of the laser-maser principle.

Richard Feynman....American.... Won (with Julian S. Schwinger and Sin-itiro Tomonaga) the Nobel Prize for physics in 1965 for research in quantum electrodynamics.

Murray Gell-Mann....American.... Proposed the eightfold way, a theoretical system of classifying elementary nuclear particles and their interactions, for which he received the Nobel Prize for physics in 1969.

Burton Richter....Samuel C.C. Ting....American.... Received the Nobel Prize for physics in 1976 for their independent discoveries of a type of elementary particle called the *Psi* or *J* particle, believed to be the smallest building block of matter.

Robert N. Noyce....American.... Developed the electronic integrated circuit on silicon chips.

MEASURING INSTRUMENTS

actinometer ..... heat of sun's rays	**hygrometer** ..... humidity of air or gas
ammeter .... electric currents	**magnetometer** ... magnetic forces
araeometer ..... liquids	**micrometer** ..... thickness
argentometer .... strength of silver solutions	**odometer** .... distance over ground
barometer ...... atmospheric pressures	**ohmmeter** ...... ohms
bolometer ...... heat	**pachymeter** ..... thickness
calorimeter ..... heat (quantity)	**pedometer** ...... distance walked
cathetometer .... small vertical distances	**photometer** ..... relative intensity of light
chronometer .... time	**pycnometer** ..... density of liquids or solids
colorimeter ..... color hues and brightness	**pyrometer** ...... high temperatures
cryometer ...... very low temperatures	**radiometer** ...... radiation
dasymeter ...... density of gases	**speedometer** .... speed
densimeter ..... specific gravities	**stereometer** ..... volume of solid bodies
dilatometer ..... expansions	**tachometer** ..... speed
dynamometer ... energy	**telemeter** .... distant objects
electrometer .... electrical forces	**torquemeter** ..... speed ranges
ergometer ...... amount of work done by muscle (muscles) over a period of time	**tribometer** ...... sliding friction
	vaporimeter ..... vapor pressure or volume
extensometer .... minute degrees of expansion	**velocimeter** ..... velocity
galvanometer .... small electric currents	**viscometer** ...... viscosity of liquids
gravimeter ...... gravity	**voltimeter** ...... voltage
hodometer ...... distance covered by wheeled vehicles	**volumeter** ...... volume of gases, liquids, or solids
hydrometer ..... specific gravity of liquids	**wattmeter** ...... electric power in watts

THE GREEK ALPHABET

A	α	Alpha		N	ν	Nu
B	β	Beta		Ξ	ξ	Xi
Γ	γ	Gamma		O	o	Omicron
Δ	δ	Delta		Π	π	Pi
E	ϵ	Epsilon		P	ρ	Rho
Z	ζ	Zeta		Σ	σ	Sigma
H	η	Eta		T	τ	Tau
Θ	θ	Theta		Υ	υ	Upsilon
I	ι	Iota		Φ	ϕ	Phi
K	κ	Kappa		X	χ	Chi
Λ	λ	Lambda		Ψ	ψ	Psi
M	μ	Mu		Ω	ω	Omega

SOME IMPORTANT PHYSICAL CONSTANTS AND OTHER USEFUL NUMERICAL DATA

Speed of light in free space . . . . c $= 2.9979 \times 10^8$ m/sec

Astronomical unit (AU) . . . . $= 93,000,000$ miles (distance from earth to sun)

Light year . . . . $= 6 \times 10^{12}$ miles

Planck's constant . . . . h $= 6.6252 \times 10^{-34}$ joule-sec

h $= \frac{h}{2\pi} = 1.0544 \times 10^{-34}$ joule-sec

Faraday constant . . . . F $= 9.652 \times 10^7$ coulombs/kmole

Density of air (0°C, 1 atm) . . . . $= 1.29$ kg/m^3

Density of water . . . . $= 1.00 \times 10^3$ kg/m^3

Density of mercury . . . . $= 1.35 \times 10^4$ kg/m^3

Avogadro number . . . . N_0 $= 6.025 \times 10^{23}$ particles per mole

Boltzmann's constant . . . . k $= 1.3804 \times 10^{-23}$ joule/°K

$= 8.617 \times 10^{-5}$ ev/°K

Universal gas constant . . . . R $= 8.3166$ joules/mole-°K

Standard volume of a perfect gas . . . . . V_0 $= 22.420$ m^3 atm/kmole

Standard atmosphere . . . . p_0 $= 1.013 \times 10^5$ newton/m^2

Acceleration due to gravity (normal) . . . g $= 9.807$ m/sec^2

Gravitational constant . . . . G $= 6.670 \times 10^{-11}$ nt-m-^{2}/kg^2

Electronic charge . . . . e $= 1.6021 \times 10^{-19}$ coulomb

Electron-volt . . . . ev $= 1.6021 \times 10^{-19}$ joule

Ratio of electron charge to mass . . . . . . e/m_e $= 1.7589 \times 10^{11}$ coulomb/kg

Electron rest mass . . . . m_e $=$ 9.10908×10^{-31} kg

5.48597×10^{-4} amu

5.11006×10^{-1} MeV

Proton rest mass . . . . m_p $=$ 1.67252×10^{-27} kg

1.00727663 amu

938.256 MeV

Neutron rest mass . . . . m_n $=$ 1.67482×10^{-27} kg

1.0086654 amu

939.550 MeV

First Bohr radius . . . . a_0 $= 5.2917 \times 10^{-11}$ m

Heat of fusion of water . . . . $=$ 7.97×10^4 cal/kg

Heat of vaporization of water . . . . $=$ 5.39×10^5 cal/kg

Ice point . . . . $= 273.15$°K

Mechanical equivalent of heat . . . . J $= 4.1855$ joules/cal

1 kg . . . . $= 5.610 \times 10^{29}$ Mev

1 electron mass . . . . $= 0.51098$ Mev

1 proton mass . . . . $= 938.21$ Mev

1 neutron mass . . . . $= 939.51$ Mev

1 atomic mass unit (amu) . . . . $= 931.14$ Mev

1 gram mass (converted to energy) . . . . $= 9 \times 10^{20}$ ergs $= 9 \times 10^{13}$ joules $=$ 2.15×10^{13} cal

1 kilowatt hour (kwh) . . . . $= 3,600,000$ joules

UNITS OF MEASURE

QUESTIONS AND ANSWERS

1. Identify the units of measure from the following descriptions.
    a) A unit of measure based on the length of the forearm from the tip of the middle finger to the elbow
    b) A unit of weight which originally referred to the weight of a seed of the carob tree in the Mediterranean area
    c) A unit of measure that originally referred to the area a yoke of oxen could plow in a single day
    d) A unit for measuring interstellar distances and is a combination of the words parallax and second (the first 2 syllables of each word)
    e) A unit of measure used to specify the distance from the end of the thumb to the end of the little finger when both are outstretched
    f) A unit of measure used to specify the height of horses

ANSWER: a) cubit b) carat c) acre d) parsec e) span f) hand.

2. What do each of the following units measure?
    a) agate
    b) carat
    c) catty
    d) ell
    e) firkin
    f) hogshead
    g) load
    h) magnum
    i) quarter

ANSWER: a) size of type b) precious stones c) tea d) cloth e) lard or butter f) liquids g) earth or gravel h) liquid i) grain.

3. Name the single unit equivalent to each of the following measurements.
    a) 4 pecks
    b) 5,280 feet
    c) 2,240 pounds
    d) 27 cubic feet
    e) 4 quarts
    f) 2.54 centimeters
    g) 640 acres
    h) 1,728 cubic inches
    i) 2 gallons
    j) 60 minims
    k) 20 short hundredweight
    l) 57.2958 degrees
    m) 0.9144 meter
    n) 1.609 kilometers
    o) 4,840 square yards

ANSWER: a) 1 bushel b) 1 mile c) 1 long ton d) 1 cubic yard e) 1 gallon f) 1 inch g) 1 square mile h) 1 cubic foot i) 1 peck j) 1 fluidram k) 1 short ton l) 1 radian m) 1 yard n) 1 mile o) 1 acre.

WEIGHTS AND MEASURES

SI Unit

Quantity	Name	Symbol
length	meter	m
mass	kilogram	kg
time	second	s
electric current	ampere	A
thermodynamic temperature	kelvin	K
amount of substance	mole	mol
luminous intensity	candela	cd

SI Unit

Quantity	Name	Symbol
area	square meter	m^2
volume	cubic meter	m^3
speed, velocity	meter per second	m/s
acceleration	meter per second squared	m/s^2
wave number	1 per meter	m^{-1}
density, mass density	kilogram per cubic meter	kg/m^3
specific volume	cubic meter per kilogram	m^3/kg
current density	ampere per square meter	A/m^2
magnetic field strength	ampere per meter	A/m
concentration (of amount of substance)	mole per cubic meter	mol/m^3
luminance	candela per square meter	cd/m^2

SI Unit

Quantity	Name	Symbol	Expression in terms of other units
frequency	hertz	Hz	s^{-1}
force	newton	N	$m \cdot kg \cdot s^{-2}$
pressure, stress	pascal	Pa	N/m^2
energy, work, quantity of heat	joule	J	$N \cdot m$
power, radiant flux	watt	W	J/s
electric charge, quantity of electricity	coulomb	C	$s \cdot A$
electric potential, potential difference, electromotive force	volt	V	W/A
capacitance	farad	F	C/V
electric resistance	ohm	Ω	V/A
electric conductance	siemens	S	A/V
magnetic flux	weber	Wb	$V \cdot s$
magnetic flux density	tesla	T	Wb/m^2
inductance	henry	H	wb/A
celsius temperature	degree Celsius	°C	K
luminous flux	lumen	lm	$cd \cdot sr$
illuminance	lux	lx	lm/m^2
activity (of a radionuclide)	becquerel	Bq	s^{-1}
absorbed dose, specific energy imparted, kerma, absorbed dose index	gray	Gy	J/kg
dose equivalent, dose equivalent index	sievert	Sv	J/kg

SI Unit

Quantity	Name	Symbol
dynamic viscosity	pascal second	$Pa \cdot s$
moment of force	newton meter	$N \cdot m$
surface tension	newton per meter	N/m
heat flux density, irradiance	watt per square meter	W/m^2
heat capacity, entropy	joule per kelvin	J/K
specific heat capacity, specific entropy	joule per kilogram kelvin	$J/(kg \cdot K)$
specific energy	joule per kilogram	J/kg
thermal conductivity	watt per meter kelvin	$W/(m \cdot K)$
energy density	joule per cubic meter	J/m^3
electric field strength	volt per meter	V/m
electric charge density	coulomb per cubic meter	C/m^3
electric flux density	coulomb per square meter	C/m^2
permittivity	farad per meter	F/m
permeability	henry per meter	H/m
molar energy	joule per mole	J/mol
molar entropy, molar heat capacity	joule per mole kelvin	$J/(mol \cdot K)$
exposure (x and gamma rays)	coulomb per kilogram	C/kg
absorbed dose rate	gray per second	Gy/s

SI Prefixes

Factor	Prefix	Symbol	Factor	Prefix	Symbol
10^{18}	exa	E	10^{-1}	deci	d
10^{15}	peta	P	10^{-2}	centi	c
10^{12}	tera	T	10^{-3}	milli	m
10^{9}	giga	G	10^{-6}	micro	μ
10^{6}	mega	M	10^{-9}	nano	n
10^{3}	kilo	k	10^{-12}	pico	p
10^{2}	hecto	h	10^{-15}	femto	f
10^{1}	deka	da	10^{-18}	atto	a

Name	Symbol	Value in SI unit
minute	min ... 1 min	$= 60$ s
hour	h ... 1 h	$= 60$ min $= 3\ 600$ s
day	d ... 1 d	$= 24$ h $= 86\ 400$ s
degree	° ... 1°	$= (\pi/180)$ rad
minute	' ... 1'	$= (1/60)° = (\pi/10\ 800)$ rad
second	'' ... 1''	$= (1/60)' = (\pi/648\ 000)$ rad
liter	1,L ... 1 L	$= 1$ dm$^3 = 10^{-3}$ m^3
metric ton	t ... 1 t	$= 10^3$ kg

LINEAR MEASURE
U.S. CUSTOMARY
12 inches = 1 foot = 0.304 8 meter[1]
3 feet = 1 yard = 0.914 4 meter[1]
5,280 feet = 1 statute mile = 1.609 kilometers
6,076.115 feet = 1 International Nautical Mile =
   1.852 kilometers[1]

---

[1]Denotes exact figures.

METRIC
10 millimeters = 1 centimeter
10 centimeters = 1 decimeter
10 decimeters = 1 meter
10 meters = 1 dekameter
10 dekameters = 1 hectometer
10 hectometers = 1 kilometer

AREA MEASURE
U.S. CUSTOMARY
144 square inches = 1 square foot = 0.092 9
   square meter
9 square feet = 1 square yard = 0.836 1 square
   meter
43,560 square feet = 1 acre = 0.404 7 hectare
640 acres = 1 square mile = 259 hectares
1 square mile = 1 section = 259 hectares
36 sections = 1 township = 932 4 hectares

METRIC
100 square millimeters = 1 square centimeter
10,000 square centimeters = 1 square meter
100 square meters = 1 are
100 ares = 1 hectare
100 hectares = 1 square kilometer

WEIGHT
U.S. CUSTOMARY (Avoirdupois)
437.5 grains = 1 ounce = 28.349 5 grams
7,000 grains = 1 pound = 0.453 592 37
   kilogram
16 ounces = 1 pound = 0.453 592 37 kilogram
2,000 pounds = 1 short ton = 0.907 2 metric ton
2,240 pounds = 1 long ton = 1.016 metric tons

METRIC
10 milligrams = 1 centigram
10 centigrams = 1 decigram
10 decigrams = 1 gram
10 grams = 1 dekagram
10 dekagrams = 1 hectogram
10 hectograms = 1 kilogram
1,000 kilograms = 1 metric ton

CAPACITY, OR VOLUME, LIQUID MEASURE
U.S. CUSTOMARY
1 gallon = 231 cubic inches = 3.785 4 liters
4 fluid ounces = 1 gill = 0.118 3 liter
4 gills = 1 pint = 0.473 2 liter
2 pints = 1 quart = 0.946 4 liter
4 quarts = 1 gallon = 3.785 4 liters

METRIC
10 milliliters = 1 centiliter
10 centiliters = 1 deciliter
10 deciliters = 1 liter
10 liters = 1 dekaliter
10 dekaliters = 1 hectoliter
10 hectoliters = 1 kiloliter

CAPACITY, OR VOLUME, DRY MEASURE
U.S. CUSTOMARY
1 bushel = 2,150.42 cubic inches = 35.239 1 liters
2 dry pints = 1 dry quart = 1.101 2 liters
8 dry quarts = 1 peck = 8.809 8 liters
4 pecks = 1 bushel = 35.239 1 liters

METRIC
1,000 cubic millimeters = 1 cubic centimeter
1,000 cubic centimeters = 1 cubic decimeter
1,000 cubic decimeters = 1 cubic meter

TROY WEIGHT
24 grains = 1 pennyweight = 1.555 17 grams
20 pennyweights = 1 ounce troy = 31.0103 47
   grams
12 ounces troy = 1 pound troy = 0.373 242
   kilogram

GUNTER'S OR SURVEYOR'S CHAIN MEASURE
7.92 in. = 1 link (li.) = 20.12 cm
66 ft. = 1 chain (ch.) = 100 li. = 20.12 m
660 ft. = 1 furlong (fur.) = 10 ch. = 201.168 m
5,280 ft. = 1 statute mile (mi.) = 8 fur. =
   1.6093 km

ENGINEER'S CHAIN
1 ft. = 1 link (li.) = 30.48 cm

100 ft. = 1 chain (ch.) = 100 li. = 30.48 m

5,280 ft. = 1 mile (mi.) = 52.8 ch. = 1.6093 km

METRIC AND U.S. EQUIVALENTS

1 angstrom (A) (light wave measurement)	0.1 millimicron
	0.000 1 micron
	0.000 000 1 millimeter
	0.000 000 004 inch
1 cable's length	120 fathoms
	720 feet
	219.456 meters
1 centimeter	0.3937 inch
1 chain (Gunter's or surveyor's)	66 feet
	20.1168 meters
1 chain (engineers)	100 feet
	30.48 meters
1 decimeter	3.937 inches
1 dekameter	32.808 feet
1 fathom	6 feet
	1,8288 meters
1 foot	0.3048 meter
1 furlong	10 chains (surveyor's)
	660 feet
	220 yards
	1/8 statute mile
	201.168 meters
1 inch	2.54 centimeters
1 kilometer	0.621 mile
	3,281.5 feet
1 league (land)	3 statute miles
	4.828 kilometers
1 link (Gunter's or surveyor's	7.92 inches
	0.201 168 meter
1 link (engineers)	1 foot
	0.305 meter
1 meter	39.37 inches
	1.094 yards
1 micron (u)	0.001 millimeter
	0.000 039 37 inch
1 mill	0.001 inch
	0.025 4 millimeter
1 mile (statute or land)	5,280 feet
	1,609 kilometers
1 international nautical mile	1.852 kilometers
	1,151 statute miles
	0.999 U.S. nautical miles
1 millimeter	0.03937 inch
1 nanometer	0.001 micrometer or
	0.000 000 039 37 inch
1 point (typography)	0.013 837 inch
	1/72 inch (approximately)
	0.351 millimeter
1 rod, pole, or perch	16 1/2 feet
	5.0292 meters
1 yard	0.9144 meter

AREAS OR SURFACES

1 acre	43,560 square feet
	4,840 square yards
	0.405 hectare
1 are	119.599 square yards
	0.025 acre
1 hectare	2.471 acres
1 square centimeter	0.155 square inch
1 square decimeter	15.5 square inches
1 square foot	929.030 square centimeters
1 square inch	6.4516 square centimeters
1 square kilometer	0.386 square mile
	247.105 acres
1 square meter	1.196 square yards
	10.764 square feet
1 square mile	258.999 hectares
1 square millimeter	0.002 square inch
1 square rod, square. pole or square perch	25.293 square meters
1 square yard	0.836 square meters

CAPACITIES OR VOLUMES

1 barrel, liquid	31 to 42 gallons
1 barrel, standard for fruits, vegetables, and other dry commodities except dry cranberries	7,056 cubic inches, 105 dry quarts, 3.281 bushels, struck measure
1 barrel, standard, cranberry	5.286 cubic inches, 86 45/64 dry quarts, 2,709 bushels, struck measure
1 bushel (U.S.) struck measure	2,150.42 cubic inches, 35.238 liters
1 bushel, heaped (U.S.)	2,747.715 cubic inches, 1,278 bushels, struck measure
1 cubic centimeter	0.061 cubic inches
1 cubic decimeter	61.024 cubic inches
1 cubic inch	0.554 fluid ounce, 4.433 fluid drams, 16.387 cubic centimeters
1 cubic foot	7.481 gallons, 28.316 cubic decimeters
1 cubic meter	1.308 cubic yards
1 cubic yard	0.765 cubic meter
1 cup, measuring	8 fluid ounces, 1/2 liquid pint
1 dram, fluid or liquid (U.S.)	1/8 fluid ounces, 0.226 cubic inch, 3.697 milliliters, 1.041 British fluid drachms
1 dekaliter	2.642 gallons, 1.135 pecks
1 gallon (U.S.)	231 cubic inches, 3.785 liters, 0.833 British gallon, 128 U.S. fluid ounces
1 gallon (British Imperial)	277.42 cubic inches, 1.201 U.S. gallons, 4.546 liters, 160 British fluid ounces
1 gill	7.219 cubic inches, 4 fluid ounces, 0.118 liter
1 hectoliter	26.418 gallons, 2.838 bushels
1 liter	1.057 liquid quarts, 0.908 dry quart, 61.024 cubic inches
1 milliliter	0.271 fluid drams, 16.231 minims, 0.061 cubic inch
1 ounce, liquid (U.S.)	1.805 cubic inch, 29.574 milliliters, 1.041 British fluid ounces
1 peck	8.810 liters
1 pint, dry	33.600 cubic inches, 0.551 liter
1 pint, liquid	28.875 cubic inches, 0.473 liter
1 quart, dry (U.S.)	67.201 cubic inches, 1.101 liters, 0.969 British quart
1 quart, liquid (U.S.)	57.75 cubic inches, 0.946 liter

1 quart (British) . . . . . .
- 0.833 British quart
- 69.354 cubic inches
- 1.032 U.S. dry quarts
- 1.201 U.S. liquid quarts

1 tablespoon . . . .
- 3 teaspoons
- 4 fluid drams
- 1/2 fluid ounce

1 teaspoon . . . .
- 1/3 tablespoon
- 1 1/3 fluid drams

WEIGHTS OR MASSES

1 assay ton . . . . 29.167 grams
1 carat . . . . 200 milligrams
- 3.086 grains
1 dram, apothecaries . . 60 grains
- 3.888 grams
1 dram, avoirdupois . . . 27 11/32 (= 27.344) grains
- 1.772 grams
1 grain . . . . 64.798 91 milligrams
1 gram . . . . 15.432 grains
- 0.035 ounce, avoirdupois
1 hundredweight, ... 112 pounds
gross or long   50.802 kilograms
1 hundredweight, ... 100 pounds
net or short   45.359 kilograms
1 kilogram. . . . . 2.205 pounds
1 microgram [μg (the . . 0.000 001 gram

Greek letter mu in combination with the letter g)]
1 milligram . . . . 0.015 grain
1 ounce, avoirdupois. . . 437.5 grains
- 0.911 troy or apothecaries ounce
- 28.350 grams
1 ounce, troy. . . . . 480 grains
- 1.097 avoirdupois ounces
- 31.103 grams
1 pennyweight . . . . 1.555 grams
1 pound, avoirdupois . . 7,000 grams
- 1.215 troy or apothecaries pound
- 453.592 37 grams
1 pound, troy . . . . 5,760 grains
- 0.823 avoirdupois pound
- 373.242 grams
1 ton, gross or long. . . . 2,240 pounds
- 1.12 net tons
- 1.016 metric tons
1 ton, metric . . . . 2,204.623 pounds
- 0.984 gross tons
- 1.102 net tons
1 ton, net or short . . . . . 2,000 pounds
- 0.893 gross ton
- 0.907 metric tons

MISCELLANEOUS UNITS OF MEASURE

ACRE: 4840 square yards, 43,560 square feet.

AGATE: approximately 5½ point (a size of type), equal to 1/14 inch.

ASTRONOMICAL UNIT (A.U.): 93,000,000 miles, approximately the distance of the earth from the sun.

BALE: a large bundle of goods.

BOARD FOOT (fbm): a unit of quantity for lumber, equal to 144 cubic inches (12 in. x 12 in. x 1 in.).

BOLT: a large roll of cloth, wallpaper, a block of timber to be cut. In cloth it equals 120 feet.

CARAT: equals 200 miligrams (used in weighing precious stones).

CATTY: weighs about 200 milligrams (used to measure tea and other materials).

CHAIN: a surveyor's measuring instrument consisting of a 100 links, equal to 66 feet.

CORD: a unit of wood cut for fuel equal to 128 cubic feet in a stack (4 x 4 x 8 ft.)

CUBIT: about 18 inches.

ELL: equals 45 inches (used to measure cloth).

FIRKIN: equals about 9 imperial gallons or about 56 pounds (used to measure lard or butter).

FORTNIGHT: a period of 14 days.

GREAT GROSS: 12 gross or 1728.

GROSS: 12 dozen or 144.

HAND: equals 4 inches (used to specify the height of a horse).

HOGSHEAD (hhd): large cask or barrel with a capacity ranging from 63 to 140 gallons.

HORSEPOWER: unit of power equal to 33,000 foot-pounds per minute.

KNOT: speed of one nautical mile per hour (measures the speed of ships).

LEAGUE: a unit of distance equal to about 3 statute miles.

LIGHT-YEAR: 5,878,000,000,000 miles, which is the distance light travels in a vacuum for a period of one year (it travels at the rate of 186,281 miles per second).

LOAD: equals 1 cubic yard (used for earth or gravel).

MAGNUM: wine bottle holding two-fifths of a gallon.

NAIL: equals 2.25 inches (used to measure cloth).

PALM: equals 3 or 4 inches.

PARSEC: a unit for measuring interstellar distances, equal to 3.26 light years.

PICA: 12-point type or a unit of 1/6 inch (used in printing).

PIN: equals 4½ gallons (used to measure liquids).

PIPE: a wine cask with a capacity of 126 gallons.

POINT: unit of type equal to approximately 1/72 inch.

PUNCHEON: equals 84 gallons (used to measure liquids).

QUARTER: equals 25 pounds (used to measure grain).

QUINTAL: 100 kilograms or 100,000 grams (a hundredweight).

QUIRE: 24-25 sheets of the same size paper equal to 1/20 of a ream.

REAM: usually 500 sheets of paper.

SCORE: a group of 20 items.

SKEIN: equals 360 feet (used to measure yarn).

SPAN: unit of length equal to 9 inches.

SQUARE: an area of 100 square feet (used to measure floor or roofing material).

STONE: British weight of 14 pounds avoirdupoids.

TIERCE: equals 42 gallons (used to measure liquids).

TUN: a large cask for liquids, especially wine, equal to 252 gallons.

MATHEMATICS, SCIENCE, AND MEDICINE

NICKNAMES OF MATHEMATICIANS, BIOLOGISTS, CHEMISTS, PHYSICISTS, AND PHYSICIANS

Archimedes . . . . Father of Experimental Science

Aristotle . . . . Father of Biology, Father of Zoology, The Learned, Pope of Philosophy

Bhaskara . . . . The Learned

Marie François Bichat . . . . Founder of Histology

Robert Boyle . . . . Father of Chemistry, Father of Scientific Chemistry

Robert Wilhelm Bunsen . . . . Father of the Bunsen Burner

Luther Burbank . . . . Plant Magician, Plant Wizard

George Washington Carver . . . . Father of Chemurgy, Plant Doctor

Baron Georges Cuvier . . . . Founder of Comparative Anatomy, Founder of Paleontology

Charles Darwin . . . . Great Naturalist

Lee De Forest . . . . Father of Radio

Democritus . . . . The Abderite, Laughing Philosopher

Abraham De Moivre . . . . Father of Analytic Trigonometry

René Descartes . . . . Father of Analytic Geometry, Father of Modern Philosophy

Diophantus . . . . Father of Algebra

Albert Einstein . . . . Father of Relativity

Euclid . . . . Father of Geometry

Pierre de Fermat . . . . Father of the Modern Theory (of Numbers)

Galen (Claudius Galenus) . . . . Father of Experimental Physiology, Great Eclectic

Robert Hutchings Goddard . . . . Father of Modern Rocketry and Space Flight

Thomas Graham . . . . Father of Colloid Chemistry

Hales . . . . Greatest of Amateur Scientists

William Harvey . . . . Father of Modern Physiology

Hippocrates . . . . Father of Modern Medicine

John Hunter . . . . Father of Scientific Surgery

Thomas Henry Huxley . . . . Storks

Edward Jenner . . . . Father of Vaccination, Father of Immunology

Friederick von Stradonitz
Kekule . . . . Father of the structure theory of organic chemistry, Father of the structure formulas of organic molecules

Antoine Laurent Lavoisier . . . . Father of Modern Chemistry

Anton van Leeuwenhoek . . . . Father of Microbiology

Gottfried Wilhelm von Leibnitz . . . . . "Aristotle of the 17th Century"

James Lind . . . . Father of Naval Hygiene

Carolus Linnaeus . . . . Beloved Botanist, Father of Modern Systematic Botany, Father of Modern Taxonomy, Little Botanist

Marcello Malpighi . . . . Father of Microscopic Anatomy

James Clerk Maxwell . . . . Founder of Electromagnetic Theory

Giovanni Battista Morgagni . . . . Father of Pathological Anatomy

Issac Newton . . . . The Priest of Nature

Hermann Oberth . . . . Father of Space Travel

J. Robert Oppenheimer . . . . Equivocal Hero of Science, Father of the Atom Bomb, Troubled Pied Piper of Los Alamos

Ambroise Paré . . . . Father of Surgery

Louis Pasteur . . . . Father of Bacteriology, Father of Vaccination, Founder of Microbiology, Founder of Preventive Medicine

Pythagoras . . . . Sage of Samos, The Samian Sage

Walter Reed . . . . Doctor in Uniform

Bertrand Russell . . . . The Passionate Skeptic

Ernest Rutherford . . . . Father of Nuclear Science

Andrey Dmitiyevich Sakharov . . . . . . Father of the (Russian) Hydrogen Bomb

Thomas Sydenham . . . . English Hippocrates, Father of Clinical Medicine

Edward Teller . . . . Father of the (American) Hydrogen Bomb

Theophrastus . . . . Father of Botany

Andreas Vesalius . . . . Father of Anatomy

Rudolf Virchow . . . . Father of Pathology, Founder of Cellular Pathology

Theodore Von Karman . . . . Father of Supersonic Flight

NATIONS AND THEIR CAPITALS

Afghanistan — Kabul
Albania — Tirana (Tirane)
Algeria — Algiers
Andorra — Andorra la Vella
Angola — Luanda
Argentina — Buenos Aires
Australia — Canberra
  Capital Territory — Canberra
  New South Wales — Sydney
  Northern Territory — Darwin
  Queensland — Brisbane
  South Australia — Adelaide
  Tasmania — Hobart
  Victoria — Melbourne
  Western Australia — Perth
Austria — Vienna
Bahamas — Nassau
Bahrain — Manama
Bangladesh — Dacca (Dhaka)
Barbados — Bridgetown
Belgium — Brussels
Belize — Belmopan
Benin — Porto-Novo
Bhutan — Thimphu
Bolivia — La Paz; Sucre
Bophuthatswana — Mmabatho
Botswana — Gaborone
Brazil — Brasilia
Bulgaria — Sofia
Burma — Rangoon
Burundi — Bujumbura
Cambodia (Kampuchea) — Phnom Penh
Cameroon — Yaoundé
Canada — Ottawa
  Alberta — Edmonton
  British Columbia — Victoria
  Manitoba — Winnipeg
  New Brunswick — Fredericton
  Newfoundland — St. John's
  Nova Scotia — Halifax
  Ontario — Toronto
  Prince Edward Island — Charlottetown
  Quebec — Quebec City
  Saskatchewan — Regina
  Yukon Territory — Whitehorse
  The Northwest Territories — Yellowknife
Cape Verde — Praia
Central African Republic — Bangui
Chad — N'Djaména
Chile — Santiago
China — Peking (Beijing)
China (Taiwan) — Taipei
Colombia — Bogotá
Comoros — Moroni
Congo — Brazzaville
Costa Rica — San José
Cuba — Havana
Cyprus — Nicosia
Czechoslovakia — Prague
Denmark — Copenhagen
  Faeroe Islands — Thorshavn
  Greenland (Kalaallit Nunaat) — Nuuk
Djibouti — Djibouti
Dominica — Roseau
Dominican Republic — Santo Domingo
Ecuador — Quito
Egypt — Cairo
El Salvador — San Salvador
Equatorial Guinea — Malabo
Ethiopia — Addis Ababa

Fiji — Suva
Finland — Helsinki
France — Paris
  Corsica — Ajaccio
  French Guiana (Guyane) — Cayenne
  French Polynesia — Papeete (on Tahiti)
  Guadeloupe — Basse-Terre
  Martinique — Fort-de-France
  Mahoré — Dzaoudzi
  New Caledonia — Nouméa
  Réunion (Bourbon) — Saint-Denis
  St. Pierre and Miquelon — St. Pierre
  Southern and Antarctic Lands — Port-au-Français
  Wallis and Futuna Islands — Mata Uta (on Uvéa)
Gabon — Libreville
The Gambia — Banjul
Germany, East — East Berlin
Germany, West — Bonn
Ghana — Accra
Greece — Athens
Grenada — St. George's
Guatemala — Guatemala City
Guinea — Conakry
Guinea-Bissau — Bissau
Guyana — Georgetown
Haiti — Port-au-Prince
Honduras — Tegucigalpa
Hungary — Budapest
Iceland — Reykjavik
India — New Delhi
Indonesia — Jakarta
Iran — Teheran (Tehran)
Iraq — Baghdad
Ireland — Dublin
Israel — Jerusalem; Tel Aviv
Italy — Rome
  Sardinia — Cagliari
  Sicily — Palermo
Ivory Coast — Abidjan (future is Yamoussoukro)
Jamaica — Kingston
Japan — Tokyo
Jordan — Amman
Kenya — Nairobi
Kiribati — Bairiki (on Tarawa Atoll)
Korea, North — Pyongyang
Korea, South — Seoul
Kuwait — Kuwait
Laos — Vientiane
Lebanon — Beirut
Lesotho — Maseru
Liberia — Monrovia
Libya — Tripoli
Liechtenstein — Vaduz
Luxembourg — Luxembourg
Madagascar — Antananarivo
Malawi — Lilongwe
Malaysia — Kuala Lumpur
Maldives — Male
Mali — Bamako
Malta — Valletta
Mauritania — Nouakchott
Mauritius — Port Louis
Mexico — Mexico City
Monaco — Monaco-Ville
Mongolia — Ulaanbaatar
Morocco — Rabat
Mozambique — Maputo
Namibia (South-West Africa) — Windhoek
Nauru — Yaren
Nepal — Kathmandu

The Netherlands — Amsterdam; The Hague
   (seat of government)
Netherlands Antilles — Willemstad, Curaçao
New Zealand — Wellington
Nicaragua — Managua
Niger — Niamey
Nigeria — Abuja
Norway — Oslo
Oman — Muscat
Pakistan — Islamabad
Panama — Panama
Papua New Guinea — Port Moresby
Paraguay — Asunción
Peru — Lima
The Philippines — Manila
Poland — Warsaw
Portugal — Lisbon
Qatar — Doha
Romania — Bucharest
Rwanda — Kigali
St. Christopher and Nevis — Basseterre
St. Lucia — Castries
St. Vincent — Kingstown
San Marino — San Marino
São Tomé and Príncipe — São Tomé
Saudi Arabia — Riyadh
Senegal — Dakar
Seychelles — Victoria
Sierra Leone — Freetown
Singapore — Singapore
Solomon Islands — Honiara
Somalia — Mogadishu (Mogadiscio)
South Africa — Cape Town (legislative capital); Pretoria (administrative capital); Bloemfontein (judicial capital)
Soviet Union — Moscow
  Armenia — Yerevan
  Azerbaijan — Baku
  Belorussia — Minsk
  Estonia — Tallinn
  Georgia — Tbilisi
  Kazakhstan — Alma-Ata
  Kirghizstan — Frunze
  Latvia — Riga
  Lithuania — Vilnius
  Moldavia — Kishinev
  Russia — Moscow
  Tadzhikistan — Dushanbe
  Turkmenistan — Ashkhabad
  Ukraine — Kiev
  Uzbekistan — Tashkent
Spain — Madrid
Sri Lanka — Colombo
Sudan — Khartoum
Suriname — Paramaribo
Swaziland — Mbabane (administrative capital); Lobamba (traditional capital)
Sweden — Stockholm

Switzerland — Bern
Syria — Damascus
Taiwan — Taipei
Tanzania — Dodoma (official capital); Dar es Salaam (actual capital)
Thailand — Bangkok
Togo — Lomé
Tonga — Nuku'alofa
Trinidad and Tobago — Port-Of-Spain
Tunisia — Tunis
Turkey — Ankara
Tuvalu — Funafuti
Uganda — Kampala
United Arab Emirates — Abu Dhabi
United Kingdom of Great Britain and Northern Ireland — London
  England — London
  Northern Ireland — Belfast
  Scotland — Edinburgh
  Wales — Cardiff
BRITISH DEPENDENCIES
Anguilla — The Valley
Bermuda — Hamilton
British Virgin Islands — Road Town
Brunei — Bandar Seri Begawan
Cayman Islands — Georgetown
Channel Islands
  Jersey — St. Helier
  Guernsey — St. Peter Port
Falkland Islands — Stanley
Gibraltar — Gibraltar
Hong Kong — Victoria
Isle of Man — Douglas
Montserrat — Plymouth
Pitcairn Island — Adamstown
Saint Helena — Jamestown
Turks and Caicos Islands — Cockburn Town
United States of America — Washington, D.C.
Upper Volta (Burkinafaso) — Ouagadougou
Uruguay — Montevideo
Vanuatu — Vila
Venezuela — Caracas
Vietnam — Hanoi
Western Samoa — Apia
Yemen — Aden
Yemen Arab Republic — San'a (Sana)
Yugoslavia — Belgrade
  Bosnia and Herzegovina — Sarajevo
  Croatia — Zagreb
  Macedonia — Skoplje
  Montenegro — Titograd
  Serbia — Belgrade
  Slovenia — Ljubljana
Zaire — Kinshasa
Zambia — Lusaka
Zimbabwe — Harare